Contemporary Authors®

NEW REVISION SERIES

ISSN 0275-7176

Contemporary Authors®

**A Bio-Bibliographical Guide to
Current Writers in Fiction, General Nonfiction,
Poetry, Journalism, Drama, Motion Pictures,
Television, and Other Fields**

NEW REVISION SERIES
volume 162

THOMSON

GALE

Detroit • New York • San Francisco • New Haven, Conn. • Waterville, Maine • London

Contemporary Authors, New Revision Series, Vol. 162

Project Editor
Amanda D. Sams

Editorial
Amy Elisabeth Fuller, Michelle Kazensky, Lisa Kumar, Mary Ruby, Rob Russell

Composition and Electronic Capture
Gary Oudersluys

Manufacturing
Drew Kalasky

This publication is a creative work fully protected by all applicable copyright laws, as well as by misappropriation, trade secret, unfair competition, and other applicable laws. The authors and editors of this work have added value to the underlying factual material herein through one or more of the following: unique and original selection, coordination, expression, arrangement, and classification of the information.

For permission to use material from the product, submit your request via the Web at http://www.gale-edit.com/permissions, or you may download our Permissions Request form and submit your request by fax or mail to:

Permissions Department
The Gale Group
27500 Drake Rd.
Farmington Hills, MI 48331-3535
Permissions Hotline:
248-699-8006 or 800-877-4253, ext. 8006
Fax 248-699-8074 or 800-762-4058

Since this page cannot legibly accommodate all copyright notices, the acknowledgments constitute an extension of the copyright notice.

While every effort has been made to secure permission to reprint material and to ensure the reliability of the information presented in this publication, The Gale Group neither guarantees the accuracy of the data contained herein nor assumes any responsibility for errors, omissions or discrepancies. The Gale Group accepts no payment for listing; and inclusion in the publication of any organization, agency, institution, publication, service, or individual does not imply endorsement of the editors or publisher. Errors brought to the attention of the publisher and verified to the satisfaction of the publisher will be corrected in future editions.

LIBRARY OF CONGRESS CATALOG CARD NUMBER 81-640179

ISBN-13: 978-0-7876-7916-3
ISBN-10: 0-7876-7916-X
ISSN 0275-7176

This title is also available as an e-book.
ISBN-13: 978-1-4144-2914-4
ISBN-10: 1-4144-2914-2
Contact your Gale Group sales representative for ordering information.

Printed in the United States of America
10 9 8 7 6 5 4 3 2 1

Contents

Preface vii

Product Advisory Board xi

International Advisory Board xii

CA Numbering System and
Volume Update Chart xiii

Authors and Media People
Featured in This Volume xv

Author Listings 1

Indexing note: All *Contemporary Authors* entries are indexed in the *Contemporary Authors* cumulative index, which is published separately and distributed twice a year.

As always, the most recent Contemporary Authors cumulative index continues to be the user's guide to the location of an individual author's listing.

Preface

Contemporary Authors (*CA*) provides information on approximately 120,000 writers in a wide range of media, including:

- Current writers of fiction, nonfiction, poetry, and drama whose works have been issued by commercial publishers, risk publishers, or university presses (authors whose books have been published only by known vanity or author-subsidized firms are ordinarily not included)

- Prominent print and broadcast journalists, editors, photojournalists, syndicated cartoonists, graphic novelists, screenwriters, television scriptwriters, and other media people

- Notable international authors

- Literary greats of the early twentieth century whose works are popular in today's high school and college curriculums and continue to elicit critical attention

A *CA* listing entails no charge or obligation. Authors are included on the basis of the above criteria and their interest to *CA* users. Sources of potential listees include trade periodicals, publishers' catalogs, librarians, and other users.

How to Get the Most out of *CA*: Use the Index

The key to locating an author's most recent entry is the *CA* cumulative index, which is published separately and distributed twice a year. It provides access to *all* entries in *CA* and *Contemporary Authors New Revision Series* (*CANR*). Always consult the latest index to find an author's most recent entry.

For the convenience of users, the *CA* cumulative index also includes references to all entries in these Gale Group literary series: *African-American Writers, African Writers, American Nature Writers, American Writers, American Writers: The Classics, American Writers Retrospective Supplement, American Writers Supplement, Ancient Writers, Asian American Literature, Authors and Artists for Young Adults, Authors in the News, Beacham's Encyclopedia of Popular Fiction: Analyses, Beacham's Encyclopedia of Popular Fiction: Biography and Resources, Beacham's Guide to Literature for Young Adults, Beat Generation: A Gale Critical Companion, Bestsellers, Black Literature Criticism, Black Literature Criticism Supplement, Black Writers, British Writers, British Writers: The Classics, British Writers Retrospective Supplement, British Writers Supplement, Children's Literature Review, Classical and Medieval Literature Criticism, Concise Dictionary of American Literary Biography, Concise Dictionary of American Literary Biography Supplement, Concise Dictionary of British Literary Biography, Concise Dictionary of World Literary Biography, Contemporary American Dramatists, Contemporary Authors Autobiography Series, Contemporary Authors Bibliographical Series, Contemporary British Dramatists, Contemporary Canadian Authors, Contemporary Dramatists, Contemporary Literary Criticism, Contemporary Novelists, Contemporary Poets, Contemporary Popular Writers, Contemporary Southern Writers, Contemporary Women Dramatists, Contemporary Women Poets, Contemporary World Writers, Dictionary of Literary Biography, Dictionary of Literary Biography Documentary Series, Dictionary of Literary Biography Yearbook, DISCovering Authors, DISCovering Authors 3.0, DISCovering Authors: British Edition, DISCovering Authors: Canadian Edition, DISCovering Authors Modules, Drama Criticism, Drama for Students, Encyclopedia of World Literature in the 20th Century, Epics for Students, European Writers, Exploring Novels, Exploring Poetry, Exploring Short Stories, Feminism in Literature, Feminist Writers, Gay & Lesbian Literature, Guide to French Literature, Harlem Renaissance: A Gale Critical Companion, Hispanic Literature Criticism, Hispanic Literature Criticism Supplement, Hispanic Writers, International Dictionary of Films and Filmmakers: Writers and Production Artists, International Dictionary of Theatre: Playwrights, Junior DISCovering Authors, Latin American Writers, Latin American Writers Supplement, Latino and Latina Writers, Literature and Its Times, Literature and Its Times Supplement, Literature Criticism from 1400-1800, Literature of Developing Nations for Students, Major Authors and Illustrators for Children and Young Adults, Major Authors and Illustrators for Children and Young Adults Supplement, Major 21st Century Writers* (eBook version), *Major 20th-Century Writers, Modern American Women Writers, Modern Arts Criticism, Modern Japanese Writers, Mystery and Suspense Writers, Native North American Literature, Nineteenth-Century Literature Criticism, Nonfiction Classics for Students, Novels for Students, Poetry Criticism, Poetry for Students, Poets: American and British, Reference Guide to American Literature, Reference Guide to English Literature, Reference Guide to Short Fiction, Reference Guide to World Literature, Science Fiction Writers, Shakespearean Criticism, Shakespeare for Students, Shakespeare's Characters for Students, Short Stories for Students, Short Story Criticism, Something About the Author, Something About the Author Autobiography Series, St. James Guide to Children's Writers, St. James Guide to Crime & Mystery Writers, St. James Guide to Fantasy Writers, St. James Guide to Horror, Ghost & Gothic Writers, St. James Guide to Science Fiction Writers, St. James Guide to Young Adult Writers, Supernatural Fiction*

Writers, Twayne Companion to Contemporary Literature in English, Twayne's English Authors, Twayne's United States Authors, Twayne's World Authors, Twentieth-Century Literary Criticism, Twentieth-Century Romance and Historical Writers, Twentieth-Century Western Writers, William Shakespeare, World Literature and Its Times, World Literature Criticism, World Literature Criticism Supplement, World Poets, World Writing in English, Writers for Children, Writers for Young Adults, and *Yesterday's Authors of Books for Children.*

A Sample Index Entry:

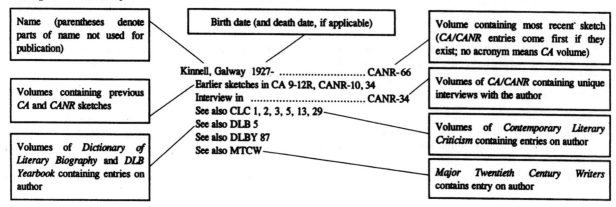

How Are Entries Compiled?

The editors make every effort to secure new information directly from the authors; listees' responses to our questionnaires and query letters provide most of the information featured in *CA*. For deceased writers, or those who fail to reply to requests for data, we consult other reliable biographical sources, such as those indexed in Gale Group's *Biography and Genealogy Master Index,* and bibliographical sources, including *National Union Catalog, LC MARC,* and *British National Bibliography.* Further details come from published interviews, feature stories, and book reviews, as well as information supplied by the authors' publishers and agents.

An asterisk (*) at the end of a sketch indicates that the listing has been compiled from secondary sources believed to be reliable but has not been personally verified for this edition by the author sketched.

What Kinds of Information Does An Entry Provide?

Sketches in *CA* contain the following biographical and bibliographical information:

- **Entry heading:** the most complete form of author's name, plus any pseudonyms or name variations used for writing

- **Personal information:** author's date and place of birth, family data, ethnicity, educational background, political and religious affiliations, and hobbies and leisure interests

- **Addresses:** author's home, office, or agent's addresses, plus e-mail and fax numbers, as available

- **Career summary:** name of employer, position, and dates held for each career post; resume of other vocational achievements; military service

- **Membership information:** professional, civic, and other association memberships and any official posts held

- **Awards and honors:** military and civic citations, major prizes and nominations, fellowships, grants, and honorary degrees

- **Writings:** a comprehensive, chronological list of titles, publishers, dates of original publication and revised editions, and production information for plays, television scripts, and screenplays

- **Adaptations:** a list of films, plays, and other media which have been adapted from the author's work

- **Work in progress:** current or planned projects, with dates of completion and/or publication, and expected publisher, when known

- **Sidelights:** a biographical portrait of the author's development; information about the critical reception of the author's works; revealing comments, often by the author, on personal interests, aspirations, motivations, and thoughts on writing

- **Interview:** a one-on-one discussion with authors conducted especially for *CA*, offering insight into authors' thoughts about their craft

- **Autobiographical essay:** an original essay written by noted authors for *CA*, a forum in which writers may present themselves, on their own terms, to their audience

- **Photographs:** portraits and personal photographs of notable authors

- **Biographical and critical sources:** a list of books and periodicals in which additional information on an author's life and/or writings appears

- **Obituary Notices** in *CA* provide date and place of birth as well as death information about authors whose full-length sketches appeared in the series before their deaths. The entries also summarize the authors' careers and writings and list other sources of biographical and death information.

Related Titles in the *CA* Series

Contemporary Authors Autobiography Series complements *CA* original and revised volumes with specially commissioned autobiographical essays by important current authors, illustrated with personal photographs they provide. Common topics include their motivations for writing, the people and experiences that shaped their careers, the rewards they derive from their work, and their impressions of the current literary scene.

Contemporary Authors Bibliographical Series surveys writings by and about important American authors since World War II. Each volume concentrates on a specific genre and features approximately ten writers; entries list works written by and about the author and contain a bibliographical essay discussing the merits and deficiencies of major critical and scholarly studies in detail.

Available in Electronic Formats

GaleNet. *CA* is available on a subscription basis through GaleNet, an online information resource that features an easy-to-use end-user interface, powerful search capabilities, and ease of access through the World-Wide Web. For more information, call 1-800-877-GALE.

Licensing. *CA* is available for licensing. The complete database is provided in a fielded format and is deliverable on such media as disk, CD-ROM, or tape. For more information, contact Gale Group's Business Development Group at 1-800-877-GALE, or visit us on our website at www.galegroup.com/bizdev.

Suggestions Are Welcome

The editors welcome comments and suggestions from users on any aspect of the *CA* series. If readers would like to recommend authors for inclusion in future volumes of the series, they are cordially invited to write the Editors at *Contemporary Authors*, Gale Group, 27500 Drake Rd., Farmington Hills, MI 48331-3535; or call at 1-248-699-4253; or fax at 1-248-699-8054.

Contemporary Authors Product Advisory Board

The editors of *Contemporary Authors* are dedicated to maintaining a high standard of excellence by publishing comprehensive, accurate, and highly readable entries on a wide array of writers. In addition to the quality of the content, the editors take pride in the graphic design of the series, which is intended to be orderly yet inviting, allowing readers to utilize the pages of *CA* easily and with efficiency. Despite the longevity of the *CA* print series, and the success of its format, we are mindful that the vitality of a literary reference product is dependent on its ability to serve its users over time. As literature, and attitudes about literature, constantly evolve, so do the reference needs of students, teachers, scholars, journalists, researchers, and book club members. To be certain that we continue to keep pace with the expectations of our customers, the editors of *CA* listen carefully to their comments regarding the value, utility, and quality of the series. Librarians, who have firsthand knowledge of the needs of library users, are a valuable resource for us. The *Contemporary Authors* Product Advisory Board, made up of school, public, and academic librarians, is a forum to promote focused feedback about *CA* on a regular basis. The seven-member advisory board includes the following individuals, whom the editors wish to thank for sharing their expertise:

- **Anne M. Christensen,** Librarian II, Phoenix Public Library, Phoenix, Arizona.

- **Barbara C. Chumard,** Reference/Adult Services Librarian, Middletown Thrall Library, Middletown, New York.

- **Eva M. Davis,** Youth Department Manager, Ann Arbor District Library, Ann Arbor, Michigan.

- **Adam Janowski, Jr.,** Library Media Specialist, Naples High School Library Media Center, Naples, Florida.

- **Robert Reginald,** Head of Technical Services and Collection Development, California State University, San Bernadino, California.

- **Stephen Weiner,** Director, Maynard Public Library, Maynard, Massachusetts.

International Advisory Board

Well-represented among the 120,000 author entries published in *Contemporary Authors* are sketches on notable writers from many non-English-speaking countries. The primary criteria for inclusion of such authors has traditionally been the publication of at least one title in English, either as an original work or as a translation. However, the editors of *Contemporary Authors* came to observe that many important international writers were being overlooked due to a strict adherence to our inclusion criteria. In addition, writers who were publishing in languages other than English were not being covered in the traditional sources we used for identifying new listees. Intent on increasing our coverage of international authors, including those who write only in their native language and have not been translated into English, the editors enlisted the aid of a board of advisors, each of whom is an expert on the literature of a particular country or region. Among the countries we focused attention on are Mexico, Puerto Rico, Spain, Italy, France, Germany, Luxembourg, Belgium, the Netherlands, Norway, Sweden, Denmark, Finland, Taiwan, Singapore, Malaysia, Thailand, South Africa, Israel, and Japan, as well as England, Scotland, Wales, Ireland, Australia, and New Zealand. The sixteen-member advisory board includes the following individuals, whom the editors wish to thank for sharing their expertise:

- **Lowell A. Bangerter,** Professor of German, University of Wyoming, Laramie, Wyoming.

- **Nancy E. Berg,** Associate Professor of Hebrew and Comparative Literature, Washington University, St. Louis, Missouri.

- **Frances Devlin-Glass,** Associate Professor, School of Literary and Communication Studies, Deakin University, Burwood, Victoria, Australia.

- **David William Foster,** Regent's Professor of Spanish, Interdisciplinary Humanities, and Women's Studies, Arizona State University, Tempe, Arizona.

- **Hosea Hirata,** Director of the Japanese Program, Associate Professor of Japanese, Tufts University, Medford, Massachusetts.

- **Jack Kolbert,** Professor Emeritus of French Literature, Susquehanna University, Selinsgrove, Pennsylvania.

- **Mark Libin,** Professor, University of Manitoba, Winnipeg, Manitoba, Canada.

- **C.S. Lim,** Professor, University of Malaya, Kuala Lumpur, Malaysia.

- **Eloy E. Merino,** Assistant Professor of Spanish, Northern Illinois University, DeKalb, Illinois.

- **Linda M. Rodríguez Guglielmoni,** Associate Professor, University of Puerto Rico—Mayagüez, Puerto Rico.

- **Sven Hakon Rossel,** Professor and Chair of Scandinavian Studies, University of Vienna, Vienna, Austria.

- **Steven R. Serafin,** Director, Writing Center, Hunter College of the City University of New York, New York City.

- **David Smyth,** Lecturer in Thai, School of Oriental and African Studies, University of London, England.

- **Ismail S. Talib,** Senior Lecturer, Department of English Language and Literature, National University of Singapore, Singapore.

- **Dionisio Viscarri,** Assistant Professor, Ohio State University, Columbus, Ohio.

- **Mark Williams,** Associate Professor, English Department, University of Canterbury, Christchurch, New Zealand.

CA **Numbering System and Volume Update Chart**

Occasionally questions arise about the *CA* numbering system and which volumes, if any, can be discarded. Despite numbers like "29-32R," "97-100" and "256," the entire *CA* print series consists of 341 physical volumes with the publication of *CA* Volume 256. The following charts note changes in the numbering system and cover design, and indicate which volumes are essential for the most complete, up-to-date coverage.

CA **First Revision**	• 1-4R through 41-44R (11 books) *Cover:* Brown with black and gold trim. There will be no further First Revision volumes because revised entries are now being handled exclusively through the more efficient *New Revision Series* mentioned below.
CA **Original Volumes**	• 45-48 through 97-100 (14 books) *Cover:* Brown with black and gold trim. 101 through 256 (156 books) *Cover:* Blue and black with orange bands. The same as previous *CA* original volumes but with a new, simplified numbering system and new cover design.
CA **Permanent Series**	• *CAP*-1 and *CAP*-2 (2 books) *Cover:* Brown with red and gold trim. There will be no further Permanent Series volumes because revised entries are now being handled exclusively through the more efficient *New Revision Series* mentioned below.
CA **New Revision Series**	• CANR-1 through CANR-162 (162 books) *Cover:* Blue and black with green bands. Includes only sketches requiring significant changes; **sketches are taken from any previously published CA, CAP, or CANR volume.**

If You Have:	You May Discard:
CA First Revision Volumes 1-4R through 41-44R and *CA Permanent Series* Volumes 1 and 2	*CA* Original Volumes 1, 2, 3, 4 and Volumes 5-6 through 41-44
CA Original Volumes 45-48 through 97-100 and 101 through 256	**NONE:** These volumes will not be superseded by corresponding revised volumes. Individual entries from these and all other volumes appearing in the left column of this chart may be revised and included in the various volumes of the *New Revision Series*.
CA New Revision Series Volumes *CANR*-1 through *CANR*-162	**NONE:** The *New Revision Series* does not replace any single volume of *CA*. Instead, volumes of *CANR* include entries from many previous *CA* series volumes. All *New Revision Series* volumes must be retained for full coverage.

A Sampling of Authors and Media People
Featured in This Volume

Fouad Ajami

Ajami is an author, a scholar, and the director of Middle East Studies at John Hopkins University. He is also known as a public speaker who makes regular appearances on television news shows for Columbia Broadcast Systems. Ajami's eloquence is widely admired, but his political analyses have sometimes met with controversy for their allegedly anti-Arab views. His most recent book, *The Foreigner's Gift: The Americans, the Arabs, and the Iraqis in Iraq,* voices his support for the American-led invasion of Iraq, arguing that the Arab world stands to benefit greatly from the removal of Saddam Hussein's tyranny.

Janet Evanovich

Evanovich is the author of a successful series of humorous detective novels featuring Jersey girl-turned-bounty hunter Stephanie Plum. Characterized by a flamboyant wardrobe, big hair, and an impertinent demeanor, Plum tracks bail jumpers for her cousin Vinnie, a bail bondsman. Evanovich's novels are noted for their mix of hardboiled mystery and farce, as well as their large cast of idiosyncratic characters. Evanovich has also written romance fiction, and recently cowrote a how-to book titled *How I Write: Secrets of a Bestselling Author.*

Elaine Feinstein

Feinstein is an English poet, novelist, short story writer, playwright, biographer, and translator. The granddaughter of Jews who fled persecution in Tsarist Russia, Feinstein retains a strong preoccupation with her background and upbringing; this fascination with her Eastern European heritage informs both her poetry and the majority of her novels. Her works also grapple with Jewish identity and what it means to be an outsider. Her most recent book is a biography of the Russian poet Anna Akhmatova, titled *Anna of All the Russias: The Life of Anna Akhmatova.*

Ralph Helfer

Helfer is a legendary Hollywood animal trainer and behaviorist who developed "affection training," a method that uses respect and kindness to develop strong bonds between humans and wild animals. During his career, Helfer worked with numerous animal celebrities, including Clarence the Cross-eyed Lion and Judy the Chimp. Helfer chronicles his eighteen-year relationship with an orphaned lion cub in *Zamba: The True Story of the Greatest Lion That Ever Lived.* He also profiles the celebrity elephant Modoc in a series of books for adults and children, the most recent being a picture book titled *The World's Greatest Elephant.*

Lois Lowry

Lowry, an award-winning author of young-adult novels, is perhaps best known for her Newbery Award-winning novels *Number the Stars* and *The Giver.* Never one to shy from controversy, her novels deal with topics ranging from the death of a sibling and the Nazi occupation of Denmark to the humorous antics of a rebellious teen named Anastasia Krupnik, and to futuristic dystopian societies. Her most recent work is a fantasy novel titled *Gossamer,* which describes a creature named the Littlest One and its work to protect a human family from nightmare-causing monsters.

Andreï Makine

Makine, a Russian-born writer who lives and writes in France, has built a vaunted reputation through numerous novels that explore life in the former Soviet Union. Despite his initial difficulties in finding a French publisher, Makine's works have earned critical acclaim. His fourth novel, *Le testament français,* won both the Prix Goncourt and the Prix Medici—a dual recognition no French writer had achieved. His most recent work in English translation is titled *The Woman Who Waited.*

Howell Raines

Raines is a Pulitzer Prize-winning journalist who served as an editor and bureau chief at the *New York Times* for nearly a quarter century. He became executive editor in 2001, and under his guidance the newspaper increased circulation and won seven Pulitzer Prizes. He resigned in 2003, in the aftermath of a scandal in which reporter Jayson Blair was proven to have engaged in the systematic plagiarism and fabrication of stories over a long period of time. Raines is the author of two memoirs, *Fly Fishing Through the Midlife Crisis* and *The One That Got Away,* both of which build upon the author's love of fishing.

Helen A. Thomas

Thomas is one of the most widely known wire service reporters in the United States. Since 1961 she has covered the White House for United Press International, and in 1974 was named White House bureau chief. In a reporting career spanning five decades she has become a legend, noted for her lively wit, her tough reporting, and her position as one of the first women to break into the male-dominated White House press corps. Her latest book is titled *Watchdogs of Democracy? The Waning Washington Press Corps and How It Has Failed the Public.*

A

AJAMI, Fouad 1946-

PERSONAL: Born 1946, in Lebanon; immigrated to the United States, 1964; became naturalized citizen. *Education:* University of Washington, Ph.D.

ADDRESSES: Office—Paul H. Nitze School of Advanced International Studies (SAIS), Johns Hopkins University, Nitze Building, 1740 Massachusetts Ave. NW, Washington, DC 20036.

CAREER: Lehrman Institute, New York, NY, former research fellow; Department of Politics and Center of International Studies, Princeton University, Princeton, NJ, faculty member; Paul Nitze School of Advanced International Studies, Johns Hopkins University, Washington, DC, associate professor and director of Middle East Studies, became Majid Khadduri Professor of Islamic Studies and director of Middle East Studies, 1980—. Author; consultant, *CBS News.*

AWARDS, HONORS: James P. Warburg postdoctoral fellowship, and Philip Lindsley Bicentennial Preceptorship, both from Princeton University; MacArthur Prize fellowship, 1982, for work on Middle East politics and culture.

WRITINGS:

The Arab Predicament: Arab Political Thought and Practice since 1967, Cambridge University Press (New York, NY), 1981, revised edition, 1992.

The Vanished Imam: Musa al Sadr and the Shi'a of Lebanon, Cornell University Press (Ithaca, NY), 1986.
Beirut: City of Regrets, photographs by Eli Reed, Norton (New York, NY), 1988.
The Dream Palace of the Arabs: A Generation's Odyssey, Pantheon (New York, NY), 1998.
The Foreigner's Gift: The Americans, the Arabs, and the Iraqis in Iraq, Free Press (New York, NY), 2006.

Contributing editor, *U.S. News and World Report.* Contributor of articles and essays to periodicals, including *New York Times Book Review, Foreign Affairs, Washington Post Book World, Foreign Policy, Politique Etrangere, Harper's,* and *New Republic.*

SIDELIGHTS: Fouad Ajami is an author, a scholar, and the director of Middle East Studies at Johns Hopkins University. He is also known as a public speaker, one who makes regular appearances on television news shows for CBS. Ajami's eloquence is widely admired, but his political analyses, both in his role as Mideast expert on the evening news and in his writings, have sometimes met with controversy.

As the recipient of a number of prestigious fellowships, including the MacArthur Foundation Award, Ajami possesses academic credentials that have never been questioned. More controversial has been the political bent of some of his writings and views, which have at times been called anti-Arab. The American-Arab Anti-Discrimination Committee has protested CBS's extensive reliance on Ajami as its Mideast expert in the face of many other able candidates. In a *Nation* review of Ajami's book *The Dream Palace of the Arabs: A Generation's Odyssey,* Andrew Rubin referred to a reported comment made by U.S. President George Bush that Ajami was "more anti-Arab than even the Israelis." However, other critics, such as Daniel Pipes of the conservative journal *Commentary,* consider Ajami expressed admiration for Ajami's avoidance of what Pipes called "the common Arab fixation on the perfidy of Israel."

Ajami's first major book, *The Arab Predicament: Arab Political Thought and Practice since 1967,* relates the panic and sense of vulnerability that Israel's 1967 victory created in the Arab world. Organized into three parts, the book renders, in part one, the conflicts among three prevalent Arab points of view—"the radical, the Ba'thist, and the fundamentalist," according to a *Choice* reviewer; in part two, Ajami explores Egypt's central role in the Middle East and the effects of the influx of oil money into the region; in part three, he covers the rise of religious fundamentalism. Elizabeth R. Hayford, writing in *Library Journal,* commented especially on Ajami's ability to "[place] Islamic fundamentalism within the broad issues of relations between ruler and ruled."

Reviews of Ajami's *The Vanished Imam: Musa al Sadr and the Shi'a of Lebanon* revealed a mix of admiration and uncertainty about Ajami's role as a distant and somewhat skeptical onlooker of Middle Eastern political events. In a lengthy review in the *New York Review of Books,* Edward Mortimer began with a description of Ajami's brief encounter in a Beirut classroom in 1963 with Musa al Sadr, an Iranian Shi'ite cleric then just beginning his rise to power. Within a year Ajami had immigrated to the United States; although he was not personally a witness to Sadr's religious and political ascent, his Lebanese sources helped him to tell the tale of the man who raised the Lebanese Shi'a from a "despised minority" to the ruling party of Lebanon.

Early in the review, Mortimer spoke of Ajami's "brilliant American academic career, built largely on incisive exposure of the follies of his fellow Arabs." The comment mirrors similar criticism by others that Ajami has capitalized on American paranoia about Muslim extremists bent on terrorist acts. However, Mortimer quickly turned away from this type of critique and praised the book's eloquence, as well as its powerful hold on the complex realities Lebanon has endured. The reviewer

stated that Ajami's use of the English language "represents one of those periodic transfusions of new blood which ensure its perennial vigor." Mortimer ascribed part of the power of Ajami's narrative to the strong feelings that underlie it: Ajami's rejection of Sadr's "activist, modernist version of Shi'ism" is not without admiration or regret; however, Ajami also laments Musa al Sadr's legacy being taken up as a hero in the Iran Revolution and having his name invoked by men like the Ayatollah Khomeini to justify violent acts. In addition, the Imam's disappearance during a 1978 visit to Muammar Al-Gaddafi in Libya gave him an otherworldly power that he as a flesh and blood man could never have matched. Reviewing *The Vanished Imam* in *Library Journal,* Hayford wrote: "What begins as a narrow study of a relatively minor figure becomes a sensitive and probing analysis of current Middle Eastern society."

In *Beirut: City of Regrets* Ajami offers a lengthy introduction and some accompanying text to what is largely a photographic essay by Eli Reed about the destruction of "the Paris of the Middle East," according to *Library Journal* reviewer David P. Snider. A *Publishers Weekly* reviewer called it "thorough, moving, and remarkably unbiased." A reviewer for the *Los Angeles Times Book Review,* however, commented that "Ajami recounts history with such a gentle spirit and understanding mind that his text does little to help us understand why the country rages with such hatred."

Ajami's 1998 work *The Dream Palace of the Arabs,* generated considerably more critical controversy than his previous works. A *Publishers Weekly* reviewer viewed it as a "cohesive and illuminating cultural history" for "even the most general reader." Periodicals with a more political focus published stronger opinions of the book, however. Andrew Rubin's review for the *Nation* stated early on that, as a Mideast expert on television, Ajami "echoes the kind of anti-Arabism that both Washington and the pro-Israel lobby have come to embrace." Rubin showed some appreciation for Ajami's thoughtful analysis of the period of literary modernism that was born in the Mideast from the early 1940s onward, but whose secular bent became impractical after the religious revolutions that swept the region. Rubin, however, vigorously protested against some of Ajami's language to describe current Arab politics, including "tribal," "atavistic," "clannish," and "backward." Rubin called this kind of language "anti-Arab orientalism." The reviewer also objected strongly to Ajami's characterization of "the struggle for a Palestinian homeland only as an internal Arab contest between modernity and tradition," which ignores "Israel's policy of systematic detentions of Palestinians, its destruction of Palestinian homes and entire villages, its ruthless attacks on refugee camps, and its torture and nightly arrests."

Daniel Pipes's review of *The Dream Palace of the Arabs* for *Commentary* echoed much of Rubin's review but drew completely opposite conclusions. Pipes acknowledged the criticisms Ajami has faced from other members of the Arab-American community; for example, renowned cultural critic Edward Said of Columbia University (whom Pipes termed Ajami's "would-be rival") has accused Ajami of having "unmistakably racist prescriptions." Pipes, on the contrary, appreciated Ajami's outspoken, straightforward, and sometimes abrupt approach to Middle Eastern subjects.

Of *The Dream Palace of the Arabs*, Pipes said: "To my taste, the early chapters of this book, in which Ajami uses poets and intellectuals to represent the political currents of the era, seem a bit contrived. As the book goes along, however, the argument becomes increasingly direct." Pipes noted particularly the final chapter of the book, "The Orphaned Peace," which critiques Arab intellectuals' rejection of the Oslo peace talks between Palestinians and Israelis. "If Fouad Ajami is right," wrote Pipes, "Arab intellectual life will continue to exalt irrationality and to honor aggression for some time to come. We may not like this, but having read [Ajami's book], we can at least begin to understand it."

Ajami stood in opposition to many Arab intellectuals when he voiced strong support for the U.S.-led invasion of Iraq in 2003. He published his views on the Iraq war in his book *The Foreigner's Gift: The Americans, the Arabs, and the Iraqis in Iraq.* It is Ajami's belief that even if the citizens of the Arab world do not appreciate it, they stand to benefit greatly from the U.S.-led military intervention because it will serve to free them from a tyranny that, otherwise, might have gone on for centuries. The author's arguments are well-stated, according to Christian Caryl in *Washington Monthly,* but the reviewer cautioned that Ajami is "deeply and personally implicated in the policies he's describing—though you could easily read this entire book without ever figuring it out." Caryl commented that Ajami "has an enviable gift for charting those invisible lines of clan, tribe, and faction that structure the Arabic-speaking world. His chapter on the feuds and alliances among the great Shi'ite families of Iraq should be required reading for all American soldiers and policy-makers."

BIOGRAPHICAL AND CRITICAL SOURCES:

PERIODICALS

American Academy of Political and Social Science Annals, November, 1987, Barbara D. Metcalf, review of *The Vanished Imam: Musa al Sadr and the Shi'a of Lebanon,* p. 175.
American Historical Review, June, 1982, review of *The Arab Predicament: Arab Political Thought and Practice since 1967,* p. 829.
American Photographer, November, 1988, Vicki Goldberg, review of *Beirut: City of Regrets,* pp. 20-21.
American Political Science Review, June, 1982, review of *The Arab Predicament,* p. 429.
America's Intelligence Wire, May 6, 2006, interview with Fouad Ajami.
Antioch Review, fall, 1986, review of *The Vanished Imam,* p. 486.
Atlantic, June, 1986, David Ignatius, review of *The Vanished Imam,* pp. 77-78.
Booklist, January 1, 1998, Grace Fill, review of *The Dream Palace of the Arabs: A Generation's Odyssey,* p. 768.
Business Week, March 4, 1991, Stanley Reed, review of *The Arab Predicament,* p. 8.
Choice, November, 1981, review of *The Arab Predicament,* pp. 43-39.
Commentary, July, 1982, Martin Kramer, review of *The Arab Predicament,* pp. 86-88; March, 1998, Daniel Pipes, review of *The Dream Palace of the Arabs;* September, 2006, Victor Davis Hanson, review of *The Foreigner's Gift: The Americans, the Arabs, and the Iraqis in Iraq,* p. 67.
Commonweal, January 31, 1986, pp. 40-41.
Current History, January, 1983, review of *The Arab Predicament,* p. 32.
Economist, December 12, 1981, review of *The Arab Predicament,* p. 105; February 7, 1987, review of *The Vanished Imam,* p. 83.
Guardian Weekly, January 22, 1989, review of *Beirut,* p. 20.
Library Journal, July, 1981, Elizabeth R. Hayford, review of *The Arab Predicament,* p. 1402; July, 1986, Elizabeth Hayford, review of *The Vanished Imam,* p. 89; July, 1988, David P. Snider, review of *Beirut,* p. 84.
Los Angeles Times Book Review, May 18, 1986, review of *The Vanished Imam,* p. 3; June 19, 1988, review of *Beirut,* p. 4.
Middle East Journal, autumn, 1981, review of *The Arab Predicament,* p. 639; spring, 1987, review of

The Vanished Imam, p. 287; summer, 1994, review of revised edition of *The Arab Predicament,* p. 561.

Modern Age, fall, 1985, review of *The Arab Predicament,* p. 365.

Nation, December 26, 1981, review of *The Arab Predicament,* p. 714; April, 1998, Andrew Rubin, review of *The Dream Palace.*

New Republic, June 13, 1981, review of *The Arab Predicament,* p. 36; May 12, 1986, Itamar Rabinovich, review of *The Vanished Imam,* pp. 30-33.

Newsweek, February 18, 1991, review of *The Arab Predicament,* p. 62.

New York Review of Books, October 9, 1986, Edward Mortimer, review of *The Vanished Imam,* pp. 17-18.

New York Times Book Review, May 25, 1986, Mary Catherine Bateson, review of *The Vanished Imam,* p. 5; July 17, 1988, Stewart Kellerman, review of *Beirut,* p. 20; July 30, 2006, Noah Feldman, review of *The Foreigner's Gift,* p. 8.

Observer, May 23, 1982, review of *The Arab Predicament,* p. 31.

Political Science Quarterly, winter, 1981, review of *The Arab Predicament,* p. 709.

Publishers Weekly, April 25, 1986, Genevieve Stuttaford, review of *The Vanished Imam,* p. 62; June 17, 1988, review of *Beirut,* p. 63; January 5, 1998, review of *The Dream Palace of the Arabs,* p. 50.

Times Literary Supplement, September 10, 1982, review of *The Arab Predicament,* p. 963.

U.S. News and World Report, November 27, 2006, Brian Duffy, "Fouad Ajami of School of Advanced International Studies at Johns Hopkins University Wins National Medal of Arts and National Humanities Medal," p. 10.

Wall Street Journal, June 2, 1988, review of *Beirut,* p. 20.

Washington Monthly, December, 1988, pp. 58-59; September, 2006, Christian Caryl, review of *The Foreigner's Gift,* p. 49.

Washington Post Book World, October 18, 1988, review of *The Vanished Imam,* p. 12; December 25, 1988, review of *Beirut,* p. 1.

Wilson Quarterly, spring, 1982, review of *The Arab Predicament,* p. 153, fall, 1986, review of *The Vanished Imam,* p. 150.

World Politics, July, 1986, review of *The Arab Predicament,* p. 611; April, 1991, Saul Newman, review of *The Vanished Imam,* p. 451.

ONLINE

Johns Hopkins University School of Advanced International Studies Web site, http://apps.sais-jhu.edu/ (February 4, 2007), biographical information on Fouad Ajami.

Just World News, http://justworldnews.org/ (May 26, 2004), Helena Cobban, "Fouad Ajami's Mea Not-Quite-Culpa."

Voice of America Web site, http://www.voanews.com/ (June 28, 2006), Judith Latham, "Author Fouad Ajami Says U.S.-Led Invasion of Iraq Was a Noble War."*

* * *

ALCORN, Randy 1954-
(Randy C. Alcorn)

PERSONAL: Born June 23, 1954, in Portland, OR; son of Arthur (a tavern owner) and Lucille (a homemaker) Alcorn; married May 31, 1975; wife's name Nanci (a homemaker); children: Karina, Angela. *Ethnicity:* "Caucasian." *Education:* Multnomah Bible College, Th. B., 1976, M.A., 1979; attended Western Seminary, 1976-77. *Religion:* Evangelical. *Hobbies and other interests:* Reading, international travel, tennis, snorkeling.

ADDRESSES: Office—39085 Pioneer Blvd., Ste. 200, Sandy, OR 97055. *E-mail*—info@epm.org.

CAREER: Good Shepherd Community Church, Boring, OR, pastor, 1977-90; Eternal Perspective Ministries, Gresham, OR, founder and director, 1991—.

WRITINGS:

Christians in the Wake of the Sexual Revolution, Multnomah (Sisters, OR), 1985, published as *Restoring Sexual Sanity,* Coral Ridge Ministries (Fort Lauderdale, FL), 2000.

(With wife, Nanci Alcorn) *Women under Stress: Preserving Your Sanity,* Multnomah (Sisters, OR), 1987.

Money, Possessions, and Eternity, Tyndale House (Wheaton, IL), 1989, revised edition, 2003.

Sexual Temptation, InterVarsity Press (Downers Grove, IL), 1989.

Is Rescuing Right? Breaking the Law to Save the Unborn, InterVarsity Press (Downers Grove, IL), 1990.

ProLife Answers to ProChoice Arguments, Multnomah (Sisters, OR), 1994.

Deadline (novel), Multnomah (Sisters, OR), 1994.

Dominion (novel), Multnomah (Sisters, OR), 1996.

Does the Birth Control Pill Cause Abortions?, privately printed, 1997.

Edge of Eternity (novel), WaterBrook (Colorado Springs, CO), 1998.

In Light of Eternity: Perspectives on Heaven, Water-Brook (Colorado Springs, CO), 1999.

Lord Foulgrin's Letters: How to Strike Back at the Tyrant by Deceiving and Destroying His Human Vermin (novel), Multnomah (Sisters, OR), 2001, revised edition, 2001.

Safely Home (novel), Tyndale House (Wheaton, IL), 2001.

(With daughters, Angela Alcorn and Karina Alcorn) *The Ishbane Conspiracy* (novel), Multnomah (Sisters, OR), 2001.

The Treasure Principle, Multnomah (Sisters, OR), 2001.

The Purity Principle, Multnomah (Sisters, OR), 2003.

The Grace and Truth Paradox, Multnomah (Sisters, OR), 2003.

The Law of Rewards, Tyndale House (Wheaton, IL), 2003.

Heaven: Biblical Answers to Common Questions, Tyndale House (Wheaton, IL), 2004.

Why Prolife?, Multnomah (Sisters, OR), 2004.

Heaven, Tyndale House (Carol Stream, IL), 2004.

(With Linda Washington) *Heaven for Kids,* Tyndale House (Carol Springs, IL), 2006.

50 Days of Heaven: Reflections that Bring Eternity to Light, Tyndale House (Carol Stream, IL), 2006.

Wait until Then, Tyndale House (Carol Springs, IL), 2007.

Deception (novel), Multnomah (Colorado Springs, CO), 2007.

Tell Me about Heaven (juvenile), illustrated by Ron Di-Cianni, Crossway Books (Wheaton, IL), 2007.

SIDELIGHTS: Randy Alcorn once told *CA:* "I have no illusions that I can accomplish anything of value apart from Christ. My desire is to be used of God to help people learn to see the invisible, to gain an eternal perspective, and to live each day with heaven in mind.

"Books I've been greatly influenced by: C.S. Lewis's *Space Trilogy, Chronicles of Narnia, Screwtape Letters,* and *Mere Christianity;* A.W. Tozer's *Knowledge of the Holy;* Francis Schaeffer's *He Is There* and *He Is Not Silent;* John Piper's *Desiring God.*"

BIOGRAPHICAL AND CRITICAL SOURCES:

PERIODICALS

Booklist, December 15, 1994, John Mort, review of *Deadline,* p. 737.

Library Journal, November 1, 1994, Henry Carrigan, Jr., review of *Deadline,* p. 64; June 1, 2000, Melanie C. Duncan, review of *Lord Foulgrin's Letters: How to Strike Back at the Tyrant by Deceiving and Destroying His Human Vermin,* p. 104.

Publishers Weekly, July 12, 1985, William Griffin, review of *Christians in the Wake of a Sexual Revolution,* p. 35.

ONLINE

Eternal Perception Ministries, http://www.epm.org (April 7, 2007).

[Sketch reviewed by ministry assistant, Linda Jeffries.]

* * *

ALCORN, Randy C.
    See ALCORN, Randy

* * *

ANDREWS, Lori B.

PERSONAL: Born 1952; female. *Education:* Yale University, B.A., (summa cum laude), J.D., 1978.

ADDRESSES: Office—Chicago-Kent College of Law, Illinois Institute of Technology, 565 West Adams St., Chicago, IL 60661-3691. *E-mail*—landrews@kentlaw.edu.

CAREER: American Bar Foundation, research fellow, 1980-92; Center for Clinical Medical Ethics, University of Chicago, senior scholar, 1989—; Chicago-Kent College of Law, Illinois Institute of Technology, became Distinguished Professor of Law, director of the Institute of Science, Law and Technology, and associate vice president. Visiting professor, Princeton University, 2002.

Taught health law courses at University of Houston Law Center, University of Chicago School of Law and School of Business; chair for Working Group on Ethical, Legal, and Social Implications of the Human Genome Project. Consultant to organizations including the World Health Organization, the Department of Health and Human Services, the Institute of Medicine of the National Academy of Sciences, and the French National Assembly. Guest on television programs, including *Nightline* and *Oprah*.

AWARDS, HONORS: Named One of the 100 Most Influential Lawyers in America, *National Law Journal*, 1991.

WRITINGS:

Birth of a Salesman: Lawyer Advertising and Solicitation, ABA Press (Chicago, IL), 1980.
The Rights of Fair Trial and Free Press, ABA Press (Chicago, IL), 1981.
Deregulating Doctoring: Do Medical Licensing Laws Meet Today's Health Care Needs?, People's Medical Society (Emmaus, PA), 1983.
New Conceptions: A Consumer's Guide to the Newest Infertility Treatments, Including In Vitro Fertilization, Artificial Insemination, and Surrogate Motherhood, St. Martin's Press (New York, NY), 1984.
(Editor) *Legal Liability and Quality Assurance in Newborn Screening*, American Bar Foundation (Chicago, IL), 1985.
State Laws and Regulations Governing Newborn Screening, American Bar Foundation (Chicago, IL), 1985.
Between Strangers: Surrogate Mothers, Expectant Fathers, and Brave New Babies, Harper & Row (New York, NY), 1989.
(Editor, with Jane E. Fullarton, Kathi E. Hanna, Neil A. Holtzman, and Arno G. Motulsky) *Assessing Genetic Risks: Implications for Health and Social Policy*, National Academy Press (Washington, DC), 1994.
Black Power, White Blood: The Life and Times of Johnny Spain (biography), Pantheon Books (New York, NY), 1996.
(Editor, with Bartha Maria Knoppers, Claude M. Laberge, and Maria Hirtle) *Human DNA: Law and Policy*, Kluwer Law International (The Netherlands), 1997.
The Clone Age: Adventures in the New World of Reproductive Technology, Henry Holt (New York, NY), 1999.

(With Dorothy Nelkin) *Body Bazaar: The Market for Human Tissue in the Biotechnology Age*, Crown (New York, NY), 2001.
Future Perfect: Confronting Decisions about Genetics, Columbia University Press (New York, NY), 2001.
(With Maxwell J. Mehlman and Mark A. Rothstein) *Genetics: Ethics, Law, and Policy*, West Group (St. Paul, MN), 2002, 2nd edition, 2006.
Sequence (novel), St. Martin's Minotaur (New York, NY), 2006.

Contributor to books, including *Behavioral Genetics and Society: The Clash of Culture and Biology*, edited by M. Rothstein and R. Carson, Johns Hopkins University Press, 1999; and *Americans with Disabilities: Exploring Implications of the Law for Individuals and Institutions*, edited by Francis and Anita Silvers, Routledge (New York, NY), 2000. Contributor of articles to journals and periodicals, including *Salon.com*, *Orgyn*, *Legal Medicine*, *Chronicle of Higher Education*, *Yale Journal of Biology and Medicine*, *Pediatrics*, *New York Times Magazine*, and *New England Journal of Medicine*.

SIDELIGHTS: Lori B. Andrews, a leading scholar in the field of health law, is known for her particular expertise in matters relating to new reproductive technologies. She has written numerous articles, book chapters, and monographs for specialists in these fields, as well as several books intended for general audiences.

Reviewers have praised the thoroughness and clarity with which Andrews explains complex medical procedures and legal implications in her books. In addition, they have noted her sensitivity to the often bewildering emotions and choices confronting infertile couples. In *New Conceptions: A Consumer's Guide to the Newest Infertility Treatments, Including In Vitro Fertilization, Artificial Insemination, and Surrogate Motherhood*, Andrews covers the physiology of infertility, the emotions it can provoke, and a range of alternative procedures available to would-be parents. Critics found the book a helpful guide. A writer for *Kirkus Reviews* hailed it as "sympathetic, informed . . . [and] distinctly ahead of others in the legal department." *Booklist*'s Micaela D. Sullivan praised it as "a sensitive and expedient text," while Karen Jackson, in *Library Journal*, especially noted Andrews's attention to the emotional issues surrounding infertility and the possible environmental hazards to reproductive health.

In a subsequent book, Andrews focuses on the increasingly controversial subject of surrogate motherhood. By the time *Between Strangers: Surrogate Mothers, Expect-*

ant Fathers, and Brave New Babies was published in 1989, Americans had become familiar with the difficult legal case involving "Baby M," a girl born to surrogate mother Mary Beth Whitehead in 1986. Whitehead had agreed to bear the child for Elizabeth and William Stern, who chose not to risk a biological pregnancy because Elizabeth Stern had multiple sclerosis, a progressive disease that pregnancy could worsen. After the baby was born, however, Whitehead changed her mind about relinquishing the infant, and a bitter legal battle ensued. The judge who decided the case in 1988 awarded custody to the Sterns but gave Whitehead liberal visitation rights. In *Between Strangers,* Andrews presents both the history of surrogate motherhood and personal stories from individuals who had made this choice. Though the book addresses the potential dilemmas that could stem from surrogate arrangements, Andrews argues that surrogacy should be permitted among consenting adults who pass medical and psychological screening tests.

Between Strangers received considerable attention from critics. Susan Chollar, in *Psychology Today,* appreciated Andrews's "intriguing insights" and thorough understanding of legal and political issues. Her book, noted Chollar, compels us to tackle issues of morality, ethics, law, and parental love. "Andrews challenges us," wrote Chollar, to weigh "whether the bond between a mother and child is qualitatively different, more permanent, or more compelling than the bond between a man and the child born of his seed." However, in the *Journal of the American Medical Association,* Myron W. Conovitz disagreed with the position Andrews takes in the book. Conovitz suggested that allowing surrogate contracts to remain unregulated may not contribute to the well-being of those involved, especially the child. Nevertheless, Conovitz found *Between Strangers* "reasonably balanced" and containing "significant facts about the surrogate movement as it has evolved in this country."

Andrews continued her analysis of pioneering reproductive technologies in *The Clone Age: Adventures in the New World of Reproductive Technology.* Although she had advocated for new high-tech solutions in her previous work, in this book she opposes the cloning of human beings. Andrews argues that cloning, which produces genetic duplicates of an animal from one or more donor cells, creates social and legal problems that society is unprepared to confront. She further suggests that cloning is fundamentally different from other reproductive innovations. Critics noted that Andrews's experience serving as chair of the Working Group on

the Ethical, Legal, and Social Implications of the Human Genome Project, from which she resigned because funding issues compromised the group's ability to function impartially, gave her an insider's perspective into the field and alerted her to the potential dangers of commercial interests' involvement in cloning. In the *New York Times Book Review,* John R.G. Turner recognized this influence, commenting that Andrews depicts research doctors and scientists in her book as "considerably greedy." Though Turner found this stance a bit harsh, and questioned Andrews's rejection of cloning as a reasonable reproductive alternative, he deemed *The Clone Age* "a fine and readable book" that is distinguished by its lucidity, humor, and sensitivity.

Andrews explores the repercussions of genetic screening in *Future Perfect: Confronting Decisions about Genetics.* As in her earlier works, she provides a realistic and readable look at the subject, pointing out the dangers associated with genetic screening as well as its benefits. Her book shows that already, genetic screening has negatively affected certain peoples' ability to gain employment and be approved for insurance. She examines the privacy issues inherent in genetic screening and shows how bias against women and ethnic minorities has already surfaced in connection with genetic screening. Noting that there are many books on this topic, a *Library Journal* reviewer nevertheless pointed out: "Andrews's legal insight and her ability to look beyond the superficial issues provide a breath of fresh air."

In addition to her many books on health law, Andrews wrote a biography of Black Panther leader Johnny Spain, who was convicted of a robbery-murder in 1966 at age seventeen and was incarcerated in San Quentin for twenty-two years. Reviewers considered Spain a fascinating subject: born to a black father and a white mother married to a white man, the boy spent his first years with his mother but was soon sent to California to be adopted by a black couple, with whom he spent an unhappy childhood. Radicalized by a prison experience exacerbated by institutionalized racism, Spain joined the Black Panthers and helped lead the organization from behind bars. After his parole in 1988, he became a community activist in San Francisco. Andrews's account of Spain's life, *Black Power, White Blood: The Life and Times of Johnny Spain,* received mixed reviews. In *Booklist,* June Vigor called the biography "gripping and inspiring," but also "uneven." A writer for *Publishers Weekly* commented that, despite describing "moments both sad and stirring," the book did not provide sufficient information about Spain's life after parole. And Paul Ruffins, writing in *Washington Post Book World,* criticized Andrews for a strong bias in favor of her subject. "Andrews . . . is so sympathetic to Spain that the book is essentially a memoir," he wrote. Noting that Andrews displayed good insights in the book but too often failed to pursue them in sufficient depth, Ruffins concluded: "Andrews is a fine stylist who makes us care about Spain and his suffering, but she diminishes her book by settling for reporting rather than analysis."

Andrews returned to her study of bioethics with *The Body Bazaar: The Market for Human Tissue in the Biotechnology Age.* This book examines the social, psychological, and economic effects that could result from commercial trade in human tissue and organs. Although the physical worth of the chemicals and minerals making up the human body was once calculated to be less than one dollar, that value has skyrocketed as more and more technologies make use of human tissue. Blood, organs, and fetal tissue are all in demand, to the extent that a black market for them exists, and crimes have been committed to obtain them. Further ethical considerations are brought up by individuals who wish to use body parts as part of their artistic projects. Andrews and her coauthor, Dorothy Nelkin, pose questions about body ownership and other such issues in *Body Bazaar.* It is "a highly readable, extraordinarily researched book," according to Elizabeth M. Whelan in *Insight on the News.*

Andrews tried her hand at fiction in 2006 with the novel *Sequence.* It concerns a geneticist, Alexandra Blake, who reluctantly complies when her government employers tell her to set aside her research projects to help locate a serial killer. Alexandra, a quirky individualist who is the daughter of a deceased Vietnam War veteran, only wants to make progress on her gene-sequencing work, but when she finally puts her mind to unraveling the case, she proves to be an effective investigator. The author shows only "workmanlike" skill as a novelist, according to a *Kirkus Reviews* writer. Davit Pitt, writing in *Booklist,* pointed to a "somewhat amateurish" quality to the dialog and certain stylistic habits of the author, but concluded that *Sequence* "generates plenty of excitement."

BIOGRAPHICAL AND CRITICAL SOURCES:

PERIODICALS

Booklist, January 1, 1984, Micaela D. Sullivan, review of *New Conceptions: A Consumer's Guide to the Newest Infertility Treatments, Including In Vitro Fertilization, Artificial Insemination, and Surrogate Motherhood,* p. 658; June 1, 1996, June Vigor, review of *Black Power, White Blood: The Life and Times of Johnny Spain,* p. 1639; April 15, 1999, William Beatty, review of *The Clone Age: Adventure in the New World of Reproductive Technology,* p. 1487; January 1, 2001, Gilbert Taylor, review of *Body Bazaar: The Market for Human Tissue in the Biotechnology Age,* p. 879; March 15, 2001, Vernon Ford, review of *Future Perfect: Confronting Decisions about Genetics,* p. 1339; March 1, 2006, David Pitt, review of *Sequence,* p. 70.

Business Wire, March 21, 2000, "Lori Andrews, 'Genetics Laureate,' Joins Metamarkets Think Tank," p. 1138.

Ethnic and Racial Studies, March, 2001, Ellis Cashmore, "Black Culture: Scholarly Interest, or Unhealthy Obsession?," p. 318.

Insight on the News, May 28, 2001, Elizabeth M. Whelan, review of *Body Bazaar,* p. 27.

Journal of the American Medical Association, February 23, 1990, Myron W. Conovitz, review of *Between Strangers: Surrogate Mothers, Expectant Fathers, and Brave New Babies,* p. 1153.

Judicature, November, 1999, Dena S. Davis, review of *The Clone Age,* p. 162.

Kirkus Reviews, November 1, 1983, review of *New Conceptions,* p. 1152; May 1, 2006, review of *Sequence,* p. 423.

Library Journal, January, 1984, Karen Jackson, review of *New Conceptions,* p. 103; June 1, 1999, Tina Neville, review of *The Clone Age,* p. 155; March 15, 2001, Tina Neville, review of *Future Perfect,* p. 100; June 1, 2006, Nanci Milone Hill, review of *Sequence,* p. 104.

New York Law Journal, September 8, 2006, Joan Ullman, review of *Sequence.*

New York Times Book Review, September 19, 1999, John R.G. Turner, review of *The Clone Age,* p. 14.

Psychology Today, June, 1989, Susan Chollar, review of *Between Strangers,* p. 76.

Publishers Weekly, May 20, 1986, review of *Black Power, White Blood,* p. 248; April 12, 1999, review of *The Clone Age,* p. 64; April 10, 2006, review of *Sequence,* p. 47.

Science News, February 28, 1998, Susan Milius, "Science Pokes Loopholes in Cloning Bans," p. 137.

Soujourners, March, 2000, Joseph Wakelee-Lynch, review of *The Clone Age,* p. 55.

Trial, July, 1999, "Genetics, Reproduction, and the Law" (interview with Lori B. Andrews), p. 20.

Washington Monthly, May, 2001, Jacob Heilbrunn, review of *Body Bazaar,* p. 56.

Washington Post, May 26, 1999, Jonathan Yardley, review of *The Clone Age,* p. C2.

Washington Post Book World, August 25, 1996, Paul Ruffins, "Another Soledad Brother," pp. 45.

ONLINE

Chicago-Kent College of Law Web site, http://www.kentlaw.edu/(February 5, 2007), biographical information about Lori B. Andrews.*

*   *   *

ARANA, Marie 1949-

PERSONAL: Born September 15, 1949, in Lima, Peru; immigrated to the United States, 1959; daughter of Jorge Enrique (an engineer) and Marie Elverine Arana; married Wendell B. Ward, Jr., December 18, 1972 (divorced, 1998); married Jonathan Yardley, March 21, 1999; children: Hilary Walsh, Adam Williamson Ward. *Education:* Northwestern University, B.A., 1971; Yale University in China, certificate of scholarship, 1976; British University, M.A., 1977.

ADDRESSES: Home—Washington, DC, and Lima, Peru. *Office*—c/o Washington Post, 1150 15th St., NW, Washington, DC 20071-0002. *E-mail*—aranam@washpost.com.

CAREER: Journalist, critic, editor, novelist. British University, Hong Kong, lecturer in linguistics, 1978-79; Harcourt, Brace, Jovanovich, New York, NY, senior editor, 1980-89; Simon & Schuster, New York, NY, senior editor and vice president, 1989-92; *Washington Post,* writer and editor, 1992-99, *Book World,* editor-in-chief, 1999—. Director and member of board of Center for Policy Research, Washington, DC, 1994-99.

MEMBER: National Association of Hispanic Journalists (member of board of directors, 1996-99), National Book Critics Circle (member of board of directors, 1996-2000).

AWARDS, HONORS: Award for excellence in editing, ABA, 1985; Christopher Award for excellence in editing, 1986; finalist, National Book Award and PEN Memoir Award, for *American Chica.*

WRITINGS:

American Chica: Two Worlds, One Childhood, Dial Press (New York, NY), 2001.

(Editor and author of introduction) *The Writing Life: Writers on How They Think and Work: A Collection from the Washington Post Book World,* Public Affairs (New York, NY), 2003.

Cellophane: A Novel, Dial Press (New York, NY), 2006.

Editor of *Studies in Bilingualism,* 1978.

SIDELIGHTS: Marie Arana spent the first several decades of her career as a journalist, editor, and critic judging the writing of others. When her own work, a memoir titled *American Chica: Two Worlds, One Childhood,* was published by Dial Press in 2001, Arana decided that it would not be reviewed in *Book World,* the respected weekly book review section she oversees for the *Washington Post.*

Arana's parents met in the 1940s when her father, Jorge Enrique Arana, was studying at the Massachusetts Institute of Technology. Her mother, Marie, was a violinist. After they married, they returned to her father's native country of Peru, where Arana was born and spent her early childhood until the family moved to the United States in 1959. As Arana describes it in *American Chica,* it was a childhood "rooted to the Andean dust" in the family's hacienda in Cartavio, Peru. Her father was working as an engineer for the multinational corporation W.R. Grace. Her mother was not welcomed into her husband's culture, and when the couple returned to the United States and settled in Summit, New Jersey, Arana would first feel the sting of those cultural differences. She relates in her memoir that on a train ride west to visit her mother's family in Wyoming, another passenger looked at her and remarked, "Well, I'll be. She's a little foreigner." In New Jersey the Aranas were the only Hispanic family. One black girl told her, "You oughta go back where you belong." With a father who went back and forth between Peru and the United States and an awareness of the cultural gap between her parents, Arana realized early on that she would have to be adaptable, sometimes filling the role befitting her dark Peruvian features and sometimes the role of an American girl with an American heritage.

Arana studied Russian language and literature at Northwestern University, where she received her degree in 1971. Her early marriage in 1972 to Wendell Ward took her to Hong Kong, where she received a certificate of scholarship in the Mandarin language through Yale University in China and a master's degree in linguistics from the British University there in 1977, while she also taught linguistics. When she returned to the United States, she worked as an editor at Harcourt, Brace, Jovanovich and at Simon & Schuster, dividing her time between New York and Washington, DC Focusing on nonfiction, she worked with such authors as Eugene McCarthy and Pat Moynihan, both former U.S. senators. She also enjoyed working on fiction and edited the works of such novelists as Stanley Elkin and Manuel Puig. By 1992 Arana had joined the *Post* as deputy book editor, and eventually she rose to editor of its weekly book review supplement, *Book World.*

Arana revealed in a *Publishers Weekly* interview with Joseph Barbato that it was a comment made on her first day on the job that marked a new beginning for her—thinking of herself as a member of a minority group. She told Barbato: "My first day on the job, the head of recruitment stopped when she saw on my forms that I was born in Lima. 'Oh, are you a minority hire?' she asked me, wondering how to put me down. 'Well, I guess you could say so,' I told her." Arana realized she was a member of a growing group of Americans, that of a minority, and she began to serve on various committees on diversity, working to get more coverage of the Hispanic population into the newspaper. As a panel moderator for the National Association of Hispanic Journalists, she realized that her sense of her own Latina identity was not easy to define. "When I was in either place, Peru or the U.S., I felt one parent was a blip," Arana told Barbato. "My own experience was of blipping in and out; of belonging and not belonging." It was a fellow panelist, the poet Judith Ortiz Cofer, who afterward encouraged her to write a memoir.

For Arana, writing *American Chica* represented more than the publication of her first book. "I had done a good job of burying the child I was. As I wrote, I found there was something very rigid and false about the armor I had built around myself. I was always the professional businesswoman who was a certain way—who would never want to have anything but a perfect life revealed," she told Barbato. Writing the book not only transformed her emotions but brought about the end of her marriage when she realized she was in love with a fellow *Post* staffer, the book critic Jonathan Yardley, who was reading each chapter as she finished it. Yardley came to realize that he was in love with her as well. Their lives changed dramatically as they left their

respective families and eventually married. All of this dramatic change was the result of writing a book she had not set out to write.

In 1996 Arana was on a one-month media fellowship at Stanford University. When she completed her project, she researched the story of Julio Cesar Arana, an infamous Peruvian rubber baron known in the early 1900s as the "Devil of Putumayo." He imposed cruel and unusual punishments on his workers, the thousands of indigenous peoples working the rubber plantations. His scandalous behavior was eventually exposed to international scrutiny by an Irish patriot named Roger Casement. Although Arana was told repeatedly by her family that he was not a relative, she nonetheless maintained the suspicion that he was. While sifting through the stacks of information she found at Stanford on this vicious man, Arana became absorbed in wondering what it might mean if he were a relative. And then she began to think about her childhood, caught between two different worlds.

When an enthusiastic book agent responded positively to sample pages of the book Arana had begun to write, she decided to take an eight-month leave of absence from her job at the *Post* in order to finish it. During that time she returned to the Peru of her early childhood to explore more fully the story of the possible ancestor. Not only did she find out that she was indeed related to Julio Cesar Arana, but she had the unsettling experience of being told by a local historian that she "had his face." It was then that she decided the book would be the story of her parents.

In her review for the *New York Times Book Review,* Wendy Gimbel characterized *American Chica* as a work that sometimes reads like "a collaboration between John Cheever and Isabel Allende. Arana's mother and father constantly lose their balance as they stumble over cultural minefields. Of free-spirited pioneer stock, the young wife feels shackled, the prisoner of Peru's demanding traditions. But her husband doesn't understand her need to turn her back on the past." Barbara Wallraff noted in her review for the *Atlantic Monthly* that "a person of a metaphorical turn of mind can read into this book the history of U.S.-Latin American relations, and if that's what you feel like doing, you'll suspect that Arana is abetting you. But the book also reads like a novel—almost. A fiction writer aiming for verisimilitude would have toned some of this material down. Surely no novelist would have had the narrator's mother marry so many times. And no one but Gabriel García Marquez would have dared to invent an adventurer uncle who lends the household a monkey and an anteater. *American Chica* tells a fantastical, spellbinding tale."

Arana noted that during the first four years of her life in Peru, a total of eighteen earthquakes shook the country. She saw those tremors, according to Donna Seaman, writing in *Booklist,* as "emblematic of the forces that jeopardized her family's attempt to span the vast divide between North and South America."

Arana became a first novelist in 2006 with publication of *Cellophane,* a blend of magical realism and realistic fiction, set in the Amazon at the height of the Great Depression. Arana's protagonist is the successful engineer and paper producer Don Victor Sobrevilla, who has carved out a fabulous estate, Floralinda, in the Amazon region of Peru. There he lives with his extended family, on the cusp of a changing world. His great desire has always been to create cellophane, not paper, and when he decides to redirect his mills to that production, "his life and those of the people around him change in unexpected ways, both humorous and tragic," according to *BookPage* contributor Harvey Freedenberg. As with the transparent product at the heart of this novel, Don Victor's decision spawns an avalanche of honesty among his family: he confesses an earlier love affair to his wife, who, in turn, tells him of her own first affair at the same time Don Victor was courting her. Characters discover honesty and transparency are not always the best policies.

Cellophane, with its butterflies appearing out of a doffed hat and strange growths on the bodies of some of the characters, invited obvious comparisons to the work of other Latin American writers of magical realism such as Isabel Allende and Gabriel Garcia Marquez. For Clark Collis, writing in *Entertainment Weekly,* however, despite the book's "richly descriptive and, at times, darkly comic tone," *Cellophane* did not live up to such a lofty comparison. Other reviewers, though, had a more positive assessment of this debut novel. Pope Brock, writing in *People,* noted that even those readers who did not like magical realism "may fall under its spell when it's this well done." Brock went on to call Arana's novel a "great book." *Booklist* contributor Donna Seaman termed the same work a "bewitching story shaped by a profound understanding of the oneness of life," while a *Kirkus Reviews* critic found it a "pleasure to

read." Further praise came from a *Publishers Weekly* reviewer who described *Cellophane* as "a tale as bawdy, raucous and dense as the jungle whose presence encroaches on every page," and from *Miami Herald* writer Fabiola Santiago, who thought it was "exquisitely written." Santiago concluded, "Arana is a finely tuned writer who knows how to harvest her worlds and bring them to the main stage, an intellectual who delivers insight and story in any genre." Liesl Schillinger, writing in the *New York Times,* was also impressed with *Cellophane,* commenting that Arana "has flown above her own history to construct a surreal but orderly pattern: a fiction that's stranger than her truth but shares its bones."

BIOGRAPHICAL AND CRITICAL SOURCES:

BOOKS

Arana, Marie, *American Chica: Two Worlds, One Childhood,* Dial Press (New York, NY), 2001.

PERIODICALS

Atlantic Monthly, June, 2001, Barbara Wallraff, review of *American Chica: Two Worlds, One Childhood,* p. 104.
Booklist, April 15, 2001, Donna Seaman, review of *American Chica,* p. 1511; November 15, 2005, Molly McQuade, "Marie Arana, Book Critic Turned First Novelist," p. 19; May 15, 2006, Donna Seaman, review of *Cellophane,* p. 21.
Entertainment Weekly, May 11, 2001, review of *American Chica,* p. 74; June 30, 2006, Clark Collis, review of *Cellophane,* p. 166.
Fort Worth Star-Telegram (Ft. Worth, TX), August 7, 2001, Rebecca Rodriguez, "Visiting the Compelling World of an 'American Chica.'"
Hispanic Magazine, September, 2001, Gigi Anders, "Marie Arana: American Chica."
Houston Chronicle (Houston, TX), August 22, 2001, Malinda Nash, "Life from Both Sides: Marie Arana Memoir Probes Her Family's Biculturalism."
Kirkus Reviews, May 15, 2006, review of *Cellophane,* p. 475.
Library Journal, April 15, 2001, Adriana Lopez, review of *American Chica,* p. 106, and Rebecca Miller, "Bridging a Bicultural Divide," p. 112; June 15, 2006, Jennifer Stidham, review of *Cellophane,* p. 54.

Miami Herald (Miami, FL), July 5, 2006, Fabiola Santiago, review of *Cellophane.*

New York Times, July 16, 2006, Liesl Schillinger, "A Wilderness of Mud," review of *Cellophane.*

New York Times Book Review, May 13, 2001, Wendy Gimbel, "Bilingual Education: Born to a Peruvian Father and an American Mother, Author Examines Her Hyphenated Life," p. 7.

People, July 3, 2006, Pope Brock, review of *Cellophane,* p. 47.

Publishers Weekly, April 2, 2001, review of *American Chica,* p. 48; June 4, 2001, Joseph Barbato, "Uniting Worlds Through Language," p. 51; April 24, 2006, review of *Cellophane,* p. 37.

ONLINE

BookPage, http://www.bookpage.com/ (December 18, 2006), Harvey Freedenberg, review of *Cellophane.*

Salon.com, http:// www.salon.com/ (July 15, 1999), Craig Offman, "Washington Post Book World Editor Steps Down."

Washington Independent Writers, http://www.washwriter.org/ (December 18, 2006), "Marie Arana."

Washington Post, http: //www.washpost.com/ (September 13, 2001), "Testimonials: Marie Arana."*

*   *   *

ARTHUR, Anthony 1937-

PERSONAL: Born January 20, 1937, in Sharon, PA; son of R.S. (in newspaper advertising) and Helen Arthur; married Carolyn Taylor, September 1, 1963; children: Reagan (daughter), Owen. *Education:* Allegheny College, B.A., 1960; Pennsylvania State University, M.A., 1963; State University of New York at Stony Brook, Ph.D., 1970.

ADDRESSES: Home—Woodland Hills, CA. *Agent*—Deborah Grosvenor, Grosvenor Literary Agency, 5510 Grosvenor Ln., Bethesda, MD 20814. *E-mail*—anthonyarth@gmail.com.

CAREER: California State University, Northridge, faculty member of English department, 1970-2002. Fulbright lecturer in Budapest, Hungary, 1980, Szeged, Hungary, 1990-91, and Dortmund, Germany, 2006.

Distinguished visiting professor, U.S. Air Force Academy, 1994-95. *Military service:* U.S. Army, Korean linguist, 1956-59.

WRITINGS:

NONFICTION

(Editor, with Peter Brier) *American Prose and Criticism, 1900-1950,* Thomson Gale (Detroit, MI), 1981.

(Editor) *Critical Essays on Wallace Stegner,* G.K. Hall (Boston, MA), 1981.

Deliverance at Los Baños, St. Martin's (New York, NY), 1985.

Forgotten Warriors: The Bushmasters, St. Martin's (New York, NY), 1987.

The Tailor-King: The Rise and Fall of the Anabaptist Kingdom of Münster, Thomas Dunne Books (New York, NY), 1999.

Literary Feuds: A Century of Celebrated Quarrels from Mark Twain to Tom Wolfe, Thomas Dunne Books (New York, NY), 2002.

(With John Broesamle) *Clashes of Will: Great Confrontations That Have Shaped Modern America,* Pearson/Longman (New York, NY), 2005, revised edition published as *Twelve Great Clashes That Shaped Modern America,* 2006.

Radical Innocent: Upton Sinclair, Random House (New York, NY), 2006.

SIDELIGHTS: Anthony Arthur's 1994 book, *The Tailor-King: The Rise and Fall of the Anabaptist Kingdom of Münster,* discusses a religious uprising that occurred in northern Germany in the year 1534. At its center was a militantly anti-Catholic group called the Anabaptists. Believing that the second coming of Christ was imminent, some nine thousand members of the sect barricaded themselves in their town and proceeded to violently impose their beliefs all who opposed them. Arthur tells in "riveting" style about the ways religious faith clashed with state authority, drawing parallels between the events of that time with those in the contemporary world, according to Steven Schroeder in *Booklist.* A *Publishers Weekly* reviewer called the book "vividly written and credibly researched" as well as "entertaining."

Literary Feuds: A Century of Celebrated Quarrels from Mark Twain to Tom Wolfe recounts the background and history of authorial sparring between such famous writers as Bret Harte and Mark Twain, Gertrude Stein and Ernest Hemingway, and Tom Wolfe and John Updike. Arthur notes in his book that his interest in writing it was not to chastise the authors involved for their infighting, but to show the often complex relationship between a writer's life and work. A *Kirkus Reviews* writer recommended it as "an amusing compendium of the vitriol and ego for which our most enduring writers somehow set aside the time."

Radical Innocent: Upton Sinclair traces the ups and downs of the life of Sinclair, who shot to fame after the 1906 publication of his book *The Jungle*. Though it was fiction, *The Jungle* was a realistic work based on Sinclair's thorough investigation into the practices of the meat-packing industry. What he revealed was enough to prompt the passage of safe-food laws, as well as to raise awareness of the horrifying conditions under which many laborers of the time were forced to work. Sinclair was paradoxical in many ways, with the actions of his life often seeming to be at odds with his professed philosophical and political beliefs. Arthur's book is "an immensely readable biography" written with "a deft, light touch," according to a *Kirkus Reviews* writer. Another enthusiastic review came from Tom Carson, who in *Los Angeles* called *Radical Innocent* "a model of good biography, uncommonly well wrought and continually interesting."

BIOGRAPHICAL AND CRITICAL SOURCES:

PERIODICALS

Booklist, September 15, 1999, Steven Schroeder, review of *The Tailor-King: The Rise and Fall of the Anabaptist Kingdom of Münster,* p. 219; October 15, 2002, Trygve Thoreson, review of *Literary Feuds: A Century of Celebrated Quarrels from Mark Twain to Tom Wolfe,* p. 377; June 1, 2006, Donna Seaman, review of *Radical Innocent: Upton Sinclair,* p. 24.
Christian Century, December 12, 2006, review of *Radical Innocent,* p. 23.
Columbia Journalism Review, July-August, 2006, Julia M. Klein, review of *Radical Innocent,* p. 58.
Financial Times, July 1, 2006, Ludovic Hunter-Tilney, review of *Radical Innocent,* p. 33.
Historian, fall, 2002, Michael A. Hakkenberg, review of *The Tailor-King,* p. 201.
Kirkus Reviews, September 1, 2002, review of *Literary Feuds,* p. 1273; March 15, 2006, review of *Radical Innocent,* p. 269.

Library Journal, September 1, 1999, Randall L. Schroeder, review of *The Tailor-King,* p. 209; October 1, 2002, Rebecca Bollen, review of *Literary Feuds,* p. 93; April 15, 2006, Diane Fulkerson, review of *Radical Innocent,* p. 85.
Los Angeles, June, 2006, Tom Carson, review of *Radical Innocent,* p. 140.
National Review, August 28, 2006, John Wilson, review of *Radical Innocent,* p. 45.
Philadelphia Inquirer, April 22, 2003, Carlin Romano, review of *Literary Feuds.*
Publishers Weekly, August 2, 1999, review of *The Tailor-King,* p. 66; March 13, 2006, review of *Radical Innocent,* p. 50.

ONLINE

Anthony Arthur Home Page, http://www.anthonyarthur. net/ (February 28, 2007).
Book Reporter, http://www.bookreporter.com/ (February 28, 2007), Toni Fitzgerald, review of *Literary Feuds.**

* * *

AUSTIN, James H. 1925-
(James Henry Austin)

PERSONAL: Born January 4, 1925, in Cleveland, OH; son of Paul Weber (an advertising artist) and Bertha Emily Austin; married Judith St. Clair, February 7, 1948; children: Scott W., Lynn St. Clair, Austin Manning, James W. *Ethnicity:* "German/English/Swiss." *Education:* Brown University, A.B. (magna cum laude), 1944; Harvard University, M.D. (cum laude), 1948. *Politics:* "Liberal Republican—Independent." *Religion:* "Unitarian/Zen Buddhist." *Hobbies and other interests:* The outdoors, fishing, gardening, pottery, calligraphy.

ADDRESSES: Home and office—Columbia, MO.

CAREER: Boston City Hospital, Boston, MA, medical intern, 1948-49, assistant resident in neurology, 1949-50; Columbia University, New York, NY, fellow in neuropathology, 1953-55; University of Oregon, Health Sciences Center (now Oregon Health Sciences University) Portland, began as associate, became professor of health sciences, 1955-67; University of Colorado Health Sciences Center, Denver, professor of neurology, 1967-

92, professor emeritus, 1992—, department chair, 1967-83; University of Idaho, Moscow, affiliate professor of philosophy, 1998; University of Missouri, Columbia, clinical professor of neurology, 2005—. *Military service:* U.S. Naval Reserve, Medical Corps, active duty, 1943-45, 1950-52.

MEMBER: American Neurological Association (member of council, 1979-82), American Academy of Neurology, Scientific and Medical Network, Sigma Xi.

AWARDS, HONORS: American Neuropathology Prize, 1959; book prize, Scientific and Medical Network, 1998, for *Zen and the Brain: Toward an Understanding of Meditation and Consciousness;* lifetime achievement award, United Leukodystrophy Foundation, 2004.

WRITINGS:

Chase, Chance, and Creativity, Columbia University Press (New York, NY), 1978.
Zen and the Brain: Toward an Understanding of Meditation and Consciousness, MIT Press (Cambridge, MA), 1998.
Zen-Brain Reflections: Reviewing Recent Developments in Meditation and States of Consciousness, MIT Press (Cambridge, MA), 2006.

Work represented in anthologies, including *America at the Millennium,* International Library of Poetry, 2000. Contributor of more than 100 articles to scientific journals.

Some of Austin's writings have been translated into Japanese and Chinese.

SIDELIGHTS: James H. Austin once told *CA:* "I've been mostly inspired by my ignorance—about creativity and about Zen. This motivated me to learn more about each topic, both through observing my inner psychophysiological processes and through library research, using journal articles and books. I enjoy making the path clearer for the next generation of seekers.

"My writing goes through a series of drafts. Only in the course of these does literary clarity emerge. At the same time, I repair my ignorance, discovering new connections.

"One pleasant surprise has been the continuing response shown to my literary construct of a person's luck coming in four different forms: 'The Varieties of Chance.' The 1974 *Saturday Review* article and the chapter on the psychology of luck in my first book continue to find their way into textbooks of college English, [such as] *Contemporary College Reader,* 1981; *Strategies—A Rhetoric and Reader,* 1988; [and] *The Sundance Writer,* 2000."

BIOGRAPHICAL AND CRITICAL SOURCES:

PERIODICALS

Best Sellers, May, 1978, review of *Chase, Chance, and Creativity.*
Boston Book Review, October, 1999, review of *Zen and the Brain: Toward an Understanding of Meditation and Consciousness,* p. 14.
Choice, July-August, 1978, review of *Chase, Chance, and Creativity.*
Library Journal, May 15, 1978, review of *Chase, Chance, and Creativity.*
Washington Post, April 9, 1978, Anthony Starr, review of *Chase, Chance, and Creativity.*

*   *   *

AUSTIN, James Henry
   See AUSTIN, James H.

*   *   *

AXFORD, Elizabeth C. 1958-
   (Elizabeth Carole Axford)

PERSONAL: Born December 21, 1958, in Van Nuys, CA; daughter of Roy A. (a professor of nuclear engineering) and Anne R. (a homemaker) Axford; married Robert J. Somers, May 5, 1979 (divorced April 24, 1984). *Ethnicity:* "Caucasian." *Education:* University of Illinois at Urbana-Champaign, B.A., 1982; San Diego State University, M.A., 1995. *Religion:* Christian. *Hobbies and other interests:* Walking, reading, film.

ADDRESSES: Home—Del Mar, CA. *Office*—Piano Press Studio, P.O. Box 85, Del Mar, CA 92014-0085; fax: 858-755-1104. *E-mail*—lizaxford@pianopress.com.

CAREER: Piano Press Studio, Miami, FL, instructor in piano and music theory, 1984-92; Piano Press Studio, Del Mar, CA, instructor in piano and music theory, 1992—. Piano Press, owner; Nashville Songwriters Association International, coordinator of regional workshops, 1990—; public speaker at camps, festivals, conferences, and other venues.

MEMBER: Nashville Songwriters Association International, National Academy of Recording Arts and Sciences, American Society of Composers, Authors, and Publishers, American Federation of Musicians, Music Teachers National Association, National Guild of Piano Teachers, Society of Children's Book Writers and Illustrators, Technology in Music Education, Academy of American Poets, California Association of Professional Music Teachers, Music Teachers Association of California, Pi Kappa Lambda.

AWARDS, HONORS: Awards of appreciation, Nashville Songwriters Association International, 1997, 2000; awards from San Diego Local Authors, 1998—.

WRITINGS:

Traditional World Music Influences in Contemporary Solo Piano Literature: A Selected Bibliographic Survey and Review, Scarecrow Press (Lanham, MD), 1997.

Merry Christmas Happy Hanukkah: A Multilingual Songbook, with compact disc, Piano Press (Del Mar, CA), 1999.

Song Sheets to Software: A Guide to Print Music Software and Web Sites for Musicians, Scarecrow Press (Lanham, MD), 2001, revised edition, 2004.

The Art of Music: A Collection of Writings, Piano Press (Del Mar, CA), Volume 1, 2001, Volume 2, 2003.

My Halloween Fun Book, Piano Press (Del Mar, CA), 2004.

My Christmas Fun Book, Piano Press (Del Mar, CA), 2006.

Songwriter and music arranger, with more than 200 published piano arrangements. Work represented in anthologies, including *The Music Box and Other Delights,* Piano Press (Del Mar, CA), 2003. Author of *"Songwriting and the Web,"* a regular feature in *NSAI Newswire,* and *"Keyboard Chops,"* a series of articles at the Internet Web site *Indie-Music.com.* Contributor to periodicals.

SIDELIGHTS: Elizabeth C. Axford once told *CA:* "I primarily do research for piano teachers and musicians, exploring the contemporary piano repertoire and Internet possibilities. These are areas which I felt needed support, in the interest of both teachers and students, as well as musicians in general.

"Most of my writing so far has involved extensive research and the compiling and organizing of information so others can access it easily. If I see a gap, I try to fill it, doing research where there is a real need. I am at the computer much of the time, but have also spent hours in libraries, at seminars and trade shows, and combing through print music and software catalogs.

"I also compose music for piano and songs, and have published over 200 piano arrangements. I have my own publishing company, Piano Press, and I intend to expand the catalog to include a variety of supplementary materials for piano students and music teachers."

BIOGRAPHICAL AND CRITICAL SOURCES:

ONLINE

Welcome to Piano Press, http://www.pianopress.com (April 7, 2007).

*   *   *

AXFORD, Elizabeth Carole
See AXFORD, Elizabeth C.

B

BAHR, Howard 1946-
(Howard Leslie Bahr)

PERSONAL: Born August 3, 1946, in Meridian, MS; son of Rose Lane. *Education:* University of Mississippi, B.A., 1976, M.A., 1980. *Religion:* Episcopal.

ADDRESSES: Home—Fayetteville, TN. *Agent*—Wendy Sherman, 450 Seventh Ave., Ste. 2307, New York, NY 10123.

CAREER: CB&Q Railroad, East St. Louis, IL, train desk clerk, 1969-70; Southern Railway, East St. Louis, yard clerk, 1969; Illinois Central Railroad, Gulfport, MS, operator and clerk, 1970-73; University of Mississippi, instructor in English, 1982-93, assistant curator of Rowan Oak (home of William Faulkner), 1982-84, curator, 1984-93; Motlow State Community College, Tullahoma, TN, assistant professor, 1993-99, associate professor of English, beginning 1999. Instructor at Northwest Mississippi Junior College, 1980, and Calhoun Community College, 1992. Public speaker, lecturer, and leader of workshops at colleges and universities throughout the South. Also worked briefly as a brakeman for Alabama, Tennessee, and Northern Railway and Missouri Pacific Railroad. *Military service:* U.S. Navy, gunner's mate, 1964-68; received Vietnam Campaign Medal with two stars and Vietnam Defense Medal.

MEMBER: Masons (past master).

AWARDS, HONORS: First place award, short story category, Southern Literary Festival, 1976; Ella Somerville Creative Writing Award for fiction, University of Mississippi, 1985; Adjutant General's Distinguished Patriot Award, Tennessee Army National Guard, 1994; William Young Boyd Military Novel Award, Naval War College and American Library Association, Harold D. Vursell Memorial Award, American Academy of Arts and Letters, and Mississippi Authors Award, Mississippi Library Association, all 1998, for *The Black Flower.*

WRITINGS:

NOVELS

The Black Flower, Nautical and Aviation (Mount Pleasant, SC), 1997.
Home for Christmas (juvenile), Nautical and Aviation (Mount Pleasant, SC), 1997.
The Year of Jubilo, Henry Holt (New York, NY), 2000.
The Judas Field, Henry Holt (New York, NY), 2006.

Contributor to books, including *Critical Essays on William Faulkner: The Sartoris Family,* edited by Arthur Kinney, 1985, and *American Literary Magazines: The Nineteenth Century,* edited by Edward E. Chielens, 1986. Author of "Mixed Train," a monthly column in *Illinois Central,* 1970-73. Contributor of short stories, articles, essays, and reviews to periodicals, including *Saturday Evening Post, Mississippi, Trains, Civil War Times Illustrated, Southern Living,* and *Faulkner Newsletter.*

SIDELIGHTS: Howard Bahr's novels *The Black Flower, The Year of Jubilo,* and *The Judas Field* all concern the Civil War in the United States. The central character in the first of the three is Bushrod Carter, a Confederate soldier enduring a long term of service. He is at once terrified and indifferent about the horrors he knows he may face in future battles. According to Margaret Flanagan in *Booklist, The Black Flower* is a bleak novel that summons up "the senseless agony of armed conflict." The author's "blend of historical fact with gut-wrenching emotion has produced a riveting novel of the Civil War, a frighteningly realistic portrait of men and women caught in an awfulness beyond their control," stated a *Publishers Weekly* reviewer.

The Year of Jubilo focuses on Gawain Harper, a former schoolteacher, as he makes his way back home to Mississippi following his service in the Confederate army. Haunted by his wartime experiences, he hopes to be able to learn to live a normal life once again. Yet even at home he finds the world forever changed. The story portrays "the ambivalence of a man desperately seeking a moral compass in the midst of anarchy and despair," commented Flanagan.

The Judas Field is set twenty years after the Civil War, yet it is still very much concerned with that conflict. Dying of cancer, Alison Sansing is compelled to revisit the Tennessee battlefield where her father and brother died. Her childhood friend Cass, who survived the battle, reluctantly accompanies her, unwilling to revisit the place where he witnessed such horror. "This beautiful novel turns the tables on our view of war," commented Bette-Lee Fox in *Library Journal*. Michele Leber, in a review for *Booklist*, called *The Judas Field* a "beautifully written portrayal of the price that war exacts."

Bahr once told *CA:* "My motivation for writing is the same one expressed by William Faulkner: to tell a story of the human heart in conflict, and to tell it as honestly and as well as I can. I do not believe any writer of fiction can do more, nor should he attempt any less. William Faulkner was the greatest of my influences, followed by Scott Fitzgerald, Loren Eisley, and Stephen Crane. Mark Twain taught me how to write humor, though I will never do it well. My advice to young writers is: Don't be afraid to imitate; it is the process through which you will eventually find your own voice. Other advice to young writers: Get a good day job (teaching is ideal); learn all you can—the names of birds and flowers, the constellations, how to clean a musket, fire a pistol, saddle a horse, change the carburetor in a Chevrolet. These kinds of things make your writing authentic and real, and they help the reader to trust you.

Don't preach. Never have contempt for your characters. Love them all, even the ones you don't like. Write every day. Never go to writing workshops or conferences unless you're being paid to speak. Stay home and write instead. Take your craft seriously, but never yourself."

BIOGRAPHICAL AND CRITICAL SOURCES:

PERIODICALS

Booklist, April 15, 1997, Margaret Flanagan, review of *The Black Flower*, p. 1385; April 1, 2000, Margaret Flanagan, review of *The Year of Jubilo*, p. 1441; July 1, 2006, Michele Leber, review of *The Judas Field*, p. 27.
Kirkus Reviews, June 1, 2006, review of *The Judas Field*, p. 531.
Library Journal, March 15, 2000, A.J. Anderson, review of *The Year of Jubilo*, p. 124; May 1, 2006, Bette-Lee Fox, review of *The Judas Field*, p. 74.
New York Times, June 18, 2000, Robert Morgan, review of *The Year of Jubilo*.
New York Times Book Review, June 18, 2000, Robert Morgan, review of *The Year of Jubilo*, p. 9; June 17, 2001, Scott Veale, review of *The Year of Jubilo*, p. 28.
Publishers Weekly, March 10, 1997, review of *The Black Flower*, p. 52; March 13, 2000, review of *The Year of Jubilo*, p. 59; May 8, 2006, review of *The Judas Field*, p. 44.

ONLINE

Book Diva, http://www.bookdiva.net/ (August 15, 2006), review of *The Judas Field*.
Book Page, http://www.bookpage.com/ (February 5, 2007), Alden Mudge, interview with Howard Bahr.
Mississippi Writers Page, http://www.olemiss.edu/ (February 7, 2007), biographical information about Howard Bahr.
Pif, http://www.pifmagazine.com/ (February 7, 2007), Michael Burgin, review of *The Year of Jubilo*.

*   *   *

BAHR, Howard Leslie
See BAHR, Howard

BAICKER-MCKEE, Carol 1958-

PERSONAL: Born 1958; children: three. *Education:* Yale University, B.A.; University of Virginia, Ph.D. *Hobbies and other interests:* "Pug lover, procrastinator, chocoholic, and all around silly person."

ADDRESSES: Home and office—Pittsburgh, PA. *E-mail*—baickermckee@adelphia.net.

CAREER: Writer, illustrator, and child psychologist.

MEMBER: Western Pennsylvania Region of Society of Children's Book Writers and Illustrators.

WRITINGS:

Mapped Out!: The Search for Snookums, illustrated by Traci O'Very Covey, Gibbs Smith (Salt Lake City, UT), 1997.
Fussbusters on the Go: Strategies and Games for Stress-Free Outings, Errands, and Vacations with Your Preschooler, Peachtree (Atlanta, GA), 2002.
Fussbusters at Home: Around-the-Clock Strategies and Games for Smoothing the Rough Spots in Your Preschooler's Day, Peachtree (Atlanta, GA), 2002.

Also author and illustrator of *Three Crabby Kids.* Author of monthly column for *Nick Jr. Family* magazine; author of blog, *Doodles and Noodles.*

ILLUSTRATOR:

Julie Stiegemeyer, *Cheep! Cheep!,* Bloomsbury (New York, NY), 2006.
Julie Stiegemeyer, *Merry Christmas, Cheeps!,* Bloomsbury (New York, NY), 2007.

SIDELIGHTS: Carol Baicker-McKee, a self-taught illustrator and clinical child psychologist, has written books for young readers as well as illustrating titles by herself and by others. A childhood interest in dioramas has inspired her creative approach as an illustrator, and her use of fabric collage gives her art a three-dimensional look. Baicker-McKee also incorporates found materials such as torn paper, clay, and wood in her illustration work.

As a writer, Baicker-McKee has penned the parent survival guides *Fussbusters on the Go: Strategies and Games for Stress-Free Outings, Errands, and Vacations with Your Preschooler* and *Fussbusters at Home: Around-the-Clock Strategies and Games for Smoothing the Rough Spots in Your Preschooler's Day.* In addition to her other writing projects, she contributes a monthly column to *Nick Jr. Family* magazine, and recommends titles for very young readers through her blog, *Doodles and Noodles.*

When she first began her writing career, Baicker-McKee thought her training in child psychology qualified her to give sensible parenting advice, but this assumption was called into question after she had children of her own. "I didn't have a clue," she confessed to Karen Macpherson of Bergen County, New Jersey's *Record.* Baicker-McKee got the ideas she includes in *FussBusters at Home* while watching other parents struggle to make their children behave while running errands. "I started off very simply, coming up with ideas for activities when parents are out and about with their kids," she explained of the book, which was described by Macpherson as "an idea-packed, lively, and humorous parenting guide." Kay Hogan Smith, writing in *Library Journal,* noted that *FussBusters on the Go* is "written with an earthy sense of humor" where "fun is the operative word."

As an illustrator, Baicker-McKee has created art to accompany picture-book texts by Julie Stiegemeyer. *Cheep! Cheep!* and *Merry Christmas, Cheeps!* feature three-dimensional chicks constructed by the illustrator using felt, terry cloth, and other household textiles. Despite the minimalist style represented in her collages, Baicker-McKee "comes up with an amazing array of expressions and comic poses," according to a *Publishers Weekly* contributor in a review of *Cheep! Cheep!* "The story comes alive through the almost 3-D collage art," wrote Linda Zeilstra Sawyer in *School Library Journal,* while a *Kirkus Reviews* critic concluded that Stiegemeyer's "chickies are cuteness in action." The Cheeps return to celebrate Christmas in *Merry Christmas, Cheeps!*

BIOGRAPHICAL AND CRITICAL SOURCES:

PERIODICALS

Kirkus Reviews, January 1, 2006, review of *Cheep! Cheep!,* p. 45.

Library Journal, October 1, 2002, Kay Hogan Smith, review of *FussBusters on the Go: Strategies and Games for Stress-Free Outings, Errands, and Vacations with Your Preschooler,* p. 121.

Publishers Weekly, February 13, 2006, review of *Cheep! Cheep!,* p. 87.

Record (Bergen County, NJ), September 1, 2002, Karen Macpherson, "Whine Coolers for Kids: Author Takes Aim at the Tough Spots," p. F4.

School Library Journal, March, 2006, Linda Zeilstra Sawyer, review of *Cheep! Cheep!,* p. 202.

ONLINE

Carol Baicker-McKee's Blog, http://www.doodlesand noodles.blogspot.com/ (December 15, 2006).

Western Pennsylvania Region of the Society of Children's Book Writers and Illustrators Web site, http://www.wpascbwi.com/ (February 20, 2007), "Carol Baicker-McKee."*

* * *

BARGER, Ralph Hubert, Jr.
   See BARGER, Ralph "Sonny"

* * *

BARGER, Ralph "Sonny" 1938-
   (Ralph Hubert Barger, Jr., Sonny Barger)

PERSONAL: Born October 8, 1938 in Modesto, CA; married first wife, Elsie (marriage dissolved); married; wife's name Sharon; children: one daughter (adopted).

ADDRESSES: Home—Phoenix, AZ. *Office*—Sonny Barger Productions, 515 E. Carefree Hwy., PMB 370, Phoenix, AZ 85085.

CAREER: Master mechanic in Phoenix, AZ; technical consultant for biker films. Appeared in films *Hell's Angels '69, Hell's Angels Forever, Gimme Shelter,* and *Hell's Angels on Wheels. Military service:* U.S. Army, 1955.

MEMBER: Hell's Angels (Cave Creek Chapter, Phoenix, AZ).

WRITINGS:

Hell's Angel: The Life and Times of Sonny Barger and the Hell's Angels Motorcycle Club (autobiography), William Morrow (New York, NY), 2000.

(With Keith and Kent Zimmerman) *Ridin' High, Livin' Free: Hell-raising Motorcycle Stories* (nonfiction), William Morrow (New York, NY), 2002.

Freedom: Credos from the Road (nonfiction), William Morrow (New York, NY), 2005.

NOVELS

(With Keith Zimmerman and Kent Zimmerman) *Dead in 5 Heartbeats* (novel), William Morrow (New York, NY), 2003.

(With Keith Zimmerman and Kent Zimmerman) *6 Chambers, 1 Bullet* (novel), William Morrow (New York, NY), 2006.

SIDELIGHTS: Ralph "Sonny" Barger has been a member of the Hell's Angels Motorcycle Club since 1957, when he formed the organization's Oakland, California, chapter. He has also served as a technical consultant for films about the Hell's Angels Motorcycle Club, including *Hell's Angels on Wheels* and *Hell's Angels '69.*

Barger's book *Hell's Angel: The Life and Times of Sonny Barger and the Hell's Angels Motorcycle Club* details his life and experiences with the notorious club. He gives details on the history and evolution of the Hell's Angels, stories about their run-ins with the law, and numerous other experiences they have encountered. "Barger paints an engrossing picture of a distinctive subculture that receives precious little literary attention," noted Mike Tribby in a *Booklist* review. *Library Journal* contributor Tim Delany described the work as an "intriguing and insightful look into the highly controversial, five-decade-old Hell's Angels Motorcycle Club."

Ridin' High, Livin' Free: Hell-raising Motorcycle Stories contains thirty-eight stories Barger collected and revised from other Hell's Angels members. Included are stories about fellow bikers such as musician David Crosby, member of Crosby, Stills and Nash; country singer Merle Haggard, and actor Steve McQueen. "The book works best when describing the simple pleasure of cruising through the American landscape at sunrise," concluded a *Publishers Weekly* reviewer.

Barger collaborated with Keith and Kent Zimmerman to write the novels *Dead in 5 Heartbeats* and *6 Chambers, 1 Bullet.* These books incorporate Barger's intimate knowledge of biker life into suspenseful plots. In *Dead in 5 Heartbeats,* a high-ranking member of the Infidelz motorcycle club is murdered, and his gang, led by Patch Kinkade, sets out to avenge his death. Reviewing for *Booklist,* Wes Lukowsky found the novel lacking in nuance but filled with "lots of testosterone" and plenty of "kicks to the groin." A *Publishers Weekly* reviewer also found that the mystery "falls flat," but added that nevertheless, "Barger's fans should love it." Kinkade's adventures continue in the sequel, *6 Chambers, 1 Bullet,* a story that finds the bikers' leader breaking into prison in order to solve the execution-style murders of some of his gang brothers.

BIOGRAPHICAL AND CRITICAL SOURCES:

BOOKS

Barger, Ralph "Sonny," *Freedom: Credos from the Road,* William Morrow (New York, NY), 2005.
Barger, Ralph "Sonny," *Hell's Angel: The Life and Times of Sonny Barger and the Hell's Angels Motorcycle Club,* William Morrow (New York, NY), 2000.

PERIODICALS

Booklist, May 15, 2000, Mike Tribby, review of *Hell's Angel,* p. 1698; September 15, 2003, Wes Lukowsky, review of *Dead in 5 Heartbeats,* p. 213.
Kirkus Reviews, August 15, 2003, review of *Dead in 5 Heartbeats,* p. 1029.
Library Journal, June 15, 2000, Tim Delaney, review of *Hell's Angel,* p. 101.
New York Times, July 3, 1980, Wayne King, "Mistrial Declared in Eight-Month Hell's Angels Trial," p. A12; August 8, 1980, Wayne King, "Barger Case over, Other Hell's Angels Face Retrial," p. A13.
Publishers Weekly, April 15, 2002, review of *Ridin' High, Livin' Free: Hell-raising Motorcycle Stories,* p. 57; August 4, 2003, review of *Dead in 5 Heartbeats,* p. 52.

ONLINE

Internet Movie Database, http://www.imdb.com/ (February 7, 2007), biographical information about Ralph "Sonny" Barger.
Let Them Talk! http://pdr.autono.net/ (February 4, 2007), Paul DeRienzo, interviews with Sonny Barger.
PopMatters, http://www.popmatters.com/ (February 7, 2007), review of *Ridin' High, Living' Free.*
Ralph "Sonny" Barger Home Page, http://sonnybarger.com (February 5, 2007).*

*   *   *

BARGER, Sonny
    See BARGER, Ralph "Sonny"

*   *   *

BARON SUPERVIELLE, Silvia 1934-

PERSONAL: Born April 10, 1934, in Buenos Aires, Argentina; immigrated to France, 1961; daughter of Andrés and Raquel Baron Supervielle. *Religion:* Roman Catholic.

ADDRESSES: Home—Paris, France.

CAREER: Writer.

WRITINGS:

La distance de sable, preface by Yves Peyré, Granit (Paris, France), 1983.
Le mur transparent, T. Bouchard (Saint-Jean-de-Losne, France), 1986.
L'or de l'incertitude (prose), José Corti (Paris, France), 1990.
(Translator into French) Jorge Luis Borges, *Les conjurés,* Jacques T. Quentin (Geneva, Switzerland), 1990.
L'eau étrangère, José Corti (Paris, France), 1993.
Le livre du retour (prose), José Corti (Paris, France), 1993.
La frontière (prose), José Corti (Paris, France), 1995.

Nouvelles cantates: Collection en lisant, en ecrivant, José Corti (Paris, France), 1995.

Un été avec Geneviève Asse, L'Echoppe (Paris, France), 1996.

Après le pas, Arfuyen (Orbey, France) 1997.

La ligne et l'ombre (prose), Seuil (Paris, France), 2000.

La rive orientale (novel), Seuil (Paris, France), 2001.

Essais pour un espace (essays), Arfuyen (Orbey, France), 2001.

Payes de voyage, Arfuyen (Orbey, France), 2004.

Une simple possibilité, Seuil (Paris, France), 2004.

La forme intermédiare (novel), Seuil (Paris, France), 2006.

Translator of work by Argentine poets into French; also translated the work of Marguerite Yourcenar into Spanish.

SIDELIGHTS: Silvia Baron Supervielle is, stated *Times Literary Supplement* contributor John Taylor, "an original, far-seeing emigrant writer who recounts her own dream deeply and honestly." Baron Supervielle, who was born in 1934 in Buenos Aires but immigrated to France when she was in her mid-twenties, has identified herself "with ancestors and explorers who sailed from Europe to the New World," according to Taylor. "Beginning in the late 1970s, she started publishing concise, elliptical poetry and richly textured prose, both focused on the implications of her exile." Included among her earlier works is *Le livre du retour,* which, according to *World Literature Today* contributor Maryann de Julio, "is at once a text, a story, and an act of recounting." "Regardless of the fact that *Le livre du retour* is most often about the particularities of reading and writing, when we read [Baron] Supervielle, we open ourselves to the marvelous," observed de Julio.

Baron Supervielle's more recent work includes *La frontière* and *Nouvelles cantates: Collection en lisant, en ecrivant,* both of which were given complimentary reviews in *World Literature Today.* Mechthild Cranston recognized *Nouvelles cantates* as a "notebook" containing biblical passages which [Baron] Supervielle highlighted and noted when reading. The author, cited Cranston, positively compared "reading her own biblical morceaux choisis" to that of "Virgil, Dante, Montaigne, [and] Beckett." "Linked by the power of language at moments of crisis, urgency, revelation, these new canticles call our attention to what is vital, essential, mysterious, anterior to all the books of our lives," concluded Cranston. De Julio's assessment of *La frontière* praised Baron Supervielle and her "poetic narrative . . . about boundaries and limits." "Supervielle allows herself a range of inventive possibility that exploits a model for writing. . . . [Readers] are moved from character as a hypothetical abstraction to the craft of abstraction itself."

Baron Supervielle's *La legne et l'ombre* "casts an elucidating light on her earlier [works] . . . [and] deserves a wide readership," observed Taylor, who summarized: "A work of full maturity, [*La ligne et l'ombre* is a] fascinating tapestry of perceptions, memories, thoughts and daydreams [that] weaves together passages set in her Parisian apartment, her house in Brittany, the streets of Buenos Aires, and her childhood summers home in Uruguay. . . . Melancholy tango lyrics are sprinkled throughout this spiritual autobiography."

Baron Supervielle told *CA:* "My writing is very much inspired by my past in Argentina and its landscape."

BIOGRAPHICAL AND CRITICAL SOURCES:

PERIODICALS

Times Literary Supplement, March 19, 1999, John Taylor, "Return Journey," p. 34; October 12, 2001, review of *La rive orientale,* p. 10.

World Literature Today, spring, 1994, Maryann de Julio, review of *Le livre du retour,* p. 343; summer, 1996, Maryann de Julio, review of *La frontière,* p. 655; summer, 1996, Mechthild Cranston, review of *Nouvelles cantates: Collection en lisant, en ecrivant,* p. 657; summer-autumn, 2002, E. Nicole Meyer, review of *La rive orientale,* p. 113.

*   *   *

BATEMAN, Teresa 1957-

PERSONAL: Born December 6, 1957 in Moscow, ID; daughter of Donald S. (a financial consultant) and Peggy L. (a homemaker) Bateman. *Ethnicity:* "White." *Education:* Ricks College, A.A.S., 1978; Brigham Young University, B.S., 1982; University of Washington, Seattle, M.A., 1987. *Religion:* Church of Jesus Christ of Latter-day Saints (Mormon).

ADDRESSES: Home—Tacoma, WA. *Office*—Brigadoon Elementary School, 3601 SW 336th St., Federal Way, WA 98023. *E-mail*—tbateman@fwps.org.

CAREER: Federal Way School District, Federal Way, WA, librarian, 1987—.

MEMBER: Society of Children's Book Writers and Illustrators, Washington Educators Association, Washington Library Media Association, Puget Sound Council.

AWARDS, HONORS: Merit award, *Society of Children's Book Writers and Illustrators* magazine, 1993, for the story "Traveling Tom and the Leprechaun"; winner of short fiction contest, *Highlights,* for "Aliens"; Paul A. Witty Short Story Award, 1997, for "Trapped in the Arctic"; Young Readers Book Award, *Scientific American,* 1997, Anne Izard Storytellers' Choice Award, 1998, award from *Storytelling World,* 1998, and Governor's Writers Award, State of Washington, 1998, all for *The Ring of Truth: An Original Irish Tale;* Parents' Choice Award, 2001, and children's choice selection, International Reading Association, 2002, both for *Farm Flu;* Gold Seal Best Book Award, Oppenheim Toy Portfolio, c. 2001, for *Farm Flu,* and 2005, for *April Foolishness;* citation among notable social studies trade books for young people, National Council for the Social Studies and Children's Book Council, 2001, for *Red, White, Blue, and Uncle Who? The Stories behind Some of America's Patriotic Symbols,* and 2005, for *April Foolishness.*

WRITINGS:

FOR CHILDREN

The Ring of Truth: An Original Irish Tale, illustrated by Omar Rayyan, Holiday House (New York, NY), 1997.

Leprechaun Gold, illustrated by Rosanne Litzinger, Holiday House (New York, NY), 1998.

Farm Flu, Albert Whitman (Morton Grove, IL), 2001.

Harp o' Gold, Holiday House (New York, NY), 2001.

The Merbaby, Holiday House (New York, NY), 2001.

A Plump and Perky Turkey, Winslow Press (Delray Beach, FL), 2001.

Red, White, Blue, and Uncle Who? The Stories behind Some of America's Patriotic Symbols, Holiday House (New York, NY), 2001.

Hunting the Daddyosaurus, Albert Whitman (Morton Grove, IL), 2002.

The Princesses Have a Ball, Albert Whitman (Morton Grove, IL), 2002.

April Foolishness, Albert Whitman (Morton Grove, IL), 2004.

The Bully Blockers Club, Albert Whitman (Morton Grove, IL), 2004.

Fluffy, Scourge of the Sea, Charlesbridge (Watertown, MA), 2005.

Hamster Camp: How Harry Got Fit, Albert Whitman (Morton Grove, IL), 2005.

Keeper of Soles, Holiday House (New York, NY), 2005.

Will You Be My Valenswine?, Albert Whitman (Morton Grove, IL) 2005.

Contributor of articles and reviews to periodicals, including *Cricket* and *Highlights.*

SIDELIGHTS: Teresa Bateman once told *CA:* "I was raised in a family of ten children. My mother made a point of reading to us at every opportunity, especially on long car trips. As a result, we are all voracious readers. There are few things that delight me more than a well-written book. Perhaps that's one of the reasons why I decided to write.

"I've always been a storyteller, When I was a teenager I had to share a bedroom with a younger sister who always 'ratted me out' to my parents when I stayed up past bedtime, reading. I used to tell her stories about a bear that lived in the closet and liked to eat succulent young things. I, naturally, was too old and stringy.

"As the years went by I continued making up stories. Now I tell them to my many nieces and nephews. Eventually I thought it would be fun to write them down and see if they were publishable. I am now the owner of an enormous stack of rejection letters. (I'm so proud . . .) However, I also have had many things published. I don't let rejection discourage me. I write because I love to write. I'd still write even if none of my stories ever got published. Writing is as much a part of me as breathing. I write each day, without fail. Some days I write a lot. Some days I write a little, but I write every day.

"One of the things I enjoy most is doing research for nonfiction articles and books. To me, research is a blast. I love going to the University of Washington Suzzalo library and pulling out microfilm, or prowling through stacks of old books. I find the strangest things that way—odd facts that tickle my fancy. Doing the research is often just as much fun as doing the writing! Being a librarian also helps. I'm surrounded by books and children every day. It's a great combination."

Bateman's first book, *The Ring of Truth: An Original Irish Tale,* is the story of Patrick O'Kelly, a peddler who tells impressive tales as a way to keep people buying his wares. Patrick makes the mistake of bragging that he can "spout better blarney" than the king of the leprechauns, which causes the king to become upset and give Patrick a ring which will force him to tell the truth. In a twist, Patrick ends up winning a blarney contest by telling the true story of his meeting with the leprechaun king. A *Kirkus Reviews* contributor wrote: "Bateman's first book is a beautifully layered, consistently sprightly take on the notion that truth is stranger than fiction," while a *Publishers Weekly* reviewer noted: "Epitomizing the best of Irish storytelling, this blithe debut pokes fun at its own blustery genre." Beth Tegart, writing for *School Library Journal,* commented: "This is a well-crafted tale told with a storyteller's touch; the language flows, and the story satisfies."

Leprechaun Gold is the story of Donald O'Dell, a kindhearted handyman who rescues a leprechaun from drowning. As a reward, the leprechaun offers Donald gold, but Donald refuses, saying he doesn't need it. The leprechaun, who refuses to take no for an answer, leaves the gold in Donald's pockets, on his doorstep, and in Donald's shoes, but each time Donald returns the gold. The leprechaun ends up tricking the lonely Donald into meeting a similarly lonely beautiful woman with golden hair and a golden heart, ensuring that Donald does receive gold. April Judge noted in a review for *Booklist:* "This well-crafted story is told in a robust, lively manner . . . a top-notch candidate for reading aloud." A *Kirkus Reviews* correspondent stated, "This charming tale has an Irish lilt that would certainly withstand an energetic reading out loud—and not just on St. Patrick's Day."

Bateman commented on her Irish themes to *CA:* "Many people ask me why I write so many Irish stories. My father says that one of our family lines goes back to Ireland. I've always loved Irish stories, and I enjoy telling them to my students. In fact, during the week of St. Patrick's Day I pick up an Irish accent that follows me around for weeks. It's usually in March that I write my best leprechaun stories.

"Writing is so much a part of me that I cannot imagine my life without it. Most important, however, writing is fun for me. It's often hard work, but it's still a lot of fun."

More recently Bateman told *CA:* "One of the things I like most about being an author is the way ideas can come out of just about any situation. I might be reading the paper, walking to school, or attending a faculty meeting when suddenly something will trigger an idea and I'm feverishly scribbling away on whatever paper is available. I've gotten ideas at banquets, at church, and even in the dentist's chair. It seems that when my mind wanders it has a specific destination waiting for me, and that destination is the story."

BIOGRAPHICAL AND CRITICAL SOURCES:

PERIODICALS

Booklist, August, 1998, April Judge, review of *Leprechaun Gold,* p. 2012.

Bulletin of the Center for Children's Books, May, 1997, review of *The Ring of Truth: An Original Irish Tale,* p. 313.

Horn Book, July-August, 1998, Nancy Vasilakis, review of *Leprechaun Gold,* p. 470.

Kirkus Reviews, February 1, 1997, review of *The Ring of Truth,* p. 218; March 15, 1998, review of *Leprechaun Gold,* p. 398.

Publishers Weekly, February 24, 1997, review of *The Ring of Truth,* p. 91.

School Library Journal, May, 1997, Beth Tegart, review of *The Ring of Truth,* p. 92; June, 1998, Kit Vaughan, review of *Leprechaun Gold,* p. 94.

*   *   *

BECKER, Jasper 1956-

PERSONAL: Born May 19, 1956, in London, England; son of Alfred (an electronics engineer) and Ilse Becker; married Ruwani Jayewardene (a development consultant), August, 1987 (divorced, 1999); married Autoaueta Beglova, May, 1999; children: Michael, Jeremy. *Education:* Attended University of Munich, 1976-77; University of London, graduated (with honors), 1978.

ADDRESSES: Home—London, England. *Agent*—Diana Finch, Ellen Levine Agency, 15 E. 26th St., Ste. 1801, New York, NY 10010-1505. *E-mail*—info@jasper becker.com

CAREER: Freelance writer. Journalist in Brussels, Belgium, 1980-83; Associated Press, Geneva, Switzerland, journalist, 1983-85; *Guardian,* London, England, journalist in London and China, 1985-91; British Broadcasting Corp. (BBC), London, journalist, 1992-94; *South China Morning Post,* Hong Kong, China, Beijing bureau chief, 1995-2002. Has appeared frequently on news programs, including *60 Minutes, Nightline, Primetime Live,* and *World News Tonight.* Becker is quoted regularly as a news analyst for television and radio news programs all over the world.

WRITINGS:

The Lost Country: Mongolia Revealed, Hodder & Stoughton (London, England), 1991.
Hungry Ghosts: China's Secret Famine, Free Press (New York, NY), 1996.
The Chinese, Free Press (New York, NY), 2000.
Rogue Regime: Kim Jong Il and the Looming Threat of North Korea, Oxford University Press (Oxford, England), 2005.
Dragon Rising: An Inside Look at China Today, National Geographic Society (Washington, DC), 2006.

Work represented in anthologies, including *Reporting the News from China,* Chatham House, 1992. Contributor to numerous periodicals, including *Vanity Fair, National Geographic, Marie Claire,* and *Travel & Leisure.*

SIDELIGHTS: Thirty million is an incomprehensible number of human beings, but it is a conservative estimate of how many Chinese peasants died from a state-caused famine between 1958 and 1962. Jasper Becker's *Hungry Ghosts: China's Secret Famine* explores this underreported tragedy.

China's communist leader Mao Tse-tung's "Great Leap Forward" was an attempt to push China past the Soviet Union, "pass England and catch up with America" all within fifteen years. Through this plan, China would become the leading nation in the world, and Mao would be the greatest leader in the world. Equal parts pseudo-science, sycophantic bureaucracy, and Mao's will-to-power allowed the starvation of so many to occur. The illusion of progress was sustained by false reports, cover-ups, and deceit.

Famine was not new to China, but historic occurrences of it were largely due to flooding and drought, and relief was difficult due to the great distances that separated villages. The 1958 famine was not localized but affected all of rural China. Mao would not admit the truth when faced with it, and he apparently did not understand until 1961 that millions had already died. Becker collected eyewitness accounts of cannibalism, stories of people feasting on cats and dogs, mice, insects, bark, leaves, and even dirt long after the peasants' grain ran out. He further noted that the same government was still in power in the late 1990s and still reluctant to admit to all that occurred during those four years.

The world outside China was blind, Becker suggested. He shows how a broad spectrum of Westerners, from economists to Maoist supporters, were misled by Chinese information that asserted there was no starvation and only bad weather was causing slight supply problems. Some Sinophiles even make Mao out as an averter of a famine rather than an instigator.

Many critics found *Hungry Ghosts* to be powerful, if somewhat gruesome. Caroline Moorehead, writing in the *New Statesman,* called it "a painstakingly readable account of the famine that engulfed China." Writing for the *Wall Street Journal,* Paul G. Pickowicz called *Hungry Ghosts* "an important, sometimes spellbinding, account." He did, however, disagree with some of Becker's conclusions, namely that "even now in the West the famine is still not accepted as a historical event." Another complaint was voiced by Richard Bernstein in the *New York Times:* "Sometimes he includes information without giving the reasons he found the information credible." Nevertheless, Bernstein admitted the book was "remarkable." A *New York Times Book Review* article by Nicholas Eberstadt claimed that Becker "has offered both a grim tribute to the dead and a challenge to our consciences."

Hungry Ghosts was officially banned by the Chinese government, but Becker's exposé of an appalling slice of modern Chinese history did not seem to hinder his journalistic career there. He has corresponded from China for London's *Guardian* newspaper, and for the British Broadcasting Corporation as well. After the publication of *Hungry Ghosts,* he became Beijing bureau chief for the *South China Morning Post,* an English-language newspaper based in Hong Kong. His next book, *The Chinese,* was published in 2000, and examines the dramatic changes that have occurred in China since the death of Mao.

Becker's title encompasses 1.25 billion people, and as he notes, China is one of the world's oldest civilizations, with a state that is "probably the oldest functioning organization in the world." He begins by sketching China's history of autocratic rulers, a preference that was long entrenched before the darkest days of Mao's Communist rule. The bulk of the book discusses the sweeping economic reforms, designed to lead China into the global marketplace, launched in late 1970s by premier Deng Xiaoping. Under Deng, China sought to change course by instituting new trade policies and fostering private enterprise. Even with the 1989 crackdown on dissidents—who opposed the political corruption that the economic reforms had only exacerbated—China continued on a path to what it called a "socialist market economy."

Becker focuses on the social impact that these changes wrought, and looks at various segments of Chinese society and discusses who has benefited from them, and who has suffered. The author's long experience as a working journalist in China gave him a wealth of anecdotal and insider source material to illustrate his theories. Rural peasantry and industrial workers have not found their fortunes vastly improved by the heady new economic climate of the 1990s, as he shows, but the burgeoning entrepreneur class and high-ranking Communist Party members have reaped extraordinary profits. Other segments of *The Chinese* discuss the particular challenges faced by intellectuals, and the endemic political corruption that still plagues the corridors of power. A *Wilson Quarterly* assessment from Jonathan Mirsky found fault with some of the book's assertions, but concluded that Becker's experiences as a reporter there yielded a certain insight to his account of China at a crossroads. "His anecdotes make the book particularly valuable," Mirsky noted. A *Publishers Weekly* reviewer also commended the work, writing: "Becker's may not be the most optimistic view of contemporary China, but it is one of the most penetrating."

In 2005, Becker switched focus from China to North Korea in his book *Rogue Regime: Kim Jong Il and the Looming Threat of North Korea*. He gives readers a look inside North Korea and the mind of its ruler, Kim Jong Il. He writes about not only the possible threat the country presents to the United States, but also the threat it presents to its own people. *Rogue Regime* gives a "frightening and depressing account" of the past and present state of the country under Kim Jong Il, wrote Jay Freeman in a review for *Booklist*. Many reviewers

found that the book presents a compelling portrait of a dangerous dictator, and is "of much interest to readers who wonder where the next war will be fought," observed a *Kirkus Reviews* contributor.

Becker once told *CA:* "My interests are Oriental cultures, Buddhism, Chinese politics, archaeology, central Asia, and international politics. These stem from twelve years as a correspondent in Brussels, Geneva, and especially Peking."

BIOGRAPHICAL AND CRITICAL SOURCES:

PERIODICALS

American Spectator, September, 2005, James R. Lilley, review of *Rogue Regime: Kim Jong Il and the Looming Threat of North Korea,* p. 76.
Asian Affairs, February, 1993, C.R. Bawden, review of *The Lost Country: Mongolia Revealed,* p. 66; October, 1996, Colina MacDougall, review of *Hungry Ghosts: China's Secret Famine,* p. 405.
Biography, fall, 2005, Carl Senna, review of *Rogue Regime,* p. 714.
Book World, April 5, 1998, review of *Hungry Ghosts,* p. 12; September 10, 2000, review of *The Chinese,* p. 6; February 4, 2001, review of *The Chinese,* p. 9; June 19, 2005, Mike Mochizuki, review of *Rogue Regime,* p. 6.
Booklist, December 15, 1996, Gilbert Taylor, review of *Hungry Ghosts,* p. 695; November 1, 2000, Julia Glynn, review of *The Chinese,* p. 513; April 15, 2005, Jay Freeman, review of *Rogue Regime,* p. 1426.
Business Week, January 15, 2001, review of *The Chinese,* p. 22.
Campaigns & Elections, July, 2006, review of *Dragon Rising: An Inside Look at China Today,* p. 58.
Chemical & Engineering News, February 26, 2001, Jean-Francois Tremblay, "A Look at China Today," p. 52.
China Quarterly, March, 1997, Frederick C. Teiwes, review of *Hungry Ghosts,* p. 212; September, 2002, Thomas P. Bernstein, review of *The Chinese,* p. 744.
Christian Science Monitor, August 11, 1997, Ann Scott Tyson, review of *Hungry Ghosts,* p. 15.
Economist, October 19, 1996, review of *Hungry Ghosts,* p. 8; June 11, 2005, review of *Rogue Regime,* p. 82.

Far Eastern Economic Review, August 20, 1992, Alan Sanders, review of *The Lost Country,* p. 30; August 15, 1996, Margaret Scott, review of *Hungry Ghosts,* p. 54; July-August, 2005, David C. Kang, review of *Rogue Regime,* p. 66.

Foreign Affairs, September, 2001, review of *The Chinese,* p. 174.

Geographical, October, 2005, Victoria James, review of *Rogue Regime,* p. 86.

Geographical Journal, July, 1998, review of *Hungry Ghosts,* p. 233.

Globe & Mail, August 20, 2005, Carl Senna, review of *Rogue Regime,* p. 9.

Guardian Weekly, July 12, 1992, review of *The Lost Country,* p. 28.

Independent Review, winter, 2000, review of *Hungry Ghosts,* p. 431.

Journal of Asian Studies, February, 1998, Lee Feigon, review of *Hungry Ghosts,* p. 181.

Kirkus Reviews, November 15, 1996, review of *Hungry Ghosts,* p. 1642; September 15, 2000, review of *The Chinese,* p. 1326; February 1, 2005, review of *Rogue Regime,* p. 158.

Library Journal, January, 1997, Jack Shreve, review of *Hungry Ghosts,* p. 117; November 15, 2000, Charles W. Hayford, review of *The Chinese,* p. 83.

London Review of Books, July 18, 1996, review of *Hungry Ghosts,* p. 3; December 15, 2005, Bruce Cummings, review of *Rogue Regime,* p. 11.

Los Angeles Times, February 2, 1997, review of *Hungry Ghosts,* p. 3; February 18, 2001, Jim Mann, review of *The Chinese,* p. 2; December 2, 2001, review of *The Chinese,* p. 19.

Middle East, December, 1993, review of *The Lost Country,* p. 41.

New Statesman, June 14, 1996, Caroline Moorehead, review of *Hungry Ghosts,* p. 44.

New Yorker, April 14, 1997, review of *Hungry Ghosts,* p. 85; April 16, 2001, review of *The Chinese,* p. 18.

New York Times, February 4, 1997, review of *Hungry Ghosts,* p. 15; February 5, 1997, Richard Bernstein, "Horror of a Hidden Chinese Famine," p. C15.

New York Times Book Review, February 16, 1997, Nicholas Eberstadt, "The Great Leap Backward," p. 6; June 1, 1997, review of *Hungry Ghosts,* p. 39; December 7, 1997, review of *Hungry Ghosts,* p. 70; August 9, 1998, review of *Hungry Ghosts,* p. 28; December 6, 1998, review of *Hungry Ghosts,* p. 97; August 7, 2005, Joshua Kurlantzick, review of *Rogue Regime,* p. 18.

Population and Development Review, March, 1997, Alphonse L. MacDonald, review of *Hungry Ghosts,* p. 186.

Publishers Weekly, January 13, 1997, review of *Hungry Ghosts,* p. 65; November 6, 2000, review of *The Chinese,* p. 78; February 21, 2005, review of *Rogue Regime,* p. 163.

Spectator, June 29, 1996, Ian Buruma, review of *Hungry Ghosts,* p. 33.

Time International, February 21, 2005, Jasper Becker, "It's Time to Disengage with Kim Jong Il," p. 21; May 23, 2005, Austin Ramzy, review of *Rogue Regime,* p. 53.

Times Higher Education Supplement, November 29, 1996, Carl Riskin, review of *Hungry Ghosts,* p. 20; February 3, 2006, James Hoare, review of *Rogue Regime,* p. 24.

Times Literary Supplement, July 10, 1992, Jeremy Swift, review of *The Lost Country,* p. 11; October 25, 1996, review of *Hungry Ghosts,* p. 3; December 22, 2000, Julia Lovell, review of *The Chinese,* p. 27.

Tribune Books (Chicago, IL), August 25, 2002, review of *The Chinese,* p. 6.

Wall Street Journal, February 7, 1997, Paul G. Pickowicz, review of *Hungry Ghosts,* p. A16.

Wilson Quarterly, winter, 2001, Jonathan Mirsky, review of *The Chinese,* p. 139.

ONLINE

Jasper Becker Home Page, http://www.jasperbecker. com (November 30, 2006).

New Humanities Reader, http://www.newhum.com/ (November 30, 2006), biography of Jasper Becker.

Open Democracy.net, http://www.opendemocracy.net/ (November 30, 2006), biography of Jasper Becker.*

*   *   *

BEDI, Ashok 1948-
(Ashok R. Bedi)

PERSONAL: Born February 10, 1948, in India; naturalized U.S. citizen; son of Ramprakash (in business) and Shanti (a homemaker) Bedi; married Usha Kamdar (a restaurant owner and chef), July 26, 1972; children: Ami, Siddhartha. *Ethnicity:* "Indian." *Education:* B.J. Medical School, Ahmedabad, India, M.B.B.S., 1970; Oxford Regional Hospital board, M.R.C., D.P.M., R.C. P.S., 1976. *Politics:* "Candidate-and-issue-specific: not party based." *Religion:* Hindu. *Hobbies and other interests:* Photography, computers.

ADDRESSES: Home—Milwaukee, WI. *Office*—1220 Dewey Ave., Wauwatosa, WI 53213; fax: 414-454-6644. *E-mail*—ashokbedi@pol.net.

CAREER: Milwaukee Psychiatric Physicians Chartered, Milwaukee, WI, private practice of psychiatry and Jungian psychoanalysis, 1980—. American Board of Psychiatry and Neurology, board-certified psychiatrist; Royal College of Physicians and Surgeons of England, diplomate in psychological medicine; Medical College of Wisconsin, clinical professor of psychiatry; Carl G. Jung Institute of Chicago, member of training faculty; C.G. Jung Foundation of New York, leader of study tours to India titled "In the Footsteps of C.G. Jung in India"; lecturer in India, the United States, and elsewhere on the spiritual and analytic dimensions of psychiatric treatment. Milwaukee Psychiatric Hospital, former clinical director; honorary psychiatrist at Aurora Psychiatric Hospital and Aurora Health Care Network; also psychiatric consultant.

MEMBER: Royal College of Psychiatrists, American Psychiatric Association (fellow).

WRITINGS:

Path to the Soul, Samuel Weiser (York Beach, ME), 2000.
(With Boris Matthews) *Retire Your Family Karma: Decode Your Family Pattern and Find Your Soul Path,* Nicholas-Hays (Berwick, ME), 2003.

Contributor to medical and psychiatric journals.

SIDELIGHTS: Ashok Bedi once told *CA:* "As a psychiatrist and psychoanalyst, in clinical practice over twenty-five years, I found that the allopathic medicine and modern psychiatry would heal the symptoms but leave the soul distressed. Something was missing in the healing and wholeness of my patients. In desperation, I dug deep into my soul and my Eastern traditions as a Hindu to find the missing piece of the jigsaw puzzle. To my pleasant surprise, when I added the Eastern wisdom to modern medicine and psychiatry, the treatment outcomes were more enduring and soulful. These experiences over the last twenty-five years prompted me to share my struggle with fellow pilgrims on the path to the soul.

"My life and clinical work are my laboratory for soul work and my writings are a faint depiction of this inner work. I scribble thoughts, feelings, and theories down in between my patient appointments, or evenings and weekends. Usually, I am dead tired and only partly conscious when I write these things down. This is fortunate, since this removes the manipulation by my ego consciousness and the whispers of the soul are amplified. Some of these whispers are captured in my writing and constitute my attempts at writing. Rather, it writes through me!"

BIOGRAPHICAL AND CRITICAL SOURCES:

PERIODICALS

Publishers Weekly, July 10, 2000, review of *Path to the Soul,* p. 59.

ONLINE

Welcome to the Path to the Soul, http://www.pathtothe soul.com (April 7, 2007).

*   *   *

BEDI, Ashok R.
   See BEDI, Ashok

*   *   *

BENEDICT, Philip 1949-
   (Philip Joseph Benedict)

PERSONAL: Born August 20, 1949, in Washington, DC; son of William Sidney (an astrophysicist) and Ruth (a physician) Benedict; married Judith Segel (an urban planner), April 4, 1970; children: Lauryn, Lily. *Education:* Cornell University, B.A., 1970; Princeton University, M.A., 1972, Ph.D., 1975.

ADDRESSES: Home—Geneva, Switzerland. *Office*—Institut d'histoire de la Réformation, Université de Genève, Geneva, Switzerland. *E-mail*—philip. benedict@ihr.unige.ch.

CAREER: Cornell University, Ithaca, NY, visiting assistant professor of history, 1975-76; University of Maryland at College Park, College Park, assistant professor of history, 1976-78; Brown University, Providence, RI, began as assistant professor, became professor of history, 1978-2005; Institut d'histoire de la Réformation, Geneva, Switzerland, professor, 2005—. Institute for Advanced Study, Princeton, NJ, member, 1983-84; Oxford University, fellow of All Souls College, 2002-03.

MEMBER: American Historical Association, American Society for Reformation Research, Society for French Historical Studies.

AWARDS, HONORS: Fulbright fellow, 1972-73; fellow of American Council of Learned Societies, 1978, and National Endowment for the Humanities, 1988-89; Guggenheim fellow, 1989-90; fellow, National Humanities Center, 1993-94; two Roelker Prizes, American Society for Reformation Research, for best article of the year on the history of sixteenth-century France; Philip Schaff Prize, American Society for Church History, and Phyllis Goodheart Gordon Prize, Renaissance Society of America, both for *Christ's Churches Purely Reformed: A Social History of Calvinism.*

WRITINGS:

Rouen during the Wars of Religion, Cambridge University Press (New York, NY), 1981.
(Editor and contributor) *Cities and Social Change in Early Modern France,* Unwin Hyman (Boston, MA), 1989.
The Huguenot Population of France, 1600-1685, American Philosophical Society (Philadelphia, PA), 1991.
(Editor and contributor) *Reformation, Revolt, and Civil War in France and the Netherlands, 1555-1585,* Royal Netherlands Academy of Arts and Sciences (Amsterdam, Netherlands), 1998.
The Faith and Fortunes of France's Huguenots, 1600-85, Ashgate (Burlington, VT), 2001.
Christ's Churches Purely Reformed: A Social History of Calvinism, Yale University Press (New Haven, CT), 2002.
(Editor and contributor) *Early Modern Europe: From Crisis to Stability,* University of Delaware Press (Newark, DE), 2005.
History through Images in the Sixteenth Century: The Wars, Massacres, and Troubles of Tortorel and Perrissin, Librairie Droz (Geneva, Switzerland), 2007.

Contributor to books. Contributor to history journals.

SIDELIGHTS: Philip Benedict once told *CA:* "I see myself as part of a generation of historians which came of age when the activism of the 1960s and the first flush of enthusiasm for social history were both strong. I continue to remain fascinated by the classic problems at the heart of historical writing in that era: the long-term patterns of economic and social change and the relationships between ideology and society."

He later added: "More recently I have also become increasingly interested in visual culture. Above all, the tragically timely subject of religious violence has preoccupied me throughout my research career."

BIOGRAPHICAL AND CRITICAL SOURCES:

PERIODICALS

Times Literary Supplement, July 17, 1981, review of *Rouen during the Wars of Religion.*

*　　*　　*

BENEDICT, Philip Joseph
See BENEDICT, Philip

*　　*　　*

BOHM-DUCHEN, Monica 1957-

PERSONAL: Born May 10, 1957, in London, England; daughter of Louis (an industrial chemist) and Dorothy (a photographer) Bohm; married Michael Duchen (a research scientist), June 25, 1978 (divorced, 2003); children: Hannah, Benjamin. *Ethnicity:* "White/Jewish." *Education:* University of London, B.A., 1979; Courtauld Institute of Art, London, M.A., 1980. *Politics:* "Left of centre." *Religion:* Jewish. *Hobbies and other interests:* Theater, cinema, travel.

ADDRESSES: Home—London, England. *E-mail*—monica.bohmduchen@btinternet.com.

CAREER: Freelance writer, lecturer, and exhibition curator, 1980—. *Exhibitions:* Organizer and curator of exhibitions, including work for Tate Gallery, National

Gallery, Open University, and Courtauld Institute of Art, London; exhibitions include "Art in Exile in Great Britain, 1933-1945," in London and Berlin, 1985-86, "After Auschwitz: Responses to the Holocaust in Contemporary Art," a touring exhibition, 1995, "Rubies and Rebels: Jewish Female Identity in Contemporary British Art," 1996-97, and "Life? or Theatre? The Work of Charlotte Salomon," Royal Academy of Arts, 1998.

MEMBER: International Association of Art Critics, Society of Authors.

WRITINGS:

Arnold Daghani, Diptych (London, England), 1987.
Thomas Lowinsky, Tate Gallery (London, England), 1990.
(With Janet Cook) *Understanding Modern Art,* Usborne Publishing (London, England), 1991.
The Nude, Scala Publications (New York, NY), 1992.
(Editor and contributor) *After Auschwitz: Responses to the Holocaust in Contemporary Art,* Lund Humphries (London, England), 1995.
(Editor, with Vera Grodzinski) *Rubies and Rebels: Jewish Female Identity in Contemporary British Art,* Lund Humphries (London, England), 1996.
Chagall, Phaidon (London, England), 1998.
The Private Life of a Masterpiece, BBC Publications (London, England), 2001.
Eva Frankfurther, 1930-1959, Peter Halban (London, England), 2001.
(Editor, with Michael P. Steinberg) *Reading Charlotte Salomon,* Cornell University Press (Ithaca, NY), 2006.

Contributor to periodicals, including *Jewish Quarterly, Jewish Renaissance, Art Monthly,* and *Modern Painters.*

SIDELIGHTS: Art historian Monica Bohm-Duchen, working in collaboration with Janet Cook, published *Understanding Modern Art.* Calling it a "stimulating read" for young people, Veronica Holliday, a reviewer in *Books for Keeps,* considered the work an "attractively produced book." Holliday also commended Bohm-Duchen and Cook's effort to encourage young people to "look carefully, think about what they see and find out about the artist" within the "context" of their work. John Holden, reviewer in *School Librarian,* called *Understanding Modern Art* "well documented and articu-

late" as well as a "useful . . . enjoyable read for fourteen and upwards." He considered the "selection of examples . . . broad and visually exciting."

In 1995 Bohm-Duchen was the curator of a traveling exhibition of art commemorating the fiftieth anniversary of the liberation of Nazi concentration camps. She gathered an extensive collection of the art included in that exhibition in her book, *After Auschwitz: Responses to the Holocaust in Contemporary Art.* Donna Seaman, a reviewer in *Booklist,* called *After Auschwitz* a "stark and harrowing" work that "depict[s] life at its bleakest." Douglas F. Smith, a reviewer in *Library Journal,* "highly recommended" the work, calling it "a fascinating if disturbing book that breaks new ground in art historical study."

Bohm-Duchen turned her attention to an individual artist with her book *Chagall.* This book focused on the "social, religious, and cultural context of Chagall's development as an artist," commented Nadine Dalton Speidel, a reviewer in *Library Journal.* The reviewer also classified *Chagall* as "recommended for public and academic libraries."

BIOGRAPHICAL AND CRITICAL SOURCES:

PERIODICALS

Booklist, June 1, 1995, Donna Seaman, review of *After Auschwitz: Responses to the Holocaust in Contemporary Art,* p. 1714.
Books for Keeps, May, 1992, Veronica Holliday, review of *Understanding Modern Art,* p. 23.
Library Journal, June 1, 1995, Douglas F. Smith, review of *After Auschwitz,* p. 112; October 1, 1998, Nadine Dalton Speidel, review of *Chagall,* p. 80.
School Librarian, August, 1992, John Holden, review of *Understanding Modern Art,* p. 116.

*   *   *

BONGIE, Laurence L. 1929-
   (Laurence Louis Bongie)

PERSONAL: Born December 15, 1929, in Turtleford, Saskatchewan, Canada; son of Louis Basil and Madalena Bongie; married Elizabeth Bryson (a professor of classical literature), July 14, 1958; children: Christopher. *Education:* University of British Columbia, B.A., 1950; University of Paris, D.Phil., 1952.

ADDRESSES: Home—Vancouver, British Columbia, Canada. *Office*—Department of French, University of British Columbia, Vancouver, British Columbia V6T 1C2, Canada.

CAREER: University of British Columbia, Vancouver, British Columbia, Canada, lecturer, 1953-54, instructor, 1954-56, assistant professor, 1956-62, associate professor, 1962-66, professor of eighteenth-century French literature, 1966-92, professor emeritus, 1992—, head of department of French, 1966-92.

MEMBER: Royal Society of Canada (fellow), Canadian Society for Eighteenth-Century Studies (honorary member), Society for Academic Freedom and Scholarship, American Society for Eighteenth-Century Studies, Eighteenth-Century Scottish Studies Society, Société Diderot, French Society for Eighteenth-Century Studies, British Columbia Society of Translators and Interpreters (founding member).

AWARDS, HONORS: Medal, Government of France, 1950; fellowships from Humanities Research Council of Canada, 1955-56, Canada Council, 1963-64, 1975-76, and Social Sciences and Humanities Research Council of Canada, 1982-83; Killam senior fellowships, 1982-83, 1987; decorated officier de l'Ordre des Palmes Académiques.

WRITINGS:

David Hume: Prophet of the Counter-Revolution, Clarendon Press (Oxford, England), 1965, Liberty Fund (Indianapolis, IN), 2000.
Diderot's Femme Savante, Voltaire Foundation (Oxford, England), 1977.
(Editor and author of introduction and notes) Etienne Bonnot de Condillac, *Les Monades,* Voltaire Foundation (Oxford, England), 1980.
The Love of a Prince: Bonnie Prince Charlie in France, 1744-1748, University of British Columbia Press (Vancouver, British Columbia, Canada), 1986.
Sade: A Biographical Essay, University of Chicago Press (Chicago, IL), 1998.
From Rogue to Everyman: A Foundling's Journey to the Bastille, McGill-Queen's University Press (Montreal, Quebec, Canada), 2005.

Contributor to language and literature journals.

SIDELIGHTS: Laurence L. Bongie is best known for his studies of Scottish philosopher David Hume and the French writer and libertine the Marquis de Sade. In *Sade: A Biographical Essay,* Bongie focuses in detail on certain aspects of Sade's life. During his lifetime the Marquis de Sade was reviled for the extreme sexual aberrations portrayed in his novels. He was also imprisoned, including in the Bastille, for nearly thirty years, for acting out those aberrations. Yet since his death in 1814, certain avant-garde literary movements and some literary historians have rehabilitated—and according to Bongie "romanticized"—Sade, praising his writings and portraying him as a champion of individual freedom rebelling against a restrictive bourgeois society. Bongie's assessment of the infamous Marquis, both as a writer and a man, is less generous.

According to Thomas L. Cooksey of *Library Journal:* "Bongie offers a valuable correction to the perception of Sade as a profound thinker, a great writer, and a martyr to liberty." Without commenting on the validity of Bongie's thesis, a *Publishers Weekly* reviewer noted: "Bongie strips Sade of . . . honorable labels. Using letters, Sade's own writings and newly found police records, he goes about his work like a detective or an investigative reporter to expose what he believes was the true Sade." Bongie ultimately concludes that the Marquis was not an original thinker, that his best work was in his letters rather than his fiction, and that the prison sentences he received, decried as unjust by some biographers, were not entirely undeserved.

Bongie's *Sade* was released shortly after another biography of Sade, Francis du Plessis Gray's *At Home with the Marquis De Sade.* Comparing the two books in the *Times Literary Supplement,* Cristina Monet felt that Sade "cannot be so easily disposed of" as Bongie's analysis would have it. Henry Hitchings, for *New Statesman,* also reviewed the two biographies together. Hitchings described Bongie's work as "the more scholarly enterprise . . . attractive." He also mentioned that Bongie is "more skeptical about de Sade's magical allure."

Bongie responded to the criticism thusly: "Robert Darnton in the *New York Review of Books* is not wrong when he identifies as a basic premise of my critical writing the less than fashionable view that there is a person behind the literary text and that it is both legitimate and useful to look for linkages between an author's life and writings. Indeed, that assumption has always gone hand in hand with the personal hope that my best research endeavors have conformed primarily to the scientific-historical model, rather than to what I sometimes uncharitably think of as the esoteric 'high-priestcraft' paradigm, a persistently trendy mode of postmodern academic discourse that under various ill-defined banners always seems to be solemnly chewing away on the conference circuit at more than it has bitten off, and, as the decades pass, taking more and more pride in saying things we all know but in a language that no one understands, the whole periodically recycled on the scrap heap of stale-dated hermeneutics and worn-out critical liturgies. I confess to an emotional bias in favor of literary scholarship that is more than a kind of linguistic scrabble. (I believe the end came for me one day when I read a French critic's comment to the effect that we must all be grateful that we know so little about the life of the great dramatist Pierre Corneille!) I rebel against the notion that our texts should be studied in isolation from the author's life and times, from the writer's presumed intentions, and even from any supposed authorial need for self-expression or for communication to an implied reader-listener.

"My bias extends also to a preference for hard facts, verifiable data, derived from primary sources—not just archival material, but from fresh and unintimidated readings of the canon and what surrounds it. I like to think of academic research as discovery-driven, problem-solving, better still as an exercise in ferreting out pretentious cant and claptrap. There is joy in playing the skeptic and contrarian while scraping away pious layers of obfuscation.

"In short, I believe that literary scholarship, as much as any other worthy area of human endeavor, requires a certain amount of plain and passionate insubordination along with periodic salutary warnings about the emperor's new clothes. To illustrate all this, what better empirical example to cite than a presumptive life-and-works linkage so fervently decried by the marquis's many admirers, whose standard Sadean exegeses tell us everything about their own individual poetics, constructs, and problematics, and so little about Sade himself, about that much worshipped archetypal exemplar of bad faith, hollow opportunism, gut-wrenching and boring pornography, derivative, banal, windy, and often incoherent thinking, so reverently mislabeled by an awestruck bevy of devotees as a messiah of great literature and brilliant philosophy?"

BIOGRAPHICAL AND CRITICAL SOURCES:

PERIODICALS

Choice, July-August, 1966, review of *David Hume: Prophet of the Counter-Revolution.*

Globe and Mail (Toronto, Ontario, Canada), January 24, 1987, Ronald Sutherland, review of *The Love of a Prince: Bonnie Prince Charlie in France, 1744-1748.*

History, October, 1967, W.H. Barber, review of *David Hume,* p. 349.

Library Journal, November 1, 1998, Thomas L. Cooksey, review of *Sade: A Biographical Essay.*

Literary Review, February, 1999, David Nokes, review of *Sade.*

Los Angeles Times Book Review, November 15, 1998, Roger Shattuck, review of *Sade.*

New Statesman, May 17, 1999, Henry Hitchings, review of *Sade.*

New York Review of Books, January 1, 1999, Robert Darnton, review of *Sade,* pp. 19-24.

New York Times, December 11, 1998, Richard Bernstein, review of *Sade.*

Publishers Weekly, November 16, 1998, review of *Sade,* p. 62.

Rain Taxi, winter, 1999-2000, Rod Smith, review of *Sade.*

Times (London, England), March 11, 1999, Malcolm Bradbury, review of *Sade.*

Times Literary Supplement, July 7, 1966, review of *David Hume;* January 9, 1987, Caroline Bingham, review of *The Love of a Prince;* May 21, 1999, Cristina Monet, review of *Sade,* pp. 9-10.

University of Toronto Quarterly, winter, 1999-2000, Christine Roulston, review of *Sade.*

Women's Review of Books, June, 1999, Gillian Gill, review of *Sade.*

*   *   *

BONGIE, Laurence Louis
    See BONGIE, Laurence L.

*   *   *

BORDOWITZ, Hank 1959-
    (Dr. Rock, C. Benjamin Issakson)

PERSONAL: Born May 22, 1959, in New York, NY; son of Eli (an educator) and Frankie (an educator) Bordowitz; married Caren Pichel, August 30, 1981;

children: Michael, Laurence, William. *Ethnicity:* "Jewish." *Education:* Rutgers University, B.A., 1989; Thomas Edison State College, M.A., 2006. *Politics:* Liberal. *Religion:* Jewish. *Hobbies and other interests:* Camping, baseball, music, computers, golf.

ADDRESSES: Home—Suffern, NY; fax: 845-368-4882. *Agent*—James Fitzgerald, The James Fitzgerald Agency, 137 E. 57th St., New York, NY 10022. *E-mail*—hank@bordowitz.com.

CAREER: Journalist, editor, and writer. WEVD, engineer, 1978-79; *Record World,* writer, editor, and chart researcher, 1979; Cannings Recording Studio, engineer, producer, and musician, 1978-81; Ben El Distributors/Crazy Eddie's Records, manager, 1981-84; Publishers Packaging Corp., managing editor of *Concert Shots, Metal Mania,* and *Rock Scene,* and senior editor of *Rock Fever, Focalpoint, Heavy Metal Hall of Fame, Hot Metal,* and *Creem Specials,* all 1985-90; *Fama,* writer and copy editor, 1992-94; *Wizard: Guide to Comics,* Congers, NY, managing editor, 1994; *Interactive Quarterly,* Montclair, NJ, editor, 1995-96; *Sheet Music,* Bedford, NY, editor, 1996-97; writer, educator, publicist, and music business consultant, 1997—; Bernard M. Baruch College of the City University of New York, instructor, entertainment business department, 1997—; Music Choice, programming consultant, 1998-2005; MCY.com, director of editorial content, 2000-01; Ramapo College of the State of New Jersey, adjunct professor, 2004—.

MEMBER: National Association of Recorded Arts and Sciences, B'nai B'rith (vice president of Music Entertainment Media Unit, 1998—), Authors Guild, Music and Entertainment Industry Educators Association.

WRITINGS:

Bad Moon Rising: The Unauthorized History of Creedence Clearwater Revival, Schirmer Books (New York, NY), 1998.
(Compiler and editor) *The U2 Reader: A Quarter Century of Commentary, Criticism, and Reviews,* foreword by John Swenson, Schirmer Books (New York, NY), 2003.
(Editor and author of introduction) *Every Little Thing Gonna Be Alright: The Bob Marley Reader,* Da Capo Press (Cambridge, MA), 2004.

The Bruce Springsteen Scrapbook, Citadel Press (New York, NY), 2004.
Turning Points in Rock and Roll: The Key Events that Affected Popular Music in the Latter Half of the 20th Century, Citadel Press (New York, NY), 2004.
Noise of the World: Non-Western Artists in Their Own Words, Soft Skull Press (Brooklyn, NY), 2004.
Billy Joel: The Life & Times of an Angry Young Man, Billboard Books (New York, NY), 2005.
Dirty Little Secrets of the Record Business: Why So Much Music You Hear Sucks, Chicago Review Press (Chicago, IL), 2006.

Contributor of foreword to *Peanuts Illustrated Songbook* Hal Leonard Books (Milwaukee, WI), 2001; and to *Baker's Biographical Dictionary of Musicians.* Scriptwriter for television and radio programs, including *Rock Quiz, Trivia Quiz, Rock Today, Metalshop,* and *The CBS Morning Show.* Television credits also include TV-1 News, Finland, and *Spike and Company Do It A Cappella,* Public Broadcasting System (PBS).

Contributor to *Music Producers,* Hal Leonard Books, 1992; *Behind the Hits,* Warner Books, 1986; *The Rolling Stone Jazz Record Guide,* Straight Arrow, 1999; *Musichound World Essential Album Guide,* Visible Ink, 1999; *Baker's Biographical Dictionary of Musicians,* Thomson Gale, 2001; *The Outlaw Bible of American Essays,* Thunder's Mouth Press, 2006; and *Best Music Writing of 2006,* Da Capo Press, 2006.

Contributor of articles and reviews to more than sixty periodicals, including *BMI Music World, Guitar Player, High Fidelity, High Times, Jazz Review, Jewish Monthly, Playboy, Sing Out!, Spin,* and *USA Weekend.* Editor, *Interactive Trader* and *Interactive Quarterly Digizine,* 1995-96. Some writings appear under the pseudonyms C. Benjamin Issakson and Dr. Rock.

SIDELIGHTS: Hank Bordowitz once told *CA:* "One of my primary passions, since before I can remember, has been music. According to my parents, I was singing long before I could talk. During school, I was also developing a talent for writing, to the point that, in third grade, the boy who sat behind me stole a work in progress, signed his name to it, and turned it in as his own. When I couldn't find the paper, I started a new one. I got an 'A.' He got a 'B-.'

"Through school, these twin passions battled like a schizophrenic hydra. I learned how to play the guitar and worked in bands through high school, dabbling in rock and jazz. I also wrote extemporanea for the school newspapers. I wrote songs for the bands. I wrote Byzantine essays for my classes that caused the dean of boys to force me to learn how to type. (I was going to take auto shop. It made me a mechanic's patsy for life.)

"At Rutgers, I studied music with the likes of Kenny Baron and Dan Goode, while majoring in journalism and spending more time at the campus radio station than in class. I met my wife during one of my regular programs. I also started writing professionally, doing record reviews for local papers.

"After interning at the late, lamented *Record World* magazine, I graduated and started seeking work in the music business. As luck would have it, the bottom had fallen out of the business that year, and no one was hiring. I went to work for a retail record chain, recorded 'demos,' got signed for a hot minute to Ze Records, and continued to write. Retail meant low pay and long hours. My record never got released. I, however, continued to build a coterie of places that would publish my work and pay me for it.

"On quitting retail for a job that didn't materialize, I went to various places looking for radio work. At several they told me they didn't have work for engineers or announcers, but they did need writers. Finally someone suggested that, if I looked for writing markets with the passion I used seeking out full-time work, I could probably do well as a writer.

"This led to a couple of years of hand-to-mouth freelancing. During this time, a friend called me and told me to get in touch with Cherry Lane Publishing, as they were starting a book line and looking for writers. I chatted with the editor up there, and he told me to come up with a proposal of four chapters and an outline for whatever band I wanted to do. Seeing no books on Creedence Clearwater Revival, I chose them, producing the four chapters and an outline during a week of intensive research at the Lincoln Center Library. Shortly after I turned in the proposal, the book line idea was dropped, but I continued to poke at the outline.

"I got a gig editing a family of hard rock magazines that eventually included *Creem* magazine special issues. I worked for the company that packaged these magazines for five years, while freelancing on various projects, including *Behind the Hits*. When the company

moved, I hung out my own shingle for a couple of years again before moving on to edit *Wizard: Guide to Comics, Interactive Quarterly,* and *Sheet Music.* During my stint with *Sheet Music,* a former editor advised me to call Schirmer Books. They had a job for which he no longer had the time, and he had recommended me for it. Again I submitted the work, but the publisher put the job on a back burner. The editor asked me if I had anything else I might want to write for him, and I offered him the Creedence Clearwater Revival proposal. He liked it, and I wound up writing *Bad Moon Rising: The Unauthorized History of Creedence Clearwater Revival.*"

In 2003, Bordowitz told *CA:* "After that was done, the same editor assigned me to research and write over 300 essays for the *Baker's Biographical Dictionary of Musicians.* As that project drew to a close and *Bad Moon Rising* came ready to hit the book stores, I was asked to become the Director of Editorial content for MCY.com, a major consumer music portal specializing in webcasts. I was ultimately responsible for every word on the site—acquiring the content, overseeing the editorial process, overseeing the proofreading. This site was very content intensive, each featured artist had several pages on the site, artists ranging from Willie Nelson to Pete Townshend to Puff Daddy to Luciano Pavarotti. The site also included the largest opera site on the web, with soundbites and synopses of dozens of operas. Unfortunately it all went crash in the dot-bomb.

"While preparing the site for re-launch, I encountered an old editor who had segued into agenting. My current agent had left the country for the Pacific Rim, so I signed on with him. We brought *The U2 Reader* to Hal Leonard, and it proved to be the right book at the right time, as Hal Leonard was looking to start a line of "Readers" and U2 was one of the bands they wanted to do. So, I researched, compiled, edited and annotated that. As that drew to a finish, my agent brought me another book, a Bruce Springsteen Scrapbook."

Bordowitz's book on Creedence Clearwater Revival, *Bad Moon Rising,* received good reviews, with Mike Tribby writing in *Booklist:* "This is must reading for CCR-philes and fans of John Fogerty's subsequent solo career." A *Publishers Weekly* contributor noted that the author "provides evenhanded treatment of highly charged issues such as the often bitter sibling rivalry and the band's protracted legal wranglings."

Bordowitz served as editor of *Every Little Thing Gonna Be Alright: The Bob Marley Reader,* which presents a series of essays written by a variety of people, from journalists and academicians to Marley's widow and noted author Alice Walker. Also included are previously published pieces. KaaVonia Hinton, writing in *Kliatt*, noted that "this book treads lesser-known waters," adding: "Readers will be both entertained and informed." *Library Journal* contributor Bill Walker wrote: "Generally well written and offering many viewpoints, this collection is a great read."

Noise of the World: Non-Western Artists in Their Own Words is an examination of world music and the various musicians who contribute to it. Based on his past interviews with many musicians who perform in a variety of genres, Bordowitz presents their quotes as statements without the accompanying questions or comments by the author. In addition to well-known performers such as Gloria Estefan, Ravi Shankar, and Paul Simon, who helped popularize world music in America, the author also interviews many lesser known musicians—at least in the United States. Writing in *Booklist*, Mike Tribby commented: "Great stuff for what the Rastas might call conscious music collections." *Library Journal* contributor Bill Walker noted that the author's "scope is impressive."

Bordowitz takes on the life of another superstar musician with his book *Billy Joel: The Life & Times of an Angry Young Man*. The author follows Joel from his youth to his struggling days playing piano bars and sleeping wherever he could. The author also discusses Joel's attempted suicide during this time, as well as his later success and his struggle with alcohol. A *Publishers Weekly* contributor referred to *Billy Joel* as "surprisingly intimate." Another reviewer noted in *Kirkus Reviews* that Bordowitz "also provides a linear history of the artist's songwriting and performances." Dave Valencia, writing in the *Library Journal*, commented that Bordowitz "offers readers a glimpse of Joel's heretofore elusive personal life."

In *Dirty Little Secrets of the Record Business: Why So Much Music You Hear Sucks*, Bordowitz examines the music industry and what he sees as its failure to provide the general public with a wide range of notable music. Instead, Bordowitz argues, they promote so-so talent on a gullible public. The author profiles various musicians, as well as record producers and executives. He also provides an in-depth look at how radio stations and record companies are run. A *Kirkus Reviews* contributor noted that Bordowitz's "research is first-rate, and he is consistently able to support his arguments."

BIOGRAPHICAL AND CRITICAL SOURCES:

PERIODICALS

Booklist, September 15, 1998, Mike Tribby, review of *Bad Moon Rising: The Unauthorized History of Creedence Clearwater Revival*, p. 183; November 15, 2004, Mike Tribby, review of *Noise of the World: Non-Western Artists in Their Own Words*, p. 540.

Kirkus Reviews, May 1, 2005, review of *Billy Joel: The Life & Times of an Angry Young Man*, p. 520; October 15, 2006, review of *Dirty Little Secrets of the Record Business: Why So Much Music You Hear Sucks*, p. 1052.

Kliatt, January, 2005, KaaVonia Hinton, review of *Every Little Thing Gonna Be Alright: The Bob Marley Reader*, p. 28.

Library Journal, November 1, 1998, Lloyd Jansen, review of *Bad Moon Rising*, p. 83; June 1, 2003, Heather McCormack, review of *The U2 Reader*, p. 125; August, 2004, Bill Walker, review of *Every Little Thing Gonna Be Alright*, p. 83; November 1, 2004, Bill Walker, review of *Noise of the World*, p. 86; July 1, 2005, Dave Valencia, review of *Billy Joel*, p. 81.

MBR Bookwatch, September, 2005, Diane C. Donovan, review of *Billy Joel*.

Publishers Weekly, October 5, 1998, review of *Bad Moon Rising*, p. 72; May 23, 2005, review of *Billy Joel*, p. 70.

ONLINE

Hank Bordowitz Home Page, http://www.bordowitz. com (November 30, 2006).

Rock'sBackPages http://www.rocksbackpages.com/ (November 30, 2006), "Hank Bordowitz," profile of author.

SFSite, http://www.sfsite.com/ (November 30, 2006), Steven H. Silver, review of *Billy Joel*.*

*   *   *

BOWEN, Rhys
See QUIN-HARKIN, Janet

BRADY, James 1928-
(James Winston Brady)

PERSONAL: Born November 15, 1928, in Brooklyn, NY; son of James Thomas (a freight solicitor in the shipping industry) and Marguerite Brady; married Florence Kelly, April 12, 1958. *Education:* Manhattan College, A.B., 1950; attended New York University, 1953-54. *Politics:* Democrat. *Religion:* Roman Catholic.

ADDRESSES: Home—East Hampton, NY; New York, NY. *Agent*—Jack Scovil, Scovil, Chichak, Galen, 381 Park Ave. S., New York, NY, 10016.

CAREER: Writer. Macy's, New York, NY, copywriter, beginning 1950; Fairchild Publications, Inc., New York, NY, Washington, DC, correspondent, 1953-58, bureau chief in London, England, 1958-59, and Paris, France, 1960-64; *Women's Wear Daily,* publisher, 1964-71, editorial director, 1968-71; Capital Cities Broadcasting Corp., vice president, 1969-71; Hearst Corp., vice president, 1971-72; *Harper's Bazaar,* New York, NY, publisher and editor, 1971-72; talk show host, 1973-74; World News Corp., New York, NY, editor of *National Star,* 1974-75, vice chair, beginning 1975; MBA Communications, Inc., editor-in-chief, 1976-77; *New York Magazine,* editor, 1977; WCBS-TV, news commentator, 1981-87; full-time writer, beginning c. 1983; CNBC, news commentator, 1997-99. *Military service:* Marine Reserve; U.S. Marine Corps Reserves, active duty, 1951-52, in Korea; became first lieutenant; Bronze Star for valor.

MEMBER: University Club.

AWARDS, HONORS: Emmy Award, New York Television Academy, 1973-74; W.Y. Boyd Literary Novel Award, 2003, for *Warning of War: A Novel of the North China Marines.*

WRITINGS:

NOVELS

Paris One, Delacorte (New York, NY), 1976.
Nielsen's Children, Putnam (New York, NY), 1978.
The Press Lord, Delacorte (New York, NY), 1981.
Holy Wars, Simon & Schuster (New York, NY), 1983.

Fashion Show; or, The Adventures of Bingo Marsh, Little, Brown (Boston, MA), 1992.
Further Lane: A Novel of the Hamptons, St. Martin's Press (New York, NY), 1997.
Gin Lane: A Novel of Southampton, St. Martin's Press (New York, NY), 1998.
The House that Ate the Hamptons: A Novel of Lily Pond Lane, St. Martin's Press (New York, NY), 1999.
A Hamptons Christmas, St. Martin's Press (New York, NY), 2000.
The Marines of Autumn: A Novel of the Korean War, St. Martin's Press (New York, NY), 2000.
Warning of War: A Novel of the North China Marines, Thomas Dunne Books (New York, NY), 2002.
The Marine: A Novel of War from Guadalcanal to Korea, Thomas Dunne Books (New York, NY), 2003.

OTHER

Superchic (nonfiction), Little, Brown (Boston, MA), 1974.
The Coldest War: A Memoir of Korea, Orion (New York, NY), 1990.
The Scariest Place in the World: A Marine Returns to North Korea (travel and memoir), Thomas Dunne Books (New York, NY), 2005.

Columnist for various periodicals, including *New York Post,* 1980-83, *Advertising Age, Parade, New York, Crain's New York Business,* and for King Features. Contributing editor, *New York,* 1973-74; editor-at-large, *Advertising Age,* beginning 1983.

ADAPTATIONS: One of Brady's novels set in the Hamptons has been adapted to film. *The Marines of Autumn: A Novel of the Korean War* was bought by Winkler Films in 2000; books have been adapted as audiobooks, including *Warning of War,* Brilliance, 2002.

SIDELIGHTS: Journalist and novelist James Brady has worked in various capacities within the publishing industry. He has held such posts as bureau chief for Fairchild Publications, Inc., publisher and editorial director of *Women's Wear Daily,* publisher and editor of *Harper's Bazaar,* and editor of Rupert Murdoch's *National Star.* He has also been a news commentator and television talk show host. However, it is as a columnist that he is most widely known. Brady's columns, which have focused on celebrities and have addressed New York society and style, have appeared in various periodicals, including the *New York Post, Advertising Age, Parade, New York, Crain's New York Business,* and *Forbes.*

Before beginning his career in the publishing industry, Brady served as a U.S. Marine Corps first lieutenant in the Korean War. Four decades later, he produced a 1990 memoir chronicling his experiences in the war. "[*The Coldest War: A Memoir of Korea*] has drawn good reviews and has been praised by combat veterans," reported Ken Gross in a 1990 issue of *People. New York Times* contributor Herbert Mitgang lauded Brady's account: "In *The Coldest War,* Mr. Brady has written a superb personal memoir of the way it was." Mitgang added: "What distinguishes Mr. Brady's book is its clarity and modesty; there is no heroic flag-waving here. Like all honest reporting about the reality of combat in any war, it leaves an antiwar aftertaste." "Brady has no trouble remembering—often in riveting detail—the shock of sudden death and common heroism, as well as the mundane facts of everyday life," praised Gross, who observed: "The book not only limns some hidden corners of combat, it also illuminates a side of Brady that few have seen."

Gross related in his 1990 review of *The Coldest War* that "[f]or a long time . . . [Brady] had tried to write about Korea as fiction, but it wouldn't work." "'The truth is often eloquent,' Brady says with a shrug. It is often more lasting as well." However, ten years after *The Coldest War* Brady did publish a work of fiction featuring the war—*The Marines of Autumn: A Novel of the Korean War.* Although written about two years after the release of *The Coldest War,* it was not published until 2000, becoming Brady's eleventh novel. For *The Marines of Autumn,* Brady fictionalized his real-life commander in the Korean War, "a captain whose leadership style extended to calmly scooping up thrown Chinese Communist hand grenades and flinging them back where they came from," related Michael Kilian in *Knight-Ridder/Tribune News Service.*

"In the largest sense *The Marines of Autumn* is about all the Marines who were sent by that grandiose horse's ass, Gen. Douglas MacArthur, up to the Chosin in the autumn of 1950, and how, frostbitten and bleeding, carrying their dead and wounded with them they clawed their way back again," wrote Kilian, indicating that "Brady . . . has given us the whole horrible experience

. . . through [the fictional Capt. Thomas Verity's] eyes." "Brady tells it like it was and tells it extremely well," proclaimed Budd Arthur in *Booklist. Library Journal* contributor Edwin B. Burgess felt, however, that in presenting the story of Verity, Brady "glorif[ies] the heroes on the ground" and also "misses no opportunity to savage MacArthur's bad judgment and overweening ambition." A *Publishers Weekly* contributor asserted that *The Marines of Autumn* "is a model of historical and moral accuracy." Brady "writes colorfully and convincingly . . . incisively mapping out the fine lines between hope and despair, heroism and cowardice." The reviewer also described Brady's novel as "powerful," "stunning," and "moving."

Brady's 1981 novel, *The Press Lord,* is "an excitingly authentic inside view of the tough and special world of New York's big newspapers," according to a *Publishers Weekly* reviewer. Brady's fourth novel is the story of Campbell Haig, the ambitious owner of a group of popular newspapers, and his acquisition of a failing New York daily and the subsequent power struggle between this newcomer and the New York newspaper establishment. It is also a novel concerned with influential people: newspaper barons, columnists, media personalities, politicians, and even the widow of a former president. "In a vibrant, vital style . . . [the author] illuminates his variegated characters," stated Mark McCaffery in *Best Sellers.* "His plot is intriguing and carefully constructed with several brilliant twists to keep the reader's attention." "What really makes this novel work, however, are not the tendrils of subterfuge that hang around the edge," noted Marilyn Willison in the *Los Angeles Times Book Review.* "It is, instead, Brady's ability to make the reader feel strongly about Campbell Haig." Another of the book's merits, added Willison, is that "Brady's innate love of newspapering comes through on every page."

In 1997 Brady published the first in a projected series of five novels highlighting the trendy social life in the Hamptons, an area in which Brady resides on a part-time basis. In successive years, Brady released *Further Lane: A Novel of the Hamptons, Gin Lane: A Novel of Southampton, The House That Ate the Hamptons: A Novel of Lily Pond Lane,* and *A Hamptons Christmas.*

In his 2002 book, *Warning of War: A Novel of the North China Marines,* Brady once again writes about the marines, this time focusing on a group caught in northern China following the bombing of Pearl Harbor as Japan invades China. Before long, the Marines, who were stationed in this remote part of China to protect Chinese business interests, find themselves battling a ruthless Japanese officer and his soldiers. Jay Freeman, writing in *Booklist,* recommended the book for its "adventure combined with a realistic portrayal of men in war." A *Kirkus Reviews* contributor referred to the novel as "shapely, an absolute natural for film." Another reviewer, writing in *Publishers Weekly,* noted: "Authentic atmospherics and crackling action are sure to keep fans turning the pages."

The Marine: A Novel of War from Guadalcanal to Korea tells the story of Colonel James Cromwell, who is serving as a military attaché in South Korea when North Korea launches its surprise invasion of June 25, 1950. Taking place during the first one hundred days of the war, the novel follows Cromwell as he joins General Douglas McArthur as he invades Inchon and moves the American forces toward Seoul. Writing in *Booklist,* George Cohen called *The Marine* "a gripping adventure story." In a review in *Marines* magazine, John Neal wrote: "The combination of historical fact and fictional points of view makes for entertaining and educational reading."

The Scariest Place in the World: A Marine Returns to North Korea resulted from a *Parade* magazine assignment that sent Brady back to South Korea fifty years after he had fought there as a young man. An *American Heritage* contributor wrote that "his account of his return is part history, part memoir, part travelogue, and part meditation on the passing of time and the inevitable disappointments of trying to retrieve the past." Roland Green, writing in *Booklist,* noted: "The contemporary scenes become most eloquent when Brady pays tribute to old comrades." A *Kirkus Reviews* contributor called *The Scariest Place in the World* "an affecting memoir . . . of service in what is still a strangely forgotten war."

BIOGRAPHICAL AND CRITICAL SOURCES:

BOOKS

Brady, James, *The Coldest War: A Memoir of Korea,* Thomas Dunne Books (New York, NY), 1990.
Brady, James, *The Scariest Place in the World: A Marine Returns to North Korea,* Thomas Dunne Books (New York, NY), 2005.

PERIODICALS

Advertising Age, November 19, 2001, Rance Crain, "Marine Corps Pins a Medal on 1st Lt. James Brady," p. 16.
American Heritage, June-July, 2005, review of *The Scariest Place in the World: A Marine Returns to North Korea,* p. 17.
Best Sellers, April, 1982, Mark McCaffery, review of *The Press Lord.*
Booklist, May 1, 2000, Budd Arthur, review of *The Marines of Autumn: A Novel of the Korean War;* March 1, 2002, Jay Freeman, review of *Warning of War: A Novel of the North China Marines,* p. 1089; May 15, 2003, George Cohen, review of *The Marine: A Novel of War from Guadalcanal to Korea,* p. 1637; April 15, 2005, Roland Green, review of *The Scariest Place in the World,* p. 1425.
Chicago Tribune, June 17, 2005, Michael Kilian, review of *The Scariest Place in the World.*
Kirkus Reviews, January 1, 2002, review of *Warning of War,* p. 5.; April 15, 2003, review of *The Marine,* p. 570; March 1, 2005, review of *The Scariest Place in the World,* p. 270.
Knight-Ridder/Tribune News Service, June 21, 2000, Michael Kilian, "Novel Takes a Look Back at the Korean War," p. K2747.
Library Journal, May 1, 2000, Edwin B. Burgess, review of *The Marines of Autumn,* p. 152; February 15, 2002, Robert Conroy, review of *Warning of War,* p. 176; July 21, 2003, "James Brady Wins W.Y. Boyd Literary Novel Award"; December 1, 2004, Barbara Hoffert, review of *The Scariest Place in the World,* p. 90; May 1, 2005, Edwin B. Burgess, review of *The Scariest Place in the World,* p. 100.
Los Angeles Times Book Review, May 30, 1982, Marilyn Willison, review of *The Press Lord.*
Marines, July-September, 2003, John Neal, review of *The Marine,* p. 38.
New York Times, June 23, 1990, Herbert Mitgang, "Two Views of Korean War, One Lofty, One Muddy," p. 15.
People, October 1, 1990, Ken Gross, "Trading Gossip for Gunfire, Columnist James Brady Writes a Powerful Korean War Memoir," p. 91.
Publishers Weekly, January 1, 1982, review of *The Press Lord;* May 1, 2000, review of *The Marines of Autumn,* p. 46, and William D. Bushnell, "Publishers Weekly Talks with James Brady," p. 47; March 4, 2002, review of *Warning of War,* p. 56; May 26, 2003, review of *The Marine,* p. 47; March 28, 2005, review of *The Scariest Place in the World,* p. 70.

ONLINE

CelebrityCafe.com, http://www.thecelebritycafe.com/ (November 30, 2006), review of *The Marines of Autumn.**

*   *   *

BRADY, James Winston
   See BRADY, James

*   *   *

BROOKHISER, Richard 1955-

PERSONAL: Born February 23, 1955, in Rochester, NY; son of Robert and Elizabeth Brookhiser; married Jeanne Safer (a psychoanalyst), September 12, 1980. *Education:* Yale University, B.A., 1977. *Politics:* Republican. *Religion:* Methodist.

ADDRESSES: Office—National Review, 215 Lexington Ave., New York, NY 10016.

CAREER: National Review, New York, NY, senior editor, 1979-85, managing editor, 1986-87, senior editor, 1988—. Speechwriter for Vice President George Bush, beginning 1982; host of the television special *Rediscovering George Washington,* aired by Public Broadcasting Service, 2002; New York Historical Society, historian curator of "Alexander Hamilton: The Man Who Made Modern America," 2004-05.

AWARDS, HONORS: D.Litt., Washington College, 2005.

WRITINGS:

The Outside Story: How Democrats and Republicans Re-elected Reagan, Doubleday (New York, NY), 1986.
(Editor) William F. Buckley, Jr., *Right Reason,* Little, Brown (Boston, MA), 1986.
The Way of the WASP: How It Made America and How It Can Save It, So to Speak, Free Press (New York, NY), 1991.

Founding Father: Rediscovering George Washington, Free Press (New York, NY), 1996.
(Editor and author of commentary) *Rules of Civility: The 110 Precepts that Guided Our First President in War and Peace,* Free Press (New York, NY), 1997.
Alexander Hamilton, American, Free Press (New York, NY), 1999.
America's First Dynasty: The Adamses, Free Press (New York, NY), 2002.
Rediscovering George Washington (television special), Public Broadcasting Service, 2002.
Gentleman Revolutionary: Gouverneur Morris, the Rake Who Wrote the Constitution, Free Press (New York, NY), 2003.
What Would the Founders Do? Our Questions, Their Answers, Basic Books (New York, NY), 2006.

Contributor to books, including *Beyond the Boom,* edited by Terry Teachout, Poseidon (Las Cruces, NM), 1990, and *Patriot Sage: George Washington and the American Political Tradition,* edited by Gary L. Gregg and Matthew Spalding, ISI Books (Wilmington, DE), 1999. Columnist for *Observer,* 1987-2007. Contributor of articles and reviews to periodicals, including *Atlantic, New York Times, New Yorker, American Heritage,* and *Time.*

SIDELIGHTS: National Review senior editor and self-described "political addict" Richard Brookhiser chronicles the 1984 U.S. presidential election campaign in his first book, *The Outside Story: How Democrats and Republicans Re-elected Reagan.* Deliberately written from the perspective of a campaign outsider, *The Outside Story,* Brookhiser writes, is meant "to focus on what the candidates say and do in public; to leave the green room and the wings and go out front, and attend, with respect, to the performance." Victor Gold, who as a staff participant had an insider's view of the race between Democrat Walter Mondale and Republican Ronald Reagan, commented in the *National Review* that it was "one of the dullest, if most bizarre, presidential campaigns in modern times." Gold went on to note, however, that Brookhiser's account of the primaries, conventions, and campaigning of 1984 is "anything but dull." Walter Goodman, writing in the *New York Times,* appreciated "Brookhiser's irreverent yet serious treatment of a prodigiously silly but deeply serious event." Other reviewers praised Brookhiser's writing style, with *New York Times Book Review* contributor Timothy Noah describing the author as "a graceful writer with a sharp eye for both the human side of his story and the interplay of ideologies."

In *The Way of the WASP: How It Made America, and How It Can Save It, So to Speak,* Brookhiser equates the WASP (white Anglo-Saxon Protestant) character with the American character and advocates a general return to WASP values. The author defines WASPs as "the whole loaf, not just the upper crust. . . . people who clip supermarket coupons as well as the ones who clip the coupons of trust funds." Those who are not white Anglo-Saxon Protestants can also be referred to as WASPs if they adhere to "the way of the WASP," which, Brookhiser asserts, consists of six related qualities: conscience, civic-mindedness, industry, success, usefulness or utility, and antisensuality. According to the author, America has turned away from these traditional values in favor of self, ambition, gratification, group-mindedness (multiculturalism), diffidence, and creativity. "Without the WASP [the United States] would be another country altogether," Brookhiser writes. "Without the continuing influence of [WASP] values, [the United States] is sure to lose its way." Brookhiser presents his thesis in a manner that *New York Times Book Review* contributor Maureen Dowd called "part essay, part data bank search, part tongue-in-cheek and part serious."

"In sum," observed Lawrence Auster in the *National Review,* "*The Way of the WASP* is a devastating refutation of the 'all-cultures-are-equal' pieties." The reviewer added that "Brookhiser gives fresh and affirmative meaning to a word normally used as a sign of disdain for America's oldest group—and for America itself." Though some reviewers did not accept the book's premise, *Times Literary Supplement* contributor Joseph Epstein commented that "Brookhiser is not wrong in his contention that [WASP] values in combination made America a wealthy, independent, and immensely impressive country." Epstein also noted that "the book, though provocative and suggestive in many ways, is more likely to prove convincing about the abandonment of the [WASP] culture than about the need to restore it." Despite expressing some reservations about *The Way of the WASP,* *New York Times* critic Christopher Lehmann-Haupt recognized Brookhiser as "an intelligent and articulate cultural critic."

Brookhiser sought to reestablish the greatness of George Washington in his self-described "moral biography," *Founding Father: Rediscovering George Washington.* In his book, he declares that, although our modern culture is saturated with images and cliches about the first president, few of us really know or appreciate Washington. Revisionist historians, intent on uncovering unsavory facts about their subjects, have recently cast him as a greedy businessman, a mediocre soldier, and an easily-swayed politician. Yet the trouble goes deeper than the contemporary taste for the sensational, believes Brookhiser. In his opinion, modern Americans have come to think that nationhood was an inevitable step in our history, but he is convinced that it might never have come about if not for Washington's firm guidance in the critical years after the American Revolution.

"In attempting to restore one great man to his proper historical place, Brookhiser does not mean to revive the Washington cult of the 19th century," advised Gary Rosen in *Commentary.* "Rather, in this slender volume, he offers a 'moral biography' of the first President: an analysis of the extraordinary but altogether human traits that made him so indispensable to the early republic." Describing Washington as a man of great physical prowess and one with a naturally fiery temper, the author shows how carefully his subject went about controlling and refining his inborn characteristics. "He urges us to emulate our first President—to curb and direct our passions, to treat our fellow citizens with civility and respect, and, above all, to perform the duties of free government no less energetically than we claim its rights," continued Rosen. "While others have busied themselves exposing and deconstructing Washington, and ascribing every conceivable injustice to him . . . it is truly refreshing to be reminded what the life of our founding father still has to teach us." Brookhiser threw more light on Washington when he edited an etiquette book that Washington studied assiduously and followed faithfully. The result is *Rules of Civility: The 110 Precepts that Guided Our First President in War and Peace.*

Another founding father is reexamined in *Alexander Hamilton: American.* Brookhiser admires Hamilton for many of the same reasons he praises Washington: his high moral standards and conduct. Ironically, Hamilton is often remembered for an ill-fated extramarital affair and his death in a duel with Aaron Burr, who sought to ruin Hamilton's reputation. Brookhiser admits that Hamilton was not as successful as Washington at controlling his passions, yet he admires the straightforward way Hamilton faced his weaknesses and sought the high road in his political career. He was the illegitimate son of a Scottish rogue; his father deserted his mother shortly after Hamilton's birth. By the age of eleven, he was an orphan, apprenticed to a merchant on the island of St. Croix. Eventually he found his way to

America, received an education at the institution that would become Columbia University, became a friend and aide to General Washington in the Continental Army, and became the first U.S. secretary of the treasury. "In this slim and elegantly written volume," wrote Richard A. Samuelson in *Commentary,* "Brookhiser sets out to show that, even at a distance of two centuries, the life of the most colorful and controversial member of the founding generation can still 'guide and caution us.'" *Booklist* contributor Gilbert Taylor echoes that enthusiasm: "[This book's] felicitous composition and insights about Hamilton's adopted American identity make it eminently readable for buffs and historians alike."

BIOGRAPHICAL AND CRITICAL SOURCES:

BOOKS

Brookhiser, Richard, *The Outside Story: How Democrats and Republicans Re-elected Reagan,* Doubleday (New York, NY), 1986.

Brookhiser, Richard, *The Way of the WASP: How It Made America and How It Can Save It, So to Speak,* Free Press (New York, NY), 1991.

PERIODICALS

American Heritage, May-June, 1996, p. 110, review of *Founding Father: Rediscovering George Washington.*

American Spectator, March, 1996, Florence King, review of *Founding Father,* p. 62; August, 1999, Terry Eastland, review of *Alexander Hamilton, American,* p. 68.

Booklist, February 15, 1996, Mary Carroll, review of *Founding Father,* p. 984; March 15, 1997, Margaret Flanagan, review of *Rules of Civility: The 110 Precepts that Guided Our First President in War and Peace,* p. 1209; January 1, 1999, Gilbert Taylor, review of *Alexander Hamilton, American,* p. 822.

Commentary, May, 1996, Gary Rosen, review of *Founding Father,* p. 69; June, 1999, Richard A. Samuelson, review of *Alexander Hamilton, American,* p. 67.

Forbes, December 2, 1996, Steve Forbes, review of *Founding Father,* p. 26.

Journal of American History, June, 1997, Dorothy Twohig, review of *Founding Father,* p. 213.

Kirkus Reviews, January 15, 1999, review of *Alexander Hamilton, American.*

Library Journal, February 1, 1999, Thomas Schaeper, review of *Alexander Hamilton, American,* p. 102.

National Review, December 31, 1985, "The Party at the Plaza," p. 123; May 9, 1986, Victor Gold, review of *The Outside Story: How Democrats and Republicans Re-elected Reagan,* pp. 48-50; January 28, 1991, Lawrence Auster, review of *The Way of the WASP: How It Made America and How It Can Save It, So to Speak,* pp. 54-55; March 11, 1996, A.J. Bocevich, review of *Founding Father,* p. 61; April 21, 1997, Reid Buckley, review of *Rules of Civility,* p. 78.

New Criterion, May, 1999, Lewis E. Lehrman, review of *Alexander Hamilton, American,* p. 31.

New Republic, November 24, 1986, Jonathan Rieder, review of *The Outside Story,* p. 40.

New Yorker, February 5, 1996, Michael Lind, review of *Founding Father,* p. 68.

New York Times, June 9, 1986, Walter Goodman, review of *The Outside Story;* January 17, 1991, Christopher Lehmann-Haupt, review of *The Way of the WASP,* p. C21.

New York Times Book Review, June 1, 1986, Timothy Noah, review of *The Outside Story,* p. 29; January 20, 1991, Maureen Dowd, review of *The Way of the WASP,* pp. 1, 34; February 18, 1996, Joseph J. Ellis, review of *Founding Father,* p. 8; April 25, 1999, Michael R. Beschloss, review of *Alexander Hamilton, American,* p. 10.

Publishers Weekly, November 9, 1990, Genevieve Stuttaford, review of *The Way of the WASP,* p. 48; January 8, 1996, review of *Founding Father,* p. 55.

Reason, March, 1996, Steven Hayward, review of *Founding Father,* p. 50.

Saturday Evening Post, May-June, 1998, Ted Kreiter, review of *Rules of Civility,* p. 54.

Times Literary Supplement, May 31, 1991, Joseph Epstein, review of *The Way of the WASP,* p. 3; June 18, 1999, C. Bradley Thompson, review of *Alexander Hamilton, American,* p. 38.

ONLINE

Richard Brookhiser Home Page, http://www.richard brookhiser.com (March 6, 2007).

C

CAMPBELL, Bonnie Jo 1962-

PERSONAL: Born September 14, 1962, in Kalamazoo, MI; daughter of Frederick Loesser and Susanna Campbell; married Christopher John Magson. *Education:* University of Chicago, B.A. (philosophy), 1984; Western Michigan University, B.A. (mathematics), 1992, M.A. (mathematics), 1995, M.F.A., 1998.

ADDRESSES: Office—P.O. Box 52, Comstock, MI 49041. *Agent*—Amanda Urban, International Creative Management, 40 W. 57th St., New York, NY 10019.

CAREER: Goulash Tours, Inc., Kalamazoo, MI, president, 1988—. Teacher of mathematics and creative writing.

AWARDS, HONORS: Short fiction award, Associated Writing Programs, 1998, for *Women and Other Animals;* Pushcart Prize, 2000, for "The Smallest Man in the World;" Reynolds Price Short Story Award, 2007, for "Boar Taint."

WRITINGS:

Women and Other Animals (short stories), University of Massachusetts Press (Amherst, MA), 1999.
(Coeditor, with Larry Smith) *Our Working Lives: Short Stories of People and Work,* Bottom Dog Press (Huron, OH), 2000.
Q Road (novel), Scribner (New York, NY), 2002.

Contributor of short stories and essays to periodicals, including *Story, Alaska Quarterly Review, Southern Review,* and *Utne Reader.* Newsletter editor, *Letter Parade,* 1985—.

SIDELIGHTS: Bonnie Jo Campbell trains donkeys and arranges bike tours to Russia and eastern Europe. Her short story collection *Women and Other Animals* was called a "bold and eloquent debut collection" by a *Publishers Weekly* reviewer, who said that Campbell's heroines are "determined, eccentric, painfully and beautifully human."

The stories feature women from rural Michigan who eat, smoke, and drink too much and work in dead-end jobs. Janet Kaye wrote in the *New York Times Book Review* that "the men they know are predators: absent, indifferent or casually brutal." Kaye called the stories "hard-hitting . . . [and] bitter but sweetened with humor." In "Gorilla Girl" a teen is able to vent her ferocity by playing a gorilla in a sideshow. A young man is seduced by the alcoholic mother of the young woman he worships in "The Perfect Lawn." In "Eating Aunt Victoria," an obese woman hides her food from the adult children of her dead lesbian lover. "Bringing Home the Bones" is the story of a Holocaust survivor who burns herself while canning vegetables, loses her leg, and then renews her relationship with her daughters.

Greg Tate wrote in *Village Voice* that Campbell "doesn't condescend to her hard-luck characters, but she confuses compassion with solemnity. There's nary a joke cracked in the whole book—little of the humor that can, at once, lay pain bare and act as its balm." *Booklist* reviewer

Donna Seaman called Campbell "a poet of survival, lust, and freedom, and the call of her powerful stories resonates long after their pages have been turned."

BIOGRAPHICAL AND CRITICAL SOURCES:

PERIODICALS

Booklist, November 15, 1999, Donna Seaman, review of *Women and Other Animals,* p. 600.
Chicago Tribune, October 27, 2002, Lucia Perillo, review of *Q Road,* p. 14.
New York Times Book Review, January 9, 2000, Janet Kaye, "More Deadly than the Male."
Publishers Weekly, October 4, 1999, review of *Women and Other Animals,* p. 62.
Village Voice, December 7, 1999, Greg Tate, "Tales of Inertia: Misery Loves Company," p. 81.

*   *   *

CAPECI, Dominic J., Jr.

ADDRESSES: Office—Missouri State University, 901 S. National Ave., Springfield, MO 65897. *E-mail*—DominicCapeci@MissouriState.edu.

CAREER: Historian, educator, and writer. Missouri State University, Springfield, MO, professor of history, then distinguished professor of history.

AWARDS, HONORS: Missouri History Book Award, 1999, for *The Lynching of Cleo Wright.*

WRITINGS:

The Harlem Riot of 1943, Temple University Press (Philadelphia, PA), 1977.
Race Relations in Wartime Detroit: The Sojourner Truth Housing Controversy of 1942, Temple University Press (Philadelphia, PA), 1982.
(With Martha Wilkerson) *Layered Violence: The Detroit Rioters of 1943,* University of Mississippi (Jackson, MI), 1991.

(Editor) *Detroit and the "Good War": The World War II Letters of Mayor Edward Jeffries and Friends,* University Press of Kentucky (Lexington, KY), 1996.
The Lynching of Cleo Wright, University Press of Kentucky (Lexington, KY), 1998.

Contributor to periodicals, including *Journal of Southern History, Journal of American History,* and *Historian.* Contributor to books, including *Encyclopedia of Race Relations,* edited by Walter Rucker and James Nathaniel Upton, Greenwood Press (Westport, CT), 2006.

SIDELIGHTS: Historian Dominic J. Capeci Jr., is the author of several books focusing on African-American history and specifically race relations. In *The Harlem Riot of 1943,* Capeci writes about a brief but deadly race riot in Harlem in which several people were killed. The author's primary purpose, however, is not only to present a case study of the riot itself but also to reflect on the economic and social conditions that had evolved over the preceding decade and had led to the riot. The author also writes about the official police and government response to the riot and its aftermath. Tony Platt, writing in *Contemporary Sociology,* noted that the author provides the reader with "a clear and detailed understanding of life in Harlem between the two World Wars." Platt added: "The riot itself is also reproduced in careful detail, with vivid impressions looting, dispassionate police, militarism, and the post-modern rhetoric of local politicians." Robert V. Haynes wrote in the *American Historical Review:* "*The Harlem Riot of 1943* is a first-rate study of a significant racial incident which contributes to a better understanding of race relations in the United States."

In his next book, the author focuses on another race riot that occurred a year prior to the Harlem riot. *Race Relations in Wartime Detroit: The Sojourner Truth Housing Controversy of 1942* recounts the story of a race riot that erupted when blacks tried to move into a new housing project specifically built for them but were opposed by nearby white neighbors. The rioters did not loot or destroy property but primarily fought among themselves and the police, leading to 109 arrests, with 106 of those arrested being black. "One of the many merits of Dominic J. Capeci's excellent book is that it shows how the Sojourner Truth incident, even more than bloodier clashes, illustrated wartime patterns of race relations," wrote Richard Polenberg in the *American Historical Review.*

Capeci collaborated with Martha Wilkerson to write about a much larger riot in Detroit the following year in their book *Layered Violence: The Detroit Rioters of 1943*. This time the focus is on what would be the most destructive race riot to occur in America up to that time. Taking place over three days in June, the riot resulted in thirty-four deaths, twenty-five blacks and nine whites. Capeci and Wilkerson present their case that this riot marked a turning point in race riots in the United States because for the first time blacks vented their anger and frustrations by mostly destroying white-owned property. W. Fitzhugh Brundage, writing in the *Journal of American History,* noted that the authors "move beyond extant scholarship on the Detroit riot by extensively using police records and court files to sketch a nuanced portrait of the rioters." *American Historical Review* contributor Roberta Senechal wrote: "A major strength of this study is the identification of riot participants and its detail on riot behavior."

The Lynching of Cleo Wright recounts an incident that led to the U.S. Justice Department's first involvement in a civil rights issue. Cleo Wright, who murdered a white woman and stabbed a police officer during his capture, was taken from a hospital in Sikestown, Missouri, where he was dying from wounds, and then lynched and burned by whites in a black neighborhood. In addition to profiles of Wright, the victim, and others involved in the incident, Capeci delves into the many social aspects of the case, including racial frustration, sexual taboo, and how participants in the lynching were protected by the social beliefs of the time. A *Publishers Weekly* contributor commented that the author's "extensive research, including interviews with survivors, is evident in his intricate and engrossing perspective." Gregor A. Preston, writing in the *Library Journal,* called the book "a detailed, scholarly analysis." In a review in the *Booklist,* Vanessa Bush referred to *The Lynching of Cleo Wright* as "excellent for high-school students studying human rights."

BIOGRAPHICAL AND CRITICAL SOURCES:

PERIODICALS

American Historical Review, April, 1978, Robert V. Haynes, review of *The Harlem Riot of 1943,* pp. 554-555; June, 1985, Richard Polenberg, review of *Race Relations in Wartime Detroit: The Sojourner*

Truth Housing Controversy of 1942, p. 781; February, 1993, Roberta Senechal, review of *Layered Violence: The Detroit Rioters of 1943,* pp. 268-269.
Booklist, June 1, 1998, Vanessa Bush, review of *The Lynching of Cleo Wright,* p. 1681.
Contemporary Sociology, November, 1978, Tony Platt, review of *The Harlem Riot of 1943,* pp. 763-764.
Historian, winter, 1994, Kenneth L. Kusmer, review of *Layered Violence,* p. 414.
Journal of American History, June, 1978, William H. Harris, review of *The Harlem Riot of 1943,* pp. 229-230; September, 1992, W. Fitzhugh Brundage, review of *Layered Violence,* pp. 719-720.
Journal of Southern History, November, 1999, Vincent Vinikas, review of *The Lynching of Cleo Wright,* pp. 907-908.
Library Journal, May 1, 1998, Gregor A. Preston, review of *The Lynching of Cleo Wright,* p. 117.
Publishers Weekly, May 18, 1998, review of *The Lynching of Cleo Wright,* p. 62.
Reviews in American History, September, 1999, Gail Williams O'Brien, review of *The Lynching of Cleo Wright,* pp. 462-469.

ONLINE

Missouri State University Web site, http://www.missouri state.edu/ (November 17, 2006), faculty profile of author.
University of Missouri Web site, http://www.umsystem. edu/ (November 17, 2006), "Missouri History Book Award."*

*   *   *

CLEMENS, Kate
See MacKEY, Mary

*   *   *

COBB, James C. 1947-
(James Charles Cobb)

PERSONAL: Born 1947. *Education:* University of Georgia, A.B., 1969, M.A., 1972, Ph.D., 1975.

ADDRESSES: Home—Hartwell, GA. *Office*—Department of History, University of Georgia, Athens, GA 30602. *E-mail*—cobby@arches.uga.edu; cobby@uga. edu.

CAREER: Historian, educator, and writer. Loganville High School, Loganville, Georgia, social studies instructor, 1969-70; University of Georgia, Athens, instructor in history and teaching fellow in history, 1972-75, B. Phinizy Spalding Distinguished Professor in the History of the American South, 1997—, chairman of the history department, 1998-2001; University of Maryland, visiting assistant professor of history, 1975-77; University of Northern Iowa, Cedar Falls, assistant professor, 1977-80, associate professor of history, 1980-81; University of Mississippi, University, associate professor, 1981-85, professor of history and southern studies, 1985-87, director of Southern Studies, 1981-87; University of Alabama, director of honors program and professor of history, 1987-89; University of Tennessee, Knoxville, Bernadotte Schmitt professor of history, 1989-97. Also advisory board member for H-Southern-Music.

MEMBER: Southern Historical Association (former president).

AWARDS, HONORS: Andrew Mellon Foundation Fellowship, Aspen Institute for Humanistic Study, 1982; E. Merton Coulter Award, 1984, for best article published in the *Georgia Historical Quarterly;* Green-Ramsdell Awards, 1988-89 and 1990-91, for best article published in the *Journal of Southern History;* McClemore Prize, Mississippi Historical Society, 1992, for outstanding book in Mississippi history; Senior Visiting Mellon Scholar, Cambridge University, May, 1995; Georgia Author of the Year Award in History, Georgia Writers Association and Kennesaw State University, 2006, for *The Brown Decision, Jim Crow, and Southern Identity.* Fellowships include University of Northern Iowa, summer research fellowship, June-August, 1978, 1981; University of Mississippi, summer research fellowships, 1982 and 1985; and the National Endowment for the Humanities, fellowship for individual research, 1985-86; Phi Eta Sigma, Phi Alpha Theta, and Phi Kappa Phi.

WRITINGS:

The Selling of the South: The Southern Crusade for Industrial Development, 1936-1980, Louisiana State University Press (Baton Rouge, LA), 1982, 2nd edition, University of Illinois Press (Urbana, IL), 1993.

(Editor, with Michael V. Namorato) *The New Deal and the South: Essays,* University Press of Mississippi (Jackson, MI), 1984.

Industrialization and Southern Society, 1877-1984, University Press of Kentucky (Lexington, KY), 1984.

The Most Southern Place on Earth: The Mississippi Delta and the Roots of Regional Identity, Oxford University Press (New York, NY), 1992.

(Editor) *The Mississippi Delta and the World: The Memoirs of David L. Cohn,* Louisiana State University (Baton Rouge, LA), 1995.

Georgia Odyssey, University of Georgia Press (Athens, GA), 1997.

Redefining Southern Culture: Mind and Identity in the Modern South (essays), University of Georgia Press (Athens, GA), 1999.

Away Down South: A History of Southern Identity, Oxford University Press (New York, NY), 2005.

The Brown Decision, Jim Crow, and Southern Identity, University of Georgia Press (Athens, GA), 2005.

(Editor, with William Stueck) *Globalization and the American South,* University of Georgia Press (Athens, GA), 2005.

Serves on the editorial boards of the "Southern Biography Series" of the Louisiana State University Press and *Southern Cultures,* both 1995—.

SIDELIGHTS: An expert on the interplay of economy, society, and culture in the American South, historian James C. Cobb is also the author of several books on these topics. In *The Selling of the South: The Southern Crusade for Industrial Development, 1936-1980,* Cobb traces the efforts of the southern states to industrialize over the half century following the Great Depression. Writing in the *Journal of American History,* David D. Lee commented: "Cobb deserves high praise for this study. Provocative and well written, it offers an historical perspective on current topics in balanced and judicious fashion." Gavin Wright noted in the *Journal of Economic History:* "It is rare to find a work of history which carries its coverage down within two years of its publication date; and rarer still to find that such a book is not mere journalism but a careful scholarly study."

Industrialization and Southern Society, 1877-1984 examines the industrialization of the southern states with a focus on the twentieth century. In the book, Cobb presents his theory that industrialization developed differently in the South as opposed to the North, where it opened up society. In the south, however, Cobb believes that industrialization served to strengthen the status quo, partly due to the South's inability to attract high-wage labor jobs. "Cobb's work is stimulating scholarship, and he has asked important questions," wrote *American Historical Review* contributor Donald Holley. Writing in the *Journal of Southern History,* Tom E. Terrill commented: "Readers will find *Industrialization and Southern Society* useful as a good place to begin to understand one of the most significant aspects of the American South."

Cobb served as editor, with Michael V. Namorato, of *The New Deal and the South: Essays,* which focuses on how the New Deal affected southern blacks, as well as the region's labor, politics, and agriculture. Holley, in the *American Historical Review,* commented that the authors "stress the limitations of the New Deal's accomplishments."

In *The Most Southern Place on Earth: The Mississippi Delta and the Roots of Regional Identity,* Cobb presents a detailed historical look at Mississippi Delta plantation life from the Antebellum period to modern times. In the process, the author closely examines the planters' dominance over plantation life until the 1990s, a dominance that kept the status quo strong in everyday life. Sydney Nathans, writing in the *Journal of Southern History,* referred to *The Most Southern Place on Earth* as a "vividly written, powerfully argued book." Nathans added: "Cobb's portrait of Delta planters is sharply critical but humanely intimate." Writing in *Reviews in American History,* Nan Elizabeth Woodruff commented: "His topics reveal the scope of the Delta's history, ranging from political and economic developments to chapters on the Blues and Mississippi writers. Combining archival work with the secondary literature, Cobb offers the first attempt to study the entire history of the Delta."

As editor of *The Mississippi Delta and the World: The Memoirs of David L. Cohn,* Cobb presents the memoir of the southern writer and essayist, a memoir that Cobb found in the Cohn collection at the University of Mississippi. The memoir begins in 1953, and its author reflects on the people in his life as well as his professional work. Martha H. Swain wrote in the *Journal of Southern History* that as editor "Cobb has imposed upon the somewhat discontinuous, sometimes obtuse, fifteen essays and has written an overview for each."

Redefining Southern Culture: Mind and Identity in the Modern South is a series of essays by the author that focuses on how southern people and society have adjusted to the realities of the modern world. He explores topics such as the urbanization changes that occurred following World War II, the changes in literature and music, and evolving race relations. As noted by Nancy B. Turner, writing in the *Library Journal,* Cobb means his look at southern cultures to "serve as an 'assault' on the prevalent theories of the South as somewhat aberrant in its evolution." Pete Daniel, writing in the *Journal of Southern History,* summed up his review by noting: "As Cobb's well-written and stimulating book makes clear, by embracing both God and the Devil, southerners tangle and knot historical threads in ways that will continue to challenge historians." *Southern Literary Journal* contributor Sally Wolff wrote: "Cobb brings to his study a great and useful range of cultural history and wonderful detail."

Cobb continues his analyses of southern society and identity in his book *Away Down South: A History of Southern Identity.* Cobb focuses primarily on history, literature, and popular culture to analyze southern identity and explore the factors that make the south "Southern." Referring to Cobb as "perhaps our best historical interpreter of the South," *Weekly Standard* contributor Edwin M. Yoder, Jr., went on to declare, "This may be his best book." Yoder added: "Not only has he done his homework, he has reflected deeply, and the result is mature (as in good wine), mellow, stylish, and tasty."

Cobb is also the editor, with William Stueck, and contributor to *Globalization and the American South.* Cobb's contribution to the book "explains that newly opened markets, improved logistical systems, and high-speed communications allow for business competition on a global scale," as noted by David A. Davis in *Southern Cultures.* According to Davis, the various authors discuss issues such as "how globalization—the process of advancing international economic and cultural exchange—affects the South, a distinct region with a reputation, somewhat undeserved, for isolationism."

BIOGRAPHICAL AND CRITICAL SOURCES:

PERIODICALS

American Historical Review, June, 1987, Donald Holley, reviews of *Industrialization and Southern Society, 1877-1984* and *The New Deal and the South: Essays,* p. 767.

Black Issues Book Review, May-June, 2006, Dara N. Byrne, review of *Away Down South: A History of Southern Identity,* p. 26.

Journal of American History, March, 1983, David D. Lee, review of *The Selling of the South: The Southern Crusade for Industrial Development, 1936-1980,* pp. 1030-1031.

Journal of Economic History, December, 1982, Gavin Wright, review of *The Selling of the South,* pp. 969-970.

Journal of Southern History, August, 1985, Tom E. Terrill, review of *Industrialization and Southern Society, 1877-1984,* pp. 456-458; May, 1994, Sydney Nathans, review of *The Most Southern Place on Earth: The Mississippi Delta and the Roots of Regional Identity,* pp. 381-383; November, 1996, Martha H. Swain, review of *The Mississippi Delta and the World: The Memoirs of David L. Cohn,* pp. 834-835; November, 2001, Pete Daniel, review of *Redefining Southern Culture: Mind and Identity in the Modern South,* p. 905.

Library Journal, August, 1999, Nancy B. Turner, review of *Redefining Southern Culture,* p. 123.

Mississippi Quarterly, winter, 1996, J.B. Smallwood, review of *The Mississippi Delta and the World,* p. 183; winter, 1999, Richard H. King, review of *Redefining Southern Culture,* p. 183.

Publishers Weekly, August 8, 2005, review of *Away Down South,* p. 228.

Reviews in American History, September, 1994, Nan Elizabeth Woodruff, review of *The Most Southern Place on Earth,* p. 449.

Southern Cultures, fall, 2005, David A. Davis, review of *Globalization and the American South,* p. 104.

Southern Literary Journal, spring, 2001, Sally Wolff, review of *Redefining Southern Culture,* p. 153.

Weekly Standard, October 31, 2005, Edwin M. Yoder, Jr., review of *Away Down South,* p. 37.

ONLINE

Humanities and Social Sciences Online, http://www.h-net.org/ (November 19, 2006), brief profile of author.

Organization of American Historians Web site, http://www.oah.org/ (November 19, 2006), brief profile of author.

University of Georgia Web site, http://www.uga.edu/ (November 19, 2006), faculty profile and curriculum vitae of author.*

COBB, James Charles
    See COBB, James C.

*   *   *

COBEN, Harlan 1962-

PERSONAL: Born January 4, 1962, in Newark, NJ; son of Carl Gerald and Barbara Coben; married Anne Armstrong (a pediatrician), November 5, 1988; children: four, including Charlotte and Benjamin. *Education:* Amherst College, B.A., 1984.

ADDRESSES: Home—Ridgewood, NJ. *Agent*—Aaron Priest Literary Agency, 708 3rd Ave., New York, NY 10017. *E-mail*—me@harlancoben.com.

CAREER: Writer. Previously worked in travel industry.

MEMBER: Mystery Writers of American, Sisters in Crime.

AWARDS, HONORS: Anthony Award for best paperback original novel, World Mystery Conference, and Edgar Award nomination, Mystery Writers of American, both 1996, both for *Deal Breaker;* Edgar Award for best paperback original mystery novel, Mystery Writers of American, Shamus Award for best paperback original novel, Private Eye Writers of America, and OLMA Award for best paperback original, American Online/ Microsoft/Internet Newsgroups, all 1997, all for *Fade Away;* Fresh Talent Award, United Kingdom, c. 1997, for *One False Move;* Edgar Allan Poe Award nomination in best novel category, Mystery Writers of America, 2002, Le Grand Prix des Lectrices de Elle for fiction, France, both for *Tell No One;* International Book of the Month, Bookspan, 2003, for *No Second Chance;* "Thumping Good Read" Award, W.H. Smith, for *Gone for Good;* Le Grand Prix des Lectrices de Elle for fiction, France, for *Tell No One.*

WRITINGS:

MYSTERY NOVELS

Play Dead, British American Publishing (Latham, NY), 1990.

Miracle Cure, British American Publishing (Latham, NY), 1991.
Tell No One: A Novel, Delacorte (New York, NY), 2001.
Gone for Good, Delacorte (New York, NY), 2002.
No Second Chance, Dutton (New York, NY), 2003.
Just One Look, Dutton (New York, NY), 2004.
The Innocent, Dutton (New York, NY), 2005.

"MYRON BOLITAR" MYSTERY NOVELS

Deal Breaker, Dell (New York, NY), 1995.
Dropshot, Dell (New York, NY), 1996.
Fade Away, Dell (New York, NY), 1996.
Back Spin, Dell (New York, NY), 1997.
One False Move, Dell (New York, NY), 1997.
The Final Detail, Dell (New York, NY), 2000.
Darkest Fear, Delacorte (New York, NY), 2000.
Promise Me, Dutton (New York, NY), 2006.

OTHER

(Editor and contributor) *Mystery Writers of America Presents Death Do Us Part: New Stories about Love, Lust, and Murder,* Little, Brown (New York, NY), 2006.

Contributor to periodicals, including the short story *"The Key to My Father"* in the *New York Times.* Books have been published in twenty-two languages.

ADAPTATIONS: Film adaptations of novels include *Tell No One,* 2006, and *Deal Breaker,* c. 2008. Books have been adapted as audiobooks, including *No Second Chance,* Books on Tape, 2003, *Just One Look,* Penguin Audio, 2004, and *Promise Me,* Brilliance Audio, 2006.

SIDELIGHTS: Harlan Coben made his mark in the 1990s with mystery novels that embrace the worlds of professional sports and high-powered media glitz. His first, *Play Dead,* concerns a Boston Celtics basketball star, David Baskin, who fakes his own death on his Australian honeymoon. His widow, supermodel Laura Ayars, investigates and finds that the people she wishes to interview about the case have a habit of turning up dead. David, meanwhile, has resurfaced, in disguise and with a new identity, playing the same position he

formerly did for the Celtics. The solution to the mystery has to do with a murder that happened thirty years earlier which was witnessed by David's brother and Laura's sister.

Library Journal contributor Marylaine Block noted that *Play Dead* is "an engrossing suspense novel"; the novel is also, Block stated, "primarily great romantic suspense" rather than a sports book. A *Publishers Weekly* contributor commented that the novel is "manipulative but otherwise engaging." Noted the reviewer: "Coben manufactures tension primarily by keeping key details out of his narrative." In *School Library Journal,* Katherine Fitch, assessing the book's appeal for young adult readers, wrote, "Coben weaves a delicate web of intrigue." Fitch went on to write: "A fast-moving thriller with a rapidly twisting plot."

Once again writing in the *School Library Journal,* Fitch found Coben's second novel, *Miracle Cure,* a "fast moving mystery." Here, the subject is the fictional development of a cure for AIDS by a pair of brilliant researchers, one of whom is murdered, as are several of their clinic's patients. When sports star Michael Silverman, a friend of the researchers, is diagnosed as HIV-positive, his wife, beautiful television journalist Sara Lowell, begins investigating the clinic murders with the help of secretly gay New York City homicide detective Max Bernstein. The suspects and other involved characters include Sara's bad-girl sister; the sisters' father, who is a research rival of the AIDS doctors; a televangelist; and a U.S. senator whose son is a patient at the AIDS clinic.

A *Kirkus Reviews* contributor questioned the high-glamour aspects of *Miracle Cure,* while *Library Journal* contributor A.J. Wright, despite calling the novel's characters "an uneasy stew of American types," declared that "Coben keeps the reader's interest by fleshing out the stereotypes a little bit and moving the plot fast enough to overcome the more incredible aspects."

Coben went on to develop a new investigative hero in later novels, which include *Deal Breaker* and the 1996 *Dropshot.* As their titles imply, the series protagonist is a sports agent; but Myron Bolitar is anything but typical. An aging child who still lives in his parents' basement despite a successful career as attorney and agent (and as basketball player before that), Bolitar plays TV-trivia games and hangs around with one Windsor Horne Lockwood III ("Win"), a lethally powerful young man of patrician ancestry who is devoted to the watching of his own X-rated home videos. The murder in *Dropshot* is that of Valerie Simpson, a former teenage tennis phenomenon who is trying for a comeback after a serious decline; she is shot dead at the Food Court of the U.S. Open, while another young prodigy, an African American former street kid named Duane Richwood, serves the ball for match point. Both Valerie and Duane were Myron's clients; thus, his involvement in the case.

Publishers Weekly contributor Maria Simson commented that the novel's "rapid-fire dialogue" reminded her of the "Fletch" novels by Gregory McDonald. "Dry humor and a self-deprecating attitude make Myron an appealing hero, and minor characters are delineated with attitude and verve," Simson wrote. Margo Kaufman, reviewing *Dropshot* for the *Los Angeles Times Book Review,* wrote that the plot twists were not surprising but that Coben's "depiction of the sports marketing scene is hilarious." *Armchair Detective* contributor Ronald C. Miller called the novel "a solid mystery with an interesting sports background, a fast-paced plot, witty dialogue, and a you'll-never-guess-whodunit denouement." He added: "Harlan Coben brings a new and exciting voice to the mystery novel."

In Coben's stand-alone novel *No Second Chance,* Dr. Marc Seidman wakes up in a hospital after being in a coma for twelve days following an attack. Also present at the attack was his wife, who was killed, and his baby daughter, who has been kidnapped. When he pays a ransom to the kidnappers, they take off with the money but do not return his daughter and then contact the doctor months later for more money. This time Seidman sets out to get his daughter back. Writing in the *South Florida Sun-Sentinel,* Oline H. Cogdill commented that the "action-laden plot spins on false endings, surprise revelations and a pathos that accentuates the story." Cogdill continued: "Coben sharply shapes the characters as realistic, flawed human beings capable of extreme courage and cowardice."

Just One Look begins with Grace Lawson finding a picture that doesn't seem to belong in a group of photos she just picked up from being developed. Nevertheless, one of the people in the picture looks like her husband, Jack, when he was a college student. Furthermore, one of the women in the picture has her faced crossed out. After revealing the picture to her husband, he quickly disappears, and Grace sets out to look for him. In the process, secrets from both her and her husband's past come to light. Connie Fletcher, writing in *Booklist,* noted the author's ability "to get readers to identify so passionately with the beleaguered principal character that they disappear into the story." A *Publishers Weekly* contributor commented that *Just One Look* "highlights the author's customary strengths (swift pacing, strong lead characters)." Joe Heim, writing in *People,* noted: "The tension doesn't build slowly; it snaps and crackles right from the get-go."

The Innocent tells the story of Matt Hunter, who, after finding out that she is pregnant, has his wife buy a cell phone with picture taking capabilities so they can record every second of their parenthood. When his wife goes on business trip he gets a phone photo sent to him of his wife seemingly having an affair with another man. Hunter, who spent four years in prison for killing another student in college during a brawl, is soon caught up in a mystery that includes a nun's murder. A *Kirkus Reviews* contributor commented that "there's a record number of jaw-dropping plot twists." A reviewer writing in *Publishers Weekly* called *The Innocent* Coben's "best book to date." *Booklist* contributor Connie Fletcher noted the novel's "intriguing start . . . [that] hurtles into a fast-paced hunter-and-hunted drama."

Coben returns to his hero Myron Bolitar in *Promise Me.* This time, after overhearing two teenage girls talk about driving drunk and getting them to promise to call him rather than do it again, Bolitar receives a call from one a few nights later and drives her to a friend's house. When the girl disappears without ever making it home, Bolitar decides it is his duty to find her. A *Kirkus Reviews* contributor wrote that the author "piles on the plot twists, false leads, violent set pieces and climactic surprises." Writing in *Booklist,* Connie Fletcher praised the novel's "melding of high suspense and high technology with a somewhat battered, very canny, questing hero." Adam B. Vary, writing in *Entertainment Weekly,* pointed out the author's "skillful pacing and truly surprising turns of plot."

Coben is also the editor of *Mystery Writers of America Presents Death Do Us Part: New Stories About Love, Lust, and Murder.* Written by members of the Mystery Writers of America, the stories are primarily about love that typically end in disaster. A *Kirkus Reviews* contributor called Coben's contribution to the anthology a "spectacular shocker." A *Publishers Weekly* reviewer wrote that "fans of quality short fiction should be satisfied."

BIOGRAPHICAL AND CRITICAL SOURCES:

PERIODICALS

Armchair Detective, spring, 1996, Ronald C. Miller, review of *Dropshot,* p. 242.

Booklist, March 1, 2004, Connie Fletcher, review of *Just One Look,* p. 1100; March 1, 2005, Connie Fletcher, review of *The Innocent,* p. 1101; April 1, 2006, Connie Fletcher, review of *Promise Me,* p. 4; July 1, 2006, David Pitt, review of *Mystery Writers of America Presents Death Do Us Part: New Stories about Love, Lust, and Murder,* p. 37.

Detroit Free Press, May 4, 2005, Ron Bernas, review of *The Innocent.*

Entertainment Weekly, April 30, 2004, Adam B. Vary, review of *Just One Look,* p. 168; April 29, 2005, Jennifer Reese, review of *The Innocent,* p. 155; April 28, 2006, Adam B. Vary, review of *Promise Me,* p. 139.

Europe Intelligence Wire, June 3, 2006, review of *Promise Me.*

Kirkus Reviews, September 1, 1991, review of *Miracle Cure,* p. 1106; March 15, 2004, review of *Just One Look,* 239; May 21, 2004, "Look'ing Good," book rankings, p. 85; March 1, 2005, review of *The Innocent,* p. 244; March 15, 2006, review of *Promise Me,* p. 263; June 15, 2006, review of *Mystery Writers of America Presents Death Do Us Part,* p. 602.

Library Journal, April 1, 1990, Marylaine Block, review of *Play Dead,* p. 136; November 1, 1991, A.J. Wright, review of *Miracle Cure,* p. 130; May 1, 2004, Jeff Ayers, review of *Just One Look,* p. 139; April 1, 2005, Jeff Ayers, review of *The Innocent,* p. 84; May 1, 2006, Jeff Ayers, review of *Promise Me,* p. 77.

Los Angeles Times Book Review, March 10, 1996, Margo Kaufman, review of *Dropshot,* p. 11.

Orlando Sentinel, May 26, 2004, Nancy Pate, review of *Just One Look.*

People, May 3, 2004, Joe Heim, review of *Just One Look,* p. 47.

PR Newswire, August 12, 2003, "Harlan Coben's *Gone for Good* voted WHSmith Thumping Good Read of the Year."

Publishers Weekly, April 6, 1990, review of *Play Dead,* p. 101; February 5, 1996, Maria Simson, review of *Dropshot,* p. 82; March 29, 2004, review of *Just One Look,* p. 36; May 10, 2004, Daisy Maryles, "It's Coben Time," p. 16; December 20, 2004, John

F. Baker, "Big Deal at Dutton for Coben," p. 10; March 7, 2005, review of *The Innocent,* p. 50; March 6, 2006, review of *Promise Me,* p. 48; June 5, 2006, review of *Mystery Writers of America Presents Death Do Us Part,* p. 40.

San Jose Mercury News, April 21, 2004, John Orr, review of *Just One Look.*

School Library Journal, October, 1990, Katherine Fitch, review of *Play Dead,* p. 150; May, 1992, Katherine Fitch, review of *Miracle Cure,* p. 151.

South Florida Sun-Sentinel (via Knight-Ridder/Tribune News Service), May 5, 2003, Oline H. Cogdill, review of *No Second Chance*; April 28, 2004, Oline H. Cogdill, review of *Just One Look;* April 27, 2005, Oline H. Cogdill, review of *The Innocent;* April 26, 2006, Oline H. Cogdill, review of *Promise Me;* August 9, 2006, Oline H. Cogdill, review of *Deal Breaker.*

Writer, September, 2006, Leslie Garisto Pfaff, "In the Gray Zone with Harlan Coben," interview with author, p. 20.

ONLINE

BookPage, http://www.bookpage.com/ (December 26, 2006), Stephanie Swilley, "Harlan Coben Tells All."

Bookreporter.com, http://www.bookreporter.com/ (December 26, 2006), Joe Hartlaub, reviews of *Promise Me, The Innocent, Just One Look,* and *Gone for Good;* Bob Rhubart, review of *No Second Chance;* also interview with author.

Harlen Coben Home Page, http://www.HarlanCoben. com (December 26, 2006).

Harlen Coben MySpace, http://www.myspace.com/harlancoben (December 26, 2006)

Internet Movie Database, http://www.imdb.com/ (December 26, 2006), information on author's film work.*

*   *   *

COOMER, Joe 1958-

PERSONAL: Born November 3, 1958, in Fort Worth, TX; son of Rufus (a business owner) and Linda (a business owner) Coomer; married Heather Hutton (an antiques dealer and writer), April 5, 1986. *Education:* Southern Methodist University, B.A., 1981.

ADDRESSES: Agent—Elaine Markson, Elaine Markson Literary Agency, Inc., 44 Greenwich Ave., New York, NY 10011.

CAREER: Writer. Owner of antiques malls in Fort Worth, TX, 1986—.

MEMBER: Texas Institute of Letters, Phi Beta Kappa.

AWARDS, HONORS: Texas Institute of Letters award for fiction and Jesse Jones Award for fiction, both 1983, both for *The Decatur Road.*

WRITINGS:

NOVELS; UNLESS OTHERWISE NOTED

The Decatur Road, St. Martin's Press (New York, NY), 1983.
Kentucky Love, St. Martin's Press (New York, NY), 1985.
A Flatland Fable, Texas Monthly (Austin, TX), 1986.
Dream House: On Building a House by a Pond (nonfiction), Faber and Faber (Boston, MA), 1992.
The Loop, Faber and Faber (Boston, MA), 1993.
Beachcombing for a Shipwrecked God, Graywolf (St. Paul, MN), 1995.
Sailing on a Spoonful of Water (memoir), Picador (New York, NY), 1997.
Apologizing to Dogs, Scribner (New York, NY), 1999.
One Vacant Chair, Graywolf Press (St. Paul, MN), 2003.
Pocketful of Names, Graywolf Press (St. Paul, MN), 2005.

ADAPTATIONS: The Loop has been optioned for film.

SIDELIGHTS: Joe Coomer's award-winning first novel, *The Decatur Road,* is set in the Appalachian hills of eastern Kentucky and was described by critic Ivan Gold in the *New York Times Book Review* as "a gentle story of mountain domesticity." Spanning some six decades, *The Decatur Road* centers primarily on the enduring relationship of Mitchell and Jenny Parks and their ongoing struggle to survive persistent hard times, with the dusty, twisted road of the title serving as a metaphor for that struggle. Coomer's subsequent novels, *Kentucky Love* and *A Flatland Fable,* received favorable reviews

and were recommended by critics, who praised their charm and powerful imagery. *Kentucky Love,* for example, was called a "story [that] charms the reader" by Phoebe-Lou Adams writing in the *Atlantic.*

In his novel *The Loop,* Coomer tells the story of Lyman, a Texas highway department employee who drives around the Fort Worth Loop at night aiding motorists and cleaning up road kill. When a parrot invades his trailer, Coomer discovers that the bird has a lot to say. Coomer sets out with the help of cute librarian Fiona to find the bird's owner, convinced that the owner can reveal the meaning of the cryptic messages repeated by the bird. A *Publishers Weekly* contributor referred to the novel as "deliciously quirky and perceptive," adding that "the denouement both heartens and satisfies."

Beachcombing for a Shipwrecked God presents three women living on a boat in Portsmouth, New Hampshire. Each woman deals with a crisis in her life, as Charlotte has in-laws that want to sue her for her son's death, Grace still grieves for—and speaks to—her dead husband, and teenage Chloe has an abusive mate. Referring to the novel as "lovely" in a review in *Booklist,* George Needham went on to call it "very cinematic." A *Publishers Weekly* contributor wrote that the author "evokes the sights, sounds and flavors of New England . . . in prose that at its best courses with the sonorous majesty of the tides."

Coomer turns to nonfiction with *Sailing on a Spoonful of Water,* a story about a sixty-year-old boat he buys and names *Yonder.* The narrative follows Coomer as he falls in love with the boat, learns how to sail it, and then must make a decision whether the costly upkeep is worth it all. John Skow, writing in *Time,* called the memoir "a quirky, relaxed account, as much family journal as boat biography." A *Publishers Weekly* contributor wrote that *Sailing on a Spoonful of Water* is "a journal filled with much caring and genuine respect."

In his novel *Apologizing to Dogs,* Coomer recounts the story of twelve antique dealers, all of them running failing stores on the same street in Fort Worth. After decades as neighbors, a mighty thunderstorm approaches in October 1986, and a stray dog named Himself begins a series of events that change the dealers' lives forever. "In a fast-paced and deeply plotted narrative where dogs hold all the secrets, Coomer neatly avoids dogma," wrote a *Publishers Weekly* contributor.

Writing in the *Library Journal*, Karen Bohrer noted: "This delightfully outrageous work will send readers searching for the author's previous books."

One Vacant Chair follows Sarah, who discovers that her husband is cheating on her and, as a result, decides to accompany her Aunt Edna to Scotland to spread the ashes of Sarah's recently deceased grandmother. Although Sarah does not know her aunt well, she soon discovers that Aunt Edna, a lunch lady at a grade school for thirty years, has a lot to say, some of which will change Sarah's life. In a review in the *Library Journal*, Joanna M. Burkhardt wrote that the author's "story shines with vivid characters in their everyday mode yet offers surprising twists." Joanne Wilkinson, writing in *Booklist*, noted Coomer's "peppery humor delivered by a most endearing cast of characters."

Coomer writes of a reclusive artist named Hannah Weed in his next novel, *Pocketful of Names*. Living on a remote island off the Coast of Maine, Hannah's life changes when a dog and then an abused teenager wash up on shore near her house. Through their influence, the solitary Hannah soon finds herself involved in the life of the surrounding community. A longtime successful artist, Hannah also learns who has been buying her art, a discovery that leads to further introspection. Joanne Wilkinson, writing in *Booklist*, commented that the author "excels at evoking the attractions of solitude versus the meaning of home and connection." A *Kirkus Reviews* contributor wrote: "Coomer demonstrates stylish moves in a reflective story that seems to take place over generations."

Coomer once told *CA:* "I wake up every morning appalled that things have changed. It's still hard to believe at midday, and by nightfall I've got to write about it. Sometimes I feel like I'm the only one who's noticed, but that's not so; I tell the same old story, different only in that I've forgotten some of the details and added my own to fill in the gaps. I find great joy in passing the story on."

BIOGRAPHICAL AND CRITICAL SOURCES:

BOOKS

Coomer, Joe, *Sailing on a Spoonful of Water,* Picador (New York, NY), 1997.

PERIODICALS

Atlantic, September, 1985, Phoebe-Lou Adams, review of *Kentucky Love,* p. 114.
Booklist, April 15, 1995, George Needham, review of *Beachcombing for a Shipwrecked God,* p. 1478; September 15, 1999, Carolyn Kubisz, review of *Apologizing to Dogs,* p. 230; September 1, 2003, Joanne Wilkinson, review of *One Vacant Chair,* p. 53; May 15, 2005, Joanne Wilkinson, review of *Pocketful of Names,* p. 1634.
Kirkus Reviews, July 1, 2003, review of *One Vacant Chair,* p. 870; April 1, 2005, review of *Pocketful of Names,* p. 370.
Library Journal, May 1, 1997, Robert F. Greenfield, review of *Sailing on a Spoonful of Water,* p. 111; September 15, 1999, Nancy Pearl, review of *Apologizing to Dogs,* p. 111; March 1, 2000, Karen Bohrer, review of *Apologizing to Dogs,* p. 152; September 15, 2003, Joanna M. Burkhardt, review of *One Vacant Chair,* p. 90; June 1, 2005, Jim Coan, review of *Pocketful of Names,* p. 114.
New York Times Book Review, January 8, 1984, Ivan Gold, review of *The Decatur Road.*
Publishers Weekly, August 31, 1992, review of *The Loop,* p. 66; April 24, 1995, review of *Beachcombing for a Shipwrecked God,* p. 61; May 5, 1997, review of *Sailing in a Spoonful of Water,* p. 185; August 30, 1999, review of *Apologizing to Dogs,* p. 51; September 15, 2003, review of *One Vacant Chair,* p. 45; May 16, 2005, review of *Pocketful of Names,* p. 38.
Time, June 23, 1997, John Skow, review of *Sailing in a Spoonful of Water,* p. 80.

ONLINE

Internet Movie Database, http://www.imdb.com/ (December 4, 2006), information on author's film work.*

*   *   *

CORMAN, Avery 1935-

PERSONAL: Born November 28, 1935, in New York, NY; married, November 5, 1967; wife's name Judy (died of cancer, November 15, 2004); children: Matthew, Nicholas. *Education:* Attended New York University.

CAREER: Writer and playwright.

WRITINGS:

(With Marcia Seligson and Mort Gerberg) *What Ever Happened to . . .?,* Price (Los Angeles, CA), 1965.

(With Marcia Seligson and Mort Gerberg) *You Have a Hang-up If . . .,* Essandess (New York, NY), 1967.

(With Marcia Seligson and Mort Gerberg) *The Everything in the World That's the Same as Something Else Book,* Simon & Schuster (New York, NY), 1969.

(With Marcia Seligson and Mort Gerberg) *More What Ever Happened to . . .?,* Price (Los Angeles, CA), 1971.

Oh, God!: A Novel, Simon & Schuster (Los Angeles, CA), 1971.

Kramer Versus Kramer: A Novel (Book-of-the-Month Club alternate selection), Random House (New York, NY), 1977.

The Bust-Out King (novel), Bantam (New York, NY), 1977.

A Conversation with Novelist Avery Corman, Author of Oh God!, Kramer v. Kramer, and The Old Neighborhood (sound recording), Encyclopedia Americana/CBS News Audio Resource Library (New York, NY), 1980.

The Old Neighborhood (novel), Linden Press/Simon & Schuster (New York, NY), 1980.

50, Simon & Schuster (New York, NY), 1987.

Prized Possessions (novel), Simon & Schuster (New York, NY), 1991.

The Big Hype (novel), Simon & Schuster (New York, NY), 1992.

A Perfect Divorce (novel), St. Martin's Press (New York, NY), 2004.

The Boyfriend from Hell (novel), St. Martin's Press (New York, NY), 2006.

Also author of plays, including *Skye,* written with Dan Rustin, music by Ben Finn, produced by the Library and Museum of the Performing Arts, 1971. Contributor of articles to periodicals, including *Esquire, Cosmopolitan, McCall's,* and *New York.*

ADAPTATIONS: Author's novels have been adapted for film, including *Oh, God!,* 1977 (plus sequels based on the same novel and titled *Oh God!: Book Two,* 1980,

and *Oh God!: You Devil,* 1984), and *Kramer Versus Kramer,* Columbia Pictures, 1979. *A Perfect Divorce* has been optioned for film by Columbia Pictures, c. 2005.

SIDELIGHTS: For years Avery Corman struggled through the anonymous apprenticeship served by most aspiring writers. He wrote plays at first, then educational films and collaborative works with friends, and supplemented it all with magazine articles. He eventually made it to the top of his profession when his novel *Oh, God!: A Novel* was purchased by Warner Brothers, produced as a major motion picture with George Burns and John Denver, and re-released as a paperback by Bantam in 1977. His next effort, *Kramer Versus Kramer: A Novel,* enjoyed the same success.

Oh, God! won appreciative reviews. The book is a comic, often satiric treatment of God's return to earth and a freelance writer's unsuccessful efforts to inform the world. The writer is rejected, acclaimed, arrested, detained in Bellevue, and dismissed by a world ecumenical board of miracle examiners. While Corman admitted that he wanted just to write a novel and prove his talent for comedy, he applied a more serious approach to his next book.

With *Kramer Versus Kramer,* Corman follows the growing relationship between Ted Kramer and his son Billy, after Joanna Kramer leaves the family and pursues her own career. Years later, Joanna launches a custody fight for Billy and wins, despite Ted's demonstrated competence as a father. "It takes a couple of topics that are both universal and timely," remarked Christopher Lehmann-Haupt, "and works them into a story told with maximum emotional effect."

Corman's 1991 novel, *Prized Possessions,* explores date rape. The young, bright, and talented Elizabeth Mason is a singer who, during her first weekend as a freshman at a prestigious school in New York, is raped by her date, Jimmy Andrews, a star tennis player at the school. Although Liz is initially reticent to reveal what happened and even places the guilt on herself, eventually the truth comes out and her family presses charges as Liz struggles to recover her equilibrium. "With Liz's story, Corman takes a tense, disturbing look at the nature of consent and raises critical questions about negative ways in which society still views female sexuality," wrote a *Publishers Weekly* contributor. In his next novel *The Big Hype,* Corman focuses on a writer, Paul Brock, who gains widespread national recognition due to the efforts of a savvy book promoter. Soon, however, Brock finds himself fighting for his artistic integrity. The novel features appearances by various real-life movie stars and writers. A *Time* contributor noted Corman's "light comic touch."

Corman examines an amicable divorce and the couple's subsequent lives and concern over their son in his novel *The Perfect Divorce.* Although Rob and Karen Burrows's son Tommy eventually makes good as an artist and the ex-couple's other relationships go awry, the two remain apart, much to the chagrin of their friends, who cannot figure out why they ever got divorced. A *Kirkus Reviews* contributor noted the "tart realism of the early scenes." Writing in *Publishers Weekly,* a reviewer commented that the author "writes with a warm and wise empathy that could strike a chord with many."

The Boyfriend from Hell focuses on freelance journalist Ronnie, who becomes involved with the handsome Richard Smith after interviewing him for an article about Satanism. After the article is published, Ronnie is given a contract to write a book about Satanism, which leads her to encounter the leader of Richard's satanic cult, Randall Cummings. Ronnie blacks out while interviewing him and finds the cult leader dead when she wakes up. Suspected by the police of killing him, Ronnie has a vision of the devil in a dream and then encounters the same face while walking down the street one day. Ronnie thinks she may be possessed and turns to her childhood Catholic priest for help as the true nature of Richard remains suspect. David Pitt, writing in *Booklist,* called *The Boyfriend from Hell* "another winner" by Corman. A *Kirkus Reviews* contributor noted the novel's "fun/creepy first chapters."

BIOGRAPHICAL AND CRITICAL SOURCES:

PERIODICALS

Booklist, April 1, 2006, David Pitt, review of *The Boyfriend from Hell,* p. 18.
Daily Variety, February 16, 2005, Claude Brodesser and Nicole LaPorte, "Corman Tome a 'Perfect' Fit for Columbia," p. 1; May 31, 2005, Michael Fleming, "Col Married to Corman Tome," p. 1.

Kirkus Reviews, July 15, 2004, review of *A Perfect Divorce,* p. 645; April 1, 2006, review of *The Boyfriend from Hell,* p. 310.
New York Times, October 7, 1977, Christopher Lehmann-Haupt, review of *Kramer Versus Kramer: A Novel,* p. C29.
Publishers Weekly, November 2, 1990, review of *The Prized Possessions,* p. 64; April 27, 1992, review of *The Big Hype,* p. 248; October 4, 2004, review of *A Perfect Divorce,* p. 72.
Time, July 27, 1992, review of *The Big Hype,* p. 73.

ONLINE

Doollee.com, http://www.doollee.com/ (December 28, 2006), information on author's plays.
Internet Movie Database, http://www.imdb.com/ (December 28, 2006), information on films based on author's novels.*

*   *   *

CORMICK, Craig 1961-

PERSONAL: Born 1961; son of Neil and Margaret Cormick; children: Hanna, Sanna, Jonas.

ADDRESSES: Office—Biotechnology Australia, GPO Box 9839, Canberra, Australian Capital Territory 2601, Australia. *E-mail*—craig.cormick@biotechnology.gov.au.

CAREER: Biotechnology Australia, Canberra, Australian Capital Territory, manager of public awareness; also works as a teacher.

MEMBER: Australian Society of Authors, Australian Journalists Association, Australian Capital Territory Writers Centre.

AWARDS, HONORS: Canberra Critics Award for literature, 1998; Australian Capital Territory Book of the Year award, 1999, for *Unwritten Histories.*

WRITINGS:

Kormak's Saga, Merino Press (Page, Australian Capital Territory, Australia), 1991.

(Editor) *Words of Grace: The Life of Grace Melbourne Baragwanath: An Oral History,* Merino Press (Page, Australian Capital Territory, Australia), 1991.

The Condensed Kalevala (folk tales), Merino Press (Page, Australian Capital Territory, Australia), 1991.

Little Red Riding-Hood: The Untold Tales, Variations on a Theme, Merino Press (Page, Australian Capital Territory, Australia), 1993.

(Editor) *Protesting the Testing: Canberra Writers Speak Out against Nuclear Testing in the Pacific,* PEN and Left Book Club (Canberra, Australian Capital Territory, Australia), 1995.

Pimplemania, Macmillan Educational, 1997.

(Coauthor) *The Hawker Primary School Dark Book,* Ginninderra Press (Charnwood, Australian Capital Territory, Australia), 1998.

Unwritten Histories (short stories), Aboriginal Studies Press (Canberra, Australian Capital Territory, Australia), 1998.

The King of Patagonia (short stories), Mockingbird (Charnwood, Australian Capital Territory, Australia), 1999.

(Editor) *John Had Really Had Enough* (short stories), Merino Press (Page, Australian Capital Territory, Australia), 1999.

(Editor) *Doing Time: Prison Poetry '99,* Pen ACT (Manuka, Australian Capital Territory, Australia), 1999.

(Editor, with Sarah St. Vincent Welch) *Time Pieces* (short stories), Ginninderra Press (Charnwood, Australian Territory, Australia), 1999.

The Monster under the Bed (juvenile), illustrated by Hanna Cormick, Ginninderra Press (Canberra, Australian Capital Territory, Australia), 1999.

Kurikka's Dreaming: The True Story of Matti Kurikka, Socialist, Utopian, and Dreamer, Simon & Schuster (New York, NY), 2000.

The Queen of Aegea (short stories), Ginninderra Press (Charnwood, Australian Capital Territory, Australia), 2001.

Dig: The Forgotten History of Burke & Wills, Ginninderra Press (Charnwood, Australian Capital Territory, Australia), 2002.

The Princess of Cups (short stories), Mockingbird (Charnwood, Australian Capital Territory, Australia), 2003.

(Editor and contributor) *Winners* (short stories by Australian authors) Ginninderra Press (Charnwood, Australian Capital Territory, Australia), 2004.

A Funny Thing Happened at 27,000 Feet . . .: Tales from Times of Terror, Mockingbird (Charnwood, Australian Capital Territory, Australia), 2005.

Shorter works include *"Good Neighbours,"* Merino Press (Page, Australian Capital Territory, Australia), 1996; *"Terra Nullius: The Unknown Land,"* Merino Press, 1997; *"The Magic Book,"* Ginninderra Press (Canberra, Australian Capital Territory, Australia), 1998; and *"Kalevala Revisited"* (folk tales), Merino Press, 2000. Editor, *BLAST* (radical arts magazine).

SIDELIGHTS: Craig Cormick is an Australian journalist, teacher, and author, who manages the public awareness program of the government-sponsored Biotechnology Australia. Cormick's award-winning collection of short stories, *Unwritten Histories,* was reviewed by Aboriginal author Anita Heiss in *Australian Book Review.* Heiss helped launch the book, which she said might be considered strange, since she has criticized many of the books written by non-Indigenous authors that have been published by Aboriginal Studies Press. Heiss said they are often written by historians, academics, and anthropologists with research grants, who lived in the communities for three weeks, months, or years with their tape recorders, notepads, and observations. Heiss commented that Cormick "has thrown a spanner in the works with *Unwritten Histories,* by producing a work that has value and benefits for educating and informing and, high on my list of pluses, entertaining."

Heiss further commented that Cormick is creative, subtle, and uses humor in portraying the role of Indigenous people since colonization, "a role that has been denied or misrepresented for so long." She called the characters in Cormick's stories "very palatable . . . some with personalities that make you laugh out loud. They are positioned at selected moments in time and across various geographic regions." Heiss concluded by saying that although she usually recommends that only books by Aboriginal authors be read in order to learn about their society, culture, and history, "it would be a disservice not to recommend this book to all."

BIOGRAPHICAL AND CRITICAL SOURCES:

PERIODICALS

Australian Book Review, April, 1999, Anita Heiss, "Storytelling," pp. 12-13.

CROUCH, Stanley 1945-

PERSONAL: Born December 14, 1945, in Los Angeles, CA; married Gloria Nixon (a sculptor), c. 1990s.

ADDRESSES: Office—New York Daily News, 450 W. 33 St., New York, NY 10001.

CAREER: Writer, playwright, columnist, music critic, musician, television commentator, and actor. Studio Watts company, 1965-67; drummer with pianist Raymond King, 1966; drummer and bandleader with various groups, including Quartet and Black Music Infinity, 1967—; Claremont College, Claremont, CA, instructor in drama, literature, and jazz history, 1969-75; Lincoln Center, New York, NY, artistic consultant and cofounder of Jazz at Lincoln Center department, 1987—; Columbia University, New York, NY, Louis Armstrong visiting professor, 2002-03. Has appeared on television and radio.

AWARDS, HONORS: Jean Stein Award, American Academy of Arts and Letters; MacArthur Foundation grant.

WRITINGS:

Ain't No Ambulances for No Nigguhs Tonight (poems), R.W. Baron (New York, NY), 1972.
Notes of a Hanging Judge: Essays and Reviews, 1979-1989, Oxford University Press (New York, NY), 1990.
The All-American Skin Game; or, The Decoy of Race: The Long and the Short of It, 1990-1994, Pantheon (New York, NY), 1995.
Always in Pursuit: Fresh American Perspectives, 1995-1997, Pantheon (New York, NY), 1998.
Don't the Moon Look Lonesome: A Novel in Blues and Swing, Pantheon (New York, NY), 2000.
The Artificial White Man: Essays on Authenticity, Basic Civitas Books (New York, NY), 2004.
Considering Genius: Writings on Jazz, Basic Civitas Books (New York, NY), 2006.

Contributor to books and anthologies, including *Black Fire,* 1968; *We Speak as Liberators: Young Black Poets,* 1970; *Black Spirits,* 1972; *The Reading Room: Writing of the Moment,* edited by Barbara Probst, Great Marsh

(New York, NY), 2000; *Police Brutality,* edited by Jill Nelson, Norton (New York, NY), 2000; and *Masters of American Comics,* Yale University Press (New Haven, CT), 2005. Staff writer and jazz critic for *Village Voice,* 1979-88; columnist for *Los Angeles Free Press, Cricket, New York Daily News,* and *SoHo Weekly News;* Contributing editor to the *New Republic,* 1990—; contributor to periodicals, including *New Yorker, New York Times,* and *Esquire.* Composer of various musical pieces, including "Future Sallie's Time," "Chicago for Bobby Seale," "The Confessions of Father None," "Flying through Wire," "Attica in Black September," and "Noteworthy Lady"; albums include *Now Is Another Time* and *Past Spirits.*

SIDELIGHTS: Stanley Crouch has performed in many roles, among them musician, jazz critic, social critic, poet, essayist, and novelist. The first book Crouch published was a volume of poetry titled *Ain't No Ambulances for No Nigguhs Tonight.* In *Library Journal,* Sandford Dorbin maintained that the publication is "God-intoxicated" and "worddrunk." Dorbin also called Crouch "wildly uneven, as you would expect a natural poet to be." Following the 1972 collection, Crouch applied his style outside the bounds of poetry and music, discussing a variety of topics in a bold manner. "Armed with an elephant's memory and a passionate knowledge of and engagement with art (blues and jazz especially, though not exclusively) and history (American, though not exclusively), Crouch delights in slaying the dragons of convention—particularly those that guard the sometimes-insular world of black intellectuals," wrote Amy Alexander on the *Salon.com* Web site.

In a review of *The All-American Skin Game, or, The Decoy of Race: The Long and the Short of It, 1990-1994* a *Boston Phoenix* contributor called it an "everything-but-the-kitchen-sink collection" of writings. The reviewer went on to note: "There's a fine line between lyricism and luster. At least, there is for Stanley Crouch, the iconoclastic culture critic." The reviewer added: "Few writers . . . juxtapose their best and worst qualities as blithely as Crouch. He has a gift for courageous phrases—tightly alliterated and rhythmically risky—that ring in the ear like a great horn line. The downside is that he doesn't always distinguish real insight from glib turns of phrase." In a *Booklist* assessment of the same volume, Bonnie Smothers remarked that Crouch "talks a lot of interesting stuff" but "is not an easy person to relate to because he is one of those 'in-your-face' thinkers whose very smugness seems meant to alienate and provoke." Alexander commented: "Crouch's troublemaking reputation was made with his first essay collection, 1990's *Notes of a Hanging Judge: Essays and Reviews, 1979-1989,* which smacked the slumbering genre of race and cultural criticism out of its 30-year torpor."

In *Notes of a Hanging Judge,* Crouch explores a variety of subjects ranging from feminism, black power, and the Third World to boxing, popular culture, and the movies of Spike Lee. Like Ralph Ellison and Albert Murray, two other writers with roots in jazz, Crouch uses music, according to *American Spectator* contributor Martha Bayles, "as a vantage point to scrutinize the rest of the world." With his essays, Crouch "sets himself apart from and above the tides of current opinion," according to Deirdre English in the *New York Times Book Review.* The author is a severe critic of political and cultural leaders who view black Americans as the helpless victims of racist oppression. The "hanging judge" in his book title is the freebooter Henry Morgan, "who sent many of his former pirate buddies to the gallows, certain that they deserved what they got," according to Crouch, who was once a black nationalist and blames the excesses of the movement and its prominent leaders for the collapse of the civil rights struggle. He scorns black proponents of separatism, anti-Semitism, and what he sees as selfish opportunism. He considers jazz to be the musical expression of a traditional "heroic optimism" among black Americans, and he praises the historic willingness of blacks "to take the field, to do battle, and to struggle up from the sink holes of self-pity." His prescription for African American progress rejects the idea of African innocence or superiority and proclaims the need for personal responsibility, education, and reasoned debate. With these recommendations, according to English, Crouch "comes off less like a hanging judge than a knowing and anxious father figure."

Crouch is severely critical of prominent figures such as Malcolm X, the "chief black heckler of the civil rights movement," and Kwame Toure (Stokely Carmichael), "the ghost of Pan-African nationalism past." He also attacks other notables, including novelist Toni Morrison and filmmaker Spike Lee. Morrison won a Pulitzer Prize for her novel, *Beloved,* but is dismissed by Crouch as a writer of "portentous melodrama." Spike Lee is characterized as a "middle-class would-be street Negro" whose acclaimed and controversial film, *Do the Right Thing,* is a "rancid fairy tale." According to Bayles,

Crouch finds Lee's "attachment to 1960s-style militance . . . the sentimental indulgence of a privileged youth ill-informed about the real problems of the black poor."

Though some critics denounced what they considered to be Crouch's personal attacks on various figures, many praised *Notes of a Hanging Judge* as insightful and refreshing. "It's rare to find both verbal virtuosity and rational coherence in the same person," noted Bayles. "For this reason alone, it's worth reading *Notes of a Hanging Judge.*" *Nation* contributor Gene Seymour observed that, while one may disagree with the author, "you have to appreciate the fact that, like any good jazz player, Crouch never repeats himself or does the predictable." Seymour also noted that Crouch's "willingness to call upon a wide range of references gives his collection a supple, almost buoyant texture." Writing in *Washington Post Book World,* David Nicholson commented: "From politics to art to jazz to the blues to literature, Crouch covers the waterfront. Throughout, he is not only provocative but perceptive and, on more than one occasion, wise. In the end it must be said that this is the kind of book you want not merely to read, but to ponder."

In 1998 readers were given another collection of Crouch's writings, *Always in Pursuit: Fresh American Perspectives, 1995-1997.* In the essays, speeches and reviews which were culled from many sources, Crouch presents "the same themes" as in previous writings, observed Bonnie Smothers in *Booklist.* "If a reader can push beyond Stanley's narrowly held opinions, there's gold to be mined from his hyperbolic riffs and rants." Smothers added: "Many pieces are entertaining, though disturbing." A *Kirkus Reviews* contributor who referred to Crouch as a "jazz guru and social/cultural critic" was impressed with Crouch's discussion of Albert Murray, Christopher Darden, and various jazz figures, but found Crouch's words on other topics to be troublesome: "Crouch sustains whole stretches of fine, sometimes expert material, but overall this 'intellectual medley' is wildly erratic, and its best verses rarely transcend its verbiage." In contrast, a *Publishers Weekly* reviewer noted "Crouch's fluid style, clearly influenced by the blues and jazz he loves, keeps his prose interesting."

Crouch's fiction debut came in 2000 with the publication of *Don't the Moon Look Lonesome: A Novel in Blues and Swing. Booklist* contributor Ellen Flexman praised the novel—the story of an interracial couple of jazz musicians struggling with "race, art, success, and family," calling it a "stylish love story" and applauding the author's ability to make his prose evoke "a blues band or a gospel choir."

In 2000 Crouch's writing was published, along with the work of others, in *The Reading Room: Writing of the Moment,* edited by Barbara Probst; and in *Police Brutality,* edited by Jill Nelson. Vanessa Bush in *Booklist* described *Policy Brutality* as "a compelling reader on the enduring evil of police brutality in a democratic society and its tacit social acceptance."

In *The Artificial White Man: Essays on Authenticity,* Crouch presents previously unpublished essays focusing on books and films as he reflects on the misogynistic aspects of the American people and their culture. In the process he discusses the works of writers such as Ernest Hemingway, Saul Bellow, and Philip Roth and the movies of filmmakers such as Quentin Tarrentino. In an interview with Joanna Rabiger in *Publishers Weekly,* Crouch commented on his book, noting that it "is a response to the balkanizing nature of social evaluation." Crouch added: "The obsession with authenticity, with being a 'real' person is everywhere, from the Democratic political convention to barbaric popular entertainment like rap, where actually being a knucklehead criminal elevates what is now known as street credibility." Harry Siegel, writing in the *Weekly Standard,* commented that the author "argues, a post-Watergate era of close examination has eroded our traditional institutions, and our popular culture now 'defines authenticity from the bottom up,' embracing 'the neo-Sam-bo' motif of hip-hop videos that reduce blacks to the manic-depressive ravings of the unhinged adolescent, a token counter to bourgeois, 'white' values." In a review in *Booklist,* Vernon Ford wrote that "Crouch exposes the cultural realities of racial authenticity." *Black Issues Book Review* contributor Herb Boyd wrote: "Those able to endure Crouch's ideological insults will find one of the nation's finest wordsmiths at work, though reading him . . . is like eating a tasty, scrumptious meal only to end up with heartburn and indigestion."

Considering Genius: Writings on Jazz is a collection of the author's writing about Jazz dating back to 1977. He discusses musicians such as John Coltrane, Thelonious Monk, and Miles Davis and presents an autobiographical essay about his love of and involvement with jazz. In a review in the *Weekly Standard,* Ted Gioia commented that "now readers have the opportunity to accompany him [Crouch] on an extended prose tour, over

the course of more than 300 pages, of the jazz world according to Crouch." Gioia added: "And with such an animated cicerone, the sights and sounds are rarely boring." Bill Ott, writing in *Booklist,* called *Considering Genius* "essential reading for jazz fans." A contributor to *Ebony* noted the author's "highly personal and 'loquacious' writing."

BIOGRAPHICAL AND CRITICAL SOURCES:

BOOKS

Crouch, Stanley, *Notes of a Hanging Judge: Essays and Reviews, 1979-1989,* Oxford University Press (New York, NY), 1990.

PERIODICALS

American Spectator, September, 1990, Martha Bayles, review of *Notes of a Hanging Judge,* pp. 35-36.
Black Issues Book Review, November-December, 2004, Herb Boyd, review of *The Artificial White Man: Essays on Authenticity,* p. 63.
Booklist, October 15, 1995, Bonnie Smothers, review of *The All-American Skin Game; or, The Decoy of Race: The Long and the Short of It, 1990-1994,* p. 370; December 1, 1997, Bonnie Smothers, review of *Always in Pursuit: Fresh American Perspectives, 1995-1997,* p. 586; April 1, 2000, Ellen Flexman, review of *Don't the Moon Look Lonesome: A Novel in Blues and Swing,* p. 129; May 15, 2000, Vanessa Bush, review of *Police Brutality,* p. 1707; November 1, 2004, Vernon Ford, review of *The Artificial White Man,* p. 447; August 1, 2006, Bill Ott, review of *Considering Genius: Writings on Jazz,* p. 24.
Boston Phoenix, April 4-11, 1996, "From the Pulpit: Stanley Crouch Offers Doses of Hectoring and Passion."
Ebony, July, 2006, review of *Considering Genius,* p. 30.
Kirkus Reviews, December 1, 1997, review of *Always in Pursuit.*
Library Journal, April 1, 1972, Sandford Dorbin, review of *Ain't No Ambulances for No Nigguhs Tonight,* p. 1328.
Nation, May 21, 1990, Gene Seymour, review of *Notes of a Hanging Judge,* pp. 710-712.
New York Times Book Review, March 11, 1990, Deirdre English, "Nobody's Victim," p. 9.

Publishers Weekly, September 11, 1995, review of *The All-American Skin Game,* p. 67; November 24, 1997, review of *Always in Pursuit,* p. 58; September 20, 2004, review of *The Artificial White Man,* p. 55, and Joanna Rabiger, "Talking Authenticity about Race," interview with author, p. 56.

Reference & Research Book News, August, 2005, review of *The Artificial White Man,* p. 237.

Washington Post Book World, April 8, 1990, David Nicholson, review of *Notes of a Hanging Judge,* p. 5.

Weekly Standard, November 15, 2004, Harry Siegel, review of *The Artificial White Man,* p. 36; July 17, 2006, Ted Gioia, review of *Considering Genius.*

ONLINE

Columbia University Center for Jazz Studies Web site, http://www.jazz.columbia.edu/bio/ (December 28, 2006), faculty profile of author.

Internet Movie Database, http://www.imdb.com/ (December 28, 2006), information on author's television appearances.

New York Daily News Web site, http://www. nydailynews.com/ (December 28, 2006), brief profile of author.

Salon.com, http://www.salon.com/ (January 19, 1999), Amy Alexander, "The Bull in the Black-Intelligentsia China Shop," profile of author*

D

DAVID, James F.
(James D. Foster)

PERSONAL: Married; children: three daughters. *Education:* Attended Seattle Pacific University; Ohio State University, M.A., Ph.D.

ADDRESSES: Home—Tigard, OR. *Office*—George Fox University, School of Behavioral and Health Sciences, 414 N. Meridian St., Newberg, OR 97132. *E-mail*—jfoster@georgefox.edu.

CAREER: Writer, psychologist, and educator. George Fox University, Newberg, OR, professor of psychology and dean of the School of Behavioral and Health Sciences, chairperson of the Undergraduate Psychology Department.

WRITINGS:

NOVELS

Footprints of Thunder, Forge (New York, NY), 1995.
Fragments, Forge (New York, NY), 1997.
Ship of the Damned, Forge (New York, NY), 2000.
Before the Cradle Falls, Forge (New York, NY), 2002.
Judgment Day, Tom Doherty Associates (New York, NY), 2005.
Thunder of Time, Forge (New York, NY), 2006.

SIDELIGHTS: James F. David is the pseudonym of psychologist and educator James D. Foster. In his first novel, *Footprints of Thunder,* a time wave exchanges pieces of the earth from the prehistoric dinosaur era with those of the present day. What results is a time quilt where, for example, there exists a space in New York City that is untouched, while adjacent to it is a meadow full of grazing dinosaurs. Other cities have disappeared altogether. The narrative follows the characters in their quest to survive, understand what is happening, and come up with a solution. Rex E. Klett, writing in the *Library Journal,* called it a "suspenseful, fantastic first novel."

Fragments is the story of a team of brainwave specialists at a university research center who try to combine the minds of five individuals who are autistic savants, each possessing a singular gift or skill. The specialists, led by research psychologist Dr. Wes Martin, are hoping to create a superconsciousness similar to that of a god, but what actually results from the experiment is devastating. The creation, named Frankie, starts a murder rampage through the town as the specialists hurry to try and destroy her. A reviewer writing in *Publishers Weekly* wrote: "David's tale is an action-packed no-brainer full of guilty pleasures for even the most cerebral reader."

Ship of the Damned is a stand-alone sequel to *Fragments.* It is based on the Philadelphia Experiment, which was a World War II attempt to make warships invisible. Dr. Wes Martin and Elizabeth Foxworth are investigating people who are all having the same dream—they are wandering on an empty ship in the desert. They discover that the ship is real—it is the U.S.S. *Norfolk,* and for fifty years it has survived in its own universe called Pot of Gold, monitored by the Office of Special Projects. The people aboard have gained psychic powers. A plan is devised to destroy the ship's generators, which are keeping it separate from the real world. A *Publishers Weekly* contributor wrote of the novel: "David crafts a great summer read, a swift amusement park ride of shipboard battles, telekinetic showdowns and potential nuclear catastrophe."

David writes of a time traveler who goes back in time to stop the serial killer who murdered his daughter in *Before the Cradle Falls.* The killer is known as the Cradle Robber because he kills babies. Portland police detective Kyle Sommers is on the killer's trail when he discovers that a time traveler is saving many of the baby victims before the Cradle Robber can kill them. Before long, Sommers is searching for the "blue man" (named because of the blue glow he emits) to see if he can save Sommers's daughter, who was killed in a tragic accident that Sommers believes was his fault. A *Publishers Weekly* contributor called the novel a "superbly paced mix of science fiction, thriller and police procedural." David Pitt, writing in *Booklist,* referred to *Before the Cradle Falls* as "a believable thriller that will appeal to both mystery and fantasy fans."

In *Judgment Day,* a fundamentalist group known as the Light in the Darkness Fellowship has acquired a spaceship from aliens to begin an exodus to a new planet and escape from the anti-Christ, who happens to be the President of the United States. In a review in *Booklist,* John Mort commented that "the climactic battle in the heavens is passionate and affecting, adding something new to the apocalyptic genre."

Thunder of Time is a sequel to David's debut novel, *Footprints of Thunder.* Although a nuclear bomb was exploded in Seattle to seal the time rifts that allow dinosaurs to roam modern-day earth, more rifts are appearing while a mysterious pyramid is found on the moon and in the Yucatan. As scientists investigate the pyramids, a third one is discovered by an eco-terrorist who wants to use it to destroy civilization and create a new world order. Writing in *Booklist,* Carl Hays noted that the author's "storytelling has markedly improved." A *Publishers Weekly* contributor referred to the novel as "action-packed."

BIOGRAPHICAL AND CRITICAL SOURCES:

PERIODICALS

Booklist, September 15, 1995, Carl Hays, review of *Footprints of Thunder,* p. 144; May 15, 2002,

David Pitt, review of *Before the Cradle Falls,* p. 1578; February 15, 2005, John Mort, review of *Judgment Day,* p. 1035; March 15, 2006, Carl Hays, review of *Thunder of Time,* p. 35.

Kirkus Reviews, August 15, 1995, review of *Footprints of Thunder,* p. 1128; May 15, 1997, review of *Fragments,* p. 737; July 1, 2000, review of *Ship of the Damned,* p. 903; April 15, 2002, review of *Before the Cradle Falls,* p. 512; March 15, 2006, review of *Thunder of Time,* p. 250.

Library Journal, September 1, 1995, Rex E. Klett, review of *Footprints of Thunder,* p. 211.

Publishers Weekly, September 4, 1995, review of *Footprints of Thunder,* p. 49; May 19, 1997, review of *Fragments,* p. 64; July 17, 2000, review of *Ship of the Damned,* p. 175; April 29, 2002, review of *Before the Cradle Falls,* p. 47; February 20, 2006, review of *Thunder of Time,* p. 135.

Science Fiction Chronicle, February, 1998, Don Dammassa, review of *Fragments,* p. 62.

ONLINE

George Fox University Web site, http://www.georgefox. edu/ (December 28, 2006), faculty profile of author as James D. Foster.

James F. David Web site, http://www.geocities.com/ Athens/Parthenon/7600/jfd.html (December 28, 2006).

SFSite.com, http://www.sfsite.com/ (December 28, 2006), Leon Olszewski, review of *Footprints of Thunder.**

*   *   *

DAWSON, Lorne L. 1954-

PERSONAL: Born March 11, 1954, in Regina, Saskatchewan, Canada; son of Donald Robert and Muriel Dawson; married; remarried, 2001; wife's name Dianne L.; children: Taylor Fletcher (first marriage). *Education:* Queen's University, Kingston, Ontario, Canada, B.A. (with honors), 1978; McMaster University, M.A., 1980, Ph.D., 1986.

ADDRESSES: Home—Waterloo, Ontario, Canada. *Office*—Department of Sociology, University of Waterloo, 200 University Ave. W., Waterloo, Ontario N2L 3G1, Canada; fax: 519-746-7326. *E-mail*—ldawson@ uwaterloo.ca.

CAREER: University of Lethbridge, Lethbridge, Alberta, Canada, assistant professor of sociology, 1989-92; University of Waterloo, Waterloo, Ontario, Canada, assistant professor, 1992-97, associate professor, 1997-2005, professor of sociology and religious studies, 2005—. Director of the Lauirer-Waterloo Ph.D. in Religious Studies.

AWARDS, HONORS: Postdoctoral fellow, Social Sciences and Humanities Research Council of Canada, 1987-89.

WRITINGS:

Reason, Freedom, and Religion: Closing the Gap between the Humanistic and Scientific Study of Religion, Peter Lang (New York, NY), 1988.
(Editor) *Cults in Context: Readings in the Study of New Religious Movements,* Canadian Scholars' Press (Toronto, Ontario, Canada), 1996, Transaction Books (New Brunswick, NJ), 1998.
Comprehending Cults: The Sociology of New Religious Movements, Oxford University Press (New York, NY), 1998, revised edition, 2006.
(Editor) *Cults and New Religious Movements: A Reader,* Blackwell (Malden, MA), 2003.
(Editor, with Douglas E. Cowan) *Religion Online: Finding Faith on the Internet,* Routledge (New York, NY), 2004.
I nuovi movimenti religiosi, Il Mulino (Bologna, Italy), 2005.

Contributor to several books, including *Misunderstanding Cults,* University of Toronto Press (Toronto, Ontario, Canada), 2000; *Cults, Religion, and Violence,* Cambridge University Press (New York, NY), 2002; *The Oxford Handbook of New Religious Movements,* Oxford University Press (New York, NY), 2004; and *Religion in Cyberspace,* Routledge (New York, NY), 2005. Contributor to periodicals, including *Journal of Contemporary Religion, Journal for the Scientific Study of Religion, Sociology of Religion,* and *Journal of the American Academy of Religion.*

SIDELIGHTS: Lorne L. Dawson once told *CA:* "While my academic articles are often theoretical and demanding, I have tried to write my books for a more general readership. I think scholars have a social obligation to

make reliable information, on often controversial subjects (e.g., why some new religions become violent), as accessible as possible. For this reason I also write newspaper articles occasionally and commonly accept invitations to speak with the media about religious issues in the news."

BIOGRAPHICAL AND CRITICAL SOURCES:

ONLINE

University of Waterloo Web site: Department of Sociology Home Page for Lorne L. Dawson, http://sociology.uwaterloo.ca/lorne_dawson.html (April 8, 2007).
University of Waterloo Web site: Faculty of Arts Home Page for Lorne L. Dawson, http://arts.uwaterloo.ca/arts/ugrad/profiles_professors/dawson (April 8, 2007).

*   *   *

DECKER, Peter R. 1934-
(Peter Randolph Decker)

PERSONAL: Born October 1, 1934 in New York, NY; son of Frank Randolph and Marjorie Decker; married Dorothy Morss, September 24, 1972; children: Karen, Christopher, Hilary. *Education:* Middlebury College, B.A., 1957; Syracuse University, M.A., 1961; Columbia University, Ph.D., 1974. *Politics:* Democrat.

ADDRESSES: *Office*—Double D Ranch, 6748 Highway 62, Ridgway, CO 81432-9796; fax: 303-861-8216; 750 Pennsylvania St., Denver, CO 80203. *E-mail*—d2ranch@aol.com.

CAREER: *Congressional Quarterly,* Washington, DC, senior writer, 1963-64; Middlebury College, Middlebury, VT, assistant to the president, 1964-67; Senator Robert Kennedy's office, Washington, staff assistant, 1967-68; Columbia University, New York, NY, instructor and lecturer, between 1972 and 1974; Duke University, Durham, NC, assistant professor, 1974-80; Double D Ranches, Ridgway, owner and operator, 1980—.

Colorado commissioner of agriculture, 1987-89. *Military service:* U.S. Army, armor, 1957-60. U.S. Army Reserve; became captain.

MEMBER: National Cattlemen's Beef Association, National Western Livestock Association, Colorado Livestock Association, Colorado Authors' League, Denver Athletic Club, Elks.

AWARDS, HONORS: Fellow of National Endowment for the Humanities at Yale University, 1977-78; humanities fellow, Rockefeller Foundation, 1979-80; D.H.L., Fort Lewis College, 2006.

WRITINGS:

Fortunes and Failures: White-Collar Mobility in Nineteenth-Century San Francisco, Harvard University Press (Cambridge, MA), 1978.
Old Fences, New Neighbors, University of Arizona Press (Tucson, AZ), 1998.
The Utes Must Go, Fulcrum Books (Golden, CO), 2005.

Contributor of articles to journals and newspapers, including *Northern Lights, Massachusetts Review, Chronicle, Community, Durango Herald,* and *Denver Post.*

SIDELIGHTS: Peter R. Decker's first book, *Fortunes and Failures: White-Collar Mobility in Nineteenth-Century San Francisco,* is a historical overview of San Francisco's transformation from a commercial port city of 30,000 people in the early 1850s to a largely industrial city of 200,000 thirty years later. Decker gives readers an account of the boom and bust cycles of the city, the origins of the merchant class and their leadership in organizing the social and political structure of the city, and the strength of the organized blue-collar workers. Writing in the *American Historical Review,* Michael Weber praised Decker's scholarship, observing that he "has made an important first attempt to combine both statistical and traditional data in studying class difference in mobility rates." Suggesting that Decker's work goes beyond a mere analysis of facts, Weber also noted that Decker "succeeded in bringing the human element to the New Urban History."

In *Old Fences, New Neighbors,* Decker explains contemporary societal shifts based on his personal experience as a cattle rancher. Decker and his wife moved from New York City to Ouray County, Colorado in the early 1970s and bought a cattle ranch. When Decker moved to Ouray, the area was a remote ranching and mining community. Over the following twenty years, the area gradually became gentrified. As Decker commented in the *Los Angeles Times Book Review,* "Today more than half of the income of Ouray County's residents is derived from dividends, interest, rest, and transfer payments. Retirees far outnumber ranchers and their employees. There are still more cattle than people, but the ratio is lessening." A *Kirkus Reviews* critic found the book highly informative, calling it "like the county it chronicles—small, but brimming with instructive examples of the hard choices facing the denizens of America's last, best places." Fred Egloff, writing in *Booklist,* explained that Decker's description of the changes in Ouray serves as a "microcosm" of the "changes caused by the gentrification that is sweeping even the more remote areas of the American West." Egloff evaluated the book as a "very interesting examination of a topical subject that raises questions that will not be resolved until tested by time and the vicissitudes of both the economy and the government."

Decker told *CA:* "I write to tell a story both to myself and to my readers; also to discover and learn more about the topic at hand, be it nonfiction or fiction. For instance, my knowledge of Native American culture was greatly enhanced by my research about the Ute tribe for *The Utes Must Go.* Likewise, I discovered a better understanding of my own hometown county after writing *Old Fences, New Neighbors.*

"I am particularly sensitive about my writing style. As a professionally trained historian, I became sensitive to and critical of much professional writing (history and other social science disciplines)—the jargon and hence limited appeal to a non-academic audience. I am particularly impressed with the historical writings of David McCullough, William Leuchtenburg, Joseph Ellis, William Chafe, and Barbara Tuchman—as much for their research as for their writing style.

"Before I write anything I have completed almost all of the research I believe is necessary for the subject. I then write from a chapter outline, nothing detailed, but enough of a guide to myself to develop the story. My research notes are organized by chapters, and I write from my notes (which include the source for a footnote where and when needed). I may find in the writing of a chapter that more research or clarification is needed, so I'll break the writing process to complete the research. I finish all the chapters, reread the manuscripts, make necessary changes, and send the draft to my editor. I am a writer who puts a great deal of faith in a good editor. I expect a close and critical reading. If I don't get it from my in-house editor, I will find (and have found) a good editor outside the publishing house.

"Like most writers, I come to a subject because of a personal interest. Beforehand, I know there is a story to be told. I may not know the ending, but I do have an idea of where the story is leading, the characters, and the setting. In the case of *The Utes Must Go,* the story had been told before, but not well and not within the context I thought appropriate. I also write a book to clarify a historical trend (*Fortunes and Failures*) and another to capture the rapid changes impacting a traditional, rural, agricultural community (*Old Fences, New Neighbors*).

"I am now attempting to write fiction, a different animal from narrative history. Some rules remain the same: use of the active voice, relating a story that will hold the interest of the reader, setting sell-described scenes, creating characters with personalities. But the use of one's imagination is critical in fiction (a real danger in narrative history) and at the same time, the writer of fiction is not tied to the dictates of historical events. History, I find, can be woven into fiction, but one must be careful not to overplay its use and application.

"In the end, writing must be fun for the writer and the reader."

BIOGRAPHICAL AND CRITICAL SOURCES:

PERIODICALS

American Historical Review, April, 1979, Michael P. Weber, review of *Fortunes and Failures: White-Collar Mobility in Nineteenth-Century San Francisco,* pp. 563-564.

Booklist, September 1, 1998, Fred Egloff, review of *Old Fences, New Neighbors,* p. 60.
Choice, October, 1978, review of *Fortunes and Failures,* p. 1132.
Kirkus Reviews, September 11, 1998, review of *Old Fences, New Neighbors,* p. 943.
Los Angeles Times Book Review, February 14, 1999, review of *Old Fences, New Neighbors,* p. 11.

*   *   *

DECKER, Peter Randolph
See DECKER, Peter R.

*   *   *

DeJEAN, Joan 1948-
(Joan Elizabeth DeJean)

PERSONAL: Born October 4, 1948, in LA. *Education:* Newcomb College, B.A., 1969; attended Leningrad State University, 1970; Yale University, M.Phil., 1972, Ph.D., 1974.

ADDRESSES: Office—Department of Romance Languages, University of Pennsylvania, Philadelphia, PA 19104. *Agent*—Alice Martell, 545 Madison Ave., Martell Agency, New York, NY 10022.

CAREER: Yale University, New Haven, CT, acting instructor, 1973-74; University of Pennsylvania, Philadelphia, assistant professor, 1974-78; Yale University, assistant professor, 1978-81; Princeton University, Princeton, NJ, associate professor, 1981-85, professor, 1985-88, Andrew W. Mellon Professor, 1987-88; University of Pennsylvania, Trustee Professor of French, 1988—.

AWARDS, HONORS: Fellow, National Endowment for the Humanities, 1977-78, 1999; Guggenheim fellow, 1987; summer fellow, German-American Academic Council Foundation, 1998; Aldo and Jeanne Scaglione Prize for French and Francophone Studies, Modern Language Association of America, 2003, for *The Reinvention of Obscenity: Sex, Lies, and Tabloids in Early Modern France;* Josephine Roberts Award, best translation or teaching edition, Society for the Study of Early Modern Women, 2003, for *Against Marriage: The Correspondence of the Grande Mademoiselle.*

WRITINGS:

Scarron's "Roman comique": A Novel of Comedy, a Comedy of the Novel, Lang (Las Vegas, NV), 1977.

Libertine Strategies: Freedom and the Novel in 17th-Century France, Ohio State University Press (Columbus, OH), 1981.

Literary Fortifications: Rousseau, Laclos, Sade, Princeton University Press (Princeton, NJ), 1984.

Fictions of Sappho, 1546-1937, University of Chicago Press (Chicago, IL), 1989.

Tender Geographies: Women and the Origins of the Novel in France, Columbia University Press (New York, NY), 1991.

The Reinvention of Obscenity: Sex, Lies, and Tabloids in Early Modern France, University of Chicago Press (Chicago, IL), 2002.

Ancients against Moderns: Culture Wars and the Making of a Fin de Siècle, University of Chicago Press (Chicago, IL), 2005.

The Essence of Style: How the French Invented High Fashion, Fine Food, Chic Cafés, Style, Sophistication, and Glamour, Simon & Schuster (New York, NY), 2005.

DeJean's writings have been widely translated.

EDITOR

(With Nancy K. Miller) *Displacements: Women, Tradition, Literatures in French,* Johns Hopkins University Press (Baltimore, MD), 1990.

(With Nancy K. Miller) Françoise de Graffigny, *Lettres d'un Péruvienne,* Modern Language Association of America (New York, NY), 1993.

(With Peggy Waller) Claire de Duras, *Ourika,* Modern Language Association of America (New York, NY), 1994.

Molière, *Le Festin de pierre/Dom Juan* (1683 Amsterdam text), Editions Droz (Geneva, Switzerland), 1998.

Against Marriage: The Correspondence of the Grande Mademoiselle, University of Chicago Press (Chicago, IL), 2002.

F.T. de Choisy, M.J. L'Héritier, and C. Perrault, *Histoire de la Marquise-Marquis de Banneville,* Modern Language Association of America (New York, NY), 2004.

Series coeditor, *"New Cultural Studies,"* University of Pennsylvania Press (Philadelphia, PA), 1989-2000, and *"Material Texts,"* University of Pennsylvania Press.*

*   *   *

DeJEAN, Joan Elizabeth
    See DeJEAN, Joan

*   *   *

DICK, Ron 1931-

PERSONAL: Born October 18, 1931, in Newcastle-upon-Tyne, England; son of Arthur John Craig (an electrical engineer) and Lilian Dick; married Pauline Lomax, October 15, 1955; children: Gary Charles, Peta Noelle Dick Enoch. *Education:* Attended Royal Air Force College, 1950-52, Royal Air Force Staff College, 1966, Joint Services Staff College, 1969, and Royal College of Defence Studies, 1972-74. *Hobbies and other interests:* Military and aviation history, restoration and flying of historic aircraft, wildlife conservation, bird-watching, traveling, hill walking, and listening to opera.

ADDRESSES: Home and office—Woodbridge, VA; fax: 703-492-8934.

CAREER: Writer, Air Force officer, aircraft pilot, and educator. Royal Air Force, career officer, 1950-88, retiring as air marshal; National Air and Space Museum, Washington, DC, Smithsonian international fellow, 1988-91; Air University, Maxwell Air Force Base, AL, visiting lecturer on the history of air power, 1991-94; writer and public speaker, 1994—. Military assignments included aerobatic pilot, pilot of historic aircraft, flying instructor, exchange flight commander, flight commander on a nuclear strike squadron, and Vulcan squadron commander in Cyprus; air attaché at British embassy in Washington, DC, 1980-83; head of British Defence Staffs in the United States, 1984-88.

MEMBER: International Association of Eagles, Royal Aeronautical Society (fellow).

AWARDS, HONORS: Clarkson Trophy and Wright Jubilee Trophy, both 1955-56, both for aerobatic flying; Companion, Order of the Bath, 1988.

WRITINGS:

Lancaster: RAF Heavy Bomber, photographs by Dan Patterson, Howell Press (Charlottesville, VA), 1996.
Messerschmitt Bf109: Luftwaffe Fighter, photographs by Dan Patterson, Howell Press (Charlottesville, VA), 1997.
Spitfire: RAF Fighter, photographs by Dan Patterson, Howell Press (Charlottesville, VA), 1997.
American Eagles: A History of the United States Air Force, photographs by Dan Patterson, Howell Press (Charlottesville, VA), 1997.
Reach and Power: The Heritage of the United States Air Force in Pictures and Artifacts, U.S. Government Printing Office (Washington, DC), 1997.
The Aviation Century, Boston Mills Press (Erin, Ontario, Canada), 2000.
Hurricane: RAF Fighter, photographs by Dan Patterson, Boston Mills Press (Erin, Ontario, Canada), 2000.

"AVIATION CENTURY" SERIES

(With Dan Patterson) *Aviation Century The Early Years,* Boston Mills Press (Erin, Ontario, Canada), 2003.
(With Dan Patterson) *Aviation Century The Golden Age,* Boston Mills Press (Erin, Ontario, Canada), 2004.
(With Dan Patterson) *Aviation Century World War II,* Boston Mills Press (Erin, Ontario, Canada), 2004.
(With Dan Patterson) *Aviation Century Wings of Change,* Boston Mills Press (Erin, Ontario, Canada), 2005.
(With Dan Patterson) *Aviation Century War & Peace in the Air,* Boston Mills Press (Erin, Ontario, Canada), 2006.

OTHER

Contributor to books, including *Oxford Companion to American Military History,* Oxford University Press (New York, NY); *The Means of Victory: RAF Bomber Command,* Charterhouse Publications (London, England), 1992; *Classic RAF Battles,* Arms & Armour Press (London, England), 1995; and *Cockpit,* Boston Mills Press (Erin, Ontario, Canada), 1998. Contributor to periodicals, including *Airsport, Flight Journal, Air and Space Smithsonian,* and *Air Power History.*

SIDELIGHTS: Ron Dick once told *CA:* "As a schoolboy in London, I spent many hours looking skyward, watching the great aerial combats of the Battle of Britain. That experience inspired me to become a pilot in the Royal Air Force, a career which captured me for thirty-eight years. Although I retired from the service in 1988, my enthusiasm for flying remained undiminished, and I found an outlet in telling others about aviation, either by lecturing or by writing.

"The compulsion to write about aviation has its roots in the fact that, as the twenty-first century approaches, most people have come to take aircraft and flying very much for granted. Most of the wonder and excitement of the early days has gone, as generations have grown up with aircraft as an everyday phenomenon. Few people pursue the thought that aviation changed the world more than any other development in the twentieth century—technologically, militarily, politically, economically, and sociologically. Not a single human being anywhere on earth is untouched by the effects of aviation. It is a story well worth the telling—full of adventure, drama, courage, disaster, success, inspiration, enterprise, unlooked for curses, and unexpected blessings. What more could an author ask?"

In addition to books about specific airplanes flown in combat during World War II, Dick is coauthor with Dan Patterson of five books in the "Aviation Century" series. In *Aviation Century The Early Years,* the authors delve into how the field of aviation developed in a specific direction, beginning the Wright brothers' first flight, on through to the planes flown in World War I and the commercial and private planes of the 1920's and 1930's. Gilbert Taylor, writing in *Booklist,* noted that the book encompasses a "limited time span but a worldwide approach."

Aviation Century The Golden Age focuses primarily on the barnstorming pilots of the 1920's and 1930's and their aircraft. Writing in *Esprit de Corps,* Norm Shannon noted that the book includes "outstanding photos, artwork and a narrative that sweeps the reader through an era of speed-kings, long-distance queens like Amy Johnson, and the magnificent machines of yesterday." *Aviation Century World War II* covers the air war of World War II beginning with the German Blitzkrieg of Poland and through to the Battle of Britain and the role the various Allied air forces played in other battles, including those in the Middle East, the Pacific, China, Burma, and India. *Esprit de Corps* contributor Bill Twatio commented: "The third volume in a remarkable series of aviation books dazzles with its unique blend of research and photography." Commenting on both volumes in his review in *Booklist,* George Cohen noted: "Any readers interested in the history of flying will treasure these profusely illustrated books."

The fourth volume in the series, *Aviation Century Wings of Change,* details the development of commercial aviation following World War II and also the many noncommercial pilots who founded flying clubs. George Cohen, once again writing in *Booklist,* commented that "this one is an absorbing history of flight." *Aviation Century War & Peace in the Air,* is the concluding volume in the "Aviation Century" series and focuses primarily on jet flight in military and civilian aviation. *Library Journal* contributor John Carver Edwards wrote that the authors "have again given us unerring history, captivating depictions of aircraft, thought-provoking sidebars, and fascinating portraits."

BIOGRAPHICAL AND CRITICAL SOURCES:

PERIODICALS

Booklist, February 1, 2004, Gilbert Taylor, review of *Aviation Century The Early Years,* p. 940; December 1, 2004, George Cohen, review of *Aviation Century The Golden Age* and *Aviation Century World War II,* p. 627; September 1, 2005, George Cohen, review of *Aviation Century Wings of Change,* p. 34; November 1, 2006, George Cohen, review of *Aviation Century War & Peace in the Air,* p. 14.

Esprit de Corps, December, 2004, Bill Twatio, review of *Aviation Century World War II,* and Norm Shannon, review of *Aviation Century the Golden Age,* p. 24.

Library Bookwatch, February, 2005, review of *Aviation Century the Golden Age* and *Aviation Century World War II.*

Library Journal, February 1, 2005, John Carver Edwards, review of *Aviation Century the Golden Age* and *Aviation Century World War II,* p. 96; October 15, 2005, John Carver Edwards, review of *Aviation Century Wings of Change,* p. 67; November 1, 2006, John Carver Edwards, review of *Aviation Century War & Peace in the Air,* p. 86.

MBR Bookwatch, January, 2006, review of *Aviation Century Wings of Change.*

Photography & Design, November, 2005, Dan Patterson, "The Aviation Century Project: A Very Large Tale," p. 42.

SciTech Book News, March, 2006, review of *Aviation Century Wings of Change.**

*   *   *

DIRIE, Waris 1965-

PERSONAL: Born 1965, in the Gallacaio region of Somalia; partner of Dana Murray (a musician), beginning 1995; children: Aleeke (son).

ADDRESSES: Home—Vienna, Austria. *Agent*—William Morrow & Co., Inc., 1350 Avenue of the Americas, New York, NY 10019.

CAREER: Writer, model, public speaker, philanthropist, and activist. United Nations Population Fund, special ambassador for the elimination of female genital mutilation, 1997—. Waris Dirie Foundation, founder; Desert Dawn Foundation, founder. Appeared in the movie *The Living Daylights,* 1987.

WRITINGS:

(With Cathleen Miller) *Desert Flower: The Extraordinary Journey of a Desert Nomad,* William Morrow (New York, NY), 1998.

Desert Dawn, Virago Press (London, England), 2003.

(With Corinna Milborn) *Desert Children,* Little, Brown (New York, NY), 2006.

Author's works have been published in eleven languages.

SIDELIGHTS: Waris Dirie is a supermodel who was born in Somalia to a nomadic family with twelve children. At age five, Dirie was subjected to female circumcision. This procedure, also termed female genital mutilation (FGM), has been performed routinely on females in various countries, particularly in Africa and the Middle East, although numerous cases are also suspected in the United States. The United Nations Population Fund (UNFPA) estimates that at least two million girls are at risk of genital mutilation each year. Eighty percent of mutilations consist of the excision of the clitoris and the labia minora. The more extreme form is infibulation, which is the excision of part or all of the external genitalia and stitching or narrowing of the vaginal opening. The infibulation rate is higher in Djibouti, Sudan, and Somalia, and carries with it a higher rate of complications. Dirie underwent this extreme type of mutilation; her sister and two of her cousins died from complications of the same procedure. Yet in those countries where the practice takes place, it is seen as highly positive, and is often a prerequisite for marriage. "They made it sound so glamorous that I enthusiastically looked forward to it, often impatiently asking my mother when it would take place," Dirie commented to Kwamboka Oyaro in *Africa News Service.* "But when it happened, it was so painful that it left a big, sick hole in my heart. Yet small girls continue to be wounded by this unnecessary and meaningless practice that only destroys. You gain nothing good; they take the good and leave the bad," Dirie stated.

In recent years, Dirie has begun to speak out in public against the practice of FGM. She has used her own experiences to educate others about the painful plight of women who are circumcised. In 1998, she published an autobiography titled *Desert Flower: The Extraordinary Journey of a Desert Nomad,* which details her childhood and early teen years in Somalia and the events that led to her success as a high-fashion and advertising model for companies such as Revlon. A number of reviewers were impressed by her story, particularly the way she described the pain caused by her circumcision and later complications. A *Kirkus Reviews* contributor wrote that *Desert Flower* "offers extraordinary firsthand insight into FGM . . . . It is also a well-told and truly engaging autobiography with an old-fashioned, Algeresque appeal." Vanessa Bush, in a *Booklist* review, also appreciated the discussion of circumcision, commenting that "the most compelling portions of Dirie's story are her graphic portrayals of the practice." A *Publishers Weekly* critic felt that "it is Dirie's remarkable lack of

narcissism or entitlement that makes her so captivating a raconteur." Raye Snover, writing in the *New York Times,* concluded: "Written with innocence and warmth, this book shows how one woman's tragedy can help others." *Desert Flower* was published in eleven languages.

Dirie continues to act as a spokesperson against FGM through her testimony, media appearances, and as a special ambassador for the UNFPA, an appointment made on September 18, 1997. In a press release made at that time, the UNFPA said Dirie planned to tour African countries to speak out against the practice and appear in public service announcements and documentary films. Dr. Nafis Sadik, UNFPA Executive Director, commented on the *United Nations Population Fund Web site,* that Dirie was tapped for the position because "she is a remarkable person and one that other women can look to for inspiration. What is best about her is that she is not some remote figure but one of the people. We hope her courage and the lesson of her life will cause others in traditional cultures to speak out against these terrible practices."

In *Desert Children,* written with journalist Corinna Milborn, Dirie revisits the topic of FGM, this time from the perspective of women and girls living in European countries. Female Genital Mutilation is not confined to more primitive tribal cultures in Africa and elsewhere, Dirie warns. She notes that more than half a million females in Europe have been subjected to FGM, or are at risk for being forced to endure the procedure. Many of these women, though living in Europe, are isolated from European culture and are unaware of the laws that protect them. They find themselves subject to their husband's authority, much as they would be if they were living in their original homeland. Often, women and girls residing in Europe are taken back to their home countries where the procedure is performed on them. Dirie advocates strongly against the practice, calling for better education of potential victims, health care professionals, and the general public. She encourages European judicial systems toward greater recognition of FGM as a crime, and for increased prosecution and punishment of those who commit it. She encourages religious leaders to speak out against FGM. Dirie also offers resources on FGM for European audiences, including summaries of known facts about the procedure, current European legislation, and organizations that offer help on the issue. Dirie "paints a vivid picture of what FGM does to a woman's body and frequently lets the victims tell in their own words of its devastating physical and psychological effects," noted a *Kirkus Reviews* contributor.

BIOGRAPHICAL AND CRITICAL SOURCES:

BOOKS

Dirie, Waris, *Desert Flower: The Extraordinary Journey of a Desert Nomad,* William Morrow (New York, NY), 1998.

PERIODICALS

Africa News Service, September 22, 2004, Kwamboka Oyaro, "Supermodel Waris Dirie's Uphill Task," profile of Waris Dirie.
Booklist, September 1, 1998, Vanessa Bush, review of *Desert Flower,* p. 37.
Europe Intelligence Wire, December 10, 2005, review of *Desert Children.*
Herizons, winter, 2007, Maggie Mortimer, "How to Stop Female Genital Mutilation," interview with Waris Dirie, p. 23.
Kirkus Reviews, July 15, 1998, review of *Desert Flower,* p. 1012; March 15, 2006, review of *Desert Children,* p. 271.
New York Times, January 3, 1999, Raye Snover, review of *Desert Flower.*
New York Times Magazine, May 9, 1999, Amy Finnerty, "The Way We Live Now: 5-9-99: Questions for Waris Dirie: The Body Politic," interview with Waris Dirie.
Publishers Weekly, August 3, 1998, review of *Desert Flower,* p. 68.
Somaliland Times, March 4, 2006, review of *Desert Children.*
Time International, July 15, 2002, Helen Gibson and Waris Dirie, "Somalia's Desert Flower: Supermodel Turned Best-Selling Author Waris Dirie Wants to Alert the World to the Plight of Her Country—and of Millions of Young Women," p. 58.
Times Newspapers of New Zealand, March 1, 2006, review of *Desert Children.*

ONLINE

United Nations Population Fund Web site, http://www. unfpa.org/ (February 6, 2007).

Waris Dirie Foundation Web site, http://www.waris-dirie-foundation.com/ (February 6, 2007), autobiography of Waris Dirie.*

*   *   *

DOENGES, Judy 1959-

PERSONAL: Born, 1959, in Elmhurst, IL; daughter of G. William and Edia Doenges. *Education:* University of Wisconsin—Madison, B.A., 1981; University of Massachusetts at Amherst, M.F.A., 1987.

ADDRESSES: Office—Department of English, 359 Eddy, Colorado State University, Fort Collins, CO 80523-1773. *E-mail*—doengeja@hotmail.com.

CAREER: Colorado State University, Fort Collins, began as assistant professor, became associate professor of English.

AWARDS, HONORS: Bakeless Literary Publication Prize, 1998, Ferro-Grumly Award and citation for notable book of the year, *New York Times Book Review,* both 1999, all for *What She Left Me;* grants and fellowships from Ohio Arts Council, National Endowment for the Arts, Artist Trust, Yaddo, MacDowell Colony, and Bread Loaf Writers' Conference.

WRITINGS:

What She Left Me (short stories and novella), University Press of New England (Hanover, NH), 1999.
The Most Beautiful Girl in the World (novel), University of Michigan Press (Ann Arbor, MI), 2006.

Contributor to periodicals, including *Georgia Review, Green Mountains Review, Permafrost, Phoebe,* and *Nimrod.*

SIDELIGHTS: Judy Doenges is the author of *What She Left Me,* an award-winning collection of stories about various disaffected people, including homosexuals, children, and substance abusers. Among the tales in this collection are "Disaster," in which a young girl watches as her babysitter's party degenerates into chaos; "Occidental," wherein a drunken Vietnam veteran mourns his mother's death; and "God of Gods," in which a butcher struggles with his homosexuality. Other stories include "The Whole Number of Families," in which a lesbian sees that her homosexuality has contributed to her mother's aloofness, "MIB," wherein a woman fails to share the zestful exuberance of her lifelong friend, a gay fashion designer; and the title tale, in which a woman reflects on her late mother, an alcoholic. *Booklist* contributor Whitney Scott affirmed that the characters in *What She Left Me* "roil with inner turmoil," and noted that "their lives touch us deeply." Another reviewer, Katherine Dieckmann, wrote in the *New York Times Book Review* that *What She Left Me* constitutes "a superb debut," and she observed that Doenges "slaps fresh life into the weary [short story] form." Dieckmann accorded special praise to both "God of Gods," which she described as a "masterly piece," and "MIB," which she deemed "an amazingly complex teen into adulthood tale of cloaked emotion."

BIOGRAPHICAL AND CRITICAL SOURCES:

PERIODICALS

Booklist, August, 1999, Whitney Scott, review of *What She Left Me,* p. 2002.
Chicago Tribune, January 30, 2000, "Up against the Rules."
New York Times Book Review, August 15, 1999, Katherine Dieckmann, "Out of the Closet, or Whatever," p. 6.
Women's Review of Books, January, 2000, Leslie Larson, "Dazed and Confused," pp. 15-16.

*   *   *

DORSEY, Tim 1961-

PERSONAL: Born 1961, in IN; married; children: two daughters. *Education:* Auburn University, B.S., 1983.

ADDRESSES: Home—Tampa, FL. *E-mail*—tad2561@yahoo.com.

CAREER: Writer, novelist, and journalist. *Alabama Journal,* Montgomery, police and courts reporter, 1983-87; *Tampa Tribune,* Tampa, FL, general assignment reporter, copy-desk editor, political reporter, 1987-94, night metro editor, night news coordinator, 1994-99.

WRITINGS:

"SERGE STORMS" SERIES; FICTION

Florida Roadkill, Morrow (New York, NY), 1999.
Hammerhead Ranch Motel, Morrow (New York, NY), 2000.
Orange Crush, Morrow (New York, NY), 2001.
Triggerfish Twist, Morrow (New York, NY), 2002.
The Stingray Shuffle, Morrow (New York, NY), 2003.
Cadillac Beach, Morrow (New York, NY), 2004.
Torpedo Juice, Morrow (New York, NY), 2005.
The Big Bamboo, Morrow (New York, NY), 2006.
Hurricane Punch, Morrow (New York, NY), 2007.

SIDELIGHTS: Writer and novelist Tim Dorsey worked as a reporter, editor, and news coordinator before becoming a full-time author. His novels are set in Florida, where he lives.

Dorsey's debut novel, *Florida Roadkill* tells the story of two con men: Serge Storms, a serial killer, and his perpetually drunk, stoned, or chemically addled sidekick, Coleman. The two are not averse to committing murder and mayhem, but in Dorsey's hands, they are curiously likable characters all the same—Serge, after all, only kills those who deserve it. In the book, Sharon, a con woman and addict, secretly videotapes dentist Dr. Veale in the back room of a strip club. In order to keep Serge and Coleman quiet about the secret tape, Veale agrees to having his hands, which are insured for five million dollars, injured. Coleman and Serge want the insurance money, which Veale hides in the car of two men who leave the club not knowing about the money. What results is a chase through the state of Florida by the two cons and others looking to get rich quick. "Dorsey's wicked sense of humor and astounding knowledge of Florida's history and legends add levity and local color to this dark tale," noted *Library Journal* contributor Thomas L. Kilpatrick.

Serge is back in Dorsey's second novel, *Hammerhead Ranch Motel.* Serge is still searching for the five million dollars he was after in *Florida Roadkill.* Serge and his new partner Lenny Lippowicz track the money and believe it is with the owner of the Hammerhead Ranch Motel. Serge and Lenny rent a room and wait for the perfect opportunity to nab the cash. While they wait, they meet the strange guests that are staying at the motel. In assessing the novel, *Mystery Net* Web site contributor Anya R. Weber stated: "Dorsey soars to glorious heights on the wings of his own absurdity."

Dorsey's third novel, *Orange Crush,* deals with Florida politics. Florida's governorship is between Marlon Conrad and Gomer Tatum. Something snaps in Conrad, and he takes off on a crazy election tour in a bright orange, second-hand Winnebago. Along the way Conrad meets some interesting people, including Serge. Opponent Tatum soon follows Conrad and eventually challenges him to a wrestling match that will decide who the next governor will be. "If 200-proof satire is your drink of choice, Dorsey is the guy you want behind the bar," concluded *Booklist* contributor Bill Ott.

In *Triggerfish Twist* Serge, Coleman, and Sharon are living on Triggerfish Lane in Tampa, Florida. Jim Davenport and his family move to Triggerfish Lane when Jim accepts a transfer from Wisconsin. Jim is a quiet man who does not like to argue or fight with anyone. He moved to the wrong street, however, if he was searching for peace and quiet. His neighbors include drug users, psychotics, and other sleazy people. Serge tries to protect Jim and his family from the other neighbors. *Book Reporter* contributor Joe Hartlaub praised: "With *Triggerfish Twist,* Dorsey has transformed himself from an author to be enjoyed to an artist whose next book will be anticipated with as much fervor as this one will be enjoyed."

Dorsey's fifth "Serge Storms" novel, *The Stingray Shuffle,* still finds Serge on the trail of the elusive five million dollars from *Florida Roadkill.* By this time, numerous others, including Russian gangsters masquerading as Latinos, have joined the hunt. *Booklist* reviewer David Pitt called the novel "a brilliantly constructed romp."

In *Torpedo Juice,* Storms comes to the aid of a vacationing retired couple who have been accosted by a thief who has broken into their hotel room to rob them, noted *Bookreporter.com* reviewer Bob Rhubart. After dispatching the robber with a unique application of an MRI machine, Storms returns to his job as social director for the No Name Pub, dispensing advice, etiquette tips, and strong liquor to a motley assortment of boozers and crazies. As the novel progresses, Serge decides that what

he needs most is a woman, and he embarks on a misguided mission to woo Molly, a librarian. Encounters with a vicious land developer and drug smugglers enliven the proceedings. "Dorsey is an undeniably funny writer, with a remarkable knack for wringing laughter out of situations that might otherwise make readers squirm," Rhubart observed.

The Big Bamboo finds Serge in a pique against Hollywood, which has abandoned Florida as a site for moviemaking and has appropriated the "weirdness" that was once the Sunshine State's greatest characteristic. To remedy the situation, Serge and Coleman head west to visit Hollywood and set them straight on Florida's benefits and to make sure the state is accurately depicted, weirdness and all, in motion pictures. Along the way, Serge exercises his personal brand of serial-killer justice, encountering numerous irritating and often despicable people who desperately need to be dispatched. Soon, though, Serge and Coleman get a lesson in the dangers and twisted personalities that populate Hollywood, encountering drug-addicted studio executives, self-absorbed directors, and high-strung starlets. To advance his agenda, Serge kidnaps a young actress and records a video ransom note, imploring Hollywood to cease some of its more egregious violations of good taste. "By putting Serge in California in his eighth novel, Dorsey's energy and affection for his characters shine," commented Oline H. Cogdill in the *South Florida Sun-Sentinel.* "Fans won't be disappointed with *The Big Bamboo,*" remarked Wanda J. Demarzo in the *Miami Herald.* "Dorsey lives up to expectations, providing plenty of murder, glib one-liners and a plot so cheerfully convoluted that when you reach the last page you won't be saying 'I knew it!'" *Library Journal* reviewer Ken St. Andre called the book "howlingly funny."

Hurricane Punch puts Serge behind the wheel of a stolen Hummer as he and Coleman ramble across the hurricane-blasted landscape of Florida. In this extended, rain-soaked road trip. Serge ruminates on Florida history, Bush administration politics, and the shortcomings of the media while dispensing his fatal justice to unsavory sorts such as price-gougers who exploit hurricane victims. "Scathing humor strips the pretense off its targets like a hurricane" in the ninth Serge Storms novel, noted a *Publishers Weekly* contributor.

BIOGRAPHICAL AND CRITICAL SOURCES:

PERIODICALS

Booklist, April 15, 1999, George Needham, review of *Florida Roadkill,* p. 1471; May 15, 2000, George

Needham, review of *Hammerhead Ranch Motel*, p. 1733; May 1, 2001, Bill Ott and Brad Hooper, review of *Florida Roadkill*, p. 1603, and Bill Ott, review of *Orange Crush*, p. 1630; February 15, 2003, David Pitt, review of *The Stingray Shuffle*, p. 1053.

Kirkus Reviews, June 1, 1999, review of *Florida Roadkill*, p. 817; May 15, 2001, review of *Orange Crush*, p. 680; March 1, 2002, review of *Triggerfish Twist*, p. 290; December 1, 2002, review of *The Stingray Shuffle*, p. 1735.

Library Journal, June 15, 1999, Thomas L. Kilpatrick, review of *Florida Roadkill*, p. 105; June 15, 2000, Thomas L. Kilpatrick, review of *Hammerhead Ranch Motel*, p. 112; June 15, 2001, Thomas L. Kilpatrick, review of *Orange Crush*, p. 102; January 1, 2005, Bob Lunn, review of *Torpedo Juice*, p. 95; February 1, 2006, Ken St. Andre, review of *The Big Bamboo*, p. 70; October 1, 2006, Ann Kim, "Prepub Mystery," review of *Hurricane Punch*, p. 55.

Miami Herald, April 26, 2006, Wanda J. Demarzo, "Serial Killer on a Serious Mission in *The Big Bamboo*," review of *The Big Bamboo*.

Publishers Weekly, July 5, 1999, review of *Florida Roadkill*, p. 58; August 30, 1999, Judy Quinn, "Roadkill the Rage in Florida," p. 23; July 31, 2000, review of *Hammerhead Ranch Motel*, p. 70; July 9, 2001, p. 49; March 1, 2002, review of *Triggerfish Twist*, p. 37; January 6, 2003, review of *The Stingray Shuffle*, p. 42; December 11, 2006, review of *Hurricane Punch*, p. 46.

Sarasota Herald Tribune, December 14, 2005, Sharyn Lonsdale, "Author with Ties to Englewood Visits McBooks," profile of Tim Dorsey, p. BCE4.

South Florida Sun-Sentinel, April 12, 2006, Oline H. Cogdill, "*The Big Bamboo:* If You Have Humor, Who Needs Plot?," review of *The Big Bamboo*.

ONLINE

Alabama Bound, http://www.alabamabound.org/ (February 6, 2007), biography of Tim Dorsey.

BookPage, http://www.bookpage.com/ (February 6, 2007), review of *Florida Roadkill*.

Bookreporter.com, http://www.bookreporter.com/ (February 6, 2007), review of *Orange Crush;* review of *Triggerfish Twist;* Bob Rhubart, review of *Torpedo Juice;* Joe Hartlaub, review of *Cadillac Beach;* biography of Tim Dorsey.

Books 'n' Bytes, http://www.booksnbytes.com/ (February 6, 2007), Harriet Klausner, reviews of *Florida Roadkill* and *Hammerhead Ranch Motel*.

HarperCollins Web site, http://www.harpercollins.com/ (February 6, 2007), interview with Dorsey.

Murder on the Beach, http://www.murderonthebeach. com/ (February 6, 2007), reviews of *Orange Crush*, *Hammerhead Ranch Motel*, and *Florida Roadkill*.

MysteryNet.com, http://www.mysterynet.com/ (February 6, 2007), Anya R. Weber, review of *Hammerhead Ranch Motel*.

Tim Dorsey Home Page, http://www.timdorsey.com (February 6, 2007).*

*   *   *

DR. ROCK
See BORDOWITZ, Hank

*   *   *

DUEY, Kathleen 1950-

PERSONAL: Born 1950. *Hobbies and other interests:* Singing, playing guitar, songwriting, horses, gardening, travel, blogging, and learning.

ADDRESSES: Home and office—Fallbrook, CA.

CAREER: Writer and novelist.

MEMBER: Authors Guild, Society of Children's Book Writers and Illustrators.

AWARDS, HONORS: Young Hoosier's Award nominee for *Train Wreck: Kansas, 1892;* Golden Duck Award for *Rex*.

WRITINGS:

"AMERICAN DIARIES" SERIES

Sarah Anne Hartford: Massachusetts, 1651, Aladdin (New York, NY), 1996.

Emma Eileen Grove: Mississippi, 1865, Aladdin (New York, NY), 1996.

Anisett Lundberg: California, 1851, Aladdin (New York, NY), 1996.

Mary Alice Peale: Philadelphia, 1777, Aladdin (New York, NY), 1996.

Willow Chase: Kansas Territory, 1847, Aladdin (New York, NY), 1997.

Ellen Elizabeth Hawkins: Mobeetie, Texas, 1886, Aladdin (New York, NY), 1997.

Alexia Ellery Finsdale: San Francisco, 1905, Aladdin (New York, NY), 1997.

Evie Peach: St. Louis, 1857, Aladdin (New York, NY), 1997.

Celou Sudden Shout: Idaho, 1826, Aladdin (New York, NY), 1998.

Summer MacCleary: Virginia, 1749, Aladdin (New York, NY), 1998.

Agnes May Gleason: Walsenberg, Colorado, 1933, Aladdin (New York, NY), 1998.

Amelina Carrett: Bayou Grand Coeur, Louisiana, 1863, Aladdin (New York, NY), 1999.

Josie Poe: Palouse, Washington, 1943, Aladdin (New York, NY), 1999.

Rosa Moreno: Hollywood, California, 1928, Aladdin (New York, NY), 1999.

Francesca Vigilucci: Washington, D.C., 1913, Aladdin (New York, NY), 2000.

Maddie Retta Lauren: Sandersville, Georgia, C.S.A, 1864, Aladdin (New York, NY), 2000.

Nell Dunne: Ellis Island, 1904, Aladdin (New York, NY), 2000.

Janey G. Blue: Pearl Harbor, 1941, Aladdin (New York, NY), 2001.

Amelina Carrett: Thibodeau, Louisiana, 1870, Aladdin (New York, NY), 2002.

Zellie Blake: Massachusetts, 1836, Aladdin (New York, NY), 2002.

WITH KAREN A. BALE; "SURVIVAL!" SERIES

Earthquake, 1906, Aladdin (New York, NY), 1998.

Cave-In: St. Claire, Pennsylvania, 1859, Aladdin (New York, NY), 1998.

Stranded: Death Valley, 1850, Aladdin (New York, NY), 1998.

Flood: Mississippi, 1927, Aladdin (New York, NY), 1998.

Blizzard: Estes Park, Colorado, 1886, Aladdin (New York, NY), 1998.

Fire: Chicago, 1871, Aladdin (New York, NY), 1998.

Titanic: April 14, 1912, Aladdin (New York, NY), 1998.

Hurricane: Open Seas, 1844, Aladdin (New York, NY), 1999.

Train Wreck: Kansas, 1892, Aladdin (New York, NY), 1999.

Swamp: Bayou Teche, Louisiana, 1851, Aladdin (New York, NY), 1999.

Forest Fire: Hinckley, Minnesota, 1894, Aladdin (New York, NY), 1999.

Hurricane: New Bedford, Massachusetts, 1784, Aladdin (New York, NY), 1999.

San Francisco Earthquake, 1906, Pocket Books (New York, NY), 1999.

Louisiana Hurricane, 1860, Pocket Books (New York, NY), 2000.

"BEASTY BUDDIES" SERIES; PICTURE BOOKS

Hogger the Hoarding Beastie, Smart Kids Publishing (Carlsbad, CA), 1999.

Moogie the Messy Beastie, Smart Kids Publishing (Carlsbad, CA), 1999.

Crassy the Crude Beastie, Smart Kids Publishing (Carlsbad, CA), 2001.

Glumby the Grumbling Beastie, Smart Kids Publishing (Carlsbad, CA), 2001.

"ALONE IN THE DARK" SERIES

Beware the Alien Invasion!, Smart Kids Publishing (Carlsbad, CA), 2000.

Boogeyman in the Basement!, Smart Kids Publishing (Carlsbad, CA), 2000.

Nowhere to Run, Nowhere to Hide!, Smart Kids Publishing (Carlsbad, CA), 2000.

Stay out of the Graveyard!, Smart Kids Publishing (Carlsbad, CA), 2000.

"UNICORN'S SECRET" SAGA

Moonsilver, illustrated by Omar Rayyan, Aladdin (New York, NY), 2001.

The Silver Thread, Aladdin (New York, NY), 2001.

The Silver Bracelet, Aladdin (New York, NY), 2002.

Mountains of the Moon, illustrated by Omar Rayyan, Aladdin (New York, NY), 2002.

The Sunset Gates, Aladdin (New York, NY), 2002.

Beyond the Sunset, Aladdin (New York, NY), 2002.

Castle Avamir, illustrated by Omar Rayyan, Aladdin (New York, NY), 2003.

True Heart, illustrated by Omar Rayyan, Aladdin (New York, NY), 2003.

The Journey Home, illustrated by Omar Rayyan, Aladdin (New York, NY), 2003.

"TIME SOLDIERS" SERIES

Rex, photography by Robert Gould, illustrations by Eugene Epstein, Big Guy Books (Carlsbad, CA), 2001.

Rex 2, photography by Robert Gould, illustrations by Eugene Epstein, Big Guy Books (Carlsbad, CA), 2001.

Patch, photography by Robert Gould, illustrations by Eugene Epstein, Big Guy Books (Carlsbad, CA), 2002.

Arthur, photography by Robert Gould, illustrations by Eugene Epstein, Big Guy Books (Carlsbad, CA), 2004.

Mummy, photography by Robert Gould, illustrations by Eugene Epstein, Big Guy Books (Carlsbad, CA), 2005.

Pony Express, photography by Robert Gould, illustrations by Eugene Epstein, Big Guy Books (Carlsbad, CA), 2006.

Samurai, photography by Robert Gould, illustrations by Eugene Epstein, Big Guy Books (Carlsbad, CA), 2006.

"SPIRIT OF THE CIMARRON" SERIES

Bonita, Penguin/Putnam (New York, NY), 2002.

Esperanza, Penguin/Putnam (New York, NY), 2002.

Sierra, Penguin/Putnam (New York, NY), 2002.

Spirit: Stallion of the Cimarron (adapted from the motion picture), Penguin/Putnam (New York, NY), 2002.

"HOOFBEATS" SERIES

Katie and the Mustang Book One, Penguin/Putnam (New York, NY), 2004.

Katie and the Mustang Book Two, Penguin/Putnam (New York, NY), 2004.

Katie and the Mustang Book Three, Penguin/Putnam (New York, NY), 2004.

Katie and the Mustang Book Four, Penguin/Putnam (New York, NY), 2004.

Lara and the Gray Mare, Penguin/Putnam (New York, NY), 2005.

Lara and the Moon-Colored Filly, Penguin/Putnam (New York, NY), 2005.

Lara and the Silent Place, Penguin/Putnam (New York, NY), 2005.

Lara at Athenry Castle, Penguin/Putnam (New York, NY), 2005.

Silence and Lily, Penguin/Putnam (New York, NY), 2007.

OTHER

Double-Yuck Magic, Morrow/Avon (New York, NY), 1991.

Mr. Stumpguss Is a Third-Grader, Morrow/Avon (New York, NY), 1992.

The Third Grade's Skinny Pig, illustrated by Gioia Fiamenghi, Avon (New York, NY), 1993.

The Big Blue Easter Egg, Nesak International (Delray Beach, FL), 1996.

The Easter Morning Surprise, Nesak International (Delray Beach, FL), 1996.

(With Karen A. Bale) *Three of Hearts,* Morrow/Avon (New York, NY), 1998.

CX Ultimate Asteroid Book: The Inside Story on the Threat from the Skies, Sagebrush (Minneapolis, MN), 1998.

(With Mary Barnes) *Freaky Facts about Natural Disasters,* Aladdin (New York, NY), 2000.

(With Ron Berry) *Allowance System Tool Kit: Easy to Use Tools that Teach Kids Money Values and Responsibilities,* Smart Kids Publishing (Carlsbad, CA), 2000.

(With Mary Barnes) *More Freaky Facts about Natural Disasters,* Aladdin (New York, NY), 2001.

Spider-Man Ultimate Picture Book, number 1, photography by Robert Gould, illustrations by Eugene Epstein, Big Guy Books (Carlsbad, CA), 2002.

Terremoto, Planeta Publishing (Miami, FL), 2002.

X-Men Ultimate Picture Book, photography by Robert Gould, illustrations by Eugene Epstein, Big Guy Books (Carlsbad, CA), 2003.

(With Robert Gould and Eugene Epstein) *100 Easy Ways to Get Your Kids Reading: A Busy Mom's Guide,* illustrations by Jacob Dubi, Big Guy Books (Carlsbad, CA), 2006.

SIDELIGHTS: Kathleen Duey began her career as a children's book author in the early 1990s with such titles as *Mr. Stumpguss Is a Third-Grader* and *The Third Grade's Skinny Pig*. In 1996 she created a series for readers in grade four to six that presents American history in a fictional adventure format. These "Diary" books, all begin and end with a diary entry. Every "American Diaries" title encompasses the events of a single day. *Mary Alice Peale: Philadelphia, 1777* chronicles the household dramas of its well-to-do title character, whose father is loyal to the English monarchy. Mary Alice's brother, meanwhile, has run off to fight with colonial independence forces. When he is injured, she secretly helps by hiding him in their barn, while the family's Philadelphia home is host to British soldiers.

In *Sarah Anne Hartford: Massachusetts, 1651*, Duey chronicles the fictional experience of a young girl in Salem, Massachusetts, during the harsh Puritan era. Sarah is distraught over her widowed father's impending marriage to the coldly righteous Mistress Goddard, and Sarah's diary entries—just two days apart—recount her tale of mischief and its consequences. On a cold winter Sunday, twelve-year-old Sarah and her friend Elizabeth disobey strict standards about Sabbath behavior, and play and laugh on the ice on their way home from church services. Caught, they are then "pilloried" as punishment, locked into stocks in the Salem town square. Cold and aching, Sarah begins to question the values of her community. "The story is exciting and the characters are sympathetic," wrote Connie Parker in the *School Library Journal*, while *Booklist*'s Karen Hutt stated that the story "personalizes the social mores and everyday life of Puritan New England."

Anisett Lundberg: California, 1851 is the story of a young girl during the California Gold Rush. Anisett's father has died, and her mother earns a living cooking for the miners. Anisett and her brother help with the work, and one day, after delivering food by mule to the camps, Anisett is kidnapped by a bitter and desperate miner after he overhears her describing an unusual rock she has found. Susan F. Marcus, writing in the *School Library Journal*, noted that the work portrays "the view of the gold-rush culture" and "highlights the courage of those who were part of it." Danger is also faced in *Willow Chase: Kansas Territory, 1847*, Duey's next title in the series. Willow is part of a wagon-train caravan full of settlers heading west across the Great Plains. Willow's mother gives one Native American man medicine for a sick child and later, while crossing the swollen Platte River with her family, Willow is swept away.

They assume she is dead and move on, but Willow is discovered by the Native American to whom her mother had shown kindness, and he gives the girl his horse with which she rejoins her family. *Booklist*'s Lauren Peterson termed the novel "a heartwarming family story with a likable protagonist."

A Texas cattle ranch is the setting for *Ellen Elizabeth Hawkins: Mobeetie, Texas, 1886*. Here, Duey's heroine writes of her desire to follow in her father's footsteps as a rancher, but is strongly discouraged from such talk because of her gender. That summer, however, a drought arrives, and with her father gone one day, Ellen's grandfather falls at their windmill; she must save him, fix the windmill blade, and drive their cattle, desperate for water, to the pastures. *School Library Journal* critic Sylvia V. Meisner called it a "satisfying story about a resourceful heroine" with "grit and determination to persevere against almost overwhelming odds."

Evie Peach: St. Louis, 1857 takes place before the American Civil War. The title character was once a slave, but their owner's last will and testament freed her and her father. They plan to buy her mother's freedom, save 750 dollars to do so, and set out for the estate where she works. Irish neighbors plot revenge for a trick Evie has played on them. They steal Evie's mother's emancipation papers, and Evie's parents are arrested as runaway slaves. Evie is their only hope. *Booklist* writer Denia Hester liked this book's "good balance of warm, winning moments and well-plotted dramatic turns." *Alexia Ellery Finsdale: San Francisco, 1905*, another title from Duey in the series, recounts the story of a young girl whose mother has died. Alexia lives in a boarding house with her gambler father. Her landlady, a self-supporting seamstress, teaches her to sew. The promise of being able to fend for herself helps Alexia make the hardest decision of her life.

Celou Sudden Shout: Idaho, 1826 tells the story of a twelve-year-old girl whose father is a fur trapper of French origin. Her mother is Shoshone, but one day Celou's mother and brother are kidnapped by hostile Crow Indians when the father is away, and Celou must follow the raiding party in order to save them. Ann W. Moore, writing in the *School Library Journal*, called it an "exciting adventure story [that] also conveys information about the Shoshone." *Summer MacCleary: Virginia, 1749*, another title from Duey, recounts the story of an indentured servant who has been accused by the daughter of the plantation owner of stealing a ring.

Summer must clear her name and solve the mystery, and she possesses, as Janet Gillen wrote in the *School Library Journal,* "redeeming qualities of strength and courage."

Duey's tales of young American girls facing danger and hardship span several decades and a variety of geographical places. *Agnes May Gleason: Walsenberg, Colorado, 1933* tells the story of a young girl whose family is on the verge of losing their dairy farm because of the Depression. Agnes's older brother has run away to find work elsewhere, and all must now work to keep the business afloat. When her father is injured, the Gleason parents travel to see a doctor, and Agnes and her siblings decide to bottle the milk and deliver it themselves one dawn. They have a hard time controlling the horses, but persevere and avoid disaster. Coop Renner, a *School Library Journal* writer, described this work as a "swiftly moving novel" with an "unusual setting and well-drawn minor characters."

Cajun country during the American Civil War era is the setting for *Amelina Carrett: Bayou Grand Coeur, Louisiana, 1863.* An orphan, Amelina lives with her war-profiteer uncle in a Cajun swamp community. After gunfire erupts, she discovers an injured Union Army soldier and helps him despite the Cajuns' strong sentiments against Northerners. Amelina even gives him her late father's clothes so that he may escape to safety. *School Library Journal* writer Gillen found this title from Duey "written with insight and sensitivity," and liked the interesting detail about "Cajun life in the Louisiana bayou"; Gillen also commended the protagonist's "courage and fortitude."

The glamorous world of early Hollywood is the setting of *Rosa Moreno: Hollywood, California, 1928.* Rosa's late father was a Mexican actor, and she and her mother are determined that Rosa will achieve stardom as well. She takes elocution lessons, visits a hair salon to achieve a set of curls similar to those of the most famous child star of the era, Shirley Temple, and auditions for film roles frequently. When she meets a female film director, Rosa thinks she might like to direct, too. "Duey portrays Rosa's life vividly and realistically," noted the *School Library Journal*'s Susan Knell, who also liked its glimpse into the rigors of child acting during this era.

The American immigrant experience is explored in *Nell Dunne: Ellis Island, 1904,* Duey's 2000 title in the series. Nell sails from Ireland to America with her fam-ily and, as her diary recounts, the journey is hardly a luxurious one: the cabins for immigrant passengers are cramped, and there are few facilities for washing. But Nell also tells of the magic she feels upon first seeing the New York City skyline. Duey, wrote *School Library Journal* critic Alison Grant, "captures the experience of thousands of immigrants seeking freedom and fortune" on the North American continent. The experiences of another immigrant group, the Japanese Americans, provide a subplot to *Janey G. Blue: Pearl Harbor, 1941.* Janey is from Kansas, but lives with her family near the Hawaii military base where her father works. She is curious about a shy quiet neighbor near her own age, Akiko Fujiwara. Janey and Akiko are thrown together in the confusion of the Japanese attack on Pearl Harbor's military installation. *School Library Journal* contributor Elaine Lesh Morgan noted that "the mood of fear and uncertainty is well maintained, and information about the attack is neatly interwoven" into Janey's tale.

Duey has created a number of ongoing series. *Bonita* is the first book in the "Spirit of the Cimarron" series, based on the animated motion picture from Dreamworks, *Spirit, Stallion of the Cimarron.* In the story, Bonita is a lovely mare separated from her owners by the dangers of war in Mexico. To survive, she joins with Paco, a burro, and Raphael, a young stallion. When a canyon flood claims Raphael's life, Bonita is accepted into a wild herd. There, she gives birth to a foal, Esperanza, who gives the name to the next book in the series. In *Esperanza,* many of the herd's female horses have survived a harsh winter, but the growing Esperanza yearns for her own life. She and a young stallion, Strider, leave the herd and face the dangers of the wilderness on their own in order to find another, better place to live. *School Library Journal* reviewer Carol Schene called the "Spirit" series books "light escapist literature" for younger readers, in which the author "includes enough action to keep the pages turning."

The "Unicorn's Secret" series tells the ongoing story of Heart Avamir and the unicorn she rescued as a young girl. In the first book of the series, *Moonsilver,* Heart and the medieval society in which she lives is introduced and outlined. She knows she was rescued from certain death as a young child by Old Simon, but her life since then has consisted of the hardscrabble struggle to survive. When she discovers an injured white horse wandering in the woods, she turns to the village healer, Rosa, for assistance and advice before discovering that the creature is a unicorn. *Booklist* reviewer Susan Dove

Lempke stated of the book that Duey "has written a beguiling story of love and healing in an easy-to-read style" geared to early readers. In the second book of the series, *The Silver Thread,* Heart must help the unicorn mother and baby she has befriended escape detection, so she hides them in a cave. When the young unicorn, Moonsilver, is shot with a poisoned arrow, Heart risks exposing them all in order to get help from Rosa, the healer. Duey once again offers "a story with dramatic tension and plenty of endearing touches," Lempke noted in another *Booklist* review. In a later book in the series, *Castle Avamir,* Heart continues searching for her lost heritage, defying a law that forbids reading among commoners to peruse a mysterious book stolen from the evil Lord Dunraven. The book mentions a Castle Avamir, which Heart hopes might hold a clue to her background. With her unicorn companion, she sets out to learn the truth about Castle Avamir. There, she is befriended by an odd little man who tells her that the children who once lived in the castle were, in the past, sent away for their own safety. Before she can learn more, Lord Dunraven and his henchmen storm the castle and take the man away as a prisoner. With little regard for her own safety, Heart decides to follow them and help if she can.

Duey's "Hoofbeats" series explores the fascination and strong relationships that girls and young women often have with horses. In *Katie and the Mustang Book One,* nine-year-old orphan Katie is taken in by the Stevenses, a childless couple. She embarks on a dull life of hard work and drudgery. Her only source of happiness and comfort is her growing connection with a mustang owned by the family. Mr. Stevens treats the animal poorly, but it slowly learns to trust people again due to Katie's kindness. Katie holds out hope for an improved life when the family decides to head west along the Oregon Trail, but her optimism is dashed when she learns that Mr. Stevens plans to put her back in an orphanage and shoot the horse she loves. Defiant and desperate, Katie takes the horse and, together with Hiram, the hired hand, heads west to find the new life no one else can give her. In response to the book, *Booklist* reviewer Kay Weissman observed that "Duey's strengths lie in attention to setting details and effective characterizations." *Lara and the Gray Mare* moves the "Hoofbeats" setting to medieval Ireland, where Lara and her family struggle against hardship, the elements, and the constant threat of raids and violence by other clans. When a mare dies while giving birth to a foal, Lara determines that she will save and nurture the young filly, even at peril to herself. Carolyn Phelan, writing in *Booklist,* called the book "excellent fare for historical fiction fans and, of course, for girls devoted to horse stories."

The "Time Soldiers" series, *School Library Journal* reviewer Tim Wadham explained, was "designed to draw video-saturated youngsters into reading through cinematic artwork." The picture books, illustrated with larger-than-life photographs and lavish art and special effects, concern a group of children called upon to perform important tasks for the good of society at various critical points throughout time. In the series book *Arthur,* the children are transported back to the time of King Arthur and his knights. There, they meet a young Arthur, accompany him through several adventures, and watch as he draws the fabled sword from the stone, securing his kingship and enduring legend. Margaret Lane, writing in *Reviewer's Bookwatch,* called *Arthur* a "truly fantastic picturebook."

Duey told *CA:* "I began writing because of two extraordinary teachers: Mrs. Elsie Frederiksen, my 4th, 5th, and 6th grade teacher in a three room schoolhouse, and Mr. William Doohan, freshman English. I know first hand that teachers and librarians change and save lives."

BIOGRAPHICAL AND CRITICAL SOURCES:

PERIODICALS

Booklist, May 15, 1996, Karen Hutt, review of *Sarah Anne Hartford: Massachusetts, 1651,* p. 1585; March 1, 1997, Lauren Peterson, review of *Willow Chase: Kansas Territory, 1847,* p. 1164; February 1, 1998, Carolyn Phelan, reviews of *Blizzard: Estes Park, Colorado, 1886* and *Earthquake,* p. 917; February 15, 1998, Denia Hester, review of *Evie Peach: St. Louis, 1857,* p. 1011; January 1, 2002, Susan Dove Lempke, review of *Moonsilver,* p. 856; March 1, 2002, Susan Dove Lempke, review of *The Silver Thread,* p. 1136; June 1, 2002, Karen Hutt, review of *Sierra,* p. 1722; September 1, 2002, Susan Dove Lempke, reviews of *Mountains of the Moon* and *The Silver Bracelet,* p. 123; June 1, 2004, Kay Weisman, review of *Katie and the Mustang Book One,* p. 1725; February 1, 2005, Carolyn Phelan, review of *Lara and the Gray Mare,* p. 960; July, 2005, Carolyn Phelan, review of *Lara at the Silent Place,* p. 1924.
Bulletin of the Center for Children's Books, May, 1996, Elizabeth Bush, review of *Sarah Anne Hartford,* pp. 297-298; April, 1998, Elizabeth Bush, review of *Earthquake,* p. 278.

Publishers Weekly, March 18, 1996, review of *Sarah Anne Hartford,* p. 70; May 17, 2004, review of *Katie and the Mustang Book One,* p. 51.

Reviewer's Bookwatch, November, 2004, Margaret Lane, review of *Arthur.*

School Library Journal, June, 1996, Connie Parker, review of *Sarah Anne Hartford,* p. 120; December, 1996, Jane Gardner Connor, review of *Mary Alice Peale: Philadelphia, 1777,* p. 122, and Susan F. Marcus, review of *Anisett Lundberg: California, 1851,* p. 122; April, 1997, Rebecca O'Connell, review of *Willow Chase,* p. 137; August, 1997, Sylvia V. Meisner, review of *Ellen Elizabeth Hawkins: Mobeetie, Texas, 1886,* p. 157; March, 1998, Peggy Morgan, review of *Blizzard: Estes Park, Colorado,* p. 211, Robin L. Gibson, review of *Evie Peach,* p. 212, and Mary M. Hopf, review of *Earthquake,* p. 212; April, 1998, Denise Furgione, review of *Alexia Ellery Finsdale: San Francisco, 1905,* p. 131; June, 1998, Ann W. Moore, review of *Celou Sudden Shout: Idaho, 1826,* p. 143; September, 1998, Joan Zaleski, reviews of *Shipwreck: The Titanic* and *Fire: Chicago, 1871,* p. 200; December, 1998, Elaine Lesh Morgan, review of *Flood: Mississippi, 1927,* p. 121, and Janet Gillen, review of *Summer MacCleary: Virginia, 1749,* pp. 121-122; January, 1999, Coop Renner, review of *Agnes May Gleason: Walsenberg, Colorado, 1933,* p. 124; September, 1999, Janet Gillen, review of *Amelina Carrett: Bayou Grand Coeur, Louisiana, 1863,* p. 222; June, 2000, Susan Knell, review of *Rosa Moreno: Hollywood, California, 1928,* p. 143; October, 2000, Alison Grant, review of *Nell Dunne: Ellis Island, 1904,* p. 156; April, 2001, Betsy Barnett, review of *Francesca Vigilucci: Washington, D.C., 1913,* p. 139; October, 2001, Elaine Lesh Morgan, review of *Janey G. Blue: Pearl Harbor, 1941,* p. 154; December, 2001, Catherine Threadgill, review of *Moonsilver,* p. 99; April, 2002, Louise L. Sherman, review of *Sierra,* p. 146; October, 2002, Elaine Ford Weischedel, review of *Zellie Blake: Lowell, Massachusetts, 1834,* p. 162, and Carol Schene, review of *Bonita,* p. 162; February, 2004, Elaine E. Knight, review of *Castle Avamir,* p. 111; October, 2004, Time Wadham, review of *Arthur,* p. 112.

ONLINE

Fantastic Fiction, http://www.fantasticfiction.co.uk/ (December 5, 2006), bibliography of Kathleen Duey.

Kathleen Duey Web site, http://www.kathleenduey.com (December 18, 2006).

Kidsreads.com, http://www.kidsreads.com/ (December 5, 2006), Tamara Penny, review of *Nell Dunne, Ellis Island, 1904.**

*   *   *

DUNLAP, Susan 1943-
   (Susan Sullivan)

PERSONAL: Born June 20, 1943, in Kew Gardens, NY; married Newell Dunlap (an editor), 1970. *Education:* Bucknell University, B.A., 1965; University of North Carolina, M.Λ.T., 1966.

ADDRESSES: Home—Albany, CA. *Agent*—Dominick Abel, 146 W. 82nd St., New York, NY 10024. *E-mail*—Suedunlap@aol.com.

CAREER: Writer, novelist, and social services professional. Department of Social Services, Baltimore, MD, social worker, 1966-67; Department of Social Services, New York, NY, social worker, 1967; Department of Social Services, Contra Costa County, CA, social worker, 1968-84; full-time writer, 1984—. Teacher of Hatha yoga.

MEMBER: Sisters in Crime (founding member; president, 1990-91).

AWARDS, HONORS: Anthony Award; Macavity Award.

WRITINGS:

FICTION

(Editor, with Robert J. Randisi) *Deadly Allies II: Private Eye Writers of America and Sisters in Crime Collaborative Anthology,* Doubleday (New York, NY), 1994.

The Celestial Buffet and Other Morsels of Murder, with a separately printed pamphlet titled *"A Tail of Two Cities: A Jill Smith Story,"* Crippen & Landru Publishers (Norfolk, VA), 2001.

Karma and Other Stories, Five Star (Waterville, ME), 2002.

Fast Friends, Severn House (Surrey, England), 2004.
A Single Eye ("*Darcy Lott*" series), Carroll & Graf (New York, NY), 2006.

"*VEJAY HASKELL*" MYSTERY SERIES

An Equal Opportunity Death, St. Martin's Press (New York, NY), 1984.
The Bohemian Connection, St. Martin's Press (New York, NY), 1985.
The Last Annual Slugfest, St. Martin's Press (New York, NY), 1986.

"*JILL SMITH*" MYSTERY SERIES

Karma, Dell Publishing (New York, NY), 1981.
As a Favor, St. Martin's Press (New York, NY), 1984.
Not Exactly a Brahmin, St. Martin's Press (New York, NY), 1985.
Too Close to the Edge, St. Martin's Press (New York, NY), 1987.
A Dinner to Die For, St. Martin's Press (New York, NY), 1987.
Diamond in the Buff, St. Martin's Press (New York, NY), 1990.
Death and Taxes, Delacorte Press (New York, NY), 1992.
Time Expired, Delacorte Press (New York, NY), 1993.
Sudden Exposure, Delacorte Press (New York, NY), 1996.
Cop Out, Delacorte Press (New York, NY), 1997.

"*KIERNAN O'SHAUGHNESSY*" MYSTERY SERIES

Pious Deception, Villard Books (New York, NY), 1989.
Rogue Wave, Villard Books (New York, NY), 1991.
High Fall, Delacorte Press (New York, NY), 1994.
No Immunity, Delacorte Press (New York, NY), 1998.

Contributor to anthologies, including *A Woman's Eye,* edited by Sara Paretsky, Delacorte Press (New York, NY), 1991.

Contributor of short stories to periodicals, including *Ellery Queen's Mystery Magazine* and *Alfred Hitchcock's Mystery Magazine.*

SIDELIGHTS: Susan Dunlap has published mystery novels featuring several popular series characters: amateur detective Vejay Haskell, police detective Jill Smith, and medical examiner turned private investigator Kiernan O'Shaughnessy. Similarities abound between the characters. For instance, all three are, in various ways, symbols of feminist independence. Vejay avoids a serious relationship, and Jill, despite a steady boyfriend, manages to maintain a sense of separation. Kiernan owns a kitchenless duplex, an Irish wolfhound, a big sport utility vehicle, and a little sports car, and employs a former football player as a housekeeper. For all three, career changes put them in a position to become investigators, though neither Jill's promotion nor Kiernan's shift of focus are nearly as extreme as the break Vejay makes with her own past. Sue Trowbridge, on the *Interbridge* Web site, called Dunlap "a true pioneer in the field of crime novels with female protagonists." A founding member and former president of Sisters in Crime, Dunlap lives in Albany, California, just north of Berkeley, the setting for her Jill Smith series.

Vejay, a former public relations executive, leaves a high-powered job and her husband to become a meter reader for Pacific Gas and Electric in the Russian River Resort north of San Francisco. Her job allows her plenty of access to people's homes and other places off-limits to most amateur sleuths. Her work as a detective begins in *An Equal Opportunity Death,* when she is accused of murdering a bartender she once dated. To clear herself, Vejay goes into action, bringing to bear the resources at her disposal as a meter reader.

"While the plotting . . . is sometimes . . . muddy," a reviewer for *Publishers Weekly* wrote of the first Vejay Haskell book, "Vejay is an interesting heroine and her mystery . . . has a pleasantly different twist." Some coincidences in the book, commented a critic in *Booklist,* "stretch the possibilities . . . but the beguiling story unfolds quickly and smoothly." Newgate Callendar of the *New York Times Book Review* wrote of *An Equal Opportunity Death* that there is "nothing in the least original" about it, yet observed that "the heroine is feistily attractive" and pronounced it a worthwhile read. Kathleen Maio of *Wilson Library Bulletin,* who called it "not a memorable mystery," concluded that the book "promises better things to come."

The Bohemian Connection takes place during a festival at the Russian River Resort, when Vejay learns that the body of a coworker's niece has been found in a sewer.

As the mystery unfolds, she finds a connection between the murder and a drug-and-prostitution ring associated with the festival itself. The story culminates with the dredging of a cesspool, which yields some surprises. A *Publishers Weekly* contributor observed that Vejay is "not well served in this obvious and unfocused plot," and a *Kirkus Reviews* writer quoted a comment from the heroine in an appraisal of the book's plot: "It was already more than I wanted to know."

The slugs in *The Last Annual Slugfest* are not bullets or punches from a boxer, but the kind of slugs one finds in the garden—only, in the Russian River Resort, they are an escargot-like delicacy. The celebration of the Slugfest, an annual slug-tasting festival, is disrupted when one of the judges, Edwina Henderson, is poisoned. As Vejay goes to work on the mystery, she discovers a conflict between Edwina and her niece over the niece's relationship with a mystery man in the past. She also learns of a controversy involving an Indian tribe's claim to the resort's property, a claim that Edwina had intended to publicize. The plot thickens when Vejay discovers that the treaty on which the claim was based is a forgery. A *Kirkus Reviews* contributor called the novel "overplotted, over-populated, overwrought, and dull," but a reviewer in *Publishers Weekly* praised the tale's resolution as "a surprise [that] caps off an entertaining story."

Dunlap was featured in a mystery writers' cookbook called *Cooking with Malice Domestic,* published in 1991. Commenting that "my view of cooking is that its main use is as a cover for poisons," Dunlap presented the recipe for Slug Pizza.

Dunlap's character Jill Smith, formerly a beat cop, has recently been promoted to homicide detective when her own series begins. As with Vejay Haskell, her surroundings are vital to her stories—in this case, the "radical chic" environment of Berkeley, California. Trowbridge called Dunlap "the Bard of Berkeley," saying that the city provides her with endless inspiration for her Jill Smith mysteries. Site of student unrest in the 1960s, Berkeley has become a refuge for wealthy liberals and eccentrics, not to mention quite a few offbeat down-and-outers, homeless people, and a number of hippie leftovers from an earlier era. Surrounding Jill is a police department filled with an assortment of temperaments and ethnicities, including beat officer Connie Pereira, aspiring physical therapist Murakawa, and jealous

Sergeant Grayson. To get a feel for the way a police department works, Dunlap told Trowbridge in the *Interbridge* interview, she participated in a ten-week class on police work, which included a "ride along" program with Berkeley officers. She also called officers with questions that arose as she was writing.

Typical of the Berkeley settings for the "Jill Smith" mysteries is that of *Karma.* Attending a ceremony featuring a self-styled Buddhist holy man, Jill is shocked when the guru suddenly falls dead before an audience—with a knife in his chest. In *As a Favor,* the murder victim is more conventional, though her role as a worker in the local welfare department could be indicative of Berkeley's liberal and left-wing politics. In any case, victim Anne Spaulding was a coworker of Jill's ex-husband Nat, who asks Jill to look into the case. Ultimately Jill discovers an intricate welfare scam behind the murder, but not before she has a series of encounters with some of Berkeley's least—and some of its most—wealthy denizens. A *Kirkus Reviews* critic called *As a Favor* a "not-very-interesting story." However, a contributor to *Publishers Weekly* praised it as an "attractive mystery with a clever twist at the end," *Library Journal* reviewer Jean B. Palmer commented on Dunlap's "lively dialogue, fast pacing, smart characters, and breezy description" of Berkeley.

Not Exactly a Brahmin finds Jill investigating the murder of wealthy philanthropist Ralph Palmerston, a perplexing case because he was admired by virtually everyone who knew him. A *Publishers Weekly* critic called it "a suspenseful, fast-paced mystery," and a *Booklist* reviewer referred to it as "an intriguing tale" in spite of somewhat "sketchy" details on police procedure. Maio of *Wilson Library Bulletin,* while professing to prefer Vejay Haskell to Jill Smith, pronounced Dunlap "one of the Great Hopes of the policewoman procedural novel."

A handicapped activist turns up drowned in *Too Close to the Edge,* a mystery involving a local gang that steals high-priced designer running shoes. At the book's climax, Jill and the killer battle it out in a helicopter above San Francisco Bay. A *Booklist* reviewer called this last scene "hair-raising," and a contributor to *Kirkus Reviews* noted that the book, despite a slow start, is "Dunlap's most accomplished work yet."

Jill is thrust into another mystery with the murder of a chef in *A Dinner to Die For.* She also has problems in her personal life as she recovers from injuries sustained in *Too Close to the Edge.* A *Booklist* reviewer noted the novel's "sparkling good humor," and a *Publishers Weekly* contributor called it "an appealing mystery with tangy details on the Bay Area's changing environs and characters." *Library Journal* reviewer Jo Ann Vicarel concluded that Dunlap "gets better with every book."

Involved in a steady relationship, Jill wants to spend more time with her lover, but mysteries such as the one in *Diamond in the Buff* keep getting in the way of her plans. The nude referred to in the title is a sunbathing dentist, who complains about a neighbor who has allegedly beaten him with a eucalyptus branch. Things get ugly when another man is thrown off his deck to his death. In spite of some unlikely coincidences, wrote a reviewer in *Publishers Weekly,* the book is a "witty police procedural." A *Kirkus Reviews* contributor commented on its "lively backdrop" of Berkeley, which along with other facets of the story, "[makes] a mundane puzzle moderately diverting and easy to take."

In *Death and Taxes,* Jill's lover, Seth Howard, also a policeman, is deep in the middle of filing his taxes when Jill learns that a notorious IRS auditor—"one of the most hated employees of the nation's most-loathed bureaucracy"—has been murdered. Naturally, it is hard for Jill to feel sympathetic for the victim in this case, but she puts her mind to solving the mystery. Although Marilyn Stasio in the *New York Times Book Review* criticized the abundance of information about taxes when compared with the "airy" details on police procedure, a *Booklist* contributor pronounced *Death and Taxes* "every bit as much fun as its predecessors."

As is often the case in "Jill Smith" mysteries, seemingly unrelated activities come together in *Time Expired:* a hostage situation, the murder of a cantankerous lawyer, and an elaborate scheme involving parking tickets. "Dunlap is a talented writer; her prose is witty, sharp, at times hilarious," observed Suzanne Manczuk in *Voice of Youth Advocates,* "yet she can be thoughtful and introspective." *Library Journal* reviewer Rex E. Klett commented that "the plot remains minimal," and a *Publishers Weekly* contributor observed that "this is no spine-tingler." But, the *Publishers Weekly* contributor concluded, "a steady buildup of credible clues and Dunlap's psychological insights move her story steadily forward."

Sudden Exposure, Dunlap told Trowbridge, was inspired by a nudity movement in Berkeley. It begins with a conflict between Sam Johnson, an over-the-hill radical

activist, and his next-door neighbor, a former Olympic diver named Bryn Wiley. Bryn claims that Sam has been shooting at her car, and things get ugly when someone shoots at Bryn's vehicle and kills a person inside it. Jill begins to investigate and discovers that things are not what they seem in Bryn's neighborhood—one neighbor, in fact, does not even officially exist. This installment in the "Jill Smith" series is, in the view of *Booklist* reviewer Emily Melton, "a clear winner, thanks to an original plot, plenty of eccentric characters, and Dunlap's trademark breezy style." Doreen Salse of *Armchair Detective* professed to have never read any of the other "Jill Smith" mysteries prior to *Sudden Exposure* but concluded: "Her transplanted Easterner musings on the peculiarities of Berkeley aside, Smith's character was interesting enough to make me curious about her other eight adventures."

The mystery in *Cop Out* hits uncomfortably close to home for Jill. For years she has worked with a private eye named Herman Ott, using him as an informant. Both Jill and Herman are renegades, which has put both at odds with Jill's police department. Therefore, when a much-admired local leader of the arts community is murdered and police suspect Herman, Jill is put into a difficult situation. She believes him to be innocent and sets out to prove her case, but in the process discovers some surprising things about the man she thought she knew. As with the neighbors in *Sudden Exposure,* no one around her in *Cop Out* is quite who he or she claims to be. A *Kirkus Reviews* contributor called the book "solid and laden with local color, but lifeless. Whatever secrets Jill uncovers, Dunlap's real preoccupation is with her heroine's conflicted relationship with her cop life and lover." By contrast, a reviewer for *Publishers Weekly* wrote: "Smith's problematic romance with the burly and emotionally needy officer Seth Howard is always lively, adding another wrinkle of color to a series marked by its vividly depicted setting and admirably controlled plots."

Like Vejay Haskell, Kiernan O'Shaughnessy made a career change, but hers was not nearly such a radical break with the past. A former medical examiner, she has become a private investigator, and her experience in forensics often helps her solve cases. In the *Interbridge* interview, Dunlap told Trowbridge that she attends autopsies and researches forensics for the series.

In *Pious Deception,* Kiernan is called in to investigate the possible suicide of a Phoenix, Arizona, man, Austin Vanderhooven. What makes the suicide seem suspect, besides the fact that the deceased was a parish priest, is the hurried destruction of the body by cremation before an autopsy can be performed. Kiernan becomes personally involved in the case, which brings back hurts from her own past, and she is forced to deal with hostile local citizens in solving the mystery. Joyce Park, on the *MysteryGuide* Web site, complimented Dunlap on her portrayal of Kiernan as a professional, and wrote, "she's among the few fictional private eyes who insist upon a written contract and evidence of previous police involvement before starting a job." Park also praised Dunlap's portrayal of the Phoenix area and wrote that the characters, at the beginning of the book, are "drawn with a cool, realistic touch." According to a contributor to *Publishers Weekly,* the beginning of the book is promising, but it turns out to be "overburdened with subplots," an impression echoed in Park's *MysteryGuide* review. Bill Ott of *Booklist,* however, wrote that "Dunlap is off to a good start here; watch for Kiernan to develop into an engaging series hero." Dunlap told Sue Trowbridge that Kiernan "doesn't want to deal with what her emotions are. She wants to put that stuff in the back of her mind . . . to look people in the face and not budge and demand an answer and just charge on with what she's doing. I find that fascinating."

In *Rogue Wave,* a sailor is washed overboard and drowned, and Kiernan is brought in to examine the corpse. As she begins the investigation, she learns that the boat's captain was responsible years before for a hit-and-run accident that rendered a local artist brain damaged. Marilyn Stasio, in the *New York Times Book Review,* described Dunlap's technique in *Rogue Wave* as "research-dissect-describe," and said that the technique "also works on the white-knuckle plot and bare-knuckle action scenes." Clarence Peterson of Chicago *Tribune Books* called Dunlap's technical expertise "extraordinary," and wrote that she "knows the West Coast . . . [and] knows how to build suspense." Peter Robertson of *Booklist* commented that "*Rogue Wave* quickly draws the reader into a tight, sleek plot."

High Fall involves the death of a stuntwoman attempting to re-create a fatal stunt from the film *Bad Companions,* shot ten years earlier. Kiernan knew the stuntwoman, and now she faces a variety of suspects who had been involved in the unfortunate motion picture. A *Kirkus Reviews* contributor commented on the "disappointing revelations at the end" but found that this was more than offset by "an engaging series of conversa-

tions, so many telling forensic details, and such a sure sense of the leading players." A *Library Journal* reviewer called it "good entertainment," and wrote: "With slick and sassy prose, Dunlap . . . moves it all forward."

No Immunity brings on a chance for Kiernan's ex-football-player housekeeper, Brad Tchernack, to do some investigating of his own. Kiernan is called away to Nevada by Jeff, a friend from medical school, who needs to know the cause of death of a woman with symptoms of Lassa fever. While she is away, Brad gets involved in the search for a missing oil man with two deaf youngsters from Panama who are showing the same Lassa fever symptoms. While Kiernan is on the run from an accusing Nevada sheriff, another private eye and a second body complicate her detective work. A *Publishers Weekly* contributor called the plot "fragmented and hard to follow." However, Stephanie Zvirin of *Booklist* wrote: "Dunlap delivers plenty of high-octane action" in this book, and readers who love the "Kiernan O'Shaughnessy" series won't be disappointed.

With *A Single Eye,* Dunlap introduces another series character: stuntwoman, Zen practitioner, and amateur detective Darcy Lott. Though Darcy is a skilled stunt professional and is physically and mentally strong, she has a distinct weakness in her fear of being alone in forests and woodlands. She is horrified during a stunt shoot that goes wrong, severely injuring a young colleague and sending Darcy herself into a terrifying plunge into a forested area. To confront this phobia, her Zen master sends her on a retreat to a Zen monastery in the California redwood forests. Darcy is also to deliver a message to the master, Leo Garson-roshi. When she arrives at the monastery, however, she finds not peace and meditation, but stress and secrets. The memory of Aeneas, a highly adept Zen student who disappeared at a retreat six years previously, has been revived when five other students from the prior retreat arrive to participate in the current one. When Garson-roshi is nearly killed by poisoned cocoa, Darcy realizes that the stakes are dangerous and deadly. Before she is through, she will have to face greed, murder, and the deepening mystery of the vanished Aeneas. "Though the whodunit is overlong and predictable, Dunlap deftly explores the conflicts between Darcy's appetite for answers and her deference to Garson-roshi," noted a *Kirkus Reviews* critic. *Booklist* reviewer Barbara Bibel called Lott "an engaging new female detective," while a *Publishers Weekly* contributor named her a "brilliant but vulnerable heroine."

BIOGRAPHICAL AND CRITICAL SOURCES:

BOOKS

Heising, Willetta L., *Detecting Women,* Purple Moon Press (Dearborn, MI), 1996.

Muller, Marcia, and Bill Pronzini, editors, *The Web She Weaves,* William Morrow (New York, NY), 1983.

Nichols, Victoria, and Susan Thompson, *Silk Stalkings,* Black Lizard (Berkeley, CA), 1988.

St. James Guide to Crime and Mystery Writers, 4th edition, St. James Press (Detroit, MI), 1996.

Twentieth-Century Crime and Mystery Writers, 3rd edition, St. James Press (Detroit, MI), 1991.

Writers Directory, 15th edition, St. James Press (Detroit, MI), 1999.

PERIODICALS

Armchair Detective, winter, 1987, review of *Not Exactly a Brahmin,* p. 93; spring, 1992, review of *Karma,* p. 237; spring, 1996, Doreen Salse, review of *Sudden Exposure,* p. 238.

Booklist, June 1, 1984, review of *An Equal Opportunity Death,* p. 1378; December 15, 1985, review of *Not Exactly a Brahmin,* p. 608; March 15, 1987, review of *Too Close to the Edge,* p. 1096; October 15, 1987, review of *A Dinner to Die For,* p. 363; August, 1989, Bill Ott, review of *Pious Deception,* p. 1948; July, 1991, Peter Robertson, review of *Rogue Wave,* p. 2033; March 15, 1992, review of *Death and Taxes,* p. 1339; May 15, 1993, review of *Time Expired,* p. 1676; April 15, 1994, review of *Deadly Allies II: Private Eye Writers of America and Sisters in Crime Collaborative Anthology,* p. 1518; September 15, 1994, Wes Lukowsky, review of *High Fall,* p. 116; February 15, 1996, Emily Melton, review of *Sudden Exposure,* p. 994; May 1, 1997, Emily Melton, review of *Cop Out,* p. 1481; April 15, 1998, Stephanie Zvirin, review of *No Immunity,* p. 1380; September 15, 2006, Barbara Bibel, review of *A Single Eye,* p. 31.

Kirkus Reviews, May 1, 1984, review of *An Equal Opportunity Death,* p. 428; August 15, 1984, review of *As a Favor,* p. 779; May 15, 1985, review of *The Bohemian Connection,* p. 449; November 15, 1985, review of *Not Exactly a Brahmin,* p. 1225; July 1, 1986, review of *The Last Annual Slugfest,* p. 977; March 15, 1987, review of *Too Close to the Edge,* p. 423; June 1, 1989, review of *Pious Deception,* p. 797; February 15, 1990, review of *Diamond in the Buff,* p. 223; March 15, 1992, review of *Death and Taxes,* p. 355; March 15, 1993, review of *Time Expired,* p. 333; June 15, 1994, review of *High Fall,* p. 807; January 1, 1996, review of *Sudden Exposure,* p. 25; March 1, 1997, review of *Cop Out,* p. 336; April 1, 1998, review of *No Immunity,* p. 450; June 15, 2002, review of *Karma and Other Stories,* p. 840; September 15, 2004, review of *Fast Friends,* p. 892; September 15, 2006, review of *A Single Eye,* p. 931.

Library Journal, October 1, 1984, Jean B. Palmer, review of *As a Favor,* p. 1865; November 1, 1987, Jo Ann Vicarel, review of *A Dinner to Die For,* p. 124; May 1, 1993, Rex E. Klett, review of *Time Expired,* p. 121; August, 1994, Rex E. Klett, review of *High Fall,* p. 137; September 1, 1995, review of *High Fall,* p. 236; March 1, 1997, Rex E. Klett, review of *Cop Out,* p. 107.

Los Angeles Times Book Review, October 8, 1989, review of *Pious Deception,* p. 10.

New York Times Book Review, October 14, 1984, Newgate Callendar, review of *An Equal Opportunity Death,* p. 46; February 9, 1986, Newgate Callendar, review of *Not Exactly a Brahmin,* p. 27; September 10, 1989, Marilyn Stasio, review of *Pious Deception,* p. 28; July 21, 1991, Marilyn Stasio, review of *Rogue Wave,* p. 25; May 10, 1992, Marilyn Stasio, review of *Death and Taxes,* p. 23; March 28, 1993, review of *Death and Taxes,* p. 24; September 18, 1994, Marilyn Stasio, review of *High Fall,* p. 34.

Publishers Weekly, May 4, 1984, review of *An Equal Opportunity Death,* p. 52; August 17, 1984, review of *As a Favor,* p. 48; May 3, 1985, review of *The Bohemian Connection,* p. 67; October 18, 1985, review of *Not Exactly a Brahmin,* p. 50; June 13, 1986, Sybil Steinberg, review of *The Last Annual Slugfest,* p. 72; January 16, 1987, Sybil Steinberg, review of *Too Close to the Edge,* p. 64; October 23, 1987, Sybil Steinberg, review of *A Dinner to Die For,* p. 48; June 23, 1989, Sybil Steinberg, review of *Pious Deception,* p. 51; January 12, 1990, Sybil Steinberg, review of *Diamond in the Buff,* p. 50; August 2, 1991, review of *A Woman's Eye,* p. 65; February 24, 1992, review of *Death and Taxes,*

p. 46; March 29, 1993, review of *Time Expired*, p. 38; August 1, 1994, review of *High Fall*, p. 74; December 18, 1995, review of *Sudden Exposure*, p. 43; February 17, 1997, review of *Cop Out*, p. 213; March 16, 1998, review of *No Immunity*, p. 58; September 25, 2006, review of *A Single Eye*, p. 48.

Tribune Books (Chicago, IL), April 5, 1992, review of *Death and Taxes*, p. 5; July 19, 1992, Clarence Peterson, review of *Rogue Wave*, p. 8.

Voice of Youth Advocates, October, 1993, Suzanne Manczuk, review of *Time Expired,* p. 215.

Washington Post Book World, July 15, 1984, Jean M. White, review of *An Equal Opportunity Death,* p. 10.

Wilson Library Bulletin, November, 1984, Kathleen Maio, review of *An Equal Opportunity Death,* p. 212; February, 1986, Kathleen Maio, review of *Not Exactly a Brahmin,* p. 49; November, 1989, Kathleen Maio, review of *Pious Deception,* p. 102.

ONLINE

Interbridge, http://www.interbridge.com/ (February 6, 2007), Sue Trowbridge, interview with Susan Dunlap.

MysteryGuide, http://www.mysteryguide.com/ (February 6, 2007), Joyce Park, review of *Pious Deception.**

E

EDWARDS, Kim 1958-

PERSONAL: Born May 4, 1958, in Killeen, TX; married Thomas Clayton, 1987; children: two daughters. *Education:* Attended Auburn Community College; Colgate University, B.A., 1981; University of Iowa, M.F.A., 1983, M.A., 1987.

ADDRESSES: Home—Lexington, KY. *Office*—University of Kentucky, Department of English, 1215 Patterson Office Tower, Lexington, KY 40506-0027. *E-mail*—Edwards@uky.edu.

CAREER: Writer, novelist, short-story writer, and educator. University of Kentucky, Lexington, KY, visiting professor, 2003, currently assistant professor. Taught in M.F.A. programs at Washington University and Warren Wilson College; spent five years teaching in Malaysia, Japan, and Cambodia.

AWARDS, HONORS: Pushcart Prize, for short story "The Way It Felt to Be Falling"; PEN/Hemingway Award finalist, for *The Secrets of a Fire King;* National Magazine Award for Excellence in Fiction; Nelson Algren Award, 1990, for short story "Sky Juice"; Whiting Writer's Award, 2000; Kentucky Literary Award for Fiction, 2005, and Barnes and Noble Discovery Award, both for *The Memory Keeper's Daughter;* recipient of grants from the National Endowment for the Arts, Pennsylvania Council on the Arts, Seaside Institute, Kentucky Arts Council, and Kentucky Foundation for Women.

WRITINGS:

The Secrets of a Fire King (short stories), W.W. Norton (New York, NY), 1997.

The Memory Keeper's Daughter (novel), Viking (New York, NY), 2005.

Contributor to periodicals, including *Paris Review, Redbook, Michigan Quarterly Review, North American Review, Iowa Woman, Threepenny Review, Chicago Tribune, Ploughshares, Anteaus, Story,* and *Zoetrope.* Author's stories have been performed at Symphony Space and broadcast on Public Radio International.

Author's works have been translated into more than fourteen languages.

ADAPTATIONS: The Memory Keeper's Daughter has been optioned for a TV film by Lifetime and Jaffe-Braunstein Films.

SIDELIGHTS: Writer and educator Kim Edwards has published many short stories in journals that include the *Paris Review, Redbook, Chicago Tribune,* and *Ploughshares.* She wrote her first short story in a fiction workshop while a student at Colgate University. "The Way It Felt to Be Falling," originally published in *Threepenny Review,* won the Pushcart Prize and is included in Edwards's first book, *The Secrets of a Fire King.* "Writing is always a process of discovery—I never know the end, or even the events on the next page, until they happen. There's a constant interplay between the imagining and shaping of the story," Edwards remarked on the *Memory Keeper's Daughter* Web site.

The Secrets of a Fire King, which Nina Sonenberg in the *New York Times Book Review* deemed an "accomplished" debut, presents stories that deal with a wide range of themes and settings. Many refer to Asia, where Edwards spent five years traveling and teaching. In "Spring, Mountain, Sea," for example, a U.S. soldier's Asian bride learns about American foods and customs from the couple's neighbors, but their response to her gift of gratitude turns her away from the American culture. In "Gold," a young man's life is affected when gold is discovered in his Malaysian village, while "The Way It Felt to Be Falling" tells how a young woman learns about her inner strength when she suddenly decides to attempt a sky dive with a friend. Chicago *Tribune Books* contributor Patricia Lear described this story as sophisticated and brilliantly constructed. "The stories are impeccable, a treasure," wrote Lear, who observed that each piece "possesses the breadth of a novel." In the *Hudson Review*, critic Tom Wilhelmus wrote: "Rich in detail and at home with abstract ideas, Kim Edwards' stories mark an impressive beginning for a talented new storyteller."

The Memory Keeper's Daughter, is Edwards's debut novel. Protagonist David Henry is a physician who overcame a difficult, impoverished background in West Virginia to become a successful orthopedic surgeon. Years later, he is still haunted by the travails of his sister, June, whose fragile health kept the family in a constant state of stress and who died of a heart condition at age twelve. At the beginning of the book, in 1964, David's life is as good as he could hope. His practice is thriving, he is married to Norah, a beautiful woman he loves very much, and the two have a child on the way. When Norah goes into labor, a harsh blizzard is threatening the Lexington, Kentucky, area, and David and Norah can only make it to the clinic, not the hospital. There, with the assistance of his nurse, Caroline, David delivers the couple's offspring. To his surprise, Norah is carrying twins. The first child, Paul, is a perfectly healthy boy. However, the second child, Phoebe, is born with Down Syndrome. Wracked with indecision, and still keenly remembering the difficulties surrounding his sister's short life, he finally asks Caroline to take Phoebe away and commit her to an institution. His intention is to save his wife and family the disrupting, draining stress caused by perpetually ill child. He tells Norah that the girl was stillborn. Caroline, unable to abandon the infant girl, instead disappears, taking Phoebe to raise as her own.

As the next twenty-five years unfold within the novel, Edwards examines the effects of these events on the two families. David struggles with the guilt of his lie and with the fact that he abandoned his daughter, the secret of her existence always looming large in the background. Norah experiences the keen grief of a mother who has lost a child. The couple's marriage deteriorates, and the family fails to come together as a whole, always driven apart by the unseen but deeply felt rift caused by Phoebe's "death." Paul grows up feeling guilt of his own at having survived, and wonders often about his lost sister. Though he had hoped for the best, David's decision brought down years of trouble on his family. Phoebe, on the other hand, living in Pittsburgh, grows happily and thrives under Caroline's love and dedicated care. For her part, Caroline's life takes an upward path, and she prospers personally and professionally. Phoebe matures into a vibrant and capable young woman, nourished by love and by Caroline's steadfast devotion. "This is what drives the story—as one family thrives, the other one deteriorates," observed by Marie Hashima Lofton on *Bookreporter. com.*

Edwards "has written a heart-wrenching book, by turns light and dark, literary and suspenseful," commented Keddy Ann Outlaw, writing in *Library Journal*. A *Publishers Weekly* reviewer concluded that "this neatly structured story is a little too moist with compassion." With this novel, "Edwards tells a moving story," commented Carolyn Kubisz in *Booklist*.

BIOGRAPHICAL AND CRITICAL SOURCES:

PERIODICALS

Booklist, May 15, 2005, Carolyn Kubisz, review of *The Memory Keeper's Daughter*, p. 1634.

Bookseller, August 4, 2006, "Viking Wins US Bestseller," p. 11.

Daily Variety, January 15, 2007, John Dempsey, "A 'Keeper' for Lifetime," p. 3.

Entertainment Weekly, August 18, 2006, "The Charts," review of *The Memory Keeper's Daughter*, p. 143.

Hudson Review, autumn, 1997, Tom Wilhelmus, review of *The Secrets of a Fire King*, p. 527.

Kirkus Reviews, April 15, 2005, review of *The Memory Keeper's Daughter*, p. 437.

Library Journal, April 15, 1997, Ellen R. Cohen, review of *The Secrets of a Fire King*, p. 122; July 1, 2005, Keddy Ann Outlaw, review of *The Memory Keeper's Daughter*, p. 66.

New York Times Book Review, April 20, 1997, Nina Sonenberg, review of *The Secrets of a Fire King*, p. 20.

Publishers Weekly, February 24, 1997, review of *The Secrets of a Fire King,* p. 64; May 15, 2005, review of *The Memory Keeper's Daughter,* p. 34.

Tribune Books (Chicago, IL), June 1, 1997, Patricia Lear, "Getting it Right," p. 4.

ONLINE

Blogcritics, http://www.blogcritics.org/ (February 24, 2007), Ginger Haycox, review of *The Memory Keeper's Daughter.*

BookBrowse, http://www.bookbrowse.com/ (April 10, 2007), interview with Kim Edwards.

Bookreporter.com, http://www.bookreporter.com/ (April 10, 2007), Marie Hashima Lofton, review of *The Memory Keeper's Daughter.*

Memory Keeper's Daughter Web site, http://www. memorykeepersdaughter.com (April 10, 2007).

W.W. Norton Web site, http://www.wwnorton.com/ (April 10, 2007), description of *The Secrets of a Fire King.*

Zoetrope: All-Story, http://www.all-story.com/ (April 10, 2007), "Kim Edwards."*

*   *   *

EHRMAN, Bart D. 1956(?)-

PERSONAL: Born c. 1956. *Education:* Wheaton College, B.A. (magna cum laude), 1978; Princeton Theological Seminary, M.Div., 1981, Ph.D. (magna cum laude), 1985.

ADDRESSES: Home—Durham, NC. *Office*—University of North Carolina, Department of Religious Studies, CB #3225, Saunders 101, Chapel Hill, NC 27599; fax: 919-962-1567. *E-mail*—behrman@email.unc.edu.

CAREER: Writer, historian, religious scholar, lecturer, and educator. Rutgers University, Department of Religion, New Brunswick, NJ, instructor, 1984-85, assistant professor, 1985-88; Princeton Theological Seminary, instructor, 1985; University of North Carolina at Chapel Hill, Department of Religious Studies, Chapel Hill, NC, assistant professor, 1988-94, associate professor, 1994-99, Director of Graduate Studies, 1996-99, Bowman and Gordon Gray Professor, 1998-2001, professor, 1999—, chair of Department of Religious Studies, 2000—, James A. Gray Distinguished Profes-

sor, 2003—. Duke University, visiting assistant professor, 1991, adjunct professor, 2000—. Guest on television and radio programs and networks, including CNN, National Public Radio, the History Channel, and A&E.

MEMBER: Carolina Speakers Bureau, North American Committee of the International Greek New Testament Project, Studiorum Novi Testamenti Societas, Society of Biblical Literature (served as president and chair of New Testament criticism section), North American Patristics Society, Academy of Distinguished Teaching Scholars, University of North Carolina at Chapel Hill.

AWARDS, HONORS: John Lupton Foundation Grant for Course Development, University of North Carolina at Chapel Hill, 1990, 1994; UNC Foundation Junior Faculty Development Award, University of North Carolina at Chapel Hill, 1990; University Research Council Grant, University of North Carolina at Chapel Hill, 1990, 1993; Faculty Fellowship, Institute for the Arts and Humanities, University of North Carolina at Chapel Hill, 1991; Society of Biblical Literature Research and Publication Grant, 1991, 1992, 2000; Undergraduate Students' Teaching Award, University of North Carolina at Chapel Hill, 1993; Brandes Seminar Course Development Award, University of North Carolina at Chapel Hill, 1994, 1997; Phillip and Ruth Hettlemann Prize for Artistic and Scholarly Achievement, University of North Carolina at Chapel Hill, 1994; Arts and Sciences Foundation Research Development Grant, University of North Carolina at Chapel Hill, 1995; University Research Council Publication Grant, University of North Carolina at Chapel Hill, 1997; University Research Council Research Grant, University of North Carolina at Chapel Hill, 1997, 2000; fellow, Institute for the Arts and Humanities, University of North Carolina at Chapel Hill.

WRITINGS:

NONFICTION

Didymus the Blind and the Text of the Gospels, Scholars Press (Atlanta, GA), 1986.

(With Gordon D. Fee and Michael W. Holmes) *The Text of the Fourth Gospel in the Writings of Origen,* Scholars Press (Atlanta, GA), 1992.

The Orthodox Corruption of Scripture: The Effect of Early Christological Controversies on the Text of the New Testament, Oxford University Press (New York, NY), 1993.

(Editor, with Michael W. Holmes) *The Text of the New Testament in Contemporary Research: Essays on the Status Quaestionis,* Eerdmans (Grand Rapids, MI), 1995.

The New Testament: A Historical Introduction to the Early Christian Writings, Oxford University Press (New York, NY), 1997, 3rd edition, 2004.

The New Testament and Other Early Christian Writings: A Reader, Oxford University Press (New York, NY), 1998, 2nd edition, 2004.

After the New Testament: A Reader in Early Christianity, Oxford University Press (New York, NY), 1999.

Jesus, Apocalyptic Prophet of the New Millennium, Oxford University Press (New York, NY), 1999.

Lost Christianities: The Battle for Scripture and the Faiths We Never Knew, Oxford University Press (New York, NY), 2003.

(Editor and translator) *The Apostolic Fathers,* Harvard University Press (Cambridge, MA), 2003.

Lost Scriptures: Books That Did Not Make It into the New Testament, Oxford University Press (New York, NY), 2003.

Truth and Fiction in the Da Vinci Code: A Historian Reveals What We Really Know about Jesus, Mary Magdalene, and Constantine, Oxford University Press (New York, NY), 2004.

(With Andrew S. Jacobs) *Christianity in Late Antiquity, 300-450 C.E.: A Reader,* Oxford University Press (New York, NY), 2004.

A Brief Introduction to the New Testament, Oxford University Press (New York, NY), 2004.

(With Bruce M. Metzger) *The Text of the New Testament: Its Transmission, Corruption, and Restoration,* 4th edition, Oxford University Press (New York, NY), 2005.

Misquoting Jesus: The Story behind Who Changed the Bible and Why, HarperSanFrancisco (San Francisco, CA), 2005, published as *Whose Word Is It? The Story Behind Who Changed the New Testament and Why,* Continuum (London, England), 2006.

Peter, Paul, and Mary Magdalene: The Followers of Jesus in History and Legend, Oxford University Press (New York, NY), 2006.

Studies in the Textual Criticism of the New Testament, Brill (Boston, MA), 2006.

The Lost Gospel of Judas Iscariot: A New Look at Betrayer and Betrayed, Oxford University Press (New York, NY), 2006.

Contributor to books, including *New Testament Textual Criticism, Exegesis, and Church History: A Discussion of Methods,* edited by B. Aland and J. Delobel, Kok Pharos (Kampen, The Netherlands), 1994; *New Testament Interpretation Today,* edited by Joel Green, Eerdmans (Grand Rapids, MI), 1996; *Eerdmans Dictionary of the Bible,* Eerdmans (Grand Rapids, MI), 1999; and *The Bible As Book,* Scriptorium (Grand Rapids, MI), 2003.

Contributor to journals and periodicals, including *Journal of Early Christian Studies, TC: A Journal of Biblical Textual Criticism, Perspectives in Religion, Studies and Documents, New Testament Studies, Journal of Biblical Literature, Biblica, Novum Testamentum, Vigiliae Christianae, Biblical Quarterly, Catholic Biblical Quarterly, Currents in Contemporary Christology, Princeton Seminary Bulletin, Critical Review of Books in Religion,* and *Biblical Theology Bulletin.*

Author of courses and lectures on audio and video tape.

Editor, *The New Testament in the Greek Fathers* monograph series (member of editorial board, 1988—, editor-in-chief, 1997); coeditor, *New Testament Tools and Studies* monograph series, 1993—.

Member of editorial board, *Critical Review of Books in Religion,* 1994-98; *Textual Criticism: An Electronic Journal,* 1995—; *Studies and Documents,* 1995—; *Pericope: Scripture as Written and Read in Antiquity,* 2001—; *New Testament Studies,* 2004—; *Journal of Early Christian Studies,* 2004—; *Early Christianity in Context,* 2004—; member of advisory board, *Electronic New Testament Manuscript Project,* 1995-99.

SIDELIGHTS: Bart D. Ehrman is a professor of religious studies at the University of North Carolina, Chapel Hill. His works typically focus on aspects of Christian history, notably on those that deal with early Christian writings and the New Testament.

"While it is well known that 'heretics' such as Marcion and Tatian tampered with the text of the New Testament . . . the fact that their proto-'orthodox' opponents also changed the New Testament's text is often overlooked," explained William L. Petersen in the *Journal of Religion.* Ehrman's 1993 work, *The Orthodox Corruption of Scripture: The Effect of Early Christological Controversies on the Text of the New Testament,* focuses on these changes, which were made by the scribes copying the texts as a way to deal with specific issues they considered heretical. An example of one of these heretical notions, from the second and third centuries, is separationism, the belief that Christ and Jesus are two separate people.

"Textual critics have long been conscious that theological concerns affected the transmission of the written texts," noted Louis William Countryman in *Church History*. "Ehrman, however, establishes a new standard of coherence and thoroughness in dealing with these issues." *Choice* reviewer F.M. Gillman praised *The Orthodox Corruption of Scripture* as a "detailed, carefully argued, and thoroughly documented study." Petersen also lauded the work, concluding: "Ehrman's study is well written. It serves a useful purpose in demonstrating how textual variants are often the result of theological prejudices and proves once again that the 'orthodox' did not hesitate to revise the received text when it did not suit their needs."

Ehrman's other books focus on similar themes and have also been well received by critics and scholars. For example, *Didymus the Blind and the Text of the Gospels*, a revision of his Princeton Theological Seminary dissertation, was lauded by Michael W. Holmes in the *Journal of Biblical Literature*. "In all, this is a superior piece of work in terms of both the importance of its findings and the potential of its methodological proposals. One looks forward to more from this author." *The Text of the New Testament in Contemporary Research: Essays on the Status Quaestionis*, edited by Ehrman and Michael W. Holmes in honor of professor Bruce M. Metzger of Princeton Theological Seminary, is a collection of essays on various aspects relating to contemporary textual criticism of the New Testament. James A. Brooks in *Religious Studies Review* called the work "an excellent supplement" to New Testament textual criticism. Daniel J. Harrington in *America* argued that the "up-to-date handbook deserves a place in all good theological libraries." Ehrman's *The Text of the Fourth Gospel in the Writings of Origen*, written with Gordon D. Fee and Michael W. Holmes, uses the surviving writings of Origen, an early Greek church father, to reconstruct a text of John. In *Religious Studies Review*, James A. Brooks lauded the work as "of inestimable value" to New Testament scholars.

Jesus, Apocalyptic Prophet of the New Millennium is aimed at a popular audience rather than religious studies scholars. In the work, Ehrman argues that much of the popular conception of Jesus is based on misleading statements made by the church or by scholars, and that it is crucial to place Jesus in context and explore the sources of information about him. Using both canonical and noncanonical sources, Ehrman argues that Jesus is best understood as an apocalyptic preacher who believed the world was coming to an end and that God would judge and destroy the evil, a portrait of Jesus similar to that first espoused by Albert Schweitzer in the early twentieth century.

Eugene O. Bowser in *Library Journal* faulted Ehrman for "wrongly giving an illusion of certainty and agreement where there is none" among historical scholars, and presenting primarily only one side of the debate. A *Publishers Weekly* critic however, concluded: "While Ehrman's provocative thesis will stir up controversy among scholars, his warm, inviting prose style and his easy-to-read historical and critical overviews make this the single best introduction to the study of the historical Jesus."

Lost Christianities: The Battle for Scripture and the Faiths We Never Knew provides a historical recounting of some of the earliest Christian groups and their conflicts with each other as they struggled to establish their particular version of Christianity as the dominant one. "With a light, vivid style, Bart D. Ehrman dramatically recounts how early Christian groups fought with each other before the fourth-century consolidation of orthodoxy," commented David C. Albertson in the *Journal of Religion*. Ehrman considers the often shaky basis for making declarations of authenticity for any ancient source, noting that materials labeled canonical or apocryphal may be one, the other, or neither, since forgery and exaggeration can enter into the designation. He explores the breadth and tremendous diversity of early Christian belief and the various groups that emerged in the early days of Christianity. Finally, he looks at the literary techniques and other strategies used by the Christian groups that succeeded in defining Christian orthodoxy in their own way. Ehrman analyzes early documents and literary categories, including gospels, epistles, and apocalypses, and "presents context, history, and commentary surrounding these important early materials," remarked Sandra Collins in *Library Journal*. A *Kirkus Reviews* critic named the book "A well-crafted, scholarly tale of forgeries, burned books, doctrinal feuds, and other episodes in the making of the New Testament and the early Church." L.W. Hurtado, writing in the *Journal of Ecclesiastical History*, concluded that "for readers with little or no previous acquaintance with the texts and developments in view here, this will provide an informed, genial and readable introduction."

In *Misquoting Jesus: The Story behind Who Changed the Bible and Why* Ehrman carefully considers the plentiful evidence that the Bible has been repeatedly changed and altered throughout its history, by both accident and design, as religious leaders and biblical guardians sought to impose their favored interpretations of biblical history and scripture. Ehrman challenges assessments of the Bible as a divinely inspired and perfect text transmitted directly from God to readers. Too many discrepancies and disagreements, errors and omissions exist in extant versions of the Bible for it to be a perfect representation of God's word. An expert in textual criticism, scholarly techniques for comparing and analyzing divergent texts, Ehrman explains the processes of textual criticism and the results that have emerged in studies of the long history of the Bible. Ehrman notes numerous instances where "scribes and editors altered the text of New Testament to avoid making Jesus look bad, to refute heresies and for sociopolitical reasons, blithely altering what they supposedly accepted as God's dictation to the mortal authors of the Christian scriptures in the process," commented Tim Callahan in *Skeptic*. Inadvertent mistakes and deliberate changes have fundamentally altered the Bible from the form it occupied in early times, according to Ehrman. "Among the things Ehrman claims were changed or added by scribes are the Lord's Prayer, the Last Supper, and the woman caught in adultery, which he says was not part of any of the four Gospels as originally written," pointed out Mark I. Pinsky in the *Orlando Sentinel*. It was these errors and inconsistencies, in fact, that severely undermined Ehrman's own religious belief and led him from born-again Christianity to disbelief. In this work, fifteen centuries of "hand-copied manuscripts and their differences are synthesized into a very provocative, readable study which any Bible student will find fascinating," commented a reviewer in *California Bookwatch*.

Peter, Paul, and Mary Magdalene: The Followers of Jesus in History and Legend contains Ehrman's analysis and scholarly consideration of the lives of three of Christ's most important followers. His analysis of the importance of these three individuals is "uncompromising in its scholarship yet utterly engaging for general readers," observed Ilene Cooper in *Booklist*. He uses historical writings, New Testament texts, and other documents to define the lives of the three. He also looks at myths and legends about the trio to explore their

importance to Christians and to the development of Christian belief, values, and passions. As part of the process, Ehrman considers "how to separate history from legend, whether it can be done at all, and whether it matters," commented a *Publishers Weekly* contributor.

In *The Lost Gospel of Judas Iscariot: A New Look at Betrayer and Betrayed,* Ehrman takes a new look at one of the most reviled figures of biblical times and offers up a positive, even uplifting interpretation of Judas's role in the earthly mission of Jesus. The Gospel of Judas is a relatively recent biblical discovery that consisted of a manuscript that offered a different interpretation of the story of Judas than that presented in the New Testament. Ehrman served as one of the scholars who authenticated the manuscript, which comes from the Gnostic tradition, and his interpretation portrays Judas not as a villain, but as a vitally important and irreplaceable agent in fulfilling Christ's divine destiny. The Gospel of Judas, according to Ehrman, "reveals a radical new understanding of Christ's mission and Judas's role in it," noted *Library Journal* reviewer C. Brian Smith. Among the twelve apostles, it was Judas alone who fully understood Christ's message, Ehrman states. Further, Ehrman notes, what is seen as Judas's betrayal was in fact an act of kindness performed in the service of Jesus and his mission on Earth. Ehrman also offers an explanation of the Gnostic tradition, the place of the Gospel of Judas within that tradition, and a thorough explication of the contents of the lost gospel. Cooper, in another *Booklist* review, called the book "a must for those interested in the subject of early Christianity," while a *Publishers Weekly* critic stated: "Ehrman's fast-paced study introduces us engagingly to the Gospel of Judas."

BIOGRAPHICAL AND CRITICAL SOURCES:

PERIODICALS

America, April 6, 1996, Daniel J. Harrington, review of *The Text of the New Testament in Contemporary Research: Essays on the Status Quaestionis,* p. 21.
Booklist, September 1, 1999, Steven Schroeder, review of *Jesus, Apocalyptic Prophet of the New Millennium,* p. 35; November 1, 2004, Ilene Cooper, review of *The Truth and Fiction in The Da Vinci Code: a Historian Reveals What We Really Know about Jesus, Mary Magdalene, and Constantine,* p. 454; November 15, 2005, Bryce Christensen,

review of *Misquoting Jesus: The Story behind Who Changed the Bible and Why*, p. 7; April 15, 2006, Ilene Cooper, review of *Peter, Paul, and Mary Magdalene: the Followers of Jesus in History and Legend*, p. 8; October 1, 2006, Ilene Cooper, "Exonerating Judas," review of *The Lost Gospel of Judas Iscariot: A New Look at Betrayer and Betrayed*, p. 27.

Books & Culture, September-October, 2006, Robert H. Gundry, "Post-Mortem: Death By Hardening of the Categories," review of *Misquoting Jesus*, p. 8.

California Bookwatch, April, 2006, review of *Misquoting Jesus*.

Choice, November, 1993, F.M. Gillman, review of *The Orthodox Corruption of Scripture*, p. 474; January, 2000, D. Ingolfsland, review of *Jesus, Apocalyptic Prophet of the New Millennium*, p. 951.

Church History, March, 1997, Louis William Countryman, review of *The Orthodox Corruption of Scripture: The Effect of Early Christological Controversies on the Text of the New Testament*, p. 81; June, 2005, Alison G. Salvesen, review of *Lost Christianities*, p. 347.

Internet Bookwatch, August, 2006, review of *After the New Testament*.

Interpretation, January, 2004, review of *Lost Scriptures: Books that Did Not Make It into the New Testament*, p. 108; January, 2004, reviews of *The New Testament and Other Early Christian Writings: A Reader* and *The New Testament: A Historical Introduction to the Early Christian Writings*, p. 108.

Journal of Biblical Literature, spring, 1989, Michael W. Holmes, review of *Didymus the Blind and the Text of the Gospels*, pp. 144-146.

Journal of Ecclesiastical History, January, 2005, L.W. Hurtado, review of *Lost Christianities*, p. 121.

Journal of Religion, October, 1994, William L. Petersen, review of *The Orthodox Corruption of Scripture*, p. 562; July, 2005, David C. Albertson, review of *Lost Christianities*, p. 477.

Kirkus Reviews, August 15, 2003, review of *Lost Christianities*, p. 1056.

Library Journal, October 1, 1999, Eugene O. Bowser, review of *Jesus, Apocalyptic Prophet of the New Millennium*, p. 99; November 15, 2003, Sandra Collins, review of *Lost Christianities*, p. 71; September 1, 2005, Charles Seymour, review of *Misquoting Jesus*, p. 147; April 1, 2006, John Jaeger, review of *Peter, Paul, and Mary Magdalene*, p. 99; October 15, 2006, C. Brian Smith, review of *The Lost Gospel of Judas Iscariot*, p. 67.

Orlando Sentinel, April 3, 2006, Mark I. Pinsky, "'Gospel Truth' Is Question for Author: Bart Ehrman Dissects What He Says Led to Mistakes in the Bible."

Publishers Weekly, July 12, 1999, review of *Jesus, Apocalyptic Prophet of the New Millennium*, p. 90; August 25, 2003, review of *Lost Christianities*, p. 58; October 11, 2004, review of *The Truth and Fiction in the Da Vinci Code*, p. 76; August 22, 2005, review of *Misquoting Jesus*, p. 59; March 13, 2006, review of *Peter, Paul, and Mary Magdalene*, p. 63; August 28, 2006, review of *The Lost Gospel of Judas Iscariot*, p. 49; November 20, 2006, Marcia Z. Nelson, "Three Authors Hit the Publishing Jackpot Bestsellers from the Academy," review of *Misquoting Jesus*, p. S8.

Religious Studies Review, January, 1994, James A. Brooks, review of *The Text of the Fourth Gospel in the Writings of Origen*, p. 62; October, 1995, James A. Brooks, review of *The Text of the New Testament in Contemporary Research*, p. 331; July, 1998, Casimir Bernas, reviews of *The New Testament: A Historical Introduction to the Early Christian Writings* and *The New Testament and Other Early Christian Writings: A Reader*, pp. 299-300.

Skeptic, winter, 2006, Tim Callahan, "The Word of the Lord?," review of *Misquoting Jesus*, p. 63.

ONLINE

Bart D. Ehrman Home Page, http://www.bartdehrman.com (February 6, 2007).

Internet Movie Database, http://www.imdb.com/ (February 6, 2007), filmography of Bart D. Ehrman.

University of North Carolina at Chapel Hill, Department of Religious Studies Web site, http://www.unc.edu/depts/rel_stud/ (February 6, 2007), biography of Bart D. Ehrman.*

*   *   *

ELLIOTT, John H. 1930-
(John Huxtable Elliott, Sir John Huxtable Elliott)

PERSONAL: Born June 23, 1930, in Reading, England; son of Thomas Charles and Janet Mary Elliott; married Oonah Sophia Butler, March 22, 1958. *Education:* Attended Eton College, 1943-48; Trinity College, Cambridge, B.A., 1952, Ph.D., 1955. *Hobbies and other interests:* Looking at buildings and pictures; travel.

ADDRESSES: Home—Oxford, England. *Office*—Oriel College, Oxford OX1 4EW, England.

CAREER: Writer, historian, art historian, and educator. Cambridge University, Cambridge, England, assistant lecturer, 1958-62, lecturer in history, 1962-67; King's College, University of London, London, England, professor of history, 1968-73; Institute for Advanced Study, Princeton, NJ, School of Historical Studies, professor, 1973-90; Oxford University, Regius Professor of Modern History, 1990-97; Oxford University, Oriel College, 1990-98. New York University, King Juan Carlos visiting professor, 1988; University of Warwick, visiting honorary professor, 2003-07. Fellow, British Academy, 1972, and American Academy of Arts and Sciences, 1977. *Military service:* British Army, 1948-49.

MEMBER: American Philosophical Society, Hispanic Society of America (corresponding member), Real Academia Sevillana de Buenas Letras, Academia Nazionale dei Lincei (foreign member).

AWARDS, HONORS: FBA, 1972; FAAAS, 1977; Visitante Illustre de Madrid, 1983; Wolfson Prize for History, 1986; Medal of Honour Universidad Internacional Menendez y Pelayo, 1987; Commander of the Order of Isabel la Católica, 1987, Grand Cross, 1996; Grand Cross Order of Alfonso X. El Sabio, 1988; Gold Medal for the Fine Arts, Spain, 1990; Cambridge University, Trinity College, honorary fellow, 1991; Eloy Antonio de Nebrija Prize, Spain, 1993; created knight bachelor, 1994; Prince of Asturias Prize for Social Sciences, Spain, 1996; Cambridge University, Oriel College, honorary fellow, 1998; Balzan Prize for History 1500-1800, 1999; Cross of St. George, 1999; Francis Parkman Prize for American History, 2007, for *Empires of the Atlantic World: Britain and Spain in America, 1492-1830.* Recipient of honorary degrees from the Universidad Autonoma de Madrid, University of Genoa, University of Portsmouth, University of Barcelona University of Warwick, Brown University, University of Valencia, University of Lleida, Universidad Complutense Madrid, College of William and Mary.

WRITINGS:

NONFICTION

The Revolt of the Catalans, Cambridge University Press (New York, NY), 1963.

Imperial Spain, 1469-1716, St. Martin's Press (New York, NY), 1963.
Europe Divided, 1559-1598, Collins (New York, NY), 1968.
Europe Divided, 1559-1598, Harper & Row (New York, NY), 1969.
Imperial Spain, 1469-1716, Penguin (New York, NY), 1970.
(Coeditor) *The Diversity of History: Essays in Honour of Sir Herbert Butterfield,* Cornell University Press (Ithaca, NY), 1970.
The Old World and the New, 1492-1650, Cambridge University Press (New York, NY), 1970.
The Discovery of America and the Discovery of Man, Oxford University Press for the British Academy (Oxford, England), 1972.
(Coauthor) *Spain: 1494-1659* (sound recording), BFA Educational Media, 1972.
El conde-duque de Olivares y la herencia de Felipe II, Universidad de Valladolid (Valladolid, Spain), Facultad de Filosofia y Letras, 1977.
(With Jose F. de la Pera) *Memoriales y Cartas del Conde Duque de Olivares,* two volumes, Alfaguara, 1978 and 1980.
(With Jonathan Brown) *A Palace for a King: The Buen Retiro and the Court of Philip IV,* Yale University Press (New Haven, CT), 1980.
(Author of essay) *Painting in Spain, 1650-1700, from North American Collections,* by Edward J. Sullivan and Nina A. Mallory, Princeton University/Princeton University Press (Princeton, NJ), 1982.
Discurso de investidura de doctor honoris causa, Universidad Autonoma de Madrid (Madrid, Spain), 1984.
Richelieu and Olivares, Cambridge University Press (New York, NY), 1984.
The Count-Duke of Olivares: The Statesman in an Age of Decline, Yale University Press (New Haven, CT), 1986.
Spain and Its World, 1500-1700: Selected Essays, Yale University Press (New Haven, CT), 1989.
(Coauthor and co-coordinator) *La Espana del Conde Duque de Olivares: Encuentro Internacional sobre la Espana del Conde Duque de Olivares celebrado en Toro los dias 15-18 de septiembre de 1987,* Universidad de Valladolid (Valladolid, Mexico), 1990.
(Editor) *The Hispanic World: Civilization and Empire: Europe and the Americas: Past and Present,* Thames and Hudson (London, England), 1991.
(Editor) *The Spanish World: Civilization and Empire, Europe and the Americas, Past and Present,* H.N. Abrams (New York, NY), 1991.

National and Comparative History: An Inaugural Lecture Delivered before the University of Oxford on 10 May 1991, Clarendon Press/Oxford University Press (Oxford, England), 1991.

Lengua e imperio en la Espana de Felipe IV, Ediciones Universidad de Salamanca, 1994.

Do the Americas Have a Common History? An Address, by J.H. Elliott, published for the Associates of the John Carter Brown Library (Providence, RI), 1998.

(Coeditor, with L.W.B. Brockliss) *The World of the Favourite,* Yale University Press (New Haven, CT), 1999.

(Coeditor, with Jonathan Brown) *The Sale of the Century: Artistic Relations between Spain and Great Britain, 1604-1655,* Yale University Press (New Haven, CT), 2002.

(With David Davies) *El Greco* (exhibition catalogue), Yale University Press (New Haven, CT), 2004.

Empires of the Atlantic World: Britain and Spain in America, 1492-1830, Yale University Press (New Haven, CT), 2006.

SIDELIGHTS: John H. Elliott is a British writer, educator, and historian who has taught at such prestigious institutions as Cambridge University, Kings College, London, and Oxford University. Knighted as a British Knight Bachelor in 1994, Elliott studies and writes about European and American history.

In *El Greco,* an exhibition catalogue accompanying a show of the painter's works at New York's Metropolitan Museum of Art, Elliott, coauthor David Davies, and numerous contributors provide eighty-three catalogue entries that cover the artist's background, history, and accomplishments as a major figure in painting. El Greco, or "The Greek," was born Domenikos Theotokopoulos in Crete, where he mastered the local style of icon painting. From there, he went to Toledo, Spain, where much theological work was being done. In Spain, he was awarded many commissions for artwork while exploring his numerous intellectual and philosophical interests. Known to be an irascible man with diverse opinions, El Greco nonetheless prospered, producing many works with religious themes as well as landscapes, portraits, and mythological subjects. In addition to shorter entries covering varied aspects of El Greco's life and work, Elliott and Davies contribute other essays that "place the artist in his time and also articulate a sense of the artist and his development," noted Robert Cahn, writing in *Library Journal.* Elliott's piece, in particular, covers the "Mediterranean milieu" where the artist worked and developed. *Booklist* reviewer Donna

Seaman observed how the verticality of El Greco's works demonstrates a reach for the divine, even as his other works strive to represent not just the natural world but transcendence. "This magnificent volume renews and deepens appreciation for a master painter for all time and all faiths," commented Seaman.

BIOGRAPHICAL AND CRITICAL SOURCES:

PERIODICALS

Booklist, January 1, 2004, Donna Seaman, review of *El Greco,* p. 805.

Library Journal, February 1, 2004, Robert Cahn, review of *El Greco,* p. 80.

*   *   *

ELLIOTT, John Huxtable
   See ELLIOTT, John H.

*   *   *

ELLIOTT, Sir John Huxtable
   See ELLIOTT, John H.

*   *   *

EMERSON, Earl 1948-
   (Earl W. Emerson)

PERSONAL: Born July 8, 1948, in Tacoma, WA; son of Ralph W. and June Emerson; married Sandra (Sandy) Evans, April 25, 1968; children: Sara, Brian, Jeffrey. *Education:* Attended Principia College, 1966-67, and University of Washington, Seattle, 1967-68.

ADDRESSES: Home—North Bend, WA. *Agent*—Dominick Abel, Dominick Abel Literary Agency Inc., 146 W. 82nd St., Ste. 1B, New York, NY 10024. *E-mail*—author@earlemerson.com.

CAREER: Writer, novelist, and firefighter. Seattle Fire Department, Seattle, WA, lieutenant, 1978—.

MEMBER: Mystery Writers of America, Private Eye Writers of America.

AWARDS, HONORS: Shamus Award, Private Eye Writers of America, 1985, for *Poverty Bay;* Edgar Award nomination

WRITINGS:

"THOMAS BLACK" SERIES; MYSTERY NOVELS

The Rainy City, Avon (New York, NY), 1985.
Poverty Bay, Avon (New York, NY), 1985.
Nervous Laughter, Avon (New York, NY), 1986.
Fat Tuesday, Morrow (New York, NY), 1987.
Deviant Behavior, Morrow (New York, NY), 1988.
Yellow Dog Party, Morrow (New York, NY), 1991.
The Portland Laugher, Ballantine (New York, NY), 1994.
The Vanishing Smile, Ballantine (New York, NY), 1995.
The Million-Dollar Tattoo, Ballantine (New York, NY), 1996.
Deception Pass, Ballantine (New York, NY), 1997.
Catfish Café, Ballantine (New York, NY), 1998.

"MAC FONTANA" SERIES; MYSTERY NOVELS

Black Hearts and Slow Dancing, Morrow (New York, NY), 1988.
Help Wanted: Orphans Preferred, Morrow (New York, NY), 1990.
Morons and Madmen, Morrow (New York, NY), 1993.
Going Crazy in Public, Morrow (New York, NY), 1996.
The Dead Horse Paint Company, Morrow (New York, NY), 1997.

OTHER MYSTERY NOVELS

Vertical Burn, Ballantine (New York, NY), 2002.
Into the Inferno, Ballantine (New York, NY), 2003.
Pyro, Ballantine (New York, NY), 2004.
The Smoke Room, Ballantine (New York, NY), 2005.
Firetrap, Ballantine (New York, NY), 2006.

Also author of novel, *Fill the World With Phantoms,* 1979.

SIDELIGHTS: Earl Emerson has brought the crime novel into the Pacific Northwest with his books set in or near Seattle, Washington. He has created two distinctive series heroes: Thomas Black, a hard-core private detective with a strong sense of justice and morals; and Mac Fontana, a small town fire chief with more than his share of extraordinary conflagrations to fight. In his *St. James Guide to Crime and Mystery Writers* essay on Emerson, John M. Muste noted that in all of Emerson's work, his prose "is clean and his narratives always move with considerable momentum. His plots are complicated, sometimes perhaps overly so, but the resolutions are clear." Muste added: "As a body of work, Emerson's novels provide an interesting setting, some relaxed humor, and a different perspective for plots that are not always entirely fresh."

Emerson's first protagonist, Thomas Black, has appeared in almost a dozen titles. Early Black stories emphasize his toughness and independence as an ex-policeman solving crimes not for financial profit but for the satisfaction of helping to right wrongs. Through the series, Black is joined in his crime-fighting efforts by an attorney named Kathy Birchfield, for whom he develops an attraction that deepens over time. From a platonic but sexually tinged relationship through the early books, Black and Birchfield move into romance and marriage, often facing dangerous situations together. "A typical Black case," wrote Muste, "begins with Kathy Birchfield coming to him with fears about the fate of a friend, or bringing him a client. The novels all contain high levels of violence, and Black himself, although adept at the martial arts, comes in for beatings; like many fictional detectives, he sometimes loses the first fight but he never loses the last one."

Emerson's works have received positive reviews. *The Portland Laugher,* for example, was cited in *Publishers Weekly* for its "superbly worked-out plot, a narrator with a likable voice, and Emerson's clean, witty prose." Another *Publishers Weekly* reviewer praised the way the detective's personal relationships "show a vulnerable side of the tough, resourceful Black." The same reviewer noted the novels' "gritty panache."

In *Catfish Café* some critics noted that Emerson departs somewhat from witty repartee to take on a more serious tone about family relationships. *Catfish Café* is about Black's investigation into a murder that might have been committed by the daughter of his one-time partner, Luther Little. Gradually, after sorting all the complicated relationships in Little's African-American family, Black surmises that the murder was the end result of an incident that occurred long ago at the café of the title. "Part social study, part whodunnit, the elegantly written *Catfish Café* does well by both," wrote Dick Lochte in the *Los Angeles Times*. A *Publishers Weekly* critic similarly noted that the murder mystery itself is not the most compelling part of the novel, which "will likely leave readers more interested in the mysteries and variety of human behavior than in explications."

Since 1978, Emerson has been employed as a professional firefighter in Seattle. This career led to the development of his second hero, Mac Fontana. Fontana heads a small fire department in a town near Seattle. Sometimes he must also moonlight as the town's sheriff, and he does so with great determination. From his debut appearance in *Black Hearts and Slow Dancing*, Fontana has proven a hit with the critics. A *Publishers Weekly* correspondent described him as "a no-nonsense and likable guy" whose actions show "that fire departments aren't just a bunch of guys and a couple of Dalmatians hanging out at the station." Another *Publishers Weekly* reviewer called *The Dead Horse Paint Company*, Fontana's fifth mystery, "deftly constructed [and] compelling." The reviewer continued: "Fontana . . . sifts through the rubble of broken lives to find a killer as Emerson constructs a brooding, engaging tale of personal and professional conflict."

Since character Fontana and author Emerson are both firefighters, some of the most vivid scenes in the Fontana books are, not surprisingly, of firefighters bravely performing their jobs. This is also the case in Emerson's standalone novels, such as *Vertical Burn*, according to a number of reviewers. In the opening scene, firefighter John Finney is caught in a blaze set off by arsonists that causes a wall to fall and kill his partner. Although Finney is not formally charged with wrongdoing, his peers suspect that he panicked during the incident and that this led to the man's death. Finney then sets out to prove his innocence and find out how the fire was started. Praising the fire scenes in the book, *Los Angeles Times* contributor Lochte felt that Emerson's descriptions were so convincing that "readers may wind up struggling to breathe," adding that the "roaring fires [are] so stunningly depicted that you can feel the heat and smell the acrid smoke." Although Michael Prager in the *Houston Chronicle* felt the story is marred by "implausibility," *Booklist* contributor Dennis Dodge called it a "thriller that delivers on thrills."

Emerson has also produced a number of other standalone mystery novels combining firefighting themes with sleuthing and detection. *Into the Inferno* brings firefighter Jim Swope and his colleagues to the scene of a truck collision on the highway. There, he meets trucker Holly Riggs, who becomes his friend and lover, and finally his ex-girlfriend and stalker. Six months later, the firefighters who responded to the accident are beginning to die from strange and horrible symptoms. Holly's sister Stephanie finds her in a coma. When Swope himself begins to show symptoms of the disease that his killed his fellow firefighters, he realizes that they were exposed to a virulent disease-causing agent at the accident scene, and that he has only a week to figure out what his affliction consists of and whether or not there is an antidote. As time ticks away, Swope and Stephanie Riggs join forces to try to find out what happened and what they are facing, and how a culture of corporate corruption impedes their progress even as Swope's condition worsens and his changes of survival become slimmer. *Booklist* reviewer David Pitt called the novel "a thoroughly captivating twist on an old theme." *Orlando Sentinel* reviewer Ann Hellmuth named Emerson "a deft writer who cleverly exploits the tension and the horror of Swope's situation." He concentrates on "character development and suspense in a cinematic tour de force that finishes with a jolting twist," commented *Library Journal* reviewer Roland Person.

Paul Wolff, the protagonist of *Pyro*, is a hard-driven Seattle firefighter known for daring acts of heroism. Below this steel-hard demeanor, however, Wolff is haunted by guilt and deeply troubled by his past. He is the son of another firefighter who was killed in an arson blaze when Paul was four years old. The death led to the breakdown of Wolff's home life, as his mother descended into alcoholism and depression and took up with an abusive man who would eventually kill her. His last family member is taken from him when his thirteen-year-old brother Neil is sent to prison for killing the man who murdered their mother. Long nursing a hatred for the arsonist responsible for his father's death, he attacks his profession with gung-ho enthusiasm and perfectionism that protects him from being affected by fire-station politics. When a series of fires begins to exhibit a familiar pattern, Wolff suspects that they are being set by the arsonist who killed his father. As the novel progresses, Wolff and the arsonist steadily zero in on each other until an explosive confrontation is inevitable. "Everything works in this engrossing story of a good man's redemptive struggle to believe in his own worth," observed a *Kirkus Reviews* contributor. With this novel, "Emerson has another four-alarm winner," stated Person in another *Library Journal* review.

Booklist reviewer David Wright noted that the novel "should appeal to a wide swath of suspense fans."

The Smoke Room combines absurd humor with the grim realities of firefighting. The novel opens with protagonist and narrator Jason Gum, a conscientious and dedicated firefighter on the fast-track to advancement, working to remedy the aftermath of a pig's 11,000-foot fall from an airplane into the upscale Seattle home of Iola Pederson. As Jason learns the hard way about his new occupation of firefighting, he undertakes a steamy affair with Iola, twenty years older than him. His dalliance leads to a dereliction of duty, and when a pair of mean-spirited colleagues decide not to report him, Jason finds himself under their highly unpleasant control. Meanwhile, Jason's firefighting partner has succumbed to temptation and stolen twelve million dollars in bearer bonds from a fire scene, hiding them in Iola's garage. Unrepentant greed and murder follow the bonds as the novel unfolds, with Jason caught in the middle, wondering how he will extricate himself from a difficult, dangerous situation. "Emerson's compelling latest defies easy categorization," remarked a *Publishers Weekly* contributor, who named the book a "consistently entertaining and always surprising yarn." *Booklist* critic David Wright called the story "laid-back and likable noir lite." In this novel, Emerson, "always reliable, surpasses everything he's done before with this sometimes painfully funny, occasionally poignant suspenser that adheres to its genre roots while achieving considerably more," commented a *Kirkus Reviews* critic.

In *Firetrap*, Seattle-based firefighter and reporter Trey Brown draws the assignment of investigating the burning of a local social club. Trey's investigation uncovers dangerous information as the trail from the burned-out club snakes along a path of conspiracy and corruption directly to the mayor's office. In the background, Trey must deal with accusations that African-American customers were abandoned to die by the Seattle Fire Department. A black man himself, Trey is keenly interested in the accusations but as a member of the fire department knows they are not true. Still, racial tensions are running high in the city. Meanwhile, Trey considers his the past troubles that have led to his estrangement from his family while navigating nascent romantic interest between him and local television journalist Jamie Estevez, who is also investigating the suspicious blaze and the city's response to it. "This is one stand-alone novel that deserves a sequel," declared David Pitt in another *Booklist* review.

BIOGRAPHICAL AND CRITICAL SOURCES:

BOOKS

St. James Guide to Crime and Mystery Writers, 4th edition, St. James Press (Detroit, MI), 1996.

PERIODICALS

Booklist, June 1, 1998, Dennis Dodge, review of *Catfish Café,* p. 1731; April 1, 2002, Dennis Dodge, review of *Vertical Burn,* p. 1309; December 1, 2002, David Pitt, review of *Into the Inferno,* p. 644; May 1, 2004, David Wright, review of *Pyro,* p. 1504; May 1, 2005, David Wright, review of *The Smoke Room,* p. 1522; April 1, 2006, David Pitt, review of *Firetrap,* p. 24.

Houston Chronicle, June 30, 2002, Michael Prager, "Smoke Eater's Serenade: Firefighting Author Writes from Experience," p. 35.

Kirkus Reviews, June 15, 1998, review of *Catfish Café,* p. 846; December 1, 2002, review of *Into the Inferno,* p. 1735; July 1, 2004, review of *Pyro,* p. 606; April 1, 2005, review of *The Smoke Room,* p. 372.

Library Journal, March 15, 2002, Roland Person, review of *Vertical Burn,* p. 108; December, 2002, Roland Person, review of *Into the Inferno,* p. 177; June 1, 2004, Roland Person, review of *Pyro,* p. 120.

Los Angeles Times, August 23, 1998, Dick Lochte, "Mysteries," p. 5; June 5, 2002, Dick Lochte, "Mysteries: Sleuth Goes to Blazes to Nab Arsonists," p. E2.

Orlando Sentinel, April 21, 2003, Ann Hellmuth, review of *Into the Inferno.*

Publishers Weekly, April 26, 1993, review of *Morons and Madmen,* p. 60; August 8, 1994, review of *The Portland Laughter,* p. 390; September 4, 1995, review of *The Vanishing Smile,* p. 52; April 29, 1996, review of *Going Crazy in Public,* p. 54; August 12, 1996, review of *The Million-Dollar Tattoo,* p. 67; May 12, 1997, review of *The Dead Horse Paint Company,* p. 61; September 1, 1997, review of *Deception Pass,* p. 100; June 1, 1998, review of *Catfish Café,* p. 48A; May 6, 2002, review of *Vertical Burn,* p. 34; December 2, 2002, review of *Into the Inferno,* p. 31; July 5, 2004, review of *Pyro,* p. 36; March 21, 2005, review of *The Smoke Room,* p. 36; February 27, 2006, review of *Firetrap,* p. 35.

ONLINE

Earl Emerson Home Page, http://www.earlemerson. com/ (February 6, 2007).

Fantastic Fiction, http://www.fantasticfiction.co.uk/ (February 6, 2007), bibliography of Earl Emerson.

Readers Room, http://www.readersroom.com/ (February 6, 2007), Rob Holden, interview with Earl Emerson.*

*   *   *

EMERSON, Earl W.
See EMERSON, Earl

*   *   *

EPSTEIN, Leslie 1938-
(Leslie Donald Epstein)

PERSONAL: Born May 4, 1938, in Los Angeles, CA; son of Philip (a screenwriter) and Lillian Epstein; married Ilene Gradman, November 1, 1969; children: Anya, Paul and Theo (twins). *Education:* Yale University, B.A., 1960, graduate study, 1963-65, D.F.A., 1967; Oxford University, diploma, 1962; University of California, Los Angeles, M.A., 1963.

ADDRESSES: Office—Creative Writing Program, College of Arts and Sciences, Boston University, 236 Bay State Rd., Boston, MA 02215. *Agent*—Lane Zachary, Zachary/Shuster/Harmsworth Agency, 1776 Broadway, Ste. 1405, New York, NY 10019. *E-mail*—leslieep@bu. edu.

CAREER: Writer, novelist, and educator. Queens College of the City University of New York, Flushing, lecturer, 1965-67, assistant professor, 1968-70, associate professor, 1970-75, professor of English, 1976-78; Boston University, Boston, MA, director of graduate creative writing program, 1978—.

MEMBER: International PEN.

AWARDS, HONORS: Rhodes scholarship, 1960-62; National Endowment for the Arts grant, 1972; Fulbright fellowship, Council for International Exchange of Scholars, 1972-73; CAPS grant, 1976-77; Guggenheim fellowship, John Simon Guggenheim Memorial Foundation, 1977-78; Most Distinguished Work of Fiction nomination, National Book Critics' Circle, 1979, and notable book citation, American Library Association, 1980, both for *King of the Jews: A Novel of the Holocaust;* Award for Distinction in Literature, American Academy and Institute of Arts and Letters; Rockefeller Institute residency, Bellagio, Italy; Ingram Merrill Foundation grant; National Endowment for the Arts grant.

WRITINGS:

NOVELS

P.D. Kimerakov, Little, Brown (Boston, MA), 1975.

King of the Jews, Coward (New York, NY), 1979, reprinted, Handsel Books (New York, NY), 2003.

Regina, Coward (New York, NY), 1982.

Pinto and Sons, Houghton Mifflin (Boston, MA), 1990.

Pandaemonium, St. Martin's Press (New York, NY), 1997.

San Remo Drive: A Novel from Memory, Handsel Books (New York, NY), 2003.

The Eighth Wonder of the World, Handsel Books/Other Press (New York, NY), 2006.

SHORT STORY COLLECTIONS

The Steinway Quintet Plus Four, Little, Brown (Boston, MA), 1976.

Goldkorn Tales, Dutton (New York, NY), 1985, published as *Goldkorn Tales: Three Novellas,* with a new foreword by Frederick Busch and a new preface by Epstein, Southern Methodist University Press (Dallas, TX), 1998.

Ice Fire Water: A Leib Goldkorn Cocktail, W.W. Norton (New York, NY), 1999.

OTHER

Contributor to periodicals, including *Atlantic Monthly, Esquire, Nation, Antaeus, Playboy, Tikkun, TriQuarterly, Yale Review, Nation, New York Times Book Review, Boston Globe, Partisan Review, Harper's,* and *Antioch Review.*

SIDELIGHTS: Leslie Epstein's first novel, *P.D. Kimerakov,* is a satire of cold war tensions between the now-defunct Soviet Union and the United States. A *New York Times Book Review,* praised the skillful characterizations and elegant style found in *P.D. Kimerakov,* but found the humor somewhat forced. However, the reviewer noted: "this defect may be a sign of Leslie Epstein's honesty: he cannot hide the essential grimness of this particular corner of history." The reviewer concluded that while Epstein's tone is at odds with his subject, "one senses in him what is rare enough at any time: the presence of a sly, appealing, grave, and humorous talent."

Epstein's next book is a collection of short fiction, *The Steinway Quintet Plus Four.* The humor in the title story comes through the voice of its narrator, Leib Goldkorn. Called "a truly enchanting character" by *New York Times* contributor Michiko Kakutani, Goldkorn personifies the dignified Jewish culture that once inhabited New York City's Lower East Side. He is the pianist in a quintet that plays in the Steinway Restaurant, once a popular meeting place for notable Jewish luminaries, but now just a relic of the past. Epstein contrasts that faded culture with New York's contemporary atmosphere of violence when two young street toughs, armed and high on drugs, terrorize the Steinway Restaurant and hold its customers and employees hostage for a ridiculous ransom. Her review highlighted the story's deft humor, but Kakutani emphasized that the author makes a powerful statement on his deeper theme as well: "In its juxtaposition of Old World culture and contemporary violence, [*The Steinway Quintet* is] an organic and wholly complete work of art."

Leib Goldkorn is also featured in the story collections, *Goldkorn Tales* and *Ice Fire Water: A Leib Goldkorn Cocktail.* Kakutani deemed the former volume an "energetic, densely patterned" work, one which illuminates "revenge and forgiveness and the stunning tricks that life can play on its victims." In *Ice Fire Water,* Epstein takes on the Holocaust, in what *Houston Chronicle* reviewer Harvey Grossinger called a "profuse, digressive, and meticulously crafted" book, which is "an uncompromising philosophical meditation that conjoins a universal human catastrophe with individual misfortune in order to comprehend the unthinkable and demoralizing horrors of history." By the time period of *Ice Fire Water,* Goldkorn is in his nineties, but his libido seems to be unflagging. He reminisces about his attempted Holocaust-era romances with Olympic figure skater-turned-movie star Sonja Henie, swimmer-turned-

movie star Esther Williams, and Brazilian movie star Carmen Miranda, and about the operetta, *A Jewish Girl in the Persian Court,* that he was trying to get produced during those years. In the present day, Goldkorn is still striving to seduce women, including real-life *New York Times* book reviewer Michiko Kakutani. "Beneath the masterful linguistic and critical performance," a reviewer commented in *Publishers Weekly,* "Epstein slyly plants speculations about survivors' accountability, the responsibility of memory, and the relativity of taboo."

Epstein's most controversial work has been his 1979 novel *King of the Jews.* In it he examines the role that some European Jews played in betraying their own people to the Nazis. The story focuses on the leader of the Judenrat, or governing council of elders, in the ghetto of a Polish industrial city. The Nazis ordered the establishment of Judenrat to control the population that they had forced into the ghettos; the councils' duties eventually included drawing up lists of passengers for the trains to the death camps. Forced to choose between their people and the Nazis, Judenrat leaders knew that if they did not supply the required quotas for the trains, the entire ghetto might be destroyed in one stroke. The ambiguity of this position led at least one Judenrat leader to take his own life. Until *King of the Jews* was published, "no work of fiction [had] opened up so fully the unbearable moral dilemma in which the Judenrat members found themselves, governing with a pistol at their heads, administering the processes of death, corrupted of course by their awful power, yet trying to preserve life when there was no real way to preserve it," Robert Alter wrote in the *New York Times Book Review.*

Epstein's protagonist in *King of the Jews* is based on Mordecai Chaim Rumkowski, the real-life elder of the ghetto in Lodz, Poland. Rumkowski remains notorious for having relished the power of his position. Like him, the fictional Isaiah Chaim Trumpelman eagerly volunteers for the position of council elder. Then he exploits his privileges, riding in a limousine or on a white stallion and even having his picture printed on the currency and stamps used in the ghetto. Many critics praised Epstein's characterization of Trumpelman for its depth. The man is depicted in larger-than-life style as someone who enjoys his role; yet Epstein also shows the elder's apparently real concern for orphans, his uncertainties, and the rationalizations that allow him to continue in his position. For example, when the grisly destination of the trains is made clear to him, he justifies his cooperation with the Nazis by saying that by sending ten Jews away, he is saving one hundred others. He even begins to think of himself as a savior, "the King of the Jews."

Epstein told *Atlantic Monthly* interviewer Daniel Smith that his novel is an accurate depiction of life in the ghetto. "In *King of the Jews* there are dozens of jokes. I don't think I made up a single one. I made up the humor of the book, but not the formal jokes. They were all taken from Jewish sources on the spot, like Ringelbaum," an inhabitant of the Warsaw ghetto who buried cans full of records about daily life there which were discovered after the war.

Taking place in the nineteenth century, Epstein's novel *Pinto and Sons,* relates the quixotic tale of Adolph Pinto, a Hungarian Jew who has immigrated to the United States to study at Harvard Medical School. After a botched experiment involving the newly discovered anesthetic ether, Pinto is expelled from Harvard. He travels to the American West, where his adventures include adopting and raising a Native American as his son, educating a tribe of Indians in mathematics and poetry, mining for gold, and attempting to discover a cure for rabies. Despite Pinto's good intentions, one catastrophe after another besets him. According to Michiko Kakutani, writing in the *New York Times,* Epstein is using "his hero's dilemmas to examine large historical and moral questions," namely, the inability of science and reason to solve basic human problems, the tendency of large man-made schemes to go awry, and the failed promise of the American dream as embodied in the frontier. Although Kakutani praised Epstein's "verbal exuberance" and his "gift for invention," she found *Pinto and Sons* "ultimately a disappointment," lacking the "moral resonance" of *King of the Jews* and sending the reader on an arbitrary "roller-coaster ride" where expectations are raised and then dashed. On the other hand, John Crowley of the *New York Times Book Review* wrote that *Pinto and Sons,* despite being too long, "is a fantastic epic of the heroic age of applied science, a fit book to put on the shelf with the great tall tales of American expansion."

Epstein's novel *Pandaemonium,* returns to the era of *King of the Jews,* the late 1930s and early 1940s, and again deals, though in less-direct fashion, with the Holocaust. It is a complex and multi-charactered book, narrated in part by a fictionalized version of Jewish actor Peter Lorre and in part by a fictionalized version of

Hollywood gossip columnist Louella Parsons. The title of the book is drawn from seventeenth-century poet John Milton's *Paradise Lost,* in which Pandaemonium is the capital of Hell, where Satan's fallen angels gather. David Freeman, writing in the *New York Times Book Review,* described the novel as "an exuberant mixture of high art and low comedy . . . a big, funny, and bold book that is a virtual catalog of literary, historical, theatrical, and cinematic devices and references." The action of *Pandaemonium* opens in Salzberg, Austria, in 1938, where director Rudolph Von Beckmann is staging an outdoor production of the classic Greek drama *Antigone.* International star Magdalena Mezaray will play the title role. Magda, a fictional creation of Epstein's, is reminiscent of both Greta Garbo and Marlene Dietrich and plays opposite male lead Peter Lorre. Lorre, who has been trapped in Hollywood in a series of mediocre films based on the exploits of the fictional Japanese detective Mr. Moto, sees this as a major career opportunity. Unfortunately, Hitler invades Austria before the production can be launched. Lorre, because he is Jewish, is soon displaced to a minor role. Magda is forced to become Hitler's consort. Von Beckman is eventually exposed as Jewish himself—the "Von" is assumed—and is sent to an internment camp. The action of the novel switches to Hollywood where Lorre, once again playing Mr. Moto for Granite Studios, futilely pursues his co-star and becomes increasingly dependent on cocaine. Fictionalized versions of real Hollywood personalities abound in the narrative and fictional events—Lorre's attempted suicide, the decapitation of Victor Granite, the kidnapping of Granite's daughter—occur in what Richard Bernstein in the *New York Times* referred to as "dizzying succession." "Von" Beckman turns up in Hollywood and, through a series of machinations, takes over production of *Mr. Moto Wins His Spurs.* Casting the newly liberated Magda opposite Lorre, Beckman transforms the movie into a kind of *Antigone* set in the Old West. Filming proceeds in the Nevada desert in the ghost town of Pandaemonium, where Beckman becomes a mini-Hitler himself, turning the town into an armed camp and ruling the production with a fascist hand. Epstein portrays the Hollywood power structure as fascist in nature, and is highly critical of the failure of Hollywood's Jewish community to respond to the Holocaust in any meaningful way.

Freeman commented of *Pandaemonium:* "There is lunatic comedy here as well as moral seriousness. Epstein blends these disparate forces with considerable panache. . . . While I was there, in Pandaemonium, I didn't want to be anywhere else."

In 2003 Epstein published *San Remo Drive: A Novel from Memory,* which is based very closely on Epstein's own family life. The narrator is Richard Jacobi, who in the 1940s and 1950s is a boy of about Epstein's age. Jacobi is the son of a director/producer who bears a striking resemblance to Epstein's father, a famous screenwriter. The first four chapters of the book are set between 1948 and 1960; in them, Jacobi's family suffers humiliation and the loss of their home on San Remo Drive when Jacobi's father is accused of being a Communist and, soon after, dies in a car crash. The remainder of the family learns to cope with life without him, and Jacobi and his brother, Barton, become adults. In this section, "Epstein conjures up Southern California in the '50s with an abundance of deftly observed and deeply evocative details," Jonathan Kirsch wrote in the *Los Angeles Times.* The second half of the book is set in the present; in it, Donna Seaman wrote in *Booklist,* Epstein "muses eloquently on the profound impact childhood memories have on both art and life." In the *New York Times,* critic Elizabeth Frank praised the novel, writing: "Losing and finding, [Epstein] shows us love between fathers and sons as the most powerful and enduring in life, capable of transcending death, time, folly, and a Hollywood childhood. In doing so he has given us, along with F. Scott Fitzgerald's *Last Tycoon,* Budd Schulberg's *What Makes Sammy Run?,* and his own *Pandaemonium,* one of the four best Hollywood novels ever written."

Epstein's next novel, *The Eighth Wonder of the World,* returns to a fascist milieu in World War II-era Italy, when Benito Mussolini ruled with a dangerous, often deranged hand. The protagonist of the novel, Amos Prince, is an American architect charged with creating a soaring monument to Mussolini and his conquests in Africa: La Vittoria, a mile-high tower and architectural wonder that will encapsulate the magnificence of fascism in a single dramatic structure. In a farcical narrative that shifts between the present day and the World War II era, Epstein tells the story of the clever and sarcastic Prince's often outlandish efforts; his interactions with Mussolini and Il Duce's primary assistant, Max Shabalian; and the ill-fated course of Mussolini's brutal dictatorship. Amos and Max are both obsessed with completing the tower, but Prince's attitudes are contaminated by intensifying anti-Semitism, while Shabalian is deeply concerned with the fate of his fellow Jews. As the two interact, Max becomes involved with Amos's family and, soon, with Prince's lovely daughter. The story unfolds in three tiers: the modern-day recollections of the now-aged Max Shabalian; Prince's increasingly virulent journal entries; and contemporary accounts of events during the war. Though the story is complicated, Epstein's "artful writing sustains a novel

as ambitious as the Babel-like tower it describes," commented a reviewer in *Publishers Weekly.*

In a more serious tragic layer of the story, Jews from around Italy gather as the construction project progresses, hoping to work on the tower and save themselves from a worse fate in the Nazi concentration camps. Shabalian develops a plan to save them from deportation into the hands of the Germans, but his efforts ultimately go awry, condemning those he had sought to rescue. "Compelling (if sometimes overdrawn) extended scenes vividly portray the accumulating madness, and Epstein offers rich expressionistic characterizations" of protagonist Amos and other real and imaginary players in his complex narrative, remarked a *Kirkus Reviews* critic.

One of the underlying themes of the novel is the prodigious mythmaking and the manipulation of image and public perception that occurred in order to make fascism, Nazism, and deadly anti-Semitism acceptable to the population. "Epstein's large, swirling, magical-realist novel of Italy in the war years, captures this era beautifully: he feels the madness of the Fascist dream at street level," when women would weep at the sight of Mussolini and declare that he was the true father of their children, commented Vince Passaro in a review in *O, the Oprah Magazine.*

Passaro called Epstein's writing "assured, evocative, and witty," and concluded that the novel "is an extraordinary artistic achievement." *Booklist* reviewer Debi Lewis observed that "a patient reader will enjoy the broad scope of this ambitious work."

BIOGRAPHICAL AND CRITICAL SOURCES:

BOOKS

Contemporary Literary Criticism, Volume 27, Thomson Gale (Detroit, MI), 1984.

PERIODICALS

Atlantic Monthly, October 20, 1999, Daniel Smith, interview with Epstein.
Booklist, October 15, 1999, Donna Seaman, review of *Ice Fire Water: A Leib Goldkorn Cocktail,* p. 417; May 15, 2003, Donna Seaman, review of *San Remo*

Drive: A Novel from Memory, p. 1644; September 1, 2006, Debi Lewis, review of *The Eighth Wonder of the World,* p. 54.

Boston Herald, May 13, 1997, James Verniere, review of *Pandaemonium,* p. 33.

Boston Magazine, November, 1982, Lee Grove, interview with Epstein, pp. 107-114; May, 1985, Lee Grove, review of *Goldkorn Tales,* pp. 98-99.

Buffalo News (Buffalo, NY), August 17, 1997, Mark Shechner, review of *Pandaemonium,* p. F8.

Harper's Magazine, August, 1985, "Atrocity and Imagination," pp. 13-16.

Houston Chronicle (Houston, TX), February 13, 2000, Harvey Grossinger, review of *Ice Fire Water,* p. 14.

Kirkus Reviews, April 15, 2003, review of *San Remo Drive,* pp. 554-555; August 1, 2006, review of *The Eighth Wonder of the World,* p. 741.

Library Journal, October 15, 1982, review of *Regina,* p. 2002; April 15, 1985, Herman Elstein, review of *Goldkorn Tales,* p. 85; October 1, 1990, Elise Chase, review of *Pinto and Sons,* p. 115; April 15, 1997, David Dodd, review of *Pandaemonium,* p. 117; September 15, 1999, Marc A. Kloszewski, review of *Ice Fire Water,* p. 114; May 1, 2003, Jim Dwyer, review of *San Remo Drive,* pp. 154; August 1, 2006, Molly Abramowitz, review of *The Eighth Wonder of the World,* p. 68.

Los Angeles Times, February 17, 1983, Elizabeth Wheeler, review of *Regina,* p. 30; December 14, 1997, Jeremy Larner, review of *Pandaemonium,* p. 4; June 15, 2003, Jonathan Kirsch, review of *San Remo Drive,* p. R2.

New York Times, April 3, 1985, Michiko Kakutani, review of *Goldkorn Tales,* p. 19; November 16, 1990, Michiko Kakutani, review of *Pinto and Sons,* p. B4; June 2, 1997, Richard Bernstein, review of *Pandaemonium,* p. B7; June 12, 2003, Dinitia Smith, review of *San Remo Drive,* p. E1; July 20, 2003, Elizabeth Frank, "You'll Never Have to Leave," p. 10.

New York Times Book Review, August 10, 1975, review of *P.D. Kimerakov,* p. 6; December 12, 1976, Michiko Kakutani, review of *The Steinway Quintet,* p. 7; February 28, 1980, Robert Alter, review of *King of the Jews,* p. 47; November 21, 1982, George Stade, review of *Regina,* p. 12; December 5, 1982, review of *Regina,* p. 46; January 1, 1984, review of *Regina,* p. 32; April 7, 1985, David Evanier, review of *Goldkorn Tales,* p. 8; May 11, 1986, review of *King of the Jews,* p. 42; December 7, 1986, Patricia T. O'Connor, review of *King of the Jews,* p. 84; November 4, 1990, John Crowley, review of *Pinto and Sons,* and Judith Shulevitz,

interview with Epstein, p. 3; June 22, 1997, David Freeman, review of *Pandaemonium,* p. 6; October 31, 1999, D.T. Max, review of *Ice Fire Water,* p. 15; January 14, 2007, Richard Lourie, "Il Duce's Architect," review of *The Eighth Wonder of the World,* p. 21.

O, the Oprah Magazine, November, 2006, Vince Passaro, review of *The Eighth Wonder of the World,* p. 238.

Present Tense, summer, 1985, Gerald Jonas, review of *Goldkorn Tales,* pp. 62-63.

Publishers Weekly, March 1, 1985, review of *Goldkorn Tales,* p. 69; September 7, 1990, Sybil Steinberg, review of *Pinto and Sons,* p. 75; March 24, 1997, review of *Pandaemonium,* pp. 59-60; August 23, 1999, review of *Ice Fire Water,* p. 47; July 17, 2006, review of *The Eighth Wonder of the World,* p. 132.

St. Louis Post-Dispatch (St. Louis, MO), August 17, 1997, Dale Singer, review of *Pandaemonium,* p. 5C.

Seattle Post-Intelligencer, June 4, 1997, review of *Pandaemonium,* p. C2.

ONLINE

Boston University Web site, http://www.bu.edu/ (April 10, 2007), biography of Leslie Epstein.

Leslie Epstein Home Page, http://www.bu.edu/english/epstein.html (April 10, 2007).

Phoenix, http://www.thephoenix.com/ (June 28, 2003), Michael Bronski, review of *San Remo Drive;* (October 31, 2006), Dana Kletter, "Fascist Dreams," review of *The Eighth Wonder of the World.*

*   *   *

EPSTEIN, Leslie Donald
See EPSTEIN, Leslie

*   *   *

ESSEX, Karen

PERSONAL: Born in New Orleans, LA. *Education:* Tulane University, B.A.; Goddard College, M.F.A.; attended Vanderbilt University graduate program.

ADDRESSES: Home—Los Angeles, CA.

CAREER: Journalist, writer, screenwriter, lecturer, biographer, educator, and producer. Blake Edwards Entertainment, Los Angeles, CA, former vice president; Force Ten Productions, former senior vice president. Works as a writing instructor. Lecturer at numerous universities and museums. Guest on television programs, including the *Today Show* and Public Broadcasting Service (PBS) programs and on radio programs on National Public Radio (NPR).

AWARDS, HONORS: Los Angeles Press Club award for entertainment journalism, 1991.

WRITINGS:

(With James L. Swanson) *Bettie Page: The Life of a Pin-up Legend* (biography), General Publishing Group (Santa Monica, CA), 1996.

NOVELS

Kleopatra, Warner Books (New York, NY), 2001.
Pharaoh: Volume II of Kleopatra, Warner Books (New York, NY), 2002.
Leonardo's Swans, Doubleday (New York, NY), 2006.

Author of screenplay for motion picture, *The Mummy, or Ramses the Damned.*

Contributor to periodicals, including *Playboy, Vogue, TV Guide, L.A. Style,* and *L.A. Weekly.*

Contributor of short stories to the *Sun: A Magazine of Ideas* and to online literary magazines.

Author's works have been translated into twenty languages.

SIDELIGHTS: Novelist and biographer Karen Essex has focused her writing career on telling the stories of iconic women. She began by telling the story, with coauthor James Swanson, of 1950s pin-up girl Bettie Page. In their book, *Bettie Page: The Life of a Pin-up Legend,* the authors expose the way the erotic model embodied the contrast between the wholesome wife/mother and the sexuality of the "bad girl." In her second book, *Kleopatra,* Essex retells the story in novel form

of the Egyptian ruler whose life, Essex maintains, has been grossly misunderstood since her defeat by the Romans. In Kleopatra, Essex saw "one of the ancient world's most brilliant and powerful rulers," as she said on the *BookPage* Web site, and she felt compelled to bring her true history to light.

Essex's first work on Bettie Page is less a biography than a "handsome, besotted tribute book," according to *New Republic* critic Margaret Talbot. Through photographs, anecdotes, and interviews with the reclusive Page herself—who was seventy-four at the time the book was written—Essex and Swanson celebrate the career of the model whose cheesecake poses seemed so scandalous in her own time but appear relatively innocent today. The book emphasizes Page's own sense of innocence and playful indulgence, laughing at the ridiculous poses her photographers concocted and refusing to see anything indecent about nudity. Talbot described Bettie Page, as portrayed in Essex and Swanson's book, as "a woman who will not be ruined by sex, but made by it." The photographs, Talbot suggested, "are not images of desire, they are images of happiness. . . . If one tingles at the sight of them, it is almost with envy." Suitably, the book reveals that Page did not end up a victim, but rather moved on to get a master's degree in English, to teach, and to work as a counselor with the Billy Graham Crusades. Nonetheless, she reported no regrets to Essex and Swanson. As Talbot concluded: "Her newfound Christian beliefs had never convinced her that she had done anything wrong in her cheesecake years. . . . There's nothing especially pathetic about her. She didn't end up as a parody of herself."

Essex and Swanson's account of Page's life after modeling ran counter to the dominant story of the 1980s that Page had descended into a shameful obscurity in the shadow of her past crimes. In the same way, Essex's fictionalized biography of Kleopatra illuminates the many ways in which mainstream history has distorted Kleopatra's life, including the widespread image of her as a sexually voracious woman who preyed upon the great men of ancient history. Writing about her book for *BookPage,* Essex commented: "Of all the women distorted by history and myth, Kleopatra is the most vivid example." Kleopatra is a victim of revisionist history, written by the winners, Essex added, saying that she was "the victim of a smear campaign by her rival and mortal enemy, Octavian." As Essex researched the history of Kleopatra, her frustration grew. She ranted to friends about the injustice, she recalled, until "a fellow writer . . . suggested that I turn my passion into a book."

Essex's corrections to Kleopatra's story begin with her name. Essex spells Kleopatra with a "K" to indicate her Greek origins; Kleopatra was not a native Egyptian, but one of the Greek rulers of Egypt. Essex allows Kleopatra's life to begin before her meeting with Mark Antony and Caesar, describing her advanced education and her participation in the politics of her family, as the daughter of Ptolemy XII, the Egyptian Pharaoh. She paints Kleopatra as a cunning and ambitious leader, learning the Egyptian language in order to win over her subjects and gain their support in her contest for power with her brother. The novel, the first of two volumes, concludes with the twenty-two-year-old Kleopatra in exile, preparing to join with Julius Caesar to regain her kingdom.

Though Essex presents Kleopatra's story as a novel, critics remarked on the historical validity of her work. A reviewer for *Publishers Weekly* remarked that "exhaustive research is evident throughout" *Kleopatra,* concluding that "even those who think they know the queen will discover new facets of her life that will engage both the intellect and the senses." Jane Baird, writing in *Library Journal,* commented that Essex's contribution to Kleopatra's story will help "create a complete portrait of the child, the woman, and the queen."

Essex's *Pharaoh: Volume II of Kleopatra* continues the story as the Egyptian ruler, now twenty-two, returns to her kingdom from her exile in Rome. Kleopatra uses her power and charisma to ally herself with Caesar and bear his son. However, when Caesar is assassinated she joins with Antony to provoke the new Roman ruler, Octavian, into a war that eventually leads to her downfall. As with Essex's first book on Kleopatra, reviewers have praised *Pharaoh,* especially noting the author's balanced portrayal of the ambitious queen. Also praising the book's "rich language" and historical accuracy, a *Publishers Weekly* critic called *Pharaoh* "an invigorating read for those interested in ancient history of simply the thrills of battles and romance."

In an online interview for *USA Today,* Essex explained that she chose the novel format "to bridge the gap . . . between the real Kleopatra and the Kleopatra that exists in the popular imagination. The general public is still stuck on that 1963 Elizabeth Taylor seductress role." Essex added that one of her biggest reasons for writing the book was "to restore this great female role model." She concluded: "So few women have had Kleopatra's

power in the world and I couldn't live with the fact that the most powerful [woman] in the world had gone down in history merely for her sexuality."

Leonardo's Swans is a fictionalized account of the lives of two prominent noble sisters in fifteenth-century Italy, Isabella and Beatrice d'Este. Elder sister Isabella is a blonde beauty, educated and accomplished, and engaged to marry aristocratic soldier Francesco Gonzaga, Marquis of Mantua. Younger, less worldly, and less beautiful Beatrice married Ludovico Sforza, a politically powerful leader from Milan. Ludovico is in the midst of an affair with his pregnant mistress Cecelia and sees Beatrice as little more than the source of his children and heirs, but Beatrice is determined to win his life. When Isabella attends Beatrice's wedding, she sees a painting by master Leonardo Da Vinci, and becomes determined that the artist must paint her portrait. As the story progresses, Ludovico becomes infatuated with Isabella, and the two carry on a torrid correspondence, perpetually separated by the Italian political climate and Francesco's jealousy. An injured and convalescing Beatrice finally wins Ludovico's love and loyalty by delivering to him an impassioned ultimatum. Isabella continues to seek a sitting from the brilliant Da Vinci, even as Beatrice declines to be painted by him. In the political background of the novel, the scheming Ludovico seeks to increase his power as he makes and sets into motion plans that will have dramatic and long-reaching effects on all players in the story, particularly the sisters. Another betrayal by Ludovico propels Beatrice toward tragedy, while Isabella grows ever more frustrated with her sister's luxury and her inability to snare Leonardo's attentions and talents. "Essex delineates the confusion of historical events and historically accurate personalities with clarity," observed a *Kirkus Reviews* critic.

Booklist reviewer Kristine Huntley called the book an "involving novel" and "powerful historical fiction." Essex's "stories of Isabella and Beatrice d'Este along with the occasional investigations of Leonardo's artworks, methods, and personality are always engrossing," commented a reviewer in *Publishers Weekly.* Loralyn Whitney, writing in *Library Journal,* named the novel a "meticulously researched fictional biography" that "brings Renaissance Italy vividly to life."

BIOGRAPHICAL AND CRITICAL SOURCES:

PERIODICALS

Booklist, November 15, 2005, Kristine Huntley, review of *Leonardo's Swans,* p. 26.

Clockworks, fall, 1999, "MFA in Creative Writing Program—Interview with Graduate Karen Essex."

Kirkus Reviews, November 1, 2005, review of *Leonardo's Swans,* p. 1156.

Library Journal, July, 2001, Jane Baird, review of *Kleopatra,* p. 122; February 1, 2006, Loralyn Whitney, review of *Leonardo's Swans,* p. 71.

New Republic, September 8, 1997, Margaret Talbot, review of *Bettie Page: The Life of a Pin-up Legend,* pp. 29-38.

Publishers Weekly, July 23, 2001, review of *Kleopatra,* p. 50; July 29, 2002, review of *Pharaoh: Volume II of Kleopatra,* p. 55; September 19, 2005, review of *Leonardo's Swans,* p. 41.

ONLINE

About.com Ancient/Classical History Web site, http://ancienthistory.about.com/ (February 6, 2007), review of *Kleopatra.*

BookBrowser, http://www.bookbrowser.com/ (February 6, 2007), Harriet Klausner, review of *Kleopatra.*

BookPage, http://www.bookpage.com/ (February 6, 2007), Karen Essex, "Reviving the real Kleopatra."

Bookreporter.com, http://www.bookreporter.com/ (September 21, 2001), Kate Ayers, interview with and biography of Karen Essex; Kate Ayers, review of *Kleopatra;* Kate Ayers, review of *Pharaoh;* Colleen Quinn, review of *Leonardo's Swans.*

Goddard College Web site, http://www.goddard.edu/ (February 6, 2007), "MFA In Creative Writing Program—Interview with Graduate Karen Essex."

MyShelf.com, http://www.myshelf.com/ (February 6, 2007), Beverly Rowe, "Author of the Month: Karen Essex," interview with Karen Essex.

Pif Magazine, http://www.pifmagazine.com/ (February 6, 2007), Jen Bergmark, interview with Karen Essex.

TimeWarner Bookmark, http://www.twbookmark.com/ (February 6, 2007), biography of Karen Essex, description of *Kleopatra.*

USA Today, http://cgi1.usatoday.com/ (August 9, 2001), transcript of online chat with Karen Essex.*

* * *

EVANOVICH, Janet 1943-
(Steffie Hall)

PERSONAL: Born April 22, 1943, in South River, NJ; married; husband's name Pete; children: Peter, Alex (daughter). *Education:* Attended Douglass College.

ADDRESSES: Home—P.O. Box 5487, Hanover, NH 03755. *E-mail*—janet@evanovich.com.

CAREER: Writer.

MEMBER: Romance Writers of America, Sisters in Crime.

AWARDS, HONORS: John Creasey Memorial, Last Laugh, and Silver Dagger award, all from Crime Writers Association; Lefty award, Left Coast Crime; Dilys award, Independent Booksellers Association; Quill Award, Mystery/Suspense/Thriller category, 2006, for *Twelve Sharp;* Golden Leaf Award, New Jersey Romance Writers.

WRITINGS:

DETECTIVE NOVELS; "STEPHANIE PLUM" SERIES

One for the Money, Scribner (New York, NY), 1994.
Two for the Dough, Scribner (New York, NY), 1996.
Three to Get Deadly, Scribner (New York, NY), 1997.
Four to Score, St. Martin's Press (New York, NY), 1998.
High Five, St. Martin's Press (New York, NY), 1999.
Hot Six, St. Martin's Press (New York, NY), 2000.
Seven Up, St. Martin's Press (New York, NY), 2001.
Three Plums in One (contains *One for the Money, Two for the Dough,* and *Three to Get Deadly*), Scribner (New York, NY), 2001.
Hard Eight, St. Martin's Press (New York, NY), 2002.
Visions of Sugar Plums, St. Martin's Press (New York, NY), 2002.
To the Nines, St. Martin's Press (New York, NY), 2003.
Ten Big Ones, St. Martin's Press (New York, NY), 2004.
Eleven on Top, St. Martin's Press (New York, NY), 2005.
Twelve Sharp, St. Martin's Press (New York, NY), 2006.
Lean Mean Thirteen, St. Martin's Press (New York, NY), 2007.
Plum Lovin', St. Martin's Press (New York, NY), 2007.

ROMANCE NOVELS; "MAX HOLT" SERIES

(As Steffie Hall) *Full House,* Second Chance at Love, 1989.

(With Charlotte Hughes) *Full Tilt,* St. Martin's Press
    (New York, NY), 2003.
(With Charlotte Hughes) *Full Speed,* St. Martin's Press
    (New York, NY), 2003.
(With Charlotte Hughes) *Full Blast,* St. Martin's Press
    (New York, NY), 2004.
(With Charlotte Hughes) *Full Bloom,* St. Martin's Press
    (New York, NY), 2005.
(With Charlotte Hughes) *Full Scoop,* St. Martin's Press
    (New York, NY), 2006.

ROMANCE NOVELS

(As Steffie Hall) *Hero at Large,* Second Chance at
    Love, 1987.
The Grand Finale, Bantam (New York, NY), 1988.
Thanksgiving, Bantam (New York, NY), 1988.
Manhunt, Bantam (New York, NY), 1988, reprinted,
    HarperTorch (New York, NY), 2005.
(As Steffie Hall) *Foul Play,* Second Chance at Love,
    1989.
Ivan Takes a Wife, Bantam (New York, NY), 1989,
    published as *Love Overboard,* HarperTorch (New
    York, NY), 2005.
Back to the Bedroom, Bantam (New York, NY), 1989,
    reprinted, HarperTorch (New York, NY), 2005.
Wife for Hire, Bantam (New York, NY), 1990.
Smitten, Bantam (New York, NY), 1990, reprinted, Har-
    perCollins (New York, NY), 2006.
The Rocky Road to Romance, Bantam (New York, NY),
    1991.
Naughty Neighbor, Bantam (New York, NY), 1992.

OTHER

Metro Girl (novel; "*Alexandra Barnaby*" series), Har-
    perCollins (New York, NY), 2004.
Motor Mouth (novel; "*Alexandra Barnaby*" series),
    HarperCollins (New York, NY), 2006.
(With Ina Yaloff and Alex Evanovich) *How I Write:
    Secrets of a Bestselling Author* (nonfiction), St.
    Martin's Griffin (New York, NY), 2006.
(With Leanne Banks) *Hot Stuff,* St. Martin's Paperbacks
    (New York, NY), 2007.

ADAPTATIONS: One for the Money was adapted for
film by TriStar.

SIDELIGHTS: Janet Evanovich is the author of a successful series of humorous detective novels set in
Trenton, New Jersey. The works feature protagonist

Stephanie Plum, a feisty Jersey girl who turns to bounty
hunting when she loses her job as a lingerie buyer.
Characterized by a flamboyant wardrobe, big hair, and
an impertinent manner, Plum tracks bail jumpers for her
cousin Vinnie, a bail bondsman. In 1994's *One for the
Money,* the novel in which she is introduced, Plum
tackles her first assignment, the capture of Joe Morelli,
a police officer and accused murderer who also happens
to be the man to whom she lost her virginity when she
was sixteen.

Reviewing *One for the Money,* Marilyn Stasio in the
New York Times Book Review delighted in a bounty-
hunting protagonist "with Bette Midler's mouth and
Cher's fashion sense." Stasio concluded: "With [Plum's]
brazen style and dazzling wardrobe, who could resist
this doll?" Calling the novel "funny and ceaselessly
inventive," Charles Champlin in the *Los Angeles Book
Review* applauded Evanovich's use of first-person narration. According to Champlin, "Stephanie's voice,
breezy and undauntable is all her own. . . . [Her] moral
seems to be that when the going gets tough, the tough
get funny." But Marvin Lachman, writing in *Armchair
Detective,* complained that "Plum's . . . voice becomes
irritating, largely due to its consistently unsophisticated
speech." In addition, calling the plot "minimal," Lachman indicated that the story "cannot sustain a book of
two hundred and ninety pages," specifically noting that
"reader suspension of disbelief is . . . threatened" by
Plum's prior relationship with Morelli. Kate Wilson, in
a mixed review in *Entertainment Weekly,* suggested that
Evanovich's inexperience as a novelist is evident in occasionally contrived dialogue, but nevertheless described
heroine Plum as "intelligent, cheery, and genuine."
Dwight Garner in the *Washington Post Book World*
characterized *One for the Money* as "a lightweight but
very funny crime novel" and a "bright, bracing book
[that] comes roaring in like a blast of very fresh air."

Evanovich's follow-up novel, *Two for the Dough,*
depicts Plum's pursuit of fugitive Kenny Mancuso. The
case is complicated by a secondary mystery involving
two dozen coffins missing from a local mortuary and
intensified by the protagonist's ongoing relationship
with Morelli, who also has an interest in the case.
Ultimately, Plum's grandmother gets involved, and, in
the words of *Times Literary Supplement* reviewer Natasha Cooper, "does her ham-fisted best to assist
Stephanie, falling into coffins, firing off bullets, and
upsetting the entire neighborhood." In the *Christian
Science Monitor,* Michelle Ross praised *Two for the
Dough,* noting: "Evanovich has created not just an im-

mediately likeable heroine, but an entire real, vibrant, and . . . colorful world. We call it wild and sassy, we call it wonderful." In the *New York Times Book Review,* Stasio again praised heroine Plum, whom she described as "the motor-mouthed Jersey girl from Trenton . . . with her pepper spray, stun gun, up-to-here hair and out-to-there attitude." An *Entertainment Weekly* reviewer, however, called the "local color . . . a bit too forcibly hued" and complained that the "dialogue has a mechanical, insular feel." A critic in *Belles Lettres* found that although "there are some great lines" in *Two for the Dough,* it "isn't as funny" as the first Plum mystery. In the *Times Literary Supplement,* however, Cooper called the work "an entertaining parody of the hard-boiled American crime novel."

The third volume in the series, *Three to Get Deadly,* details Plum's search for "Uncle Mo," a candy store owner and local hero who skipped out on a concealed weapons charge. A reviewer in *Library Journal* noted that *Three to Get Deadly* brings "more fast and funny action from a winning writer." Stasio, in an assessment in the *New York Times Book Review,* called the novel "another rollicking chapter in the madcap career of . . . Evanovich's sassy bounty hunter." A *Publishers Weekly* reviewer appreciated the way the heroine "muddles through another case full of one-liners as well as corpses," and concluded that "the redoubtable Stephanie is a character crying out for a screen debut."

In the fourth "Stephanie Plum" mystery, *Four to Score,* Stephanie is called on to find a waitress who has jumped bail after a car-theft charge. *Four to Score* includes some familiar characters as well as a supporting cast of eccentrics. *New York Times Book Review* contributor Stasio again praised Evanovich's work, calling this novel a "brashly funny adventure."

High Five, the next volume in the series, became Evanovich's first hardcover bestseller. Its plot involves a missing uncle, a stalker, some photos of body parts in garbage bags, and Stephanie's adventures—or misadventures—working odd jobs when her bounty-hunting business slows down. The novel "deftly combines eccentric, colorful characters, wacky humor, and nonstop . . . action," observed Wilda Williams in *Library Journal.* "The action never stops," noted a *Publishers Weekly* reviewer, who praised the book's "snappy" dialogue and sharply-drawn characters. No less popular was *Hot Six,* in which Stephanie agrees to help her mentor, Ranger, clear himself after being accused of killing

Homer Ramos, a drug and gun dealer. Admiring the book as a "lunatic tapestry of nonstop action" and bizarre yet funny characters, a writer for *Publishers Weekly* concluded that "Evanovich just keeps getting better."

In *Seven Up,* which *New York Times Book Review* critic Stasio described as "pure, classic farce—Jersey girl style," Stephanie goes after Eddie DeChooch, an aging mobster who happens to be dating her grandmother. Though a reviewer for *Publishers Weekly* found this effort less successful than its predecessor, *Booklist* contributor GraceAnne A. DeCandido hailed it as both hilarious and sensitive to all of its characters, even the unattractive Eddie. "No character, no matter how broadly draw, stays a caricature for long," wrote DeCandido, who added that "it's difficult to read Evanovich in public places, so frequently do chuckles turn into belly laughs."

Evanovich's 2003 offering, *To The Nines,* finds Stephanie on the silly, sexy, and sometimes terrifying case of missing Indian contract worker, Samuel Singh. Her cousin and employer, Vinnie, has teamed her up with the always intriguing Ranger, who continues to provide romantic competition for Stephanie's temporary roommate, Joe Morelli. There is a serial killer on the loose and Stephanie, the recipient of sinister floral deliveries, appears to be on his list. This least likely of bounty hunters finds herself in Las Vegas as the plot thickens around Evanovich's trademark host of lively characters. Her sidekicks, office manager Connie and ex-prostitute turned bounty hunter Lulu, provide entertainment to rival that of the Elvis and Tom Jones impersonators Stephanie inevitably encounters. The Plum family is reliably eccentric with appearances from Grandma Mazur and Stephanie's mom, who has reached her limit while housing Stephanie's pregnant unwed sister, Valerie.

A *Publishers Weekly* reviewer called *To The Nines* "nonstop, zany adventure." Although Marianne Fitzgerald of *Library Journal* maintained that the trip to Las Vegas is an unsatisfactory deviation from the usual New Jersey stomping grounds, she recommended this installment to those "clamoring for their Stephanie fix." A *Kirkus Reviews* contributor stated: "The plot is—as usual—a shambles" but went on to acknowledge that "the people and their dialogue are as sharp and funny as ever," which may have contributed to the book's nine-week stint as a best-selling hardcover.

In the tenth episode of the series, *Ten Big Ones,* Stephanie hunts down more elusive, idiosyncratic bail jumpers, including a woman who held up a Frito-Lay truck for corn chips, bringing a quick end to her "no-carb" diet, and a man arrested for urinating on his neighbor's rose bushes. Early in the novel, Stephanie finds herself in hot water when she witnesses a convenience store robbery and, because she can identify the culprits, becomes a target for a local street gang. She seeks cover at Ranger's apartment, intensifying the Morelli-Ranger romantic drama.

While *Entertainment Weekly* contributor Karen Karbo felt that the book "clearly suffers from book-a-year syndrome," a *Publishers Weekly* reviewer related that "Evanovich is at her best in her tenth Stephanie Plum adventure," which, according to the reviewer, "reads like the screenplay for a 1930s screwball comedy: fast, funny, and furious." In a *People* review, contributor Samantha Miller expressed "one quibble" with the book: "*Ten Big Ones* wraps up so abruptly that readers might feel payoff-deprived." Overall, however, Miller praised Evanovich, commenting that the author's series "is as addictive as Fritos—and ten books in, not losing any of its salty crunch." *Booklist* contributor Stephanie Zvirin found that "the strain of keeping her formula fresh and funny shows." However, Zvirin concluded: "Fortunately, a dynamite finish—unexpected and very funny—saves the day." Even reviewers who were not impressed by the book's plot were often compelled to praise the author for her usual cast of amusing and eccentric characters.

Next in the series is *Eleven on Top,* which finds Stephanie tiring of the rough treatment she receives from her criminal clients. In a bold career move, Stephanie leaves her cousin's bounty-hunting business and gets a job at a button factory, then a dry cleaning business. When neither enterprise works out, and after her car is blown to bits, Stephanie gets a job at a fast-food restaurant, which ends when the store is blown up as well. On top of the constant explosions around her, Stephanie keeps receiving creepy, threatening notes from a stalker, who is obviously keeping tabs on her whereabouts. When Stephanie's stalker runs over Joe with a car, Stephanie joins Lula, who has taken over her duties, in hunting criminals and trying to solve the mystery that has come way too close to her personal life for comfort.

"Each Stephanie Plum book is better than the one before," wrote Harriet Klausner in a review of *Eleven on Top* on her Review Archive Web site. "Janet Evanov-ich is a creative writer who brilliantly spins slapstick into life-threatening events," Klausner concluded. While a *Publishers Weekly* reviewer felt that the lead character of the series "stumbles out of the gate due to some forced humor," the reviewer added that she "eventually hits her usually entertaining stride." Other reviewers found the book humorous from start to finish. GraceAnne A. DeCandido commented in *Booklist* that the eleventh book in the series is "brimming with lines that will have readers howling with laughter," adding that "it's wonderful to watch both a beloved character and a cherished author grow." In a review for the *ABC Wide Bay Qld* Web site, Sue Gammon expressed disappointment with the tenth book, commenting that *Ten Big Ones,* "while enjoyable, was also fairly predictable." After reading *Eleven on Top,* however, Gammon acknowledged that "Evanovich is back on top form with this light-hearted and funny episode in the perils of Plum."

In *Twelve Sharp,* "Evanovich uses all of her considerable arsenal" of plot and storytelling techniques to create a tale focused on Stephanie Plum's bounty hunting partner and sometime lover, Ranger Manoso, noted GraceAnne A. DeCandido in *Booklist.* Unable to make a romantic decision between the quietly powerful Ranger and police office Joe Morelli, Stephanie is astonished when a woman who claims to be Ranger's wife suddenly storms into her life. The alleged Carmen Manoso warns Stephanie away from Ranger, but shortly afterward is found shot to death in an SUV outside Plum's bond agency. Worse, reports are surfacing that Ranger has kidnapped his ten-year-old daughter, Julie, from the girl's mother and stepfather in Florida. Stephanie discovers that it is not Ranger who committed the act, but a deranged impersonator and identity thief intent on acquiring all aspects of Ranger's life, including Stephanie herself. Evanovich "finds exactly the tight tone of danger-laden farce for Stephanie's duel with the false Ranger," noted a *Kirkus Reviews* critic. The author is "one of the very few writers whose skill can turn what should be serious moments into boisterously funny scenes. And her technique shines in *Twelve Sharp,* commented Oline H. Cogdill in the *South Florida Sun-Sentinel.* "The boundaries of good taste are deliciously stretched; low-brow comedy becomes an art in Evanovich's hands," Cogdill remarked.

With *Metro Girl,* Evanovich steps away from the "Stephanie Plum" series to concentrate on a new series hero, Alexandra "Barney" Barnaby. The first novel tells of Alexandra's search for her missing brother, who has run afoul of an exiled Cuban warlord. In the second book in the series, *Motor Mouth,* Alexandra, an engineer and racing enthusiast, works as a spotter for NASCAR driver Sam Hooker, helping him to avoid trouble on the track during races. She and Sam are also estranged lovers, whose relationship suffered a rift when he was caught in a one-night stand with a sales clerk. Alexandra retains her professionalism and continues to work as Sam's spotter, but otherwise she has little contact with him. When Sam loses a close race, Alexandra believes that the opposing team cheated, and the search begins for an electronic device that gives the other side an illegal upper hand. The stakes get even higher when a murder is discovered and the villains take an interest in stopping Alexandra and Sam from ferreting out their secret. Evanovich plumbs NASCAR trivia and lore to fill in the background of a story based firmly in the big-money, high-RPM world of professional racing. The protagonists "find themselves in one outrageously hilarious situation after another," commented DeCandido in another *Booklist* review, concluding that Evanovich "appears to have another winner on her hands."

After a solid and successful career as a novelist, Evanovich has acquired considerable insight on the process of writing and publishing. She shares this information in *How I Write: Secrets of a Bestselling Author,* cowritten with Ina Yaloff and daughter Alex Evanovich. While coauthor Yaloff covers some of the nuts-and-bolts basics of writing, Evanovich offers expert commentary and answers to questions readers and hopeful writers have posed to her on her Web site. She explains in detail her techniques for writing dialogue, accurate crime scenes, storylines and plots. Her real-world examples also amount to a great deal of background and inside information on the creation and writing of the "Stephanie Plum" novels. Though reviewer Ilene Cooper, writing in *Booklist,* felt that much of Evanovich's advice can be found in other forms in other resources. "What you can't find in most writers' guides is her inimitable voice and a wealth of examples" drawn from her own successful novels, Cooper stated. "Learning how bestselling author Janet Evanovich writes might not guarantee success to all those aspiring writers out there, but she does offer much constructive advice beyond the usual 'show, don't tell' offerings in the plethora of how-to-write books on the market," noted *Bookreporter.com* reviewer Roz Shea.

BIOGRAPHICAL AND CRITICAL SOURCES:

PERIODICALS

Armchair Detective, summer, 1995, Marvin Lachman, review of *One for the Money,* p. 287.

Belles Lettres, January, 1996, review of *Two for the Dough,* p. 15.
Booklist, May 1, 2000, GraceAnne A. DeCandido, review of *Hot Six,* p. 1622; May 1, 2001, Bill Ott, review of *Hot Six,* p. 1598, GraceAnne A. DeCandido, review of *Seven Up,* p. 1628, and "Story behind the Story: Stephanie Plum as Indiana Jones," p. 1629; May 1, 2004, Stephanie Zvirin, review of *Ten Big Ones,* p. 1506; March 15, 2005, Shelley Mosley, review of *Full Bloom,* p. 1272; May 15, 2005, GraceAnne A. DeCandido, review of *Eleven on Top,* p. 1612; July 1, 2006, GraceAnne A. DeCandido, review of *Twelve Sharp,* p. 7; September 1, 2006, Ilene Cooper, review of *How I Write: Secrets of a Bestselling Author,* p. 36; September 15, 2006, GraceAnne A. DeCandido, review of *Motor Mouth,* p. 5; December 15, 2006, GraceAnne A. DeCandido, review of *Plum Lovin',* p. 5.
Christian Science Monitor, July 25, 1996, Michelle Ross, review of *Two for the Dough,* p. 21.
Detroit Free Press, June 21, 2006, Marta Salij, "Evanovich is as Sharp as Ever in Latest Plum Adventure," review of *Twelve Sharp.*
Entertainment Weekly, November 11, 1994, Kate Wilson, review of *One for the Money,* p. 68; February 23, 1996, review of *Two for the Dough,* p. 119; June 15, 2004, Karen Karbo, review of *Ten Big Ones,* p. 172; June 23, 2006, J.P. Mangalindan, review of *Twelve Sharp,* p. 73.
Kirkus Reviews, June 1, 2003, review of *To the Nines,* p. 781; May 15, 2005, review of *Eleven on Top,* p. 565; June 1, 2006, review of *Twelve Sharp,* p. 548; September 15, 2006, review of *Motor Mouth,* p. 922.
Kliatt, July, 2005, Mary Purucker, review of *Full Bloom,* p. 53.
Library Journal, December, 1996, review of *Three to Get Deadly,* p. 151; June 1, 1999, Wilda Williams, review of *High Five,* p. 186; May 1, 2000, Wilda Williams, review of *Hot Six,* p. 158; June 1, 2001, Wilda Williams, review of *Seven Up,* p. 224; July, 2003, Marianne Fitzgerald, review of *To the Nines,* p. 130; June 1, 2004, Rex E. Klett, review of *Ten Big Ones,* p. 107.
Los Angeles Times Book Review, November 20, 1994, Charles Champlin, review of *One for the Money,* p. 8.
New York Times Book Review, September 4, 1994, Marilyn Stasio, review of *One for the Money,* p. 17; January 21, 1996, Marilyn Stasio, review of *Two for the Dough,* p. 31; February 16, 1997, Marilyn Stasio, review of *Three to Get Deadly,* p. 28;

July 19, 1998, Marilyn Stasio, review of *Four to Score,* p. 20; June 27, 1999, Marilyn Stasio, review of *High Five,* p. 26; July 22, 2001, Marilyn Stasio, review of *Seven Up,* p. 22; June 22, 2005, Edward Wyatt, "For This Author, Writing is Only the Beginning," profile of Janet Evanovich, p. E1.

People, June 21, 2004, Samantha Miller, review of *Ten Big Ones,* p. 49.

Publishers Weekly, November 25, 1996, review of *Three to Get Deadly,* p. 59; June 21, 1999, review of *High Five,* p. 60; July 5, 1999, "A High Five Family," p. 23; November 8, 1999, "Good Seven for *High Five,*" p. 14; May 1, 2000, review of *Hot Six,* p. 52; May 7, 2001, review of *Seven Up,* p. 227; June 23, 2003, review of *To the Nines,* p. 50; June 7, 2004, review of *Ten Big Ones,* pp.35-36; July 5, 2004, Daisy Maryles, "It's 10 for the Money," review of *Ten Big Ones,* p. 13; March 14, 2005, review of *Full Bloom,* p. 51; May 30, 2005, review of *Eleven on Top,* p. 43; May 22, 2006, review of *Twelve Sharp,* p. 33; December 18, 2006, review of *Plum Lovin',* p. 43.

South Florida Sun-Sentinel, June 21, 2006, Oline H. Cogdill, "*Twelve Sharp:* Plum Tale Darker, but Still Juicy," review of *Twelve Sharp.*

Times Literary Supplement, March 15, 1996, Natasha Cooper, review of *Two for the Dough,* p. 24.

Washington Post Book World, August 28, 1994, Dwight Garner, review of *One for the Money,* p. 6.

ONLINE

ABC Wide Bay Qld Web Site (Australia), http://www.abc.net.au/ (February 6, 2007), Sue Gammon, review of *Eleven on Top.*

All About Romance, http://www.likesbooks.com/ (September 18, 1998), Lorna Jean, "Quickie with Janet Evanovich on Her Stephanie Plum Series," interview with Janet Evanovich.

BookPage.com, http://www.bookpage.com/ (February 6, 2007), Bruce Tierney, "Janet Evanovich: Mystery Maven Keeps Readers Coming Back for More," interview with Janet Evanovich; "Meet the Author: Janet Evanovich," biography of Janet Evanovich.

Bookreporter.com, http://www.bookreporter.com/ (February 6, 2007), Roz Shea, review of *Two for the Dough;* Roz Shea, review of *Three to Get Deadly;* Roz Shea, review of *Four to Score;* Roz Shea, review of *High Five;* Roz Shea, review of *Hot Six;* Roz Shea, review of *Seven Up* Roz Shea, review of *Hard Eight;* Roz Shea, review of *Visions of Sugar Plums;* Maggie Harding, review of *To the Nines;* Roz Shea, review of *Ten Big Ones;* Roz Shea, review of *Metro Girl;* Roz Shea, review of *Eleven on Top;* Roz Shea, review of *Twelve Sharp;* Roz Shea, review of *How I Write;* Roz Shea, review of *Motor Mouth;* Roz Shea, review of *Plum Lovin'.*

Fantastic Fiction, http://www.fantasticfiction.co.uk/ (February 6, 2007), bibliography of Janet Evanovich.

Harriet Klausner's Review Archive, http://harrietklausner.wwwi.com/ (February 6, 2007), Harriet Klausner, review of *Eleven on Top.*

Janet Evanovich Home Page, http://www.evanovich.com (February 6, 2007).

Writers Write, http://www.writerswrite.com/ (February 6, 2007), Claire E. White, "A Conversation with Janet Evanovich."*

*　　*　　*

EVANS, Lee
See FORREST, Richard

F

FARRANT, M.A.
See FARRANT, M.A.C.

*   *   *

FARRANT, M.A.C. 1947-
(M.A. Farrant, Marion Alice Coburn Farrant)

PERSONAL: Born April 5, 1947, in Sydney, Australia; daughter of William Derbyshire Gibson and Nancy Eloise Whitehouse; married Garret Coburn, January 15, 1968 (divorced, 1971); married Terry Farrant, December 20, 1974; children: Bill, Anna. *Ethnicity:* "Anglo-Saxon." *Education:* Attended Simon Fraser University and University of Victoria. *Politics:* "Left." *Religion:* "Not in the organized sense."

ADDRESSES: Agent—Carolyn Swayze, Box 39588, White Rock, British Columbia V4N 4M2, Canada. *E-mail*—macfarrant@shaw.ca.

CAREER: Writer. Visiting writer in residence at several universities in Australia, 1998; guest speaker at other institutions, including University of Victoria and Simon Fraser University; gives frequent readings from her works at festivals, libraries, schools, and other venues throughout Canada and elsewhere; judge of writing contests; frequent guest on Canadian media programs. Worked as a social worker, child care worker, tap dancer, and bookkeeper.

MEMBER: Writers Union of Canada, Federation of British Columbia Writers, Sidney and North Saanich Arts Council.

AWARDS, HONORS: First prize, fiction category, British Alternative Writing and Design Contest, 2002, and award for best fiction title, *January,* 2003, both for *Darwin Alone in the Universe;* first prize, nonfiction category, *Grain,* 2002, for "We Keep the Party Going"; Memoirink Prize, 2005, for "Traveling Garbage"; grants from Canadian Department of Foreign Affairs and International Trade, Canada Council, and British Columbia Arts Council.

WRITINGS:

Sick Pigeon (fiction), Thistledown Press (Saskatoon, Saskatchewan, Canada), 1991.
Raw Material (short stories), Arsenal Pulp Press (Vancouver, British Columbia, Canada), 1993.
Altered Statements (short stories), Arsenal Pulp Press (Vancouver, British Columbia, Canada), 1995.
Word of Mouth (short stories), Thistledown Press (Saskatoon, Saskatchewan, Canada), 1996.
What's True, Darling (short stories), Polestar Book Publishers (Custer, WA), 1998.
Girls around the House (linked stories), Polestar Book Publishers (Custer, WA), 1999.
Gifts (short stories), limited edition, Reference West (Victoria, British Columbia Canada), 1999.
Darwin Alone in the Universe (short-short stories), Polestar Book Publishers (Custer, WA), 2003.
My Turquoise Years: A Memoir (novel), Douglas & McIntyre (Vancouver, British Columbia, Canada), 2004.
The Breakdown So Far, Talonbooks (Vancouver, British Columbia, Canada), 2007.

Contributor to chapbooks and anthologies, including *The Concrete Forest,* edited by Hal Niedviecki, McClelland & Stewart (Toronto, Ontario, Canada), 1998;

Tesseracts 7, edited by Paula Johanson and Jean-Louie Trudel, Tesseracts Books (Edmonton, Alberta, Canada), 1998; *Exact Fare Only: Good, Bad, and Ugly Rides on Public Transit,* edited by Grant Buday, Anvil Press (Vancouver, British Columbia, Canada), 2000; *All Wound Up: Alternative Writing from British Columbia,* Ripple Effect Press (Vancouver, British Columbia, Canada), 2002; and *Penguin Anthology of Canadian Humour,* edited by Will Ferguson, Penguin, 2006. Correspondent for *Geist,* 1996-2003, and *Adbuster's.* Contributor of short stories and reviews to periodicals, including *NeWest Review, Fiddlehead, Chatelaine, Maclean's, Prism International, Monday, Exile, Malahat Review, Ottawa Citizen,* and *Vancouver Sun.*

ADAPTATIONS: Sick Pigeon was adapted as a television feature and broadcast by the Bravo! Network, 1995. *Girls around the House, What's True, Darling,* and other short stories have been dramatized and broadcast on Canadian radio programs. A miniseries based on Farrant's novel *My Turquoise Years* was broadcast by the Canadian Broadcasting Corporation in 2004.

SIDELIGHTS: M. A.C. Farrant is a Canadian author of short fiction. The stories in *Raw Material* "offer strikingly different responses to fragmentation in contemporary culture," according to Jeanette Lynes in *Canadian Literature.* Describing the boredom of suburban life and middle-class culture, the stories draw on those of Franz Kafka and Lewis Carroll, and, as Lynes observed, the book "provides a carefully honed, fresh perspective."

Altered Statements is a collection of satirical vignettes about modern society, with riffs on runaway dogs, estrogen-fueled grandmothers, and meetings of Shopaholics Anonymous. The book is "imaginative and amusing, but with a disturbing bite," according to Susan Patrick in *Canadian Book Review Annual.* Donna Nurse wrote in *Quill and Quire* that Farrant's "unusual blend of parody and science fiction sweeps the reader along at a breathless pace."

Word of Mouth is "more serious in tone and content" than Farrant's previous books, according to Claire Wilkshire in *Canadian Book Review Annual,* and has a more ordered structure than either *Raw Material* or *Altered Statements.* The book essentially consists of two novellas, the first starring Sybilla, a nineteen-year-old welfare mom; the second examines a woman's relationship with her family, told from many different points of view. In *Quill and Quire,* Jamie Kastner wrote that the book "feels more like conversation than literature, a testament to Farrant's success at rendering the spoken word on paper."

In *What's True, Darling,* Farrant presents twenty short pieces that, according to a *Publishers Weekly* reviewer, "play the English language like a fine instrument while bemusing the sophisticated reader."

Girls around the House features what a *Publishers Weekly* reviewer called "jaunty, interconnected stories," narrated by former hippie Marion, who with her husband is struggling to keep control of her three almost-adult children. At the same time, she is also host to her bridge-playing mother-in-law. With stories about stocking up on condoms and beer for her kids, hiding her good underwear and favorite cheese from them, and about how she and her husband miss the "independence, wealth and the Open Road" they had imagined they would experience once their children grew up, the book's "saving grace is [Marion's] sense of irony and willingness to take responsibility for her frustrations," according to *Publishers Weekly.*

Darwin Alone in the Universe is a collection of very short stories that offer the author's unique perspectives on the concept of change and how people respond to it, as Farrant herself explained in her introduction to the book. Her characters seem to begin as ordinary—even boring—people nudged by the author toward the brink of absurdity, but never quite pushed over the edge. The result, wrote Margaret Gunning in *January* magazine, "defies analysis." The vignettes hover between the real and the fantastic, and satire unpredictably gives way to glimpses of reflection and open-minded curiosity. Gunning compared the collection to "an unexpected gift, funny, strange. . . ."

My Turquoise Years: A Memoir is actually a coming-of-age novel set in Canada in the 1960s. Whereas *Darwin Alone in the Universe* offers more than forty quick looks at the way people interact with change, *My Turquoise Years* is a long-form exploration of how change—or the anticipation of change—affects a teenage girl and the family with whom she lives. Marion has lived with her aunt since she was five years old, abandoned by her mother though visited frequently by her seafaring father. An impending visit from her distant birth-mother turns Marion's life upside down and propels her extended foster family into a frenzy of activities designed to make a good impression. *Library Journal* contributor Jan Brue Enright called *My Turquoise Years* a "touching" and "humorous" look at growing in Canada.

BIOGRAPHICAL AND CRITICAL SOURCES:

PERIODICALS

Bloomsbury Review, September, 1995, review of *Altered Statements,* p. 28.

Books in Canada, November, 1991, review of *Sick Pigeon,* p. 43; October, 1993, review of *Raw Material,* p. 29; November, 1995, review of *Altered Statements,* p. 36.

Boulevard, January, 2000, Joseph Blake, feature article about *Girls around the House.*

Canadian Book Review Annual, 1994, p. 185; 1996, Susan Patrick, review of *Altered Statements,* and Claire Wilkshire, review of *Word of Mouth,* p. 183; 1997, review of *What's True, Darling,* p. 207.

Canadian Literature, spring, 1995, Jeanette Lynes, review of *Raw Material,* p. 181; autumn, 1997, Sharon R. Wilson, review of *Altered Statements,* p. 137.

Canadian Materials, November, 1991, review of *Sick Pigeon,* p. 360.

Focus, March, 2005, Sara Cassidy, feature article about *My Turquoise Years.*

Focus on Women, February, 2000, Marie Savage, feature article about *Girls around the House.*

January, July, 2003, Margaret Gunning, review of *Darwin Alone in the Universe.*

Library Journal, June 15, 2004, Jan Brue Enright, review of *My Turquoise Years: A Memoir,* p. 70.

Publishers Weekly, February 16, 1996, reviews of *What's True, Darling* and *Girls around the House,* p. 204.

Quill and Quire, October, 1991, review of *Sick Pigeon,* p. 33; July, 1993, review of *Raw Material,* p. 45; July, 1995, Donna Nurse, review of *Altered Statements,* p. 50; September, 1996, Jamie Kastner, review of *Word of Mouth,* p. 65.

Small Press, spring, 1992, review of *Sick Pigeon,* p. 78.

Vancouver Sun, October 8, 1996, interview by Malcolm Perry.

*   *   *

FARRANT, Marion Alice Coburn
See FARRANT, M.A.C.

*   *   *

FARREN, Mick 1943-

PERSONAL: Born September 3, 1943, in Cheltenham, Gloucestershire, England; married Joy Hebdich, 1967 (divorced, 1979); married Elizabeth Volck, 1979. *Education:* Attended St. Martin's School of Art.

ADDRESSES: Home—Los Angeles, CA. *Agent*—Abner Stein, 10 Roland Gardens, London SW7 3PH, England.

CAREER: Writer, novelist, artist, musician, and screenwriter. Singer in musical group Deviants, 1967-69.

WRITINGS:

SCIENCE FICTION NOVELS

The Texts of Festival, Hart-Davis (London, England), 1973, Avon (New York, NY), 1975.

The Feelies, Big O, 1978, Ballantine (New York, NY), 1990.

The Song of Phaid the Gambler (*"Phaid the Gambler"* series), New English Library (London, England), 1981, published in two volumes as *Phaid the Gambler,* Ace (New York, NY), 1986, and *Citizen Phaid,* Ace (New York, NY), 1987.

Protectorate, New English Library, 1984, Ace (New York, NY), 1985.

Corpse, New English Library (London, England), 1986, published as *Vickers,* Ace (New York, NY), 1988.

Their Master's War, Ballantine (New York, NY), 1987.

The Long Orbit, Ballantine (New York, NY), 1988.

Exit Funtopia, Sphere (London, England), 1989.

The Armageddon Crazy, Ballantine (New York, NY), 1989.

Mars: The Red Planet, Ballantine (New York, NY), 1990.

Necrom, Ballantine (New York, NY), 1991.

"DNA COWBOYS" SERIES; SCIENCE FICTION NOVELS

The Quest of the DNA Cowboys, Mayflower (St. Albans, England), 1976.

The Synaptic Manhunt, Mayflower (St. Albans, England), 1976.

The Neural Atrocity, Mayflower (St. Albans, England), 1977.

The Last Stand of the DNA Cowboys, Sphere (New York, NY), 1989.

The DNA Cowboys Trilogy (contains *The Quest of the DNA Cowboys, Manhunt,* and *The Neural Atrocity,* Do-Not Press (London, England) 2003.

"NOSFERATU" SERIES; HORROR NOVELS

The Time of Feasting, Tor (New York, NY), 1996.
Darklost, Tor (New York, NY), 2000.

More than Mortal, Tor (New York, NY), 2001.
Underland, Tor (New York, NY), 2002.

OTHER NOVELS

The Tale of Willy's Rats, Mayflower (St. Albans, England), 1975.
Jim Morrison's Adventures in the Afterlife (fantasy fiction), St. Martin's Press (New York, NY), 1999.
Kindling ("Flame of Evil" series), Tor (New York, NY), 2004.
Conflagration ("Flame of Evil" series), Tor (New York, NY), 2006.

EDITOR

Get on Down, Futura (London, England), 1976.
(With Peter Marchbank) *Elvis in His Own Words,* Omnibus Press (London, England), 1977.
(With Colin Cross and Paul Kendall) *Encyclopedia of British Beat Groups and Solo Artists of the Sixties,* Omnibus Press, 1980.
(With David Dalton) *The Rolling Stones: In Their Own Words,* Putnam (New York, NY), 1983.

Editor of *It* and *Nasty Tales,* both 1970-73; consulting editor, *New Musical Express,* 1975-77.

OTHER

(With Edward Barker) *Watch Out Kids,* Open Gate Books (London, England), 1972.
(With George Snow) *Rock 'n' Roll Circus: The Illustrated Rock Concert,* Pierrot Publishing (London, England), 1978.
(With Roy Carr) *Elvis Presley: The Complete Illustrated Record,* Crown (New York, NY), 1982.
The Black Leather Jacket, Plexus (London, England), 1985, Abbeville (New York, NY), 1986.
(With Dirk Vellenga) *Elvis and the Colonel,* Delacorte (New York, NY), 1988.
The Hitchhiker's Guide to Elvis, Collector's Guide (Burlington, Ontario, Canada), 1994.
Conspiracies, Lies and Hidden Agendas (nonfiction), Renaissance Books (Los Angeles, CA), 1999.
Give the Anarchist a Cigarette (memoir), Jonathan Cape (London, England), 2001.

Gene Vincent: There's One in Every Town (biography), Do-Not Press (London, England), 2004.

Screenwriter of *Black Leather Jacket,* a documentary based on Farren's nonfiction book of the same title, and *Fear in the Dark,* a documentary on horror films, 1991. Writer for television series *The Adventures of the Galaxy Rangers,* including episodes "Edge of Darkness," "The Magnificent Kiwi," "Rogue Arm," "Scarecrow's Revenge," "Lord of the Sands," and "Tower of Combat."

SIDELIGHTS: Mick Farren is an eclectic writer whose publications include both science fiction novels and works on popular culture. Farren, a former lead vocalist with the pop band the Deviants, worked in editorial capacities for various music publications, including *It* and *Nasty Tales,* in the 1970s, the decade when he also began publishing science fiction.

Among Farren's most prominent works in the science fiction genre are *The Quest of the DNA Cowboys, The Synaptic Manhunt,* and *The Neural Atrocity.* This trio of mid-1970s publications concern the DNA Cowboys, marauders roaming an Earth in which human needs are ministered by a decidedly unstable computer that occasionally produces gaping holes in the very fabric of reality. In these novels the DNA Cowboys battle villains and overcome extraordinary catastrophes while attempting to determine the origins of various reality breakdowns. In 1989, Farren revived the DNA Cowboys in *The Last Stand of the DNA Cowboys,* wherein the heroes must combat a burgeoning squad of malcontents bent on occupying the gaps in reality.

Farren's other science fiction tales include *The Feelies,* a zany account in which corpses are transformed into historical figures; *The Song of Phaid the Gambler* (also published in two volumes as *Phaid the Gambler* and *Citizen Phaid*), which details the various exploits of an adventurer in the far future; and *Necrom,* the story of a dissipated rock singer who is transported into another dimension which includes a quasi-parallel Earth in which he discovers his resemblance to a notorious political assassin.

Farren has also produced several pop-culture publications, including three nonfiction books—*Elvis Presley: The Complete Illustrated Record, Elvis and the Colonel,* and *The Hitchhiker's Guide to Elvis*—devoted to the legendary rock 'n' roll performer whose career, spanning from the 1950s to the 1970s, included many film performances as well as concerts and popular recordings.

Farren continued to explore different genres in the 1990s. In 1996 he published *The Time of Feasting,* a gothic horror about modern-day vampires and the first of the four-part "Nosferatu" series, in which the space-faring Nephilim create a series of supernatural races on Earth. A *Publishers Weekly* critic called the work "an uncommonly brisk dark fantasy." The series continued with *Darklost,* which concerns an encounter between the Nosferatu and elements of H.P. Lovecraft's famous Cthulhu mythos. In the third volume, *More than Mortal,* Farren brings his vampires into contact with Taliesin, also known as Merlin, the powerful wizard from Arthurian legend. Disturbed in his tomb by archaeological excavations in England, Merlin reappears and threatens to upset the balance of supernatural power among the various paranormal races on earth. In the final book of the series, *Underland,* larger elements of the subterranean Cthulhu race are at work as government agents of the National Security Agency's Paranormal Warfare Facility seek Nosferatu Victor Renquist's help to challenge and claim the supernatural powers of the Cthulhu as their own. PWF director Walker Grael also reveals the astonishing fact that Nazis discovered an underground world beneath the arctic ice in 1947, and have been operating in flying saucers from that base ever since. Renquist is charged with leading a team of agents to the base, where he finds a race that worships Dhrakuh, the Serpent, an enormous central mind with connections to the Nephilim that birthed all of earth's paranormal races. A *Kirkus Reviews* critic called the novel "overburdened, but a daring mix of Jules Verne and the vampire genre." A reviewer in *Publishers Weekly* named it a "fiendishly inventive book."

In 1999 Farren published a nonfiction, A-Z guide on conspiracy theories called *Conspiracies, Lies, and Hidden Agendas. Jim Morrison's Adventures in the Afterlife,* also published in 1999, is a fantasy novel featuring "an all-star cast including Moses, Jesus Christ, Dylan Thomas, and Doc Holiday," according to a *Publishers Weekly* reviewer. *Gene Vincent: There's One in Every Town* is a biography of early bad-boy rocker Vincent, which a *Bookwatch* reviewer called an "impressive biographical sketch."

Kindling is the first book of a futuristic science fantasy series set on an alternate Earth-like world in which the powerful Mosul Empire, allied with planetary Tauten and Marmeluke warlords and worshipers of gods Ignir and Aksura, drive to overtake and control the rest of the world. Defying the rapacious and destructive advance of the Mosul Empire is the quartet of paranormal beings called The Four, who can combine themselves and their abilities into a single powerful being capable of standing against the Mosul and their supernatural allies. The Four consists of Argo Weaver, a pugnacious country boy; Cordelia Blakeny, an aristocratic young woman with special talents; Raphael Vega, a conscripted Spanish soldier and hero sent out as cannon fodder against the Mosul; and Jessamine, concubine for a Tauten military leader. Together, they inhabit a world of constant warfare and suppressed magic, based in the kingdom of Albany, a stronghold of Earth resistance in Eastern America. Assisted by Yancy Slide, an Albany Ranger who is reputed to be a demon, the Four engage the Mosul's supernatural forces while the Albany Rangers drive back the physical invasion force. "Farren alternates scenes of action, sex, and brutality as the four follow separate trails to their inevitable union," noted a *Kirkus Reviews* critic, who called the novel "fast-moving, if sometimes incoherent." *Library Journal* reviewer Jackie Cassada remarked favorably on the novel's "fascinating characters and vivid descriptions."

Conflagration, Farren's second book about the Four, finds the characters victorious over the first invading wave of Mosul. However, they also discover that the Mosul queen, Jeakqual-Ahrach, has created a pair of twin beings with ferocious supernatural powers who are intended to battle the Four. Another Mosul attack is foiled, and the members of the Four accompany American Prime Minister Jack Kennedy on a diplomatic mission to England. As they work to convince the Norse Union to join them in the fight against the Mosul, the members of the Four face magical challenges in a raucous, carefree London atmosphere of sex, parties, drugs, and music. The kidnapping of a member of the four ups the stakes considerably, sending the three remaining members to Paris, where they must face the strength of the magical twins created by the Mosul queen. A *Kirkus Reviews* contributor called the book "an edgy mixture of fantasy, erotica, and alternate history." The world's struggle against "a nearly unstoppable colonial force that Farren's fantastic alternate history portrays is altogether gripping," commented Regina Schroeder in *Booklist.*

BIOGRAPHICAL AND CRITICAL SOURCES:

BOOKS

Farren, Mick, *Give the Anarchist a Cigarette,* Jonathan Cape (London, England), 2001.

Watson, Noelle, and Paul E. Schellinger, editors, *Twentieth-Century Science-Fiction Writers,* 3rd edition, St. James Press (Detroit, MI), 1991.

PERIODICALS

Booklist, August, 2004, Regina Schroeder, review of *Kindling,* p. 1912; May 15, 2006, Regina Schroeder, review of *Conflagration,* p. 37.
Bookwatch, January, 2005, review of *Gene Vincent: There's One in Every Town.*
Kirkus Reviews, October 1, 2002, review of *Underland,* p. 1415; June 15, 2004, review of *Kindling,* p. 562; May 1, 2006, review of *Conflagration,* p. 442.
Library Journal, March 15, 2003, Michael Rogers, review of *The DNA Cowboys Trilogy,* p. 122; August, 2004, Jackie Cassada, review of *Kindling,* p. 73; June 15, 2006, Jackie Cassada, review of *Conflagration,* p. 62.
Publishers Weekly, March 20, 1978, review of *Rock 'n' Roll Circus,* p. 65; November 29, 1985, Genevieve Stuttaford, review of *The Black Leather Jacket,* p. 40; January 18, 1991, Penny Kaganoff, review of *Necrom,* p. 54; October 21, 1996, review of *The Time of Feasting,* p. 69; September 27, 1999, review of *Jim Morrison's Adventures in the Afterlife,* p. 70; July 9, 2001, review of *More than Mortal,* p. 51; October 28, 2002, review of *Underland,* p. 55; April 24, 2006, review of *Conflagration,* p. 43.
Spectator, October 6, 2001, Julie Burchill, review of *Give the Anarchist a Cigarette,* p. 67.

ONLINE

Internet Movie Database, http://www.imdb.com/ (February 6, 2007), filmography of Mick Farren.*

*   *   *

FEINSTEIN, Elaine 1930-

PERSONAL: Born October 24, 1930, in Bootle, Lancashire, England; daughter of Isidore and Fay Cooklin; married Arnold Feinstein (an immunologist), July 22, 1957 (died, 2002); children: Adam, Martin, Joel. *Education:* Newnham College, Cambridge, B.A., 1952, M.A., 1955.

ADDRESSES: Agent—Gill Coleridge, Rogers, Coleridge & White, 20 Powis Mews, London W11 1JN, England; (plays and film) Lemon Unna & Durbridge, 24-32 Pottery Lane, London W11 4LZ, England. *E-mail*—elainefeinstein@compuserve.com.

CAREER: Cambridge University Press, London, England, editorial staff member, 1960-62; Bishop's Stortford Training College, Hertfordshire, England, lecturer in English, 1963-66; University of Essex, Wivenhoe, England, assistant lecturer in literature, 1967-70; freelance writer, 1971—. Writer-in-residence, British Council in Singapore, 1993, and for the British Council in Tromsoe. Has also worked as a journalist.

MEMBER: Poetry Society, Eastern Arts Association, Royal Society of Literature (fellow).

AWARDS, HONORS: Arts Council grants, 1970, 1979, 1981; Daisy Miller Prize, 1971, for fiction; Kelus poetry prize, 1978; Cholmondeley Poets Award, 1990; D.Litt., Leicester University, England, 1990.

WRITINGS:

POETRY

In a Green Eye, Goliard Press (London, England), 1966.
The Magic Apple Tree, Hutchinson (London, England), 1971.
At the Edge, Sceptre Press (Northamptonshire, England), 1972.
The Celebrants and Other Poems, Hutchinson (London, England), 1973.
Some Unease and Angels: Selected Poems, Green River Press (University Center, MI), 1977, second edition, Hutchinson (London, England), 1982.
The Feast of Euridice, Faber (London, England), 1981.
Badlands, Hutchinson (London, England), 1986.
City Music, Hutchinson (London, England), 1990.
Selected Poems, Carcanet (Manchester, England), 1994.
Daylight, Carcanet (Manchester, England), 1997.
Gold, Carcanet (Manchester, England), 2000.

NOVELS

The Circle, Hutchinson (London, England), 1970.

The Amberstone Exit, Hutchinson (London, England), 1972.

The Glass Alembic, Hutchinson (London, England), 1973, published as *The Crystal Garden,* Dutton (New York, NY), 1974.

The Children of the Rose, Hutchinson (London, England), 1974.

The Ecstasy of Dr. Miriam Garner, Hutchinson (London, England), 1976.

The Shadow Master, Hutchinson (London, England), 1977, Simon & Schuster (New York, NY), 1978.

The Survivors, Hutchinson (London, England), 1982.

The Border, Hutchinson (London, England), 1984.

Mother's Girl, Dutton (New York, NY), 1988.

All You Need, Hutchinson (London, England), 1989.

Loving Brecht, Hutchinson (London, England), 1992.

Dreamers, Macmillan (London, England), 1994.

Lady Chatterley's Confession, Macmillan (New York, NY), 1995.

Dark Inheritance, Women's Press (London, England), 2001.

PLAYS

"Breath" (teleplay), *Play for Today,* British Broadcasting Corp. (BBC), 1975.

Echoes (radio play), 1980.

A Late Spring (radio play), 1982.

"Lunch" (teleplay), *BBC-2 Playhouse,* 1982.

A Captive Lion (radio play), 1984.

The Diary of a Country Gentlewoman (twelve-part television series, based on the novel by Edith Holden), ITV, 1984, also known as *Country Diary of an Edwardian Lady.*

Maria Tsvetayeva: A Life (radio play), 1985.

A Brave Face (teleplay), 1985.

A Day Off (radio play; based on the novel by Storm Jameson), 1986.

If I Ever Get on My Feet Again (radio play), 1987.

Lear's Daughters, first produced in London, England, 1987.

The Chase (teleplay), 1988.

A Passionate Woman (teleplay; series), 1989.

The Man in Her Life (radio play), 1990.

Foreign Girls (radio play), 1993.

Winter Meeting (radio play), 1994.

Also author of radio play *Women in Love* (based on the novel by D.H. Lawrence); and a radio adaptation of her own novel *Lady Chatterly's Confession.*

OTHER

(Editor) *Selected Poems of John Clare,* University Tutorial Press (London, England), 1968.

(Translator) *The Selected Poems of Marina Tsvetayeva,* Oxford University Press (London, England), 1971, second revised edition, Oxford University Press (New York, NY), 1993.

Matters of Chance (short stories), Covent Garden Press (London, England), 1972.

(Translator) *Three Russian Poets: Margarita Aliger, Yunna Moritz, and Bella Akhmadulina,* Carcanet Press (Manchester, England), 1979.

(Editor, with Fay Weldon) *New Stories Four,* Arts Council of Great Britain (London, England), 1979.

The Silent Areas (short stories), Hutchinson (London, England), 1980.

Bessie Smith (biography), Viking (New York, NY), 1986.

A Captive Lion: The Life of Marina Tsvetayeva, Dutton (New York, NY), 1987.

(Translator, with Antonina W. Bouis) Nika Turbina, *First Draft: Poems,* M. Boyars (London, England), 1988.

(Editor) *PEN New Poetry,* Quartet (London, England), 1988.

Lawrence and the Women: The Intimate Life of D.H. Lawrence, HarperCollins (New York, NY), 1993, published as *Lawrence's Women: The Intimate Life of D.H. Lawrence,* HarperCollins (London, England), 1993.

Pushkin, Weidenfeld & Nicolson (London, England), 1998, published as *Pushkin: A Biography,* Ecco Press (Hopewell, NJ), 1999.

(Editor) *After Pushkin* (poetry), Carcanet Press (Manchester, England), 1999.

Ted Hughes: The Life of a Poet, Norton (New York, NY), 2001.

Collected Poems and Translations, Carcanet (Manchester, England), 2002.

Anna of All the Russias: The Life of Anna Akhmatova, Knopf (New York, NY), 2006.

Contributor to periodicals, including *Times Literary Supplement.*

SIDELIGHTS: Elaine Feinstein is an English poet, novelist, short story writer, playwright, biographer, and translator. Such diversity of interest and talent is relatively rare. The granddaughter of Jews who fled persecution in Tsarist Russia, Feinstein retains a strong preoccupation with her background and upbringing; this fascination with her Eastern European origins informs both her poetry and the majority of her novels. As Jennifer Birkett noted in *Contemporary Women Poets,* "landscapes of exile, suffering, and loss" characterize Feinstein's verse.

Dictionary of Literary Biography contributor Peter Conradi called Feinstein "a writer who has made fragmentation and deracination her special topics," adding that she "has developed a language of formidable efficiency for evoking each, and for searching for authentication in the teeth of each. If her earliest books defamiliarized the ordinary world and the domestic self, her later books appropriately domesticated the exotic." *New Yorker* essayist George Steiner likewise noted that a "pulse of narrative and of dramatic voice is vivid in [Feinstein's] verse."

Feinstein was born in Bootle, Lancashire, and brought up in the industrial town of Leicester in the English Midlands. Her father owned a factory, and his success with it fluctuated dramatically. Although her family was never destitute, Feinstein experienced some genteel poverty in her childhood. An only child, she was raised to respect religion, but it was only after World War II that she came to realize what being Jewish meant for her. Feinstein noted in her essay in the *Contemporary Authors Autobiography Series* (*CAAS*) that her childhood sense of security "was exploded, once and for all, at the war's end, when I read what exactly had been done to so many children, as young as I was, in the hell of Hitler's camps. You could say that in that year I became Jewish for the first time. That is not something I regret. But no doubt the knowledge of human cruelty damaged me. For a very long time afterwards, I could feel no ordinary human emotion without testing it against that imagined experience, and either suspecting it or dismissing it." Conradi put it another way. After the war, he wrote, Feinstein came "to an understanding of the degree to which being Jewish could mean to suffer and live in danger."

Feinstein was educated with a grant provided by the Butler Education Act of 1944, receiving both her bachelor and master's degrees from Cambridge University. In 1957, two years after leaving Cambridge, she married Arnold Feinstein, an immunologist. For several years she devoted herself to rearing the couple's three sons, but she was also able to work as an editor for Cambridge University Press and as a part-time English

lecturer at several colleges. Her first volume of poetry, *In a Green Eye,* was published in 1966. According to Deborah Mitchell in the *Dictionary of Literary Biography,* the book "already shows an unassuming sureness of diction and imagery. . . . The poems are simple and generously affectionate—she is always anxious to do justice to whomever she is 'portraying' as well as to express her own relationship with the individual. There is also an unsentimental recognition that, in human relationships, people are tied to one another, pushing and pulling toward and away from one another in mutual dependency."

For a time in the late 1960s Feinstein joined a poetry group in an effort to clarify her approach and better understand her own poetic voice. The group helped her to do this in an oblique way: she came to disagree with its insistence on "Englishness" as a motivating characteristic. Conradi suggested that members of the group "wished to de-Europeanize themselves, to make a cult of and to explore the history of their particular Englishness. This helped [Feinstein] define herself against any such cult, as a person who had never definitely 'settled' in England, and whose roots, if she had them and was not nomadic, were certainly not to be discovered in a nationalist version of 'Little England.'" Thereafter Feinstein's work began to explore her ancestry and heritage as well as the horrors inflicted on modern Jews. Her poetry was especially influenced by the verse of Marina Tsvetayeva, a Russian author of the early twentieth century.

Feinstein once told *CA:* "I began to write poetry in the '60s very *consciously* influenced by American poets; at a time when the use of line, and spacing, to indicate the movement of poetry, was much less fashionable than it is now among young British poets. It was my translations from the Russian of Marina Tsvetayeva, however, that gave me my true voice, or at least made me attend to a strength and forward push, *against* and *within* a formal structure, that I could have only learnt from Tsvetayeva herself. In the wholeness of her self-exposure, she opened a whole world of experience. Without her, I should never have written novels, still less plays."

Feinstein's early novels "came out of domestic and personal experience whose woes and wonders they to some degree make lyrical," to quote Conradi. A favorite early theme of Feinstein's is a woman's search for identity within and outside of familial relationships. Both *The Circle* and *The Amberstone Exit* feature young women so mired in domestic or family responsibilities that they cannot fully explore themselves.

Many critics agree that the death of Feinstein's parents in 1973 marks the beginning of Feinstein's movement into new thematic territory. Conradi stated: "It was about this time that she began to enquire into Jewish history more systematically and enlarge her reading. A wish to make her characters more securely substantial also entered into this investigation; the result was not merely more substantial characterization, but also more satisfying mythmaking."

"In a complex process," Mitchell wrote, "Feinstein has combined traditional myths with myths she has created out of themes that arose originally from direct reactions to her personal experience and that have been gradually clarified and set into a broader historical perspective." In works such as *The Shadow Master, The Ecstasy of Dr. Miriam Garner,* and *The Border,* Feinstein leaves not only the boundaries of England but the constraints of realism; characters confront the drama of Jewish history, and one way or another it begins to control their lives. Conradi observed that in many of Feinstein's novels "someone falls dangerously ill, sick beyond the reach even of modern pharmacy, and it is often the past which can be said figuratively to have sickened them, and which has returned to get them." In the *New Statesman,* Clapp contended that this obsession with the past is represented by ghostly visitations. "Now the spectres have been unleashed," Clapp concluded, "and, though it's not easy to give whole-hearted assent to their original necessity, the open acknowledgment of their presence brings remarkable release."

One of Feinstein's best-known novels is *The Survivors,* a multi-generational story of two Jewish families who flee Odessa for turn-of-the-century Liverpool. In the *Times Literary Supplement,* Peter Lewis described the families: "The Gordons are extremely well-to-do and middle-class, and have been assimilated to a considerable extent into English social life. The Katz family is working class, belongs to the Liverpool equivalent of a ghetto (within a slum area), and is orthodox in religion." The tale revolves around a marriage between the Gordon and Katz families, and the subsequent offspring of that union. Lewis noted a good probability that Feinstein "has transmuted her family and personal history into fiction in *The Survivors,* which is full of insights into the changing patterns of Jewish life during this century." *Listener* contributor John Mellors found more to praise than just the novel's story, however. "It is the poet's precision and verbal fastidiousness which make *The Survivors* far more than just another family chronicle," Mellors wrote. Neil Philip offered a similar opinion in

British Book News. The Survivors, concluded Philip, "is an exceptional novel: intimate, engrossing, economical, yet covering sixty years, two world wars and immense social change. It is Elaine Feinstein's remarkably sure grip on her material which enables her to treat such large themes, to encompass three generations, to manage such a large cast, without losing sight of the personal, the individual, the sense of the minute as well as the year. . . . Fiction as rich and rewarding as this is rare."

In her 1989 novel, *All You Need,* Feinstein chose a very contemporary setting—London in the late 1980s—and a highly cosmopolitan cast of characters—successful businessmen, television producers, literary stars—and produced a work in which the focus is less on the past than it is on the present and near future. The main character is a suburban homemaker named Nell who moves to London with her teenage daughter after her husband is arrested and sent to jail for somewhat mysterious reasons. Like her previous novels, *All You Need* focuses on the self-discovery and reawakening of the female protagonist. Unlike Feinstein's previous work, however, this one employs the reawakened protagonist as an observer of the contemporary British cultural scene, rather than as a psychological and spiritual conduit to the past. For this reason, most critics were somewhat disappointed by *All You Need. Observer* contributor Jan Dalley called the book "good-natured but rather bland," and Nicci Gerrard, writing in the *New Statesman*—while generally liking the novel—missed "the elegiac notes that make Elaine Feinstein's earlier works so haunting."

From the contemporaneity of *All You Need* Feinstein then examined—in *Dreamers*—Vienna in the Habsburg period of the mid-nineteenth century. This novel presents an intellectual and thematic portrait of the time and place, focusing on how Jews lived and contributed to the society and culture of central Europe at a time when anti-Semitism was becoming institutionalized. As Ruth Padel summarized the novel's themes in the *New Statesman,* Feinstein examines questions such as: "How should Jews live in a liberalising Christian empire, with anti-Semitism rising as Jews contribute to everything the city values? Disguise themselves, or keep marks of difference? Converting, as Heine did, is useless. Assimilation is never enough. Hitler's dream backlights everything." The novel depicts various responses to these questions, following a wide range of characters during a fifteen-year period. Padel noted that in *Dreamers* "you get Vienna through its ideas, soldiers, prostitutes, poets, bankers, singers, cooks, social injustices and changes—until the closing paragraph. There, the two themes—political change in nineteenth-century Europe and the *impasse* of its Jews—merge in a last shot." She concluded that the "novel is beautifully plotted, but moments of relationship, and of meditation on them, are where [Feinstein's] lyric perception always soars."

In 1993 Feinstein wrote a biography of D.H. Lawrence titled *Lawrence and the Women: The Intimate Life of D.H. Lawrence.* This study focuses on the women in his life and his troubled relationships with them. Two years later she wrote a sequel to one of Lawrence's most famous novels, *Lady Chatterley's Lover,* called *Lady Chatterley's Confession.* Writing in the *Times Literary Supplement,* Miranda Seymour concluded that "Feinstein, with sturdy pragmatism, recognizes that sex would never have kept this relationship [between the eponymous heroine and Mellors, her upper-class paramour] alive for long and that, without it, Lady Chatterley is a lost woman. It is not a romantic conclusion to the story but it is a perfectly convincing one." Craig Brown argued in the *Spectator* that Feinstein did not appear to grasp some of the comedy of Lawrence's original. He concluded: "Lawrence, who always had more of an eye for Mellors' manhood than Lady C's womanhood, would not, I think, approve of Feinstein's novel. On the other hand, it is far more plausible as a sequel than anything he would have written."

Feinstein's novels and short stories have eclipsed the attention given to her early verse, but she has drawn praise and respect in British literary circles for her poetry. Mitchell noted that "the poems come from a familiar world but there is nothing cozy or reassuringly safe about Feinstein's domesticity," Mitchell wrote, adding that Feinstein's "poems are faithful to the actual experience described . . . but she is less interested, finally, in realism for its own sake than in the 'making strange' of familiar experience to enable the reader to recognize its importance once more." Perhaps not surprisingly, Feinstein's talents have led her not only to write poetry, but to translate the work of other poets as well.

Feinstein's interest in the poet Maria Tsvetayeva, whom she called "my teacher of courage," has continued for more than twenty years. Feinstein has not only translated Tsvetayeva's poetry, she also wrote a biography titled *A Captive Lion: The Life of Marina Tsvetayeva.* In a

Spectator review, Peter Levi contended that the work "as it now stands is like the ultimate Tsvetayeva poem, a painful extension of the painful life, with its final focus on a nail used for tethering horses from which she hung herself. It is not the kind of truth one enjoys hearing." Most critics praised Feinstein's English translations from the Russian—a difficult undertaking given the disparities between the two languages. Levi observed that some of the resultant works "are magnificent poems that do not look like translations at all, they are so good." According to Ellendea Proffer in the *New York Times Book Review,* readers "can only be grateful for her work in bringing this difficult poet [Tsvetayeva] into English, and certainly it can be said that these are the best translations available."

Feinstein's 1999 book *Pushkin* focuses her attention on Russian poet Alexander Pushkin, who is sometimes referred to as the Russian Shakespeare. Feinstein obtained new information from recently discovered Russian documents about his life in this up-to-date biography. Harry V. Williams, writing for *Library Journal,* found that Feinstein used these materials and, along with liberal quotes form Pushkin's own work, wrote "a very readable volume." The biography is "utterly professional, and seeking to open the window on to Pushkin's genius for those who are not readers of Russian," wrote Hugh Barnes in the *New Statesman.* A reviewer for *Russian Life* praised Feinstein's work, calling it "an easy-reading, objective . . . and yet loving biography."

Feinstein tackled the life of Ted Hughes, husband of Sylvia Plath and poet in his own right, in the 2001 book *Ted Hughes: The Life of a Poet.* Feinstein knew Hughes (they were contemporaries at Cambridge) and did not place judgment on him for any responsibility he may have had in Plath's suicide or in the murder-suicide of his mistress and their child. Instead, as a reviewer for the *Economist* wrote, she "manages to avoid being sucked into the vortex of blame and sensationalism." Sympathetic to Hughes and the relationships surrounding him, Feinstein chose to remain "detached." *New York Times* contributor Brooke Allen also stated that the book is an "engaging . . . and convincing narrative that manages to blend honesty with sympathy." Critical of Feinstein's detachedness from the subject because she did not delve too deeply into the mixed up love affair, *New Criterion* writer Jeffery Meyers called *Ted Hughes* "brief, superficial and deeply disappointing." Allen, however, felt that *Ted Hughes* is "the measured, gentle biography that needed to be written [about Plath and

Hughes's relationship]," concluding that Feinstein's portrayal of Hughes was "sensitive and discreet."

Noting Feinstein's background, Robert Hanks said in the *Daily Telegraph* that she "has the CV for the job" to help make sense of the myths and the truths in Ted Hughes's life. Although Hanks felt that Feinstein's insight on Hughes's poetry is new, he did call her "a sound critic" and asserted that the book is "not gratuitous." *Guardian* critic Blake Morrison summed up Feinstein's work as "pleasingly brief, even-tempered and unsensationalist."

In *Anna of All the Russias: The Life of Anna Akhmatova,* Feinstein explores the life and career of Tsvetayeva's fellow poet. Together, wrote Olga Grushin in the *New York Times Book Review,* these two contemporaries became "the two greatest female poets in Russian literature." Like Tsvetayeva, Akhmatova led a tragic life: her ex-husband Nikolai Gumilyov was summarily shot by Bolshevik revolutionaries in 1921, and her son Lev spent years in Soviet prison camps. "Her early fame as a poet and [as] a legendary beauty of bohemian pre-revolutionary St. Petersburg," Grushin concluded, "gave way to decades of forced silence and official denunciations." She was condemned as bourgeois by the Soviet cultural ministry and was barred from publishing her work for more than a quarter of a century. Despite these trials, explained a *Kirkus Reviews* contributor, Akhmatova "surviv[ed] the revolution and Soviet terror to secure a triumphant legacy." "Only after Stalin's death did she experience slow rehabilitation," declared Carlin Romano in the *Philadelphia Enquirer,* "receiving a small dacha from the state, admiration from younger Russian poets like Josef Brodsky, and international literary fame." "Feinstein's magisterial translations of Akhmatova's poetry," the *Kirkus Reviews* writer stated, "further enrich this portrait of a mythic personality as vulnerable as she was implacable." "Feinstein," concluded Anne Applebaum, writing for the *Spectator,* "has done English-speaking readers a great favour by making Akhmatova's life story, and therefore her poetry, more accessible to us than ever before."

Despite her work as a biographer, it is still Feinstein's fiction and verse that has drawn so much attention. Discussing this, Conradi felt that Feinstein's "impressive progress as a novelist can be seen . . . as an emancipation of prose from a provincial sense of its limits," a discovery the author gleaned from her work on Tsvetayeva. Feinstein "wants to write novels which

move her readers, as the great novels of the past have done," added the critic, "and to involve them in the fate of her characters so that they will care about what happens to them." Addressing herself to Feinstein's poetic contributions, Mitchell wrote: "The mature achievement of her verse has been recognized by a small number of diverse critics, [although] . . . the very individuality which is so refreshing in her work, as well as its diversity, has puzzled a sometimes parochial English reading public." Nevertheless, concluded Mitchell, Feinstein is "something of a rarity among writers—equally at home in verse and fiction, being too well aware of the distinct qualities of each form to make one an adjunct of the other. The cross-fertilization between narrative and lyric means that she is continually developing new and enriching approaches to writing poetry."

BIOGRAPHICAL AND CRITICAL SOURCES:

BOOKS

Contemporary Authors Autobiography Series, Volume 1, Thomson Gale (Detroit, MI), 1984.
Contemporary Literary Criticism, Volume 36, Thomson Gale (Detroit, MI), 1986.
Contemporary Women Poets, St. James Press (Detroit, MI), 1997.
Dictionary of Literary Biography, Thomson Gale (Detroit, MI), Volume 14: *British Novelists since 1960,* 1983, Volume 40: *Poets of Great Britain and Ireland since 1960,* 1985.
Schmidt, Michael, and Grevel Lindop, editors, *British Poetry since 1960,* Carcanet Press (Manchester, England), 1972.
Schmidt, Michael, and Peter Jones, editors, *British Poetry since 1970,* Carcanet Press (Manchester, England), 1980.

PERIODICALS

Biography, fall, 2005, Stephen Schwartz, review of *Anna of All the Russias: The Life of Anna Akhmatova,* p. 699; summer, 2006, Orlando Figes, review of *Anna of All the Russias,* p. 506.
Booklist, February 15, 2006, Donna Seaman, review of *Anna of All the Russias,* p. 36.
British Book News, July, 1982, Neil Philip, review of *The Survivors.*

Choice, October, 1999, R. Gregg, review of *Pushkin,* p. 336; March, 2002, W.J. Martz, review of *Ted Hughes: The Life of a Poet,* p. 1236.

Contemporary Review, September, 1999, review of *Pushkin,* p. 165.

Daily Telegraph (London, England), February 19, 2000, Gillian Pachter, "Sunlight Lends Dust the Lustre of Sequins: Gillian Patcher Marvels at the Work of Poetic Alchemy," p. 3; November 3, 2001, Robert Hanks, "We Were Just Kids."

Economist, November 14, 1998, review of *Pushkin,* p. 13; November 20, 1999, review of *After Pushkin,* p. 101; November 17, 2001, review of *Ted Hughes;* August 13, 2005, "Lady in Red: Anna Akhmatova," p. 72.

Globe and Mail (Toronto, Ontario, Canada), November 27, 1999, review of *Pushkin,* p. D21.

Guardian (London, England), October 27, 2001, Blake Morrison, "Keeper of a Stubborn Faith," p. 8.

Harper's, April, 2006, John Leonard, "New Books," p. 83.

Kirkus Review, April 15, 1999, review of *Pushkin,* p. 594; January 1, 2006, review of *Anna of All the Russias,* p. 27.

Library Journal, May 1, 1999, Harry V. Williams, review of *Pushkin,* p. 76; February 1, 2006, Stacy Shotsberger Russo, review of *Anna of All the Russias,* p. 78.

Listener, March 11, 1982, John Mellors, review of *The Survivors.*

London Review of Books, May 13, 1999, review of *Pushkin,* p. 27.

New Criterion, March, 2002, Jeffrey Meyers, review of *Ted Hughes,* p. 72.

New Statesman, September 15, 1989, Nicci Gerrard, review of *All You Need,* p. 34; August 12, 1994, Ruth Padel review of *Dreamers,* p. 39; January 8, 1999, Hugh Barnes, review of *Pushkin,* p. 57.

New Yorker, April 29, 1985, George Steiner, review of *The Border.*

New York Times, January 23, 2000, Emily Barton, review of *Pushkin,* p. 21; February 3, 2002, Brooke Allen, "In Sylvia's Shadow," p. 12.

New York Times Book Review, December 27, 1987, Ellendea Proffer, review of *A Captive Lion: The Life of Marina Tsvetayeva,* p. 22; March 19, 2006, Olga Grushin, "Not Silenced," review of *Anna of All the Russias.*

Observer (London, England), September 24, 1989, Jan Dalley, review of *All You Need.*

Philadelphia Inquirer, June 27, 2006, Carlin Romano, "A Poet Who Gave Voice to Russia's Suffering."

Publishers Weekly, April 19, 1999, review of *Pushkin,* p. 54; January 2, 2006, review of *Anna of All the Russias,* p. 46.

Russian Life, June-July, 1999, review of *Pushkin,* p. 53.

Spectator, March 7, 1987, Peter Levi, review of *A Captive Lion;* December 16, 1995, Craig Brown, review of *Lady Chatterley's Confession;* November 14, 1998, William Scammell, review of *Pushkin,* p. 44; July 2, 2005, Anne Applebaum, "A Truly Russian Icon," review of *Anna of All the Russias,* p. 30.

Times (London, England), October 24, 2001, Erika Wagner, review of *Ted Hughes,* p. 11.

Times Literary Supplement, February 26, 1982, Peter Lewis, review of *The Survivors;* October 13, 1995, Miranda Seymour, review of *Lady Chatterley's Confession;* January 29, 1999, Donald Rayfield, review of *Pushkin,* p. 29; March 10, 2000, Andrew Kahn, review of *After Pushkin,* p. 24; April 21, 2000, Conor O'Callaghan, review of *Gold,* p. 26; March 9, 2001, Natasha Cooper, review of *Dark Inheritance,* p. 24.

Virginia Quarterly Review, spring, 2002, review of *Ted Hughes,* p. 66.

Wall Street Journal, July 15, 1999, Nina Khrushcheva, review of *Pushkin,* p. A16.*

*   *   *

FISCHER, John
See FLUKE, Joanne

*   *   *

FISCHER, R.J.
See FLUKE, Joanne

*   *   *

FLORIAN, Douglas 1950-

PERSONAL: Born March 18, 1950, in New York, NY; son of Harold (an artist) and Edith Florian; married November 3, 1985; wife's name Marie; children: five. *Education:* Queens College of the City University of New York, B.A., 1973; attended School of Visual Arts, 1976.

ADDRESSES: Home—New York, NY. *Office*—500 W. 52nd St., New York, NY 10019. *E-mail*—laugheteria@aol.com.

CAREER: Author and illustrator, 1971—. Lecturer at elementary schools. *Exhibitions:* Work exhibited at Society of Illustrators show, 1993.

AWARDS, HONORS: Outstanding Science Trade Book for Children designation, National Science Teachers Association/Children's Book Council, 1987, for *A Winter Day,* and 1992, for *Vegetable Garden;* Parents' Choice Award for story book, 1991, for *An Auto Mechanic;* Gold Medal for poetry, National Parenting Publications Awards, 1994, Lee Bennett Hopkins Award for poetry, 1995, and American Library Association Notable Book citation, all for *Beast Feast;* Reading Magic Award, *Parenting,* 1994, for *Bing Bang Boing;* International Board on Books for Young People honor list inclusion, for *Discovering Seashells;* Claudia Lewis Award for Poetry, 2001, for *Mammalabilia;* Gryphon Award, Center for Children's Books, 2004, for *Bow Wow Meow Meow;* named Children's Book Council Young People's Poetry Poet, 2006.

WRITINGS:

FOR CHILDREN; SELF-ILLUSTRATED

A Bird Can Fly, Greenwillow (New York, NY), 1980.
The City, Crowell (New York, NY), 1982.
People Working, Crowell (New York, NY), 1983.
Airplane Ride, Crowell (New York, NY), 1984.
Discovering Butterflies, Scribner (New York, NY), 1986.
Discovering Trees, Scribner (New York, NY), 1986.
Discovering Frogs, Scribner (New York, NY), 1986.
Discovering Seashells, Scribner (New York, NY), 1986.
A Winter Day, Greenwillow (New York, NY), 1987.
A Summer Day, Greenwillow (New York, NY), 1988.
Nature Walk, Greenwillow (New York, NY), 1989.
Turtle Day, Crowell (New York, NY), 1989.
A Year in the Country, Greenwillow (New York, NY), 1989.
A Beach Day, Greenwillow (New York, NY), 1990.
City Street, Greenwillow (New York, NY), 1990.
Vegetable Garden, Harcourt (San Diego, CA), 1991.
At the Zoo, Greenwillow (New York, NY), 1992.
Monster Motel: Poems and Paintings, Harcourt (San Diego, CA), 1993.
Bing Bang Boing: Poems and Drawings, Harcourt (San Diego, CA), 1994.
Beast Feast, Harcourt (San Diego, CA), 1994.

On the Wing: Bird Poems and Paintings, Harcourt (San Diego, CA), 1996.
In the Swim: Poems and Paintings, Harcourt (San Diego, CA), 1997.
Insectlopedia: Poems and Paintings, Harcourt (San Diego, CA), 1998.
Laugh-eteria: Poems and Drawings, Harcourt (San Diego, CA), 1999.
Winter Eyes: Poems and Paintings, Greenwillow (New York, NY), 1999.
Lizards, Frogs, and Polliwogs: Poems and Paintings, Harcourt (San Diego, CA), 2000.
Mammalabilia: Poems and Paintings, Harcourt (San Diego, CA), 2000.
A Pig Is Big, Greenwillow (New York, NY), 2000.
Summersaults: Poems and Paintings, Greenwillow (New York, NY), 2002.
Autumnblings: Poems and Paintings, Greenwillow (New York, NY), 2003.
Bow Wow Meow Meow: It's Rhyming Cats and Dogs: Poems and Paintings, Harcourt (San Diego, CA), 2003.
Omnibeasts: Animal Poems and Paintings, Harcourt (Orlando, FL), 2004.
Zoo's Who: Poems and Paintings, Harcourt (Orlando, FL), 2005.
Handsprings: Poems and Paintings, Greenwillow (New York, NY), 2006.
Comets, Stars, the Moon, and Mars: Space Poems and Paintings, Harcourt (Orlando, FL), 2007.

"HOW WE WORK" SERIES

An Auto Mechanic, Greenwillow (New York, NY), 1991.
A Carpenter, Greenwillow (New York, NY), 1991.
A Potter, Greenwillow (New York, NY), 1991.
A Chef, Greenwillow (New York, NY), 1992.
A Painter, Greenwillow (New York, NY), 1993.
A Fisher, Greenwillow (New York, NY), 1994.

ILLUSTRATOR:

(With Kristin Linklater) *Freeing the Natural Voice,* Drama Books, 1976.
Dorothy O. Van Woerkom, *Tit for Tat,* Greenwillow (New York, NY), 1977.
Thomas M. Cook and Robert A. Russell, *Introduction to Management Science,* Prentice-Hall (Englewood Cliffs, NJ), 1979.

Mirra Ginsburg, adaptor, *The Night It Rained Pancakes*, Greenwillow (New York, NY), 1980.

Bill Adler, *What Is a Cat?: For Everyone Who Has Ever Loved a Cat*, Morrow (New York, NY), 1987.

Mary Lyn Ray, *A Rumbly Tumbly Glittery Gritty Place*, Harcourt (San Diego, CA), 1993.

Tony Johnston, *Very Scary*, Harcourt (San Diego, CA), 1995.

Contributor of illustrations to periodicals, including *New Yorker, New York Times, Nation, Travel & Leisure*, and *Across the Board*.

OTHER

See for Your Self ("Meet the Author" series), Richard C. Owen (Katonah, NY), 2005.

SIDELIGHTS: Although he has been writing and illustrating children's books for many years, Douglas Florian did not receive special attention until he moved from writing nonfiction to creating self-illustrated collections of nonsense verse. The silly poems and imaginative artwork in books such as *Beast Feast, Mammalabilia: Poems and Paintings, Insectlopedia: Poems and Paintings,* and the seasonal self-illustrated *Autumnblings* and *Summersaults*, have prompted some reviewers to compare Florian to Ogden Nash, a famous writer of free verse. Other well-known poet/illustrators that have been compared to Florian include Jack Prelutsky, Shel Silverstein, and John Ciardi.

The son of artist Hal Florian, Douglas Florian decided to follow in his father's footsteps at age ten. As Florian later recalled on *Embracing the Child* online: "I studied drawing with many teachers, but my first was my father. He taught me to love nature in all of its forms." At age fifteen, Florian attended a summer painting course at New York's School of Visual Arts and he enjoyed the experience so much that he decided to make art his career. "When I walked into the school's large studio filled with paint-encrusted easels, vivid palettes, and the smell of linseed oil," Florian explained in a Harcourt Brace publicity release, "I knew then and there I was going to be an artist." He later attended Queens College, studying under the Caldecott award-winning illustrator Marvin Bileck. "He taught me to treat a drawing like a person: with love and affection," Florian noted in *Embracing the Child.*

Florian soon discovered that desire alone was not enough to make it as an artist. The hard work of honing his skills did not pay off until he was twenty-one years old and saw his first drawings published in the *New York Times.* He continued to produce work for a variety of magazines, but eventually grew tired of working to meet deadlines. When his illustrations for Mirra Ginsburg's *The Night It Rained Pancakes* earned praise from critics, Florian turned his focus to children's books. He began working on a series of nonfiction titles, teaching children about nature in one volume of his "Discovering" series and introducing them to adult occupations such chef and auto mechanic in another.

Despite these first efforts, it would ultimately be Florian's self-illustrated poetry collections that earned the author/artist the most praise. When asked how he made the transition to verse, he explained on *Embracing the Child:* "One day at a flea market, I bought a book of poems called *Oh, That's Ridiculous,* edited by William Cole. The poems in that book were so funny that I was inspired to write some of my own. A few early poems wound up in my book *Monster Motel: Poems and Paintings,* and others in *Bing Bang Boing: Poems and Drawings.*"

Florian received praise for both these early nonsense verse collections. With *Monster Motel* the author created fourteen poems about remarkable creatures, including the "Gazzygoo" and the "Fabled Feerz," accompanying each with pen-and-ink and watercolor illustrations. "Similar in style to the works of Jack Prelutsky," Kay Weisman remarked in *Booklist,* "this will make an excellent choice for youngsters." *School Library Journal* contributor Lauralyn Persson concluded in her review of *Monster Motel* that "Florian's seemingly simple watercolors grow more intriguing with each new book." In a *School Library Journal* review of *Bing Bang Boing,* Kathleen Whalin complimented Florian's "control of the medium," comparing his work to that of Ciardi.

Discussing his initial attraction to verse forms with *Booklist* interviewer Gillian Engberg, Florian noted: "I didn't want to be tied down to the literal." "I just felt that I wanted to be able to flex my imagination a little bit more—," the poet added, "to use my so called poetic license (I get it renewed every six months by the way)." Asked how he handles children's questions about breaking the rules of grammar, spelling, and writing, Florian replied: "I tell them that they should do whatever they have to do to make their poems better, even if it means putting words upside down, or backwards, or spelling words wrong, or using bad grammar. . . . The only rule in poetry is that it has to work."

Following his own instructions for writing children's verse, Florian has produce an award-winning series of books about creatures big and small in *Beast Feast.* A collection of lighthearted poems that feature animals of all types, *Beast Feast* took a great deal of effort on Florian's part to complete. "I actually wrote eighty poems and painted more than fifty watercolors for the book," the author/illustrator said in his publicity release, "and then my editor and I picked the ones we like the best. We wanted *Beast Feast* to be absolutely first-rate."

Earning its author the National Parenting Publications Gold Medal award for poetry along with the Lee Bennett Hopkins Award for poetry in 1995, *Beast Feast* includes twenty-one carefully selected poems and illustrations. A *Kirkus Reviews* contributor described the work as "subtle, sophisticated, and quite charming." The poems in the collection rely on alliteration and puns based on animal names that invite the verses to be read aloud to children. "Florian's distinctive, full-page watercolors are as playful as his verse," a *Publishers Weekly* reviewer noted, calling the book an "ideal read-aloud." Also remarking on the useful factual information about animals that Florian incorporates into his poems, Lee Bock commented in *School Library Journal* that Florian "knows what children find funny" and deemed *Beast Feast* "a wonderful book."

Florian followed *Beast Feast* with *On the Wing: Bird Poems and Paintings, In the Swim: Poems and Paintings, Insectlopedia, Mammalabilia,* and *Lizards, Frogs, and Polliwogs: Poems and Paintings. On the Wing* offers readers twenty-one poems that focus on a variety of birds, while *In the Swim* presents the same number of poems about water-loving creatures. Writing in *Booklist,* Carolyn Phelan claimed that the appeal of *On the Wing* "lies in its fluent wordplay and generous use of humor in both the poetry and the paintings." Commenting on *In the Swim, Horn Book* contributor Roger Sutton reported that "these clipped verses splash with mischief and wit." In a review of the same book, *School Library Journal* critic Ellen D. Warwick observed: "What's unusual here is the sheer, unforced playfulness, the ease and fluidity informing both verse and pictures."

Continuing his nature theme in *Insectlopedia,* Florian again collects twenty-one short poems, this time entertaining young readers with the uniqueness of dif-

ferent types of bugs. Covering everything from worms and beetles to termites and mayflies, Florian's poems received high praise from reviewers, particularly with regard to his efforts to capture the spirit of the verse in his accompanying watercolor illustrations. "Readers may not be able to stop looking at the inventive watercolor-and-collage illustrations," predicted a *Publishers Weekly* reviewer, the critic going on to add that Florian's "silly, imaginative verses . . . (almost) match the exquisite pictures in playfulness and wit." Phelan, writing in *Booklist,* stated that "the clever artwork, deftly constructed, and the entertaining collection of insect and arachnid verse it illustrates will delight readers." "There are other books of poetry about insects and lots of collections of humorous verses about animals," concluded *School Library Journal* critic Carolyn Angus, "but none match *Insectlopedia.*"

Similar high marks were awarded to both *Mammalabilia* and *Lizards, Frogs, and Polliwogs.* Through the twenty-one poems in *Mammalabilia,* Florian covers a wide-range of animals, both familiar and exotic, among them an aardvark, a fox, and a tapir. Citing in particular the author/illustrator's unique gouache artwork, *New York Times* reviewer Cynthia Zarin remarked that Florian's "combination of . . . winsome pictures and often inspired text transforms the animals he scrutinizes into boarders at his own personal bestiary: they're Florianized." Describing the book as an "irresistible homage to mammal memorabilia," a *Publishers Weekly* critic noticed that the poet's "humor is eccentric, but just right for his target audience." Comparing *Mammalabilia* to its creator's earlier successes *Insectlopedia* and *On the Wing, Booklist* contributor John Peters found the book "ideal for reading aloud, to one listener or to a crowd."

Taking up the cause of reptiles and amphibians, Florian combines short, playful verse with watercolor illustrations to produce *Lizards, Frogs, and Polliwogs.* Constructing poems and pictures that feature such unlikely creatures as geckoes, Gila monsters, and skinks, the author/illustrator again reaped warm words from critics. "This one stands up to the rest," remarked *School Library Journal* reviewer Nina Lindsay, the critic going on to say that, "beautifully designed, this title is as irresistible as Florian's others." A contributor to *Publishers Weekly* pointed out that, in addition to the "mischievous reptile lore that will make young readers laugh," Florian has added a new dimension to his artwork. "These frogs and friends don't necessarily jump out at readers," according to the critic, "but continually take them by surprise."

Animals, animals, and more animals—from slugs to lizards, to sharp-toothed sharks—make an appearance in *Zoo's Who*, while creatures more familiar to young readers take a bow in *Bow Wow Meow Meow: It's Raining Cats and Dogs*. As expected, Florian's fans can continue to indulge in the "simple joys of playing with language and imagery," as a *Kirkus Reviews* writer assured readers of the twenty-one verses in *Zoo's Who*, and *Christian Science Monitor* reviewer Jenny Sawyer praised the poet for his "laugh-out-loud linguistic cleverness." While household pets prove endearing in *Bow Wow Meow Meow*, their wildhearted cousins—wolves and predatory big cats—illustrate the species' more exaggerated characteristics in several of the twenty-one poems included. Noting that the collection is typical of Florian's high standards, Joanna Rudge Long made particular note of the illustrations in the book. "Luscious with offbeat color, [and] composed with wit and grace, Florian's art not only illustrates his verse, it's a pleasure as pure design," Long noted in *Horn Book*, praising *Bow Wow Meow Meow* as a celebration of pets and their people. Some of the most popular animal verses from Florian's books—including *Bow Wow Meow Meow*—are also collected in *Omnibeasts: Animal Poems and Paintings*, which gives children new to Florian's art a healthy dose of whimsical wordplay topped by his colorful art.

Florian moves from the earth's residents to its four seasons in the poetry collections *Winter Eyes, Handsprings, Summersaults,* and *Autumnblings,* all which pair humorous verse and engaging art. In *Winter Eyes* he treats readers to forty-eight short poems that explore the bright and dark sides of the last season of the year. Some verses focus on the joys of cold-weather activities such as sledding, skating, and ice fishing, the poet nonetheless echoing the complaints of some that winter is just too cold and lasts too long. Noting the volume's "appealing" artwork, *New York Times* contributor Tiana Norgren added in her review of *Winter Eyes* that "the beautiful washes of watercolor that make the snow, ice, thawed earth, and pink sunset sky so convincing are punctuated by cheerful penciled patches of bright orange, blue, and hot pink." In a *School Library Journal* review, Shawn Brommer predicted that "this book will be as welcome as a warm cup of cocoa after a long day of making snowmen and turning figure eights." *Horn Book* reviewer Roger Sutton found "the rhymes are just predictable enough—without being boring—to make [*Winter Eyes*] . . . a good choice for newly independent readers."

Florian allows readers to enjoy warmer weather in both *Handsprings*, which a *Kirkus Reviews* writer described

as a "thoughtful but humorous look at the joys of spring," and *Summersaults*. In twenty-eight poems that a *Publishers Weekly* contributor described as "overflowing . . . with inventive verses celebrating the delights and discontents of summer," *Summersaults* brims with images of those lazy, crazy days: from flies and fleas and grasshoppers to a refreshing bite of watermelon to a day spent at the beach or skateboarding with friends. "Each poem distills one aspect of summer life into a small, polished shell full of rich vocabulary," noted a *Kirkus Reviews* writer, the critic adding that *Summersaults* "is children's poetry at its best." Scrolling further through the seasons, *Autumnblings* begins the move to fall, as patchwork words and engaging rhymes are as animated as windblown autumn leaves. In *School Library Journal* Susan Scheps noted the "childlike style of the various-sized watercolor and colored-pencil paintings" Florian pairs with his playful verse, while GraceAnne A. DeCandido cited the use of varied typefaces as well as the author/illustrator's talent for "Using rhyme, meter, and . . . puns to good effect," in her *Booklist* review of *Autumnblings*.

Children attracted to the rhymes of "Shel Silverstein and Jack Prelutsky and other purveyors of nonsense" are bound to enjoy *Laugh-eteria*, according to *School Library Reviewer* Barbara Chatton. In this collection of short verse, Florian takes on topics familiar to children, including school, dinosaurs, and eating strange foods. "Kids won't have to force their laughter while reading Florian's . . . pithy verses," observed a *Publishers Weekly* critic. Writing in *Booklist*, Phelan remarked: "Often clever, occasionally gross, the short rhymes appeal to an elementary-school child's sense of humor."

In *A Pig Is Big*, a picture book designed for younger readers, Florian explores the concept of size as a pig is compared to larger and larger objects. On each page, a pig shows his relative size next to other things, beginning with a hat before moving on to other animals and concluding with the entire universe. While admitting that the later pages feature vocabulary that might be out of a preschooler's grasp, a *Publishers Weekly* contributor nonetheless felt the book's "presentation is clever and humorous, well suited for elementary school children prepared to grasp the size of [the] universe." "Florian's illustrations, watercolors with colored pencils, expand the text to make this a satisfying book," claimed Phelan.

Called "one of the most remarkable contemporary versers for young readers" by *Bulletin of the Center for*

Children's Books contributor Deborah Stevenson, Florian continues to build upon his well-established reputation as a poet who understands how to delight children and present poetry in an way that appeals to them. Appreciated for his illustrations as well as his verse, he persists, according to critics, in taking both his art work and poetry to new levels. "While it's never possible to have too much good poetry, children's literature is particularly blessed with a fullness in this area," continued Stevenson, adding: "Florian is one of those blessings."

BIOGRAPHICAL AND CRITICAL SOURCES:

PERIODICALS

Booklist, March 15, 1993, Kay Weisman, review of *Monster Motel: Poems and Paintings,* p. 1351; September 15, 1993, Carolyn Phelan, review of *A Painter;* February 15, 1994; August, 1994; March 15, 1996, Carolyn Phelan, review of *On the Wing: Bird Poems and Paintings,* p. 1258; March 15, 1998, Carolyn Phelan, review of *Insectlopedia: Poems and Paintings,* p. 1240; March 15, 1999, Carolyn Phelan, review of *Laugh-eteria,* p. 1340; March 15, 2000, Gillian Engberg, interview with Florian, p. 1382; March 15, 2000, John Peters, review of *Mammalabilia: Poems and Paintings,* p. 1380; September 15, 2000, Carolyn Phelan, review of *A Pig Is Big,* p. 247; April 1, 2002, Gillian Engberg, review of *Summersaults: Poems and Paintings,* p. 1330; February 1, 2003, Gillian Engberg, review of *Bow Wow Meow Meow: It's Raining Cats and Dogs,* p. 994; August, 2003, GraceAnne A. DeCandido, review of *Autumnblings: Poems and Paintings,* p. 1985; October 15, 2004, Diane Foote, review of *Omnibeasts: Animal Poems and Paintings,* p. 407; March 15, 2005, Ilene Cooper, review of *Zoo's Who: Poems and Paintings,* p. 1290; March 15, 2006, Hazel Rochman, review of *Handsprings: Poems and Paintings,* p. 48.

Bulletin of the Center for Children's Books, December, 1992, p. 110; July-August, 1994, p. 355; November, 1994, p. 77; May, 2002, review of *Summersaults,* p. 322; April, 2003, review of *Bob Wow Meow Meow,* p. 312; September, 2003, Deborah Stevenson, review of *Autumnblings,* p. 13; May, 2005, review of *Zoo's Who,* p. 381; March, 2006, April Spisak, review of *Handsprings,* p. 311.

Christian Science Monitor, November 15, 2005, Jenny Sawyer, review of *Zoo's Who,* p. 16.

Horn Book, December, 1980, p. 632; July, 1997, Roger Sutton, review of *In the Swim,* p. 470; November, 1999, Roger Sutton, review of *Winter Eyes: Poems and Paintings,* p. 752; March, 2000, review of *Mammalabilia,* p. 204; May, 2001, Martha V. Parravano, review of *Lizards, Frogs, and Polliwogs,* p. 342; July-August, 2002, Joanna Rudge Long, review of *Summersaults,* p. 478; May-June, 2003, review of *Bow Wow Meow Meow,* p. 363; November-December, 2003, Joanna Rudge Long, review of *Autumnblings,* p. 759; May-June, 2005, Martha V. Parravano, review of *Zoo's Who,* p. 336; March-April, 2006, Joanna Rudge Long, review of *Handsprings,* p. 201.

Kirkus Reviews, March 1, 1983, review of *People Working;* April 15, 1994, review of *Beast Feast;* March 1, 2002, review of *Summersaults,* p. 333; March 15, 2003, review of *Bow Wow Meow Meow,* p. 466; July 15, 2003, review of *Autumnblings,* p. 963; April 1, 2005, review of *Zoo's Who,* p. 416; February 15, 2006, review of *Handsprings,* p. 182.

New York Times, November 21, 1999, Tiana Norgren, review of *Winter Eyes,* p. 41; November 19, 2000, Cynthia Zarin, review of *Mammalabilia,* p. 46; December 3, 2000, Allison Steele, review of *A Pig Is Big,* p. 85.

Publishers Weekly, April 1, 1983, review of *People Working,* p. 60; March 7, 1994, review of *Beast Feast;* March 9, 1998, review of *Insectlopedia,* pp. 69-70; April 19, 1999, review of *Laugh-eteria,* p. 73; March 13, 2000, review of *Mammalabilia,* p. 84; October 9, 2000, review of *A Pig Is Big,* p. 87; March 12, 2001, review of *Lizards, Frogs, and Polliwogs,* p. 90; April 29, 2002, review of *Summersaults,* p. 70; February 10, 2003, review of *Bow Wow Meow Meow,* p. 187; June 30, 2003, review of *Autumnblings,* p. 77.

School Library Journal, August, 1982, Mary B. Nickerson, review of *The City,* p. 96; June, 1993, Lauralyn Persson, review of *Monster Motel;* May, 1994; Lee Bock, review of *Beast Feast;* September, 1994, Tom S. Hurlburt, review of *A Fisher,* p. 207; November, 1994, Kathleen Whalin, review of *Bing Bang Boing;* May, 1997, Ellen D. Warwick, review of *In the Swim,* p. 119; April, 1998, Carolyn Angus, review of *Insectlopedia,* pp. 115-116; June, 1999, Barbara Chatton, review of *Laugh-eteria,* p. 114; September, 1999, Shawn Brommer, review of *Winter Eyes,* p. 212; April, 2000, Barbara Chatton, review of *Mammalabilia,* p. 119; April, 2001, Nina

Lindsay, review of *Lizards, Frogs, and Polliwogs,* p. 129; May, 2003, Susannah Price, review of *Bow Wow Meow Meow,* p. 136; October, 2003, Susan Scheps, review of *Autumnblings,* p. 149; October, 2004, Lee Bock, review of *Omnibeasts,* p. 140; April, 2005, Margaret Bush, review of *Zoo's Who,* p. 122; April, 2006, Kirsten Cutler, review of *Handsprings,* p. 124.

ONLINE

Bulletin of the Center for Children's Books Online, http://alexia.lis.uiuc.edu/puboff/bccb/ (July 7, 2001), Deborah Stevenson, "True Blue: Douglas Florian."

Children's Book Council Web site, http://www.cbcbooks.org/ (March 8, 2007), interview with Florian.

Douglas Florian Home Page, http://www.douglasflorian.com (March 8, 2006).

Embracing the Child, http://www.eyeontomorrow.com/ (June 30, 2001), "Meet Douglas Florian."

Storybook Art, http://storybookart.com/ (July 7, 2001), "Douglas Florian."

OTHER

Florian, Douglas, "Artist/Author at a Glance" (publicity release), Harcourt, c. 1994.

* * *

FLUKE, Joanne 1943-
(John Fischer, R.J. Fischer, a joint pseudonym, Jo Gibson, Chris Hunter, Gina Jackson, Kathryn Kirkwood)

PERSONAL: Born 1943, in MN; married to a television writer; children: five. *Education:* Degree in clinical psychology. *Hobbies and other interests:* Reading, target shooting, cooking, painting, and hosting murder mystery parties for friends.

ADDRESSES: Home—Southern CA. *E-mail*—Gr8Clues@aol.com.

CAREER: Writer. Has also worked as a counselor with adults and young adults.

MEMBER: Mystery Writers of America, Sisters in Crime, Authors' Guild.

WRITINGS:

ADULT NOVELS

The Stepchild, Dell (New York, NY), 1980.
The Other Child, Dell (New York, NY), 1983.
Winter Chill, Dell (New York, NY), 1984.
Cold Judgment, Dell (New York, NY), 1985.
Vengeance Is Mine, Dell (New York, NY), 1986.
(As John Fischer) *High Stakes,* Pocket Books (New York, NY), 1986.
(As John Fischer) *Station Break,* Pocket Books (New York, NY), 1987.
Video Kill, Pocket Books (New York, NY), 1989.
Final Appeal, Pocket Books (New York, NY), 1989.
Dead Giveaway, Pocket Books (New York, NY), 1990.
Fatal Identity, Zebra Books (New York, NY), 1993.
Deadly Memories, Zebra Books (New York, NY), 1995.
(As Chris Hunter) *Eyes,* Zebra Books (New York, NY), 1996.
(As Gina Jackson) *Caitlyn's Cowboy* (romance), Zebra Books (New York, NY), 1999.
(As Gina Jackson) *Cookies and Kisses* (romance), Zebra Books (New York, NY), 2000.

"HANNAH SWENSON" MYSTERIES

The Chocolate Chip Cookie Murder, Kensington (New York, NY), 2000.
The Strawberry Shortcake Murder, Kensington (New York, NY), 2001.
Blueberry Muffin Murder, Kensington (New York, NY), 2002.
Lemon Meringue Pie Murder, Kensington (New York, NY), 2003.
Fudge Cupcake Murder, Kensington (New York, NY), 2004.
Sugar Cookie Murder, Kensington (New York, NY), 2004.
Peach Cobbler Murder, Kensington (New York, NY), 2005.
Cherry Cheesecake Murder, Kensington (New York, NY), 2006.

YOUNG ADULT NOVELS; UNDER NAME JO GIBSON

The Dead Girl, Zebra Books (New York, NY), 1993.
The Crush, Zebra Books (New York, NY), 1994.

The Crush II, Zebra Books (New York, NY), 1994.
Slay Bells, Zebra Books (New York, NY), 1994.
My Bloody Valentine, Zebra Books (New York, NY), 1995.
The Seance, Zebra Books (New York, NY), 1996.
Wicked, Zebra Books (New York, NY), 1996.
Dance of Death, Scholastic (New York, NY), 1996.

ROMANCES; UNDER PSEUDONYM KATHRYN KIRKWOOD

A Match for Melissa, Zebra Books (New York, NY), 1998.
A Season for Samantha, Zebra Books (New York, NY), 1999.
A Husband for Holly, Zebra Books (New York, NY), 1999.
A Valentine for Vanessa, Zebra Books (New York, NY), 2000.

COAUTHOR, WITH HUSBAND; HUMOR; WRITTEN UNDER JOINT PSEUDONYM R.J. FISCHER

Baby's Guide to Raising Mom, Pinnacle (New York, NY), 1997.
Doggy Do's (and Don'ts), Pinnacle (New York, NY), 1997.
Where Would I Be without You, Mom?, Pinnacle (New York, NY), 1998.

OTHER

Contributor to *Winter Kittens,* Zebra (New York, NY), 1999, and *A Match for Mother,* Zebra (New York, NY), 1999.

Also contributor, as Joanne Fluke, to the anthology *Sugar and Spice,* Zebra (New York, NY), 2006.

SIDELIGHTS: Joanne Fluke has written suspense novels, mysteries, humorous nonfiction, and romances, under her own name and several pseudonyms. She has also written for young adults. Fluke once told *CA:* "I enjoy writing for young adults. I dislike novels that 'talk down' to teenagers and are over-simplified. I believe that teenagers and adults share common motivations, fears, and dreams. I also believe that any reader, regardless of age, enjoys a carefully plotted, intriguing story."

Typical of her adult suspense fiction is *Wicked,* published under the pseudonym Jo Gibson. In this novel, author Eve Carrington and her boyfriend, an aspiring writer, attend an elite authors' workshop together. There, Eve becomes entangled in a strange and dangerous rivalry with another writer, Angela Adams. Eve is also threatened by a psychotic killer in the novel a *Library Journal* contributor called "involving, fast-paced, and appropriately chilling."

Fluke creates a more homespun style of mystery with *The Chocolate Chip Cookie Murder,* published under her own name and the first book in the "Hannah Swenson" series of mysteries. In this book readers meet Hannah, a cookie entrepreneur who sets up shop in her Minnesota hometown after her father's death. The Cookie Jar, Swenson's café, becomes a popular spot. After a truck driver is found shot to death behind her shop, Hannah helps her brother-in-law, a deputy sheriff, track down the killer. The plot is "satisfyingly packed with plot twists and red herrings," in the opinion of a *Publishers Weekly* reviewer, and by the time it concludes, readers have also learned several delicious new cookie recipes. "This mystery is pleasant and easy to take," commented Rex E. Klett for *Library Journal.* A *Kirkus Reviews* contributor called it "a modestly entertaining debut with some delectable recipes as a bonus." The *Publishers Weekly* contributor also noted: "The Pecan Chews recipe is especially recommended."

In the sequel, *The Strawberry Shortcake Murder,* Hannah acts as a judge in a televised baking contest. The murder of one of the other judges—a known wife beater—disrupts the proceedings, and once again Hannah investigates. Rex Klett, writing in *Library Journal,* called *The Strawberry Shortcake Murder* "a comfortable, cozy read." A *Publishers Weekly* contributor wrote: "Add the ingredients of a cleverly crafted mystery and a realistic portrayal of smalltown life, and you have a superior cozy sure to leave readers satisfied . . . but hungry for more."

Blueberry Muffin Murder finds Hannah supplying cookies for the Lake Eden Winter Carnival when a popular television cooking host named Connie MacIntyre, who treats her staff and others badly, is murdered via blunt trauma to the head. When Hannah's friend, Janie Burkholtz, who worked for Connie, becomes a prime suspect, Hannah decides to find the real killer, despite being warned off the case by detective Mike Kingston, who is also one of Hannah's love interests. A *Kirkus*

Reviews contributor noted that Hannah puts "herself in peril repeatedly as she breaks into hotel rooms, steals keys, [and] pays after-hours visits to deserted shopping malls." A *Publishers Weekly* reviewer wrote that "a vivid picture of the small lake town and a well-crafted mystery provide the ingredients for yet another tempting feast that should satisfy all fans."

Hannah investigates the murder of flirtatious Rhonda Scharf in *Lemon Meringue Pie Murder*. Rhonda had inherited the Voelker property from her aunt and her body is found in the house's basement. With the rare blessing to investigate from her boyfriend, detective Kingston, Hannah enlists the help of her other boyfriend, Norman Rhoades, to solve the case. "As always, the whodunit pales before the larger question: Will Norman or Mike, or possibly both of them, pop the question," wrote a *Kirkus Reviews* contributor. A *Publishers Weekly* contributor noted that the author also provides "enticing recipes for cookies and other treats."

When the body of Lake Eden's sheriff turns up in the dumpster, Hannah is on the case in the mystery *Fudge Cupcake Murder*. Rex E. Klett, writing in the *Library Journal*, referred to the mystery as "dependable entertainment." *Sugar Cookie Murder* features Hannah investigating who murdered Martin Dubinski's wife of two days during a Christmas party. The former Las Vegas show girl is murdered with a cake cutter belonging to Hannah's mother. "Hannah still proves she's smarter than Mike [Kingston] gives her credit for," wrote a *Kirkus Reviews* contributor. A *Publishers Weekly* contributor noted the "wacky and delightful characters."

Peach Cobbler Murder begins with Shawna Lee, a rival of Hannah's for detective Mike Kingston's affection, opening a bakery that competes successfully with Hannah's own store. When Shawna is murdered, Hannah avoids being a prime suspect because she is at church attending her business partner's wedding along with most of the other residents of Lake Eden. However, Mike Kingston was not at the wedding. When Mike becomes a potential suspect, Hannah begins an investigation. A *Kirkus Reviews* contributor called *Peach Cobbler Murder* Fluke's "tastiest [mystery] yet."

In *Cherry Cheesecake Murder*, Hannah remains single, despite two marriage proposals, one from detective Mike Kingston and the other from dentist Norman Rhoades, made to her in *Peach Cobbler Murder*. When

an old college friend, Ross Barton, comes to town as a Hollywood producer, he enlists much of Hannah's family, including her mother, sister, and niece, for the film project. Tragedy strikes, however, when the film's director, Dean Lawrence, appears to accidentally shoot himself while instructing the movie's leading man in how to use a prop pistol, all of which is caught on film. Hannah, however, is suspicious and her investigation turns up foul play. A *Kirkus Reviews* contributor noted that the author "lavishes . . . attention on the mechanics of location shooting."

BIOGRAPHICAL AND CRITICAL SOURCES:

PERIODICALS

Booklist, February 15, 2001, Jenny McLarin, review of *The Strawberry Shortcake Murder,* p. 1118.
Kirkus Reviews, March 15, 2000, review of *The Chocolate Chip Cookie Murder,* p. 339; January 1, 2002, review of *Blueberry Muffin Murder,* p. 19; February 1, 2003, review of *Lemon Meringue Pie Murder,* p. 186; August 1, 2004, review of *Sugar Cookie Murder,* p. 716; February 15, 2005, review of *Peach Cobbler Murder,* p. 200; January 15, 2006, review of *Cherry Cheesecake Murder,* p. 63.
Library Journal, August, 1996, review of *Wicked,* p. 60; April 1, 2000, Rex E. Klett, review of *The Chocolate Chip Cookie Murder,* p. 135; March 1, 2001, Rex Klett, review of *The Strawberry Shortcake Murder,* p. 133; March 1, 2002, Rex E. Klett, review of *Blueberry Muffin Murder,* p. 144; March 1, 2004, Rex E. Klett, review of *Fudge Cupcake Murder,* p. 112; November 1, 2004, Rex E. Klett, review of *Sugar Cookie Murder,* p. 60; March 1, 2005, Rex E. Klett, review of *Peach Cobbler Murder,* p. 71.
Locus, December, 1993, review of *The Dead Girl,* p. 52.
Publishers Weekly, March 27, 2000, review of *The Chocolate Chip Cookie Murder,* p. 56; April 3, 2000, review of *The Chocolate Chip Cookie Murder,* p. 65; January 29, 2001, review of *The Strawberry Shortcake Mystery,* p. 68; February 4, 2002, review of *Blueberry Muffin Murder,* p. 56; January 13, 2003, review of *Lemon Meringue Pie Murder,* p. 44; September 6, 2004, review of *Sugar Cookie Murder,* p. 49; September 4, 2006, review of *Sugar and Spice,* p. 39.
Science Fiction Chronicle, June, 1994, review of *The Crush,* p. 39.

ONLINE

Hannah Swensen Mysteries Home Page, http://www. murdershebaked.com (March 7, 2007).*

* * *

FOERSTER, Richard 1949-

PERSONAL: Born October 29, 1949, in New York, NY; son of Alfons (a mechanic) and Elizabeth (a homemaker) Foerster; married Valerie Malinowski, October 28, 1972 (divorced, 1985). *Ethnicity:* "German American." *Education:* Fordham University, B.A., 1971; University of Virginia, M.A., 1972; Manhattanville College, teacher certification, 1975. *Politics:* Democrat. *Religion:* Episcopalian. *Hobbies and other interests:* Gardening.

ADDRESSES: Home—York Beach, ME. *Office*— Chautauqua Literary Journal, P.O. Box 613, Chautauqua, NY 14722. *E-mail*—rafoerster@aol.com.

CAREER: Clarence L. Barnhart, Inc., Bronxville, NY, assistant editor, 1973-76; teacher of advanced English, Bronxville, 1975; Prentice-Hall, Educational Books Division, Englewood Cliffs, NJ, language arts editor and department head, 1976-79; *Chelsea* magazine, New York, NY, associate editor, 1978-94, editor, 1994-2001; *Chautauqua Literary Journal,* Chautauqua, NY, editor, 2002—. University of Maine at Farmington, adjunct professor of creative writing, 1994, 2002, 2003; Writers' Center at Chautauqua, writer in residence, summers, 1993, 1994, 1996, 1998, 2002, 2004.

MEMBER: PEN American Center, National Book Critics Circle, Society for the Arts, Religion and Contemporary Culture (fellow).

AWARDS, HONORS: "Discovery"/*Nation* award for poetry, 1985; Brodie Herndon Memorial Prize, Poetry Society of Virginia, 1988, 1991; R.T. McDonald Award, California State University Foundation, 1990; Bess Hokin Prize, *Poetry* magazine, 1992; fellow of National Endowment for the Arts, 1995, and Maine Arts Commission, 1997; Amy Lowell poetry traveling scholarship, 2000-01; fellowships from MacDowell Colony,

1985, Virginia Center for the Creative Arts, 1987, 1988, 1991, 1995, 2006, Yaddo, 1992, 1996, 1997, Hawthornden Castle, 1993, Fundación Valparaiso, 1997 and 2007, Camargo Foundation, 1999, Tasmanian Writers' Centre, 2002, and La Napoule Arts Foundation, 2004.

WRITINGS:

Sudden Harbor (poetry), Orchises Press (Alexandria, VA), 1992.
Patterns of Descent (poetry), Orchises Press (Alexandria, VA), 1993.
Trillium (poetry), BOA Editions (Rochester, NY), 1998.
Double Going (poetry), BOA Editions (Rochester, NY), 2002.
The Burning of Troy (poetry), BOA Editions (Rochester, NY), 2006.

Also author of poetry chapbooks *"The Hours,"* Red Hydra Press (Tuscaloosa, AL), 1993; and *"Transfigured Nights"* also author of study guides for Holt, Rinehart & Winston, 1989, 1993. Work represented in anthologies. Contributor to periodicals, including *Nation, New Criterion, Southwest Review, Kenyon Review, TriQuarterly,* and *New England Review.*

SIDELIGHTS: Richard Foerster once told *CA:* "When I discovered writing as a means of artistic expression, I knew it would remain my life's work. Though I tried prose, I nevertheless failed at sustaining plots and characters over many pages, so the option of becoming a short-story writer, novelist or playwright was soon denied me. But in the lyric—whether pure or mixed with narrative—I found the vehicle for developing and sustaining a voice with which I could engage the world."

While Foerster has contributed poetry to periodicals for several years, it wasn't until 1992 that he published his first full-length collection, *Sudden Harbor.* With this work, the author established himself as a strong new voice. In the view of Robert Phillips of *Small Press,* this collection "should make clear Foerster's claim not only as one of the best of the New Formalists, but as one of the best poets of his generation." Peter Josyph, writing in *Library Journal,* called Foerster's "persona . . . intensely vulnerable . . . never precious; his elegant language is never obscure."

Robert B. Shaw, writing about *Sudden Harbor* in *Poetry,* saw Foerster as "a kind of memoirist, but his manner is distinctively his own. . . . His treatments, one might say, are less historical than archetypal." In the author's recounting of his early years as the son of German parents who moved to America, Foerster avoids "the customary cliches about the immigrant experience. The images [his poems] offer instead are more potent and primal."

Foerster's work "confirm[s] poetry's artfulness, its antiquities and classicisms," according to critic Joel Lipman of *Small Press.* Reviewing Foerster's second collection, *Patterns of Descent,* Lipman found value in the author's themes of sexuality and death, which he called "rhapsodic," and "at times masked and allusive." In *Patterns,* Foerster makes full use of the rural Maine environment he calls home. The book "is filled with images of water and water birds, growing plants, and flowers," observed *Booklist* reviewer Whitney Scott. Scott wrote that "Covenant," a poem in memory of a friend's deceased son, describes "'A hawk is soaring in tightening loops,' then 'stoops' into a pattern of descent towards its prey. This ancient ritual is compared to the future of a parent 'hurled/in grief's inhabitable hell.'" "Yet if Foerster's subjects are often bleakly existential, his tone is seldom gloomy," wrote Ben Howard in an issue of *Poetry.* "By turns reflective, wistful, and melancholy, his poems maintain an observant equanimity in the presence of transience."

In 1998 Foerster produced *Trillium,* a book that "should be in every poetry collection," *Library Journal* critic Tim Gavin suggested. Michael Scharf, while also citing Foerster's talent, gave more qualified praise for *Trillium* in his *Poetry* review: It "is the clear product of heightened senses and formal acumen, and often makes for gentle, enjoyable company. Though clearly enamored of the world, it never quite comes into its own, or compels us into its ken." However, John Hoppenthaler, writing for *Arts and Letters* commented, "Foerster *is* a nature poet of the first order," and P.H. Liotta of the *Journal* said, "The turn Foerster has taken in this book represents both a remarkable departure and an accommodating unity with his previous work."

A reviewer writing for *Publishers Weekly* said that Foerster's 2002 book *Double Going* "draws consoling connections between experience and the imagination, literature, myth." Ryan Stellabotte went into more depth on the Fordham University Web site: "the finely wrought poems in this powerful volume bear the weight of memories and losses, of childhood confusions and adult longings, and often bring an understanding that is neither facile nor sentimental."

Foerster recently told *CA:* "For me the writing of poetry is akin to playing a musical instrument or blowing glass. It is a transformative process, turning breath into patterns of sound that assume a shapeliness on the page. Recently I've been writing poems that probe the nature of deity in regard to the certainty of mortality."

BIOGRAPHICAL AND CRITICAL SOURCES:

PERIODICALS

American Book Review, March-April, 2003, Wayne Miller, review of *Double Going.*
Arts and Letters, spring, 1999, John Hoppenthaler, review of *Trillium,* p. 152.
Booklist, November 15, 1993, Whitney Scott, review of *Patterns of Descent,* p. 598.
Journal, autumn, 1998, P.H. Liotta, review of *Trillium,* p. 146.
Library Journal, May 1, 1992, Peter Josyph, review of *Sudden Harbor,* p. 85; June 15, 1998, Tim Gavin, review of *Trillium,* p. 82
Poetry, October, 1993, Robert B. Shaw, review of *Sudden Harbor,* p. 47; November, 1994, Ben Howard, review of *Patterns of Descent,* p. 109; February, 1999, Michael Scharf, review of *Trillium,* p. 322.
Publishers Weekly, November 19, 2001, review of *Double Going.*
Small Press, winter, 1993, Robert Phillips, review of *Sudden Harbor,* p. 55; spring, 1994, Joel Lipman, review of *Patterns of Descent,* p. 107.

ONLINE

Fordham University Web site, http://www.fordham.edu/ (May 15, 2007), Ryan Stellabotte, review of *Double Going.*

* * *

FORREST, Richard 1932-2005
(Lee Evans, Richard Stockton Forrest, Rebecca Morgan, Stockton Woods)

PERSONAL: Born May 8, 1932, in Orange, NJ; died of complications from pulmonary disorder, March 14, 2005; son of Williams Kraemer and Georgia Forrest;

married Frances Anne Reese, December 20, 1952 (divorced, May, 1955); married Mary Bolan Brumby (a nurse), May 11, 1955 (died, 1996); married Patricia Whitton, June 28, 1999; children: (first marriage) Richard; (second marriage) Christopher, Remley, Katherine, Mongin, Bellamy. *Education:* Attended New York Dramatic Workshop, 1950, and University of South Carolina, 1953-55. *Politics:* Democrat. *Religion:* Unitarian Universalist.

CAREER: Writer, playwright, and manager. Playwright, 1955-58; Lawyers Title Insurance Corp., Richmond, VA, state manager, 1958-68; Chicago Title Insurance Co., Chicago, IL, vice president, 1969-72; freelance writer, 1972-2005. Vice president of Connecticut Board of Title Underwriters. *Military service:* U.S. Army, Rangers, 1951-53; served in Korea; became staff sergeant.

MEMBER: Mystery Writers of America.

AWARDS, HONORS: Edgar Allan Poe Award, Mystery Writers of America, 1975, for *Who Killed Mr. Garland's Mistress?;* Porgie Award for best original paperback, *West Coast Review of Books,* for *The Laughing Man.*

WRITINGS:

MYSTERY NOVELS

Who Killed Mr. Garland's Mistress?, Pinnacle Books (New York, NY), 1974.
The Killing Edge, Tower Publications (New York, NY), 1980.
Lark, New American Library (New York, NY), 1986.

"LYON AND BEA WENTWORTH" MYSTERY SERIES

A Child's Garden of Death, Bobbs-Merrill (New York, NY), 1975.
The Wizard of Death, Bobbs-Merrill (New York, NY), 1977.
Death Through the Looking Glass, Bobbs-Merrill (New York, NY), 1978.
The Death in the Willows, Holt (New York, NY), 1979.
Death at Yew Corner, Holt (New York, NY), 1981.
Death under the Lilacs, St. Martin's Press (New York, NY), 1985.

Death on the Mississippi, St. Martin's Press (New York, NY), 1989.
The Pied Piper of Death, St. Martin's Press (New York, NY), 1997.
Death in the Secret Garden, Severn House (Sutton, England), 2004.
Death at King Arthur's Court, Severn House (Sutton, England), 2005.

UNDER PSEUDONYM STOCKTON WOODS

The Laughing Man, Fawcett (New York, NY), 1980.
Game Bet, Fawcett (New York, NY), 1981.
The Man Who Heard Too Much, Fawcett (New York, NY), 1983.
(With Mary Forrest) *The Complete Nursing Home Guide* (nonfiction), Facts on File (New York, NY), 1990.
(With Mary Forrest) *Retirement Living* (nonfiction), Facts on File (New York, NY), 1991.

"SIGN" MYSTERY SERIES FOR ADULTS WITH LIMITED READING SKILLS

Sign of the Beast, NTC/Contemporary Publishing (Chicago, IL), 1998.
Sign of Blood, NTC/Contemporary Publishing (Chicago, IL), 1998.
Sign of Terror, NTC/Contemporary Publishing (Chicago, IL), 1999.

Author of the serials *The Disappearing Airplane* and *Murder in the Big Apple,* both 1999, both twenty episode mystery stories, both published in *Asashi Weekly* (a bilingual Japanese newspaper in Tokyo, Japan).

Author of the plays *Cry for the Spring, The Meek Cry Loud,* and *The Sandhouse.*

Author of the *"Lexi Lane Nautical Mystery"* series under the pseudonym Rebecca Morgan and the *"Randy Holden Aeronautical Adventure"* series under the pseudonym Lee Evans.

Contributor of short stories to periodicals, including *Northeast Magazine, Ellery Queen Mystery Magazine,* and *Mystery Monthly.*

Several editions of Forrest's work have been published in Finnish, French, German, Italian, and Swedish. His manuscript collection is part of the Twentieth-Century Archives at Mungar Memorial Library, Boston University, Boston.

SIDELIGHTS: Richard Forrest's crime novels combine the classic puzzle plotting of traditional mysteries with the element of corruption common in detective novels. His portrayal of human pain on an individual and personal level further distinguishes his work from that of previous authors. Susan Baker, writing in *Twentieth-Century Crime and Mystery Writers,* noted that "Forrest presents this mixture [of mystery novels, detective novels, and individual human pain] in consistently graceful prose and adds reasonably restrained moments of sex and violence." Most of Forrest's novels are about Lyon Wentworth, a children's book author and former English professor. He is also a keen amateur mystery-solver who works with the chief of the Murphysville police, Rocco Herbert, whom he met in the military while serving in Korea. Wentworth's wife, Bea, is a successful, independent politician and feminist. Her access to inside information frequently comes in handy during her husband's investigations. Bea's aide is Kimberly Ward, who led welfare mothers in a protest, met Mrs. Wentworth, and stayed to work for her. Forrest's characters intentionally do not fit into neat stereotypes. Rather, his work calls the reader's attention to the assumptions of stereotypes rather than perpetuate them. Wentworth's relationship with Herbert, for example, is not characterized by the macho exchanges one might expect based on their history together; both Wentworth and Herbert display brains and brawn. Forrest's mobsters are not stereotypical pinstriped goons, either. One of them reads Proust and another has created a home in the style and spirit of a Japanese haven. His characters are not created to lecture readers, but to make subtle social comments.

In describing Wentworth's children's books, Forrest's work tells us something about the author's own reasons for writing and the appeal of the murder mystery genre. Wentworth's doctoral dissertation was written on the subject of violence in Victorian children's literature. Baker observed: "Not surprisingly, then, he is conscious of the power of literature to exorcize fears, to render private terrors manageable." Wentworth's books, like Forrest's novels, tell stories of victory over monsters. Forrest, however, came to writing along a different path than Wentworth, who studied and then taught literature

before dedicating himself to a writing career. Forrest once told *CA* that he "spent early years as a playwright until [a] growing family made business a necessity. Resigned [my] position as vice president of major insurance company on [my] fortieth birthday to write full time—why not?"

Baker summed up Forrest's work as "well-written, with thoroughly realized backgrounds and persuasively likeable characters. Occasionally in the earliest books, the machinery of planning creaks a bit too obviously, but the care and craft with which Forrest approaches his writing have led to increasing subtlety. There is nothing slapdash here; above all, Richard Forrest writes *thoughtful* mysteries, socially conscious and emotionally satisfying."

In *Death at Yew Corner,* Bea has lost her bid for re-election, but finds herself embroiled in the investigation of the death of her former philosophy teacher, found murdered at a hospital. Bea then discovers more murders, seemingly connected to labor racketeering. Before the story concludes, she faces the challenge of solving a locked-room murder. *New York Times* reviewer Newgate Callendar called the novel a "neat, well-plotted, expertly written job." *The Pied Piper of Death* finds Bea reinstalled as a U.S. senator. This time, Lyon Wentworth is involved in investigating the murder of Markham Swan, a writer who was researching the history of the wealthy Piper family but who ends up dead on the family's vast estate. As the investigation unfolds, disturbing stories of Swan's infidelity emerge, and the story takes unexpected turns involving Civil War memorabilia and family tragedy. GraceAnne A. DeCandido, writing in *Booklist,* commented that "The writing is stylish and the plotting swift and well knit: a pleasure." *Death in the Secret Garden* brings a rash of diverse deaths to the sleepy small town of Murphysboro, Connecticut. Pregnant teenager Boots Anderson is found shot dead in the state forest, and her ex-lover, car salesman Eddy Rashish, is killed by her grief-stricken father. Congressman Bill Tallman dies in the midst of clandestine sex with escort Ashley Towers. Brash church secretary Barbara Sykes is shot to death in her office. Police chief Rocco Herbert and the Wentworths search through a variety suspects, including a mentally ill Vietnam veteran, a local Lothario, and a church official, but none emerge as likely murderers. As the investigation continues, the state governor becomes convinced that Bea Wentworth is her husband's lover and sets out to destroy Bea's career and reputation. A *Kirkus Reviews* critic observed that "nobody will complain that Forrest doesn't keep the pot boiling or season the stew with occasional clues." *Booklist* contributor Emily Melton called the novel a "cleverly plotted procedural."

BIOGRAPHICAL AND CRITICAL SOURCES:

BOOKS

Twentieth-Century Crime and Mystery Writers, 3rd edition, St. James Press, 1991.

PERIODICALS

Booklist, September 1, 1997, GraceAnne A. DeCandido, review of *The Pied Piper of Death,* p. 63; December 1, 2004, Emily Melton, review of *Death in the Secret Garden,* p. 639.
Kirkus Reviews, January 15, 2005, review of *Death in the Secret Garden,* p. 85; January 1, 2006, review of *Death at King Arthur's Court,* p. 18.
New York Times, March 8, 1981, Newgate Callender, review of *The Death at Yew Corner.**

*   *   *

FORREST, Richard Stockton
     See FORREST, Richard

*   *   *

FOSTER, James D.
     See DAVID, James F.

*   *   *

FREDERICK, K.C. 1935-

PERSONAL: Born 1935, in Detroit, MI.

ADDRESSES: Home—Boston, MA.

CAREER: Writer, teacher. Teacher in the Boston, MA area.

AWARDS, HONORS: Pushcart Prize, 1986, for "Everybody's Got a Hungry Heart"; National Endowment for the Arts fellowship, 1993.

WRITINGS:

NOVELS

Country of Memory, Permanent Press (Sag Harbor, NY), 1998.
The Fourteenth Day, Permanent Press (Sag Harbor, NY), 2000.
Accomplices, Permanent Press (Sag Harbor, NY), 2003.
Inland, Permanent Press (Sag Harbor, NY), 2006.

Work represented in anthologies, including *Best American Short Stories,* 1970, 1973, 1974, 1976, 1977, and 1991; contributor of short fiction to periodicals, including *Epoch, Shenandoah, Kansas Quarterly, Ascent, Beloit Fiction Journal,* and *Ohio Review.*

SIDELIGHTS: K.C. Frederick has won several awards for his short fiction, including a Pushcart Prize. In 1998, he published a Kafkaesque first novel titled *Country of Memory.* Petir, the novel's protagonist, has a job denying claims for an insurance company in a fictional Eastern European country on which the sun rarely shines. He is being stalked by a peasant who lost a leg in an accident and wants to get even with Petir over the denial of his insurance claim. If this is not worry enough, an old acquaintance of Petir's—a childhood friend who is now a transvestite—asks Petir to stand in for him in a rendezvous with a mysterious woman. Conformist Petir uncharacteristically accepts the assignment, only to find out later that his acquaintance has been found murdered in women's clothing near a refugee camp on the outskirts of town. As the stalker draws closer, Petir seeks solace from the mysterious woman and from his ex-wife who now lives with her lesbian lover. The chaotic events in his current life serve to illuminate a suppressed memory from his childhood—his mother sending him out of the house only to blow it up with herself, his father, and his grandmother inside. Petir wins escape from both inner and outer turmoil through a final confrontation with the embittered peasant.

James Saynor, reviewing the novel for the *New York Times Book Review,* called *Country of Memory* "almost a pastiche of the twentieth-century Eastern European novel—a digest of quiet desperation, mining a vein of literary style from Kafka to Kundera." Saynor added that the novel "has an odd depressive exuberance. It amounts to Old World gloom described with irrepressible New World bounce." The critic noted the author's technique, dubbing Frederick "a fitful storyteller; the narrative pressure of his novel comes and goes in spurts, like water in an Eastern European plumbing system."

In *The Fourteenth Day,* a country has been torn apart by the events known as The Thirteen Days, and now three survivors are thrown together to face the future.

Accomplices is the story of Stivan and Anya, survivors of a five-year-old revolution in an unnamed European country. She had nursed him through his injuries and a coma that resulted from an automobile accident. Years later, he attempts to forge a romantic relationship with Anya, now suffering from breast cancer. Stivan provides refuge to Anya's brother, limousine driver Leni, who is hiding from his boss, Raffi, because Raffi's mistress died of a drug overdose while she was with Leni. Stivan, a translator, works for a priest, only to discover that he is smuggling immigrants into the country. The plot is a combination of love story and politically charged drama. A *Kirkus Reviews* contributor described it as being "a complex portrait of the intricacies of emerging freedom."

Inland is set in 1959 in the American Midwest. Ted Riley is a graduate student and English teacher whose focus does not extend to the complexities and threats of the outside world during the McCarthy era, and whose concern for his own mother's illness is also limited. He lost his first love, Sally, in a plane crash, and now falls for free spirit Dori, who, like Ted, loves horror films. Ted also becomes friendly with library worker Andrew Kesler, a Polish immigrant and alleged homosexual, whose stories and demeanor sometimes make Ted uncomfortable. Ted's life has the potential to become more exciting when a government recruiter suggests that he become a spy. A *Publishers Weekly* reviewer praised Frederick's handling of the period atmosphere and concluded by noting "the ever-present undertone of paranoia mixed with melancholy."

BIOGRAPHICAL AND CRITICAL SOURCES:

PERIODICALS

Kirkus Reviews, September 15, 1998, review of *Country of Memory;* June 1, 2003, review of *Ac-*

complices, p. 770; October 15, 2006, review of *Inland,* p. 1034.

Library Journal, October 15, 1998, Lawrence Rungren, review of *Country of Memory,* p. 97.

New York Times Book Review, December 13, 1998, James Saynor, review of *Country of Memory,* p. 30.

Publishers Weekly, July 14, 2003, review of *Accomplices,* p. 54; September 11, 2006, review of *Inland,* p. 35.*

*   *   *

FRIEDMAN, Benjamin M. 1944-

PERSONAL: Born August 5, 1944, in Louisville, KY; son of Norbert and Eva Friedman; married Barbara Cook; children: John, Jeffrey. *Education:* Harvard University, A.B. (summa cum laude), 1966, A.M., 1969, Ph.D., 1971; King's College, Cambridge, M.Sc., 1970.

ADDRESSES: Home—Cambridge, MA. *Office*—Harvard University, Department of Economics, Littauer Center 127, Cambridge, MA 02138. *E-mail*—bfriedman@harvard.edu.

CAREER: Writer, editor, educator, and economist. Federal Reserve Bank of New York, New York, NY, research assistant, 1968; Federal Reserve Bank of Boston, Boston, MA, staff consultant, 1968-69, consultant to the president, 1969-71; Federal Reserve, assistant to the director of the division of research and statistics, 1969, staff member of the federal open market committee subcommittee on the directive, 1969-70; Morgan Stanley and Co., economist, 1971-72; Harvard University, Cambridge, MA, assistant professor, 1972-76, associate professor, 1976-80, professor of economics, 1980-89, William Joseph Maier Professor of Political Economy, 1989—, economics department chair, 1991—, director of undergraduate studies.

MEMBER: Phi Beta Kappa.

AWARDS, HONORS: John Henry Williams Prize, Harvard University, 1966; Marshall Scholar, 1966-68; junior fellow, Harvard University Society of Fellows, 1968-71; David Horowitz Prize, Bank of Israel, 1982; George S. Eccles Prize, Columbia University Graduate

School of Business, 1989, for *Day of Reckoning: The Consequences of American Economic Policy under Reagan and After;* John R. Commons Award, 2005, for achievements in economics and service to the economics profession.

WRITINGS:

Economic Stabilization Policy: Methods in Optimization, American Elsevier (New York, NY), 1975.

Monetary Policy in the United States: Design and Implementation, Association of Reserve City Bankers (Chicago, IL), 1981.

Day of Reckoning: The Consequences of American Economic Policy under Reagan and After, Random House (New York, NY), 1988.

Implications of Increasing Corporate Indebtedness for Monetary Policy, Group of Thirty (New York, NY), 1990.

(With Jonas Agell and Mats Persson) *Does Debt Management Matter?,* Oxford University Press (New York, NY), 1992.

Risks and Impediments to U.S. Economic Expansion, Cambridge Energy Research Associates (Cambridge, MA), 2003.

Deficits and Debt in the Short and Long Run, National Bureau of Economic Research (Cambridge, MA), 2005.

The Moral Consequences of Economic Growth, Knopf (New York, NY), 2005.

What Remains from the Volcker Experiment?, National Bureau of Economic Research (Cambridge, MA), 2005.

EDITOR AND CONTRIBUTOR

New Challenges to the Role of Profit, Lexington Books (Lexington, MA), 1978.

The Changing Roles of Debt and Equity in Financing U.S. Capital Formation, University of Chicago Press (Chicago, IL), 1982.

Corporate Capital Structures in the United States, University of Chicago Press (Chicago, IL), 1985.

Financing Corporate Capital Formation, University of Chicago Press (Chicago, IL), 1986.

(With Frank H. Hahn) *Handbook of Monetary Economics,* American Elsevier (New York, NY), 1990

Should the United States Privatize Social Security?, MIT Press (Cambridge, MA), 1999.

(And author of introduction) James J. Heckman and Alan B. Krueger, *Inequality in America: What Role for Human Capital Policies?,* MIT Press (Cambridge, MA), 2003.

Harvard Magazine, director, 1984-90, incorporator, beginning 1991.

Contributor to periodicals, including *Journal of Political Economy, Review of Economics and Statistics, New England Economic Review, Journal of Money, Credit, and Banking, Journal of Finance, Harvard Business Review, New York Times, Wall Street Journal, New York Review of Books,* and *Challenge.*

OTHER

Contributor to *The New Palgrave: A Dictionary of Economics,* volume 1, edited by Eatwell, Milgate, and Newman, Macmillan, 1987.

SIDELIGHTS: Benjamin M. Friedman, an investment banking expert and Harvard University professor, is the author of *Day of Reckoning: The Consequences of American Economic Policy under Reagan and After,* in which he explores the fiscal strategy known as "Reaganomics" and its potential negative effects on the nation's finances. Supply-side economics, which was instituted in the early 1980s by President Ronald Reagan, involves reducing taxes in order to stimulate economic activity. However, Friedman writes, this was intended to be accompanied by a decrease in government spending. When this failed to occur, the government budget deficit began increasing, approaching 2.8 trillion dollars in 1988. This debt, combined with the expectation of future deficit, resulted in higher interest rates, which discouraged investment in domestic exports, while encouraging the government to borrow abroad. In this manner, the U.S. was rapidly becoming a nation of "tenants," rather than "owners," which, according to the author, would ultimately conflict with the nation's collective self-image. Because the U.S. could no longer compete in the world market, the author predicted in *Day of Reckoning* an end to "the material basis for the progress that has marked Americans' perceptions of themselves and their society since its very beginnings." He expected not only a decrease in the standard of living in the U.S., but also a loss of American sovereignty on the international front. Friedman urged the government to begin paying its debt, even though the task would not be easily accomplished without causing a recession or a depression. He recommended new taxes—either a consumption tax or a three percent income tax increase—and cuts in social security and defense spending in order to help reduce the deficit. The author concluded the work with a warning: "If we do not correct America's fiscal course, our children and our children's children will have the right to hold us responsible." *Los Angeles Times Book Review* contributor James Flanigan called *Day of Reckoning* "a work of scholarship that offers an economic education in itself." Christopher Lehmann-Haupt, writing in the *New York Times,* praised the book as "a lucid discussion of vital issues. . . . Every citizen ought to read it."

In *The Moral Consequences of Economic Growth,* Friedman offers a "compelling argument that rising incomes make us not just richer people, but better ones," commented Megan McArdle in *Reason.* When times are good and economic growth is stable, society is more able to attend to social programs, tends to give more to charitable causes, and is less concerned with competition and "catching up" with others who may have more. "The real benefit of growth, Friedman argues, is that it encourages a wide range of social virtues, including dedication to democracy, tolerance of diversity, social mobility, and commitment to fairness," noted Michael Mandel in *Business Week.* Conversely, in times of economic downturns, when money is tight and jobs are scarce, society tends to move inward, and individuals are more apt to protect their assets at the expense of others. Nativist and racist movements flourish in such times, when distrust of outsiders is high and individuals can easily come to believe that their resources are being exploited or appropriated by others. Friedman sees the Ku Klux Klan and the Nazis as extreme examples of groups that rise during economic stagnation and down times. To prevent such from occurring, and to ensure a consistent level of economic growth and application of coincident moral behavior, "Friedman argues that governments everywhere should focus policy on creating the broad prosperity that will allow their societies to become more open, tolerant, and generous," remarked McArdle. *Cato Journal* contributor Will Wilkinson assessed Friedman's work as demonstrating strong positive and negative characteristics, stating that the book "is magnificent and flawed. It is a work of astounding scholarship and exhilarating intellectual imagination as

well as disappointing partisanship and theoretical fragility." However, other reviewers, such as Kenneth G. Elzinga in *Books & Culture,* called it an "important book on an important subject." The author "has, without question, an impressive command of worldwide economic/technological history, and this book is a treasure trove of arresting details," remarked Dan Seligman in *Commentary. Booklist* contributor Mary Whaley commended Friedman's "scholarly and valuable approach to sophisticated economic and moral challenges," while a *Publishers Weekly* reviewer concluded that Friedman's work is a "lucid, judiciously reasoned call for renewed attention to broad-based economic advancement."

BIOGRAPHICAL AND CRITICAL SOURCES:

BOOKS

Friedman, Benjamin M., *Day of Reckoning: The Consequences of American Economic Policy under Reagan and After,* Random House (New York, NY), 1988.

PERIODICALS

Booklist, October 15, 2005, Mary Whaley, review of *The Moral Consequences of Economic Growth,* p. 24.
Books & Culture, January-February, 2006, Kenneth G. Elzinga, "Why Growth is Good," review of *The Moral Consequences of Economic Growth,* p. 34.
Business Week, November 7, 2005, Michael Mandel, "What's So Good about Growth," review of *The Moral Consequences of Economic Growth,* p. 144.
Cato Journal, winter, 2006, Will Wilkinson, review of *The Moral Consequences of Economic Growth,* p. 201.
Commentary, December, 2005, Dan Seligman, "Good and Plenty," review of *The Moral Consequences of Economic Growth,* p. 78.
Economist, November 12, 2005, "Why the Rich Must Get Richer; Economic Growth," review of *The Moral Consequences of Economic Growth,* p. 87.
Europe Intelligence Wire, October 11, 2006, "Harvard Economist to Speak at Rotman School on *Moral Consequences of Economic Growth.*
Library Journal, September 15, 2005, Lawrence R. Maxted, review of *The Moral Consequences of Economic Growth,* p. 74.

Los Angeles Times Book Review, October 16, 1988, James Flanigan, review of *Day of Reckoning,* p. 1.

New Yorker, October 31, 2005, review of *The Moral Consequences of Economic Growth,* p. 87.

New York Times, October 24, 1988, Christopher Lehmann-Haupt, review of *Day of Reckoning,* p. 19.

New York Times Book Review, October 23, 1988, Adam Smith, review of *Day of Reckoning,* p. 41.

Publishers Weekly, September 5, 2005, review of *The Moral Consequences of Economic Growth,* p. 53.

Reason, July, 2006, Megan McArdle, "The Virtue of Riches: How Wealth Makes Us More Moral," review of *The Moral Consequences of Economic Growth,* p. 53.

ONLINE

Harvard University Department of Economics Web site, http://www.economics.harvard.edu/ (January 2, 2007), biography of Benjamin M. Friedman.*

G

GALVIN, Brendan 1938-

PERSONAL: Born October 20, 1938, in Everett, MA; son of James Russell (a letter carrier) and Rose Galvin; married Ellen Baer, August 1, 1968; children: Kim, Peter, Anne Maura. *Education:* Boston College, B.S., 1961; Northeastern University, M.A., 1964; University of Massachusetts at Amherst, M.F.A., 1967, Ph.D., 1970.

ADDRESSES: Home—Durham, CT; Truro, MA. *Office*—Department of English, East Carolina University, Bate Building 2202, Greenville, NC 27858-4353; fax: 252-328-4889.

CAREER: Writer and educator. Northeastern University, Boston, MA, instructor in English, 1963-65; Slippery Rock State College, Slippery Rock, PA, assistant professor of English, 1968-69; Central Connecticut State University, New Britain, assistant professor, 1969-74, associate professor, 1974-80, professor of English, 1980—; East Carolina University, Greenville, NC, professor of English and Whichard Distinguished Chair in the Humanities. Founder and director of Connecticut Writers Conference; visiting writer, Connecticut College, 1975-76; affiliated with Wesleyan-Suffield Writer-Reader Conference, 1977-78, Martha's Vineyard Poetry Seminar, 1986; Coal Royalty Visiting Chair in creative writing, University of Alabama, Tuscaloosa, spring, 1993; Windham Robertson Visiting Writer in Residence, Hollins College; visiting writer, Loyola University-New Orleans; visiting writer, Western Carolina University.

AWARDS, HONORS: Fine Arts Work Center fellowship, 1971; National Endowment for the Arts creative writing fellowship, 1974, 1988; Artist Foundation fellowship, 1978; New England Film Festival, first prize, 1978, for *Massachusetts Story;* Connecticut Commission on the Arts fellowship, 1981, 1984; Guggenheim fellow, 1988; Sotheby Prize, Arvon Foundation, 1988; Levinson Prize, *Poetry* magazine, 1989; O.B. Hardison, Jr., Poetry Prize, Folger Shakespeare Library, 1991; Outstanding Academic Book, American Library Association, 1993, for *Saints in Their Ox-Hide Boat;* Charity Randall Citation, International Poetry Forum, 1994; Iowa Poetry Prize, 1997, for *Hotel Malabar;* National Book Award finalist, 2005, for *Habitat: New and Selected Poems, 1965-2005;* Aiken Taylor Award, *Sewanee Review,* for the work of a career.

WRITINGS:

POETRY

The Narrow Land, Northeastern University Press (Boston, MA), 1971.

The Salt Farm, Fiddlehead (Fredericton, New Brunswick, Canada), 1972.

No Time for Good Reasons, University of Pittsburgh Press (Pittsburgh, PA), 1974.

The Minutes No One Owns, University of Pittsburgh Press (Pittsburgh, PA), 1977.

Atlantic Flyway, University of Georgia Press (Athens, GA), 1980.

Winter Oysters, University of Georgia Press (Athens, GA), 1983.

A Birder's Dozen, Ampersand Press (Princeton, NJ), 1984.

Seals in the Inner Harbor, Carnegie-Mellon University Press (Pittsburgh, PA), 1985.

Raising Irish Walls (chapbook) Ampersand Press (Princeton, NJ), 1989.

Wampanoag Traveler: Being, in Letters, the Life and Times of Loranzo Newcomb, American and Natural Historian, Louisiana State University Press (Baton Rouge, LA), 1989.

Great Blue: New and Selected Poems, University of Illinois Press (Champaign, IL), 1990.

Early Returns, Carnegie-Mellon University Press (Pittsburgh, PA), 1992.

Saints in Their Ox-Hide Boat, Louisiana State University Press (Baton Rouge, LA), 1992.

Islands (chapbook) Druid City Press (Tuscaloosa, AL), 1993.

Sky and Island Light, Louisiana State University Press (Baton Rouge, LA), 1995.

Hotel Malabar, University of Iowa Press (Iowa City, IA), 1998.

The Strength of a Named Thing, Louisiana State University Press (Baton Rouge, LA), 1999.

Place Keepers, Louisiana State University Press (Baton Rouge, LA), 2003.

Habitat: New and Selected Poems, 1965-2005, Louisiana State University Press (Baton Rouge, LA), 2005.

Ocean Effects, Louisiana State University Press (Baton Rouge, LA), 2007.

OTHER

Massachusetts Story (documentary film script), produced by Gordon Massingham, 1978.

Today You Will Meet the Love of Your Life (poetry video), Connecticut Public TV, 1987–88

Also author of books on poetic theory. Contributor to periodicals, including *American Review, Atlantic, Connecticut English Journal, Georgia Review, Harper's, Hudson Review, Massachusetts Studies in English, Nation, New Republic, New Yorker, Paris Review, Ploughshares, Poetry, Sewanee Review, Hollins Critic,* and *Shenandoah.* Editor, with George Garrett, *Poultry: A Magazine of Voice,* 1981—.

SIDELIGHTS: Brendan Galvin told *CA:* "I began writing little stories on the kitchen floor when I was maybe nine or ten, using Disney characters in badly plotted one-pagers, and in high school received my first rejection when the faculty advisor to the student newspaper didn't believe I'd written the poems I submitted. I was a tackle on the football team, and I think he thought I took them from someone on the bus to school.

"Later, as a biology major at Boston College, I sometimes wrote at the back of a laboratory while my peers cut into a turtle's plastron to get at its terrified heart. Biology gave me a vocabulary I use in my poems without self-consciousness, so it's not unusual for me to use a word like 'meniscus.'

"I was accepted at two dental schools, but decided on a master's degree in English, instead. At Northeastern University I took a poetry-writing course with Wallace Stevens scholar Samuel French Morse, who encouraged me to try for publication, and in the following year the *Atlantic* accepted two poems. I continued to write and publish at the University of Massachusetts, where I earned an M.F.A. in Creative Writing and a Ph.D., with a dissertation on Theodore Roethke.

"Robert Frost, Theodore Roethke, Robert Lowell, James Dickey, Elizabeth Bishop, James Wright, Richard Wilbur, Galway Kinnel, and D.H. Lawrence are just a few of the poets I admire deeply and keep returning to in my reading. In addition I read a lot of fiction and history, natural history, and folklore.

"I continue to write about the natural world I live in at my home in the woods above a Cape Cod salt marsh. I accept the fact that my poems are 'under peopled,' but am not perplexed by it. In many respects I'm a private person to whom the politics of literary reputation seem both a waste of time and an appalling example of our present-day lack of shame.

"Around the time I turned fifty, I walked into my study one afternoon and the autumn sun was falling through the skylight onto my open notebook. A pen was lying beside the notebook. Sounds like a scene from a bad movie, I know, but my first thought was, 'That's the most beautiful sight in the world!' I wonder how many people my age feel that way about the tools of their trade. That moment convinced me I'd chosen the right life, and I'm still deeply pleasured by feeling the poem grow under my fingertips. I believe the world exists so that writers can write about it."

Galvin's poetry is characterized by a sense of geographic place and personal heritage, and a keen interest in the landscapes, the fauna and flora, of the world about him. Some of his specific themes have included the country versus the city, the exploitation of workers, and the victimization of children. More generally, Galvin can be seen as a poet who celebrates the beauty of the natural world, making use of images from that world to explore human relationships: familial, interpersonal, social, and historical. Writing in a precise yet lyrical free verse, influenced by his early work in metric forms, Galvin's voice interweaves the literary with the conversational, often borrowing from the local speech patterns of his native Cape Cod. He also makes use of scientific terminology, reflecting his lifelong interest in the natural sciences. His imagery tends to be realistic, firmly rooted in the direct experience of the senses, particularly the visual. Additional elements that make Galvin's poetry distinctive are its use of serio-comic effects and traditional narrative techniques.

Galvin's first book, *The Narrow Land,* deals with seasons along the Atlantic Coast. His second, *The Salt Farm,* broadens his range of topics, including poems about animals, the loss of loved ones, and the burning of an abandoned factory. In both books, Galvin's preference for the rural over the urban, the beauties of nature over "the paranoia of supermarkets," is clearly expressed.

By the mid-seventies, Galvin had established his poetic reputation with publication in such major venues as *Harper's, Atlantic Monthly,* and the *New Yorker.* His third book, and first major collection, *No Time for Good Reasons,* brought together forty-six poems, the best of ten years' work. It received critical praise for its inventiveness, its organic use of language, and its sense of humor. In his next collection, *The Minutes No One Owns,* Galvin further developed his vision and deepened the texture of his language. Both of these books, as their titles indicate, are concerned with the passage of time, another of Galvin's recurrent themes.

Galvin's fifth collection, *Atlantic Flyway,* presents an example of why he has described his own work as "under peopled." Birds play a significant role in poems throughout this book, and human characters are often described in avian terms. Galvin also begins to explore his own heritage in *Atlantic Flyway,* including poems about a journey in search of his ancestral home, about his grandfather, and about the Irish potato famine.

Wampanoag Traveler: Being, in Letters, the Life and Times of Loranzo Newcomb, American and Natural Historian further demonstrates Galvin's interest in his-

tory and natural history, and as the author has stated, involved research in both fields. It also extends his narrative approach to poetry by creating an entire book-length story set in the eighteenth century. *Wampanoag Traveler* relates the tale of Loranzo Newcomb, who gathers seeds and other specimens in the New World for shipment to the Royal Society in England. It is told in fourteen sections, each an imaginary letter written by Newcomb, thirteen to the Society and a final letter addressed directly to the reader. Snake bites, hummingbirds, a trained alligator, and fiddler crabs are among the subjects covered, every one serving as a starting point for Newcomb's ponderings on a variety of themes, from unrequited love to the destruction of the environment. In the final letter, a discussion of apples, Galvin examines the question of history itself. Writing in *Poetry,* Ben Howard criticized the book for a lack of thematic unity, and stated: "Galvin's project is ambitious, but the power of the book lies less in its grand design than in its compelling local effects." Glyn Maxwell, in the *Times Literary Supplement,* attributed the success of the poem to "Newcomb's voice, the intelligence and humanity that Galvin breathes into this lonesome scientist."

Composed of sixty poems from eight previous collections, along with twenty new poems, *Great Blue: New and Selected Poems* provides a representative selection of Galvin's work. In the title poem of the book, a near-mystical parallel is drawn between the great blue heron and Galvin's mother, both of whom are seen as guardian spirits. Here one can also find poems about animals, folklore, nature, art, history, holiday rituals, Galvin's Irish ancestry, and other subjects. In *Shenandoah,* X.J. Kennedy praised the collection as "tightly-winnowed" and praised the works's "forthrightness, intensity and originality." Writing in *Prairie Schooner,* Philip Paradis described *Great Blue* as "an outstanding collection by a major contemporary poet," and stated that "Galvin's style with its lyricism, earthiness, penchant for irony, and realistic clear-sightedness suggests he is certainly acquainted with the wellsprings of Irish poetry."

In *Saints in Their Ox-Hide Boat,* Galvin returns to the book-length story format of *Wampanoag Traveler.* This tale centers on an actual historical character, his own namesake, the sixth-century Irish monk, Brendan the Navigator. Background for the poem relies heavily on the medieval *Voyage of St. Brendan,* which tells of a small fishing boat, manned by Brendan and other monks, that may well have sailed all the way to the New World. Galvin's version, however, is primarily a fictitious account, in which he creates personalities for Brendan and the other monks and adds adventures of his own. The premise of the book is that Brendan, as an old man, is dictating an account of his voyage to a young scribe in order to correct misconceptions about it. Phoebe-Lou Adams, writing in the *Atlantic Monthly,* stated: "Mr. Galvin's highly distinctive style blends legend, folktale, psychological reconstruction, and gritty commonplace into its own poetic coherence." Fred Chappel in the *Georgia Review* remarked: "This work is a true narrative poem even by my persnickety standards, and a fascinating story it is."

In *The Strength of a Named Thing,* the "poems are offerings to our attention, and with what sheer pleasure they enlarge our spirit and sensibility," commented Thomas Reiter in *Hollins Critic.* For Galvin, "naming as an expression of the quality or value inherent in a person, thing, or locale is at the heart of this book. Naming confers identity," Reiter observed. Naming "becomes a way of creating and holding wisdom strongly in place in a community, a locality," and naming serves to "rescue an object from anonymity," Reiter commented. Reiter concluded that the volume of poems is "indispensable."

Hotel Malabar is Galvin's third book-length narrative poem and a winner of the Iowa Poetry Prize in 1997. The story revolves around events at a Cape Cod resort hotel during the summer of 1976. The narrative structure centers on monologues delivered by the diverse cast of characters. A. Norton Parlin is the hotel's owner, an elderly man who has given a series of taped interviews to Sheila, one of a trio of federal agents investigating Parlin's potential treason when he managed a Central American banana plantation. Mac, the hotel's maintenance man and groundskeeper, and Gorencamp, the chief of operations, also contribute their perspectives. The last character is Fermin, an herbalist from India, who serves as Parlin's personal health consultant. "The craft of the fiction writer is everywhere evident, witness the distinctiveness given each speaker by imagery, syntax, cadence, and tone," observed Reiter in another *Hollins Critic* review. As the agents investigate, they uncover evidence of Parlin's connections to the Nazis during World War II, but rather than the major act of treason involved in sending intelligence data on Canal Zone maneuvers to Germany, Parlin's actual involvement turns out to be much more mundane. *Hotel Malabar* stands as an ingenious and compelling performance, a one-of-a-kind enactment of American bad dreams," commented Reiter. "Here Galvin is at the height of his narrative powers."

Galvin once wrote: "I grew up on Cape Cod and in a suburb of Boston, and these two poles have affected my work strongly, in that my poems are full of imagery from the sea, the land, austere and muted, of the outer Cape, and the urban blight that infects humans who come in contact with it, especially through their work, most of which is unfulfilling and worthless." Elsewhere, he has written "the true risk [in writing poetry] is presenting felt expressions of the way things are, statements that move the inner life of the hearer because they offer him a truth deeper than one he previously knew."

George Garrett noted in the *Dictionary of Literary Biography* that "whether he is being serious or funny, or, as is usual, a combination of both, it appears that Galvin is facing up to the desperate elements in nature as well as in social and private situations; he is working out crucial events with strokes both bold and delicate."

BIOGRAPHICAL AND CRITICAL SOURCES:

BOOKS

Christina, Martha, editor, *OuterLife: The Poetry of Brendan Galvin,* Ampersand Press (Princeton, NJ), 1991.
Contemporary Authors Autobiography Series, Volume 8, Thomson Gale (Detroit, MI), 1991.
Contemporary Poets, 6th edition, St. James Press (Detroit, MI), 1996.
Critical Survey of Poetry, Salem Press (Englewood Cliffs, NJ), 1982.
Dictionary of Literary Biography, Volume 5: *American Poets since Word War II,* Thomson Gale (Detroit, MI), 1980.

PERIODICALS

Atlantic Monthly, June, 1992, Phoebe-Lou Adams, review of *Saints in Their Ox-Hide Boat,* p. 128.
Georgia Review, fall, 1990, review of *Wampanoag Traveler: Being, in Letters, the Life and Times of Loranzo Newcomb, American and Natural Historian,* p. 540; summer, 1992, Fred Chappell, review of *Saints in Their Ox-Hide Boat,* p. 376.
Hollins Critic, October, 1998, Thomas Reiter, review of *Hotel Malabar,* p. 19; June, 2000, Thomas Reiter, review of *The Strength of a Named Thing,* p. 20.

Poetry, June, 1977, review of *No Time for Good Reasons,* p. 167; September, 1990, Ben Howard, review of *Wampanoag Traveler,* p. 353; January, 1993, Ben Howard, review of *Saints in Their Ox-Hide Boat,* p. 229; February, 1998, Christian Wiman, review of *Sky and Island Light,* p. 289.

Prairie Schooner, spring, 1993, Philip Paradis, review of *Great Blue: New and Selected Poems,* p. 168.

Publishers Weekly, December 30, 1996, review of *Sky and Island Light,* p. 61; October 25, 1999, review of *The Strength of a Named Thing,* p. 78.

Shenandoah, winter, 1991, review of *Great Blue,* p. 115.

ONLINE

East Carolina University Department of English Web site, http://www.ecu.edu/english/ (January 2, 2007), biography of Brendan Galvin.*

* * *

GARBER, Eric
See HOLLERAN, Andrew

* * *

GASH, Jonathan
See GRANT, John

* * *

GAUNT, Graham
See GRANT, John

* * *

GEORGE, Elizabeth 1949-
(Susan Elizabeth George)

PERSONAL: Born February 26, 1949, in Warren, OH; daughter of Robert Edwin (a conveyor salesman) and Anne (a registered nurse) George; married Ira Jay Toibin (a business manager), May 28, 1971 (divorced, November, 1995); married Tom McCabe (a retired firefighter).

Education: Foothill Community College, A.A., 1969; University of California, Riverside, B.A., 1970; California State University, Fullerton, M.S., 1979; attended the University of California Berkeley. *Politics:* Democratic. *Religion:* "Recovering from Catholicism." *Hobbies and other interests:* Reading, theater, movies, skiing, photography, gardening.

ADDRESSES: Home—Seattle, WA.

CAREER: Writer, novelist, and educator. Mater Dei High School, Santa Ana, CA, teacher of English, 1974-75; El Toro High School, El Toro, CA, teacher of English, 1975-87; Coastline Community College, Costa Mesa, CA, teacher of creative Writing, beginning 1988; Irvine Valley College, Irvine, CA, teacher of creative writing, 1989; University of California, Irvine, teacher of creative writing, 1990. Teacher of intensive writing seminars for the University of Oklahoma and Book Passage, Corte Madera, CA; visiting professor, University of British Columbia, Vancouver, Canada, and Exeter College, Oxford University, Oxford, England; Maui Writer's Retreat, creative writing instructor.

AWARDS, HONORS: Award for teacher of the year, Orange County Department of Education, 1981; Anthony and Agatha awards for best first novel, both 1989, Le Grand Prix de Litterature Policiere, 1990, and Edgar and Macavity Award nominations, all for *A Great Deliverance;* MIMI award (Germany), for *Well-Schooled in Murder.* Recipient of honorary degree from California State University, Fullerton.

WRITINGS:

A Great Deliverance, Bantam (New York, NY), 1988.
Payment in Blood, Bantam (New York, NY), 1989.
Well-Schooled in Murder, Bantam (New York, NY), 1990.
A Suitable Vengeance, Bantam (New York, NY), 1991.
For the Sake of Elena, Bantam (New York, NY), 1992.
Missing Joseph, Bantam (New York, NY), 1993.
Playing for the Ashes, Bantam (New York, NY), 1994.
In the Presence of the Enemy, Bantam (New York, NY), 1996.
Deception on His Mind, Bantam (New York, NY), 1997.
The Evidence Exposed (short stories), Hodder & Stoughton (London, England), 1999.

In Pursuit of the Proper Sinner, Bantam (New York, NY), 1999.

A Traitor to Memory, Bantam Books (New York, NY), 2001.

Remember, I'll Always Love You, ASAP Publishing (Mission Viejo, CA), 2001.

I, Richard: Stories of Suspense, Bantam (New York, NY), 2002.

(Editor) *Crime from the Mind of a Woman,* Coronet (London, England), 2002, published as *A Moment on the Edge: 100 Years of Crime Stories by Women,* HarperCollins (New York, NY), 2004.

A Place of Hiding, Bantam (New York, NY), 2003.

Write Away: One Novelist's Approach to Fiction and the Writing Life, HarperCollins (New York, NY), 2004.

With No One as Witness, HarperCollins (New York, NY), 2005.

What Came before He Shot Her, HarperCollins (New York, NY), 2006.

Contributor to anthologies, including *Sisters in Crime,* Volume 2, Berkley Books (New York, NY), 1990; *Women on the Case,* Bantam (New York, NY), 1996; and *Murder and Obsession,* Random House (New York, NY), 1999.

A collection of George's manuscripts is housed at the Mugar Memorial Library, Boston University.

ADAPTATIONS: Twelve of George's Inspector Lynley novels have been adapted by the BBC and WGBH Boston and aired on PBS's Mystery! Series, including *A Great Deliverance,* 2001; *Well-Schooled in Murder,* 2002; *Payment in Blood,* 2002; *For the Sake of Elena,* 2002; *Missing Joseph,* 2002; *Playing for the Ashes,* 2003; *In the Presence of the Enemy,* 2003; *A Suitable Vengeance,* 2003; *Deception on His Mind,* 2003; *In Pursuit of the Proper Sinner,* 2004; *A Traitor to Memory,* 2004; *A Cry for Justice,* 2004; and *If Wishes Were Horses,* 2004. The character of Inspector Lynley has also appeared in other episodes of the PBS *Mystery* series not based on George's novels.

SIDELIGHTS: American writer Elizabeth George has won wide acclaim with her popular crime novels featuring a team of Scotland Yard sleuths. The author's depiction of British life is so accurate that even many of her readers in Great Britain have assumed that she is British. In fact, she was born in Ohio and raised in California. Her fascination with the classic British

mystery genre led her to try her own hand at it. Her first book, *A Great Deliverance,* featured an aristocratic inspector, Thomas Lynley; his aggressive, working-class assistant, Detective Sergeant Barbara Havers; and Lynley's best friend, independent forensic pathologist Simon St. James, who team together to investigate the beheading of a wealthy family's patriarch. In a *Publishers Weekly* article by Lisa See, George was quoted as saying that *A Great Deliverance* "wasn't a good book. . . . It was a clunky, old-fashioned, Agatha Christie-style mystery where St. James took everyone into the library and explained the crime. But it *was* a finished book." *A Great Deliverance* also won the prestigious Anthony and Agatha awards.

George followed *A Great Deliverance* with *Payment in Blood,* in which Lynley and Havers are sent to a Glasgow estate to investigate the death of a playwright pierced through the neck with a lengthy dagger. Lynley and Havers discover that the murderer must have passed through a neighboring room, one occupied on that fateful evening by an aristocratic woman with whom Lynley is in love. With Lynley distracted by romance, Havers assumes responsibility for their inquiry, which points to yet another aristocrat, an aging stage director of great prominence. Carolyn Banks, in her review of *Payment in Blood* in the *Washington Post,* noted the novel's "wonderfully drawn tensions and bonds between the characters," and she commended George for her skilled manipulation of crime-story conventions such as "the isolated old house [and] the tangled histories of the players."

In George's next mystery, *Well-Schooled in Murder,* Lynley and Havers must investigate the murder of a young boy found nude at a churchyard near his prestigious public school. The duo's probe leads to the uncovering of various criminal and scandalous activities, including blackmail, sadism, and suicide. *Washington Post Book World* contributor Jean M. White called *Well-Schooled in Murder* "a bewitching book, exasperatingly clever, and with a plot that must be peeled layer by layer like an onion." Marilyn Stasio, in her assessment of crime fiction for the *New York Times Book Review,* noted the "sensationalistic plot" of *Well-Schooled in Murder* and proclaimed George "a gifted storyteller."

In *A Suitable Vengeance,* George casts protagonist Lynley into a setting of domestic conflict. He has arrived at his mother's home in Cornwall to introduce his fiancée to her. Accompanying the couple are some of Lynley's friends, including Simon St. James and his sister, Sidney St. James. Shortly into the novel, Sidney engages in a surprisingly violent clash with her lover, Justin. Lynley's brother, a drug addict, soon arrives to further disturb matters. Then a newspaper editor is found dead. Lynley, while trying to resolve a long estrangement from his mother, must begin an investigation into the death. That inquiry leads to the uncovering of further drug use and the particularly malicious activities of a London woman. Margaret Cannon, writing in the Toronto *Globe and Mail,* deemed *A Suitable Vengeance* "a superior story," and described George as "an elegant craftswoman." Another enthusiast, Charles Champlin, wrote in the *Los Angeles Times Book Review* that with *A Suitable Vengeance* George gives readers a "sumptuous, all-out reading experience."

George continues to develop her characters with each new book. Her skill in plotting also becomes more finely honed with each successive title, according to numerous reviewers. Discussing *For the Sake of Elena,* the author's fifth book in another *Los Angeles Time Book Review* piece, Champlin noted that "like P.D. James, whom she comes as close to resembling as anyone now writing, [George] concocts an intricate timetable plot with a guess-again finale." He further noted, however, that "her larger interests are in character delineation, relationships closely observed, and social issues exposed. . . . The new book sustains the high standard Elizabeth George has set for herself." *Belles Lettres* reviewer Jane Bakerman called *For the Sake of Elena* "suspenseful, literate but readily accessible to a wide range of readers, thoughtful and thought provoking . . . an elegant novel."

Playing for the Ashes, about the mysterious death of a star cricket player, received praise from Emily Melton in *Booklist:* "George is a gifted writer who spins rich, colorful, mesmerizing, multifaceted stories that combine an absorbing mystery with provocative insights into her characters' innermost thoughts and emotions. . . . Readers will be astounded by the ease with which she weaves complex relationships and provocative moral, emotional, and ethical questions into the compelling plot. Another tour de force from one of today's best storytellers."

"Elizabeth George is arguably the finest writer working in the mystery genre today," wrote Margo Kaufman in a *Los Angeles Times Book Review* assessment of *In the Presence of the Enemy,* George's eighth novel. The plot concerns the kidnapping of the illegitimate daughter of a conservative politician. Havers ends up brutally beaten in her attempts to save the child. The story is lengthy, and James Hynes expressed in the *Washington Post* that *In the Presence of the Enemy* "is the longest, slowest, dullest book" he had ever read. Yet Jessica Cleerdin, a contributor to the *Star-Ledger,* found it an "interesting" plot, one greatly enhanced by the author's "realistic" style. Cleerdin continued: "Her crisp, precise writing mirrors that of news articles, adding a sense of urgency as the plot unfolds."

Barbara Havers takes center stage in the next installment of the series, *Deception on His Mind.* Off-duty while recovering from injuries incurred in the previous book, Havers tags along when her Pakistani neighbors head to a seaside town to try to settle some racial tensions there. Havers soon becomes involved in investigating the murder of a Pakistani in the town. In this story, the author "goes beyond her usual sensitive portrayal of the players, examining the nature of a different culture, how that dovetails with a murder investigation, and the role racism plays in the operations," explained Carol Kreck of the *Denver Post.* Lynley, St. James, and the other regular characters are present only in the first eleven pages of the book, and Havers "does very well by herself," according to Kreck. Typically, Havers has much to endure, including disciplinary action and a possible demotion for her independent actions in the case.

George continued her trend toward more intricate plotting with *In Pursuit of the Proper Sinner,* a story involving murder and sexual perversion among Britain's upper class. The investigation is complicated by lingering anger and mistrust between Lynley and Havers, due to events that took place in the previous novel. *Library Journal* reviewer Francine Fialkoff commented that George "may have gone overboard with her penchant for complex plotting," and further noted that "Lynley's moral agonies are becoming tedious." Other reviewers found *In Pursuit of the Proper Sinner* yet another fine achievement from George. Stephanie Zvirin, writing in *Booklist,* stated that "George delivers infinitely more than the requisite deception and murder," and assured that the book is "masterfully plotted, thoughtful, and bursting with clever complications." A *Publishers Weekly* reviewer also praised George for combining a taut mystery with fine character development, and doing so "with an engaging mix of subtlety and bravado. The multifaceted surprise ending to the taut, suspenseful plot is the juiciest plum in this can't-put-down novel."

A Traitor to Memory is a "sprawling epic" that takes in "classical music, cybersex, and vehicular homicide," according to a *Publishers Weekly* writer. George again demonstrated her willingness to be innovative in this novel, which uses multiple viewpoints to tell the story. A central figure is a young man who has spent most of his life performing as a prodigy of the violin. Suddenly he finds himself unable to play a note. The key to his musical paralysis leads through several decades and murders. *Booklist* reviewer Connie Fletcher commented that despite its length of more than seven hundred pages, *A Traitor to Memory* manages to "fairly zip along, keeping the reader on the knife's edge of suspense, thanks to George's skill." Fletcher rated the book "first rate suspense with a stunner of an ending." *Library Journal* writer Jane la Plante found the introspection of the violinist ultimately "tedious and creepy," but the *Publishers Weekly* reviewer praised the book as "ambitious" and called the author's narrative "consistently inventive."

In *A Place of Hiding,* Inspector Lynley steps aside briefly to let series costars Simon St. James and his wife Deborah take the spotlight. An unexpected visit from Cherokee River, the brother of Deborah's American friend and roommate China River, reveals that China has been arrested for murder. She is being held on the island of Guernsey, charged with murdering wealthy Guy Brouard, an influential philanthropist. Brouard and his wife Ruth have painful connections to the Holocaust. They were working with a World War II hero who lived on the island to put together a war museum to honor those who were victimized by the Nazis during the island's occupation. Simon and Deborah accompany Cherokee to Guernsey to try to exonerate China and uncover the identity of the real murderer. Unexpected twists and shocking discoveries await the protagonists as the story darkly unspools. *Entertainment Weekly* reviewer Tina Jordan concluded: "This is mystery writing at its most complex and intelligent."

With No One as Witness concerns the brutal, ritualistic death of a teenage boy which is linked to three other similar deaths. Because all of the victims were black males, and because connections to a serial killer were made very late in the investigation, Scotland Yard Assistant Commissioner Sir David Hillier fears that there will be accusations of racism leveled at the department. To combat this image, Hillier promotes black officer Winston Nkata to sergeant and involves him prominently in public meetings and press briefings. Lynley, Nkata, and constable Barbara Havers eventually identify the

victims and link them to Colossus, a group for troubled youths run by a staff with questionable backgrounds. Further links are found between the young men and a magic shop with ties to a group called MABIL, which stands for Men and Boys in Love, and which supports sexual encounters between adult males and boys. Before the story's end, the director of Colossus will have a close encounter with the killer, and Lynley will experience a loss that will profoundly change his life forever. "George deftly depicts the palaver and predicaments of middle-and working-class Brits in this dark, chilling tale of desperation and revenge," commented *Booklist* reviewer Alison Block.

What Came before He Shot Her proceeds from the devastating events of *With No One as Witness,* chronicling the events and characters that led to Lynley's tremendous loss. Twelve-year-old Joel, his teenage sister Ness, and brother Toby Campbell are three mixed-race siblings suffering through a difficult upbringing after their father is murdered and their mother institutionalized. Their Aunt Kendra takes them in, and although she means well, she does not have the means to raise three children. Ness and Joel fight to adjust and survive in their dangerous new surroundings in North Kensington, while Joel helps protect younger, developmentally challenged brother Toby. Despite his good intentions and earnest attempts to help, Joel's decisions are usually followed by tragedy. Ness's involvement with a vicious, jealous drug dealer endangers Ness and the family. After run-ins with the law, Ness ends up in jail. "The bad luck stretches all the way to Belgravia, where Inspector Thomas Lynley's wife Helen meets Joel and a handgun on her doorstep," reported a *Kirkus Reviews* critic. A *Publishers Weekly* reviewer called the novel "an outstanding and explosive addition to a popular series." The story demonstrates George "at the top of her form," commented Jane la Plante in the *Library Journal.* "This is a riveting installment in a superb series—far more than just plain good," commented Zvirin in another *Booklist* review.

In her long literary career, George has also turned her hand to editing. Her *A Moment on the Edge: 100 Years of Crime Stories by Women* assembles twenty-six tales spanning more than eight decades and representing a variety of mystery genre types, including locked-room mysteries, psychological studies, detective tales, and white-collar crime stories. Authors represented include mystery stalwarts Ngaio Marsh, Ruth Rendell, Minette Walters, and Dorothy Sayers, along with other authors not strictly associated with the mystery genre, such as

Joyce Carol Oates and Nadine Gordimer. George includes concise introductory notes on each author, and pens a "lively, informative introduction" to the entire collection, noted Jane la Plante in the *Library Journal*. The book is, "from start to finish, a first-rate anthology," Stephanie Zvirin concluded in a *Booklist* review.

A teacher as well as an author, George offers sage lessons to beginning writers in *Write Away: One Novelist's Approach to Fiction and the Writing Life*. In the book, George's "pedantry is of the pleasant variety, meant not to bury potential writers but to encourage them," observed Bethanne Kelly Patrick on *Bookreporter.com*. Taking examples from her own books as well as from major literary works, George describes in detail the conceptual and creative process she uses to write the popular Lynley novels and her other books. She explains how she determines her characters' traits in a "character map" before she even starts on her first draft. She emphasizes the value of discipline for writers and the irreplaceable practice of simply getting words down on paper or screen. She encourages writers to enjoy the entire process of creating, rather than focusing on what comes after the "having written," when the book or story is completed. She also realistically assesses the odds against new writers, and endorses finding pleasure and fulfillment in the writing, whether or not it will eventually result in publication. Throughout the book, George "may have been describing what works for her, but her energy and excitement made me want to discover what works best for me," Patrick commented.

George remarked on her work in the *St. James Guide to Crime and Mystery Writers*: "My novels tend to harken back to the Golden Age of the detective story in that they attempt to reflect the glamour of Dorothy L. Sayers's type of writing rather than the grim reality of present day dissections of murder. Nonetheless, the issues they revolve around are very much part of contemporary life." In that same book, Jane S. Bakerman summarized that George's popularity results from her skillful use of "an intriguing range of continuing characters who are interesting individually as well as in their interactions with one another, gripping plots, well-drawn descriptive passages, and plenty of gore. The crimes depicted in these novels are horrific not only in physical detail but also in their psychological impact upon the cast of characters—and upon the readers. Strongly sexual undercurrents color and inform all these factors. With sharp realism but without exploitation, then, George notes and capitalizes upon the human fascination with sex and violence. Crime writers often

focus on these subjects, of course, but not many display the control George commands."

BIOGRAPHICAL AND CRITICAL SOURCES:

BOOKS

St. James Guide to Crime and Mystery Writers, 4th edition, St. James Press (Detroit, MI), 1996.

PERIODICALS

Atlantic Monthly, November, 2006, review of *What Came before He Shot Her,* p. 125.
Belles Lettres, fall, 1992, Jane Bakerman, review of *For the Sake of Elena,* p. 28.
Booklist, May 15, 1994, Emily Melton, review of *Playing for the Ashes,* p. 1645; July, 1999, Stephanie Zvirin, review of *In Pursuit of the Proper Sinner,* p. 1893; December 15, 1999, review of *In Pursuit of the Proper Sinner* (audio version), p. 798; May 1, 2000, Karen Harris, review of *In Pursuit of the Proper Sinner* (audio version), pp. 1626-1627; May 1, 2001, Connie Fletcher, review of *A Traitor to Memory,* p. 1632; May 15, 2004, Stephanie Zvirin, review of *A Moment on the Edge: 100 Years of Crime Stories by Women,* p. 1601; February 1, 2005, Stephanie Zvirin, review of *With No One as Witness,* p. 917; August 1, 2006, Allison Block, review of *What Came before He Shot Her,* p. 8.
Books, summer, 1998, review of *Deception on His Mind,* p. R3.
Christian Science Monitor, March 27, 1997, review of *In the Presence of the Enemy,* p. B2; July 31, 1997, Michele Ross, review of *Deception on His Mind,* p. B2, Robin Whitten, review of *In the Presence of the Enemy,* p. B4.
Clues: A Journal of Detection, fall-winter, 2000, Carl D. Malmgren, "Truth, Justice, the American Way: Martha Grimes and Elizabeth George," p. 47.
Denver Post, July 13, 1997, Carol Kreck, review of *Deception on His Mind,* p. E6.
Entertainment Weekly, December 12, 1997, Tom De Haven, review of *In the Presence of the Enemy,* p. 77; December 24, 1999, review of *In Pursuit of the Proper Sinner,* p. 144; August 10, 2001, Mark Harris, "Lady Thrillers: Four Popular Women of Mystery Introduce New Chapters in the Lives of Their Hard-boiled Heroines"; August 8, 2003, Tina Jordan, review of *A Place of Hiding,* p. 78; March

18, 2005, Mark Harris, review of *With No One as Witness*, p. 74; October 20, 2006, Tina Jordan, review of *What Came before He Shot Her*, p. 87.

Globe and Mail (Toronto, Ontario, Canada), August 4, 1990; September 25, 1999; review of *In Pursuit of the Proper Sinner*, p. D15.

Kirkus Reviews, February 1, 2005, review of *With No One as Witness*, p. 151; August 1, 2006, review of *What Came before He Shot Her*, p. 755.

Knight-Ridder/Tribune News Service, August 6, 1997, Lynn Carey, "Elizabeth George Reveals Why Britain's the Setting for Her Best-Selling Mysteries," p. 806.

Library Journal, July, 1999, Francine Fialkoff, review of *In Pursuit of the Proper Sinner*, p. 141; June 1, 2001, Jane la Plante, review of *A Traitor to Memory*, p. 214; February 1, 2004, Joyce Kessel, audiobook review of *A Place of Hiding*, p. 143; August, 2004, Jane la Plante, review of *A Moment on the Edge*, p. 61; March 15, 2005, Jane la Plante, review of *With No One as Witness*, p. 78; April 15, 2006, Douglas C. Lord, review of *With No One as Witness*, p. 123; September 1, 2006, Jane la Plante, review of *What Came before He Shot Her*, p. 136.

Los Angeles Times, June 9, 1996, Dennis McLellen, "Murder She Writes," p. E1.

Los Angeles Times Book Review, August 13, 1989, Charles Champlin, "Bloody Sunday," review of *Payment in Blood*, p. 8; July 12, 1992, Charles Champlin, review of *For the Sake of Elena*, p. 8; May 12, 1996, Margo Kaufman, review of *In the Presence of the Enemy*, p. 11; October 31, 1999, review of *In Pursuit of the Proper Sinner*, p. 11.

New York Times, August 26, 1992, Herbert Mitgang, review of *For the Sake of Elena*, p. B2; August 17, 1994, Sarah Lyall, "Making the List," p. C16; December 14, 1999, Mel Gussow, "Golly! A Yank Wrote Those Oh-So-British Mysteries?," p. B1; April 10, 2005, Dwight Garner, "Inside the List," review of *With No One as Witness*.

New York Times Book Review, November 12, 1989, Josh Rubins, review of *Payment in Blood*, p. 58; August 12, 1990, Marilyn Stasio, review of *Well-Schooled in Murder*, p. 21; June 20, 1993, Marilyn Stasio, review of *Missing Joseph*, p. 21; April 21, 1996, Marilyn Stasio, review of *In the Presence of the Enemy*, p. 39; August 10, 1997, Marilyn Stasio, review of *Deception on His Mind*, p. 18.

People, October 11, 1999, Pam Lambert, review of *In Pursuit of the Proper Sinner*, p. 49; August 6, 2001, review of *A Traitor to Memory*, p. 53.

Philadelphia Inquirer, October 18, 2006, Maxine Clarke, review of *What Came before He Shot Her*.

Publishers Weekly, May 23, 1994, review of *Playing for the Ashes*, p. 80; March 11, 1996, Lisa See Kendall, "Elizabeth George: An American in Scotland Yard: Each Novel Has Outperformed the Last," profile of Elizabeth George, p. 38; August 2, 1999, review of *In Pursuit of the Proper Sinner*, p. 71; June 4, 2001, review of *A Traitor to Memory*, p. 60; February 21, 2005, review of *With No One as Witness*, p. 161; August 7, 2006, review of *What Came before He Shot Her*, p. 31.

School Library Journal, January, 1998, Susan H. Woodcock, review of *Deception on His Mind*, p. 136.

Star-Ledger, March 24, 1996, Jessica Cleerdin, review of *In the Presence of the Enemy*, p. 6.

Swiss News, March, 2006, review of *With No One as Witness*, p. 60.

Wall Street Journal, August 9, 1994, Tom Nolan, review of *Playing for the Ashes*, p. A10; July 25, 1997, Tom Nolan, review of *Deception on His Mind*, p. A12; August 24, 1999, review of *In Pursuit of the Proper Sinner*, p. A16.

Washington Post, August 29, 1989, Carolyn Banks, "Lord Lynley's Well-Staged Return," review of *Payment in Blood*, p. E3; February 29, 1996, James Hynes, "The Really Big Sleep," review of *In the Presence of the Enemy*, p. C2.

Washington Post Book World, July 15, 1990, Jean M. White, "Beneath the Old Ivy," review of *Well-Schooled in Murder*, p. 11; October 17, 1999, Katy Munger, review of *In Pursuit of the Proper Sinner*, p. 13.

ONLINE

BookPage, http://www.bookpage.com/ (January 2, 2007), Jay MacDonald, "The Other Side of the Story," interview with Elizabeth George.

Bookreporter.com, http://www.bookreporter.com/ (January 2, 2007), biography of Elizabeth George; Kathy Weissman, review of *What Came before He Shot Her*; Barbara Lipkien Gershenbaum, review of *With No One as Witness*; Terry Miller Shannon, review of *A Moment on the Edge*; Barbara Lipkien Gershenbaum, review of *A Place of Hiding*; Bethanne Kelly Patrick, review of *Write Away: One Novelist's Approach to Fiction and the Writing Life*.

Elizabeth George Web site, http://www.elizabethgeorge online.com (January 2, 2007).

Internet Movie Database, http://www.imdb.com/ (January 2, 2007), filmography of Elizabeth George.

MyShelf.com, http://www.myshelf.com/ (October, 1999), "October 1999's Author of the Month: Elizabeth George," profile of Elizabeth George.*

*   *   *

GEORGE, Susan Elizabeth
    See GEORGE, Elizabeth

*   *   *

GIBSON, Jo
    See FLUKE, Joanne

*   *   *

GIRZONE, Joseph F. 1930-
    (Joseph Francis Girzone)

PERSONAL: Born May 15, 1930, in Albany, NY; son of Peter Joseph and Margaret Rita Girzone. *Education:* St. Bonaventure University, B.A., 1951; received theology degree from Catholic University of America, 1955; graduate study at Fordham University.

ADDRESSES: Home—Albany, NY.

CAREER: Writer, public speaker, and Catholic priest. Entered Carmelite Order, 1948; ordained Catholic priest, 1955; high school teacher in New York and Pennsylvania, 1955-64; St. Albert's Seminary, Middletown, NY, faculty member, 1960-61; pastor at churches in New York, 1964-81; Our Lady of Mt. Carmel Church, Amsterdam, NY, pastor, 1974-81; writer, 1981—. Founder, the Joshua Foundation, 1995. Worked as computer salesman for Olivetti Corporation. Director of Dominican Third Order of Religious Lay People, 1964-76; member of New York State Bishops' Advisory Commission for Criminal Justice, beginning in 1973; chair of Schenectady County, New York, Human Rights Commission, 1973-74; vice-chair of Title III advisory board for New York State Office of Aging, 1974-76; member of Roman Catholic Diocesan Peace and Justice Commission, beginning in 1976; member of board of directors of Schenectady Joint Commission of Christians and Jews; president of Amsterdam Community Concerts. Co-owner of senior citizens newspaper *Golden Age Sentinel.* Public speaker and retreat organizer.

AWARDS, HONORS: Liberty Bell Award, American Bar Association, 1974; Citizen of the Age of Enlightenment Award, Society for Creative Intelligence, 1976.

WRITINGS:

Kara: The Lonely Falcon (young adult), Richelieu Court (Albany, NY), 1979.
Who Will Teach Me? (nonfiction), Richelieu Court (Albany, NY), 1982.
Gloria: Diary of a Teenage Girl (young adult), Richelieu Court (Albany, NY), 1982.
Joshua (novel), Richelieu Court (Albany, NY), 1983.
Joshua and the Children: A Parable (novel), Macmillan (New York, NY), 1989.
(Author of preface) Myles Connolly, *Mr. Blue,* Richelieu Court (Albany, NY), 1990.
The Shepherd (novel), Macmillan (New York, NY), 1992.
Joshua in the Holy Land (novel), Macmillan (New York, NY), 1993.
Never Alone: A Personal Way to God, Doubleday (New York, NY), 1994.
(Author of introduction) Denis McBride, *Impressions of a Life: Stories of Jesus,* Ligouri (Ligouri, MO), 1994.
Joshua and the City, Doubleday (New York, NY), 1995.
What Is God?, Doubleday (New York, NY), 1996.
Joey: The True Story of One Boy's Relationship with God, Doubleday (New York, NY), 1997.
A Portrait of Jesus, Doubleday (New York, NY), 1998.
Joshua: The Homecoming, Doubleday (New York, NY), 1999.
(Editor) *Jesus, His Life and Teachings: As Recorded by His Friends, Matthew, Mark, Luke, and John,* Doubleday (New York, NY), 2000.
The Parables of Joshua, Doubleday (New York, NY), 2001.
The Messenger: A Parable, Doubleday (New York, NY), 2002.
Trinity: A New Living Spirituality, Doubleday (New York, NY), 2002.
Joshua in a Troubled World, Doubleday (New York, NY), 2005.
My Struggle with Faith, Doubleday (New York, NY), 2006.
Joshua's Family, Doubleday (New York, NY), 2007.

ADAPTATIONS: The following works were adapted as audio cassettes: *Kara: The Lonely Falcon,* 1991; *Joshua in the Holy Land,* 1992; *The Shepherd,* 1992; and *Jesus: His Life and Teachings,* 2001. *Joshua* was adapted as a feature film, 2002.

SIDELIGHTS: Active in the priesthood for more than twenty years, Joseph F. Girzone is the author of several best-selling novels—including *Joshua* and its sequel, *Joshua and the Children: A Parable*—about the return of Jesus Christ to present-day Earth. Also the author of two children's books and the parents' handbook *Who Will Teach Me?,* Girzone turned to full-time writing after being advised by his doctor to retire from active parish work.

Girzone was ordained a Catholic priest in 1955 and, for nearly ten years, taught high school in New York and Pennsylvania. He served as pastor of several Catholic churches in upstate New York until 1974, when he became pastor of Our Lady of Mt. Carmel Church in Amsterdam, NY. Involved in community as well as parish life, Girzone served in organizations concerned with human rights, aging, and criminal justice while carrying out his formal religious duties. But in 1981, his stressful schedule began to take its toll on his health, and he decided to leave his parish work. Because he was unwilling to accept a pension before his official retirement age, however, Girzone made an agreement with his diocese to support himself through writing and lecturing. Already the author of one book, an allegorical work for children titled *Kara: The Lonely Falcon,* Girzone completed three more books by the end of 1981: *Who Will Teach Me?, Gloria: Diary of a Teenage Girl,* a novel for young adults about a teenager's encounter with bone cancer; and *Joshua.*

A popular speaker, Girzone became inspired to write *Joshua* while on a lecture tour. The novel is based on what Girzone imagined would have happened if Jesus Christ had returned to Earth in the 1980s. "I'd always had the feeling that there was something wrong in the way the Christian message was being passed on to people," he said in a *WB* interview. "There were so many troubled and bruised Christians and that just didn't make sense, because Jesus was always talking about the peace that He came to bring." Girzone wanted to write a novel conveying Jesus's message to a modern audience and addressing the often legalistic and divisive aspects of organized religion he believed might be alienating both Christians and non-Christians from Christ's teachings.

Girzone's resulting work introduced Joshua, a simple woodcarver who settles in a small New York town and spreads his message among its residents, whose characters are based on Girzone's hometown friends and acquaintances. Joshua begins visiting churches of all denominations, preaching against the sometimes prejudiced and exclusive practices of Christianity while conveying his knowledge of God as the source of inner peace, strength, and freedom. Having aroused the anger of the clergy with his reproaches, Joshua is summoned to Rome to explain his views to Vatican officials, before whom the nature of his true identity is revealed.

After completing *Joshua,* Girzone found himself running out of money and unable to interest a publisher in the manuscript. He was determined to publish his novel, however, even at his own expense, and upon learning that the twelve-dollar per page printing cost would be drastically reduced if he were to put the manuscript on computer disk, he decided to do so. His brother-in-law recommended an Olivetti personal computer for the task and Girzone, finding no Olivetti dealerships in his area, petitioned the company to hire him. By 1983, Girzone not only had published his book, but also, according to William Griffin in *Publishers Weekly,* had become one of Olivetti's top salesmen.

Girzone's next challenge lay in marketing *Joshua* to bookstores, which he found reluctant to risk stocking privately printed books. Girzone marketed his book himself, selling it to leaders of religious retreats, whose participants bought and recommended the book to others. After contacting numerous bookstore owners and managers, Girzone finally persuaded Gary Mele, a Waldenbooks district sales manager, to read *Joshua.* Impressed, Mele placed three copies in several of his district's stores, where they sold immediately. Through word-of-mouth praise, the book became a best-seller, first locally, and then nationally, when *Joshua*'s increasing sales prompted the Waldenbooks chain to distribute it throughout the country in 1985. The novel's growing sales attracted the interest of a Macmillan subsidiary; since the book's 1987 acquisition by Macmillan, more than half a million copies have been sold.

Joshua perhaps owes its immense but quiet renown—it became a best-seller without the usual aid of major book reviews or a massive publicity campaign—to the enthusiastic personal recommendations of its early readers, a diverse worldwide group including Hindus and Jews, clergy and statesmen, believers and nonbelievers. Others point to Girzone's inspirational message of love as the source of its popularity. "A lot of healing has taken place among people who have been touched by the book," Girzone told Griffin in *Publishers Weekly.* "It seems to me almost as if God wanted *Joshua* to be written. To get it done, He had to kick me out of the mainstream of the Church, keep me away from ecclesiastical structure, and give me the freedom to do it."

In 1989 Girzone followed his grass-roots success with a sequel, the parable *Joshua and the Children,* in which Joshua returns again, this time to a community—often compared to Northern Ireland—torn apart by violence and religious conflict. A stranger to the townspeople, Joshua recognizes that many of the town's adults are too emotionally involved in the destructive power struggle to change their ways, so he befriends children from each of the village's warring parties. Joshua shows his young friends how to trust and love one another in the face of terrorism and fear, imbuing them with his powerful legacy of healing and joy.

Girzone again reached a wide audience with *Joshua and the Children,* and like *Joshua,* it also became a best-seller. "I really feel that writing is the perfect outlet for my work as a priest," he commented, speaking of his books' success in *WB.* "You reach a lot more people by writing books. And you get a chance to explain what you want to explain in a lot more depth and in a way that lasts. . . . As you can see, the message of Christ will always be relevant to the people of every age. Basically, [Joshua's] message is the same message that Jesus brought us 2,000 years ago," the author concluded. "It's there in all its simplicity and always will be."

Girzone followed with two additional volumes in his Joshua series. *Joshua in the Holy Land* places the eponymous character in the contemporary Middle East, where, wandering about the desert, he finds and returns a lost lamb to a prominent sheik, whom he then befriends. After Joshua miraculously heals a snakebite suffered by the sheik's granddaughter, he begins his mission to bring peace to the embattled region. Joshua successfully effects reconciliation among Christians, Jews, and Moslems through the Children of Peace, a popular movement that reforms governments and society as it gains strength and numbers. Girzone's mysterious protagonist reappears in *Joshua and the City,* set in a modern metropolis where Joshua confronts and ameliorates various social problems, including prostitution, drug addiction, and poverty. Through his kindness and good works, Joshua becomes an inspiration in the life of a young prostitute who attempts to proposition him; a depressed wealthy woman and her husband; and several troubled African-American youths.

Joshua came to the big screen in 2002 via a feature film adaptation with Tony Goldwyn in the title role. The movie had a limited release and received mixed reviews, but its timing coincided with two new Girzone books, *The Parables of Joshua* and *The Messenger: A Parable.* The former revisits Joshua as he retells Jesus' parables with a modern twist. As Girzone writes in the introduction, "I have heard the most callous people comment with such great piety on the parables that I could not help but wonder if we haven't made parables pleasant-sounding fables about human situations past, but with no present-day meaning." Thus the environment, materialism, abortion, and capital punishment all become topics of Girzone's book. While John Mort in *Booklist* wondered if such messages needed contemporizing—"don't even the irreligious feel that the stories of the prodigal son or the rich man are great life lessons?"—a *Publishers Weekly* contributor thought that "fans of Girzone will be delighted by another Joshua read, although it's not quite up to par." *The Messenger* presents a new character, Francis, as a modern-day messenger of God who confronts hostility from the institutional Catholic Church, which perceives him as threatening to their own agendas. This book, which "appears to be a barely disguised autobiographical tale of Girzone's own life," as a *Publishers Weekly* critic commented, does not measure up to *Joshua*'s "fresh, folksy" appeal.

In a nonfiction work, *Never Alone: A Personal Way to God,* Girzone shares his own struggles and offers hope in the unconditional love of God. According to Dennis M. Doyle in a *Commonweal* review, Girzone "defines spirituality as a 'mystical friendship with Jesus' requiring that 'we open ourselves to God, and show a willingness to follow his grace in our lives.'" Girzone also asserts the importance of prayer and observes the surprising accountability that comes with such newfound freedom. A *Publishers Weekly* reviewer described *Never Alone* as an "easy-to-read, but by no means simplistic book." A *Kirkus Reviews* critic praised Girzone's "humanity and insight," concluding that Christians and non-Christians alike "will find much of value here."

Joshua in a Troubled World finds the wise and gentle Joshua experiencing distrust and prejudice in the post-9/11 world. As he travels around Washington, DC, Joshua attracts the attention of the FBI with his appearance as a person of Middle Eastern background. Twice taken in for questioning and followed doggedly, Joshua continues his mission in the nation's capital, visiting a number of prominent Middle Eastern Muslims, Christians, and Jews, and organizing them into a loose coalition of peace-seekers. When these influential individuals visit their home countries, they bring their native spiritual and political leaders into the fold, resulting in a new and strongly felt declaration of peace among the members of the diverse religions. *Library Journal* reviewer Tamara Butler observed that readers would find this and all other Joshua novels a "kinder and gentler alternative" to other popular religious series that portray Jesus's return in more violent, apocalyptic terms.

Though Girzone has provided religious inspiration to thousands through his years as a priest and via his numerous books, he admits that he has also experienced times of spiritual conflict and doubt. In *My Struggle with Faith,* Girzone offers a "beautifully crafted reflection on the Christian faith and struggle," commented Anthony J. Elia in the *Library Journal.* He considers directly and in-depth the "central spiritual quandaries shared by many," Elia observed. Girzone looks at sometimes troubling, sometimes confusing issues such as literal versus metaphorical interpretations of the Bible; religion versus science; various misconceptions about Jesus and his life, and the most fundamental question of all, the existence of God. He also discusses more direct issues, noted Jeanette Leardi in the *Dallas Morning News,* such as priestly celibacy and marriage, religious activism and evangelism in the context of a democracy, and independence of bishops and other religious leaders from dictates handed down by the Vatican. At the core of the book, Girzone explores the doubt, disbelief, and depression that were attendant on his search for his core beliefs, and his "various struggles to reconcile his personal faith with the tenets and workings of today's Vatican," Leardi stated. A *Publishers Weekly* writer concluded: "In his simple, readable prose, Girzone paints a beautiful portrait of faith."

BIOGRAPHICAL AND CRITICAL SOURCES:

BOOKS

Bestsellers 90, Issue 1, Thomson Gale (Detroit, MI), 1990.
Girzone, Joseph F., *The Parables of Joshua,* Doubleday (New York, NY), 2001.

PERIODICALS

Booklist, January 1, 2001, John Mort, review of *The Parables of Joshua,* p. 869; May 15, 2001, Nancy Spillman, review of *Jesus, His Life and Teachings:*
As Recorded by His Friends, Matthew, Mark, Luke, and John, p. 1765; October 1, 2002, Ray Olson, review of *Trinity: A New Living Spirituality,* p. 288; November 15, 2004, John Mort, review of *Joshua in a Troubled World,* p. 531.
Business Wire, November 8, 2004, "TBN Announces the Broadcast Television Premiere of the Inspirational Film *Joshua* Slated to Debut Thanksgiving Day at 2 p.m. and 7 P.M. PST."
Commonweal, September 9, 1994, Dennis M. Doyle, review of *Never Alone: A Personal Way to God,* p. 21.
Dallas Morning News, September 20, 2006, Jeanette Leardi, "Reviews of Religious Books and Web Sites," review of *My Struggle with Faith.*
Fort Worth Star-Telegram, April 18, 2002, Robert Philpot, movie review of *Joshua.*
Kirkus Reviews, January 1, 1994, review of *Never Alone,* p. 35.
Library Journal, April 1, 2002, Melanie C. Duncan, review of *The Messenger,* p. 86; February 1, 2005, Tamara Butler, review of *Joshua in a Troubled World,* p. 60; May 15, 2006, Anthony J. Elia, review of *My Struggle with Faith,* p. 106.
People, November 6, 1989, Lucinda Smith, "Father Joseph Girzone's Joshua Parables Put a Best-selling End to His Quiet Retirement," p. 75.
Publishers Weekly, October 6, 1989, William Griffin, "PW Interviews: Joseph F. Girzone," p. 78; March 14, 1994, review of *Never Alone,* p. 29; March 27, 2000, "For the Easter Basket," p. 78; January 15, 2001, review of *The Parables of Joshua,* p. 68; February 18, 2002, review of *The Messenger,* p. 74; August 26, 2002, review of *Trinity,* p. 63; November 29, 2004, review of *Joshua in a Troubled World,* p. 21; March 13, 2006, review of *My Struggle with Faith,* p. 61.
WB, November/December, 1989, interview with Joseph F. Girzone.

ONLINE

Beliefnet, http://www.beliefnet.com/ (January 2, 2007), Michael G. Maudlin, "Joseph Girzone's Penance," review of *Jesus: His Life and Teaching.*
HarperCollins Religious Web site, http://www.harper collinsreligious.com/ (January 2, 2007), biography of Joseph F. Girzone.
Internet Movie Database, http://www.imdb.com/ (January 2, 2007), filmography of Joseph F. Girzone.*

GIRZONE, Joseph Francis
    See GIRZONE, Joseph F.

*   *   *

GLANCY, Diane 1941-

PERSONAL: Original name, Helen Diane Hall; born March 18, 1941, in Kansas City, MO; daughter of Lewis and Edith Hall; married Dwane Glancy, May 2, 1964 (divorced, March 31, 1983); children: David, Jennifer. *Ethnicity:* Native American/European. *Education:* University of Missouri, B.A., 1964; Central State University, Edmond, OK, M.A., 1983; University of Iowa, M.F.A., 1988. *Religion:* Christian.

ADDRESSES: Home—Prairie Village, KS. *Office*—Department of English, Macalester College, 1600 Grand, St. Paul, MN 55105. *E-mail*—glancy@ macalester.edu.

CAREER: Macalester College, St. Paul, MN, began as assistant professor, became professor of English, 1988—. Oklahoma State Arts Council, artist in residence, 1982-92; U.S. Information Agency, lecturer in Syria and Jordan.

AWARDS, HONORS: Fellowship of Writers' Workshop, University of Iowa; Pegasus Award, Oklahoma Federation of Writers, 1984, for *Brown Wolf Leaves the Res and Other Poems;* named laureate for the Five Civilized Tribes, 1984-86; Lakes and Prairies Award, *Milkweed Chronicle,* 1986, for *One Age in a Dream;* Oklahoma Theater Festival Award, 1987, for *Segwohi;* Five Civilized Tribes Playwriting Prize, 1987, for *Weebjob;* Aspen Summer Theater Award, 1988, for *Stickhorse;* Capricorn Poetry Prize, 1988, for *Iron Woman;* Charles Nilon Minority Fiction Award, 1990, for *Trigger Dance;* fellowship from the National Education Association and Minnesota State Arts Board, and National Endowment for the Arts poetry fellowship, both 1990; North American Indian Prose Award, University of Nebraska Press, and American Book Award, Before Columbus Foundation, both 1992, for *Claiming Breath;* National Endowment for the Humanities grant, 1992; Native American fellow of Sundance Institute at University of California, Los Angeles, 1998; McKnight fellowship/ Loft Award of Distinction in Creative Prose, 1999; Many Voices fellowship, Playwrights Center, Min-

neapolis, 2001; Thomas Jefferson teaching/scholarship Award, Macalester College, 2001; Cherokee Medal of Honor, Cherokee Honor Society, 2001; Stevens Poetry Award, National Federation of State Poetry Societies, 2001; grant from National Endowment for the Arts, 2003; Juniper Prize, 2004, for *Primer of the Obsolete.*

WRITINGS:

SHORT STORIES

Trigger Dance, Fiction Collective Two (Boulder, CO), 1990.
Firesticks: A Collection of Stories, University of Oklahoma Press (Norman, OK), 1993.
Monkey Secret, TriQuarterly Books (Evanston, IL), 1995.
The Voice that Was in Travel: Stories, University of Oklahoma Press (Norman, OK), 1999.
The Dance Partner: Stories of the Ghost Dance, Michigan State University Press (East Landing, MI), 2005.

NOVELS

The Only Piece of Furniture in the House: A Novel, Moyer Bell (Wakefield, RI), 1996.
Pushing the Bear: A Novel of the Trail of Tears, Harcourt Brace (New York, NY), 1996.
Flutie, Moyer Bell (Wakefield, RI), 1998.
The Closets of Heaven: A Novel of Dorcas, the New Testament Seamstress, Chax Press (Tuscon, AZ), 1999.
Fuller Man, Moyer Bell (Wakefield, RI), 1999.
The Man Who Heard the Land, Minnesota Historical Society Press (Saint Paul, MN), 2001.
The Mask Maker, University of Oklahoma Press (Norman, OK), 2002.
Designs of the Night Sky, University of Nebraska Press (Lincoln, NE), 2002.
Stone Heart: A Novel of Sacajawea, Overlook Press (Woodstock, NY), 2003.

POETRY

Traveling On, Myrtlewood Press (Tulsa, OK), 1982.
Brown Wolf Leaves the Res and Other Poems, Blue Cloud Quarterly Press (Marvin, SD), 1984.

One Age in a Dream, illustrated by Jay Moon, Milkweed Editions (Minneapolis, MN), 1986.

Offering: Aliscolidodi, Holy Cow! Press (Duluth, MN), 1988.

Iron Woman, New Rivers Press (Moorhead, MN), 1990.

Lone Dog's Winter Count, West End Press (Albuquerque, NM), 1991.

Boom Town, Black Hat (Goodhue, MN), 1995.

Primer of the Obsolete, Chax Press (Tuscon, AZ), 1998.

(Ado)ration, Chax Press (Tuscon, AZ), 1999.

The Relief of America, Northwestern University Press (Evanston, IL), 2000.

Stones for a Pillow, Chax Press (Tucson, AZ), 2001.

The Shadow's Horse, University of Arizona Press (Tuscon, AZ), 2003.

Rooms: New and Selected Poems, Salt Publishers (Cambridge, England), 2005.

Asylum in the Grasslands, University of Arizona Press (Tucson, AZ), 2006.

PLAYS

Segwohi, produced in Tulsa, OK, 1987.

Testimony, produced in Tulsa, OK, 1987.

Webjob, produced in Tulsa, OK, 1987.

Stick Horse, produced in Aspen, CO, 1988.

The Lesser Wars, produced in Minneapolis, MN, 1989.

Halfact, produced in San Diego, CA, at Modern Language Association Conference, 1994.

War Cries: A Collection of Plays, introduction by Kimberly Blaeser (includes *"Webjob," "Stick Horse," "Bull Star," "Halfact," "Segwohi," "The Truth Teller," "Mother of Mosquitos," "The Best Fancy Dancer the Pushmataha Pow Wow's Ever Seen,"* and *"One Horse"*), Holy Cow! Press (Duluth, MN), 1997.

American Gypsy: Six Native American Plays, University of Oklahoma (Norman, OK), 2002.

Also author of plays *Stone Heart: Everybody Loves a Journey West, Jump Kiss,* and *The Woman Who Was a Red Deer Dressed for a Deer Dance.*

OTHER

Drystalks of the Moon (poetry and prose), Hadassah Press (Tulsa, OK), 1981.

Claiming Breath (essays), University of Nebraska Press (Lincoln, NE), 1992.

(Editor, with C.W. Truesdale) *Two Worlds Walking: Short Stories, Essays, and Poetry by Writers with Mixed Heritages,* New Rivers Press (New York, NY), 1994.

The West Pole (poetry and prose), University of Minnesota Press (Minneapolis, MN), 1997.

The Cold-and-Hunger Dance (poetry and prose), University of Nebraska Press (Lincoln, NE), 1998.

(Editor, with Mark Nowak) *Visit Teepee Town: Native Writings after the Detours,* Coffee House Press (Minneapolis, MN), 1999.

In-between Places (essays), University of Arizona Press (Tuscon, AZ), 2004.

Contributor to books, including *I Tell You Now: Autobiographical Essays by Native American Writers,* edited by Brian Swann and Arnold Krupat, University of Nebraska Press (Lincoln, NE), 1987; *Talking Leaves,* edited by Craig Lesley, Bantam (New York, NY), 1991; *Stiller's Pond: New Fiction from the Midwest,* edited by Jonis Agee, Roger Blakely, and Susan Welch, New Rivers Press (Moorhead, MN), 1991; *Earth Song, Sky Spirit: Short Stories of Contemporary Native American Experience,* edited by Clifford Trafzer, Doubleday (New York, NH), 1993; and *Freeing the! First Amendment: Critical Perspectives on Freedom of Expression,* edited by Robert Jensen and David Allen, New York University Press (New York, NY), 1995.

SIDELIGHTS: Diane Glancy is a poet, playwright, short story writer, essayist, and novelist who often explores the quest for spirituality among mixed-race characters. One-eighth Cherokee herself, Glancy identifies with the Native American and mixed-blood characters she writes about, and like some other contemporary Native American writers, she experiments with genres and styles in an attempt to give expression to the reality of mixed-blood peoples. "The difference in Glancy's writing has to do with her attempts to construct Native American texts by combining oral and written traditions, fusing the visual and verbal, mixing poetry and prose, and experimenting with the arrangement of the text on the page," noted Julie LaMay Abner in the *Dictionary of Literary Biography.* Though not all of her experiments are successful, Glancy has won numerous awards for her writings and critical applause for her deeply felt, poetic depictions of marginalized characters. Wendy Murray Zoba, writing in *Books and Culture,* commented on Glancy's quiet childhood, noting that eventually, Glancy "found the one voice that held the others together. Or the voice found her. It came through her writing. The result has been a body of work that defies literary convention." Zoba continued: "If she is hard to categorize, she has nevertheless found readers."

Known first as a poet, Glancy began to garner significant critical attention with the publication of collections of short stories and autobiographical poem-essays. *Firesticks: A Collection of Stories* centers on Native American characters in contemporary, urban settings who, critics noted, are hard to distinguish from non-Native Americans in their troubled and dreary lives. "Glancy invests her prose with tremendous emotional resonance . . . in tales that often seem more like poems than conventional short stories," observed a reviewer for *Publishers Weekly. The Cold-and-Hunger Dance,* a collection of essays and poems, shares with the earlier volume an emphasis on "the importance of the written word and the act of writing," observed Mary B. Davis in *Library Journal.* In the pieces gathered here, Glancy explores the tangle of emotions evoked by witnessing ceremonies held by tribes other than her own, and universalizes her personal experience as the child of parents with differing cultural backgrounds. In pursuit of melding her Christian beliefs with her Nativist spirituality, Glancy reworks several Native legends to "bizarre" effect, according to a reviewer for *Publishers Weekly.*

Like *The Cold-and-Hunger Dance, Claiming Breath* is a collection of short, related, autobiographical pieces that often meld genres. Often inspired by long stretches traveling across Oklahoma, the author muses on marriage and divorce, the uncanny influence of her Cherokee grandmother on her identity, and attempts to reconcile Native American spiritualism with her own Christian-based beliefs. The result is a "wildly uneven grab-bag in the form of a journal," according to a critic for *Kirkus Reviews,* who found "fresh language and banality, fine prose-poetry and self-indulgence," side by side in *Claiming Breath.* Nevertheless, the volume may serve as a model for those who advocate journal writing as "a road to self-actualization," this critic concluded.

The West Pole is another unusual collection of autobiographical prose and poetry musings on Glancy's attempts to define her identity as a Native American writer. But, like *Claiming Breath,* critics found the pieces of mixed value. "Glancy has a gift for language," observed *Library Journal* contributor Vicki Leslie Toy Smith, "but . . . she seems to stop writing before she has exhausted a subject." Similarly, a reviewer for *Publishers Weekly* found the collection "at best only

sporadically rewarding," though Glancy's efforts at "deftly blending Indian beliefs and mythology with European Christianity" are "refreshing" compared to the angrier and more divisive sentiments found in much other Native American writing.

In her first novel, *Pushing the Bear: A Novel of the Trail of Tears,* Glancy retells the grueling tale of the thousands of Cherokee Indians who were forced to leave their home lands in North Carolina, Alabama, Georgia, and Tennessee and walk to reservations in Oklahoma. The journey has gone down in history as the Trail of Tears, because so many people died along the way from exposure and disease. Glancy's historical novel centers on a young woman and her family, with numerous secondary characters including soldiers who enforced the march, white clergy, and Indians of all ages whose sufferings are recounted in the first-person. Critics focused much of their attention on Glancy's successful incorporation of a wealth of historical material relating to the forced march, and the evocative voice of her myriad characters to tell "an exquisitely sad tale," in the words of *Booklist* reviewer Kathleen Hughes. "The voices that comprise the narrative are vigorous, and the period details convincing but not obtrusive," wrote a *Kirkus Reviews* contributor. Moreover, *Pushing the Bear* exemplifies, according to a reviewer for *Publishers Weekly,* "the Cherokee conception of story as the indestructible chain linking people, earth and ancestry—a link that becomes, if not unmitigated salvation, then certainly a salve to the spirit."

Almost simultaneously with the publication of *Pushing the Bear,* Glancy published another novel, *The Only Piece of Furniture in the House,* a coming-of-age story that, in its focus on the spiritual life of its protagonist, set the pattern for future novels by the author. In this novel, Rachel Hume grows up as the second-oldest of nine children born to a deeply religious mother and her itinerant railway worker husband in the American South and Southwest. When Rachel meets and marries Jim, a soldier, her new life in military housing tests her religious faith as she is surrounded by people who daily break the rules she has learned to live by. In the midst of a postpartum depression, Rachel returns to her childhood home only to realize she must learn to face the world or give up her marriage. A reviewer for *Publishers Weekly* made special note of Glancy's "expressive prose [which] evocatively captures the intriguing complexity of life in the Bible Belt South."

Like *The Only Piece of Furniture in the House,* the protagonist of *Flutie* is an adolescent girl struggling to reconcile her powerful spiritual life with the realities of her emotionally and materially deprived surroundings. A contributor for *Kirkus Reviews* observed that "Glancy demonstrates a strong and very particular gift for catching the way in which spiritual yearnings work on an untutored mind." In this novel, Flutie Moses sees stories in everything and everyone around her, but can hardly speak to anyone with whom she is not intimate, and thus much of the narrative is given over to accounts of Flutie trying to speak. "This quite beautiful novel proves unexpectedly moving in the ways Glancy finds to write the sounds of silence," reported GraceAnne A. DeCandido in *Booklist*. Flutie's visions lead her toward a Cherokee spiritualism that is unavailable to the rest of her family, and in a book she gains inspiration from the legend of Philohela, whose brother-in-law cut out her tongue to prevent her from accusing him of raping her. With her newfound powers of speech, Flutie graduates from high school and prepares to attend college to follow her dream of studying geology. The result is "a story of great emotional honesty and power," observed Carolyn Ellis Gonzalez in *Library Journal*.

As in her earlier novels, the protagonist of *Fuller Man* is a young woman predominantly struggling with the role of religious faith in her life. Halley Willie, her sister Nearly, and her brother Farley each must find his or her own way among the battles between their devout mother and skeptical father. "In single images, remarks and disjunct scenes, as if from a journalist's notebook, Halley lays out each important moment of her maturation, from grade school to middle age," as she teeters between faith and doubt, according to a reviewer for *Publishers Weekly*. Like *The Only Piece of Furniture in the House*, the journey toward spiritual healing in the form of fundamentalist Christianity documented by Glancy's narrative in *Fuller Man* was noted by critics for its sympathetic treatment, a rare find in contemporary American literature. While the contributor to *Kirkus Reviews* found Glancy's efforts marred by her unusual, sometimes "cryptic," storytelling methods, "Glancy's determination to plumb an unfashionable question in fiction—how faith or the lack of it shapes and sustains our lives—is admirable."

The Man Who Heard the Land and *The Mask Maker* approach fiction from a more poetic angle than Glancy's previous novels. In the first, a teacher of environmental literature turns to his Native American roots to begin to get through his depression. The results, according to Mary Margaret Benson in her *Library Journal* review "are mixed: his life is still troubled . . . but he has a fuller understanding of himself." *The Mask Maker*, which Debbie Bogenschutz in *Library Journal* called a "truly dynamic" experiment, tells the story of a mixed-blood Native American mother, who deals with her feelings and emotions through the traditional artwork of the mask. Glancy accompanies her text with Bible passages and the thoughts of the main character in her own voice, each featured on the side of the page.

Designs of the Night Sky falls somewhere between a collection of stories and a novel; main character Ada works in a library and reads accounts of the Trail of Tears. Confronting problems in her own life and delving into historical accounts of tragedy, Ada seeks comfort in Christianity and at the Dust Bowl roller rink. The novel changes back and forth between the historical forced migration of the Cherokee and Ada's life and the stories of her family members. Debbie Bogenschutz in her *Library Journal* review called the book "an engaging novel," while a critic for *Kirkus Reviews* considered the book, perhaps in spite of its non-traditional format, "at its core a probing, honest tale." Howard Meredith, writing for *World Literature Today,* noted: "In every sense, this is Glancy's most ambitious endeavor."

In 2003, Glancy took on the challenge of presenting historical heroine Sacajawea's story in a novel format. Though it had been done before, Glancy's approach gave the story a new twist; while using a second-person voice to give Sacajawea's perspective on the Lewis and Clark expedition, Glancy featured excerpts from the Louis and Clark journals on a second column on the page. The narrative is two-fold; one gives the historical perspective of the white explorers, the other the thoughts of a young Native American woman. Sacajawea, a Shoshone woman who had been kidnapped by the Hidatasa tribe and then sold to a Canadian trapper as his second wife, was pregnant with the trapper's child when she served as a translator for the expedition. Glancy's depiction of Sacajawea neglects none of her strength of character; Margaret Flanagan wrote in *Booklist* that "Sacajawea is blessed with an inner vision that puts an earthy and vibrant spin on each individual experience and encounter." A reviewer for *Publishers Weekly* thought that many of Sacajawea's responses were "predictable;" however, the critic concluded, "Glancy's sharply observed details and lyrical stylings make for a lively, thought-provoking read"; a critic for *Kirkus Reviews* considered the book "a brilliantly artistically ambitious retelling." In *Library Journal*, Debbie Bogenschutz reported that "the interest in this retelling lies in the contrast between the two parties' journals"; Anne G. Myles in *North American Review* similarly commented, "This doubling is the narrative's most distinctive and difficult feature, as Glancy executes it literally, graphically on the page." Myles continued, "Such readerly dislocation is surely part of the point: we find ourselves, like the protagonist, out of our element; we have to work out for ourselves what kind of authority two incommensurable perspectives have within the novel and within our understanding of the truth."

Glancy defines herself as a Native American writer, and her fiction and nonfiction writings alike treat the consequences of that self-definition, especially for her spiritual life. Admiring critics have pointed to the evocative language she uses to create characters besieged by inner lives whose expression is not welcome in the worlds they inhabit, which are marked by poverty in the material, emotional, and spiritual senses. "Her work is a refreshingly honest depiction of contemporary American Indian life with common themes that are easily accessible to Indian and non-Indian readers alike: mixed-bloodedness, heritage, colonialism, middle age, feminism, divorce, death, power, and survival," wrote Abner in the *Dictionary of Literary Biography*. While some critics have found her autobiographical collections of short prose and poetry less satisfying than her novels, the journal-like musings found in *Claiming Breath* and *The West Pole* have been valued by other critics as a model for readers seeking identity and self-worth in times of trouble.

Glancy told *CA:* "I think language places us in the world. Language is the land on which I live. There is a Native American belief that our stories can't be separated from the land, but in the case of the Cherokee, who were removed from the original place of their stories in the southeast and forced to march west on the 1838 Trail of Tears, something else has to occur: a belief that the stories move also, or that we carry them within us. In other words, the land is an attitude or place located in the mind. Therefore, there is a geography of thought, an abstract geography which the language of writing establishes. Otherwise, we are left without stories."

BIOGRAPHICAL AND CRITICAL SOURCES:

BOOKS

Dictionary of Literary Biography, Volume 175: *Native American Writers of the United States,* Thomson Gale (Detroit, MI), 1997.

Native North American Almanac, Thomson Gale (Detroit, MI), 1994.

Notable Native Americans, Thomson Gale (Detroit, MI), 1995.

PERIODICALS

Booklist, August, 1996, Kathleen Hughes, review of *Pushing the Bear: A Novel of the Trail of Tears,* p. 1881; March 15, 1998, GraceAnne A. DeCandido, review of *Flutie,* p. 1201; December 15, 2000, Donna Seaman, review of *Flutie,* p. 787; January 1, 2003, Margaret Flanagan, review of *Stone Heart: A Novel of Sacajawea,* p. 847.

Books and Culture, May, 2001, Wendy Murray Zoba, "The Voice that Found Her," p. 32.

Kirkus Reviews, January 15, 1992, review of *Claiming Breath,* p. 90; June 15, 1996, review of *Pushing the Bear,* p. 843; February 15, 1998, review of *Flutie,* p. 212; September 1, 1999, review of *Fuller Man,* p. 1331; September 15, 2002, review of *Designs of the Night Sky,* p. 1348; November 15, 2002, review of *Stone Heart,* p. 1642.

Library Journal, February 1, 1989, Rhoda Carroll, review of *Offering: Aliscolidodi,* p. 66; December, 1990, Debbie Tucker, review of *Trigger Dance,* p. 162; March 1, 1992, Jessica Grim, review of *Claiming Breath,* p. 91; April 1, 1993, Debbie Bogenschutz, review of *Firesticks: A Collection of Stories,* p. 134; July, 1996, Starr E. Smith, review of *Pushing the Bear,* p. 158; November 1, 1996, Janet Ingraham, review of *The Only Piece of Furniture in the House,* p. 106; March 15, 1997, Vicki Leslie Toy Smith, review of *The West Pole,* p. 70; March 1, 1998, Carolyn Ellis Gonzalez, review of *Flutie,* p. 127; November 15, 1998, review of *Flutie,* p. 67; September 1, 2001, Mary Margaret Benson, review of *The Man Who Heard the Land,* p. 233; March 1, 2002, Debbie Bogenschutz, review of *The Mask Maker,* p. 138; September 1, 2002, Nancy Pearl and Jennifer Young, "Native Voices, Old and New," p. 244; September 15, 2002, Howard Miller, review of *American Gypsy: Six Native American Plays,* p. 62; November 1, 2002, Debbie Bogenschutz, review of *Designs of the Night Sky,* p. 128; January, 2003, Debbie Bogenschutz, review of *Stone Heart,* p. 154.

New York Times Book Review, April 11, 1993, Angie Jabine, review of *Firesticks,* p. 29; October 1, 1995, Dwight Garner, review of *Monkey Secret,*

p. 32; January 5, 1997, Alexandra Lange, review of *The Only Piece of Furniture in the Room,* p. 18; May 17, 1998, Elizabeth Gaffney, review of *Flutie,* p. 40.

North American Review, November-December, 2003, Anne G. Myles, "Writing the Go-Between," pp. 53-58.

Publishers Weekly, February 1, 1993, review of *Firesticks,* p. 76; June 17, 1996, review of *Pushing the Bear,* p. 47; October 7, 1996, review of *The Only Piece of Furniture in the House,* p. 59; February 10, 1997, review of *The West Pole,* p. 76; March 16, 1998, review of *Flutie,* p. 55; August 31, 1998, review of *The Cold-and-Hunger Dance,* p. 57; May 31, 1999, review of *Visit Teepee Town: Native Writing after the Detours,* p. 89; August 23, 1999, review of *The Voice that Was in Travel,* p. 45; December 23, 2002, review of *Stone Heart,* p. 43; October 6, 2003, review of *The Shadow's Horse,* p. 81.

World Literature Today, July-September, 2003, Howard Meredith, review of *Designs of the Night Sky,* p. 151.

*　　*　　*

GLATZER, Hal 1946-

PERSONAL: Born January 31, 1946, in New York, NY; son of Harold (an attorney) and Glenna (an English teacher) Glatzer; married Kathleen Francovic (a director of surveys), August 22, 1992. *Education:* Syracuse University, B.A., 1967; University of Hawaii, M.A., 1979; graduate study at Hilo College. *Politics:* Democrat. *Hobbies and other interests:* Playing banjo, guitar, fiddle, mandolin, autoharp, and dulcimer in the style of traditional mountain music and Bluegrass; reading, watching television, gardening.

ADDRESSES: Home—San Francisco, CA.

CAREER: Writer, journalist, editor, musician, and computer consultant. *Honolulu Advertiser,* Hilo, HI, bureau chief, 1971; *Orchid Isle* (magazine), Hilo, editor, 1971-74; KITV-News, Hilo, reporter, 1975; Oceanic Cablevision, Honolulu, HI, news director, 1976; television producer in Honolulu and Seattle, WA, 1976; *People,* New York, NY, Hawaii correspondent, 1976-80; *The Printout,* Honolulu, editor, 1979-80; Words and Pictures, Seattle, chief executive officer, 1980; computer consultant in Seattle, 1980; *Software News,* Westborough, MA, West Coast correspondent, 1983; Key Thinkers, Inc., Oakland, CA, partner, 1985. Curator of an exhibit of sheet music from Broadway and Tin Pan Alley. Former member of Big Island Committee on Crime Prevention. Delegate for the Democratic Convention in Kansas City, MO, 1974.

MEMBER: American Association for the Advancement of Science, Union of Concerned Scientists, Institute of Electrical and Electronic Engineers, Computer Press Association (vice president, 1985-87), Hawaii Professional Writers, Art Deco Society of California (served as director), Mystery Writers of America, Sisters in Crime.

AWARDS, HONORS: Media Award, American Cancer Society, 1978.

WRITINGS:

Kamehameha County (journalistic novel), Friendly World Enterprises (Pepeekeo, HI), 1974.
Introduction to Word Processing, Sybex (Berkeley, CA), 1981.
The Birds of Babel: Satellites for a Human World, H.W. Sams (Indianapolis, IN), 1983.
Who Owns the Rainbow? Conserving the Radio Spectrum, H.W. Sams (Indianapolis, IN), 1984.
The Trapdoor, 1986.
Murder on the Kona Coast, 1987.
Too Dead to Swing: A Katy Green Mystery, John Daniel (Santa Barbara, CA), 2002.
A Fugue in Hell's Kitchen, Perseverance Prese/John Daniel & Co. (McKinleyville, CA), 2004.
The Last Full Measure, John Daniel & Co. (McKinleyville, CA), 2006.

Contributor to local magazines and to *Christian Science Monitor.*

Author of short stories adapted to audio plays, starring Mark Markheim, the Hollywood hawkshaw, including "A Dead Body's a Deal-Breaker" and "Vengeance in Vegas."

ADAPTATIONS: Too Dead to Swing was originally performed as an audio play for Audio-Playwrights in 2000.

SIDELIGHTS: Hal Glatzer is a former journalist who has turned to writing mystery fiction. His novel *Too Dead to Swing: A Katy Green Mystery,* for example, was originally performed as an audio-play. However, Glatzer constructed the book as though it were a newly discovered unpublished novel from the 1940s by an author named Hannah Dobryn. In all the Katy Green novels published to date, Glatzer pays particular attention to creating an accurate voice and outlook for Katy. "My technique for doing this is to think of them as having been written by someone else, a woman called Hannah Dobryn, who is writing in the years just after WWII, when the pre-war years were still a fresh memory," Glatzer remarked in an interview on the *Fugue in Hell's Kitchen* Web site. "This enables me to keep the setting in mind, and frees me to imagine how a woman of Katy's generation would write."

In *Too Dead to Swing,* the story centers around an all-girl 1940s swing band. When one of the members is attacked, musician and amateur sleuth Katy Green joins the band. As the group travels by train, members of the band are murdered one by one. *Library Journal* reviewer Rex E. Klett wrote that the novel's "simple, easy-going style" was engaging and recommended *Too Dead to Swing* to fans of Forties noir mysteries.

A Fugue in Hell's Kitchen finds swing musician Katy giving violin lessons in order to make a living in New York, where male musicians always get the best band jobs and playing gigs. Soon, Emily finds herself embroiled in helping her friend, Chinese immigrant Amalia Chen, defend herself against accusations of theft. A professor at the Meyers Conservatory, Amelia had recently checked a priceless autographed Nicholas Paganini manuscript out of the conservatory's library. The manuscript is stolen from her cello case during a radio performance, but is later inexplicably returned. When the library discovers that the returned manuscript is a forgery, Amalia is accused of stealing the original. Arrested and jailed, Amalia suffers the prejudice and discrimination facing Asians on the cusp of World War II. While helping her friend by searching for the manuscript, Katy also investigates the death of the conservatory's dean, Iris Meyers, and the librarian. "Lively, likable Katy and a colorful array of suspects add up to some breezy, nostalgic fun," commented a *Kirkus Reviews* critic.

In *The Last Full Measure,* set in the days before the Pearl Harbor attack, Katy is invited by her musician friends Lillian and Ivy to play aboard the luxury cruise ship Lurline on a trip to Hawaii. Katy gladly joins the ship's all-female band, the "Swingin' Sarongs." Fronting the group is Hawaiian singer Roselani Akau, an eclectic musician who combines native Hawaiian music with the swing standards of the day. Katy achieves a major victory when she convinces noted composer Phillip DeMorro to join the Sarongs for some sets aboard ship. The arrival of Roselani's twin brother Bill, a competitive surfer, intrigues almost everyone on the Lurline, especially since Bill and Lillian are clearly lovers. Katy, meanwhile, seeks companionship among a group of Japanese-American military men, particularly Shunichi "Danny Boy" Ohara. Katy is astonished when Lillian reveals to her that she and Bill plan to dig up a valuable Akau family treasure buried somewhere in Hawaii. Before this plan can unfold, however, Bill is murdered and, in an atmosphere of virulent anti-Japanese prejudice, Danny Boy is arrested as a suspect. Katy knows that Danny Boy is not the murderer, and sets out to locate the real murderer and bring him, or her, to justice. The author "portrays the life of working musicians (or, more often, looking-for-work musicians) with authority and charm," observed a writer in *Publishers Weekly.* "Glatzer's ambitious mix of mystery and history hits all the right notes," remarked a *Kirkus Reviews* contributor.

Glatzer told *CA:* "I am an eclectic radical thinker. . . . I believe in God and Mankind. I do not believe in owning land. I believe in beating swords into ploughshares and spears into pruning hooks. I do not study war."

BIOGRAPHICAL AND CRITICAL SOURCES:

PERIODICALS

Booklist, April 15, 1982, review of *Introduction to Word Processing,* p. 1052; May 1, 2001, review of *Too Dead to Swing: A Katy Green Mystery,* p. 1617.

Book World, October 3, 1982, review of *Introduction to Word Processing,* p. 11.

California Bookwatch, May, 2006, "Perseverance Press," review of *The Last Full Measure.*

Journalism Quarterly, summer, 1985, review of *Who Owns the Rainbow? Conserving the Radio Spectrum,* p. 425; autumn, 1985, review of *The Birds of Babel,* p. 675.

Kirkus Reviews, December 15, 2003, review of *A Fugue in Hell's Kitchen,* p. 1425; February 1, 2006, review of *The Last Full Measure,* p. 113.

Library Journal, March 1, 2002, Rex E. Klett, review of *Too Dead to Swing,* p. 143; March 1, 2004, Rex E. Klett, review of *A Fugue in Hell's Kitchen,* p. 111.

New York Times, August 23, 1992, "Weddings; Kathleen Francovic and Hal Glatzer."

Publishers Weekly, December 4, 2000, review of *Too Dead to Swing,* p. 32; January 30, 2006, review of *The Last Full Measure,* p. 43.

San Francisco Review of Books, September, 1982, review of *Introduction to Word Processing,* p. 30.

ONLINE

A Fugue in Hell's Kitchen Web site, http://www.fuguemystery.com/ (January 2, 2007), interview with Hal Glatzer.

Audio Playwrights Web site, http://www.audio-play.com/ (January 2, 2007).

BookLoons, http://www.bookloons.com/ (January 2, 2007), Mary Ann Smith, review of *A Fugue in Hell's Kitchen.*

Last Full Measure Web site, http://www.lastfullmeasure.info/ (January 2, 2007), biography of Hal Glatzer.

MyShelf.com, http://www.myshelf.com/ (January 2, 2007), Nancy Mehl, review of *Too Dead to Swing.*

MysteryReader.com, http://www.themysteryreader.com/ (January 2, 2007), Jennifer Monahan Winberry, review of *Too Dead to Swing.*

Too Dead to Swing Web site, http://www.toodeadtoswing.com/ (January 2, 2007), biography of Hal Glatzer.*

*   *   *

GOLDMAN, Judy 1942-
(Judy Ann Goldman)

PERSONAL: Born in 1942, in Rock Hill, SC; married; children: one son, one daughter.

ADDRESSES: Home—Charlotte, NC. *Agent*—Marly Rusoff & Associates, Inc., P.O. Box 524, Bronxville, NY 10708.

CAREER: Queens College, New York, NY, creative writing instructor; Duke University, Durham, NC, writing workshop instructor; National Public Radio, Charlotte, NC, commentator; guest on media programs, including *Poetry Live.*

AWARDS, HONORS: Roanoke-Chowan Award for Poetry; Gerald Cable Poetry Award, for *Wanting to Know the End;* Fortner Writer and Community Award; Sir Walter Raleigh Award for Fiction and Mary Ruffin Poole Award for Best First Work of Fiction, both for *The Slow Way Back.*

WRITINGS:

Holding Back Winter (poems), St. Andrews Press (Laurinburg, NC), 1987.
Wanting to Know the End (poems), Silverfish Review Press, 1993.
Collected Essays, Warren Publishing (Davidson, NC), 1994.
The Slow Way Back (novel), William Morrow (New York, NY), 1999.
Early Leaving (novel), William Morrow (New York, NY), 2004.

Work represented in anthologies. Contributor of poems and essays to periodicals, including *Southern Review, Gettysburg Review, Shenandoah, Kenyon Review, Ohio Review, Crazy Horse,* and *Prairie Schooner.*

SIDELIGHTS: Judy Goldman published several books of poetry and essays before writing her debut novel, *The Slow Way Back,* a story of three generations of women in a Southern Jewish family. The story evolved from personal essays Goldman had delivered on National Public Radio. It tells of radio therapist Thea McKee, who is married to a Gentile, while her sister, Mickey, is devoted to her faith and their father. As a girl, Thea sensed that family secrets were being hidden when her mother reacted violently to the child trying on her wedding dress. In addition, her father always favored her sister over Thea. When Thea is in middle age, a packet of letters comes into her possession, written in Yiddish by her Grandma Bella in the 1930s. They hold the key to the family's long-hidden secrets. A *Publishers Weekly* contributor described Goldman as being "a touching storyteller and an astute observer of human nature."

The narrator of Goldman's next novel, *Early Leaving,* is film critic Kathryne Smallwood, who has enjoyed an upper-middle-class life in Charlotte, North Carolina, until her eighteen-year-old son, Early, kills a black teen and attempts to hide his crime by setting the body and the boy's car on fire. Kathryne is tormented by not knowing whether she was in some way responsible for Early's actions. She and her husband have been having marital problems, and he is having an affair. She considers whether Early was overly influenced by his friend, Chip, and whether Early was drinking or doing drugs. Ultimately it appears that her indulgence of her son was a negative factor. Other themes include liberal attitudes toward racism, conflict avoidance, and the need to balance protection of children with teaching them responsibility. *Library Journal* reviewer Eleanor J. Bader called *Early Leaving:* "Masterfully written and fast-paced."

BIOGRAPHICAL AND CRITICAL SOURCES:

PERIODICALS

Booklist, September 1, 2004, Deborah Donovan, review of *Early Leaving,* p. 60.
Kirkus Reviews, July 1, 2004, review of *Early Leaving,* p. 595.
Library Journal, October 15, 1999, Molly Abramowitz, review of *The Slow Way Back,* p. 105; August, 2004, Eleanor J. Bader, review of *Early Leaving,* p. 67.
Publishers Weekly, August 30, 1999, review of *The Slow Way Back,* p. 54.

ONLINE

Austin Chronicle Online, http://www.austinchronicle. com/ (October 1, 1999), Katherine Catmull, review of *The Slow Way Back.*
Judy Goldman Home Page, http://www.judygoldman. com (November 24, 2006).
Rebecca's Reads.com, http://www.rebeccasreads.com/ (November 24, 2006), interview.*

*   *   *

GOLDMAN, Judy Ann
    See GOLDMAN, Judy

*   *   *

GOMEZ, Alberto Perez
    See PÉREZ-GÓMEZ, Alberto

GOODMAN, Allegra

PERSONAL: Daughter of Lenn (a professor of philosophy) and Madeleine (a geneticist, epidemiologist, and dean) Goodman; married David Karger (a professor of computer science); children: four. *Education:* Graduated from Harvard University (magna cum laude), 1989; Stanford University, Ph.D., 1997.

ADDRESSES: Home—Cambridge, MA.

CAREER: Writer, novelist, and educator. Conducts occasional workshops, seminars, and writing classes.

AWARDS, HONORS: Whiting Foundation Award, 1991, for *Total Immersion; New York Times* Notable Book of the Year Award, for *The Family Markowitz;* Edward Lewis Wallant Award for Jewish fiction and National Book Award finalist, both for *Kaaterskill Falls; Salon. com* award for fiction; named one of the twenty best writers under forty by the *New Yorker.*

WRITINGS:

Total Immersion (stories), Harper & Row (New York, NY), 1989.
The Family Markowitz (stories), Farrar, Straus (New York, NY), 1996.
Kaaterskill Falls (novel), Thorndike Press (Thorndike, ME), 1998.
Paradise Park (novel), Dial Press (New York, NY), 2001.
Intuition (novel), Dial Press (New York, NY), 2006.

Contributor to periodicals, including *Commentary, Good Housekeeping, Slate, American Scholar,* and the *New Yorker.*

ADAPTATIONS: Intuition was adapted to audio cassette.

SIDELIGHTS: Allegra Goodman began her writing career when she sold her first story to *Commentary* magazine at age seventeen; her first collection of stories was published on the day she graduated from Harvard. Within months, she married classmate David Karger, and the couple moved to California, where they attended Stanford and began a family. They returned to Cambridge with their two sons when David accepted a position as an assistant professor at the Massachusetts Institute of Technology.

The eleven stories in Goodman's first collection, *Total Immersion,* were called "exhilarating" by a *Publishers Weekly* contributor, who noted that the characters "are observant Jews living in a believably rendered Oxford, England, or Honolulu, Hawaii. While committed to fixed principles, these people must adapt to a shifting, alien, and seductive world." A *Kirkus Reviews* contributor called the volume a "light, amusing work, impressive in its pan-shots and sharp, short needling." *Library Journal* critic Alice Shane named *Total Immersion* a "dazzling collection of short stories, replete with razor-sharp perceptions and a sense of high comedy."

The Family Markowitz is a collection of ten stories, all but one previously published in either the *New Yorker* or *Commentary.* A *Publishers Weekly* contributor wrote that Goodman "combines delicious comic set pieces with deeper meditations and conversations on Jewish identity, God, frazzled relationships amid the breakdown of family life." The installments span approximately ten years in the lives of three generations of a family, including memorable moments, the usual misunderstandings, and the affection, tensions, loneliness, and other emotions that become apparent under close scrutiny. *Booklist* contributor Donna Seaman called the characters "real people everyone can relate to." "The writing is so deft and affectionate, the skewed perceptions so familiar, the dialogue rings so painfully true and is so funny that the stories often feel lighter than they are," wrote Naomi Glauberman in the *Los Angeles Times Book Review.*

The book begins with the death of Rose Markowitz's second husband, Maury Rosenberg, in New York City. Rose's family now consists of her two sons, Ed and Henry. Ed, a professor teaching at Georgetown University, is married to Sarah and is the father of four children; he has little time to spare for his mother and little understanding of his college-age children. One daughter is a vegetarian, and another, Miriam, is a Harvard Medical School student who embraces orthodoxy and is strictly kosher. Henry, who is unmarried and in therapy as he grapples with his sexual identity, brings his mother to Venice, California, where he works in an art gallery. But after a few years of listening to her harping, Henry drops her off at a senior citizens' facility and heads to Oxford, England, to manage a Laura Ash-

ley store. Rose's regular visitor becomes Alma Renquist, a graduate student who interviews her for a thesis. Glauberman called Goodman "brilliant at capturing the clutter of both interior and exterior life—her characters often say one thing while their minds are elsewhere." Claire Messud wrote in a *New York Times Book Review* article that *The Family Markowitz* "has great consistency and charm. One of the characters reflects that 'there must be a way to draw with human sight. There has to be a rule for finding significant details, a method of selective focus.' And this is Ms. Goodman's own project: the stories' details are selective and significant, and draw upon the wealth of Jewish culture out of which Ms. Goodman writes. It is their weight and accuracy that make the collection so entertaining." Among the stories in the volume are "The Four Questions," about a Passover dinner, "Mosquitoes," which finds Ed at an interfaith conference in rural Minnesota, and "The Persians," in which Ed and Sarah shop for an appropriate book to be given as a bat mitzvah gift to the daughter of friends. *Salon.com* critic Dwight Garner felt that Goodman's "unfussy, matter-of-fact style borrows from Grace Paley and Philip Roth, but in *The Family Markowitz . . .* Goodman sounds like nobody else. You move through these smart and slyly funny stories . . . with an increasing appreciation of her deep-seated talent."

Kaaterskill Falls, Goodman's first novel, takes place between the years 1976 and 1978. It is a story about three families who belong to a Washington Heights community of Orthodox Jews led by Rav Elijah Kirshner. Each summer the families go with their rabbi to the Catskills in upper New York State to vacation. In failing health, Rav Kirshner is faced with choosing which of his sons, Isaiah or Jeremy, will inherit the religious community. The loyal but dull Isaiah, with the help of his wife, Rachel, has served as his father's secretary, while the older son, Jeremy, is a scholar who favors the secular over the religious world. Another family includes Isaac Shulman and his wife, Elizabeth, who are the parents of five daughters. Elizabeth, who longs to have something of her own, receives permission from Elijah to open a small kosher grocery in Kaaterskill, New York. The third family is headed by Andras Melish, a character *New Leader* reviewer Tova Reich called "perhaps the most interesting in the book."

Salon.com reviewer Laura Green felt that in *Kaaterskill Falls,* "the broad canvas does mute the reader's response to individual characters; we feel interest in many, but allegiance to none. To the extent that Goodman chooses a primary consciousness, it's Elizabeth's; most readers will easily sympathize with her desire for 'the quick and subtle negotiations of the outside world.' But Goodman refuses to make *Kaaterskill Falls* a story of individual triumph over stifling communal norms." Ruth R. Wisse wrote in *Commentary:* "Like the teaching of Rav Kirshner, this novel points in contradictory directions, inward to the specifically Jewish and outward to the embrace of America. Goodman's description of the difficult succession from the Rav to his younger son quite brilliantly suggests how and why in contemporary Jewish life Orthodoxy can become 'ultra-Orthodoxy,' how behavior becomes stricter, more defensive, more rigid. And the personal rivalry between the brothers Jeremy and Isaiah hints at why the cultural rivalry between the secular and religious branches of American Jewry is unlikely to go away." Alice McDermott, writing in *Commonweal,* called the novel "a tapestry, a panoramic view of a community, a people, and a place."

The protagonist-narrator of Goodman's next novel, *Paradise Park,* is Sharon Spiegelman, a nonpracticing Jew from Boston who winds up in Hawaii in 1974 with her folk-dancing partner, Gary, a flaky, older graduate student who has dragged Sharon up and down the West Coast as he works for liberal causes. *Entertainment Weekly* contributor Lisa Schwarzbaum noted that "Sharon is a notable departure from Goodman's family-oriented heroines—a young woman estranged from blood relatives. Her parents are divorced, her brother dead, and her spiritual interests grow as much from her need to create family out of friends, lovers, and workmates as they do out of a hunger in her soul." The man Sharon worships eventually dumps her at a flea-bag hotel in Waikiki, the bill for which he fails to pay, and skips to Fiji with a wealthy German woman. Sharon, who is on a perpetual quest to find God, now has reality to deal with and works at a number of jobs, including catching cockroaches that are then electroplated and sold. Her new Christian Hawaiian boyfriend, Kekui, is banished from his family because of their relationship, and they spend a year growing pot in a plot of jungle owned by the government. Sharon also works at a number of more usual jobs—as a temp secretary, a cashier in a restaurant called Mambo Zippy's, and as a practice patient for medical students. She lives in the house of a drug dealer, in a monastery where she must be silent for four months, and in a co-op house where she has to fight her biologist roommates for the right to keep her cat.

"In typical picaresque style, Goodman builds a broad depiction of society by pitting her heroine against a vast succession of people and institutions," wrote Joyce Hackett in the *Boston Review.* "She renders a perfect-pitch portrait of the lost generation of 1970s hippies, both the zealous, earnest grandiosity with which they intended to remake the world and the aimless desolation induced by repudiating one set of conventional ties after another. . . . The funniest parts of this very funny book are Goodman skewering the pettiness and reductionism of so much of human spiritual searching."

The novel's title comes from the name of a bird park Sharon visits with her boyfriend of the moment, a thuggish marine. She compares the birds who bounce off the mesh ceilings that confine them in their beautiful, contrived forest with the birds she observed flying free on a remote island where she worked for a summer counting red-footed boobies with ornithologists. But even the peace of that paradise dissolved when the tiny red mites that feasted on the birds migrated to the heads of the humans.

For a time, Sharon embraces Christianity and then Buddhism, but she finally meets people who arrange for her to spend the summer at a Hasidic girls' school in Bellevue, Washington. After the summer, she goes to Brooklyn with one of the students, where she meets Mikhail, a Russian-born Orthodox Jew and pianist. They marry, and ultimately she reconnects with her parents. "Like a snow globe shaken hard, Spiegelman floats around in the events of her life until inertia causes her to settle," wrote Neal Wyatt in *Booklist.* A *Publishers Weekly* reviewer felt that "readers will finish the novel feeling that, given faith in the ultimate goodness of life, things can turn out all right."

"As a narrator Sharon proves sympathetic and compelling, her story a kind of stressed-out confession full of run-on sentences," stated Emily White in the *Voice Literary Supplement.* "Because she barely trusts herself, she often doubles back, tries to explain, directly beseeches the reader, 'Let me tell you,' as if we might not allow her to finish. Allegra Goodman's great achievement in *Paradise Park* is the way Sharon forms a subtle, needy, and highly active relationship with the reader." Melanie Rehak commented in *Harper's Bazaar* that "*Paradise Park* can be exhausting at times—Sharon, frankly, can be a bit exasperating—but Goodman's talent for channeling voices makes us eager to see the character through to the end." Writing in the *Washington Post Book World,* Carolyn See praised the first two hundred pages of the novel. "The charm . . .

here has to do with the dissonance between Sharon's 'seeking' self as she remembers it and the utter pain-in-the-rear she was in real life." "Long winded and often comically clueless, the protagonist of *Paradise Park* may not be a very heroic heroine, but she's an endearingly human one in her neverending search for self-knowledge," wrote Judith Wynn in the *Boston Herald.*

"Books of spiritual searching are not new, of course," wrote Maude A. McDaniel in the *World and I,* "but a seeker like Sharon is surely out of the ordinary in the literary world. Yet in her vernacular, yes, even shallow, approach to the whole matter of finding God, she breaks new ground. Goodman may be no Dostoyevsky, but in this case, Goodman is more than good enough." In a *New York Times Book Review* article, Jennifer Schuessler wrote that "the challenge with a questing first-person narrator is to give him or her a voice the reader wants to follow into the wilderness of a made-up world, and one that allows us to see more of the tale than the teller does. Think Huck Finn or Holden Caulfield. . . . Sharon's got the voice all right; the novel is a bright bauble of clear, rain-washed prose and low-key humor." *Commentary* contributor John Podhoretz felt that "Allegra Goodman's willingness to experiment with new voices, and new ways of telling her brilliantly conceived stories of Jews in conflict with modernity, only makes us hungry for more." *Time* reviewer Paul Gray concluded: "Like Saul Bellow and Philip Roth before her, Goodman has achieved a breakthrough book by discovering and recording a thoroughly uninhibited narrative voice."

With her novel *Intuition,* Goodman offers a "delicate analysis of how an ethics scandal filters through the sensibility of brilliant and brilliantly realized characters," commented Jennifer Reese in *Entertainment Weekly.* "It's a tricky operation that Goodman performs with the precision of a scientist, and the flair of an artist at the top of her game." The story centers on four cancer researchers at the cash-strapped Philpot Institute in Cambridge, MA. The institute's director, Marion Mendelssohn, is a careful and cautious scientist. Her codirector and philosophical opposite, Sandy Glass, is a brash, outgoing doctor and administrator with excellent political and people skills. Cliff and Robin are post-doctoral researchers at the institute, embroiled in an on-again, off-again relationship and laboring under the stress of high-stakes research. As the lab's work grinds on with little progress, Cliff's experiments suddenly show astonishing results when a previously ineffective virus appears to have the effect of shrinking tumors in mice.

Recognizing the huge potential of Cliff's findings—medically, financially, and as a career-making discovery—Mendelssohn encourages caution and further study. Glass, on the other hand, wants to announce the discovery immediately before the results are replicated or confirmed, thinking it better to be in error than to risk having another laboratory claim the process first. Glass courts the media and touts the breakthrough, but in the background, Robin makes a disturbing discovery of her own: the possibility that Cliff's discovery is a sham, his results fabricated or, at best, exaggerated. When the effects of this discovery come crashing down on the institute in the form of scandal and congressional investigations, the lives of all four characters are irrevocably changed. "Goodman's sympathetic yet floundering characters are compelling, their conflicts provocative, and her writing spellbinding" as the story of their conflict and quandary unfolds, stated *Booklist* reviewer Donna Seaman. Goodman's portrayal of the characters and their situation unfolds in a "riveting, calibrating narrative revelation while preserving the ambiguities of scientific dispute," remarked Zackary Sholem Berger in *Forward.* "This is moral fiction without moralizing," Berger concluded. "In deft, tight, and wonderfully playful prose," Goodman "creates characters whose strengths and weaknesses intertwine in close encounters at home, at work, at synagogue, and at play" commented reviewer Sally Vallongo in the *Toledo Blade.* A *New Yorker* reviewer commented favorably on the "aesthetic delicacy of Goodman's writing." Goodman "draws tender but unflinching portraits" of her characters, observed a *Publishers Weekly* reviewer, deriving a "truly humanist novel from the supposedly antiseptic halls of science."

BIOGRAPHICAL AND CRITICAL SOURCES:

PERIODICALS

America's Intelligence Wire, April 14, 2006, Rhonda Shafner, "Allegra Goodman Talks about Her New Novel about a Cancer Research Laboratory," profile of Allegra Goodman.

Atlanta Journal-Constitution, March 11, 2001, David Kirby, "Books: Flighty Truth-Seeker in 'Paradise' Would Be Right at Home in '60s," p. D4.

Book, March, 2001, Chris Barsanti, review of *Paradise Park,* p. 76.

Booklist, September 15, 1996, Donna Seaman, review of *The Family Markowitz,* p. 203; July, 1998, Vanessa Bush, review of *Kaaterskill Falls,* p. 1856;

January 1, 2000, Karen Harris, review of *Kaaterskill Falls,* p. 948; February 1, 2001, Neal Wyatt, review of *Paradise Park,* p. 1039; December 15, 2005, Donna Seaman, review of *Intuition,* p. 5.

Boston Herald, March 25, 2001, Judith Wynn, "On the Road to 'Paradise'—Flighty Heroine Recounts Her Odyssey to Adulthood," p. 58.

Boston Review, April-May, 2001, Joyce Hackett, review of *Paradise Park,* p. 34.

Commentary, December, 1998, Ruth R. Wisse, review of *Kaaterskill Falls,* p. 67; May, 2001, John Podhoretz, review of *Paradise Park,* p. 70.

Commonweal, November 6, 1998, Alice McDermott, review of *Kaaterskill Falls,* p. 16.

Entertainment Weekly, March 16, 2001, Lisa Schwarzbaum, "The Wanderer: A Boom in Fiction by Jewish-American Women Continues with Allegra Goodman's Vital *Paradise Park,*" p. 60; March 3, 2006, Jennifer Reese, "Lab Dances: In Allegra Goodman's *Intuition,* a Team of Cancer Researchers Turn on One Another," review of *Intuition,* p. 104.

Forward, April 7, 2006, Zackary Sholam Berger, "Allegra Goodman's Science Fiction," review of *Intuition.*

Harper's Bazaar, March, 2001, Melanie Rehak, "Holy Daze," p. 336.

Houston Chronicle, June 24, 2001, Harvey Grossinger, "Allegra Goodman Heroine Learns a Song of Sharon," p. 21.

Kirkus Reviews, March 15, 1989, review of *Total Immersion,* p. 403.

Kliatt, September, 2006, Nola Theiss, audiobook review of *Intuition,* p. 50.

Library Journal, May 15, 1989, Alice Shane, review of *Total Immersion,* p. 88; August, 1996, Molly Abramowitz, review of *The Family Markowitz,* p. 116; June 15, 1998, Beth E. Andersen, review of *Kaaterskill Falls,* p. 105; August, 1999, Joyce Kessel, review of *Kaaterskill Falls,* p. 163; January 1, 2001, Yvette Olson, review of *Paradise Park,* p. 154; January 1, 2006, Starr E. Smith, review of *Intuition,* p. 96.

Los Angeles Times Book Review, February 16, 1997, Naomi Glauberman, "Life Is Elsewhere," p. 10.

Nation, November 23, 1998, Tom LeClair, review of *Kaaterskill Falls,* p. 27.

New Leader, October 5, 1998, Tova Reich, review of *Kaaterskill Falls,* p. 18.

New Yorker, March 20, 2006, "Briefly Noted," review of *Intuition,* p. 149.

New York Times, June 26, 1997, Sara Rimer, "A Fiction Writer without Neuroses?," p. C1; March 5, 2006, Sue Halpern, "Scientific Americans," review of *Intuition;* March 21, 2006, Gina Kolata, "Writer Depicts Scientists Risking Glory for Truth and Truth for Glory," review of *Intuition,* p. F3.

New York Times Book Review, September 10, 1989, Randi Hacker, review of *Total Immersion,* p. 26; October 22, 1996, Michiko Kakutani, review of *The Family Markowitz,* p. B2; November 3, 1996, Claire Messud, "The Autumn of the Matriarch," p. 14; August 21, 1998, Michiko Kakutani, review of *Kaaterskill Falls,* p. 40; August 30, 1998, Daphne Merkin, review of *Kaaterskill Falls,* p. 13; March 11, 2001, Jennifer Schuessler, "Looking for Love: Abandoned in Hawaii, the Heroine of Allegra Goodman's Novel Embarks on a Spiritual Quest," p. 10; June 3, 2001, review of *Paradise Park,* p. 26.

Publishers Weekly, March 24, 1989, review of *Total Immersion,* p. 58; July 15, 1996, review of *The Family Markowitz,* p. 54; May 25, 1998, review of *Kaaterskill Falls,* p. 62; July 27, 1998, Ivan Kreilkamp, "Allegra Goodman: A Community Apart," p. 48; January 1, 2001, review of *Paradise Park,* p. 64; December 5, 2005, review of *Intuition,* p. 29; April 3, 2006, audiobook review of *Intuition,* p. 67.

School Library Journal, October, 2001, Jan Tarasovic, review of *Paradise Park,* p. 194.

Time, March 26, 2001, Paul Gray, "Portnoy, Move Over: Allegra Goodman's Breakthrough Novel Follows a Flower Child on Her Comic Quest for Enlightenment," p. 72.

Toledo Blade, March 26, 2006, Sally Vallongo, "Characters Shine in New Novel of Scientific Intrigue," review of *Intuition.*

U.S. News & World Report, March 12, 2001, Marc Silver, "Like Jane Austen, Only Jewish," p. 82.

Vogue, August, 1998, Mary Cantwell, review of *Kaaterskill Falls,* p. 142.

Voice Literary Supplement, March, 2001, Emily White, "Escape Clause."

Wall Street Journal, August 14, 1998, Pearl K. Bell, review of *Kaaterskill Falls,* p. W7; March 16, 2001, Bella Stander, review of *Paradise Park,* p. W8.

Washington Post Book World, March 2, 2001, Carolyn See, "Seeking Is Believing," p. C06; February 26, 2006, Ron Charles, interview with Allegra Goodman, p. 3; February 26, 2006, Geraldine Brooks, "Experimenting with the Truth," review of *Intuition,* p. 3.

World and I, June, 2001, Maude A. McDaniel, "A Flake for All Seasons," p. 246.

ONLINE

Allegra Goodman Home Page, http://theory.lcs.mit.edu/ ˜karger/allegra.html (January 7, 2007).

BookPage, http://www.bookpage.com/ (January 2, 2007), Alden Mudge, "Coming of Age on the Rollicking Road to Paradise," interview with Allegra Goodman.

Bookreporter.com, http://www.bookreporter.com/ (March 3, 2006), Joni Rendon, interview with Allegra Goodman; (January 2, 2007), review of *Paradise Park,* and Joni Rendon, review of *Intuition.*

Bookslut.com, http://www.bookslut.com/ (May, 2006), Barbara J. King, "Allegra Goodman's World of Science," review of *Intuition.*

Powells.com, http://www.powells.com (January 2, 2007), Dave Weich, interview with Allegra Goodman.

Salon.com, http://www.salon.com/ (November 5, 996), Dwight Garner, review of *The Family Markowitz;* (July 31, 1998) Laura Green, review of *Kaaterskill Falls.**

*   *   *

GORE, Ariel 1971-

PERSONAL: Born in 1971; children: Maia. *Education:* Mills College, B.A.; University of California at Berkeley, M.A.

ADDRESSES: Home and office—P.O. Box 12525, Portland, OR 97212. *E-mail*—arielgore@earthlink.net.

CAREER: Hip Mama (magazine), Oakland, CA, founder and editor, 1994—

WRITINGS:

The Hip Mama Survival Guide: Advice from the Trenches on Pregnancy, Childbirth, Cool Names, Clueless Doctors, Potty Training, Toddler Avengers, Domestic Mayhem, Support Groups, Right Wing Losers, Work, Day Care, Family Law, the Evil Patriarchy, Collection Agents, Nervous Breakdowns, Hyperion (New York, NY), 1998.

The Mother Trip: Hip Mama's Guide to Staying Sane in the Chaos of Motherhood, illustrated by Susan Forney, Seal Press (New York, NY), 2000.

(Editor, with Bee Lavender) *Breeder: Real-Life Stories from the New Generation of Mothers,* illustrated by Jonny Thief, foreword by Dan Savage, Seal Press (New York, NY), 2001.

Atlas of the Human Heart (memoir), Seal Press (New York, NY), 2003.

(With daughter, Maia Swift) *Whatever, Mom: Hip Mama's Guide to Raising a Teenager,* Seal Press (Emeryville, CA), 2004.

(Editor) *The Essential Hip Mama: Writing from the Cutting Edge of Parenting,* Seal Press (Emeryville, CA), 2004.

The Traveling Death and Resurrection Show (novel), HarperSanFrancisco (San Francisco, CA), 2006.

How To Become a Famous Writer before You're Dead: Your Words in Print and Your Name in Lights, Three Rivers Press (New York, NY), 2007.

Contributor to books. Author of a blog.

SIDELIGHTS: Ariel Gore is the creator of the parenting magazine *Hip Mama* and its offshoot, *The Hip Mama Survival Guide: Advice from the Trenches on Pregnancy, Childbirth, Cool Names, Clueless Doctors, Potty Training, Toddler Avengers, Domestic Mayhem, Support Groups, Right Wing Losers, Work, Day Care, Family Law, the Evil Patriarchy, Collection Agents, Nervous Breakdowns,* a book on parenting for the nineties and beyond. After dropping out of high school in Palo Alto, California, and attaining her GED, Gore traveled across Europe and Asia. In Italy she gave birth to Maia, a daughter fathered by a man with whom she had lived for a time in an abandoned building in Amsterdam. When Gore returned to the United States, she lived with her parents. When she found that she could not support herself and her daughter, she went on public assistance for six years, which allowed her to earn journalism degrees at Mills College and the University of California.

Gore was a nontraditional journalist whose ideas about parenting were very different from those found in mainstream parenting magazines. She began *Hip Mama* as a senior project for her journalism program. "A bunch of friends were over and we were making spaghetti and I said: 'I wonder if we have a peer group,'" recalled Gore to Lori Eickmann of the *Chicago Tribune.* When Gore realized that she was not alone in her lifestyle and values, she suspected that she might have a large potential audience of nontraditional parents collecting government benefits. The quarterly magazine, which debuted in 1994, contains a wide variety of material, including practical articles on parenting and dealing with the welfare system, personal experience pieces, reviews, artwork, and recipes. "It's not really servicey, it's a support-group-type thing," Gore told Eickmann. "I try to balance political stuff, solid parenting information and literature, so that it's another voice." Many articles are contributions from the magazine's subscribers. Feminist Mary Kay Blakely is quoted in the *Chicago Tribune* as saying: "Our image of the welfare mom is shattered when we read *Hip Mama*. Ariel speaks honestly about the issues of motherhood."

Although at first reluctant to go on the internet with her periodical, in 1997 Gore took *Hip Mama* online because so many people asked her to do it. Low-income mothers had access to the internet through public libraries and colleges and universities, and the online magazine soon became a clearinghouse for information on the rapidly changing welfare laws in this country. Gore says she knows from firsthand experience that she could not support herself and her daughter and attend college at the same time. Without welfare help, she would not be where she is today—a college graduate able to support her family.

While finishing her master's degree, Gore wrote a proposal for a parenting book based on the material in her magazine. When Hyperion bought *The Hip Mama Survival Guide,* Gore was elated. Writing while Maia was at school or asleep at night, Gore gathered the voices of her peer group. The title reflects many of Gore's topics, but there are others. She is honest about the pluses and minuses of being on public assistance and addresses many of the issues facing low-income and single mothers. She writes on subjects that include avoiding guilt over such things as having a little too much to drink while pregnant and what a modern young mom should do about those body piercings before going into labor.

In reviewing *The Mother Trip: Hip Mama's Guide to Staying Sane in the Chaos of Motherhood* for the *Library Journal,* Linda Beck commented: "What looks to be a breezy . . . certainly untraditional book about motherhood is really worthwhile." Gore writes of the isolation, heartbreak, and delight of motherhood, interjecting personal anecdotes and her opinions regarding motherhood in America.

As the success of both the print magazine and *Hip Mama Online* grew, Gore gave control of the Web site to Bee Lavender, who is coeditor of Gore's *Breeder: Real-Life Stories from the New Generation of Mothers.* Contributors are young women from all economic situations, with various sexual preferences, married and not. Many of the stories are poignant, while others are humorous. Beck wrote that "here are women who chose to follow their dreams without trading on others." A *Publishers Weekly* contributor noted "the recurrent themes sounded by these Gen-X voices—alienation, economic insecurity and the importance of health insurance."

Atlas of the Human Heart is Gore's memoir in which she traces her travel, at the age of sixteen, to Hong Kong, and the years as a student, smuggler, squatter, and actress she spent as she moved on to Tibet, Nepal, India, Amsterdam, and England. She comments on the violent nature of her relationship with her child's father, Maia's birth in Italy, and her return to California with her newborn daughter.

Gore's first work of fiction is *The Traveling Death and Resurrection Show,* the story of Frances Catherine, or "Frankka," a stigmatic who can cause her palms to bleed when she is hungry. *Booklist* contributor Kristine Huntley wrote that the story "limns one woman's complicated relationship with her religion and her personal faith." Frankka keeps her secret until she is in college, where she shares it with Tony, and the two concoct a religious-themed traveling theater that eventually includes other performers, such as a bearded lady, trapeze artist, levitating drag queen, psychic, and fire eater. Problems arise when the evangelical community protests what they perceive to be sacrilege after the show is reviewed in the *Los Angeles Times.* In a *Library Journal* review, Eleanor J. Bader called the novel "a savvy rebuke of religious bigotry and a fun, fast, memorable read."

BIOGRAPHICAL AND CRITICAL SOURCES:

BOOKS

Gore, Ariel, *Atlas of the Human Heart,* Seal Press (New York, NY), 2003.

PERIODICALS

Booklist, April 1, 2003, Beth Leistensnider, review of *Atlas of the Human Heart,* p. 1359; February 1, 2006, Kristine Huntley, review of *The Traveling Death and Resurrection Show,* p. 28.

Chicago Tribune, April 13, 1997, Lori Eickmann, interview.

Library Journal, May 15, 2000, Linda Beck, review of *The Mother Trip: Hip Mama's Guide to Staying Sane in the Chaos of Motherhood,* p. 112; May 1, 2001, Linda Beck, review of *Breeder: Real-Life Stories from the New Generation of Mothers,* p. 114; August, 2003, Shelley Cox, review of *Atlas of the Human Heart,* p. 96; January 1, 2006, Eleanor J. Bader, review of *The Traveling Death and Resurrection Show,* p. 96.

National Review, September 14, 1998, Wendy Shalit, review of *The Hip Mama Survival Guide: Advice from the Trenches on Pregnancy, Childbirth, Cool Names, Clueless Doctors, Potty Training, Toddler Avengers, Domestic Mayhem, Support Groups, Right Wing Losers, Work, Day Care, Family Law, the Evil Patriarchy, Collection Agents, Nervous Breakdowns,* p. 68.

Publishers Weekly, March 26, 2001, review of *Breeder,* p. 81; January 9, 2006, review of *The Traveling Death and Resurrection Show,* p. 29.

OTHER

Annabelle, http://www.annnabellemagazine.com/ (November 26, 2006), interview.

Ariel Gore Home Page, http://www.arielgore.com (November 26, 2006).

Bookslut, http://www.bookslut.com/ (May 3, 2005), Elizabeth Klein, "An Interview with Ariel Gore."

Here, http://www.heremagazine.com/ (November 26, 2006), Katie Haegele, "Somewhere to Run To: An Interview with Ariel Gore."

Hip Mama Online, http://www.hipmama.com (November 26, 2006).

The New Homemaker, http://www.newhomemaker.com/ (November 26, 2006), Lynn Siprelle, "Ariel Gore: A *TNH* Interview."*

*   *   *

GRANT, John 1933-

(Jonathan Gash, Graham Gaunt, Jonathan Grant)

PERSONAL: Born September 30, 1933, in Bolton, Lancastershire, England; son of Peter Watson (a mill worker) and Anne (a mill worker) Grant; married Pam- ela Richard (a nurse), February 19, 1955; children: Alison Mary, Jacqueline Clare, Yvonne. *Education:* University of London, M.B., B.S., 1958; Royal College of Surgeons and Physicians, M.R.C.S., L.R.C.P., 1958; also earned D.Path., D.Bact., D.H.M., M.D., and D.T. M.H. *Hobbies and other interests:* Music ("I play a few instruments; choral music"), history, antiques.

ADDRESSES: Home—England.

CAREER: General practitioner in London, England, 1958-59; pathologist in London and Essex, England, 1959-62; clinical pathologist in Hannover and Berlin, Germany, 1962-65; University of Hong Kong, Hong Kong, lecturer in clinical pathology and head of division, 1965-68; microbiologist in Hong Kong and London, 1968-71; University of London, School of Hygiene and Tropical Medicine, London, head of bacteriology unit, 1971-88. *Military service:* British Army, Medical Corps; attained rank of major; served in Germany.

MEMBER: International College of Surgeons (fellow), Royal Society of Tropical Medicine (fellow).

AWARDS, HONORS: Creasy Award, Crime Writers' Association, 1977, for *The Judas Pair.*

WRITINGS:

"LOVEJOY" MYSTERIES; UNDER PSEUDONYM JONATHAN GASH

The Judas Pair, Harper (New York, NY), 1977.

Gold by Gemini, Harper (New York, NY), 1978.

The Grail Tree, Harper (New York, NY), 1979.

Spend Game, Collins (London, England) 1980, Ticknor & Fields (New Haven, CT), 1981.

The Vatican Rip, Collins (London, England), 1981, Ticknor & Fields (New Haven, CT), 1982.

The Sleepers of Erin, Dutton (New York, NY), 1983.

Firefly Gadroon, St. Martin's Press (New York, NY), 1984.

The Gondola Scam, St. Martin's Press (New York, NY), 1984.

Pearlhanger, St. Martin's Press (New York, NY), 1985.

The Tartan Sell, St. Martin's Press (New York, NY), 1986, published as *The Tartan Ringers,* Collins (London, England), 1986.

Moonspender, St. Martin's Press (New York, NY), 1987.

Jade Woman, St. Martin's Press (New York, NY), 1989.

The Very Last Gambado, St. Martin's Press (New York, NY), 1990.

The Great California Game, St. Martin's Press (New York, NY), 1991.

The Lies of Fair Ladies, St. Martin's Press (New York, NY), 1992.

Paid and Loving Eyes, St. Martin's Press (New York, NY), 1993.

The Sin within Her Smile, Viking (New York, NY), 1994.

The Grace in Older Women, Viking (New York, NY), 1995.

The Possessions of a Lady, Viking (New York, NY), 1996.

The Rich and the Profane, Macmillan (London, England), 1998, Viking (New York, NY), 1999.

A Rag, a Bone, and a Hank of Hair, Viking (New York, NY), 2000.

Every Last Cent, Macmillan (London, England), 2001, Viking (New York, NY), 2002.

The Ten Word Game, St. Martin's Minotaur, 2004.

"DR. CLARE BURTONALL" MYSTERIES; UNDER PSEUDONYM JONATHAN GASH

Different Women Dancing, Viking (New York, NY), 1997.

Prey Dancing, Viking (New York, NY), 1998.

Die Dancing, Macmillan (London, England), 2000, Viking (New York, NY), 2001.

Bone Dancing, Allison & Busby (London, England), 2003.

Blood Dancing, Allison & Busby (London, England), 2006.

OTHER

(Under pseudonym Jonathan Gash) *Member of Parliament,* M. Joseph (London, England), 1974.

Terminus (play), produced at Chester Festival, England, 1976.

(Under pseudonym Graham Gaunt) *The Incomer,* Doubleday (New York, NY), 1982.

(Under pseudonym Jonathan Grant) *Mehala, Lady of Sealandings,* 1993.

(Under pseudonym Jonathan Gash) *The Year of the Woman,* Allison & Busby (London, England), 2004.

(Under pseudonym Jonathan Gash) *Finding Davey* (juvenile), Allison & Busby (London, England), 2005.

Screenwriter of various "Lovejoy" television episodes; contributor of poems to *Record;* contributor to *Journal of the Lancashire Dialect Society* and to books, including *Winter's Crimes 11,* edited by George Hardinge, St. Martin's Press (New York, NY), 1979; *The Year's Best Mystery and Suspense Stories,* edited by Edward D. Hock, Walker (New York, NY), 1982; *Winter's Crimes 18,* edited by Hilary Hale, Macmillan (London, England), 1986; *Winter's Crimes 21,* edited by Hilary Hale, Macmillan (London, England), 1989; and *1st Culprit: A Crime Writers' Association Annual,* St. Martin's Press (New York, NY), 1993.

ADAPTATIONS: Grant's Lovejoy novels were adapted for the television series *Lovejoy,* produced by the British Broadcasting Corporation (BBC-TV) and starring Ian McShane.

SIDELIGHTS: Novelist John Grant, known to his fans by the nom de plume Jonathan Gash, is the creator of the widely successful "Lovejoy" mystery series. Grant's experiences of the 1970s, working in the antique stalls of London during his days as a medical student, inspired a lifelong interest in antiques, as well as his budding career as a novelist. Antiques would figure prominently in the stories featuring Grant's Lovejoy, who first appeared in the 1977 novel *The Judas Pair.* Encouraged by the success of that first novel, which won the Crime Writers' Association's Creasy Award, Grant continued his literary endeavors.

Protagonist Lovejoy is an English antiques dealer, and not a typical hero. He is often broke, is unethical in his business dealings, is a great lover of women, and is devoted to antiques. His heroism lies in his dedication to what he does and his constant pursuit of the truth.

In reviewing *The Grace in Older Women,* which finds Lovejoy cavorting with more mature ladies, *Booklist* reviewer Emily Melton commented that Grant "has the formula for success down pat, but he's never repetitive—each story is more outrageously fun and funny than the last." Melton wrote that with *The Possessions of a Lady,* "Grant offers up another hilarious tale featuring one of the most appealing eccentrics in crime fiction." In her review of the twentieth Lovejoy mystery,

The Rich and the Profane, Jenny McLarin noted in *Booklist* that "seemingly thousands of ancillary characters are involved in an astonishing variety of scams, schemes, thefts, and affairs," while a *Publishers Weekly* reviewer called Grant "in top form."

In *A Rag, a Bone, and a Hank of Hair,* Lovejoy's research to verify the authenticity of green gemstones leads him to another mystery, as the antiquing sleuth discovers his old partner has died mysteriously. A *Publishers Weekly* reviewer wrote that "the pace is more than leisurely, with many a detour to natter about antiques. . . . Fans will chuckle all the way." "Lovable rogue Lovejoy has found a permanent home on the shady side of the antiques trade," noted Bill Ott in his *Booklist* appraisal, adding that aficionados of Grant's series "will have a ball this time."

In the novel *The Ten Word Game,* Lovejoy steals his own Rembrandt forgery and is kidnapped and taken aboard a Russian cruise ship whose passengers are antiques collectors and experts. His kidnappers want him to steal authentic treasure, and Lovejoy, who is tolerant of forging, but who opposes stealing, is busy running from the thugs who would have him lift Old Masters from the Hermitage Museum, aided by his only ally, Margaret Dainty. A *Kirkus Reviews* contributor wrote that "the plot is goofy from the get-go, but the talk and erudition are first-rate." "As always in this series, readers will learn much about art and antiques along the way," noted Connie Fletcher in *Booklist,* who described this installment as being "a beautifully written, riveting mystery romp."

Following his retirement from the practice of medicine in 1988, Grant, still writing as Gash, developed a second series featuring cardiologist Clare Burtonall. In *Different Women Dancing,* Clare's life is one of hospital routine and marriage to a wealthy realtor involved in shady schemes. She witnesses an accident and becomes involved with Bonn, a fellow witness who is a former seminary student-turned-male prostitute. A *Publishers Weekly* reviewer described Bonn as "a kind of Candide, innocent and charismatic, a rising star in the underworld of sex for hire and the syndicate of which he is a part." *Booklist* reviewer David Pitt compared Grant's new series to the Lovejoy books, noting that the Clare Burtonall books promised to be "a lot rougher." Writing in the *Library Journal,* contributor Rex E. Klett praised *Different Women Dancing* as being "told with the author's accustomed panache."

Clare has become a sometime customer of Bonn, and readers find her drawn into his world of drugs and violence, in the novel *Prey Dancing.* A *Publishers Weekly* reviewer noted of the novel that, "in edgy, slangy, and original prose, [Grant] captures his quirky cast and unusual settings to create entertainment of the first rank." *Booklist* reviewer Emily Melton dubbed *Prey Dancing* "brilliantly written, mysterious, menacing, and filled with unforgettable characters . . . another winner in an extraordinary new series."

BIOGRAPHICAL AND CRITICAL SOURCES:

PERIODICALS

Booklist, March 15, 1995, Emily Melton, review of *The Grace in Older Women,* p. 1283; August, 1996, Emily Melton, review of *The Possessions of a Lady,* p. 1886; April 15, 1997, David Pitt, review of *Different Women Dancing,* p. 1404; July, 1998, Emily Melton, review of *Prey Dancing,* p. 1864; February 15, 1999, Jenny McLarin, review of *The Rich and the Profane,* p. 1045; February 15, 2000, Bill Ott, review of *A Rag, a Bone, and a Hank of Hair,* p. 1088; December 15, 2003, Connie Fletcher, review of *The Ten Word Game,* p. 729.

Kirkus Reviews, April 1, 1994, review of *The Sin within Her Smile,* p. 438; April 1, 1995, review of *The Grace in Older Women,* p. 432; June 15, 1996, review of *The Possessions of a Lady,* p. 860; May 1, 1997, review of *Different Women Dancing,* p. 681; December 1, 2003, review of *The Ten Word Game,* p. 1384.

Library Journal, June 1, 1997, Rex E. Klett, review of *Different Women Dancing,* p. 154.

New York Times Book Review, March 19, 1989, Newgate Callendar, review of *Jade Woman,* p. 29; July 18, 1993, Marilyn Stasio, review of *Paid and Loving Eyes,* p. 17; June 29, 1997, Marilyn Stasio, review of *Different Women Dancing,* p. 22; April 4, 1999, Marilyn Stasio, review of *The Rich and the Profane,* p. 20.

Publishers Weekly, March 13, 1995, review of *The Grace in Older Women,* p. 62; July 1, 1996, review of *Possessions of a Lady,* p. 45; April 7, 1997, review of *Different Women Dancing,* p. 76; July 6, 1998, review of *Prey Dancing,* p. 54; March 15, 1999, review of *The Rich and the Profane,* p. 50; February 14, 2000, review of *A Rag, a Bone, and a Hank of Hair,* p. 177.

ONLINE

Who Dunnit, http://www.who-dunnit.com/ (November 27, 2006), Alan Paul Curtis, review of *The Ten Word Game,* brief biography.*

GRANT, Jonathan
   See GRANT, John

* * *

GRASEMANN, Ruth Barbara
   See RENDELL, Ruth, Baroness of Babergh

* * *

GRIPPANDO, James 1958-
   (James M. Grippando)

PERSONAL: Born January 27, 1958, in Waukegon, IL; married; wife's name Tiffany. *Education:* University of Florida, B.A. (with high honors), J.D. (with honors). *Hobbies and other interests:* Cycling, in-line skating, golf, sailing.

CAREER: Admitted to the Florida Bar; law clerk to Honorable Thomas Clark, U.S. Court of Appeals, 1983; worked as a trial attorney in Miami, FL, 1984-96.

MEMBER: Mystery Writers of America, Phi Beta Kappa.

AWARDS, HONORS: University of Florida Outstanding Leadership Award, University of Florida; named an "Emerging Leader under 40," *Florida Trend;* Best Novels of 1998 citation, *Bookman News,* for *The Advocate.*

WRITINGS:

"SWYTECK" SERIES

The Pardon, HarperCollins (New York, NY), 1994.
Beyond Suspicion, HarperCollins (New York, NY), 2002.
Last to Die, HarperCollins (New York, NY), 2003.
Hear No Evil, HarperCollins (New York, NY), 2004.
Got the Look, HarperCollins (New York, NY), 2006.
When Darkness Falls, HarperCollins (New York, NY), 2007.

OTHER

The Informant, HarperCollins (New York, NY), 1996.
The Abduction, HarperCollins (New York, NY), 1998.
Found Money, HarperCollins (New York, NY), 1999.
Under Cover of Darkness, HarperCollins (New York, NY), 2000.
A King's Ransom, HarperCollins (New York, NY), 2001.

Contributor to textbooks, journals and to periodicals, including *Mystery Scene.*

ADAPTATIONS: Books adapted for audio include *Under Cover of Darkness* (ten cassettes), read by Richard Poe, Recorded Books, 2000; *A King's Ransom* (four cassettes), read by John Bedford Lloyd, Harper, 2001; *Beyond Suspicion* (unabridged; seven cassettes), read by L.J. Ganser, Recorded Books, 2002; *Last to Die* (ten CDs), read by Nick Sullivan, BBC Audiobooks America, 2003; *Hear No Evil* (CDs), read by Nick Sullivan, BBC Audio Books America, 2004; and *Got the Look* (ten CDs), read by Nick Sullivan, BBC Audiobooks America, 2006.

SIDELIGHTS: Crime and suspense author James Grippando was a trial lawyer and partner at one of Florida's leading law firms before bringing his knowledge of crime to writing mystery novels.

Grippando's novel *The Informant* involves a series of seemingly unrelated and gruesome killings across the United States. An informant has begun to leak clues to a reporter at a Miami paper, but the anonymous caller demands cash for the information, which the FBI agrees to provide. The informant claims to think exactly like the killer and to be able to predict the killer's next move. In the meantime the reporter and one FBI agent, Victoria Santos, cross paths. Unlike many on the case, Santos is convinced that the informant and the killer are separate individuals. A *Publishers Weekly* contributor described it as possessing "an unusually cerebral and low-key beginning to a thriller, emphasizing procedures, forensics, and professional ethics rather than shock or even suspense." After the question regarding the identity of informant and killer is resolved, the *Publishers Weekly* contributor continued, Grippando moves the story into the more familiar territory of the thriller genre. In what Stasio called "a nice flair for the grotesque," Grippando picks up the pace and features additional murders by sharks and pythons. The final climax takes place on a cruise ship and brings all of the main characters together.

Grippando writes about the manipulative and many-layered world of politics in *The Abduction*. It is the year 2000, and Allison Leahy is the first female in the United States to run for president. Opposing her is an African-American candidate named Lincoln Howe. Howe's granddaughter, Kristen, has just been mysteriously abducted, and Leahy experienced a similar tragedy years ago when her newly-adopted baby girl was abducted and never returned. Leahy is torn as to whether to become involved in the investigation of Kristen's disappearance, and she wonders whether the recent abduction is a manipulative plot by her political opponents. Others wonder whether Leahy's supporters orchestrated the abduction. Leahy ends up working with Kristen's mother to investigate the abduction, and the actions of both women cause repercussions in the political arena.

Grippando's *Found Money* offers a "cautionary tale of greed, family secrets, and the dangers of getting what you wish for," according to a *Publishers Weekly* critic. Main character Ryan learns that his recently deceased father had two million dollars hidden in the attic, the money obtained through blackmail. Ryan decides to do nothing about the money until he can learn more about its origin, which leads to a flurry of investigations by the FBI and other officials. In the meantime, after Amy Parkins receives a 200,000 dollar cash gift that she traces back to Ryan's deceased father, Ryan and Amy work together to uncover a conspiracy involving corporations and high-level political figures.

A serial killer is pursued by rookie FBI agent Andie Henning in *Under Cover of Darkness*. The story begins with Beth, wife of Seattle attorney Gus Wheatley, disappearing without a trace, and without taking anything with her, after which other young women turn up dead. A *Publishers Weekly* contributor wrote: "The most successful component of this story is Gus Wheatley's growing awareness of his emotional separation from his family."

A King's Ransom finds Florida lawyer Nick Rey dealing with a ransom demand after his father, Matthew, a fisherman involved in a Nicaraguan seafood business, is kidnapped while in Colombia. As the facts surface, it appears that Matthew was under suspicion for dealing drugs and also had an insurance policy for exactly the amount of the ransom demand. A *Publishers Weekly* reviewer wrote: "Grippando's experience as a trial lawyer shows in his depiction of Nick's frantic legal moves to clear his family's name."

In 1994 Grippando began a mystery series featuring the character of Miami attorney Jack Swyteck. In *Beyond Suspicion,* the second book in the series, Jack discovers that his former girlfriend, Jessie Merrill, and her doctor, faked a medical condition that condemned her to death in the very near future. Jessie then sold a three million dollar insurance policy for half that amount. She retains Jack, who wins the case when Viatical Solutions, owned by the Russian mob, sues to recover their loss. It is after the case is decided that Jack learns that both he and the Russians have been had. When Jessie is killed, there are a number of suspects, including Jack, now in a shaky marriage to Cindy.

Jack's jazz musician buddy Theo Knight asks Jack to defend his brother, Tatum, formerly a hit man, in *Last to Die*. Tatum was once contacted by Sally Fenning, who wanted to hire him to kill her, and now she has been found dead. Her will stipulates that her fortune is to go to the last survivor of the six people she names, none of whom she ever really liked. In order to clear Tatum, Jack must uncover the facts surrounding Sally's death, as well as that of her daughter, who at the age of four was drowned by an intruder. In *Hear No Evil,* Jack defends a naval officer who has been accused of murdering her husband at Guantanamo Bay. David Pitt commented in a *Booklist* review that this story is "a tight, smartly constructed mystery that will keep readers on the edge of their seats."

Jack is in a relationship with Mia Salazar in *Got the Look,* but discovers that she is married when her husband declines to pay a ransom after Mia is kidnapped. Mia is in a terrifying situation, and Jack works to free her with Andie Henning, whose personal life is now falling apart. In a *Booklist* review, Joanne Wilkinson commented on Grippando' "great feel for pacing," adding that he "writes highly effective, gripping action scenes that will leave readers in suspense until the final page."

Grippando told *CA:* "I love to write. That's why I do it. I spent four years writing a novel that was never published, and I have never once looked back on it as a waste of time. I enjoyed the process, and that's the one piece of advice I give all aspiring writers—keep it fun."

BIOGRAPHICAL AND CRITICAL SOURCES:

PERIODICALS

Booklist, August, 1996, Wes Lukowsky, review of *The Informant,* p. 1854; February 15, 1998, Mary Carroll, review of *The Abduction,* p. 998; May 1, 2000, David Pitt, review of *Under Cover of Darkness,* p. 1617; March 15, 2001, David Pitt, review of *A King's Ransom,* p. 1332; July, 2002, David Pitt, review of *Beyond Suspicion,* p. 1796; May 1, 2003, David Pitt, review of *Last to Die,* p. 1544; May 1, 2004, David Pitt, review of *Hear No Evil,* p. 1508; November 1, 2005, Joanne Wilkinson, review of *Got the Look,* p. 4.

Kirkus Reviews, July 1, 2002, review of *Beyond Suspicion,* p. 903; May 15, 2003, review of *Last to Die,* p. 701; July 15, 2004, review of *Hear No Evil,* p. 648; November 15, 2005, review of *Got the Look,* p. 1205.

Library Journal, April 1, 1997, p. 145; March 15, 1998, Susan A. Zappia, review of *The Abduction,* p. 93; January, 1999, Susan A. Zappia, review of *Found Money,* p. 150; June 1, 2000, Susan A. Zappia, review of *Under Cover of Darkness,* p. 196; April 15, 2001, Craig Shufelt, review of *A King's Ransom,* p. 131; September 1, 2002, Joel W. Tscherne, review of *Beyond Suspicion,* p. 212; June 15, 2003, Joel W. Tscherne, review of *Last to Die,* p. 100; December 1, 2005, Jeff Ayers, review of *Got the Look,* p. 112.

Publishers Weekly, July 22, 1996, review of *The Informant,* p. 227; February 9, 1998, review of *The Abduction,* pp. 71-72; January 11, 1999, review of *Found Money,* p. 57; June 5, 2000, review of *Under Cover of Darkness,* p. 70; April 16, 2001, review of *A King's Ransom,* p. 44; July 29, 2002, review of *Beyond Suspicion,* p. 50; May 19, 2003, review of *Last to Die,* p. 49; August 2, 2004, review of *Hear No Evil,* p. 52; November 7, 2005, review of *Got the Look,* p. 51.

ONLINE

Bookreporter.com, http://www.bookreporter.com/ (June 1, 2001), interview; (December 27, 2006), Ann Bruns, review of *A King's Ransom;* Joe Hartlaub, reviews of *Beyond Suspicion, Hear No Evil, Got the Look;* Judy Gigstad, review of *Last to Die.*

James Grippando Home Page, http://www.james grippando.com (December 15, 2006).*

*   *   *

GRIPPANDO, James M.
   See GRIPPANDO, James

H

HABERMAS, Juergen
   See HABERMAS, Jürgen

*   *   *

HABERMAS, Jürgen 1929-
   (Juergen Habermas)

PERSONAL: Born June 18, 1929, in Düsseldorf, Germany; son of Ernst and Grete Habermas; married Ute Wesselhoeft (a teacher), 1955; children: Tilmann, Rebekka, Judith. *Education:* Attended University of Göttingen and University of Zurich; University of Bonn, Ph.D., 1954; attended University of Marburg, 1961.

ADDRESSES: Home—Starnberg, Germany.

CAREER: Free-lance journalist, 1954-56; Institut für Sozialforschung, Frankfurt, West Germany (now Germany), research assistant, 1956-59; University of Heidelberg, Heidelberg, West Germany, professor of philosophy, 1961-64; University of Frankfurt am Main, Frankfurt am Main, Germany, professor of philosophy and sociology, 1964-71, honorary professor, 1975-82, adjunct professor, 1982-94, professor emeritus, 1994—. Max-Planck-Institut zur Erforschung der Lebensbedingungen der Wissenschaftlich-technischen Welt, director, 1971-80; Max-Planck-Institut für Sozialwissenschaften, director, 1980-81. Princeton University, Christian Gauss Lecturer, 1971; Cornell University, Messenger Lecturer, 1984; Harvard University, Tanner Lecturer, 1986; University of California, Berkeley, Howison Lecturer, 1988; National University, Seoul, Korea, Seonam

Lecturer, 1996; University of Marburg, Christian Wolff Lecturer, 2001; visiting professor at Northwestern University, beginning 1994, and New York University, beginning 1999; guest lecturer at other institutions, including New School for Social Research, Wesleyan University Middletown, CT, University of California, Santa Barbara, Haverford College, University of Pennsylvania, Collège de France, and Collège de Philosophie, Paris, France.

MEMBER: Academia Europaea (distinguished member), German Academy for Language and Poetry (distinguished member), American Academy of Arts and Sciences (honorary member), British Academy of Science (foreign member), Serbian Academy of Science (foreign member), Russian Academy of Science (foreign member).

AWARDS, HONORS: Hegel-Preis, City of Stuttgart, West Germany, 1973; Sigmund-Freud-Preis, German Academy for Language and Poetry,1976; honorary doctorate, New School for Social Research, 1980; Adorno-Preis, City of Frankfurt am Main, 1980; Geschwister-Scholl Prize, City of Munich, West Germany, 1985; Wilhelm-Leuschner Medal of Landes Hessen, 1985; Förderpreis für deutsche Wissenschaftler, Gottfried Wilhelm Leibniz-Programm der Deutschen Forschungsgemeinschaft, 1986; Sonning Prize (Copenhagen, Denmark), 1987; honorary doctorates from Hebrew University of Jerusalem, University of Buenos Aires, and University of Hamburg, 1989, University of Utrecht, 1990, Northwestern University, 1991, University of Athens, 1993, and University of Tel Aviv, 1995; Karl Jaspers Prize, University of Heidelberg, 1995; honorary doctorate from University of Bologna, 1996,

Sorbonne, University of Paris, 1997, and Cambridge University, 1999; Hessischer Kulturpreis, 1999; Helmholtz Medal, Berlin-Brandenburg Academy of Science, 2000; honorary doctorate, Harvard University, 2001; Frankfurt Book Fair Peace Prize, 2001; Prinz von Asturien Preis für Socialwissenschaften, 2003; Kyoto Prize for Philosophy, 2004; Holberg-Preis, 2005; Bruno Kreisky Prize (Vienna, Germany), 2006.

WRITINGS:

NONFICTION; IN ENGLISH TRANSLATION

Strukturwandel der Öffentlichkeit: Untersuchungen zu einer Kategorie der bürgerlichen Gesellschaft, Luchterhand (Neuwid am Rhein, Germany), 1962, new edition, Suhrkamp (Frankfurt, Germany), 1990, translation by Thomas Burger and Frederick G. Lawrence published as *The Structural Transformation of the Public Sphere: An Inquiry into a Category of Bourgeois Society,* MIT Press (Cambridge, MA), 1989.

Theorie und Praxis: Sozialphilosophische Studien, Luchterhand (Neuwid am Rhein, Germany), 1963, revised edition, Suhrkamp (Frankfurt, Germany), 1971, translation by John Viertel published as *Theory and Practice,* Beacon Press (Boston, MA), 1973.

Zur Logik der Sozialwissenschaften, J.C.B. Mohr (Tübingen, Germany), 1967, enlarged edition, Suhrkamp (Frankfurt, Germany), 1970 translation by Shierry Weber Nicholsen and Jerry A. Stark published as *On the Logic of the Social Sciences,* MIT Press (Cambridge, MA), 1988.

Erkenntnis und Interesse, Suhrkamp (Frankfurt, Germany), 1968, translation by Jeremy J. Shapiro published as *Knowledge and Human Interests,* Beacon Press (Boston, MA), 1971.

Toward a Rational Society: Student Protest, Science, and Politics (contains three essays from *Protestbewegung und Hochschulreform* [also see below] and three essays from *Technik und Wissenschaft als "Ideologie"* [also see below]), translated by Jeremy J. Shapiro, Beacon Press (Boston, MA), 1971.

Philosophisch-politische Profile, Suhrkamp (Frankfurt, Germany), 1971, translation by Frederick G. Lawrence published as *Philosophical-Political Profiles,* MIT Press (Cambridge, MA), 1983.

Legitimationsprobleme im Spätkapitalismus, Suhrkamp (Frankfurt, Germany), 1973, translation by Thomas McCarthy published as *Legitimation Crisis,* Beacon Press (Boston, MA), 1975.

Communication and the Evolution of Society, introduced and translated by Thomas McCarthy, Beacon Press (Boston, MA), 1979.

(Editor) *Stichworte zur geistigen Situation der Zeit,* Suhrkamp (Frankfurt, Germany), 1979, translation and introduction by Andrew Buchwalter published as *Observations on "The Spiritual Situation of the Age": Contemporary German Perspectives,* MIT Press (Cambridge, MA), 1984.

Theorie des kommunikativen Handelns, Suhrkamp (Frankfurt, Germany), 1981, translation by Thomas McCarthy published as *The Theory of Communicative Action,* Beacon Press (Boston, MA), 1984.

Moralbewusstsein und kommunikatives Handeln, Suhrkamp (Frankfurt, Germany), 1983, translation by Christian Lenhardt and Shierry Weber Nicholsen published as *Moral Consciousness and Communicative Action,* introduction by Thomas McCarthy, MIT Press (Cambridge, MA), 1990.

Vorstudien und Erganzungen zur Theorie des kommunikativen Handelns, Suhrkamp (Frankfurt, Germany), 1984, translation by Barbara Fultner published as *On the Pragmatics of Social Interaction: Preliminary Studies in the Theory of Communicative Action,* MIT Press (Cambridge, MA), 2001.

Der Philosophische Diskurs der Moderne, Suhrkamp (Frankfurt, Germany), 1985, translation by Frederick G. Lawrence published as *The Philosophical Discourse of Modernity: Twelve Lectures,* MIT Press (Cambridge, MA), 1987.

Autonomy and Solidarity: Interviews, edited and introduced by Peter Dews, Verso (London, England), 1986.

Nachmetaphysisches Denken: Philosophische Aufsätze, Suhrkamp (Frankfurt, Germany), 1988, translation by William Mark Hohengarten published as *Postmetaphysical Thinking: Philosophical Essays,* MIT Press (Cambridge, MA), 1992.

The New Conservatism: Cultural Criticism and the Historians' Debate, edited and translated by Shierry Weber Nicholsen, introduction by Richard Wolin, MIT Press (Cambridge, MA), 1989.

Jürgen Habermas on Society and Politics: A Reader, Beacon Press (Boston, MA), 1989.

Vergangenheit als Zukunft (interview by Michael Haller), Pendo, 1991, translation and edition by Max Pensky published as *The Past as Future: Vergangenheit als Zukunft,* foreword by Peter Hohendahl, University of Nebraska Press (Lincoln, NE), 1994.

Faktizität und Geltung, Suhrkamp (Frankfurt, Germany), 1992, translation by William Rehg published as *Between Facts and Norms: Contributions to a Discourse Theory of Law and Democracy,* MIT Press (Cambridge, MA), 1996.

Justification and Application: Remarks on Discourse Ethics, translated by Ciaran Cronin, MIT Press (Cambridge, MA), 1993.

Die Normalität einer Berliner Republik: Kleine Politische Schriften VIII, Suhrkamp (Frankfurt, Germany), 1995, translation by Steven Rendall published as *A Berlin Republic: Writings on Germany,* introduction by Peter Uwe Hohendahl, University of Nebraska Press (Lincoln, NE), 1997.

Die Einbeziehung des Anderen, Suhrkamp (Frankfurt, Germany), 1996, translation edited by Ciaran Cronin and Pablo De Greiff published as *The Inclusion of the Other: Studies in Political Theory,* MIT Press (Cambridge, MA), 1998.

Von sinnlichen Eindruck zum symbolischen Ausdruck, Suhrkamp (Frankfurt, Germany), 1997, translation by Peter Dews published as *The Liberating Power of Symbols: Philosophical Essays,* MIT Press (Cambridge, MA), 2001.

On the Pragmatics of Communication, edited by Maeve Cooke, MIT Press (Cambridge, MA), 1998.

Die postnationale Konstellation: Politische Essays, Suhrkamp (Frankfurt, Germany), 1998, translation by Max Pensky published as *The Postnational Constellation: Political Essays,* also edited and introduced by Pensky, MIT Press (Cambridge, MA), 2001.

Warheit und Rechtfertigung: Philosophische Aufsätze, Suhrkamp (Frankfurt, Germany), 1999, translation and edition by Barbara Fultner published as *Truth and Justification,* MIT Press (Cambridge, MA), 2003.

Die Zukunft der menschlichen Natur, Suhrkamp (Frankfurt, Germany), 2001, translation published as *The Future of Human Nature,* Polity Press (Cambridge, England), 2003.

Religion and Rationality: Essays on Reason, God, and Modernity, edited and introduced by Eduardo Mendieta, MIT Press (Cambridge, MA), 2002.

Giovanna Borradori, interviewer, *Philosophy in a Time of Terror: Dialogues with Jürgen Habermas and Jacques Derrida,* University of Chicago Press (Chicago, IL), 2003.

Der gespaltene Westen: Kleine Politische Schriften X, Suhrkamp (Frankfurt, Germany), 2004, translation and edition by Ciaran Cronin published as *The Divided West,* Polity Press (Cambridge, England), 2006.

IN GERMAN

Das Absolut und die Geschichte: Von der Zwiespaltigkeit in Schellings Denken, University of Bonn (Bonn, West Germany), 1954.

Student und Politik: Eine soziologische Untersuchung zum politischen Bewusstsein Frankfurter Studenten, edited by Frank Benseler, Luchterhand (Neuwid am Rhein, Germany), 1961.

Technik und Wissenschaft als "Ideologie," Suhrkamp (Frankfurt, Germany), 1968.

(Editor) *Antworten auf Herbert Marcuse,* Suhrkamp (Frankfurt, Germany), 1968.

(Editor) Friedrich Wilhelm Nietzsche, *Erkenntnistheoretische Schriften,* Suhrkamp (Frankfurt, Germany), 1968.

Protestbewegung und Hochschulreform, Suhrkamp (Frankfurt, Germany), 1969.

Arbeit, Erkenntnis, Fortschritt, Munter (Amsterdam, Netherlands), 1970.

(With Niklas Lumann) *Theorie der Gessellschaft oder Sozialtechnologie,* Suhrkamp (Frankfurt, Germany), 1971.

(Editor) *Kultur and Kritik: Verstreute Aufsätze,* Suhrkamp (Frankfurt, Germany), 1973.

Zwei Reden, Suhrkamp (Frankfurt, Germany), 1974.

Zur Rekonstruktion des historischen Materialismus, Suhrkamp (Frankfurt, Germany), 1976.

(Editor, with Rainer Doebert and Gertrud Nunner-Winkler) *Entwicklung des Ichs,* Kiepenheur & Witsch (Cologne, Germany), 1977.

Politik, Kunst, Religion: Essays über zeitgenöss, Redam (Stuttgart, Germany), 1978.

Kleine Politische Schriften I-IV, Suhrkamp (Frankfurt, Germany), 1981.

Die Neue Unübersichtlichkeit: Kleine Politische Schriften V, Suhrkamp (Frankfurt, Germany), 1985.

Eine Schadensabwicklung: Kleine Politische Schriften VI, Suhrkamp (Frankfurt, Germany), 1988.

Die Hachholende Revolution: Kleine Politische Schriften VII, Suhrkamp (Frankfurt, Germany), 1990.

Texte und Kontexte: Philosophische Aufsätze, Suhrkamp (Frankfurt, Germany), 1991.

Erläuterungen zur Diskursethik, Suhrkamp (Frankfurt, Germany) 1991.

Zeit der Übergänge: Kleine Politische Schriften IX, Suhrkamp (Frankfurt, Germany), 2001.

Kommunikatives Handeln und detranszendentalisierte Vernunft, Reclam (Stuttgart, Germany), 2001.

Zeitdiagnosen: Zwölf Essays, Suhrkamp (Frankfurt, Germany), 2003.

Zwischen Naturalismus und Religion: Philosophische Aufsätze, Suhrkamp (Frankfurt, Germany), 2005.

Also contributor to books.

SIDELIGHTS: One of Germany's best-known contemporary social theorists, Jürgen Habermas "owes his great eminence to his efforts to reestablish German philosophy's lost connection to social practice and to put it on a durable . . . basis," wrote Michael Rosen in the *Times Literary Supplement.* And, said Philip G. Altbach in *Christian Century,* "his writings have had a major impact on German liberal and radical thought and on the development of the student movement [of the 1960s] as well."

An advocate of Immanuel Kant's thesis that knowledge cannot be explicated with total objectivity because of the subjective conditions under which it is studied, Habermas rejects the positivist theory that all learning can be objectively verified by the empirical sciences; he asserts, reported Donald Capps in *Christian Century,* "that a radical critique of knowledge is possible only as social theory." "During the early stages of the student movement," observed Bertram Schefold in *Cambridge Review,* "his arguments against positivism provided an ideological weapon in the struggle for a democratic university reform."

According to Altbach, Habermas is concerned that higher education has become the servant of industrial capitalism and no longer contributes effectively to the growth of science. "Habermas feels," wrote Altbach, "that the only way to deal with this situation is to democratize the university so that its own participants—notably the students and junior faculty—can bring pressure to bear against this technological role and can press for the involvement of the universities in criticism of the society."

Theorie und Praxis: Sozialphilosophische Studien, Habermas's first major work, explains how theory is related to action and how the subject was approached in the past. *Erkenntnis und Interesse,* which Capps described as "an illumination . . . of the philosophical poverty of contemporary scientific theory," serves as an introduction to Habermas's subsequent collection *Toward a*

Rational Society: Student Protest, Science, and Politics, an account of the author's ideas about social change. Several critics praised the book's usefulness in helping readers to understand the role of higher education in society. Altbach similarly noted that the book "is a stimulating and important work," but pointed out that Habermas's "use of sociological and philosophical jargon sometimes makes this volume almost incomprehensible." Nevertheless, summarized James J. Conlin in *Best Sellers,* "it is a work to reread with profit for, although it lacks over-all unity and misses its aim of a sketch of society, this small book contains thought-provoking ideas about society and man's condition in it."

BIOGRAPHICAL AND CRITICAL SOURCES:

BOOKS

Douramanis, Demetrios, *Mapping Habermas: From German to English, 1952-1955; A Bibliography of Primary Literature,* Edition Eurotext, 1995.

Ealy, Steven D., *Communication, Speech, and Politics: Habermas and Political Analysis,* University Press of America (Washington, DC), 1981.

Habermas, Jürgen, *Autonomy and Solidarity: Interviews,* edited and introduced by Peter Dews, Verso (London, England), 1986.

Habermas, Jürgen, *Justification and Application: Remarks on Discourse Ethics,* translated by Ciaran Cronin, MIT Press (Cambridge, MA), 1993.

Held, David, *Introduction to Critical Theory: Horkheimer to Habermas,* Hutchinson (London, England), 1980.

Horster, Detlef, *Habermas: An Introduction* with contributions by Willem van Reijen, translated from German by Heidi Thompson, Pennbridge Books (Philadelphia, PA), 1992.

Keat, Russell, *The Politics of Social Theory: Habermas, Freud, and the Critique of Positivism,* University of Chicago Press (Chicago, IL), 1981.

Kelly, Michael, editor, *Critique and Power: Recasting the Foucault/Habermas Debate,* MIT Press (Cambridge, MA), 1994.

Kortian, Garbis, *Metacritique: The Philosophical Argument of Jürgen Habermas,* translated by John Raffan, with an introductory essay by Charles Taylor and Alan Montefiore, Cambridge University Press (New York, NY), 1980.

McCarthy, Thomas A., *The Critical Theory of Jürgen Habermas,* MIT Press (Cambridge, MA, 1978.

Nordquist, Joan, compiler, *Jürgen Habermas: A Bibliography,* Reference and Research Services (Santa Cruz, CA), 1986.

Rasmussen, D.M., *Reading Habermas,* Basil Blackwell (Oxford, England), 1990.

Sensat, Julius, Jr., *Habermas and Marxism: An Appraisal,* Sage Publications (Beverly Hills, CA), 1979.

Thinkers of the Twentieth Century, 2nd edition, St. James Press (Detroit, MI), 1987.

Thompson, John B., and David Held, editors, *Habermas, Critical Debates,* MIT Press (Cambridge, MA), 1982.

White, Stephen K., *The Recent Work of Jürgen Habermas: Reason, Justice, and Modernity,* Cambridge University Press (New York, NY), 1988.

PERIODICALS

Best Sellers, November 15, 1970, James F. Conlin, review of *Toward a Rational Society: Student Protest, Science, and Politics.*

Cambridge Review, May 7, 1971.

Choice, July, 1972; June, 1974; September, 1979; June, 1984; February, 1988.

Christian Century, November 25, 1970; September 29, 1971.

Times Literary Supplement, June 5, 1969; February 26, 1971; December 17, 1971; February 11, 1972; October 4, 1974; November 28, 1980; May 18, 1984; October 5, 1984; February 13, 1987.

*　　*　　*

HALL, Steffie
See EVANOVICH, Janet

*　　*　　*

HARDWICK, Gary 1960-
(Gary C. Hardwick, Gary Clifford Hardwick)

PERSONAL: Born May 4, 1960, in Detroit, MI; son of Willie Steve and Mary Louise Hardwick; married Susan Annette Hall, July 2, 1988; children: Bailey Alexander. *Education:* University of Michigan, B.A., 1982; Wayne State University, J.D., 1985. *Religion:* Baptist.

CAREER: Writer, attorney, screenwriter, director, actor, comic, and novelist. Admitted to the Bar of Michigan, 1985. U.S. Bankruptcy Court for eastern district Michigan, Detroit, law clerk to presiding justice, 1985-87; Michigan Consolidated Gas Company, attorney, 1988-90; U.S. Department of Justice, Los Angeles, CA, U.S. Trustee, 1990—. Disney Studios fellow. Actor in films, including *The Brothers.*

MEMBER: American Bar Association, Michigan Bar Association, California Bar Association, Wolverine County Bar Association, Association for Corporate Counsel.

WRITINGS:

NOVELS

Cold Medina, Dutton (New York, NY), 1996.
Double Dead, Dutton (New York, NY), 1997.
Supreme Justice, William Morrow (New York, NY), 1999.
Color of Justice, William Morrow (New York, NY), 2002.
The Executioner's Game, William Morrow (New York, NY), 2005.

SCREENPLAYS

Trippin', October Films, 1999.
(And director) *The Brothers,* Screen Gems, 2001.
(Cowriter, and director) *Deliver Us from Eva,* USA Films, 2003.
(And producer and director) *Universal Remote,* USA Films, 2007.

Also author of scripts for television series, including *Hangin' with Mr. Cooper,* 1992, *Where I Live,* ABC, 1993, *South Central,* FOX, 1994, *Me and the Boys* (also producer), ABC, 1994, *In the House* (also producer), NBC/UPN, 1995, *Matt Waters* (also producer), CBS, 1996, and *Spawn Animated,* HBO.

SIDELIGHTS: Television scriptwriter, attorney, screenwriter, director, and mystery novelist Gary Hardwick brings his life experience to his suspenseful stories of crime in the streets of Detroit. Hardwick grew up in

Detroit and loved above all to watch television and to write—in fact, they are still his favorite pastimes. But he opted for a career in law, performing stand-up comedy to pay the bills while he was in law school. Hardwick actually wrote his first novel when he was nineteen, but did not write another until many years later since, in his words, "young people don't have a lot to say—life experiences come later." He eventually moved to Los Angeles where he has worked as a television scriptwriter and produced the sitcom *In the House.*

Hardwick, an African-American, is the author of what may be the first legal thriller to feature a black protagonist. The author's novels have sold well, particularly in Detroit, and Hardwick explained that "I paint Detroit in realistic terms. . . . it's really two cities: wealthy and poor and both cities, both the haves and have-nots, are black."

Hardwick's first novel, *Cold Medina,* takes place during a close Detroit mayoral race. In the midst of intense politicking, a serial killer—who turns out to be white—is murdering and mutilating the bodies of African American drug lords, bringing race relations in the city to a near frenzy. Additionally, a new cocaine-like drug called cold medina has been unleashed on the streets, provoking extremely aggressive behavior. A *Publishers Weekly* contributor called the book "a fast paced, suspenseful chiller," and commented on the "intriguing situations and offbeat characters" Hardwick weaves within his storyline.

Hardwick sets his next novel in Detroit as well, again among crime and politics. In *Double Dead,* the city's mayor is murdered by two assassins, bringing to light the mayor's extramarital affair. The mayor's mistress manages to escape with her murdered lover's briefcase, which may hold the key to the crime. In the meantime the case is investigated by county prosecutor Jesse King, who is opposed by lawyer and ex-lover Karen Blake. As the mayor's murder is investigated, it becomes clear that the victim had been involved in questionable dealings and relationships. When Blake is murdered and King is framed for her killing, he and the deceased mayor's mistress team up in an effort to clear their own names and solve the case.

Danny Cavanaugh, the protagonist of *Color of Justice,* is a white man raised in a black community in Detroit, where he now works as a police officer. Prone to violence, Cavanaugh works in the city's Special Crimes Unit, tackling some of the toughest, ugliest cases. Cavanaugh is brought in to investigate the torture/murder of a prominent African American couple, John and Lenora Baker. He discovers that the Bakers were the force behind an Internet start-up, NewNubia.com, that had led to financial ruin for many of Detroit's wealthiest African Americans. As more murders occur, Cavanaugh realizes that the killer is targeting light-skinned blacks, those who usually have more success associating with the white community. Complicating matters is Cavanaugh's troubles with his black live-in girlfriend, Vinny; members of a race-based group, the Castle Society; and a reformed convict preacher, whose three adult children are pursuing him to settle scores from their abusive childhoods. The book "features compelling scenes of racial conflict and personal strife," noted a *Publishers Weekly* reviewer, while *Booklist* contributor Connie Fletcher found that Hardwick offers an "unflinching picture of how race plays out on the streets and in the police." A *Kirkus Reviews* critic called Hardwick's story "a perceptive study of the prejudices that await light-skinned blacks, particularly those who could pass for white."

The Executioner's Game, a political thriller, opens with the unexpected death of U.S. Secretary of Commerce Donald Howard in the jungles of the Congo. Howard had been in the African nation to observe the plight of AIDS sufferers, which moves him emotionally and makes him determined to seek U.S. assistance for the area. Howard is shocked by his Secret Service protector Alex Deavers's indifference to the suffering around him. Before Howard can leave Africa, an explosive is detonated in the vehicle he and Deavers are traveling in, killing Howard. Protagonist Luther Green is a hardened military veteran and survivor of the streets, currently working as a coldly effective CIA agent. All of his experience does not prepare him for the shocking assignment to kill Deavers, his mentor from the CIA academy, who is found to not be a Secret Service agent and who is suspected of killing Howard. Green does not believe his longtime friend is a killer, but in deference to his sense of duty, he sets off to fulfill his mission. Doubts and second-thoughts plague him, however, as he tracks the elusive Deavers before a final confrontation in Green's native Detroit. Hardwick "writes crackling scenes and vivid dialogue," commented a *Kirkus Reviews* contributor. He "brings us a well-developed, well-paced story," one that "reaches into the psychological and emotional life of the hero, giving insight into the double-timing, dangerous and distrusting world of undercover work," remarked Tanu T. Henry in *Black Issues Book Review.*

Hardwick is the screenwriter and director of a number of successful motion pictures. *The Brothers* follows the romantic adventures of four childhood friends in Los Angeles, now adults and successful and affluent in their own careers. The story revolves around the four men and their difficulties with women. Jackson avoids commitment, while Terry feels more than ready to settle down and get married. Derrick, on the other hand, feels trapped and strangled by his marriage, and Brian is so frustrated that he entertains the idea of swearing off dating black women forever. As the men traverse their individual situations, developments unfold that teach them important lessons about their relationships and the women in their lives. "Hardwick is far less interested in scoring sociological points than in revving up his audience with rude hilarity and outrageous situations. And he pretty much pulls it off" with an appealing cast and considerable humor, noted reviewer Robert W. Butler in the *Kansas City Star.*

Deliver Us from Eva pits three men against the strong-willed older sister of the women in their lives. Eva Dandridge is a tough professional woman who serves as a protector of her younger sisters Kareenah, Jacqui, and Bethany. Eva's strong influence over her sisters' lives and decisions frustrates their husbands and boyfriends. At Eva's urging, Kareenah puts off having children with her husband Tim; Bethany refuses to move in with her policeman boyfriend Mike unless they are married; and Jacqui follows Eva's advice in her marriage to postal worker Darrell. The three men hatch a plan to remove Eva's unwanted presence from their lives, hiring smooth ladies' man Ray Adams to court her and thereby distract her from her sisters' affairs. Ray assumes the challenge—and a challenge it is, at least until the unexpected happens, and Ray and Eva begin falling in love. The "well-cast relationship comedy-drama is played too broadly in the early going, but gradually settles into a more appealing groove as a glossy date-movie," commented Joe Leydon in *Variety. Hollywood Reporter* critic Frank Scheck noted that "the film ultimately proves itself a reasonably diverting lark." As director and screenwriter, Hardwick "delivers the goods for a moderately budgeted romantic comedy of solid entertainment aspirations," remarked *Film Journal International* reviewer Doris Toumarkine.

BIOGRAPHICAL AND CRITICAL SOURCES:

PERIODICALS

Black Issues Book Review, May-June, 2005, Tanu T. Henry, review of *The Executioner's Game,* p. 69.
Booklist, December 1, 2001, Connie Fletcher, review of *Color of Justice,* p. 632.
Daily Variety, February 5, 2003, Joe Leydon, review of *Deliver Us from Eva,* p. 6.
Film Journal International, February, 2003, Doris Toumarkine, review of *Deliver Us from Eva,* p. 31.
Hollywood Reporter, September 24, 2001, Zorianna Kit and Chris Gardner, "Union Perfect for USA's *Eva,*" p. 3; September 26, 2001, Zorianna Kit, "Getting Eva," review of *Deliver Us from Eva,* p. 1; February 3, 2003, Frank Scheck, review of *Deliver Us from Eva,* p. 9.
Kansas City Star, March 22, 2001, Robert W. Butler, review of *The Brothers.*
Kirkus Reviews, November 1, 2001, review of *Color of Justice,* p. 1519; December 15, 2004, review of *The Executioner's Game,* p. 1156.
Publishers Weekly, November 20, 1995, review of *Cold Medina,* p. 65; November 12, 2001, review of *Color of Justice,* p. 36; December 6, 2004, review of *The Executioner's Game,* p. 43.
Variety, May 17, 1999, Dennis Harvey, review of *Trippin',* p. 54; March 19, 2001, Robert Koehler, review of *The Brothers,* p. 30; February 3, 2003, Joe Leydon, review of *Deliver Us from Eva,* p. 32.

ONLINE

Filmbug.com, http://www.filmbug.com/ (January 2, 2007), biography of Gary Hardwick.
Gary Hardwick Home Page, http://www.garyhardwick.com (January 2, 2007).
Internet Movie Database Web site, http://www.imdb.com/ (January 2, 2007), filmography of Gary Hardwick.*

*   *   *

HARDWICK, Gary C.
See HARDWICK, Gary

HARDWICK, Gary Clifford
  See HARDWICK, Gary

                    *   *   *

HAVEN, Kendall 1946-
  (Kendall F. Haven)

PERSONAL: Born September 24, 1946, in Asheville, NC; son of Girard E. (a nonprofit director) and May F. Haven; married Roni Berg (a graphic designer), August 9, 1986. *Ethnicity:* "Caucasian." *Education:* U.S. Military Academy, B.S., 1968; Oregon State University, M.S., 1974, Ph.D., 1975. *Religion:* "Not particularly." *Hobbies and other interests:* "The coastal zone where worlds collide, waves crash, and life begins."

ADDRESSES: Home and office—Fulton, CA. *E-mail*—kendallhaven@sbcglobal.net.

CAREER: U.S. Army Satellite Systems Test and Development, civilian employee, 1972-74; Oregon State University, Corvallis, teacher of oceanography and hydrodynamics, 1974-75; Lawrence Livermore Laboratory, Livermore, CA, worked in Energy and Environment Division, 1975-77; Lawrence Berkeley Laboratory, Berkeley, CA, senior research scientist and director of Regional Environmental Studies Group, 1977-83; freelance writer and professional storyteller, 1984—. University of California, Berkeley, teacher of coastal zone management classes, 1982-84; teacher of storytelling classes at colleges and universities, 1991—, including Chapman University, California State University, Boise State University, University of Nevada, Las Vegas, University of South Carolina, the Citadel, East Tennessee State University, and University of Phoenix. "Tell Me a Story" (concert series), creator, producer, and host, 1985-88; Bay Area Storytelling Festival, chair, 1987-90; *Inside Story* (storytelling newsletter), publisher, 1991-93; National Whole Language Umbrella Storytelling Action Group, founder, 1994, chair, 1994—; Sonoma Storytelling Festival, cofounder; presenter at hundreds of workshops, conferences, and storytelling performances. Recordings include *Voices and Bully,* released by Contra Costa Crisis and Suicide Intervention Service, 1986; *Reluctant Heroes,* StoryStreet Productions, 1987; *Frog Pond Blues,* American Cancer Society, 1988; *Getting Along,* JTG of Nashville, 1988; *Dinosaur Tales,* StoryStreet Productions, 1988; *The Baby Sitter,* Institute of Mental Health Initiatives, 1990;

Neighborhood Magic, StoryStreet Productions, 1990; *Fathers and Sons,* StoryStreet Productions, 1991; and *The Adventures of Christina Valentine* (radio play), Children's Television Resource and Education Center, 1992. *Military service:* U.S. Army, 1964-68, Signal Corps, 1968-73; became captain.

MEMBER: National Storytelling Association (member of board of directors, 1995-99), Society of Children's Book Writers and Illustrators, Authors Guild, Authors League of America.

AWARDS, HONORS: Named western regional teller, National Storytelling Festival, 1986; winner of regional storytelling competitions, American Library Association, 1986 and 1988; award from California Conference of Local Mental Health Directors, 1987, for the stories "Voices" and "Bully"; winner of national storytelling competition, General Mills Corp., 1987; California Special Recognition Award, California Division, American Cancer Society, 1989, for the story "Frog Pond Blues"; named "notable recording artist," American Library Association, 1989 and 1992; Public Radio Silver Program Award, Corporation for Public Broadcasting, 1992, for the radio drama, *The Adventures of Christina Valentine;* Silver Award, best educational program, International Festival Association, 1993; *Storytelling World* Awards, 1995, 1996, 1997, 2000, 2001, 2003, and 2004; grants from Child Assault Prevention Training Center of Northern California, Solano County Park System, Gerbode Foundation, and Institute of Mental Health Initiatives.

WRITINGS:

JUVENILE

The Killer Brussel Sprouts, with audio cassette, JTG of Nashville (Nashville, TN), 1992.
Marvels of Science: 50 Fascinating Five-Minute Reads, Libraries Unlimited (Englewood, CO), 1992.
Getting Along (short stories), JTG of Nashville (Nashville, TN), 1994.
Amazing American Women: 40 Fascinating Stories of American Her-story, Libraries Unlimited (Englewood, CO), 1995.
Great Moments in Science: Readers Theater and Experiments, Libraries Unlimited (Englewood, CO), 1996.

Stepping Stones to Science: True Tales and Awesome Activities, Libraries Unlimited (Englewood, CO), 1997.

Marvels of Math: Fascinating Reads and Awesome Activities, Libraries Unlimited (Englewood, CO), 1998.

Bedtime Stories, StoryStreet, 1998.

New Years to Kwanzaa: Original Stories of Celebration, Fulcrum (Golden, CO), 1999.

Close Encounters with Deadly Dangers: Riveting Reads and Classroom Ideas, Libraries Unlimited (Englewood, CO), 1999.

The Land of Oulaf (novel), StoryStreet, 1999.

The Science and Math Bookmark Book: 300 Fascinating, Fact-Filled Bookmarks, Libraries Unlimited (Englewood, CO), 1999.

(Coauthor) *The 100 Most Popular Scientists for Young Adults: Biographical Sketches and Professional Paths,* Libraries Unlimited (Englewood, CO), 1999.

Worm Holes, Warp Drive, Monoliths, and Monsters: The Amazing Science of Science Mysteries, Fulcrum (Golden, CO), 2000.

Voices of the Revolution (stories), Libraries Unlimited (Englewood, CO), 2000.

That's Weird! Awesome Science Mysteries, Fulcrum (Golden, CO), 2001.

Voices of the American Civil War: Stories of Men, Women, and Children Who Lived through the War between the States, Teachers Ideas Press (Westport, CT), 2002.

Alexander Graham Bell: Inventor and Visionary, Franklin Watts (New York, NY), 2003.

Women at the Edge of Discovery: 40 True Science Adventures, Libraries Unlimited (Westport, CT), 2003.

100 Greatest Science Inventions of All Time, Libraries Unlimited (Westport, CT), 2005.

Wonders of the Sea: Merging Ocean Myth and Ocean Science, Libraries Unlimited (Westport, CT), 2005.

Wonders of the Land: Merging Earth Science with Earth Myth, Libraries Unlimited (Westport, CT), 2006.

100 Greatest Science Discoveries of All Time, Libraries Unlimited (Westport, CT), 2007.

OTHER

Write Right: Teaching Creative Writing Using Storytelling Techniques, Libraries Unlimited (Englewood, CO), 1999.

Super Simple Storytelling, Libraries Unlimited (Englewood, CO), 2000.

Get It Write! Creating Lifelong Writers, from Expository to Narrative, Teachers Ideas Press (Portsmouth, NH), 2004.

Contributor to books, including *Launching a Scientist,* National Storytelling Press, 1995. Contributor to magazines, including *National Storytelling, GRIT, Journal of the Whole Language Umbrella, Kid Connection,* and *Teacher in Focus National.* Contributing editor, *California Reader.*

SIDELIGHTS: Kendall Haven once told *CA:* "I am the only graduate of West Point to ever become a full-time professional storyteller. I am also the only full-time storyteller in this country with a doctorate in science. That unconventional beginning for a performing storyteller has given me a unique perspective on the architecture of stories and on the process of storytelling.

"My doctorate is in oceanography. Through the late 1970s and early 1980s, I worked as a senior research scientist at Lawrence Berkeley Laboratory, conducting coastal environmental assessments for the Department of Energy. In a great career upheaval, I shifted to being a full-time storyteller.

"That shift was mandated by the realization of how powerful stories are. I'd take my nephew to the park, planning to wear him out on the climbing structures and train. Eventually, exhausted myself, I'd give up and flop into the sprawling sandpit to make up stories for him. It turned out that's what he really wanted all along.

"Those made-up stories in the park drew crowds. Kids are natural story magnets, drawn by the strong vibrational and electrical fields of a story-telling, or by their long-range story radar, always sifting the air for the flowing pulse and rhythm of a story. I'd begin a story and kids would materialize from all over the park. Some would boldly plop down right in front and ask me to start over. They had missed the beginning. Others would cautiously pretend to play with a nearby leaf to have an excuse for lingering within easy earshot.

"Then the adults who brought those kids to the park would scurry over to see what was going on in the sandbox. Others would wander by to see what the crowd was all about and, time after time, they stayed to listen. No one scoffed, 'Oh, just a story,' and left. They stayed and listened.

"I began to see how powerfully attractive the specific form, architecture, and process of stories and storytelling are. I began to see how hungry for stories most humans are and that the unique form and structure of stories seem to resonate at the deepest core of the human psyche. I began to realize that most humans are on story-deficit, desperately *needing* to soak up the majesty, wisdom, and joy of told stories—that is, personally, orally delivered information in the specific architecture of a story.

"Then I found out you could actually get paid to tell stories. That was the day I joined the burgeoning ranks of professional storytellers.

"Why do I spend all my time telling and writing stories? Because there is no more powerful and profound medium for human communication. There is no aspect of factual, conceptual, social, or emotional endeavor that cannot be more effectively and convincingly communicated through a story.

"I have spent almost twenty years watching and studying the line-by-line success of live performances of stories by storytellers and comparing what I have learned there to what I see in published, narrative stories. I have been able to bring concepts, lessons, and wisdom from two worlds—live storytelling and story writing—to bear on my work. The results have given me monumental insights on the essential architecture of a story and on how listeners and readers receive, interpret, and internalize a story.

"My writing process is straightforward and simple. One of the story truths I have learned is that stories are always about characters, not events. (That is, readers are captivated by interesting characters, while plot and action *alone* always leave them unsatisfied and bored.) To uncover any story is to investigate the story character's deepest and most hidden truths. I have to dig for the hidden motives, desires, goals, quirks, habits, and traits that make the character compelling. My job as a writer is to develop a character fully, so that the character's wants and goals, risks and conflicts, and struggles loom in vivid, multi-dimensional, larger-than-life detail in the minds of my readers. Once that task is accomplished, the rest is editorial detail.

"Because of my background in science, my work as a touring master storyteller, and my deep knowledge of story structure and architecture, it has been natural for

me to tackle nonfiction stories describing the flow of historical events. I am fascinated by history, and especially by military history. I find that, as a culture, our sense of history and of our place in it is steadily and dangerously diminishing. It is as though we live in a perpetual, floating present which simply *is,* with no connected historical context or development that led to this particular present. History is last week's television episode. Ancient history is last quarter's corporate report, or last season's hit situation comedy. Yet there exists a fascinating world of high-stakes struggles, dilemmas, risks, and dramas that lie scattered in the path of our collective past. It is a joy for me to wade through this history and ferret out what really happened. It is an even greater joy to find a way to relate that history using the fullest power and allure of the form of a story."

BIOGRAPHICAL AND CRITICAL SOURCES:

PERIODICALS

Appraisal: Science Books for Young People, winter, 1995, review of *Marvels of Science: 50 Fascinating Five-Minute Reads,* p. 32; fall, 1998, review of *Stepping Stones to Science: True Tales and Awesome Activities,* p. 44.

Book Report, January-February, 1996, Lesley S.J. Farmer, review of *Amazing American Women: 40 Fascinating Five-Minute Reads,* p. 51; May-June, 1996, Patsy Launspach, review of *Amazing American Women,* p. 48; September-October, 1996, Frances M. Ramsey, review of *Great Moments in Science: Experiments and Readers Theatre,* p. 59; November-December, 1999.

Bulletin of the Center for Children's Books, February, 1998, review of *Stepping Stones to Science,* p. 227.

Curriculum Review, February, 1998, review of *Stepping Stones to Science,* p. 13; March, 1999, review of *Close Encounters with Deadly Dangers: Riveting Reads and Classroom Ideas,* p. 15.

Knowledge Quest, March-April, 1999, review of *Marvels of Math: Fascinating Reads and Awesome Activities,* p. 49.

Library Talk, September-October, 1994, review of *Marvels of Science,* p. 58.

School Library Journal, September, 1994, Gwen Porter, review of *Marvels of Science,* p. 147.

School Media Quarterly, fall, 1994, review of *Marvels of Science,* p. 67.

Science Books and Films, January-February, 1998, review of *Stepping Stones to Science,* p. 16; July-August, 1999, review of *Close Encounters with Deadly Dangers,* p. 168.

Voice of Youth Advocates, October, 1996, review of *Great Moments in Science: Readers Theater and Experiments,* p. 242; April, 1999, review of *Marvels of Math,* p. 57.

ONLINE

Kendall Haven: Award-Winning Author and Master Storyteller, http://www.kendallhaven.com (April 9, 2007).

* * *

HAVEN, Kendall F.
See HAVEN, Kendall

* * *

HEIGHTON, Steven 1961-

PERSONAL: Born August 14, 1961, in Toronto, Ontario, Canada. *Education:* Queen's University, B.A., 1985, M.A., 1986.

ADDRESSES: Home—Kingston, Ontario, Canada. *Agent*—Anne M'Dermid & Associates, 92 Willcocks St., Toronto, Ontario M5S 1C8, Canada. *E-mail*—sheighton@kos.net.

CAREER: Writer, novelist, poet, essayist, short-story writer, editor, translator, and educator. English as a Second Language teacher, Osaka, Japan, 1985; freelance writer, 1988—. Writer-in-residence, St. Mary's University, 1992; writer-in-residence, Berton House, Dawson City, 2001; writer-in-residence, Concordia University, Montreal, 2002-03; Jack McClelland writer-in-residence, University of Toronto, Massey College, 2004; poetry instructor, summer literary seminars, St. Petersburg, Russia. Frequent presenter at writing workshops and seminars.

AWARDS, HONORS: Air Canada Award, 1989; Gerald Lampert Award for best poetry debut, 1990, for *Stalin's Carnival;* first prize in short fiction, *Prism International,*

1991; *Stand* magazine short story competition prize-winner, 1991; gold medal for fiction, National Magazine Awards, 1992; Journey Prize finalist, 1992; Trillium Award finalist, 1993, for *Flight Paths of the Emperor;* Governor General's Award finalist, 1995, for *The Ecstasy of Skeptics;* W.H. Smith Award nomination, 1998, for *Flight Paths of the Emperor;* Petra Kenney Award for poetry, 2002; *Publishers Weekly* book of the year distinction, 2002, for *The Shadow Boxer;* Award for Excellence in the Arts, Kingston Arts Council, 2004; McEwan College Book of the Year finalist, 2006, for *Afterlands; New York Times Book Review* Editors' Choice award, for *Afterlands;* Pushcart Prize nomination.

WRITINGS:

Stalin's Carnival (poetry), Quarry Press (Kingston, Ontario, Canada), 1989.
Foreign Ghosts (poetry), Oberon Press (Ottawa, Ontario, Canada), 1989.
Flight Paths of the Emperor (short stories), Porcupine's Quill (Erin, Ontario, Canada), 1992.
The Ecstasy of Skeptics (poetry), Anansi (Concord, Ontario, Canada), 1994.
On earth as it is (short stories), Porcupine's Quill (Erin, Ontario, Canada), 1995.
The Admen Move on Lhasa: Writing and Culture in a Virtual World (essays), Anansi (Concord, Ontario, Canada), 1996.
The Shadow Boxer (novel), Knopf Canada (Toronto, Ontario, Canada), 2000, Houghton Mifflin (Boston, MA), 2002.
The Address Book, House of Anansi Press (Toronto, Ontario, Canada), 2004.
(Associate editor, with Helen Tsiriotakis) *Musings: An Anthology of Greek-Canadian Literature,* edited by Tess Fragoulis, Vehicule Press (Montreal, Quebec, Canada), 2004.
Afterlands (novel), Alfred A. Knopf (Toronto, Ontario, Canada), 2005, Houghton Mifflin (Boston, MA), 2006.

Contributor to anthologies, including *The Journey Prize Anthology,* McClelland & Stewart, 1992; *Best English Short Stories,* Heinemann, 1992; *Best of Best Stories: 1986-1995,* Minerva, 1995; *Best Canadian Stories,* Oberon, 1989, 1992, and 1995; *Writing Home,* edited by Constance Rooke, M&S, 1997; *Turn of the Story,* edited by Joan Thomas and Heidi Harms, Anansi, 1999; *Lost Classics,* edited Ondaatje, Redhill, Spalding, and

Spalding, Knopf, 2000; *The Reader,* edited by Carolyn Meyer and Bruce Meyer, Prentice Hall, 2001; *The Notebooks,* edited by Michelle Berry and Natalee Caple, Doubleday, 2002; and *The New Canon,* edited by Carmine Starnino, Vehicule, 2005.

Contributor to periodicals, including *Brick, Malahat Review, Exile, Stand, Critical Quarterly, Nimrod, Agni, Literary Review, Northwest Review, Revue Europe, Quadrant, Independent on Sunday, Poetry* and *Chelsea Hotel. Quarry* magazine, editor, 1991-94. Heighton's works have been translated into nine languages.

SIDELIGHTS: Steven Heighton is a Canadian writer who has distinguished himself in both poetry and fiction. He began his literary career in 1989 with *Stalin's Carnival,* a poetry collection that Maurice Mierau, writing in *Books in Canada,* described as "a promising if uneven debut." In the central portion of this volume, Heighton explores the psychology of Soviet dictator Joseph Stalin, and he even presents English renderings of works attributed to the onetime leader. Mierau proclaimed the Stalin-related verse "interesting and uneven," and he concluded that "Heighton is already an ambitious and very accomplished writer."

In 1992 Heighton published *Flight Paths of the Emperor,* a collection of short stories that Ann Copeland, in her *Books in Canada* appraisal, found "sophisticated and elegantly told." Some of the tales in this volume reflect Heighton's experiences as a teacher in Japan during the late 1980s. "A Man away from Home Has No Neighbors," for example, concerns a Japanese soldier's love for a Chinese peasant, and "An Apparition Play" relates a father's alienation from his daughter while in Japan to conduct a burial service. Another tale, "On Strikes and Errors in Japanese Baseball," chronicles an attempt to uncover information on the atomic bombing of Hiroshima. Copeland proclaimed *Flight Paths of the Emperor* to be "a memorable collection," and she praised it as being "larger and deeper than any one of its fascinating parts." Another reviewer, Mark Ford, wrote in the *Times Literary Supplement* that Heighton's tales "are nearly all vivacious, purposeful, and entertaining." Tom McCarthy noted in the London *Observer:* "Technically, the best pieces are little short of brilliant."

Heighton followed *Flight Paths of the Emperor* with *The Ecstasy of Skeptics,* an ambitious collection of poems expressing both the Apollonian and Dionysian aspects of his own life. "As you might guess, this is ambitious stuff," acknowledged Scott Ellis in *Books in Canada,* adding that "Heighton almost always pulls it off." Bert Almon wrote in the *Canadian Book Review Annual* that *The Ecstasy of Skeptics* "arouses more skepticism than ecstasy," and he contended that "this is not a powerful collection of poems." He conceded, however, that "Heighton has talent."

After issuing *The Ecstasy of Skeptics,* Heighton produced his *On earth as it is,* his second collection of short stories. Notable tales in this volume include "Translations of April," wherein a translator relates tales written by a dead loved one, and "To Everything a Season," in which, as Sheryl Halpern observed in *Books in Canada,* eight individuals "play out the different seasons of lovemaking and leavetaking." Stephen Smith, in his *Quill & Quire* assessment, summarized the tales in *On earth as it is* as "real and rooted and vital," and Tamas Dobozy added in *Canadian Literature* that "the book delivers." Henry Hitchings noted in the *Times Literary Supplement* that "Heighton explores the failure of our attempts to communicate—both with others and with ourselves—and the way reality cannot sustain the fantasies we attempt to imprint on it."

Heighton next published *The Admen Move on Lhasa: Writing and Culture in a Virtual World,* a collection of essays on subjects ranging from the essence of art to the nature of contemporary life. Zsuzsi Gartner, writing in *Quill & Quire,* deemed Heighton's book "passionate, honest, and somewhat noble." Lawrence Mathews, in his *Essays on Canadian Writing* analysis, praised it as "passionate, generous-spirited, . . . blessedly anachronistic." Patricia Morley, who concluded that "some of the individual pieces attempt more than they achieve," nonetheless considered Heighton to be "an accomplished writer of fiction and poetry," and she added, in her *Canadian Book Review Annual* consideration, that *The Admen Move on Lhasa* "is ambitious in scope and brilliant in parts."

Among Heighton's other writings is *The Shadow Boxer,* a novel about an aspiring writer who attempts to complete his first novel while overcoming both personal inadequacies and family problems. *Times Literary Supplement* reviewer Margaret Stead called *The Shadow Boxer* "an energetic, fluent and interesting novel," and a *Publishers Weekly* critic hailed it as "remarkable."

Heighton turned again to the novel form with *Afterlands,* based on the true-life story of a group of arctic explorers trapped for months on a drifting, ever-shrinking ice floe. In 1871, during an expedition to the North Pole, the ship Polaris was caught in ice off the coast of Greenland. In an attempt to lighten the vessel's load and free it from the ice, nineteen passengers and crewmembers were offloaded to an ice floe. Then, inexplicably, they were abandoned by the Polaris, beginning a six-month ordeal of survival as the floe drifted through frigid northern waters. In telling the story, Heighton "brilliantly riffs off" the events recorded in the diary and memoir of Lt. George Tyson, a real-life figure who endured the hardships on the ice floe and became the de facto leader of the group, noted a *Publishers Weekly* critic. Among the other characters portrayed by Heighton are Tukulito, also known as Hannah, a married woman who served as the group's Esquimau translator, and Kruger, a belligerent German sailor whose infatuation with Hannah and conflict with Tyson caused additional troubles for the hard-pressed group of survivors. "The extended flashback that describes the six-month misadventure is a numbingly dramatic, visually stunning tour de force," commented a *Kirkus Reviews* critic, who also noted that the novel contains "tremendous sequences and images." Heighton also relates stories of the survivors' lives after rescue, showing how memories of even long-term traumatic experiences can be unreliable, and "how casually events can be interpreted in many different ways," noted Colleen Mondor in *Booklist.* Reviewer Lorna Dolan, writing in the *Financial Times,* commented that Heighton's "retelling of the hard months of hunger, cold and isolation is compelling, vividly imagined, and written in rich and precise prose." The *Publishers Weekly* reviewer concluded that "this novel's scale, its delight in detail, and its psychological insight make it an exceptionally satisfying adventure."

BIOGRAPHICAL AND CRITICAL SOURCES:

PERIODICALS

Booklist, January 1, 2006, Colleen Mondor, review of *Afterlands,* p. 55.

Books in Canada, January, 1990, Maurice Mierau, "Man of Steel," pp. 46-47; December, 1992, Ann Copeland, "Senses of Strangeness," pp. 38-39; April, 1995, Scott Ellis, "The New Lyricism," pp. 49-50; September, 1995, Sheryl Halpern, "Lingering Refrains," pp. 35-36.

Canadian Book Review Annual, 1995, Bert Almon, review of *The Ecstasy of Skeptics,* p. 3173; 1998, Patricia Morley, review of *The Admen Move on Lhasa: Writing and Culture in a Virtual World,* p. 268.

Canadian Literature, fall-winter, 1993, Jim Snyder, "Claims of Loneliness," pp. 158-160; summer, 1998, Tamas Dobozy, "Approaching Earth," pp. 176-178.

Essays on Canadian Writing, spring, 1998, Lawrence Mathews, "Beautiful Downtown Lhasa," pp. 167-171.

Financial Times, June 10, 2006, Lorna Dolan, "In Brief," review of *Afterlands,* p. 53.

Kirkus Reviews, December 15, 2001, review of *The Shadow Boxer;* December 1, 2005, review of *Afterlands,* p. 1247.

Library Journal, December, 2001, Jim Dwyer, review of *The Shadow Boxer,* p. 172.

Observer (London, England), February, 1997, Tom McCarthy, "Change at Japan for All Points West," p. 17.

Publishers Weekly, February 18, 2002, review of *The Shadow Boxer,* p. 77; November 21, 2005, review of *Afterlands,* p. 26.

Quill & Quire, December, 1992, Stephen Smith, "Remarkable First Flight," p. 15; July, 1995, Stephen Smith, review of *On earth as it is,* p. 51; March, 1997, Zsuzsi Gartner, "Life Is Short and Literature Matters," p. 74.

Times Literary Supplement, February 7, 1997, Mark Ford, review of *Flight Paths of the Emperor,* p. 21; September 19, 1997, Henry Hitchings, "Rudderless in Kathmandu," p. 21; August 11, 2000, Margaret Stead, "Leaving the Soo," p. 24.

ONLINE

Steven Heighton Home Page, http://www.steven heighton.com (January 2, 2007).

Vancouver International Writers and Readers Festival 2004 Web site, http://www.writersfest.bc.ca/2004 festival/ (January 2, 2007), biography of Steven Heighton.

Writers Union of Canada Web site, http://www.writers union.ca/ (January 2, 2007), biography of Steven Heighton.*

*   *   *

HELFER, Ralph 1937-

PERSONAL: Born 1937, in Chicago, IL; married Toni Ringo (deceased); married Suzzi Matua (a safari guide); children: (first marriage) Tana.

ADDRESSES: Home—Newport Beach, CA; Kenya. *Office*—Eden International, P.O. Box 25971, Los Angeles, CA 90025; Eden International Safaris & Treks, P.O. Box 7101, City Square 00200, Nairobi, Kenya. *E-mail*—ralphhelfersafaris@hotmail.com.

CAREER: Animal behaviorist, safari leader, and writer. Motion picture and television stuntman, 1950s; Africa USA (wild animal ranch), Soledad Canyon, CA, owner, c. 1960s-70s; Marine World Africa USA, Vallejo, CA, owner; Enchanted Village (theme park), Buena Park, CA, owner, c. 1970s; Gentle Jungle (wild animal training company), founder and director, 1980s; Eden International (safari company), Los Angeles, CA, founder and director. Supplied wild animals for motion pictures, including *The Island of Dr. Moreau, Quest for Fire,* and *Clarence, the Cross-eyed Lion,* and for television shows, including *Gentle Ben, Daktari,* and *Star Trek.*

AWARDS, HONORS: Eighteen PATSY Awards for work with animals.

WRITINGS:

NONFICTION

The Beauty of the Beasts: Tales of Hollywood's Wild Animal Stars, J.P. Tarcher (Los Angeles, CA), 1990.
Modoc: The True Story of the Greatest Elephant That Ever Lived, HarperCollins (New York, NY), 1997.
Mosey: The Remarkable Friendship of a Boy and His Elephant, Orchard (New York, NY), 2002.
Zamba: The True Story of the Greatest Lion That Ever Lived, HarperCollins (New York, NY), 2005.
The World's Greatest Elephant (picture book), illustrated by Ted Lewin, Philomel (New York, NY), 2006.

ADAPTATIONS: Savage Harvest, based on a story by Ralph Helfer and Ken Noyle, was produced as a film, 1981; *Modoc: The True Story of the Greatest Elephant That Ever Lived* was optioned for film by Tig Productions.

SIDELIGHTS: Ralph Helfer is a legendary Hollywood animal trainer and behaviorist who developed "affection training," a method that uses respect and kindness to develop strong bonds between humans and wild animals. During his career, Helfer worked with numerous animal celebrities, including Clarence the Cross-eyed Lion and Judy the Chimp.

Helfer published his first book, *The Beauty of the Beasts: Tales of Hollywood's Wild Animal Stars,* in 1990. In the work, he recounts his experiences working with a variety of animals, including C.J., an orangutan, and Gentle Ben, a black bear. Genevieve Stuttaford, writing in *Publishers Weekly,* stated that "animal lovers will be charmed and entertained by Helfer's menagerie."

Modoc: The True Story of the Greatest Elephant That Ever Lived is actually two biographies in one, as Helfer tells the story of a circus elephant as well as her inseparable human companion. Bram Gunterstein, whose father was an animal trainer for a German circus, was born in 1896, the same night that Modoc was born on the Guntersteins' farm. The pair grew up together, and when the circus was sold to an American circus owner, Bram stowed away aboard the ship that would carry the elephant to the United States. A typhoon sank the ship in the Bay of Bengal, and Bram and Modoc were among the only survivors. The duo traveled through India until they were eventually found by the circus owner, who assigned Bram to act as Modoc's trainer in America. After a period of great success with the Ringling Brothers circus, Modoc was sold without Bram's knowledge and vanished for nearly two decades. A production company owned by Helfer eventually found the elephant living on a farm in the Ozarks and reunited her with Bram. According to a reviewer in *Publishers Weekly,* "sentimentalists and animal lovers should flock to this story," and *Booklist* contributor Nancy Bent deemed *Modoc* "a truly fascinating book."

Helfer revisits the tale of Modoc in two more-recent works, *Mosey: The Remarkable Friendship of a Boy and His Elephant* and the picture book *The World's Greatest Elephant.* Written for a young-adult audience, *Mosey* was described as "an unusual but engaging combination of adventure-survival story and boy-and-his-pet tale" by *Booklist* contributor Chris Sherman. In *The World's Greatest Elephant,* Helfer recounts the remarkable story of Bram and Modoc for young readers. "Helfer's impeccable pacing keeps the suspense high as he builds the emotional connection between his two heroes—one human, one animal," noted a critic in *Publishers Weekly.* Several reviewers, including *Booklist* critic Hazel Rochman, offered particular praise for the dramatic illustrations by Ted Lewin. "His gorgeous, watercolor double-page spreads show the . . . rescue drama, but even more stunning are the depictions of the bond between the lifelong friends," Rochman stated. According to *School Library Journal* contributor Margaret Bush, Helfer's "bold and heartwarming adventure tale should have wide appeal."

Helfer chronicles his eighteen-year relationship with a gentle giant in *Zamba: The True Story of the Greatest Lion That Ever Lived*. In the work, the animal behaviorist describes his efforts to turn an orphaned lion cub into a top Hollywood attraction using the revolutionary principles of "affection training." According to Judy McAloon, writing in *School Library Journal*, "the many stories, both humorous and touching, make this a fascinating book." Helfer "beautifully expresses a simple philosophy so many have trouble following: respect for all living creatures, given and returned," noted an appreciative critic in *Kirkus Reviews*.

BIOGRAPHICAL AND CRITICAL SOURCES:

BOOKS

Helfer, Toni Ringo, *The Gentle Jungle*, Brigham Young University Press (Provo, UT), 1980.

PERIODICALS

Booklist, September 15, 1997, Nancy Bent, review of *Modoc: The True Story of the Greatest Elephant That Ever Lived*, p. 196; July, 2002, Chris Sherman, review of *Mosey: The Remarkable Friendship of a Boy and His Elephant*, p. 1840; July, 2005, Nancy Bent, review of *Zamba: The True Story of the Greatest Lion That Ever Lived*, p. 1884; February 1, 2006, Hazel Rochman, review of *The World's Greatest Elephant*, p. 48.
Bulletin of the Center for Children's Books, April, 2006, Elizabeth Bush, review of *The World's Greatest Elephant*, p. 356.
Childhood Education, fall, 2002, Irene A. Allen, review of *Mosey*, p. 50.
Kirkus Reviews, May 15, 2005, review of *Zamba*, p. 575; February 1, 2006, review of *The World's Greatest Elephant*, p. 1323.
Library Journal, July 1, 2005, Ann Forister, review of *Zamba*, p. 117.
People, August 8, 2005, Lisa Kay Greissinger, review of *Zamba*, p. 46.
Publishers Weekly, March 9, 1990, review of *The Beauty of the Beasts: Tales of Hollywood's Wild Animal Stars*, p. 56; August 4, 1997, Paul Nathan, "If You Like Androcles," p. 36; September 1, 1997, review of *Modoc*, p. 90; June 13, 2005, review of *Zamba*, p. 46; April 10, 2006, review of *The World's Greatest Elephant*, p. 71.
School Library Journal, July, 2002, Vicki Reutter, review of *Mosey*, p. 136; January, 2006, Judy McAloon, review of *Zamba*, p. 174; February, 2006, Margaret Bush, review of *The World's Greatest Elephant*, p. 120.
Voice of Youth Advocates, December, 1998, review of *Modoc*, p. 380; August, 2002, review of *Mosey*, p. 192.

ONLINE

Eden International Safaris & Treks Web site, http://www.edeninternationalsafaris.net/ (January 25, 2007).
Talking Animals Web site, http://www.talkinganimals.net/ (January 20, 2007), Duncan Strauss, "African Safari: Kenya Imagine Seeing So Many Animals—and So Close?"*

* * *

HENLEY, Patricia 1947-

PERSONAL: Born June 9, 1947, in Terre Haute, IN; daughter of Joseph (a telecommunications engineer) and Virginia (a homemaker) Cowgill; married Charles King Henley, August, 1968 (divorced, July, 1977); married S.K. Robisch (a professor of American literature), May 22, 1993; children: Kathleen O'Neal Odom, Charles Michael. *Education:* Johns Hopkins University, M.A., 1974. *Politics:* "Democratic Party." *Religion:* Catholic.

ADDRESSES: Home—West Lafayette, IN. *Office*—Purdue University, Department of English, Heavilon Hall, West Lafayette, IN 47906. *E-mail*—phenley15@hotmail.com.

CAREER: Writer, novelist, short-story writer, and educator. Purdue University, West Lafayette, IN, professor of English, 1987—. Volunteer, St. Thomas Aquinas Center.

AWARDS, HONORS: Montana First Book Award, Montana Arts Council, 1986, for *Friday Night at the Silver Star;* Best American Short Stories 1990, 1990, for *The Secret of Cartwheels;* National Book Award finalist, 1999, for *Hummingbird House;* IMPAC Dublin Literary Prize nomination, 2000, for *Hummingbird House; New Yorker* Best Fiction Award finalist.

WRITINGS:

Learning to Die: Poems, Three Rivers Press (New York, NY), 1979.

Friday Night at Silver Star: Stories, Graywolf Press (St. Paul, MN), 1986.

The Secret of Cartwheels: Short Stories, Graywolf Press (St. Paul, MN), 1992.

Back Roads, Carnegie Mellon University (Pittsburgh, PA), 1996.

Hummingbird House (novel), MacMurray & Beck (Denver, CO), 1999.

Worship of the Common Heart: New and Selected Stories, MacMurray & Beck (Denver, CO), 2000.

In the River Sweet (novel), Pantheon (New York, NY), 2002.

Contributor to anthologies, including *The Best American Short Stories* and *The Pushcart Anthology.*

SIDELIGHTS: Among poet and fiction-writer Patricia Henley's critically praised works is her 1999 debut novel *Hummingbird House.* Set in Central America in the late 1980s, the novel features protagonist Kate Banner, a Michigan midwife who has spent the last eight years in Nicaragua. Worn out with her work and traumatized by the death around her, she decides it is time to leave. Kate moves to Guatemala, where she stays in a house with a group of activist friends. With Father Dixie Ryan, a struggling priest, she opens Hummingbird House, a clinic and school for Guatemalan children. In researching her novel, Henley spent five months traveling around Guatemala interviewing refugees, activists, and Indian women.

On the whole, *Hummingbird House* was well received, and was a finalist for the prestigious National Book Award. A reviewer for *Booklist* called the book "a strongly written and wrenching tale of self-sacrifice" and wrote that "Henley has written a strongly political first novel that avoids being merely a polemic only because she has managed to make Kate a sympathetic, believable character whose thoughts and reactions seem both honest and realistic."

Other works by Henley include *Worship of the Common Heart: New and Selected Stories,* which contains nineteen stories penned over two decades. Praising Henley as "an unusual writer of true distinction," *Book* contributor Ann Collette noted that the stories feature women from all walks of life engaged in change; "immediate in their impact, these stories distinguish themselves from the bland sameness that characterizes much of contemporary short fiction," the critic maintained. In the *Library Journal,* Lisa Nussbaum cited Henley's "folksy, down-to-earth style and likable, flawed characters," while in *Publishers Weekly* a critic noted that "post-hippie attitudes . . . [such as] a disdain for conventional mores, a preference for relationships with like-minded free spirits and an appreciation for nature" characterize *Worship of the Common Heart.*

The protagonist of Henley's novel *In the River Sweet* is Ruth Anne Bond, a fifty-year-old Hoosier woman living in the small town of Tarkington, IN. She is comfortably set in her Midwest lifestyle, a dedicated Catholic, and a devoted wife and mother. She works as the town librarian, while her husband, Johnny, runs a restaurant. When her daughter Laurel declares herself to be a lesbian, Ruth Anne struggles to reconcile her religious beliefs against homosexuality with her strong love for her daughter. Soon, Ruth Anne is reeling from another blow to her complacent lifestyle: she receives an e-mail from a young Vietnamese man who identifies himself as Tin Tran, the illegitimate son that Ruth Anne gave up for adoption years ago when she was working at a French convent in Vietnam. Tin, also living in the Midwest, is getting married, and wants to meet with Ruth Anne to get acquainted with the mother he never knew. Facing a multitude of conflicting emotions and vivid memories from her past, Ruth Anne considers her options, wondering how she will break her secret to her husband and daughter, and worrying that her past indiscretions will destroy her life in the present. "The moral dilemmas attendant upon living with such a secret are sensitively treated and readers' sympathies for each of the troubled characters will be fully engaged," commented a reviewer in *Publishers Weekly.* A *Kirkus Reviews* critic called the novel "sentimental, but readable and sincere all the same." Henley "has crafted a story with solid characters who command our attention," remarked Christine Thomas in the *San Francisco Chronicle.* "Despite some jolts along the road," Thomas concluded,

"*In the River Sweet* remains remarkably captivating, a provoking meditation on the contradictions of strength and vulnerability that lie within us all."

BIOGRAPHICAL AND CRITICAL SOURCES:

PERIODICALS

Book, November, 2000, Ann Collette, review of *Worship of the Common Heart: New and Selected Stories,* p. 75.

Booklist, March 15, 1999, Nancy Pearl, review of *Hummingbird House,* p. 1289; February 1, 2000, Donna Seaman, review of *Hummingbird House,* p. 1011; August, 2002, Eileen Hardy, review of *In the River Sweet,* p. 1919.

Kirkus Reviews, July 1, 2002, review of *In the River Sweet,* p. 904.

Kliatt, September, 2004, Nola Theiss, review of *In the River Sweet,* p. 21.

Library Journal, June 15, 1986, Peter Bricklebank, review of *Friday Night at Silver Star: Stories,* p. 78; October 15, 2000, Lisa Nussbaum, review of *Worship of the Common Heart,* p. 107; November 1, 2004, Nancy Pearl, "A Bushel and a Peck of Hoosier Reads," review of *In the River Sweet,* p. 135.

New York Times, October 13, 2002, Carol Doup Muller, "Books in Brief; Fiction," review of *In the River Sweet.*

New York Times Book Review, July 6, 1986, W.D. Wetherell, review of *Friday Night at Silver Star,* p. 17; January 31, 1993, David Wong Louie, review of *The Secret of Cartwheels,* p. 6; November 7, 1999, Jeannie Pyun, review of *Hummingbird House,* p. 26; December 24, 2000, Jeff Waggoner, review of *Worship of the Common Heart,* p. 14.

Publishers Weekly, April 25, 1986, review of *Friday Night at Silver Star,* p. 89; August 14, 2000, review of *Worship of the Common Heart,* p. 328; September 30, 2002, review of *In the River Sweet,* p. 48.

San Francisco Chronicle, December 29, 2002, "A Catholic Mom with a Secret Past," Christine Thomas, review of *In the River Sweet,* p. RV-5.

Washington Post Book World, December 15, 2002, Aoibheann Sweeney, "Sea of Troubles," review of *In the River Sweet,* p. 3.

ONLINE

Amazon.com, http://www.amazon.com/ (May 18, 2000), "Amazon.com talks to Patricia Henley."

IdentityTheory.com, http://www.identitytheory.com/ (December 18, 2002), Robert Birnbaum, interview with Patricia Henley.

Patricia Henley Home Page, http://www.patriciahenley. com (January 2, 2007).

Powells.com, http://www.powells.com/ (January 2, 2007), "Of Cairns & Gratitude," autobiography of Patricia Henley.*

*   *   *

HICKMAN, Tracy 1955- (Tracy Raye Hickman)

PERSONAL: Born November 26, 1955, in Salt Lake City, UT; son of Harold R. (a professor) and Joan P. (a receptionist) Hickman; married Laura Curtis (an author), June 17, 1977; children: Angel, Curtis, Tasha, Jarod. *Education:* Attended Brigham Young University. *Religion:* Church of Jesus Christ of Latter-Day Saints. *Hobbies and other interests:* Video, music, guitar, piano, singing, models, movies, computer games, television production, and animation.

ADDRESSES: Home—St. George, UT. *Agent*—Jonathan Lazear, The Lazear Agency Inc., 800 Washington Ave. N., Ste. 660, Minneapolis, MN 55401.

CAREER: Writer, novelist, game designer, and screenwriter. TSR, Inc., Lake Geneva, WI, game designer, 1981-86, consultant, 1986—. Church of Jesus Christ of Latter-Day Saints (Mormons), missionary in Hawaii and Indonesia, 1975-77. Creator of adventure games, including "Indiana Jones and the Temple of Doom," "Pharaoh," "Lost Tomb of Martek," "Oasis of the White Palm," "Ravenloft" and "Ravenloft II," and numerous versions of "Dragonlance." Worked variously as a supermarket stocker, theater projectionist and manager, glass worker, television assistant director, and drill press operator.

WRITINGS:

"DRAGONLANCE CHRONICLES" SERIES; WITH MARGARET WEIS

Dragons of Autumn Twilight (also see below), TSR (Lake Geneva, WI), 1984.

Dragons of Winter Night (also see below), TSR (Lake Geneva, WI), 1985.

Dragons of Spring Dawning (also see below), TSR (Lake Geneva, WI), 1985.

Dragonlance Chronicles (contains *Dragons of Autumn Twilight, Dragons of Winter Night,* and *Dragons of Spring Dawning*), poetry by Michael Williams, illustrations by Denis Beauvais and Jeffrey Butler, TSR (Lake Geneva, WI), 1988.

Dragonlance: The Second Generation, poetry by Michael Williams, illustrations by Ned Dameron, TSR (Lake Geneva, WI), 1994.

Dragons of Summer Flame, poetry by Michael Williams, TSR (Lake Geneva, WI), 1995.

"DRAGONLANCE LEGENDS" TRILOGY; WITH MARGARET WEIS

Time of the Twins (also see below), TSR (Lake Geneva, WI), 1986.

War of the Twins (also see below), TSR (Lake Geneva, WI), 1986.

Test of the Twins (also see below), TSR (Lake Geneva, WI), 1986.

The Dragonlance Legends (contains *Time of the Twins, War of the Twins,* and *Test of the Twins*), poetry by Michael Williams, illustrated by Valerie Valusek, TSR (Lake Geneva, WI), 1988.

"DRAGONLANCE TALES"; EDITOR, WITH MARGARET WEIS, AND CONTRIBUTOR

Magic of Krynn, TSR (Lake Geneva, WI), 1986.

Kender, Gully Dwarves, and Gnomes, TSR (Lake Geneva, WI), 1987.

Love and War, TSR (Lake Geneva, WI), 1987.

The Reign of Istar, TSR (Lake Geneva, WI), 1992.

The Cataclysm, TSR (Lake Geneva, WI), 1992.

The War of the Lance, TSR (Lake Geneva, WI), 1992.

The Dragons of Krynn, TSR (Lake Geneva, WI), 1994.

"WAR OF SOULS" SERIES; WITH MARGARET WEIS

Dragons of a Fallen Star, TSR (Renton, WA), 1999.

Dragons of a Fallen Sun, TSR (Renton, WA), 2000.

Dragons of a Lost Star, TSR (Renton, WA), 2001.

Dragons of a Vanished Moon, Wizards of the Coast (Renton, WA), 2002.

"DARKSWORD" SERIES; WITH MARGARET WEIS

Forging the Darksword, Bantam (New York, NY), 1988.

Doom of the Darksword, Bantam (New York, NY), 1988.

Triumph of the Darksword, Bantam (New York, NY), 1988.

Legacy of the Darksword, Bantam (New York, NY), 1997.

"ROSE OF THE PROPHET" TRILOGY; WITH MARGARET WEIS

Will of the Wanderer, Bantam (New York, NY), 1989.

The Paladin of the Night, Bantam (New York, NY), 1989.

The Prophet of Akhran, Bantam (New York, NY), 1989.

"DEATH GATE CYCLE"; WITH MARGARET WEIS

Dragon Wing, Bantam (New York, NY), 1990.

Elven Star, Bantam (New York, NY), 1990.

Fire Sea, Bantam (New York, NY), 1991.

Serpent Mage, Bantam (New York, NY), 1992.

The Hand of Chaos, Bantam (New York, NY), 1993.

Into the Labyrinth, Bantam (New York, NY), 1993.

The Seventh Gate, Bantam (New York, NY), 1994.

"STARSHIELD" SERIES; WITH MARGARET WEIS

Starshield Sentinels, Ballantine (New York, NY), 1996, published as *The Mantle of Kendis Dai,* Ballantine (New York, NY), 1997.

Nightsword, Ballantine (New York, NY), 1998.

"BRONZE CANTICLES" SERIES; WITH WIFE, LAURA HICKMAN

Mystic Warrior, Aspect, 2004.

Mystic Quest, Aspect, 2005.

Mystic Empire, Aspect, 2006.

OTHER

(Editor, with Margaret Weis) *Leaves from the Inn of the Last Home: The Complete Krynn Source Book,* TSR (Lake Geneva, WI), 1987.

(With Margaret Weis) *Dragonlance Adventures* (game manual), TSR (Lake Geneva, WI), 1987.

(With Margaret Weis) *The Art of Dragonlance,* edited by Mary Kirchoff, TSR (Lake Geneva, WI), 1987.

(Editor, with Margaret Weis) *The History of Dragonlance: Being the Notes, Journals, and Memorabilia of Krynn,* compiled and designed by Maryls Heeszel, TSR (Lake Geneva, WI), 1995.

The Immortals, ROC (New York, NY), 1996.

Margaret Weis and Tracy Hickman Present Treasures of Fantasy, Harper (New York, NY), 1997.

(Editor, with Margaret Weis) *Heroes and Fools: Tales of the Fifth Age,* TSR (Renton, WA), 1999.

(With Margaret Weis) *Realms of Dragons: The Worlds of Weis and Hickman,* edited by Denise Little, Harper (New York, NY), 1999.

(With Margaret Weis) *More Leaves of the Inn of the Last Home,* edited by Elizabeth Baldwin, TSR (Renton, WA), 2000.

(With Margaret Weis) *Well of Darkness* (book 1 of "Sovereign Stone" trilogy), EOS (New York, NY), 2000.

(Editor, with Margaret Weis) *Rebels and Tyrants: Tales of the Fifth Age,* Wizards Publishing (Renton, WA), 2000.

(Editor, with Margaret Weis and Patrick McGilligan) *The Best of Tales,* Wizards Publishing (Renton, WA), 2000.

(With Margaret Weis) *Dragons of a Lost Star,* Wizards of the Coast, 2001.

ADAPTATIONS: Mystic Warrior was adapted to audiocassette.

SIDELIGHTS: Novelist and screenwriter Tracy Raye Hickman was introduced to role-playing games by his wife, Laura, and was soon so taken with the activity that he began designing games himself. When he approached TSR Inc., a game publisher and the maker of "Dungeons & Dragons," with his ideas in the early 1980s, he met Margaret Weis, with whom he has since collaborated on dozens of fantasy novels. With *The Immortals,* published in 1996, Hickman began his solo foray into novel writing, while still continuing his successful collaborations with Weis.

Hickman and Weis's novels feature clashes between good and evil forces in worlds populated by wizards, elves, dragons, and a variety of other beings, including humans. They followed their popular "Dragonlance" and "Darksword" novels with their longest series, the seven-volume "Death Gate Cycle," which portrays a universe whose inhabitants find their lives threatened by both natural forces and warring factions. A *Publishers Weekly* critic, reviewing the fourth Death Gate novel, *Serpent Mage,* noted that "the worlds created by Hickman and Weis become more attractively complex with each book of the series." By the arrival of the final entry, *The Seventh Gate,* some reviewers were less impressed with their efforts; a *Publishers Weekly* commentator thought all but the most devoted fans would "find that incomprehensible . . . landscapes and tedious prose make this volume both dizzying and dull." *Booklist* contributor Roland Green, however, contended that *The Seventh Gate* provided the series with "perhaps the most powerful conclusion in Weis and Hickman's considerable body of work." He praised the duo for their storytelling ability and their use of "classic fantasy elements."

In the late 1990s Weis and Hickman embarked on a new series, "Starshield." In the first entry, *The Mantle of Kendis-Dai* (first published as *Sentinels*), the survival of an interstellar civilization hinges on the recovery of an ancient relic, the eponymous mantle owned by the world's chief god. Merinda Neskat, a woman searching for the mantle, encounters a lost band of Earth astronauts led by Jeremy Griffiths, who aid her in the quest. *Booklist* contributor Roland Green praised the volume's pace, writing style, and "excellent" character portrayals, although a *Publishers Weekly* reviewer asserted that "ludicrous dialogue . . . and particularly cheesy characterizations spoil this introduction to a potentially intriguing universe." The next book in the series, *Nightsword,* finds Jeremy, having acquired the mantle, now in love with Merinda and seeking to beat various villains in a race to find the all-powerful weapon of the title. Once again, a *Publishers Weekly* critic faulted Weis and Hickman's work, saying they were "trying to revive characters already sagging" in the series opener. On the other hand, Jackie Cassada declared in *Library Journal* that *Nightsword* and its predecessor showed the collaborators at "the top of their storytelling form." In *Booklist,* Green opined that *Nightsword* "mostly delivers on the promise made by *The Mantle of Kendis-Dai*" that Weis and Hickman would provide "another excellent adventure saga."

In 2000 the collaborators began their "Sovereign Stone" trilogy with *Well of Darkness,* which involves political intrigue between two sons of a king in a realm inhabited by elves and dwarves as well as humans; one son and his magician ally manage to touch off a war. A *Publish-*

ers *Weekly* reviewer averred that Hickman and Weis are "not much more than good plain cooks as stylists, but here they are writing at an entirely respectable level."

Hickman's first solo book, *The Immortals,* is set in the near future, when efforts to cure AIDS have produced an even worse disease, whose sufferers are rounded up and sent to camps, ostensibly for quarantine but actually for elimination. The prisoners eventually rise up against their oppressors with the aid of a wealthy businessman who has infiltrated one of the camps in an attempt to find his homosexual son. A *Publishers Weekly* commentator applauded Hickman's new twist on "a classic SF theme" and praised his handling of character and setting. *The Immortals,* the reviewer added, "represents a radical departure for the author. . . . He's to be commended for his daring and vision."

With the first book in the "Bronze Canticles" series, *Mystic Warrior,* Hickman forged a literary relationship with a new collaborator: his wife, Laura Hickman. A biographer on the *Tracy Hickman* Web site noted that writing novels together is the fulfillment of a "long-time dream" for the couple. In terms of working with his wife rather than long-time collaborator Margaret Weis, Hickman stated in an interview on *SFFWorld.com:* "Every partnership is unique: they have their different strengths and ways of making it work. The important thing, however, is to put the integrity of the work first—before egos. If you are asking 'what is best for the book' and stop asking 'what is best for me' in a collaboration, you'll have much better success both with the book and the collaboration."

Mystic Warrior tells the story in which the separate universes of goblins, humans, and the faerie converge. The world of humans is controlled by ruthless dragons, and newlywed blacksmith Galen Arvad finds himself connected to the faerie and goblin realms through his dreams. Sharing this connection are a faerie Seeker, who lives in a world in constant war with mystical creatures, and a goblin who lives among the vast machines left behind by a race of immense Titans. As the three struggle to understand the nature of their connection, they begin to understand that the magic that threads through their worlds is much bigger than themselves and that it will have profound effects on their lives and on the joint fate of their universes. A *Publishers Weekly* reviewer called the novel an "impressive and provocative fantasy" as well as a "fine example of socially conscious and unpredictable imaginative fiction."

The second book in the series, *Mystic Quest,* takes up the story of the three worlds nearly a quarter century after the events in the first book, focusing on the sons and daughters of the earlier protagonists. Humans are in rebellion against the repressive dragons using the Deep Magic rediscovered by Galen Arvad. In the human world, Arvad's sons, Caelith and Jorgan, undertake a quest to find the legendary lost city of the gods, Calsandria. Faerie princess Aislynn becomes a mystic in training and joins a quest of her own to find an important lost city in her realm. In the goblin's world, wizard Thux also strikes off to locate a fabled city, this one containing secrets to making the Titans' gigantic robots work. A reviewer in *MBR Bookwatch* called the Hickmans' book "an enthralling fantasy novel with plenty of action and fully developed characters. *Mystic Quest* is fantasy at its very best." The gates between the faerie, human, and goblin worlds finally open in the concluding volume of the trilogy, *Mystic Empire.* Once the access between worlds is created, the three disparate universes and their inhabitants must find common ground and a way to coexist peacefully. A *Publishers Weekly* critic commented favorably on the authors' "lyrical writing" in this volume.

Hickman, an active member of the Church of Jesus Christ of Latter-Day Saints, once told *CA* that his religious faith provides the "moral foundation reflected most strongly in my work." "The heart of any writing is the story," Hickman continued. "While technique and discipline are essential to a writer, these elements are without substance unless, at the base, there is the simple tale. Nothing can compensate for a lack of plot."

BIOGRAPHICAL AND CRITICAL SOURCES:

PERIODICALS

Booklist, August, 1994, Roland Green, review of *The Seventh Gate,* p. 2030; November 15, 1996, Green, review of *Sentinels,* p. 576; June 1, 1997, Green, review of *Legacy of the Darksword,* p. 1669; May 15, 1998, Green, review of *Nightsword,* p. 1608.
Kliatt, November, 2004, Hugh Flick, Jr., audiobook review of *Mystic Warrior,* p. 48.
Library Journal, May 15, 1997, Susan Hamburger, review of *Legacy of the Darksword,* p. 106; May 15, 1998, Jackie Cassada, review of *Nightsword,* p. 118; April 15, 2004, Jackie Cassada, review of *Mystic Warrior,* p. 128.

MBR Bookwatch, April, 2005, review of *Mystic Quest.*

Publishers Weekly, August 17, 1990, Sybil Steinberg, review of *Elven Star,* p. 55; January 6, 1992, review of *Serpent Mage,* p. 52; October 18, 1993, review of *Into the Labyrinth,* p. 67; January 17, 1994, review of *The Second Generation,* p. 420; July 25, 1994, review of *The Seventh Gate,* p. 38; April 22, 1996, review of *The Immortals,* p. 63; October 21, 1996, review of *Sentinels,* p. 75; April 27, 1998, review of *Nightsword,* p. 51; September 4, 2000, review of *Well of Darkness,* p. 91; March 15, 2004, review of *Mystic Warrior,* p. 59; March 21, 2005, review of *Mystic Quest,* p. 40; March 6, 2006, review of *Mystic Empire,* p. 50.

ONLINE

Dragoncon.org, http://www.dragoncon.org/ (January 2, 2007), biography of Tracy Hickman.

SFFWorld.com, http://www.sffworld.com/ (May 21, 2006), interview with Tracy Hickman.

Tracy Hickman Home Page, http://www.trhickman.com (January 2, 2007).*

* * *

HICKMAN, Tracy Raye
    See HICKMAN, Tracy

* * *

HOBBS, Will 1947-
    (William Carl Hobbs)

PERSONAL: Born August 22, 1947, in Pittsburgh, PA; son of Gregory J. and Mary Hobbs; married Jean Loftus (a former teacher and literary agent), December 20, 1972. *Education:* Stanford University, B.A., 1969, M.A., 1971. *Hobbies and other interests:* Hiking in the mountains and canyons, white water rafting, archaeology, natural history.

ADDRESSES: Home—Durango, CO.

CAREER: Educator and author of children's books. Pagosa Springs, CO, and Durango, CO, public schools, taught middle school and high school reading and English, 1973-89; writer, 1990—.

MEMBER: Authors Guild, Phi Beta Kappa.

AWARDS, HONORS: Notable Trade Book in the Field of Social Studies designation, National Council for the Social Studies/Children's Book Council (NCSS/CBC), 1988, and Colorado Blue Spruce Young Adult Book Award, 1992, both for *Changes in Latitudes;* NCSS/CBC Notable Trade Book in the Field of Social Studies designation, 1989, Best Books for Young Adults designation, American Library Association (ALA), 1989, and Teachers' Choice citation, International Reading Association (IRA), and Regional Book Award, Mountains and Plains Booksellers Association, both 1990, all for *Bearstone;* Pick of the Lists choice, American Booksellers Association (ABA), 1991, ALA Best Books for Young Adults and Best Books for Reluctant Young-Adult Readers citations, 1992, included among ALA 100 Best Young-Adult Books of the Past Twenty-five Years, 1994, and California Young Readers Medal, 1995, all for *Downriver;* ALA Best Books for Young Adults designation, 1993, for *The Big Wander;* ABA Pick of the Lists choice and ALA Best Books for Young Adults designation, both 1993, and Spur Award, Western Writers of America, and Colorado Book Award, all for *Beardance;* NCSS/CBC Notable Trade Book in the Field of Social Studies designation, 1995, for *Kokopelli's Flute;* ALA Top-Ten Best Books for Young Adults choice and Quick Picks for Reluctant Young-Adult Readers choice, and NCSS/CBC Notable Trade Book in the Field of Social Studies designation, all 1996, Spur Award, and Colorado Book Award, all for *Far North;* ABA Pick of the Lists choice, 1997, and Edgar Allan Poe Award, Mystery Writers of America, 1998, both for *Ghost Canoe;* ABA Pick of the Lists designation, 1997, and Colorado Center for the Book Award, 1998, both for *Beardream;* IRA Young-Adult Choice selection, 1998, for *River Thunder;* ALA Best Books for Young Adults and Quick Picks for Reluctant Young Adult Readers designations, ABA Pick of the Lists choice, and IRA Teachers' Choice selection, all 1998, all for *The Maze;* ALA Best Books for Young Adults and Quick Picks for Reluctant Young Adult Readers selections, ABA Pick of the Lists choice, and NCSS/CBC Notable Children's Trade Book in the Field of Social Studies designation, all 1999, all for *Jason's Gold;* National Science Teachers Association (NSTA) Outstanding Science Trade Book for Students designation and Children's Literature Young-Adult Choice designation, both 2003, both for *Wild Man Island;* NSTA Outstanding Science Trade Book for Students designation, 2004, for *Jackie's Wild Seattle;* IRA Notable Books for a Global Society designation and Southwest Book Award, both 2007, both for *Crossing the Wire;* nominations for numerous state readers' choice awards.

WRITINGS:

YOUNG-ADULT NOVELS

Changes in Latitudes, Atheneum (New York, NY), 1988.
Bearstone, Atheneum (New York, NY), 1989.
Downriver, Atheneum (New York, NY), 1991.
The Big Wander, Atheneum (New York, NY), 1992.
Beardance, Atheneum (New York, NY), 1993.
Kokopelli's Flute, Simon & Schuster (New York, NY), 1995.
Far North, Morrow (New York, NY), 1996.
Ghost Canoe, Morrow (New York, NY), 1997.
River Thunder, Delacorte (New York, NY), 1997.
The Maze, Morrow (New York, NY), 1998.
Jason's Gold, Morrow (New York, NY), 1999.
Down the Yukon, HarperCollins (New York, NY), 2001.
Wild Man Island, HarperCollins (New York, NY), 2002.
Jackie's Wild Seattle, HarperCollins (New York, NY), 2003.
Leaving Protection, HarperCollins (New York, NY), 2004.
Crossing the Wire, HarperCollins (New York, NY), 2006.
Go Big or Go Home, HarperCollins (New York, NY), 2008.

Contributor of articles to periodicals, including *Horn Book, ALAN Review, Journal of Youth Services in Libraries, Journal of Adolescent and Adult Literacy, Book Links, Signal, Voices from the Middle, Voice of Youth Advocates,* and numerous state journals.

PICTURE BOOKS

Beardream, illustrated by Jill Kastner, Simon & Schuster (New York, NY), 1997.
Howling Hill, illustrated by Jill Kastner, Morrow (New York, NY), 1998.

ADAPTATIONS: Hobbs's novels have been adapted for audiocassette by Recorded Books, Bantam Doubleday Dell Audio, and Listening Library. *Bearstone* was adapted as a play by Karen Glenn, published in *Scholastic Scope,* January 14, 1994. *Jason's Gold* and *Down the Yukon* were adapted as plays published in *READ* magazine.

SIDELIGHTS: The wilderness-based novels of author Will Hobbs, which include *Bearstone, Kokopelli's Flute, Far North,* and *Down the Yukon* have been well received by both his young-adult fans and reviewers. A large part of Hobbs's success as a writer is due to the fact that he knows what his audience—predominately middle-school and high school boys—likes. A former English teacher, Hobbs noted in the *Colorado Reading Council Journal* that "if kids come to care about and identify with the characters in stories, they will also learn more about and ultimately care more about preserving the treasures of our natural world." Since his first novel appeared in 1988, Hobbs has seen his readership grow, with the result that almost all of his books have remained in print due to the demands of each new generation of fans.

Born in Pittsburgh, Pennsylvania, Hobbs and his family moved to the Panama Canal Zone when the future author was less than a year old. His father's Air Force career was behind several family moves, including stints in Virginia, Alaska, California, and Texas. Having siblings made the moves easier because all four of the Hobbs children were involved in scouting and had a love of the out-of-doors inspired by their parents.

Although Hobbs hiked and backpacked in many regions, it was the Southwest that most captured his imagination, and he spent several summers during high school and college as a guide and camp director at New Mexico's Philmont Scout Ranch. In 1973, after graduating from Stanford University, he and his wife Jean moved to a remote area of southwestern Colorado, near the San Juan Mountains and the Weminuche Wilderness, and now looks out from his writing desk at snow-capped mountain peaks.

In beginning his writing career in his early thirties, Hobbs was inspired by his local surroundings, and his first novel, *Bearstone,* is set in the Weminuche Wilderness near the Hobbs family's Colorado home. Published after eight years' worth of work, *Bearstone* focuses on Cloyd, a Ute Indian boy who has been sent by his tribe in Utah to spend the summer with an old rancher named Walter. Angry and hostile, Cloyd distrusts the old man's affection. While exploring the mountains near Walter's ranch, Cloyd discovers a Native American burial site and a small bearstone. Inspired by his discovery, the boy renames himself Lone Bear and learns how to "live in a good way," as his grandmother has taught him. An incident concerning a hunter who illegally kills a grizzly bear forces Cloyd to decide between revealing the truth and getting revenge or keeping silent. Cloyd's story continues in *Beardance,* as he rides into the mountains with Walter in search of a lost gold mine. Then they hear that a mother grizzly has been sighted with her three cubs. While searching for the cubs, Cloyd meets a wildlife biologist with the same goal; after the mother bear is reported killed, the boy risks his life in an effort to save the orphaned grizzly cubs and remains alone in the mountains despite winter's approach.

In praising *Bearstone, School Library Journal* contributor George Gleason described Hobbs's first novel as "far above other coming-of-age stories." Hobbs's young protagonist's "first experiences with spirit dreams are particularly well done," wrote *Horn Book* critic Elizabeth S. Watson in a review of *Beardance,* while Merlyn Miller observed in the *Voice of Youth Advocates* that the novel "weaves Native American legends with real adventure. Not only is Cloyd connected with his ancestry," Miller added, "but he's focused with courage, determination, and strength."

The main characters in *Beardance* and *Bearstone* return in Hobbs's first picture book, *Beardream.* Illustrated by Jill Kastner, *Beardream* describes how a boy called Short Tail awakens an oversleeping grizzly bear from hibernation, and how, in ancient times, the Ute people learned the bear dance from the bears. In an author's note at the end of *Beardream,* Hobbs stated: "It is my belief that future generations of the human family will have greater and greater need for the inspiration of native wisdom, which sees humankind not apart from nature, but as a part of nature." In the *Journal of Adolescent and Adult Literacy,* a critic recommended that the picture book be read aloud in order that the listener may "experience the beautiful . . . language that is a hallmark of Hobbs's work."

Hobbs's second novel—and the first of his books to see print—*Changes in Latitudes* was inspired by a photograph Hobbs saw in *National Geographic* that depicted a sea turtle swimming underwater. Curious as to what it would be like to swim with the turtles, Hobbs developed a story in which imaginative readers can take that swim with the turtles while also gaining compassion for

endangered species. In the novel, sixteen-year-old Travis is the oldest of three siblings. Cynical and self-absorbed, he tries to hide from his problems by withdrawing into his own "cool" world. Vacationing in Mexico with their mother, the teen and his younger brother, Teddy, learn about the plight of the region's sea turtles. When Teddy dies attempting to rescue some turtles, Travis learns to deal with adversity and discovers that strength is gained by overcoming, rather than running away, from setbacks. Nancy Vasilakis, writing in *Horn Book,* wrote that, in *Changes in Latitudes,* Hobbs "neatly balances the perilous situation of these ancient lumbering sea creatures against the breakdown of [Travis's] . . . family." The critic also commended the author for his "sensitive ear for the language of the young."

Having rowed his own whitewater raft through the rapids of the Grand Canyon ten times, Hobbs is familiar with the dangers and the beauty of the journey, and he shares this with readers in *Downriver.* Narrated by Jessie, a fifteen-year-old girl who has been sent away from home, the novel follows seven teens on a raft trip down the Grand Canyon. Jessie and the rest of the group—known as the "Hoods in the Woods"—leave their leader behind and take off on their own, making their own decisions and coping with the consequences. *Downriver* "is exquisitely plotted, with nail-biting suspense and excitement," wrote George Gleason in a review for *School Library Journal,* while in *Booklist* Candace Smith commended the book's rafting scenes. "The scenery description is beautiful and the kids are believable," concluded Mary Ojibway in her enthusiastic review of *Downriver* for *Voice of Youth Advocates.*

Returning in *River Thunder,* Jessie gets the chance to row through the Grand Canyon by herself. Unexpectedly high water on the Colorado forces Jessie and the rest of the Hoods in the Woods gang to confront their fears when raging rapids threaten. Deborah Stevenson, reviewing *River Thunder* for the *Bulletin of the Center for Children's Books,* described the novel's adventure sequences as "terrific and involving," while in *School Library Journal* Joel Shoemaker wrote that Hobbs's "descriptions deliver high-volume excitement sure to entice many readers."

Although he has experienced first-hand many of the adventures he writes about in his young-adult novels, Hobbs's descriptions of hang gliding in *The Maze* are based on time spent with friends who fly, watching them jump off cliffs and soar. Hobbs sets his story in the

Maze, a remote region of Canyonlands National Park in Utah, an area noted for its beauty. Like Icarus, young protagonist Rick Walker attempts to fly out of his own personal labyrinth, a life of foster homes and dead ends. "Rick is a richly-textured character," noted Sarah K. Herz in her *Voice of Youth Advocates* review of the novel. Todd Morning, writing in *School Library Journal*, asserted that "what sets this book apart is the inclusion of fascinating details about the condors and hang gliding, especially the action-packed description of Rick's first solo flight above the canyons." "Hobbs spins an engrossing yarn, blending adventure with a strong theme," wrote *Horn Book* writer Mary M. Burns, and Morning deemed *The Maze* "an adventure story [readers] . . . can't put down."

A sea-kayaking trip in southeast Alaska with his wife inspired the setting for Hobbs's novel *Wild Man Island.* As readers meet fourteen-year-old Andy Galloway, the book's narrator, Andy has come to the end of an enjoyable guided sea-kayaking vacation. Now, while preparing to return home, he takes his kayak and decides to make a quick, two-mile trip to Hidden Falls, the place where his archaeologist dad accidentally met his death years before. When a freak storm arises, Andy and his craft are washed ashore on a wild, remote island. Hunger, cold, and roaming grizzly bears threaten the teen's life until a Newfoundland dog befriends him and leads Andy to a cave that turns out to be the home of a strange, man that seems to be a Neolithic holdover but ultimately reveals his true history. "Hobbs resolves the story's complexities in ways that protect the characters' integrity," commented Joel Shoemaker in *School Library Journal,* while in the *Journal of Adolescent and Adult Literacy* James Blasingame wrote that the novel's "conflicts are resolved in a satisfying conclusion." *Wild Man Island* features the "short, pithy chapters" guaranteed to "attract readers, reluctant and otherwise," according to Burns, and in *Kirkus Reviews* a critic commended the novel as "a rugged, satisfying episode for outdoorsy readers."

Jackie's Wild Seattle takes its name from a wildlife rehabilitation center in Seattle, Washington, where fourteen-year-old Shannon and little brother Cody come to spend their summer vacation. During their stay, the siblings become involved in their Uncle Neal's work with animals, and after Neil is injured, quickly learn how to work with the injured and orphaned coyotes, bear cubs, raccoons, and birds of prey they find in the city. Commenting on Hobbs's back story—Cody is still haunted by the fall of Manhattan's Twin Towers, which

he witnessed from a cliff near his New Jersey home, a *Kirkus Reviews* writer deemed the novel an "absorbing story about animal rehabilitation, the state of the world, fear, achievement, and trust." Writing that "this exciting, poignant, and beautifully developed story covers a crucial few weeks for several people whose lives intertwine to change and benefit all," Mary R. Hoffman added in her *School Library Journal* review that *Jackie's Wild Seattle* "will reach deep into the hearts of young readers."

A meeting with a teacher from Craig a town on Prince of Wales Island, Alaska, inspired Hobbs's novel *Leaving Protection.* The teacher, who had earned her way through college working on her father's fishing boat, now invited the popular novelist to work on her family's boat, and write a novel about life on a salmon trawler. In the novel, when sixteen-year-old Robbie Daniels leaves his home in Port Protection for the nearby fishing town of Craig, he hopes to find work as a deck hand on a commercial fishing boat during king salmon season. Therefore, the teen can hardly believe his good fortune when legendary fisherman Tor Torsen hires him on. Out on the open ocean, alone with Tor, Robbie discovers the reason for his seeming good luck: his mysterious captain is not only fishing, he is searching along the coastline for the historic metal plaques that were buried by early Russian explorers laying claim to Alaska. After Robbie learns how valuable these possession plaques are, Tor's wrath and a violent storm at sea put his courage and wit to the ultimate test. *Leaving Protection* is a "nautical thriller [that] brims with detail about the fishing life," wrote a *Publishers Weekly* contributor, adding that the novel's "climactic finale involving a dramatic and fateful storm at sea [is] grippingly rendered." Reviewing Hobbs's book for *School Library Journal,* Jeffrey Hastings praised *Leaving Protection* as "straightforward outdoor fiction laced with bracing action and heady suspense."

A timely novel that focuses on the problem of illegal immigration in America, *Crossing the Wire* introduces readers to fifteen-year-old Victor Flores, a Mexican teen who, since his father's tragic death, has become the main breadwinner to his mother and four younger siblings. Unable to support his family through farming, Victor attempts the dangerous trip north across the border, encountering fast-moving trains, mountain and desert crossings, drug smugglers, border guards, and unscrupulous men hoping to take advantage of the teen's desperation. In *Kirkus Reviews* a critic wrote that "Hobbs has created a pageturning adventure set squarely in the real world," adding that the novelist "offers no easy answers." In an author's note, Hobbs wrote that he wrote *Crossing the Wire* to "put a human face" to the quandary of the Mexicans risking all to find a better life in America. Noting that the novel is "gritty and realistic," Paula Rohrlick concluded in her *Kliatt* review that, whatever their personal opinions regarding the immigration question, readers "will . . . appreciate Victor's desperation, determination, and courage."

Hobbs weaves elements of fantasy into his characteristic Western setting in *Kokopelli's Flute*. Thirteen-year-old Tepary Jones and his dog, Dusty, journey to the ruins of an ancient Anasazi cliff house overlooking the canyons near the boy's home on a seed farm in New Mexico. Hoping to see a total eclipse of the full moon from this remote location, Tep soon realizes that he is not alone when he surprises looters searching for Anasazi artifacts. Picking up an ancient Anasazi flute made of eagle bone that the looters had dropped in their hurry to escape, the teen is pulled into the grip of an ancient magic which transforms him each night into a bushy-tailed woodrat. With the help of Dusty, Tep is able to track down the looters and also obtains the medicinal herbs needed to save his mother from a deadly sickness. Hobbs "blends fantasy with fact so smoothly that the resulting mix can be consumed without question," wrote Darcy Schild in a *School Library Journal* review of the popular novel, while in *Voice of Youth Advocates* Nancy Zachary called *Kokopelli's Flute* "an engaging and delightful tale."

In *Far North* Hobbs leads readers up into the rugged wilderness of Canada's Northwest Territories. Gabe Rogers, almost sixteen years old and fresh from Texas, enrolls in a boarding school in Yellowknife in order to be closer to his father, who works on nearby diamond exploration rigs. Gabe's roommate, Raymond Providence, a native teen from a remote Dene village, decides to quit school after only a few months, and on a flight home in a small bush plane both Raymond and Gabe end up stranded on the banks of the Nahanni River. The boys' winter survival story was described by *Horn Book* contributor Mary M. Burns as "a thrill-a-minute account" of a battle "against seemingly impossible odds." According to Burns, *Far North* "is not just another page-turner; there are deeper issues addressed," such as the differences between the two boys' cultures. Calling the novel a "classic Hobbs adventure," Diane Tuccillo wrote in *Voice of Youth Advocates* that in *Far North* "characters are well-drawn, and excitement and energy penetrate their entire trek."

Hobbs ventures into mystery with *Ghost Canoe*, winner of an Edgar Allan Poe award for best young-adult mystery. Set in 1874, along the storm-tossed coast of Washington's Olympic Peninsula, this story follows fourteen-year-old Nathan MacAllister, the son of a lighthouse keeper. When a mysterious shipwreck leaves behind a set of unexplained footprints on the shore, Nathan suspects something is amiss. Writing in *School Library Journal*, Gerry Larson called *Ghost Canoe* "a winning tale that artfully combines history, nature, and suspense." In the *Bulletin of the Center for Children's Books*, Elizabeth Bush noted that although the book's mystery is predictable, there is enough action "to keep the pages flipping."

Also set in the past—this time amid the Klondike gold rush of 1897-98—*Jason's Gold* follows Jason Hawthorn as he races to catch up to his older brothers who have taken off for the gold fields in Canada's Yukon. Along the way he meets a not-yet-famous Jack London, the author of *White Fang*, and develops a romantic relationship with traveling performer Jamie Dunavant. Mostly he travels alone, with King, a husky he rescues from a madman. In *Jason's Gold* Hobbs creates an action-packed adventure story filled with vivid descriptions of bone-chilling cold, personal courage, and friendship, and he continues Jason's saga in *Down the Yukon*. As the book begins, Jason's brother Ethan loses the family sawmill business to Cornelius Donner in a poker game. Now sixteen years old, Jason is determined to regain the sawmill. Together with Ethan and girlfriend Jamie, he decides to compete in a canoe race to Nome in which the winner will receive 20,000 dollars in prize money. Unfortunately, ne'er-do-well Donner, who swindled the business from Ethan, has also entered the race; now he and his henchmen manage to sabotage the brothers' canoe. "The ending, though predictable, features an appropriate twist," remarked *Booklist* critic Catherine Andronik in her review of *Down the Yukon*, while *School Library Journal* reviewer Vicki Reutter deemed the novel "more exciting than its predecessor."

Commenting on his decision to write for a teen audience, Hobbs noted on his home page: "My first hope for my novels is that they tell a good story, that the reader will keep turning the pages and will hate to see the story end. Beyond that, I hope to be inspiring a love for the natural world. I'd like my readers to appreciate and to care more about what's happening to wild creatures, wild places, and the diversity of life."

BIOGRAPHICAL AND CRITICAL SOURCES:

BOOKS

Encyclopedia of Children's Literature, Continuum (New York, NY), 2001.
Gallo, Donald R., editor, *Speaking for Ourselves Too,* National Council of Teachers of English, 1993.
Hobbs, Will, *Beardream,* Simon & Schuster (New York, NY), 1997.
Hobbs, Will, *Ghost Canoe,* Morrow (New York, NY), 1997.
Writers for Young Adults, edited by Ted Hipple, Scribner (New York, NY), 1997, pp. 121-129.

PERIODICALS

ALAN Review, fall, 1994.
Booklist, March 1, 1991, Candace Smith, review of *Downriver,* p. 1377; October 15, 1992, p. 424; May 1, 1997; September 1, 1997, p. 106; September 1, 1998, p. 126; February 15, 2000, Jeanette Larson, review of *Ghost Canoe* (audiobook), p. 1128; March 15, 2000, review of *Jason's Gold,* p. 1340; April 1, 2001, Catherine Andronik, review of *Down the Yukon,* p. 1482; November 15, 2001, Anna Rich, review of *Down the Yukon,* p. 589; April 15, 2002, review of *Wild Man Island,* p. 1395; June 1, 2003, Traci Todd, review of *Jackie's Wild Seattle,* p. 1776; May 1, 2006, Jennifer Mattson, review of *Crossing the Wire,* p. 83.
Bulletin of the Center for Children's Books, April, 1997, Elizabeth Bush, review of *Ghost Canoe,* p. 285; July, 1997, Deborah Stevenson, review of *River Thunder,* pp. 397-398; May, 2003, review of *Jackie's Wild Seattle,* p. 363; July-August, 2006, Maggie Hommel, review of *Crossing the Wire,* p. 500.
California Reader, winter, 1992, pp. 15-16.
Colorado Reading Council Journal, spring, 1993, pp. 7-9.
Five Owls, fall, 2001, reviews of *Kokopelli's Flute, The Maze, Downriver,* and *Beardance,* p. 2.
Horn Book, May-June, 1988, p. 358; January-February, 1993, p. 91; January-February, 1994, Elizabeth S. Watson, review of *Beardance,* p. 70; March-April, 1996; November-December, 1996, p. 745; September-October, 1998, Mary M. Burns, review of *The Maze,* p. 609; July-August, 2002, Mary M. Burns, review of *Wild Man Island,* p. 462.

Journal of Adolescent and Adult Literacy, September, 1997, review of *Beardream,* p. 83; May, 2000, Joel Taxel, review of *The Maze,* pp. 780-781; February, 2003, James Blasingame, review of *Wild Man Island,* pp. 442-443.
Journal of Youth Services in Libraries, spring, 1995.
Kirkus Reviews, March 15, 1997, p. 462; March 15, 2002, review of *Wild Man Island,* p. 413; March 15, 2003, review of *Jackie's Wild Seattle,* p. 468; March 15, 2004, review of *Leaving Protection,* p. 270; March 1, 2006, review of *Crossing the Wire,* p. 154.
Kliatt, September, 1999, p. 8; March, 2002, Claire Rosser, review of *Wild Man Island,* p. 11; July, 2002, Michele Winship, review of *Down the Yukon,* p. 20; March, 2003, Claire Rosser, review of *Jackie's Wild Seattle,* p. 12; May, 2003, Claire Rosser, review of *Wild Man Island,* p. 235; March, 2004, Paula Rohrlick review of *Leaving Protection,* p. 25; July, 2004, Myrna Marler, review of *Far North,* p. 192; March, 2006, Paula Rohrlick, review of *Crossing the Wire,* p. 12.
Publishers Weekly, February 12, 1988, p. 88; February 1, 1991, pp. 80-81; November 2, 1992, p. 72; October 12, 1998, review of *Howling Hill,* p. 77; April 12, 2004, review of *Leaving Protection,* p. 67.
School Library Journal, March, 1988, pp. 212, 214; September, 1989, p. 272; March, 1991, George Gleason, review of *Downriver,* p. 212; November, 1992, p. 92; December, 1993, p. 134; October, 1995, p. 134; April, 1997, Leda Schubert, review of *Beardream,* p. 104; September, 1997, Joel Shoemaker, review of *River Thunder,* p. 217; October, 1998, Virginia Golodetz, review of *Howling Hill,* p. 102; May, 2001, Vicki Reutter, review of *Down the Yukon,* p. 150; May, 2002, Joel Shoemaker, review of *Wild Man Island,* p. 154; May, 2003, Mary R. Hofmann, review of *Jackie's Wild Seattle,* p. 153; April, 2004, Jeffrey Hastings, review of *Leaving Protection,* p. 156; December, 2006, Larry Cooperman, review of *Crossing the Wire,* p. 70.
Voice of Youth Advocates, August, 1991, Mary Ojibway, review of *Downriver,* pp. 171-172; December, 1992, p. 279; December, 1993, p. 292; February, 1996, p. 372; February, 1997, p. 328; October, 1997, Cindy Lombardo, review of *River Thunder,* p. 244; February, 1999, Sarah K. Herz, review of *The Maze,* p. 434; June, 2001, review of *Down the Yukon,* p. 122; June, 2002, review of *Wild Man Island,* p. 118; August, 2003, review of *Jackie's Wild Seattle,* p. 224; October, 2004, Tim Brennan,

review of *Leaving Protection,* p. 202; April, 2006, Walter Hogan, review of *Crossing the Wire,* p. 46.

ONLINE

Will Hobbs Home Page, http://www.willhobbsauthor. com (January 15, 2007).

*   *   *

HOBBS, William Carl
  See HOBBS, Will

*   *   *

HOCHSCHILD, Adam 1942-

PERSONAL: Born October 5, 1942, in New York, NY; son of Harold K. (in business) and Mary (an artist) Hochschild; married Arlie Russell (a sociologist and author), June 26, 1965; children: David, Gabriel. *Education:* Harvard University, A.B. (cum laude), 1963. *Politics:* "Non-denominational progressive."

ADDRESSES: Home—San Francisco, CA. *Agent*—Georges Borchardt, Inc., 136 East 57th St., New York, NY 10022.

CAREER: Freelance writer, 1965—; *San Francisco Chronicle,* San Francisco, CA, reporter, 1965-66; *Ramparts* (magazine), San Francisco, writer and editor, 1966-68, 1973-74; *Mother Jones* (magazine), San Francisco, cofounder, 1974, editor and writer, 1976-81, 1986-87. Presidential campaign staff member for Sen. George McGovern, 1972; commentator for National Public Radio in Washington, DC, 1982-83; regents lecturer at University of California at Santa Cruz, 1987; commentator for Public Interest Radio in New York, NY, 1987-88; University of California at Berkeley graduate school of journalism, lecturer and writing instructor, 1992—. Fulbright lecturer in India, 1997-98. *Military service:* U.S. Army Reserve, 1964-70.

MEMBER: National Writers Union, National Book Critics Circle, Media Alliance, PEN.

AWARDS, HONORS: Certificate of Excellence from Overseas Press Club of America, 1981, for *Mother Jones* article on South Africa; Bryant Spann Memorial Prize,

Eugene V. Debs Foundation, 1984, for *Mother Jones* article on El Salvador; *Half the Way Home: A Memoir of Father and Son* was named a Notable Book of the Year for 1986 by the *New York Times Book Review* and the American Library Association; Thomas M. Storke International Journalism Award, World Affairs Council, 1987; *The Unquiet Ghost: Russians Remember Stalin* was named a Notable Book of the Year for 1995 by the *New York Times Book Review* and *Library Journal;* Madeline Dane Ross Award, Overseas Press Club of America, 1995, for *The Unquiet Ghost;* PEN/Spielvogel-Diamonstein Award for the Art of the Essay, for *Finding the Trapdoor: Essays, Portraits, Travels;* Mark Lynton History Prize of the J. Anthony Lucas Awards, Duff Cooper Prize, Lionel Gelber Prize, and California Book Awards Gold Medal, all for *King Leopold's Ghost: A Story of Greed, Terror, and Heroism in Colonial Africa;* Lannan Literary Award for Nonfiction, 2005; *Los Angeles Times* Book Prize in History, Lionel Gelber Prize, and California Book Awards Gold Medal, PEN USA Literary Award for Research Non-Fiction, all for *Bury the Chains: Prophets and Rebels in the Fight to Free an Empire's Slaves.*

WRITINGS:

Half the Way Home: A Memoir of Father and Son, Viking (New York, NY), 1986.
The Mirror at Midnight: A South African Journey, Viking (New York, NY), 1990.
The Unquiet Ghost: Russians Remember Stalin, Viking (New York, NY), 1994.
Finding the Trapdoor: Essays, Portraits, Travels, Syracuse University Press (Syracuse, NY), 1997.
King Leopold's Ghost: A Story of Greed, Terror, and Heroism in Colonial Africa, Houghton Mifflin (Boston, MA), 1998.
(Editor, with Allan Forsyth) Boris Sergievsky, *Airplanes, Women and Song: Memoirs of a Fighter Ace, Test Pilot and Adventurer,* Syracuse University Press (Syracuse, NY), 1998.
Bury the Chains: Prophets and Rebels in the Fight to Free an Empire's Slaves, Houghton Mifflin (Boston, MA), 2005.

Contributor of articles and reviews to periodicals, including *Harper's, New Republic, Village Voice, Nation, Washington Monthly, New York Review of Books, New York Times, New Yorker, Granta,* and *Los Angeles Times.* Member of board of directors, *Nuclear Times,* 1982-89.

SIDELIGHTS: A cofounder and former editor of *Mother Jones* magazine, Adam Hochschild has earned a considerable reputation for his reporting on issues of national and international importance. His books *The Mirror at Midnight: A South African Journey, The Unquiet Ghost: Russians Remember Stalin,* and *King Leopold's Ghost: A Story of Greed, Terror, and Heroism in Colonial Africa,* focus on apartheid, Stalin's concentration camps, and the conquest of the Congo by King Leopold II of Belgium. Hochschild's autobiography, *Half the Way Home: A Memoir of Father and Son,* recounts his troubled relationship with his father.

Half the Way Home is "by turns nostalgic and regretful, lyrical and melancholy," wrote *New York Times* reviewer Michiko Kakutani. She added that Hochschild "creates a deeply felt portrait of a man and a boy" narrated with "Proustian detail and affection." "Mr. Hochschild illuminates, with rare tact, the situations of fathers and sons," concluded Mary Gordon in the *New York Times Book Review,* "and he avoids the traps of sentimentality and rancor both."

Hochschild's grandfather, Berthold Hochschild, came from Germany to New York in 1886, where he was one of the founders of a company that eventually became AMAX, Inc., a worldwide mining empire. The Hochschilds rejected their Jewish heritage to better assimilate into the white Gentile majority. Clinching his acceptance into the WASP elite, Berthold's son Harold married Mary Marquand, a white Protestant with excellent social and political connections, when he was forty-nine and she was forty-one. A year later they had a son, Adam.

An only child, Adam Hochschild grew up with all the servants, fine homes, travel, and quality education wealth could provide, and also with all the expectations his anxious parents could place on him. In Gordon's words, Harold Hochschild "believed that the world was a difficult place and that his son was born to run it." Recognized for his benevolence, sound judgment, and irrefutable reason, Harold Hochschild raised his son with the same quiet reserve and emotional detachment he employed with business associates. But although such authoritative tactics worked smoothly with business executives, they came across to Harold's son as domineering, patriarchal, and intimidating. Adam Hochschild's mother adored both her husband and son, but while young Adam was encouraged by her devotion, he also felt betrayed by her failure to intercede on his behalf. "For," as Gordon explained, "he had to believe the justice of his father's criticisms if the mother who adored him went along with them."

Hochschild's break from his father's authority and his parents' world began after a visit to the mines owned by the company his father headed in central Africa. Concern over racial injustice there and in the United States led Hochschild as a young man to join the civil rights movement. A political activist during the 1960s, Hochschild demonstrated against the Vietnam War and joined the leftist ranks of the alternative press, eventually helping to found *Mother Jones,* named after labor organizer Mary Harris Jones. The self-proclaimed "magazine for the rest of us," *Mother Jones* brought leftist politics to a large and diverse audience.

The differences between Adam and Harold Hochschild on the surface seem apparent, critics point out, but they are in fact difficult to define. While Adam Hochschild fairly clearly led the life of a 1960s radical, Harold Hochschild was not a stereotypical ruthless entrepreneur. The company the elder Hochschild directed had major holdings in central and southern Africa, where the mines often ran under the oppressive contract labor system, yet, like his peace-activist son, he publicly opposed the Vietnam War. Though he had had many business contacts in China before 1949, he supported the Communist Revolution there. And, unlike many other corporate tycoons, as an ecologist he brought about some of the most effective environmental legislation in New York State. His fatherly disapproval, then, was not so much of his son's political and social beliefs as of his ways of expressing those beliefs. As Richard Eder noted in the *Los Angeles Times Book Review,* Harold Hochschild's criticism grew "out of concern that Adam was wasting his life."

That Adam Hochschild can so readily illustrate his and his father's similarities as well as their differences adds credibility and depth to his story in critics' eyes. Gordon observed, for example, that "it would indeed have been easy [for Hochschild] to present himself as the hero of the piece and his father as the villain, but he does not." Also adding depth, according to reviewers, is Hochschild's realistic portrayal of the relative peace he and his father attained during the last few years of the elder Hochschild's life. "*Half the Way Home* isn't only a story of flight. It's also a story of a son's reconciliation with his father," Suzanne Gordon wrote in the *Washington Post Book World.* Hochschild remembers fondly that eventually his father, as noted by Kakutani, "even hands out gift subscriptions [to *Mother Jones,*] as an unspoken gesture that he approves, perhaps even takes pride, in his son's vocation." Like other critics, Kakutani noted with relief that there "are no tearful reconciliation scenes between father and son—just as there were never any declarations of overt hostility." The reconciliation takes place quietly, the reviewer observed, and "by the time Harold Hochschild lies dying in a hospital bed, Adam has been able to move toward an acceptance of this difficult man, and even to acknowledge his own love."

Critics compared Hochschild's book favorably with other parent-child reminiscences. Roger W. Fromm, writing in the *Library Journal,* deemed the book "an honest, sensitive, fascinating portrait of a father-son relationship that is unique, yet one of universal experience." *Newsday* contributor Merin Wexler praised *Half the Way Home* as "an intriguing memoir, gently told," adding that Hochschild's book contains memories which are "in themselves remarkable, but his telling makes them doubly so."

Based on his awareness that his family's fortune was derived from mining operations in the African nation of Zambia, Hochschild visited southern Africa while in college. Later visits to the region and extensive research into its history led to Hochschild's *The Mirror at Midnight,* which combines history, travelogue, and personal interviews to create "one of the most illuminating books ever written on contemporary South Africa," noted Genevieve Stuttaford for *Publishers Weekly.* During a long journey across the country, Hochschild spoke to the head of a South African neo-Nazi group, members of a rugby team, and to a racially-mixed schoolteacher who had spent time in prison. Their various insights into South African politics and society give a panoramic view of life in that troubled country.

The Unquiet Ghost was inspired by Hochschild' travel to Russia to visit the sites of several former Soviet prison camps and to speak to those people who spent time as prisoners in these camps or worked there as guards. During the reign of Soviet dictator Joseph Stalin, millions of Russians were arrested and imprisoned as "enemies of the state" and sent to prison camps in the vast Siberian wilderness. Many millions died during their ordeal, while others spent years in hard labor for crimes involving no more than thinking the wrong thoughts in a totalitarian state. Hochschild, explained

Robert Legvold in *Foreign Affairs,* "went to see how people a half-century after the horror now related to it, particularly how its perpetrators and prey now feel." Hochschild found that information about Stalin and his crimes had been suppressed by the communist authorities for decades. He told *Progressive* interviewer Linda Rocawich that "the standard history text used in every Soviet high school . . . had ten lines about Stalin—the man who was absolute ruler of the country for twenty-five years. It had absolutely nothing about the Great Purge, in which nineteen million people were arrested and seven million executed outright. It completely skipped over the famines caused by the collectivization of agriculture, in which another, six, seven, eight million died. There was this vacuum, this silence, and the scale of the silence just awed me." Many former prisoners were reluctant to speak about their time in the camps and suppressed memories of that time in their lives. Former guards denied the horrors that prisoners had undergone. "This haunting and powerful report," noted a *Publishers Weekly* contributor, "reveals that the dictator's legacy persists in widespread denial, amnesia, numbness and pervasive fear." "Ultimately," wrote Gilbert Taylor in *Booklist,* "[Hochschild's] contribution is to seek out witnesses of Stalinism and preserve their ruthlessly realistic testimony."

In *King Leopold's Ghost,* Hochschild recounts another example of ruthless power and bloody mass murder, this time the conquest of the Congo by Belgian King Leopold II in 1885. The barbaric war of conquest, and the violence with which Leopold ruled his colony, drew the outraged attention of the world. The king's troops dismembered captured enemy troops, forced civilians into slavery to work collecting wild rubber, and slaughtered many others who dared to protest. "Hochschild's superb, engrossing chronicle," wrote a *Publishers Weekly* reviewer, "focuses on one of the great, horrifying and nearly forgotten crimes of the century." According to Gail M. Gerhart in *Foreign Affairs,* "Hochschild has assembled the most remarkable facts and dramatis personae, added a keen appreciation for sociopolitical nuances . . . and produced a splendid new popular history." A *Booklist* reviewer called *King Leopold's Ghost* an "impressively researched history."

Bury the Chains: Prophets and Rebels in the Fight to Free an Empire's Slaves is a history of the end of slavery in the British Empire, which it could be said began with the meeting of a dozen abolitionists, most of them Quakers, in London on May 22, 1787. These abolitionists organized opposition to slavery that included a boycott of slave-produced sugar. Most of the slaveholders were British, but the slaves were primarily Africans who were shipped to work on the plantations of the Caribbean. There they grew crops such as cotton, coffee, and sugar to be consumed by the British. They were cruelly treated, beaten, and even killed by their masters. The first major slave revolt, in 1791, was in French St. Domingue, later Haiti, and its success led to the abolishing of slavery by France. The British tried to capture the colony but were defeated by the former slaves. England outlawed slavery in 1833, thirty years before the United States. "Hochshild is a marvellous writer," concluded Leonard Kennedy in *Catholic Insight.* "This is another fascinating and outstanding work."

Hochschild told *CA:* "I seem to be one of these people who writes a book on a totally different subject each time. I also tend to get stuck between books, and to think I'm never going to find the right subject for the next one. Although when I do find each subject, I realize that, in one way or another, it is something that's been obsessing me for a long time, even if I haven't recognized it before . . . I find that there's a sort of magnetic attraction that takes over, that pulls me towards certain people, episodes, bits of history. A person or a situation that seems to embody some moral dilemma."

BIOGRAPHICAL AND CRITICAL SOURCES:

BOOKS

Hochschild, Adam, *Half the Way Home: A Memoir of Father and Son,* Viking (New York, NY), 1986.

PERIODICALS

Booklist, January 15, 1994, Gilbert Taylor, review of *The Unquiet Ghost: Russians Remember Stalin,* p. 896; March 15, 1999, review of *King Leopold's Ghost: A Story of Greed, Terror, and Heroism in Colonial Africa,* p. 1297; September 1, 2004, Vanessa Bush, review of *Bury the Chains: Prophets and Rebels in the Fight to Free an Empire's Slaves,* p. 2.

Catholic Insight, May, 2006, Leonard Kennedy, review of *Bury the Chains,* p. 44.

Economist, February 5, 2005, review of *Bury the Chains,* p. 76.

Foreign Affairs, July-August, 1994, Robert Legvold, review of *The Unquiet Ghost,* p. 176; March, 1999, Gail M. Gerhart, review of *King Leopold's Ghost,* p. 158.

Geographical, May, 2005, Mark Lynas, review of *Bury the Chains,* p. 75.

Journal of British Studies, January, 2006, Hugh Dubrulle, review of *Bury the Chains,* p. 179.

Library Journal, May 15, 1986, Roger W. Fromm, review of *Half the Way Home: A Memoir of Father and Son,* p. 61; November 15, 2004, Frederick J. Augustyn, Jr., review of *Bury the Chains,* p. 70.

Los Angeles Times Book Review, June 15, 1986, Richard Eder, review of *Half the Way Home,* p. 3.

Nation, February 14, 2005, Daniel Lazare, review of *Bury the Chains,* p. 23.

Newsday, July 6, 1986, Merin Wexler, review of *Half the Way Home;* March 20, 1994.

New York Times, June 21, 1986, Michiko Kakutani, review of *Half the Way Home,* p. 11; September 1, 1998, Michiko Kakutani, review of *King Leopold's Ghost,* p. B6.

New York Times Book Review, June 15, 1986, Mary Gordon, review of *Half the Way Home,* p. 7; November, 25, 1990, Geoffrey Wheatcroft, review of *The Mirror at Midnight: A South African Journey,* p. 10; March 27, 1994, Paul Goldberg, review of *The Unquiet Ghost,* p. 6; April 21, 1997, p. 50; September 20, 1998, Jeremy Harding, review of *King Leopold's Ghost,* p. 8.

Progressive, July, 1994, Linda Rocawich, interview, p. 31.

Publishers Weekly, October 5, 1990, Genevieve Stuttaford, review of *The Mirror at Midnight,* p. 83; January 17, 1994, review of *The Unquiet Ghost,* p. 386; July 20, 1998, review of *King Leopold's Ghost,* p. 195; January 3, 2005, review of *Bury the Chains,* p. 48.

Washington Post Book World, May 11, 1986, Suzanne Gordon, review of *Half the Way Home.*

ONLINE

BookPage Online, http://www.bookpage.com/ (December 2, 2006), Alden Mudge, "Power to the People" (interview).

Guardian Online, http://books.guardian.co.uk/ (February 12, 2005), Robin White, review of *Bury the Chains.*

Houghton Mifflin Web site, http://www.houghtonmifflin books.com/ (December 2, 2006), biography.

Mother Jones Online, http://www.motherjones.com/ (January 10, 2005), Dave Gilson, "Bury the Chains: An Interview with Adam Hochschild."

Salon.com, http://www.salon.com/ (September 9, 1998, Zachary Karabell, review of *King Leopold's Ghost.*

San Francisco Chronicle Online, http://www.sfgate.com/ (September 27, 1998), Luc Sante, review of *King Leopold's Ghost.**

*   *   *

HOLLERAN, Andrew 1943(?)-
(Eric Garber)

PERSONAL: Born c. 1943 in Aruba. *Education:* Attended Harvard University, the University of Iowa, and the University of Pennsylvania. *Religion:* Roman Catholic.

ADDRESSES: Home—Gainesville, FL.

CAREER: Writer, novelist, editor, educator, and short-story writer. American University, instructor in creative writing, 2000. *Military service:* U.S. Army, served in West Germany (now Germany) during the 1960s.

AWARDS, HONORS: Ferro-Grumley Award for best gay novel, 1997, for *The Beauty of Men.*

WRITINGS:

NOVELS

Dancer from the Dance, Morrow (New York, NY), 1978, Perennial (New York, NY), 2001.
Nights in Aruba, Morrow (New York, NY), 1983, Perennial (New York, NY), 2001.
The Beauty of Men, Morrow (New York, NY), 1996.
Grief, Hyperion (New York, NY), 2006.

OTHER

(Author of introduction) Larry Kramer, *The Normal Heart,* New American Library (New York, NY), 1985.
Ground Zero (essays), Morrow (New York, NY), 1988.

(Author of afterword) George Stambolian, editor, *Men on Men 4,* Dutton (New York, NY), 1992.
In September, the Light Changes: The Stories of Andrew Holleran, Hyperion (New York, NY), 1999.
(Author of introduction) Donald Weise, editor, *Fresh Men 2: New Voices in Gay Fiction,* Carroll & Graf (New York, NY), 2005.

Contributor of short stories to anthologies, including *Aphrodisiac: Fiction from Christopher Street,* Coward, McCann (New York, NY), 1980; *First Love/Last Love: New Fiction from Christopher Street,* edited by Michael Denneny, Charles Ortleb, and Thomas Steele, Putnam (New York, NY), 1985; and *Men on Men 3,* edited by Stambolian, Plume (New York, NY), 1990. Work also represented in *Hometowns: Gay Men Write about Where They Belong,* edited by John Preston, Plume, 1992.

Contributor of essays to anthologies, including *The Christopher Street Reader,* edited by Denneny, Ortleb, and Steele, Coward, McCann, 1983; *Personal Dispatches: Writers Confront AIDS,* edited by John Preston, St. Martin's (New York, NY), 1988; and *A Member of the Family,* edited by Preston, Dutton, 1992.

Contributor to periodicals, including *Christopher Street, Village Voice,* and *Tribe.*

SIDELIGHTS: Eric Garber, who writes under the pseudonym Andrew Holleran, is acknowledged as one of the foremost authors in the modern gay literary movement. His work is significant in this arena because of his early success during a decidedly different era—that of an urban pre-AIDS homosexual subculture—and because of his continuation in chronicling the ravages that the fatal epidemic has wrought on the gay community. Holleran's first work, the novel *Dancer from the Dance,* depicts a heady atmosphere of casual sex and a yearning for true commitment. The follow-up, *Nights in Aruba,* written as AIDS began to irrevocably change lifestyles and attitudes, brought to light the traumas engendered by "coming out" to family as well as the separate realization that a new celibacy had taken the place of promiscuity. The cycle was completed with *The Beauty of Men,* a novel that explored the effect of advancing age on a veteran of the once-wild New York club scene. A collection of essays titled *Ground Zero* further explores the theme of radical and irreversible change that swept through gay culture during the 1980s. Little personal information is available about Holleran, who chooses to remain anonymous. However, the author admitted in a 1983 interview that much of his writing is autobiographical in nature.

Dancer from the Dance, published in 1978, was seen by many as one of the early "post-Liberation" novels. Following some notorious clashes with police on the streets of New York City in the summer of 1969, a movement took root among both gays and lesbians. Openly identifying themselves as homosexual, they organized politically and actively campaigned for the repeal of laws and attitudes that forced them to hide their sexuality. In New York City as well as in many other urban centers, a distinct gay culture emerged, and one of its effects was a vivid nightlife scene of bars, discos, and recreational drug use. In this atmosphere, widespread promiscuity was acceptable, either as an end to itself or as part of the search for "Mr. Right."

Dancer from the Dance is the fictionalized account of a young man's entrance into—and ultimate dissatisfaction with—this aspect of gay life. Holleran sketches the protagonist, Anthony Malone, as a distinct type: youthful, handsome, savvy, and completely intoxicated by the free climate. His education is guided by another archetype, the older, flamboyant, and sage Sutherland. *Dancer from the Dance* depicts the narcissism and glamour that sometimes preoccupied gay men, many of whom saw the book as an affirmation and celebration of their distinct community experience. As Malone becomes a "circuit queen," making the rounds of Manhattan parties and discos, Holleran offers a commentary on the sadness of gay life through Sutherland, who voices a serious interpretation of the inherent melancholy behind the "anything-goes" mood. In the end, the disillusioned Malone swims off into the night, realizing that his day in the limelight of narcissism will only last a short time.

Dancer from the Dance received considerable critical attention for a first novel. Writing in the *New Republic,* Paul Robinson called the novel "beautifully written, singleminded and at once evocative and hilarious." John Lahr, reviewing the work for the *New York Times Book Review,* noted that an "erotic heat percolates through these pages" and lauded Holleran's characterization of Malone as "a mystery that remains deliciously unsolved."

Nights in Aruba, the pseudonymous author's second work, was published in 1983. This quieter, more reflective novel centers around the dual life that its protago-

nist, Paul, leads between his fast-paced, promiscuous "out" life in New York City and his extended visits to aging parents in Florida. Admittedly bored by the hijinks of sex and drugs in the Manhattan disco scene, Paul's development centers around his coming to terms with his homosexuality, his Catholic upbringing, and his relationship with his parents. Although the spectre of AIDS does not figure into *Nights in Aruba,* Paul's growing maturity and contemplative nature reflect the significant changes which had begun to take root in the gay community with the realization that casual sex could now mean death. The protagonist is no longer just a beautiful and fleeting face in the night, but rather a character with a concrete and universally commonplace past. At the time of the novel's publication, Holleran noted in a *Publishers Weekly* interview that he considered *Nights in Aruba* a continuation of *Dancer from the Dance.* He also discussed the often-difficult autobiographical nature of his writing. "I tried to keep a distance while being very personal," he admitted, "to avoid being a man in the seat next to you on an airplane, yammering and yammering."

Nights in Aruba received less critical attention than Holleran's inaugural novel. Barbara Pepe, writing in the *Village Voice,* noted that Holleran's peripheral characters in the follow-up to *Dancer from the Dance* "are caricatured in the same stark, spare, sometimes cruel style." She commented that *Nights in Aruba*'s "bittersweet complacency is the obvious resolution to" the protagonist's disjointed search for love and truth in the first work. *New York Times Book Review* critic Caroline Seebohm also praised Holleran's characterizations, while faulting the author's occasional repetition of phrase. She remarked that *Nights in Aruba* "lacks both the intensity and flashing wit of the earlier book," but concluded by stating that Holleran, having "thoroughly plundered" the ghost of his past, perhaps "can travel lighter."

Ground Zero, Holleran's third volume, appeared in 1988. A collection of essays that were originally published in the New York periodicals *Christopher Street* and *Village Voice,* they are ruminations on the crisis that has decimated and irrevocably altered the gay community. The work's title reflects the catastrophic element that the age of AIDS has introduced upon the author's milieu, but he also reflects upon the disease's effect on the larger community of its victims who are not gay. Holleran comments on the compulsory maturity that the epidemic has forced upon gay culture, and rails against the belief that this has been a painful yet ultimately positive metamorphosis. Other essays in the book discuss the writers Henry James and George Santayana as well as coming to terms with the lost friends and shared history of the era depicted in *Dancer from the Dance*. In a review of *Ground Zero* for *Time*, R.Z. Sheppard found that Holleran has a grasp of "the first law of writing about personal misfortune: appalling facts, tersely put, speak for themselves." Sheppard further praised Holleran's "keen, ironic intelligence." The essays also elicited praise from Brendan Lemon, who critiqued *Ground Zero* for the *Nation*. Lemon contended that the spectre of AIDS "has killed neither Holleran's *bel esprit* nor his acute lyrical sense," noting that the end result of the "uniquely gifted personal essayist's" collection is "tonic. . . . Even the author seems restored."

Lark, the protagonist of Holleran's 1997 novel *The Beauty of Men,* "could be *Dancer*'s narrator or, indeed, its hero 15 years later," declared *Booklist* reviewer Ray Olson. Lark's friends have all died from AIDS, or suicide inspired by anxiety over AIDS. Lark himself lives in Florida, where he divides his time between daily visits to his quadriplegic mother and making the rounds of the local gay pickup spots. He is obsessed by the loss of his youth and ashamed of that obsession, as so many of his comrades never got the chance to grow old. Holleran commented to *Publishers Weekly* interviewer Bill Goldstein: "*The Beauty of Men* is a reflective novel, but about a man who is not able to reflect successfully. It's about his cell, his prison. I don't think his mind helps him. He seems to be intelligent, but he doesn't see. Lark seems a mystery to me. His depression is continuous, but I didn't want to explain it."

Olson found Lark to be "pathetic," and made note that "only Holleran among gay novelists could make riveting reading out of an entire novel focused on him—which is precisely what Holleran, still a gorgeous writer, has done." A *Publishers Weekly* writer credited Holleran with creating a "profoundly sad, elegant and insightful new novel." Lark is "a chillingly emblematic Everyman, failing to find meaning and purpose in a world devastated by AIDS. Holleran's trademark prose—lush, carefully cadenced and keenly observed—creates a mesmerizingly claustrophobic world where the trapped elderly residents of Lark's mother's nursing home, the lonely men Lark encounters in his fruitless search for love and the overwhelming anonymity of suburban America have equal power to break the heart." *New York Times Book Review* contributor Alan Hollinghurst declared that *The Beauty of Men* offers something of

great significance to any reader, whatever their sexual orientation might be: the description of "a modern atrophy of the spirit, and what I think Mr. Holleran wants to identify as a particularly American stupefaction and emptiness. From Lark's lost life he distills a reluctant but persuasive poetry."

Short stories written over a wide span of years were collected in the 1999 book *In September, the Light Changes: The Stories of Andrew Holleran.* As in Holleran's other work, the overriding concerns in these stories are loss of health, youth, and friends; yet *New York Times Book Review* writer Peter Parker found *In September* "less dispiriting" than *The Beauty of Men.* "None of the stories could be described as comic, yet they do contain some very funny moments. A number of them consist largely of conversations in which Holleran's sharp ear for the cadences, vocabulary, and preoccupations of his characters' language instantly brings them alive." The author's observations on gay life are "unflinching, provocative, witty and shrewd," in Parker's estimation. A *Publishers Weekly* reviewer voiced some reservations, finding that Holleran's stories were "sometimes predicable in their lyricism" and "are capably fashioned but do not break new ground"; and a *Booklist* writer called the pieces in the collection "hit-or-miss, ranging in quality from the banal to the brilliantly constructed." Roger W. Durbin in the *Library Journal* gave a more ringing endorsement to *In September,* declaring it to be full of "poignancy, ribald humor, pensiveness, keen discernment, and unsettling apprehension. . . . What ultimately shines . . . is a seasoned, indomitable spirit."

Grief, Holleran's 2006 novel and his first in ten years, explores the "pain of a generation of gay men who have survived the AIDS epidemic and reached middle age yearning for fidelity, tenderness, and intimacy," observed a reviewer in *Publishers Weekly*. The novel's unnamed protagonist has spent twelve years in Florida caring for his ailing mother. After her death, he accepts a teaching position in Washington, DC, in order to get away and start life over. He rents a room in an architecturally gorgeous townhouse owned by a celibate, middle-aged gay man who is "slowly and quietly grieving over the loss of youthful energy, attractiveness, and prowess," noted Brad Hooper in *Booklist*. Though the narrator and his landlord share a superficial relationship and have much in common through many friends and acquaintances lost to AIDS, they know they will never form a true bond of intimacy and caring. The narrator finds himself engrossed in a volume of letters by Mary

Todd Lincoln, whose profound grief after the death of her husband Abraham Lincoln never abated the remainder of her life. The narrator sees much in common with himself and Mrs. Lincoln, as he strongly regrets not coming out to his mother before her death. Even stronger is the mixed grief and guilt he feels for surviving the 1980s and 1990s while so many of his friends perished from AIDS. Grief, the narrator discovers, is something that everyone must face at sometime or another, but it is the reaction to it, and the ability to overcome it, that gives hope even in its darkest hours.

Grief "astonishes" with its direct, unwavering look at "our growing older and the losses we experienced so early in our lives," commented Greg Mitchell in *Publishers Weekly*. "Holleran exquisitely captures the many nuances of loss," remarked Thom Geier in *Entertainment Weekly*. Throughout the story, "Holleran's prose is unerringly marvelous," commented Paul Russell, writing in the *Lambda Book Report*. A writer in *Kirkus Reviews* named *Grief* "a haunting, exquisite novel about the nature of loss, grief, and the illusion of intimacy" and "a quiet story well told." For *Advocate* critic Chris Freeman, the novel stands as "an intellectually and emotionally satisfying meditation on aging, loss, love, and American history." *Salon.com* reviewer Laura Miller concluded: "*Grief* is a short novel, but like a single note struck on a perfect silver bell, it carries far."

BIOGRAPHICAL AND CRITICAL SOURCES:

BOOKS

Contemporary Literary Criticism, Volume 38, Thomson Gale (Detroit, MI), 1986.

Levin, James, *The Gay Novel in America,* Garland Publishing (New York, NY), 1991.

Nelson, Emanuel S., editor, *Contemporary Gay American Novelists,* Greenwood Press (Westport, CT), 1993.

PERIODICALS

Advocate, July 4, 2006, Chris Freeman, "Good Grief," review of *Grief,* p. 57.

Booklist, June 1, 1996, Ray Olson, review of *The Beauty of Men,* p. 1643; June 1, 1999, Michael Spinella, review of *In September, the Light Changes: The Stories of Andrew Holleran,* p. 1786; May 15, 2006, Brad Hooper, review of *Grief,* p. 23.

Entertainment Weekly, June 9, 2006, Thom Geier, review of *Grief,* p. 143.

Kirkus Reviews, April 1, 2006, review of *Grief,* p. 314.

Lambda Book Report, summer, 2006, Paul Russell, review of *Grief,* p. 13.

Library Journal, June 1, 1999, Roger W. Durbin, review of *In September, the Light Changes,* p. 182; June 1, 2006, Debbie Bogenschutz, review of *Grief,* p. 107.

Nation, November 21, 1988, Brendan Lemon, review of *Ground Zero,* p. 538.

New Republic, September 30, 1978, Paul Robinson, review of *Dancer from the Dance,* p. 33.

New York Times, June 3, 2006, Bill Goldstein, "Writer of Gay Classic Evokes Mrs. Lincoln," review of *Grief,* p. B7.

New York Times Book Review, January 14, 1979, John Lahr, review of *Dancer from the Dance,* p. 15; September 25, 1983, Caroline Seebohm, review of *Nights in Aruba,* p. 14; August 28, 1988, Robert Minkoff, review of *Ground Zero,* p. 19; June 30, 1996, Alan Hollinghurst, review of *The Beauty of Men,* p. 7; July 25, 1999, Peter Parker, "The Party's Over: A Collection of Stories about Gay Men in the Wane of the Century," review of *In September, the Light Changes,* p. 25.

Publishers Weekly, June 3, 1983, review of *Nights in Aruba,* p. 64; July 29, 1983, review of *Dancer from the Dance,* p. 72; April 29, 1996, review of *The Beauty of Men,* p. 49; May 3, 1999, review of *In September, the Light Changes,* p. 66; April 3, 2006, Greg Mitchell, review of *Grief,* p. 10, and review of *Grief,* p. 36; May 8, 2006, Michael Scharf, "Coming to Grief: PW Talks with Andrew Holleran," p. 44.

Time, July 18, 1988, review of *Ground Zero,* p. 68.

Village Voice, October 25, 1983, review of *Nights in Aruba,* p. 52.

ONLINE

Matt and Andrej Koymasky Web site, http://andrej koymasky.com/ (May 31, 2003), biography of Andrew Holleran.

Salon.com, http://www.salon.com/ (July 29, 2006), Laura Miller, "Andrew Holleran's *Grief,*" review of *Grief.**

*   *   *

HOND, Paul

PERSONAL: Born in Baltimore, MD.

ADDRESSES: Home—New York, NY. *Agent*—Barbara J. Zitwer Agency, 525 West End Ave., Ste. 7H, New York, NY 10024.

CAREER: Writer.

WRITINGS:

The Baker: A Novel, Random House (New York, NY), 1997.
Mothers and Sons: A Novel, Random House (New York, NY), 2005.

SIDELIGHTS: Paul Hond is the author of *The Baker: A Novel,* which chronicles the life of Mickey Lerner, a middle-aged, Jewish baker who lives in Baltimore, Maryland, in the late 1960s. Mickey is going through the breakup of his marriage to French violinist Emi, who seems more devoted to her career than she is to their relationship. In addition, Mickey finds himself growing increasingly distant from his teenaged son, Ben. But Mickey's life is dramatically altered when his wife is fatally shot during a riot following the assassination of civil rights activist Martin Luther King, Jr. Mickey tries to overcome his grief by traveling to Paris, his wife's birthplace. Once there, he makes the acquaintance of another baker, one who inspires Mickey to resume his own career in baking. Meanwhile, Ben has been left in charge of the family's bakery in Baltimore. Among the youth's problems is the conduct of his best friend, the bakery's delivery driver, who has become involved with low-level criminals. Even Mickey's problems fail to neatly resolve themselves after he returns to Baltimore, for the city is still rife with racial tension in the wake of King's death.

Michael Lowenthal dubbed the novel a "highbrow potboiler" in his *New York Times* appraisal. A *Publishers Weekly* contributor declared that Hond delineates the racial and ethnic tensions in Mickey's community "with an emotional depth, lyricism and power that signal an auspicious debut."

Hond's second book is *Mothers and Sons: A Novel.* Twenty-seven-year-old Moss Messinger lives a sad, single life in New York, pestered by pigeons, unable to commit to his girlfriend, Danielle, dependent on his friends, and getting by writing restaurant reviews. He also misses his mother, Nina, who conceived him with

a stranger, raised him until he was nineteen, and then left for Europe to play jazz piano, eventually marrying and moving to California. Friends include Boris, who became a millionaire with his *LittleEinstein.com* sperm bank. Boris tries to help Moss by offering him a review of an upscale new eatery and the use of his Maine retreat. But these attempts fail. Moss's abandonment by his mother prevents him from ever growing up, and her reappearance only further complicates his life. In reviewing the novel for the *Library Journal,* Joanna M. Burkhardt noted that the novel "is well crafted, and Hond convincingly captures the range of emotions encountered in everyday life."

BIOGRAPHICAL AND CRITICAL SOURCES:

PERIODICALS

Kirkus Review, January 15, 2005, review of *Mothers and Sons: A Novel,* p. 74.
Library Journal, May 1, 2005, Joanna M. Burkhardt, review of *Mothers and Sons,* p. 74.
New York Times, May 10, 1998, Michael Lowenthal, review of *The Baker: A Novel.*
Publishers Weekly, January 26, 1998, review of *The Baker,* p. 67; February 21, 2005, review of *Mothers and Sons,* p. 156.
Washington Post, April 15, 2005, Carolyn See, review of *Mothers and Sons,* p. C3.*

*   *   *

HOPKINS, Ellen L. 1955-

PERSONAL: Born March 26, 1955, in Long Beach, CA; daughter of Albert and Valeria Wagner; married Jerry Vancelette (divorced); married John Hopkins (a TV news assignment editor), October 19, 1991; children: Jaysen Vancelette, Cristal Thetford, Kelly Foutz. *Education:* Attended University of California—Santa Barbara. *Politics:* "Rabid Democrat." *Religion:* Lutheran. *Hobbies and other interests:* Hiking, biking, skiing, gardening, camping, fishing, and sports.

ADDRESSES: Home—Washoe Valley, NV. *Office*—Juniper Creek Publishing, P.O. Box 2205, Carson City, NV 89702. *E-mail*—ellenhopkins@charter.net.

CAREER: Author, poet, freelance writer, 1992—. Valley Video, owner, 1980-85; *Tahoe Truckee Reader,* reporter, editor, 1992-96; *Northern Nevada Family*

Magazine, editor, contributor, 2000-02; Juniper Creek Publishing, Inc., Carson City, NV, and *Three Leaping Frogs,* children's newspaper, publisher.

MEMBER: Society of Children's Book Writers and Illustrators (SCBWI), Reno MOMS, Holy Cross Lutheran Church Choir, Blue Tahoe Schutzhund Club, New Writers of the Purple Sage.

AWARDS, HONORS: SCBWI Charlotte's Web pin for outstanding contributions to children's literature by a new author, 2001; Sierra Arts Foundation professional artist award, 2001 and 2004; American Library Association (ALA) Quick Picks for Reluctant Young Adult Readers selection, New York Public Library Books for the Teen Age selection, and National Book Award nominee, 2006, all for *Crank;* Nevada Writers Hall of Fame Silver Pen Award, 2006; ALA Best Book for Young Adults nominee, 2007, for *Burned.*

WRITINGS:

NONFICTION

Air Devils: Sky Racers, Sky Divers, and Stunt Pilots, Perfection Learning (Logan, IA), 2000.
Orcas, High Seas Supermen, Perfection Learning (Logan, IA), 2000.
Tarnished Legacy: The Story of the Comstock Lode, Perfection Learning (Logan, IA), 2001.
Into the Abyss: A Tour of Inner Space, Perfection Learning (Logan, IA), 2001.
The Thunderbirds: The U.S. Air Force Aerial Demonstration Squadron, Capstone Press (Mankato, MN), 2001.
The Golden Knights: The U.S. Army Parachute Team, Capstone Press (Mankato, MN), 2001.
Fly Fishing, Capstone Press (Mankato, MN), 2002.
Freshwater Fishing, Capstone Press (Mankato, MN), 2002.
Canopies in the Clouds, Perfection Learning (Logan, IA), 2002.
Countdown to Yesterday, Perfection Learning (Logan, IA), 2002.
United States Air Force, Heinemann Library (Crystal Lake, IL), 2003.
United States Air Force Fighting Vehicles, Heinemann Library (Crystal Lake, IL), 2003.
United States Special Operations Forces, Heinemann Library (Crystal Lake, IL), 2003.

All for Our Country: Check out Nevada!, Juniper Creek Publishing (Carson City, NV), 2003.
Light Shows: Comets, Meteors & Asteroids, Perfection Learning (Logan, IA), 2003.
Mysteries of Space, Perfection Learning (Logan, IA), 2003.
Are We Alone? The Case for Extraterrestrial Life, Perfection Learning (Logan, IA), 2003.
Inside a Star, Perfection Learning (Logan, IA), 2003.
Telescopes: Exploring the Beyond, Perfection Learning (Logan, IA), 2003.
Storming the Skies: The Story of Katherine and Marjorie Stinson, Pioneer Women Aviators, Avisson Press (Greensboro, NC), 2004.

Contributor of articles to local, regional, and national periodicals.

YOUNG ADULT FICTION

Crank, Simon & Schuster (New York, NY), 2004.
Burned, McElderry Books (New York, NY), 2006.
Impulse, McElderry Books (New York, NY), 2007.
Glass, McElderry Books (New York, NY), 2007.

SIDELIGHTS: Ellen L. Hopkins is the author of high-interest books for juvenile readers on nonfiction topics as well as highly acclaimed young adult novels such as *Crank, Burned,* and *Impulse.* Hopkins raised a family, had her own business, and worked as a journalist and editor before turning her hand to book-length freelancing. Her debut title was the year 2000 *Air Devils: Sky Racers, Sky Divers, and Stunt Pilots,* which recounts the history of flight and covers such topics as dirigibles, early airplanes, military planes, and even airplane pylon races. According to *Booklist* contributor Catherine Andronik, the work is "easy to read, contemporary, and not condescending." In her next publication, *Orcas, High Seas Supermen,* Hopkins brings to readers the world of the Orca, or killer whale. Information about whale habitat, survival mechanisms, and communication is interspersed with color and black-and-white photographs, diagrams, and sidebars. Noting that whale lifestyles are "expertly explained," *Booklist* critic Roger Leslie concluded: "Always captivating, this book is sure to please" Orca fans.

Hopkins wrote a score of nonfiction works before she published her first young adult novel, taking inspiration from her own daughter's addiction to methamphetamine for the 2004 title *Crank,* written in free verse. The book details the devastation wrought by the drug called crank on the life of sixteen-year-old Kristina, who calls herself Bree when under the influence of it. This alter ego takes over when Kristina's boring home life smothers her, and drugs—to which she is introduced on a visit to her estranged father—throw her into the arms of boys both good and bad, resulting in an unwanted pregnancy. Though her family helps Kristina through the pregnancy and subsequent adoption, Hopkins allows for no easy happy endings, for, as with many addicts, Kristina returns to her crank habit after the birth. A *Kirkus Reviews* critic called *Crank* a "powerful and unsettling" novel, whose "hypnotic and jagged free verse wrenchingly chronicles" Kristina's plight. Similar praise came from *School Library Journal* contributor Sharon Korbeck, who found the novel "a stunning portrayal of a teen's loss of direction and realistically uncertain future." For *Kliatt* contributor Claire Rosser, *Crank* was a "devastating story." Rosser went on to note: "We aren't used to YA novels that end in such despair, but we have to face the truth that many addicts do not recover." Likewise, *Booklist* reviewer Gillian Engberg felt "readers won't soon forget smart, sardonic Kristina . . . [or] her chilling descent into addiction." A *Publishers Weekly* contributor further commended Hopkins for "creat[ing] a world nearly as consuming and disturbing as the titular drug."

Another sixteen-year-old girl is at the center of Hopkins's second young adult novel, *Burned.* With this work, Hopkins turns her attention from drugs to the influence of religion and domestic violence on a teen's life. Once again using free verse, Hopkins presents young Pattyn, whose first-person narrative details the repression and violence she experiences as a female member of the Mormon Church and the daughter of an alcoholic, abusive father. Sent to her aunt's desert ranch as a form of punishment for questioning her father and her religion, Pattyn matures with her newfound freedom and has a love affair with a young boy which ends in pregnancy. A critic for *Kirkus Reviews* called this novel "sharp and heartbreaking." Other reviewers also had high praise for the work. Writing in *Booklist,* Frances Bradburn found *Burned* a "troubling but beautifully written novel," while *School Library Journal* contributor Kathy Lehman observed that Hopkins "has masterfully used verse to re-create the yearnings and emotions of a teenage girl trapped in tragic circumstances."

Hopkins once commented: "As a freelance writer for a number of years, I became infatuated with several subjects and decided to carry them to the audience that most needs/deserves inspiration: children. Many of my books are hi/lo, a particular challenge, but stimulating reluctant readers is especially rewarding.

"With my current projects, I am pushing into new arenas, guaranteed to keep me busy for years to come. In addition to my husband, I am grateful for the support of mentors and peers within the writing community, especially the Society of Children's Book Writers and Illustrators. I am also fortunate to work with some of the best editors in the business. Finally, belief in myself and my God-given talent keeps me striving to succeed and excel."

BIOGRAPHICAL AND CRITICAL SOURCES:

PERIODICALS

Booklist, July, 2000, Catherine Andronik, review of *Air Devils: Sky Racers, Sky Divers, and Stunt Pilots,* p. 2016; November 1, 2000, Roger Leslie, review of *Orcas, High Seas Supermen,* p. 528; November 15, 2004, Gillian Engberg, review of *Crank,* p. 595; June 1, 2006, Frances Bradburn, review of *Burned,* p. 62.

Bulletin of the Center for Children's Books, June, 2006, Deborah Stevenson, review of *Burned,* p. 455.

Horn Book Guide, fall, 2001, review of *The Thunderbirds: The U.S. Air Force Aerial Demonstration Squadron* and *The Golden Knights,* p. 393; spring, 2002, review of *Fly Fishing* and *Freshwater Fishing,* p. 166.

Kirkus Reviews, October 1, 2004, review of *Crank,* p. 96; April 1, 2006, review of *Burned,* p. 348.

Kliatt, May, 2000, review of *Air Devils,* p. 38; September, 2004, Claire Rosser, review of *Crank,* p. 21.

Publishers Weekly, November 1, 2004, review of *Crank,* p. 63.

School Library Journal, November, 2004, Sharon Korbeck, review of *Crank,* p. 145; May, 2005, Elizabeth Stumpf, review of *Storming the Skies: The Story of Katherine and Marjorie Stinson, Pioneer Women Aviators,* p. 152; July, 2006, Kathy Lehman, review of *Burned,* p. 105.

Voice of Youth Advocates, April, 2005, Valerie Ott, review of *Crank,* p. 14.

ONLINE

Ellen Hopkins Home Page, http://www.ellenhopkins. com (November 20, 2006).*

HORSLEY, Kate 1952-

PERSONAL: Born April 17, 1952, in Richmond, VA; daughter of Joseph C. (a physician) and Alice Cabell (an artist) Horsley; married Rhodes Green Lockwood, November 15, 1981 (divorced); married Morgan Davie; children: (first marriage) Aaron Heath Parker. *Ethnicity:* "Anglo." *Education:* University of Richmond, B.A.; Western Kentucky University, M.A.; University of New Mexico, Ph.D., 1984. *Politics:* Socialist. *Religion:* Zen Buddhist. *Hobbies and other interests:* Cello, drawing.

ADDRESSES: Office—Albuquerque Technical Vocational Institute, Arts and Sciences, 525 Buena Vista SE, Albuquerque, NM 87108.

CAREER: Albuquerque Technical Vocational Institute, English instructor, 1987—, chair of English department, 1998-2000. Creative writing workshop instructor.

AWARDS, HONORS: City of Albuquerque Citizenship Award, 1994; Albuquerque Bravo Award, Albuquerque Arts Alliance, 1996; Western States Arts Federation Award for Fiction, 1996, for *A Killing in New Town;* New Mexico Press Women's Award, 1996.

WRITINGS:

Crazy Woman, La Alameda Press (Albuquerque NM), 1992.
A Killing in New Town, La Alameda Press (Albuquerque NM), 1996.
Confessions of a Pagan Nun: A Novel, Shambhala Press (Boston, MA), 2001.
Careless Love; or, The Land of Promise, University of New Mexico Press (Albuquerque NM), 2003.
The Changeling of Finnistuath: A Novel, Shambhala (Boston, MA), 2003, published as *The Changeling: A Novel,* 2005.
Black Elk in Paris: A Novel, Trumpeter Books (Boston, MA), 2006.

SIDELIGHTS: Kate Horsley created a character caught in a world of fierce cultural conflict in her first novel, *Crazy Woman.* The novel follows the story of Sara Franklin, who is captured by the Apaches. Sara must first learn to survive as a slave and then as a woman who must earn the respect and trust of the tribe. Horsley

explores the idea of captivity from the point of view of a woman in both her native culture and in her life among the Indians.

A Killing in New Town also profiles the life of a strong woman in a period of cultural change and conflict. Eliza Pelham lives in a town divided between the Old Town, where the railroad was supposed to help support the indigenous people, and the New Town, where the whites built their hotels and businesses, and then had the railroad stop there. Eliza, a woman grown tired of small-town closed-mindedness, dreams of living in the open country. In her loneliness and depression, Eliza seeks escape through alcohol and an affair. Her life is suddenly transformed by the kidnapping of her two children. She sets out to find them with her unlikely allies, Bridle O'Doonan, the consumptive saloon girl, and an Eastern-educated Apache, Robert Youngman. "The most unforgettable section of the book comes with Eliza's quest for her kidnapped children that leads to a small mining camp in the mountains. No one is accountable for their actions, and whiskey, gambling, prostitution and death by gunfire are the only constants," wrote David Farmer in the *Dallas Morning News.* A reviewer for *Publishers Weekly* stated: "The title implies a murder story, and though the story is about murder, Horsley's intention is a double meaning that refers largely to the 'killing' that settlers hope to make in New Town. Small daily details and larger ideas make this unconventional western a truly compelling blend of adventure, Southwestern mythology and reality."

Horsley's *Confessions of a Pagan Nun: A Novel* is set in fifth-century Ireland. Although Christianity is already the dominant religion throughout Western Europe, Ireland still clings to its pagan beliefs. This novel is a fictional memoir of Gwynneve who, after losing her mother, joins a troupe of traveling entertainers and later apprentices herself for many years to Giannon, one of the last surviving Druids. Later in life, though remaining secretly unbaptized, she enters a convent where her literacy gets her a job as a translator of Christian theology. At St. Bridget's convent, Gwynneve copies the gospels and the writings of Saint Augustine—with whom she carries on a running intellectual battle—in the script she learned from Giannon. She also records her recollections of village and convent life for posterity.

Gwynneve contrasts the waning Druid influence and the emergent Christianity as she tells her story. One religious concept melds into the other. But she is not blind to the disappointing materialism the church brings with it. As Michael D. Langan wrote in the *Buffalo News:* "In the end, Gwynneve is alone. . . . She recognizes the consolation of nature, but lacks a full understanding of the new Christian law of love." Wendy Bethel commented in the *Library Journal:* "Her story is not just that of a strong woman making her way in a hostile world. It is also the story of what happens to a country when a new religion takes the place of the old. A beautiful and thought-provoking book." "Poetically written and marvelously researched, the novel offers complex theological arguments wrapped in a compelling story about memorable characters," wrote *Booklist* contributor Patricia Monaghan.

The Changeling of Finnistuath: A Novel is the story of Grey, a fourteenth-century Irish peasant who is raised as a boy after her father declares that if his eighth child is another girl, he will kill her. Grey's mother, who believes in fairies as well as what the priests teach her, convinces herself that Grey could be a changeling, treats her with the special consideration due an only son, and tells her that she must always conceal her body. Grey learns the truth when she experiences menarche, but she continues to live as a male. She later becomes a monastery whore, an unwed mother, and ultimately a warrior. She also survives the havoc wreaked by the Black Plague. Bethel reviewed this novel, calling it "an unusual and beautiful story."

Black Elk in Paris: A Novel is based on a true story. One of two Native Americans to come to Paris in 1888 with Buffalo Bill Cody for the Universal Exposition and unveiling of the Eiffel Tower is Choice, or Black Elk. The narrator, Philippe Normand, is a doctor and friend of Madou Balise, the young daughter of a bourgeois family. Madou becomes infatuated with Choice, a quiet man she perceives as being wise and serene. The family, however, considers him a savage and threatens to have him institutionalized. *Reviewer's Bookwatch* contributor Willis M. Buhle described the book as being "an engaging and entertaining novel."

Recording a period of dramatic historical change within a work of fiction has proven inspiring for Horsley, who told *CA:* "The powerful and challenging times in history compel me to look at the human struggle from the point of view of the average man or woman—the person who, though average, reacts with integrity and strength to seemingly crushing events or pervasive ignorance." Horsley also said: "I want to try to communicate the truth in a powerful and absorbing way that encourages compassion and integrity. I want to do for readers what writers have done for me—made me feel that I was not alone and given me a worthwhile means of escape from this cynical world: entertainment that absorbs and challenges. . . . Writers such as Hesse, Tolkein, and Kerouac have influenced my quest for depth and freedom in my own writing."

BIOGRAPHICAL AND CRITICAL SOURCES:

PERIODICALS

Booklist, September 9, 1996, review of *A Killing in New Town,* p. 79; June 1, 2001, Patricia Monaghan, review of *Confessions of a Pagan Nun: A Novel;* February 1, 2006, Deborah Donovan, review of *Black Elk in Paris: A Novel,* p. 29

Buffalo News, September 2, 2001, Michael D. Langan, review of *Confessions of a Pagan Nun,* p. F7.

Dallas Morning News, April 6, 1997, David Farmer, review of *A Killing in New Town,* p. 8J.

Kirkus Reviews, January 1, 2006, review of *Black Elk in Paris,* p. 9.

Library Journal, August, 2001, Wendy Bethel, review of *Confessions of a Pagan Nun,* p. 161; March 15, 2004, Wendy Bethel, review of *The Changeling of Finnistuath: A Novel,* p. 106; February 15, 2006, Wendy Bethel, review of *Black Elk in Paris,* p. 107.

Publishers Weekly, September 9, 1996, review of *A Killing in New Town,* p. 79; January 5, 2004, review of *The Changeling of Finnistuath,* p. 41; November 28, 2005, review of *Black Elk in Paris,* p. 22.

Reviewer's Bookwatch, May, 2006, Willis M. Buhle, review of *Black Elk in Paris.*

School Library Journal, November, 2001, Christine C. Menefee, review of *Confessions of a Pagan Nun,* p. 191.*

*   *   *

HUBER, Peter W. 1952-
(Peter William Huber)

PERSONAL: Born November 3, 1952, in Toronto, Ontario, Canada; immigrated to United States, 1970, naturalized citizen, 1985; son of Theodore and Dorothy Huber; married Andrea Grodsky (a dance critic), July

21, 1982; children: Sophie Anne, Michael Joseph, Stephen Anthony. *Education:* Massachusetts Institute of Technology, S.B. and S.M., 1974, Ph.D., 1976; Harvard University, J.D. (summa cum laude), 1982.

ADDRESSES: Home—5029 Edgemoor Ln., Bethesda, MD 20814. *Office*—Manhattan Institute, 52 Vanderbilt Ave., New York, NY 10017. *E-mail*—pwhuber@ verizon.net.

CAREER: Massachusetts Institute of Technology, Cambridge, assistant professor, 1976-78, associate professor of mechanical engineering, 1978-83, Carl Richard Soderberg Associate Professor, 1980-82; U.S. Court of Appeals, District of Columbia Circuit, Washington, DC, law clerk to Judge Ruth Bader Ginsburg, 1982-83; U.S. Supreme Court, Washington, DC, law clerk to Justice Sandra Day O'Connor, 1983-84; Onek, Klein & Farr (law firm), Washington, DC, associate, 1985; Science Concepts, Inc., Washington, DC, senior associate, 1985—; Manhattan Institute for Policy Research, New York, NY, senior fellow, 1985—; private practice of law in Washington, DC, beginning in 1985; Kellogg, Huber, Hansen, Todd & Evans (law firm), partner; Telecom Policy and Analysis: A Kellogg, Huber Consulting Group, chair. Consultant to Antitrust Division of U.S. Department of Justice; consultant in engineering, telecommunications, and liability; Digital Power Capital, Washington, DC, cofounding partner; ICx Technologies, cofounder and chief technology advisor. Appeared on television programs, including *McNeil-Lehrer News Hour* and *Face the Nation.*

MEMBER: American Nuclear Society, Society for Risk Analysis, Pi Tau Sigma.

WRITINGS:

The Geodesic Network, U.S. Department of Justice (Washington, DC), 1987.
Liability: The Legal Revolution and Its Consequences, Basic Books (New York, NY), 1988.
Sandra Day O'Connor, Chelsea House (New York, NY), 1990.
Galileo's Revenge: Junk Science in the Courtroom, Basic Books (New York, NY), 1991.
(Editor, with Robert E. Litan) *The Liability Maze: The Impact of Liability Law on Safety and Innovation,* Brookings Institution (Washington, DC), 1991.

(With Michael K. Kellogg and John Thorn) *Federal Telecommunications Law,* Little, Brown (Boston, MA), 1992, revised edition, Aspen Law & Business (Gaithersburg, MD), 1999.
(Coauthor) *The Geodesic Network II: 1993 Report on Competition in the Telephone Industry,* Geodesic, 1992.
(Editor, with Kenneth R. Foster and David E. Bernstein) *Phantom Risk: Scientific Inference and the Law,* MIT Press (Cambridge, MA), 1993.
Orwell's Revenge: The 1984 Palimpsest, Maxwell Macmillan International (New York, NY), 1994.
(With Michael K. Kellogg and John Thorn) *Federal Broadband Law,* Little, Brown (Boston, MA), 1995.
(With Michael K. Kellogg and John Thorn) *The Telecommunications Act of 1996: Special Report,* Little Brown (Boston, MA), 1996, also published as *Special Report: The Telecommunications Act of 1996,* Aspen Law & Business (Gaithersburg, MD), 1996.
(With Kenneth R. Foster) *Judging Science: Scientific Knowledge and the Federal Courts,* MIT Press (Cambridge, MA), 1997.
Law and Disorder in Cyberspace: Abolish the FCC and Let Common Law Rule the Telecosm, Oxford University Press (New York, NY), 1997.
Hard Green: Saving the Environment from the Environmentalists: A Conservative Manifesto, Basic Books (New York, NY), 1999.
(With Mark P. Mills) *The Bottomless Well: The Twilight of Fuel, the Virtue of Waste, and Why We Will Never Run Out of Energy,* Basic Books (New York, NY), 2005.

Contributor to journals, magazines, and newspapers, including *Harvard Law Review, Yale Law Journal, Wall Street Journal, Washington Post, National Review, City Journal,* and *Commentary.* Columnist, *Forbes.* Contributing editor of *Regulation,* 1984—, and *Legal Times,* 1987; member of board of editors of *Harvard Law Review,* 1980-82.

SIDELIGHTS: Peter W. Huber, an alumni of Harvard Law School and Massachusetts Institute of Technology (from which he received a doctorate in mechanical engineering), specializes in antitrust policy and the telecommunications industry. The conservative legal scholar has not only contributed to such notable publications as *Harvard Law Review, Wall Street Journal,* and *Forbes,* but has also authored, coauthored, and coedited a number of books. Among them are works directly associated with his chosen profession—publications profiling legal issues in the telecommunications industry. However, Huber has also produced titles discussing the use of science in America's legal system, and, more remote from his primary field of expertise, two books confronting common stances taken by environmentalists, *Hard Green: Saving the Environment from the Environmentalists: A Conservative Manifesto* and *The Bottomless Well: The Twilight of Fuel, the Virtue of Waste, and Why We Will Never Run Out of Energy,* the latter of which attempts to dispel fears of a looming energy crisis.

Typical of Huber's studies of the legal system is the 1991 *Galileo's Revenge: Junk Science in the Courtroom.* That publication is, according to a *JAMA* review by Laurence R. Tancredi, "a superb diatribe against the current legal system that allows plaintiffs' lawyers to trump up cases based on frivolous scientific grounds and to produce extraordinary awards." *New York Times Book Review* contributor Elisabeth Rosenthal wrote: "By combining legal history, psychology and sociology, Mr. Huber perceptively traces how the situation got out of hand." Huber primarily outlines "individual cases" but also discusses "the role of legal theory" and his recommendations on how to "improve the court process," related Tancredi. "Readers can take pleasure in his tempered yet passionate appeal," commented a *Publishers Weekly* critic. Tancredi judged: "*Galileo's Revenge* is well written, highly entertaining, and a very important contribution to our understanding of how junk science is used in the courts." Tancredi continued, "Huber's examples are legion, and they make fascinating reading." According to Rosenthal: "The book's most serous flaw is that Mr. Huber makes his case powerfully in the first 100 pages—and the makes it over and over again. While the many case studies make good reading, the editorials interspersed among them are at best unnecessary (we get the point) and are often painfully rambling and repetitive."

Huber revisited the relationship between the legal system and science in a book he coauthored with Kenneth R. Foster—*Judging Science: Scientific Knowledge and the Federal Courts.* In a *Science* review of the 1997 release, Michael D. Green summarized: "[Huber] has been an outspoken and prominent critic of the tort system, especially its performance in the arenas of science and new technology. He is widely credited with popularizing the phrase 'junk science,' although his

work has been dismissed by many academics. The present book lacks the tendentious rhetoric that characterized his earlier work and, perhaps as a result of the collaboration of his former critic Kenneth Foster, is far more balanced, careful, and nuanced." While Green generally complimented the book, he felt that the book's "coverage of some critical issues is meager" and "some of the authors' criticism is [not entirely] fair."

"While much of *Judging Science* is a clear and easy-to-read primer on falsifiability, reliability, and validity, the authors consistently relate their review directly to the challenges facing a sitting judge," informed Matthew Schall in *Library Quarterly.* Schall stated that the authors "use the 1993 Supreme Court case of Daubert v. Merrel Dow Pharmaceuticals to describe the complex relationship between scientific testimony and the American judicial system."

With his 1999 release, *Hard Green,* Huber "challenges much that is now accepted dogma about environmentalism," observed *Electricity Daily* contributor Kennedy Maize, declaring *Hard Green* "a needed antidote." Huber asserts that society can "protect the environment from real dangers and still enjoy the luxuries of modern industrial society," stated *Chicago Tribune* critic Steve Chapman, who recognized that "most of his arguments will find favor with conservatives." In *Hard Green,* Huber analyzes many established arguments about what destroys and what supports the environment, exposing them as inaccurate myths. Huber, who believes that preserving the quantity of wilderness is a top priority, explains why big cities and technology support a healthy environment and why solar power and organic farming are counterproductive in protecting the environment.

"One might wish that Huber had packed *Hard Green* with more hard data, but his thesis remains compelling," assessed *National Review* contributor Christopher Rapp. Likewise, Chapman judged: "Though Huber's pithy dismissals of environmentalist bogeymen spare the reader from being drowned in scientific data, they occasionally sound glib and insubstantial." However, Chapman also found "*Hard Green . . .* an unusual book, one that moves the environmental debate a bit beyond the trenches that the right and the left have been defending for two decades. Those in either camp who approach *Hard Green* with a halfway open mind may find that after reading Huber, the idea of a new approach no longer sounds so crazy." Similarly, James Freeman concluded in *USA Today:* "After reading Huber's *Hard*

Green, you'll find it hard not to agree with him." Freeman urged, "So, the first chance you get, buy a copy." Freeman further remarked: "Huber explains with clear logic what so many of us have felt in our guts."

Huber examines the reality of depleting energy and oil reserves in the 2004 work, *The Bottomless Well,* a "free-market-oriented, techno-optimist manifesto," according to a *Publishers Weekly* reviewer. Coauthored with Mark P. Mills, the book posits the notion that mankind will continue to find new energy sources as old ones disappear. The authors contend that America's conspicuous consumption of energy is in fact positive, for it gives humanity the wherewithal to find new sources of energy. As with Huber's *Hard Green,* the authors of *The Bottomless Well* also challenge environmentalist and conservationist concepts; for example, they argue that more energy-efficient equipment will not reduce the consumption of oil, but instead only heighten demand for energy. A contributor for *Oil and Gas Investor* commented that "Mills and Huber see their job as puncturing myths and stirring up optimism, occasionally in their zeal running the risk of repetition." More specifically, the *Publishers Weekly* contributor faulted the authors for a lack of data to substantiate their claims, and concluded that *The Bottomless Well* was "an intriguing but incomplete vision of energy policy." Similarly, Jerry Taylor, writing in the *National Review,* noted: "Huber and Mills indeed draw blood, but for all of the clever insights therein (and there are many), there is also much in *The Bottomless Well* that is confused and flatly wrong." A more positive assessment came from *Booklist* contributor George Cohen, who concluded: "Readers with prior knowledge of this complicated subject will appreciate their conclusions the most."

BIOGRAPHICAL AND CRITICAL SOURCES:

PERIODICALS

Booklist, December 14, 2004, George Cohen, review of *The Bottomless Well: The Twilight of Fuel, the Virtue of Waste, and Why We Will Never Run Out of Energy,* p. 693.

Chicago Tribune, February 13, 2000, Steve Chapman, "A Worthwhile Attempt to Advance the Debate on Environmental Protection."

Choice, July-August, 2005, R.J. Barthelmie, review of *The Bottomless Well,* p. 2018.

Electricity Daily, April 17, 2000, Kennedy Maize, "Earth Day and Disingenuous Greens."

Harvard Business Review, March, 2005, John T. Landry, review of *The Bottomless Well,* p. 28.

JAMA: The Journal of the American Medical Association, February 26, 1992, Laurence R. Tancredi, review of *Galileo's Revenge,* p. 1136.

Jewish World Review, January 24, 2000, Linda Chavez, "Agreeing with Bubba . . . This Time."

Library Quarterly, April, 1999, Matthew Schall, review of *Judging Science,* p. 277.

National Resources Journal, summer, 2005, Micha Gisser, review of *The Bottomless Well,* pp. 778-782.

National Review, May 22, 2000, Christopher Rapp, review of *Hard Green;* April, 25, 2005, Jerry Taylor, "High Priests of Energy," review of *The Bottomless Well,* p. 56.

New York Times, January 22, 2000, John Tierney, "The Big City Urban Sprawl As a Way to Save Trees."

New York Times Book Review, October 13, 1991, Elisabeth Rosenthal, "Tarnished Testimony."

Oil and Gas Investor, November, 2005, "Is the End of Oil Nigh?," review of *The Bottomless Well,* p. S293.

Publishers Weekly, July 12, 1991, review of *Galileo's Revenge,* p. 57; December 13, 2004, review of *The Bottomless Well,* p. 57.

Science, November 28, 1997, Michael D. Green, review of *Judging Science,* p. 1574.

USA Today, January 19, 2000, James Freeman, "Saving Earth from Environmentalists."

Weekly Standard, March 20, 2000, Robert Royal, "Right Green: Toward a Conservative Theory of Environmentalism."

ONLINE

Digital Power Group Web site, http://www.digitalpower group.com/ (November 20, 2006), "Peter W. Huber."

Manahattan Institute Web site, http://www.manhattan institute.org/ (November 20, 2006), "Peter Huber."*

*   *   *

HUBER, Peter William
See HUBER, Peter W.

HUGHES, Dean 1943-
(D.T. Hughes)

PERSONAL: Born August 24, 1943, in Ogden, UT; son of Emery T. (a government worker) and Lorraine Hughes; married Kathleen Hurst (a teacher and educational administrator), November 23, 1966; children: Tom, Amy, Robert. *Education:* Weber State College, B.A. (cum laude), 1967; University of Washington, M.A., 1968, Ph.D., 1972; postdoctoral study at Stanford University, summer, 1975, and Yale University, summer, 1978. *Politics:* Democrat. *Religion:* Mormon. *Hobbies and other interests:* Theater, jazz, travel, golf, skiing, collecting kaleidoscopes.

CAREER: Roosevelt Hotel, Seattle, WA, bellman, 1967-72; Central Missouri State University, Warrensburg, MO, associate professor of English, 1972-80; Brigham Young University, Provo, UT, part-time visiting professor, 1980-82; writer, part-time editor, and consultant, 1980—. Guest author, speaker, and workshop leader at writing conferences.

MEMBER: Children's Literature Association, Society of Children's Book Writers, Authors Guild, Authors League of America.

AWARDS, HONORS: National Endowment for the Humanities summer seminar stipend, 1975 and 1978; Outstanding Faculty Achievement Award, Central Missouri State University, 1980; *Honestly, Myron* was selected one of the "Best Books for Kids" by Children's Book Committee; *Booklist* Editor's Choice Award, 1989, for *Family Pose.*

WRITINGS:

"NUTTY" SERIES

Nutty for President, illustrated by Blanche Sims, Atheneum (New York, NY), 1981.
Nutty and the Case of the Mastermind Thief, Atheneum (New York, NY), 1985.
Nutty and the Case of the Ski-Slope Spy, Atheneum (New York, NY) 1985.
Nutty Can't Miss, Atheneum (New York, NY), 1987.
Nutty Knows All, Atheneum (New York, NY), 1988.

Nutty, the Movie Star, Atheneum (New York, NY), 1989.
Nutty's Ghost, Atheneum (New York, NY), 1993.
Re-Elect Nutty!, Atheneum (New York, NY), 1994.

"LUCKY" SERIES

Lucky Breaks Loose, Deseret (Salt Lake City, UT), 1990.
Lucky's Crash Landing, Deseret (Salt Lake City, UT), 1990.
Lucky's Gold Mine, Deseret (Salt Lake City, UT), 1990.
Lucky Fights Back, Deseret (Salt Lake City, UT), 1991.
Lucky's Mud Festival, Deseret (Salt Lake City, UT), 1991.
Lucky the Detective, Deseret (Salt Lake City, UT), 1992.
Lucky's Tricks, Deseret (Salt Lake City, UT), 1992.
Lucky's Cool Club, Deseret (Salt Lake City, UT), 1993.
Lucky in Love, Deseret (Salt Lake City, UT), 1993.
Lucky Comes Home, Deseret (Salt Lake City, UT), 1994.

"CHILDREN OF THE PROMISE" SERIES

Rumors of War, Deseret (Salt Lake City, UT), 1997.
Since You Went Away, Deseret (Salt Lake City, UT), 1997.
Far from Home, Deseret (Salt Lake City, UT), 1998.
When We Meet Again, Deseret (Salt Lake City, UT), 1999.
As Long as I Have You, Deseret (Salt Lake City, UT), 2000.
So Much of Life Ahead: A Novel, Bookcraft (Salt Lake City, UT), 2005.

"HEARTS OF THE CHILDREN" SERIES

The Writing on the Wall: A Novel, Bookcraft (Salt Lake City, UT), 2001.
Troubled Waters: A Novel, Bookcraft (Salt Lake City, UT), 2002.
How Many Roads? A Novel, Bookcraft (Salt Lake City, UT), 2003.
Take Me Home: A Novel, Bookcraft (Salt Lake City, UT), 2004.

WILLIAMS FAMILY TRILOGY

Under the Same Stars, Deseret (Salt Lake City, UT), 1979, revised edition, 2005.

As Wide as the River, Deseret (Salt Lake City, UT), 1980, revised edition, 2005.

Facing the Enemy, Deseret (Salt Lake City, UT), 1982, revised edition, 2005.

OTHER

Along the Sideroad, Nelson, Foster & Scott, 1973.

Romance and Psychological Realism in William Godwin's Novels, Arno, 1981.

Hooper Haller (young adult novel), Deseret (Salt Lake City, UT), 1981.

Honestly, Myron (juvenile novel), illustrated by Martha Weston, Atheneum (New York, NY), 1982.

Switching Tracks (juvenile novel), Atheneum (New York, NY), 1982.

Millie Willenheimer and the Chestnut Corporation (juvenile novel), Atheneum (New York, NY), 1983.

Jenny Haller (young adult novel), Deseret (New York, NY), 1983.

Brothers (novel), Deseret (Salt Lake City, UT), 1986.

The Mormon Church: A Basic History (nonfiction), Deseret (Salt Lake City, UT), 1986.

Theo Zephyr (juvenile), Atheneum (New York, NY), 1987.

Cornbread and Prayer, Deseret (Salt Lake City, UT), 1988.

Family Pose (young adult novel), Atheneum (New York, NY), 1989, published as *Family Picture,* Scholastic (New York, NY), 1990.

Jelly's Circus (juvenile), Aladdin Books (New York, NY), 1989.

Big Base Hit, illustrated by Dennis Lyall, Knopf (New York, NY), 1990.

Championship Game, illustrated by Dennis Lyall, Knopf (New York, NY), 1990.

Line Drive, illustrated by Dennis Lyall, Knopf (New York, NY), 1990.

Making the Team, illustrated by Dennis Lyall, Knopf (New York, NY), 1990.

Pressure Play, illustrated by Dennis Lyall, Knopf (New York, NY), 1990.

Rookie Star, illustrated by Dennis Lyall, Knopf (New York, NY), 1990.

What a Catch!, illustrated by Dennis Lyall, Knopf (New York, NY), 1990.

Winning Streak, Bullseye (New York, NY), 1990.

All Together Now, illustrated by Dennis Lyall, Knopf (New York, NY), 1991.

Defense!, illustrated by Dennis Lyall, Knopf (New York, NY), 1991.

Kickoff Time, illustrated by Dennis Lyall, Knopf (New York, NY), 1991.

Play-Off, illustrated by Dennis Lyall, Knopf (New York, NY), 1991.

Safe at First, illustrated by Dennis Lyall, Knopf (New York, NY), 1991.

Stroke of Luck, illustrated by Dennis Lyall, Knopf (New York, NY), 1991.

Superstar team, illustrated by Dennis Lyall, Knopf (New York, NY), 1991.

Up to Bat, illustrated by Dennis Lyall, Knopf (New York, NY), 1991.

Backup Goalie, illustrated by Dennis Lyall, Knopf (New York, NY), 1992.

Nothing but Net, illustrated by Dennis Lyall, Knopf (New York, NY), 1992.

Point Guard, illustrated by Dennis Lyall, Knopf (New York, NY), 1992.

Psyched!, illustrated by Dennis Lyall, Knopf (New York, NY), 1992.

Total Soccer, illustrated by Dennis Lyall, Knopf (New York, NY), 1992.

Victory Goal, illustrated by Dennis Lyall, Knopf (New York, NY), 1992.

(With Tom Hughes) *Baseball Tips,* illustrated by Dennis Lyall, Random House (New York, NY), 1993.

End of the Race, Atheneum (New York, NY), 1993.

Go to the Hoop!, illustrated by Dennis Lyall, Knopf (New York, NY), 1993.

(As D.T. Hughes) *Lullaby and Goodnight* (true crime), Pocket Books (New York, NY), 1993.

On the Line, illustrated by Dennis Lyall, Knopf (New York, NY), 1993.

Quick Moves, illustrated by Dennis Lyall, Knopf (New York, NY), 1993.

Shake Up, illustrated by Dennis Lyall, Knopf (New York, NY), 1993.

One-Man Team, Knopf (New York, NY), 1994.

Second-Team Star, Knopf (New York, NY), 1994.

Dog Detectives and Other Amazing Canines (juvenile nonfiction), Random House (New York, NY), 1994.

K-9 Crime Busters, Random House (New York, NY), 1994.

The Trophy, Knopf (New York, NY), 1994.

Find the Power!, Bullseye Books (New York, NY), 1994.

(With others) *Great Stories from Mormon History,* Deseret (Salt Lake City, UT), 1994.

Quarterback Hero, Bullseye Books (New York, NY), 1994.

Backup Soccer Star, Bullseye Books (New York, NY), 1995.

(With others) *We'll Bring the World His Truth: Missionary Adventures from around the World,* Deseret (Salt Lake City, UT), 1995.

Team Picture (sequel to *Family Pose*), Atheneum (New York, NY), 1996.

Brad and Butter Play Ball (juvenile), illustrated by Layne Johnson, Random House (New York, NY), 1998.

No Fear, Atheneum (New York, NY), 1999.

Now We're Talking, Atheneum (New York, NY), 1999.

Grand Slam, Atheneum (New York, NY), 1999.

Bases Loaded, Atheneum (New York, NY), 1999.

No Easy Out, Atheneum (New York, NY), 1999.

Home Run Hero, Atheneum (New York, NY), 1999.

Play Ball, Atheneum (New York, NY), 1999.

Take Your Base, Atheneum (New York, NY), 1999.

Team Player, Atheneum (New York, NY), 1999.

A igreja mormon: historia basica, Deseret (Salt Lake City, UT), 2001.

Soldier Boys, Atheneum Books for Young Readers (New York, NY), 2001.

Midway to Heaven: A Novel, Deseret (Salt Lake City, UT), 2004.

All Moms Go to Heaven: Reflections, Deseret (Salt Lake City, UT), 2005.

Search and Destroy, Atheneum Books for Young Readers (New York, NY), 2005.

Saboteur: A Novel of Love and War, Deseret (Salt Lake City, UT), 2006.

Contributor to books by others, including *Monsters, Ghoulies, and Creepy Creatures,* edited by Lee Bennett Hopkins, A. Whitman, 1977, and *Merrily Comes Our Harvest In,* edited by Lee Bennett Hopkins, 1978; contributor of articles, reviews, and poems to numerous periodicals, including *Dickens Studies Newsletter, Blackwater Review, Dialogue, English Journal, Averett Journal,* and *Cricket.*

ADAPTATIONS: Books adapted for audio include *Troubled Waters,* 2002, *How Many Roads?,* 2003, and *So Much of Life Ahead,* 2005, all Bookcraft (Salt Lake City, UT).

SIDELIGHTS: Dean Hughes is a prolific and versatile writer who has written nonsense poetry, historical novels, a scholarly monograph, sports novels, children's

stories, and young adult novels. A native of Utah, Hughes often profiles Mormons in his novels. His *Under the Same Stars* and *As Wide as the River* trace the life of the fictitious Williams family, early Mormons driven out of Jackson County, Missouri, because of their religious practices. *Facing the Enemy* completes the trilogy.

Hughes has written more than twenty sports novels. Most of these are found within three series: "The Angel Park Hoop Stars," "The Angel Park Soccer Stars," and "The Angel Park All-Stars." Critics have commented that Hughes distinguishes his plots with in-depth characters and realistic descriptions. In two of his baseball books, *Big Base Hit* and *Making the Team,* "readers witness respect, consideration, and personal growth" in the characters, according to Janice C. Hayes in the *School Library Journal.*

Another novel for young readers, *Honestly, Myron,* concerns a fifth-grader who wants to be a great man like Abraham Lincoln. The boy begins telling the truth at all times and soon finds himself in many sticky situations. *Switching Tracks,* unlike most of Hughes's other juvenile novels, is written in a serious tone. It describes the anguish of a young teen as he deals with the suicide of his father and the comfort he finds from an older gentleman in his neighborhood. A critic in *Kirkus Reviews* described Hughes's treatment of the "guarded relationship" as "touching but never sentimental or predictable."

Hughes has also written a series based on a fifth-grader named Nutty Nutshell. In *Nutty for President,* William Bilks is another fifth-grader who persuades Nutty, the class "goof off," to run for school president. During the campaign, William discovers Nutty's hidden talents, transforming Nutty from a bumbler into a confident leader. A critic for *Kirkus Reviews* described *Nutty for President* as "a standout in its class . . . snappy [and] well-grounded." In the *School Library Journal,* Steve Matthews commented that "the school setting and student interaction is well portrayed with recognizable character types."

Hughes's experience as a bellman at a hotel in Seattle became the basis for his young adult novel *Family Pose.* The book is about David, a runaway orphan who is befriended by Paul, a hotel bellman and recovering alcoholic. Because of his experiences in the foster care system, David is very reluctant to seek help or tell anyone about himself. A dedicated group of hotel workers, however, gradually helps bring David out of his shell. The novel was praised by a critic for *Kirkus Reviews* as being a "moving and memorable story" because of its "lovingly drawn characters and strong central relationship." These sentiments were echoed in *Horn Book* by Ethel R. Tichwell, who wrote that "the growing affection between Paul and David [is] well presented and gives the book considerable emotional impact." In the *New York Times Book Review,* Betsy Hearne noted that "the detailed setting and the subtly unfolded observation of each character in *Family Pose* give readers the uncanny sense of a life crisis relived."

Soldier Boys is a novel for young adult readers about two young men in uniform. Dieter Hedrick, a thirteen-year-old farm boy from Bavaria, is a Hitler Youth leader, and Spence Morgan, a farm boy from Utah, is a United States paratrooper. The story traces the events in the life of each as history leads up to World War II's Battle of the Bulge, when both young men experience fear and loss. The tragic high point of the novel is the meeting of the two on a snow-covered Belgian hill. Peter D. Sieruta wrote in *Horn Book:* "This book may linger in the reader's mind for quite some time."

A *Kirkus Reviews* contributor called *Search and Destroy* "simply written and taut." Rick Ward is a hopeful writer who joins the army in order to broaden his experiences. He is sent to Vietnam, where he is one of a six-member "search and destroy" team that hunts down and kills the enemy. Befriended by Preacher, an older man who teaches him compassion for the people of the country, Rick goes from day to day just trying to stay alive. Paula Rohrlick wrote in *Kliatt* that in addition to Hughes's antiwar message, "the special bond of soldiers who are willing to die for each other comes across clearly too."

Hughes once told *CA:* "In 1980 I took a leave of absence from teaching and wrote full time. I wrote and sold five books in that year. I extended my leave, and now I plan to stay with full-time writing, although I do some editing and teach technical writing. I try to raise serious questions for young readers, often in the context of a humorous book. How does America elect its leaders? Is honesty really possible? Can you avoid greed in business? These are some of the kinds of questions I have tried to get young people thinking about. Some of my books are about Mormons, but I don't think they are only *for* Mormons."

Hughes added: "I think I'm gradually becoming known as the Nutty author. I am getting quite a few letters from young readers these days, and most of them mention that they like the books I've written about Nutty. Part of the reason may be that the Bantam Skylark editions—along with adoptions by children's book clubs—have taken those books to more readers than ever before. I also think that something about Nutty and his friend William Bilks seems both fun and real to kids who spend their days in school.

"Each time a new book comes out I add it to a shelf in my family room. I now have fifteen up there, with more on the way. That's very exciting and satisfying to me. I'm consulting less and writing more these days. I still hope that one day soon I'll be able to make a full-time living writing only fiction. But if I never do, I still have a great deal of freedom compared to people who go to work each day, and to me creating novels, while it is hard work, never seems like a job."

BIOGRAPHICAL AND CRITICAL SOURCES:

BOOKS

Twentieth-Century Young-Adult Writers, St. James Press (Detroit, MI), 1994.

PERIODICALS

Booklist, February 1, 2006, Ed Sullivan, review of *Search and Destroy,* p. 44.
Book Report, May-June, 2002, Judith Beavers, review of *Soldier Boys,* p. 56.
Horn Book, September, 1989, Ethel R. Tichwell, review of *Family Pose;* January-February, 2002, Peter D. Sieruta, review of *Soldier Boys,* p. 77; January-February, 2006, Betty Carter, review of *Search and Destroy,* p. 81.
Kirkus Reviews, May 1, 1981, review of *Nutty for President;* July 15, 1982, review of *Switching Tracks;* April 1, 1989, review of *Family Pose;* November 1, 2001, review of *Soldier Boys,* p. 1551; December 1, 2005, review of *Search and Destroy,* p. 1275.
Kliatt, January, 2002, Paula Rohrlick, review of *Soldier Boys,* p. 6; January, 2006, Paula Rohrlick, review of *Search and Destroy,* p. 8.

New York Times Book Review, May 21, 1989, Betsy Hearne, review of *Family Pose.*

Publishers Weekly, December 3, 2001, review of *Soldier Boys,* p. 60; September 15, 2003, review of *How Many Roads?,* p. S8; August 23, 2004, review of *Take Me Home: A Novel,* p. S16.

School Library Journal, February, 1982, Steve Matthews, review of *Nutty for President;* June, 1990, Janice C. Hayes, reviews of *Big Base Hit* and *Making the Team;* November, 2001, Todd Morning, review of *Soldier Boys,* p. 158; January, 2006, Jane G. Connor, review of *Search and Destroy,* p. 134.

ONLINE

Dean Hughes Home Page, http://www.deanhughes.net (December 26, 2006).

Meridian, http://www.meridianmagazine.com/ (December 13, 2001), Stephen Wunderli, review of *Soldier Boys.**

*   *   *

HUGHES, D.T.
See HUGHES, Dean

*   *   *

HUNTER, Chris
See FLUKE, Joanne

I-J

ISAACS, Ronald H. 1947-
    (Ronald Howard Isaacs)

PERSONAL: Born September 10, 1947, in Toronto, Ontario, Canada; U.S. citizen; son of David (in sales) and Gertrude (a homemaker) Isaacs; married, June 20, 1971; wife's name Leora W.; children: Keren, Zachary. *Ethnicity:* "Jewish." *Education:* Jewish Theological Seminary of America, B.H.L., 1969, M.A., 1971, Rabbi, 1974; Columbia University, B.A., 1969, M.A., 1971, Ed.D., 1979. *Hobbies and other interests:* Sports memorabilia, music.

ADDRESSES: Office—Temple Sholom, 594 N. Bridge St., Bridgewater, NJ 08807; fax: 908-707-9055.

CAREER: Rabbi, educator, radio host, and writer. Voices Four (Hebrew liturgical folk-rock ensemble), cofounder and performer, 1969-73; Greenburgh Hebrew Center, Dobbs Ferry, NY, principal and youth director, 1973-75; Temple Sholom, Bridgewater, NJ, rabbi, 1975—, and codirector of Temple Sholom Hebrew High School. Rutgers University, visiting lecturer, 1976-82; Jewish Theological Seminary of America, adjunct lecturer, 2002. United Synagogue of Conservative Judaism, Kadima rabbi for Northern New Jersey Region, 1982-92; Coalition for the Advancement of Jewish Education, board member, 1992-94; Northern New Jersey Rabbinical Assembly, vice president, 1995-96; Rabbinical Assembly of America, chair of publications committee, 2001. Lovin' Company (Hebrew liturgical folk-rock ensemble), founder and performer, 1980-82; WCTC-Radio, host of *Jewish American Hour,* 1990-94; recorded the albums *Arbaah Kolote: The Voices Four,* released by Monitor Recordings in 1969, and *Our Rock*

and Our Redeemer, Monitor Recordings, 1971. Camp Ramah in the Poconos, head of music and coordinator of Ramah Family Camp and Shabbat Plus Adult Learning Program, summers, 1988-2001. United Way of Somerset Valley, board member, 1990-93; Human Relations Council of Bridgewater, board member, 1999—; Bridgewater Police Department, member of Committee of Chaplains, 2001—.

MEMBER: Faith in Action (board member, 1999—).

AWARDS, HONORS: D.H.L., Jewish Theological Seminary of America, 2001.

WRITINGS:

(With wife, Leora Isaacs) *Jewish Expressions: My Holiday Activity Book,* Ktav Publishing House (Jersey City, NJ), 1986.
The Jewish Instructional Games Book, New York Board of Jewish Education (New York, NY), 1986.
Shabbat Delight: A Celebration in Stories, Songs, and Games, Ktav Publishing House (Jersey City, NJ), 1987.
(With Leora Isaacs) *Reflections: A Jewish Grandparents' Gift of Memories,* Jason Aronson (Northvale, NJ), 1987.
The Jewish Family Game Book for the Sabbath and Festivals, Ktav Publishing House (Jersey City, NJ), 1989.
The Bride and Groom Handbook, Behrman House (West Orange, NJ), 1990.
(With Leora Isaacs) *Gleanings: Four Shavuot Scripts,* Leeron Publishers (Bridgewater, NJ), 1990.

(With Leora Isaacs) *Loving Companions: Our Jewish Wedding Album,* Jason Aronson (Northvale, NJ), 1991.

(With Kerry M. Olitzky) *The Jewish Mourner's Handbook,* Ktav Publishing House (Jersey City, NJ), 1992.

Rites of Passage: Guide to the Jewish Life Cycle, Ktav Publishing House (Jersey City, NJ), 1992.

(With Kerry M. Olitzky) *The Discovery Haggada,* Ktav Publishing House (Jersey City, NJ), 1992.

(With D. Pressman) *Shma Kolaynu: A High Holy Day Youth Machzor,* Ktav Publishing House (Jersey City, NJ), 1992.

(With Kerry M. Olitzky) *A Glossary of Jewish Life,* Jason Aronson (Northvale, NJ), 1992.

(With Kerry M. Olitzky) *The How-to Handbook for Jewish Living,* Ktav Publishing House (Jersey City, NJ), Volume 1, 1993, Volume 2, 1996.

Becoming Jewish: A Handbook for Conversion, Ktav Publishing House (Jersey City, NJ), 1993.

(With S. Arlen and R. Wagner) *Chain of Life: A Curricular Guide,* Coalition for the Advancement of Jewish Education (New York, NY), 1993.

The Jewish Information Source Book: A Dictionary and Almanac, Jason Aronson (Jersey City, NJ), 1993.

(With Leora Isaacs) *Jewish Family Matters: A Leader's Guide,* United Synagogue of Conservative Judaism (New York, NY), 1994.

(With D. Pressman) *Siddur Shir Chadash for Youth and Family,* Ktav Publishing House (Jersey City, NJ), 1994.

(With Kerry M. Olitzky) *Doing Mitzvot: Mitzvah Projects for Bar/Bat Mitzvah,* Ktav Publishing House (Jersey City, NJ), 1994.

(With Kerry M. Olitzky) *Sacred Celebrations: A Jewish Holiday Handbook,* Jason Aronson (Northvale, NJ), 1994.

(With Kerry M. Olitzky) *Critical Documents of Jewish History: A Sourcebook,* Jason Aronson (Northvale, NJ), 1995.

Lively Student Prayer Services: A Handbook of Teaching Strategies, Ktav Publishing House (Jersey City, NJ), 1995.

(With Kerry M. Olitzky) *Sacred Moments: Tales of the Jewish Life Cycle,* Jason Aronson (Northvale, NJ), 1995.

Derech Eretz: Pathways to an Ethical Life, United Synagogue Department of Youth (New York, NY), 1995.

Critical Jewish Issues: A Book for Teenagers, Ktav Publishing House (Jersey City, NJ), 1996.

The Jewish Book of Numbers, Jason Aronson (Northvale, NJ), 1996.

Words for the Soul: Jewish Wisdom for Life's Journey, Jason Aronson (Jersey City, NJ), 1996.

Mitzvot: A Sourcebook for the 613 Commandments, Jason Aronson (Northvale, NJ), 1996.

Madrich LeGabbai: A Gabbai's How-to Manual, Ktav Publishing House (Jersey City, NJ), 1996.

Close Encounters: Jewish Views of God, Jason Aronson (Northvale, NJ), 1996.

Sacred Seasons: A Sourcebook for the Jewish Holidays, Jason Aronson (Northvale, NJ), 1997.

Every Person's Guide to Jewish Prayer, Jason Aronson (Northvale, NJ), 1997.

Sidra Reflections: Guide to Sidrot and Haftarot, Ktav Publishing House (Jersey City, NJ), 1997, leader's guide, 1998.

(With Kerry M. Olitzky) *Rediscovering Judaism: Bar and Bat Mitzvah for Adults; A Course of Study,* Ktav Publishing House (Jersey City, NJ), 1997.

Jewish Bible Almanac, Jason Aronson (Northvale, NJ), 1997.

Miracles: A Jewish Perspective, Jason Aronson (Northvale, NJ), 1997.

Jewish Music: Its History, People, and Song, Jason Aronson (Northvale, NJ), 1997.

Divination, Magic, and Healing: The Book of Jewish Folklore, Jason Aronson (Northvale, NJ), 1998.

Ascending Jacob's Ladder: Jewish Views of Angels, Demons, and Evil Spirits, Jason Aronson (Northvale, NJ), 1998.

The Jewish Book of Etiquette, Jason Aronson (Northvale, NJ), 1998.

Judaism, Medicine, and Healing, Jason Aronson (Northvale, NJ), 1998.

(Editor) *The Jewish Sourcebook on the Environment and Ecology,* Jason Aronson (Northvale, NJ), 1998.

Messengers of God: A Jewish Prophets Who's Who, Jason Aronson (Northvale, NJ), 1998.

Every Person's Guide to Shabbat, Jason Aronson (Northvale, NJ), 1998.

Every Person's Guide to Shavuot, Jason Aronson (Northvale, NJ), 1998.

Every Person's Guide to Death and Dying in the Jewish Tradition, Jason Aronson (Northvale, NJ), 1999.

Exploring Jewish Ethics and Values, Ktav Publishing House (Jersey City, NJ), 1999.

Every Person's Guide to Jewish Philosophy and Philosophers, Jason Aronson (Northvale, NJ), 1999.

(With Kerry M. Olitzky) *I Believe: The Thirteen Principles of Faith: A Confirmation Textbook,* Ktav Publishing House (Jersey City, NJ), 1999.

Reaching for Sinai: How-to Handbook for Celebrating a Meaningful Bar/Bat Mitzvah, Ktav Publishing House (Jersey City, NJ), 1999.

Every Person's Guide to the High Holy Days, Jason Aronson (Northvale, NJ), 1999.

The Tabernacle, the Temple, and Its Royalty, Jason Aronson (Northvale, NJ), 1999.

Every Person's Guide to Holiness: The Jewish Perspective, Jason Aronson (Northvale, NJ), 1999.

Every Person's Guide to Jewish Blessings, Jason Aronson (Northvale, NJ), 1999.

Entering the Biblical Text: Exploring Jewish Values in the Torah, Ktav Publishing House (Jersey City, NJ), 2000.

Beginnings: Raising a Jewish Child, United Synagogue of Conservative Judaism (New York, NY), 2000.

The Bible: Where Do You Find It, and What Does It Say?, Jason Aronson (Northvale, NJ), 2000.

Every Person's Guide to Jewish Law, Jason Aronson (Northvale, NJ), 2000.

Animals in Jewish Thought and Tradition, Jason Aronson (Northvale, NJ), 2000.

Every Person's Guide to Jewish Sexuality, Jason Aronson (Northvale, NJ), 2000.

Every Person's Guide to the Book of Proverbs and Ecclesiastes: Biblical Wisdom for the Twenty-first Century, Jason Aronson (Northvale, NJ), 2000.

Every Person's Guide to Sukkot, Shemini Atzeret, and Simchat Torah, Jason Aronson (Northvale, NJ), 2000.

Every Person's Guide to Purim, Jason Aronson (Northvale, NJ), 2000.

Every Person's Guide to Hanukkah, Jason Aronson (Northvale, NJ), 2000.

Every Person's Guide to Passover, Jason Aronson (Northvale, NJ), 2000.

The Talmud: What Does It Say and Where Can You Find It?, Jason Aronson (Northvale, NJ), 2000.

Every Person's Guide to What's Kosher and What's Not, Jason Aronson (Northvale, NJ), 2000.

Ask the Rabbi: The Book of Answers to Jewish Kids' Questions, Jason Aronson (Northvale, NJ), 2000.

Every Person's Guide to Aggadah, Jason Aronson (Northvale, NJ), 2000.

Building the Faith: A Book of Inclusion for Dual-Faith Families, Federation of Jewish Men's Clubs (New York, NY), 2001.

Understanding the Hebrew Prophets, Ktav Publishing House (Jersey City, NJ), 2001.

Defending the Faith: Trials and Great Debates in Jewish History, Ktav Publishing House (Jersey City, NJ), 2001.

Can You Believe It: Amazing Jewish Facts and Curiosities, Jason Aronson (Northvale, NJ), 2001.

Ethics for Everyday Living: Jewish Wisdom for the Twenty-first Century, Jason Aronson (Northvale, NJ), 2001.

Every Person's Guide to the Book of Psalms, Jason Aronson (Northvale, NJ), 2001.

Exploring the Jewish Prophets, Ktav Publishing House (Jersey City, NJ), 2001.

(With Kerry M. Olitzky) *The Third "How-to" Handbook for Jewish Living,* Ktav Publishing House (Jersey City, NJ), 2002.

Let My People Go: An Instant Lesson on World Slavery, Torah Aura (Los Angeles, CA), 2002.

Legends of Biblical Heroes: A Sourcebook, Jason Aronson (Northvale, NJ), 2002.

A Taste of Text: An Introduction to the Talmud and Midrash, UAHC Press (New York, NY), 2003.

Ask the Rabbi: The Who, What, When, Where, Why, and How of Being Jewish, Jossey-Bass (San Francisco, CA), 2003.

The Jewish Traveller's Handbook, Ktav Publishing House (Jersey City, NJ), 2003.

Life's Little Book of Big Jewish Advice, Ktav Publishing House (Jersey City, NJ), 2004.

Gates of Heaven: A Handbook for Unveilings and Visiting the Cemetery, Ktav Publishing House (Jersey City, NJ), 2004.

Essential Judaism in a Nutshell, Ktav Publishing House (Jersey City, NJ), 2004.

Amazing Jewish Facts: Can You Believe It?, Rowman & Littlefield Publishers (Lanham, MD), 2004.

Count Your Blessings: 100 Blessings a Day, Ktav Publishing House (Jersey City, NJ), 2004.

(With Kerry M. Olitzky) *The Complete How To Handbook for Jewish Living,* Ktav Publishing House (Jersey City, NJ), 2004.

Kosher Living: It's More than Just the Food, Jossey-Bass (San Francisco, CA), 2005.

Questions Christians Ask the Rabbi, Ktav Publishing House (Jersey City, NJ), 2005.

A Taste of Torah: An Introduction to Thirteen Challenging Bible Stories, URJ Press (New York, NY), 2006.

A Service of Comfort: Afternoon and Evening Prayers with Spiritual Reflections for the House of Mourning, Ktav Publishing House (Jersey City, NJ), 2007.

Author of sourcebooks for Kadima Encampments, 1982-92. Creator of *The Pocket Size Ungame: Spiritual Version,* released by Ungame Co., 1983. Contributor to periodicals, including *Kol Kadima, United Synagogue Jewish Living Now, Pedagogic Reporter, Jewish Education,* and *Impact.* Member of editorial board, *Shofar.*

SIDELIGHTS: Ronald H. Isaacs once told *CA:* "I write as I prepare to teach my courses for our own Hebrew high school and adult education programs. I try to write for a couple of hours each day and generally choose a topic which I have always enjoyed teaching or reading about, but which I would like to research further."

Isaacs has produced a wide range of books as guides for those of the Jewish faith, as well as for those interested in the Jewish religion. His books often reflect his own personal emphasis on asking questions, typified by an "Ask the Rabbi" in-box that he provides for his own congregation and students. For example, in *Ask the Rabbi: The Who, What, When, Where, Why, and How of Being Jewish,* the author addresses a wide range of complex questions concerning Judaism. However, he also includes less serious queries, such as the question some have asked concerning why so many comedians are Jewish. A *Publishers Weekly* contributor commented that, "as a basic, accessible introduction to Judaism, it is . . . a handy guide for all readers." Ilene Cooper, writing in *Booklist,* referred to the book as "an essential guide for Jews and others who want to know more about Jewish practices."

Isaacs addresses deeper philosophical topics in his *Close Encounters: Jewish Views of God.* In this book, the author discusses various Jewish beliefs about understanding God. In the process, he encompasses such topics as the *Bible,* mysticism, and various rabbinic literature. A *Publishers Weekly* contributor wrote that the author "has an ability to break down difficult concepts into succinct segments, creating an accessible reference guide for the lay reader." Isaacs also addresses the lay reader in his book *Every Person's Guide to Jewish Philosophy and Philosophers,* which Hayim Y. Sheynin called "notable for its inclusiveness" in a review for the *Library Journal.*

The author has also written several "fact books" about Judaism. For example, in the *Jewish Bible Almanac,* he provides, as he writes, "curious facts, oddities, unusual statistics, and biblical information." The book includes information on topics such as capital punishment in Judaism. Eugene O. Bowser, writing in the *Library Journal,* noted that the author "does provide a handy sampling of a very broad range of subjects in an excellently accessible style for the complete neophyte."

In his 2006 book, *Questions Christians Ask the Rabbi,* Isaacs addresses more than 200 questions he has been asked by Christians, primarily via his Web site. As expected, many of the questions concern Jesus and his divinity, but others focus on Jewish holidays and dietary laws. A *Reference & Research Book News* contributor noted that the author takes "a concise but accessible, family-friendly approach" in answering the questions.

BIOGRAPHICAL AND CRITICAL SOURCES:

BOOKS

Isaacs, Ronald H., *Jewish Bible Almanac,* Jason Aronson (Northvale, NJ), 1997.

PERIODICALS

Booklist, October 15, 2003, Ilene Cooper, review of *Ask the Rabbi: The Who, What, When, Where, Why, and How of Being Jewish,* p. 402.
Library Journal, April 15, 1997, Robert A. Silver, review of *Sacred Seasons: A Sourcebook for the Jewish Holidays,* p. 86; April 1, 1998, Eugene O. Bowser, review of *Jewish Bible Almanac,* p. 96; December, 1998, Sheynin, Hayim Y. Sheynin, review of *Every Person's Guide to Jewish Philosophy and Philosophers,* p. 114; January 1, 2001, Graham Christian, review of *Every Person's Guide to Purim,* p. 117.
Publishers Weekly, November 8, 1993, review of *The How-to Handbook for Jewish Living,* p. 48; August 15, 1994, review of *Sacred Celebrations: A Jewish Holiday Handbook,* p. 56; October 14, 1996, review of *Close Encounters, Jewish Views about God,* p. 76; December 8, 1997, review of *Miracles: A Jewish Perspective,* p. 68; March 9, 1998, review of *Judaism, Medicine, and Healing,* p. 63; July 31, 2000, review of *Every Person's Guide to Jewish Sexuality,* p. 34; August 25, 2003, review of *Ask the Rabbi,* p. 57.
Reference & Research Book News, November, 2006, review of *Questions Christians Ask the Rabbi.*
Shofar, spring, 2004, review of *Ask the Rabbi: The Who, What, When, Where, Why, and How of Being Jewish,* p. 191.

*   *   *

ISAACS, Ronald Howard
    See ISAACS, Ronald H.

*   *   *

ISSAKSON, C. Benjamin
    See BORDOWITZ, Hank

JACKSON, Gina
    See FLUKE, Joanne

*   *   *

JAMISON, Cheryl Alters 1953-

PERSONAL: Born June 17, 1953, in Illinois; daughter of Marcellus M. and Betty E. Alters; married Bill Jamison (a writer), 1985; children: Heather Jamison Neale (stepdaughter). *Education:* Illinois State University, B.S., 1975; University of Illinois at Springfield, M.A., 1977.

ADDRESSES: Home—Tesuque, NM.

CAREER: Writer.

AWARDS, HONORS: James Beard Award, 1994, for *Smoke and Spice,* and 1995, for *The Border Cookbook.*

WRITINGS:

WITH HUSBAND, BILL JAMISON

The Insider's Guide to Sante Fe, 2nd revised edition, Harvard Common (Harvard, MA), 1990, 4th revised edition published as *The Insider's Guide to Sante Fe, Taos, and Albuquerque,* 2000.

The Rancho de Chimayo Cookbook: The Traditional Cooking of New Mexico, Harvard Common (Boston, MA), 1991.

Texas Home Cooking, Harvard Common (Boston, MA), 1993.

Smoke and Spice: The Joy of Real Backyard Barbecue, Harvard Common Press (Boston, MA), 1994, revised edition published as *Smoke & Spice: Cooking with Smoke, The Real Way To Barbecue,* 2003.

The Border Cookbook: Authentic Home Cooking of the American Southwest and Northern Mexico, Harvard Common (Boston, MA), 1995.

Best Places to Stay in Mexico, 3rd edition, Houghton (Boston, MA), 1995.

Best Places to Stay in Hawaii, 3rd edition, Houghton (Boston, MA), 1995.

Sublime Smoke: Bold New Flavors Inspired by the Old Art of Barbecue, Harvard Common (Boston, MA), 1996.

The Insider's Guide to Santa Fe, Taos, and Albuquerque, 4th edition, Harvard Common (Boston, MA), 1996.

Best Places to Stay in the Caribbean, 4th edition, Houghton (Boston, MA), 1996.

Born to Grill: An American Celebration, illustrated by Sara Love, Harvard Common (Boston, MA), 1998.

American Home Cooking: Over Three Hundred Recipes Celebrating Our Rich Tradition of Home Cooking, Broadway Books (New York, NY), 1999.

A Real American Breakfast: The Best Meal of the Day, Any Time of the Day, William Morrow (New York, NY), 2002.

Chicken on the Grill: 100 Surefire Ways to Grill Perfect Chicken Every Time, William Morrow (New York, NY), 2004.

Grilling for Friends: Surefire, Fun Food for Great Grill Parties, William Morrow (New York, NY), 2006.

The Big Book of Outdoor Cooking and Entertaining: Spirited Recipes and Expert Tips for Barbecuing, Charcoal and Gas Grilling, Rotisserie Roasting, Smoking, Deep-Frying, and Making Merry, William Morrow (New York, NY), 2006.

SIDELIGHTS: Cheryl Alters Jamison is a cookbook and entertainment writer who has collaborated with her husband Bill Jamison on numerous cookbooks focusing primarily on American food and outdoor cooking. For example, *American Home Cooking: Over Three Hundred Recipes Celebrating Our Rich Tradition of Home Cooking* provides tips on cooking a wide range of American favorites, from deviled eggs and stratas to game foods and pancakes. Writing in *Booklist* about *American Home Cooking,* Barbara Jacobs noted: "Is [it] . . . the definitive word on U.S. gastronomy? A case could be made." A *Publishers Weekly* contributor noted: "The Jamisons authoritatively articulate the pastiche of multicultural influences that characterize American regional cuisine, enabling readers to rediscover national (and regional) culinary treasures."

The Jamisons are big fans of outdoor cooking, which they address in several of their books, including *Born to Grill: An American Celebration.* The authors begin by instructing readers on the proper way to build and outdoor fire for grilling and then, along with their recipes, offer advice on the best condiments, many of them homemade. "Such meticulous attention to detail makes this a superior resource," wrote Mark Knoblauch in *Booklist*. A *Forbes* contributor simply stated: "This is it: the Bible of the [grill]." In another outdoor cookbook, titled *Smoke and Spice: The Joy of Real Backyard Barbecue*, the authors provide 300 barbecue recipes largely based on slow cooking over smoldering wood or other types of fires. Barbara Jacobs, writing in *Booklist*, noted that "no detail is too unimportant" for the authors.

In their 2002 book *A Real American Breakfast: The Best Meal of the Day, Any Time of the Day*, the Jamisons provide approximately three hundred breakfast recipes along with a colorful mix of photos and old-time restaurant menus. A *California Bookwatch* contributor called *A Real American Breakfast* "a lively, fun cookbook." Referring to the book as "immensely appealing," Judith Sutton wrote in *Booklist* that the book is "as much a social history as a cookbook."

BIOGRAPHICAL AND CRITICAL SOURCES:

PERIODICALS

Booklist, March 15, 1994, Barbara Jacobs, review of *Smoke and Spice: The Joy of Real Backyard Barbecue*, p. 1314; October 15, 1995, Barbara Jacobs, review of *The Border Cookbook: Authentic Home Cooking of the American Southwest and Northern Mexico*, p. 375; April 15, 1998, Mark Knoblauch, review of *Born to Grill: An American Celebration*, p. 1408; October 15, 1999, Barbara Jacobs, review of *American Home Cooking: 400 Spirited Recipes Celebrating Our Rich Traditions of Home Cooking*, p.14; May 1, 2000, Bill Ott and Brad Hooper, review of *The Insider's Guide to Santa Fe, Taos, and Albuquerque*, p. 1595.

California Bookwatch, October, 2006, review of *A Real American Breakfast: The Best Meal of the Day, Any Time of the Day*.

Forbes, May 4, 1998, review of *Born to Grill*, p. S140.

Inside MS, spring, 2001, Marsha Berman, review of *Born to Grill*, p. 48.

Library Journal, April 15, 1998, Judith C. Sutton, review of *Born to Grill*, p. 109; October 15, 1999, Judith C. Sutton, review of *American Home Cooking*, p. 98; February 15, 2002, Judith Sutton, review of *A Real American Breakfast*, p. 173.

New York Times Book Review, June 2, 2002, Dwight Garner, review of *A Real American Breakfast: The Best Meal of the Day, Any Time of the Day*, p. 6.

Publishers Weekly, August 21, 1995, review of *The Border Cookbook*, p. 62; April 1, 1996, review of *Sublime Smoke*, p. 71; March 2, 1998, review of *Born to Grill*, p. 63; August 2, 1999, review of *American Home Cooking*, p. 77; January 21, 2002, review of *A Real American Breakfast*, p. 83.

Texas Monthly, October, 1995, Patricia Sharpe, review of *The Border Cookbook*, p. 130.

Whole Earth, fall, 1998, Daphne Derven, review of *Born to Grill*, p. 111.

ONLINE

Cooking with the Jamisons, http://www.cookingwiththejamisons.com/ (April 5, 2007).

Global Gourmet, http://www.globalgourmet.com/ (April 5, 2007), "A Conversation with Cheryl Alters Jamison and Bill Jamison, Authors of *American Home Cooking*."*

*   *   *

JOHNS, Janetta
   See QUIN-HARKIN, Janet

*   *   *

JONES, Gareth Stedman 1942-

PERSONAL: Born December 17, 1942, in London, England; son of Lewis (a teacher) and J.O. Stedman Jones; children: two sons (one by Sally Alexander and one by Miri Rubin). *Education:* St. Paul's School, Lincoln College, Oxford, B.A. (with first class honors), 1964; Nuffield College, Oxford, D.Phil., 1970. *Politics:* Socialist. *Hobbies and other interests:* Country walks, collecting old books, cricket.

ADDRESSES: Home—Cambridge, England. *Office*—King's College, Cambridge CB2 1ST, England. *Agent*—Margaret Hanbury Literary Agency, 27 Walcot Square, London SE11 4UB, England. *E-mail*—gsj@kings.cam.ac.uk.

CAREER: Educator, historian and writer. Oxford University, Nuffield College, Oxford, England, research fellow, 1967-70; St. Antony's College, Oxford, senior associate member, 1971-72; Goethe University, Frankfurt, Germany, Humboldt Stiftung, 1973-74; King's College, Cambridge, England, fellow, 1976—; Cambridge University, Cambridge, university lecturer in history, 1979-86, reader in history of social thought, 1986-97, codirector of the Center for History and Economics, 1991—, professor of political science, 1997—. Visiting professor at several institutions, including University of California at Santa Cruz, 1982, Columbia University, New York, NY, 1986, Göttingen University, Germany, 1993, and Johns Hopkins University, Baltimore, MD, 1994. Senior research fellow at United Nations University World Institute for Development and Economic Research (UNU-WIDER), 1990-91; Directeur d'Etudes Associé at the Ecole des Hautes Etudes en Sciences Sociales, Paris, France, 1997; scholar in residence at the Centre for British Studies, University of California, Berkeley, 2005.

AWARDS, HONORS: Humboldt Award, West Germany, 1973-74.

WRITINGS:

Outcast London, Oxford University Press (Oxford, England), 1971.
(Editor, with Raphael Samuel) *Culture, Ideology, and Politics: Essays for Eric Hobabawn,* Routledge & Kegan Paul (Boston, MA), 1982.
Languages of Class: Studies in English Working Class History, Cambridge University Press (New York, NY), 1984.
(Editor, with David Feldman) *Metropolis, London: Histories and Representations since 1800,* Routledge (New York, NY), 1989.
(Editor, with Ian Patterson) Charles Fourier, *The Theory of Four Movements,* Cambridge University Press (New York, NY), 1996.
(Editor, with Alison Light and Sally Alexander) Raphael Samuel, *Island Stories: Unravelling Britain,* Verso (New York, NY), 1998.
(Author of introduction and notes) Karl Marx and Friedrich Engels, *The Communist Manifesto,* Penguin (New York, NY), 2002.
An End to Poverty? A Historical Debate, Columbia University Press (New York, NY), 2004.

Contributor of articles to periodicals, including *New Left Review, Modern Occasions, Times Literary Supplement, New Statesman,* and *History Workshop Journal.* Joint founder and joint editor of *History Workshop Journal,* 1976—.

SIDELIGHTS: Gareth Stedman Jones is a historian with a special interest in economics. In his book *An End to Poverty? A Historical Debate,* the author traces ideas surrounding globalization and poverty back two centuries to the French Revolution and follows the debate through to the beginning of the twentieth century and World War I. He considers how economic theorist Adam Smith and writers such as Thomas Paine thought and wrote about ending poverty. Stedman Jones also explores how certain Christian evangelicals and Malthusian theorists did not believe in the growing social idea that poverty could be eliminated and railed against social-aid programs that they believed would lead to over-breeding of the poor.

An End to Poverty? A Historical Debate has been widely praised by critics. "Jones offers a lucid, erudite exploration of a fertile topic in European intellectual history," wrote a *Publishers Weekly* contributor. Some reviewers also noted that the author's goal was to relate the past debate to current world problems concerning poverty. For example, David Feldman, writing in *History Today* noted: "Stedman Jones recommends that in the present we return to the republican legacy to combine commercial society with inclusive citizenship and greater equality." Commenting on the "moral" of Stedman Jones's book, Sheri Berman wrote in the *World Policy Journal:* "If Stedman Jones's tale in particular has anything to teach us, it is that moderate, 'social democratic' reforms have their best hope of success in a world that is peaceful and optimistic, where people are not scared by radical and destabilizing socioeconomic change (and therefore amenable to political extremism) and a belief in the 'commonality of mankind' and a commitment to the less fortunate is able to flourish."

BIOGRAPHICAL AND CRITICAL SOURCES:

PERIODICALS

Contemporary Review, December, 2004, review of *An End to Poverty? A Historical Debate,* p. 382.
History Today, December, 1998, review of *Island Stories: Unraveling Britain,* p. 56; August, 2005, David Feldman, review of *An End to Poverty?,* p. 56.
Kirkus Reviews, September 1, 2005, review of *An End to Poverty?,* p. 957.
Publishers Weekly, August 15, 2005, review of *An End to Poverty?,* p. 43.

World Policy Journal, spring, 2006, Sheri Berman, review of *An End to Poverty?,* p. 63.

ONLINE

Centre for History and Economics, King's College, University of Cambridge Web site, http://www-histecon.kings.cam.ac.uk/ (April 5, 2007), profile of Stedman Jones.

* * *

JONES, Matthew F. 1956-

PERSONAL: Born December 1, 1956, in Newton, MA; son of Charles W. and Ruth H. Jones; married Karen Shapero Jones; children: Reuben Isaih. *Education:* Hartwick College, B.A. (cum laude), 1977; Syracuse University School of Law, J.D. (magna cum laude), 1980. *Politics:* Independent. *Hobbies and other interests:* Running, swimming, cross country skiing, canoeing.

ADDRESSES: Home—Newton, MA. *Agent*—Suzanne Gluck, International Creative Management, 40 W. 57th St., New York, NY 10019.

CAREER: Writer. Lynchburg College, Lynchburg, VA, writer-in-residence, 1995; University of Virginia, Charlottesville, VA, workshop leader, 1996; Randolph-Macon Woman's College, Lynchburg, VA, writer-in-residence, 1997-98. Also practiced law.

WRITINGS:

NOVELS

The Cooter Farm, Hyperion (New York, NY), 1991.
The Elements of Hitting, Hyperion (New York, NY), 1994.
A Single Shot, Farrar, Straus (New York, NY), 1996.
Blind Pursuit, Farrar, Straus (New York, NY), 1997.
Deepwater, Bloomsbury (New York, NY), 1999.
Boot Tracks, Europa Editions (New York, NY), 2006.

ADAPTATIONS: Deepwater was adapted for film by David S. Marfield and released by Halcyon Entertainment, 2005.

SIDELIGHTS: Matthew F. Jones took an unusual road to his career as a writer. Jones, who grew up on a dairy farm in upstate New York, studied political science as an undergraduate and later earned a law degree with high honors. But Jones seemed predestined to become a novelist. While practicing as a lawyer, he was involved in an accident that nearly paralyzed him and made him realize what he wanted to do with his life. During his long year of recovery, never having taken a writing course, he wrote his first novel, the story of a dysfunctional family living on an upstate New York farm. Jones' work, which can be difficult to categorize from book to book, has been noted for its character-driven plotting, realism blended to a deep sense of spiritualism, uniqueness, and sharp eye for detail. Jones incorporates in his fiction elements of suspense, psychological intrigue, human conflict, suffering, absurdity, and the struggle between mankind's desire to do good against the obstacles in life that would lead him from it.

The Cooter Farm is narrated in the voice of ten-year-old Ollie Cooter, who desperately wishes for a normal family life. Ollie's father, Scooter, used to be a track star but has been reduced in later life to a hypochondriac who sells bull semen for a living. Scooter's malicious brother Hooter (nicknamed for his harsh laugh) runs the farm, as their father is senile and incapable of making decisions. Another brother, Looter (named for his propensity to steal), stays high on marijuana and dates women from a nearby commune. Hooter has been regularly raping his much younger sister, thirteen-year-old Mary Jean, who also lives at the farm. Through Mary Jean, Ollie becomes more aware of the evil that Hooter conceals. Mary Jean convinces Ollie that Hooter can only be stopped by enlisting The Power, a force that lives in a local abandoned house. When the children call upon The Power events backfire and present new and unimagined horrible possibilities.

Critics responded favorably to Jones' debut. Sharon Lloyd Stratton, writing in the *Richmond Times-Dispatch,* called *The Cooter Farm* "strong and memorable . . . a truly amazing first novel," while Michael Griffin, writing in the *Orlando Sentinel* applauded the naivete and the "heart" of the child narrator, comparing Jones' characters to those typical of a Charles Dickens novel. Curt Schleir, reviewing the book in the *Florida Times-Union,* hailed the novel as "the debut of a major new talent," as did *Library Journal* contributor Thomas L. Kilpatrick, who called Jones' debut "a bold first novel" and dubbed Jones "a bright young writer." *Entertainment Weekly* contributor Gene Lyons declared *The Cooter Farm* "an altogether remarkable debut," comparing the book to the work of Joyce Carol Oates and John Irving. *San Francisco Chronicle* critic Charles Shackett remarked that the novel is "so funny and fast reading that the seriousness of the conflicts sneaks up on the reader." Shackett concluded that the novel "is a fine debut for Matthew Jones."

In his 1994 novel *The Elements of Hitting,* Jones' protagonist is again the product of a dysfunctional and tormented family. Walter Innis is facing a mid-life crisis: his wife is leaving him and he cannot hold his job as a used car salesman. Walter's father, a former star baseball pitcher who injured his pitching arm throwing rocks at a sailboat while taking part in a foolish bet, is dying in a nursing home. Walter remembers family life becoming increasingly worse following his father's injury: his father drank and beat his mother, and his mother eventually had an affair with her rich employer Henry Truxton. Walter's mother was later found dead in a lake bordering the home of Truxton, a man now running for political office twenty years later. Believing that Truxton was responsible for his mother's death, Walter sets out with his best friend, a good-hearted but not exactly principled lawyer, to try and wreck his political campaign. Against all odds, circumstances occur that appear to alleviate Walter's miseries. He is approached by a former college sweetheart, Jeannie, who is trying unsuccessfully to coach her son's Little League team in his hometown. Even though he never excelled at the game, Walter, having learned baseball at the hands of his father, is an obvious choice for coach. Walter goes on to find possible love with Jeannie and to believe that life is not quite as hopeless as he believed.

According to Denney Clements, writing in the *Wichita Eagle,* Jones notably captures the absurd and painful aspects of life with this novel, even while sending the message that those with the courage to go on may find some meaning and hope in life. Griffin, writing again for the *Orlando Sentinel,* commented on Jones' skill at making the story "a baseball book that breaks the mold," while a *Kirkus Reviews* contributor declared: "Jones packs plenty of humor, pathos and plot into a story that literally ends with a bang." *Washington Post Book World* contributor Chris Bohjalian favorably assessed the novel, concluding: "At its core, is an often haunting and occasionally beautiful story of one man's attempt to rebuild his life with two strikes against him."

Suspense, murder, and human despair characterize Jones' third novel, *A Single Shot.* John Moon lives in a remote, upstate New York town, and he has been left by his wife and child and is simply trying to scratch out a living for himself by working odd jobs and hunting. Moon is poaching for deer one morning and is hot on the tracks of a wounded buck that he has been following for hours. The buck takes off in a different direction than expected, and when Moon hears a rustle in the woods, he fires. To his horror he finds he has killed a teenage girl. Later he discovers her belongings in a nearby cave, including 100,000 dollars in cash that he decides to keep to lure his wife and son back to his household. In the meantime he struggles with guilt and initially hides the body in his freezer. The money actually belongs to some malevolent individuals in town who come looking for Moon and instigate a final suspenseful showdown in the forest, where Moon is attempting to give the corpse a proper burial. The criminals cause plenty of chaos in the neighborhood, ransacking the home of Moon's best friend, who turns out to be involved in the underlying murder and robbery and later shoots himself in distress.

Daniel Woodrell, reviewing the book for the *Washington Post Book World,* remarked on the effectiveness of Jones' portrayal of Moon and the taut disintegration of Moon's psyche which occurs over the seven-day span of the novel, asserting that Jones "has in concocted a literary thriller of sorts, for the requisite mayhem and intrigue are present. But it is a satisfyingly dour and deterministic novel, the doom stacking scene by scene toward a startling, macabre, and inevitable result." *Philadelphia Enquirer* reviewer Michael Harrington remarked that "Jones is remarkably adept at detailing the way both nature and necessity turn against Moon. . . . Scenes of gruesomely detailed violence alternate with exquisitely described natural beauty." A contributor to *Publishers Weekly* called the book "gritty and claustrophobic," and characterized it as being written with "great economy, surprising pathos, and a keen sense of the grotesque." In a *New York Times* review, Christopher Lehmann-Haupt assessed the novel as a "harrowing literary thriller," and commented that "Mr. Jones . . . has created in a powerful blend of love and violence, of the grotesque and the tender."

Jones continued writing in the suspense thriller genre with *Blind Pursuit.* In this 1997 novel, the daughter of a yuppy couple living in a wealthy exurb of Albany, New York, is abducted. A police investigation later leads the parents to suspect their neighbors, a respected couple with whom they attend church. As Jones unearths the mystery and motivations behind the deep secrets of some of these characters, it turns out that the suspect raped and murdered his own daughter and that his wife knew about and concealed his crime. The author also explores the parents' guilt as they agonize over not spending enough time with their daughter and leaving her with a nanny whose background they had not extensively checked into. A reviewer from the *San Francisco Chronicle* called the book a riveting effort propelled by "sadistic yet mesmerizing energy." Susan Salter Reynolds, writing in the *Los Angeles Times,* offered high praise for Jones' literary talent, asserting that *Blind Pursuit* is "a smorgasbord of agonies, and Jones cuts deeply, acutely, into each one of them." Reynolds further praised Jones' characterizations, asserting that this "author is so attentive to voice, to every wavering indecision, that the dialogue at times reads like a taped transcription. At first, this is frustrating, but then, like eyes adjusting to darkness, your hearing registers the precision of this method." *Booklist* contributor David Pitt felt that the abductor's identity was the least of many surprises in the novel and called *Blind Pursuit* "an extremely well constructed (and sometimes quite moving) mystery," while a *Kirkus Reviews* contributor observed that the novel contains "relentless, lean-and-mean page-turner plotting and a grimly satisfying ending."

A fifth novel by Jones, *Deepwater,* appeared in 1999 and was adapted for film in 2005. As the novel opens, a young drifter by the name of Nat Banyon finds himself in the rural town of Deepwater and is soon hired by an older man, Herman Finch, to paint the hotel Finch operates. As a contributor to *Publishers Weekly* remarked, the novel soon becomes "an inspired tale of suspicious strangers, a secret love affair and one man's slide into madness." Banyon is attracted to Finch's alluring young wife, Iris, and the two soon begin a love affair. Meanwhile, Banyon's relationship with Finch also develops, according to a review by Bob Lunn in *Library Journal,* into "a complicated bond that is equal parts antagonism and friendship, suspicion and fear." Finch seems to have a sinister hold over the Deepwater community and Banyon experiences a deepening sense of alarm as he notices uncanny similarities between his own physical appearance and old photographs of Finch and of Finch's seeming omnipotence. A contributor to *Publishers Weekly* commented that the tale was "told exceedingly well" and added Jones "creates tension with remarkable economy and intricacy in a sinister narra-

tive that ultimately reveals itself as a powerful expression of loneliness, dangerous passions and the quest for identity." *Booklist* Bill Ott wrote that despite a conventional opening, "in the hands of a writer who knows how to wring the sex out of a hot night, we're just as compelled as poor Nat to keep going in the wrong direction. Jones varies the formula just enough by giving the wrong guy a full-dress personality and forging an almost spiritual link between hunter and hunted."

After a break from writing novels, Jones published *Boot Tracks* in 2006. Charlie Rankin is free after a four-year jail term for stealing forty-some dollars and a few candy bars from a hospital vending machine. He is not free, however, to move on with his life. With a sense of obligation to his jail mate and protector, nicknamed "The Buddha," Rankin is ordered to kill a man for him out of vengeance. In the process he couples with ex-porn star LuAnn and a relationship develops. Rankin's own sanity begins to crumble as he struggles with his loyalty to "The Buddha" and his off-center sense of morality.

Reviews for *Boot Tracks* were mostly positive. Writing in *Booklist,* Ott noted that the ex-con just out of prison was not a new premise, but that "Jones does it proud in this powerful tale." Hannah Tucker, reviewing the book in *Entertainment Weekly,* called the book "a brooding character study of a man who's morally compromised." A contributor to *Kirkus Reviews* called the book "dark but illuminating novel," and stated that it is "a nightmare thriller with the power to haunt."

Jones once told *CA:* "The world, I would say, doesn't necessarily accept people with open arms. It puts up obstacles. Indifferently challenges people to get around them. I find, in my writing, very few universal truths, only individuals trying to survive as best they can with whatever tools God has granted them."

BIOGRAPHICAL AND CRITICAL SOURCES:

BOOKS

Writers Directory, 22nd edition, St. James Press (Detroit, MI), 2006.

PERIODICALS

American Libraries, April, 1996, review of *A Single Shot,* p. 74.

Armchair Detective, fall, 1996, review of *A Single Shot,* p. 503.

Booklist, October 15, 1991, review of *The Cooter Farm,* p. 408; March 15, 1994, Bill Ott, review of *The Elements of Hitting,* p. 1327; April 1, 1996, Mary Ellen Quinn, review of *A Single Shot,* p. 1343; June 1, 1997, David Pitt, review of *Blind Pursuit,* p. 1666; August, 1999, Bill Ott, review of *Deepwater,* p. 2034; June 1, 2006, Bill Ott, review of *Boot Tracks,* p. 43.

Bookwatch, July, 2006, review of *Boot Tracks.*

Chicago Tribune, June 8, 1997, review of *Blind Pursuit,* p. 6.

Drood Review of Mystery, September, 2000, review of *Deepwater,* p. 17.

Entertainment Weekly, January 31, 1992, Gene Lyons, review of *The Cooter Farm,* p. 52; July 11, 1997, Alexandra Jacobs, review of *A Single Shot,* p. 60; May 26, 2006, Hannah Tucker, review of *Boot Tracks,* p. 111.

Florida Times-Union, January 26, 1992, Curt Schleir, review of *The Cooter Farm.*

Kirkus Reviews, November 1, 1991, review of *The Cooter Farm,* p. 1365; February 15, 1994, review of *The Elements of Hitting,* p. 164; February 1, 1996, review of *A Single Shot,* p. 162; March 15, 1997, review of *Blind Pursuit,* p. 407; September 1, 1999, review of *Deepwater,* p. 1333; April 1, 2006, review of *Boot Tracks,* p. 314.

Kliatt, November, 1997, review of *A Single Shot,* p. 8.

Library Journal, January, 1992, Thomas L. Kilpatrick, review of *The Cooter Farm,* p. 175; April 1, 1996, Darryl Dean James, review of *A Single Shot,* p. 117; April 15, 1997, Mark Annichiarico, review of *Blind Pursuit,* p. 118; November 1, 1999, Bob Lunn, review of *Deepwater,* p. 124.

Los Angeles Times, January 19, 1992, review of *The Cooter Farm,* p. 6; May 12, 1996, review of *A Single Shot,* p. 10; July, 1996; August 10, 1997, Susan Salter Reynold, review of *Blind Pursuit,* p. 2.

New York Times, April 22, 1996, Christopher Lehmann-Haupt, review of *A Single Shot,* p. B2.

New York Times Book Review, April 10, 1994, Diane Cole, review of *The Elements of Hitting,* p. 24; July 13, 1997, Frederick Busch, review of *Blind Pursuit,* p. 16; November 21, 1999, David L. Ulin, review of *Deepwater,* p. 74.

Orlando Sentinel, January 26, 1992, Michael Griffin, review of *The Cooter Farm;* April 24, 1994, Michael Griffin, review of *The Elements of Hitting.*

People, August 12, 1996, Pam Lambert, review of *A Single Shot,* p. 32.

Philadelphia Enquirer, August 10, 1997, Michael Harrington, review of *A Single Shot.*

Publishers Weekly, November 1, 1991, review of *The Cooter Farm,* p. 74; February 21, 1994, review of *The Elements of Hitting,* p. 234; April 14, 1997, review of *A Single Shot,* p. 72; May 12, 1997, review of *Blind Pursuit,* p. 60; August 9, 1999, review of *Deepwater,* p. 339.

Richmond Times-Dispatch, March 1, 1992, Sharon Lloyd Stratton, review of *The Cooter Farm.*

San Francisco Chronicle, June 14, 1992, Charles Shackett, review of *The Cooter Farm,* p. 7; October 3, 1997, review of *Blind Pursuit.*

Virginia Quarterly Review, winter, 1995, review of *The Elements of Hitting,* p. 23; winter, 1998, review of *Blind Pursuit,* p. 24.

Washington Post Book World, May 16, 1994, Chris Bohjalian, review of *The Elements of Hitting;* July 7, 1996, Daniel Woodrell, review of *A Single Shot,* p. 6.

Wichita Eagle, April 3, 1994, Denney Clements, review of *The Elements of Hitting.*

ONLINE

Internet Movie Database, http://www.imdb.com/ (March 4, 2007), author profile.*

K

KALFUS, Ken 1954-

PERSONAL: Born April 9, 1954, in Bronx, NY; son of Martin (a businessman) and Ida Kalfus; married Inga Saffron (a journalist), May 2, 1991; children: Sky. *Education:* Attended Sarah Lawrence College, 1972-74, and New York University, 1974-76.

CAREER: Journalist and author, 1990—.

AWARDS, HONORS: National Book Award nomination, 2006, for *A Disorder Peculiar to the Country.*

WRITINGS:

(Editor and author of introduction) Christopher Morley, *Christopher Morley's Philadelphia,* illustrated by Walter Jack Duncan and Frank H. Taylor, Fordham University Press (Bronx, NY), 1990.
Thirst (stories), Milkweed Editions (Minneapolis, MN), 1998.
Pu-239 and Other Russian Fantasies (stories), Milkweed Editions (Minneapolis, MN), 1999.
The Commissariat of Enlightenment: A Novel, Ecco (New York, NY), 2003.
A Disorder Peculiar to the Country: A Novel, Ecco (New York, NY), 2006.

SIDELIGHTS: Journalist Ken Kalfus grew up in Long Island, New York, but has lived around the world in locations as diverse as Belgrade, Dublin, and Moscow. Accordingly, his debut collection of short stories, titled *Thirst,* offers an eclectic and varied treat for the reader,

according to several reviewers. Kalfus was contacted by Milkweed Editions when an editor there read Kalfus's writing in *Harper's.* In response to the editor's request, Kalfus submitted several stories, and the editor's choices were published in book form. According to critic Mary Ann Grossmann of the *St. Paul Pioneer Press,* the author's stories reflect his international experiences. *Voice Literary Supplement* critic Dwight Garner commented on the author's outlook, concluding that Kalfus is the "rare writer whose travels haven't colored his prose with cosmopolitan cynicism." Garner compared Kalfus to Hemingway in his ability to "let moments speak for themselves."

Thirst, according to Grossmann, contains the common themes of human dislocation and situational uncertainty. Kalfus admits that uncertainty is central to both his writing style and personal outlook. Grossmann joined other critics in finding the theme of uncertainty particularly effective in the short story "A Line Is a Series of Points." The story allows readers a glimpse into the psyche of refugees who have been homeless for so long that wandering has become a way of life; it is based on Kalfus's observations of Muslim refugees who had been forced out of a Bosnian village by Serbs. Kalfus was struck by the sense of denationalization that he observed, and the sense that such people could have "come from anywhere."

A *Publishers Weekly* reviewer praised *Thirst* for being "skilled and versatile" and for alternating between "postmodern playfulness and darker realism." This reviewer liked the daring aspect of some of the stories, as well as the element of surprise in the collection. Among the stories are "Cats in Space," which features suburban teenagers who set a cat adrift in a hot air balloon and later rescue the animal; "Night and Day You Are the One," which features a sleep-deprived character who walks back and forth between two different worlds in the same city; the title story, which finds an Irish au pair and a Moroccan student becoming romantically involved in Paris; and "The Joy and Melancholy Baseball Trivia Quiz," which suggests deeper meanings behind sports statistics.

Applauding Kalfus for subtly showing the reader that "sometimes the really significant truths are those found closest to home," Garner called *Thirst* the most effective debut book he had seen in a year. James Held of the *Philadelphia Inquirer* advised the reader to "unexpect the expected," and gave the author credit for capturing the humor inherent in our pursuits of deeper questions, such as "knowing and being." Ron Carlson, writing in the *New York Times Book Review,* described Kalfus's style as one where the reader is never completely comfortable and the stories are laced with "fundamental strangeness."

After living in Russia for four years, Kalfus published a second collection of five short stories and one novella titled *Pu-239 and Other Russian Fantasies.* The stories in this collection take place in Russia at various times between Joseph Stalin's regime and the present. "What is most wonderful about the variety of these stories is Kalfus's restraint," commented *Review of Contemporary Fiction* contributor Paul Maliszewski. "While Kalfus is an American author, this is not Russia as seen through American eyes," Maliszewski continued. Similarly, Paul Richardson wrote in *Russian Life:* "It is exceptionally difficult for a foreigner to write fiction about Russia and get it right. Ken Kalfus gets it right. Again and again." In the book's title story, readers meet Timofey, a nuclear engineer who learns that he has absorbed fatal amounts of radiation. In an effort to leave his family with some means of support after he dies, Timofey attempts to sell weapons-grade plutonium on the black market. His clientele, however, ignorantly assume that the powder he offers is an illicit drug. In "Anzhelika 13," a young girl begins menstruating on the day of Joseph Stalin's death and associates the biological event with Russia's mourning.

"Kalfus shows a striking talent for transcultural understanding, and for depicting the very strange," noted a *Publishers Weekly* contributor in a review of *Pu-239 and Other Russian Fantasies.* "Kalfus is a rare writer of fiction whose passages of description feel like action," wrote Laura Miller for *Salon.com.* "It's as if he were injecting his readers with a serum that renders them, in a rush, intimately familiar with the texture of the Russian experience," Miller acknowledged. "Hopefully, it won't be long before readers see a novel from this master storyteller," remarked Veronica Scrol in *Booklist,* and upon hearing of the pending publication of Kalfus's first novel, Miller wrote: "Ah, something at last to look forward to in the next millennium."

The Commissariat of Enlightenment: A Novel begins in pre-revolutionary Russia in the year 1910. Eminent author Leo Tolstoy is dying in a railway station in the small Russian town of Astapavo. Nikolai Grisbin, a young and ambitious cinematographer for a French newsreel company, joins the throng of media that congregate in the tiny town in hopes of capturing on film Tolstoy's last moments on Earth. On the way to Astapavo, Grisbin meets Professor Vorobev, a scientist and embalmer who wishes to embalm Tolstoy's body with his self-proclaimed revolutionary preservation skills, to which he attests by presenting a preserved rat. While in Astapavo, Grisbin meets revolutionary communists Joseph Stalin and Vladimir Lenin. Stalin, who is quietly collecting political allies, convinces Grisbin to use his cinematic skills for propaganda purposes. After the revolution and Lenin's rise to power, in the year 1919, Grisbin changes his name to Astapov and goes to work for the Commissariat of Enlightenment, a Russian agency dealing in political propaganda. Here Grisbin truly realizes the dark power of film as he takes part in manipulating and controlling images and stories, ultimately determining what will become Russia's political history. When Lenin is close to death, Professor Vorobev is called on to preserve his body. The novel ends at the collapse of the Soviet Union.

"Told in supple, witty prose, the story exhibits all the vigorous intelligence and vision readers have come to expect from Kalfus," stated a *Publishers Weekly* reviewer of *The Commissariat of Enlightenment.* "It's not moral complexity or clashes of opinion that interest Ken Kalfus, but the driving force of single ideas, the questioning, gives a relentless impetus to the narrative that makes this novel compelling to read," remarked Barry Unsworth in the *New York Times Book Review.* Unsworth continued: "Some scenes of action and description are realized so vividly that they almost have the force of hallucination." In the *Houston Chronicle,* Evan Miles Williamson revealed one of the novel's problems: "Rather than let the reader draw conclusions from the events being dramatized, Kalfus repeatedly clubs readers over the head with his thesis: History is manipulable, and our culture is controlled by the propaganda machines of the media." Summing up popular opinion of the book, and making the prevalent comparison of Kalfus to revered Russian writer Nikolai Gogol, a *Kirkus Reviews* contributor called the book "a brilliant fusion of satire, science fiction, and political commentary," adding, "Gogol is probably tearing his hair out, wishing he'd dreamed this up." Remarking on his development as a writer since the publication of *Thirst,* Kalfus revealed to Garner in a *Salon.com* interview, "I certainly felt that when I was writing those stories that aiming for spareness in my work was a way of avoiding screwing it up with things that weren't relevant. I think my style has become a bit more lush. I think I'm more confident."

The theme that runs through *A Disorder Peculiar to the Country: A Novel* is hate, represented by how hate is expressed by Joyce and Marshall Harriman toward each other. Headed for divorce, both are elated on September 11, 2001—she because his office is high in the south tower of the World Trade Center, and he because he thinks she is on Flight 93. Neither have died, however, and they live through a volatile year before their divorce is finalized. *Washington Post* reviewer Jonathan Yardley commented: "Marriage as metaphor for larger conflict is scarcely new, but Ken Kalfus has put a new and singularly imaginative twist on it." Elizabeth Kiem wrote in a review for the *San Francisco Chronicle Online* that this story "juxtaposes New York's anxiety in the months after the disaster with the downward spiral of a disintegrating marriage. It's an analogy that asserts itself bluntly and relentlessly."

BIOGRAPHICAL AND CRITICAL SOURCES:

PERIODICALS

Bloomsbury Review, September, 1999, review of *Pu-239 and Other Russian Fantasies,* p. 13.

Book, March-April, 2003, Beth Kephart, review of *The Commissariat of Enlightenment: A Novel,* pp. 78-79.

Booklist, August, 1999, Veronica Scrol, review of *Pu-239 and Other Russian Fantasies,* p. 2027; January 1, 2003, review of *The Commissariat of Enlightenment,* pp. 847-848; June 1, 2006, Frank Caso, review of *A Disorder Peculiar to the Country: A Novel,* p. 37.

Choice, March, 1999, review of *Thirst,* p. 1266.

Entertainment Weekly, February 14, 2003, review of *The Commissariat of Enlightenment,* p. 76.

Esquire, November, 1999, *Pu-239 and Other Russian Fantasies,* p. 82.

Harper's, February, 2003, John Leonard, review of *The Commissariat of Enlightenment,* pp. 67-68.

Hungry Mind Review, fall, 1999, review of *Pu-239 and Other Russian Fantasies,* p. 32.

Kirkus Reviews, July 15, 1999, review of *Pu-239 and Other Russian Fantasies,* p. 1074; December 1, 2002, review of *The Commissariat of Enlightenment,* p. 1720; May 1, 2006, review of *A Disorder Peculiar to the Country,* p. 429.

Library Journal, August, 1999, Jim Dwyer, review of *Pu-239 and Other Russian Fantasies,* p. 144; June 1, 2006, Joshua Cohen, review of *A Disorder Peculiar to the Country,* p. 108.

New Statesman, August 21, 2006, Natasha Tripney, review of *A Disorder Peculiar to the Country,* p. 51.

New York, July 17, 2006, Daniel Asa Rose, review of *A Disorder Peculiar to the Country,* p. 64.

New Yorker, November 22, 1999, review of *Pu-239 and Other Russian Fantasies,* p. 202; August 7, 2006, review of *A Disorder Peculiar to the Country,* p. 89.

New York Times Book Review, July 26, 1998, Ron Carlons, review of *Thirst,* p. 9; September 26, 1999, review of *Pu-239 and Other Russian Fantasies,* p. 10; October 3, 1999, review of *Thirst,* p. 104; December 5, 1999, reviews of *Pu-239 and Other Russian Fantasies,* p. 77, and *Thirst,* p. 105; February 2, 2003, Barry Unsworth, review of *The Commissariat of Enlightenment.*

Philadelphia Inquirer, June 28, 1998, James Held, review of *Thirst.*

Publishers Weekly, April 27, 1998, review of *Thirst,* p. 45; July 12, 1999, review of *Pu-239 and Other Russian Fantasies,* p. 72; January 6, 2003, review of *The Commissariat of Enlightenment,* p. 37; April 3, 2006, review of *A Disorder Peculiar to the Country,* p. 34.

Review of Contemporary Fiction, spring, 2000, Paul Maliszewski, review of *Pu-239 and Other Russian Fantasies,* p. 183; summer, 2003, Tim Feeney, review of *The Commissariat of Enlightenment,* p. 138.

Russian Life, January, 2000, Paul Richardson, review of *Pu-239 and Other Russian Fantasies,* p. 58.

St. Paul Pioneer Press, August 30, 1998, Mary Ann Grosmann, review of *Thirst.*

Times Literary Supplement, July 9, 1999, review of *Thirst,* p. 23.

Voice Literary Supplement, June, 1998, Dwight Garner, review of *Thirst,* pp. 73-74.

Washington Post, August 1, 2006, Jonathan Yardley, review of *A Disorder Peculiar to the Country,* p. C3.

Yale Review, October, 2001, review of *Pu-239 and Other Russian Fantasies,* p. 129.

ONLINE

Houston Chronicle Online, http://www.chron.com/ (March 23, 2003), Eric Miles Williamson, review of *The Commissariat of Enlightenment.*

Mostly Fiction, http://mostlyfiction.com/ (December 27, 2006), Mary Whipple, review of *The Commissariat of Enlightenment.*

Philadelphia Inquirer Online, http://www.philly.com/ (November 14, 2006), Bruce E. Beans, review of *A Disorder Peculiar to the Country.*

PIF, http://www.pifmagazine.com/ (December 27, 2006), Ryan Boudinot, "Interview with Ken Kalfus."

Salon.com, http://www.salon.com/ (December 27, 2006), Laura Miller, review of *Pu-239 and Other Russian Fantasies,* Dwight Garner, "The Salon Interview: Ken Kalfus."

San Francisco Chronicle Online, http://sfgate.com/ (July 21, 2006), Elizabeth Kiem, review of *A Disorder Peculiar to the Country.*

Seattle Times Online, http://seattletimes.nwsource.com/ (December 27, 2006), Mark Lindquist, review of *A Disorder Peculiar to the Country.*

SignOnSanDiego.com, http://www.signonsandiego.com/ (July 23, 2006), Gordon Hauptfleisch, review of *A Disorder Peculiar to the Country.*

Stranger Online, http://www.thestranger.com/ (December 27, 2006), Evan Sult, review of *Pu-239 and Other Russian Fantasies.**

*   *   *

KARLEN, Neal 1959-
(Neal Stuart Karlen)

PERSONAL: Born June 25, 1959, in Minneapolis, MN; son of Markle and Charlotte Hope Karlen. *Education:* Brown University, B.A. (magna cum laude), 1982. *Religion:* Jewish.

ADDRESSES: E-mail—neal@nealkarlen.com.

CAREER: Newsweek, New York, NY, staff writer and reporter, 1982-86; *Rolling Stone,* New York, staff writer, 1986-90; *New York Times,* New York, staff writer, 1990—. *America Tonight* and *Off Tenth,* Columbia Broadcasting System, New York, on-air essayist; British Broadcasting Corporation, documentary correspondent. University of Minnesota School of Journalism and Mass Communications, instructor of writing and magazine production, 1997-2005.

MEMBER: Phi Beta Kappa.

AWARDS, HONORS: American Historical Society prize, Brown University, 1982; Minnesota State Arts Board grant for nonfiction writing, 1991.

WRITINGS:

The Emperor's New Clothes (libretto), produced in 1990.

(With Henny Youngman) *Take My Life, Please,* William Morrow (New York, NY), 1991.

Babes in Toyland: The Making and Selling of a Rock and Roll Band, Times Books (New York, NY), 1994.

(With Nanci Donnellan) *The Babe in Boyland: The Fabulous Sports Babe,* ReganBooks (New York, NY), 1996.

(With Jenny McCarthy) *Jen-X: Jenny McCarthy's Open Book,* ReganBooks (New York, NY), 1997.

Slouching toward Fargo: A Two-Year Saga of Sinners and St. Paul Saints at the Bottom of the Bush Leagues with Bill Murray, Darryl Strawberry, Dakota Sadie, and Me, ReganBooks (New York, NY), 1999.

Shanda: The Making and Breaking of a Self-Loathing Jew (memoir), Simon & Schuster (New York, NY), 2004.

Contributor to anthologies, including *The Complete Armchair Book of Baseball,* Scribner, 1997, and *Fishing with Fathers,* Penguin, 2005. Contributor to periodicals, including the *New York Times, Washington Post, Esquire, GQ,* and *Spy.* Columnist for the *Minneapolis-St. Paul Magazine,* 1990—.

SIDELIGHTS: With *Babes in Toyland: The Making and Selling of a Rock and Roll Band,* former *Rolling Stone* writer Neal Karlen looks at the rise of Babes in Toyland, one of the few successful all-female "grunge" rock bands. "Digging beneath the hardcore surface of this alternative scene," explained *Rolling Stone* writer Matt Damsker, "he unearths the fragile egos of musicians who sleep together in single hotel rooms, play on borrowed equipment and scrape together cash and emotional capital—against all odds of making it." "Karlen is sometimes more interested in his subjects' reputation than in their talent," declared a *Kirkus Reviews* critic, "so the content of their music gets scant attention." He also documents the struggle of their agent Tim Carr, who made a place for them at Warner Music—a major recording label—and then set out to make them famous quickly. By the time they joined the 1993 Lollapalooza tour, explained Karlen in a *Mademoiselle* article, the three members of Babes in Toyland—Kat Bjelland, Lori Barbero, and Maureen Herman—"hadn't even yet processed that Beavis and Butt-Head, the animated nitwits of MTV's top-rated show, had just screened their video and given the band their highest on-air recommendation: 'They're *cool!* These girls *rock!*'"

However, some reviewers argued that Karlen's portrayal of the rise of the band Babes in Toyland at times appears to be the story of its fall as well. "Though Karlen is clearly a fan of the band," stated *New York* magazine reviewer Walter Kirn, "his account of the tedious, idiotic hoo-ha surrounding its rise to fame is depressing." Throughout the recording of their first album for Warner, *Fontanelle*, Damsker explained, "Babes in Toyland frittered away expensive studio time, weathering a brief breakup and near-constant emotional breakdowns." The band's original bassist, Michelle Leon, left the band after her boyfriend's death. Bjelland feuded with Courtney Love, a former friend and leader of the grunge band Hole, and she married (and later divorced) an Australian punk rocker named Stuart Spasm. "Karlen's hyperrhetoric sometimes intrudes," concluded the *Kirkus Reviews* critic, "but he isn't oblivious to the ironies in Warner's effort to sell the Babes without sacrificing their street credibility."

Slouching toward Fargo: A Two-Year Saga of Sinners and St. Paul Saints at the Bottom of the Bush Leagues with Bill Murray, Darryl Strawberry, Dakota Sadie, and Me is the result of an assignment for *Rolling Stone*, the purpose of which was to dig up dirt on the St. Paul Saints, and particularly on its owner, Bill Murray. But Karlen had difficulty writing negatively about the team, its management, and the players, who included Darryl Strawberry, tainted by drug and tax problems but who was signed and gave new life to the team. Other characters who receive warm praise are president and promotor Mike Veek and player J.D. Drew. A *Publishers Weekly* contributor wrote: "Readers not acquainted with the independent leagues will appreciate the portrayal of life on baseball's back roads."

The word "shanda" in Yiddish means disgrace or shame, and in his memoir, *Shanda: The Making and Breaking of a Self-Loathing Jew,* Karlen writes of his participation in, rejection of, and reacceptance of his religion. Karlen was born to an Orthodox Jewish family and planned on becoming a rabbi, but his rejection included making fun of his Jewishness and telling Jewish jokes on stage. He reversed his attitude after meeting and studying with Hasidic rabbi Manis Friedman, who taught him the true meaning of his faith. A *Kirkus Reviews* contributor wrote that "the descriptions of their visits serve as a model for person-to-person transmission of a faith and culture."

BIOGRAPHICAL AND CRITICAL SOURCES:

BOOKS

Karlen, Neal, *Shanda: The Making and Breaking of a Self-Loathing Jew,* Simon & Schuster, 2004.

PERIODICALS

Entertainment Weekly, November 15, 1996, Kate Meyers, review of *The Babe in Boyland: The Fabulous Sports Babe,* p. 66.
Kirkus Reviews, May 15, 1994, review of *Babes in Toyland: The Making and Selling of a Rock and Roll Band,* p. 686.
Library Journal, June 1, 1999, Paul M. Kaplan, review of *Slouching toward Fargo: A Two-Year Saga of Sinners and St. Paul Saints at the Bottom of the Bush Leagues with Bill Murray, Darryl Strawberry, Dakota Sadie, and Me,* p. 124; September 15, 2004, Stephen Joseph, review of *Shanda: The Making and Breaking of a Self-Loathing Jew,* p. 63.
Mademoiselle, October, 1993, interview, pp. 180-184, 221-222.
Newsweek, September 20, 2004, Marc Peyser, "A Bacon Sandwich Was Just the Beginning: A Fast Chat with Neal Karlen," p. 9.
New York, August 22, 1994, Walter Kirn, review of *Babes in Toyland,* p. 47.

Publishers Weekly, March 29, 1999, review of *Slouching toward Fargo,* p. 77; August 16, 2004, review of *Shanda,* p. 60.

Rolling Stone, October 6, 1994, Matt Damsker, review of *Babes in Toyland,* p. 37.

ONLINE

Jewish Daily Forward Online, http://www.forward.com/ (October 29, 2004), Lev Raphael, review of *Shanda.*

Neal Karlen Home Page, http://www.nealkarlen.com (December 27, 2006).*

*   *   *

KARLEN, Neal Stuart
  See KARLEN, Neal

*   *   *

KASICH, John R. 1952-

PERSONAL: Surname rhymes with "basic"; born May 13, 1952, in McKees Rocks, PA; son of John (a mail carrier) and Anne (a homemaker) Kasich; married Mary Lee Griffith (divorced); married Karen Waldbillig (a communications consultant), March 22, 1997; children: (second marriage) Emma, Reese (twin daughters). *Education:* Ohio State University, B.A., 1974. *Politics:* Republican. *Religion:* Christian. *Hobbies and other interests:* Reading, golf, travel.

ADDRESSES: Home—Westerville, OH. *Office*—Lehman Brothers Holding, Inc., 745 7th Ave., New York, NY 10019.

CAREER: Politician, news commentator. Ohio State Senate, Columbus, OH, administrative assistant, 1975-77, state senator, 1979-82; United States House of Representatives, Washington, DC, Republican representative from Ohio's Twelfth District, 1983-2001, chair of the budget committee, member of the national security committee; Lehman Brothers Holding, Inc., New York, NY, managing director of investment banking division, 2001—. *Heartland with John Kasich,* Fox News, host, 2001—. Guest on television programs, including *Larry*

King Live, CNN; *Meet the Press,* NBC; and *60 Minutes,* CBS; *The O'Reilly Factor,* Fox News, guest host. Serves on the board of advisors of the Washington Legal Foundation

AWARDS, HONORS: Named "one of the most fascinating men in politics," *George* magazine, 1997; named as one of the "one hundred people for the next century," *Newsweek,* 1997.

WRITINGS:

Courage Is Contagious: Ordinary People Doing Extraordinary Things to Change the Face of America, Doubleday (New York, NY), 1998.

Stand for Something: The Battle for America's Soul, Warner Books (New York, NY), 2006.

Author and coauthor of government reports.

ADAPTATIONS: Stand for Something was adapted for audio (three CDs), Time Warner AudioBooks, 2006.

SIDELIGHTS: Former United States Representative John R. Kasich, a Republican elected from Ohio's Twelfth District in the early 1980s, built a political reputation as a fiscal conservative at a time of intense debate over matters of taxes and spending. Increasingly visible and influential as a member of the national security committee and the chair of the house budget committee, the nine-term congressman became a national spokesperson for conservative values. He wrote *Courage Is Contagious: Ordinary People Doing Extraordinary Things to Change the Face of America,* a book profiling Americans who exemplify self-reliance and civic responsibility.

In information published on his former House of Representatives Web site, Kasich defined himself as a compassionate but hard-headed reformer. He cited his work on the Balanced Budget Act of 1997 and welfare reform measures as prime achievements that he hoped would relieve American citizens of heavy tax burdens while promoting more fair spending policies. He stressed his commitment to ending corporate welfare, government tax breaks to businesses, and excessive defense spending.

Kasich's view is that solutions will come from communities and families, rather than from Washington. This is the theme of his *Courage Is Contagious.* The book profiles Americans whom Kasich considers heroic because of their volunteer activities. These people include Amber Coffman, a teenager who created a program to distribute sandwiches to homeless people, and Albert Lexie, a shoeshiner at Pittsburgh's Children's Hospital who, over a period of twenty years, donated thousands of dollars of his tips to the hospital.

Upon leaving Congress, Kasich took a position with Lehman Brothers and also appeared as host of the television program *Heartland with John Kasich* for Fox News. In his second book, *Stand for Something: The Battle for America's Soul,* Kasich expresses his opinion that core values, including "honesty, integrity, personal responsibility, faith, humility, accountability, compassion, [and] forgiveness," must be renewed in order to repair America. *Booklist* contributor Vanessa Bush wrote that Kasich "is certain to provoke speculation about future campaign ambitions with this book."

BIOGRAPHICAL AND CRITICAL SOURCES:

PERIODICALS

Booklist, March 15, 2006, Vanessa Bush, review of *Stand for Something: The Battle for America's Soul,* p. 9.

Cincinnati Post, February 16, 1999, James Lileks, review of *Courage Is Contagious: Ordinary People Doing Extraordinary Things to Change the Face of America,* p. 10A.

Publishers Weekly, March 13, 2006, review of *Stand for Something,* p. 56.

Reference & Research Book News, August, 2006, review of *Stand for Something.*

OTHER

John Kasich Home Page, http://www.johnkasich.com (December 28, 2006).*

*   *   *

KELLOGG, Steven 1941-
    (Steven Castle Kellogg)

PERSONAL: Born October 26, 1941, in Norwalk, CT; son of Robert E. and Hilma Marie Kellogg; married Helen Hill, 1967; children: (stepchildren) Pamela, Melanie, Kimberly, Laurie, Kevin, Colin. *Education:* Rhode Island School of Design, B.F.A., 1963; graduate study at American University.

ADDRESSES: Home—P.O. Box 280, Essex, NY 12936.

CAREER: Author and illustrator of children's books; artist. American University, Washington, DC, instructor in etching, 1966; has also taught printmaking and painting. *Exhibitions:* Works exhibited at American Institute of Graphic Arts Book Show, Children's Book Showcase, and at Bologna International Children's Book Fair.

AWARDS, HONORS: Dutch Zilveren Griffel, 1974, for *Can I Keep Him?;* Christopher Award, 1976, for *How the Witch Got Alf;* Irma Simonton Black Award, Bank Street College of Education, 1978, for *The Mysterious Tadpole;* American Book Award finalist, 1980, and Georgia Children's Picture Storybook Award, University of Georgia College of Education, and Little Archer Award, University of Wisconsin-Oshkosh Department of Library Services, both 1982, all for *Pinkerton, Behave!;* Parents' Choice Award, Parents' Choice Foundation, 1982, for *Tallyho, Pinkerton!,* and 1986, for *Best Friends;* Michigan Young Reader's Award, Michigan Council of Teachers of English, 1983, for *The Island of the Skog;* Boston Globe/Horn Book Illustration Award Honor Book, 1985, and Utah Children's Informational, and Young Adult's Book Award, 1988, both for *How Much Is a Million?* by David M. Schwartz; David McCord Children's Literature citation, Framingham (MA) State College/International Reading Association (IRA), 1987, for significant contribution to excellence in books for children; Regina Medal, Catholic Library Association, 1989; *Horn Book* Honor Book designation, 1994, for *If You Made a Million* by Schwartz; New England Booksellers Award, 1996; Bank Street College of Education Best Children's Books of the Year designation, 1996, and IRA Children's Choice designation, 1997, both for *Frogs Jump!* by Alan Brooks; Jo Osborn Medal, 1997; IRA Children's Choice designation, ALA Notable Book designation, and Utah Children's Book Award list, all 1997, all for *Rattlebang Picnic* by Margaret Mahy; ALA Notable Children's Book designation, for *Jack and the Beanstalk;* Capitol Choice designation, 1997, for *The Three Pigs;* Children's Literature Choice listee, 1998, and Buckeye Children's Book Award listee (OH), 2001, both for *Library Lil* by Suzanne Williams; designations for American Library Association Notable Books for Children, Child Study Association of America Children's Book of the Year, *New York Times* Outstanding Book of the Year, and *School Library Journal* Best Book of the Year; Notable Children's Book in the Language Arts designation, National Council of Teachers of English, 2000, for *The Three Sillies;* Capitol Choices honor, 2000, Bank Street

College of Education Best Children's Books of the Year designation and Children's Literature Choice designation, both 2001, Michigan Reader's Choice Award, 2003, and Volunteer State Book Award, 2004, all for *The Baby BeeBee Bird* by Diane Redfield Massie; Delaware Diamonds Reading list, 2001-02, for *The Missing Mitten Mystery;* Rhode Island School of Design Professional Achievement Award, 2003; *Boston Globe/ Horn Book* Nonfiction Award, 2006, for *If You Decide to Go to the Moon* by Faith McNulty.

WRITINGS:

FOR CHILDREN; SELF-ILLUSTRATED

The Wicked Kings of Bloon, Prentice-Hall (Englewood Cliffs, NJ), 1970.
Can I Keep Him?, Dial (New York, NY), 1971.
The Mystery Beast of Ostergeest, Dial (New York, NY), 1971.
The Orchard Cat, Dial (New York, NY), 1972.
Won't Somebody Play with Me?, Dial (New York, NY), 1972.
The Island of the Skog, Dial (New York, NY), 1973.
(Reteller) *There Was an Old Woman,* Parents' Magazine Press (New York, NY), 1974.
Much Bigger than Martin, Dial (New York, NY), 1976.
The Mysterious Tadpole, Dial (New York, NY), 1977, twenty-fifth anniversary edition revised with new illustrations, 2002.
Pinkerton, Behave!, Dial (New York, NY), 1979.
A Rose for Pinkerton, Dial (New York, NY), 1981.
Tallyho, Pinkerton!, Dial (New York, NY), 1982.
Ralph's Secret Weapon, Dial (New York, NY), 1983.
(Reteller) *Paul Bunyan: A Tall Tale,* Morrow (New York, NY), 1984.
(Reteller) *Chicken Little,* Morrow (New York, NY), 1985.
(Reteller) *Pecos Bill,* Morrow (New York, NY), 1986.
Best Friends, Dial (New York, NY), 1986.
Aster Aardvark's Alphabet Adventures, Morrow (New York, NY), 1987.
Prehistoric Pinkerton, Dial (New York, NY), 1987.
(Reteller) *Johnny Appleseed,* Morrow (New York, NY), 1988.
(Reteller) *Jack and the Beanstalk,* Morrow (New York, NY), 1991.
(Reteller) *Mike Fink,* Morrow (New York, NY), 1992.
The Christmas Witch, Dial (New York, NY), 1992.
(Reteller) *Yankee Doodle,* Aladdin Books (New York, NY), 1994.

(Reteller) *Sally Ann Thunder Ann Whirlwind Crockett: A Tall Tale,* Morrow (New York, NY), 1995.
(Reteller) *I Was Born About 10,000 Years Ago: A Tall Tale,* Morrow (New York, NY), 1996.
(Reteller) *The Three Little Pigs,* Morrow (New York, NY), 1997.
(Reteller) *A-Hunting We Will Go!,* Morrow (New York, NY), 1998.
(Reteller) *The Three Sillies,* Candlewick Press (Cambridge, MA), 1999.
(Reteller) *Give the Dog a Bone,* SeaStar Books (New York, NY), 2000.
A Penguin Pup for Pinkerton, Dial (New York, NY), 2001.
Pinkerton and Friends: A Steven Kellogg Treasury (omnibus), Dial (New York, NY), 2004.

"COLOR" STORIES

The Mystery of the Missing Red Mitten, Dial (New York, NY), 1974, revised edition published as *The Missing Mitten Mystery,* 2000.
The Mystery of the Magic Green Ball, Dial (New York, NY), 1978.
The Mystery of the Flying Orange Pumpkin, Dial (New York, NY), 1980.
The Mystery of the Stolen Blue Paint, Dial (New York, NY), 1982.

ILLUSTRATOR:

George Mendoza, *Gwot! Horribly Funny Hairticklers,* Harper (New York, NY), 1967.
James Copp, *Martha Matilda O'Toole,* Bradbury Press (Englewood Cliffs, NJ), 1969.
Eleanor B. Heady, *Brave Johnny O'Hare,* Parents' Magazine Press (New York, NY), 1969.
Mary Rodgers, *The Rotten Book,* Harper (New York, NY), 1969.
Miriam Young, *Can't You Pretend?,* Putnam (New York, NY), 1970.
Hilaire Belloc, *Matilda Who Told Lies and Was Burned to Death,* Dial (New York, NY), 1970.
Ruth Loomis, *Mrs. Purdy's Children,* Dial (New York, NY), 1970.
Fred Rogers, *Mister Rogers' Songbook,* Random House (New York, NY), 1970.
Peggy Parish, *Granny and the Desperadoes,* Macmillan (New York, NY), 1970.

Anne Mallett, *Here Comes Tagalong,* Parents' Magazine Press (New York, NY), 1971.

Jan Wahl, *Crabapple Night,* Holt (New York, NY), 1971.

Aileen Friedman, *The Castles of the Two Brothers,* Holt (New York, NY), 1972.

Jan Wahl, *The Very Peculiar Tunnel,* Putnam (New York, NY), 1972.

Jeanette Franklin Caines, *Abby,* Harper (New York, NY), 1973.

Joan Lexau Nodset, *Come Here, Cat,* Harper (New York, NY), 1973.

Doris Herold Lund, *You Ought to See Herbert's House,* F. Watts (New York, NY), 1973.

Liesel Moak Skorpen, *Kisses and Fishes,* Harper (New York, NY), 1974.

Jean Van Leeuwen, *The Great Christmas Kidnapping Caper,* Dial (New York, NY), 1975.

Margaret Mahy, *The Boy Who Was Followed Home,* F. Watts (New York, NY), 1975.

Cora Annett, *How the Witch Got Alf,* F. Watts (New York, NY), 1975.

Alice Bach, *The Smartest Bear and His Brother Oliver,* Harper (New York, NY), 1975.

Hilaire Belloc, *The Yak, the Python, the Frog,* Parents' Magazine Press (New York, NY), 1975.

Judith Choate, *Awful Alexander,* Doubleday (New York, NY), 1976.

Lou Ann Bigge Gaeddert, *Gustav the Gourmet Giant,* Dial (New York, NY), 1976.

Edward Bangs, *Steven Kellogg's Yankee Doodle,* Parents' Magazine Press (New York, NY), 1976.

Alice Bach, *The Most Delicious Camping Trip Ever,* Harper (New York, NY), 1976.

Alice Bach, *Grouchy Uncle Otto,* Harper (New York, NY), 1977.

Carol Chapman, *Barney Bipple's Magic Dandelions,* Dutton (New York, NY), 1977, new edition, 1988.

Alice Bach, *Millicent the Magnificent,* Harper (New York, NY), 1978.

Marilyn Singer, *The Pickle Plan,* Dutton (New York, NY), 1978.

Mercer Mayer, *Appelard and Liverwurst,* Four Winds Press (New York, NY), 1978.

Douglas F. Davis, *There's an Elephant in the Garage,* Dutton (New York, NY), 1979.

William Sleator, *Once, Said Darlene,* Dutton (New York, NY), 1979.

Susan Pearson, *Molly Moves Out,* Dial (New York, NY), 1979.

Julia Castiglia, *Jill the Pill,* Atheneum (New York, NY), 1979.

Jean Marzollo, *Uproar on Hollercat Hill,* Dial (New York, NY), 1980.

Trinka Hakes Noble, *The Day Jimmy's Boa Ate the Wash,* Dial (New York, NY), 1980.

Amy Ehrlich, *Leo, Zack and Emmie,* Dial (New York, NY), 1981.

Mercer Mayer, *Liverwurst Is Missing,* Four Winds Press (New York, NY), 1981.

Alan Benjamin, *A Change of Plans,* Four Winds Press (New York, NY), 1982.

Cathy Warren, *The Ten-Alarm Camp-Out,* Lothrop (New York, NY), 1983.

Jane Bayer, *A, My Name Is Alice,* Dial (New York, NY), 1984.

Trinka Hakes Noble, *Jimmy's Boa Bounces Back,* Dial (New York, NY), 1984.

David M. Schwartz, *How Much Is a Million?,* Lothrop (New York, NY), 1985.

Carol Purdy, *Iva Dunnit and the Big Wind,* Dial (New York, NY), 1985.

Amy Ehrlich, *Leo, Zack, and Emmie Together Again,* Dial (New York, NY), 1987.

Trinka Hakes Noble, *Jimmy's Boa and the Big Splash Birthday Bash,* Dial (New York, NY), 1989.

David M. Schwartz, *If You Made a Million,* Lothrop (New York, NY), 1989.

Deborah Guarino, *Is Your Mama a Llama?,* Scholastic (New York, NY), 1989.

Reeve Lindbergh, *The Day the Goose Got Loose,* Dial (New York, NY), 1990.

Tom Paxton, *Engelbert the Elephant,* Morrow (New York, NY), 1990.

Amy Ehrlich, *Parents in the Pigpen, Pigs in the Tub,* Dial (New York, NY), 1993.

Peter Glassman, *The Wizard Next Door,* Morrow (New York, NY), 1993.

James Thurber, *The Great Quillow,* Harcourt (San Diego, CA), 1994.

Mark Twain, *The Adventures of Huckleberry Finn,* Morrow (New York, NY), 1994.

Margaret Mahy, *The Rattlebang Picnic,* Dial (New York, NY), 1994.

Laura Robb, editor, *Snuffles and Snouts,* Dial (New York, NY), 1995.

Alan Brooks, *Frogs Jump!: A Counting Book,* Scholastic (New York, NY), 1996.

Suzanne Williams, *Library Lil,* Dial (New York, NY), 1997.

Bill Martin, Jr., *A Beasty Story,* Silver Whistle/Harcourt (San Diego, CA), 1999.

Diane Redfield Massie, *The Baby Beebee Bird,* Harper-Collins (New York, NY), 2000.

Joanne Ryder, *Big Bear Ball,* HarperCollins (New York, NY), 2002.

David M. Schwartz, *Millions to Measure,* HarperCollins (New York, NY), 2003.

Trinka Hakes Noble, *Jimmy's Boa and the Bungee Jump Slam Dunk,* Dial (New York, NY), 2003.

Robert Kinerk, *Clorinda,* Silver Whistle/Harcourt (San Diego, CA), 2003.

J. Fred Coots and Haven Gillespie, *Santa Claus Is Comin' to Town,* HarperCollins (New York, NY), 2004.

Faith McNulty, *If You Decide to Go to the Moon,* Scholastic (New York, NY), 2005.

Dennis Haseley, *The Invisible Moose,* Dial (New York, NY), 2006.

Robert Kinerk, *Clorinda Takes Flight,* Simon & Schuster (New York, NY), 2007.

ADAPTATIONS: Author's works have been adapted into other media by Weston Woods, including: *Chicken Little* (video, film), *The Day Jimmy's Boa Ate the Wash* (video, film, filmstrip/cassette), *How Much Is a Million?* (video, film), *Is Your Mama a Llama?* (video, film), *Island of the Skog* (video, film, filmstrip/cassette), *The Mysterious Tadpole* (video, film, filmstrip/cassette), *Pinkerton, Behave!* (filmstrip/cassette), *Yankee Doodle* (video, film, filmstrip/cassette), and *If You Made a Million* (video).

SIDELIGHTS: While award-winning author and illustrator Steven Kellogg is perhaps best known as the author of the beloved picture book *The Mysterious Tadpole,* he has also created popular children's picture books about Pinkerton the Great Dane, a series of "color" mysteries for younger readers, and adaptations of American legends featuring Paul Bunyan, Pecos Bill, Johnny Appleseed and Mike Fink. As a *Publishers Weekly* reviewer pointed out, "one reason for the popularity Kellogg enjoys is that children sense he's laughing with them when they explore his tenderly comic, always surprising stories and pictures."

Noted for his humorous texts and his detailed, action-filled drawings, Kellogg has also illustrated works for many other children's authors, among them Hilaire Belloc, Mercer Mayer, Trinka Hakes Noble, Tom Paxton, David M. Schwartz, James Thurber, Joanne Ryder, Faith McNulty, and Margaret Mahy. His collaborations with Schwartz, which include *How Much Is a Million?, If You Made a Million,* and *Millions to Measure,* showcase his ability to synthesize abstract elements in what *School*

Library Journal reviewer Kathleen Kelly Macmillan described as "trademark whimsical illustrations." Praising Kellogg's artwork for another nonfiction picture book, McNulty's award-winning *If You Decide to Go to the Moon,* as "impressive," a *Publishers Weekly* reviewer added that the illustrator's "sweeping spreads of realistic space-and-moonscapes strike just the right balance of beauty and eeriness" in bringing to life McNulty's environmental "call to action." In his art for Robert Kinerk's *Clorinda,* a picture book that finds a Rubenesque bovine pursuing her dream of becoming a ballet dancer, "Kellogg's costumed dancers, human and livestock both, likewise cavort across the pages with characteristic verve," according to a *Kirkus Reviews* writer. In similar fashion, the title character in Dennis Hasley's *The Invisible Moose* is portrayed in a similarly ludicrous situation—wandering the streets of Manhattan—providing Kellogg's young fans with a picture book that a *Publishers Weekly* reviewer dubbed "a winsome and witty collaboration."

Born in Connecticut in 1941, Kellogg was combining his artistic and storytelling talents from an early age, drawing pictures for his younger sisters while telling them tales to accompany his artwork. He especially enjoyed drawing animals, and he papered his room with many such pieces; one of his favorite growing-up fantasies was to be hired by *National Geographic* magazine to draw animals on location in Africa. Kellogg was encouraged in his childhood ambitions by his grandmother, who taught the boy about the animal inhabitants of the wooded areas near his home.

Kellogg continued to draw and paint throughout his high-school years, and after graduation he won a scholarship to study at the Rhode Island School of Design. One of the highlights of his time there was a semester spent in Florence, Italy, where he was able to study the original drawings of the great artists of the Italian Renaissance. After graduating, he enrolled in graduate courses at the American University in Washington, DC, and by 1966, he was teaching an etching class there.

While in graduate school, Kellogg married Helen Hill and gained the six stepchildren who have since served as inspiration for many of his drawings. At about the same time, Kellogg began work on his original picture books *The Orchard Cat* and *The Island of the Skog.* He also illustrated George Mendoza's *Gwot! Horribly Funny Hairticklers.* Several other illustration projects followed, including James Copp's *Martha Matilda O'Toole* and Eleanor B. Heady's *Brave Johnny O'Hare,* before Kellogg's first solo effort, *The Wicked Kings of Bloon,* was published in 1970. In between his self-authored projects, Kellogg has continued to collaborate with other writers, creating art for books such as the award-winning *The BeeBee Bird* by Diane Redfield Massie and *A Beasty Story* by Bill Martin, Jr.

When it was released in 1971, *Can I Keep Him?* gained its author/illustrator an even wider audience and also attracted critical praise. As Kellogg later admitted to Pamela Lloyd in *How Writers Write,* this story about a little boy who begs his mother to allow him to keep the stray animals he finds is "a little bit autobiographical." Animals also figure in *The Orchard Cat,* about a cat who discovers he would rather make friends than follow his mother's cynical, power-hungry advice. *Won't Somebody Play with Me?* is another early work, this time focusing on a little girl who must find a way to fill the time until she is allowed to open her birthday presents.

The Mystery of the Missing Red Mitten follows Annie through the many scenarios she imagines for her lost mitten: including serving as the heart for a snowman, or the hat for a hawk. As Kellogg's illustrations consist of black-and-white line drawings, the mitten adds a splash of red as it appears in all the young girl's imaginative incarnations. The success of *The Mystery of the Missing Red Mitten* prompted Kellogg to create several other color-related titles, such as *The Mystery of the Magic Green Ball, The Mystery of the Flying Orange Pumpkin,* and *The Mystery of the Stolen Blue Paint.*

First published in 1977, Kellogg's *The Mysterious Tadpole* quickly won over a generation of young children, and it would do the same thing twenty-five years later when, in 2002, Kellogg re-released the story with a revised plot and new illustrations. Cited by several reviewers as a modern classic, the story begins when a boy receives a tadpole his uncle has brought home from Scotland. Named Alphonse, the tiny amphibian quickly outgrows his original container, and within a short time the creature is large enough to take over the swimming pool and even overwhelms Louis's school. Alphonse's metamorphosis becomes clear to all when it is learned that he was caught along the shore of Scotland's famous Loch Ness. Praising the new edition of the book in *Booklist,* Carolyn Phelan wrote that Kellogg brings to life Louis's humorous efforts to deal with his ungainly pet in "new illustrations [that] are bigger, bolder, brighter, and brimming with lively details."

Kellogg's popular Pinkerton character was introduced in 1979 in the pages of *Pinkerton, Behave!* Inspired by the author/illustrator's family's Great Dane of the same name, *Pinkerton, Behave!* chronicles the dog's misadventures in obedience class. Barbara Elleman declared in her *Booklist* review of the book that "Kellogg wittily captures expressions and movements of animal and human," while his "bright, lively colors and spare use of narrative blend to help make this a splendid comedic success." In *A Rose for Pinkerton* the Great Dane meets Rose the cat, a critter based on another of the Kellogg family's pets. *Tallyho, Pinkerton!* finds Pinkerton and Rose entangled in a humorous fox hunt, while the Great Dane is tempted by dinosaur bones during a chaotic visit to a natural history museum in *Prehistoric Pinkerton.* After dreaming that he is the father of a penguin egg in *A Penguin Pup for Pinkerton,* the hapless Great Dane creates chaos all over town when he mistakes toy balls for real eggs. In the words of *School Library Journal* reviewer Lisa Dennis in a review of the last-named book, "Pinkerton's back—and his new adventures are as outrageous and entertaining as ever."

While much of Kellogg's inspiration has come from his own family, the author/illustrator has also been inspired by larger-than-life characters recalled from his childhood. In *Paul Bunyan: A Tall Tale,* for example, he retells the story of the famed woodsman and his blue ox named Babe, bringing all to life in illustrations that Millicent Lenz described in the *Dictionary of Literary Biography* as "splendidly fitting." Critics were equally appreciative of *Pecos Bill,* in which Kellogg chronicles several of the Texas hero's adventures, including his marriage to cowgirl Slewfoot Sue. Kellogg expands his collection of tall tales with *Johnny Appleseed, Mike Fink, Sally Ann Thunder Ann Whirlwind Crockett,* and *I Was Born About 10,000 Years Ago.* In the last-named book, in which five narrators relate the special—and unlikely—roles they played in events dating back to Adam and Eve's departure from Eden, Kellogg "has pulled out all the stops," according to *Horn Book* contributor Mary M. Burns. Praising Kellogg's art for "lighting up every page," *Booklist* contributor Carolyn Phelan noted that his "expansive, effervescent illustrations interpret the boastful stories with zest, imagination, and wit."

Traditional folktales have also provided the author/illustrator with inspiration, leading to picture books such as *There Was an Old Woman, Chicken Little, The Three Little Pigs, Jack and the Beanstalk,* and *A-Hunting We Will Go!* Another traditional tale, *The Three Sillies,* introduces an exasperated young man who believes that his sweetheart and her family are the three silliest people in the entire world . . . that is, until he meets three other individuals who are even sillier. Calling the picture book "a rollicking farce," a *Publishers Weekly* critic added that Kellogg's "riotous ink-and-watercolor illustrations spill over with preposterous particulars." The author/illustrator's "bizarre use of language and grammar makes [*The Three Sillies*] . . . feel like oral storytelling at its best," added Marta Segal in a *Booklist* review.

"I try to blend illustrations and the words so that each book is a feast for the eye and ear," Kellogg noted on his home page. "I want the time that the reader shares with me and my work to be an enjoyable experience— one that will encourage a lifetime of association with pictures, words, and books."

BIOGRAPHICAL AND CRITICAL SOURCES:

BOOKS

Children's Literature Review, Volume 6, Thomson Gale (Detroit, MI), 1984.

Cummings, Pat, editor and compiler, *Talking with Artists,* Bradbury Press (New York, NY), 1992.

Dictionary of Literary Biography, Volume 61: *American Writers for Children since 1960: Poets, Illustrators, and Nonfiction Authors,* Thomson Gale (Detroit, MI), 1987.

Lloyd, Pamela, *How Writers Write,* Methuen (London, England), 1987.

St. James Guide to Children's Writers, 5th edition, St. James Press (Detroit, MI), 1999.

Silvey, Anita, editor, *Children's Books and Their Creators,* Houghton Mifflin (Boston, MA), 1995.

PERIODICALS

Booklist, November 15, 1979, p. 506; May 15, 1989, Barbara Elleman, interview with Kellogg, pp. 1640-1641; October 15, 1996, Carolyn Phelan, review of *I Was Born About 10,000 Years Ago: A Tall Tale,* p. 422; August, 1998, Shelle Rosenfeld, review of *A-Hunting We Will Go!,* p. 2011; October 1, 1998, Irene Wood, review of *Chicken Little,* p. 348; September 15, 1999, Linda Perkins, review of *A Beasty Story,* p. 268; November 1, 1999,

Marta Segal, review of *The Three Sillies,* p. 535; October 15, 2000, Ilene Cooper, review of *The Missing Mitten Mystery,* p. 435; December 1, 2000, Michael Cart, review of *Give the Dog a Bone,* p. 715; December 15, 2000, Amy Brandt, review of *The Baby BeeBee Bird,* p. 827; September 1, 2001, Kay Weisman, review of *A Penguin Pup for Pinkerton,* p. 116; November 1, 2002, Carolyn Phelan, review of *The Mysterious Tadpole,* p. 508; February 1, 2003, Carolyn Phelan, review of *Millions to Measure,* p. 994; November 1, 2003, Ilene Cooper, review of *Clorinda,* p. 513; February 1, 2006, Gillian Engberg, review of *The Invisible Moose,* p. 44.

Bulletin of the Center for Children's Books, November, 2005, Elizabeth Bush, review of *If You Decide to Go to the Moon,* p. 148.

Connecticut, December, 1989.

Early Years, January, 1986, "Steven Kellogg . . . Teachers' Co-Conspirator."

Horn Book, November-December, 1990; January-February, 1994, Maeve Visser Knoth, review of *Parents in the Pigpen, Pigs in the Tub,* p. 62; November-December, 1994, Ann A. Flowers, review of *The Great Quillow,* p. 727; January, 2000, review of *The Three Sillies,* p. 87; September, 2001, Robin Smith, review of *A Penguin Pup for Pinkerton,* p. 574; March-April, 2003, Danielle J. Ford, review of *Millions to Measure,* p. 227; November-December, 2004, review of *Santa Claus Is Comin' to Town,* p. 657; September-October, 2005, Vicky Smith, review of *If You Decide to Go to the Moon,* p. 605; January-February, 2007, Steven Kellogg, transcript of *Boston Globe/Horn Book* Award acceptance speech, p. 25.

Kirkus Reviews, February 1, 2003, review of *Millions to Measure,* p. 238; August, 15, 2003, review of *Jimmy's Boa and the Bungee Jump Slam Dunk,* p. 1077; September 15, 2003, review of *Clorinda,* p. 1176; September 1, 2005, review of *If You Decide to Go to the Moon,* p. 979; February 15, 2006, review of *The Invisible Moose,* p. 183.

Publishers Weekly, April 16, 1982, p. 71; December 13, 1999, review of *The Three Sillies,* p. 82; April 29, 2002, review of *Big Bear Ball,* p. 68; October 13, 2003, review of *Clorinda,* p. 77; November 14, 2005, review of *If You Decide to Go to the Moon,* p. 67; March 27, 2006, review of *The Invisible Moose,* p. 78.

School Library Journal, November 1, 1998, Nancy A. Gifford, review of *A-Hunting We Will Go!,* p. 107; September, 1999, Pat Leach, review of *A Beasty Story,* p. 195; September, 2000, Julie Cummins,

The Baby BeeBee Bird, p. 205; November, 2000, Joy Fleishhacker, review of *Give the Dog a Bone,* p. 144; August, 2001, Lisa Dennis, review of *A Penguin Pup for Pinkerton,* p. 155; April, 2002, Sylvia Veicht, review of *Is Your Mama a Llama?,* p. 76; March, 2003, Kathleen Kelly Macmillan, review of *Millions to Measure,* p. 224; November, 2003, Kristin de Lacoste, review of *Clorinda,* p. 102; October, 2005, DeAnn Tabuchi, review of *If You Decide to Go to the Moon,* p. 141; March, 2006, Wendy Woodfill, review of *The Invisible Moose,* p. 192.

Times Literary Supplement, July 18, 1980.

ONLINE

Children's Literature: Meet Authors and Illustrators Web site, http://www.childrenslit.com/ (March 8, 2007), "Steven Kellogg."
Steven Kellogg Home Page, http://www.stevenkellogg.com (March 8, 2007).

*   *   *

KELLOGG, Steven Castle
   See KELLOGG, Steven

*   *   *

KIRKWOOD, Kathryn
   See FLUKE, Joanne

*   *   *

KLAUSE, Annette Curtis 1953-

PERSONAL: Born June 20, 1953, in Bristol, England; immigrated to United States, 1968; daughter of Graham Trevor (a radiologist) and Mary Frances Curtis; married Mark Jeffrey Klause (a library assistant), August 11, 1979. *Education:* University of Maryland, B.A., 1976, M.L.S., 1978. *Hobbies and other interests:* Reading science fiction, fantasy, and horror; collecting first editions, limited editions, and chapbooks of science fiction, fantasy, and horror; attending science-fiction conventions.

ADDRESSES: Home—Hyattsville, MD.

CAREER: Fiction writer and librarian. Montgomery County, MD, Department of Public Libraries, worked variously for library contracting companies, 1981—, substitute librarian, 1981-82; Silver Spring Community Libraries Department of Public Libraries, Silver Spring, MD, children's librarian I, 1981; Kensington Park Community Library, Kensington Park, MD, part-time children's librarian I, 1982-84; Bethesda Regional Library, Bethesda, MD, full-time children's librarian I, 1984-89; Olney Community Library, Olney, MD, head of children's services, 1989-91; Kensington Park Community Library, head of children's services, 1991-92; Aspen Hill Community Library, Rockville, MD, head of children's services, beginning 1992.

MEMBER: American Library Association, Association of Library Services to Children, Young Adult Library Services Association.

AWARDS, HONORS: American Library Association (ALA) Best Book for Young Adults, and Best Book for Reluctant Readers designations, *School Library Journal* Best Book designation, *Booklist* Best Book and Editor's Choice designations, and Best Book of the Year Honor Book, Michigan Library Association Young-Adult Division, all 1990, Maryland Library Association Black-Eyed Susan award for grades six through nine, 1992-93, California Young Reader Medal in young-adult category, and Sequoyah Young-Adult Book Award, Oklahoma Library Association, both 1993, and South Carolina Library Association Young Adult Award, all for *The Silver Kiss;* ALA Notable Book for Children designation, *Booklist* Editor's Choice designation, *School Library Journal* Best Books designation, and New York Public Library's 100 Best Children's Books designation, all 1993, all for *Alien Secrets.*

WRITINGS:

The Silver Kiss, Delacorte (New York, NY), 1990.
Alien Secrets, Delacorte (New York, NY), 1993.
Blood and Chocolate, Delacorte (New York, NY), 1997.
Freaks: Alive, on the Inside!, Margaret K. McElderry Books (New York, NY), 2006.

Short fiction included in anthologies, such as *Short Circuits,* edited by Donald Gallo, Delacorte, 1992. Poetry published in *Takoma Park Writers 1981,* Downcounty Press, 1981; *Cat's* magazine; *Aurora; Visions;*

and others. Contributor of articles to professional journals; contributor of book reviews to *School Library Journal,* 1982-94.

ADAPTATIONS: Klause's novels have been adapted as audiobooks by Recorded Books, including *Blood and Chocolate,* 2005, and *Freaks,* Recorded Books, 2006. *Blood and Chocolate* was adapted for film by Ehren Kruger, released by Sony, 2007.

SIDELIGHTS: A professional librarian, Annette Curtis Klause broke new ground in young-adult literature with *The Silver Kiss,* a book described as "sexy, scaring, and moving," by *Bulletin of the Center for Children's Books* critic Roger Sutton. A vampire love story, Klause's first novel was praised as a darkly seductive thriller with heart and a message; it has been followed by several other novels, including *Alien Secrets, Blood and Chocolate,* and *Freaks: Alive, on the Inside!* Discussing her work, which has caused some measure of controversy due to its violence and sexual content, Klaus once commented: "What I really want to do with my books is change the way readers look at themselves and the world around them. To confirm the right to be different." Indeed, the outsider theme takes center stage in each of Klause's novels.

Born in Bristol, England, in 1953, Klause developed a fascination with all things grisly at an early age. "My mother read and sang to me," the writer explained. "But my daddy used to sit me on his lap and tell me the plots to gangster and monster movies. I knew all about Boris Karloff, Bela Lugosi, Jimmy Cagney, and Edward G. Robinson before I ever saw any of their movies." Klause's father encouraged his daughter's off-beat imagination still further by letting her speak to "Willoughby," a little boy who, the man pretended, lived down his throat.

When she was seven years old, Klause and her family moved north to Newcastle-upon-Tyne. As she recalled, her first experience with creative writing occurred a year or so later, when she was incapacitated with a twisted ankle. Bedridden, the girl wrote a poem about her mother ironing and decided from then on to save all her poetry in a notebook. Soon she was writing and illustrating her own books, mostly about a cat and its kittens. At age ten Klause and a neighborhood friend began making up plays and performing them on a tape recorder. "The plays usually involved some kind of humorous mistake," Klause recalled, "like a woman calling up a plant nursery instead of a nursery school for her child."

In addition to plays and poetry, Klause also began experimenting with horror fiction, penning a work she titled *The Blood Ridden Pool of Solen Goom.* Each of the chapters of this fantabulous work ended with ". . . and more blood flowed into the blood ridden pool of Solen Goom." Through middle school she read fantasy and science-fiction books, in addition to the works of Mark Twain and, as she got older, the beatnik books of Jack Kerouac. "I wanted desperately to be a beatnik," Klause remembered. She discovered her first vampire novel at age fourteen, Jane Gaskell's *The Shiny Narrow Grin,* and this book would inspire her first novel many years later. "I was smitten by the pale young man who appeared in a few suspenseful scenes," Klause recalled, "and became mesmerized with the whole concept of vampires."

Initially, Klause responded to her fascination with vampires by writing "a pretentious, over-written, dreadful sequence of poems interspersed with prose called *The Saga of the Vampire,*" as she later admitted. While pretentious, these early writings proved invaluable for Klause when she finally sat down to write her first novel.

Relocating to Washington, DC, during middle school and high school, Klause continued writing poetry. In college she studied toward a profession as a librarian, taking poetry workshops but moving to short stories once she graduated and started working as a librarian. When Klause finally began sending her work out to magazines, she collected numerous rejection letters. As she began to develop her voice and her audience, several of her poems and a short story were published in anthologies and small magazine reviews.

Ultimately, a writing workshop with children's writer Larry Callen turned Klause's focus to young adults. "I knew I wanted to write for young people," she recalled. Klause soon graduated from short stories and, with the help and encouragement of Callen, set to work on a novel. "I wanted to write for teenagers, so I thought back to what I liked to read at that age. In a way, I stole from myself with *The Silver Kiss,* because I looked at my old writing notebooks and found the vampire poem I had written as a teenager, and I realized I had some good ideas in that poem. So I just borrowed them." Although the main characters were lifted from Klause's own adolescent poems, the plot of the novel is contemporary and, according to some critics, is daring for a young-adult title.

The story of a seventeen-year-old girl named Zoe whose world is in turmoil, *The Silver Kiss* blends horror, suspense, and romantic longing. Zoe's mother is dying of cancer, her father is too upset to provide consolation to his daughter, and her best friend is moving away. A series of murders have also rocked Zoe's town; women have been found with their throats slashed and their bodies drained of blood. However, she still goes to her favorite park at night to think and dream, and there Zoe meets the eerily handsome, silver-haired boy who will change her life. Simon, as Zoe comes to learn, is a vampire. Alive for centuries, he is trailing his brother, a fellow vampire who, in addition to being responsible for the town's current rash of murders, also brutally killed the brothers' mother three centuries ago. Simon has tracked his brother through the ages, seeking vengeance. Drawn to Zoe, he feels a glimmer of life because of this attraction and his friendship helps the girl better understand her own feelings about her mother's imminent death. In the process, Zoe learns to cope with her own loneliness and fears. Helping Simon locate his brother, Zoe also aids her supernatural friend in ending his own tormented existence. The pull between Zoe and Simon is strongly sensual, full of the dark passions of the vampire legend.

The Silver Kiss "was a couple of years in the writing," Klause acknowledged. "Then another two for rewriting and marketing. A couple of editors liked it early on, but told me that the vampire was much more convincing than Zoe. Which is understandable: I sympathize more with the Simon character, the outsider." Finally, a former editor of *School Library Journal,* for whom Klause had written reviews and who had since moved into an editorial position at New York City publisher Delacorte, read the manuscript and decided to publish it. "He called me at work," the novelist/librarian recalled, "and I figured here was another rejection. When he said Delacorte wanted to publish it, I thought I would float away."

Even before its 1990 release, Klause's novel caused a stir. Molly Kinney, a contributor to *School Library Journal,* called the work "a well-drawn, powerful, and seductive novel," adding that its "climax is a roller-coaster ride in reality, the macabre, death, and love."

Klause blends science fiction and mystery in her second book, *Alien Secrets.* "With *The Silver Kiss* I needed to do some preliminary research into vampire lore, but I had read so much of it already that I was fairly well steeped in it," the writer explained. "With *Alien Secrets* it was completely different. I had to create an entire new world. I had to extrapolate what life would be like when the story takes place—what events had occurred on Earth and how people would think and act in my new world. I had to do astronomical research to find out how people would travel through space, in what sequence and through which galaxies. And I had to track down a likely star that might have habitable planets around it." Unlike some hard-science fiction, Klause's novel does not contain a lot of complex, scientific jargon or data; at heart, it is a mystery and another outsider story. "That is the trick," Klause explained. "To do all this research so that I am completely immersed in my make-believe world to the point where the reader believes in it as well. You don't use all the research. It's like an iceberg. It's the stuff below the surface that makes the setting real."

Alien Secrets follows the adventures of Puck, a thirteen-year-old Earthling who is on her way to visit her parents on the planet Shoon. Expelled from a private school in England, Puck is carrying plenty of emotional luggage with her. Aboard the space ship taking her back to her parents she meets Hush, a native of Shoon. Hush has problems as well: someone has pilfered the precious statue Hush was entrusted with returning to his planet. Together the two teens search the spaceship to find the statue, become caught up in all sorts of intrigues involving murder and smuggling, and finally learn how to work through their emotional problems, helping each other reach greater self-understanding in the process. "It's *Murder on the Orient Express,* space style," deemed Roger Sutton in a review of the novel for the *Bulletin of the Center for Children's Books.*

"*Alien Secrets* demonstrates Klause's versatility and affirms her talent," Donna L. Scanlon wrote in the *Voice of Youth Advocates,* adding that the author "assembles a sympathetic and well rounded cast of characters." Susan L. Rogers, reviewing the book for *School Library Journal,* cited the story's multicultural themes, noting that Puck's "experiences with alien friends and enemies provide lessons applicable to the changing relationships between races and ethnic groups here on Earth as well." Similarly, Maeve Visser Knoth maintained in *Horn Book* that Klause "uses her setting to explore themes of imperialism and oppression of native peoples" in her "rich, exciting story."

Characteristically, Klause began her third novel, *Blood and Chocolate,* by researching her subject—werewolves—in depth, as a sort of psychic preparation. "I like to howl for a few minutes before starting to write it," she admitted, "just to get in the mood. I am asked to speak at schools quite frequently, to talk about my books and writing. At one assembly, I had the entire student body start to howl with me. It was very therapeutic."

In *Blood and Chocolate* the main character, Vivian Gandillon, is a teenager in a family of werewolves, part of a pack that secretly live among humans in a Maryland suburb. Competitive, vain, and totally unimpressed with the other werewolves her own age, she falls for Aiden, a human teen at her high school. As Vivian wrestles with the decision of whether or not to tell Aiden what she is, a brutal murder threatens her pack's secrecy. Caught between two worlds and pressured by pack leader Gabriel to become his consort, Vivian is forced to deal with her divided sense of loyalty, her story related in what a *Publishers Weekly* contributor deemed "darkly sexy prose and suspenseful storytelling." Reviewing the novel for *Booklist*, Stephanie Zvirin wrote that *Blood and Chocolate* "can be read as feminist fiction, as smoldering romance, as a rites of passage novel, or as a piercing reflection on human nature," while *Horn Book* writer Lauren Adams remarked that Klause imbues her werewolf characters with "all the unbounded heat and urgency of prime adolescence."

The title of *Freaks* describes the central protagonists of Klause's 2006 novel, which follows the quest of seventeen-year-old Abel Dandy to escape his life in a traveling sideshow, as well as the attentions of fellow "freak" Phoebe the Dog-Faced Girl. An outsider in the carnival world of 1899 due to the fact that he lacks a physical abnormality, Abel is led on his adventurous quest by a strange Egyptian woman who appears in his dreams, pleading to be rescued. Traveling the freak-show circuit as part of Dr. Mink's Monster Menagerie, with Phoebe's hairy-faced younger brother, Apollo, in tow, Abel discovers the cruelty with which many disabled and deformed children are treated, and learns that, in the broader spectrum of society, his family and friends have been living one step away from the asylum.

While remarking on the sexually suggestive language in *Freaks, Booklist* contributor Gillian Engberg wrote that Klause's "vibrant, affectionately drawn cast of characters (including a seductive mummy); and the exuberant, often bawdy language" are sure to attract teen readers. In *Kirkus Reviews* a writer noted that because the story's "unusual setting . . . is treated with respect and affec-

tion," the book serves readers as an "unexpectedly comfortable coming-of-age tale." Also praising the novel's coming-of-age theme, *School Library Journal* contributor Sharon Rawlins noted that Klause's "gripping and sensual, but never explicitly sexual, tale is a fascinating mixture of fantasy and reality." "The fascination of human oddities will draw readers to this novel," predicted an equally enthusiastic *Kliatt* reviewer, the critic adding that "intrepid Abel's varied adventures will keep them turning the pages."

Regarding the thematic content of her novels, Klause explained that she does not start out with a theme or message; instead, she allows them to grow naturally out of the story. "I always felt like an outsider growing up," she once noted. "I was the one with red hair, the one always staring out the window. I am interested in outsiders and what we can all learn from them. In my vampire book, Simon is definitely the outsider, but Zoe learns from him. It's the same with Puck and Hush. The alien helps Puck to come to terms with herself. I call it my outsider-as-catalyst theory." "You can't force the theme," the writer continued. "It has to come naturally. Because of my background as the odd kid out in England and a foreigner in the United States, I find I often deal with the positive aspects of difference. Different is good. People contribute to life and society in different ways, but everybody has something to contribute."

BIOGRAPHICAL AND CRITICAL SOURCES:

BOOKS

Twentieth-Century Young Adult Writers, St. James Press (Detroit, MI), 1994.

PERIODICALS

Booklist, June 1, 1997, Stephanie Zvirin, review of *Blood and Chocolate,* p. 1694; February 1, 2006, Gillian Engberg, review of *Freaks: Alive, on the Inside!,* p. 49.
Bulletin of the Center for Children's Books, September, 1990, review of *The Silver Kiss,* p. 10; September, 1993, review of *Alien Secrets,* p. 15; January, 2006, April Spisak, review of *Freaks,* p. 235.
Horn Book, September-October, 1993, review of *Alien Secrets,* pp. 599-600; July-August, 1997, Lauren Adams, review of *Blood and Chocolate,* p. 59.

Kliatt, January, 2006, Paula Rohrlick, review of *Freaks,* p. 9.

Kirkus Reviews, December 1, 2005, review of *Freaks,* p. 1276.

New York Times Book Review, April 21, 1991, p. 33.

Publishers Weekly, July 27, 1990, review of *The Silver Kiss,* p. 236; July 5, 1993, review of *Alien Secrets,* p. 74; May 26, 1997, review of *Blood and Chocolate,* p. 86; January 2, 2006, review of *Freaks,* p. 64.

School Library Journal, September, 1988, pp. 120-123; September, 1990, review of *The Silver Kiss,* p. 255; September, 1993, review of *Alien Secrets,* p. 233; January, 2006, Sharon Rawlins, review of *Freaks,* p. 136.

Voice of Youth Advocates, April, 1993, review of *Alien Secrets,* p. 20; August, 1993, pp. 165-166; April, 1998, review of *Blood and Chocolate,* p. 37.*

*   *   *

KNEALE, Matthew 1960-
(Matthew Nicholas Kerr Kneale)

PERSONAL: Born November 24, 1960, in London, England; son of Nigel (a playwright) and Judith (a writer) Kneale; married Shannon Russell, September, 2000. *Education:* Magdalen College, Oxford University, B.A., 1982. *Hobbies and other interests:* Travel, long-distance hill and mountain walking, cycling.

ADDRESSES: Agent—Deborah Rogers, Rogers, Coleridge & White, 20 Powys Mews, London W11 1JN, England.

CAREER: Writer, photographer. Teacher of English as a foreign language in Tokyo, 1982-83, and in Rome; tutor of English and history. Freelance photographer.

MEMBER: Society of Authors.

AWARDS, HONORS: Winner of Somerset Maugham Award, 1988, for *Whore Banquets;* winner of John Llewellyn Rhys Award, 1993, for *Sweet Thames;* speaker at Adelaide Festival, 1994, Singapore Festival, 1995; and Tasmania and Melbourne Festivals, 2000; shortlisted for Booker Prize, 2000, and winner of Whitbread Book of the Year Award, 2000, Prix Relay du Roman d'Evasion, 2002, all for *English Passengers.*

WRITINGS:

NOVELS

Whore Banquets, Gollancz (London, England), 1987, published as *Mr. Foreigner,* Weidenfeld & Nicolson (London, England), 2002.

Inside Rose's Kingdom, Gollancz (London, England), 1989.

Sweet Thames, Sinclair-Stevenson (London, England), 1992, Black Swan Books (Redding Ridge, CT), 1994.

English Passengers, Nan A. Talese (New York, NY), 2000.

Small Crimes in an Age of Abundance, Nan A. Talese (New York, NY), 2005.

SIDELIGHTS: Matthew Kneale's *English Passengers* is a sweeping historical novel of the colonization of Tasmania by the British in the nineteenth century. One portion of the story concerns an English minister, Geoffrey Wilson, who sails to Tasmania in 1857; in an effort to defend Biblical literalism against Charles Darwin and his theory of evolution, he wants to prove that the Garden of Eden was located there. Joining him is a doctor, Thomas Potter, who is looking for the skulls of Tasmanian aborigines in an attempt to prove his theory about the differences between the races. They are both oblivious to the fact that their ship's captain, the roguish Illiam Quillian Kewley, is a smuggler. The novel flashes both back and forward in time to portray the devastating effects of British settlement on the aboriginal population. There are about twenty first-person narrators, chief among them a proud and tough aborigine named Peevay.

"*English Passengers* feels a bit too much like two separate novels," observed Adam Hochschild in the *New York Times Book Review,* "because one stream of its action is essentially foreordained and tragic, the other unpredictable and comic. . . . The ship-of-fools strand of the plot has a particularly satisfying finish when Dr. Potter meets the end he deserves, one deliciously appropriate to his quest for specimens. But Captain Kewley alone is worth the price of admission, as he bribes and connives his way around the world." Reviewing the work for the London *Times,* Ruth Scurr called the work a "dashing historical novel" that is "grand in conception." *Booklist* contributor Neal Wyatt lauded Kneale for "a deliciously sly and clever wit" and "elegant precision" in his storytelling, making the book "a delight to read." The multiple narrators, he added, remain distinct and allow for differing views of the same occurrences. A *Publishers Weekly* reviewer noted that even with the numerous narrators, the story does not become confusing. The reviewer pronounced *English Passengers* "a rich tale" and "an impressive epic." A *Kirkus Reviews* commentator deemed it "original," "knowledgeable," and "very moving."

Kneale has remarked that while he has a passion for travel, he did not go to Tasmania until he was researching *English Passengers,* which he was inspired to write by a desire to portray the horrors wrought by British imperialism, and to explore the shockingly racist "scientific" theories that developed in the mid-nineteenth century. Earlier, he told *CA:* "I contracted a severe case of the travel bug sometime early on in life and till now have visited some seventy countries and all seven continents. I have also spent a year living in both Tokyo and, later, Rome. The areas I feel I have got to know best are Italy, Latin America, Australia, and Asia. My strangest journey was probably in Indonesian New Guinea, where I walked and stayed with the Dani people, who are only recently emerged from the Stone Age. My saddest journey was in China in June, 1989, where I found myself a witness to the quiet bravery of the student demonstrators. All this journeying about, together with a study of history, has left me with a fascination with how cultures work, and their seemingly limitless ability to believe that they alone have found the right and normal way of going about things. My first novel, *Whore Banquets,* was based on my year in Tokyo, and is a study of cultural miscomprehensions. . . . *Sweet Thames* is set in London in 1849, and is a wry look at Victorian English thinking, from the starting point of an obsessively ambitious drainage engineer whose wife vanishes in the middle of a cholera epidemic."

Kneale moves forward in time and looks at different aspects of travel in his 2005 title, *Small Crimes in an Age of Abundance,* "twelve stories linked by the theme of wrongdoing and the suppression of conscience," as a contributor for the *Bookseller* described the work. In one tale, an English family on vacation in China discover their own prejudices; another story finds an American in central Asia suddenly cast in a different role than the staid and boring one he assumes at home; another story examines the attempt of a couple to find romance and peace in Tuscany, with unexpected results. Still other stories stay closer to home, but with equally

ironic outcomes. Reviewing the collection in the *Spectator,* Olivia Glazebrook felt that "several of the stories have a sinister footnote." However, Glazebrook was unimpressed with this attempt by Kneale, concluding that it "may be an interesting exercise, but it is a lifeless read." However, Robert E. Brown, reviewing the same collection in *Library Journal,* had a higher assessment, noting that the stories were "well wrought and intriguing." Kneale told the *Bookseller* contributor his reason for choosing the short story form: "I've travelled a lot, but never found a way of getting down in fiction the multiple perspectives that travel gives you." The twelve stories of *Small Crimes in an Age of Abundance* represent Kneale's attempt at such a multi-faceted viewpoint. The author explained in *Bookseller* he arranged the stories to resemble a novel in form "so that readers should feel that they have travelled through it," receiving "a cumulative emotional charge."

BIOGRAPHICAL AND CRITICAL SOURCES:

PERIODICALS

Booklist, March 15, 2000, Neal Wyatt, review of *English Passengers,* p. 1327; February 1, 2005, Neal Wyatt, review of *Small Crimes in an Age of Abundance,* p. 942.

Bookseller, November 25, 2004, "Kneale's Stories of Twelve Bad Deeds," p. 26.

Canberra Times (Canberra, Australia), February 7, 1989, review of *Inside Rose's Kingdom.*

Cosmopolitan, January 5, 1987, review of *Whore Banquets*; June, 1989, review of *Inside Rose's Kingdom.*

Daily Telegraph, February 6, 1987, review of *Whore Banquets*; May 6, 1989, review of *Inside Rose's Kingdom*; September 12, 1992, review of *Sweet Thames.*

Evening Standard (London, England), July 23, 1992, review of *Sweet Thames.*

Financial Times, January 31, 1987, review of *Whore Banquets.*

Guardian (London, England), January 30, 1987, review of *Whore Banquets*; April 17, 1989, review of *Inside Rose's Kingdom.*

Independent (London, England), February 10, 1987, review of *Whore Banquets.*

Independent on Sunday (London, England), August 2, 1992, review of *Sweet Thames.*

Kirkus Reviews, February 15, 2000, review of *English Passengers,* p. 195; February 1, 2005, review of *Small Crimes in an Age of Abundance,* p. 140.

Library Journal, March 15, 2000, review of *English Passengers,* p. 127; February 1, 2005, Robert E. Brown, review of *Small Crimes in an Age of Abundance,* p. 73.

Literary Review, April, 1987, review of *Whore Banquets;* March, 1989, review of *Inside Rose's Kingdom.*

New Statesman, March 27, 1987, review of *Whore Banquets.*

New York Times Book Review, May 28, 2000, Adam Hochschild, review of *English Passengers.*

Observer (London, England), February 1, 1987, review of *Whore Banquets;* August 16, 1992, review of *Sweet Thames.*

Philadelphia Inquirer, September 5, 2000, review of *English Passengers.*

Publishers Weekly, February 14, 2000, review of *English Passengers,* p. 174; January 10, 2005, review of *Small Crimes in an Age of Abundance,* p. 36.

Spectator, August 8, 1992, review of *Sweet Thames;* March 5, 2005, Olivia Glazebrook, review of *Small Crimes in an Age of Abundance,* p. 49.

Sunday Telegraph, February 2, 1987, review of *Whore Banquets.*

Sunday Times, July 19, 1992, review of *Sweet Thames.*

Time Out, April 5, 1989, review of *Inside Rose's Kingdom;* August 5, 1992, review of *Sweet Thames.*

Times (London, England), March 16, 2000, Ruth Scurr, review of *English Passengers.*

Times Literary Supplement, January 30, 1987, review of *Whore Banquets;* March 30, 1989, review of *Inside Rose's Kingdom;* August 8, 1992, review of *Sweet Thames.*

ONLINE

Bookreporter.com, http://www.bookreporter.com/ (March 24, 2000), "Matthew Kneale"; (November 20, 2006), Ann Bruns, review of *English Passengers.*

ContemporaryWriters.com, http://www.contemporary writers.com/ (November 20, 2006), "Matthew Kneale."

Guardian Online, http://books.guardian.co.uk/ (January 18, 2001), Emma Yates, "Five Minutes with Matthew Kneale."

Salon.com, http://www.salon.com/ (February 21, 2001), Laura Miller, review of *English Passengers.**

*   *   *

KNEALE, Matthew Nicholas Kerr
   See KNEALE, Matthew

KORDA, Michael 1933-
   (Michael Vincent Korda)

PERSONAL: Born October 8, 1933, in London, England; son of Vincent (an artist and art director) and Gertrude (an actress) Korda; married Carolyn Keese, April 16, 1958 (divorced); married Margaret Mogford; children: (first marriage) Christopher Vincent. *Education:* Magdalene College, Cambridge, B.A., 1958.

ADDRESSES: Home—Duchess County, NY.

CAREER: Columbia Broadcasting System, Inc. (CBS-TV), New York, NY, script reader, 1957; Simon & Schuster, Inc. (publishers), New York, 1958-2005, began as editorial assistant, became editor-in-chief. *Military service:* Royal Air Force, 1952-54.

MEMBER: American Horse Shows Association, National Society of Film Critics.

WRITINGS:

Male Chauvinism! How It Works, Random House (New York, NY), 1973.

Power! How to Get It, How to Use It, Random House (New York, NY), 1975.

Success! How Every Man and Woman Can Achieve It, Random House (New York, NY), 1977.

Charmed Lives: A Family Romance, Random House (New York, NY), 1979.

Worldly Goods (novel), Random House (New York, NY), 1982.

Queenie (biographical novel), Linden Press/Simon & Schuster (New York, NY), 1985.

The Fortune (novel), Summit (New York, NY), 1988.

Curtain (novel), Summit (New York, NY), 1991.

The Immortals: A Novel, Poseidon Press (New York, NY), 1992.

Man to Man: Surviving Prostate Cancer, Random House (New York, NY), 1996.

Another Life: A Memoir of Other People, Random House (New York, NY), 1999.

Country Matters: The Pleasures and Tribulations of Moving from a Big City to an Old Country Farmhouse, HarperCollins (New York, NY), 2001.

Making the List: A Cultural History of the American Bestseller, 1900-1999, Barnes & Noble (New York, NY), 2001.

Horse People: Scenes from the Riding Life, HarperCollins (New York, NY), 2003.

Marking Time: Collecting Watches and Thinking about Time, Barnes & Noble (New York, NY), 2004.

Ulysses S. Grant: The Unlikely Hero, Atlas/HarperCollins (New York, NY), 2004.

(With wife, Margaret Korda) *Horse Housekeeping: Everything You Need to Know to Keep a Horse at Home,* HarperCollins (New York, NY), 2005.

(With Margaret Korda) *Cat People,* HarperCollins (New York, NY), 2005.

Journey to a Revolution: A Personal Memoir and History of the Hungarian Revolution of 1956, HarperCollins (New York, NY), 2006.

Ike: An American Hero, HarperCollins (New York, NY), 2007.

Contributor of articles to magazines, including *Popular Photography, Vogue, Self, Newsweek, Harper's Bazaar, Publishers Weekly,* and *Glamour.*

ADAPTATIONS: *Queenie* was optioned for television; *Curtain* was adapted to audio by Simon & Schuster, 1991.

SIDELIGHTS: As a former editor-in-chief of the book-publishing firm Simon & Schuster, Michael Korda proved time and again his ability to recognize, edit, and successfully market best-sellers. In addition, Korda has demonstrated his own creative talents by writing several best-selling books himself.

Korda began his career at Simon & Schuster in 1958 as an editorial assistant. While performing the "donkey-work" associated with his entry-level position, Korda told *New York* magazine, he discovered that hard work, longevity, and a knowledge of the reading public's desires were vital to success in the publishing industry. A penchant for controversy and self-promotion also helped thrust Korda into the spotlight during the 1960s and 1970s, when he took the initiative to publish books other editors declined because of their questionable subject matter.

Korda embarked on a writing career in 1973 with the publication of *Male Chauvinism! How It Works.* The book, which analyzes male chauvinism and suggests ways women might cope with the phenomenon, was not well-received by reviewers. "If American men are as sniveling and insecure as Korda says they are," noted

Newsweek critic Maureen Orth, "maybe women ought to forget logic and proceed with karate." Korda's next book, *Power! How to Get It, How to Use It,* fared no better with critics but quickly topped the best-seller lists. Describing office behavior as carefully as an anthropologist, Korda offered advice on ways to maximize one's power position through judicious arrangement of office furniture, proper placement of a handkerchief, and adherence to a Machiavellian code of ethics. Calling it a "sad book," Richard Reeves, writing in the *New York Times Book Review,* described *Power!* as a "guidebook for the upwardly mobile and the numb-lipped amoral . . . Talent? Work? Kindness? There is no place for them in the 'Power!' strategy."

Breaking away from the self-help format, Korda turned to the details of his own family history to produce *Charmed Lives: A Family Romance.* A well-regarded biography, the book focuses on Korda's father, Vincent, and his uncles, Zoltan and Alexander Korda. As a youth, Korda idolized Alexander, who became a legendary figure in the motion picture industries of England and the United States. Critics praised Korda's account of his famous family but the book sold only moderately well. Lauding Korda's "vivid sense of detail and characterization," *Washington Post Book World* critic Peter Bogdanovich found that the book demonstrated the author's "poetic understanding of what the world is like and what really matters in it." *Time* critic Richard Schickel compared Korda's memoir to one of Alexander Korda's renowned films, calling it "warm, well-structured, humorous, a little larger and more romantic than life, but underneath it all, shrewdly observed." Praising Korda's style in the *New York Times Book Review,* Anatole Broyard observed that the writer "has found a tone that is wryly loving and tenderly ironical. He is warm without being sentimental; admiring, but with just the right degree of irreverence."

Korda chronicled the life of another famous relative—actress Merle Oberon, wife of Alexander Korda—in the fictionalized biography *Queenie.* Full of scandalous details and thinly veiled references to famous Hollywood personalities, the book quickly became a best-seller, and was sold to television for mini-serialization. Critical reception was typical of the sort usually bestowed upon the genre. Calling the novel "derivative and predictable," Christopher Schemering characterized it in the *Washington Post Book World* as "part Harlequin, part gothic, and part Carol Burnett movie skit." Lamenting the publication of "yet another novel about an impossibly beautiful woman whose overwhelming ambition propels her to the summit of an ineffably empty world littered with the carcasses of the unfortunate men she has left behind," Joy Fielding, writing in the Toronto *Globe and Mail* conceded that "perhaps one cannot escape the cliches of a Hollywood novel because Hollywood itself is such a cliche." Critiquing the book in the *New York Times Book Review,* Marcelle Thiebaux found that "the glitz, the flesh, [and] the treachery," set against glamorous international settings supplied "crisp entertainment and enough action for weeks of prime-time viewing."

Adding to his canon of fictionalized accounts of the lives of the rich and famous with novels such as *Worldly Goods, The Fortune,* and *Curtain,* Korda continued to find success and popularity. Anthony Holden, writing in *Spectator,* called Korda "one of the established modern masters of 'faction' . . . he is brilliantly adept at adding fictional flesh to biographical bones." Korda raised the celebrity stakes even higher with *The Immortals: A Novel,* a fictionalized account of the relationship and mysterious deaths of John F. Kennedy and Marilyn Monroe. Critics responded to the controversial book with mixed reviews. Diana McLellan praised the novel in the *Washington Post Book World,* referring to it as "a new kind of mythic reality: part history, part speculation, part old but tasty gossip, part complete fiction, all woven into a seamlessly inventive whole." Joe Queenan, on the other hand, described the book's numerous faults in the *New York Times Book Review.* Queenan wrote that it is "a structural mess" with "hopeless dialogue" and "a seemingly pointless subplot about the mob." He concluded: "This is the single greatest failing of Mr. Korda's book—not that it makes its subjects seem wretched, but that it makes them seem drab."

After working for forty-seven years as editor-in-chief at Simon & Schuster, Korda retired in 2005. In an interview with the *Washington Post* he stated: "I felt it was time to get off the stage, or at least into the wings." Shortly thereafter, he wrote *Journey to a Revolution: A Personal Memoir and History of the Hungarian Revolution of 1956,* a book described by a *Publishers Weekly* contributor as "part hard-nosed history lesson, part affectionate celebration of Hungary and Hungarian culture, and part sepia-tinged memoir." The book chronicles the twelve-day revolution against Communist authorities in Hungary side-by-side with Korda's own account of his idealistic road trip to provide aid to the ultimately failed struggle. While noting that the historical portion of the book offered little new insight into the context of the revolution, reviewers found Korda's

personal reflections to be compelling. An *Economist* critic noted that Korda's "lively eyewitness account recalls the chaos and excitement of revolutionary Budapest," and Allison Block wrote in *Booklist* that "Hungarians have long been revered for their charisma and charm, qualities Korda displays in this compelling account."

BIOGRAPHICAL AND CRITICAL SOURCES:

BOOKS

Contemporary Popular Writers, St. James Press (Detroit, MI), 1997.
Korda, Michael, *Charmed Lives: A Family Romance,* Random House (New York, NY), 1979.
Korda, Michael, *Man to Man: Surviving Prostate Cancer,* Random House (New York, NY), 1996.
Korda, Michael, *Country Matters: The Pleasures and Tribulations of Moving from a Big City to an Old Country Farmhouse,* HarperCollins (New York, NY), 2001.
Korda, Michael, *Journey to a Revolution: A Personal Memoir and History of the Hungarian Revolution of 1956,* HarperCollins (New York, NY), 2006.

PERIODICALS

Booklist, August 1, 2006, Allison Block, review of *Journey to a Revolution,* p. 32.
Economist, October 21, 2006, "Hands up for Freedom: The Hungarian Uprising has Inspired a New Generation of Books," review of *Journey to a Revolution,* p. 95.
Globe and Mail (Toronto, Ontario, Canada), April 20, 1985, Joy Fielding, review of *Queenie.*
Kirkus Reviews, July 1, 2006, review of *Journey to a Revolution,* p. 665.
Library Journal, September 15, 2006, Maria C. Bagshaw, "Failed Illusions: Moscow, Washington, Budapest, and the 1956 Hungarian Revolt," review of *Journey to a Revolution,* p. 71.
Newsweek, September 15, 1975, Maureen Orth, review of *Male Chauvinism! How It Works.*
New York, April 1, 1985, author profile and interview.
New York Times Book Review, September 21, 1975, Richard Reeves, review of *Power! How to Get It, How to Use It;* November 4, 1979, Anatole Broyard, review of *Charmed Lives,* p. 7; April 28,

1985, Marcelle Thiebaux, review of *Queenie*; September 13, 1992, Joe Queenan, review of *The Immortals: A Novel*, p. 9.

Publishers Weekly, July 31, 2006, review of *Journey to a Revolution*, p. 63.

Spectator, May 11, 1991, Anthony Holden, review of *Curtain.*

Time, November 5, 1979, Richard Schickel, review of *Charmed Lives,* p. 106.

Washington Post, November 3, 2005, Hillel Italie, "Longtime Simon & Schuster Editor to Step Down," p. C03.

Washington Post Book World, October 28, 1979, Peter Bogdanovich, review of *Charmed Lives*; April 28, 1985, Christopher Schemering, review of *Queenie,* p. 4; September 28, 1992, Diana McLellan, review of *The Immortals,* p. B4.*

*   *   *

KORDA, Michael Vincent
See KORDA, Michael

*   *   *

KOTZ, Nathan Kallison
See KOTZ, Nick

*   *   *

KOTZ, Nick 1932-

(Nathan Kallison Kotz)

PERSONAL: Born September 16, 1932, in San Antonio, TX; son of Jacob (a physician) and Tybe Kotz; married Mary Lynn Booth (a freelance writer), August 12, 1960; children: Jack Mitchell. *Education:* Dartmouth College, A.B., 1955; attended London School of Economics, 1955-56.

ADDRESSES: Home—Broad Run, VA.

CAREER: Journalist and writer. *Des Moines Register,* Des Moines, Iowa, reporter, 1958-64, Washington correspondent, 1964-70; *Washington Post,* Washington, DC, reporter, beginning 1970. Distinguished adjunct

professor, American University School of Communications. *Military service:* U.S. Marine Corps Reserve, 1956-58; became first lieutenant.

MEMBER: National Press Club, Sigma Delta Chi.

AWARDS, HONORS: Raymond Clapper Awards, 1966, 1968; Pulitzer Prize for national reporting, 1968; the first Robert Kennedy Memorial Award in journalism, 1969; Olive Branch Award, Editors' Organizing Committee, 1989, for *Wild Blue Yonder: Money, Politics, and the B-1 Bomber*; National Magazine Award.

WRITINGS:

Let Them Eat Promises: The Politics of Hunger in America, introduction by George S. McGovern, Prentice-Hall (Englewood Cliffs, NJ), 1969.

The Unions, Simon & Schuster (New York, NY), 1972.

(With wife, Mary Lynn Kotz) *A Passion for Equality: George A. Wiley and the Movement,* Norton (New York, NY), 1977.

Wild Blue Yonder: Money, Politics, and the B-1 Bomber, Pantheon (New York, NY), 1988.

Judgment Days: Lyndon Baines Johnson, Martin Luther King, Jr., and the Laws That Changed America, Houghton Mifflin (Boston, MA), 2005.

Contributor to *Look, Harper's, Nation, Progressive, New York Times, Washington Monthly,* and other publications.

SIDELIGHTS: In *Let Them Eat Promises: The Politics of Hunger in America,* Pulitzer Prize-winning journalist Nick Kotz "paints an appalling picture of political persiflage, bureaucratic ineptitude and moral obtuseness," stated John Leonard in the *New York Times.* "His is investigative reportage of the highest order, telling us what we need to know" about how the government has allowed hunger to become widespread in the United States. As *Atlantic* contributor Edward Weeks observed, Kotz's "well-written, firmly documented, coolly indignant book is too disturbing and too factual to be brushed off as another troublemaker. It strikes at the most persistent mismanagement in our federal system." Leonard further noted: "There isn't an aspect of this 'dismal story' that Mr. Kotz neglects," and as a result "his conclusions are compelling."

Kotz conducts a similar investigation in *Wild Blue Yonder: Money, Politics, and the B-1 Bomber.* In this book, which *Washington Post Book World* contributor Arthur T. Hadley called "well-researched and superbly documented," Kotz "describes the 20-year gestation of the B-1 bomber, from President Eisenhower's first 'no,' through endless crass political maneuvering, to President Reagan's final 'yes.'" "Apart from its scope and detail," wrote Sheila Tobias in the *New York Times Book Review,* "the book's strength lies in the subtlety of its argument. By rooting the story of the B-1 in that of its predecessor," the critic continued, the author "gives himself three decades of bomber politics to discuss." Harry G. Summers, Jr., explained in his *Los Angeles Times Book Review* critique that "Kotz found the fundamental flaw" of the B-1 program "in the very concept of strategic bombing itself." As a result, Summers noted, "in one sense, Kotz's 'Wild Blue Yonder' is a history of that campaign [for strategic bombing], a campaign that spanned 30 years and seven Presidents. But in a broader sense, it is an indictment of our entire process for the conception, design, production and deployment of those weapons systems upon which our national security and our survival itself depends." *Wild Blue Yonder,* wrote Tobias, "is not just another tale of waste, fraud and abuse. Nor does the author merely rail against the military-industrial complex. Mr. Kotz makes clear that bomber politics . . . is the result of a skew in our economy that has given one sector of the aerospace industry, in collaboration with its military partners, an unhealthy power."

In his 2005 book, *Judgment Days: Lyndon Baines Johnson, Martin Luther King, Jr., and the Laws That Changed America,* Kotz explores the complex relationship between the former President of the United States and the assassinated civil rights leader. In the process, he writes about the African-American civil rights movement beginning in the 1960s and how Johnson and King worked together to create the Civil Rights Act of 1964 and the Voting Rights Act of 1965. Kotz also presents his case that the movement's efforts may have had very different effects, and not necessarily beneficial ones, if it were not for the way these two leaders interacted despite the growing tensions between the two over the Vietnam War near the end of King's life. Vernon Ford, writing in *Booklist,* commented that the author "traces the synergy of nonviolent civil disobedience with keen political acumen." Writing in the *Black Issues Book Review,* Lee A. Daniels noted that the book is important "for understanding more . . . about the course the black freedom struggle . . . took from the mid-1960s on." A *Kirkus Reviews* contributor wrote that Kotz has

delivered "a piquant reminder that great social progress occurs when the powerful collaborate rather than joust." Lee C. White, writing in the *Recorder,* referred to the book as a "compelling story." White went on to write: "Kotz has produced a valuable and very readable rendering of how two widely diverse people contributed to a remarkable legislative achievement. It takes a master storyteller to create a suspenseful narrative when the outcome is known to all."

BIOGRAPHICAL AND CRITICAL SOURCES:

PERIODICALS

America, May 23, 2005, Donals P. Kommers, review of *Judgment Days: Lyndon Baines Johnson, Martin Luther King, Jr., and the Laws That Changed America,* p. 24.

Atlantic, February, 1970, Edward Weeks, review of *Let Them Eat Promises: The Politics of Hunger in America.*

Black Issues Book Review, March-April, 2005, Lee A. Daniels, review of *Judgment Days,* p. 54; September-October, 2005, Fred Beauford, "Affirmative Action: 40th Anniversary," p. 42, brief mention of *Judgment Days.*

Booklist, December 15, 2004, Vernon Ford, review of *Judgment Days,* p. 694.

Christian Century, October 18, 2005, Leon Howell, review of *Judgment Days,* p. 53.

Christianity Today, October, 2006, Mark Noll, review of *Judgment Days,* p. 142.

Esquire, December, 2005, Charles P. Pierce, review of *Judgment Days,* p. 80.

First Things: A Monthly Journal of Religion and Public Life, August-September, 2005, James Nuechterlein, review of *Judgment Days,* p. 32.

Jet, May 30, 2005, review of *Judgment Days,* p. 14.

Kirkus Reviews, November 15, 2004, review of *Judgment Days,* p. 1080.

Library Journal, August 1, 1977, James Levin, review of *A Passion for Equality: George A. Wiley and the Movement,* p. 1633; November 15, 2004, Karl Helicher, review of *Judgment Days,* and article "Civil Rights Partners," interview with author, pp. 71-72.

Los Angeles Times Book Review, April 17, 1988, Harry G. Summers, Jr., review of *Wild Blue Yonder: Money, Politics, and the B-1 Bomber.*

Management Review, January, 1973, review of *The Unions,* p. 71.

National Catholic Reporter, January 21, 2005, Joe Feuerherd, review of *Judgment Days,* p. 6.

New York Times, January 15, 1970, John Leonard, review of *Let Them Eat Promises;* February 6, 2005, Samuel G. Freedman, review of *Judgment Days.*

New York Times Book Review, March 6, 1988, Sheila Tobias, review of *Wild Blue Yonder.*

Political Science Quarterly, winter, 2005, James H. Meriwether, review of *Judgment Days,* p. 676.

Publishers Weekly, November 29, 2004, review of *Judgment Days,* p. 29; January 31, 2005, Dermot McEvoy, "Nick Kotz: Civil Rights Revisited," interview with author, p. 45.

Recorder, August 19, 2005, Lee C. White, review of *Judgment Days.*

Social Work, May, 1978, Francis P. Purcell, review of *A Passion for Equality,* pp. 256-257.

Technology and Culture, January, 1990, I.B. Holley, review of *Wild Blue Yonder,* p. 187.

Washington Post Book World, March 13, 1988, Arthur T. Hadley, review of *Wild Blue Yonder.*

PERIODICALS

Nick Kotz Home Page, http://www.nickkotz.com (December 28, 2006).*

L

LAMAR, Jake 1961-

PERSONAL: Born March 27, 1961, in Bronx, NY; son of Jacob Virgil, Sr. (a teacher and in business) and Joyce Marie (a personnel administrator) Lamar; married; wife's name Dorli, September 11, 1999. *Education:* Harvard University, B.A. (cum laude), 1983.

ADDRESSES: Home—Paris, France. *Agent*—Kristine Dahl, International Creative Management, 40 West 57th St., New York, NY 10019.

CAREER: Time, New York, NY, staff writer and associate editor, 1983-89; freelance writer, 1989—. Adjunct lecturer at University of Michigan, 1993.

AWARDS, HONORS: Lyndhurst Prize, 1992, for *Bourgeois Blues: An American Memoir.*

WRITINGS:

Bourgeois Blues: An American Memoir (nonfiction), Summit Books (New York, NY), 1991.
The Last Integrationist, Crown (New York, NY), 1996.
Close to the Bone, Crown (New York, NY), 1998.
If 6 Were 9, Crown (New York, NY), 2001.
Rendezvous Eighteenth, St. Martin's Minotaur (New York, NY), 2003.
Ghosts of Saint-Michel, St. Martin's Minotaur (New York, NY), 2006.

Author of essays, including "Behind Enemy Lines: Post-War Notes of an American in Paris" and "The Road to Rendezvous Eighteenth." Contributor to magazines and newspapers, including *Esquire, New York Times,* and *Details.*

SIDELIGHTS: Jake Lamar is a Bronx-born, Harvard-educated author who has made his home in Paris, France, since 1993. His first book, *Bourgeois Blues: An American Memoir,* is a memoir that focuses on his relationship with his father and on their lives as African American men in the United States. On the merits of this book, Lamar was awarded the Lyndhurst Prize. As he explained in an interview for *Paris through Expatriate Eyes,* the grant is "very obscure but a lot of famous writers have won it: Cormac McCarthy, Richard Ford, Toni Morrison, Alice Walker but no one knows about it. . . . You can't apply for it. Someone calls you out of the blue and tells you that you've won all of this money." The grant provided forty thousand dollars a year for three years. Lamar decided to spend a year in Paris but fell in love with the city and has continued to live and write there since that time.

Like his memoir, much of Lamar's fiction revolves around the perplexing issues facing young black professionals in modern society. His first novel, *The Last Integrationist,* is set in the near future and features African American attorney general Melvin Hutchinson, an ultra-conservative who favors televised executions and draconian boot camps for drug offenders. As Melvin seeks the U.S. vice presidency, he must come to terms with the white power brokers who back him as well as his own conflicted picture of himself. *Salon.com* reviewer Megan Harlan noted that Lamar "employs both empathy and a tough, critical eye in observing his large cast of characters," and concluded that *The Last Integrationist* "is a rare, intelligent, provocative novel on race in America." A *Publishers Weekly* reviewer called the book a "richly imagined . . . novel that features a lot of fine writing about race in America." Gene Lyons, reviewing the book in *Entertainment Weekly,* deemed Lamar "a fearless young talent to keep your eye on."

Lamar's *Close to the Bone* "examines the broader question of what is a person, of how identity is influenced by race, sex, and relationships," to quote Vanessa Bush in *Booklist*. Using the O.J. Simpson murder trial as a backdrop, the novel explores the lives of three black men who each face challenges in their personal and professional lives. *BookBrowser* contributor Lee Meadows characterized the work as "a wonderfully adult story of appealing characters driven by the memories of their past and their hopes for the future." A *Powells.com* reviewer stated that Lamar "cuts through the controversies surrounding the African American experience" with his tale of identity and interracial love. In her *Library Journal* review, Ellen Flexman praised *Close to the Bone* as "a sensitive and romantic look at race and relationships in the 1990s."

Lamar turned to the mystery format for his third novel, *If 6 Were 9*. The protagonist, Clay Robinette, finds his comfortable marriage and position in academia threatened when he agrees to help a colleague beat a murder rap. Unfortunately, Clay recognizes the victim as a student with whom he has just had an affair. Inevitably, scandal erupts and it is Clay who faces suspicion both in the workplace and at home. A *Publishers Weekly* critic described the book as "part mystery, part academic satire and part socioracial examination." Wes Lukowsky in *Booklist* noted that Lamar "brings to his first thriller the same sensitivity to racial issues evident in his earlier work." Gavin McNett of the New York Times wrote: "*If 6 Were 9* is a page-turner of a murder mystery with a clear, breezy style. The book is also a wicked black comedy in both senses of the phrase—it's both caustically funny and a shrewd take on racial politics." And a *Kirkus Reviews* contributor stated: "The real strength here lies in [Lamar's] often feckless, always candid, deeply unheroic hero, hollow yet irresistibly human."

Rendezvous Eighteenth is Lamar's first novel set Paris. The title refers to a colorful, sometimes dangerous part of the city where the author makes his home. In the story, Ricky Jenks is an American expatriate content with his low-key life as a piano player. When his cousin appears with a request for help finding his missing wife, Ricky's peaceful existence is upended. In addition to telling a lively mystery story, "the African-American scene in Paris is dissected and laid bare" in this book, according to *Bookloons* reviewer Mary Ann Smyth.

Lamar's next novel, *Ghosts of Saint-Michel*, also illuminates the expatriate life in Paris. This story concerns Marva Dobbs, a 62-year-old American woman whose soul food restaurant is a huge success in the French capital. Marva's affair with Hassan, a young Algerian who works for her, has unexpected consequences when he is accused of being a terrorist. Marva and Hassan drop out of sight, and Marva's daughter, the Parisian police, and spies from various persuasions all go on the hunt for them. Lamar "writes of Paris with charm and authority," noted a *Kirkus Reviews* writer.

Discussing his choice to live in Paris in an interview with *Paris through Expatriate Eyes*, Lamar reflected: "Here I find that writers are appreciated just for being writers. Writing in and of itself is respected. And I think that in America it's only rich and successful writers that are respected. In France everybody from the baker to the literary critic respects people who write books and care about literature. That's a very nice thing for someone who is dedicated to the craft but not famous."

BIOGRAPHICAL AND CRITICAL SOURCES:

PERIODICALS

Black Issues Book Review, March-April, 2004, Melissa Ewey Johnson, review of *Rendezvous Eighteenth*, p. 48.

Booklist, December 1, 1998, Vanessa Bush, review of *Close to the Bone*, p. 651; December 1, 2000, Wes Lukowsky, review of *If 6 Were 9*, p. 696; October 15, 2003, Bill Ott, review of *Rendezvous Eighteenth*, p. 394.

Entertainment Weekly, April 5, 1996, Gene Lyons, review of *The Last Integrationist*, p. 77.

Kirkus Reviews, January 1, 1996, review of *The Last Integrationist*; November 15, 2000, review of *If 6 Were 9*, p. 1578; October 1, 2003, review of *Rendezvous Eighteenth*, p. 1202; May 1, 2006, review of *Ghosts of Saint-Michel*, p. 430.

Library Journal, December, 1998, Ellen Flexman, review of *Close to the Bone*, p. 157.

New York Times, January 28, 2001, Gavin McNett, review of *If 6 Were 9*.

People, June 26, 2006, review of *Ghosts of Saint-Michel*, p. 49.

Publishers Weekly, November 6, 1995, review of *The Last Integrationist*, p. 81; February 5, 1996, review of *The Last Integrationist*, p. 36; November 2, 1998, review of *Close to the Bone*, p. 69; December 4, 2000, review of *If 6 Were 9*, p. 56; October 20, 2003, review of *Rendezvous Eighteenth*, p. 38.

ONLINE

BookBrowser, http://www.bookbrowser.com/ (January 21, 2001), Lee Meadows, review of *Close to the Bone.*

Bookloons, http://www.bookloons.com/ (January 5, 2006), review of *Rendezvous Eighteenth.*

Jake Lamar's Home Page, http://www.jakelamar.com/ (December 31, 2005).

New Mystery Reader, http://www.newmysteryreader.com/ (January 5, 2006), Dana King, review of *Ghosts of Saint-Michel.*

Paris through Expatriate Eyes, http://www.paris-expat.com/ (December 31, 2005), interview with Jake Lamar.

Paris Voice, http://www.parisvoice.com/ (December, 2003/January, 2004), review of *Rendezvous Eighteenth.*

Powells.com, http://www.powells.com/biblio/ (January 21, 2001), review of *Close to the Bone.*

St. Petersburg Times Online, http://www.sptimes.com/ (January 5, 2007), review of *Ghosts of St. Michel.*

Salon.com, http://www.salon.com/08/sneakpeeks/ (January 21, 2001), Megan Harlan, review of *The Last Integrationist.**

*   *   *

LANSKY, Vicki 1942-

PERSONAL: Born January 6, 1942, in Louisville, KY; daughter of Arthur (a men's clothing industry executive) and Mary (a homemaker) Rogosin; married S. Bruce Lansky (a publisher and literary agent), June 13, 1967 (divorced, 1983); children: Douglas, Dana. *Education:* Connecticut College, B.A., 1963. *Hobbies and other interests:* Tending plants, swimming, travel.

ADDRESSES: Office—Book Peddlers, 2828 Hedberg Dr., Minnetonka, MN 55305. *E-mail*—Vickilee@aol.com.

CAREER: Writer and publisher. Sportswear buyer for Lord & Taylor and Mercantile Stores, New York, NY, 1965-69; freelance photographer, 1968-72; Childbirth Education Association, Minneapolis, MN, teaching assistant, 1971-74; Meadowbrook Press, Wayzata, MN, founder, treasurer, and executive vice president in charge of operations, 1974-83; Book Peddlers (publisher), Minnetonka, MN, founder and owner, 1983—. *Practical Parenting* (newsletter), editor and publisher, 1979-88. Associated Press Broadcast Features, daily radio commentator, 1981-82; appeared on television programs, including *Donahue, Oprah, Live with Regis and . . .,* and *Today.* Pillsbury/Green Giant Consumer Advisory Panel, past member; spokesperson for American Plastics Council, 1993, 3M Company, 2005, and others. Member of advisory board, Catholic Charities Office for Divorced and Separated, Parenthood Cable TV, National Parenting Center, and Children's Rights Council.

AWARDS, HONORS: Parents Choice Award, 1990, for *Vicki Lansky's Divorce Book for Parents;* Best New Product Introduction selection, Juvenile Products Manufacturers Association, 1993, for *Games Babies Play.*

WRITINGS:

(With others) *Feed Me! I'm Yours,* Meadowbrook Press (Deephaven, MN), 1974, revised edition, illustrated by Kathy Rogers, 1994, 4th edition, 2004.

The Taming of the C.A.N.D.Y. (Continuously Advertised, Nutritionally Deficient Yummies!) Monster: A Cookbook, Meadowbrook Press (Deephaven, MN), 1978, published with illustrations by Lynn Johnston, Book Peddlers (Deephaven, MN), 1988, 3rd edition, 1999.

Dear Babysitter, edited by Kathryn Ring, Meadowbrook Press (Deephaven, MN), 1982, published as *Dear Babysitter Handbook,* Bantam Books (New York, NY), 2001.

Vicki Lansky's Practical Parenting Tips, illustrated by Kathryn Ring, Meadowbrook Press (Deephaven, MN), 1982, revised edition published as *Practical Parenting Tips: Over 1,500 Helpful Hints for the First Five Years,* Fine Communications (New York, NY), 2003.

Toilet Training, Bantam Books (New York, NY), 1984, revised edition published as *Toilet Training: A Practical Guide to Daytime and Nighttime Training,* 1993, 3rd edition, Book Peddlers (Minnetonka, MN), 2002.

Welcoming Your Second Baby, Bantam Books (New York, NY), 1984, revised edition, Book Peddlers (Deephaven, MN), 2005.

Vicki Lansky's Practical Parenting Tips for the School-Age Years, Bantam Books (New York, NY), 1985.

Traveling with Your Baby, Bantam Books (New York, NY), 1985.

Getting Your Baby to Sleep (and Back to Sleep), Bantam Books (New York, NY), 1985, published with audiocassette and compact disc as *Getting Your Child to Sleep—and Back to Sleep,* Book Peddlers (Deephaven, MN), 2004.

Birthday Parties, Bantam Books (New York, NY), 1986, published as *Vicky Lansky's Birthday Parties,* Book Peddlers (Deephaven, MN), 1989, published as *Birthday Parties: Best Party Tips and Ideas for Ages 1-8,* 1995.

The Best of Vicki Lansky's Practical Parenting, Book Peddlers (Deephaven, MN), 1987.

Fat-Proofing Your Kids, Bantam Books (New York, NY), 1987, published as *Fat-Proofing Your Children . . . So That They Never Become Diet-Addicted Adults,* 1988.

101 Ways to Tell Your Child "I Love You," illustrated by Kaye Pomeranc White, Contemporary Books (Chicago, IL), 1988.

Vicki Lansky's Divorce Book for Parents: Helping Your Children Cope with Divorce and Its Aftermath, New American Library (New York, NY), 1989, 3rd edition, Book Peddlers (Deephaven, MN), 1996.

Baby-Proofing Basics: How to Keep Your Child Safe, 1991, 2nd edition, Book Peddlers (Minnetonka, MN), 2002.

101 Ways to Make Your Child Feel Special, illustrated by Kaye Pomeranc White, Contemporary Books (Chicago, IL), 1991.

Another Use for . . . 101 Common Household Items, illustrated by Martha Campbell, Book Peddlers (Deephaven, MN), 1991.

101 Ways to Say "I Love You," Simon & Schuster (New York, NY), 1991.

Games Babies Play: From Birth to Twelve Months, Book Peddlers (Deephaven, MN), 1993.

Don't Throw That Out!: A Pennywise Parent's Guide to Creative Uses for over 200 Household Items, Book Peddlers (Deephaven, MN), 1994.

101 Ways to Be a Special Mom, illustrated by Kaye Pomeranc White, Contemporary Books (Chicago, IL), 1995.

101 Ways to Be a Special Dad, illustrated by Kaye Pomeranc White, Contemporary Books (Chicago, IL), 1995.

Baking Soda: Over 500 Fabulous, Fun, and Frugal Uses You've Probably Never Thought Of, illustrated by Martha Campbell, Book Peddlers (Deephaven, MN), 1995, 2nd edition, 2004.

Transparent Tape: Over 350 Super, Simple, and Surprising Uses You've Probably Never Thought Of, illustrated by Martha Campbell, Book Peddlers (Deephaven, MN), 1995, 2nd edition, 2005.

(Coauthor) *Healthy Pregnancy, Healthy Babies: A Guide to Prenatal and Baby Care,* Publications International (Lincolnwood, IL), 1995.

Trouble-Free Travel with Children: Helpful Hints for Parents on the Go, 1995.

(Coauthor) *Complete Pregnancy and Baby Book: A Guide to Prenatal, Infant, and Toddler Care,* Publications International (Lincolnwood, IL), 1996.

101 Ways to Spoil Your Grandchild, illustrated by Rondi Collette, Contemporary Books (Chicago, IL), 1996.

The Bag Book: Over 500 Great Uses—and Reuses—for Paper, Plastic, and Other Bags to Organize and Enhance Your Life, illustrated by Martha Campbell, Book Peddlers (Minnetonka, MN), 2000.

Best New Baby Tips, Book Peddlers (Minnetonka, MN), 2001.

Vinegar: Over 400 Various, Versatile, and Very Good Uses You've Probably Never Thought Of, illustrated by Martha Campbell, Book Peddlers (Minnetonka, MN), 2004.

Sunday newspaper columnist, Minneapolis *Star and Tribune,* 1985-86; columnist, *Sesame Street Parents,* c. 1987-97. Contributing editor, *Family Circle,* 1988—.

FOR CHILDREN

Koko Bear's New Potty, illustrated by Jane Prince, Bantam Books (New York, NY), 1986.

Koko Bear's New Babysitter, illustrated by Jane Prince, Bantam Books (New York, NY), 1987.

A New Baby at Koko Bear's House, Bantam Books (New York, NY), 1987.

Vicki Lansky's Kids Cooking, Scholastic, Inc. (New York, NY), 1987.

Koko Bear's Big Earache, illustrated by Jane Prince, Bantam Books (New York, NY), 1988.

Sing Along as You Ride Along (with audiocassette), Scholastic, Inc. (New York, NY), 1988.

Sing Along Birthday Fun (with audiocassette), Scholastic, Inc. (New York, NY), 1988.

Vicki Lansky's Microwave Cooking for Kids, Scholastic, Inc. (New York, NY), 1991.

It's Not Your Fault, Koko Bear: A Read-Together Book for Parents and Young Children during Divorce, illustrated by Jane Prince, Book Peddlers (Minnetonka, MN), 1998.

SIDELIGHTS: In 1974 Vicki Lansky and several other mothers from a local Childbirth Education Association chapter wrote a baby food cookbook for new mothers. Although she believed the book to have commercial appeal, no publisher was interested in it. Undaunted, Lansky and her husband turned their back porch into their own publishing company, Meadowbrook Press, and began producing *Feed Me! I'm Yours* for distribution. Their creative promotional efforts and numerous appearances on television talk shows eventually propelled the book to bestseller status as America's best-selling baby and toddler cookbook.

As her children grew older, Lansky found the struggle to maintain good nutritional habits intensifying. Saturday-morning television commercials for junk food fueled her children's desire for processed foods during favorite cartoon programs, and Lansky realized that one way to counter this offensive was with tasty alternative recipes with child appeal. In *The Taming of the C.A.N. D.Y. (Continuously Advertised, Nutritionally Deficient Yummies!) Monster: A Cookbook* she provides parents with practical ways to improve their children's eating habits. The book rose quickly to the number-one spot on the *New York Times* trade paperback bestseller list.

Drawing on her growing reputation as a savvy parent, in 1979 Lansky began publishing *Practical Parenting,* a bimonthly newsletter consisting of articles and tips on childrearing issues. Remaining in publication until the late 1980s, the newsletter grew into a nationally syndicated radio feature and sparked a series of practical parenting books. Lansky designed each book to cover a single topic, providing a quick and easy source of information for inexperienced parents. Lansky explained to Sue MacDonald in the *Cincinnati Enquirer* that "a lot of these books [are] a replacement for the support group" because new parents often lack parents in close proximity and mothers frequently avoid asking friends of family for child-rearing advice.

In the books she has published during her long career—first with Meadowbrook Press and more recently with Book Peddlers—Lansky sometimes pairs a book for parents with a children's book on the same topic. For example, *Welcoming Your Second Baby* is intended to prepare parents for the issues that arise when a new baby arrives in a single-child household. The book's chapter headings take the form of questions that commonly trouble expectant parents, such as caring for a new infant without neglecting an older sibling or

handling special issues like adoption, blended families, and even newborn death. For children, her related picture book *A New Baby at Koko's House* is designed to appeal to the older sibling via an entertaining story, while also supporting the adult reader by including parent-focused tips on each page.

As Lansky once noted: "I continue to be fascinated by the world of household trivia, the challenges of book publishing, . . . the changing world of divorce social services, computer online services as well as desktop publishing and, of course, the ever evolving nature of the human condition and relationships.

"I feel very lucky to be around at this point in time. I doubt that I could have made a living with this type of material seventy-five years ago and I am not sure of the need for it seventy-five years hence. Despite the fact that my titles have probably sold over six million copies, I have no illusions about the literary value of my work. There is none. But I have touched many people's lives and hopefully made it a little better or easier for them."

BIOGRAPHICAL AND CRITICAL SOURCES:

PERIODICALS

Booklist, September 1, 1978, review of *The Taming of the C.A.N.D.Y. (Continuously Advertised, Nutritionally Deficient Yummies!) Monster: A Cookbook,* p. 11; July, 1983, reviews of *Toilet Training* and *Welcoming Your Second Baby,* p. 1503; March 1, 1985, review of *Vicki Lansky's Practical Parenting Tips for the School-Age Years,* p. 915; September 1, 1985, review of *Getting Your Baby to Sleep (and Back to Sleep),* p. 13; December 15, 1985, review of *Vicki Lansky's Practical Parenting Tips,* p. 635; April 1, 1988, review of *The Taming of the C.A.N. D.Y. (Continuously Advertised, Nutritionally Deficient Yummies!) Monster,* p. 1298; September 15, 1990, review of *Welcoming Your Second Baby,* p. 126; June 1, 1991, review of *Baby-Proofing Basics: How to Keep Your Child Safe,* p. 1846, and review of *Getting Your Child to Sleep—and Back to Sleep,* p. 1850; February 15, 1994, Jo Peer-Haas, review of *Don't Throw That Out!: A Pennywise Parent's Guide to Creative Uses for Over 200 Household Items,* p. 1045; February 15, 1995, Mike Tribby, review of *Baking Soda: Over 500*

Fabulous, Fun, and Frugal Uses You've Probably Never Thought Of, p. 1046; February 15, 1999, Barbara Jacobs, review of *The Taming of the C.A.N.D.Y. (Continuously Advertised, Nutritionally Deficient Yummies!) Monster,* p. 1022.

Bookwatch, January, 1993, review of *Practical Parenting Tips: Over 1,500 Helpful Hints for the First Five Years,* p. 12; April, 1993, review of *Games Babies Play: From Birth to Twelve Months,* p. 12.

Children's Bookwatch, June, 1993, review of *101 Ways to Be a Special Dad,* p. 8; January, 1998, review of *It's Not Your Fault, Koko Bear,* p. 1.

Cincinnati Enquirer, August 3, 1984, Sue MacDonald, interview with Lansky.

Library Journal, July, 1978, review of *The Taming of the C.A.N.D.Y. (Continuously Advertised, Nutritionally Deficient Yummies!) Monster,* p. 1408; March 15, 1985, Kari D. Anderson, review of *Vicki Lansky's Practical Parenting Tips for the School-Age Years,* p. 58; May 15, 1989, Marcia G. Fuchs, review of *Vicki Lansky's Divorce Book for Parents: Helping Your Children Cope with Divorce and Its Aftermath,* p. 80; May 15, 1991, Linda Beck, review of *Baby-Proofing Basics,* p. 103.

Los Angeles Times, July 25, 1982, review of *Dear Babysitter,* p. 12.

New York Times, November 12, 1995, Laurel Graeber, review of *Trouble-Free Travel with Children: Helpful Hints for Parents on the Go.*

New York Times Book Review, April 2, 1978, review of *Feed Me! I'm Yours,* p. 41; November 26, 1989, review of *Vicki Lansky's Divorce Book for Parents,* p. 26.

Parents, May, 1990, reviews of *Toilet Training,* p. 226, and *Koko Bear's New Potty,* p. 228.

Party and Paper Retailer, February, 1996, "Birthday Parties: Best Party Tips and Ideas," p. 44.

Publishers Weekly, January 16, 1978, review of *The Taming of the C.A.N.D.Y. (Continuously Advertised, Nutritionally Deficient Yummies!) Monster,* p. 98; October 10, 1980, Sally A. Lodge, review of *Best Practical Parenting Tips,* p. 72; June 29, 1984, review of *Welcoming Your Second Baby,* p. 103; April 2, 2001, Sally A. Lodge, "Growing-Up Books Come of Age," p. 23.

Reading Teacher, February, 1981, review of *The Taming of the C.A.N.D.Y. (Continuously Advertised, Nutritionally Deficient Yummies!) Monster,* p. 585.

School Library Journal, June, 1998, Kathy Piehl, review of *It's Not Your Fault, Koko Bear,* p. 130.

Small Press, summer, 1991, review of *A New Baby at Koko Bear's House,* p. 57.

Special Delivery, fall, 1999, Kamal Bridge, reviews of *A New Baby at Koko Bear's House* and *Welcoming Your Second Baby,* p. 25.

Us, June 27, 1978.

Washington Post Book World, March 5, 1978, review of *Feed Me! I'm Yours* and *The Taming of the C.A.N.D.Y. (Continuously Advertised, Nutritionally Deficient Yummies!) Monster,* p. F4.

Whole Earth, spring, 1995, review of *Trouble-Free Travel with Children,* p. 111.

ONLINE

Book Peddlers Web site, http://www.bookpeddlers.com/ (March 10, 1007).

Practical Parenting Home Page, http://www.practicalparenting.com/ (January 27, 2006).

*　　*　　*

LEAMING, Barbara

PERSONAL: Born in Philadelphia, PA; daughter of James F. and Muriel Leaming; married David Packman (a professor), February 21, 1975. *Education:* Smith College, B.A.; New York University, Ph.D.

ADDRESSES: Home—CT. *Agent*—Wallace & Sheil Agency, Inc., 177 E. 70th St., New York, NY 10021.

CAREER: Former professor of theater and film at Hunter College of the City University of New York, New York, NY; writer.

WRITINGS:

BIOGRAPHIES

Grigori Kozintsev, Twayne (Boston, MA), 1980.

Polanski: The Filmmaker as Voyeur, Simon & Schuster (New York, NY), 1981, published as *Polanski: His Life and Films,* Hamish Hamilton (London, England), 1982.

Orson Welles: A Biography, Viking Penguin (New York, NY), 1985.

If This Was Happiness: A Biography of Rita Hayworth, Viking (New York, NY), 1989.

Bette Davis: A Biography, Simon & Schuster (New York, NY), 1992.

Katherine Hepburn, Crown (New York, NY), 1995.

Marilyn Monroe, Crown (New York, NY), 1998.

Mrs. Kennedy: The Missing History of the Kennedy Years, Free Press (New York, NY), 2001.

Jack Kennedy: The Education of a Statesman, W.W. Norton (New York, NY), 2006.

Contributor of articles to periodicals, including *Vanity Fair* and the *New York Times Magazine.*

SIDELIGHTS: Biographer Barbara Leaming's *Polanski: The Filmmaker as Voyeur* details the life and work of the controversial filmmaker who fled the United States while being tried for statutory rape in 1977. Leaming traces Roman Polanski's years as an abandoned child in World War II Europe. She also analyzes the possible influence his tragic experiences—such as the murder of his wife, actress Sharon Tate, by Charles Manson's clan—may have had on his work, including the gruesome *Macbeth* and the pessimistic *Chinatown. Los Angeles Times* critic Irwin R. Blacker viewed the biography as "an insightful and useful study of both the artist and his work." A reviewer for the *Fort Worth Star-Telegram* reached a similar conclusion, calling *Polanski* "an appreciative but hardly gentle study."

Leaming once told *CA:* "I am a professor of film history and aesthetics. Both the [Grigori] Kozintsev and Polanski books were written out of my long-term study of Soviet and East European cinema and culture. I also have a special interest in the relationship between American film and its cultural context."

Leaming explored such a relationship in her next biography, turning her attention to the legendary cinematic giant Orson Welles. The appearance of *Orson Welles: A Biography* was timely, for it was published within weeks of his death in 1985. Reviewer Louis Parks saw it as a triumph in the *Houston Chronicle:* "The book is not only timely, it is also unusual and fascinating, an exceptionally intimate, personal look at a remarkable public figure. Leaming achieves what all biographers want but few manage—she gets at her subject from the inside."

Initially, when Leaming approached Welles to write his authorized biography, he refused. She pursued him for a number of years, all the while accumulating information on him from a multitude of sources. Leaming was on the verge of composing an unauthorized biography when Welles decided to speak. The meetings to follow were not mere interviews, for it is said by various reviewers that Welles slowly opened his soul to Leaming. According to Leaming, it is the achievement of such closeness which has made her work a success. Parks quoted Leaming: "If Orson Welles had died without talking, the private man just never would have appeared. There were hints (of him) in things people told me, but he just wasn't there. . . . That legend of his is so entrenched—a larger-than-life figure, arrogant and terrifying, unreachable and cold. But when you know him, he's shy and vulnerable. He's the most approachable, warm, amusing person you can imagine. It's something I would never have known if Orson hadn't decided to take the chance."

The fact that Leaming was able to get so close to Welles is viewed favorably by some critics and skeptically by others. Whereas *Financial Times* critic Nigel Andrews professed that Leaming "obtained near limitless access to the Master, and has repaid the privilege with a biography that is as revealing, confiding and sumptuously wide-ranging as any autobiography," Jay Scott noted in the Toronto *Globe and Mail:* "Leaming wooed and won the recalcitrant Welles and, at the same time, one suspects, fell in love with him. . . . We are told in [others' biographies of Welles] that Welles could charm birds out of trees; he certainly charmed Leaming out of her critical faculties and with a few exceptions she accepts his memories as Holy Writ and his rationalizations as fact." Other reviewers express opinions similar to Scott's, asserting that Leaming was so taken in by Welles that he moved her to plead for all of his life's mistakes. *Detroit News* commentator Bruce Cook called it a "singular lack of objectivity" and believed Welles found the ideal biographer, "so protective of him that very often she seems more an amanuensis than a biographer." Nevertheless, in spite of this, Cook felt the biography is a "good and wonderfully readable book." Others are also pleased with Leaming's work. According to David Elliott in the *Chicago Sun Times,* "Welles is alive in [Leaming's] book as he has never been before in print. . . . Here is Welles as a talking, eating, sexing, stirringly emotive man. . . . Leaming should have spent more time on the films and plays, a little less with 'look what I found' stuff (courtesy of Welles, mostly) on his prodigious sex life. But for the first time his wives, and not just Rita Hayworth, are more than mere appendages. . . . Leaming has written the best of the Welles books, full of body heat, and a generosity that rarely blunts insight." Sarah Bradford, writing in *Spectator,* believed Welles's life was told in a "fascinating, skillfully assembled biography."

In her next two books, Leaming looked at two other film legends: Welles's former wife and World War II pin-up girl Rita Hayworth, and the combative Bette Davis, flamboyant star of the Warner Brothers studio during the 1940s. Both women, according to Leaming, were products of abusive childhoods, and both of them reflected this damage in their later histories. Both Davis and Hayworth were unable to keep their public images—Hayworth as a "sex kitten," Davis as a feisty, strong-willed feminist—from influencing their off-screen lives.

Rita Hayworth, according to *If This Was Happiness: A Biography of Rita Hayworth,* was sexually abused by her sometime dance partner and father, Eduardo Cansino, who recruited his teenaged daughter to work with him in his nightclub act. "According to Ms. Leaming," wrote Susan Braudy in the *New York Times Book Review,* "her father's abusive treatment was the key to her emotional development and led to a lifetime of disastrous relationships." Hayworth married five times: the first, at age 18, to a much older man who exploited her, stated Braudy, by "threaten[ing] her with physical abuse and disfigurement," and "offer[ing] her to any man he thought would advance her career." Her second husband was Orson Welles, who married her in 1943. However, Welles was unable to meet Hayworth's emotional needs and soon sought solace outside the marriage. Three other marriages—to Prince Aly Khan, heir to the throne of the Aga Khan, to the singer Dick Haymes, and to the director James Hill—also ended in divorce. Hayworth became an alcoholic and in 1980 was diagnosed with Alzheimer's disease. Her daughter, Princess Yasmin Khan, cared for her until her death in 1987.

Many critics celebrated Leaming's convincing portrayal of Hayworth. "The meticulous research," stated Braudy, "makes the painful story of Hayworth's personal problems vivid, which may diminish some envy of her public successes. The book teaches a harder lesson: Rita Hayworth's tortured childhood . . . shaped her. . . . Hollywood did not destroy her." "Leaming's prose can gush," declared Paul Gray in *Time,* ". . . and regularly descends to write-by-the-numbers cliche. But the material is poignant, another reminder of the chasm that can exist between public images and private pain." Hayworth "claimed to have been happy with Welles," Gray concluded, "at least before his infidelities became too blatant. 'If this was happiness,' Welles told Leaming years later, 'imagine what the rest of her life had been.'"

Leaming also presents Bette Davis as a person haunted by her childhood. Davis's father, a Boston lawyer, deserted his family when Bette was ten years old. Bette's mother, Ruthie, compensated by pushing her older daughter into an acting career and making personal sacrifices to maintain Bette's schooling. "When Bette ultimately achieved success," wrote James Kotsilibas-Davis in the *Washington Post Book World,* "Ruthie would exact her toll, living like a queen on her daughter's earnings." In part because of these troubles, Davis evolved into a woman and an actress who practiced what *Los Angeles Times Book Review* contributor David Elliott called "empress tactics." Elliott continued: "A friend said later, 'She began to imitate herself as an actress and to refuse to know that she was doing that.'" Davis's self-destructive practices helped to end all four of her marriages—including those to abusive husbands such as William Grant Sherry and Gary Merrill—and to alienate her daughter. "Leaming's biography," declared Richard Christiansen in the *Chicago Tribune,* "walks delicately between pity and scorn for its subject. The author records the traumas Davis inflicted on her daughter B.D., yet she carefully notes the deep pain that B.D., a born-again Christian, inflicted on her mother with the publication of *My Mother's Keeper,*" her tell-all vituperative autobiography.

After the Davis biography, Leaming turned her attention to one of Davis's contemporaries, Katherine Hepburn, the most celebrated actress of her generation. Although Hepburn granted Leaming an interview, *Katherine Hepburn* is an unauthorized biography, its contents not approved by its subject. Describing her single meeting with Hepburn, Leaming stated: "She was so smart and so perceptive, irresistible. She would go so far in the interview and then be deliberately contrary if she thought she wasn't controlling it." Some critics suggested that in *Katherine Hepburn* Leaming reveals significant aspects of the star's character that have not been previously portrayed. Both in her own biographical writings and in her film personnas, Hepburn emerges as a self-determined and spirited woman, a feminist model of her day. According to Ellis Nassour, writing in *Back Stage:* "Leaming uncovers a Katherine Hepburn in stark contrast with the independent, opinionated, fearless Kate." Delving back two generations, Leaming shows how Hepburn's tragic family background shaped her life. It was a family plagued by suicides, five in all; Hepburn discovered her own brother's body after he hanged himself. It is Leaming's contention that these suicides were instrumental in shaping Hepburn's character, particularly her choice of men. Wary of committing to and losing a man, Hepburn had numerous affairs with married men, such as director John Ford and Spencer Tracy, who were not really available. Leaming depicts Tracy as an abusive and domineering alcoholic who often manipulated Hepburn, and Hepburn herself as a woman far less self-assured than her public image would have us believe. Yet despite its often critical frankness, Leaming's biography is more an insightful and sympathetic portrait than a sordid expose. "As feisty and fascinating as Hepburn herself," stated Ilene Cooper of *Booklist,* "Leaming's book catches all the angles of light reflected through the prism of a fascinating life." Lisa Schwarzbaum, writing in *Entertainment Weekly,* felt that "Leaming's great accomplishment in *Katherine Hepburn* is to make the Great Kate come alive as a regular woman and to tell that story with an empathy and acuity desperately rare in the biographies of stars."

For her sixth film biography, Leaming chose a subject about whom countless biographies, memoirs, and other books had already appeared: Marilyn Monroe. Could Leaming find anything new or worthwhile to say about the blonde bombshell that had not already been said? The answer to this question, as well as critical response to Leaming's *Marilyn Monroe,* varies greatly. According to *Booklist* critic Brad Hooper, "Leaming . . . has lots to say, and she's worth listening to. . . . We come away from Leaming's detailed, explicit, sympathetic picture with more understanding of Monroe's demons and more comprehension of her talents." A *People* reviewer commented: "Leaming does not dwell on rumor and gossip about Monroe's life and death. Instead, basing her account on dozens of interviews and thousands of primary documents, she brings new insight—and a woman's perspective—to Monroe's professional and psychological struggles." Yet other reviewers felt that Leaming's book offered little information of value about Monroe. "This survey of the tragically brief life and career of the 1950s sex symbol," observed Stephen Rees in a *Library Journal* review, "devotes so much space to the men in Monroe's life (Joe DiMaggio, Arthur Miller, Laurence Olivier, Elia Kazan, and many others) that she almost becomes a background player in her own drama. . . . Leaming shows little interest in Monroe's actual film work and provides little information on her involvement with the Kennedys." Similarly, a *Publishers Weekly* reviewer noted: "Leaming relays the precise dates when Monroe signed contracts, called in sick, filmed for half a day, etc. It's an approach that does little to explain Monroe's dynamic screen presence, her warmth and charm."

Leaming turned from biographies of film stars to celebrities of another sort, the Kennedys, in a pair of books profiling John F. Kennedy and his wife, Jacque-

line Kennedy. The 2001 *Mrs. Kennedy: The Missing History of the Kennedy Years* takes on the question of the role Jackie played in the Kennedy White House, "arguing that Jackie played a key part in her husband's presidency," according to *Time* critic Laura Miller. As with many of the female film stars she has profiled, Leaming once again goes to Jackie Kennedy's childhood and youth to explain her later actions. Leaming portrays a troubled childhood with a mother that largely rejected her; this later made Jackie keep an emotional distance between herself and others. As First Lady, Leaming asserts, Jackie used her social skills to make the president—youthful and politically naive—seem more mature and august than he in fact was. Miller did not think that Leaming made her case for a Jackie Kennedy who was intimately involved in decision-making. Miller concluded: "However gracefully [Jackie] intervened in shaping the public face of [JFK's] Administration, her efforts, even by Leaming's highly sympathetic account, were intermittent at best." Likewise, Sally Bedell Smith, writing in the *New York Times Book Review,* felt Leaming "repeatedly misses the mark." However, Ilene Cooper, writing in *Booklist,* observed that whether the reader accepts Leaming's thesis or not, the author "has clearly done her research, and she tells a darn good story." Similarly, a *Publishers Weekly* reviewer thought Leaming "provides a fascinating glimpse into the psychodynamics of one of the 20th century's most famous marriages." A critic for *Kirkus Reviews* had much higher praise, describing *Mrs. Kennedy* as "admirably detailed, stunningly successful, and likely to become the definitive biography of the Kennedy marriage."

With *Jack Kennedy: The Education of a Statesman,* Leaming focuses on the president and his ties to England. Jeff Broadwater, writing in *History,* thought this was a "serious book with a provocative thesis: John F. Kennedy brought to the White House a distinctive approach to foreign policy derived from his deep ties to Great Britain." While still a youth, Kennedy witnessed firsthand—as the son of the then U.S. ambassador to Great Britain—the failed attempts at appeasing Hitler prior to World War II. He also made lasting friendships with men who would later hold important office in England. Leaming also demonstrates how Kennedy learned much about foreign policy from Prime Minister Harold Macmillan. Broadwater felt that Leaming gave "an intriguing human face on the fabled 'special relationship' between the United States and the United Kingdom" in this work. For Geoffrey Wheatcroft, writing in the *New York Times,* Leaming "has written what is in part an absorbing and enjoyable book; whether her thesis really stands up is another matter." Less positive was the review of a *Publishers Weekly* contributor who felt that Leaming "overreaches and overstates in her first attempt at political biography." On the other hand, *Library Journal* reviewer William D. Pederson felt the book was "engagingly written . . . [and] provides new insights into JFK's behavior." Further praise came from a *Kirkus Reviews* critic who found the same work "thoroughly well written and constructed, with fresh views on the Kennedy presidency and the difficult path that led to Camelot."

BIOGRAPHICAL AND CRITICAL SOURCES:

BOOKS

Leaming, Barbara, *Orson Welles: A Biography,* Viking Penguin (New York, NY), 1985.

PERIODICALS

Back Stage, December 1, 1995, Ellis Nassour, review of *Katherine Hepburn,* p. 30.

Biography, summer, 2006, Geoffrey Wheatcroft, review of *Jack Kennedy: The Education of a Statesman,* p. 526.

Book, November-December, 2001, Penelope Mesic, review of *Mrs. Kennedy: The Missing History of the Kennedy Years,* p. 57.

Booklist, March 1, 1995, Ilene Cooper, review of *Katherine Hepburn,* p. 1139; September 1, 1998, Brad Hooper, review of *Marilyn Monroe,* p. 4; September 1, 2001, Ilene Cooper, review of *Mrs. Kennedy,* p. 2.

Canberra Times (Canberra, Australia), August 5, 2006, "Limits in JFK's Getting of Winston."

Chattanooga Times, February 13, 1982, review of *Polanski: The Filmmaker as Voyeur.*

Chicago Sun Times, September 8, 1985, David Elliott, review of *Orson Welles: A Biography.*

Chicago Tribune, May 17, 1992, Richard Christiansen, review of *Bette Davis: A Biography,* p. 3.

Contemporary Review, March, 1986, review of *Orson Welles.*

Detroit Free Press, October 13, 1985, review of *Orson Welles;* November 9, 2001, John Smyntek, review of *Mrs. Kennedy.*

Detroit News (Detroit, MI), October 13, 1985, Bruce Cook, review of *Orson Welles.*

Entertainment Weekly, May 12, 1995, Lisa Schwarzbaum, review of *Katherine Hepburn,* p. 56.

Financial Times, October 19, 1985, Nigel Andrews, review of *Orson Welles.*

Fort Worth Star-Telegram, February 14, 1982, review of *Polanski.*

Globe and Mail (Toronto, Canada), October 5, 1985, Jay Scott, review of *Orson Welles;* November 2, 1985, review of *Orson Welles.*

History, summer, 2005, Jeff Broadwater, review of *Jack Kennedy,* p. 113.

Houston Chronicle, October 20, 1985, Louis Parks, review of *Orson Welles.*

Kirkus Reviews, September 15, 1998; review of *Marilyn Monroe;* September 1, 2001, review of *Mrs. Kennedy,* p. 1268; April 15, 2006, review of *Jack Kennedy,* p. 393.

Library Journal, October 15, 1998, Stephen Rees, review of *Marilyn Monroe,* p. 73; September 1, 2001, Cynthia Harrison, review of *Mrs. Kennedy,* p. 196; April 1, 2006, William D. Pederson, review of *Jack Kennedy,* p. 104.

Los Angeles Times, April 11, 1982, Irwin R. Blacker, review of *Polanski;* September 9, 1985, review of *Orson Welles.*

Los Angeles Times Book Review, May 17, 1992, David Elliott, review of *Bette Davis,* pp. 2, 8.

New Republic, March 17, 1986, review of *Orson Welles.*

New York Review of Books, June 10, 1982, review of *Polanski.*

New York Times, September 6, 1985, review of *Orson Welles;* April 16, 1995, review of *Katherine Hepburn;* June 25, 2006, Geoffrey Wheatcroft, "A Special Relationship," review of *Jack Kennedy.*

New York Times Book Review, September 15, 1985, review of *Orson Welles;* November 19, 1989, Susan Braudy, review of *If This Was Happiness: A Biography of Rita Hayworth,* pp. 7, 9; November 5, 2001, Sally Bedell Smith, review of *Mrs. Kennedy,* p. 14.

Observer (London, England), November 18, 2001, Andrew Rawnsley, "I'm Not All Right, Jack," review of *Mrs. Kennedy.*

Orlando Sentinel (Orlando, FL), November 23, 2001, Loraine O'Connell, review of *Mrs. Kennedy.*

People, May 1, 1995, review of *Katherine Hepburn,* p. 28; November 23, 1998, review of *Marilyn Monroe,* p. 47; December 3, 2001, David Cobb Craig, review of *Mrs. Kennedy,* p. 45.

Philadelphia Inquirer, December 12, 2001, Donald Newlove, review of *Mrs. Kennedy.*

Publishers Weekly, March 13, 1995, review of *Katherine Hepburn,* p. 53; October 26, 1998, review of *Marilyn Monroe,* p. 53; September 3, 2001, review of *Mrs. Kennedy,* p. 71; August 3, 2006, review of *Jack Kennedy,* p. 59.

Reference & Research Book News, August, 2006, review of *Jack Kennedy.*

Seattle Times (Seattle, WA), April 11, 1982, review of *Polanski.*

Spectator, April 3, 1982, review of *Polanski,*; November 9, 1985, Sarah Bradford, review of *Orson Welles*; November 17, 2001, Sarah Bradford, review of *Mrs. Kennedy,* p. 49.

Time, October 7, 1985, review of *Orson Welles*; December 4, 1989, Paul Gray, review of *If This Was Happiness,* pp. B8, 97; October 22, 2001, Laura Miller, review of *Mrs. Kennedy,* p. 78.

Times Literary Supplement, November 28, 1986, review of *Orson Welles.*

Village Voice, October 15, 1985, review of *Orson Welles.*

Village Voice Literary Supplement, March, 1982, review of *Polanski.*

Washington Post Book World, September 17, James Kotsilibas-Davis, review of *Bette Davis,* 1992, p. 8.*

* * *

LEBERT, Benjamin 1982-

PERSONAL: Born January 9, 1982, in Freiberg, Germany. *Education:* Castle Nueseelen Boarding School.

ADDRESSES: Home—Munich, Germany.

CAREER: Writer for young-adult supplement of *Süddeutsche Zeitung,* Munich, Germany.

WRITINGS:

NOVELS

Crazy, translated from German by Carol Brown Janeway, Knopf (New York, NY), 2000.

Der Vogel is ein Rabe, Goldmann (Munich, Germany), 2005, English translation by Peter Constantine published as *The Bird Is a Raven,* Knopf (New York, NY), 2005.

ADAPTATIONS: Crazy was adapted for film by producers Jakob Claussen and Thomas Wobke, directed by Hans-Christian Schmid, and won numerous awards in Germany.

SIDELIGHTS: Benjamin Lebert, sometimes called a *wunderkind* in the world of contemporary German literature, achieved immediate success with the publication of his coming-of-age novel, *Crazy.* Written when the author was only fifteen, the book was an overnight sensation among German youth. By the end of 2001 it had sold over 300,000 copies in Germany alone, and its American publication marked another milestone for Lebert, who was then eighteen. The novel was eventually translated into twenty-five languages.

The protagonist of this semi-autobiographical novel also bears the name Benjamin Lebert, and, like the author, he is handicapped and a school dropout. *Crazy* tells the story of a boy who has failed at several boarding schools and has now entered a new one in a last-ditch attempt to graduate. He soon acquires several colorful friends who join him in a mutual journey of self-discovery, experimenting with drugs, sex, smoking, and alcohol while reflecting often on the meaning of their lives. Benni, as he is called, joins his friends on several escapades, including a raid on the girls' dorm and a forbidden trip to Munich. Despite his growing feeling of belonging, Benni in the end does not improve his grades and is forced to leave the school.

In an interview with Simon Hattenstone in the *Guardian,* Lebert said that he started writing monster stories around the age of nine and began *Crazy* during weekends at home from school. He told Hattenstone that through writing, "you can invent your own world. There's a kind of purity. . . . You have to be very honest and very close to yourself." He indicated that he was angered to find that some reviewers thought the book was actually written by his father, a journalist. His former teachers, he said, had little confidence in his writing abilities: "They said I was a loser. . . . But I feel in some way everyone is not a loser. Everyone is brave in some way."

Lebert's rise to fame began when German author Maxim Biller read one of Lebert's pieces in a youth supplement to a German newspaper and faxed it to his own publishing house, which later decided to publish and promote *Crazy*. The book's often-mentioned similarities to J.D. Salinger's *Catcher in the Rye* prompted Lebert to remark to Allison Linn in an interview in *Book:* "Without *Catcher in the Rye*, this book never would have been written." Linn noted that "Lebert has clearly captured the hearts of so many German teens in part because he so unabashedly revealed his insecure and sensitive side in the novel—the child still trapped in the teen-ager."

Many reviews of *Crazy* mentioned Lebert's obvious potential as a writer. In the *New York Times Book Review*, Jeffrey Eugenides commented on the book's tendency to "blather on and on" as "Lebert's band of schoolboys wax philosophic," and criticized the "sketchy characterization" and "unjustified behavior" evident in the story. But Eugenides also found that "on a purely linguistic level [Lebert] writes clearly and adequately." Max Brzezinski, writing in the *Antioch Review*, called the book "cliché-ridden" and "superficial," but acknowledged that it "shows genuine promise." Hattenstone concluded that "*Crazy* is a beautiful book about someone grasping freedom for the first time." *Booklist* reviewer Kristine Huntley commented: "Lebert's voice is enticing from the first page, and his witty but simple observations make this book an impressive first novel from a talented young writer."

Lebert's next book, *Der Vogel is ein Rabe*, published in English translation as *The Bird Is a Raven*, is a short novel that depicts a long conversation between people who meet on a train. The narrator, Paul, is initially friendly to Henry, a stranger with whom he shares a berth. He is soon overwhelmed, however, by Henry's frank talk about his troubled relationships, his violent impulses, and his sexual inhibitions. Evaluating *The Bird Is a Raven* for the *New York Times Book Review*, Etelka Lehoczky credited the young author with having a well-realized "master plan" in a book that has "a sense of delicately balanced tension." A *Kirkus Reviews* writer called *The Bird Is a Raven* a "jagged, lyrical . . . gem" that "shines darkly."

BIOGRAPHICAL AND CRITICAL SOURCES:

PERIODICALS

Antioch Review, winter, 2001, Max Brzezinski, review of *Crazy*, p. 111.

Booklist, February 15, 2000, Kristine Huntley, review of *Crazy*, p. 1052; November 1, 2005, Kristine Huntley, review of *The Bird Is a Raven*, p. 24.
Guardian (London, England), July 31, 2000, Simon Hattenstone, "Portrait: Flawed Genius," p. 8.
Kirkus Reviews, November 1, 2005, review of *The Bird Is a Raven*, p. 1160.
Library Journal, April 1, 2000, Judith Kicinski, review of *Crazy*, p. 130; February 1, 2006, Christopher Korenowsky, review of *The Bird Is a Raven*, p. 72.
Los Angeles Times, April 28, 2000, Heller McAlpin, "Thoughtful Teens Populate Young Writer's Coming-of-Age Tale," p. E3.
New York Times Book Review, May 14, 2000, Jeffrey Eugenides, "Pup Fiction," p. 12; January 29, 2006, Etelka Lehoczky, review of *The Bird Is a Raven*.
Publishers Weekly, March 20, 2000, review of *Crazy*, p. 73; October 17, 2005, review of *The Bird Is a Raven*, p. 42.
School Library Journal, August, 2000, Sheryl Fowler, review of *Crazy*, p. 212.

OTHER

Book, http://www.bookmagazine.com/ (May-June, 2000), profile of Leber and excerpt from *Crazy*.*

*   *   *

LEE, Kathryn Louise
    See LEE, Katie

*   *   *

LEE, Katie 1919-
    (Kathryn Louise Lee)

PERSONAL: Born October 23, 1919, in Aledo, IL; daughter of Zanna Park (an architect) and Ruth (a designer and decorator) Lee; married Charles V. Eld (an air force officer), November 6, 1942 (divorced, July, 1945); married Gene A. Bush, 1958 (divorced, May, 1962); children: (first marriage) Ronald Charles. *Ethnicity:* "Scottish/Irish/English." *Education:* University of Arizona, B.F.A., 1942. *Politics:* Liberal. *Religion:* "Agnostic/pagan." *Hobbies and other interests:* "Free rivers that run un-dammed."

ADDRESSES: Home and office—Jerome, AZ. *E-mail*—katydid@swiftwireless.com.

CAREER: Performer, researcher, and writer, c. 1954—. Katydid Books and Music, Jerome, AZ, principal. Singer and actress on television and radio programs, including *Gildersleeve Show,* National Broadcasting Co.; *Halls of Ivy, Railroad Hour,* and *Pacific Telephone Show.* Appeared in movies and videos, on German, British, Japanese, and Dutch television shows, on National Public Radio, and on *Morning Edition* with Rene Montagne. Record albums, cassettes, and compact discs include *Songs of Couch and Consultation,* 1957; *Life Is Just a Bed of Neuroses,* RCA Victor, 1960; *Spicy Songs for Cool Knights,* Specialty, c. 1961; *Folk Songs of the Colorado River,* Folkways, 1961; *The Best of Katie Lee,* Horizon Records, 1962; *The Slolom Truth Ski Songs,* privately recorded, 1964; *Love's Little Sisters,* Katydid Records, 1975; *Ten Thousand Goddam Cattle,* Katydid Books and Music, 1977; *Fenced!,* Katydid Books and Music, 1979; (with Ed Stabler) *Katie Lee and Ed Stabler Sing the Poems of His Knibbs and the Badger,* Katydid Books and Music, 1992; *Colorado River Songs,* Katydid Books and Music, 1998; and *Glen Canyon River Journeys,* Katydid Books and Music, 1998. Performed in clubs and coffeehouses across the United States, 1954-78. Also affiliated with the television special *The Last Wagon,* about cowboys Gail Gardner and Billy Simon. Glen Canyon Institute, member of advisory board.

MEMBER: Earth Island Institute, American Society of Composers, Authors, and Publishers, Screen Actors Guild, American Federation of Musicians, American Federation of Television and Radio Artists, Wilderness Society, National Parks Association, Great Old Broads for Wilderness, Southwest Center for Biodiversity, Colorado River Rats, Utah Environmental Congress, Southern Utah Wilderness Alliance, Grand Canyon River Guides, Grand Canyon, Private Boosters Association, Jerome Historical Society, Zeta Phi Eta.

AWARDS, HONORS: CINE Golden Eagle, Council on International Nontheatrical Events, 1972, for *The Last Wagon;* David Brower Award for outstanding environmental activism, Glen Canyon Institute, 2001; First Culture Treasure Keepers of Canyon Country Award, Center for Sustainable Environment, Northern Arizona University, 2002; Ward Roylance Award for commitment to arts and outdoor education, Entrada Institute, 2003.

WRITINGS:

Ten Thousand Goddam Cattle: A History of the American Cowboy in Song, Story, and Verse, illustrated by William Moyers, Northland Press (Flagstaff, AZ), 1976, reprinted, University of New Mexico Press (Albuquerque, NM), 2001.

All My Rivers Are Gone: A Journey of Discovery through Glen Canyon, introduction by Terry Tempest Williams, Johnson Books (Boulder, CO), 1998, updated edition published as *Glen Canyon Betrayed,* Fretwater Press (Flagstaff, AZ), 2006.

Sandstone Seduction (memoir), foreword by Ellen Meloy, Johnson Books (Boulder, CO), 2004.

Work represented in anthologies, including *Sisters of the Earth,* edited by Lorraine Anderson, Vintage Press (New York, NY), 1991; *Jack Ruby's Kitchen Sink,* edited by Tom Miller, National Geographic Adventure Press (Washington, DC), 2000; *Grand Canyon Women,* edited by Betty Leavengood, Pruett Publishing (Boulder, CO); *When in Doubt Go Higher,* edited by M. John Fayhee, Mountain Sports Press (Boulder, CO); and *Hell's Half Mile,* edited by Michael Engelhard, Breakaway Books (Moab, UT). Contributor to periodicals, including *Arizona Historical Quarterly, Mountain Gazette, American Whitewater Journal, Wild Earth, Boatman's Quarterly Review, Waiting List,* and *Hidden Passage.* Photographer for *Arizona Highways,* 1954-60.

SIDELIGHTS: Katie Lee is a singer, actress, and writer who has written about the American West. Her career as a performer, which began in 1948, included appearances in the early 1950s on various radio and television programs, including programs hosted by Dave Garroway and Jack Paar. In the mid-1950s to 1960s, she played in nightclubs in New York City, Miami, and Chicago, and she began touring as a singer and lecturer in a program devoted to folk songs related to the Colorado River in 1970. She also made several recordings.

Lee's writings include *Ten Thousand Goddam Cattle: A History of the American Cowboy in Song, Story, and Verse,* wherein she relates the cowboy's role in American culture and recounts her efforts to locate Old Dolores, a town mentioned in a song by James Grafton Rogers. John I. White, writing in *American West,* described *Ten Thousand Goddam Cattle* as a book "about southwestern people as well as their songs," and he predicted that the volume "should quickly find a place besides other good collections of songs by and about . . . the American cowboy." A *Music Educator's Journal* reviewer, meanwhile, concluded that Lee's book provides "a realistic picture of life on the prairie."

Lee is also the author of *All My Rivers Are Gone: A Journey of Discovery through Glen Canyon,* in which she recalls her experiences on the Colorado River prior to the damming that created Lake Powell. A *Publishers Weekly* critic noted that Lee "successfully evokes the magnificent trails, beaches and waterfalls . . . of the canyon," and a *Library Journal* reviewer observed that Lee "writes poetically and soulfully."

Several years ago Lee told *CA:* "I am now eighty years old! (Young!) My efforts to restore Glen Canyon (lying dead under Reservoir Fowell) will continue until my death. Nothing and no one human would have dammed it in the first place, but humans with vision and dedication will un-dam it soon! Our rivers are the life blood of this planet. They must run to keep us and the planet from dying!"

BIOGRAPHICAL AND CRITICAL SOURCES:

BOOKS

Lee, Katie, *All My Rivers Are Gone: A Journey of Discovery through Glen Canyon,* Johnson Books (Boulder, CO), 1998, updated edition published as *Glen Canyon Betrayed,* Fretwater Press (Flagstaff, AZ), 2006.
Lee, Katie, *Sandstone Seduction,* Johnson Books (Boulder, CO), 2004.

PERIODICALS

American West, September-October, 1977, review of *Ten Thousand Goddam Cattle: A History of the American Cowboy in Song, Story, and Verse,* p. 63.
Library Journal, November 1, 1998, Thomas K. Fry, review of *All My Rivers Are Gone: A Journey of Discovery through Glen Canyon,* p. 121.
Music Educators Journal, January, 1978, review of *Ten Thousand Goddam Cattle,* p. 129.
Publishers Weekly, October 19, 1998, review of *Ten Thousand Goddam Cattle,* p. 63.

OTHER

Rusho, W.L., *Glen Canyon Remembered* (video), Tower Productions (Salt Lake City, UT), 2006.

*   *   *

LEMANN, Nicholas 1954-

PERSONAL: Surname is pronounced "lemon"; born August 11, 1954, in New Orleans, LA; son of Thomas B. (a lawyer) and Barbara M. (a psychologist) Lemann; married Dominique A. Browning (an editor), May 20, 1983 (divorced); married Judith Shulevitz (an editor), November, 1999; children: Four children, including Alexander B. and Theo. *Education:* Harvard University, B.A., 1976. *Religion:* Jewish.

ADDRESSES: Home—Pelham, NY. *Office*—Columbia University, Graduate School of Journalism, 2950 Broadway, New York, NY 10027. *Agent*—Amanda Urban, International Creative Management, 40 W. 57th St., New York, NY 10019. *E-mail*—nl2124@columbia.edu.

CAREER: Writer, editor. *Washington Monthly,* Washington, DC, managing and contributing editor, 1976—; *Texas Monthly,* Austin, TX, associate, contributing, and executive editor, beginning 1978; *Washington Post,* Washington, DC, reporter, 1979-81; *Atlantic Monthly,* Boston, MA, national correspondent, beginning 1983; affiliated with *New Yorker,* New York, NY, 1999—; Graduate School of Journalism, Columbia University, New York, NY, dean, 2003—.

AWARDS, HONORS: Los Angeles Times Book Award for History, 1991, for *The Promised Land: The Black Migration and How It Changed America.*

WRITINGS:

(Editor, with Charles Peters) *Inside the System,* Prentice-Hall (Engelwood Cliffs, NJ), 1978, 4th edition, Holt (New York, NY), 1979.
The Fast Track: Texans and Other Strivers (essays; includes "Sherwood Blount's First Million," "Big Oil," "Little Oil," "The Split," and "The Medical Center"), W.W. Norton (New York, NY), 1981.

Out of the Forties (nonfiction), Texas Monthly (Austin, TX), 1983.

The Promised Land: The Great Black Migration and How It Changed America (nonfiction), Knopf (New York, NY), 1991.

The Big Test: The Secret History of the American Meritocracy, Farrar, Straus and Giroux (New York, NY), 1999.

Redemption: The Last Battle of the Civil War, Farrar, Straus and Giroux (New York, NY), 2006.

Contributor to periodicals.

SIDELIGHTS: A journalist who has held positions at the *Washington Post* and *Atlantic Monthly,* Nicholas Lemann has also distinguished himself as an accomplished writer of nonfiction. His first work to receive critical attention was *The Fast Track: Texans and Other Strivers,* a collection of essays that focuses on a variety of ambitious people, including a Texas real-estate mogul, a prominent heart surgeon, and the founding mother of Off-Off-Broadway theater. Lemann's thesis, speculated R.J. Davis in the *Washington Post,* "is that the lust for cash is the least of the many fuels that propel the wheels of commerce; far more important is the desire to do something that one does well." Reviewers responded favorably to *The Fast Track; New Republic* contributor Anne Tyler, for instance, deemed it "an absorbing collection—a crisply written, clear-eyed study of America's travels upward." And though Davis assessed that the book was lacking in cohesiveness, he remarked that "we shall doubtless be hearing more of Nicholas Lemann in the future."

Lemann's next work, *Out of the Forties,* provides a glimpse of the past through a selection of photographs from the 1940s. Lemann chose the pictures from a collection of 85,000 that were commissioned by Standard Oil (now Exxon) as part of a campaign designed to bolster the company's image. The photographs document a wide variety of American experiences and are judged by Lemann as "perhaps the best portrayal of the middle and late 1940s in any medium," quoted *Washington Post Book World* critic Jonathan Yardley. Some reviewers commented that the pictures alone would have made for an engaging book: a young girl observes her father fixing the family car; wide-eyed teenagers in New Jersey watch their first television set; cowboys play cards in a Texas bunkhouse; a farmer and his family lounge on a service-station porch in North Carolina. Yet rather than let the images stand unaccompanied, Lemann found and interviewed some of the people that appeared in them and included their stories in *Out of the Forties.*

The result, Yardley declared, is an "unusually appealing and provocative book" in which the photographs are used "as the starting point from which to explore the validity of . . . nostalgia" as well as to illustrate the changes that took place in America between the 1940s and 1980s. "In this antidote to sentimental memoirs," wrote *New York Times Book Review* contributor Peter Davis, "Nicholas Lemann manages to mingle nostalgia with bitterness, anger with pride in a fashion reminiscent of Michael Lesy's now semiclassic *Wisconsin Death Trip.*" Davis also commented on the power of the photographs, judging that "the images assault, caress, beckon, haunt."

The 1940s also serve as a launching point for Lemann's highly acclaimed best-seller *The Promised Land: The Great Black Migration and How It Changed America,* which chronicles the large black population shift from the rural South to the urban North that began in that period. Much of the impetus for this movement is credited to the advent of the mechanical cotton picker in the mid-1940s, a machine that did the work of fifty people and one that made the sharecropper system obsolete. Many Southern blacks—approximately four million between 1940 and 1970—subsequently migrated North in search of jobs and a better life. Lemann begins his narrative by following several typical black families from the Mississippi Delta town of Clarksdale to Chicago, outlining their hopes of finding the "promised land." While this migration eventually gave rise to a sizable black middle-class, a number of blacks fared no better in the city than they did as sharecroppers. Often poverty and racism kept them relegated to ghettos where crime was rampant, families and other institutions unstable, well-paying jobs scarce, and the quality of life akin to that in some Third World countries.

Against this personal and historical background, Lemann details how public policymakers in Washington, DC, attempted to address the problems faced by many urban blacks. He describes, for instance, how President Lyndon Johnson's War on Poverty program impacted the ghettos and the individuals who lived in them. Some federal efforts worked, such as the Head Start program for impoverished preschool children and the creation of government jobs. But attempts to improve life within inner cities—to establish what was called at the time "gilded ghettos"—were largely unsuccessful because, as Seymour Martin Lipset observed in *Times Literary Supplement,* "Blacks do not want a 'gilded ghetto'; they want to get out of the ghetto." While the failure of government programs to eradicate the social problems of the black urban poor and the rise of conservatism discouraged policymakers from attempting larger efforts, Lemann argues that the government simply did not go far enough.

Although the problems that continue to face those in the primarily black urban "underclass" are unwieldy, Lemann believes they are not unsolvable. His optimistic, thorough, and personal approach won the favor of many critics. "Lemann reminds the reader that certain conditions in black America remain intolerable. As a result, he stirs one's conscience," wrote Christopher Lehmann-Haupt in the *New York Times.* Lipset remarked that *The Promised Land* "reads like a novel; or rather like a series of short stories, which enable the reader to understand the lives of the characters in them." *Washington Post Book World* critic Jonathan Yardley termed the book "purposeful and original" and C. Vann Woodward, writing in *New York Times Book Review,* stated that Lemann "has fulfilled an important and neglected need. Furthermore, he has done this with skill and devotion, and his book deserves wide attention." Lipset concluded that "on very rare occasions, a book can turn a nation's social and political outlook around. This one is good enough to do it."

In *The Big Test: The Secret History of the American Meritocracy,* Lemann describes the history and social impact of the educational testing industry. College-admissions tests such as the SAT were developed in the 1930s, intended to make college admissions more a matter of natural intelligence rather than social connections. Yet the tests seemed to perpetuate the system they were intended to break up. Lemann discusses the great anxiety modern students feel about taking the test, knowing that their scores may have a significant influence on the quality of school they are admitted to, the quality of job they will go on to obtain, and the quality of their entire life. In an interview for *People Weekly,* Lemann was quoted as saying: "One thing I find horrifying is the test-preparation craze. . . . There's a new tier emerging—prepping as early as seventh grade, hiring a 500-dollar-an-hour tutor or someone who will help write your admissions application essay for 3,000 dollars. It's a way for those with money to manipulate the system in their kids' favor."

A reviewer for *Business Week* called *The Big Test* "one of the most astute and disquieting efforts of the season.

What begins as a chronicle of the evolution of standardized testing ends as a penetrating commentary on today's frantic skirmish for a place in the professional upper middle class. Lemann shows how our educational system, 'one of the United States' great original social contributions,' has become a giant—and somewhat rigged—slot machine. . . . *The Big Test* is a very enjoyable read." *Booklist* reviewer Mary Carroll, in discussing *The Big Test,* noted: "[Lemann] . . . infuses a potentially dry topic with life and energy" and called the book "a fascinating subject, fascinatingly studied."

Lemann's 2006 work, *Redemption: The Last Battle of the Civil War,* is a study of how Southern whites attempted to redeem their defeat in the Civil War by suppressing black freedom through terror and political chicanery. Much of Lemann's book focuses on the actions of the racial supremacist White Leaguers in Louisiana and Mississippi. Writing in the *New York Times Book Review,* Sean Wilentz felt the author "simplifies too much" in his narrative, yet also observed that the book "offers a vigorous, necessary reminder of how racist reaction bred an American terrorism that suppressed black political activity and crushed Reconstruction in the South." *Library Journal* contributor Thomas J. Davis felt that Lemann "personalizes the gruesome racial politics from which U.S. apartheid and its legacies emerged with the nation's acquiescence" by his use of the private papers of those involved, including the well-intentioned Republican governor of Mississippi, Adelbert Ames. A reviewer for *Publishers Weekly* had praise for Lemann's chronicle, noting that the author "delivers an engrossing but painful account of a disgraceful episode in American history." Similar praise came from a *Kirkus Reviews* critic who called *Redemption* "a sobering account of the true end of Reconstruction, long suppressed in favor of the self-serving fairy tale peddled by the victors."

BIOGRAPHICAL AND CRITICAL SOURCES:

PERIODICALS

America, August 31, 1991, review of *The Promised Land: The Great Black Migration and How It Changed America,* p. 124.

American Spectator, June, 1991, review of *The Promised Land,* pp. 9, 14.

Atlantic Monthly, October 2006, review of *Redemption: The Last Battle of the Civil War,* p. 126.

Black Enterprise, February, 1992, review of *The Promised Land,* p. 244.

Booklist, August, 1999, Mary Carroll, review of *The Big Test: The Secret History of the American Meritocracy,* p. 1982; September 15, 2006, Vanessa Bush, review of *Redemption,* p. 19.

Business Week, October 25, 1999, review of *The Big Test,* p. 15.

Center Magazine, November-December, 1983, review of *Out of the Forties,* p. 18.

Christian Century, December 12, 2006, review of *Redemption,* p. 23.

Commentary, August, 1991, review of *The Promised Land,* p. 62; October, 1999, review of *The Big Test,* pp. 57-60.

Daily News (New York, NY), April 16, 2003, "New York City Journalism Graduate School Gets Dean."

Economist, April 6, 1991, review of *The Promised Land,* p. 86.

Esquire, February, 1991, review of *The Promised Land,* p. 31.

Fortune, October 25, 1999, review of *The Big Test,* p. 68.

Glamour, March, 1991, review of *The Promised Land,* p. 206.

Journal of American History, March, 1992, review of *The Promised Land,* p. 1510.

Journal of Regional Science, November, 1991, review of *The Promised Land,* p. 494.

Kirkus Reviews, July 1, 2006, review of *Redemption,* p. 666.

Library Journal, February 15, 1991, review of *The Promised Land,* p. 207; September 1, 1999, review of *The Big Test,* p. 211; July 1, 2006, Thomas J. Davis, review of *Redemption,* p. 90.

Nation, April 22, 1991, review of *The Promised Land,* p. 528.

National Catholic Reporter, November 22, 1991, review of *The Promised Land,* p. 37.

National Review, August 26, 1991, review of *The Promised Land,* p. 39.

Nation's Cities Weekly, April 22, 1991, review of *The Promised Land,* p. 3.

New Leader, April 8, 1991, review of *The Promised Land,* p. 14.

New Republic, June 13, 1981, Anne Tyler, review of *The Fast Track: Texans and Other Strivers,* pp. 31-32; May 17, 1991, review of *The Promised Land,* p. 35.

New Statesman, August 23, 1991, review of *The Promised Land,* p. 36.

Newsweek, March 18, 1991, review of *The Promised Land,* p. 62.

New York, October 11, 1999, review of *The Big Test,* p. 104.

New York Review of Books, March 28, 1991, review of *The Promised Land,* p. 11.

New York Times, February 21, 1991, Christopher Lehmann-Haupt, review of *The Promised Land,* p. C18; August 11, 2006, Katharine Q. Seelye, "2 Editors Resign at Web Site Linked to Journalism Review," p. C3.

New York Times Book Review, July 31, 1983, Peter Davis, review of *Out of the Forties,* pp. 9, 20; February 24, 1991, C. Vann Woodward, review of *The Promised Land,* pp. 1, 24; October 24, 1999, review of *The Big Test,* p. 6; September 10, 2006, Sean Wilentz, "A Less Perfect Union," review of *Redemption.*

People Weekly, August 22, 1983, review of *Out of the Forties,* p. 10; November 22, 1999, "Testing, Testing," interview with Lemann, p. 187.

Progressive, June, 1991, review of *The Promised Land,* p. 40.

Public Interest, summer, 1991, review of *The Promised Land,* p. 3.

Publishers Weekly, May 15, 1981, review of *The Fast Track,* p. 53; January 11, 1991, review of *The Promised Land,* p. 87; November 22, 1991, review of *The Promised Land,* p. 15; August 30, 1999, review of *The Big Test,* p. 61; November 1, 1999, review of *The Big Test,* p. 50; May 29, 2006, review of *Redemption,* p. 46.

Reason, October, 1991, review of *The Promised Land,* p. 60.

Tikkun, November-December, 1991, review of *The Promised Land,* p. 85.

Time, March 11, 1991, review of *The Promised Land,* p. 72; October 4, 1999, review of *The Big Test,* p. 100.

Times Literary Supplement, May 31, 1991, Seymour Martin Lipset, review of *The Promised Land,* p. 5.

Tribune Books (Chicago, IL), February 17, 1991, review of *The Promised Land,* pp. 1, 4.

USA Today Magazine, July, 1991, review of *The Promised Land,* p. 96.

U.S. News and World Report, March 4, 1991, review of *The Promised Land,* p. 55; April 22, 1991, review of *The Promised Land,* p. 23; October 25, 1999, review of *The Big Test,* p. 16.

Washington Monthly, May, 1991, review of *The Promised Land,* p. 51; September, 2006, John Meacham, review of *Redemption,* p. 54.

Washington Post, May 25, 1981, R.J. Davis, review of *The Fast Track,* p. E7.

Washington Post Book World, June 19, 1983, Jonathan Yardley, review of *Out of the Forties,* pp. 3, 7; March 10, 1991, Jonathan Yardley, review of *The Promised Land,* p. 3.

Yale Review, spring, 1984, review of *Out of the Forties,* p. 438.

ONLINE

Columbia University Journalism School Web site, http://www.jrn.columbia.edu/ (January 29, 2007), "Nicholas Lemann."

PEN American Center Web site, http://www.pen.org/ (January 29, 2007), "Nicholas Lemann."*

*   *   *

LEVY, Andrew 1962-
(Andrew Gordon Levy)

PERSONAL: Born November 5, 1962, in Mount Holly, NJ; son of Walter (a telecommunications consultant) and Claire Levy; married Siobhan McEvoy, August 12, 1998; children: Aedan. *Ethnicity:* "White." *Education:* Brown University, B.A., 1984; Johns Hopkins University, M.A., 1986; University of Pennsylvania, Ph.D., 1991. *Politics:* Independent. *Religion:* Jewish.

ADDRESSES: Home—Indianapolis, IN. *Office*—Department of English, Butler University, Indianapolis, IN 46208; fax 317-940-9930. *E-mail*—alevy@butler.edu.

CAREER: Writer, educator. Edgewood Teleservices, Plainsboro, NJ, systems analyst and software designer, 1984-86; Philadelphia College of Pharmacy and Science (now University of the Sciences), Philadelphia, PA, adjunct professor, 1989-92; Butler University, Indianapolis, IN, assistant professor, 1992-96, associate professor, 1996-98, Edna Cooper Professor of English, 1998—, codirector of Writers' Studio, 1993-95 and 1997—, director of Fellows Program at Writers' Studio, 1993—. Speaker at colleges and universities, including University of Louisville, University of Pennsylvania, University of Maryland—St. Mary's City, and University of California—Davis.

WRITINGS:

The Culture and Commerce of the American Short Story (monograph), Cambridge University Press (New York, NY), 1993.

(With Fred Leebron) *Creating Fiction: A Writer's Companion,* Harcourt (San Diego, CA), 1995.

(Editor, with Fred Leebron and Paula Geyh) *Postmodern American Fiction: A Norton Anthology,* Norton (New York, NY), 1997.

The First Emancipator: The Forgotten Story of Robert Carter, the Founding Father Who Freed His Slaves, Random House (New York, NY), 2005.

Contributor to *The Americanization of the Holocaust,* edited by Hilene Flanzbaum, Johns Hopkins University Press (Baltimore, MD), 1998; *Falling toward Grace,* edited by Kent Calder and Susan Neville, Indiana University Press (Bloomington, IN), 1998; and *The American Century: Art and Culture, 1950-2000,* edited by Lisa Phillips, Norton (New York, NY), 1999. Contributor of stories, articles, and reviews to periodicals, including *Kansas Quarterly, Postmodern Culture, Harper's,* and *Nineteenth-Century Literature.* Associate editor, *Boulevard,* 1986—.

SIDELIGHTS: An English professor and author of several books on American literature and writing, Andrew Levy delved into American history for his 2005 *The First Emancipator: The Forgotten Story of Robert Carter, the Founding Father Who Freed His Slaves.* Carter, "scion of the most powerful slaveholding family in colonial Virginia," according to *Journal of Southern History* contributor Kirt Von Daacke, freed 450 of his slaves in 1791, taking to heart the principles of the new-found nation while others merely debated the issue. This was the largest single freeing of slaves until Abraham Lincoln signed the Emancipation Proclamation over seventy years later. Levy employed private documents from the period, including letters and diaries, to portray the philosophical and religious thinking that compelled Carter to his momentous action. *Booklist* contributor Vanessa Bush found *The First Emancipator* "absorbing" as well as "well researched and thoroughly fascinating." Von Daacke also had praise for the work, noting that despite certain faults of interpretation, "Levy's work remains significant for its treatment of Carter's religious journey from elite Anglicanism to evangelical Christianity." Similarly, Melvin Patrick Ely, writing in the *Washington Post Book World,* thought "Levy's careful reading of Carter family papers yields a vivid narrative of the future emancipator's evolution." A *Frontlist.com* contributor also commended Levy's biographical study, concluding: "Drawing on years of painstaking research, written with grace and fire, *The First Emancipator* is a portrait of an unsung hero who has finally won his place in American history. It is an astonishing, challenging, and ultimately inspiring book."

BIOGRAPHICAL AND CRITICAL SOURCES:

PERIODICALS

Booklist, April 15, 2005, Vanessa Bush, review of *The First Emancipator: The Forgotten Story of Robert Carter, the Founding Father Who Freed His Slaves,* p. 1426.
Journal of Southern History, August, 2006, Kirt Von Daacke, review of *The First Emancipator,* p. 656.
Washington Post Book World, April 24, 2005, Melvin Patrick Ely, review of *The First Emancipator,* p. 3.

ONLINE

Andrew Levy Home Page, http://blue.butler.edu/~alevy (January 31, 2007).
Butler University, Department of English Web site, http://www.butler.edu/ (January 29, 2007), "English Faculty: Andrew Levy."
Frontlist.com, http://www.frontlist.com/ (January 29, 2007), review of *The First Emancipator.**

*   *   *

LEVY, Andrew Gordon
   See LEVY, Andrew

*   *   *

LEWIS, John Royston
   See LEWIS, Roy

*   *   *

LEWIS, J.R.
   See LEWIS, Roy

*   *   *

LEWIS, Roy 1933-
   (J.R. Lewis, John Royston Lewis, David Springfield)

PERSONAL: Born January 17, 1933, in Rhondda, Glamorganshire, Wales; son of John Harold (a miner) and Ellen Lewis; married Gwendoline Hutchings (a teacher), February, 1955 (divorced, 1984); children: Mark, Yvette, Sarah. *Education:* University of Bristol, LL.B., 1954; University of Exeter, diploma in education, 1957; called to the Bar, London, England, 1965; University of Durham, M.A., 1978. *Hobbies and other interests:* Watching rugby on television.

ADDRESSES: Home—South Stainmore, Westmorland, England.

CAREER: Teacher and writer. Managing director of publishing companies, including Templar North Publications Limited, Casdec Limited, and Felton Press; Okehampton Secondary School, Devon, England, teacher, 1957-59; Cannock Chase Technical College, Staffordshire, England, lecturer, 1959-61; Cornwall Technical College, Redruth, Cornwall, England, lecturer, 1961-63; Plymouth College of Technology, Devon, England, lecturer, 1963-67; Her Majesty's inspector of schools, Newcastle, England, 1967-75; New College, Durham, England, vice-principal, 1975-81; Wigan College of Technology, Wigan, England, principal, 1981-90. *Military service:* Royal Artillery, 1954-56.

MEMBER: Chartered Institute of Secretaries and Administrators, fellow, 1983; international president, 1988.

WRITINGS:

MYSTERY NOVELS

A Lover Too Many, Collins (London, England), 1969, World (Cleveland, OH), 1971.
A Wolf by the Ears, Collins (London, England), 1970, World (Cleveland, OH), 1972.
Error of Judgment, Collins (London, England), 1971.
The Fenokee Project, Collins (London, England), 1971.
A Secret Singing, Collins (London, England), 1972.
A Fool for a Client, Collins (London, England), 1972.
Blood Money, Collins (London, England), 1973.
Of Singular Purpose, Collins (London, England), 1973.
A Question of Degree, Collins (London, England), 1974.
Double Take, Collins (London, England), 1975.
A Part of Virtue, Collins (London, England), 1975.
Witness My Death, Collins (London, England), 1976.
Distant Banner, Collins (London, England), 1976.

Nothing but Foxes, Collins (London, England), 1977, St. Martin's Press (New York, NY), 1979.

An Uncertain Sound, Collins (London, England), 1978, St. Martin's Press (New York, NY), 1980.

An Inevitable Fatality, Collins (London, England), 1978.

A Violent Death, Collins (London, England), 1979.

A Certain Blindness, Collins (London, England), 1980, St. Martin's Press (New York, NY), 1981.

A Relative Distance, Collins (London, England), 1981.

Seek for Justice, Collins (London, England), 1981.

Dwell in Danger, St. Martin's Press (New York, NY), 1982.

A Gathering of Ghosts, Collins (London, England), 1982, St. Martin's Press (New York, NY), 1983.

A Limited Vision, Collins (London, England), 1983, St. Martin's Press (New York, NY), 1984.

Once Dying, Twice Dead, St. Martin's Press (New York, NY), 1984.

Most Cunning Workmen, Collins (London, England), 1984, St. Martin's Press (New York, NY), 1985.

A Blurred Reality, St. Martin's Press (New York, NY), 1985.

A Trout in the Milk, St. Martin's Press (New York, NY), 1986.

Premium on Death, Collins (London, England), 1986, St. Martin's Press (New York, NY), 1987.

Men of Subtle Craft, Collins (London, England), 1987, St. Martin's Press (New York, NY), 1988.

The Salamander Chill, Collins (London, England), 1988, St. Martin's Press (New York, NY), 1989.

A Necessary Dealing, Collins (London, England), 1989.

The Devil Is Dead, St. Martin's Press (New York, NY), 1990.

A Kind of Transaction, HarperCollins (London, England), 1991.

A Wisp of Smoke, HarperCollins (London, England), 1991, St. Martin's Press (New York, NY), 1992.

A Secret Dying, HarperCollins (London, England), 1992, St. Martin's Press (New York, NY), 1993.

Bloodeagle, HarperCollins (London, England), 1993, St. Martin's Press (New York, NY), 1994.

The Cross Bearer, HarperCollins (London, England), 1994, St. Martin's Press (New York, NY), 1995.

Angel of Death, St. Martin's Press (New York, NY), 1995.

A Short-Lived Ghost, St. Martin's Press (New York, NY), 1995.

Suddenly as a Shadow, HarperCollins (London, England), 1997.

The Ghost Dancers, HarperCollins (London, England), 1997.

The Shape-Shifter, HarperCollins (London, England), 1998.

A Form of Death, Allison & Busby (London, England), 2000.

Assumption of Death, Constable (London, England), 2000.

Dead Secret, Carroll & Graf (New York, NY), 2001.

The Nightwalker, Allison & Busby (London, England), 2002.

The Ways of Death, Constable, 2002.

Phantom, Allison & Busby (London, England), 2002.

Dead Man Running, Allison & Busby (London, England), 2003.

Headhunter, Carroll & Graf (New York, NY), 2004.

Grave Error, Carroll & Graf (New York, NY), 2005.

Death Squad, Allison & Busby (London, England), 2007.

UNDER NAME J.R. LEWIS

Law of the Retailer: An Outline for Students and Business Men, Allman (London, England), 1964, published as *Law for the Retailer,* Jordan (Bristol, England), 1974.

Cases for Discussion, Pergamon Press (New York, NY), 1965.

An Introduction to Business Law, Allman (London, England), 1965.

Law in Action, Allman (London, England), 1965.

Questions and Answers on Civil Procedure, Sweet and Maxwell (London, England), 1966.

Building Law, Allman (London, England), 1966.

Democracy: The Theory and the Practice, Allman (London, England), 1966.

Managing within the Law, Allman (London, England), 1967.

(With John Anthony Holland) *Principles of Registered Land Conveyancing,* Butterworth (London, England), 1967.

Company Law, Allman (London, England), 1967.

Revision Notes for Ordinary Level British Constitution, Allman (London, England), 1967.

Civil and Criminal Procedure, Sweet and Maxwell (London, England), 1968.

Landlord and Tenant, Sweet and Maxwell (London, England), 1968.

Outlines of Equity, Butterworth (London, England), 1968.

(With Anne Redish) *Mercantile and Commercial Law,* Heinemann (London, England), 1969.

Law for the Construction Industry, Macmillan (London, England), 1975.

Administrative Law for the Construction Industry, Macmillan (London, England), 1976.

The Teaching of Public Administration in Further and Higher Education, Joint University Council for Social and Public Administration (London, England), 1979.

The Victorian Bar, 1837-1882, R. Hale (London, England), 1980.

Certain Private Incidents, Templar North (Wigan, England), 1980.

The Victorian Bar, R. Hale (London, England), 1982.

The Maypole, Wigantech (Wigan, England), 1983.

OTHER

(Under pseudonym David Springfield) *The Company Executive and the Law,* Heinemann (London, England), 1970.

Writer for radio program *Brought to Justice.* Contributor to *Legal Executive.*

SIDELIGHTS: Roy Lewis has written numerous nonfiction books but is better known as the author of more than fifty crime novels with several very different protagonists. Many of Lewis's novels feature Inspector Crow of Scotland Yard and are set in the Welsh or English countryside. Crow displays what a *Publishers Weekly* critic termed a "wry overview of English country life in decline." William Weaver, writing in the *St. James Guide to Crime and Mystery Writers,* called Crow "a likeable, laconic protagonist." Lewis has also written several mysteries about Eric Ward, a police officer who became a lawyer when his eyesight went bad due to glaucoma. "Lewis's novels featuring Ward," wrote a *Booklist* critic, "are sensitively written and deeply moving." In addition, Lewis has written several novels about a timid archaeologist named Arnold Landon, whose cases involve British historical sites. A *Publishers Weekly* critic noted that although Landon loses his wits around women, "as an investigator he's canny enough to keep us enthralled." With this handful of recurring protagonists, Lewis has demonstrated his skill at developing characters readers are interested in following. "Lewis's strongest virtues," wrote Weaver, "are his grasp of character—his people are seldom eccentric, but lively, unexpected, even quirkish—and his unfailing sense of place, of atmosphere, whether he is

writing about a Welsh building site (*Distant Banner*), the legal world (*A Fool for a Client*), or the well-to-do bourgeoisie of Durham."

Library Journal reviewer Rex E. Klett recommended *A Form of Death* for its "clear, practiced prose, cleverly twisted plotting, sustained tension, and detailed police procedure." Ward is practicing law in what he regards as a pathetic practice, catering to low-life clients. He is left alone when his younger and extremely wealthy wife travels to Singapore on a business trip accompanied by what Klett called "a very attentive corporate lawyer." In her absence, Ward becomes entangled with a troubled, high-class prostitute who is soon murdered. In an effort to save his reputation, Ward begins an investigation that leads him on a deadly trail of drugs and deceit. Marilyn Stasio commented in her review of the book for the *New York Times Book Review:* "Lewis smartly moves the hero in and out of his bind while making his devotion to his shady waterfront clientele entirely understandable." Emily Melton, writing for *Booklist,* called the book "a literate, thoughtful examination of human nature combined with a grimly suspenseful police procedural."

Dead Secret finds Landon and his team digging in Northumberland's ancient Pentire Woods. Another team, investigating a peat bog at the edge of Wolfcleugh Woods, finds a desiccated body there. A land-development company looking to plow roads and build houses in the woods owned by Steven Brand-Ruckley comes into conflict with an environmental group. Meanwhile Landon finds another body; this time, it is that of a young student from New Zealand, who is distantly related to Brand-Ruckley. A critic for *Kirkus Reviews* commented that the book offers an "interesting background and convoluted plot, though not quite enough of likable, curmudgeonly Detective Chief Inspector Culpeper—and a bit too much of nebbishy Arnold."

In *The Devil Is Dead,* Landon makes a grisly discovery at the site of an abandoned church. It is the body of an intinerant gypsy, horribly butchered and abandoned. Landon is subsequently threatened by the members of a cult known to favor blood sacrifice, but when he contacts the local authorities to discuss his suspicions that the cult members are involved in the killing, his fears are dismissed offhandedly. Landon is later the victim of a horrendous assault. Sybil Steinberg, writing in *Publishers Weekly,* called *The Devil Is Dead* an "intelligent, nicely textured mystery [that] gathers speed and races to a thrilling conclusion."

Landon's adventures continue in *Bloodeagle,* which finds the archaeologist inspecting the excavation site for a new bridge. He is to ensure that no artifacts will be destroyed or disturbed by the construction. Soon, however, the local police turn to him for help with their investigation of a killing that involved a bloody technique known to have been used by the ancient Vikings. As the case is unraveled, the murderer's connections to the Vikings and to a more contemporary group are probed. This "absorbing" novel provides readers with a "surprising but satisfying" resolution, according to Emily Melton in *Booklist.* A *Publishers Weekly* reviewer commented less favorably on the book, noting that while many of the author's stories are "crisply plotted," this one is "overwrought." In *The Cross Bearer,* the author's fiftieth book, Landon and his sidekick, bookstore owner and novelist Jane Wilson, set out in search of an ancient treasure of the Knights Templar, a fourteenth-century order of religious knights.

Arnold Landon's sixteenth adventure, titled *Grave Error,* finds the timid archaeologist testifying in court about the authenticity of a cauldron, reputed to be a Celtic artifact, that is stolen and sold on the black market. Although Landon finds the cauldron to be authentic, his expertise is undermined by James MacLean, a professor with considerably more personal style than Landon possesses. Landon ends up disgraced. A *Publishers Weekly* reviewer commented that while this story's plot is not inherently suspenseful, "the book's strength lies in the relationships among the characters." David Pitt, writing in *Booklist,* commented that crime and archaeology "continue to mix well" in Lewis's work.

Lewis once told *CA:* "I maintain an interest in law and now write articles on legal history. Many of these are concerned with scandals in Victorian society. I have also read pieces on law and life in Victorian Northumberland on the radio program *Brought to Justice.* Fiction remains an escape, but Victorian studies now take up more of my time."

BIOGRAPHICAL AND CRITICAL SOURCES:

BOOKS

St. James Guide to Crime and Mystery Writers, 4th edition, St. James Press (Detroit, MI), 1996.

PERIODICALS

Booklist, April 15, 1979, review of *Nothing but Foxes,* p. 1274; January 15, 1984, review of *A Limited Vision,* p. 717; September 1, 1984, review of *Once Dying, Twice Dead,* p. 26; February 15, 1994, Emily Melton, review of *Bloodeagle,* p. 1063; March 15, 2001, Emily Melton, review of *A Form of Death,* p. 1358; February 1, 2006, David Pitt, review of *Grave Error,* p. 35.

Kirkus Reviews, November 15, 1983, review of *A Limited Vision,* p. 1184; April 15, 2001, review of *Dead Secret,* p. 546; December 1, 2005, review of *Grave Error,* p. 1258.

Library Journal, April 1, 2001, Rex E. Klett, review of *A Form of Death,* p. 136; January 1, 2006, Roland Person, review of *Grave Error,* p. 80.

Listener, December 23, 1976, review of *A Distant Banner,* p. 853; May 4, 1978, review of *An Uncertain Sound,* p. 586.

New York Times Book Review, December 19, 1971, review of *A Lover Too Many,* p. 23; July 26, 1981, Newgate Callendar, review of *A Certain Blindness,* p. 22; January 16, 1983, Newgate Callendar, review of *Dwell in Danger,* p. 26; September 18, 1983, review of *A Gathering of Ghosts,* p. 45; January 15, 1984, Newgate Callendar, review of *A Limited Vision,* p. 29; April 15, 2001, Marilyn Stasio, review of *A Form of Death,* p. 20.

Publishers Weekly, January 15, 1979, review of *Nothing but Foxes,* p. 117; October 2, 1982, review of *Dwell in Danger,* p. 43; November 11, 1983, review of *A Limited Vision,* p. 44; June 22, 1984, review of *Once Dying, Twice Dead,* p. 90; August 31, 1990, Sybil Steinberg, review of *The Devil Is Dead,* p. 51; November 9, 1992, review of *A Secret Dying,* p. 76; December 6, 1993, review of *Bloodeagle,* p. 59; December 12, 1994, review of *The Cross Bearer,* p. 52; December 19, 2005, review of *Grave Error,* p. 45.

Times Literary Supplement, January 22, 1970, review of *A Lover Too Many,* p. 93; June 11, 1970, review of *A Wolf by the Ears,* p. 642; April 30, 1971, review of *Error of Judgment,* p. 511; December 31, 1971, review of *The Fenokee Project,* p. 1638; June 15, 1973, review of *Blood Money,* p. 697; January 25, 1974, review of *Of Singular Purpose,* p. 88; September 6, 1974, review of *A Question of Degree,* p. 960; February 6, 1976, review of *A Part of Virtue,* p. 150; January 7, 1977, review of *A Distant Banner,* p. 19; May 20, 1977, p. 631; July

18, 1980, review of *A Certain Blindness*, p. 823; December 31, 1982, review of *A Gathering of Ghosts*, p. 1448.*

* * *

LIGHTNER, David L. 1942-
(David Lee Lightner)

PERSONAL: Born May 13, 1942, in Bethlehem, PA. *Education:* Pennsylvania State University, B.A., 1963; University of Pennsylvania, A.M., 1964; Cornell University, Ph.D., 1969.

ADDRESSES: Office—Department of History and Classics, University of Alberta, Edmonton, Alberta T6G 2H4, Canada. *E-mail*—david.lightner@ualberta.ca.

CAREER: University of Illinois at Chicago Circle, Chicago, assistant professor of history, 1969-70; St. Olaf College, Northfield, MN, assistant professor, 1970-74; City College of the City University of New York, New York, NY, research assistant, 1974-75; University of Connecticut, Storrs, assistant professor, 1975-77; University of Alberta, Edmonton, Alberta, Canada, assistant professor, 1977-82, associate professor, 1982-2006, professor of history, 2006—.

MEMBER: American Historical Association, Organization of American Historians, Economic History Association, Canadian Association of University Teachers.

WRITINGS:

Labor on the Illinois Central Railroad, 1852-1900: The Evolution of an Industrial Environment, Arno Press (New York, NY), 1977.

(Editor) *Asylum, Prison, and Poorhouse: The Writings and Reform Work of Dorothea Dix in Illinois,* Southern Illinois University Press (Carbondale, IL), 1999.

Slavery and the Commerce Power: How the Struggle against the Interstate Slave Trade Led to the Civil War, Yale University Press (New Haven, CT), 2006.

Contributor to periodicals, including *Journal of Southern History, Journal of Supreme Court History, Journal of the Early Republic, Southern Studies,* *Canadian Review of American Studies, Civil War History, Illinois Historical Journal, Journal of Transport History, Mid-America,* and *Lincoln Herald.*

SIDELIGHTS: David L. Lightner's first book, *Labor on the Illinois Central Railroad, 1852-1900: The Evolution of an Industrial Environment,* is a revision of the Ph.D. dissertation that he submitted to Cornell University in 1969. The book explores the "day-to-day relations of workers and managers . . . [and] the way in which labor fit into the business environment," wrote Paul V. Black in *Business History Review.* "Lightner's study of the nineteenth-century Illinois Central is the first major published work to fill this gap." In the book, Lightner discusses many issues, including wages, promotion and discipline, based on surviving sources, mainly correspondence between top executives. Black noted the limitations of having only these sources but also noted that, despite these limitations, "the book shows evidence of painstaking research, a vivid writing style, and a lively personal involvement with the subject. It is a major contribution in a neglected area of business and labor history."

Asylum, Prison, and Poorhouse: The Writings and Reform Work of Dorothea Dix in Illinois is a collection of Dorothea Dix's writings. Dix was a nineteenth-century reformer who crusaded primarily for humane, hospitalized care for the mentally ill. In 1846, Dix focused on Illinois, presenting documents to the legislature that described the conditions at the state penitentiary at Alton, and urged the state body to establish a mental hospital. Many newspaper articles written by Dix during this time are collected in the volume. Lightner introduces each article and includes detailed notes. "Lightner successfully acquaints his readers with Dix the polemicist, reformer, and philanthropist," wrote Mary Ellen Curtin in the *Times Literary Supplement.* "He has edited three of Dix's most impassioned pleas for change and has written an incisive assessment of her mixed legacy."

BIOGRAPHICAL AND CRITICAL SOURCES:

PERIODICALS

Business History Review, summer, 1978, Paul V. Black, review of *Labor on the Illinois Central Railroad, 1852-1900: The Evolution of an Industrial Environment,* pp. 307-308.

Times Literary Supplement, October 15, 1999, Mary Ellen Curtin, review of *Asylum, Prison, and Poorhouse: The Writings and Reform Work of Dorothea Dix,* p. 37.

*　　*　　*

LIGHTNER, David Lee
    See LIGHTNER, David L.

*　　*　　*

LITTELL, Robert 1935-

PERSONAL: Born January 8, 1935, in the Brooklyn, NY; married; children: two sons. *Education:* Graduated from Alfred University, 1956.

CAREER: Writer. Former Eastern Europe and Soviet affairs editor for *Newsweek. Military service:* U.S. Naval Reserve; became lieutenant junior grade.

AWARDS, HONORS: Edgar Allan Poe Award for best first mystery novel from Mystery Writers of America, Gold Dagger Award from Crime Writers Association, and Critics Award (England), all 1974, all for *The Defection of A.J. Lewinter;* Los Angeles Times Book Prize in Mystery/Thriller, 2006, for *Legends: A Novel of Dissimulation.*

WRITINGS:

NOVELS

The Defection of A.J. Lewinter, Houghton (Boston, MA), 1973.
Sweet Reason, Houghton (Boston, MA), 1974.
The October Circle, Houghton (Boston, MA), 1975.
Mother Russia, Harcourt (New York, NY), 1978.
The Debriefing, Harper (New York, NY), 1979.
The Amateur, Simon & Schuster (New York, NY), 1981.
The Sisters, Bantam (New York, NY), 1986.
The Revolutionist, Bantam (New York, NY), 1988.
The Once and Future Spy, Bantam (New York, NY), 1990.
An Agent in Place, Bantam (New York, NY), 1991.

The Visiting Professor, Faber (London, England), 1993, Random House (New York, NY), 1994.
Walking Back the Cat, Random House (New York, NY), 1996.
The Company: A Novel of the CIA, Overlook Press (Woodstock, NY), 2002.
Legends: A Novel of Dissimulation, Overlook Press (Woodstock, NY), 2005.
Vicious Circle: A Novel of Complicity, Overlook Press (Woodstock, NY), 2006.

OTHER

(Editor) *The Czech Black Book* (translation of *Sedm prazskych dnu,*), Praeger (New York, NY), 1969.
(With Richard Z. Chesnoff and Edward Klein) *If Israel Lost the War,* Coward-McCann (New York, NY), 1969.
(With Diana Maddox) *The Amateur* (screenplay; based on Littell's novel of the same title), Twentieth Century-Fox, 1982.
(With Shimon Peres) *For the Future of Israel,* Johns Hopkins University Press (Baltimore, MD), 1998.

Also author of four other screenplays.

SIDELIGHTS: Robert Littell is "one of the best writers" of his genre, according to George Kelley in the *St. James Guide to Crime and Mystery Writers.* He is the author of more than ten novels and a number of screenplays, and has collaborated with other writers on nonfiction works as well.

While working as an Eastern Europe and Soviet affairs editor for *Newsweek,* Littell edited the translation of a series of reports and testimonies detailing the Soviet invasion of Czechoslovakia in 1968. Published as *The Czech Black Book,* the material was collated privately by historians of the Czechoslovak Academy of Sciences. The book records—through newspaper reports, public resolutions, radio and television broadcasts, posters, and cartoons—the seven days from August 21 through August 27, when more than five hundred thousand Soviet and satellite troops occupied Czechoslovakia and met with staunch citizen resistance. *New York Times* critic Christopher Lehmann-Haupt determined that the book would prove "useful as a reference work," and Tad Szulc, writing in the *New York Times Book Review,* declared the volume a "precious contribution" to other literature on the history of Czechoslovakia.

In 1970 Littell left his post with *Newsweek* to become a novelist and moved to France with his wife and two small sons. *The Defection of A.J. Lewinter* was the first result of his labors, and it quickly garnered critical and popular acclaim. In the novel, Littell calls upon his expertise in Soviet affairs to weave a suspense tale about an American missile engineer who defects to the Russians. An elaborate power play ensues when both countries—and the reader—are introduced to the likelihood that "A.J. Lewinter" is a hoax. A *Spectator* reviewer described *The Defection of A.J. Lewinter* as making the point that "all the mayhem of intelligence work relates . . . to the rules of the intelligence game itself."

Littell followed *The Defection of A.J. Lewinter* with *Sweet Reason,* a black comedy describing a U.S. Navy destroyer's tour of duty off the coast of an unnamed Asian country. The book attempts to expose, according to Lehmann-Haupt, the absurdities of modern, Vietnam-type warfare. The *New York Times* critic found the novel to be "considerably less than profound." David Wilson wrote in a review for the *Times Literary Supplement,* that, while the novel is at times funny and sharp-witted, altogether it is an awkward combination of "dry satire and knockabout farce."

Returning to his sphere of political expertise, Littell next wrote *The October Circle,* a novel about a group of Bulgarian expartisans who protest the 1968 Soviet invasion of Czechoslovakia. Alarmed Bulgarian Party bureaucrats begin to "erase the events staged by the circle," and even begin eliminating members of the group as well, a reviewer explained in *Newsweek.* Overall, critics responded favorably to Littell's story, despite its dark premise. *Christian Science Monitor* contributor Diana Rowan noted that *The October Circle* is a sharp and "entertaining adventure."

Lehmann-Haupt said that while the plot of *The October Circle* seems typical of other novels written during or about the Cold War, "the images in which the story unfolds is something else." A *Newsweek* critic expressed similar satisfaction, lauding the novel's "constantly surprising imagery." And Marvin Levin, writing about *The October Circle* in the *New York Times Book Review,* concluded that the author's technique is "impressionistic."

In talking to journalist and *Chicago Tribune Book World* contributor Helen Dudar about his next novel, *Mother Russia,* Littell acknowledged that this was the book that almost finished his writer's life in France. "Financially, I was down to the wire," he stated in a *Chicago Tribune Book World* interview. The author recalled that publisher Harcourt Brace Jovanovich did little to promote the book and that, despite excellent reviews, the novel was virtually without sales. A black comedy that examines social and political deviants in the Soviet Union, *Mother Russia* introduces Robespierre Isayevich Pravdin, an imaginative hustler who is enlisted by the KGB to help destroy a Nobel Prize-winning Soviet writer's reputation. Littell has "tackled the absurdities of the police state," in his other works, wrote contributor James N. Baker in a review for *Newsweek,* "but never more effectively" than with this work.

The commercial success of *The Debriefing* salvaged Littell's novel-writing aspirations. Similar to *The Defection of A.J. Lewinter* in plot and spirit, the novel deals with a Cold War defector, this time a Russian whose American debriefing officer must penetrate Russia to investigate whether his charge is real or "planted." Critic Newgate Callendar, reviewing the novel for the *New York Times Book Review,* called it "superior entertainment." Similarly, *Newsweek* contributor Walter Clemons declared that the author has written the novel with "elegance."

Even greater critical and commercial success met Littell's sixth fiction offering, *The Amateur,* which introduces Charlie Heller, a CIA cryptologist bent on avenging his fiancée's murder by West German terrorists. When Heller's superiors refuse to support his assassination plans, he blackmails them into providing token field training and assistance; yet they, along with the terrorists, want him dead. Critic Anatole Broyard wrote in the *New York Times* that part of *The Amateur*'s appeal is the fact that "its hero is an amateur in a world of professionals."

The Sisters is regarded by some critics as the author's best novel. The book introduces two CIA covert operation agents dubbed "the sisters." When they discover a Soviet "sleeper," an undercover agent who lives normally until called upon to conduct a mission, the sisters decide "to use the agent," Kelley explained, "to commit a crime for which the Russians will be blamed." Meanwhile, the Russians know that their sleeper spy has been compromised and they move to remedy the situation. Critic Peter Andrews, writing in the *New York Times Book Review,* called *The Sisters* "slick." Writing in the *New York Review of Books,* contributor Thomas

R. Edwards found that with *The Sisters,* Littell demonstrates a strong "imagination." *The Sisters,* Kelley concluded, is a "classic spy novel."

Littell's next novel was 1988's *The Revolutionist.* In this tale of the Russian Revolution, some of the characters and events from the author's other novels return. The novel follows the life of Alexander Til, who leaves America in 1917 to participate in the Russian Revolution. The author "captures the senseless brutality of the system," observed Kelley.

In *Walking Back the Cat* Littell posits a Soviet deep-cover operation set up during the Cold War on a New Mexican Indian reservation and only now activated to begin assassinating a series of Americans. Mafia manipulation of the tribe's casino operations complicates efforts to uncover the Soviet operation and its ultimate purpose. "Playful characterizations" propel the reader forward through a complex storyline, noted one *Publishers Weekly* critic.

Littell's most commercially successful book to date is *The Company: A Novel of the CIA,* which was a best-seller in the summer of 2002. The sweeping narrative covers fifty years of CIA operations, from Berlin at the outset of the Cold War to the end of the century. Littell mixes true events and historic figures with fictional characters—three CIA agents and a KGB operative—in a story that weighs the moral and personal implications of espionage. One *Publishers Weekly* reviewer characterized *The Company* as "gung-ho, hard-drinking, table-turning fun." In a review for the *New York Times Book Review,* contributor James J. Uebbing concluded that "there is plenty here to amuse anyone."

In 2006 Littell published another novel, *Vicious Circle: A Novel of Complicity,* set in the Middle East. The plot focuses on Rabbi Isaac Apfulbaum, who is taken hostage by an Islamic Fundamentalist doctor just days before Arab and Israeli representatives are set to sign an unprecedented agreement. Government officials and various spies are called in to help broker an agreement, and tension is high because of the stakes at hand. In the meantime, the rabbi and doctor are surprised by the unexpected bond they feel toward each other. Critics lauded Littell for his work on the novel overall, citing its fairness toward entities polarized by politics and religion. *Vicious Circle* is a "sharply observed, remarkably evenhanded" book, remarked one *Kirkus Reviews* contributor. Others commented on the author's ability

to combine disparate elements into one story deftly. The novel demonstrates a compelling combination of "stark beauty and ugliness," wrote *Booklist* contributor David Wright.

BIOGRAPHICAL AND CRITICAL SOURCES:

BOOKS

Contemporary Literary Criticism, Volume 42, Thomson Gale (Detroit, MI), 1987.
St. James Guide to Crime and Mystery Writers, 4th edition, St. James Press (Detroit, MI), 1996.

PERIODICALS

America, May 3, 1969, review of *The Czech Black Book,* p. 546; June 2, 1973, review of *The Defection of A.J. Lewinter,* p. 522.
American Libraries, January, 1986, review of *The Sisters,* p. 10; February, 2002, Bill Ott, review of *The Company: A Novel of the CIA,* p. 65.
Annals of the American Academy of Political and Social Science, September, 1969, review of *The Czech Black Book,* p. 202.
Armchair Detective, spring, 1993, review of *An Agent in Place,* p. 13.
Best Sellers, April 1, 1969, review of *The Czech Black Book,* p. 7; May 15, 1973, review of *The Defection of A.J. Lewinter,* p. 92; October, 1978, review of *Mother Russia,* p. 205; July, 1979, review of *The Debriefing,* p. 125.
Book, November, 2002, review of *The Company,* p. 56.
Booklist, January 1, 1976, review of *The October Circle,* p. 614; May 15, 1978, review of *Mother Russia,* p. 1476; May 15, 1979, review of *The Debriefing,* p. 1423; March 15, 1981, review of *The Amateur,* p. 999; November 15, 1985, review of *The Sisters,* p. 450; February 1, 1988, review of *The Revolutionist,* p. 889; April 1, 1990, review of *The Once and Future Spy,* p. 1505; January 1, 1994, Denise Perry Donavin, review of *The Visiting Professor,* p. 806; May 15, 1997, Bill Ott, review of *Walking Back the Cat,* p. 1567; February 1, 2002, Bill Ott, review of *The Company,* p. 927; May 1, 2005, David Wright, review of *Legends: A Novel of Dissimulation,* p. 1528; August 1, 2006, David Wright, review of *Vicious Circle: A Novel of Complicity,* p. 51.

BookPage, May, 2002, review of *The Company,* p. 9; September, 2002, review of *The Company,* p. 23.

Books, August, 1988, review of *The Revolutionist,* p. 20; September, 1991, review of *An Agent in Place,* p. 22; September, 1992, review of *An Agent in Place,* p. 26; November, 1993, review of *The Visiting Professor,* p. 25; spring, 2003, review of *The Company,* p. 20.

Bookseller, July 26, 2002, Philip Jones, review of *The Company,* p. 35.

Books of the Times, July, 1979, review of *The Debriefing,* p. 313; August, 1981, review of *The Amateur,* p. 348.

Book World, March 30, 1969, review of *The Czech Black Book,* p. 7; March 25, 1973, review of *The Defection of A.J. Lewinter,* p. 15; March 31, 1974, review of *Sweet Reason,* p. 4; August 2, 1981, review of *The Amateur,* p. 10; March 2, 1986, review of *The Sisters,* p. 1; December 15, 1991, review of *An Agent in Place,* p. 7; May 15, 1994, review of *The Visiting Professor,* p. 4; April 14, 2002, review of *The Company,* p. 1; March 16, 2003, review of *The Company,* p. 11; April 20, 2003, review of *The Once and Future Spy,* p. 10.

British Book News, January, 1982, review of *The Amateur,* p. 8.

Chicago Tribune Book World, November 25, 1979, Helen Dudar, "Behind the Cover," p. 2.

CHOICE, May, 1969, review of *The Czech Black Book,* p. 420.

Christian Science Monitor, November 6, 1969, "Gaston's Ghastly Green Thumb," p. 3; May 9, 1973, review of *The Defection of A.J. Lewinter,* p. 10; March 22, 1976, review of *The October Circle,* p. 22; June 29, 1979, Joel Rosenkranz, review of *The Debriefing,* p. 19.

Drood Review of Mystery, May, 2002, review of *The Company,* p. 16.

Economist, August 30, 1969, review of *The Czech Black Book,* p. 39; August 10, 2002, review of *The Company.*

Encounter, October, 1969, review of *The Czech Black Book,* p. 73.

Entertainment Weekly, May 17, 2002, "The Week," p. 68.

Esquire, May, 1973, review of *The Defection of A.J. Lewinter,* p. 66.

Globe & Mail (Toronto, Ontario, Canada), July 13, 2002, review of *The Company,* p. 15; April 5, 2003, review of *The Company,* p. 21.

Guardian Weekly, June 26, 1969, review of *The Czech Black Book,* p. 16; December 29, 1973, review of *The Defection of A.J. Lewinter,* p. 17.

Harper's, October, 2006, John Leonard, review of *Vicious Circle,* p. 79.

January Magazine, May, 2005, Ali Karim, "Robert Littell: A Legend in His Own Time."

Journal of Politics, November, 1970, review of *The Czech Black Book,* p. 1015.

Kirkus Reviews, January 1, 1973, review of *The Defection of A.J. Lewinter,* p. 20; December 15, 1973, review of *Sweet Reason,* p. 1376; November 1, 1975, review of *The October Circle,* p. 1252; April 1, 1978, review of *Mother Russia,* p. 390; May 15, 1979, review of *The Debriefing,* p. 594; February 1, 1981, review of *The Amateur,* p. 163; March 1, 1981, review of *The Amateur,* p. 290; December 1, 1985, review of *The Sisters,* p. 1281; February 15, 1988, review of *The Revolutionist,* p. 230; March 15, 1990, review of *The Once and Future Spy,* p. 369; January 1, 1994, review of *The Visiting Professor,* p. 11; May 1, 1997, review of *Walking Back the Cat,* p. 666; January 1, 2002, review of *The Company,* p. 11; March 15, 2005, review of *Legends,* p. 308; July 15, 2006, review of *Vicious Circle,* p. 693.

Kliatt, spring, 1977, review of *The October Circle,* p. 6; spring, 1981, review of *The Debriefing,* p. 10; spring, 1982, review of *The Amateur,* p. 13; January, 1990, review of *The Revolutionist,* p. 12; July, 2003, review of *Walking Back the Cat,* p. 6; January, 2004, Susan Offner, review of *The Defection of A.J. Lewinter,* p. 46; July, 2004, John E. Boyd, review of *The Sisters,* p. 56.

Ladies' Home Journal, September, 1979, Carol Eisen Rinzler, review of *The Debriefing,* p. 7.

Library Journal, May 1, 1969, review of *The Czech Black Book,* p. 1885; March 15, 1970, review of *Left and Right with Lion and Ryan,* p. 1188; January 1, 1973, review of *The Defection of A.J. Lewinter,* p. 87; January 1, 1974, review of *Sweet Reason,* p. 66; November 15, 1975, review of *The October Circle,* p. 2173; May 15, 1978, review of *Mother Russia,* p. 1082; July 1979, review of *The Debriefing,* p. 1489; May 1, 1981, Robin W. Winks, review of *The Amateur,* p. 994; February 1, 1986, Barbara Conaty, review of *The Sisters,* p. 93; May 1, 1988, Ann Donovan, review of *The Revolutionist,* p. 90; January, 1994, Cynthia Johnson, review of *The Visiting Professor,* p. 163; May 1, 1997, David Keymer, review of *Walking Back the Cat,* p. 141; December, 2001, Barbara Conaty, review of *The Company,* p. 173; January, 2003, Michael Rogers, review of *The Once and Future Spy,* p. 166; April 1, 2003, Mark Pumphrey, review of *The Company,* p. 148; May 15, 2003, Michael Rogers, review of *The Sisters,* p. 134; December, 2003, Michael Rogers, review of *The Amateur* and *The Defection of A.J. Lewinter,* p. 174; August, 2004, Michael Rogers, review of *The Debriefing,* p. 131; October 15, 2006, Barbara Conaty, review of *Vicious Circle,* p. 53.

Listener, January 10, 1980, review of *The Debriefing,* p. 62; April 17, 1986, review of *The Sisters,* p. 29.

Los Angeles Times, June 9, 2002, review of *The Company,* p. 11.

MBR Bookwatch, September, 2005, Diane C. Donovan, review of *Legends.*

New Leader, June 23, 1969, review of *The Czech Black Book,* p. 21; May-June, 2005, Tova Reich, review of *Legends,* p. 40.

New Republic, May 30, 1981, reviews of *The Amateur* and *The Debriefing,* p. 38.

New Statesman, June 25, 1976, review of *The October Circle,* p. 856.

Newsweek, March 12, 1973, review of *The Defection of A.J. Lewinter,* p. 94; February 18, 1974, review of *Sweet Reason,* p. 99; January 19, 1976, review of *The October Circle,* p. 74; July 3, 1978, James N. Baker, review of *Mother Russia,* p. 79; July 23, 1979, Walter Clemons, review of *The Debriefing,* p. 77; March 10, 1986, Peter S. Prescott, review of *The Sisters,* p. 76; May 13, 2002, Andrew Nagorski, review of *The Company,* p. 55.

New Yorker, June 13, 2005, John Updike, review of *Legends,* p. 174.

New York Review of Books, May 8, 1986, Thomas R. Edwards, review of *The Sisters,* p. 12.

New York Times, April 28, 1969, Christopher Lehmann-Haupt, review of *The Czech Black Book,* p. 39; February 15, 1973, Christopher Lehmann-Haupt, review of *The Defection of A.J. Lewinter,* p. 41; February 20, 1974, Christopher Lehmann-Haupt, review of *Sweet Reason,* p. 35; February 13, 1976, Christopher Lehmann-Haupt, review of *The October Circle,* p. 31; July 2, 1979, Christopher Lehmann-Haupt, review of *An Agent in Place,* p. 15; September 2, 1979, Newgate Callendar, review of *The Debriefing,* p. 21; March 15, 1981, review of *The Debriefing,* p. 35; May 10, 1981, Michael Malone, review of *The Amateur,* p. 15; May 13, 1981, Anatole Broyard, review of *The Amateur,* p. 17; January 31, 1982, review of *The Amateur,* p. 31; January 30, 1986, Christopher Lehmann-Haupt, review of *The Sisters,* p. 23; February 2, 1986, Peter Andrews, review of *The Sisters,* p. 9; May 26, 1988, Christopher Lehmann-Haupt, review of *The Revolutionist,* p. 16; May 5, 1990, Herbert Mitgang, review of *The Once and*

Future Spy, p. 12; December 4, 1991, Herbert Mitgang, review of *An Agent in Place,* p. 2.

New York Times Book Review, May 4, 1969, Tad Szulc, review of *The Czech Black Book,* p. 3; March 4, 1973, review of *The Defection of A.J. Lewinter,* p. 42; February 15, 1976, Martin Levin, review of *The October Circle,* p. 20; September 2, 1979, Newgate Callendar, review of *The Debriefing,* p. 21; March 15, 1981, review of *The Debriefing,* p. 35; May 10, 1981, Michael Malone, review of *The Amateur,* p. 15; January 31, 1982, review of *The Amateur,* p. 31; February 2, 1986, Peter Andrews, review of *The Sisters,* p. 9; May 22, 1988, Meredith Tax, review of *The Revolutionist,* p. 20; May 27, 1990, Newgate Callender, review of *The Once and Future Spy,* p. 27; August 11, 1991, review of *The Once and Future Spy,* p. 28; December 29, 1991, Newgate Callender, review of *An Agent in Place,* p. 23; August 3, 1997, James F. Clarity, review of *Walking Back the Cat,* p. 16; May 12, 2002, James J. Uebbing, review of *The Company,* p. 25; August 21, 2005, Neil Gordon, review of *Legends.*

Observer (London, England), June 22, 1969, review of *The Czech Black Book,* p. 26; September 23, 1973, review of *The Defection of A.J. Lewinter,* p. 36; March 23, 1975, review of *Sweet Reason,* p. 30; June 13, 1976, review of *The October Circle,* p. 27; December 12, 1976, review of *The October Circle,* p. 26; March 6, 1977, review of *Sweet Reason,* p. 29; August 16, 1981, review of *The Amateur,* p. 23; March 23, 1986, review of *The Sisters,* p. 26; June 10, 1990, review of *The Once and Future Spy,* p. 54; June 17, 1990, review of *The Once and Future Spy,* p. 59; June 30, 1991, review of *An Agent in Place,* p. 52; December 5, 1993, review of *The Visiting Professor,* p. 22; January 22, 1995, review of *The Visiting Professor,* p. 21; November 17, 2002, review of *The Company,* p. 19; December 29, 2002, review of *The Company,* p. 16.

People Weekly, June 8, 1981, review of *The Amateur,* p. 24; April 28, 1986, Campbell Geeslin, review of *The Sisters,* p. 17; June 28, 2004, "The Men We Became," p. 51.

Philadelphia Inquirer, July 5, 2005, Sandy Bauers, review of *Legends.*

Publishers Weekly, February 10, 1969, review of *The Czech Black Book,* p. 67; May 12, 1969, review of *The Czech Black Book,* p. 61; November 26, 1973, review of *The Defection of A.J. Lewinter,* p. 39; December 31, 1973, review of *Sweet Reason,* p. 22; November 17, 1975, review of *The October Circle,* p. 94; March 27, 1978, review of *Mother Russia,*

p. 66; May 14, 1979, review of *The Debriefing,* p. 205; January 9, 1981, review of *The Debriefing,* p. 72; March 13, 1981, Barbara A. Bannon, review of *The Amateur,* p. 75; December 18, 1981, review of *The Amateur,* p. 69; November 29, 1985, Sybil Steinberg, review of *The Sisters,* p. 37; April 22, 1988, Sybil Steinberg, review of *The Revolutionist,* p. 62; April 20, 1990, Sybil Steinberg, review of *The Once and Future Spy,* p. 57; January 3, 1994, review of *The Visiting Professor,* p. 69; May 12, 1997, review of *Walking Back the Cat,* p. 57; March 23, 1998, review of *For the Future of Israel,* p. 85; February 18, 2002, review of *The Company,* p. 71; November 18, 2002, review of *The Defection of A.J. Lewinter,* p. 44; April 14, 2003, review of *The Sisters,* p. 51; June 2, 2003, review of *The Sisters,* p. 34; May 23, 2005, review of *Legends,* p. 59; August 1, 2005, review of *Legends,* p. 61; July 31, 2006, review of *Vicious Circle,* p. 51.

Reason, January, 1989, Martin Morse Wooster, review of *The Revolutionist,* p. 52.

Rolling Stone, March 11, 1976, review of *The Defection of A.J. Lewinter,* p. 73.

Saturday Review, March 29, 1969, review of *The Czech Black Book,* p. 21.

Spectator, September 15, 1973, review of *The Defection of A.J. Lewinter,* p. 346.

Times Educational Supplement, December 3, 1993, Brian Morton, review of *The Visiting Professor,* p. 28.

Times Literary Supplement, July 24, 1969, review of *The Czech Black Book,* p. 796; May 2, 1975, David Wilson, review of *Sweet Reason,* p. 492; July 23, 1976, review of *The October Circle,* p. 905; January 29, 1982, review of *The Amateur,* p. 104; February 5, 1982, review of *The Amateur,* p. 147; June 14, 1991, Savkar Altinel, review of *An Agent in Place,* p. 26; December 3, 1993, review of *The Visiting Professor,* p. 20; March 8, 1996, review of *Walking Back the Cat,* p. 24; April 4, 2003, Alex Danchev, review of *The Company,* p. 21.

Tribune Books (Chicago, IL), April 17, 1988, review of *The Revolutionist,* p. 7; May 27, 1990, review of *The Once and Future Spy,* p. 4; March 20, 1994, review of *The Visiting Professor,* p. 7; May 4, 2003, review of *The Company,* p. 6.

Wall Street Journal, June 13, 1988, Martin Morse Wooster, review of *The Revolutionist,* p. 13.

Washington Post, August 11, 1979, Rod MacLeish, review of *The Debriefing,* p. 3.

West Coast Review of Books, September, 1978, review of *Mother Russia,* p. 36.

ONLINE

Fantastic Fiction, http://www.fantasticfiction.co.uk/ (January 8, 2007), biography of Robert Littell.

Grumpy Old Bookman Blog, http://grumpyoldbookman. blogspot.com/ (July 21, 2005), review of *Legends.**

*   *   *

LORD, Graham 1943-

PERSONAL: Born February 16, 1943, in Umtali, Rhodesia (now Zimbabwe); son of Harold (a business-man) and Ida Lord; married Jane Carruthers, 1962 (marriage ended); partner of Juliet Lewis (an artist); children: Mandy, Kate. *Education:* Churchill College, Cambridge, B.A. (with honors), 1965. *Hobbies and other interests:* Books, films, music, and travel.

ADDRESSES: E-mail—pelicans@caribsurf.com.

CAREER: Writer, biographer, novelist, columnist, and journalist. *Cambridge News,* Cambridge, England, reporter, 1964; *Sunday Express,* London, England, reporter, 1965-69, literary editor and books columnist, 1969-92; reporter and writer for the *Daily Telegraph,* London *Times,* and *Daily Mail,* 1992—.

WRITINGS:

NOVELS

Marshmallow Pie, Coward-McCann (New York, NY), 1970.

A Roof under Your Feet, Macdonald (London, England), 1973.

The Spider and the Fly, Hamilton (London, England), 1974, Viking (New York, NY) 1975.

God and All His Angels, Hamilton (London, England), 1976, Viking (New York, NY), 1977.

The Nostradamus Horoscope, Hutchinson (London, England), 1981.

Time Out of Mind, Hamilton (London, England), 1986.

A Party to Die For, Warner (London, England), 1997.

Sorry, We're Going to Have to Let You Go, Little, Brown (London, England), 1999.

OTHER

Ghosts of Solomon's Mines: Mozambique and Zimbabwe: A Quest (autobiography), Sinclair-Stevenson (London, England), 1991.

Just the One: The Wives and Times of Jeffrey Bernard, Sinclair-Stevenson (London, England), 1992.

James Herriot: The Life of a Country Vet (biography), Carroll & Graf (New York, NY), 1997.

Dick Francis: A Racing Life, Little, Brown (London, England), 1999.

Arthur Lowe, Orion (London, England), 2002.

Niv: The Authorized Biography of David Niven, Thomas Dunne Books/St. Martin's Press (New York, NY), 2005.

John Mortimer: The Devil's Advocate, Orion (London, England), 2005, published as *John Mortimer: The Secret Lives of Rumpole's Creator,* Thomas Dunne Books (New York, NY), 2006.

Raconteur (a short story magazine), editor, 1994-96. Contributor to *Triangles,* edited by Alex Hamilton, Hutchinson (London, England), 1973, *The Thirteenth Ghost Book,* edited by James Hale, Barrie & Jenkins (London, England), 1977, *The After-Midnight Ghost Book,* edited by James Hale, Hutchinson (London, England), 1980, and *The Mystery Guild Anthology,* edited by John Waite, Book Club Associates/Constable (London, England), 1980.

Author's works have been translated into French, Italian, Dutch, Portuguese, German, Russian, and Chinese.

SIDELIGHTS: Graham Lord once told *CA* that writing novels "is cheaper than booze and more effective than psychiatry, and like both should be firmly resisted as far as possible." Indeed, Lord, a former Fleet Street reporter and literary editor, has produced a number of novels beginning in 1970. But his writing also embraces biography, notably of several British celebrities.

In 1992 Lord produced a close look at a famous journalist in *Just the One: The Wives and Times of Jeffrey Bernard.* A columnist for *Spectator,* Bernard had for years chronicled his life in what critic Laurie Taylor characterized in *New Statesman & Society* as a "suicide note in weekly installments." When he announced his plans to examine Bernard, Lord wrote in *Just the One,* "some suggested . . . this book would be superfluous since Bernard had written his own life story in his column.

They were wrong . . . there were numerous secret corners of his life that he had kept hidden." Still, *New Statesman & Society* reviewer Taylor remained among the skeptics. In her review of *Just the One,* she criticized Lord for taking on as a subject a man who "did, after all, invent the 'Jeffrey Bernard' of his columns," and suggested that there is "something desperately absurd about trying to show with cold biographical evidence . . . that he somehow got it wrong."

Lord went head-to-head with another British icon in 1997's *James Herriot: The Life of a Country Vet.* Herriot's celebrity, of course, transcends the boundaries of the United Kingdom—in fact, it was Lord's 1972 *Sunday Express* review of *It Shouldn't Happen to a Vet* that helped propel Herriot into the literary world. The unassuming Yorkshire veterinarian caused a sensation with his subsequent bestsellers, including *All Creatures Great and Small.* Herriot—a pseudonym of James "Alf" Wight—died in 1995, and in Lord's volume the life and work of the man are recounted from his hardscrabble youth in Glasgow, Scotland, to his clinic where Herriot practiced for more than fifty years.

In what *Library Journal* reviewer Diane Premo called "a warm, candid portrait," Lord assesses the impact of Herriot's fame, revealing his subject as "modest and self-effacing in the extreme." Nor does the biographer hesitate to point out the literary embellishments that distinguished Herriot the character from Alf Wight the inspiration. The Yorkshire vet—who, Lord reveals, had a nervous breakdown and was also plagued by debt—and his counterparts—wife "Helen" and partners "Siegfried" and "Tristan," "none of whom shines under Lord's scrutiny," according to a *Kirkus Reviews* critic—were not exactly as depicted in books and the popular public television series. Reading this, some Herriot fans were disappointed, while others, including the *Kirkus Reviews* contributor, found value in the way Lord analyzes "the simple, direct style Wight brought to his homey material."

Niv: The Authorized Biography of David Niven is Lord's official biography of debonair British actor, David Niven. Lord begins from the vantage point of knowing that Niven himself had written two successful autobiographies, and that the actor's stories of his life were frequently exaggerated. In this context, Lord "sets out to gently correct the record," commented a *Publishers Weekly* reviewer. As a biographer, Lord "chose well with Niven, who lived a hugely entertaining life if not necessarily a profound one," remarked Bruce Handy in the *New York Times Book Review.* He details Niven's early days in Hollywood and his struggles to establish himself as an actor, with considerable coverage of Niven's nearly fifty years as a comforting presence on the British and American screen. Lord recounts how Niven left Hollywood to serve during World War II, at perhaps considerable damage to his then-developing acting career. He discusses some of Niven's most notable films, including the *Pink Panther, Around the World in Eighty Days, Casino Royale,* and *Separate Tables,* which earned Niven an Oscar in 1959. Among the nuggets of Hollywood trivia served by Lord is the fact that Niven and Bette Davis were originally cast to play the leads in the *African Queen,* roles later made famous by Humphrey Bogart and Katharine Hepburn; he was once considered for the role of James Bond; and he turned down lead roles in *Lolita* and *My Fair Lady,* which went to James Mason and Rex Harrison, Handy reported. Lord also covers many personal details of Niven's life, including his numerous liaisons with famous Hollywood starlets, including Merle Oberon, Rita Hayworth, Marilyn Monroe, and Ava Gardner; his two marriages, the second of which was brittle and unhappy; and his declining health and eventual death from Lou Gehrig's disease. The *Publishers Weekly* contributor concluded that throughout Lord's biography, Niven's "reputation as a lovable raconteur remains untarnished, even by the truth."

Throughout his career, Lord has developed a reputation as a contentious biographer who persisted in writing about his subjects even when they objected, and who sought to expose aspects of their lives they would have preferred to keep hidden. This perception of Lord-as-biographer became an impediment when he undertook a biography of English writer and barrister John Mortimer, the creator of famed fictional barrister Rumpole of the Bailey. At first, Lord received Mortimer's cooperation in creating an official biography, but later the writer withdrew his permission and support. Undaunted, Lord proceeded to write an unauthorized biography, published as *John Mortimer: The Devil's Advocate* in Great Britain and as *John Mortimer: The Secret Lives of Rumpole's Creator* in the United States. Lord covers Mortimer's youth, his development as a law professional and as a writer, and his status as creator of one of crime fiction's most enduring characters. He also delves into less savory aspects of Mortimer's life, including his reputation as a womanizer, his personality quirks, his tendency to inflate stories of his past, and his legal championing of pornography in Britain that Lord feels contributed to the country's moral decay.

Though some critics recognized the depth of detail and research in the biography, they also saw Lord's approach as being somewhat vengeful. "Rumbustious yet censorious, prurient yet perceptive about his subject's qualities as a prolific novelist, playwright and scriptwriter, the result is the work of a rejected suitor, bent on a degree of revenge," observed Jeremy Lewis in the *Sunday Times.* A *Kirkus Reviews* critic remarked, however, that Lord's biography offers "breathless prose and many juicy revelations—an absorbing read."

BIOGRAPHICAL AND CRITICAL SOURCES:

BOOKS

Lord, Graham, *Just the One: The Wives and Times of Jeffrey Bernard,* Sinclair-Stevenson (London, England), 1992.

PERIODICALS

Booklist, October 15, 1997, Margaret Flanagan, review of *James Herriot: The Life of a Country Vet,* p. 371.

Bookseller, August 26, 2005, "In the Dock: Lord Creates a Rumpus about Rumpole," review of *John Mortimer: The Devil's Advocate,* p. 39.

Kirkus Reviews, September 15, 1997, review of *James Herriot,* p. 61; September 1, 2004, review of *Niv: The Authorized Biography of David Niven,* p. 850; June 1, 2006, review of *John Mortimer: The Secret Life of Rumpole's Creator,* p. 559.

Library Journal, October 15, 1997, Diane Premo, review of *James Herriot,* p. 61; February 15, 1998, Linda Bredengerd, review of *James Herriot,* p. 183; September 15, 2002, Theresa Connors, audiobook review of *Dick Francis: A Racing Life,* p. 111.

New Statesman, September 12, 2005, Celia Brayfield, "A Biographer Scorned," review of *John Mortimer: The Devil's Advocate,* p. 52.

New Statesman & Society, November 27, 1992, Laurie Taylor, review of *Just the One,* p. 40.

New York Times Book Review, January 9, 2005, Bruce Handy, "*Niv:* Blithe Spirit," review of *Niv.*

Observer (London, England), August 28, 2005, Caroline Boucher, "Trash Rumpole at Your Peril," review of *John Mortimer: The Devil's Advocate.*

Publishers Weekly, September 13, 2004, review of *Niv,* p. 65; April 10, 2006, review of *John Mortimer: The Secret Lives of Rumpole's Creator,* p. 53.

Spectator, November 9, 2002, Jonathan Cecil, "The Man Who Hated Being Typecast—And Was," review of *Arthur Lowe,* p. 80; November 15, 2003, Hugh Massingberd, "It's Being so Cheerful that Keeps Me Going," review of *Niv,* p. 52.

Sunday Times (London, England), August 21, 2005, Jeremy Lewis, review of *John Mortimer: The Devil's Advocate.*

ONLINE

Graham Lord Home Page, http://www.graham-lord.com (December 17, 2006).

*   *   *

LOTT, Bret 1958-

PERSONAL: Born October 8, 1958, in Los Angeles, CA; son of Wilman Sequoia (a corporative executive) and Barbara (a banker) Lott; married Melanie Kai Swank (an office manager), June 28, 1980; children: Zebulun Holmes, Jacob Daynes. *Education:* California State University, B.A., 1981; University of Massachusetts—Amherst, M.F.A., 1984.

ADDRESSES: Office—Southern Review, Louisiana State University, Baton Rouge, LA 70803. *E-mail*—rlott2@lsu.edu

CAREER: Writer, novelist, educator, and editor. Big Yellow House, Santa Barbara, CA, cook's trainer, 1977-79; RC Cola, Los Angeles, CA, salesman, 1979-80; *Daily Commercial News,* Los Angeles, reporter, 1980-81; Ohio State University, Columbus, instructor in remedial English, 1984-86; College of Charleston, Charleston, SC, professor of English, 1986-2004; Vermont College of Norwich, faculty member, 1994-2000; editor, the *Southern Review,* Louisiana State University, 2004—.

MEMBER: Associated Writing Programs, National Council on the Arts, Poets and Writers.

AWARDS, HONORS: Syndicated fiction project award from PEN/National Endowment for the Arts, for "I Owned Vermont"; Ohio Arts Council fellow in literature,

1986; South Carolina Arts Commission fellow in literature, 1987-88; South Carolina syndicated fiction project award, 1987, for "Lights"; Pushcart Prize, Pushcart Press, 2000; Chancellor's medal, University of Massachusetts, 2000; National Media award, National Down Syndrome Congress, 2000; Fulbright senior American scholar, Bar Ilan University, Tel Aviv, Israel, 2006-07.

WRITINGS:

The Man Who Owned Vermont (novel), Viking (New York, NY), 1987.

A Stranger's House (novel), Viking (New York, NY), 1988.

A Dream of Old Leaves (short stories), Viking (New York, NY), 1989.

Jewel (novel), Pocket Books (New York, NY), 1991, reprinted, Pocket Books (New York, NY), 1999.

Reed's Beach, Pocket Books (New York, NY), 1993.

How to Get Home (novella and stories), John F. Blair (Winston-Salem, NC), 1996.

Fathers, Sons, and Brothers: The Men in My Family (essays), Harcourt (New York, NY), 1997.

The Hunt Club (novel), Villard (New York, NY), 1998.

(Editor, with W. Scott Olsen) *A Year in Place,* University of Utah Press (Salt Lake City, UT), 2001.

A Song I Knew by Heart (novel), Random House (New York, NY), 2004.

The Difference between Women and Men (short stories), Random House (New York, NY), 2005.

Before We Get Started: A Practical Memoir of the Writer's Life, Ballantine Books (New York, NY), 2005.

(Editor) *The Best Christian Short Stories,* WestBow Press (Nashville, TN), 2006.

Short stories included in anthology *Twenty under Thirty,* Scribner, 1986. Contributor of fiction to periodicals, including *Missouri Review, Michigan Quarterly Review, Iowa Review, Yale Review, Yankee, Seattle Review, Redbook,* and *Confrontation;* contributor of literary reviews to periodicals, including *New York Times Book Review, Los Angeles Times,* and *Michigan Quarterly Review.*

SIDELIGHTS: Bret Lott is a writer of short stories and novels, a professor, and editor of the *Southern Review.* Respected in his field, Lott was appointed as a member of the National Council on the Arts, the advisory body of the National Endowment for the Arts, in 2006. But Lott's life experiences range widely. He has worked in sales, experience which he brings to bear in his first novel, *The Man Who Owned Vermont.* Rick Wheeler, a Massachusetts soft drink salesman who both knowingly and unknowingly sabotages his marriage, is the protagonist of the book. With a life and marriage that fall short of his expectations, Rick is often sullen and self-defeating. On one occasion he refuses to stop the car to let his pregnant wife find a bathroom, and her subsequent miscarriage—along with the guilt and blame—trigger a growing breach that culminates in separation. Only then, as Rick tries to connect with others in order to fill the emptiness, does he recognize his complicity in the gradual disintegration of the relationship. Critics responded positively to the book, citing the author's ability to demonstrate the feelings and actions of real people in fiction. "Lott knows how ordinary people work and love (or try to love)," wrote Michiko Kakutani in a review for the *New York Times.*

Writing in *Time* magazine, one critic perceived Wheeler's story as a tale of ordinary human courage. "Given every reason to surrender, he struggles on," the reviewer reflected. *The Man Who Owned Vermont* "manages to capture ordinary life's poetic—and tragic—moments," contributor Lori B. Miller observed in the *New York Times Book Review.* "Mr. Lott's . . . storytelling . . . is subtle but powerful."

A book of personal essays about his family, *Fathers, Sons, and Brothers: The Men in My Family* was published in 1997. Lott presents the reader with fifteen stories that relate events and anecdotes about him and his family members while reflecting on the connections that exist between them, and how they have changed over time. For example, in the story "Learning Sex," Lott tells of the time his wife and he broached the sensitive subject with their son. Lott relates that experience to his own parents' difficulties approaching the same subject with him. Lott's essay collection appealed to many readers and critics. *Fathers, Sons, and Brothers* contains many "honest and affecting essays," wrote Brian McCombie in a review for *Booklist.* Other reviewers, however, thought that Lott's stories may be too familiar and therefore not as insightful as they could be. The author "treats experiences all too common to male readers," noted *Library Journal* contributor William Gargan.

Lott presents a different kind of family dynamic in his first thriller novel, *The Hunt Club.* Fifteen-year-old Huger Dillard, the protagonist, helps his blind uncle run a primitive backwoods hunting club for wealthy patrons, largely physicians, from Charleston, South Carolina. Huger serves as his uncle's eyes, but nothing prepares them for the Saturday when they find a headless corpse, labeled with a cardboard sign identifying the deceased as Dr. Charles Middleton Simons, and identifying the murderer as his wife. But she is later found hanged in a hotel room. From this harrowing beginning, the story proceeds as Huger and his uncle find themselves in real danger, with someone after their apparently worthless Carolina swampland. *Booklist* reviewer Joanne Wilkinson noted that the book is promoted as a thriller, but "at the heart of this wonderfully well written novel is a haunting coming-of-age story." Critic Thomas L. Kilpatrick, writing in the *Library Journal,* called the book "a good read with action, suspense, and a hint of Southern folklore."

In 1999 Lott's literary career, for many years low-key, received a tremendous boost when his 1991 novel, *Jewel,* was reprinted as a mass market paperback and selected as part of Oprah Winfrey's TV book club. The novel tells the story of Jewel Hilburn, a devoted Mississippi wife and mother. Her sixth child, Brenda Kay, is born with Down Syndrome, and a once-tranquil family life is thrown into turmoil. Jewel is fiercely determined that Brenda Kay will have the best care possible, and the girl becomes the family's entire focus. Many of the other characters' own dreams and ambitions wither in the face of this new reality, including husband Leston's hopes of owning a lumber yard. Jewel's decision to move the family to California to ensure Brenda Kay's education, however, ignites conflict between her and Leston that even love and compassion for the child cannot overcome. Lott "expertly realizes a stubborn, faithful mother and her phenomenally unselfish, supportive family," commented a *Publishers Weekly* reviewer.

A Song I Knew by Heart is a "highly emotional depiction of grief," commented Joanne Wilkinson in *Booklist.* Naomi, a widow in her seventies, has already suffered the profound grief of the loss of her spouse, Eli, whom she had known since childhood. She is devastated when her son, Mahlon, is killed in a car accident. As Naomi and widowed daughter-in-law Ruth endure the bitter pain together, Naomi decides to return to her childhood home in South Carolina. Ruth, with no ties left to keep her in the north, accompanies her. Together, the two women, bound by death, face aspects of their pasts, endure the dreadful present, and look toward a better future. Wilkinson called the book an "achingly tender portrait."

In his collection *The Difference between Women and Men,* "the universe of Bret Lott's stories is the uncertainty of family life," noted reviewer Edith Alston in the *Weekly Standard.* In one story, a man uses an unfortunate turn of phrase while traveling in a car with his wife. Upon reaching home, he discovers that his marriage of twenty-seven years is now in jeopardy. Many of Lott's tales "eerily border the edge of an alternate universe," Alston commented. When a man admits an affair to his wife in another story, he is confident that the two of them will be able to get through the difficult situation. However, he is unaware that, in his wife's view and in reality, he has already begun to vanish, bit by bit. "The Train, the Lake, the Bridge" is the "real jewel" of the collection, Alston stated, "a ghost story without ghosts" in which haunting events from the narrator's Depression-era boyhood in New England figure prominently. In "Rose," Lott revisits the characters, settings, and events of William Faulkner's extraordinary short story, "A Rose for Emily." The "characters Lott plays witness to inhabit today's world, where marriage and parenthood are fragile states," noted Alston.

As a writer of essays, novels, and short stories, Lott has considerable experience in the literary world. With *Before We Get Started: A Practical Memoir of the Writer's Life,* he offers a collection of advice and insight geared toward the neophyte writer. Lott approaches the subject of writing by "focusing on creativity and guiding the writer to certain realities of the craft," noted Loree Davis in the *Library Journal.* A combination of memoir and instruction, Lott's book recounts the difficulties from his early days as a writer, prior to being selected as an Oprah writer, when he had to balance the needs of his family with a teaching job that drained time from his writing schedule. He encourages writers to pay attention to the weight and importance of every word in a story, and to work hard to make time to write even in a frenetically busy life. Writers new to the craft will "appreciate the heartfelt supportiveness of his counsel," stated a *Publishers Weekly* critic, as well as his handling of the world of writing and publishing "with resounding candor and sincerity."

Lott told *CA:* "Though I'd always enjoyed writing—whether letters, or essays for school—the idea of being a writer never really occurred to me until I was a senior in college, after first having been a forestry major, then a marine biology major, then quitting school to work as a salesman, then coming back to school with the notion of teaching high school. But finally, in my senior year,

my teacher John Herman suggested I go on for a master's degree, which I did. At the University of Massachusetts—Amherst I studied under Jay Neugeboren and James Baldwin, and my first stories started appearing in *Writer's Forum,* the *Yale Review,* and the *Iowa Review.* After graduation I got a job teaching five sections of remedial English each quarter at Ohio State University. Even though we had our first child then, and even though I was teaching so much, I managed to sneak down to the basement of our apartment each morning at about 4:30 to write for a couple of hours before my wife, Melanie, and Zeb woke up. In that way I was able to complete *The Man Who Owned Vermont.*

"All my writings, whether short stories or novels, are about working people—people who have to sort through their personal lives and problems while working to pay bills and put food in the refrigerator. I think this comes from the fact that my family is a working one. (I was the first person to go to college in the Lott family in three generations.) My brothers and sister and wife and in-laws and most friends all work forty hours a week; that seems real to me—not a professor's life or a writer's life that so many people imagine is glamorous and full of interesting activities. And so writing is for me my own work, my job, what I do. And though it is work, I still have a blast every time I sit down at my desk, imagining the lives of other people and putting them down on paper. In the *Georgia Review,* Steven Corey called *The Man Who Owned Vermont* 'a delicate and wise view of working and loving in modern America.' These are indeed the themes I want to write about, the concerns I want to capture in my fiction."

Lott later added: "The longer I write—the more books I write, the more sentences I put together, the more single words I pick to use—the harder the whole thing gets. I don't mean this to be gloomy or off-putting. It's just that I am constantly in touch, and more so with every book I write, with my shortcomings, what I cannot do. My lack of vocabulary, of imagination, of insight and artistry. I mean this. When I was writing my first book, the whole world was available: I didn't know what I couldn't do, and for that reason the adventure of writing back then was a joyful one, a surprise every day. Now I am in middle age, and the surprises are deeper ones, more rewarding ones, because I know what I am up against, and still I am here, and still I am writing. The biggest surprise is realizing continually how little I know, and yet still feeling the need to find out more, to discover why these characters in my stories do what they do.

"I have my whole life been trying to write books that oppose the cynical, jaded perspective so very much of our culture has adopted as the air we have no choice but to breathe. I am not consciously thinking to write books that are attempts to be sincere, to be honest, to be straightforward and to tell the truth. But this is all I know to do, and the effect I want to have, then, is to let people know there is hope, and that we are not shackled to the bleak and horizonless viewpoint it seems so much literary fiction hands us. I don't think it ought to be a surprise to anyone that I am a practicing Christian, that I believe Christ was who He said He was, and that the hope He holds out to us all is woven into the very fabric of who I am. There is hope. That's the effect I want my books to have on my readers."

BIOGRAPHICAL AND CRITICAL SOURCES:

PERIODICALS

Another Chicago Magazine, fall, 1998, review of *Fathers, Sons, and Brothers: The Men in My Family*, p. 257.

Antioch Review, summer, 1987, review of *The Man Who Owned Vermont*, p. 375.

Bloomsbury Review, May, 1997, review of *Fathers, Sons, and Brothers*, p. 19.

Book World, November 7, 1993, review of *Reed's Beach*, p. 11; July 6, 1997, review of *Fathers, Sons, and Brothers*, p. 8; May 17, 1998, review of *The Hunt Club*, p. 7.

Booklist, May 15, 1987, review of *The Man Who Owned Vermont*, p. 1408; June 15, 1988, review of *A Stranger's House*, p. 1708; August, 1989, review of *A Dream of Old Leaves*, p. 1946; September 15, 1991, review of *Jewel*, p. 121; August, 1996, Jim O'Laughlin, review of *How to Get Home*, p. 1882; May 1, 1997, Brian McCombie, review of *Fathers, Sons, and Brothers*, p. 1474; February 1, 1998, Joanne Wilkinson, review of *The Hunt Club*, p. 899; March 15, 1999, review of *The Hunt Club*, p. 1316; February 15, 2004, Joanne Wilkinson, review of *A Song I Know by Heart*, p. 1003; November 15, 2004, Donna Seaman, review of *Before We Get Started: A Practical Memoir of the Writer's Life*, p. 530; June 1, 2005, Joanne Wilkinson, review of *The Difference between Women and Men*, p. 1753.

Books & Culture, September-October, 2005, Susan Wise Bauer, review of *The Difference between Women and Men*, p. 31.

Christianity Today, June, 2005, Lauren F. Winner, "A Jewel of a Writer," July, 2005, Cindy Crosby, "Lyrical Storytelling," p. 59.

Georgia Review, fall, 1987, review of *The Man Who Owned Vermont*, p. 639.

Globe & Mail (Toronto, Canada), June 12, 1999, review of *Jewel*, p. 4.

Kirkus Reviews, April 1, 1987, review of *The Man Who Owned Vermont*, p. 503; June 1, 1988, review of *A Stranger's House*, p. 784; May 15, 1989, review of *A Dream of Old Leaves*, p. 722; August 15, 1991, review of *Jewel*, p. 1034; July 15, 1993, review of *Reed's Beach*, p. 881; June 15, 1996, review of *How to Get Home*, p. 848; March 15, 1997, review of *Fathers, Sons, and Brothers*, p. 442; January 15, 1998, review of *The Hunt Club*, p. 72; February 15, 2004, review of *A Song I Knew by Heart*, p. 148; April 15, 2005, review of *The Difference between Women and Men*, p. 441.

Kliatt, May, 1999, review of *The Hunt Club*, p. 58.

Library Journal, June 1, 1987, James B. Hemesath, review of *The Man Who Owned Vermont*, p. 129; September 1, 1988, Michele Leber, review of *A Stranger's House*, p. 183; June 1, 1989, M.J. Simmons, review of *A Dream of Old Leaves*, p. 146; September 15, 1991, Thomas L. Kilpatrick, review of *Jewel*, p. 110; July, 1996, Ellen R. Cohen, review of *How to Get Home*, p. 167; June 15, 1997, William Gargan, review of *Fathers, Sons, and Brothers*, p. 69; January, 1998, Thomas L. Kilpatrick, review of *The Hunt Club*, p. 142; March 15, 2001, Joyce Sparrows, review of *A Year in Place*, p. 84; September 15, 2003, review of *Jewel*, p. 112; March 1, 2004, Robin Nesbitt, review of *A Song I Know by Heart*, p. 108; January 1, 2005, Loree Davis, review of *Before We Get Started*, p. 112; May 1, 2005, Susanne Wells, review of *The Difference between Women and Men*, p. 79.

Los Angeles Times, August 21, 1988, review of *A Stranger's House*, p. 1; February 11, 1990, review of *A Stranger's House*, p. 8; August 25, 1996, review of *How to Get Home*, p. 10.

Massachusetts Review, spring, 1988, Roger Sale, review of *The Man Who Owned Vermont*, p. 74.

New York Times, June 6, 1987, Michiko Kakutani, review of *The Man Who Owned Vermont*, p. 12; August 18, 1988, Caryn James, review of *A Stranger's House*, p. 20.

New York Times Book Review, July 12, 1987, Lori B. Miller, review of *The Man Who Owned Vermont*, p. 20; May 8, 1988, review of *The Man Who Owned Vermont*, p. 42; September 11, 1988, Isabel Eberstadt, review of *A Stranger's House*, p. 33;

September 10, 1989, Eils Lotozo, review of *A Dream of Old Leaves,* p. 26; March 1, 1992, Judith Freeman, review of *Jewel,* p. 21; November 8, 1992, review of *Jewel,* p. 64; February 13, 1994, James Polk, review of *Reed's Beach;* August 4, 1996, Barbara Quick, review of *How to Get Home,* p. 18; July 6, 1997, Andrea Cooper, review of *Fathers, Sons, and Brothers,* p. 15; March 29, 1998, Robert Polito, review of *The Hunt Club,* p. 9; June 18, 2000, review of *Fathers, Sons, and Brothers,* p. 28.

Publishers Weekly, May 1, 1987, Sybil Steinberg, review of *The Man Who Owned Vermont,* p. 54; March 4, 1988, review of *The Man Who Owned Vermont,* p. 107; June 9, 1989, Sybil Steinberg, review of *A Dream of Old Leaves,* p. 54; December 8, 1989, review of *A Stranger's House,* p. 52; August 23, 1991, review of *Jewel,* p. 46; August 31, 1992, review of *Jewel,* p. 72; August 16, 1993, review of *Reed's Beach,* p. 85; June 17, 1996, review of *How to Get Home,* p. 48; April 14, 1997, review of *Fathers, Sons, and Brothers,* p. 61; December 1, 1997, review of *The Hunt Club,* p. 43; November 22, 2004, review of *Before We Get Started,* p. 52; May 16, 2005, review of *The Difference between Women and Men,* p. 36.

Quill and Quire, December, 1989, review of *A Dream of Old Leaves,* p. 29.

School Library Journal, November 1, 1998, Pam Spencer, review of *The Hunt Club,* p. 161.

Southern Living, September, 2005, Valerie L. Kramer, review of *The Difference between Women and Men,* p. 215.

Time, July 27, 1987, review of *The Man Who Owned Vermont,* p. 65.

Today's Christian Woman, March-April, 2006, Janice Byrd, review of *A Song I Knew by Heart,* p. 63.

Tribune Books (Chicago, IL), August 7, 1988, review of *A Stranger's House,* p. 6; October 29, 1989, review of *A Dream of Old Leaves,* p. 6; November 24, 1991, review of *Jewel,* p. 6; November 22, 1992, review of *Jewel,* p. 8.

Village Voice, October 3, 1989, review of *A Dream of Old Leaves,* p. 56.

Virginia Quarterly Review, winter, 2006, Wade Edwards, review of *The Difference between Women and Men,* p. 281.

Weekly Standard, August 15, 2005, Edith Alston, review of *The Difference between Women and Men,* p. 39.

Wilson Library Bulletin, September, 1987, Ben Davis, review of *The Man Who Owned Vermont,* p. 101.

Writer, July, 2005, Steve Weinberg, review of *Before We Get Started,* p. 48.

ONLINE

College of Charleston Faculty Award Winners, http://www.cofc.edu/ (January 8, 2007), biography of Bret Lott.

Louisiana State University Highlights, http://www.lsu.edu/ (fall, 2004), "Celebrated Author Takes over Editorship of Historic Literary Publication."

National Endowment for the Arts, http://www.nea.gov/ (December 11, 2006), "U.S. Senate Confirms Appointment of Six New Members to National Council on the Arts."

Southern Review, http://www.lsu.edu/thesouthernreview/ (January 8, 2007), "President Bush Nominates *Southern Review* Editor and Director to National Council on the Arts."*

*   *   *

LOWRY, Lois 1937-
(Lois Hammersberg Lowry)

PERSONAL: Born March 20, 1937, in Honolulu, HI; daughter of Robert E. (a dentist) and Katharine Hammersberg; married Donald Grey Lowry (an attorney), June 11, 1956 (divorced, 1977); married Martin Small; children: Alix, Grey (deceased), Kristin, Benjamin. *Education:* Attended Brown University, 1954-56; University of Southern Maine, B.A., 1972; graduate study. *Religion:* Episcopalian.

ADDRESSES: Home—Cambridge, MA. *Agent*—Phyllis Westberg, Harold Ober Associates, 425 Madison Ave., New York, NY 10017.

CAREER: Children's book author and photographer, 1972—.

MEMBER: Society of Children's Book Writers and Illustrators, PEN New England, PEN American Center, Authors Guild, Authors League of America, MacDowell Colony (fellow).

AWARDS, HONORS: Children's Literature Award, International Reading Association (IRA), Notable Book designation, American Library Association (ALA), and MA and CA state children's choice awards, all 1978, all for *A Summer to Die;* Children's Book of the Year citation, Child Study Association of America, and ALA Notable Book designation, both 1979, both for *Anastasia Krupnik;* ALA Notable Book designation, 1980, and International Board on Books for Young People Honor List citation, 1982, both for *Autumn Street;* ALA Notable Book designation, 1981, and American Book Award nomination in juvenile paperback category, 1983, both for *Anastasia Again!;* ALA Notable Book designation, 1983, for *The One-Hundredth Thing about Caroline;* Children's Book of the Year designation, Child Study Association of America, 1986, for *Us and Uncle Fraud;* NJ state children's choice award, 1986, for *Anastasia, Ask Your Analyst; Boston Globe/Horn Book* Award, Golden Kite Award, Society of Children's Book Writers and Illustrators, and Child Study Award, Children's Book Committee of Bank Street College, all 1987, all for *Rabble Starkey;* Christopher Award, 1988; Newbery Medal, ALA, National Jewish Book Award, and Sidney Taylor Award, National Jewish Libraries, all 1990, all for *Number the Stars;* Newbery Medal, 1994, for *The Giver;* Children's Choice citation, IRA/ Children's Book Council, 1997, for *See You Around, Sam!;* Hope S. Dean Memorial Award, 2003.

WRITINGS:

JUVENILE NOVELS

A Summer to Die, illustrated by Jenni Oliver, Houghton Mifflin (Boston, MA), 1977.

Find a Stranger, Say Goodbye, Houghton Mifflin (Boston, MA), 1978.

Anastasia Krupnik, Houghton Mifflin (Boston, MA), 1979.

Autumn Street, Houghton Mifflin (Boston, MA), 1979.

Anastasia Again!, illustrated by Diane deGroat, Houghton Mifflin (Boston, MA), 1981.

Anastasia at Your Service, illustrated by Diane deGroat, Houghton Mifflin (Boston, MA), 1982.

Taking Care of Terrific, Houghton Mifflin (Boston, MA), 1983.

Anastasia, Ask Your Analyst, Houghton Mifflin (Boston, MA), 1984.

Us and Uncle Fraud, Houghton Mifflin (Boston, MA), 1984.

The One Hundredth Thing about Caroline, Houghton Mifflin (Boston, MA), 1985.

Anastasia on Her Own, Houghton Mifflin (Boston, MA), 1985.

Switcharound, Houghton Mifflin (Boston, MA), 1985.

Anastasia Has the Answers, Houghton Mifflin (Boston, MA), 1986.

Rabble Starkey, Houghton Mifflin (Boston, MA), 1987.

Anastasia's Chosen Career, Houghton Mifflin (Boston, MA), 1987.

All about Sam, illustrated by Diane deGroat, Houghton Mifflin (Boston, MA), 1988.

Number the Stars, Houghton Mifflin (Boston, MA), 1989, reprinted, Yearling (New York, NY), 2005.

Your Move, J.P.!, Houghton Mifflin (Boston, MA), 1990.

Anastasia at This Address, Houghton Mifflin (Boston, MA), 1991.

Attaboy, Sam!, illustrated by Diane deGroat, Houghton Mifflin (Boston, MA), 1992.

The Giver, Houghton Mifflin (Boston, MA), 1993.

Anastasia, Absolutely, Houghton Mifflin (Boston, MA), 1995.

See You Around, Sam!, Houghton Mifflin (Boston, MA), 1996.

Stay!: Keeper's Story, illustrated by True Kelley, Houghton Mifflin (Boston, MA), 1997.

Looking Back: A Book of Memories, Houghton Mifflin (Boston, MA), 1998.

Zooman Sam, Houghton Mifflin (Boston, MA), 1999.

Gathering Blue, Houghton Mifflin (Boston, MA), 2000.

Gooney Bird Greene, illustrated by Middy Thomas, Houghton Mifflin (Boston, MA), 2002.

The Silent Boy, Houghton Mifflin (Boston, MA), 2003.

The Messenger, Houghton Mifflin (Boston, MA), 2004.

Gooney Bird and the Room Mother, illustrated by Middy Thomas, Houghton Mifflin (Boston, MA), 2005.

Gossamer, Houghton Mifflin (Boston, MA), 2006.

Gooney the Fabulous, illustrated by Middy Thomas, Houghton Mifflin (Boston, MA), 2007.

OTHER

Black American Literature (textbook), J. Weston Walsh (Portland, ME), 1973.

Literature of the American Revolution (textbook), J. Weston Walsh (Portland, ME), 1974.

(Photographer) Frederick H. Lewis, *Here in Kennebunkport,* Durrell (Kennebunkport, ME), 1978.

(Author of introduction) *Dear Author: Students Write about the Books That Changed Their Lives,* Conari Press, 1998.

(And photographer) *Looking Back: A Photographic Memoir* (autobiography), Houghton Mifflin (Boston, MA), 1998.

Contributor of stories, articles, and photographs to periodicals, including *Redbook, Yankee,* and *Down East.*

ADAPTATIONS: *Find a Stranger, Say Goodbye* was adapted as the *Afterschool Special* television film "I Don't Know Who I Am," produced 1980. *Taking Care of Terrific* was adapted as a segment of the television series *Wonderworks,* 1988. *Anastasia at Your Service* was adapted as an audiobook for Learning Library, 1984. *Anastasia Krupnik* was adapted as a filmstrip, Cheshire, 1987. *The Giver* was adapted as a film by Todd Alcott and directed by Vadim Perelman for Twentieth Century-Fox, c. 2007. *Gooney Bird Greene and Her True-Life Adventures,* a dramatization by Kent R. Brown, was adapted from *Gooney Bird Greene* and published by Dramatic Publishing, 2005. Several of Lowry's novels have been adapted as audiobooks by Listening Library.

SIDELIGHTS: Lois Lowry, an award-winning author of young-adult novels, is perhaps best known for the Newbery Award-winning novel *Number the Stars* and her futuristic trilogy consisting of *The Giver, Gathering Blue,* and *Messenger.* Never one to shy from controversy, her novels deal with topics ranging from the death of a sibling and the Nazi occupation of Denmark to the humorous antics of a rebellious teen named Anastasia Krupnik, and to futuristic dystopian societies. Although Lowry's books explore a variety of settings and characters, she distills from her work a single unifying theme: "the importance of human connections," as she wrote on her home page.

In 1937, when Lowry was born, her father, a military dentist and career army officer, was stationed at Schofield Barracks near Pearl Harbor in Honolulu, Hawaii. The family separated with the onset of World War II, Lowry's father serving out his tour of duty while Lowry and her mother stayed with her mother's family in the Amish country of Pennsylvania. "I remember all these relatively normal Christmases with trees, presents, turkeys, and carols, except that they had this enormous hole in them because there was never any father figure," the author recalled in an interview for *CA.* This deep sense of loss is "probably why I've written a terrific father figure into all of my books—sort of a fantasy of mine while growing up." Her grandmother was not especially fond of children, but her grandfather adored her, and Lowry escaped the absolute trauma of war under the shelter of his affection. Much later, Lowry's wartime experience inspired her fourth novel, *Autumn Street.*

In her first novel, *A Summer to Die,* Lowry portrays an adolescent's effort to deal with her older sister's illness and eventual death. When the Chalmers family moves to the country for the summer, thirteen-year-old Meg and fifteen-year-old Molly are forced to share a room. Already jealous of her older sister, Meg becomes increasingly argumentative and resentful when Molly's recurring nosebleeds demand much of her parents' attention. As her sister's condition deteriorates, Meg realizes that Molly is slowly dying of leukemia. For friendship, she turns to Will Banks, an elderly neighbor who encourages the teen's interest in photography, and Ben and Maria, a hippie couple who invites Meg to photograph the birth of their child.

A Summer to Die was well received by critics. Lowry's "story captures the mysteries of living and dying without manipulating the reader's emotions, providing understanding and a comforting sense of completion," observed Linda R. Silver in *School Library Journal.* In fact, Lowry's tale of Meg and Molly was drawn from life; her older sister, Helen, died of cancer when Lowry was twenty-five years old. Despite its inspiration, the author has maintained that "very little of [*A Summer to Die*] was factual, except the emotions." Even so, "when my mother read the book she recognized the characters as my sister and me," Lowry added. "She knew that the circumstances in the book were very different, but the characters had great veracity for her."

"Until I was about twelve I thought my parents were terrific, wise, wonderful, beautiful, loving, and well-dressed," Lowry once confessed. "By age twelve and a half they turned into stupid, boring people with whom I did not want to be seen in public. . . . That happens to all kids, and to the kids in my books as well." These same childhood memories, combined with Lowry's experiences as a parent, inspire her most popular character: Anastasia Krupnik, the spunky, rebellious, and irreverent star of books such as *Anastasia, Ask Your Analyst!, Anastasia on Her Own,* and *Anastasia at Your Service.* In the first book of the series, *Anastasia Krupnik,* the ten-year-old heroine faces numerous comic crises, including a crush on a boy who is continually dribbling an imaginary basketball, and the coming arrival of a new sibling. With the passing of each crisis Anastasia gains new insight into herself, and by the book's close she is prepared to move on to a new level of maturity. "Anastasia's feelings and discoveries should be familiar to anyone who has ever been ten," noted Brad Owens in the *Christian Science Monitor,* "and . . . Lowry has a sensitive way of taking problems seriously without ever being shallow or leaning too far over into despair."

The broad audience appeal sparked by the first "Anastasia" book has prompted Lowry to write several other novels that follow the coming of age of her diminutive heroine. In *Anastasia at Your Service* Anastasia is now twelve years old and tackling a summer job serving as maid to a rich, elderly woman. When the woman turns out to be a classmate's grandmother, the girl must deal with the embarrassment of working for the family of a well-to-do peer. "Despite differences the girls become friends; and with the help of Anastasia's precocious brother Sam, they generate a plot that is rich, inviting, and very funny," noted Barbara Elleman in a *Booklist* review of *Anastasia at Your Service*.

The popular Anastasia has gone on to appear in over a dozen more titles, among them *Anastasia Has the Answers, Anastasia's Chosen Career,* and *Anastasia Again!* As a lovestruck thirteen year old plying the personal ads, she generates confusion in *Anastasia at This Address,* showcasing what a *Publishers Weekly* reviewer described as her "headstrong, inventive, endearing in irrepressible" self, while her unwitting tampering of the U.S. mail in *Anastasia Absolutely* prompts a "moral crisis" that results in what *Horn Book* reviewer Maeve Visser Knoth predicted would be "light, satisfying reading" for Anastasia's many fans.

"I have the feeling she's going to go on forever—or until I get sick of her," Lowry once remarked of the fictional Anastasia. While the final book in the series, *Anastasia Absolutely,* was published in 1995, the popular heroine's family has been introduced to younger readers via her little brother in the books *Attaboy Sam!, See You around, Sam!* and *Zooman Sam.* In *Zooman Sam,* Sam is on the cusp of learning to read. Acquiring the skill will allow him to be someone special, he believes: specifically, the Chief of Wonderfulness. To help him along, his mother makes Sam a special "Zooman Sam" jumpsuit for him to dress up in during Future Job Day at his nursery school (there was not enough room on the garment to fit the word "zookeeper"). With dreams of being a zookeeper, a special job indeed in a room full of children dreaming of more mundane occupations, Sam feels honored when his teacher tells him that she will let him stand at the head of the circle and tell about a different zoo animal each day for six weeks. With his budding reading skills, Sam is delighted to take on the task and enjoys the attention that comes with it. "Lowry gets everything about Sam just right," wrote Stephanie Zvirin in *Booklist,* while *Horn Book* reviewer Roger Sutton observed that the author "spins interesting variations on her theme," and wraps the book up with "a swell . . . surprise."

Again directed for younger readers, the title character in Lowry's chapter book *Gooney Bird Greene* is the newest arrival to the second grade and the most eccentric person the other students have ever seen. Leaning toward flamboyant dress (a pair of cowboy boots and pajamas one day, a polka-dot shirt and tutu the next), Gooney Bird is also a master storyteller in a small package. She delights in relating tales such as her "absolutely true" adventures of how she flew in from China on a flying carpet, how she got her "diamond earrings" (actually gumball machine trinkets) from a noble prince, and how she earned her oddball name. Encouraged in these tall tales by her teacher, Mrs. Pidgeon, Gooney Bird spins out her imaginative saga, prompting her fellow students to create and tell their own stories. In the process, the entire class—and the book's reader—learns important lessons in storytelling and constructing a compelling and believable narrative. GraceAnne A. DeCandido, writing in *Booklist,* called *Gooney Bird Greene* a "laugh-out-loud" story that serves as "quite a debut" for its young heroine. The book's message and the "cleverly titled stories could spark children's interest in writing their own stories," wrote Janet B. Bair in *School Library Journal.* Peter D. Sieruta, reviewing Lowry's story for *Horn Book,* observed that Gooney Bird is "not always convincing as a character, but she's a fine storyteller, and her message to her classmates—that they, too, have stories to share—is a good one."

Like Anastasia before her, Gooney Bird reappears in several other titles. Still impressing members of Mrs. Pidgeon's second-grade class with her storytelling, she also rises to the challenge of improving her vocabulary in *Gooney Bird and the Room Mother,* arranging a special treat for the school's Thanksgiving celebration as well. Gooney morphs from raconteur to moralist in *Gooney the Fabulous* when her teacher asks each student to write a story inspired by a reading of Aesop's fables. Reviewing *Gooney Bird and the Room Mother,* Kristine M. Casper dubbed the book "a fast-paced read" in her *School Library Journal* review, the critic adding that Lowry's efforts to encourage vocabulary-building is effectively integrated into the story. Hazel Rochman wrote in *Booklist* that Mrs. Pidgeon's Thanksgiving Day lessons "are fun" and that Lowry's story "builds to a tense, beautiful climax." Once more "Gooney takes the lead," announced Ilene Cooper in a *Booklist* review of *Gooney the Fabulous,* the critic adding that the author "nicely individualizes her characters and gets readers interested" in Gooney and her second-grade world.

Although her "Anastasia" and "Gooney Bird Greene" stories have been popular lighthearted fare, much of

Lowry's success as a novelist has come through her willingness to explore challenging and sometimes controversial teen-oriented topics. For example, she documents an adopted child's search for her biological mother in *Find a Stranger, Say Goodbye*. Although neither Lowry nor any of her children are adopted, she recognized that the subject was an important one that, at the time, was the subject of little focus. "Maybe it's because of having watched my own kids go through the torture of becoming adults . . . that I think those kinds of issues are important and it's important to deal with them in a sensitive and compassionate way," the author once noted.

Based on a factual account, *Number the Stars* is an historical novel set against the backdrop of Nazi-occupied Denmark. In this 1990 novel—the first of Lowry's books to receive the Newbery honor—ten-year-old Annemarie Johansen and her family are drawn into the resistance movement. As narrated by Annemarie, the book follows the family's efforts to shuttle Jews from Denmark into neutral Sweden during World War II, an activity that helped ensure the survival of nearly all of Denmark's Jewish population. The book "avoids explicit description of the horrors of war, yet manages to convey without oversimplification the sorrow felt by so many people who were forced to flee their homeland," wrote a *Children's Literature Review* critic. As quoted in *School Library Journal*, Newbery Awards Committee chair Caroline Ward commented that in *Number the Stars* "Lowry creates suspense and tension without wavering from the viewpoint of Annemarie, a child who shows the true meaning of courage."

Lowry received a second Newbery Medal for her 1993 novel *The Giver*. A radical departure from her previous works, the novel introduces readers to a futuristic utopian world wherein every aspect of life—birth, death, families, career choices, emotions, even the weather—is strictly controlled in order to create a safe and comfortable community where humans can live with no fear of violence. Living in this community, twelve-year-old Jonas is looking forward to an important rite of passage: the ceremony in which he, along with all children his age, is to be assigned a life's vocation. Skipped during the ceremony, Jonas is ultimately selected for a unique position when he is assigned to become the new Receiver, a prestigious and powerful person charged with holding all the memories of the community. During his apprenticeship to the current Receiver, an elderly man whom Jonas calls The Giver, the boy begins learning about the things—memories, emotions, and knowl-

edge—that the community has given up in favor of peace. At first, these memories are pleasant: images of snow, colors, feelings of love. But Jonas soon encounters the darker aspects of human experience—war, death, and pain—and discovers that elderly or infirm community members who are "Released" are actually being euthanized. This discovery leads the boy to escape from the community with his young foster brother Gabriel.

Lowry ends *The Giver* with an interestingly ambiguous ending in which readers are left unsure of the boys' fate. In a companion novel, *Gathering Blue*, she describes a technologically primitive world in which, as she states in her author's note, "disorder, savagery, and self-interest" rule. As in *The Giver*, a child is chosen to play a special role in this society. In this world, the child is Kira. Born with a twisted leg—a condition that would normally have resulted in her being put to death as a baby—Kira was somehow allowed to live. Now a talented seamstress, she is chosen to be The Threader, a person whose duty it is to create the robe of The Singer. This garment depicts the history of the world and is used in the society's annual ritual of the Gathering. As The Threader, Kira begins to learn the dark secrets prompting her society's rules and must ultimately make a life-altering choice.

Many reviewers praised both *The Giver* and *Gathering Blue* for their sensitive handling of serious themes, a *Publishers Weekly* reviewer hailing *Gathering Blue* as a "dark, prophetic tale with a strong medieval flavor." Kay Bowes, writing in *Book Report*, called that same novel "thought-provoking" and "challenging," while a *Horn Book* writer wrote that *Gathering Blue* "shares the thematic concerns of *The Giver* . . . [but] adds a layer of questions about the importance of art in creating and, more ominously, controlling community." Ellen Fader, writing in *School Library Journal*, concluded that with *Gathering Blue* "Lowry has once again created a fully-realized world," adding that "readers won't forget these memorable characters or their struggles in an inhospitable world."

Messenger continues the story begun in *The Giver* and *Gathering Blue*. Entering the forest sanctuary of "The Village" as a young refugee, Matty has come to love his new home and respect the community's shared values. Now a teen, he has been guided toward adulthood by a blind man named Seer. Increasingly politically aware as he matures, Matty senses that a change has come over those in The Village whom he once respected; rather than welcoming newcomers, most in the community have become greedy and jealous. Unwilling to share their good fortune, they are now determined to wall themselves off from the rest of the world. A young man named Leader, guide of The Village (in fact, Jonah from *The Giver*), is also concerned about this change. When Village members vote to prohibit the influx of more outsiders, Matty is sent by Leader to find Seer's daughter Kira (from *Gathering Blue*). Making his way through the harsh forest environment outside the Village, the teen hopes to reunite Kira with her father before the opportunity is lost forever. Although Kira is lame and the journey to Seer is arduous, she selflessly refuses to take advantage of Matty's skill as a healer because use of this power seems to cause Matty harm.

Calling *Messenger* "simply and beautifully written" in her review for the *New York Times Book Review,* Hazel Rochman noted the book's position as the third volume in Lowry's loosely knit trilogy. Rereading both *The Giver* and *Gathering Blue,* she noted that these two volumes contain "unresolved endings." While Lowry's unwillingness to create a strong resolution in her futuristic novels might be problematic for some reviewers, "others [have] applauded." "While *Messenger* may tie the three stories together just a little too neatly," Rochman added, "it is still far from a sweet resolution. Up to the last anguished page, Lois Lowry shows how hard it is to build community," leaving readers with the same frustration that her main characters experience. "Lowry's many fans will welcome this return to the fascinating world she has created," wrote Paula Rohrlick in a *Kliatt* review of *Messenger,* the critic also citing "the provocative issues she raises" in the suspenseful novel. "Lowry's skillful writing imbues the story with a strong sense of foreboding," concluded Marie Orlando in a review of the novel for *School Library Journal,* while in *Kirkus Reviews* a critic predicted that "readers will be absorbed in thought and wonder long after" the final page of *Messenger* is turned.

In *The Silent Boy* Lowry again takes up a solemn theme, introducing Katy Thatcher, Kate's physician father, and their life in a small New England town during the early part of the twentieth century. Peggy Stoltz, a local girl who helps on the Thatcher farm, is Katy's best friend. Peggy has a brother named Jacob, as well as a sister named Nell who works on the farm next to the Thatchers' place. Jacob, considered an "imbecile," or "touched in the head," is a gentle thirteen year old who never speaks but has a profound ability to handle and com-

municate with animals. After Katy knits together a tenuous friensship with Jacob, she begins to sense the wonder in his affinity with animals. Meanwhile, the girl has trouble dealing with the realities of country life, with her upcoming tenth birthday, and with the arrival of a new baby in her family. Nell also expects a baby, the result of a relationship with her employers' son. Ultimately, things come to a head after Jacob disappears with Nell's unwanted and unnamed infant and the baby then turns up dead. Katy cannot believe that the sensitive and gentle Jacob could commit an act of murder, even one that, in his mind, may have been completely acceptable or even desirable. Jacob is eventually incarcerated in an asylum, leaving Katy haunted by the tragedy of his life. "Lowry's graceful, lively prose is dense with historical details," remarked Gillian Engberg in a *Booklist* review of *The Silent Boy.* Ellen Fader, writing in *School Library Journal,* noted of the novel that "Lowry excels in developing strong and unique characters and in showing Katy's life in a small town that changes around her as the first telephones and automobiles arrive." The novel's storyline "balances humor and generosity with the obstacles and injustice of Katy's world," a *Publishers Weekly* reviewer wrote, while a *Kirkus Reviews* writer deemed the novel "a tragedy deftly foreshadowed."

While *The Giver* and its sequels was classified by several reviewers as science fiction, in her novel *Gossamer* Lowry steps clearly into the realm of fantasy. Dubbed "spellbinding" by a *Publishers Weekly* contributor, the story introduces Littlest One, a young creature who, as a member of a race of dream givers, is learning to practice her ancestral art. In touching the objects that make up a certain human's day, dream givers collect threads of memories, sounds, and images, using these to weave together the dreams that fill the minds of the sleeping. Working with experienced teacher Thin Elderly, Littlest is assigned to practice her art in the home of an elderly foster mother, where she comes in contact with John, the woman's troubled young charge. As her skills develop, the dream giver creates images that reflect the healthy relationship developing between John and his foster mother, but as part of her work she must also fight off the efforts of the Sinisteeds, who find in John the perfect vehicle for their horrific nightmares. Reviewing *Gossamer,* the *Publishers Weekly* contributor cited Lowry for her "exquisite, at times mesmerizing writing," while Lauralyn Persson wrote in *School Library Journal* that the author's "carefully plotted fantasy has inner logic and conviction." Noting that *Gossamer* is "written with Lowry's characteristic elegance and economy, and with her usual attentiveness to the internal consistency of her imaginary world," James Hynes concluded in his *New York Times Book Review* appraisal that the novel is "enormously entertaining and . . . very moving."

While many of Lowry's children's books draw on pleasant memories and experiences from their author's past, as her career has stretched through the years from parenthood to grandparenthood, she has continued to collect experiences, both tragic and joyful. She sifts through this lifetime of remembrances and attempts and in *Looking Back: A Book of Memories.* locates threads of stories and patterns in these experience. More like a visit from a favorite friend than an autobiography, *Looking Back* is "much more intimate and personal than many traditional memoirs," according to *School Library Journal* contributor Barbara Scotto, while a *Publishers Weekly* reviewer observed of the book that "a compelling and inspirational portrait of the author emerges from these vivid snapshots of life's joyful, sad, and surprising moments."

BIOGRAPHICAL AND CRITICAL SOURCES:

BOOKS

American Women Writers, 2nd edition, St. James Press (Detroit, MI), 2000.

Authors and Artists for Young Adults, Volume 32, Thomson Gale (Detroit, MI), 2000.

Beacham's Guide to Literature for Young Adults, Beacham Publishing (Osprey, FL), 1990, Volume 4, 1990, Volume 6, 1994.

Chaston, Joel D., *Lois Lowry,* Twayne (New York, NY), 1997.

Children's Literature Review, Thomson Gale (Detroit, MI), Volume 6, 1984, Volume 46, 1997, Volume 72, pp. 192-206.

Dictionary of Literary Biography, Volume 52: *American Writers for Children since 1960: Fiction,* Thomson Gale (Detroit, MI), 1987, pp. 249-261.

Green, Carol Hurd, and Mary Grimley Mason, editors, *American Women Writers,* Volume 5, Continuum Publishing (New York, NY), 1994.

Lowry, Lois, *Looking Back: A Book of Memories,* Houghton Mifflin (Boston, MA), 1998.

St. James Guide to Young-Adult Writers, 2nd edition, St. James Press (Detroit, MI), 1999.

Silvey, Anita, editor, *Children's Books and Their Creators,* Houghton Mifflin (Boston, MA), 1995.

Something about the Author Autobiography Series, Volume 3, Thomson Gale (Detroit, MI), 1986, pp. 131-146.

PERIODICALS

Book, May-June, 2003, review of *Gooney Bird Greene,* p. 31.

Booklist, October 15, 1979, Barbara Elleman, review of *Anastasia Krupnik,* p. 354; September 1, 1982, Barbara Elleman, review of *Anastasia at Your Service,* p. 46; September 1, 1987, review of *Anastasia's Chosen Career,* pp. 66-67; March 1, 1990, Ilene Cooper, review of *Your Move, J.P.!,* p. 1345; April 1, 1991, Stephanie Zvirin, review of *Anastasia at This Address,* p. 1564; October 1, 1995, Carolyn Phelan, review of *Anastasia, Absolutely,* p. 761; November 1, 1997, Ellen Mandel, review of *Stay!: Keeper's Story,* p. 472; November 1, 1998, Carolyn Phelan, review of *Looking Back,* p. 490; July, 1, 1999, Stephanie Zvirin, review of *Zooman Sam,* p. 1947; September 15, 1999, review of *Looking Back,* p. 254; June 1, 2000, Ilene Cooper, review of *Gathering Blue,* p. 1896; September 1, 2002, GraceAnne A. DeCandido, review of *Gooney Bird Greene,* p. 125; April 15, 2003, Gillian Engberg, review of *The Silent Boy,* p. 1462; February 15, 2004, Hazel Rochman, review of *Messenger,* p. 1056; March 1, 2005, Hazel Rochman, review of *Gooney Bird and the Room Mother,* p. 1197; February 15, 2006, Hazel Rochman, review of *Gossamer,* p. 99; January 1, 2007, Ilene Cooper, review of *Gooney the Fabulous,* p. 81.

Book Report, May, 1999, review of *Looking Back,* p. 73; January 2001, Kay Bowes, review of *Gathering Blue,* p. 58.

Books for Keeps, January, 2002, review of *Gathering Blue,* p. 26.

Bulletin of the Center for Children's Books, January, 1980, Zena Sutherland, review of *Anastasia Krupnik,* p. 99; May, 1984, Zena Sutherland, review of *Anastasia, Ask Your Analyst,* p. 169; March, 1990, Ruth Ann Smith, review of *Your Move, J.P.!,* p. 169; April, 1993, p. 257; September, 1995, Deborah Stevenson, review of *Anastasia, Absolutely,* pp. 20-21; November, 1996, p. 105; January, 1998, Janice Del Negro, review of *Stay!,* p. 165; January, 1999, Janice Del Negro, review of *Looking Back,* p. 174; September, 1999, review of *Zooman Sam,* p. 21; June, 2004, Krista Hutley, review of *Messenger,* p. 427; July-August, 2006, April Spisak, review of *Gossamer,* p. 507.

Catholic Library World, September, 1999, review of *See You Around, Sam,* p. 33.

Children's Bookwatch, March, 1999, review of *Looking Back,* p. 6; December, 1999, review of *Zooman Sam,* p. 4; March, 2001, review of *Looking Back,* p. 8.

Children's Literature (annual), 2004, Don Latham, "Discipline and Its Discontents: A Foucauldian Reading of 'The Giver,'" pp. 134-151.

Christian Science Monitor, January 14, 1980, Brad Owens, review of *Anastasia Krupnik,* p. B6; March 1, 1985, Lyn Littlfield Hoopes, review of *Us and Uncle Fraud,* p. 65; May 1, 1987, Betsy Hearne, "Families Shaped by Love, Not Convention," pp. B3-B4.

Five Owls, April, 1989, pp. 59-60; September-October, 1993, Gary D. Schmidt, review of *The Giver,* pp. 14-15; March, 2001, review of *Gathering Blue,* p. 92.

Horn Book, August, 1977, Mary M. Burns, review of *A Summer to Die,* p. 451; December, 1979, Ann A. Flowers, review of *Anastasia Krupnik,* p. 663; October, 1981, Mary M. Burns, review of *Anastasia Again!,* pp. 535-536; September-October, 1985, Ann A. Flowers, review of *Anastasia on Her Own,* pp. 556-557; May-June, 1986, Mary M. Burns, review of *Anastasia Has the Answers,* pp. 327-328; July-August, 1987, Ann A. Flowers, review of *Rabble Starkey,* pp. 463-465; May-June, 1989, Mary M. Burns, review of *Number the Stars,* p. 371; March-April, 1990, Ethel R. Twitchell, review of *Your Move, J.P.!,* pp. 201-202; July-August, 1990, Shirley Haley-James, "Lois Lowry"; November-December, 1993, Patty Campbell, "The Sand in the Oyster," pp. 717-721; July-August, 1994, Lois Lowry, "Newbery Medal Acceptance," pp. 414-422, Walter Lorraine, "Lois Lowry," pp. 423-426; November-December, 1995, Maeve Visser Knoth, review of *Anastasia, Absolutely,* p. 761; September-October, 1996, Roger Sutton, review of *See You Around, Sam!,* p. 597; January-February, 1998, Roger Sutton, review of *Stay!,* pp. 76-77; January, 1999, Peter D. Sieruta, review of *Looking Back,* p. 87; September, 1999, Roger Sutton, review of *Zooman Sam,* p. 613; September, 2000, Roger Sutton, review of *Gathering Blue,* p. 573; September-October, 2002, Peter D. Sieruta, review of *Gooney Bird Greene,* pp. 575-577; May-June, 2004, Betty Carter, review of *Messenger,* p. 332; July-August, 2006, review of *Gossamer,* p. 446.

Instructor, May, 1999, review of *The Giver,* p. 16; May, 1999, review of *See You Around, Sam,* p. 16; May, 2001, review of *The Giver,* p. 37.

Journal of Adolescent and Adult Literacy, September, 2004, Lori Atkins Goodson, review of *The Silent Boy,* p. 75, and Jo Ann Yazzie, review of *Messenger,* p. 80.

Journal of Youth Services in Libraries, fall, 1996, pp. 39-40, 49.

Junior Bookshelf, August, 1979, Mary Hobbs, review of *A Summer to Die,* pp. 224-225; August, 1980, p. 194.

Kirkus Reviews, April 1, 1986, review of *Anastasia Has the Answers,* pp. 546-547; March 1, 1987, review of *Rabble Starkey,* p. 374; March 15, 1991, review of *Anastasia at This Address,* p. 396; March 1, 1993, review of *The Giver,* p. 301; October 15, 1997, review of *Stay!,* p. 1584; July 15, 1999, review of *Zooman Sam,* p. 1135; March 15, 2003, review of *The Silent Boy,* p. 472; April 1, 2004, review of *Messenger,* p. 333; April 1, 2005, review of *Gooney Bird and the Room Mother,* p. 420; March 1, 2006, review of *Gossamer,* p. 235.

Kliatt, March, 2004, Paula Rohrlick, review of *Messenger,* p. 12.

New York Times Book Review, May 21, 1989, Edith Milton, "Escape from Copenhagen," p. 32; October 31, 1993, Karen Ray, review of *The Giver,* p. 26; January 14, 1996, Michael Cart, review of *Anastasia, Absolutely,* p. 23; October 15, 1998, review of *Looking Back,* p. 1534; February 14, 1999, review of *Looking Back,* p. 27; November 19, 2003, Elizabeth Spires, review of *Gathering Blue,* p. 57; May 16, 2004, Hazel Rochman, "Something's Rotten in Utopia," p. 17; May 14, 2006, James Hynes, review of *Gossamer,* p. 21.

Observer (London, England), October 21, 2001, review of *Gathering Blue,* p. 16.

Publishers Weekly, November 8, 1985, review of *Switcharound,* p. 60; February 21, 1986, interview with Lowry, pp. 152-153; March 13, 1987, p. 86; March 15, 1991, review of *Anastasia at This Address,* p. 58; July 28, 1997, review of *Stay!,* p. 75; August 24, 1998, review of *Looking Back,* p. 58; April 5, 1999, review of *Stay!,* p. 243; September 13, 1999, review of *Zooman Sam,* p. 85; July 31, 2000, review of *Gathering Blue,* p. 96; March 24, 2003, review of *The Silent Boy,* p. 76, and Ingrid Roper, interview with Lowry, p. 77; March 6, 2006, review of *Gossamer,* p. 74.

Reading Teacher, March, 2001, review of *Gathering Blue,* p. 638.

School Librarian, February, 1995, pp. 31-32.

School Library Journal, May, 1977, Linda R. Silver, review of *A Summer to Die,* pp. 62-63; April, 1980, Marilyn Singer, review of *Autumn Street,* pp. 125-

126; March, 1981, p. 109; October, 1981, Marilyn Kaye, review of *Anastasia Again!*, p. 144; October, 1983, Kathleen Brachmann, review of *The One Hundredth Thing about Caroline*, p. 160; February, 1986, Maria B. Salvadore, review of *Switcharound*, p. 87; September, 1987, Dudley B. Carlson, review of *Anastasia's Chosen Career*, p. 180; August, 1988, Trev Jones, review of *All about Sam*, p. 96; March, 1989, Louise L. Sherman, review of *Number the Stars*, p. 177; May, 1992, Marcia Hupp, review of *Attaboy, Sam!*, p. 114; October, 1996, Starr LaTronica, review of *See You Around, Sam!*, p. 102; October, 1997, Eva Mitnick, review of *Stay!*, p. 134; September, 1998, Barbara Scotto, review of *Looking Back*, p. 221; September, 1999, review of *Zooman Sam*, p. 193; August, 2000, Ellen Fader, review of *Gathering Blue*, p. 186; November, 2002, Janet B. Bair, review of *Gooney Bird Greene*, pp. 129-130; April, 2003, Ellen Fader, review of *The Silent Boy*, pp. 164-165; April, 2004, Marie Orlando, review of *Messenger*, p. 50; May, 2005, Kristine M. Casper, review of *Gooney Bird and the Room Mother*, p. 90; May, 2006, Lauralyn Persson, review of *Gossamer*, p. 132.

Signal, May, 1980, pp. 119-122.

Voice of Youth Advocates, August, 1985, p. 186; April, 1988, p. 26; August, 1993, p. 167; December, 1995, p. 304; April, 1999, review of *Looking Back*, p. 76; August, 1999, review of *Looking Back*, p. 164; April, 2001, review of *Gathering Blue*, p. 12; February, 2005, review of *Messenger*, p. 443.

Washington Post Book World, May 9, 1993, p. 15.

ONLINE

Books 'n' Bytes, http://www.booksnbytes.com/ (May 28, 2003), Harriet Klausner, review of *Gathering Blue*.

Lois Lowry Home Page, http://www.loislowry.com (March 17, 2007).

Rambles Online, http://www.rambles.net/ (May 28, 2003), Donna Scanlon, review of *Gathering Blue*.

OTHER

Good Conversation!: A Talk with Lois Lowry (video), Tim Podell Productions, 2002.

*　　*　　*

LOWRY, Lois Hammersberg
See LOWRY, Lois

M

MacARTHUR, Brian Roger
    See MacARTHUR, Brian

*   *   *

MacARTHUR, Brian 1940-
    (Brian Roger MacArthur)

PERSONAL: Born February 5, 1940; son of S.H. and M. MacArthur; married Peta Deschampsneufs, 1966 (divorced, 1971); married Bridget Trahair, 1975 (divorced, 1993); married Maureen Waller, 2000; children: two daughters. *Education:* Leeds University, B.A. *Hobbies and other interests:* Reading and travel.

ADDRESSES: Home—London, England.

CAREER: Writer, historian, editor, and journalist. Worked as a reporter for *Yorkshire Post,* 1962-64, *Daily Mail,* 1964-66, and *Guardian,* 1966-67; *Times,* London, England, education correspondent, 1967-70, associate editor, beginning 1991; *Times Higher Education Supplement,* founding editor, 1971-76, executive editor, 1981-82; *Home News,* editor, 1976-78; *Evening Standard,* London, department editor, 1978-79; *Sunday Times,* London, chief assistant to editor, 1979-81, junior department editor, 1982-84, joint deputy editor, 1987-91; *Western Morning News,* editor, 1984-85; *Today,* editor-in-chief, 1985-87.

MEMBER: Garrick Club.

AWARDS, HONORS: Honorary M.A. from Open University, 1976.

WRITINGS:

(With Richard Bourne) *The Struggle for Education, 1870-1970: A Pictorial History of Popular Education and the National Union of Teachers,* Schoolmaster Publishing (London, England), 1970.

(Editor) *New Horizons for Education: A Symposium on the Future as Britain Enters Its Second Century of State Education,* Council for Educational Advancement (London, England), 1970.

Beyond 1980: The Evolution of British Higher Education, International Council for Educational Development (New York, NY), 1975.

Eddy Shah: Today and the Newspaper Revolution, David & Charles (North Pomfret, England), 1988.

(Editor) *Despatches from the Gulf War,* Bloomsbury (London, England), 1991.

Deadline Sunday: A Life in the Week of the Sunday Times, Hodder & Stoughton (London, England), 1991.

(Editor) *The Penguin Book of Twentieth-Century Speeches,* Viking (New York, NY), 1992, 2nd revised edition, Penguin (New York, NY), 1999.

(Editor) *The Penguin Book of Speeches: An Anthology of Great Oratory through the Ages,* Viking (New York, NY), 1993.

(Editor) *The Penguin Book of Historic Speeches,* Viking (New York, NY), 1996.

(Editor) *Requiem: Diana, Princess of Wales, 1961-1997: Memories and Tributes,* Arcade (New York, NY), 1997.

What Future for Quality Newspapers?, Ditchley Foundation (Oxfordshire, England), 1997.

De Beauvoir Town Millennium Scrapbook: A Moment in Time—Captured by Its People, De Beauvoir Scrapbook Association (London, England), 1999.

(Editor) *The Penguin Book of Twentieth-Century Protest,* Viking (New York, NY), 1999.

Surviving the Sword: Prisoners of the Japanese in the Far East, 1942-45, Random House (New York, NY), 2005.

SIDELIGHTS: Brian MacArthur is a writer whose journalistic work has spanned several decades and includes a career at the London *Times* as well as a notorious run as the editor-in-chief of *Today,* a short-lived British tabloid. In addition, he has written and edited several books with topics ranging from Great Britain's educational system to the fast-paced life of a journalist, and has compiled several volumes of significant speeches from history. Other topics benefiting from MacArthur's interest include the media coverage of the First Gulf War, writings in memory of the late Princess Diana, and a volume recounting the sufferings endured by Allied military forces in Japanese prisoner of war camps.

MacArthur was born on February 5, 1940. His education included elementary schools like Brentwood School and Helsby Grammar School. MacArthur graduated from Leeds University with a B.A. and immediately began work as a journalist with the British papers. In his 1991 publication *Deadline Sunday: A Life in the Week of the Sunday Times,* he explores the weekly chores and assignments involved in the production of a newspaper. Cutting from one center of action to another, MacArthur presents not only the harried pace of a journalist but the excitement that it entails. In between the moments of decision or action, he uses quotes from his fellow journalists on journalistic ethics. The book also features quips from columnists on the commitment it takes to be a dedicated journalist in such a fast-paced environment. MacArthur himself knows the cost of such a quick pace: He has worked for more than a dozen newspapers and has attempted to balance that pace with his personal life.

Perhaps the most personal of MacArthur's work is *Eddy Shah: Today and the Newspaper Revolution,* which chronicles the disastrous launching of the *Today* tabloid and the author's own role in it. Working at the *Western Times,* MacArthur was wooed away from his job there by Eddy Shah, a charismatic businessman. Shah persistently pursued MacArthur for the role of editor-in-chief of *Today,* and on May 17, 1985, MacArthur accepted the position. Eight months later *Today* was published. Almost immediately MacArthur found

himself faced with printing technology that proved unreliable and inefficient, as well as a shortness of staff and financial problems. In addition to the instability of the paper's printing technology, MacArthur was faced with the same instability from Shah, a man who had no set vision for *Today,* either in political viewpoint or marketing focus. *Today* folded after only one year.

MacArthur's recollection of his experiences as editor-in-chief of *Today* not only addresses his own relationship with Shah, but also explore the relationship between technology and the newspaper business. *Eddy Shah* was praised for its fairness and its author credited for his balanced portrayal of a story which affected him personally. "MacArthur, one infers, is saddened by his experience," commented *Observer* contributor Dennis Hackett. "'No single person can tell the story of Eddy Shah and the first year of Today,' he writes. But much can be gained here from reading between the lines and forming one's own conclusion from the evidence fairly presented."

Continuing to write about the information industry, MacArthur explores the effect of the media on the Gulf War in his editorship of 1991's *Despatches from the Gulf War.* The volume collects many pieces done by CNN and other media covering the war, among them articles in which correspondents describe the experience of viewing hundreds of deceased Iraqis on the Mutla Ridge. In addition to the physical horrors of war, the journalist includes selections on Iraqi leader Saddam Hussein and his political leverage as compared to that possessed by other Middle Eastern leaders. MacArthur garnered praise for his diverse collection. "The book is a varied and vivid recollection of the desert storm; a reminder of the effort that went into it, and of the cost—not least in the U.S.—that is still being paid," commented Esmond Wright in a critique of the volume for *Contemporary Review.*

In 1993, twenty-three years after he cowrote his first book, MacArthur produced *The Penguin Book of Speeches: An Anthology of Great Oratory through the Ages.* This volume, a collection of speeches throughout history, is one of several such anthologies, the first of which was 1992's *The Penguin Book of Twentieth-Century Speeches.* Many selections from *Twentieth-Century Speeches* serve as testimony to the growth of socialism and the women's movement. The conflicts between communism and fascism are also threaded throughout the selections. MacArthur's collection focuses in particular on the wars that permeated the century, collecting the oratory of Adolf Hitler, speeches on Vietnam, and Tony Benn's speech delivered from the House of Commons against a second Gulf war.

The juxtaposition of speeches reflecting the antiwar stance of the twentieth century with patriotic speeches railing against human rights abuses elicited praise from critics. Rather than detract from each other and diminish the poignancy of individual speeches, MacArthur's selections were deemed by reviewers to work well together as records of significant historical movements. Ferdinand Mount wrote in a review for the *Times Literary Supplement* that "there are plenty of incidental pleasures to be had from the odd juxtapositions of speakers and the reminders of the long ancestry of some memorable phrases—Lloyd George in the Norway debate, advising Churchill not to 'allow himself to be converted into an air-raid shelter to keep the splinters from hitting his colleagues,' fifty years before John Major said the same of Norman Lamont."

The issue of human rights also figures prominently in MacArthur's 1999 volume *The Penguin Book of Twentieth-Century Protest,* which begins with Ida B. Wells's speech attacking the lynching of African Americans in 1900. The announcement by Chinese students that they would enter into a hunger strike is included as well. This particular announcement preceded the Tiananmen Square massacre in 1989. The apartheid movement is criticized via Donald Woods' eulogy of murdered South African leader Steve Biko. Arthur Koestler's speech against capital punishment, specifically against women, rounds out the human rights movement within the book.

Toward the end of *The Penguin Book of Twentieth-Century Speeches* is the eulogy presented by the Earl of Spencer at the funeral of Princess Diana, a royal figure who met a tragic death in 1997. MacArthur would further explore the life and death of Diana in his book *Requiem: Diana, Princess of Wales, 1961-1997: Memories and Tributes.* Here he collects editorials, memoirs, and poems all written after the British princess's death as the result of a motor vehicle accident. *Requiem* reports on the phenomenon that allowed the princess to be both held in awe by the public because of her royal stature and cherished as a public advocate and friend to those in need.

In *Surviving the Sword: Prisoners of the Japanese in the Far East, 1942-45,* MacArthur focuses his journalistic attention on a difficult aspect of World War II his-

tory, the brutal abuse of prisoners of war in Japanese custody. Thousands of British, Australian, and American troops were captured by the Japanese in the early years of the war. These Far East Prisoners of War, or Fepows, were routinely and consistently subjected to torture and ghastly living conditions in Japanese forced-labor camps. Medical treatment was practically non-existent. Men too sick or injured to stand were forced to sit and work. Starvation, disease, and sadistic beatings were a daily reality, and prisoners were often killed at a whim. MacArthur tells of the horrors endured by the prisoners while being forced to build the Burma Railway, and he also recounts the true story of the famed Bridge on the River Kwai. The tales of the Fepow's hideous treatment by the Japanese are stark and unvarnished, made all the more vivid by a focus on the travails of individual prisoners. Yet MacArthur also uncovers some stories of unexpectedly humane treatment of prisoners, as well as instances of heroic endurance and self-sacrifice that clearly illustrated the character of the prisoners and their will to survive. "27 percent of the Japanese prisoners died in captivity compared with 4 percent of Germany's; this fact alone is damning," noted reviewer Richard Garrett on *Asian Review of Books on the Web.* MacArthur presents a harrowing recounting of the prisoners' barbaric treatment in a story that tells of "cruelty and depravity and of heroism, gallantry and most important, survival against almost (but not quite) overwhelming odds," commented a critic in *Contemporary Review. Booklist* reviewer Gilbert Taylor called the story as presented by MacArthur, "a tough history to face but a moving memorial to the men it remembers."

BIOGRAPHICAL AND CRITICAL SOURCES:

PERIODICALS

American Heritage, November-December, 2005, "Allied Prisoners of the Japanese: A Recent Volume Gives the Horrifying Details," review of *Surviving the Sword: Prisoners of the Japanese in the Far East, 1942-45,* p. 22.

Booklist, June 1, 1993, Gilbert Taylor, review of *The Penguin Book of Twentieth-Century Speeches,* p. 1772; July, 2005, Gilbert Taylor, review of *Surviving the Sword,* p. 1894.

Christian Science Monitor, December 3, 1993, Merle Rubin, review of *The Penguin Book of Twentieth-Century Speeches,* p. 12.

Contemporary Review, February, 1992, Esmond Wright, review of *Despatches from the Gulf War,* p. 107; October, 2005, review of *Surviving the Sword,* p. 253.

Economist, November 21, 1992, review of *The Penguin Book of Twentieth-Century Speeches,* p. 107.

Observer (London, England), November 13, 1988, review of *Eddy Shah: Today and the Newspaper Revolution,* p. 43; December 29, 1991, review of *Deadline Sunday,* p. 43; November 30, 1997, review of *Requiem: Diana, Princess of Wales, 1961-1997: Memories and Tributes,* p. 17.

Spectator, March 5, 2005, Sibylla Jane Flower, "Bad Presentation of a Good Cause," review of *Surviving the Sword,* p. 51.

Times Literary Supplement, November 15, 1991, review of *Deadline Sunday,* p. 16; December 11, 1992, Ferdinand Mount, review of *The Penguin Book of Twentieth-Century Speeches,* p. 10.

ONLINE

Asian Review of Books on the Web, http://www.asianreviewofbooks.com/ (October 9, 2005), Richard Garrett, review of *Surviving the Sword.*

Penguin UK Web site, http://www.penguin.co.uk/ (December 17, 2006), biography of Brian MacArthur.*

*   *   *

MACKEY, Mary 1945-
(Kate Clemens)

PERSONAL: Born January 21, 1945, in Indianapolis, IN; daughter of John Edward (a physician) and Jean (an art museum director) Mackey; married Rob Colwell, December, 1965 (marriage ended); companion of Angus Wright (a professor). *Education:* Harvard University, B.A. (magna cum laude), 1966; University of Michigan, M.A., 1967, Ph.D., 1970; studied Russian in the U.S.S.R., 1969. *Hobbies and other interests:* Swimming, canoeing, backpacking, travel.

ADDRESSES: Home—Berkeley, CA. *Office*—Department of English, California State University, 6000 J St., Sacramento, CA 95819. *Agent*—Barbara Lowenstein, 250 W. 57th St., New York City, NY 10107. *E-mail*—mackeym@csus.edu.

CAREER: Indianapolis Star, Indianapolis, IN, feature writer, 1965; Sonoma State University, Rohnert Park, CA, instructor in English, c. 1971; California State University, Sacramento, CA, assistant professor, 1972-76, associate professor, 1976-80, professor of English, 1980—, and writer in residence; Ariel Press, founder, 1973. Indiana University, visiting professor, 1975; visiting lecturer at Smithsonian Institution and Harvard University; taught film and poetry courses in the Dominican Republic under the auspices of the U.S. State Department. Freelance script writer and sound technician for commercial and educational films. Bay Area Book Council, member of advisory board, 1992—.

MEMBER: PEN American Center West (president, 1989-92), National Book Critics Circle, Feminist Writers Guild (founder and member of national steering committee), Writers Guild of America, Bay Area Book Reviewers Association, PEN Oakland (member of governing board, 1999—).

AWARDS, HONORS: Woodrow Wilson fellowship, 1966-67; fellow, Virginia Center for the Creative Arts, 1999.

WRITINGS:

Immersion (novella), Shameless Hussy Press (Berkeley, CA), 1972.

Split Ends (poetry), Ariel Press (Columbus, OH), 1974.

Silence (screenplay), 1974.

One Night Stand (poetry), Effie's Press (Emeryville, CA), 1977.

(Editor, with Mary MacArthur) *Chance Music* (anthology), Gallimaufry (Cambridge, MA), 1977.

Skin Deep (poetry), Gallimaufry (Cambridge, MA), 1978.

As Old as You Feel (television documentary special), Columbia Broadcasting System, 1978.

McCarthy's List (novel), Doubleday (New York, NY), 1979.

McCarthy's List (screenplay), Warner Bros., 1979.

Dark Oceans (screenplay), 1980.

The Last Warrior Queen (novel), Putnam (New York, NY), 1983.

A Grand Passion (novel), Simon & Schuster (New York, NY), 1986.

The Dear Dance of Eros (poetry), Fjord Press (Seattle, WA), 1987.

The Kindness of Strangers (novel), Simon & Schuster (New York, NY), 1988.

Season of Shadows (novel), Bantam (New York, NY), 1991.

The Year the Horses Came (part one of *"Earthsong Trilogy"*), Harper (San Francisco, CA), 1993.

The Horses at the Gate (part two of *"Earthsong Trilogy"*), Harper (San Francisco, CA), 1996.

The Fires of Spring (part three of *"Earthsong Trilogy"*), Onyx, 1998.

(With Renee De Palma) *The Spy* (screenplay), 2000.

(With Renee De Palma) *Running from Orion*, 2000.

October at Fools Hope (novel), Fjord Press (Seattle, WA), 2001.

(Under pseudonym Kate Clemens) *Stand-in* (novel), Kensington Books (New York, NY), 2003.

(Under pseudonym Kate Clemens) *Sweet Revenge* (novel), Kensington Books (New York, NY), 2004.

Breaking the Fever (poetry), Marsh Hawk Press (East Rockaway, NY), 2006.

The Notorious Mrs. Winston (novel), Berkley Books (New York, NY), 2007.

Contributor to periodicals, including *New Age Journal, Saturday Evening Post, Yellow Silk, Ms., New American Review, Chiron Review, Salon, Poetry Now, San Jose Mercury News,* and *Harvard Advocate.*

Mackey's works have been translated into several foreign languages, including Japanese, Hebrew, and Finnish.

SIDELIGHTS: Mary Mackey's first novel, *McCarthy's List,* is a dark comedy about a paranoid schizophrenic woman wrongly sentenced to death. It details the wrongs done her by various men in her life and suggests, according to *New York Times Book Review* writer Michael Malone, that at certain times madness might be "a perfectly rational adjustment to an insane situation." Malone found Mackey's imagination "inventive" and praised her "crisp style that only occasionally trips over its own nimbleness."

The Kindness of Strangers is the story of Viola Kessler, a veteran of the German vaudeville stage. Spanning the years from 1912 to 1976, the novel includes worldwide celebrities and political figures as characters. Viola's rise to prominence on the stage ends when she becomes involved in a political scandal. Years later, her daughter Kathe enjoys great success as a television star in New York. In her old age, Viola is concerned for her headstrong granddaughter, Mandy, who is captivated by the Hollywood movie industry. Karen Stabiner of the *Los Angeles Times Book Review* described the book as a "predictable framework fleshed out with engrossing details."

Mackey's "Earthsong Trilogy" is set in Europe, beginning in the year 4372 B.C. The plots of the three novels are based upon the archaeological work of Marija Gimbutas, whose research has uncovered a peaceful, Goddess-worshiping civilization believed to have been destroyed by Indo-European nomads from the steppes. All three novels feature the visionary queen Marrah, whose life spans the earliest incursions of the violent, nomadic people into her unprepared culture. In *The Year the Horses Came,* Marrah rescues a strange-looking foreigner named Stavan, who is a member of the warlike Hansi people. The sequels describe Marrah's and Stavan's efforts to save the Motherpeople from being overrun by the Hansi—a task that requires the Motherpeople to become more warlike themselves. "The most touching moments come with the Motherpeople's realization that to survive, they too must learn to kill, a dilemma that is not new to us but wrenching still," observed Alix Madrigal in the *San Francisco Sunday Examiner and Chronicle.* The critic added that the trilogy "isn't all history or politics—or polemics, for that matter. It's a good, fast-moving story, with plenty of action and adventure, a large and vivid cast of characters and a tender love story or two." A *Publishers Weekly* correspondent likewise commended Mackey's work for "plenty of historical detail and a bountiful array of vibrant characters."

Mackey once told *CA:* "Nearly thirty years ago, Shameless Hussy Press published my short novel *Immersion.* As far as the editor and I can discover, mine was the first novel published by a feminist press at the beginning of what came to be called the Women's Movement. Set in the rain forests of Costa Rica, *Immersion* was only eighty pages long, written in a poetic, highly complex, avant-garde style, yet it contained most of the themes that I would explore in my next eight novels and in many of my subsequent collections of poetry.

"Stated as succinctly as possible, these themes are: concern for the ecological integrity of the planet; exploration of issues of gender and power; relationships (harmonious and inharmonious) between men and women; and the conflict (or at times the resolution of conflicts) between logic and emotion, the scientific world view and the religious world view, the mystical and the experiential.

"At the same time I was writing *McCarthy's List,* I was writing a great deal of poetry about the position of women in America. I strove to craft my poems not into sermons or political tracts, but into intense lyric moments filled with images. In order to read San Juan de la Cruz and Pablo Neruda in the original, I learned Spanish. The influence of these two poets still resonates in my poetry, and I am immeasurably indebted to them as well as to Anna Akhmatova, Walt Whitman, Adrienne Rich, Seamus Heaney, and Marge Piercy. Although I am probably most widely known as a novelist, my first love has always been poetry.

"In some ways my writing has changed a great deal, and in other ways it has been remarkably consistent. In the late 1970s, influenced by Merlin Stone's *When God Was a Woman,* Charlene Spretnak's *Lost Goddess of Early Greece,* and the novels of Mary Renault, I wrote *The Last Warrior Queen,* a fictional reworking of the Sumerian myth of the descent of the goddess Inanna into the underworld. In this novel I explored the implications of a pre-patriarchal civilization where women had temporal and spiritual power. I also looked at the emotional and erotic possibilities of relationships between men and women when they treated each other as partners rather than adversaries.

"Many years later in the summer of 1991, I discovered *The Language of the Goddess* and *The Civilization of the Goddess* by archaeologist Marija Gimbutas. Inspired by Gimbutas's research (which indicated that Europe actually may have been occupied by relatively peaceful cultures which were earth-centered, in which partnership relationships between men and women was the norm, and in which women had both spiritual and political power), I set out to write the three novels of the 'Earthsong Trilogy': *The Year the Horses Came, The Horses at the Gate,* and *The Fires of Spring.*

"Since the category of 'visionary fiction' has only recently come into currency, readers have sometimes mistaken these novels for genre fantasy instead of meticulously researched visions of a different world view. Others have been disturbed by the prospect that God might be seen as female (an idea I have always found intriguing, although my personal conviction is that the Divine is beyond gender).

"I have written and I continue to write because I am perpetually fascinated with the infinite variety of the world and its people. I seek to entertain my readers, to move them, to leave them—when they come to the end of one of my novels or poems—a little different than they were when they began."

BIOGRAPHICAL AND CRITICAL SOURCES:

BOOKS

Contemporary Authors Autobiography Series, Volume 27, Thomson Gale (Detroit, MI), 1997.

PERIODICALS

Booklist, January 1, 1996, Whitney Scott, review of *The Horses at the Gate,* p. 790.
Los Angeles Times Book Review, December 9, 1979, review of *McCarthy's List,* June 12, 1983, review of *The Last Warrior Queen;* June 19, 1988, Karen Stabiner, review of *The Kindness of Strangers,* p. 8.
New Age Journal, February, 1996, review of *The Horses at the Gate,* pp. 47-48.
New York Times Book Review, October 14, 1979, Michael Malone, review of *McCarthy's List,* pp. 15, 28.
Publishers Weekly, August 17, 1998, review of *The Fires of Spring,* p. 69.
San Francisco Chronicle, August 22, 1993, Alix Madrigal, "Culture Clash in the Neolithic Era," pp. 3, 8.
San Francisco Sunday Examiner and Chronicle, January 7, 1996, Alix Madrigal, "The Ancient Matriarchy Confronts Invading Warriors," p. 3.
Washington Post Book World, July 3, 1988, review of *The Kindness of Strangers,* p. X8.

ONLINE

Mary Mackey: Author, http://www.csus.edu/indiv/m/mackeym (March 8, 2007).

*   *   *

MAKINE, Andreï 1957-

PERSONAL: Born 1957.

ADDRESSES: Home—Paris, France.

CAREER: Author.

AWARDS, HONORS: Prix Goncourt and Prix Medici, both 1995, both for *Le testament français.*

WRITINGS:

La fille d'un héros de l'Union soviétique, R. Laffont (Paris, France), 1990, translated as *A Hero's Daughter,* Arcade Publishing (New York, NY), 2003.

Confession d'un porte-drapeau déchu, Belfond (Paris, France), 1992, translated as *Confessions of a Fallen Standard-Bearer,* Arcade Publishing (New York, NY), 2000.

Au temps du fleuve Amour, Editions du Felin (Paris, France), 1994, translated as *Once upon the River Love,* Arcade Publishing (New York, NY), 1998.

Le testament français, Mercure de France (Paris, France), 1995, translated as *Dreams of My Russian Summers,* Arcade Publishing (New York, NY), 1997.

Le crime d'Olga Arbyelina, Mercure de France (Paris, France), 1998, translated as *The Crime of Olga Arbyelina,* Arcade Publishing (New York, NY), 1999.

Requiem pour l'Est, Mercure de France (Paris, France), 2000, translated as *Requiem for a Lost Empire,* Arcade Publishing (New York, NY), 2001.

La musique d'une vie, Seuil (Paris, France), 2001, translated as *Music of a Life,* Arcade Publishing (New York, NY), 2002.

La terre et le ciel de Jacques Dorme, Mercure de France (Paris, France), 2003, translated as *The Earth and Sky of Jacques Dorme,* Arcade Publishing (New York, NY), 2005.

La femme qui attendait, Seuil (Paris, France), 2004, translated as *The Woman Who Waited,* Arcade Publishing (New York, NY), 2006.

Cette France qu'on oublie d'aimer, Flammarion (Paris, France), 2006.

SIDELIGHTS: Andreï Makine, a Russian-born writer who lives in France and mainly writes in French, has built a vaunted reputation through numerous novels that explore life in the former Soviet Union. "No writer alive can reconstruct the Soviet past with the poignancy of Makine," commented Barbara Hoffert in a *Library Journal* review of Makine's second novel, *Confessions of a Fallen Standard-Bearer.* Critics praise Makine's insightful treatment of human consciousness, but they also marvel at his beautifully wrought prose in a language that is not his native one.

Makine's first book, *La fille d'un héros de l'Union soviétique,* became an enormous hit when it was published in France, though it was initially spurned by French publishers. Julie K.L. Dam reported in *Time* magazine that Makine "had to go to great lengths just to get published. The literati initially couldn't accept a Russian writing in French, so he rewrote his first two novels in Russian and presented the French originals as translations. He even posed as his ghost French translator." Nevertheless, the work met with critical acclaim after its publication. It tells the story of Ivan Demidov, a Soviet soldier who survives World War II only to struggle amid the squalor and famine of post-war Russia. His daughter, Olya, eventually becomes a tool of the KGB, much to the chagrin of her father. The English translation of the novel, *A Hero's Daughter,* was finally published in 2003. Writing in *Library Journal,* Barbara Hoffert commented that Makine's first novel "nicely foreshadows his future successes in both style and content." Likewise, a *Publishers Weekly* contributor felt that Makine's inexperience shows in the novel, remarking that "Ivan and Olya are less fully realized characters than walking metaphors for Soviet exploitation." Nevertheless, the critic added, the book displays "the seeds of the powerful social criticism that flowers in Makine's more mature novels."

Makine's second novel, *Confession d'un porte-drapeau déchu* (published in English as *Confessions of a Fallen Standard-Bearer*), further established his reputation. Here again Makine explores the difficulties of life in the post-World War II Soviet Union, this time following two families as they face poverty and heartache in a small vilalge. Tobin H. Jones, in an article for the *French Review,* commented that *Confession d'un porte-drapeau déchu* "is a novel to read for the insights it can offer into both the construction and the inscription of cultural and social identity. It also surfaces ways of art by which the writer of contemporary fiction covers the writings of others amidst the disorientation born of conflict among opposing social and ideological structures. But most of all, this novel is one to read quite simply because it is so powerfully and sensitively written." Jones continued: "*Confession d'un porte-drapeau déchu* echoes Makine's preoccupation with disillusionment seen in [*La fille d'un héros de l'Union soviétique*]. . . . In this work, Makine has created an unpretentious but poetic narrative whose power lies in its evocation of generations and the discovery of the past as a means to understand the loss of self and to create from the loss endured the foundations of a new consciousness."

Anglophone reviewers were again entranced by Makine's third novel, published in English as *Once upon the*

River Love. Barbara Hoffert, in a review for *Library Journal,* commented: "this delicate, beautifully rendered little work reads like a precursor to the magisterial *Dreams of My Russian Summers.*" Richard Bernstein, in a long review for the *New York Times Book Review,* explained: "Mr. Makine overdoes it in places . . . But this is a minor fault. *Once upon the River Love* marks a further development in what is turning out to be an exciting literary career. Mr. Makine leaves us with that rare sense of having been drenched, entombed like a Siberian village under the heavy snow, in an entirely unfamiliar, exotic world, captured and held there so that it will long linger in the memory." A *Publishers Weekly* reviewer agreed: "Makine has given American readers another unforgettable novel, which wears its exoticism on its sleeve, commands respect and defies imitation."

Makine's fourth novel, *Le testament français,* was received with great enthusiasm in France, where it won both the Prix Goncourt and the Prix Medici—a dual recognition no French writer had ever achieved. This novel eventually became the first of Makine's works to be translated into English, in 1997 as *Dreams of My Russian Summers.* A *New York Times* reviewer commented: "Makine employs a highly poetic voice to blend memory and imagination, merging the particular realities of Soviet life with a timeless evocation of a sensitive adolescence. Skillfully constructed and elegantly written, the novel records a series of eventful recollections that never descend to the trivial or the anecdotal." A *Publishers Weekly* reviewer remarked that the novel's portrayal of the grandmother "makes this latest installment in the great European tradition also one of the toughest and, ultimately, one of the most hopeful." Lisa Rohrbaugh, writing for the *Library Journal,* agreed: "Makine has fashioned a deeply felt, lyrically told tale."

Makine's 1998 novel, *Le crime d'Olga Arbyelina,* also received praise when it was translated into English in 1999 as *The Crime of Olga Arbyelina. Publishers Weekly* commented: "Makine's novel possesses the feverish beauty of a hothouse culture in its final efflorescence." Hoffert, reviewing the book for *Library Journal,* reiterated her delight in Makine's "luminous, hypnotic prose that is a bit like a drug itself." She added that "the description of Russia on the verge of revolution is gripping and the ending a melancholy shock well worth the wait."

The critical acclaim for Makine's work continued to grow with his next two novels, *Requiem for a Lost Empire* and *Music of a Life. Requiem for a Lost Empire*

returns to familiar Makine elements—former soldiers dealing with memories of war and desparing of the present, female characters who are cynically used and abused by their men and their government, and striking prose. Writing in the *Review of Contemporary Fiction,* Jason Picone commented that "despite the horrific subject matter, this is yet another profoundly humanistic novel from Makine, who continues to earn the sky-high literary comparisons (Proust, Balzac, Tolstoy, Dostoyevsky) thrust upon him." *Booklist* critic Michael Spinella concurred, calling the novel "a magnificent saga of horrific events rendered in masterful prose." *Music of a Life* is a dense, compact work that follows an accomplished pianist who is forced to hide his ability in the brutal, politically poisonous atmosphere of post-war Russia. A *Kirkus Reviews* contributor lauded Makine's "matchless delicacy and economy," while Hoffert, again writing in *Library Journal,* remarked that "though it resonates with the same themes" as the author's previous works, "this new novel feels entirely fresh and necessary." Francis Henry King, writing in the *Spectator,* noted that "when I describe Andrei Makine as a great writer, this is no journalistic exaggeration but my wholly sincere estimate of a man of prodigious gifts."

The Earth and Sky of Jacques Dorme serves as the concluding volume in a trilogy of novels (including *Dreams of My Russian Summers* and *Requiem for a Lost Empire*) set in post-war Russia. The title character is a French pilot who has escaped a German POW camp and ventured to Stalingrad. There, he has a brief romance with a woman, Alexandra. She ultimately bears his child, but their romance is doomed by the war, and the child grows up in an orphanage. A *Kirkus Reviews* contributor commented that "nobody surpasses Makine as a maker of stunning [visuals] . . . which subtly underscore his narrative's plangent romantic momentum." King, writing again in the *Spectator,* remarked: "At one point [Makine] refers to the clash between truth and lies in the Soviet Union as not a single, vast war but a multiplicity of little ones. His technique is constantly to move nimbly backwards and forwards to illuminate now one of these little wars and now another with devastating brilliance."

The Woman Who Waited, which a *Publishers Weekly* reviewer called "a sensuously styled, elegiac tale set in the mid-1970s," features Vera, a Russian woman who has waited thirty years for her fiance to return from the war. The narrator, a younger man, views Vera with derision for her apparent self-delusion in devoting her life to the mistaken belief that her fiance will indeed return. However, as he learns more about Vera's past, the narrator revises his assessment of her. Once again, critics responded to Makine's effort with enthusiasm. *Spectator* reviewer Simon Baker noted: "In this short, beautiful work, translated with great style by Geoffrey Strachan, Andrei Makine demonstrates the versatility of intellect and prose that can turn a simple story into something textured and substantial." Sebastian Harcombe, writing in the *New Statesman,* praised the author's ability to render his homeland in stunning detail: "He is possessed of an astonishing ability to recollect events, feelings and scenes long gone; and the further he travels away from the land of his youth, the keener his retrospective recall becomes." Praising Makine's achievement, a *Kirkus Reviews* contributor called the author "one of Europe's most lavishly gifted writers."

BIOGRAPHICAL AND CRITICAL SOURCES:

PERIODICALS

Booklist, October 1, 2000, Michael Spinella, review of *Confessions of a Fallen Standard-Bearer,* p. 323; July, 2001, Michael Spinella, review of *Requiem for a Lost Empire,* p. 1982; August, 2003, Michael Spinella, review of *A Hero's Daughter,* p. 1956; February 1, 2006, Frank Caso, review of *The Woman Who Waited,* p. 30.

French Review, October, 1996, Tobin H. Jones, review of *Le testament français,* pp. 147-148; March, 1998, Tobin H. Jones, review of *Confession d'un porte-drapeau déchu,* pp. 677-678.

Kirkus Reviews, June 1, 1998, review of *Once upon the River Love,* p. 763; June 15, 2002, review of *Music of a Life,* p. 831; June 15, 2003, review of *A Hero's Daughter,* p. 827; December 15, 2004, review of *The Earth and Sky of Jacques Dorme,* p. 1159; January 15, 2006, review of *The Woman Who Waited,* p. 56.

Library Journal, June 23, 1997, p. 67; July, 1997, Lisa Rohrbaugh, review of *Dreams of My Russian Summers,* p. 126; July 1998, Barbara Hoffert, review of *Once upon the River Love,* pp. 137-138; August, 1999, Barbara Hoffert, review of *The Crime of Olga Arbyelina,* p. 140; October 1, 2000, Barbara Hoffert, review of *Confessions of a Fallen Standard-Bearer,* p. 148; July, 2001, Barbara Hoffert, review of *Requiem for a Lost Empire,* p. 125; July, 2002, Barbara Hoffert, review of *Music of a*

Life, p. 120; July, 2003, Barbara Hoffert, review of *A Hero's Daughter,* p. 124; February 1, 2005, Janet Evans, review of *The Earth and Sky of Jacques Dorme,* p. 69; February 1, 2006, Jenn B. Stidham, review of *The Woman Who Waited,* p. 72.

New Statesman, May 1, 2006, Sebastian Harcombe, "Buried Memories," review of *The Woman Who Waited,* p. 54.

New Yorker, September 7, 1998, review of *Once upon the River Love,* p. 89.

New York Review of Books, November 20, 1997, Tatyana Tolstaya, "Love Story," p. 4.

New York Times, July 15, 1998, Richard Bernstein, "In a Land Where Love Had No Place," p. E10.

New York Times Book Review, August 17, 1997, review of *Dreams of My Russian Summers,* p. 8; September 6, 1998, William Boyd, "Rowing from Siberia to Brighton Beach," p. 8; December 10, 2000, Richard Lourie, "This Boy's Life," review of *Confessions of a Fallen Standard-Bearer,* p. 23.

Publishers Weekly, July 7, 1997, Herbert R. Lottman, "From Russia—and France—with Love," p. 18; July 23, 1997, review of *Dreams of My Russian Summers,* p. 67; June 1, 1998, review of *Once upon the River Love,* p. 46; July 26, 1999, review of *The Crime of Olga Arbyelina,* p. 59; July 16, 2001, review of *Requiem for a Lost Empire,* p. 157; June 10, 2002, review of *Music of a Life,* p. 39; July 28, 2003, review of *A Hero's Daughter,* p. 80; December 20, 2004, review of *The Earth and Sky of Jacques Dorme,* p. 34; January 16, 2006, review of *The Woman Who Waited,* p. 36.

Review of Contemporary Fiction, spring, 2002, Jason Picone, review of *Requiem for a Lost Empire,* p. 125; spring, 2003, Laird Hunt, review of *Music of a Life,* p. 138.

Spectator, December 30, 1995, Anita Brookner, "Prize-winning Novels from France," p. 32; November 2, 2002, Francis Henry King, "Harmony Triumphantly Achieved," review of *Music of a Life,* p. 61; May 1, 2004, Digby Durrant, "Decline and Fall of a Russian Hero," review of *A Hero's Daughter,* p. 36; April 16, 2005, Francis Henry King, "The End of a Noble Masterpiece," review of *The Earth and Sky of Jacques Dorme,* p. 43; June 17, 2006, Simon Baker, "Coming out of the Cold," review of *The Woman Who Waited.*

Time, November 27, 1995, Julie K.L. Dam; September 28, 1998, John Skow, review of *Once upon the River Love,* p. 90.

Times Literary Supplement, January 19, 1996, Dan Gunn, "The Chosen Country," p. 11.

Washington Post Book World, March 12, 2006, Michael Dirda, "A Callow Young Intellectual Pines for a

Woman Whose Depths He Can't Even Imagine," review of *The Woman Who Waited,* p. 15.

ONLINE

Daily Telegraph Online, http://www.telegraph.co.uk/ (accessed March 28, 2004), "A Writer's Life: Andreï Makine," interview with author.*

* * *

MARTIN, Charles 1942-

PERSONAL: Born June 25, 1942, in Bronx, NY; son of Charles Justus (a salesman) and Kathleen (a homemaker) Martin; married Leslie Barnett, 1965 (marriage ended), married Johanna Keller (an arts journalist); children: Gregory, Emily. *Education:* Fordham University, A.B., 1964; State University of New York—Buffalo, M.A., 1985, Ph.D., 1997.

ADDRESSES: Home—New York, NY and Syracuse, NY. *E-mail*—martinchaf@aol.com.

CAREER: Educator. Notre Dame College of Staten Island, teacher of English, 1968-70; Queensborough Community College, Bayside, NY, instructor, then associate professor, then professor of English, 1970—; teacher at Syracuse University. Teacher in the Johns Hopkins Writing Seminars, Baltimore, MD, 1987-94; teacher at Sewanee Writers Conference, West Chester Conference on Form and Narrative in Poetry, and Unterberg Center; poet in residence at Cathedral of Saint John the Divine, New York, NY, 2005—.

MEMBER: Academy of American Poets, Poetry Society of America.

AWARDS, HONORS: Pulitzer Prize nomination and National Book Critics Circle Award nomination, both 1987, both for *Steal the Bacon;* Pulitzer Prize nomination, 1996, for *What the Darkness Proposes;* Pushcart Prize, 2001; Lenore Marshall Award finalist, Academy of American Poets, and Pulitzer Prize nomination, both for *Starting from Sleep: New and Selected Poems;* Harold Morton Landon Translation Award, Academy of American Poets, 2004, for *Metamorphoses;* Award for Literature, American Academy of Arts and Letters, 2005; Bess Hokin Award from *Poetry;* grants from National Endowment for the Arts and Ingram-Merrill.

WRITINGS:

Room for Error, University of Georgia Press (Athens, GA), 1978.
(Translator) *The Poems of Catullus,* Abattoir (Omaha, NE), 1979, revised edition, Johns Hopkins University Press (Baltimore, MD), 1990.
Passages from Friday, Abattoir (Omaha, NE), 1983.
Steal the Bacon, Johns Hopkins University Press (Baltimore, MD), 1987.
Fulvio Testa: Watercolors, March 6-31, 1990, Claude Bernard Gallery (New York, NY), 1990.
Catullus: A Critical Study, Yale University Press (New Haven, CT), 1992.
What the Darkness Proposes, Johns Hopkins University Press (Baltimore, MD), 1996.
Starting from Sleep: New and Selected Poems, Overlook Press (Woodstock, NY), 2002.
(Translator and author of notes) Ovid, *Metamorphoses,* Norton (New York, NY), 2004.

Contributor to periodicals, including *Parnassus, Hudson Review, New Yorker,* and *Poetry.*

SIDELIGHTS: According to *Dictionary of Literary Biography* contributor Richard Moore, American poet Charles Martin "is known among his fellow poets . . . as a writer of wit, lyrical delicacy, and compelling form, who has developed an artistic language with which he can deal with fundamental questions in American life." Martin's oeuvre, which ranges from translations of the classical Roman poet Catullus to offbeat, quirky modernist and surrealistic works in the style of Franz Kafka, Theodore Roethke, Matthew Arnold, and Alfred Lord Tennyson, has attracted much favorable critical attention. In the late 1980s, his collection *Steal the Bacon* was nominated for several major book awards, including the Pulitzer Prize and the National Book Critics Circle Award. "The distinguished record of his publications and the honors he has won," declared Moore, "attest to his growing reputation."

"From the beginning," Moore maintained, "Martin has been committed to ambitious projects that combine bookish parody with personal experience and social concern." Martin began his career as a poet while working at Notre Dame College of Staten Island in the late 1960s and early 1970s, when a series of his poems appeared in the journal *Poetry*. Martin later moved to Queensborough Community College, where he would continue to work as a professor of English. His earliest works were parodic in form, and a selection of these appeared in the collection *Room for Error*. "Caught up in the apparently arbitrary, almost surrealistic associations," explained Moore of one poem, "The Rest of the Robber Barons," "one hardly notices the elaborate rhyme scheme (abacdcdb), which is precisely kept for the rest of the poem, and the subtly varied meter. The effect—one might call it 'irony of treatment'—is complex."

Other works in *Room for Error* continue Martin's odd mixture of parody and seriousness. "Thus, 'Four for Theodore Roethke,' a poem in ironic celebration of the married life, becomes a precise parody of Roethke's well-known marriage poem 'Four for Sir John Davies,'" states Moore. Another poem cycle, "Institutional Life," consists of twelve sequential sonnets evoking an surrealistic atmosphere "suggestive of a mental hospital and Franz Kafka's fictive bureaucracies," the *Dictionary of Literary Biography* contributor explained. "It is also an outrageous, funny parody of Homer's *Odyssey*. . . . At times the sequence has a 'pop' carnival atmosphere, which is also very characteristic of Martin." "The original meaning of *satire* was 'a dish of mixed ingredients,'" continued Moore, "and once the reader's initial confusion settles, the elements of Martin's mixture work well together."

Martin also takes elements from classical and English literature—as well as from his experiences teaching English as a second language—in his translations of the Roman poet Catullus as well as in his books *Passages from Friday* and *Steal the Bacon. The Poems of Catullus* was a landmark volume, not only for Martin personally, but also for classical studies. "The Roman poet had already been so copiously and so variously translated and at so many levels of competence," explained Moore, "that one at first wonders what Martin could possibly add. But with his combination of metrical fascination and modernist experimentation, he may have produced the most memorable Catullus of his generation." *Passages from Friday* (incorporated in its entirety in *Steal the Bacon*) tells the story of Robinson Crusoe "from the point of view of Crusoe's man Friday," Moore states. "First Martin had to invent a language for Friday to speak: seventeenth-century, archaic, broken English—but in regular iambic qua-

trains." "Martin has plans for future poetry projects," Moore declared. "Judging by what he has already produced—its techniques, ambition, and inspiration—important things are to be expected."

Martin received a Pulitzer Prize nomination for his 2002 collection, *Starting from Sleep: New and Selected Poems*. The work includes sonnets, translations, and excerpts from his long narrative "Passages from Friday." "In this indispensable overview of more than thirty years in which his mastery of craft has graced contemporary subjects," remarked *Antioch Review* critic Ned Balbo, "Martin offers a wholly original voice to which his measured lines bring dignity and feeling." According to George Held, writing in the *Philadelphia Inquirer*, "*Starting from Sleep* shows how a poet with a fund of knowledge about classical culture who is alert to contemporary issues can employ traditional forms to treat his thoughts about both the ancients and the moderns."

In 2004, Martin published an award-winning translation of Ovid's epic *Metamorphoses*, a collection of myths told in verse. According to Rodney G. Dennis in the *Harvard Review*, Martin's translation "is a substantial achievement—the poem is in fifteen books, each composed of the 700 to 900 lines dictated by the capacity of papyrus rolls in antiquity. Martin is a good poet and a good scholar. His blank verse, the meter used most often, is graceful and smooth." Eric Ormsby, writing in the *New Criterion*, praised the work, stating, "Martin doesn't attempt to duplicate Ovid's hexameter but employs a basic pattern of iambic pentameter which he subtly varies, interrupting the cadence at moments so that it hesitates or seems to stumble, then allowing it suavely to unfurl." Dennis added that Martin's version offers "passages that show [his] own verbal strength moving effectively along with Ovid's intentions, and the sum of it all is extremely good."

BIOGRAPHICAL AND CRITICAL SOURCES:

BOOKS

Dictionary of Literary Biography, Volume 120: *American Poets since World War II, Third Series*, Thomson Gale (Detroit, MI), 1992.
Oxford Companion to Twentieth-Century Poetry in English, Oxford University Press (New York, NY), 1994.

PERIODICALS

Antioch Review, summer, 2003, Ned Balbo, review of *Starting from Sleep: New and Selected Poems,* p. 586.

Classical Journal, April, 1994, review of *Catullus: A Critical Study,* p. 408.

Classical Review Annual, 1994, review of *Catullus,* p. 40.

Classical World, July, 1993, review of *Catullus,* p. 524.

Harvard Review, June, 2006, Rodney G. Dennis, review of *Metamorphoses,* p. 186.

London Review of Books, October 8, 1992, review of *Catullus,* p. 16.

New Criterion, November, 2004, Eric Ormsby, "A Song and a Mistake," review of *Metamorphoses,* p. 61.

Philadelphia Inquirer, April 6, 2003, George Held, "Poetry, Translations with a Hint of Satire from Defiant Formalist," review of *Starting from Sleep.*

Publishers Weekly, September 30, 1996, review of *What the Darkness Proposes,* p. 84.

Religious Studies Review, October, 1993, review of *Catullus,* p. 349.

Sewanee Review, April, 1994, review of *Catullus,* p. R37.

Washington Post Book World, December 4, 1994, review of *Catullus,* p. 16.

ONLINE

Charles Martin Home Page, http://www.charlesmartin poet.com (January 1, 2007).*

*　　*　　*

McDONOUGH, Yona Zeldis 1957-

PERSONAL: Born June 26, 1957, in Chadera, Israel; daughter of Chayym (a writer) and Malcah (a painter) Zeldis; married Paul A. McDonough (a photographer), November 2, 1985; children: two. *Education:* Vassar College, A.B., 1979; Columbia University, M.A., 1982. *Religion:* Jewish.

ADDRESSES: Home—Brooklyn, NY. *E-mail*—pmcdonough1@nyc.rr.com.

CAREER: Freelance writer, c. 1983—. Presenter of workshops for children, including presentation, with mother, Malcah Zeldis, at Museum of Jewish Heritage, New York City, 2000.

MEMBER: American Society of Journalists and Authors, Society of Children's Book Illustrators, National Writers Union.

WRITINGS:

Coping with Social Situations: A Handbook of Correct Behavior, Rosen Publishing (New York, NY), 1984.

Coping with Beauty, Fitness, and Fashion: A Girl's Guide, Rosen Publishing (New York, NY), 1987.

(With Howard Yahm) *Tying the Knot: A Couple's Guide to Emotional Well-being from Engagement to the Wedding Day,* Penguin (New York, NY), 1990.

Frank Lloyd Wright, Chelsea House (New York, NY), 1992.

Eve and Her Sisters: Women of the Old Testament, paintings by mother, Malcah Zeldis, Greenwillow Press (New York, NY), 1994.

(Author of text) *Moments in Jewish Life: The Folk Art of Malcah Zeldis,* Friedman/ Fairfax (New York, NY), 1996.

Anne Frank, illustrated by Malcah Zeldis, Holt (New York, NY), 1997.

God Sent a Rainbow, and Other Bible Stories, paintings by Malcah Zeldis, Jewish Publication Society (Philadelphia, PA), 1997.

(With Howard Yahm) *Between "Yes" and "I Do": Resolving Conflict and Anxiety during Your Engagement,* Carol Publishing (Secaucus, NJ), 1998.

(Editor) *The Barbie Chronicles: A Living Doll Turns Forty,* Touchstone (New York, NY), 1999.

Sisters in Strength: American Women Who Made a Difference, illustrated by Malcah Zeldis, Holt (New York, NY), 2000.

The Dollhouse Magic, illustrated by Diane Palmisciano, Holt (New York, NY), 2000.

Who Was Harriet Tubman?, illustrated by Nancy Harrison, Grosset & Dunlap (New York, NY), 2002.

Peaceful Protest: The Life of Nelson Mandela, illustrated by Malcah Zeldis, Walker & Company (New York, NY), 2002.

(Editor) *All the Available Light: A Marilyn Monroe Reader,* Simon & Schuster (New York, NY), 2002.

The Four Temperaments, Doubleday (New York, NY), 2002.

A Doll Named Dora Anne, illustrated by DyAnne DiSalvo-Ryan, Grosset & Dunlap (New York, NY), 2002.

Who Was Wolfgang Amadeus Mozart?, illustrated by Carrie Robbins, Grosset & Dunlap (New York, NY), 2003.

Who Was Louis Armstrong?, illustrated by John O'Brien, Grosset & Dunlap (New York, NY), 2004.

In Dahlia's Wake: A Novel, Doubleday (New York, NY), 2005.

The Doll with the Yellow Star, illustrated by Kimberly Bulcken Root, Holt (New York, NY), 2005.

Who Was John F. Kennedy?, illustrated by Jill Weber, Grosset & Dunlap (New York, NY), 2005.

The Life of Benjamin Franklin: An American Original, illustrated by Malcah Zeldis, Holt (New York, NY), 2006.

Hammerin' Hank: The Story of Hank Greenberg, illustrated by Malcah Zeldis, Walker & Company (New York, NY), 2006.

SIDELIGHTS: The works of Yona Zeldis McDonough cover a broad range of subjects, from biographies and chapter books for young readers to both fiction and nonfiction for adults. "In the past," McDonough once noted, "I wrote books for young adults with great verve and interest, partly because I always felt connected to the adolescent in me. Now that I have a child . . . I find I am interested in going back even further, and have been working on manuscripts for very young children."

In *Tying the Knot: A Couple's Guide to Emotional Well-being from Engagement to the Wedding Day*, coauthored with psychotherapist Howard Yahm, McDonough examines the conflicts and fun that accompany an impending marriage and recommends ways of dealing with the stress that such emotional ups and downs inevitably cause. The authors based the volume in part on their own experiences and in part on interviews with about fifty couples. McDonough's "advice throughout," Mary Ann Wasick stated in *Library Journal*, "is that couples should . . . make final decisions that fulfill their own expectations, not those of others." "Chummy and useful," added *Booklist* contributor Deanna Larson-Whiterod, "this handbook should be wrapped and given alongside pretty wedding party books at every bridal shower."

Eve and Her Sisters: Women of the Old Testament, illustrated by McDonough's mother, artist Malcah Zeldis, brings the lives of Biblical women to young people in a picture-book format. "McDonough's tales," noted a *Publishers Weekly* contributor, "maintain the reverence of the originals and also highlight feminist-seeming issues in a voice accessible to children." Zeldis's pictures attracted favorable comment from several critics. Her

"bright bubblegum colors," stated Ilene Cooper in *Booklist*, ". . . make for pictures that are full of energy." And Patricia Dooley, reviewing *Eve and Her Sisters* for *School Library Journal*, declared that "Zeldis's primitive paintings are brightly colored and child-like, with some amusing details and touches (pink lambs with blue faces)."

In another book for young readers, *The Dollhouse Magic*, McDonough reveals the lives of two young girls growing up during the Great Depression of the 1930s. Jane and Lila are captivated by a beautiful doll house that sits in the window of an elderly woman's house, and their interest eventually causes old Miss Whitcomb to emerge from her house and speak to them. In a story about friendship across the generations, McDonough has created what *Booklist* contributor Carolyn Phelan called "an appealing beginning chapter book, particularly for doll fans."

A doll is also featured in *The Doll with the Yellow Star*, published in 2005. The book tells the story of eight-year-old Claudine, a young Jewish girl living in France during World War II. After the country is occupied by Nazi Germany, all Jews are forced to wear yellow stars, and life for Claudine and her family gradually gets more difficult. Claudine sews a yellow star on her doll's clothing, but she eventually loses her doll after her parents send her to the United States to protect her. Claudine is eventually reunited with her father. Writing in *School Library Journal*, Teri Markson praised the book as "nicely written and generously illustrated with watercolors." Similarly, a *Publishers Weekly* contributor noted: "While the prose slips into woodenness at times, the events keep the pages turning, and McDonough's emotional acuity always shines through."

In *Anne Frank* and *Frank Lloyd Wright*, McDonough examines two very different personalities and their respective accomplishments. Jeanette Larson, writing in *School Library Journal*, called McDonough's biography of the American architect Wright "a well-researched, interesting, and balanced biography," and concluded: "McDonough examines her subject's life and discusses both his brilliance and his foibles." *Booklist* reviewer Hazel Rochman and *Bulletin of the Center for Children's Books* contributor Betsy Hearne agreed that *Anne Frank* provides a valuable introduction to the young Dutch Jewish girl who died in a Nazi concentration camp during World War II, and whose diary has become standard reading in many junior high and high schools. But, stated Rochman, *The Diary of Anne Frank* tells young readers nothing about the background of Anne Frank's life—about the Holocaust that resulted in the deaths of millions of Jews across Europe. "There is nothing about how most children died—in the ghettos, massacres, transports, camps," Rochman declared. "We can hold on to her uplifting message that she believes that people 'are really good at heart.'" "With the Holocaust introduced at early stages in the curriculum these days," Hearne added, McDonough's biography "will be helpful in setting the stage for children's inevitable meeting with an international icon." "If there is a demand in your library for books that introduce the Holocaust to younger children" Rochman concluded, "then this is a good place to start."

In a trio of picture books aimed at elementary-school students and illustrated by Malcah Zeldis, McDonough chronicled a Founding Father of America, a famous baseball player, and an iconic African leader. *The Life of Benjamin Franklin: An American Original* features the early American scientist and statesman, while *Hammerin' Hank: The Story of Hank Greenberg* examines the life of one of the first Jewish baseball stars in the United States. Ilene Cooper, reviewing the latter book for *Booklist,* remarked that "the life of baseball star Hank Greenberg deserves to be celebrated, and this solid, chronological telling does just that." In *Peaceful Protest: The Life of Nelson Mandela,* McDonough tells the story of the South African activist who spent nearly three decades in prison before becoming the country's first black president. *Booklist* critic Hazel Rochman noted that the book offers "more depth and detail than most biographies on Mandela for this age level." McDonough has also written a series of illustrated biographies for young readers about such figures as Harriet Tubman, Wolfgang Amadeus Mozart, Louis Armstrong, and John F. Kennedy.

Other books by McDonough include *The Barbie Chronicles: A Living Doll Turns Forty,* in which she collects a variety of essays by writers including Anna Quindlen, Ann DuCille, Erica Jong, and Carol Shields that span the gamut of opinion about the doll created in 1959 and known to girls everywhere. Calling the authors "well chosen," a *Publishers Weekly* contributor added that McDonough's book "artfully explores the world that created Barbie, the childhood selves the authors remember and the meaning behind one of our era's most controversial pieces of plastic."

The Four Temperaments is McDonough's first novel for adults. It features Ginny Valentine, a ballerina who has

affairs with an older musician, Oscar Kornblatt—and with his son, Gabriel. Two other main characters are Oscar's wife, Ruth, and Gabriel's wife, Penelope. Kristine Huntley, writing in *Booklist,* commented that "the enthralling narrative pulls the reader in and doesn't let go." A *Publishers Weekly* reviewer called the novel "uneven" but added that "McDonough has a knack for building solid characters."

McDonough followed this novel for adults with another, *In Dahlia's Wake: A Novel.* Set in Brooklyn, the novel charts the challenges faced by a couple mourning the loss of their only child, a daughter named Dahlia. The girl's parents, Rick and Naomi, react to their heartache in different ways—Rick by having an affair, Naomi by channeling her grief into volunteer work. A *Publishers Weekly* reviewer criticized the novel's "contrived plotting and stock characters," but *Booklist* contributor Huntley praised the work as "a gripping, involving read."

BIOGRAPHICAL AND CRITICAL SOURCES:

PERIODICALS

Booklist, November 15, 1989, Deanna Larson-Whiterod, review of *Tying the Knot: A Couple's Guide to Emotional Well-being from Engagement to the Wedding Day,* p. 625; May 15, 1994, Ilene Cooper, review of *Eve and Her Sisters: Women of the Old Testament,* p. 168; October 1, 1997, Hazel Rochman, review of *Anne Frank,* p. 335; November 15, 2000, Carolyn Phelan, review of *The Dollhouse Magic,* p. 642; March 1, 2001, Stephanie Zvirin, review of *Anne Frank,* p. 1280; August, 2002, Kristine Huntley, review of *The Four Temperaments,* p. 1922; November 15, 2002, Hazel Rochman, review of *Hammerin' Hank: The Story of Hank Greenberg,* p. 599; March 15, 2005, Kristine Huntley, review of *In Dahlia's Wake,* p. 1266; March 1, 2006, Ilene Cooper, review of *Hammerin' Hank,* p. 96.

Bulletin of the Center for Children's Books, January, 1998, Betsy Hearne, review of *Anne Frank,* p. 166.

Library Journal, December, 1989, Mary Ann Wasick, review of *Tying the Knot,* p. 148.

Publishers Weekly, April 18, 1994, review of *Eve and Her Sisters,* p. 62; July 28, 1997, review of *Anne Frank,* p. 73; September 20, 1999, review of *The Barbie Chronicles,* p. 65; July 8, 2002, review of

The Four Temperaments, p. 32; March 7, 2005, review of *In Dahlia's Wake*, p. 51; December 12, 2005, review of *The Doll with the Yellow Star*, p. 66.

School Library Journal, February, 1992, Jeanette Larson, review of *Frank Lloyd Wright*, p. 116; May, 1994, Patricia Dooley, review of *Eve and Her Sisters*, p. 109; October, 1997, Marcia W. Posner, review of *Anne Frank*, p. 120; October, 2005, Teri Markson, review of *The Doll with the Yellow Star*, p. 120.*

*   *   *

McGINN, Colin 1950-

PERSONAL: Born 1950. *Education:* Studied psychology at Manchester University; studied philosophy at Oxford University

ADDRESSES: Office—Department of Philosophy, P.O. Box 248054, University of Miami, Coral Gables, FL 33124-4670. *E-mail*—cmcginn@mail.as.miami.edu.

CAREER: Writer and philosopher. University College, London, England, professor, 1974-85; Oxford University, Wilde Reader in Mental Philosophy; Rutgers University, professor of philosophy, 1988-2006; University of Miami, 2006—, professor of philosophy.

AWARDS, HONORS: John Locke Prize, Oxford University, 1973.

WRITINGS:

The Character of Mind, Oxford University Press (New York, NY), 1982, revised edition published as *The Character of Mind: An Introduction to the Philosophy of Mind*, Oxford University Press, 1997.

The Subjective View: Secondary Qualities and Indexical Thoughts, Clarendon Press (New York, NY), 1983.

Wittgenstein on Meaning: An Interpretation and Evaluation, B. Blackwell (New York, NY), 1984.

Mental Content, B. Blackwell (New York, NY), 1989.

The Problem of Consciousness: Essays toward a Resolution, B. Blackwell (Cambridge, MA), 1991.

Moral Literacy: or, How to Do the Right Thing, Hackett Publishing Co. (Indianapolis, IN), 1992.

The Space Trap, Duckworth (London, England), 1992

Problems in Philosophy: The Limits of Inquiry, Blackwell (Cambridge, MA), 1993.

Minds and Bodies: Philosophers and Their Ideas, Oxford University Press (New York, NY), 1997.

Ethics, Evil, and Fiction, Clarendon Press (New York, NY), 1997.

Knowledge and Reality: Selected Essays, Clarendon Press (New York, NY), 1999.

The Mysterious Flame: Conscious Minds in a Material World, Basic Books (New York, NY), 1999.

Logical Properties: Identity, Existence, Predication, Necessity, Truth, Oxford University Press (New York, NY), 2000.

The Making of a Philosopher: My Journey through Twentieth-Century Philosophy, HarperCollins (New York, NY), 2002.

Mindsight: Image, Dream, Meaning, Harvard University Press (Cambridge, MA), 2004.

Consciousness and Its Objects, Oxford University Press (New York, NY), 2004.

The Power of Movies: How Screen and Mind Interact, Pantheon Books (New York, NY), 2005.

Shakespeare's Philosophy, HarperCollins (New York, NY), 2006.

SIDELIGHTS: Colin McGinn's writings explore the dynamics of the mind in relation to the self, the body, and the material world. McGinn's arguments and observations regarding particular aspects of the philosophy of language and consciousness and psychology are viewed by many critics as enlightening, innovative and challenging. Of McGinn's first book, *The Character of Mind*, Brian O'Shaughnessy, writing for the *London Review of Books*, maintained: "Colin McGinn's admirable book manages to give a comprehensive picture of the state of play in the subject at the present time." O'Shaughnessy championed the discussion of the self above all other aspects of the book. "Perhaps the most impressive part of the book is the discussion of the self. McGinn approaches this topic in a novel way, suggesting that we interpret the familiar enough search for criteria of personal identity as in effect an inquiry into the nature of the self." O'Shaughnessy, in concluding, suggested that McGinn brings a duality to his writing. "If science is a hunter, philosophy is at once hunter and conservationist. Both forces are well represented in McGinn. Natural wonder rather than mystification, the desire to explain and connect rather than the drive to reduce: that is what one finds on every page of this brilliant book."

According to Edward Wilson Averill's review of *The Subjective View: Secondary Qualities and Indexical Thoughts* in *Philosophical Review,* "McGinn seeks to give clear accounts of two ways in which the world is subjectively represented; its representation in the experience of secondary qualities and in the having of indexical thoughts." A contributor in *Choice,* however, commended McGinn's book for its originality. "Although subjective qualities and indexicals have often been treated separately, McGinn develops a unified theory that treats the perception of secondary qualities and the conceptualization of experience in indexical terms as subjective modes of representation."

W. Taschek, in a review for *Choice,* commented on the basic argument presented in McGinn's *Wittgenstein on Meaning: An Interpretation and Evaluation.* "The book's primary aim is to put forward an alternative and more accurate interpretation of Wittgenstein's later views, arguing *pace* Kripke that Wittgenstein does not formulate a skeptical paradox aimed at challenging the factual or objective status of following a rule; and, consequently, that Wittgenstein does not develop, as part of his positive view, a skeptical or antirealist solution to this challenge. McGinn finds more that is importantly right, but also some problems."

Richard H. Schlagel, in his review of *Mental Content* in the *Review of Metaphysics,* asserted: "Despite the author's imaginative analyses, the book has two main weaknesses. First while externalism, like naive realism, has a certain commonsense plausibility, it does not offer an account of the status of the perceptual macroworld, or the difference between this world and the scientific microworld." Quite apart from Schlagel's review, K. Quillen, writing in *Choice,* commended McGinn's work: "Original and provocative, this comprehensive treatment of mental content will be welcomed and debated by philosophers of mind."

Times Literary Supplement critic Daniel C. Dennett considered *The Problem of Consciousness: Essays toward a Resolution* to be "an expression and discussion of the unanswered questions about consciousness, which he [McGinn] gives every evidence of understanding quite well." R.G. Crowder, writing in *Choice,* accepted the book's importance but does not recommend it to a general audience. "For those readers who take the granted from the 'obvious' reality of consciousness poses a problem for the embodiment of mind in a physical system (perhaps most professional philosophers),

the tight arguments here may be illuminating. For others . . . the broad scholarship and close reasoning here may seem misdirected."

In a *Times Literary Supplement* review of *Moral Literacy; or, How to Do the Right Thing,* Owen Flanagan commented: "*Moral Literacy* is a primer on how to think rationally about real-life moral problems, about our treatment of animals, abortion, violence, sex, drugs, and censorship. Colin McGinn succeeds in keeping abstract arguments to a minimum." Later in the review, Flanagan commended McGinn's techniques and his attention to detail. "McGinn is a master of the imaginary thought experiment, and his attention to some of the neglected details of trees in his woods is illuminating—for example, the discussion of tabloid journalism and censorship."

In 1992 McGinn made his first foray into fiction writing. His first fictional effort, *The Space Trap,* received an ambivalent review from David Papineau in *Times Literary Supplement.* Papineau applauded McGinn's comedy but noted McGinn's lack of originality. "His concern is not to expose human shortcomings, but to articulate the experience of geographical dislocation. . . . McGinn has a genuine gift for comic writing. But he will be better able to use it for his own purposes once he has found his own voice."

Of *Problems in Philosophy: The Limits of Inquiry,* Peter van Inwagen in *Philosophical Review* reported: "In this fascinating book, Colin McGinn offers an empirical theory to explain the futility of philosophy (not his phrase)."

Ethics, Evil, and Fiction is a philosophical exploration of fictional representations of moral character. Nicola Bradbury, in the *Modern Language Review* stated: "Such resistance and such confidence characterize this work in ways that may be helpful to students of philosophy seeking clarity, but raise many questions for anyone more familiar with literary criticism."

A reviewer of *The Mysterious Flame: Conscious Minds in a Material World,* writing in *Economist,* asserted: "Mr. McGinn concludes that the riddle of consciousness is too hard for humans. No doubt there is an answer but humans don't have the nose to find it." However, the reviewer does offer firm commendation of McGinn's likeable style. "Even so, he remains readable throughout.

Aiming at a general readership, he introduces a number of other philosophical problems which he thinks can't be solved either . . . and he enlivens proceedings by exploring various futuristic possibilities, illustrated with frequent references to 'Star Trek' and other popular science fictions." McGinn's accessible style received similar praise in Galen Strawson's review in the *New York Times Book Review.* Strawson suggested that McGinn's book "seems in places designed to annoy professional philosophers. But it was not written for them. It is an introductory, popular work, and its looseness and dash are excellent teachers, constantly provoking questions and objections."

In 2002, having established his reputation as a prolific writer and respected thinker, McGinn published a memoir, *The Making of a Philosopher: My Journey through Twentieth-Century Philosophy.* In it, he traces his roots from his teenage years in Blackpool, England, through his college days at the University of Manchester and the University of Oxford, to his challenging early days as a young academic, and then to his long stint as a professor at Rutgers University. Reviewing the book in the *New York Times Book Review,* Mary Lefkowitz commented: "By showing us what it is like to be a philosopher in action, McGinn lets us see for ourselves that philosophical issues are exciting and important. The kind of analytic philosophy that he practices leads to moral literacy because it encourages clarity of thought. In that way, if only in that way, it has real practical value. That is one of the many things McGinn teaches us by telling us his own story." A *Kirkus Reviews* contributor also recommended the memoir, calling it a "playful memoir offering an amusing view of academic philosophy's day-to-day tussle, as well as a clear introduction to the author's thought."

In two books published in 2004, *Mindsight: Image, Dream, Meaning* and *Consciousness and Its Objects,* McGinn returned to writing about philosophical concepts. In *Mindsight,* written for a popular audience, he examines the qualities of dreams, imagination, perceptions, and beliefs, arguing that modern philosophy has lost sight of the importance of imagination as an intellectual force. In *Consciousness and Its Objects,* a book written for professional philosophers, McGinn explores the nature of consciousness and the problems it poses to philosophers seeking to understand the human mind.

McGinn offers another book for general readers in 2005's *The Power of Movies: How Screen and Mind Interact.* In the book, he compares movies to dreams, suggesting that films engage us because our experience in watching them is similar to what happens when we dream. He also argues that both dreams and movies provide important releases for the mind. Praising the book as "a brisk and often scintillating discourse," a *Kirkus Reviews* contributor remarked that "McGinn's observations will resonate with thoughtful moviegoers."

Shakespeare's Philosophy is another general-interest work by McGinn. Here, the author examines the philosophical elements of six of William Shakespeare's plays. McGinn argues that Shakespeare should be seen as both a playwright and philosopher. "Most interesting is McGinn's earnest delight in rediscovering Shakespeare's characters," commented a *Publishers Weekly* reviewer, who added that the book makes its points "without seeming at all dusty." A *Kirkus Reviews* contributor also praised the book, noting that McGinn "brings to Shakespeare studies a philosophical perspective often either absent or amateurishly handled."

BIOGRAPHICAL AND CRITICAL SOURCES:

PERIODICALS

Choice, February, 1984, review of *The Subjective View: Secondary Qualities and Indexical Thoughts,* p. 833; February, 1986, W. Taschek, review of *Wittgenstein on Meaning: An Interpretation and Evaluation,* p. 879; December, 1989, K. Quillen, review of *Mental Content,* p. 645; October, 1991, R.G. Crowder, review of *The Problem of Consciousness: Essays toward a Resolution,* p. 357; February, 1998, S. Satris, review of *Ethics, Evil, and Fiction,* p. 1002.

Economist, May 1, 1999, "Are We Just Not Clever Enough to Understand the Mind?," p. 79.

Kirkus Reviews, March 1, 2002, review of *The Making of a Philosopher: My Journey through Twentieth-Century Philosophy,* p. 313; October 1, 2005, review of *The Power of Movies: How Screen and Mind Interact,* p. 1065; September 15, 2006, review of *Shakespeare's Philosophy,* p. 940.

London Review of Books, April 1, 1983, Brian O'Shaughnessy, "Persons," pp. 15-17.

Modern Language Review, January, 1999, Nicola Bradbury, review of *Ethics, Evil, and Fiction,* p. 151.

New Statesman & Society, July 17, 1992, Boyd Tonkin, "Moral Literacy: How to Do the Right Thing," p. 49.

New York Times Book Review, July 11, 1999, Galen Strawson, "Little Gray Cells," p. 13; May 19, 2002, Mary Lefkowitz, "Analyze This, This and This: Colin McGinn's Memoir Describes the Intense Life of a Philosopher," p. 16.

Philosophical Review, April, 1985, Edward Wilson Averill, review of *The Subjective View,* pp. 296-299; April, 1996, Peter van Inwagen, review of *Problems in Philosophy,* pp. 253-256.

Publishers Weekly, April 26, 1999, review of *The Mysterious Flame,* p. 71; October 2, 2006, review of *Shakespeare's Philosophy,* p. 50.

Review of Metaphysics, December, 1990, Richard H. Schlagel, review of *Mental Content,* pp. 427-429.

Times Literary Supplement, May 24, 1985, Avishal Margalit, "Going by the Rules," p. 587; May 10, 1991, Daniel C. Dennett, "The Brain and Its Boundaries," p. 10; July 10, 1992, David Papineau, "Another Englishman at Large," p. 22; December 25, 1992, Owen Flanagan, "Ways of Being Good," p. 20.*

*   *   *

McPHEE, Jenny 1962(?)-

PERSONAL: Born c. 1962; daughter of John (an author) and Pryde (a photographer) McPhee; married; children: two sons. *Education:* Williams College, Williamstown, MA.

ADDRESSES: Agent—Kimberly Witherspoon, InkWell Management, 521 Fifth Avenue, 26th Floor, New York, NY 10175.

CAREER: Writer and translator.

WRITINGS:

(Translator with Martha McPhee) Pope John Paul II, *Crossing the Threshold of Hope,* Knopf (New York, NY), 1994.

(Translator) Paolo Maurensig, *Canone Inverso,* Henry Holt (New York, NY), 1998.

(Translator with Richard Fremantle) Franco Quadri, *Robert Wilson,* Rizzoli (New York, NY), 1998.

(With Laura McPhee and Martha McPhee) *Girls: Ordinary Girls and Their Extraordinary Pursuits,* Random House (New York, NY), 2000.

The Center of Things (novel), Doubleday Publishing (New York, NY), 2001.

No Ordinary Matter (novel), Free Press (New York, NY), 2004.

SIDELIGHTS: Jenny McPhee's father is the esteemed essayist John McPhee, and her sister Martha McPhee is an award-winning novelist. McPhee entered the world of publishing gradually, beginning as a translator. She later collaborated on a nonfiction book about the lives of American girls with Martha as well as with their sister Laura, a successful and prizewinning photographer. Then she struck out on her own, publishing her debut novel, *The Center of Things* in 2001.

The McPhee sisters decided to embark on a study of the great things American girls were accomplishing after hearing so much bad news about girls' lives. Despite the media focus on the number of problems girls were facing, the sisters found that girls were also succeeding at everything from football, science, and investments, to chess, ballet, and music. McPhee told Jennifer Wolcott the *Christian Science Monitor,* "It wasn't as if we had to go searching. . . . Girls like this are everywhere. For every one we found, we could have found 50,000 more like her. We're just not used to celebrating our girls in this country."

Attempting to present a geographically diverse portrait, the McPhee sisters traveled the country seeking girls whose accomplishments stood out not because they were so unusual, but because they reflected the achievements of girls in general. In *Girls: Ordinary Girls and Their Extraordinary Pursuits,* they tell the stories of a teenage novelist, a seven-year-old competitive chess champion, a professional child harpist, and a New Yorker who works as a camp counselor in Bosnia. McPhee told a contributor to the *Christian Science Monitor,* "I think all the time about these girls and what they accomplish. . . . Some of them have terrible troubles, but they don't let that stop them from putting all their energies into their interests."

Reviewers generally welcomed this contribution to literature about girls. Mary Carroll in *Booklist,* called the book "a celebration of young American women." Jean Hanff KoreLizt, reviewing *Girls* for *Harper's Bazaar,* described the book as "stunning," and "a nuanced, resonant snapshot of American girlhood at the turn of the millennium." Sandra Isaacson in *Library Journal* suggested that the girls chosen for the book are not so ordinary, but rather very talented and driven; and concluded: "This work is interesting but falls short of being dynamic because of its brevity." A reviewer for *Publishers Weekly,* however, maintained that "these endearing portraits of young athletes, artists and adventurers help expand the limits of the possible."

The release of *Girls* was shortly followed by the publication of McPhee's first novel, *The Center of Things. The Center of Things* tells the story of a single, plain, not-so-young tabloid reporter who becomes obsessed with Nora Mars, a former movie diva about whom she is assigned to write an obituary. The reporter, Marie Brown, is also obsessed with physics, an interest she indulges with "freelance intellectual" Marco Trentadue, whom she meets at the library. Meanwhile, her research into the life of Mars leads her to consider a tryst with the actress's third husband, Rex Mars. Among all these other longings, Marie reveals a desire to give up tabloid journalism and become a science writer.

A reviewer for *Publishers Weekly* said of *The Center of Things:* "It takes guts for a debut novelist to mix such disparate subjects as abstruse science, philosophy, movies, and the single life in New York City, but McPhee takes the risk with brio and acquits herself with élan." Dennis Overbye, reviewing the book for the *New York Times Book Review,* also found that the unusual combination worked: "McPhee . . . knows how to keep things light. All her cosmic vamping adds a teasing hint of intellectual relief to a tale of tangled lives that for all its complexity might seem a shade cartoonish told straight out." Judith Kicinski, in *Library Journal,* called McPhee "a talented, graceful, and often sardonic writer," saying that with *The Center of Things,* "John McPhee should be proud of his daughter." The *Publishers Weekly* critic similarly noted the family connection, concluding: "While the McPhee name may be the initial drawing card here, the novel's off beat charm will distinguish Jenny McPhee as an accomplished writer with her own distinctive style."

In her second novel, 2004's *No Ordinary Matter,* McPhee offers a story of two sisters, Lillian and Veronica Moore, who go searching for details about their father's death twenty-five years earlier. Their father died in a car crash, but the sisters don't know where he was going when he died, or where he is buried. The sisters' mother, now living in New Zealand, refuses to answer their questions about their father, so they hire a private detective. Complicating matters are Lillian's

pregnancy, Veronica's romance with the same unemployed actor who is the father of Lillian's unborn child, and questions about whether their father was really their father—and whether they are really sisters. While noting that the novel is a melodramatic farce, critics responded enthusiastically to the book. A *Kirkus Reviews* contributor, for instance, called the novel "absurdly improbable" but also remarked that it is "a witty spoof, nicely put together and hard to put down." Similarly, *Booklist* reviewer Kaite Mediatore noted that, "on the surface, this novel's premise shouldn't work" but then added that in the end, the book "reads like a Shakespearean comedy." A *Publishers Weekly* reviewer termed the novel a "guilty pleasure," while *Library Journal* contributor Beth E. Anderson commented that McPhee "successfully pulls off this souped-up, big-hearted soap."

BIOGRAPHICAL AND CRITICAL SOURCES:

PERIODICALS

Book, July, 2001, Beth Kephart, review of *The Center of Things,* p. 66.

Booklist, October 15, 1998, Bonnie Johnston, review of *Canone Inverso,* p. 400; November 1, 1998, Jack Helbig, review of *Robert Wilson,* p. 461; October 1, 2000, Mary Carroll, review of *Girls: Ordinary Girls and Their Extraordinary Pursuits,* p. 295; June 1, 2001, Kristine Huntley, review of *The Center of Things,* p. 1847; June 1, 2004, Kaite Mediatore, review of *No Ordinary Matter,* p. 1702.

Commonweal, January 13, 1995, Peter Steinfels, review of *Crossing the Threshold of Hope,* pp. 21-22.

Entertainment Weekly, August 17, 2001, Gillian Flynn, review of *The Center of Things,* p. 66; June 11, 2004, Jennifer Reese, "A Family 'Matter': Though Her Sister Is a Novelist and Dad Is John McPhee, She's Making a Name for Herself," p. 130.

Harper's Bazaar, October, 2000, Jean Hanff KoreLitz, "Family Portrait," p. 234.

Kirkus Reviews, April 15, 2004, review of *No Ordinary Matter,* p. 354.

Library Journal, October 1, 2000, Sandra Isaacson, review of *Girls,* p. 130; July, 2001, Judith Kicinski, review of *The Center of Things,* p. 125; May 15, 2004, Beth E. Anderson, review of *No Ordinary Matter,* p. 115.

New York Times Book Review, July 22, 2001, Dennis Overbye, "Quantum Fizz," p. 7.

People Weekly, August 27, 2001, synopsis of *The Center of Things,* p. 43.

Publishers Weekly, September 25, 2000, "Women and Girls of Stature," p. 107; June 11, 2001, review of *The Center of Things,* p. 55; May 17, 2004, review of *No Ordinary Matter,* p. 33.

Times Literary Supplement, November 11, 1994, Peter Hebblethwaite, "Professor in Slippers," p. 32.

Washington Post, July 15, 2001, "Getting Physical," p. T4.

ONLINE

Book Page Fiction Review, http://www.bookpage.com/ (October 7, 2001), Deborah Hopkinson, review of *The Center of Things.*

Calendar Live, http:// www.calendarlive.com/ (September 2, 2001), Mark Rozzo, review of *The Center of Things.*

Christian Science Monitor Online, http://www. csmonitor.com/ (January 24, 2001), Jennifer Wolcott, "American Girls: 'We're Doing Just Great, Thanks.'"

Media Bistro, http://www.mediabistro.com/ (October 7, 2001), Diana Michele Yap, review of *The Center of Things.*

Rain Taxi, http://www.raintaxi.com/ (November 20, 2001), Rumaan Alam, review of *The Center of Things.*

Salon.com http://www.salon.com/ (October 7, 2001).

Zoetrope All Story, http://www.all-story.com/ (October 7, 2001).*

*　　*　　*

MILLER, George Wayne
　See MILLER, G. Wayne

*　　*　　*

MILLER, G. Wayne 1954-
　(George Wayne Miller)

PERSONAL: Born June 12, 1954, in Melrose, MA; son of Roger Miller (an airplane mechanic) and Mary Maraghey; married Alexis Magner (a writer and daily features editor of *Providence Journal*); children: Rachel, Katy, Cal. *Education:* Harvard University, 1976.

ADDRESSES: Office—Providence Journal, 75 Fountain St., Providence, RI 02902. *E-mail*—pascoagwriter@yahoo.com.

CAREER: Journalist and author. *North Adams Transcript,* North Adams, MA, reporter, 1977-78; *Cape Cod Times,* Hyannis, MA, staff writer, 1978-81; *Providence Journal,* staff writer, writing committee chairman, and book reviewer, 1981—; *TheCambridgeCompany,* founder. Online serial fiction writer, 1999.

MEMBER: Jesse Smith Memorial Library (chairman).

AWARDS, HONORS: Prize for feature writing, American Society of Newspaper Editors; finalist for the Pulitzer Prize, 2004, for coverage of the 2003 Rhode Island night club fire.

WRITINGS:

Thunder Rise, Arbor House/Morrow (New York, NY), 1989.

The Work of Human Hands: Hardy Hendren and Surgical Wonder at Children's Hospital, Random House (New York, NY), 1993.

Coming of Age: The True Adventure of Two American Teens, Random House (New York, NY), 1995.

Toy Wars: The Epic Struggle between G.I. Joe, Barbie, and the Companies That Make Them, Times Books (New York, NY), 1998.

King of Hearts: The True Story of the Maverick Who Pioneered Open-Heart Surgery, Time Books (New York, NY), 2000.

Men and Speed: A Wild Ride through NASCAR's Breakout Season, PublicAffairs (New York, NY), 2002.

The Xeno Chronicles: Two Years on the Frontier of Medicine Inside Harvard's Transplant Research Lab, PublicAffairs (New York, NY), 2005.

SIDELIGHTS: G. Wayne Miller grew up in a Boston suburb, attended parochial school, and then went to a Massachusetts preparatory school where hockey was his focus. He did not make it onto the varsity team, which crushed his dreams of playing for the Boston Bruins. Instead, he became more involved in his writing and realized he had been interested in it since the third grade. Miller started writing regularly, and recalled in his Web site biography, "What I really liked to do, and it's still my first love, is fiction."

Miller graduated from Harvard University in 1976, and started working as a reporter for the *North Adams Transcript* a few months later. He was surprised that he got this job, stating in his Web site biography: "God know why I was hired, for I had zero experience"; he had not taken a single journalism class in college. A short time later he began working as a staff writer at the *Cape Cod Times,* eventually moving to the same position at the *Providence Journal,* where he continues to work.

Miller's interest in early Stephen King novels inspired him to seriously begin writing fiction. Several of his horror and mystery stories were published in magazines, hardcover collections of short stories, and paperback collections. He sold his first novel, *Thunder Rise,* in 1988 to publisher William Morrow. It tells the tale of a divorced man, who, along with his daughter, moves from New York to a small New England town. His daughter and other children in the town begin having nightmares and develop flu-like symptoms that cannot be treated medically, but a local Quidneck Indian with psychic powers claims to know the cause and the cure. *Thunder Rise* received mixed reviews, critic Sybil Steinberg remarking in a *Publishers Weekly* review that the book was an "occasionally awkward but generally well-paced and effective thriller." A *Kirkus* reviewer found that Miller "shows promise in scenes untied to his horror theme, especially in the warmth of his father-daughter dialogue, though even here he should have pushed harder on his delete key." In spite of the mixed reviews, Miller was pleased with the outcome, stating in his Web site biography that *Thunder Rise* is "an entertaining book with several of my favorite fictional characters, and my daughters think it's cool, which is good enough for me."

After the publication of *Thunder Rise,* an editor at Random House who had worked with Miller wrote asking if he had any ideas for nonfiction books. This inquiry led to Miller's first nonfiction book, *The Work of Human Hands: Hardy Hendren and Surgical Wonder at Children's Hospital,* a biography of Dr. Hardy Hendren, the chief of surgery at Children's Hospital in Boston. The book discusses new procedures developed by Hendren and his colleagues, pediatric advances, and the patients they have saved. Throughout the book Miller describes the successful story of Lucy Moore, a child born with VATER syndrome, a maldevelopment of the intestinal, genital, and cardiac systems.

Miller's third book, *Coming of Age: The True Adventure of Two American Teens,* was published in 1995 by Random House. Three years previous, in 1992, Miller began shadowing the lives of the Burrillville, Rhode Island, High School senior class of 1993. Miller especially focuses on Dave Bettencourt, publisher of a radical underground newspaper. In this book, Miller describes the adventures that these teens go through, and how their lives and experiences are different from those of their parents during their own teen years.

Miller's fourth book, *Toy Wars: The Epic Struggle between G.I. Joe, Barbie, and the Companies That Make Them,* started as a long-term project for the *Providence Journal.* It took five years to write the book, the longest project he had every worked on. It began in 1992, where as a staff writer for the *Journal* he set out to write a biography of the toy soldier, G.I. Joe. The biography turned into *Toy Wars,* a story of the battle between toy manufacturers. The main focus is on Hasbro and assorted problems within the company. According to Miller, after Hasbro became a publicly traded company they became more concerned with profits and stock prices than with making a high-quality toy. According to a *Publishers Weekly* critic, Miller is "a shrewd writer who wrings every ounce of drama from his five-year behind-the-scenes account."

King of Hearts: The True Story of the Maverick Who Pioneered Open-Heart Surgery was published in 2000 by Times Books. It is the biography of heart surgeon C. Walton Lillehei of the University of Minnesota, who created open-heart surgery and the heart-lung machine. *King of Hearts* tells the story of children with congenital heart defects and how researchers and doctors used experimental efforts and surgical techniques to repair these children's hearts. A reviewer in *Publishers Weekly* claimed: "Miller's fast-paced and scrupulously researched account reveals both the exhilaration and the tragedy of Lillehei's story."

In a 2002 interview published on his Home Page, Miller described how he came to write *Men and Speed: A Wild Ride through NASCAR's Breakout Season.* "It grew out of a brainstorming lunch I had in the fall of 1999 with my longtime editor at Random House, Jon Karp. . . . [O]ne of the objectives of our brainstorming was to find a topic that would permit not only a literary approach but also have a good chance of selling with some intensity. I had come up with a list of 20 or so topics, and Jon went through it, stopping on NASCAR. This is it! he said." While he knew little about the sport of autoracing, Miller researched the sport heavily and gained tremendous access to NASCAR professionals. In the resulting book, Miller explains the reasons for NASCAR's huge popularity, from the speed and danger of the sport to the drivers' willingness to remain accessible to their fans. *Library Journal* reviewer Eric C. Shoaf praised the book as a "readable" one that "captures the many nuances of the American fascination with NASCAR racing."

For *The Xeno Chronicles: Two Years on the Frontier of Medicine Inside Harvard's Transplant Research Lab,* Miller returned to the field of medicine. The title refers to xenotransplantation, the process of transplanting organs from one species into the body of another. The goal of such research is to make it possible to safely transplant animal organs into humans, but many people are opposed to such research, including animal rights activists opposed to what they view as the exploitation of innocent animals for human gain. Reviewers lauded the book as a clear-eyed, balanced treatment of a provocative and controversial subject. A *Science News* contributor called the book a "vivid, personalized account," while *Library Journal* reviewer Kathy Arsenault commented that "Miller's flair for a dramatic story and a brilliant cast of characters make this a gripping read."

In addition to his nonfiction publishing and journalism career, Miller also founded and operates *TheCambridge-Company,* a writing, editing, design, and publishing service that does custom work in traditional book form.

BIOGRAPHICAL AND CRITICAL SOURCES:

PERIODICALS

Booklist, January 1, 1993, William Betty, review of *The Work of Human Hands: Hardy Hendren and Surgical Wonder at Children's Hospital,* p. 780; January 1, 1998, David Rouse, review of *Toy Wars: The Epic Struggle between G.I. Joe, Barbie, and the Companies That Make Them,* p. 755; January 1, 2000, William Betty, review of *King of Hearts: The True Story of the Maverick Who Pioneered Open-Heart Surgery,* p. 848; June 1, 2005, Donna Chavez, review of *The Xeno Chronicles: Two Years on the Frontier of Medicine Inside Harvard's Transplant Research Lab,* p. 1734.

Business Week, February 16, 1998, William C. Symonds, review of *Toy Wars,* p. 17.

Entertainment Weekly, June 23, 1995, Suzanne Ruta, review of *Coming of Age: The True Adventure of Two American Teens,* p. 48.

Forbes, January 24, 2000, review of *Brave Heart,* p. 170.

Kirkus Reviews, July 15, 1989, review of *Thunder Rise,* p. 1023; December 1, 1997, review of *Toy Wars,* p. 1755.

Library Journal, January, 1993, Kelly Jo Houtz, review of *The Work of Human Hands,* p. 156; January, 2000, Kathleen Arsenault, review of *King of Hearts,* p. 146; June 1, 2002, Eric C. Shoaf, review of *Men and Speed: A Wild Ride through NASCAR's Breakout Season,* p. 160; July 1, 2005, Kathy Arsenault, review of *The Xeno Chronicles,* p. 112.

New York Times, March 7, 1993, Gloria Hochman, review of *The Work of Human Hands,* p. 8.

Publisher Weekly, August 4, 1989, Sybil Steinberg, review of *Thunder Rise,* p. 82; December 7, 1992, review of *The Work of Human Hands,* p. 47; May 15, 1995, review of *Coming of Age,* p. 67; December 22, 1997, review of *Toy Wars,* p. 46; December 20, 1999, review of *The Work of Human Hands,* p. 65; April 11, 2005, review of *The Xeno Chronicles,* p. 41.

Science News, September 10, 2005, review of *The Xeno Chronicles,* p. 175.

Washington Monthly, May, 1998, James Surowiecki, review of *Toy Wars,* p. 46.

OTHER

G. Wayne Miller Home Page, http://www.gwaynemiller. com (March 21, 2000).

Men and Speed Web site, http://www.menandspeed.com (January, 2002).

*   *   *

MOATS, Lillian 1946-

PERSONAL: Born August 23, 1946, in Detroit, MI; father an architect; mother an artist; married J.P. Somersaulter (marriage ended); married Michael Moats, 1979; children: (second marriage) David Julian. *Education:* Attended Barnard College, 1964-65; University of Michigan, B.F.A., 1968; University of Wisconsin, M.S., 1970.

ADDRESSES: Home—Downers Grove, IL.

CAREER: Pajon Arts Ltd., Downers Grove, IL, film-making partner, 1973-93; self-employed artist and writer, 1993—.

AWARDS, HONORS: Special jury award (with J.P. Somersaulter), Chicago International Children's Film Festival, for body of work; more than forty other national and international film festival awards (with Somersaulter), including five awards from Chicago International Film Festival, all for art films.

WRITINGS:

(And illustrator) *The Gate of Dreams* (fairytales for children and adults), Cranbrook Press (Bloomfield Hills, MI), 1993, revised edition, 1996.
Legacy of Shadows (fictionalized memoir), Three Arts Press (Downers Grove, IL), 1999.
Speak, Hands (memoir), Three Arts Press (Downers Grove, IL), 2006.

Author (and artist and director, with J.P. Somersaulter) of more than twenty art films.

SIDELIGHTS: Lillian Moats and her partner, J.P. Somersaulter, have written and directed more than twenty art films for children and adults, most of them animated. Some are original stories and others are adaptations of classical folk and fairy tales. Some have been televised by the British Broadcasting Corporation and dubbed for transmission in Europe and Scandinavia. Some are collected in the Museum of Modern Art, and others have been shown at film festivals around the world, including Australia, Scotland, Italy, Spain, Denmark, India, Yugoslavia, and Iran, as well as at the Art Institute of Chicago and the Museum of Contemporary Art.

Moats once told *CA:* "My interests since childhood have been in art and writing. The concept of craftsmanship has been integral to both, since I was raised in a family of artists and artisans. For almost twenty years, I made animated art films as a vocation with my partner J.P. Somersaulter, while I painted portraits as an avocation. My need to write was secondary to artwork until a prolonged and severe emotional breakdown in my late twenties put me in touch with issues and themes that I could only express with enough precision in the verbal realm. Subjects too painful and personal to address outright at that time found symbolic expression in my original fairy tales.

"My personal understanding of fairy tales is built upon a foundation of insight from Bruno Bettelheim's writings. I am indebted to that renowned child psychologist and fairy tale scholar—first for writing *The Uses of Enchantment* for all of us—and later for encouraging me to publish my fairy tales. Three of these comprise my first book *The Gate of Dreams*. I illustrated *The Gate of Dreams* with silhouettes and (in the hardcover first edition) with oil vignettes. Artisans figure heavily in these symbolic stories. This made them particularly appropriate for publication by Cranbrook Press, which was very active in the Arts and Crafts Movement.

"There was a change in my relationship to writing in the late 1980s when I began to compose on a computer. The ease of moving sentences and paragraphs enabled me to see instantly the results of complex editing. This made writing feel much more like the visual and plastic arts which had always been more pleasurable to me in terms of process. Because of this, and because of my deepening interest in complex psychological subjects, my priorities reversed. In the last several years, writing has become what I must do. I returned to drawing and painting primarily to enhance my writing.

"My second book, *Legacy of Shadows,* is a fictionalized memoir that evolved from my exploration of the mysterious impact of family history on individual psychology. It traces the lives of three women whose stories indelibly blend into one during the span of three generations. My motivation for writing it was the realization that each of us is deeply directed by the legacy for unresolved emotion passed from generation to generation."

Moat later told *CA:* "My third book *Speak, Hands* picks up in time a few years after the end of *Legacy of Shadows*. Though both are psychological mysteries, the two books are quite different in style and focus. *Speak, Hands* is a deep meditation on the subjects of hands, memory, and the unconscious.

"Recently I returned to painting to express political concerns."

BIOGRAPHICAL AND CRITICAL SOURCES:

BOOKS

Moats, Lillian, *Speak, Hands,* Three Arts Press (Downers Grove, IL), 2006.

MONTERO, Mayra 1952-

PERSONAL: Born 1952, in Cuba.

ADDRESSES: Home—Puerto Rico.

CAREER: Author and journalist.

AWARDS, HONORS: Sonrisa Vertical Prize for erotic fiction, 2000, for *Púrpura profundo.*

WRITINGS:

Veintitrés y una tortuga, illustrated by Juan Alvarez O'Neill, Instituto de Cultura Puertorriqueña (San Juan, Puerto Rico), 1981.

La trenza de la hermosa luna, Anagrama (Barcelona, Spain), 1987.

Del rojo de su sombra, Tusquets (Barcelona, Spain), 1992, translated by Edith Grossman as *The Red of His Shadow,* HarperCollins (New York, NY), 2001.

Tú, la oscuridad, Tusquets (Barcelona, Spain), 1995, translated by Edith Grossman as *In the Palm of Darkness,* HarperCollins (New York, NY), 1997.

Como un mensajero tuyo, Tusquets (Barcelona, Spain), 1998, translated by Edith Grossman as *The Messenger,* HarperFlamingo (New York, NY), 1999.

Ultima noche que pasé contigo, [Barcelona, Spain], translated by Edith Grossman as *The Last Night I Spent with You,* HarperCollins (New York, NY), 2000.

Púrpura profundo, Tusquets (Barcelona, Spain), 2000, translated by Edith Grossman as *Deep Purple,* HarperCollins (New York, NY), 2003.

El capitán de los dormidos, Tusquets (Barcelona, Spain), 2002, translated by Edith Grossman as *Captain of the Sleepers,* Farrar, Straus and Giroux (New York, NY), 2005.

Son de Almendra, Alfaguara (Guaynabo, Puerto Rico), 2005, translated by Edith Grossman as *Dancing to Almendra,* Farrar, Straus and Giroux (New York, NY), 2007.

Author of weekly column for *El Nuevo Día* newspaper, Puerto Rico.

SIDELIGHTS: Mayra Montero is a Cuban-born author of novels and short stories. A resident of Puerto Rico since the mid-1960s, she is also a highly regarded journalist. Known for incorporating sexually explicit scenes into her fiction, Montero also takes pride in fashioning a distinctly Caribbean tone in her work. In an interview with *School Library Journal,* Montero discussed the influence of the Caribbean on her work: "You could say . . . that the Caribbean is in a way the spirit, the thread of all my stories. There are smells, music, color, noises, Caribbean flavors. The Caribbean and its circumstances have an extremely overpowering presence for those of us who write from these islands."

Montero's first work of fiction to be translated into English was the novel *Tú, la oscuridad,* which was published as *In the Palm of Darkness* in 1997. Edith Grossman, the acclaimed translator of this and several other novels by Montero, has also translated the works of such noted writers as Gabriel García Marquez and Mario Vargas Llosa. A *New Yorker* reviewer called the novel a "dazzling, original fugue on love and extinction," while in *Booklist* reviewer Brian Kenney commented that "with enormous skill, Montero weaves together several tales to create a brief and suspenseful story of contemporary Haiti."

In the Palm of Darkness finds American herpetologist Victor Grigg searching for the nearly extinct blood frog on the Mont des Enfants Perdus ("Mountain of Lost Children"), a region near Port au Prince. His elderly guide, Thierry Adrien, tells Victor tales about his own life in the town of Jeremie, his family, and the mysteries of Haiti. Adrien relates the fate of his father, a zombie hunter, who was found dead with the skin stripped from his body. Dr. Emile Boukaka, a surgeon and leader of a voodoo sect, is also an expert on frogs; he claims that Agwe Taroyo, the god of waters, has summoned the frogs to the bottom of the sea. As Grigg and Adrien explore the region in search of the purple frog, their camp is trashed, and they discover a plant biologist working in the area whose feet have been cut off. Working on the mountain, the domain of a chieftain who warns all to keep away, Grigg's quest for the frog is overshadowed by voodoo and violence.

Montero "confronts the modern Western way of knowing with an older, more universal kind," Richard Eder commented in his *Los Angeles Times Book Review* appraisal of *In the Palm of Darkness.* "Through the two men's doomed endeavor, through Thierry's tales and premonitions, and through Victor's increasingly distraught brooding about his childhood and marriage, the reader is taken on a double journey." Zofia Smardz praised Montero's prose in the *New York Times Book Review,* calling *In the Palm of Darkness* "a resplendent piece of writing that brings a mysterious and murderous country throbbingly to life." In a *Library Journal* review, Janet Ingraham dubbed the novel "a shocking, absorbing, beautifully written tale," while a *Publishers Weekly* reviewer added that, "thanks to Grossman's lovely translation, American readers can now enjoy this author's formidable talent."

In 1920, a bomb exploded in a Havana, Cuba, theater while the world-famous Italian tenor Enrico Caruso was performing on stage. Caruso fled in fear, suspecting that the Sicilian "Black Hand" was after him. In *The Messenger,* Montero takes this fact and speculates as to what happened next. The story is told by Aida Cheng, daughter of a Chinese father and Afro-Cuban mother, as well as by Aida and Caruso's daughter, Enriqueta, thirty years later. Chapter titles are taken from the libretto of Verdi's opera *Aida,* prefiguring the fact that the couple's fate is doomed, as was that of Verdi's Aida and Rhadames. Caruso and Aida meet and become lovers when she helps him escape after the bombing. Her godfather, José de Calazan Bangoche, is a priest of the Santeria religion who speaks to the gods and foresees the future through a magic chain called the *ekukele,* or messenger. José knows what is to come and tries to prevent his goddaughter from saving the opera star.

In reviewing *The Messenger, Booklist* reviewer Lee Reilly called some of the minor characters "lively" while maintaining that neither Aida nor Enriqueta "are by themselves interesting." However, in *World Literature Today,* reviewer Lucrecia Artalejo commented on Montero's feminist slant, noting that Caruso is painted as "the very portrait of agony and despair due to his obsessions: a tremendous dread of losing his voice, and a fear of being killed by the Sicilian Black Hand. . . . His lack of physical and emotional stability contrasts with both Aida's determination to protect him and her endurance." "Montero's visions of intercontinental culture-clash, star-crossed lovers, and historical violence fully justify the operatic treatment she provides," opined a *Publishers Weekly* reviewer. Janice P. Nimura wrote of *The Messenger* in the *New York Times Book Review* that it is "a haunting duet that mixes Afro-Cuban ritual, Chinese folklore, opera, and documented history."

Montero's 2000 novel, *The Last Night I Spent with You,* focuses on a married couple who decide to go on a vacation after the marriage of their daughter. During the

course of the trip—a cruise—troubles in the form of infidelities permeate their relationship, resulting in a sexually explicit novel that *Booklist* contributor Bonnie Johnston called "intensely passionate and disturbing." "Montero's deadpan humor sharpens her account of the passions of her middle-aged protagonists," added a *Publishers Weekly* reviewer, "and she adroitly establishes [the couple's] . . . separate viewpoints in her flexible, hypnotic prose."

In *The Red of His Shadow,* published in English in 2001, Montero delves into the mysterious world of voodoo. Set on the Caribbean island of Hispaniola, home to the nations of Haiti and the Dominican Republic, the novel centers on Zulé, a young voodoo priestess threatened by a past association with a voodoo priest, Similá. Critics lauded Montero for her exploration of the world of voodoo and her handling of the themes of love, jealousy, and political treachery. Writing in the *New York Times Book Review,* Jana Giles noted, "Moving between flashbacks to Zulé's youth and scenes of the present, Montero skillfully inserts voodoo rituals into the narrative as she draws out a tale of doomed passion and fatal pride."

Deep Purple, published in English in 2003, tells the story of a longtime music critic, Agustin Caban, who is commissioned by his newspaper to write his erotic memoirs. He dutifully relates his numerous affairs with musicians of both sexes—and even with an occasional animal. A *Publishers Weekly* reviewer praised Montero's "arch, literate writing" and called the novel "a delectable treat from start to finish." The original Spanish-language version of the novel won the Sonrisa Prize for erotic fiction in 2000.

Montero's next novel, *Captain of the Sleepers,* published in English in 2005, is set on the Puerto Rican island of Vieques in the 1950s, when the U.S. Navy took over much of the island for a military training base. This period also witnessed the rise of a nationalist movement in Puerto Rico. The novel's main characters, Andres and J.T.—the latter an American pilot who is the "captain" of the title—look back at their lives at mid-century from the vantage point of old age. In 1950, J.T. had an affair with Andres's mother, and the repercussions of this affair have reverberated through the ensuing decades. As with Montero's previous novels, critics praised *Captain of the Sleepers* for its lush narrative, frank sexuality, and emotional complexity. "Exquisite flashes of lust and corrosive jealousy, among the adults and young Andres alike, vivify the narrative," commented a reviewer in *Publishers Weekly.* Likewise, Hilda Llorens, writing in the *Women's Review of Books,* remarked: "Montero tells a brilliant story, skillfully using the past to narrate a tale of the present. With delicate and forceful prose, she evokes feelings of heartbreak and rage."

BIOGRAPHICAL AND CRITICAL SOURCES:

PERIODICALS

Booklist, April 1, 1997, review of *Tú, la oscuridad,* p. 1284; May 15, 1997, Brian Kenney, review of *In the Palm of Darkness,* p. 1561; January 1, 1998, *In the Palm of Darkness,* p. 730; April 1, 1999, Lee Reilly, review of *The Messenger,* p. 1386; June 1, 2000, Bonnie Johnston, review of *The Last Night I Spent with You,* p. 1860.
Kirkus Reviews, April 15, 1997, review of *In the Palm of Darkness,* p. 589.
Library Journal, April 1, 1997, Janet Ingraham, review of *In the Palm of Darkness,* p. 128; May 1, 1999, Lawrence Olszewski, review of *The Messenger,* p. 111; June 1, 2000, Yvette Olson, review of *The Last Night I Spent with You,* p. 200.
Los Angeles Times Book Review, May 18, 1997, Richard Eder, "Voodoo Child," p. 2.
New Yorker, August 25, 1997, review of *In the Palm of Darkness,* p. 160.
New York Times Book Review, June 15, 1997, Zofia Smardz, "A Nice Place for Extinction," p. 22; August 2, 1998, review of *In the Palm of Darkness,* p. 28; June 20, 1999, Janice P. Nimura, review of *The Messenger,* p. 16; August 12, 2001, Jana Giles, review of *The Red of His Shadow,* p. 29.
Observer (London, England), November 23, 1997, review of *In the Palm of Darkness,* p. 17.
Publishers Weekly, March 31, 1997, review of *In the Palm of Darkness,* p. 61; March 22, 1999, review of *The Messenger,* p. 69; April 10, 2000, review of *The Last Night I Spent with You,* p. 72; June 2, 2003, review of *Deep Purple,* p. 35; February 2, 2004, John F. Baker, "Author Moves, with Translator," p. 14; July 25, 2005, review of *Captain of the Sleepers,* p. 42.
School Library Journal, August, 2002, "Chatting with Mayra Montero: The Celebrated Author's Latest Novel, El capitan de los dormidos (The Captain of the Sleepers), Is Receiving Critical Praise Internationally. Here Is What Montero Had to Say to Criticas," p. S8.
Washington Post Book World, December 25, 2005, "The Writing Life: A Prize-winning Translator and a Distinguished Cuban Novelist Share Ideas on How They Work," p. 10.
Women's Review of Books, March-April, 2006, Hilda Llorens, "The Power of Secrets," review of *Captain of the Sleepers,* p. 28.
World Literature Review, autumn, 1999, Lucrecia Artalejo, review of *The Messenger,* p. 708.

ONLINE

HarperCollins Web site, http://www.harpercollins.com/ (January 2, 2007), author profile.*

*   *   *

MONTGOMERY, Marion 1925-
(Marion H. Montgomery, Jr.)

PERSONAL: Born April 16, 1925, in Thomaston, Upson County, GA; son of Marion H. and Lottie Mae Montgomery; married Dorothy Carlisle, January 20, 1951; children: Priscilla Montgomery Jensen, Lola Dean, Marion H. III, Heli, Ellyn Montgomery Byrd. *Education:* University of Georgia, A.B., 1950, M.S., 1953; attended University of Iowa, 1956-58. *Politics:* "Independent conservative." *Religion:* "Anglo Catholic."

ADDRESSES: Home and office—Crawford, GA.

CAREER: University of Georgia, Athens, assistant director of university press, 1950-52, business manager of *Georgia Review,* 1951-53; Darlington School for Boys (now Darlington School), Rome, GA, instructor, 1953-54; University of Georgia, instructor, 1954-60, assistant professor, 1960-67, associate professor, 1967-70, professor of English, 1970-87, professor emeritus, 1987—. Converse College, writer in residence, 1963. *Western Review,* managing editor, 1957-58. *Military service:* U.S. Army, 1943-46; became sergeant.

AWARDS, HONORS: Eugene Saxton Memorial Award, Harper and Brothers (publisher), 1960; Georgia Writers Association, award for fiction, 1964, for *Darrell,* award for poetry, 1970, for *The Gull and Other Georgia Scenes;* poetry award, *Carlton Miscellany,* 1967; Stanley W. Lindberg Award, 2001; Gerhart Niemeyer Award, Intercollegiate Studies Institute, 2003; Earhart Foundation grant.

WRITINGS:

FICTION

The Wandering of Desire (novel), Harper and Brothers (New York, NY), 1962.

Darrell (novel), Doubleday (New York, NY), 1964.

Ye Olde Bluebird (novella), New College Press (Sarasota, FL), 1967.

Fugitive (novel), Harper & Row (New York, NY), 1974.

Work represented in anthologies, including *Best American Short Stories,* edited by Martha Foley, 1971. Contributor of short stories to periodicals.

POETRY

Dry Lightening, University of Nebraska Press (Lincoln, NE), 1960.

Stones from the Rubble, Argus Books (New York, NY), 1965.

The Gull and Other Georgia Scenes, University of Georgia Press (Athens, GA), 1969.

Contributor to anthologies, including *Best Poems of 1958.* Contributor of poetry to periodicals.

OTHER

Ezra Pound: A Critical Essay, Eerdmans (Grand Rapids, MI), 1970.

T.S. Eliot: An Essay on the American Magus, University of Georgia Press (Athens, GA), 1970.

The Reflective Journey toward Order: Essays on Dante, Wordsworth, Eliot, and Others, University of Georgia Press (Athens, GA), 1974.

Eliot's Reflective Journey to the Garden, Whitston Publishing (Troy, NY), 1979.

The Prophetic Poet and the Spirit of the Age, Sherwood Sugden (La Salle, IL), Volume 1: *Why Flannery O'Connor Stayed Home,* 1981, Volume 2: *Why Poe Drank Liquor,* 1983, Volume 3: *Why Hawthorne Was Melancholy,* 1984.

Possum, and Other Receipts for the Recovery of "Southern" Being, University of Georgia Press (Athens, GA), 1987.

The Trouble with You Innerleckchuls, Christendom College Press (Front Royal, VA), 1988.

The Men I Have Chosen for Fathers: Literary and Philosophical Passages, University of Missouri Press (Columbia, MO), 1990.

Liberal Arts and Community: The Feeding of the Larger Body, Louisiana State University Press (Baton Rouge, LA), 1990.

Virtue and Modern Shadows of Turning: Preliminary Agitations, University Press of America (Lanham, MD), 1990.

Romantic Confusions of the Good: Beauty as Truth, Truth Beauty, Rowman & Littlefield (Lanham, MD), 1997.

Concerning Intellectual Philandering: Poets and Philosophers, Priests, and Politicians, Rowman & Littlefield (Lanham, MD), 1998.

The Truth of Things: Liberal Arts and the Recovery of Reality, Spence Publishing (Dallas, TX), 1999.

Making: The Proper Habit of Our Being: Essays Speculative, Reflective, Argumentative, St. Augustine's Press (South Bend, IN), 2000.

Romancing Reality: Homo Viator and the Scandal Called Beauty, St. Augustine's Press (South Bend, IN), 2001.

John Crowe Ransom and Allen Tate: At Odds about the Ends of History and the Mystery of Nature, McFarland and Co. (Jefferson, NC), 2003.

Eudora Welty and Walker Percy: The Concept of Home in Their Lives and Literature, McFarland and Co. (Jefferson, NC), 2003.

On Matters Southern: Essays about Literature and Culture, 1964-2000, edited by Michael M. Jordan, McFarland and Co. (Jefferson, NC), 2005.

Hillbilly Thomist: Flannery O'Connor, St. Thomas, and the Limits of Art, two volumes, McFarland and Co. (Jefferson, NC), 2006.

With Walker Percy at the Tupperware Party: In Company with Fyodor Dostoevsky, Gabriel Marcel, T.S. Eliot, Flannery O'Connor, and Others, St. Augustine's Press (South Bend, IN), 2007.

SIDELIGHTS: Marion Montgomery's fiction often contrasts characters who are leaving the rural South for success in the city with those who, having achieved that success, are trying to recapture their rural beginnings. This particular theme comes from Montgomery's interest in the Agrarian writers of the thirties who advocated an artistic return to the land in order to establish a mutually supportive culture and agriculture.

Montgomery's novel *The Wandering of Desire* reflects his interests in agrarian themes, telling the story of two men, Wash Mullis and Doc Blalock, and their ultimately failed attempts to conquer the land. Writing about Montgomery's work in the *Dictionary of Literary Biography,* Thomas Landers noted that the novel "is a complex work in which the diversity of characters and actions . . . suggests the author's wide knowledge of his region and its lore." Walker Percy, reviewing *The Wandering of Desire* in *Commonweal* called the work "a chronicle, a country epic, a first novel sprung forth whole and entire with full Faulknerian panoply of legends, yarns, family tales, and a command of country epithet unsurpassed since *The Hamlet.*"

Discussing Montgomery's second novel *Darrell,* Landers said that the work "is simpler in its plot structure than *The Wandering of Desire.* . . ." In *Darrell,* Landers commented, the "action is uncomplicated and is rendered sequentially. Indeed the novel is Montgomery's only conventional fictional narrative." In this novel Montgomery tells the tale of a country-born and country-raised man called Darrell, who convinces his aged grandmother to move with him from their small town to the city. The two end up settling, not in the heart of the city, but on its perimeter, in the Atlanta suburbs. Eventually, Darrell's obsession to fulfill the wish of a dying girl, Sandra Lee, to visit the Atlanta zoo, leads both of them to their deaths in a motorcycle crash. Landers concluded: "Beneath this straightforward plot—which is no more than a situation out of which grows the final tragic consequence—the reader finds a statement of Montgomery's view of urban life. Suburbia is rendered as kind of a banal hell in which people are manipulated by forces beyond their control." O.B. Emerson, writing in *Critique: Studies in Modern Fiction,* said of *Darrell:* "With his clear voice, insight, and vision, Marion Montgomery is one of the most appealing spokesmen for the new South as well as the old." And in *Best Sellers,* Luke M. Grande assessed the book as "one of those flawless works of art being turned out by Southern writers as only they, apparently, can." He made note of Montgomery's "technical skill," calling him "an accomplished storyteller," and praised "his penetrating vision of the tragicomedy of life with rare effectiveness."

In 1974 Montgomery published *Fugitive,* which Landers considered to be "his most overtly Agrarian" work. *Fugitive* tells the story of Walt Mason, a successful songwriter in Nashville, who moves to the small town of Weaverton, Tennessee, in search of rural simplicity. The town, however, is far from the idyllic country community Mason seeks. Like other cities, Weaverton is plagued by commercialism and a dependence on technology. According to Landers, *Fugitive* will present "some difficulties for the critic or reader who expects a conventional plot composed of sequential events." Montgomery's style in this novel includes numerous digressions, the relevance of which may not be immediately apparent to the reader. The work demands from the reader, said Landers, "a willing suspension of disbelief." *New York Times Book Review* contributor Shirley Ann Grau found Montgomery's *Fugitive* "difficult, crabbed, full of half-disclosed meanings." For Grau "the experimental structure . . . makes unnecessary demands on the reader," and she found that this "desperately serious literary venture" "leaves the impression of a simple story complicatingly told." Thomas H. Landess of the *Georgia Review* cited Montgomery as "one of a handful of writers whose work belies the prophecies of sociological critics that the epoch of significant Southern fiction has come to and end," and deemed *Fugitive* "a work as ambitious in its own way as anything yet attempted by a Southerner of his generation." And although he found the book's shifting point of view "tricky," and expressed the concern that Montgomery "here is so bold in his aspirations that throughout the novel the reader spends much of his time wondering if the action, however skillfully rendered, can possibly bear the burden of the author's weighty thematic substance." He concluded: "The work is extraordinarily successful, which is to say that it represents a substantial literary achievement." Landess summarized: "what Montgomery has written here is the American success story played backwards, a tale of a hero who leaves fame and fortune in the city to seek a humdrum life on the farm. . . . For these and many other reasons his trip is well worth the time and trouble, however tortuous the turns in the road. I suspect that this is the first novel of a kind, and as such it deserves our most serious and respectful attention."

BIOGRAPHICAL AND CRITICAL SOURCES:

BOOKS

Contemporary Literary Criticism, Volume 7, Thomson Gale (Detroit, MI), 1977.

Dictionary of Literary Biography, Volume 6: *American Novelists since World War II,* Second Series, Thomson Gale (Detroit, MI), 1980.

PERIODICALS

American Literature, January, 1971, review of *T.S. Eliot: An Essay on the American Magus,* p. 594.

Best Sellers, May 15, 1964, Luke M. Grande, review of *Darrell.*

Critique, Volume 8, number 1, 1965, O.B. Emerson, review of *Darrell.*

Georgia Review, spring, 1967, review of *Stones from the Rubble,* p. 135; summer, 1974, Thomas H. Landess, review of *Fugitive,* p. 212; fall, 1985, review of *The Prophetic Poet and the Spirit of the Age,* p. 629.

Modern Age, spring, 2001, John Attarian, review of *The Truth of Things: Liberal Arts and the Recovery of Reality,* p. 167; spring, 2006, Patrick J. Walsh, review of *Eudora Welty and Walker Percy: The Concept of Home in Their Lives and Literature,* p. 166.

National Review, August 11, 1970, review of *T.S. Eliot,* p. 852.

New Republic, July 27, 1974, review of *Fugitive,* p. 32.

New York Times Book Review, June 9, 1974, Shirley Ann Grau, review of *Fugitive,* p. 4.

Poetry, October, 1966, review of *Stones from the Rubble,* p. 48.

Review of Politics, spring, 2001, Kurt J. Miyazaki, review of *The Truth of Things: Liberal Arts and the Academy,* p. 414.

Sewanee Review, spring, 1965, review of *Darrell,* p. 333.

Times Literary Supplement, January 1, 1971, review of *T.S. Eliot,* p. 10.

Weekly Standard, April 10, 2006, Patrick J. Walsh, review of *On Matters Southern: Essays about Literature and Culture, 1964-2000.*

*   *   *

MONTGOMERY, Marion H., Jr.
See MONTGOMERY, Marion

*   *   *

MORGAN, Rebecca
See FORREST, Richard

N

NANCE, John
See NANCE, John J.

* * *

NANCE, John J. 1946-
(John Nance)

PERSONAL: Born July 5, 1946, in Dallas, TX; son of Joseph Turner (an attorney) and Margrette Z. (an English professor and published poet) Nance; married Benita Priest (a school development specialist), July 26, 1968; children: Dawn Michelle, Bridgitte Cathleen, Christopher Sean. *Education:* Southern Methodist University, B.A., 1968, J.D., 1969; U.S. Air Force Undergraduate Pilot Training, distinguished graduate, 1971; also attended the University of Hawaii.

ADDRESSES: Home and office—University Place, WA. *Agent*—Wieser & Wieser, 25 E. 21st St., New York, NY 10010.

CAREER: Writer, journalist, columnist, pilot, and lawyer. *Park Cities North Dallas News,* writer, columnist, and aviation writer, 1957-64; KAIM-AM/FM, Honolulu, HI, announcer and newsperson, 1964-65; WFAA-AM/FM/TV, Dallas, TX, radio and television newsperson, 1966-70; NEWSCOM News Service, Dallas, news director, 1969-70; admitted to the Bar of the State of Texas, 1970; attorney in private practice, 1970—; Braniff International Airlines, Dallas, pilot, 1975-82; Alaska Airlines, Seattle, WA, pilot, 1985—, professional leave, 1987-93; Simulator Training

Incorporated (flight school), Seattle, pilot training consultant and instructor, 1986-92; EMEX Corporation, Tacoma, WA, airline safety analyst and consultant, 1986—; ABC Radio and Television Network, aviation analyst, 1994; *Good Morning America,* ABC, aviation editor, 1995; Nance & Carmichael, PC (law firm), Austin, TX, partner, 1997. Executive Transport Incorporated, president, 1979-85; Preventative Products Incorporated, vice-president of development, 1983-88. Congressional Office of Technology Assessment, consultant, 1987; Foundation for Issues Resolution in Science and Technology, founding board member, 1987-89; National Patient Safety Foundation at American Medical Association, member of board; consultant and analyst on aviation and earthquake safety for major television and radio news networks, including American Broadcasting Companies (ABC), National Broadcasting Company (NBC), Columbia Broadcasting System (CBS), Cable News Network (CNN), Public Broadcasting Service (PBS), National Public Radio (NPR), United Press International (UPI), Associated Press (AP), and British Broadcasting Corporation (BBC), 1984-95; guest appearances on nationally broadcast television shows, including *Good Morning America, Today, This Morning, Macneil-Lehrer Report, Oprah, CBS Evening News,* and *Nova,* 1984—; professional speaker on health care and medical fields, corporate, managerial, aviation, seismic, and other topics, 1988—; ABC News (exclusive), aviation analyst, 1995—; *Good Morning America,* aviation editor, 1996—. *Military service:* U.S. Air Force, 1970-75; pilot and aircraft commander, 1971-75; entered associate reserve, 1975; present rank, lieutenant colonel. Served in Vietnam War as pilot, 1971-74; project officer, Cockpit Resource Management and Aircrew Flight Safety Program Development and Education, 97th Military Aircraft Squadron, 1988-93; activated and deployed to Operation Desert Storm (Persian Gulf

War), 1990-91; Individual Mobilization Augmentee, Randolph AFB, Texas, affiliated with Crew Resource Management (CRM) education, 1993-95.

MEMBER: American Bar Association, Authors Guild of America, Texas Bar Association, Reserve Officers Association, Screen Actors Guild, Writers Guild, Phi Alpha Delta, Delta Chi.

AWARDS, HONORS: Washington Governor's Outstanding Author Award, 1987, for *Blind Trust;* Pacific Northwest Writers Conference Lifetime Achievement Award, 1996.

WRITINGS:

NONFICTION

Splash of Colors: The Self-Destruction of Braniff International, Morrow (New York, NY), 1984.
Blind Trust, Morrow (New York, NY), 1986.
On Shaky Ground, Morrow (New York, NY), 1988.
What Goes Up, Morrow (New York, NY), 1991.
Golden Boy: The Harold Simmons Story, Eakin Press (Austin, TX), 2003.

NOVELS

Final Approach, Crown (New York, NY), 1990.
Scorpion Strike, Crown (New York, NY), 1992.
Phoenix Rising, Crown (New York, NY), 1994.
Pandora's Clock, Doubleday (New York, NY), 1995.
Medusa's Child, Doubleday (New York, NY), 1997.
The Last Hostage, Doubleday (New York, NY), 1998.
Blackout, Putnam (New York, NY), 2000.
Headwind, Putnam (New York, NY), 2001.
Turbulence, Putnam (New York, NY), 2002.
Fire Flight, Simon & Schuster (New York, NY), 2003.
Skyhook, Putnam (New York, NY), 2003.
Saving Cascadia, Simon & Schuster (New York, NY), 2005.
Orbit, Simon & Schuster (New York, NY), 2006.

OTHER

Contributor to *Transportation Safety in an Age of Deregulation,* edited by Leon N. Moses and Ian Savage, Oxford University Press (New York, NY), 1989.

Contributor to periodicals, including *Los Angeles Times, USA Today, San Francisco Chronicle,* and *Professional Pilot. Braniff Inflight Magazine,* columnist, 1987-89.

ADAPTATIONS: Pandora's Clock was released as a television miniseries by NBC, 1996; *Medusa's Child* was released as a television miniseries by ABC, 1997. Several of the author's books have been adapted for audio, including *Orbit.*

SIDELIGHTS: John J. Nance's background as a journalist, lawyer, and experienced military and commercial pilot has made him a highly respected analyst of the aviation industry and has led him to write numerous nonfiction and fiction books about airline safety and other societal issues. Born in Dallas, Texas, in 1946, Nance was interested in flying and writing at a young age, becoming the aviation writer for his neighborhood newspaper when he was thirteen. While earning an undergraduate and law degree as an ROTC scholar at Southern Methodist University, Nance worked full-time as a radio broadcast journalist. After receiving a degree in air law and passing the Texas Bar Exam, Nance attended the U.S. Air Force Undergraduate Pilot Training at Williams Air Force Base in Arizona, where he was cited as a distinguished graduate. He later served as a pilot and aircraft commander for the U.S. Air Force, flying thirty-five missions in Vietnam. In 1975 Nance left active duty and joined the reserves, serving as an aircraft commander. He was promoted to lieutenant colonel—a rank he still holds—in 1989. Nance worked as a commercial pilot for Braniff International Airlines for seven years, until the corporation went bankrupt in 1982. Byron Acohido in the *Seattle Times* once noted how Nance's career has given him a unique advantage as an aviation analyst: "Reporters gravitate to Nance because he's a rare specimen: an articulate, knowledgeable and well-connected member of the aviation community who owes allegiance to no one save his conscience." Acohido quoted a member of the aviation community, who stated: "Most pilots have a hard time communicating about flying," and added: "John has background in law, and he's a wordsmith. He can express our feelings without offending people."

Nance wrote his first book after losing his position as a pilot for Braniff when they went into bankruptcy. *Splash of Colors: The Self-Destruction of Braniff International* focuses on the executive decisions to dramatically expand the company after the federal government deregulated the airline industry in 1978, an action that minimized governmental intervention in the airlines, allowing companies to grow rapidly and engage in competitive cost-cutting practices that some people argued would affect safety. Unforeseen increases in fuel prices and interest rates on the money Braniff had borrowed for its expansion ultimately led to financial disaster for the company. Mark Potts, in a review of *Splash of Colors* in the *Washington Post,* praised Nance's coverage of the plight of both the workers and the executives of Braniff and called the book "one of the best chronicles of corporate tragedy."

In his next book, *Blind Trust,* Nance explores the importance of the individual aviation employee, whom he cites as a key factor in risk management in modern-day air travel. Analyzing a number of tragic airplane crashes, Nance identifies issues in the airline industry that need to be addressed in order to minimize aviation safety problems caused by human error. Many of the dangers he discusses stem from deregulation; companies hired inexperienced pilots to fly unfamiliar routes and forced pilots to work longer hours. In order to cut costs and offer low passenger fares in further attempts to compete with other airlines, companies also minimized the maintenance of planes and replaced experienced employees with lower-paid newcomers. The industry's new concern with growth, Nance claims, led airline corporations to ignore the effect these changes had on workers and their performance in relation to air safety. Nance concludes in *Blind Trust* that eighty-five percent of all airline disasters are due to "stressed-out pilots, overworked air traffic controllers, less-than-vigilant government investigators and cost-conscious maintenance crews." He suggests that government officials and airline executives should put more effort into understanding and remedying these problems. "Deregulation," the author says in the book, "has retarded dramatically and dangerously the spread of a very basic understanding: People will make mistakes; these mistakes can be anticipated through human-factors and human-performance research and investigation; and what the industry can learn from such research can be applied in direct practical ways to prevent those predictable mistakes from causing crashes and killing passengers."

Critics praised Nance for his clear and insightful presentation in *Blind Trust.* Paul Sonnenburg in the *Los Angeles Times Book Review* noted Nance's "discerning aircraft accident analyses—models of deftly sketched detail, compassionate perception of human behavior, and shrewd synthesis of complex relationships and

perspectives." Douglas B. Feaver, in his review for the *Washington Post,* called Nance's book "one of the best and most troubling aviation safety books of recent years."

In addition to his nonfiction works, Nance has become well known as a writer of suspense novels. Such bestsellers as *Medusa's Child* and *Blackout* have helped establish Nance as "arguably the king of the modern-day aviation thriller," as a *Publishers Weekly* reviewer wrote.

In *Pandora's Clock,* the author presents a claustrophobic worst-case scenario: a commercial airplane passenger afflicted with a doomsday virus. *Medusa's Child,* a 1996 release, takes the reader through twelve hours aboard a cargo plane sabotaged with a nuclear device capable of obliterating half the Atlantic seaboard. As the bomb's timer ticks down, the crew struggles to disarm the weapon even as the plane approaches a hurricane. *People* contributor Cynthia Sanz wrote that the author "skillfully ratchets up the suspense."

Nance published *The Last Hostage* in 1998, an on-flight hostage drama that provides "a thrilling ride," according to J.D. Reed in *People. Library Journal* reviewer Maria Perez-Stable remarked that the novel's "fast-moving plot has more twists than a corkscrew." With *Blackout,* FBI agent Kat Bronsky and news reporter Robert MacCabe team up to investigate why numerous jumbo jets are falling from the sky. In each case a mysterious, blinding flash has preceded the crash, and a corporate jet is in the vicinity of each disaster. The finger is pointed at terrorists bent on disabling the U.S. air industry by orchestrating air tragedies. To *Booklist* critic Gilbert Taylor, *Blackout* delivers "a glorified chase scene stretched from Hong Kong to Idaho." A *Publishers Weekly* contributor noted that the author "continues to craft brilliantly hair-raising in-flight emergency scenes" culminating in "a rousing, well-developed finale that comes together smoothly on final approach."

In his novel *Turbulence,* Nance writes about a potential airline hijacking with a twist. During a flight from London to Capetown, the passengers of an airliner become increasingly upset with the pilot, the incompetent Phil Knight, and chief flight attendant, Judy Jackson. The near revolt is brought about by a clash between the inept and spiteful Jackson and Dr. Brian Logan, who blames the airline company for the death of his wife and child. To complicate matters further, the

CIA believes that the plane may also contain a weapon that is targeted for use on a European capital, sparking a debate on whether or not it should be shot down. A *Publishers Weekly* contributor wrote that Nance does "the job of spurring the plot to ever higher excitement."

Headwind features a story about an ex-U.S. President who is arrested in Europe for crimes supposedly committed by the CIA during his tenure. It is up to a small-time lawyer and two pilots who commandeer an airplane to save him. Noting the novels "white-knuckle flying sequences," Ronnie H. Terpening also wrote in the *Library Journal* that the novel "crackle[s] with tension." A *Publishers Weekly* contributor commented: "Flair-raising near-disaster in the air, high courtroom drama and a strong international cast of characters make this surefire bestseller a nonstop read."

Nance changes his formula slightly in his novel *Fire Flight,* which is more about smoke jumping and a mystery rather than the in-flight suspense the author usually writes. The story follows pilot Clark Maxwell, who comes out of retirement only to be involved in a crash that kills his copilot and a hotshot smoke jumper. Clark suspects that the crash, caused when the wings fell off the plane, was due to negligence or sabotage, a suspicion further supported when another pilot friend is killed in a similar scenario. As a result, Clark sets out to discover the truth. "With its lively cast and rich plot, this is Nance's best book in years," wrote a *Publishers Weekly* contributor. Several critics also noted the author's ability to build suspense. In her review in *Booklist,* Mary Frances Wilkens commented that the author "successfully melds a timely topic, forest fires, with his specialty, pulse-pounding airborne excitement." In his review in the *Library Journal,* Robert Conroy wrote that the author "has crafted an exciting and compelling story."

In *Skyhook,* Ben Cole, an aviation expert, and April Rosen, boss of a cruise line, find themselves involved in a plot that could cause the destruction of Skyhook, a secret government computer program that helps rescue planes that are experiencing flight problems. A *Kirkus Reviews* contributor called *Skyhook* a "thoroughly entertaining thriller about secrets, lies (bureaucratic sort), and little guys beating the odds." A *Publishers Weekly* reviewer wrote: "Nance offers his usual abundance of authentic aviation detail as well as a few final twists."

Nance features a natural disaster in *Saving Cascadia.* The story revolves around a resort built on Cascadia Island off the coast of Washington. The construction goes on despite warnings that the island is in store for a natural catastrophe of tremendous proportion, due to the fact that Cascadia Island is located on a large seismic fault. When an earthquake occurs during the resort's grand opening, it is followed by a tsunami with seventy-foot waves headed for the island and threatening to wipe out both the island's tourists and residents. "Nance does it again, thrill upon thrill," wrote a *Kirkus Reviews* contributor. A *Publishers Weekly* contributor commented that the author "builds suspense to a fever pitch in this all-too-credible nail-biter."

Orbit takes place in the year 2009 and features Kip Dawson, who has won the right to fly on the American Space Adventure ship to orbit the earth. However, once in space, the ship is hit by a rock that kills the pilot, meaning that Kip must fly the ship back to earth by himself. Meanwhile, Kip's efforts are being sabotaged by a NASA director out to destroy any thoughts of future civilian space programs. "*Orbit* ranks among Nance's best," wrote Robert Conroy in the *Library Journal.*

Nance once told *CA:* "As an author, I'm a communicator with a journalist's responsibility for balance and accuracy, a storyteller's passion to entertain and excite, and an advocate's determination to educate and motivate. I'm very privileged to have gained an audience that seems to enjoy both my nonfiction and fiction, and I'm determined to remain scrupulously faithful to their expectations by structuring the truth (without embellishment) into dynamic, human terms, and by telling exciting tales against the background of strict reality."

BIOGRAPHICAL AND CRITICAL SOURCES:

BOOKS

Nance, John J., *Blind Trust,* Morrow (New York, NY), 1986.

PERIODICALS

Booklist, June 1, 1994, Dennis Winters, review of *Phoenix Rising,* p. 1771; January 1, 2000, Gilbert Taylor, review of *Blackout,* p. 834; February 15, 2003, George Cohen, review of *Skyhook,* p. 1018; September 15, 2003, Mary Frances Wilkens, review of *Fire Flight,* p. 181; February 1, 2005, George Cohen, review of *Saving Cascadia,* p. 946; February 15, 2006, George Cohen, review of *Orbit,* p. 51.

Kirkus Reviews, February 15, 2002, review of *Turbulence,* p. 214; February 15, 2003, review of *Skyhook,* p. 262; September 15, 2003, review of *Fire Flight,* p. 1150; January 1, 2005, review of *Saving Cascadia,* p. 14.

Library Journal, March 15, 1998, Maria Perez-Stable, review of *The Last Hostage,* p. 95; March 1, 2001, Ronnie H. Terpening, review of *Headwind,* p. 132; November 1, 2003, Robert Conroy, review of *Fire Flight,* p. 125; February 15, 2006, Robert Conroy, review of *Orbit,* p. 109.

Los Angeles Times Book Review, January 26, 1986, Paul Sonnenburg, review of *Blind Trust,* p. 1.

People, March 31, 1986, Cynthia Sanz, review of *Medusa's Child,* p. 93; March 2, 1998, J.D. Reed, review of *The Last Hostage,* p. 38.

Publishers Weekly, May 10, 1991, review of *What Goes Up,* 270; March 23, 1992, review of *Scorpion Strike,* p. 60; January 6, 1997, review of *Medusa's Child,* p. 64; January 12, 1998, review of *The Last Hostage,* p. 46; January 3, 2000, review of *Blackout,* p. 60; February 12, 2001, review of *Headwind,* p. 182; April 15, 2002, review of *Turbulence,* p. 42; March 24, 2003, review of *Skyhook,* p. 60; September 8, 2003, review of *Fire Flight,* p. 52; February 14, 2005, review of *Saving Cascadia,* p. 55.

Seattle Times, January 16, 1989, Byron Acohido, profile of author, p. F1.

Washington Post, September 24, 1984, Mark Potts, review of *Splash of Colors: The Self-Destruction of Braniff International,* p. D6; January 21, 1986, Douglas B. Feaver, review of *Blind Trust.*

ONLINE

Bookreporter.com, http://www.bookreporter.com/ (March 3, 2000), "John J. Nance," interview with author.

Simon & Schuster Web site, http://www.simonsays.com/ (April 15, 2007), brief profile of the author.*

*   *   *

NASLUND, Sena Jeter

PERSONAL: Born in Birmingham, AL; married John C. Morrison (a physicist), 1995; children: (previous marriage) Flora. *Education:* Attended Birmingham-Southern College; University of Iowa, Ph.D.

ADDRESSES: Home—Louisville, KY.

CAREER: University of Louisville, Louisville, KY, writer-in-residence; Spalding University, Louisville, program director of the brief residency MFA in writing program.

AWARDS, HONORS: Lawrence Fiction Prize; awards from National Endowment for the Arts, Kentucky Arts Council, and Kentucky Foundation for Women; Harper Lee Award, Southeastern Library Association Fiction Award; Kentucky Poet Laureate.

WRITINGS:

Ice Skating at the North Pole: Stories, Ampersand Press (Bristol, RI), 1989.

The Animal Way to Love (novel), Ampersand Press (Bristol, RI), 1993.

Sherlock in Love: A Novel, David Godine (Boston, MA), 1993.

The Disobedience of Water: Stories and Novellas, David Godine (Boston, MA), 1999.

Ahab's Wife; or, The Star-Gazer: A Novel, William Morrow (New York, NY), 1999.

Four Spirits: A Novel, William Morrow (New York, NY), 2003.

(Editor, with Kathleen Driskell) *High Horse: Contemporary Writing by the MFA Faculty of Spalding University,* Fleur-de-Lis Press (Louisville, KY), 2005.

Abundance: A Novel of Marie Antoinette, William Morrow (New York, NY), 2006.

Contributor to literary journals. *Louisville Review,* founder and editor; *Fleur-de-lis,* founder and editor.

ADAPTATIONS: Books adapted for audio include *Ahab's Wife; or, The Star-Gazer: A Novel; Four Spirits: A Novel* (unabridged; fifteen CDs), Sound Library, BBC Audiobooks America; and *Abundance: A Novel of Marie Antoinette,* read by Susanna Burney (abridged; ten CDs), Harper Audio.

SIDELIGHTS: After her earliest short fiction appeared in literary journals, Sena Jeter Naslund published the collection *Ice Skating at the North Pole: Stories.* The individual stories share certain characteristics, according to *Library Journal* reviewer Marcia Tager, including "a recurring motif" of music or musical instrument; a calamity that damages or threatens a woman's life, and an exploration of "what it means to live, love, work, and make music in the world as it exists for us all." *Publishers Weekly* reviewer Sybil Steinberg noted Naslund's realistic portrayals of women and their lives, predicting that "her idiosyncratic characters might be advantageously transplanted to a longer work."

Naslund's *Sherlock in Love: A Novel* was commended by critics, including *Library Journal* contributor Barbara Hoffert, as the one among several recent Sherlock Holmes spinoffs that "comes closest to achieving the style of [Sir Arthur Conan] Doyle's original work." The novel represents an "attempt to close the one case in which Holmes failed to bring a miscreant to justice," Tobin Harshaw reported in the *New York Times Book Review*. In Naslund's version, Holmes has died and Dr. Watson is attempting to write a biography of his old friend. When he publishes a newspaper advertisement requesting background information from Holmes's former contacts, he is assailed by all manner of anonymous threats to his safety and invasions of his security arrangements. When he follows clues to this unexpected mystery backward in time, Watson uncovers characters from Holmes's past, including a woman who had masqueraded as a male violinist and a love affair that could surprise die-hard fans of Conan Doyle. In her *Booklist* review, Donna Seaman described *Sherlock in Love* as a "cleverly plotted, cheerfully risque adventure," replete with "entertaining . . . historical references."

If *Sherlock in Love* was "elegant," as Hoffert asserted, then so are the stories in *The Disobedience of Water: Stories and Novellas*—"a bit quirkier, a bit more modern, but just as satisfying in their own way." In this collection, a *Publishers Weekly* contributor reported: "Plot matters less to Naslund than voice, sympathy, setting and tone." Seaman wrote in *Booklist*: "Each tale begins as though the reader has just opened a door or turned a corner and walked into a conversation."

After listening to audio versions of classics such as *Moby-Dick* and *Huckleberry Finn* with her daughter during a long drive, Naslund came up with the idea for her next book, *Ahab's Wife; or, The Star-Gazer: A Novel*. In an interview with Leslie Haynesworth for *Publishers Weekly,* Naslund related: "It irked me a bit to be aware that these two candidates for the title 'Great American Novel' had almost no women in them. Half the human race ignored, yet their vision was considered among the most complete, the greatest." Naslund decided to write the story of Moby Dick through the eyes of Una, a young woman who disguises herself as a cabin boy and sets sail on a whaling ship. Una endures a series of horrific adventures, including marriage to a madman, before eventually meeting, and marrying Captain Ahab. Linda Simon, in *World and I,* wrote: "*Ahab's Wife* is nothing less than artful and satisfying fiction: a compelling history of a heroic woman." A *Publishers Weekly* reviewer commented that "Una is a character who is destined to endure."

Four Spirits: A Novel is a historical novel that focuses on the civil rights movement of the 1960s, a time when vicious dogs and fire hoses were used freely by authorities such as Bull Connor to control protestors in the South while Martin Luther King preached nonviolence to his followers. Among the factual events Naslund uses to portray the turmoil of the time is the 1963 deaths of the "Four Spirits" of the title, four black girls who died when their Birmingham, Alabama, church was bombed. A number of vignettes feature characters who ultimately are brought together in their struggle against segregation. *Booklist* contributor Brad Hooper noted that this results in "a smoothly flowing composite narrative of how life was led at the time and how it was irreparably altered." The main protagonist is Stella Silver, a white college student who is moved to act after witnessing the open celebration of the assassination of President John F. Kennedy by her Birmingham neighbors. Stella takes a position teaching at a black school, along with her friends Stella and wheelchair-bound Cat, thereby putting her own life at risk. "Told in beautifully crafted prose, this is a moving, historically accurate tale of a time of social transformation," concluded *Library Journal* reviewer Starr E. Smith.

Abundance: A Novel of Marie Antoinette is a fictional memoir in which Naslund reveals the life of the Austrian princess whose life was ended at the age of thirty-eight by the blade of the guillotine. A *Publishers Weekly* reviewer wrote: "With vivid detail and exquisite narrative technique, Naslund exemplifies the best of historical fiction." A fourteen-year-old Mary Antoinette was sent from Austria to France by her mother, Archduchess Maria Teresa, to marry Louis Auguste, the Dauphin of France, just one year her senior. The marriage took place four years later and was intended to unite the two countries. As Naslund relates her story, she notes King Louis XVI's impotence and preference to hunt rather than consummate the marriage for many years, their family life and children, and the fashions and culture of the time. Marie's fear for her children and husband as the first rumblings of the French Revolution are felt reflect her love for them. "The author injects humanity into the two as, over the years, they become parents and grow into their authority," commented Emily Chenoweth in *People*. The Affair of the Diamond Necklace, the false accusation that Marie committed adultery with a cardinal is also incorporated into the story. *Entertainment Weekly* reviewer Tina Jordan wrote: "Naslund's writing is opulent and fabulous, as encrusted with detail as one of Marie's shimmering dresses." "Naslund has done her homework, and imagined her complex, bewitching protagonist in persuasive depth and detail," wrote a *Kirkus Reviews* critic. "The result is an exemplary historical novel."

BIOGRAPHICAL AND CRITICAL SOURCES:

PERIODICALS

Booklist, October 1, 1993, Donna Seaman, review of *Sherlock in Love: A Novel*, p. 257; April 15, 1999, Donna Seaman, review of *The Disobedience of Water: Stories and Novellas*, p. 1516; August, 1999, Grace Fill, review of *Ahab's Wife; or, The Star-Gazer: A Novel*, p. 1988; July, 2003, Brad Hooper, review of *Four Spirits: A Novel*, p. 1846; September 1, 2006, Mary Ellen Quinn, review of *Abundance: A Novel of Marie Antoinette*, p. 57.

Entertainment Weekly, October 8, 1999, review of *Ahab's Wife; or, The Star-Gazer*, p. 66; October 6, 2006, Tina Jordan, review of *Abundance*, p. 74.

Kirkus Reviews, August 1, 2003, review of *Four Spirits*, p. 984; July 1, 2006, review of *Abundance*, p. 652.

Library Journal, October 15, 1989, Marcia Tager, review of *Ice Skating at the North Pole: Stories*, p. 104; September 15, 1993, Barbara Hoffert, review of *Sherlock in Love*, p. 105; September 1, 1999, Starr E. Smith, review of *Ahab's Wife; or, The Star-Gazer*, p. 234; August, 2003, Starr E. Smith, review of *Four Spirits*, p. 133; August 1, 2006, Anna M. Nelson, review of *Abundance*, p. 72.

Nation, December 13, 1999, Tom LeClair, review of *Ahab's Wife; or, The Star-Gazer*, p. 44.

Newsweek, September 27, 1999, Laura Shapiro, review of *Ahab's Wife; or, The Star-Gazer*, p. 67.

New York Times Book Review, November 21, 1993, Tobin Harshaw, review of *Sherlock in Love*, p. 24; October 15, 2006, Liesl Schillinger, review of *Abundance*, p. 15.

People, November 29, 1999, review of *Ahab's Wife; or, The Star-Gazer*, p. 63; November 17, 2003, Annette Gallagher Weisman, review of *Four Spirits*, p. 46; October 30, 2006, Emily Chenoweth, review of *Abundance*, p. 45.

Publishers Weekly, August 25, 1989, Sybil Steinberg, review of *Ice Skating at the North Pole*, p. 58; September 13, 1993, p. 98; March 8, 1999, review of *The Disobedience of Water*, p. 48; August 9, 1999, review of *Ahab's Wife; or, The Star-Gazer*, p. 340; September 27, 1999, Leslie Haynesworth, interview with Sena Jeter Naslund, p. 65; July 14, 2003, review of *Four Spirits*, p. 53; May 29, 2006, review of *Abundance*, p. 32.

School Library Journal, January, 2004, Robert Saunderson, review of *Four Spirits*, p. 164.

Time, October 25, 1999, Pico Iyer, review of *Ahab's Wife; or, The Star-Gazer*, p. 128.

World and I, January, 2000, Linda Simon, review of *Ahab's Wife; or, The Star-Gazer*, p. 260.

ONLINE

Blogcritics.org, http://blogcritics.org/archives/2006/02/01/003222.php (February 1, 2006), G.L. Hauptfleisch, review of *Four Spirits*.

Mostly Fiction, http://www.mostlyfiction.com/ (February 21, 2007), interview with Sena Jeter Naslund.

Sena Jeter Naslund Home Page, http://www.senajeternaslund.com (February 21, 20007).*

* * *

NISSEL, Angela 1974-

PERSONAL: Born 1974, in Philadelphia, PA; daughter of Jack and Gwen (a nurse) Nissel. *Education:* University of Pennsylvania, B.A., 1998.

ADDRESSES: Home—Philadelphia, PA.

CAREER: Writer. Cofounder and site manager of *Okayplayer.com*, 1999—. Previously worked as a temporary receptionist in a law office and at the Internal Revenue Service.

AWARDS, HONORS: Best New Web site, Online Hip-Hop Awards, 2001, for *Okayplayer.com*.

WRITINGS:

MEMOIRS

The Broke Diaries: The Completely True and Hilarious Misadventures of a Good Girl Gone Broke, Villard Books (New York, NY), 2001.
Mixed: My Life in Black and White, Villard Books (New York, NY), 2006.

Also served on the writing staff of the television series *Scrubs,* writer, 2002-04, story editor, 2004-06, and consulting producer, c. 2006—.

ADAPTATIONS: *The Broke Diaries* is being adapted as a sitcom for television.

SIDELIGHTS: According to a *Publishers Weekly* contributor, Angela Nissel's first book, *The Broke Diaries: The Completely True and Hilarious Misadventures of a Good Girl Gone Broke,* calls to mind Helen Fielding's *Bridget Jones's Diary.* But Nissel's work is an autobiography, the reviewer noted, which includes "a series of biting, funny entries" detailing Nissel's everyday struggle to get herself through the medical anthropology program at the University of Pennsylvania on student loans, part-time jobs, and lots of ingenuity.

The daughter of a single mother, Nissel accepted occasional help from her mother, but that did little to defray her financial burden. Nissel decided to create an online diary emphasizing the often humorous situations created by her quest for food and rent money. In her diary she posted entries on everything from crashing funerals for free food to how to stretch your laundry budget (by doing without certain items of clothing). Nissel's Web site eventually became the second most popular online site at the University of Pennsylvania campus, and the author began to shop around for a publisher.

The Broke Diaries, the book Nissel put together from the entries at her Web site, roughly spans the length of her senior year in college. Among the entries is one describing the horror of going to the store to purchase one package of ramen noodles only to find she was two cents short; another describes her first experience at a check-cashing store. "What makes the book special is her biting and often downright bizarre humor in the face of circumstances that would otherwise be anything *but* funny," observed Derek M. Jennings on the *Independent Weekly* Web site. Other critics found Nissel's tales of broke-ness were humorous reminders of their own college days. Jennifer Weiner, writing on the *Philadelphia Inquirer* Web site, remarked that the main audience for *The Broke Diaries* would likely be drawn "from the ranks of the overeducated and underpaid," but added: "It's for anyone who ever scoured the campus for the one washing machine that accepted fake quarters; ducked a call from an irate creditor by feigning illness, absence or death; or accepted a date less for the romance than for the prospect of free food."

With the occurrence of numerous layoffs around the country in 2001, Jennings predicted a new audience for Nissel's book: "They'll buy up this book with their severance pay to get a glimpse at the shape of things to come. Broke people will be the Next Big Thing. Trendy. Respected. Understood. Chic." Jennings added: "And the broke shall inherit the earth."

In her next book, *Mixed: My Life in White and Black,* Nissel tells of her experiences as the child of a white father, who left the family when she was eight, and a black mother. Brought up by her mother, who was once a member of the radical Black Panthers and later became a nurse, Nissel relates her difficulties coming to terms with her situation as she spends time with both her black and white extended families, but not feeling like she really belonged either one. The author also writes of her time at college and short stint as an exotic dancer. Noting the author's "candor," Alyssa Lee also wrote in *Entertainment Weekly* that the Nissel tells a story "that's as poignant as it is painfully funny." Several other critics also commented on Nissel's ability to look on the humorous side of her life. For example, a *Publishers Weekly* contributor noted that "Nissel's writing is very funny and very sharp." Brad Hooper, writing in *Booklist,* called *Mixed* "a touching, intimate testimonial."

BIOGRAPHICAL AND CRITICAL SOURCES:

BOOKS

Newsmakers, Issue 4, Thomson Gale (Detroit, MI), 2006.
Nissel, Angela, *The Broke Diaries: The Completely True and Hilarious Misadventures of a Good Girl Gone Broke,* Villard Books (New York, NY), 2001.

Nissel, Angela, *Mixed: My Life in Black and White,* Villard Books (New York, NY), 2006.

PERIODICALS

Booklist, February 1, 2006, Brad Hooper, review of *Mixed,* p. 22.

Entertainment Weekly, February 24, 2006, Allyssa Lee, review of *Mixed,* p. 67.

Kirkus Reviews, January 15, 2006, review of *Mixed,* p. 76.

Publishers Weekly, January 22, 2001, review of *The Broke Diaries,* p. 309; January 30, 2006, review of *Mixed,* p. 57.

School Library Journal, June, 2006, Shannon Seglin, review of *Mixed,* p. 194.

ONLINE

Angela Nissel Home Page, http://www.angelanissel.com (April 16, 2007).

Independent Weekly Online, http://www.indyweek.com/ (April 11, 2001), Derek M. Jennings, "The Broke Column."

Philadelphia Inquirer Online, http://www.philly.com/ (May 9, 2001), Jennifer Weiner, "College Tales of a Lone Grit, and True Grit."

USA Today Online, http://www.usatoday.com/ (June 18, 2001), Tara McKelvey, "Dear Diary: Ramen Noodles Rule!"*

O

OATLEY, Keith 1939-

PERSONAL: Born March 16, 1939, in London, England; son of Harold and Winifred Oatley; married Sally Gass, June 9, 1961; children: Simon, Grant. *Education:* Clare College, Cambridge, B.A., 1961; University College, London, Ph.D., 1965; also studied at Imperial College, London, 1964-65.

ADDRESSES: Home—Brighton, England. *Office*—Department of Human Development and Applied Psychology, University of Toronto, 252 Bloor St. W., HDAP, Toronto M5S 1V6, Canada. *E-mail*—keith. oatley@utoronto.ca; koatley@oise.utoronto.ca.

CAREER: Psychologist, educator, and writer. National Physical Laboratory, Teddington, Middlesex, England, senior scientific officer, 1965-66; University of Sussex, Brighton, England, lecturer in experimental psychology, beginning 1967-86; University of Toronto, Canada, associate professor in the Department of Psychology, 1971-72 and 1977-78, professor of applied cognitive psychology, 1991—, chair of the Department of Human Development and Applied Psychology, 1999-2002; University of Glasgow, Scotland, professor of cognitive psychology, 1986-90. Also served in the Committee of Mathematical Biology, University of Chicago, and Department of Psychology, University of Toronto.

MEMBER: Experimental Psychology Society, Royal Society of Canada (fellow), British Psychological Society (fellow), International Society for Research on Emotions (president, 1992-96).

AWARDS, HONORS: Commonwealth Writer's Prize, best first book, 1994, for *The Case of Emily V.*

WRITINGS:

NONFICTION

Brain Mechanisms and Mind, Dutton (New York, NY), 1972.

Perceptions and Representations: The Theoretical Bases of Brain Research and Psychology, Methuen (London, England), 1978.

Selves in Relation: An Introduction to Psychotherapy and Groups, Methuen (London, England), 1984.

Best Laid Schemes: The Psychology of Emotions, Cambridge University Press (New York, NY), 1992.

(With Jennifer M. Jenkins) *Understanding Emotions,* Blackwell (Cambridge, MA), 1996, 2nd revised edition (with Jenkins and Dacher Kelter), 2006.

(Editor, with Jennifer M. Jenkins and Nancy L. Stein) *Human Emotions: A Reader,* Blackwell (Cambridge, MA), 1998.

Emotions: A Brief History, Blackwell (Malden, MA), 2004.

Contributor to psychology journals and to *Nature, Animal Behavior,* and *Medical and Biological Engineering.* Also series editor for Cambridge University Press Series *"Studies of Emotion and Social Interaction."*

NOVELS

The Case of Emily V., Secker & Warburg (London, England), 1993.

Natural History, Viking (New York, NY), 1998.

SIDELIGHTS: Trained as a psychotherapist and interested in wide range of associated research, including physiological psychology, visual perception, and epidemiological psychiatry, Keith Oatley has also written widely about science in both nonfiction and fiction formats. Among his nonfiction books is *Best Laid Schemes: The Psychology of Emotions,* which focuses on how emotions function within the human cognitive systems. Referring to the book as "distinctive, important and enjoyable," *British Journal of Psychology* contributor Fraser Watts also wrote: "The material treated in this book is sufficiently broad and unusual to be controversial, though personally I find it welcome and refreshing." Oatley also coauthored with Jennifer M. Jenkins the book *Understanding Emotions,* as well as the second, revised edition with Jenkins and Dacher Kelter. The book focuses on modern understanding of human emotions based on current scientific theory and empirical research. The authors discuss such aspects of emotion as emotional development in childhood, how emotions affect people individually, and mental health both in childhood and adulthood. The book also includes lists of supplemental readings.

In his first novel *The Case of Emily V.,* Oatley presents a mystery featuring a collaboration between the great fictional detective Sherlock Holmes and the founding father of psychiatry Sigmund Freud. The story is told by Holmes, Dr. Watson, and Freud's patient Emily V. and revealed through a series of documents that are footnoted by a modern-day psychologist. The case revolves around Emily's belief that she killed her abusive guardian. Writing in the *Library Journal,* Jo Ann Vicarel commented that the author's "Victorian-style prose reflects that era." Most critics had high praise for Oatley's debut novel. Referring to *The Case of Emily V.* as "subtle and insightful," a *Publishers Weekly* contributor also wrote that the author's "rendition of the Baker Street duo will be a pleasant surprise." Writing on the *Kevin's Corner* Blog, Kevin R. Tipple commented that the author "provide[s] the reader an excellent mystery of depth and substance."

Natural History is an historical novel about the battle to stop the spread of cholera. Oatley tells the story of physician John Leggate's attempts to track the disease's spread in hopes of finding a way to prove his theories and prevent another epidemic. In the process, he meets and falls in love with musician Marian Brooks, which complicates his scientific efforts because the local newspaper editor is also in love with Marian and writes scathing reports decrying John's research. A *Resource Links* contributor noted that *Natural History* "engrosses and informs a reader all at the same time." Writing on the *Bookloons* Web site, Sally Selvadurai commented: "Enjoy it for an entertaining look at nineteenth century English society: its attitudes and mores, the complexities of romance, and a window into the world of medicine."

BIOGRAPHICAL AND CRITICAL SOURCES:

PERIODICALS

British Journal of Psychology, August, 1994, Fraser Watts, review of *Best Laid Schemes: The Psychology of Emotions,* p. 438.
Library Journal, October 1, 2006, Jo Ann Vicarel, review of *The Case of Emily V.,* p. 52.
Publishers Weekly, September 11, 2006, review of *The Case of Emily V.,* p. 37.
Reference & Research Book News, November, 2006, review of *Understanding Emotions.*
Resource Links, June, 1997, review of *The Case of Emily V.,* p. 235; October, 2000, review of *Natural History,* p. 49.

ONLINE

BookLoons, http://www.bookloons.com/ (April 16, 2007), Sally Selvadurai, review of *A Natural History.*
Keith Oatley Home Page, http://hdap.oise.utoronto.ca/oatley/index.htm (April 16, 2007).
Kevin's Corner Blog, http://www.hollywoodcomics.com/~kevin/index.html/ (September 3, 2006), Kevin R. Tipple, review of *The Case of Emily V.*
University of Toronto Human Development and Applied Psychology Web site, http://hdap.oise.utoronto.ca/ (April 16, 2007), author's faculty Home Page.*

*　　*　　*

ØKLAND, Einar 1940-
(Einar Andreas Økland, Einar Okland)

PERSONAL: Born January 17, 1940, in Valestrand (some sources cite Sveio), Norway; son of Bernt Martin and Sigrun Økland; married Liv Marit Nordbö, July 13, 1963; children: Siri, Ask. *Ethnicity:* "Caucasian." *Education:* University of Oslo, Ph.D., 1965.

ADDRESSES: Home and office—Valevåg, Norway; fax: +47-5374-2413.

CAREER: Rönvik Psyk., Bodö, Norway, clinical psychologist, 1965-66; University of Oslo, Oslo, Norway, teacher of psychology, 1966; freelance writer, Valevaag, Norway, 1967—. Det Norske Samlaget (Oslo, Norway), publisher's head advisor, 1985—.

AWARDS, HONORS: Grants from Norwegian Ministry of Culture and Norwegian Society of Authors; awards for children's books; Norwegian Society of Literary Critics' Prize, 1978; Ascheoug Prize, 1988; Dobloug Prize, 2000; Samlags prisen, 2000; Kari Skjönsbergs pris, 2006.

WRITINGS:

Ein gul dag (poetry), Cappelen (Oslo, Norway), 1963.
Mandragora (poetry), Samlaget (Oslo, Norway), 1966.
Svart i det grøne (short stories), Samlaget (Oslo, Norway), 1967.
Vandreduene: Lyriske stykke, Samlaget (Oslo, Norway), 1968.
(With Dag Solstad) *Georg: Sit du Godt?,* Samlaget (Oslo, Norway), 1968.
(Editor, with Paal-Helge Haugen and Tor Obrestad) *Moderne prosa: Arbeidsbok frå eit litteraturseminar,* Samlaget (Oslo, Norway), 1968.
Amatør-album: Lyrisk landskaps roman med figurar (novel; title means "An Amateur's Album"), Samlaget (Oslo, Norway), 1969.
Aberfan, Samlaget (Oslo, Norway), 1969.
Galskap: Underholdningsroman (novel; title means "Madness"), Samlaget (Oslo, Norway), 1971.
Gull-alder: Lyrikk—prosa—dramatikk (novel; title means "A Golden Age"), Samlaget (Oslo, Norway), 1972.
Stille stunder: Manns gaman, Samlaget (Oslo, Norway), 1974.
Det blir alvor (short stories), illustrated by Kari Bøge, Samlaget (Oslo, Norway), 1974.
Bronsehesten: Folkeminne (poetry; title means "The Bronze Horse"), Samlaget (Oslo, Norway), 1975.
(Editor, with Olav Angell and Jan Erik Vold) *Jazz i Norge,* Gyldendal (Oslo, Norway), 1975.
Kven veit? Seint i April, tidleg i mai: Forteljing, illustrated by Kari Bøge, Samlaget (Oslo, Norway), 1976.

Statsministerens sko, og andre tekster, Norske bokklubben (Oslo, Norway), 1976.
Ingenting meir, illustrated by Finn Graff, Pax (Oslo, Norway), 1976.
Snakk med dr. Ost, illustrated by Kari Bøge, Samlaget (Oslo, Norway), 1977.
På frifot: Blanda vers (poetry), illustrated by Oddvar Torsheim, Gyldendal (Oslo, Norway), 1978.
Romantikk: Folkeminne (poetry; title means "Nostalgia"), Samlaget (Oslo, Norway), 1979.
Skrive frukter: Epistlar, artiklar, småstykke frå norsk litteratur, 1963-1978 (essays; title means "Fruits of Writing"), Gyldendal (Oslo, Norway), 1979.
Ein god dag (juvenile), illustrated by Wenche Øyen, Samlaget (Oslo, Norway), 1979.
Ei ny tid (juvenile), illustrated by Wenche Øyen, Samlaget (Oslo, Norway), 1981.
(Editor) *Høydepunkt* (juvenile), Volume 1: *Egne tekster utvalgt og kommentart av 34 norske forfattere,* Tiden (Oslo, Norway), 1981.
Fra Aksel Sandemose til Sigurd Evensmo, Gyldendal (Oslo, Norway), 1981.
Snøsteinen, Samlaget (Oslo, Norway), 1982.
Nå igjen: Artiklar, comentariar, innlegg, intervju o.a. (essays; title means "Once More"), Samlaget (Oslo, Norway), 1982.
Egg til alle (juvenile), illustrated by Jonj Stroem, Aschehoug (Oslo, Norway), 1982.
Her er ingen papegøye: Ei sann historie frå Bergen, illustrated by Bernard Stoltz, Samlaget (Oslo, Norway), 1984.
Blå roser: Folkeminne (poetry; title means "Blue Roses"), Samlaget (Oslo, Norway), 1985.
Mellom himmel og jord: Vers vrette og vrange, illustrated by Bernard Stoltz, Samlaget (Oslo, Norway), 1986.
(With Jorunn Veiteberg) *Reklamebildet: Norske annonsar og plakatar frå århundreskriftet til i dag,* Samlaget (Oslo, Norway), 1986.
Walkman: Tolv dagar musikk, illustrated by Wenche Øyen, Samlaget (Oslo, Norway), 1986.
Mange års røynsle med pil og boge: 99 dikt (poetry), with recording of readings by the author, Samlaget (Oslo, Norway), 1988.
Brev merke på norsk post: Eit utval av reklamemerke, julemerke, propaganda, utstillingsmerke o.a., Samlaget (Oslo, Norway), 1988.
Måne over Valestrand: Essays og epistlar, Samlaget (Oslo, Norway), 1989.
Per Krohg som illustratør: Eit utval henta frå bøker, tidsskrift, plakatar, annonsar, notar, postkort o.a., Samlaget (Oslo, Norway), 1989.

Når ikkje anna er sagt: Folkeminne (poetry), illustrated by Bernard Stoltz, Samlaget (Oslo, Norway), 1991.

Siste time: Ni ulike historier, Samlaget (Oslo, Norway), 1992.

I staden for roman eller humor: Essay, artiklar, epistlar, Samlaget (Oslo, Norway), 1993.

Dikt i samling, 1963-1993 (poetry), Samlaget (Oslo, Norway), 1993.

Heile tida heile tida (poetry), Samlaget (Oslo, Norway), 1994.

(Editor and author of foreword) *Elias Blix' beste,* Samlaget (Oslo, Norway), 1995.

Norske bokomslag, 1880-1980, Samlaget (Oslo, Norway), 1996.

Frå helling via hylling til halling: Essay, artiklar, epistlar, Samlaget (Oslo, Norway), 1997.

Suarte norske (poetry), Samlaget (Oslo, Norway), 1997.

Etter Brancusi: Nye dikt (poetry), Samlaget (Oslo, Norway), 1999.

(With Holger Koefoed) *Th. Kittelsen: Kjente og ukjente sider ved kunstneren,* Stenersen (Oslo, Norway), 1999.

I tilfelle nokon spør (essays, articles, letters, and other prose), Samlaget (Oslo, Norway), 2001.

Poetiske gleder (poetry), Samlaget (Oslo, Norway), 2003.

Den blanke bjølla (short stories), Samlaget (Oslo, Norway), 2005.

Krattet på badet (poetry), Samlaget (Oslo, Norway), 2006.

Other writings include *Du er så rar,* 1973; *Den blå ringen,* 1975; *Slik er det,* 1975; *Sikk-sakk,* 1978; and *Dikt i utval,* 2002. Work represented in anthologies. Contributor to periodicals. Affiliated with the periodical *Profil* in the 1960s and with the literary journal *Basar.*

SIDELIGHTS: Einar Økland once told *CA:* "Because I have never divorced, never driven a car, never practiced any form of sport or gymnastics, I have lived a healthy and successful life with plenty of peace and quiet here on my small farm on the western coast of Norway and [in] a lot of travels in Norway and abroad. I consider myself a poet. My lifelong interests—apart from family, friends, and books—are fishing, cooking, jazz music, and graphic arts. I struggle to keep my amateur status whatsoever I do."

More recently he added: "My father died when I was seven and I felt lonely, alienated, and miserable for many years afterward. But I was already a passionate

reader by then and expanded my reading whenever possible. Much of my motivation for writing stems from these circumstances. Among my recognizable influences I dare mention ordinary people's way of talking, the Bible, the poetry of William Butler Yeats, Berthold Brecht, Pablo Neruda, H. Martinson.

"My writing process: spontaneity first, then storing, inspection, editing, and rewriting. Most of my writing has been done between breakfast and lunch.

"A lot of my inspirations come from being asked to write a contribution for a magazine, a yearbook, an anthology, or a special occasion. I love to honor unexpected, crazy requests that should not have been made. When choosing my own subjects I do so with minimal insight and with no other motivating force than curiosity or longing.

"In 1968 I discovered that I did not want to be self-centered and to 'express myself,' so I stopped that—and still my writings could be personal and engaging. I prefer nonfiction to fiction, and in 1974 I wrote my last novel. Those are the most prominent changes to my writings. I never sought to find my own style or my own voice. Instead of narrowing my approach I always liked to fan out in different forms, formats, themes, moods. I go for variations and differences in my writing because I consider both my readers and myself to be basically rich and multi-faceted."

BIOGRAPHICAL AND CRITICAL SOURCES:

BOOKS

Karlsen, Ole, editor, *Ein orm i eit auge: Om Einar Økland's forfatterskap,* Cappelen Aladémisk Forlag (Oslo, Norway), 1997.

Tusvik, Sverre, and Guri Vesaas, editors, *Einar Økland 50,* Samlaget (Oslo, Norway), 1990.

*   *   *

OKLAND, Einar
See ØKLAND, Einar

*   *   *

ØKLAND, Einar Andreas
See ØKLAND, Einar

O'SHEA, Stephen

PERSONAL: Born in Toronto, Ontario, Canada.

ADDRESSES: Home—Providence, RI.

CAREER: Writer, journalist, translator, and historian. Paris correspondent for periodicals, including *Variety, Elle,* and *Interview.*

WRITINGS:

Back to the Front: An Accidental Historian Walks the Trenches of World War I, Douglas & McIntyre (Vancouver, British Columbia, Canada), 1996, Walker and Co. (New York, NY), 1997.

The Perfect Heresy: The Revolutionary Life and Death of the Medieval Cathars, Walker and Co. (New York, NY), 2000.

Sea of Faith: The Shared Story of Christianity and Islam in the Medieval Mediterranean World, Walker and Co. (New York, NY), 2006, published as *Sea of Faith: Islam and Christianity in the Medieval Mediterranean World,* Douglas & McIntyre (Vancouver, British Columbia, Canada), 2006.

SIDELIGHTS: Stephen O'Shea's *Back to the Front: An Accidental Historian Walks the Trenches of World War I* was inspired by his 1985 winter hike across one of the bloodiest battlefields of World War I, a conflict that lasted four years and left ten million dead. "This is not military history," noted Susan Adams in *Forbes.* "Rather, it is the past as seen through the eyes of a curious traveler, refreshingly aware of his failings and the irony of his surroundings. . . . This is a great read."

Paris-based journalist O'Shea found the earth of World War I's Western Front still marked by a continuing line of trenches and was amazed to find rusting bullets, unexploded shells, and disintegrating gas masks littering the landscape. Beginning the next summer, he walked the length of the front, 450 miles from Belgium's North Sea coast to the border of France and Switzerland. He visited the Langemarck cemetery near Ypres, Belgium, where 44,000 Germans are buried, many of them not-yet-fully trained student volunteers who were mowed down by British machine guns. O'Shea observed the museums, monuments, burial grounds, and vaults that contained the bones of the dead as he walked from village to village. Over the next ten years, O'Shea also read all the literature that pertained to the war and considered the role of his own family members in the conflict. His Irish grandfathers fought for the British, and he lost two great-uncles.

Library Journal contributor Mark E. Ellis commented that "what does emerge from his narrative is a shocking description of what happened on the battlefields." O'Shea writes that generals who lost up to 100,000 men in one month began new offensives the next month, using the same tactics. He also writes of the individual battles, notably in Verdun, Somme, and Argonne. "What is most compelling about his re-creations of the great battles is the way he interweaves them with the landscape of today," noted John Bemrose in *Maclean's.* "Everywhere he looks, O'Shea discovers absurdity, as though the assembly-line slaughter had undermined the meaningfulness of human life right down to the present." *Booklist* critic Gilbert Taylor wrote: "With this ambulant meditation and protest against militarism, O'Shea has created a high-stature addition to the classic works about the Great War." A *Publishers Weekly* contributor noted that O'Shea "displays a poet's gift of description and a sorrowful, contemplative pacifism in expressing the horror and futility of the Great War."

In writing *The Perfect Heresy: The Revolutionary Life and Death of the Medieval Cathars,* O'Shea spent two years in the south of France researching the rise and fall of the heretical group founded in the twelfth century and whose members were slaughtered by the Church. He begins in Albi, at the imposing cathedral built of red stone by Bishop Bernard de Castanet, one of the officials of the Catholic Church who had seen their power threatened by Catharism, a medieval variation of Gnostic Christianity. Loren Rosson III wrote in the *Library Journal* that "at times, the book reads like a historical novel." *History* contributor John E. Weakland considered why this book, "not designed to replace scholarly works," was necessary. He concluded that "the answer lies in the brilliant narrative of O'Shea, whose gripping tale is filled with a cast of truly memorable heroes and villains who are introduced to the reader in a series of biographical sketches at the beginning of the book."

"Who were these Cathars who inspired such fanatical cruelty?" wondered Joshua Levin in *Forbes.* "Not much of a menace to anyone, really. The Cathar faith stemmed from the same paradox that fuels every dualistic gnostic heresy, to wit: If God is so good, how come the world is so crummy? The Cathars' theological solution made the body and all the material world the Devil's dominion, while leaving the human spirit and Heaven in God's hands."

The geographical base of the French Cathars was what is now Languedoc, but the Cathars could also be found in Germany and Italy. They practiced vegetarianism and believed in tolerance, pacifism, and gender equality. Their spiritual leaders, called the Perfect, drew followers from the Catholic Church, which the Cathars said represented a false religion. Because of their beliefs, they shunned material goods. They also rejected the sacraments, the concept of hell, and the account of Christ's crucifixion. During this period, the aristocracy of Northern Europe lived luxuriously. Popes begged the noblemen of the region to remove the heretics, to no avail, and St. Dominic was sent on a preaching tour. The turning point came when papal legate Peter of Castelnau was killed by a henchman of the Count of Toulouse. The abbott Arnauld Amaury led an army of some 40,000 knights and soldiers down the Rhône Valley in 1209, to stop first at Béziers, where the entire town of 20,000 people was slaughtered, including faithful Catholics and a newborn baby. Amaury is credited with having said: "Kill them all. God will recognize his own." Thus began the Albigensian crusade, during which the heretics were murdered, often by being burned alive.

This continued for half a century, during which time the Inquisition was established by Pope Innocent III to find and kill any remaining Cathars who might have been missed. A *Publishers Weekly* contributor noted that O'Shea suggests that this "enabled the expansion of the French monarchy into the formerly independent region of Languedoc and created the first modern police state." *Spectator* writer Susan Lowry stated that "this was a Christian jihad waged against Christians, a horrific spin-off from the better-known but even more gruesome Crusades to "liberate" the Holy Land, still celebrated as glorious exploits in children's picture books."

Wendy Orent reviewed *The Perfect Heresy* in the *Guardian,* noting that "in the nineteenth century, the subject drew writers—many of them cranks—attracted to the story of the faith's demise." Among these was Napoleon Peyrat, anticlerical liberal and talented fabulist, whose 1870s account, although largely fabricated, still is accepted as truth in some circles. "His Cathars were

heroic, the forefathers of progress in the darkness of Catholic totalitarianism," wrote Orent. "His heretics hoarded an immense treasure—spiritual and material—at Montsegur, and managed, before their incineration, to hide it in the foothills of the Pyrenees. And Esclarmonde of Foix, a high-born Cathar Perfect who may have debated with St. Dominic, was transformed, in Peyrat's narrative, into an Occitan Joan of Arc, a virginal high priestess."

Peyrat's interpretations were incorporated into French fable, literature, fantasy, and occult belief. Following World War I, the myths of the Cathars spread beyond France, and Languedoc became the subject of the writings of many, including Simone Weil, who wrote as Emile Novis and considered the site to be a moral utopia, and Maurice Magre, who in the 1920s and 1930s wrote two Cathar novels in which he rewrote Peyrat's version of history, portraying the Perfect as Buddhists.

In 1930, Magre met German student Otto Rahn in Paris and then introduced him to his associates in the Pyrenees. Rahn wrote *Crusade against the Grail* in 1933, in which he portrayed the Cathars as pagans and the guardian of the Grail as the feminine Esclarmonde of Foix. Rahn returned to Germany, joined the SS, and published *The Court of Lucifer.* Following World War II, the Nazis and Cathars were linked by former Vichy collaborators who said that Hitler was part of the Cathar secret society. The story was adapted as the plots of the "Indiana Jones" films, beginning with *Raiders of the Lost Ark.*

During the 1960s, the Pyrenees became home to a variety of groups, including Dutch Rosicrucians, Belgian neo-gnostics, and French hippies. The area was visited by archeologists, neo-pagans, and the curious, and became the subject of books, both fiction and nonfiction, including *The Holy Blood and The Holy Grail,* by Michael Baigent, Richard Leigh, and Henry Lincoln. "The trio made Catharism a mass phenomenon and turned the international Glastonbury Arthurian followers on to a new medieval romance," noted Orent. "The writers took the legacy of Magre, Roche, and others and wrote a thoroughly entertaining occult detective story, marketed, however, as nonfiction." This fictional account tells that a priest found the treasure, sold some of it, and blackmailed the Vatican. The plot also puts forth the idea that Jesus was a king who married Mary Magdalene.

Orent noted that the commercialization of the Cathars has extended to businesses in the region, including real estate, restaurants, and wineries, and that there are more than 5,000 Web sites that benefit from the Cathar name. Orent wrote that "the medieval heresy, which the Catholic Church thought it had so successfully quelled, has, thanks to fabulists, cranks, wishful thinkers, and romantics, proved remarkably enduring."

J.L. Nelson wrote in the *London Review of Books* that "O'Shea devastatingly exposes the political interests of the Crusaders, the recurrent manifestations of their hypocrisy, the acts of horrific violence perpetrated on fellow Christians as well as on heretics." *Booklist* reviewer Margaret Flanagan called *The Perfect Heresy* "a riveting chronicle of a shameful episode in medieval church history."

Lowry stated that O'Shea "writes with the enthusiasm and immediacy of a contemporary chronicler, with the occasional, rather startling use of modern slang: at one point Innocent III makes 'an historic flip-flop'; Mary Magdalene 'was never associated with Lady Luck.' O'Shea even contrives to have some fun. . . . By contrast, his accounts of battles, massacres, and burnings are starkly moving. The book is unputdownable." Lowry continued: "The Crusade is placed squarely in its wider historical context: the author believes that, far from being an aberration or footnote to the general awfulness of the Middle Ages, it marked an important turning point, a crossroads." In a *Washington Post Book World* review, Rene Weis called O'Shea "a graceful and passionate writer."

In *Sea of Faith: The Shared Story of Christianity and Islam in the Medieval Mediterranean World,* O'Shea carefully explores the tumultuous history of Christian and Muslim coexistence in the Mediterranean. In a narrative that covers more than a thousand years, O'Shea looks at how the two religious groups have fought fiercely between themselves, but also lived in peace for long periods of time. The author considers seven major battles between Muslims and Christians, discusses the significance and repercussions of each, and reflects on how each battle helped shape the spiritual and religious fiber of the post-Crusades world. In addition to his coverage of warfare and conflict, he also describes several periods of convivencia, described by a *Kirkus Reviews* contributor as "the practice of Muslims and Christians living together in harmony," during which commerce and culture thrived. O'Shea adds a modern element to his story via firsthand descriptions of the current state of ancient battlegrounds, as well as buildings, towns, and other structures.

"O'Shea's marvelous accomplishment offers an unparalleled glimpse of the struggles of each religion to establish dominance in the medieval world," as well as the means of cooperation they established while coexisting within the same territory, noted a *Publishers Weekly* reviewer. Mick Herron, writing in *Geographical,* named *Sea of Faith* an "important, intelligent, absorbingly well-written account" of the history of Islamic and Christian life in the ancient Mediterranean region. The book is a "gripping account of Christianity and Islam's last tortured millennium of combat and coexistence," noted the *Kirkus Reviews* contributor. Anthony Elia, writing in the *Library Journal,* called O'Shea's book "well written" and "a rich chronicle of historical detail, military confrontation, and political machinations."

BIOGRAPHICAL AND CRITICAL SOURCES:

PERIODICALS

Booklist, May 15, 1997, Gilbert Taylor, review of *Back to the Front: An Accidental Historian Walks the Trenches of World War I,* p. 1560; August, 2000, Margaret Flanagan, review of *The Perfect Heresy: The Revolutionary Life and Death of the Medieval Cathars,* p. 2082.

California Bookwatch, February, 2007, review of *Sea of Faith: The Shared Story of Christianity and Islam in the Medieval Mediterranean World.*

Forbes, October 20, 1997, Susan Adams, review of *Back to the Front,* p. 324; June 12, 2000, Joshua Levine, review of *The Perfect Heresy,* p. 442.

Geographical, September, 2006, Mick Herron, "Sibling Rivalry Writ Large on the Shores of the Medieval Mediterranean," review of *Sea of Faith,* p. 91.

Guardian (London, England), October 7, 2000, Wendy Orent, review of *The Perfect Heresy,* p. 1.

History, fall, 2000, John E. Weakland, review of *The Perfect Heresy,* p. 35.

Kirkus Reviews, April 15, 2006, review of *Sea of Faith,* p. 396.

Library Journal, May 15, 1997, Mark E. Ellis, review of *Back to the Front,* p. 86; August, 2000, Loren Rosson III, review of *The Perfect Heresy,* p. 112; June 1, 2006, Anthony Elia, review of *Sea of Faith,* p. 126.

London Review of Books, June 7, 2001, J.L. Nelson, review of *The Perfect Heresy,* p. 28.

Maclean's, February 10, 1997, John Bemrose, review of *Back to the Front,* p. 59.

New Yorker, August 6, 2001, Joan Acocella, review of *The Perfect Heresy,* p. 82.

New York Times, October 23, 2000, Richard Bernstein, review of *The Perfect Heresy,* p. B7.

Publishers Weekly, May 12, 1997, review of *Back to the Front,* p. 70; July 31, 2000, review of *The Perfect Heresy,* p. 85; January 23, 2006, review of *Sea of Faith,* p. 119; April 10, 2006, review of *Sea of Faith,* p. 67.

Reference & Research Book News, November, 2006, review of *Sea of Faith.*

Spectator, December 16, 2000, Suzanne Lowry, review of *The Perfect Heresy,* p. 79.

Times Literary Supplement, February 9, 2001, R.I. Moore, review of *The Perfect Heresy,* p. 10.

Washington Post Book World, August 26, 2001, Rene Weis, review of *The Perfect Heresy,* p. T08.*

P

PEARL, Esther Elizabeth
See RITZ, David

*   *   *

PÉREZ-GÓMEZ, Alberto 1949-
(Alberto Perez Gomez, Alberto Perez-Gomez)

PERSONAL: Born December 24, 1949, in Mexico City, Mexico; son of Jorge (an aeronautical engineer) and Angela Pérez; children: Alejandra, Beatriz. *Ethnicity:* "Hispanic." *Education:* Instituto Politécnico Nacional de México, diploma (architectural theory), 1970; National Polytechnic Institute of Mexico, diploma (architectural engineering; with honors), 1971; Cornell University, diploma (urban development and history of architecture), 1972; University of Essex, M.A., 1975, Ph.D., 1979.

ADDRESSES: Office—School of Architecture, Macdonald-Harrington Bldg., McGill University, 815 Sherbrooke St. W., Montreal, Quebec H3A 2K6, Canada; fax: 514-398-7372. *E-mail*—alberto.perez-gomez@mcgill.ca.

CAREER: Instituto Politécnico Nacional, Mexico City, Mexico, lecturer in vocational education, 1969-71, lecturer in architecture, 1972-73; Architectural Association School of Architecture, London, England, instructor in design, 1975-77; University of Toronto, Toronto, Ontario, Canada, lecturer, 1977-78, assistant professor of architecture, 1978-79; Syracuse University, Syracuse, NY, assistant professor, 1979-80, associate professor of architecture, 1980-81; University of Houston, Houston, TX, associate professor of architecture, 1981-83; Carleton University, Ottawa, Ontario, associate professor of architecture and director of School of Architecture, 1983-86; McGill University, Montreal, Quebec, Canada, visiting professor, 1986, Saidye Rosner Bronfman Professor of the History of Architecture, 1987—. Universidad Anáhuac, part-time lecturer, 1972-73; Polytechnic of Central London, instructor, 1976-77; University of Essex, lecturer, 1977; frequent visiting lecturer at universities and colleges in the United States, Canada, Mexico, and Western Europe. Member of Canadian Commonwealth Scholarship and Fellowship Committee, 1986-88; Canadian Centre for Architecture, member of advisory board, 1986—; Institut de Recherche en Histoire de l'Architecture, director, 1990-93; *Journal of Architectural Education,* member of editorial board.

MEMBER: Mexican Academy of Architecture (fellow), Sociedad de Arquitectos Mexicanos, Asociación de Ingenieros Arquitectos del Estado de México, Royal Architectural Institute of Canada.

AWARDS, HONORS: Alice Davies Hitchcock Book Award, Society of Architectural Historians, 1983, for *Architecture and the Crisis of Modern Science.*

WRITINGS:

Eclosion (poetry; title means "Blooming"), privately printed (Mexico), 1967.
Iber (prose poem), privately printed (Mexico), 1968.
Le teoria de la arquitectura (title means "The Theory of Architecture"), Instituto Politécnico Nacional (Mexico City, Mexico), 1969.

La genesis y superación del funcionalismo en arquitectura (title means "The Origins and Limitations of Functionalism in Architecture"), Limusa-Wiley (Mexico City, Mexico), 1980.

Architecture and the Crisis of Modern Science, MIT Press (Cambridge, MA), 1983.

Polyphilo; or, the Dark Forest Revisited: An Erotic Epiphany of Architecture, MIT Press (Cambridge, MA), 1992.

(Editor, with Louise Pelletier) *Architecture, Ethics and Technology,* McGill-Queen's University Press (Montreal, Quebec, Canada), 1994.

(With Louse Pelletier) *Anamorphosis: An Annotated Bibliography with Special References to Architectural Representation,* McGill-Queen's University Press (Montreal, Quebec, Canada), 1995.

Architectural Representation and The Perspective Hinge, MIT Press (Cambridge, MA), 1997.

(Editor, with Ulrich Franzen and Kim Shkapich) *Education of an Architect: A Point of View, the Cooper Union School of Art and Architecture,* Monacelli Press (New York, NY), 1999.

Built upon Love: Architectural Longing after Ethics and Aesthetics, MIT Press (Cambridge, MA), 2006.

Author of introduction, *Ordonnance for the Five Kinds of Columns after the Method of the Ancients,* by Claude Perrault, University of Chicago Press, 1990. Series editor (with Stephen Parcell), *"CHORA: Intervals in the Philosophy of Architecture,"* McGill-Queen's University Press, 1994-2004. Contributor of articles and reviews to architecture journals and newspapers, including *Fifth Column, Modernity and Popular Culture,* and *Urban Design and Preservation Quarterly.*

Some of Pérez-Gómez's writings were translated into French and (without authorization) Korean.

SIDELIGHTS: Alberto Pérez-Gómez once told *CA:* "My current focus is on the nature of architectural theory and its history, the problem of the city as urban stage and its modern deterioration, and issues concerning theoretical projects in architecture. Particularly crucial is the understanding of architecture in relation to contemporary art and philosophy and to the problems of modern culture at large."

BIOGRAPHICAL AND CRITICAL SOURCES:

PERIODICALS

Times Literary Supplement, August 3, 1984, review of *Architecture and the Crisis of Modern Science,* p. 876.

PEREZ-GOMEZ, Alberto
See PÉREZ-GÓMEZ, Alberto

* * *

PETERSON, Merrill D. 1921-
(Merrill Daniel Peterson)

PERSONAL: Born March 31, 1921, in Manhattan, KS; son of William Oscar (a minister) and Alice Peterson; married Jean Humphrey, May 24, 1944 (deceased, 1995); children: Jeffrey, Kent. *Education:* Attended Kansas State College (now University), 1939-41; University of Kansas, A.B., 1943; Harvard University, Ph.D., 1950. *Hobbies and other interests:* American painting (both historical and contemporary) and wood engraving; photography.

ADDRESSES: Home—Charlottesville, VA.

CAREER: Historian, educator, and writer. Brandeis University, Waltham, MA, 1949-55, began as instructor, became assistant professor; Princeton University, NJ, assistant professor and Bicentennial Preceptor in History, 1955-58; Brandeis University, 1958-62, began as associate professor, became professor of history and chairman of School of Social Science; University of Virginia, Charlottesville, Thomas Jefferson Foundation Professor of History, 1962-87, professor emeritus, 1987—, chairman of department, 1966-72, dean of faculty, 1981-85; Mary Ball Washington Professor of American History, University College Dublin, 1988-89. Poynter fellow, Indiana University, 1975; lecturer at Mercer University, 1975, Salzburg Seminar in American Studies, 1975, Louisiana State University, Fleming Lectures, 1980. Chairperson and executive director of Thomas Jefferson Commemoration Commission, 1993-94. *Military service:* U.S. Navy, 1943-46; became lieutenant junior grade.

MEMBER: American Academy of Arts and Sciences (fellow), American Historical Association, Society of American Historians (fellow), American Antiquarian Society, Virginia Historical Society, Massachusetts Historical Society, Phi Beta Kappa.

AWARDS, HONORS: Bancroft Prize, Columbia University, and Gold Medal of the Jefferson Memorial Association, both 1960, both for *The Jefferson Image in* the American Mind; Guggenheim fellowship, 1962-63; Center for Advanced Study in the Behavioral Sciences fellowship, 1968-69; L.H.D., Washington College, 1976; National Endowment for the Humanities fellow and National Humanities Center fellow, both 1980-81; L.D., Marietta College, 1982; Phi Beta Kappa Book Award, 1994; Virginia Foundation for Humanities 20th Anniversary Award, 1994; Virginia Foundation for Humanities 20th Anniversary Award, 1994; Pulitzer Prize finalist, 1995, for *Lincoln in American Memory;* National First Freedom Award, Freedom Council, 1997; Lifetime Achievement Award, Library of Virginia, 2005.

WRITINGS:

The Jefferson Image in the American Mind, Oxford University Press (New York, NY), 1960.
(Editor, with Leonard Levy) *Major Crises in American History,* two volumes, Harcourt (New York, NY), 1962.
(Editor) *Democracy, Liberty and Property: State Constitutional Convention Debates of the 1820s,* Bobbs-Merrill (Indianapolis, IN), 1966.
Thomas Jefferson: A Profile, Hill & Wang (New York, NY), 1967.
Thomas Jefferson and the New Nation: A Biography, Oxford University Press (New York, NY), 1970.
James Madison: A Biography in His Own Words, Harper (New York, NY), 1974.
(Editor) *The Portable Thomas Jefferson,* Viking (New York, NY), 1975.
Adams and Jefferson: A Revolutionary Dialogue, University of Georgia Press (Athens, GA), 1976.
Olive Branch and Sword: The Compromise of 1833, Louisiana State University Press (Baton Rouge, LA), 1981.
(Editor) *Thomas Jefferson: Writings,* Library of America (New York, NY), 1984.
(Editor) *Thomas Jefferson: A Reference Biography,* Scribner (New York, NY), 1984.
The Great Triumvirate: Webster, Clay, and Calhoun, Oxford University Press (New York, NY), 1987.
(Editor, with Robert Vaughan) *The Virginia Statute for Religious Freedom: Its Evolution and Consequences in American History,* Cambridge University Press (New York, NY), 1988.
(Editor) *Visitors to Monticello,* University Press of Virginia (Charlottesville, VA), 1989.
(Editor) *The Political Writings of Thomas Jefferson,* Thomas Jefferson Memorial Foundation (Charlottesville VA), 1993.

Lincoln in American Memory, Oxford University Press (New York, NY), 1994.
Jefferson Memorial: An Essay, U.S. Department of the Interior (Washington, DC), 1998.
Coming of Age with the New Republic, 1938-1950, University of Missouri Press (Columbia, MO), 1999.
John Brown: The Legend Revisited, University of Virginia Press (Charlottesville, VA), 2002.
"Starving Armenians": America and the Armenian Genocide, 1915-1930 and After, University of Virginia Press (Charlottesville, VA), 2004.

Contributor to scholarly journals.

SIDELIGHTS: Merrill D. Peterson once told *CA:* "I became interested in American history as I was reaching for intellectual maturity at the time of the Second World War. Actually it was less an interest in history than in what American thought and experience could contribute to an understanding of American democracy and its future. Perhaps I was involved in my own 'search for a usable past,' though the concept was as yet unknown to me. Vernon L. Parrington's *Main Currents in American Thought* was an important influence, while the works of Lewis Mumford opened exciting vistas, quite beyond Marx, for the study of American society and culture. Such reading steered me into the special program in the History of American Civilization at Harvard. There Perry Miller was most influential, for he added the scholarly discipline of the history of ideas without in any way diminishing my intellectual fascination with the subject or my deeper moral commitment. It was probably inevitable that I should, having learned the methods of a Miller, return to the quest of a Parrington; and so it is that my work has focused on Jefferson and the career of American democracy. In recent years I have followed my biographical bent with studies of the second generation of American statesmen and of Lincoln's career in American thought and imagination."

New York Times Book Review contributor Henry Steele Commager called *Thomas Jefferson: Writings,* edited by Peterson, "the largest and most skillfully edited single-volume of Jefferson ever published, one that contains almost three times the documents and letters in the *Portable Thomas Jefferson* Mr. Peterson gave us a decade ago."

Peterson gained widespread recognition with his first book *The Jefferson Image in the American Mind,* which focused on the posthumous reputation of this American founding father. John A Woods, writing in the *English Historical Review,* referred to the book as "remarkable." *American Literature* contributor Merle Curti called it "a major contribution to American intellectual history." Nearly a decade later, Peterson wrote *Thomas Jefferson and the New Nation: A Biography,* which *Political Science Quarterly* contributor Jacob E. Cooke wrote is "characterized by . . . interpretive balance and narrative skill."

Olive Branch and Sword: The Compromise of 1833 focuses on the political maneuverings that brought about the Compromise of 1833, which resolved a crisis of the Union caused by South Carolina's nullification of the protective tariff. Richard B. Latner, writing in the *Journal of Southern History,* called the book "a detailed explanation of the background, formulation and consequences of the compromise as well as a case study in the art of political compromise." *Journal of Economic History* contributor Sidney Ratner noted that the book "brings to the attention of economic historians the human elements in all the economic transactions and some of their unanticipated consequences."

Peterson writes about three legendary politicians, orators, and writers in *The Great Triumvirate: Webster, Clay, and Calhoun.* Commenting in the *New England Quarterly,* Irving H. Bartlett noted that the author "has given us a big book on national politics from 1812 to 1852, focused on the three major players of the period who dominated the 'second generation of American statesmanship.'" *Journal of American History* contributor Michael J. Birkner called *The Great Triumvirate* "absorbing reading" and noted that "a broad lay readership will relish" the book.

In *Lincoln in American Memory,* the author "traces in rich, learned detail the efforts of six generations of Americans to get right with Lincoln." as noted by Geoffrey C. Ward in *American Heritage.* A *Publishers Weekly* contributor wrote: "With insightful detail, University of Virginia historian Peterson . . . richly catalogues the resounding image, for scholars and civil society alike, of the martyred president."Phillip Shaw Paludan, writing in the *Historian,* commented that the book's "strength is its broad sweep." Paludan went on to note: "Memory can be evoked through books of course, but it also can be called forth by poetry, dreams, statues, paintings, advertising, and music," adding: "Peterson's cast includes all these."

John Brown: The Legend Revisited "trace[s] Brown's myth by combing the substantial iconography and bibliography, both scholarly and popular, accrued since

his death in 1859," according to William Cheek and Aimee Lee Cheek writing in the *Journal of Southern History.* In a review in the *Virginia Magazine of History & Biography,* Mark Wahlgren Summers commented that the book "fills a need, as its namesake certainly does, and its focus is narrow, sharp, and clear."

The author was inspired to write *"Starving Armenians": America and the Armenian Genocide, 1915-1930 and After* after spending time in Armenia at the age of seventy-six as part of the Peace Corps. Simon Payaslian, writing in the *Middle East Journal,* noted: "Peterson altogether ignores US policy in the 19th century, limiting his discussion to the American missionaries and humanitarian response to the massacres in the 1890s."

BIOGRAPHICAL AND CRITICAL SOURCES:

PERIODICALS

American Heritage, February-March, 1995, Geoffrey C. Ward, review of *Lincoln in American Memory,* p. 14.

American Historical Review, February, 1983, William W. Freehling, review of *Olive Branch and Sword: The Compromise of 1833,* p. 182.

American Literature, January, 1961, Merle Curti, review of *The Jefferson Image in the American Mind,* pp. 469-470.

American Quarterly, summer, 1961, Emory G. Evans, review of *The Jefferson Image in the American Mind,* p. 200.

English Historical Review, April, 1972, John A. Woods, review of *The Jefferson Image in the American Mind,* p. 435.

Historian, winter, 1994, Phillip Shaw Paludan, review of *Lincoln in American Memory,* p. 393.

Journal of American History, March, 1978, Stephen G. Kurtz, review of *Adams and Jefferson,* p. 1089; March, 1983, Harry L. Watson, review of *Olive Branch and Sword,* pp. 967-968; December, 1988, Michael J. Birkner, review of *The Great Triumvirate: Webster, Clay, and Calhoun,* pp. 959-962; June, 2005, Keith Pomakoy, review of *"Starving Armenians": America and the Armenian Genocide, 1915-1930 and After,* p. 261.

Journal of Economic History, December, 1982, Sidney Ratner, review of *Olive Branch and Sword,* pp.946-947.

Journal of Southern History, May, 1971, review of *Thomas Jefferson and the New Nation,* pp. 288-290; February, 1983, Richard B. Latner, review of

Olive Branch and Sword, pp. 120-121; May, 2004, William Cheek and Aimee Lee Cheek, review of *John Brown,* p. 435.

Middle East Journal, winter, 2005, Simon Payaslian, review of *Starving Armenians,* p. 132.

New England Quarterly, September, 1988, Irving H. Bartlett, review of *The Great Triumvirate,* pp. 455-456.

New York Times Book Review, July 7, 1985, Henry Steele Commager, review of *Thomas Jefferson: Writings,* p. 19.

New York Times, November 8, 1987, Donald B. Cole, review of *The Great Triumvirate;* June 26, 1994, David S. Reynolds, review of *Lincoln in American Memory.*

Political Science Quarterly, June, 1972, Jacob E. Cooke, review of *Thomas Jefferson and the Nation,* pp. 324-325.

Publishers Weekly, March 7, 1994, review of *Lincoln in the American Memory,* p. 58.

Reviews in American History, September, 1988, John Ashworth, review of *The Great Triumvirate,* pp. 385-389.

Virginia Magazine of History & Biography, Volume 110, issue 4, 2002, Mark Wahlgren Summers, review of *John Brown: The Legend Revisited,* p. 49.

ONLINE

Inside UVA Online, http://www.virginia.edu/insideuva/ (December 11, 2006), "Peterson Wins Lifetime Achievement Award."*

*   *   *

PETERSON, Merrill Daniel
  See PETERSON, Merrill D.

*   *   *

PINNEY, Thomas 1932-

PERSONAL: Born April 23, 1932, in Ottawa, KS; son of John J. and Lorene Pinney; married Sherrill Ohman, September 1, 1956; children: Anne, Jane, Sarah. *Education:* Beloit College, B.A., 1954; Yale University, Ph. D., 1960.

ADDRESSES: Home—Pomona, CA. *Office*—Department of English, Pomona College, Claremont, CA 91711.

CAREER: Hamilton College, Clinton, NY, instructor in English, 1957-61; Yale University, New Haven, CT, instructor in English, 1961-62; Pomona College, Claremont, CA, assistant professor, 1962-67, associate professor, 1967-73, professor of English, beginning in 1973, Spalding Professor, William M. Keck Distinguished Service Professor and chairperson of department, 1984—, professor emeritus.

AWARDS, HONORS: Guggenheim fellow, 1966, 1984; grants from American Council of Learned Societies, 1973 and 1984; Mellon fellow, Pomona College, 1974; National Endowment for the Humanities fellow, 1980; IACP Cookbook Award, Beer and Spirits category, International Association of Culinary Professionals, 2006, for *A History of Wine in America: From Prohibition to the Present;* Mellon Emeritus fellowship, 2006.

WRITINGS:

(Editor) George Eliot, *Essays,* Columbia University Press (New York, NY), 1963.

(Editor, with John Clive) Thomas Babington Macaulay, *Selected Writings of Thomas Babington Macaulay,* University of Chicago Press (Chicago, IL), 1972.

(Editor) Thomas Babington Macaulay, *The Letters of Thomas Babington Macaulay,* Cambridge University Press (New York, NY), Volume I: *1807-February, 1831,* 1974, Volume II: *March, 1831-December, 1833,* 1974, Volume III: *January, 1834-August, 1841,* 1976, Volume IV: *September, 1841-December, 1848,* 1977, Volume V: *January, 1849-December, 1855,* 1981, Volume VI: *January, 1856-December, 1859,* 1981.

A Short Handbook and Style Sheet, Harcourt (New York, NY), 1977.

(Editor) Thomas Babington Macaulay, *The Selected Letters of Thomas Babington Macaulay,* Cambridge University Press (New York, NY), 1983.

(Editor) Rudyard Kipling, *Kipling's India: Uncollected Sketches, 1884-1888,* Schocken (New York, NY), 1985.

(Editor) Rudyard Kipling, *The Day's Work,* Oxford University Press (New York, NY), 1987.

(Editor) Rudyard Kipling, *Kipling in California,* Friends of the Bancroft Library, University of California (Berkeley, CA), 1989.

A History of Wine in America: From the Beginnings to Prohibition, University of California Press (Berkeley, CA), 1989.

(Editor) Rudyard Kipling, *The Letters of Rudyard Kipling,* University of Iowa Press (Iowa City, IA), Volume 1: *1872-1889,* Volume 2: *1890-1899,* Volume 3: *1900-1910,* Volume 4: *1911-1919,* Volume 5: *1920-1930,* Volume 6: *1931-1936,* 1990–2004.

(Editor) Rudyard Kipling, *Rudyard Kipling: Something of Myself and Other Autobiographical Writings,* Cambridge University Press (New York, NY), 1990.

(Editor, and author of introduction and notes) Rudyard Kipling, *The Jungle Play,* Penguin (New York, NY), 2000.

(Editor, with Rosalind Kennedy) Rudyard Kipling, *Kipling Down Under: Rudyard Kipling's Visit to Australia, 1891: A Narrative with Documents,* Xlibris, 2000.

(Editor, with David Alan Richards) Rudyard Kipling, *Kipling and His First Publisher: Correspondence of Rudyard Kipling with Thacker, Spink and Co., 1886-1890,* Rivendale Press (High Wycombe, Bucks, England), 2001.

A History of Wine in America: From Prohibition to the Present, University of California Press (Berkeley, CA), 2005.

John Ignatius Bleasdale, Book Club of California (San Francisco, CA), 2006.

Contributor to *Book of California Wine,* by Ernest Born, University of California Press (Berkeley, CA), 1984.

SIDELIGHTS: English scholar Thomas Pinney collected a great many of the writings, and especially the letters, of both Thomas Babington Macaulay and Rudyard Kipling. A series of volumes collecting the letters of the former were written over a period from 1974 to 1981, and his six-volume series that collects the Kipling letters was published from 1990 to 2004. Covering the period from 1872 to 1936, the letters provide insight into the world in which Kipling lived and wrote and the people of the period. The volumes contain photographs and drawings by Kipling, who had received instruction as a child and whose father was an artist. An extensive index makes the series more accessible. Jeffrey Meyers, who reviewed the third and fourth volumes in *English Literature in Transition 1880-1920,* wrote that Pinney "has labored heroically to produce in his exemplary notes a concise social and political history of Edwardian and early Georgian England. . . . Kipling's letters also cast new light on his writing. He mentions the early influence of Walt Whitman and the stylistic discipline (shared with Hemingway) that came from sending telegraphic dispatches."

Pinney is also a wine scholar, having published two very well-received volumes on the history of wine in the United States, divided into two periods and published fifteen years apart. They include *A History of Wine in America: From the Beginnings to Prohibition* and *The History of Wine in America: From Prohibition to the Present.* Pinney discusses wine not only in terms of how the grapes are grown and the wine created, but also the part it has played in American culture. He provides precise statistics as to the growth of the industry in California, and also covers other wine-growing regions of the country. Michael Franz reviewed the most recent volume for *Wine Review Online,* noting that both "are impressive accomplishments, and not least among their virtues is the fact that they are such pleasures to read."

BIOGRAPHICAL AND CRITICAL SOURCES:

PERIODICALS

Booklist, June 1, 2005, Mark Knoblauch, review of *A History of Wine in America: From Prohibition to the Present,* p. 1736.

English Literature in Transition 1880-1920, winter, 2004, Jeffrey Myers, reviews of *The Letters of Rudyard Kipling,* Volume 3: *1900-1910,* and Volume 4: *1911-1919,* p. 94; winter, 2006, D.H. Stewart, reviews of *The Letters of Rudyard Kipling,* Volume 5: *1920-1930,* and Volume 6: *1931-1936,* p. 63.

Library Journal, June 1, 2005, John Charles, review of *A History of Wine in America,* p. 164.

Spectator, December 18, 2004, Juliet Townsend, reviews of *The Letters of Rudyard Kipling,* Volume 5: *1920-1930,* and Volume 6: *1931-1936,* p. 89.

ONLINE

Wine Review Online, http://www.winereviewonline.com/franz_wine_books_06.cfm/ (January 24, 2006), Michael Franz, review of *A History of Wine in America.**

POINTS, Larry G. 1945-
  (Larry Gene Points)

PERSONAL: Born January 14, 1945, in Dodge City, KS; son of Gene Earl and Helen Louise Points; married Beverly Ann Watts (a school teacher and administrator), December 23, 1981; children: Kristy, Kara. *Education:* Southeast Missouri State University, B.S., 1966.

ADDRESSES: Home and office—Delmar, MD. *E-mail*—larry@seacritters.com.

CAREER: Mt. Rainier National Park, Longmire, WA, park ranger, 1969-70; Hopewell Furnace National Historic Site, Elverson, PA, supervisory park ranger, 1970-74; Assateague Island National Seashore, Berlin, MD, chief of park interpretation, 1974-2001. Deputy mayor of Delman, MD. Speaker at schools. *Military service:* U.S. Army, 1967-69; served in Thailand.

MEMBER: Assateague Costal Trust, Mid-Atlantic Marine Education Association, Maryland Reading Association.

AWARDS, HONORS: Conservation Award, Isaac Walton League, 1973; several agency awards from National Park Service.

WRITINGS:

(With Andrea Jauck) *Assateague: Island of the Wild Ponies,* Macmillan (New York, NY), 1993, revised and updated edition, Sierra Press (Mariposa, CA), 1997.
(With Andrea Jauck) *Ribbons of Sand: Exploring Atlantic Beaches,* Panorama International Publications (Mariposa, CA), 1997.
(With Andrea Jauck) *Barrier Islands Are for the Birds,* Sierra Press (Mariposa, CA), 2000.

SIDELIGHTS: In addition to his career serving as a park ranger in several prominent U.S. national parks, Larry G. Points has also published children's nature books in collaboration with fellow naturalist Andrea Jauck. In *Assateague: Island of the Wild Ponies* Points introduces readers to the beaches, marshes, forests, and coastal regions of the barrier island located off the coast of Maryland and Virginia. Based on knowledge gained while Points served as chief of Park Interpretation on the National Park Service site, the book provides an intimate view of the remote region, and features photographs—many taken by Points himself—that capture the overwhelming beauty to be seen throughout the park.

Points once commented: "I grew up in Cape Girardeau, Missouri, on the Mississippi River and at the edge of the Ozarks. This afforded me the opportunity to experience the outdoors and develop interests that would lead to a career in that realm. Following graduation from my hometown college in 1966, I joined the National Park Service and received training to be a park ranger at the Grand Canyon. Following a two-year interlude with the military, I rejoined the park service for a year of additional training at Mt. Rainier National Park in Washington state. Then I transferred east to Hopewell Furnace National Historic Site in Pennsylvania, where I served as the park's chief of interpretation and resource management. In 1974 I transferred to Assateague Island National Seashore where I spent the next twenty-seven years of my career, retiring in early 2001.

"At Assateague Island I served as the chief of park interpretation and directed the development of a wide variety of educational services. These included ranger-guided programs, children's activities, visitor centers, nature trails, audio-visual resources, and exhibits of all kinds. My professional writing began with a variety of publications intended for visitors to help them achieve understanding of park resources. In the late 1980s I embarked with a fellow park naturalist, Andrea Jauck, on the creation of an extensive series of wayside (outdoor) exhibits for Assateague Island. This work involved researching images and graphics, and writing text.

"Andrea and I worked so well together on the exhibits that we decided to privately coauthor a series of nonfiction children's books on subjects of the Atlantic seashore. We knew what interested children and their families and attempted to answer the most common questions they had. We were particularly interested in presenting photographs to support the text and are pleased to say that, in the current era of digital images and computer manipulation, the images in our books are "the real stuff": i.e., un-retouched 35mm photos actually taken by a variety of nature photographers in the field."

BIOGRAPHICAL AND CRITICAL SOURCES:

PERIODICALS

Booklist, March 15, 1993, Deborah Abbott, review of *Assateague: Island of the Wild Ponies,* p. 1353.

Childhood Education, fall, 2000, review of *Barrier Islands Are for the Birds,* p. 45.
School Library Journal, June, 1993, Charlene Strickland, review of *Assateague,* p. 98.

ONLINE

Larry Points Home Page, http://www.seacritters.com (February 18, 2007).*

*   *   *

POINTS, Larry Gene
  See POINTS, Larry G.

*   *   *

POLK, William R. 1929-
  (William Roe Polk)

PERSONAL: Born March 7, 1929, in Fort Worth, TX; son of George Washington and Adelaide Polk; married Joan Cooledge, December 15, 1950 (divorced December, 1960); married Ann Cross, June 9, 1962 (divorced 1975); married Baroness Elisabeth von Oppenheimer, December 29, 1981; children: (first marriage) Milbry Catherine, Alison Elizabeth; (second marriage) George W. IV, Eliza Forbes. *Education:* Attended University of Chile, 1945-46; Harvard University, B.A. (Magna Cum Laude), 1951, Ph.D., 1958; American University of Beirut, graduate study, 1951-52; Oxford University, B.A. (honors), 1955, M.A., 1959.

ADDRESSES: Home—France.

CAREER: Writer, historian, editor, and educator. Harvard University, Cambridge, MA, assistant professor of Middle Eastern studies, 1955-61; U.S. Department of State, Washington, DC, member of Policy Planning Council, 1961-65; University of Chicago, Chicago, IL, professor of Middle Eastern history and founder and director of Center for Middle Eastern Studies, 1965-74; Adlai Stevenson Institute of International Affairs, Chicago, president, 1967-73. Currently senior director, W.P. Carey Foundation. Advisory editor, Beacon Press, 1956-60; senior editor and member of board of directors, Arlington Books, Inc., 1959-61. Lecturer in United

States and abroad. Member of board of directors of Hyde Park Bank & Trust Co., Microfilm Data System, Moore International, Rabia Ltd., and W.P. Carey Foundation

MEMBER: Council on Foreign Relations, Middle East Institute (member of board of governors, 1962—), Middle East Studies Association of North America (member of board of directors), Academy on Public Policy (fellow).

AWARDS, HONORS: Four Rockefeller Foundation fellowships, 1951-55; Guggenheim fellowship, 1961-62.

WRITINGS:

What Arabs Think (published with *American Business and the Arab World* by W. Jack Butler), Foreign Policy Association (New York, NY), 1952.
(With David M. Stamler and Edmund Asfour) *Backdrop to Tragedy: The Struggle for Palestine,* Beacon Press (Boston, MA), 1957.
(Editor, with others) *Studies on the Civilization of Islam,* Beacon Press (Boston, MA), 1962.
(Editor and author of introduction) *Developmental Revolution: North Africa, Middle East, South Africa,* Middle East Institute (Washington, DC), 1963.
The Opening of South Lebanon, 1788-1840: A Study of the Impact of the West on the Middle East, Harvard University Press (Cambridge, MA), 1963.
The United States and the Arab World, Harvard University Press (Cambridge, MA), 1965, 5th edition published as *The Arab World Today,* 1991.
(Editor, with Richard L. Chambers) *Beginnings of Modernization in the Middle East: The Nineteenth Century,* University of Chicago Press (Chicago, IL), 1968.
Passing Brave, Knopf (New York, NY), 1972.
(Translator and author of introduction) *The Golden Ode,* University of Chicago Press (Chicago, IL), 1974.
The Elusive Peace: The Middle East in the Twentieth Century, St. Martin's Press (New York, NY), 1979.
Neighbors and Strangers: The Fundamentals of Foreign Affairs, University of Chicago Press (Chicago, IL), 1997.
Polk's Folly: An American Family History, Doubleday (New York, NY), 2000.
Understanding Iraq: The Whole Sweep of Iraqi History, from Genghis Khan's Mongols to the Ottoman Turks to the British Mandate to the American Occupation, HarperCollins (New York, NY), 2005.

The Birth of America: From before Columbus to the Revolution, HarperCollins (New York, NY), 2006.

(With George S. McGovern) *Out of Iraq: A Practical Plan for Withdrawal Now,* Simon & Schuster (New York, NY), 2006.

Also editor of and contributor to *Perspective of the Arab World,* 1956. Contributor to a report, *"Ideology and Foreign Affairs,"* prepared for the U.S. Senate Committee on Foreign Relations. Contributor to *Bulletin of the Atomic Scientists, Foreign Affairs Quarterly,* the *Atlantic,* and other journals.

SIDELIGHTS: Author, historian, and educator William R. Polk is an internationally recognized expert on Middle Eastern affairs. Polk's professional affiliations have included Harvard University and the University of Chicago, as well as the U.S. Department of State. His book-length assessment of the Middle East, published as *The Arab World Today,* has been published in five editions since it was first printed in 1965. Polk's *Neighbors and Strangers: The Fundamentals of Foreign Affairs* was deemed "a wise, learned, and graceful work" by David C. Hendrickson in *Foreign Affairs.* Hendrickson further called the book "a superb introduction to the origin and logic of the principal areas of transaction among political collectives—defense, trade, espionage, and diplomacy." In *Library Journal,* James Holmes characterized *Neighbors and Strangers* as "a lively and thought-provoking account strongly recommended for academic libraries."

Polk is a member of a distinguished American family of Scotch-Irish origin that includes former president James K. Polk and a host of other military, academic, and business leaders. In *Polk's Folly: An American Family History,* the author profiles his forebears from the earliest immigrants—who landed in Maryland in 1680—to his brother, a journalist who was murdered in 1948. In between, Polk documents his family's success as plantation owners; James K. Polk's commendable presidency, during which the United States won the Mexican War; and Polk family contributions to the Civil War in both the Union and Confederate armies. To quote David Herbert Donald in the *New York Times Book Review,* Polk "demonstrates that the Polks are an underestimated clan, whose members have been involved in nearly every stage of American development and have participated with bravery and determination in every one of the country's wars." Noting that the earliest American generations of the Polk family are not well-documented, and that other generations failed to keep good records

of themselves, Donald cited William R. Polk for his attempts to reconstruct his ancestors' lives based upon histories of what was happening around them. "His method has enabled him to produce a spirited, broad-scale saga of an American family we ought to remember," Donald declared. *Library Journal* correspondent Dale F. Farris likewise praised Polk for his "passionate search for notables in his complex family tree," concluding that *Polk's Folly* is "a fascinating, entertaining saga that illuminates American history."

A former U.S. State Department advisor, Polk is interested in international affairs, particularly those involving Iraq and U.S. involvement in that embattled country. In *Understanding Iraq: The Whole Sweep of Iraqi History, from Genghis Khan's Mongols to the Ottoman Turks to the British Mandate to the American Occupation,* Polk outlines Iraqi history from ancient times to the present, with considerable attention paid to defining eras in the country's history. He discusses the earliest history of Iraq and its development into an Islamic state. He looks at the British influence during the years from 1917 to 1958; at the development of revolutionary Iraq from 1958 to 1991, when it was ruled by military leaders such as Saddam Hussein; and the most recent shift in the country's identity, American Iraq, from 1991 to the present. Polk also considers Iraq's future as it emerges from the turmoil of war, political upheaval, and outside interference. "The thrust of Mr. Polk's history lesson is not gentle: America is blundering in Iraq out of historical ignorance," observed a commentator in the *Economist.* Reviewer Fred Rhodes, writing in the *Middle East,* noted that "*Understanding Iraq* is an important book, spelling out the lessons of history in a compelling and absorbing narrative." *Foreign Affairs* reviewer L. Carl Brown called Polk's book a "sober and informed account of Iraq's history, culminating in a compelling critique of the U.S. intervention there." Polk's six-decade career in diplomatic and academic circles "grants him unique authority on his subject and puts this book head and shoulders above other analyses," commented Brendan Driscoll in *Booklist.* A *Kirkus Reviews* commentator called Polk's work on Iraq "learned, constantly engaging and full of pointed lessons for those wondering why the war has not ended, peace has not come, and no one in Iraq save Halliburton seems liberated."

In keeping with his attitudes and scholarly interests in Iraq, Polk has also helped craft suggestions for America's withdrawal from the difficult and worsening situation in that country. *Out of Iraq: A Practical Plan for Withdrawal Now,* written with former Democratic senator and presidential candidate George S. McGovern, contains a detailed, phased withdrawal plan designed to allow America to withdraw from Iraq within six months. Polk and McGovern criticize the American occupation of Iraq as scandalously wasteful of lives and resources, damaging to the American economy and irreversibly destructive to the members of the military who have served there. They strongly disagree with Republican desires to "stay the course" in Iraq, noting that American presence there increases the likelihood of terrorist attacks on U.S. concerns. Polk and McGovern endorse an immediate withdrawal of troops and resources. Their plan includes a two-year commitment to help Iraq rebuild; the training and deployment of a national Iraqi police force; and the establishment of a U.S. embassy to start rebuilding relations with Iraq. *Library Journal* reviewer Nader Entessar called Polk and McGovern's work a "crisp and cogently argued book," and "essential reading for anybody who wants to cut through the maze of confusion" around U.S. policy in Iraq.

With *The Birth of America: From before Columbus to the Revolution*, Polk offers a history of the earliest days of the United States in a "fluent account of British America from colonization to the imperial crisis of the 1760s and 1770s," commented Gilbert Taylor in *Booklist*. Polk carefully considers the physical realities and hardships of early colonization, and makes clear distinctions between those colonists who came willingly from Europe and those who were forced here as slaves from Africa. He discusses issues such as colonial conflicts with native populations, the establishment of working economies in the new world, commerce-based and slave-based economic systems, and the beginning of the American Revolution. Polk's work is "packed with impeccable scholarship and insightful analysis," commented a *Kirkus Reviews* critic. A *Publishers Weekly* contributor called Polk "a masterful storyteller who takes us into a strange world and helps us to understand it."

BIOGRAPHICAL AND CRITICAL SOURCES:

PERIODICALS

Booklist, April 15, 2005, Brendan Driscoll, review of *Understanding Iraq: The Whole Sweep of Iraqi History, from Genghis Khan's Mongols to the Ottoman Turks to the British Mandate to the American Occupation*, p. 1427; February 15, 2006, Gilbert Taylor, review of *The Birth of America: From before Columbus to the Revolution*, p. 34; October 15, 2006, Vanessa Bush, review of *Out of Iraq: A Practical Plan for Withdrawal Now*, p. 19.

Choice, January, 2006, C.E. Farah, review of *Understanding Iraq*, p. 914.

Economist, July 2, 2005, review of *Understanding Iraq*, p. 74.

Foreign Affairs, spring, 1981, John C. Campbell, review of *The Arab World*, p. 960; March-April, 1998, David C. Hendrickson, review of *Neighbors and Strangers: The Fundamentals of Foreign Affairs*, p. 150; May-June, 2005, L. Carl Brown, review of *Understanding Iraq*, p. 148.

Kirkus Reviews, March 1, 2005, review of *Understanding Iraq*, p. 280; February 1, 2006, review of *The Birth of America*, p. 124.

Library Journal, September 1, 1997, James Holmes, review of *Neighbors and Strangers*, p. 201; January, 2000, Dale F. Farris, review of *Polk's Folly: An American Family History*, p. 133; October 15, 2006, Nader Entessar, review of *Out of Iraq*, p. 76.

Middle East, March 21, 2005, review of *Understanding Iraq*, p. 47; January, 2006, Fred Rhodes, review of *Understanding Iraq*, p. 64.

Middle East Journal, autumn, 2006, Judith S. Yaphe, review of *Understanding Iraq*, p. 802.

New York Times Book Review, January 16, 2000, David Herbert Donald, "A Family Affair," review of *Polk's Folly*, p. 18.

Publishers Weekly, January 9, 2006, review of *The Birth of America*, p. 40.

ONLINE

Blogcritics, http://www.blogcritics.org/ (May 9, 2006), review of *Understanding Iraq*.

History News Network Web site, http://hnn.us/ (June 19, 2006), interview with William R. Polk.

Informed Comment, http://www.juancole.com/ (May 26, 2004), biography of William R. Polk.

William R. Polk Home Page, http://www.williampolk.com (January 10, 2007).

*　　*　　*

POLK, William Roe
See POLK, William R.

Q

QUIN-HARKIN, Janet 1941-
(Rhys Bowen, Janetta Johns, Janet Elizabeth Quin-Harkin)

PERSONAL: Born September 24, 1941, in Bath, England; immigrated to the United States in 1966; daughter of Frank Newcombe (an engineer) and Margery (a teacher) Lee; married John Quin-Harkin (a retired sales manager), November 26, 1966; children: Clare, Anne, Jane, Dominic. *Education:* University of London, B.A. (with honors), 1963; graduate study at University of Kiel and University of Freiburg. *Religion:* Roman Catholic. *Hobbies and other interests:* Tennis, travel, drama, music, sketching, and hiking.

ADDRESSES: Home and office—San Rafael, CA. *Agent*—Fran Lebowitz, Writers House, Inc., 21 W. 26th St., New York, NY 10010. *E-mail*—rhysbowen@comcast.net; rhys@rhysbowen.com.

CAREER: Writer, novelist, and educator. British Broadcasting Corp. (BBC), London, England, studio manager in drama department, 1963-66; teacher of dance and drama, 1971-76. Worked for Australian Broadcasting, Sydney, Australia. Founder and former director of San Raphael's Children's Little Theater. Writing teacher at Dominican College, San Rafael, 1988-95.

MEMBER: Mystery Writers of America (regional president, Northern California chapter, 2001), Sisters in Crime, American Association of University Women, Society of Children's Bookwriters.

AWARDS, HONORS: Children's Book Showcase selection, Children's Book Council, Outstanding Books of the Year citation, *New York Times*, American Institute of Graphic Arts Children's Book Show citation, and Best Books of the year citation, *School Library Journal, Washington Post,* and *Saturday Review,* all 1976, all for *Peter Penny's Dance;* Children's Choice citation, 1985, for *Wanted: Date for Saturday Night;* Award for Best Screenplay, Marin Arts Council, 1995; Barry Award nomination, 1999, for *Evan Help Us;* Agatha Award nomination for best short story, 2001, for "The Seal of the Confessional"; Agatha Award for best novel, Herodotus Award, best first historical novel, Reviewer's Choice, best historical novel, and Mary Higgins Clark Award nomination, all 2002, all for *Murphy's Law;* Agatha Award nomination and Reviewer's Choice Award nomination, 2003, for *The Death of Riley;* Anthony Award, World Mystery Convention, Bruce Alexander Memorial Award, best historical novel, Freddy Award, Sleuthfest, FL, and Macavity Award nomination, all 2004, all for *For the Love of Mike;* Anthony Award, World Mystery Convention, 2004, for short story, "Doppelganger"; Edgar Allan Poe Award nomination, Mystery Writers of America, 2005, all for *Evan's Gate;* Anthony Award nomination, 2005, for short story "Voodoo"; Macavity Award nomination, best historical mystery, 2006, for *In Like Flynn.*

WRITINGS:

CHILDREN'S BOOKS

Peter Penny's Dance, illustrated by Anita Lobel, Dial (New York, NY), 1976.
Benjamin's Balloon, Parents' Magazine Press (New York, NY), 1979.
Septimus Bean and His Amazing Machine, illustrated by Art Cumings, Parents' Magazine Press (New York, NY), 1980.

Magic Growing Powder, illustrated by Cumings, Parents' Magazine Press (New York, NY), 1981.

Helpful Hattie, illustrated by Susanna Natti, Harcourt (San Diego, CA), 1983.

Three Impossible Things, Parents' Magazine Press (New York, NY), 1991.

Billy and Ben: The Terrible Two, illustrated by Carol Newsom, Bantam (New York, NY), 1992.

YOUNG ADULT NOVELS

Write Every Day, Scholastic (New York, NY), 1982.

(Under pseudonym Janetta Johns) *The Truth about Me and Bobby V.,* Bantam (New York, NY), 1983.

Tommy Loves Tina, Berkley/Ace (New York, NY), 1984.

Winner Takes All, Berkley/Ace (New York, NY), 1984.

Wanted: Date for Saturday Night, Putnam (New York, NY), 1985.

Summer Heat, Fawcett (New York, NY), 1990.

My Phantom Love, HarperCollins (New York, NY), 1992.

On My Own, HarperCollins (New York, NY), 1992.

Getting Personal: Becky, Silhouette Books (New York, NY), 1994.

The Apartment, HarperCollins (New York, NY), 1994.

The Sutcliffe Diamonds, HarperCollins (New York, NY), 1994.

The Boy Next Door, Bantam (New York, NY), 1995.

Fun, Sun, and Flamingoes, Pocket Books (New York, NY), 1997.

Who Do You Love, Bantam (New York, NY), 1999.

Love Potion, Avon (New York, NY), 2000.

"SWEET DREAMS" SERIES

California Girl, Bantam (New York, NY), 1981.

Love Match, Bantam (New York, NY), 1982.

Ten-Boy Summer, Bantam (New York, NY), 1982.

Daydreamer, Bantam (New York, NY), 1983.

The Two of Us, Bantam (New York, NY), 1984.

Exchange of Hearts, Bantam (New York, NY), 1984.

Ghost of a Chance, Bantam (New York, NY), 1984.

Lovebirds, Bantam (New York, NY), 1984.

101 Ways to Meet Mr. Right, Bantam (New York, NY), 1985.

The Great Boy Chase, Bantam (New York, NY), 1985.

Follow That Boy, Bantam (New York, NY), 1985.

My Secret Love, Bantam (New York, NY), 1986.

My Best Enemy, Bantam (New York, NY), 1987.

Never Say Goodbye, Bantam (New York, NY), 1987.

"ON OUR OWN" SERIES

On Our Own, Bantam (New York, NY), 1986.

The Graduates, Bantam (New York, NY), 1986.

The Trouble with Toni, Bantam (New York, NY), 1986.

Out of Love, Bantam (New York, NY), 1986.

Old Friends, New Friends, Bantam (New York, NY), 1986.

Best Friends Forever, Bantam (New York, NY), 1986.

"SUGAR AND SPICE" SERIES

Flip Side, Ballantine (New York, NY), 1987.

Tug of War, Ballantine (New York, NY), 1987.

Surf's Up, Ballantine (New York, NY), 1987.

The Last Dance, Ballantine (New York, NY), 1987.

Nothing in Common, Ballantine (New York, NY), 1987.

Dear Cousin, Ballantine (New York, NY), 1987.

Two Girls, One Boy, Ballantine (New York, NY), 1987.

Trading Places, Ballantine (New York, NY), 1987.

Double Take, Ballantine (New York, NY), 1988.

Make Me a Star, Ballantine (New York, NY), 1988.

Big Sister, Ballantine (New York, NY), 1988.

Out in the Cold, Ballantine (New York, NY), 1988.

Blind Date, Ballantine (New York, NY), 1988.

It's My Turn, Ballantine (New York, NY), 1988.

"HEARTBREAK CAFÉ" SERIES

No Experience Required, Fawcett (New York, NY), 1990.

The Main Attraction, Fawcett (New York, NY), 1990.

At Your Service, Fawcett (New York, NY), 1990.

Catch of the Day, Fawcett (New York, NY), 1990.

Love to Go, Fawcett (New York, NY), 1990.

Just Desserts, Fawcett (New York, NY), 1990.

"FRIENDS" SERIES

Starring Tess and Ali, HarperCollins (New York, NY), 1991.

Tess and Ali and the Teeny Bikini, HarperCollins (New York, NY), 1991.

Boy Trouble for Tess and Ali, HarperCollins (New York, NY), 1991.

Tess and Ali, Going on Fifteen, HarperCollins (New York, NY), 1991.

"SENIOR YEAR" SERIES

Homecoming Dance, HarperCollins (New York, NY), 1991.
New Year's Eve, HarperCollins (New York, NY), 1991.
Night of the Prom, HarperCollins (New York, NY), 1992.
Graduation Day, HarperCollins (New York, NY), 1992.

"BOYFRIEND CLUB" SERIES

Ginger's First Kiss, Troll Communications (Mahwah, NJ), 1994.
Roni's Dream Boy, Troll Communications (Mahwah, NJ), 1994.
Karen's Perfect Match, Troll Communications (Mahwah, NJ), 1994.
Ginger's New Crush, Troll Communications (Mahwah, NJ), 1994.
Queen Justine, Troll Communications (Mahwah, NJ), 1995.
Roni's Two-Boy Trouble, Troll Communications (Mahwah, NJ), 1995.
No More Boys, Troll Communications (Mahwah, NJ), 1995.
Karen's Lesson in Love, Troll Communications (Mahwah, NJ), 1995.
Roni's Sweet Fifteen, Troll Communications (Mahwah, NJ), 1995.
Justine's Babysitting, Troll Communications (Mahwah, NJ), 1995.
The Boyfriend Wars, Troll Communications (Mahwah, NJ), 1995.

"TGIF!" SERIES

Sleepover Madness, Pocket Books (New York, NY), 1995.
Friday Night Fright, Pocket Books (New York, NY), 1995.
Four's a Crowd, Pocket Books (New York, NY), 1995.
Forever Friday, Pocket Books (New York, NY), 1995.
Toe-Shoe Trouble, Pocket Books (New York, NY), 1996.
Secret Valentine, Pocket Books (New York, NY), 1996.

"SISTER, SISTER" SERIES

Cool in School, Pocket Books (New York, NY), 1996.
You Read My Mind, Pocket Books (New York, NY), 1996.

Also author of *One Crazy Christmas and 5 to Come.*

UNDER NAME RHYS BOWEN; "CONSTABLE EVANS MYSTERIES"

Evans Above, St. Martin's Press (New York, NY), 1997.
Evan Help Us, St. Martin's Press (New York, NY), 1998.
Evanly Choirs, St. Martin's Press (New York, NY), 1999.
Evan and Elle, St. Martin's Press (New York, NY), 2000.
Evan Can Wait, St. Martin's Press (New York, NY), 2001.
Evans to Betsy, St. Martin's Press (New York, NY), 2002.
Evan's Gate, St. Martin's Press (New York, NY), 2004.
Evan Blessed, St. Martin's Press (New York, NY), 2005.
Evanly Bodies, St. Martin's Press (New York, NY), 2006.

UNDER NAME RHYS BOWEN; "MOLLY MURPHY" SERIES

Murphy's Law St. Martin's Press (New York, NY), 2001.
Death of Riley St. Martin's Press (New York, NY), 2002.
For the Love of Mike, St. Martin's Press (New York, NY), 2003.
In Like Flynn, St. Martin's Press (New York, NY), 2005.
Oh Danny Boy, St. Martin's Press (New York, NY), 2006.
In Dublin's Fair City, St. Martin's Press (New York, NY), 2007.

OTHER

(Contributor) *Chandler Reading Program,* five volumes, edited by Lawrence Carillo and Dorothy McKinley, Noble & Noble, 1967–72.

CONTEMPORARY AUTHORS • New Revision Series, Volume 162

Madam Sarah (adult historical novel), Fawcett (New York, NY), 1990.

Fool's Gold (adult historical novel), HarperCollins (New York, NY), 1991.

Amazing Grace (adult historical fiction), HarperCollins (New York, NY), 1993.

The Secrets of Lake Success (based on the NBC mini-series, created by David Stenn), Tor Books (New York, NY), 1993.

Trade Winds (based on the NBC mini-series, created by Hugh Bush), Schoolfield/Caribbean Productions, 1993.

Her Royal Spyness (mystery novel), Berkley Prime Crime (New York, NY), 2007.

Also author of several documentaries and four radio plays and scripts, including *Dandelion Hours,* for the BBC, 1966. Contributor to anthologies, including *Unholy Orders,* 2000, *The World's Finest Mystery and Crime Stories: Fifth Annual Collection,* 2004, and *Fifty Years of Crime and Suspense.* Contributor to periodicals, including *Scholastic* and *Mother's Journal.* Author's works have been translated into other languages.

SIDELIGHTS: Janet Quin-Harkin is the popular and prolific author of more than one hundred books, most of which are geared for teen readers. Quin-Harkin's series include "Sweet Dreams," "Sugar and Spice," "Heartbreak Café," and "On Our Own," among others, comprising books of standard length with a fixed group of characters involved in "the sort of lives that Middle America leads," as Quin-Harkin once said in describing her work. According to the author, the "Sweet Dreams" series opened up a new direction in publishing, providing books that were cheap enough for the readers themselves to purchase and thus making teen readers independent from the choices of parents and librarians. These books were also designed to be more upbeat than the usual young adult contributions, which dealt, according to Quin-Harkin, with "the darker side of reality." In the 1990s, Quin-Harkin turned to writing mystery novels for adults under the name Rhys Bowen. These mysteries feature the character Evan Evans of the North Wales Police.

Criticized by some as lacking in substance, and praised by others as an encouragement for reluctant readers, teen books such as those Quin-Harkin has built a career on are an important part of juvenile publishing, accounting for hundreds of thousands of sales annually. Quin-Harkin's books tell what happens when a teen and her best friend break up, when a family moves, or when parents are divorced. Most often there are young men involved: guys a girl wants to date, or loves from afar, or beats at tennis. Quin-Harkin writes about the concerns of teenage girls of the 1980s and 1990s; relevance is her watchword, and she has built an enormous and faithful readership as a result.

Born in Bath, England, Quin-Harkin began writing for fun at an early age; she had published her first short story by age sixteen. Her own teen years were quite placid, as she attended an all-girls school where academics rather than sports or romance were emphasized. The usual emotional upheavals of a young woman were thus largely postponed until Quin-Harkin attended college, earning a B.A. with honors from the University of London. For the first few years after graduation, Quin-Harkin worked for the British Broadcasting Corporation as a studio manager and also as a writer of radio and television plays. Such writings were "fairly highbrow," as the author described them. She then moved to Australia, where she met her husband while working for the Australian Broadcasting Company. The couple married in 1966 and moved to the United States. Settling in the San Francisco Bay area, Quin-Harkin balanced the role of mother and writer. She worked initially for a textbook company and helped develop new primary reading texts more relevant for contemporary urban children than the traditional primer stories of Dick and Jane.

Work on textbooks set Quin-Harkin to writing for herself again, and her first book was published in 1976. *Peter Penny's Dance* is a picture book for children, inspired by the lyrics from an old English folk song: "I've come to claim a silver pound because I've danced the world around." Peter is a sailor who would rather dance a reel than scrub the decks, and who sets off to dance around the world. He finds adventure in France, Africa, China, and America, but Peter finally dances home, to claim the hand of his beloved Lavinia, the captain's daughter. Everything about this first title was easy for Quin-Harkin: the story seemed to come of itself and the manuscript found a home on the second try. Zena Sutherland of the *Bulletin of the Center for Children's Books* called the tale "a bouncy, bonny book," and many critics praised the illustrations by Anita Lobel. Of the book's exciting conclusion, *Horn Book* reviewer Ethel L. Heins wrote: "In a splendid finale, reminiscent of *Around the World in Eighty Days,* Peter arrived back in England in the nick of time and skipped his way straight to the church and into the arms of his overjoyed bride." *Peter Penny's Dance* went on to win numerous awards. This early successful start, was followed by several years without sales, as Quin-Harkin continued to raise her family while struggling to work at her craft. Then several early titles were sold to Parents Magazine Press—*Benjamin's Balloon, Septimus Bean and His Amazing Machine,* and *Magic Growing Powder*—which established Quin-Harkin as a picture book author.

In 1981 came a turning point in the author's career, when her agent called to ask if she could do a teen novel in a hurry. A trip to the local bookstore provided the author with a bundle of similar books which she studied carefully, and then she sat down to turn out sample chapters of her own teen fiction. These samples evolved into *California Girl,* the first in Bantam's "Sweet Dreams" series. In *California Girl,* Jenny is a sixteen-year-old swimmer with Olympic aspirations. When her coach moves to Texas, Jenny's family follows so that she can continue training. But Texas is a far cry from Jenny's former home state; here she is regarded as strange because of her devotion to her athletic dreams. She soon finds a friend, however: Mark is an injured football player who supports her swimming, helping her train, and the finale comes with Jenny competing in the Nationals for a berth in the Olympics. Along the way is a crew of supporting characters: the scheming cheerleader who wants her former boyfriend back, Jenny's rather unsympathetic mother, and an empty-headed girlfriend. Becky Johnson in *Voice of Youth Advocates* noted that "the story is fast-moving and the main character is serious-minded and independent." Johnson also felt, however, that the supporting cast of characters lacked meaningful depth: "This gets high marks for readability but could have had more realistic character development." However, Ella B. Fossum, writing in the *School Library Journal,* thought the book was "a cut above the usual teenage love story" because of the added complications and insightful details of Jenny's Olympic aspirations.

The second book in the series, *Love Match,* also involves an athletic theme, when Joanna refuses to try to ensure Rick's affection by allowing him to beat her at tennis. While a *Bulletin of the Center for Children's Books* reviewer concluded that the book had "little substance" because of its formulaic plot—girl meets boy, loses boy, wins boy in the end—Joe McKenzie in the *School Library Journal* commented that "readers will figure it all out early too, but many of them won't care," because of the sympathetic nature of the leading character, Joanna. This blend of a sympathetic and generally well-drawn and independent main character, along with a formulaic plot, has formed the heart of much of Quin-Harkin's teen writing. Most of the titles fall into the category of escapist reading, "predictable but palatable," as Ilene Cooper of *Booklist* noted in a review of *Daydreamer,* a further title in the "Sweet Dreams" series. Maureen Ritter, however, writing in *Voice of Youth Advocates* about *Daydreamer,* emphasized the readability factor and noted that the book was "perfect for a hi/lo reader," and that aside from divorced parents, the main character, Lisa, "does not suffer from the traumas that most YA novel characters do; only the necessary conflicts needed for growth."

Other titles in the series have also earned mixed praise: Plots that have just enough individuality to set them apart. Kathy Fritts in the *School Library Journal* noted that "funny scenes and a fast pace" set *101 Ways to Meet Mr. Right* "a notch above average," and Elaine Patterson, reviewing the same book in *Kliatt,* commented that "girls of all ages" would identify with the main character's "fears, fantasies, and flops" as she searches for the true love that is under her nose all the time. While critics may disagree about the relative merits of such books, readers pronounced them successes; one book in the "Sweet Dreams" series, *Ten-Boy Summer,* sold over half a million copies. In this work, central characters Jill and Toni determine to liven up their junior-year summer by breaking up with their respective boyfriends, and then betting on who will be the first to have dated ten boys. Sally Estes of *Booklist* found the book's premise "a bit farfetched, perhaps, but light and lively enough to attract nondemanding readers of teenage romances." Similarly, Susan Levine wrote in the *Voice of Youth Advocates* that *Ten-Boy Summer* "satisfies its requirements of a fast, uncomplicated, lightly romantic story with a happy ending."

Series writing has its pitfalls, according to Quin-Harkin, the largest of which is slipping into cliché. The author becomes so familiar with the set of characters that it is easy to use stock dialogue or responses instead of always being on guard to search for the most appropriate wording. Quin-Harkin generally writes a 200-page book every two months, and many of these are told in the first person. "On the whole, first person is very effective because it doesn't ever become overly dramatic," Quin-Harkin noted, adding: "And of course, when you're first person, you're right there with the character and it's very immediate." Her experience in radio and television also informs her work, making for strong dialogue and pictorial writing. Quin-Harkin thinks in terms of scenes rather than chapters, a technique that gives her books a fast pace. She reaches back to her own feelings as a teenager for inspiration, and has also used the experiences of her four children and their friends as they traversed their teen years.

If cliché is one pitfall in series books, boredom for the writer can be another. According to Quin-Harkin, the "Sugar and Spice" series went on far longer than she wanted. The adventures of the two cousins, Chrissy and Cara, became somewhat stale after several books, but the series was so popular that Quin-Harkin was forced to continue with it, writing some twenty installments. Bouncy Chrissy, a cheerleader type from a small town in Iowa, has come to live in San Francisco with her serious, ballet-studying cousin, Caroline (or Cara). *Flip Side* inaugurated the series and introduced the city and country cousins in a situation in which they both yearn for the other's boyfriend but are too nice to do anything about it. *School Library Journal* contributor Kathy Fritts called the book "a winner," while Laurel Ibey, writing in the *Voice of Youth Advocates,* concluded that everyone who read *Flip Side* would "find it full of fun!" Another adventure in the "Sugar and Spice" series takes urban Cara to Chrissy's Iowa farm in *Nothing in Common.* Fritts asserted that a "fast pace, wonderful scenes of family and farm life, lots of action, and plenty of boy-girl mix and match make it a sure hit." Cara finally decides to give up dancing in *The Last Dance,* which Juli Lund in the *Voice of Youth Advocates* praised for the fact that it "did not have a perfect 'happy ending,' but instead realistically portrayed not-so-perfect actual life."

Other series books from Quin-Harkin include those from "On Our Own" and "Heartbreak Café." "Heartbreak Café," contains only six books; each is told from the point of view of one of the people involved with the rundown café, which is a hangout for teens with problems. With *No Experience Required,* Quin-Harkin features heroine Debbie Leslie, whose parents have just divorced. Debbie manages to get a position at the Heartbreak Café, but Joe, the grandson of the owner, figures the wealthy kid won't last a month. Debbie sets out to prove him wrong and turns out to be one of Quin-Harkin's archetypal feisty and headstrong female characters. A *Publishers Weekly* reviewer, commenting on *No Experience Required,* noted that "Quin-Harkin's skilled storytelling effectively blends wry humor with universal concerns." The "On Our Own" series is a spin-off from "Sweet Dreams," following some of those main

characters on their way into college. Jill has been accepted to an exclusive out-of-state school, but Toni has to defer college plans because of her father's heart attack. Plagued by a miserable roommate, Jill is finally rescued by a visit from Toni, who tells the girl off. First-time college experiences inaugurated this mini-series, and a *Publishers Weekly* reviewer noted that such experiences "ring true." Other commentators found problems with the series. A *Voice of Youth Advocates* reviewer, Kaye Grabbe, objected to what she considered "little character development," noting that Jill "never seems like much of a real person." In a *Voice of Youth Advocates* review of *The Graduates,* Sandra Dayton maintained, "it is unfortunate that the shallow dialogue and narrative read so very quickly," but said that the book is "worthwhile for the exposure of so many real problems of college freshmen."

A series geared at pre-teens is "Friends," which follows the relationship between two girls, Alison and Tess, over the four summers they spend together in a small resort town. Tess is newly arrived in the town in the first book of the series, *Starring Tess and Ali,* and Alison forms a quick friendship with her. Trouble arises, however, with remarks Tess makes about how overprotective Ali's mother is. Ali is upset by such remarks until she learns the root of them: Tess's mother has recently deserted the family and envy and spite are undoubtedly contributing to the girl's behavior. A *Publishers Weekly* reviewer noted, in a review of *Starring Tess and Ali,* that younger readers might resent the "juvenile tone" of the book, but that Quin-Harkin had created a "compassionate protagonist whose heretofore compliant ways are undergoing thoughtful reevaluation."

Quin-Harkin has also written many non-series teen books, perhaps the best known being *Wanted: Date for Saturday Night,* in which the central problem is finding a date for shy Julie for the freshman formal. Along the way, Julie manages to join the "in" crowd, only to discover they are shallow and no fun. Reviews again were mixed. Carolyn Gabbard Fugate in the *School Library Journal* found that "the characterizations of Julie and the minor characters are excellent," and concluded that the book was "a good, solid addition to a junior or senior high-school library." Zena Sutherland of the *Bulletin of the Center for Children's Books,* however, concluded that the book had "a formula plot and cardboard characters," while Kaye Grabbe in *Voice of Youth Advocates* commented on the book's "improbable story" and "shallow characterizations." *Wanted* went on to win a Children's Choice award as well as a large readership.

Another stand-alone book from Quin-Harkin is *Summer Heat,* in which teen protagonist Laurie Beth, on the verge of graduating from high school, must choose between two suitors and two completely different lifestyles. A *Publishers Weekly* reviewer commented favorably on this title, noting that "love certainly plays an important role in [Laurie Beth's] decision—but so does her new-found sense of self-worth—and that's what makes this story so refreshing." Other non-series efforts include *The Sutcliffe Diamonds,* which romance readers will "devour," according to Elaine M. McGuire in the *Voice of Youth Advocates;* and *The Apartment,* which a *Voice of Youth Advocates* contributor described as a story of "three girls from very different backgrounds [who] share an apartment during a pivotal period in their lives."

In the mid-1990s Quin-Harkin began writing for adults, particularly in the mystery series featuring North Welsh police constable Evan Evans. The Evans books, penned under the pseudonym Rhys Bowen, are set in the village of Llanfair, which is similar to a village Quin-Harkin used to visit during summer vacations as a child. Speaking to Jo Peters of *BookBrowser* about her childhood visits to an aunt in Wales, Quin-Harkin explained: "My fictitious village of Llanfair is a combination of two villages where I had relatives and stayed in my summer holidays. . . . It was an uncomplicated time of long walks, afternoons at a nearby beach and chapel on Sundays."

With the first book in the series, *Evans Above,* Quin-Harkin sets the scene and main characters in place for a series to grow and prosper. When his policeman father is killed in the line of duty, young Evans, a North Wales constable, is assigned to the village of Llanfair, where there are far too many Evanses. Constable Evans becomes, in local parlance, Evans the Law, to distinguish him from the butcher, Evans the Meat, the dairyman, Evans the Milk, or the postman, Evans the Post. But Llanfair proves to be anything but tranquil. Two hikers presumably fall to their deaths on Mount Snowdon on the same day, while a third is soon discovered in a cave with his throat cut. Up to his ears in crime, Evans is also pursued by the eligible young ladies of the village, Betsy the Bar (the local barmaid), and Bronwen the Book (a teacher). Reviewing this debut novel in the series, Judy McAloon in the *School Library*

Journal praised the book's "well-crafted plot, nicely drawn characters, [and] strong sense of place," concluding that young adult readers would enjoy both the book's setting and protagonist, "a hero who is young enough to feel self-conscious with women." Rex E. Klett, writing in the *Library Journal,* noted the book's "straightforward plotting, tempered with unique characterization and subtle humor," and a writer for *Kirkus Reviews* also found much to like in this "pleasingly unpretentious debut."

Constable Evans makes return performances in *Evan Help Us, Evanly Choirs, Evan and Elle,* and *Evan Can Wait.* In the second novel in the series, Evans is pursued by yet another female, a single woman who moves into the village with her daughter. Murder soon intrudes into this domestic comedy, however, when Colonel Arbuthnot, a yearly visitor from London who claims to have found the ruins of Camelot near the village, is found dead. The same fate also awaits returning villager Ted Morgan, who has plans to turn a local mine into a theme park. Investigating the case, Evans finds a connection between the two murders and the new femme fatale, a trail that leads him to London and back. "Bowen's quiet humor and her appreciation for rural village life make this a jewel of a story," wrote a contributor to *Publishers Weekly. Booklist* contributor GraceAnne A. DeCandido called the setting for the novel "ineffably quaint and impossibly charming," going on to say that the novel was as "satisfying as a Guinness pint." Marilyn Stasio, writing in the *New York Times Book Review,* echoed such a sentiment, noting that "the pleasure of visiting Llanfair is that nothing, not even murder, can ruffle its placid composure."

In his third outing, *Evanly Choirs,* Constable Evans is persuaded to add his voice to the local choir in its preparations for the *eisteddfod,* a music festival held in a nearby town. Into the mix comes famous opera star Ifor Llewellyn and his wife, Margaret, taking a restful vacation in Llanfair. The famous opera singer is persuaded to join the male chorus, but becomes a large pain in the neck to most people in the village. No matter; soon his tenor voice is stilled for good when the opera star is found dead one morning. Evans is on the trail while his choirmates struggle to maintain a competitive edge. "Between his singing debut and his bumpy romance with the schoolteacher, Evan sorts through a humorous series of false confessions to catch the real killer," wrote a contributor for *Publishers Weekly,* who concluded: "Ultimately, it's Bowen's keen sense of small-town politics and gossip that will keep her fans turning pages." A writer for *Kirkus Reviews* claimed it is the book's "cozily intimate style, and modest, down-home hero," which make for "satisfying entertainment," a feature also noted by *Booklist* contributor Jenny McLarin, who called this "charming tale . . . [a] perfect book to curl up with on a rainy day."

Feminine competition once again plays a part in the goings on in Llanfair in the fourth series entry, *Evan and Elle*. When eligible widow Madame Yvette opens a French restaurant in the village, she wins the stomachs and hearts of not a few, including the good constable. But he resists all efforts to be parted from his real sweetheart, ever-true Bronwen. When the Madame's restaurant is burned down, Evan is forced to get closer. At first, suspicion leads to Welsh extremists responsible for a string of arsons in the area, but a body found in the ashes turns the investigation into a homicide. The trail leads first to the southern coast of England and then on to France, as Evan and his sidekick, Sergeant Watkins, unravel the mystery. "This is a slight confection of a mystery," noted a reviewer for *Publishers Weekly*, "sweetened with the author's obvious affection for her characters, as well as for all things Welsh." *Booklist* critic Jenny McLarin also reflected upon the lightness of the story line, but further commented, "It hardly matters, though, because the strength of this series is not plot but those staples of the British cozy, village ambience and eccentric characters." McLarin concluded that *Evan and Elle* is as "light and sweet as a crepes suzette." Karen G. Anderson in *January Magazine* concluded: "The book turns out to be as complex and delicious as one of Mme. Yvette's celebrated recipes."

The fifth book in the series, *Evan Can Wait*, features two plot lines that slowly begin to connect as Evans delves into the mysterious death of film producer/director Grantley Smith, whose crew has come to Llanfair on an assignment. His body is found drowned in a slate mine, and Evans then begins to examine the relationships between the various crew members for possible clues. A new story develops as Evans learns of art fraud and a murder that occurred years before that involved the mines, where a painting—one of several items from the National Gallery stored in the mines during World War II—was stolen. Critics lauded both the setting and the characters in this installment. "The author creates a vivid background for the novel by weaving in descriptive details about the area, the deadly mines, and the quickly changing weather," noted Pam

Johnson in a review for the *School Library Journal*. A *Publishers Weekly* reviewer wrote that the author's "great strength is her endearing Welsh characters, from the modest Evan to such amusing locals as the saucy barmaid and the rival chapel preachers." In the *Library Journal*, Rex Klett called *Evan Can Wait* "an exciting addition to the series."

Evan's Gate finds the constable involved in his eighth case. Now working as a plainclothes detective, Evans is investigating the disappearance of a young girl named Ashley Sholokhov, who may have been abducted from a local beach by her Russian father. When Evans makes the grisly discovery of a child's skeleton while digging outside a cottage he's renovating, he begins to suspect that the dead child is somehow related to Ashley's case and the long-ago disappearance of another child named Sarah. Though Evans's bosses want him to concentrate on finding Ashley's father, he can't let go of the possible connection to Sarah and her family, all of whom have come back to Wales for the first time since Sarah's death to attend a birthday party for Tomos Thomas, the girl's eighty-year-old grandfather. *Booklist* reviewer Sue Bowen remarked favorably on the novel's "fine sense of place," as well as its "compelling dual storyline" and "cast of sympathetic, well-drawn characters." *Library Journal* reviewer Rex E. Klett called the novel "an attractive series addition." Bowen "delivers an enchanting portrait of Wales with genuine, flawed characters, a modicum of humor and plenty of red herrings," remarked a *Publishers Weekly* contributor.

Evan and Bronwen are set to tie the knot in *Evan Blessed*. After hauling Bronwen's belongings to the couple's mountainside cottage, Evan is approached by a hiker, Paul Upfield, who says he has lost track of his seventeen-year-old girlfriend on the mountains slopes after the two had an argument. A police search turns up no trace of the young woman, but the ominous discovery of an underground dungeonlike bunker, seemingly a perfect place to stow a captive, adds urgency to the search. As the police struggle to find information from the burgeoning summer tourist crowd, Evan begins to receive strange clues couched in the form of sheet music. The case becomes personal when Bronwen herself vanishes, and additional musical clues arrive suggesting that she has been abducted. Bowen "builds tension with every page simply by making Evan and Bronwen . . . so likable and resourceful that you pull for them all the way," commented a *Kirkus Reviews* critic.

Evanly Bodies, the tenth book in the Evans series, puts the now-married Evans in partnership with an abrasive and none-too-bright senior officer, Detective Inspector Bragg. Chafing against the arrangement and intolerant of Bragg's glaring stupidity, Evans struggles to keep his wits about him while investigating the murder of the head of the University of Wales History Department. The professor, unpopular with students and faculty alike and keenly disliked by his wife, was shot with an antique Japanese pistol through the open window of his kitchen. Bragg suspects the wife in the killing, but she claims to have been out walking the dog at the time. Before Bragg or Evans can act, another person is shot with the same weapon. In conjunction with the murder investigation, Evans searches for Jamilla, a British-born Pakistani girl who was soon to be sent back to Pakistan for an unwanted arranged marriage. A third person is shot with the old pistol, and when Evans locates Jamilla, he also finds the vital clue to solving the shootings. *Booklist* reviewer David Pitt mused that reading this installment of the Evans series "is like getting together with an old, dear friend." A *Kirkus Reviews* contributor called the novel's murder mystery plot "derivative, but the wider playing field for the clever, appealing Evans brings both his social and detective skills to the fore." A *Publishers Weekly* reviewer concluded: "Bowen sparkles in this cleverly concocted puzzler."

Asked why she turned from writing young adult novels to mysteries, Quin-Harkin told Peters: "My hundredth book was approaching. I had put my kids through college and we had paid off the house. And, quite frankly, I felt that I had written enough for young people. I decided it was now time to write what I liked to read—and that was mysteries, with a strong sense of place. So I took a gamble, a new name and started back at square one as a mystery writer. I haven't regretted it for a second."

With the first of her "Molly Murphy" novels, Quin-Harkin embarked on a new series of historical cozy mysteries, also under her pseudonym of Rhys Bowen. The debut novel, *Murphy's Law,* set in 1901, follows the determined and resourceful Molly as she flees her Irish homeland after killing Justin, a local laird who had tried to rape her. Boarding a ship for England, Molly encounters Kathleen O'Conner, who begs her to take her children to her husband Seamus in New York, since she is forbidden to board the ship because of her tuberculosis. Molly agrees, assumes O'Conner's identity for the trip, and soon she and the children are consigned to the misery of a cramped and unpleasant transatlantic crossing. On board, Molly is accosted by the brutish and unpleasant O'Malley, who apparently knew Kath-

leen O'Conner. Upon arrival at Ellis Island, O'Malley is found stabbed to death, and police detective Daniel Sullivan seeks answers from Molly and the solution to the man's murder. A *Kirkus Reviews* contributor called Molly "a charming if pushy heroine who eventually earns Sullivan's appreciation." Rex E. Klett, writing in the *Library Journal,* commended the novel's "strong focus, great characters, and authentic period descriptions." Bowen "conveys a nice sense of place and period in this debut of a new historical series with its spunky, 19th-century Irish heroine," remarked a *Publishers Weekly* critic.

In *Death of Riley,* Molly accepts a job as a companion to the aged Miss Van Woekem. During the course of her duties, Molly becomes aware of a man who appears to be investigating a neighbor. The man, Paddy Riley, owns an investigation agency, and Molly convinces him to let her come to work in his office. To her chagrin, however, she is not involved in any investigations, but is instead relegated to duties as a cleaning lady. Upon arriving at work one morning, however, she discovers Riley badly wounded and near death, and the assailant hurriedly leaving the office. When Riley dies, Molly decides to investigate his murder on her own, and in the process assumes responsibility for Riley's business. *Booklist* reviewer Sue O'Brien called Molly a "smart, feisty, independent heroine," and noted that early twentieth-century New York is "realistically portrayed, along with the Irish immigrant experience, in this appealing series."

For the Love of Mike finds Molly successfully established in Reilly's investigation business. She finds much of her work, such as tracking down straying spouses, to be tedious, and seeks a way to change the focus of her business. To this end, she lands an assignment to look into the theft of clothing designs from garment maker Mostel and Klein. Whoever is stealing the designs is selling them to competitor Lowenstein so he can get the new fashions produced and on sale before Mostel and Klein can take advantage of their own work. Molly undertakes a lesson in the sewing business and learns first-hand about the difficult, often cruel conditions of garment sweatshops as they existed in the early 1900s. A second assignment arrives in a letter from Irish countryman Major Favisham, who hires Molly to find his daughter Katherine, who has recently left Ireland for New York. As Molly continues her work, surprising and dangerous connections arise between the two cases. Meanwhile, new romance may be blossoming with labor leader Jacob Singer, in competition with Molly's first

American heartthrob, police captain Daniel Sullivan. A *Kirkus Reviews* critic observed that "Molly grows ever more engaging against a vibrant background of New York's dark side at the turn of the century."

Oh Danny Boy sets Molly to work helping her beloved Daniel clear himself of accusations that he accepted a bribe. Molly believes that Daniel was framed by someone who wanted him off the case of the East Side Ripper, a vicious killer of prostitutes. Molly's concern for Daniel becomes even more complicated when she realizes that their single night of unrestrained passion has left her pregnant. An abortion is considered and rejected, as Molly searches for solutions to her predicament, to Daniel's legal mess, and to the murderous Ripper. Complicating matters is the disappearance of Molly's closest friend, Letitia Blackwell. In the course of her investigation, Molly joins forces with police matron Sabella Goodwin, who is also looking into the Ripper case. Soon, they determine that the slain women were not prostitutes. In fact, one of the victims is Letitia. They do discover that each had a connection to Coney Island, which will be key in determining the Ripper's identity. Bowen "deserves kudos for her recreation of early 20th-century New York," noted a *Publishers Weekly* reviewer.

BIOGRAPHICAL AND CRITICAL SOURCES:

BOOKS

Authors and Artists for Young Adults, Volume 6, Thomson Gale (Detroit, MI), 1991.

PERIODICALS

Booklist, September 1, 1982, Sally Estes, review of *Ten-Boy Summer,* p. 37; May 15, 1983, Ilene Cooper, review of *Daydreamer,* p. 1221; August, 1998, GraceAnne A. DeCandido, review of *Evan Help Us,* p. 1972; April 15, 1999, Jenny McLarin, review of *Evanly Choirs,* p. 1446; December 15, 1999, Jenny McLarin, review of *Evan and Elle,* p. 759; August, 2001, GraceAnne A. DeCandido, review of *Murphy's Law,* p. 2095; January 1, 2002, GraceAnne A. DeCandido, review of *Evans to Betsy,* p. 816; November 1, 2002, Sue O'Brien, review of *Death of Riley,* p. 476; March 15, 2004, Sue O'Brien, review of *Evan's Gate,* p. 1269;

February 1, 2005, GraceAnne A. DeCandido, review of *In Like Flynn,* p. 944; February 15, 2006, David Pitt, review of *Oh Danny Boy,* p. 51; May 1, 2006, David Pitt, review of *Evanly Bodies,* p. 22.

Bulletin of the Center for Children's Books, October, 1976, Zena Sutherland, review of *Peter Penny's Dance,* p. 30; March, 1982, review of *Love Match,* p. 136; June, 1985, p. 192.

Horn Book, June, 1976, Ethel L. Heins, review of *Peter Penny's Dance,* p. 281.

Kirkus Reviews, November 15, 1997, review of *Evans Above;* April 28, 1999, review of *Evanly Choirs;* August 15, 2001, review of *Murphy's Law,* p. 1164; December 15, 2001, review of *Evans to Betsy,* p. 1723; October 1, 2002, review of *Death of Riley,* p. 1427; October 1, 2003, review of *For the Love of Mike,* p. 1201; May 15, 2005, review of *Evan Blessed,* p. 564; February 1, 2005, review of *In Like Flynn,* p. 149; January 15, 2006, review of *Oh Danny Boy,* p. 62; June 1, 2006, review of *Evanly Bodies,* p. 547.

Kliatt, spring, 1982, p. 10; spring, 1983, p. 5; fall, 1985, Elaine Patterson, review of *101 Ways to Meet Mr. Right,* p. 16.

Library Journal, December, 1997, Rex E. Klett, review of *Evans Above,* p. 159; March 1, 2000, Rex E. Klett, review of *Evan and Elle,* p. 128; January 1, 2001, Rex E. Klett, review of *Evan Can Wait,* p. 162; October 1, 2001, Rex E. Klett, review of *Murphy's Law,* p. 145; March 1, 2002, Rex E. Klett, review of *Evans to Betsy,* p. 144; November 1, 2002, Rex E. Klett, review of *Death of Riley,* p. 132; December, 2003, Rex E. Klett, review of *For the Love of Mike,* p. 171; April 1, 2004, Rex E. Klett, review of *Evan's Gate,* p. 128; February 1, 2005, Rex E. Klett, review of *In Like Flynn,* p. 57.

New York Times Book Review, October 25, 1998, Marilyn Stasio, "Crime," p. 43.

Publishers Weekly, May 24, 1991, review of *Starring Tess and Ali,* p. 58; August 17, 1998, review of *Evan Help Us,* p. 52; April 5, 1999, review of *Evanly Choirs,* p. 226; January 10, 2000, review of *Evan and Elle,* p. 48; November 13, 2000, review of *Evan Can Wait,* p. 88; September 3, 2001, review of *Murphy's Law,* p. 67; February 18, 2002, review of *Evans to Betsy,* p. 79; November 18, 2002, review of *Death of Riley,* p. 45; November 3, 2003, review of *For the Love of Mike,* p. 57; March 29, 2004, review of *Evan's Gate,* p. 42; February 28, 2005, review of *In Like Flynn,* p. 45; January 16, 2006, review of *Oh Danny Boy,* p. 40; June 19, 2006, review of *Evanly Bodies,* p. 43; January 22, 2007, review of *In Dublin's Fair City,* p. 165.

School Library Journal, November, 1981, Ella B. Fossum, review of *California Girl,* p. 110; March, 1982, Joe McKenzie, review of *Love Match,* p. 160; March, 1985, p. 181; September, 1985, p. 180; January, 1988, Kathy Fritts, reviews of *Flip Side* and *Nothing in Common,* p. 95; May, 1998, Judy McAloon, review of *Evans Above,* p. 175; May, 2001, Pam Johnson, review of *Evan Can Wait,* p. 175.

Voice of Youth Advocates, December, 1981, Becky Johnson, review of *California Girl,* p. 34; December, 1982, Susan Levine, review of *Ten-Boy Summer,* p. 35; December, 1983, Maureen Ritter, review of *Daydreamer,* p. 281; June, 1985, p. 134; August-October, 1986, p. 156; December, 1986, p. 231; April, 1988, Laurel Ibey, review of *Flip Side,* p. 35; October, 1994, p. 215; December, 1994, p. 279.

ONLINE

BookBrowser, http://www.bookbrowser.com/ (April 15, 2007), Jo Peters, interview with Rhys Bowen.
January Magazine, http://www.januarymagazine.com/ (April 15, 2007), Karen G. Anderson, review of *Evan and Elle.*
Rhys Bowen Home Page, http://home.comcast.net/ ˜rhysbowen (April 15, 2007).
Rhys Bowen's Mystery Home Page, http://www. rhysbowen.com (April 15, 2007).

* * *

**QUIN-HARKIN, Janet Elizabeth
See QUIN-HARKIN, Janet**

R

RAINES, Howell 1943-
(Howell Hiram Raines)

PERSONAL: Born February 5, 1943, in Birmingham, AL; son of W.S. (a builder) and Bertha Raines; married Susan Woodley (a photographer), March 22, 1969; married second wife; wife's name Krystyna; children: Ben Hayes, Jeffrey Howell. *Education:* Birmingham-Southern College, B.A., 1964; University of Alabama, Tuscaloosa, M.A., 1973.

ADDRESSES: Home—St. Petersburg, FL. *Agent*—Russell & Volkening, Inc., 551 Madison Ave., New York, NY 10017.

CAREER: Writer, editor, and journalist. *Birmingham Post-Herald,* Birmingham, AL, reporter, 1964-65; WBRC-TV, Birmingham, AL, staff writer, 1965-67; *Tuscaloosa News,* Tuscaloosa, AL, reporter, 1968-69; *Birmingham News,* Birmingham, AL, film critic, 1970-71; *Atlanta Constitution,* Atlanta, GA, political editor, 1971-74; *St. Petersburg Times,* St. Petersburg, FL, political editor, beginning 1976; *New York Times,* Atlanta bureau chief, beginning 1979, London bureau chief, 1987-88, Washington bureau chief, 1988-93, editorial page editor, 1993-2001, executive editor, 2001-03. Guest on television programs, including the *Colbert Report.*

AWARDS, HONORS: Pulitzer Prize for "Grady's Gift," a personal reflection published in the *New York Times Magazine,* 1992.

WRITINGS:

(Contributor) Herbert Alexander, editor, *Campaign Money* (nonfiction), Free Press (New York, NY), 1976.

Whiskey Man (novel), Viking (New York, NY), 1977, reprinted, University of Alabama Press (Tuscaloosa, Al), 2000.

My Soul Is Rested (oral history), Putnam (New York, NY), 1977.

Fly Fishing Through the Midlife Crisis (memoir), Morrow (New York, NY), 1993.

The One That Got Away (memoir), Scribner (New York, NY), 2006.

Contributor to periodicals, including the *Atlantic Monthly* and the *Guardian* (Manchester, England).

SIDELIGHTS: Once the top editor of one of America's stalwart newspapers, Howell Raines is a Pulitzer-Prize-winning journalist, prominent memoirist, and noted editor. During nearly a quarter-century career with the *New York Times,* Raines served as chief of many of the paper's satellite bureaus, as editor of the *Times'* influential editorial page, and as finally as the executive editor. In 2003, Raines resigned from the paper in the aftermath of a scandal in which a young reporter, Jayson Blair, was proven to have engaged in systematic, long-term plagiarism and fabrication in the stories he wrote and published in the *Times.* In a lengthy article in *Atlantic Monthly,* Raines explained his perspective and took responsibility for the errors in the Blair case. However, under Raines's guidance, the *New York Times* had entered a new phase of prosperity, increasing circulation, reenergizing its mission, and winning a prestigious and record-breaking assortment of seven Pulitzer Prizes in 2002.

Raines is an avid fisherman, and two of his significant works of memoir and self-analysis reflect the wisdom and trappings of dedicated anglers. In *Fly Fishing*

Through the Midlife Crisis, published in 1993 as Raines turned fifty years old, provides Raines's reminiscences on his initiation into the fishing culture, and includes ruminations on notable fishing gear as well as genuine angling tips. Along with the fishing advice, however, comes more serious discussion, as the author addresses some of the most significant themes confronting men at midlife: "mortality, loyalty (and divorce, its near cousin), and betrayal of friends and the true self," noted a reviewer in *Publishers Weekly.* Much of the book centers on Raines's friendship with Dick Blalock, an irascible, overweight, deeply involved expert fly fisherman who served as Raines's guide and mentor. Hal Espen, writing in the *New York Times Book Review,* called the book "funny, sweet, rueful and charming, an antic paean to fishing lore and the companionable pleasures of the foolish business of casting a line with like-minded fools, some of them holy." For Raines, those who fish are seeking an experience that is transcendental, even magical. "It's hard to find books that fall into that category as well," concluded Jim Tharpe in *Nieman Reports,* "but when Raines is at his best in this book it's a word that comes to mind."

"Whatever else one might say about Howell Raines, the truest thing about the erstwhile editor of the *New York Times* is that he is one heck of a writer," commented Frank Wilson in the *Philadelphia Inquirer.* "Every sentence on every page of his new memoir, *The One That Got Away,* is beautifully shaped and cadenced." *The One That Got Away,* written in the aftermath of his departure from the *New York Times,* covers Raines's ideas on journalism, his professional defeat, and the irreplaceable joys of fly fishing in native streams as well as far-flung waters. In his work, Raines proves that he is a "lovely and witty writer whose guiding metaphors involve the fly-fisherman's mantra of catch and release and whose ultimate thesis is the glory of unplanned circumstances, including those of a romantic variety," remarked James Warren in *Washington Monthly.* "Skillfully drawing parallels between the deceptions practiced by fishermen, journalists, and politicians, Raines describes his love of the unpredictability of fishing and of life," observed *Booklist* reviewer Vanessa Bush. Throughout the book, noted a *Kirkus Reviews* contributor, Raines "comes across as self-deprecating and learned, fierce and confident; his writing is as brisk and bracing as the early-morning air on a remote salmon stream."

BIOGRAPHICAL AND CRITICAL SOURCES:

BOOKS

Raines, Howell, *Fly Fishing Through the Midlife Crisis,* Morrow (New York, NY), 1993.

Raines, Howell, *The One That Got Away,* Scribner (New York, NY), 2006.

PERIODICALS

American Prospect, October 7, 2002, Nicholas Confessore, "Bad News: What the Right Doesn't Understand about Howell Raines," p. 12.
Atlantic Monthly, May, 2004, Howell Raines, "My Times."
Booklist, January 1, 2006, Vanessa Bush, review of *The One That Got Away,* p. 21.
Kirkus Reviews, February 15, 2006, review of *The One That Got Away,* p. 174.
New York, May 8, 2006, Philip Weiss, "Fishing with Howell," profile of Howell Raines, p. 36.
New York Times Book Review, June 11, 2006, Hal Espen, "I'd Rather Be . . .," review of *The One That Got Away,* p. 18.
Nieman Reports, winter, 1993, Jim Tharpe, review of *Fly Fishing Through the Midlife Crisis,* p. 72.
Philadelphia Inquirer, July 5, 2006, Frank Wilson, review of *The One That Got Away.*
Publishers Weekly, August 23, 1993, review of *Fly Fishing Through the Midlife Crisis,* p. 55.
Time, May 29, 2006, Lev Grossman and Richard Lacayo, "Five Memoirs That Are Worth Your Time," review of *The One That Got Away,* p. 71.
Washington Monthly, June, 2006, James Warren, "Big Fish Story: In Howell Raines's Telling, His Only Mistake Was Caring Too Much," review of *The One That Got Away,* p. 36.

ONLINE

Slate, http://www.slate.com/ (May 13, 2003), Jack Shafer, "Defending Howell Raines: He Didn't Catch Jayson Blair. You Didn't Either," profile of Howell Raines.*

*   *   *

RAINES, Howell Hiram
See RAINES, Howell

*   *   *

RAYFIEL, Thomas 1958-

PERSONAL: Born 1958. *Education:* Grinnell College, graduated 1980.

CAREER: Writer, novelist, and screenwriter.

NOVELS

Split Levels, Simon & Schuster (New York, NY), 1994.
Colony Girl, Farrar, Straus (New York, NY), 1999.
Eve in the City, Ballantine (New York, NY), 2003.
Parallel Play, Random House (New York, NY), 2007.

OTHER

(With Arthur Joffe) *Harem* (screenplay), 1985.

Also author of serial novel *Lutwidge Finch,* published online in *zingmagazine.*

Contributor of short stories to periodicals, including *Grand Street, Quarterly, GQ,* and *Antioch Review.*

SIDELIGHTS: In Thomas Rayfiel's first novel, *Split Levels,* the author takes on suburbia under the guise of his protagonist, Allen Stanley, a thirty-something who returns to his home town under less-than-ideal circumstances. The town holds little in the way of pleasant memories for Stanley, who left after his sister's suspicious disappearance and his mother's accidental death shortly thereafter. Things have not improved: his father is found in the bathtub with his wrists slashed. Stanley encounters past acquaintances, an amorous neighbor, the police (who view him as a possible suspect in his father's death), and an attractive teenage girl. Critics praised Rayfiel's skillful dialogue and his mystery-writer style. The ending and the discovery of the person responsible for framing Stanley for his father's murder will, according to Gilbert Taylor in *Booklist,* leave "mystery buffs . . . satisfied."

Rayfiel's second novel, *Colony Girl,* is set in a Christian religious settlement called the Colony, in the cornfields near Arhat, Iowa. Eve is fifteen years old and torn between her existence at the Colony and the world beyond. The Colony is overseen by Gordon, the sect's founder, who has recently withdrawn, choosing to watch cable television while he deals with his own devils. Eve, a previous favorite of Gordon, takes a summer job as a flag person on a highway crew and falls in love with her new friend Joey, as well as Joey's father, Herb.

Gordon announces his plans to marry Serena, Eve's best girlfriend, which pushes Eve to dedicate herself to destroying the cult's leader.

Gordon was described by *Commonweal* critic Valerie Sayers as a "wonderfully vivid character." Rayfiel manages to avoid casting the sect leader as a villain, despite his penchant for sex and drugs. Eve's character is at times touched with wisdom beyond her years, and has the simplicity that children bring to things. Sayers also noted that although Eve is "an interesting soul," she never really "finds her voice," and felt that the novel's resolution is not up to the promise hinted at throughout.

Eve returns in Rayfiel's next novel, *Eve in the City.* Having left the religious colony where she grew up, Eve, now seventeen years old, lives and works in New York City. To her disadvantage, she lacks proper identification to find a legitimate job (she has, for example, no last name; no one else at the Colony had last names, either, since nobody in the Bible had them). To survive, she takes a job as a cocktail waitress at an illegal after-hours bar run by a Russian immigrant named Viktor. During an early morning walk home from work, Eve sees a man and a woman who may be fighting, kissing, or having sex—she cannot be sure of what she saw. When the man collapses with a knife in his gut, however, she is certain she saw a murder. She reports what she witnessed to the police, and in the process meets an attractive detective. Her life is further complicated when an artist friend takes intimate pictures of her, hangs prints of the pictures in the subway to attract graffiti, and displays the results as art in a prominent gallery exhibition. At the show, Eve takes an interest in a moody artist, even as she entertains a marriage proposal from green-card seeking Viktor and tries to further her own development as an individual and as a woman. A *Kirkus Reviews* critic called the novel "an enviably intelligent piece of writing." Eve remains a flawed but "likable heroine whom readers will want to follow further as she moves toward a brighter future," observed Beth Leistensnider in *Booklist.*

In *Parallel Play,* twenty-seven-year-old Eve has married and become a mother in a novel that a *Kirkus Reviews* contributor called "part anti-romantic comedy, part meditation on postpartum miseries and the joys of motherhood." Married to amiable, mild-manner Harvey, a doctor, Eve has not had sex with him in a year and worries that he might be having an affair. Meanwhile, she pines for ex-boyfriend Mark, a bodybuilding bad boy and carpenter. Worse, Eve struggles to reconcile her emotions and desires with the fact that she now has a child for whom she must be responsible. Resentful of the burden imposed by her baby, Ann, she also feels guilty because she is not the type of exemplary mom she sees on television and at the park. When Mark reappears in her life, facing his own difficult marriage, Eve has to confront her past feelings for him while deciding how to cope with her current situation. Slowly, Eve begins to realize how much Ann means to her and recognizes the importance of her family. "Eve remains a complex character with conflicting feelings whose voice sustains the novel," commented a *Publishers Weekly* reviewer.

BIOGRAPHICAL AND CRITICAL SOURCES:

PERIODICALS

Booklist, March 1, 1994, Gilbert Taylor, review of *Split Levels,* p. 1184; August, 1999, Ellie Barta-Moran, review of *Colony Girl,* p. 2028; August, 2003, Beth Leistensnider, review of *Eve in the City,* p. 1957.

Commonweal, October 22, 1999, Valerie Sayers, review of *Colony Girl,* p. 16.

Hudson Review, winter, 1995, Thomas Filbin, review of *Split Levels,* pp. 650-651.

Kirkus Reviews, September 1, 2003, review of *Eve in the City,* p. 1097; November 1, 2006, review of *Parallel Play,* p. 1098.

Library Journal, August, 1999, Yvette Weller Olson, review of *Colony Girl,* p. 142.

New York Times Book Review, May 29, 1994, Marilyn Stasio, review of *Split Levels,* p. 15; September 21, 2003, Richard Eder, "Not in Iowa Anymore," review of *Eve in the City.*.

Publishers Weekly, February 7, 1994, review of *Split Levels,* p. 16; August 2, 1999, review of *Colony Girl,* p. 73; September 22, 2003, review of *Eve in the City,* p. 85; October 16, 2006, review of *Parallel Play,* p. 30.

ONLINE

Grinnell College Web site, http://www.grinnell.edu/ (September 20, 2001), "Writers Who Are Alumni of Grinnell College."*

RAYFIELD, Donald 1942-
(Patrick Donald Rayfield)

PERSONAL: Born February 12, 1942, in Oxford, England; son of Harry Heron (an accountant) and Joan Rachel (a professor) Rayfield; married Rosalind Moore, July 27, 1963; children: Harriet, Gabriel, Barnaby. *Education:* Magdalene College, Cambridge, B.A., 1963, Ph. D., 1977. *Politics:* "Liberal with a small 'l.'" *Hobbies and other interests:* Breeding otters and wallabies, propagating shrubs, language study (especially languages of eastern Europe and the Near East).

ADDRESSES: Office—Department of Russian, Queen Mary College, University of London, Mile End Rd., London E1 4NS, England. *E-mail*—d.rayfield@qmul. ac.uk.

CAREER: University of Queensland, Brisbane, Australia, lecturer in Russian, 1964-66; Queen Mary College, University of London, 1967—, began as lecturer, became professor of Russian and Georgian, professor emeritus.

AWARDS, HONORS: Awarded the Order of the British Empire by Queen Elizabeth II, 2003, for services to Slavic studies.

WRITINGS:

(Translator and author of introduction) Nadezhda Mandel' shtam, *Ch.42,* Menard Press (London, England), 1973.

(Translator and author of introduction) Osip Mandel' shtam, *The Goldfinch,* Menard Press (London, England), 1973.

Chekhov: Evolution of His Art, Barnes & Noble (New York, NY), 1975.

(Translator) Galaktion Tabidze, *Ati Leksi* (title means "Ten Poems"), Ganatleba, 1975.

The Dream of Lhasa: The life of Nikolay Przhevalsky (1839-88) Explorer of Central Asia, Ohio State University Press (Athens, OH), 1976.

(Editor) Victor X., *The Confessions of Victor X,* Grove Press (New York, NY), 1985.

The Cherry Orchard: Catastrophe and Comedy, Twayne (New York, NY), 1994.

The Literature of Georgia: A History, Oxford University Press (New York, NY), 1994, 2nd revised edition, Curzon Press (London, England), 2000.

(Editor and translator) *The Chekhov Omnibus: Selected Stories,* Everyman (Dent, England), 1994.

Anton Chekhov: A Life, HarperCollins (London, England), 1997, Henry Holt (New York, NY), 1998.

(Translator and author of introduction) Ilia Chavchavadze, *King Dimitri's Sacrifice,* Tbilisi, 1998.

Understanding Chekhov: A Critical Study of Chekhov's Prose and Drama, University of Wisconsin Press (Madison, WI), 1999.

(Editor, with O.E. Makarova) *Dnevnik A.S. Suvorin, 1834-1912,* Garnett Press (London, England), 2000.

(Editor, with others) *The Garnett Book of Russian Verse: An Anthology with English Prose Translation,* Garnett Press (London, England), 2000.

Stalin and His Hangmen: The Tyrant and Those Who Killed for Him, Random House (New York, NY), 2004.

(Editor) *Comprehensive Georgian-English Dictionary,* Garnett Press (London, England), 2006.

Work represented in anthologies, including *The Elek Book of Oriental Verse* and *Cambridge Essays in Drama.* Contributor to literature and Slavic studies journals.

SIDELIGHTS: Donald Rayfield is a professor of Russian whose books have been instrumental in broadening the knowledge of Eastern European history. Among his later works is *Stalin and His Hangmen: The Tyrant and Those Who Killed for Him,* in which he studies the policies and tendencies of Stalin and his followers, most of whom needed no urging to use violence. Rayfield traces Stalin's history from his days as a seminary student to his rise as a tyrant who was responsible for the deaths of approximately ten million in his war against the peasants and hundreds of thousands of free thinkers in the 1930s. He comments on Stalin's ability to attract the kind of people who were willing to act on his behalf. "Rayfield's book shows us the whole pyramid of murderers with Stalin at the apex and his coterie of banal, mediocre yes-men in the layer just below, down to the bottommost stratum of sadists who did the actual killing," wrote Roger Cooke in *Sarmatian Review.* A *Contemporary Review* contributor noted: "The continuing fear of a Stalinist revival in Russia is one reason for this book." Cooke concluded: "We need a book like Rayfield's every year."

Rayfield once commented: "Academics usually write books for the wrong reasons. They become obsessed with minutiae, polemics, and the search for authority.

Readers and publishers should help them by insisting on the Pushkinian virtues of 'brevity, clarity, and simplicity,' and the Chekhovian standards of 'feeling, sense, and taking time.' Readers might also call for a return to multilingual standards, so that the art of translation might revive from its present insular inertia and make up for its deficient inspiration."

BIOGRAPHICAL AND CRITICAL SOURCES:

PERIODICALS

Contemporary Review, September, 2004, review of *Stalin and His Hangmen: The Tyrant and Those Who Killed for Him,* p. 190.

Library Journal, January 1, 2005, David Lee Poremba, review of *Stalin and his Hangmen,* p. 130.

Publishers Weekly, December 13, 2004, review of *Stalin and His Hangmen,* p. 59.

Sarmation Review, September, 2005, Roger Cooke, review of *Stalin and His Hangmen,* p. 1150.

ONLINE

School of Modern Languages, Queen Mary College, University of London Web site, http://www.modern-languages.qmul.ac.uk/ (December 29, 2006), biography.*

*   *   *

RAYFIELD, Patrick Donald
  See RAYFIELD, Donald

*   *   *

RENDELL, Ruth, Baroness of Babergh 1930-
  (Ruth Barbara Grasemann, Barbara Vine)

PERSONAL: Born February 17, 1930, in London, England; daughter of Arthur (a teacher) and Ebba (a teacher) Grasemann; married Donald Rendell, 1950 (divorced, 1975; remarried, 1977; deceased, c. 1999); children: Simon. *Education:* Educated in Essex, England. *Hobbies and other interests:* Reading, walking, opera.

ADDRESSES: Home—London, England. *Agent*—PFD, Drury House, 34-43 Russell St., London WC2B 5HA, England.

CAREER: Writer, novelist, short-story writer, and journalist. Express and Independent Newspapers, West Essex, England, reporter and subeditor for the Chigwell *Times,* 1948-52. Member of British House of Lords.

AWARDS, HONORS: Edgar Allan Poe Award, Mystery Writers of America, 1975, for story "The Fallen Curtain," 1976, for collection *The Fallen Curtain and Other Stories,* 1984, for story "The New Girlfriend," and 1986, for novel *A Dark-Adapted Eye;* Gold Dagger Award, Crime Writers Association, 1977, for *A Demon in My View,* 1986, for *Live Flesh,* and 1987, for *A Fatal Inversion;* British Arts Council bursary, 1981; British Arts Council National Book Award, 1981, for *The Lake of Darkness;* Popular Culture Association Award, 1983; Silver Dagger Award, Crime Writers Association, 1984, for *The Tree of Hands;* Angel Award for fiction, 1988, for *The House of Stars; Sunday Times* award for Literary Excellence, 1990; Gold Dagger Award, Crime Writers Association, 1991, for *King Solomon's Carpet;* Cartier Diamond Dagger Award for a lifetime's achievement in the field, Crime Writers Association, 1991; named Commander of the British Empire, 1996; Grand Master Award, Mystery Writers of America, 1997; named Baroness Rendell of Babergh, 1997; *Mystery Ink* Gumshoe Award for Lifetime Achievement, 2004; Crime Writers Association; *Sunday Times* Literary Award.

WRITINGS:

MYSTERY NOVELS

To Fear a Painted Devil, Doubleday (Garden City, NY), 1965.
Vanity Dies Hard, John Long (London, England), 1966, published as *In Sickness and in Health,* Doubleday (Garden City, NY), 1966.
The Secret House of Death, John Long (London, England), 1968, Doubleday (Garden City, NY), 1969.
One Across, Two Down, Doubleday (Garden City, NY), 1971.
The Face of Trespass, Doubleday (Garden City, NY), 1974.
A Demon in My View, Doubleday (Garden City, NY), 1977.

A Judgment in Stone, Hutchinson (London, England), 1977, Doubleday (Garden City, NY), 1978.
Make Death Love Me, Doubleday (Garden City, NY), 1979.
The Lake of Darkness, Doubleday (Garden City, NY), 1980.
Master of the Moor, Pantheon (New York, NY), 1982.
The Killing Doll, Pantheon (New York, NY), 1984.
The Tree of Hands, Pantheon (New York, NY), 1984.
Live Flesh, Pantheon (New York, NY), 1986.
Heartstones, Harper (New York, NY), 1987.
Talking to Strangers, Hutchinson (London, England), 1987, published as *Talking to Strange Men,* Pantheon (New York, NY), 1987.
The Bridesmaid, Mysterious Press (New York, NY), 1989.
Going Wrong, Mysterious Press (New York, NY), 1990.
The Crocodile Bird, Crown (New York, NY), 1993.
Ginger and the Kingsmarkham Chalk Circle, Phoenix (London, England), 1996.
The Keys to the Street, Random House (New York, NY), 1996.
Bloodlines: Long and Short Stories, Wheeler (Rockland, MA), 1997.
Whydunit (Perfectly Criminal 2), Severn House (London, England), 1997.
Thornapple, Travelman (London, England), 1998.
A Sight for Sore Eyes: A Novel, Crown (New York, NY), 1999.
Adam and Eve and Pinch Me, Crown (New York, NY), 2001.
The Rottweiler, Crown (New York, NY), 2004.
Thirteen Steps Down, Crown Publishers (New York, NY), 2004.
The Water's Lovely, Crown Publishers (New York, NY), 2007.

"INSPECTOR WEXFORD" SERIES; MYSTERY NOVELS

From Doon with Death (also see below), John Long (London, England), 1964, Doubleday (Garden City, NY), 1965.
Wolf to the Slaughter, John Long (London, England), 1967, Doubleday (Garden City, NY), 1968.
A New Lease of Death (also see below), Doubleday (Garden City, NY), 1967, published as *Sins of the Fathers,* Ballantine (New York, NY), 1970.
The Best Man to Die, John Long (London, England), 1969, Doubleday (Garden City, NY), 1970.
A Guilty Thing Surprised, Doubleday (Garden City, NY), 1970.

No More Dying Then, Hutchinson (London, England), 1971, Doubleday (Garden City, NY), 1972.

Murder Being Once Done, Doubleday (Garden City, NY), 1972.

Some Lie and Some Die, Doubleday (Garden City, NY), 1973.

Shake Hands Forever, Doubleday (Garden City, NY), 1975.

A Sleeping Life, Doubleday (Garden City, NY), 1978.

Put On by Cunning, Hutchinson (London, England), 1981, published as *Death Notes,* Pantheon (New York, NY), 1981.

The Speaker of Mandarin, Pantheon (New York, NY), 1983.

An Unkindness of Ravens, Pantheon (New York, NY), 1985.

The Veiled One, Pantheon (New York, NY), 1988.

Kissing the Gunner's Daughter, Mysterious Press (New York, NY), 1992.

Simisola, Random House (New York, NY), 1995.

Road Rage, Crown (New York, NY), 1997.

Harm Done, Crown (New York, NY), 1999.

The Babes in the Wood, Crown (New York, NY), 2002.

End in Tears, Crown (New York, NY), 2006.

STORY COLLECTIONS

The Fallen Curtain and Other Stories, Hutchinson (London, England), 1976, published as *The Fallen Curtain: Eleven Mystery Stories by an Edgar Award-Winning Writer,* Doubleday (Garden City, NY), 1976.

Means of Evil and Other Stories, Hutchinson (London, England), 1979, published as *Five Mystery Stories by an Edgar Award-Winning Writer,* Doubleday (Garden City, NY), 1980.

The Fever Tree and Other Stories, Hutchinson (London, England), 1982, Pantheon (New York, NY), 1983, published as *The Fever Tree and Other Stories of Suspense,* Ballantine (New York, NY), 1984.

The New Girlfriend and Other Stories, Hutchinson (London, England), 1985, published as *The New Girlfriend and Other Stories of Suspense,* Pantheon (New York, NY), 1986.

(Editor) *A Warning to the Curious: The Ghost Stories of M.R. James,* Hutchinson (London, England), 1986.

Collected Short Stories, Hutchinson (London, England), 1987, published as *Collected Stories,* Pantheon (New York, NY), 1988.

The Copper Peacock and Other Stories, Mysterious Press (New York, NY), 1991.

Blood Lines: Long and Short Stories, Crown (New York, NY), 1996.

Piranha to Scurfy and Other Stories, Vintage (New York, NY), 2002.

Contributor of short stories to *Ellery Queen's Mystery Magazine.*

UNDER PSEUDONYM BARBARA VINE

A Dark-Adapted Eye, Viking (New York, NY), 1985.

A Fatal Inversion, Bantam (New York, NY), 1987.

(With others) *Yes, Prime Minister: The Diaries of the Right Honorable James Hacker,* Salem House Publishers, 1988.

The House of Stairs, Harmony Books (New York, NY), 1989.

Gallowglass, Harmony Books (New York, NY), 1990.

King Solomon's Carpet, Harmony Books (New York, NY), 1992.

Anna's Book, Harmony Books (New York, NY), 1993.

No Night Is Too Long, Harmony Books (New York, NY), 1994.

The Brimstone Wedding, Harmony Books (New York, NY), 1996.

The Chimney Sweeper's Boy, Harmony Books (New York, NY), 1998.

Grasshopper, Harmony Books (New York, NY), 2000.

The Blood Doctor, Shaye Areheart Books (New York, NY), 2002.

The Minotaur, Shaye Areheart Books (New York, NY), 2005.

OTHER

"People Don't Do Such Things," Tales of the Unexpected, Independent Television (ITV), 1985.

(With Colin Ward) *Undermining the Central Line,* Chatto & Windus (London, England), 1989.

(With photographs by Paul Bowden) *Ruth Rendell's Suffolk* (nonfiction), Hutchinson (London, England), 1992.

(Editor) *The Reason Why: An Anthology of the Murderous Mind,* Crown (New York, NY), 1996.

Contributor to anthologies, including *Haunted Houses: The Greatest Stories,* edited by Martin H. Greenberg, 1983; *Haunting Women,* edited by Alan Ryan, Avon

Books (New York, NY), 1988; *Scare Care,* edited by Graham Masterson, St. Martin's Press (New York, NY), 1989; *The New Gothic: A Collection of Contemporary Gothic Fiction,* edited by Patrick McGrath and Bradford Morrow, Random House (New York, NY), 1991; *I Shudder at Your Touch,* edited by Michelle Slung, ROC (New York, NY), 1992; *Little Deaths,* edited by Ellen Datlow, Dell (New York, NY), 1995; *Crossing the Border: Tales of Erotic Ambiguity,* edited by Lisa Tuttle, 1998; *The Mammoth Book of 20th Century Ghost Stories,* edited by Peter Haining, Carroll & Graf (New York, NY), 1998; *Mistresses of the Dark: Twenty-Five Macabre Tales by Master Storytellers,* edited by Stefan R. Dziemianowicz, Denise Little, and Robert E. Weinberg, 1998; and *The Mammoth Book of Haunted House Stories,* edited by Peter Haining, Carroll & Graf (New York, NY), 2000.

Author's works have been translated into fourteen languages.

ADAPTATIONS: A Judgment in Stone was filmed as *The Housekeeper,* Rawfilm/Schulz Productions, 1987; several of Rendell's Wexford mysteries have been adapted for British television and subsequently aired on the Arts and Entertainment network's "Masters of Mystery" series; numerous Ruth Rendell and Barbara Vine short stories and novels have been adapted to film and television as stand-alone programs and as part of the "Ruth Rendell Mysteries" series, including *An Affair in Mind,* 1988, *A Guilty Thing Surprised,* 1988, *Shake Hands Forever,* 1988, *Tree of Hands,* 1989, *No More Dying Then,* 1989, *The Veiled One,* 1989, *The Best Man to Die,* 1990, *Put on by Cunning,* 1990, *A New Lease of Death,* 1991, *Murder Being Once Done,* 1991, *From Doon with Death,* 1991, *Talking to Strange Men,* 1992, *A Fatal Inversion,* 1992, *The Speaker of Mandarin,* 1992, *Kissing the Gunner's Daughter,* 1992, *Gallowglass,* 1993, *Vanity Dies Hard,* 1995, *The Secret House of Death,* 1996, *Simisola,* 1996, *Road Rage,* 1998, *Lake of Darkness,* 1999, *The Fallen Curtain,* 1999, *Harm Done,* 2000, and *No Night is Too Long,* 2002.

SIDELIGHTS: Ruth Rendell is a prolific author who, writing under her own name and the pseudonym Barbara Vine, has enthralled both the general public and literary critics with her skillfully written mysteries and suspenseful stories. She has the ability, according to *Dictionary of Literary Biography* contributor Patricia A. Gabilondo, to render tales that could be considered formulaic, into something "always suspenseful and viscerally compelling." In her first novel, the author introduced Chief Inspector Reginald Wexford, a proper Englishman whose town of Kingsmarkham, Sussex, is plagued by many murders. Wexford has been the subject of numerous sequels and has won much praise for his creator for the deft characterizations, clever plots, and surprising endings that mark these books. While the Wexford books are straightforward police procedural novels, the books Rendell publishes under the Vine pseudonym are more gothic, often involving twisted psychology to produce edgy thrillers. David Lehman of *Newsweek* commented that "few detective writers are as good at pulling such last-second rabbits out of their top hats—the last page making us see everything before it in a strange, new glare."

Rendell's Wexford character is middle-aged, happily married, and the father of two grown daughters. His extensive reading allows him to quote from a wide range of literature during his murder investigations, but despite his erudition, Wexford is not cynical, eccentric, or misanthropic as are many literary detectives. His well-adjusted manner serves as contrast to the many strange mysteries he investigates. Social differences are frequently illuminated in these mysteries, and Rendell has been singled out as particularly skillful at portraying England's social stratification, even in the details of her descriptions of architectural features. Gabilondo mused: "Her meticulous description of setting serves to create atmosphere and, more important, to communicate the intimate relation between the physical and the psychological, especially in terms of the way that landscapes, whether urban or rural, take on the imprints of sociological change and personal conflict."

Wexford is also notable for his philosophical turn of mind and his keen empathy for his fellow man, in whatever the circumstances. His sensitivity makes him quite desirable to the women he encounters, yet Wexford remains determinedly devoted to his wife. Wexford's greatest disdain is for the "inanities of modernity," wrote Gabilondo. "Through Wexford's often ironic eye, Rendell paints a remarkably specific portrait of the changes that have occurred in English life—the encroachment of suburban sprawl, the banal homogenization of consumer culture, the dispossessed youth, the problems with unemployment, and the growing complexities of civil bureaucracies. Able to see both sides of any issue, as well as to grasp the essential poignancy of the human condition, Wexford finds himself often at odds with his official role, for his reliance on intuition and the imagination usually runs counter to the official line, offering a rich resource of dramatic tension," concluded Gabilondo. Wexford's open-mindedness is contrasted with the more narrow vision and rigid morality of his partner, Inspector Michael Burden. Unlike many series characters, Wexford and Burden age and go through many significant changes as the series progresses.

Rendell's early Wexford mysteries dealt frequently with desire and taboo, while in her later books she takes on social issues in a more direct manner. Feminism, ecoterrorism, and other modern concerns are examined, not always in a flattering light. In *A Sleeping Life,* gender-identity conflicts figure prominently in the murder case, while Wexford's daughter becomes involved in a radical feminist group. Rendell actually drew the ire of real-life feminist groups after the publication of *An Unkindness of Ravens,* which features a man-hating group called Action for the Radical Reform of Intersexual Attitudes (ARRIA). Members of the group vow to carry weapons and refrain from marriage; it even seems that some members advocate the murder of a man as an initiation rite. The author also ruffled feathers with *Kissing the Gunner's Daughter,* which challenges the popular notion that class stratification is much less meaningful in Britain than it has been in the past. Racism is addressed in *Simisola,* another Wexford novel; the problems of urban and suburban sprawl are considered in *Road Rage;* and the subject of wife-beating is approached in *Harm Done.*

The Babes in the Wood finds Inspector Wexford on the trail of teenage brother and sister Giles and Sophie Dade, who have come up missing, along with their babysitter, Joanna Troy, after heavy storms and torrential rains flood the Sussex countryside. Fears arise that the trio died in the floodwaters, but when the babysitter's body is discovered alone in her car, there is reason to hope that the children are still alive. As time passes, the likelihood of finding them alive grows dimmer, until the sudden and unexpected reappearance of the girl. Her return prompts as many questions as it answers, particularly where she has been and what has happened to her brother. Wexford's investigation reveals dreadful family secrets, shocking revelations about Giles and Sophie, and answers that are not revealed until the book's final pages. Throughout, "Rendell's gift for intelligent, coolheaded storytelling remains undiminished," commented Mark Harris in *Entertainment Weekly.*

End in Tears explores the sometimes criminal lengths that hopeful parents will go to in order to conceive, find, or acquire a child. Rendell also delineates the predatory element that will manipulate and exploit this primal desire for offspring. Teenage mother Amber Marshalson is found dead outside her home, her head bashed in with a brick. Sometime later, her pregnant friend Megan Bartlow is killed in a dingy row house. Inspector Wexford, dismayed by the moral decay he sees represented by the burgeoning numbers of teen pregnancies, steps in to investigate the murders of the young women. Suspicion focuses on several potential murderers, including a pair of sinister twins, a heavily tattooed and pierced ex-boyfriend, and a tall, thin man in a hooded jacket. Even Amber's grieving father, her hostile stepmother, and the wealthy parents of her baby's father are not above suspicion. Complicating Wexford's attitude in the case is his daughter Sylvia's willingness to serve as surrogate mother for her ex-husband Neil and his new wife Naomi. In this book, Rendell still "proves a master at rendering the joys and sorrows of human relationships," stated *Booklist* reviewer Allison Block. A *Kirkus Reviews* critic called the story "average for Rendell's distinguished list of whodunits, which makes it just a whisker below state of the art."

Various types of psychological torment are central in Rendell's other books. *A Judgment in Stone* portrays an illiterate woman whose inability to read has led to a life of shame, isolation, and regression. *The Killing Doll* features Dolly Yearman, a schizophrenic whose delusions eventually lead her to murder. *Live Flesh* is told from the point of view of a convicted murderer and rapist, who lives in a strange symbiotic relationship with the police officer he crippled with a gunshot wound. In *The Bridesmaid,* the Pygmalion myth is turned inside out as a beautiful girl is shown to be marred by her mental instability. Despite her flaws, she becomes the object of sexual obsession for Philip; eventually, she brings him to the brink of murder. One of the author's most ambitious novels is *The Keys to the Street,* which uses the concentric circles and paths of London's Regent Park to follow the interconnected threads of human lives, particularly that of a well-to-do man who lives on the streets in the wake of a family tragedy and a young woman struggling to assert her independence. Although it may be the author's "most compassionate and most complex treatment of the human condition," according to Gabilondo, it left "most reviewers disappointed in her failure to bring all the strands together. The effectiveness of the structure, however, lies in this intentional failure to make everything connect. In Rendell's psychological thrillers, those avenues of emotional connection, like the misaligned arcs of Regent's Park, often do not meet, frustrating the hopes and dreams of her characters' lives." A very positive assessment of the book was offered by Emily Melton in *Booklist,* however; she wrote that it is "at once tragic, shocking, satisfying, and hopeful," and added: "Without a doubt, Rendell ranks with today's finest writers, and this book is one of her best. . . . Superbly written and beautifully constructed, the story is unique, powerful, and provocative."

Adam and Eve and Pinch Me is a "gem from the British master," wrote a *Publishers Weekly* reviewer, filled with characters "so vivid they live beyond the frame of the novel." At the center of the plot is Minty Knox, a woman in her thirties who works in a dry-cleaners and is obsessed with germs and cleanliness. Her hygiene phobias, as well as the ghosts she imagines she sees, figure prominently in a plot that is "intricate but brisk," according to the writer, "a literary page-turner, both elegant and accessible." *Booklist* reviewer Connie Fletcher called the book "madly absorbing," and advised: "Rendell's characters are fully drawn, and we become completely caught up in their struggles." Discussing her writing with a *Publishers Weekly* interviewer, Rendell commented: "I do write about obsession, but I don't think I have an obsession for writing. I'm not a compulsive writer. I like to watch obsession in other people, watch the way it makes them behave."

The Rottweiler focuses on a bestial serial killer stalking the streets of London, garroting his victims and stealing small keepsake items from their bodies. The killer earned his sobriquet from bite marks on the neck of his first victim, which he is chagrined to note were not inflicted by him. When items taken from the killer's victims begin to surface in Inez Ferry's antique shop, the police believe that the killer is one of the several boarders living in rooms above the shop. However, their investigation fails to uncover which of the eccentric residents shares his or her skin with the brutal Rottweiler. "The various characters involved including Inez herself are . . . brilliantly drawn," remarked Antonia Fraser in *Spectator.* When Rendell reveals the Rottweiler's identity a third of the way through the book, the reader's relationship with the story changes to one of knowledge tinged with dread, waiting for the killer to strike again while hoping the authorities will make an arrest before more victims die. *Entertainment Weekly* reviewer Tina Jordan called the novel "classic Rendell, macabre and fast-paced." The novel is "unusually three-dimensional for a mystery novel, with a set of characters

who engage interest on their own merits," remarked Janet Maslin in the *New York Times Book Review.* "Whether they turn out to be linked to the Rottweiler's evil streak is almost a secondary matter," Maslin observed. *Orlando Sentinel* reviewer Ann Hellmuth concluded: "Ruth Rendell is the perfect storyteller, never resorting to cliches and tired formats but transfixing and enthralling with intelligent writing, clever plotting, and character development."

Obsession fuels the pathological behaviors of the characters in *Thirteen Steps Down.* Mix Cellini is an exercise-machine repairman who nurses twin obsessions: one for local supermodel Nerissa Nash, who he believes will eventually marry him, and one for another local hero, serial killer Harold Christie. Mix rents an attic room from bitter, snobbish widow Gwendolen Chawcer, who has seen her better days along with St. Blaise House, her crumbling London mansion. Gwendolen nurses a long-time obsession of her own, a romantic attachment to Dr. Stephen Reeves, who treated her dying mother 1953 and who courted her for a bit. She has not seen Reeves in almost a half century, but when she learns that his wife has died, she foresees a reunion that Reeves does not expect. Mix and Gwendolen thoroughly despise each other, but their animosity adds a frisson to their embattled relationship that mutual respect or affection would not provide. Within this volatile psychological atmosphere, madness will arise, control will be lost, and murders will occur. *New York Times Book Review* critic Marilyn Stasio called the book a "profoundly unnerving psychological suspense novel about a young man gripped by obsessions that can lead only to madness and murder." Rendell's novel offers "vivid characters, a plot addictive as crack, and a sense of place unequaled in crime fiction," remarked a *Publishers Weekly* critic.

In addition to her many novels, Rendell is also the author of numerous well-received short stories that have appeared in anthologies and collections over the years. *The Copper Peacock and Other Stories* "delights with its fine-tuned psychological effects," commented a *Publishers Weekly* reviewer. In the book's title story, Bernard is a writer who borrows a friend's apartment to find the solitude needed to work on a book. He takes an interest in the lovely Judy, the maid who cleans the apartment and fixes his lunch. Curiously, she exhibits increasingly severe bruises and injuries as time goes on, and Bernard is stunned when she gives him an ugly but expensive peacock-shaped bookmark. The story's "denouement is a master stroke," the *Publishers Weekly* critic stated. "The Fish Sitter" posits human prey for the dwellers in an aquarium. A cat-based mystery finds a regal feline ascending to her proper place in the royal hierarchy after the death of another cat. In "Mother's Help," a handsome and charming father enlists his children's help in disposing of unwanted wives. Chief Inspector Wexford appears in "An Unwanted Woman," wherein he tries to help a moody and unnerving teenage runaway.

"Rendell is one of the finest writers of our time," stated *Booklist* reviewer Emily Melton, and her story collection *Blood Lines: Long and Short Stories,* is "a must-have collection by one of the world's most talented authors," Melton concluded. Rendell explores a wide field of psychological aberration in the stories, including the shame that results from obsession in "Clothes," the search for love and companionship in "The Strawberry Tree," and anger resulting from damaged egos in "The Man Who Was the God of Love." She uncovers the humanity inherent in her characters, but does not shy away from the inhumanity that sometimes dwells deep within as well. "For all the stories' differences, however, Rendell's hand remains rock-steady throughout," observed Pam Lambert in a *People* review. A *Publishers Weekly* critic noted that in these stories, "Rendell's deft touch and keen insight (and sometimes wry wit) can wring abject horror from even the smallest vignette."

With the books written under her penname of Barbara Vine, Rendell manages to "escape the strictures of the detective novel and concentrate on the darker peculiarities of human nature," observed Katie Owen in *New Statesman.* In *The Blood Doctor,* for example, Martin Nanther, a biographer and once the fourth Lord Nanther, undertakes a biography of his great-grandfather Henry, the first Lord Nanther, who was awarded a hereditary peerage by Queen Victoria in recognition for his research into hemophilia and his services as royal physician. Martin's life is complicated by the recent loss of the privileges and benefits of his title when the House of Lords opts to eliminate hereditary peerages. As the novel progresses, Martin learns that he and his wife's failure to conceive a child is the result of faulty genes, and that if they want to have a child, they will have to turn to modern science and genetic manipulation to create a baby designed to their specifications. Meanwhile, his research uncovers numerous unpleasant things about his great-grandfather Henry, the "architect of a crime that has outlived him for generations," and parallels with his own life and marital troubles, according to a

Kirkus Reviews writer, who named the book a "dense, dazzling exploration of the biographer as detective, and of the truism that blood will tell."

In *The Minotaur,* also written under the Vine pseudonym, young Swedish nurse Kerstin Kvist is hired to care for John Cosway, a once-brilliant mathematical genius who has seemingly succumbed to schizophrenia. Living with John at Lydstep Old Hall is his harridan mother and four odious middle-aged sisters. As Kerstin interacts with John, she begins to realize that his troubles are not caused by mental illness, but by heavy doses of brain-addling drugs. John, she finds, is the owner of Lydstep Old Hall, and it behooves the mother and sisters to keep him incapacitated so that they can continue to live there as long as they wish. A considerable sum of money is also tied up in John's name. A plot is underway, she realizes, to strip John Cosway of his rightful home and fortune, and soon this plot brings murder down to Lydstep. *Booklist* reviewer Connie Fletcher called the novel "very satisfying reading." A *Kirkus Reviews* critic stated: "Using the conventions of a Victorian pastiche, Vine presents as satisfying a family of monsters as you're likely to find. It's like watching a house of cards collapse in exquisite slow-motion." Vine, concluded *Detroit Free Press* critic Ron Bernas, "is one of the best, a writer of literate thrillers that never fail to draw in readers, even though they know where she's going."

Gabilondo concluded: "Rendell's greatest contribution, in addition to her gifts as a storyteller, has been to track the social and the psychological circulation of that vast system—political, familial, cultural, and genetic—in which people are forced to play out their lives, through a body of work that takes readers not into the cozy drawing rooms of traditional English mystery but into the lives and psyches of men and women in a vividly contemporary Britain."

BIOGRAPHICAL AND CRITICAL SOURCES:

BOOKS

Contemporary Literary Criticism, Thomson Gale (Detroit, MI), Volume 28, 1984, Volume 48, 1988, Volume 50, 1988.

Dictionary of Literary Biography, Thomson Gale (Detroit, MI), Volume 87: *British Mystery and Thriller Writers since 1940,* 1989, Volume 276: *British Mystery and Thriller Writers since 1960,* 2003.

Mystery and Suspense Writers: The Literature of Crime, Detection, and Espionage, Scribner (New York, NY), 1998.

PERIODICALS

Advertiser (Adelaide, Australia), July 27, 2002, Katharine England, review of *The Blood Doctor,* p. W13.

America's Intelligence Wire, December 9, 2005, Jill Lawless, "Queen of Suspense Ruth Rendell Tackles Celebrity and Murder in *Thirteen Steps Down,*" profile of Ruth Rendell.

Antioch Review, winter, 1997, review of *The Keys to the Street,* p. 122.

Belles Lettres: A Review of Books by Women, spring, 1994, Lorraine E. McCormack, review of *The Crocodile Bird,* p. 13.

Booklist, December 1, 1994, Emily Melton, review of *No Night is Too Long,* p. 635; October 1, 1995, Emily Melton, review of *The Brimstone Wedding,* p. 213; March 1, 1996, Emily Melton, review of *Blood Lines: Long and Short Stories,* p. 1077; August, 1996, Emily Melton, review of *The Keys to the Street,* p. 1856; August, 1997, Emily Melton, review of *Road Rage,* p. 1848; December 1, 1998, Emily Melton, review of *A Sight for Sore Eyes: A Novel,* p. 620; April 15, 1999, review of *Kissing the Gunner's Daughter,* p. 1458; August, 1999, review of *A Judgment in Stone,* p. 2025; September 1, 1999, Stephanie Zvirin, review of *Harm Done,* p. 8; November 1, 1999, Karen Harris, review of *A Sight for Sore Eyes,* p. 551; June 1, 2000, Mary McCay, review of *Harm Done,* p. 1922; August, 2000, Bill Ott, review of *Grasshopper,* p. 2077; November 1, 2000, Connie Fletcher, review of *Piranha to Scurfy and Other Stories,* p. 493; November 15, 2001, Connie Fletcher, review of *Adam and Eve and Pinch Me,* p. 524; May 15, 2002, Stephanie Zvirin, review of *The Blood Doctor,* p. 1556; September 1, 2003, Stephanie Zvirin, review of *The Babes in the Wood,* p. 7; July, 2005, Connie Fletcher, review of *Thirteen Steps Down,* p. 1877; December 1, 2005, Connie Fletcher, review of *The Minotaur,* p. 7; May 1, 2006, Allison Block, review of *End in Tears,* p. 39.

Bookseller, June 10, 2005, review of *Thirteen Steps Down,* p. 13; December 2, 2005, Frances Harvey, review of *End in Tears,* p. 15.

British Medical Journal, July 29, 2000, Judy Jones, "Concern Mounts over Female Genital Mutilation," p. 262; November 30, 2002, Jeff Aronson, review of *The Blood Doctor,* p. 1307.

Detroit Free Press, March 15, 2006, Ron Bernas, review of *The Minotaur.*

Entertainment Weekly, February 14, 1992, review of *Gallowglass,* p. 50; July 17, 1998, Darcy Lockman, review of *The Chimney Sweeper's Boy,* p. 78; April 23, 1999, "The Week," review of *A Sight for Sore Eyes,* p. 58; March 15, 2002, review of *Adam and Eve and Pinch Me,* p. 72; October 31, 2003, Mark Harris, review of *The Babes in the Wood,* p. 77; November 19, 2004, Tina Jordan, review of *The Rottweiler,* p. 88; September 30, 2005, Jennifer Reese, "Mistress of the Dark: In *Thirteen Steps Down,* Ruth Rendell Pulls off the Almost-Perfect Crime Novel," review of *Thirteen Steps Down,* p. 96; December 30, 2005, Jennifer Reese, "Literature of the Year," review of *Thirteen Steps Down,* p. 148; July 21, 2006, Jennifer Reese, "Deep 'End,'" review of *End in Tears,* p. 74.

Europe Intelligence Wire, October 20, 2002, Katie Owen, review of *The Babes in the Wood;* November 2, 2002, Rachel Simhon, review of *The Babes in the Wood;* July 29, 2005, Graham Chalmers, "In Conversation: Ruth Rendell, Cedar Court Hotel, Harrogate," interview with Ruth Rendell.

Independent (London, England), August 18, 2001, Jane Jakeman, review of *Adam and Eve and Pinch Me,* p. 9; June 15, 2002, Jane Jakeman, "Where Does Ruth Rendell End and 'Barbara Vine' Begin?," p. 30.

Kirkus Reviews, May 15, 2002, review of *The Blood Doctor,* p. 698; July 15, 2003, review of *The Babes in the Wood,* p. 942; July 1, 2005, review of *Thirteen Steps Down,* p. 706; January 15, 2006, review of *The Minotaur,* p. 61; May 15, 2006, review of *End in Tears,* p. 500.

Library Journal, March 15, 1998, Francine Fialkoff, review of *The Chimney Sweeper's Boy,* p. 97; February 1, 1999, Caroline Mann, review of *A Sight for Sore Eyes,* p. 122; August, 1999, Michael Rogers, review of *Some Lie and Some Die,* p. 149; September 1, 1999, Francine Fialkoff, review of *Harm Done,* p. 237, and Michael Rogers, review of *Murder Being Once Done,* p. 238; October 1, 1999, Sandy Glover, review of *A Sight for Sore Eyes,* p. 150; May 15, 2000, Danna Bell-Russel, review of *Harm Done,* p. 142; June 15, 2000, Michael Rogers, review of *A Judgment in Stone,* p. 122; October 15, 2000, Zaheera Jiwaji, review of *Grasshopper,* p. 105; December, 2000, Jane la Plante, review of *Piranha to Scurfy and Other Stories,* p. 194; February 15, 2001, Michael Rogers, review of *The Fallen Curtain and Other Stories,* p. 206; December, 2001, Caroline Mann, review of

Adam and Eve and Pinch Me, p. 175; June 15, 2002, Caroline Mann, review of *The Blood Doctor,* p. 98; October 1, 2003, Caroline Mann, review of *The Babes in the Wood,* p. 122; August 1, 2005, Jane la Plante, review of *Thirteen Steps Down,* p. 71; January 1, 2006, Rebecca Vnuk, review of *The Minotaur,* p. 106; June 15, 2006, Caroline Mann, review of *End in Tears,* p. 64.

New Statesman, September 6, 1996, Carol Birch, review of *The Keys to the Street,* p. 47; October 30, 1998, Francis Gilbert, review of *A Sight for Sore Eyes;* July 3, 2000, Nicola Upson, "Crime Waves," review of *Grasshopper,* p. 58; June 10, 2002, Katie Owen, "Novel of the Week," review of *The Blood Doctor,* p. 53; October 4, 2004, Rebecca Gowers, "Murky Depths," review of *Thirteen Steps Down,* p. 54.

New Statesman & Society, March 12, 1993, Bill Greenwell, review of *Anna's Book,* p. 38; August 20, 1993, Julie Wheelwright, review of *The Crocodile Bird,* p. 40; May 20, 1994, Wendy Brandmark, review of *No Night is Too Long,* p. 39; April 5, 1996, Patricia Craig, review of *The Brimstone Wedding,* p. 39.

Newsweek, September 21, 1987, David Lehman, review of *Talking to Strange Men,* p. 77.

New Yorker, November 7, 2005, review of *Thirteen Steps Down,* p. 139.

New York Times Book Review, October 13, 1996, Marilyn Stasio, review of *The Keys to the Street,* p. 29; September 7, 1997, Marilyn Stasio, review of *Road Rage,* p. 34; April 4, 1999, Marilyn Stasio, review of *A Sight for Sore Eyes,* p. 20; November 21, 1999, Marilyn Stasio, review of *Harm Done,* p. 80; March 3, 2002, Marilyn Stasio, review of *Adam and Eve and Pinch Me,* p. 21; August 4, 2002, Marilyn Stasio, review of *The Blood Doctor,* p. 19; November 18, 2004, Janet Maslin, "A Killer Is on the Loose, but Life's Demands Continue," review of *The Rottweiler;* November 27, 2005, Marilyn Stasio, "Killer in the Attic," review of *Thirteen Steps Down;* March 26, 2006, Marilyn Stasio, "The Madman in the Attic," review of *The Minotaur,* p. 15; July 23, 2006, Marilyn Stasio, "Unhappy Families," review of *End in Tears,* p. 22.

Orlando Sentinel, December 29, 2004, Ann Hellmuth, review of *The Rottweiler.*

People, February 6, 1984, review of *The Fever Tree,* p. 12; April 7, 1986, Campbell Geeslin, review of *The New Girlfriend,* p. 16; July 20, 1987, Campbell Geeslin, review of *Heartstones,* p. 12; October 18, 1992, William A. Henry, III, review of *Anna's Book,* p. 40; July 15, 2006, Pam Lambert, review of *Blood Lines,* p. 41.

Publishers Weekly, March 9, 1990, review of *Gallowglass,* p. 53; August 17, 1990, review of *Going Wrong,* p. 50; August 16, 1991, review of *The Copper Peacock,* p. 49; March 2, 1992, review of *King Solomon's Carpet,* p. 51; June 21, 1993, review of *Anna's Book,* p. 87; December 19, 1994, review of *No Night is Too Long,* p. 47; April 22, 1996, review of *Blood Lines,* p. 61; July 29, 1996, review of *Keys to the Street,* p. 73; July 7, 1997, review of *Road Rage,* p. 53; March 23, 1998, review of *The Chimney Sweeper's Boy,* p. 80; February 8, 1999, review of *A Sight for Sore Eyes,* p. 197; October 18, 1999, review of *Harm Done,* p.73; August 28, 2000, review of *Grasshopper,* p. 50; November 13, 2000, review of *Piranha to Scurfy and Other Stories,* p. 89; January 28, 2002, review of *Adam and Eve and Pinch Me,* p. 274, and interview with Ruth Rendell, p. 275; June 24, 2002, review of *The Blood Doctor,* p. 43; September 29, 2003, review of *The Babes in the Wood,* p. 46; August 15, 2005, review of *Thirteen Steps Down,* p. 37; January 16, 2006, review of *The Minotaur,* p. 39; May 29, 2006, review of *End in Tears,* p. 40.

San Jose Mercury News, December 19, 2003, John Orr, review of *The Babes in the Wood.*

School Library Journal, March, 1997, Judy McAloon, review of *The Keys to the Street,* p. 216.

Seattle Times, February 10, 2002, Adam Woog, review of *Adam and Eve and Pinch Me,* p. J11.

Spectator, June 1, 2002, Charlotte Joll, "Trying to Climb the Family Tree," review of *The Blood Doctor,* p. 37; October 4, 2003, Antonia Fraser, "And Now for My Next Trick . . ." review of *The Rottweiler,* p. 55; April 9, 2005, Anita Brookner, "A Nest of Ungentle Essex Folk," review of *The Minotaur,* p. 36; November 26, 2005, Harriet Waugh, "Recent Crime Novels," review of *End in Tears,* p. 49; November 4, 2006, Andrew Taylor, "Looking on the Dark Side," review of *The Water's Lovely.*

Telegraph (London, England), November 4, 2005, "Her Dark Materials," interview with Ruth Rendell.

Time, May 5, 1986, William A. Henry, III, review of *The New Girlfriend,* p. 74; August 18, 1986, William A. Henry, III, review of *A Dark-Adapted Eye,* p. 72; August 17, 1987, William A. Henry, III, review of *A Dark-Adapted Eye,* p. 64; February 1, 1988, William A. Henry, III, review of *Talking to Strange Men,* p. 65; August 8, 1988, William A. Henry, III, review of *The Veiled One,* p. 74; June 19, 1989, review of *The House of Stairs,* p. 65; July 2, 1990, Stefan Kanfer, review of *Gallowglass,* p. 67.

ONLINE

Internet Movie Database, http://www.imdb.com/ (February 10, 2007), filmography of Ruth Rendell.*

* * *

RHODES, Richard 1937-
(Richard Lee Rhodes)

PERSONAL: Born July 4, 1937, in Kansas City, KS; son of Arthur (a mechanic for Missouri Pacific Railroad) and Georgia Rhodes; married Linda Iredell Hampton, August 29, 1960 (divorced, April 27, 1974); married Mary Magdalene Evans, November 26, 1976 (divorced); married Ginger Kay Untrif, October 3, 1993; children: (first marriage) Timothy James, Katherine Hampton. *Education:* Yale University, B.A. (cum laude), 1959.

ADDRESSES: Home—CA. *Agent*—Morton Janklow, Janklow & Nesbit Associates, 445 Park Ave., New York, NY 10022.

CAREER: Writer and journalist. *Newsweek,* New York, NY, writer trainee, 1959; Radio Free Europe, New York, NY, staff assistant, 1960; Westminster College, Fulton, MO, instructor in English, 1960-61; Hallmark Cards, Inc., Kansas City, MO, book editing manager, 1962-70; *Harper's,* New York, NY, contributing editor, 1970-74; *Playboy,* Chicago, IL, contributing editor, 1974-80; *Rolling Stone,* New York, NY, contributing editor, 1988-93. Writer-in-residence, Kansas City Regional Council for Higher Education, 1972; visiting fellow, Defense and Arms Control Studies Program, Massachusetts Institute of Technology, 1988-89; visiting scholar, History of Science Department, Harvard University, 1989-90; advisor, Alfred P. Sloan Foundation, 1990—; affiliate, Center for International Security and Cooperation, Stanford University, 2004—. *Military service:* U.S. Air Force Reserve, 1960-65; surgical technician.

AWARDS, HONORS: Playboy editorial award, 1972; Guggenheim fellowship, 1974-75; National Endowment for the Arts fellowship, 1978-79; Ford Foundation fellowship, 1981-83, 1985; Alfred P. Sloan Foundation fellowship, 1985, 1988, 1991-94, 2001-06; winner of National Book Award, 1987, National Book Critics Circle Award for general nonfiction, 1988, and Pulitzer Prize for general nonfiction, 1988, all for *The Making*

of the Atomic Bomb; L.H.D., Westminster College, Fulton, MO, 1988; MacArthur Foundation fellowship, Program on Peace and International Cooperation, 1990-91; *Dark Sun: The Making of the Hydrogen Bomb* was named by *Publishers Weekly* as one of the best books of 1995 and was one of three finalists for the 1996 Pulitzer Prize in History; *Los Angeles Times* Book Award nomination for biography, 2004, for *John James Audubon: The Making of an American.*

WRITINGS:

NONFICTION

The Inland Ground: An Evocation of the American Middle West, Atheneum (New York, NY), 1970.
The Ozarks, Time-Life (New York, NY), 1974.
Looking for America: A Writer's Odyssey, Doubleday (Garden City, NY), 1979.
The Making of the Atomic Bomb, Simon & Schuster (New York, NY), 1986.
Farm: A Year in the Life of an American Farmer, Simon & Schuster (New York, NY), 1989.
A Hole in the World: An American Boyhood, Simon & Schuster (New York, NY), 1990, 10th-anniversary edition with new preface and epilogue, University of Kansas Press (Lawrence, KS), 2000.
Making Love: An Erotic Odyssey, Simon & Schuster (New York, NY), 1992.
Nuclear Renewal: Common Sense about Energy, Whittle/Viking (New York, NY), 1993.
Dark Sun: The Making of the Hydrogen Bomb, Simon & Schuster (New York, NY), 1995.
How to Write: Advice and Reflections, Morrow (New York, NY), 1995.
(With wife, Ginger Rhodes) *Trying to Get Some Dignity: Stories of Triumph over Childhood Abuse,* Morrow (New York, NY), 1996.
Deadly Feasts: Tracking the Secrets of a Terrifying New Plague, Simon & Schuster (New York, NY), 1997.
(Editor) *Visions of Technology: A Century of Vital Debate about Machines, Systems, and the Human World,* Simon & Schuster (New York, NY), 1999.
Why They Kill: The Discoveries of a Maverick Criminologist, Knopf (New York, NY), 1999.
Masters of Death: The SS-Einsatzgruppen and the Invention of the Holocaust, Knopf (New York, NY), 2002.
John James Audubon: The Making of an American, Knopf (New York, NY), 2004.

Arsenals of Folly: Nuclear Weapons in the Cold War, Knopf (New York, NY), 2007.

NOVELS

The Ungodly: A Novel of the Donner Party, Charter-house (New York, NY), 1973.
Holy Secrets, Doubleday (New York, NY), 1978.
The Last Safari, Doubleday (New York, NY), 1980.
Sons of the Earth, Coward (New York, NY), 1981.

OTHER

(Editor and author of introduction) Robert Serber, *The Los Alamos Primer: The First Lectures on How to Build an Atomic Bomb,* University of California Press (Berkeley, CA), 1992.
(Author of introduction) Rachel Fermi and Esther Samra, *Picturing the Bomb: Photographs from the Secret World of the Manhattan Project,* Abrams (New York, NY), 1995.
(Editor) John James Audubon, *The Audubon Reader,* Knopf (New York, NY), 2006.

Author of television documentaries *The Loss of Innocence,* National Educational Television, 1965, and *The Osage River: Another Kind of Wilderness,* KCPT-TV, 1973. Contributor to books, including *The Literary Journalists,* edited by Norman Sims, Ballantine (New York, NY), 1984, and *Writing in an Era of Conflict,* Library of Congress (Washington, DC), 1990. Contributor to periodicals, including *American Heritage, Chicago Sun-Times, Chicago Tribune Book World, Esquire, Harper's, Journal of the American Medical Association, New Yorker, New York Times Book Review, Playboy, Reader's Digest,* and *Redbook.*

ADAPTATIONS: *Deadly Feasts* was adapted for audio cassette by Simon & Schuster Audio, 1997; *Visions of Technology* was adapted for audio cassette.

SIDELIGHTS: Journalist Richard Rhodes has produced a large body of work encompassing both fiction and nonfiction, and a wide variety of subject matter, but he has won particular acclaim for his writings on nuclear weapons. *The Making of the Atomic Bomb,* published in 1987, brought Rhodes the National Book Award, the National Book Critics Circle Award, and the Pulitzer Prize—"the literary world's Triple Crown," as a *Best-*

sellers 1990 contributor put it. While noted for writing about explosives, Rhodes has written books on numerous other topics, including farming, sexual passion, and his own troubled childhood.

One of Rhodes's early assignments almost never came to light. Editor Dick Kluger, impressed by the young writer, asked Rhodes to produce a literary study on the American Midwest. "Rhodes froze in fear," reported a *Dictionary of Literary Biography* contributor. "Unable to exorcise the demons of his nightmarish childhood, he felt he had no right to speak." Still, Rhodes attempted two chapters, both "flat, uninspired, and pedestrian," according to the *Dictionary of Literary Biography* contributor. Then a friend invited Rhodes to a coyote hunt in Kansas. Seeing the carnage inflicted on the canines, and the unfeeling reaction of the people watching, awakened an impulse in Rhodes. He returned home, got "thoroughly drunk," re-read Ernest Hemingway's *Death in the Afternoon,* and began to produce what would become his signature style of literary journalism. His essay on the coyote hunt, "Death All Day in Kansas," was published in *Esquire* and became the cornerstone for Rhodes's first full-length book, *The Inland Ground: An Evocation of the American Middle West.*

This work, wrote a *Dictionary of Literary Biography* contributor, "is a running commentary [on] the people of the American Middle West, their customs and follies, their anxieties and delights, their morals and philosophies." Rhodes, the contributor continued, "celebrates their decency, goodness, ingenuity, and inherent loyalty. Along the way, however, he discovers an egregious darkness in the heart. Mindless slaughter, callous indifference, conspicuous waste—this is, he reminds readers, the American character."

Rhodes followed his debut book with several novels and articles for periodicals. An established writer, Rhodes then turned his attention to the atomic bomb. He first became interested in the subject while writing a profile of atomic scientist J. Robert Oppenheimer that would later be collected in *Looking for America: A Writer's Odyssey.* In 1976 Rhodes received a grant to research a novel set in Los Alamos, the site of the work that produced the first atomic bomb. He soon concluded, however, that this story did not need to be fictionalized to be fascinating, so he spent several years in research and writing to produce a nonfiction work. *The Making of the Atomic Bomb* chronicles the evolution of atomic physics, from early experiments with the atom around the turn of the twentieth century, through the creation of the bombs that were dropped on Hiroshima and Nagasaki to end World War II, to the post-World War II work on the hydrogen bomb. The book provides many details about the scientists involved in these ventures—including Oppenheimer, Enrico Fermi, Ernest Rutherford, and Niels Bohr—and background on the era in which they lived.

New York Times Book Review contributor William J. Broad recommended the book as a work that "offers not only the best overview of the century's pivotal event, but a probing analysis of what it means for the future." He praised Rhodes, calling him an "intelligent layman," for approaching the subject without preconceived ideas or moralizing. "Short on heroes and villains, his book is populated instead with complex figures in a compelling plot," Broad wrote. *Chicago Tribune Book World* reviewer Priscilla Johnson McMillan also found much reason for enthusiasm: "If the story Rhodes has to tell is in many ways a tragic one, his telling of it is a tour de force. Writing with lucidity and with stunning economy, he places abstractions within our grasp and renders sound judgments about the science of the bomb and the men and women who made it." *New York Times* critic John Gross, however, thought many of Rhodes's portrayals of scientists were superficial and some of his phrasing was awkward. In spite of those reservations, Gross did find that several passages provide evidence of Rhodes's dramatic skill. "His account of Trinity, the first atomic test in New Mexico in July 1945, is particularly compelling; reading it, you find the tension building as though the outcome were still in doubt (as in a larger sense, no doubt, it still is)," Gross wrote. Gross also saw in Rhodes's work "a tendency to look for scientific solutions to what are essentially political problems. But at least he forces you to debate the issues, and his narrative has a consistent moral edge." *The Making of the Atomic Bomb* brought Rhodes a sweep of the major book awards of 1987-88.

Rhodes followed his atomic chronicle with an agricultural one. *Farm: A Year in the Life of an American Farmer* is a detailed study of a Missouri farm family. Rhodes reportedly filled forty-two notebooks with observations that he then boiled down into *Farm*'s 336 pages. Rhodes gave the family the pseudonym Bauer and also changed the names of some of the sites in the book to preserve his subjects' privacy. This did not prevent him, however, from offering a truthful portrait of a demanding and financially precarious endeavor, ac-

cording to several reviewers. "*Farm* gets as close to the sweat and slim profit margins of an uncertain occupation as any suburban slicker could imagine," wrote R.Z. Sheppard in *Time*. Rhodes won praise not only for the wealth of material he presented, but also for how he presented it. "Rhodes generally affects the no-nonsense, unadorned tone of the farmers, but his occasional lyricisms are not inappropriate," a *Publishers Weekly* contributor observed. *New York Times Book Review* critic Maxine Kumin commented that "Rhodes brings empathy and intelligence to his subject," while Sheppard described the book as a "near perfect piece of reportage."

Rhodes once noted that writing *Farm* was like going home; he had spent his adolescence at a boys' home—the Andrew Drumm Institute—located on a farm near Independence, Missouri. His time on the farm, however, was preceded by a harrowing childhood in an abusive home, and Rhodes dealt with this period of his life in *A Hole in the World: An American Boyhood*. Rhodes was barely a year old when his mother committed suicide; several years later, his father married a woman who perpetrated shocking acts of cruelty upon Rhodes and his older brother, Stanley. She fed them little, forbade them to bathe, and imposed bizarre and complicated rules on them. When they broke one of these rules, she would kick, slap, or beat them, sometimes using a broom handle, a spike heel, or a belt as a weapon of punishment. Their father, meanwhile, was a passive witness. The boys were able to escape their horrendous situation and go to the Drumm Institute only after Stanley reported the abuse to police.

In *Time,* R.Z. Sheppard described the book as "painful to read and hard to put down," and found Rhodes's story ultimately inspiring, with his winning a scholarship to Yale University and subsequently becoming a very successful writer. Similarly, Christopher Lehmann-Haupt noted in *New York Times* that reading the book, "one marvels at the tenacity of the human spirit." He also praised the "spring-fed clarity" of Rhodes's prose. *New York Times Book Review* commentator Russell Banks, however, expressed reservations about how Rhodes tells his tale. He "portrays his stepmother and his father almost too simplistically, as if they were characters without motivation, without an inner life," Banks mused. "The stepmother does seem quite mad," the critic added, "but . . . she cannot have been without an inner life or—given what we know of parents who abuse their children—without some history of having suffered herself." The book also leaves unresolved the puzzle of why the boys' father did nothing to stop the abuse, Banks added.

Rhodes explores a different aspect of his life in *Making Love: An Erotic Odyssey.* He recounts his sexual experiences in detail, including his homoerotic explorations with other boys at the Drumm Institute, his loss of virginity to a prostitute, his two marriages, and his liaison with his then-current partner, a woman he referred to as "G" (in 1993 he married Ginger Untrif). Lehmann-Haupt, reviewing the book for the *New York Times,* found that Rhodes's story occasionally fails to ring true, but that if his effort "never brings him close to solving the mystery of love, it is a courageous enough assault on eros to leave no hollow proprieties intact." Martin Amis, however, writing in the *New York Times Book Review,* thought the book "a cataract of embarrassment" and believed he saw why few writers, as Rhodes notes in the book's preface, have dealt with sex outside of fiction: "A widespread fear of writing a book like *Making Love* would perhaps be reason enough." *New Republic* contributor Katha Pollitt deemed the work frequently clichéd, sexist, and self-absorbed, giving little credence to Rhodes's assertion that he views the women in his life as fully rounded individuals; ostensibly to avoid identifying them, he tells little about any nonsexual aspect of his partners, but the absence of this information "managed to make sex simultaneously vague and mechanical," Pollitt commented.

Rhodes returned to nuclear topics in *Nuclear Renewal: Common Sense about Energy.* In this 1993 work he lays out an argument for increased use of nuclear energy, contending that it is inexpensive, efficient, and, contrary to the statements of many environmentalists, quite safe. James Ridgeway, reviewing the book for *Audubon,* was not swayed; he observed that Rhodes "airily dismisses" the disaster at the Chernobyl nuclear plant, and also felt that Rhodes discounts the genuine and widespread concern and opposition that nuclear power aroused. All in all, the book is a "flippity tract," Ridgeway concluded. A *Scientific American* commentator, though, found Rhodes "informed and articulate, his eye on the telling detail," and thought he "made a concise and attractive case for a new beginning with fission power." At any rate, "we will surely gain from seriously renewed discussion," the reviewer stated.

Rhodes published two books in 1995. In *How to Write: Advice and Reflections,* he shares insights into his creative process. *Washington Post* critic Carolyn See

pronounced the book "a remarkable work of self-revelation" and commended Rhodes as being "generous . . . with his mind and his heart." *Los Angeles Times Book Review* contributor Frederick Busch called *How to Write* "as useful a study of the craft, of the professional conduct of a writing career, as I've seen."

Rhodes's other 1995 publication was the eagerly awaited follow-up to *The Making of the Atomic Bomb.* In *Dark Sun: The Making of the Hydrogen Bomb* the author chronicles the efforts to develop ever more destructive weapons from 1939 onward. His account includes extensive coverage of espionage and politics, as well as science. For instance, he was able to use Soviet documents released after the end of the cold war, as well as U.S. Federal Bureau of Investigation files, to tell the stories of spies such as Klaus Fuchs, who leaked U.S. nuclear secrets to the Soviets. He also provides a detailed analysis of the political environment that produced the arms race.

Dark Sun was one of three finalists for the 1996 Pulitzer Prize in History. Writing in *Commentary,* Walter A. McDougall found *Dark Sun* for the most part praiseworthy, but disagreed with Rhodes's analyses of some topics. "Rhodes asserts that as early as 1949, 'a degree of mutual deterrence had already been installed between the United States and Soviet Union,'" McDougall continued: "If that is so . . . then clearly the arms race amounted to insane 'overkill.'" However, Rhodes, McDougall claimed, provides little evidence to support this assertion. McDougall also took issue with Rhodes's casting of U.S. military officers as villains who caused the arms race. "Richard Rhodes has thought deeply and well about the conundrums of politicized science in a democracy, and has the skill to convey his wisdom to a general audience," McDougall acknowledged. "But his blanket condemnation of U.S. military strategies in the perilous age of the cold war suggests, at a minimum, insufficient research into the diplomatic and military documents of those conflicts, and into the literature of nuclear deterrence." Some other reviewers did not voice such reservations, though. *Time* contributor Richard Stengel termed *Dark Sun* "epic and fascinating," while *Science* contributor Hans A. Bethe praised "the thorough research that is the basis of this book." Bethe added: "The book is full of suspense. Its only fault is that it kept me from doing other work."

Danger of another sort is the focus of *Deadly Feasts: Tracking the Secrets of a Terrifying New Plague.* This book examines the phenomenon of protinaceous infectious diseases, from its early identification in 1913 Germany to its best-known latter-day incarnation, as spongiform encephalopathy (in bovine form, "mad cow disease"). As Rhodes's mad-cow study comes to light, offered Phoebe-Lou Adams in *Atlantic,* "the book becomes truly alarming." This slow-acting virus infects the brains of its victims, and seem to defy all attempts at eradication. In the mid-1990s an outbreak of mad cow disease threatened herds in Europe. Because of ineffective action by the British government, says the author, spongiform encephalopathy is in a position "to reach not only beef eaters but consumers of any other meat, including those in the United States," as Adams described it. "In cinematic fashion," a *Publishers Weekly* contributor remarked, "Rhodes creates a complex, colorful and sometimes gory medical documentary."

Given his brutalized childhood, Rhodes has recognized a theme in his writings. As he was quoted in *First Things:* "Most of my books have examined human violence in one form or another, always for the purpose of discovering what causes such violence and how it might be prevented, mitigated, or at least survived." In that spirit, Rhodes produced *Why They Kill: The Discoveries of a Maverick Criminologist.* The maverick in question is Lonnie Athens, himself a survivor of childhood abuse. Athens, a Seton Hall University criminologist, eschews statistics in favor of in-depth interviews with the most violent of criminals. He has identified violent criminals as victims of abusive childhoods, but it does not stop there. "People become violent, Athens concluded, through a long, slow process he calls violentization, an awkward term that means simply that people learn to be violent," as Paul Chance wrote in a *Psychology Today* article.

Violentization involves four kinds of experiences, Chance continued: brutalization, subjugation, violent coaching and criminal activity. "In other words, their world teaches them to be violent." Then what of abused children who, like Athens and Rhodes, did not turn out savage? Athens reasons that in those cases at least one of the elements of violentization is missing.

Rhodes tests Athens's theory against such well-known criminals as boxer Mike Tyson, a convicted rapist; Lee Harvey Oswald, the acknowledged assassin of President John F. Kennedy; and Cheryl Crane, who at age fourteen stabbed to death the lover of her mother, actress Lana Turner. "The author champions Athens as a pioneering genius battling a criminological establish-

ment that ascribes violent crime to psychopathology or antecedent social conditions," remarked a *Publishers Weekly* contributor. "I confess that before reading *Why They Kill,* I had never heard of Athens," noted *First Things* reviewer John DiIulio, Jr. "There are many first-rate ethnographies of violent felons behind bars and on the streets, but Rhodes has done a service by bringing Athens' work to light." Chance added, however, that the book "crashes" when the author "stops quoting Athens and starts flying solo" with the case studies of the celebrities. Chance also castigated Rhodes for pointing a finger at conservative Christianity as a factor in the childhood of violent criminals. "For the record," remarked Chance, "recent empirical studies of child-rearing practices indicate that, if anything, Christian fundamentalists make exceptionally loving, capable parents." And while calling *Why They Kill* "not a flashy book," *Booklist* contributor David Pitt recommended this volume as "a serious, intelligent, and altogether mesmerizing portrait of evil and the people who fight it."

Rhodes has applied his journalistic eye toward fiction as well as fact. In *The Last Safari,* the author presents a murder mystery set in Africa. Rhodes's fourth novel, *Sons of the Earth,* focuses on Reeve "Red" Wainwright, a former astronaut who became a hero by piloting a crippled spacecraft home from the moon. His sudden celebrity destroys his marriage and drives him to alcoholism; eventually, however, he achieves a more stable success by forming a solar energy corporation and writing a best-selling book on the subject. When Wainwright's teenaged son is kidnapped, the ex-astronaut must raise 500,000 dollars in gold in a few hours. David Quammen wrote in the *New York Times Book Review:* "As a conventional cliffhanger and as a systematic contemplation of the uses and costs of fame in our idolatrous society, *Sons of the Earth* succeeds respectably. But what is most compelling about the book is its ghoulish and timely portrait of the villain, a fame-starved misfit named Karl Loring Grabka." Quammen continued: [In Grabka, Rhodes has] "created a villain who calls to mind that particular sort of covetous predation which apparently brought Mark David Chapman out of the darkness toward John Lennon . . . and John Warnock Hinckley toward, first, actress Jodie Foster and then Ronald Reagan." Quammen also remarked that "the texture of [Grabka's] tawdry and disconnected life [is] portrayed in a chillingly convincing and concrete way." The reviewer noted: "*Sons of the Earth* has great worth."

In *Masters of Death: The SS-Einsatzgruppen and the Invention of the Holocaust,* Rhodes examines the gathering momentum of Nazi movement toward the Final Solution with a focus on the sections of Eastern Europe occupied by the Germans. Using both official documents and first-person accounts, the author explores the psychology of ordinary men becoming barbaric executioners and examines the technology that led to efficient factories of mass murder for Soviet Jews and numerous others. Frederic Krome stated in the *Library Journal* that Rhodes "provides a detailed examination of the organization, motivations, and activities of the SS-Einsatzgruppen, which killed thousands of Jews in the wake of Hitler's invasion of the Soviet Union." A *Kirkus Reviews* contributor wrote: "Though the explorations in mass psychology may not convince all readers, Rhodes exposes the industrial logic that underlies modem genocide."

Jay Freeman, writing in *Booklist,* called *Masters of Death* "grotesquely fascinating," adding: "In Rhodes' chilling account, victims beg, shriek, and writhe in agony while their executioners exult." In a review in *Shofar,* Hilary Earl commented: "The book's greatest strength is that for the first time in English, using some primary sources, but mostly summarizing existing work, Rhodes provides an accessible and graphic narrative of genocidal murder on the eastern front." *Canadian Journal of History* contributor Lawrence D. Stokes wrote: "Curiously enough, at least in Anglo-American historiography Richard Rhodes has written the first book-length narrative (previous accounts have largely only reproduced the reports by the EG [SS-Einsatzgruppen] to their Berlin headquarters) which focuses primarily upon this initial phase of the Shoah (= 'utter destruction')."

For the biography *John James Audubon: The Making of an American,* Rhodes had in-depth access to the Audubon's letters and journals, as well as a host of other primary sources. "Rhodes's portrait reveals a self-made man in a self-made nation, where perpetual reinvention was the norm," wrote Peter Cashwell in *OnEarth.* The biography covers the famous naturalist's entire life, beginning with his scandalous boyhood as the child of a French sea captain and a chamber maid. In addition to recounting many of Audubon's failed ventures in business and art, Rhodes explores Audubon's love of birds from his youth to his coming to America, where he becomes its foremost bird naturalist. Susan Hunt, writing in *Birder's World,* commented that she had viewed Audubon's capture and killing of birds as horrendous but noted that the author paints a "more sympathetic picture of Audubon" by being "convincing about Audu-

bon's love for birds." Writing in the *Economist,* a reviewer noted that Rhodes "sets Audubon in the political context of the day." *Smithsonian* contributor Carey Winfrey called the biography "masterful."

Rhodes also served as editor of *The Audubon Reader.* Donna Seaman, writing in *Booklist,* noted that the collection "presents an invaluable and stirring collection of Audubon's zestful letters, vital biographies . . . and zestful journal excerpts." *Weekly Standard* contributor Robert Finch wrote: "Throughout the essays in this work, there are wonderful observations, not only of birds, but also of the landscape, the characters, and the culture of young America in the early decades of the 19th century." The reviewer went on to comment that the letters "make this collection most valuable." adding that, "in making the authentic Audubon of his letters available in a readily accessible form, Rhodes has made a major contribution to our understanding of Audubon's mind and character."

BIOGRAPHICAL AND CRITICAL SOURCES:

BOOKS

Bestsellers 1990, Thomson Gale (Detroit, MI), 1990.
Dictionary of Literary Biography, Volume 185: *American Literary Journalists, 1945-1995,* Thomson Gale (Detroit, MI), 1997, pp. 241-252.
Rhodes, Richard, *A Hole in the World: An American Boyhood,* Simon & Schuster (New York, NY), 1990.
Rhodes, Richard, *Making Love: An Erotic Odyssey,* Simon & Schuster (New York, NY), 1992.
Rhodes, Richard, *How to Write: Advice and Reflections,* Morrow (New York, NY), 1995.
Sims, Norman, editor, *The Literary Journalists,* Ballantine (New York, NY), 1984.

PERIODICALS

Agricultural History, April, 1997, review of *Dark Sun: The Making of the Hydrogen Bomb,* p. 560; winter, 1999, review of *Farm: A Year in the Life of an American Farmer,* p. 128.
American Scientist, March, 1999, review of *Visions of Technology: A Century of Vital Debate about Machines, Systems, and the Human World,* p. 178;

January-February, 2005, Paul Lawrence Farber, review of *John James Audubon: The Making of an American*, p. 74.

Atlantic, May, 1997, Phoebe-Lou Adams, review of *Deadly Feasts: Tracking the Secrets of a Terrifying New Plague*, p. 120.

Audubon, November-December, 1993, James Ridgeway, review of *Nuclear Renewal: Common Sense about Energy*, pp. 123-126; November-December, 2004, Fred Baumgarten, review of *John James Audubon*, p. 94.

Barron's, September 1, 1997, review of *Deadly Feasts*, p. 39.

Birder's World, October, 2005, Susan Hunt, review of *John James Audubon*, p. 70.

Booklist, February 15, 1997, Donna Seaman, review of *Deadly Feasts*, p. 970; December 15, 1998, review of *Visions of Technology*, p. 714; September 15, 1999, David Pitt, review of *Why They Kill: The Discoveries of a Maverick Criminologist*, p. 203; April 15, 2002, Jay Freeman, review of *Masters of Death: The SS-Einsatzgruppen and the Invention of the Holocaust*, p. 1379; March 15, 2006, Donna Seaman, review of *The Audubon Reader*, p. 11.

Books, June, 1997, review of *Deadly Feasts*, p. 16.

Books & Culture, July, 1999, review of *Visions of Technology*, p. 42; September-October, 2006, Cindy Crosby, review of *John James Audubon*, p. 24.

Business Week, March 31, 1997, review of *Deadly Feasts*, p. 19.

Canadian Journal of History, August, 2003, Lawrence D. Stokes, review of *Masters of Death*, p. 342.

Chicago Tribune Book World, July 5, 1981, Priscilla Johnson McMillan, review of *The Making of the Atomic Bomb*.

Commentary, October, 1995, Walter A. McDougall, review of *Dark Sun*, pp. 52-55; August, 1997, Laura Maneulidis, review of *Deadly Feasts*, p. 61.

Economist, April 25, 1998, review of *Deadly Feasts*, p. 83; August 7, 2004, review of *John James Audubon*, p. 69.

Entertainment Weekly, October 15, 1999, review of *Why They Kill*, p. 74.

First Things, March, 2000, John DiIulio, Jr., review of *Why They Kill*, p. 84.

Fortune, October 11, 1999, review of *Why They Kill*, p. 84.

Futurist, August, 1999, review of *Visions of Technology*, p. 45.

Globe and Mail (Toronto, Ontario, Canada), October 16, 1999, review of *Why They Kill*, p. D25.

Kirkus Reviews, February 15, 1997, review of *Deadly Feasts*, p. 283; January 15, 1999, review of *Visions of Technology*, p. 128; August 1, 1999, review of *Why They Kill*, p. 1209; April 1, 2002, review of *Masters of Death*, p. 475; June 1, 2004, review of *John James Audubon*, p. 529.

Kliatt, July, 2006, Raymond Puffer, review of *John James Audubon*, p. 33.

Lancet, May 31, 1997, Paul Bendheim, review of *Deadly Feasts*, p. 1632.

Library Journal, March 15, 1997, review of *Deadly Feasts*, p. 86; January, 1999, Dayne Sherman, review of *Visions of Technology*, p. 145; September 15, 1999, review of *Why They Kill*, p. 97; May 1, 2002, Frederic Krome, review of *Masters of Death*, p. 117.

Los Angeles Times Book Review, August 20, 1995, Frederick Busch, review of *How to Write: Advice and Reflections*, pp. 3, 10; October 26, 1997, review of *Deadly Feasts*, p. 5; October 17, 1999, review of *Why They Kill*, p. 7.

Nature, April 10, 1997, review of *Deadly Feasts*, p. 565; May 20, 1999, review of *Visions of Technology*, p. 219.

New Republic, November 9, 1992, Katha Pollitt, review of *Making Love*, pp. 38-41.

New Scientist, February 6, 1999, review of *Visions of Technology*, p. 48.

New Statesman, August 23, 1999, review of *Visions of Technology*, p. 39.

New Yorker, April 14, 1997, review of *Deadly Feasts*, p. 82.

New York Times, February 3, 1987, John Gross, review of *The Making of the Atomic Bomb*, p. C14; October 11, 1990, Christopher Lehmann-Haupt, review of *A Hole in the World*, p. C22; September 21, 1992, Christopher Lehmann-Haupt, review of *Making Love*, p. C16; September 27, 1999, review of *Why They Kill*, p. E8.

New York Times Book Review, August 9, 1981, David Quammen, review of *Sons of the Earth*, p. 12; February 8, 1987, William J. Broad, review of *The Making of the Atomic Bomb*, pp. 1, 39; September 24, 1989, Maxine Kumin, review of *Farm*, pp. 1, 30; October 28, 1990, Russell Banks, review of *A Hole in the World*, p. 14; August 30, 1992, Martin Amis, review of *Making Love*, pp. 1, 21; March 16, 1997, review of *Deadly Feasts*, p. 9; June 1, 1997, review of *Deadly Feasts*, p. 38; February 8, 1998, review of *Farm*, p. 28; May 17, 1998, review of *Deadly Feasts*, p. 48; September 19, 1999, review of *Why They Kill*, p. 13.

OnEarth, winter, 2005, Peter Cashwell, review of *John James Audubon*, p. 40.

Psychology Today, November, 1999, Paul Chance, review of *Why They Kill*, p. 79.

Publishers Weekly, August 25, 1989, review of *Farm,* p. 52; February 10, 1997, review of *Deadly Feasts,* p. 75; February 15, 1999, review of *Visions of Technology,* p. 99; August 16, 1999, review of *Why They Kill,* p. 71; April 8, 2002, review of *Masters of Death,* p. 216.

Science, September 8, 1995, Hans A. Bethe, review of *Dark Sun,* pp. 1455-1457.

Science Books and Films, November, 1999, review of *Visions of Technology,* p. 259.

Science News, December 18, 2004, review of *John James Audubon,* p. 403.

Scientific American, February, 1994, review of *Nuclear Renewal,* pp. 120-121.

Shofar, summer, 2004, Hilary Earl, review of *Masters of Death,* p. 141.

Smithsonian, December, 2004, Carey Winfrey, "Birds and Beasts: A New Book on Audubon," p. 11.

Time, September 25, 1989, R.Z. Sheppard, review of *Farm: A Year in the Life of an American Farmer,* pp. 81-82; October 29, 1990, R.Z. Sheppard, review of *A Hole in the World,* p. 102; August 21, 1995, Richard Stengel, review of *Dark Sun,* p. 66.

Times Literary Supplement, August 15, 1997, review of *Deadly Feasts,* p. 25.

Tribune Books (Chicago, IL), May 18, 1997, review of *Deadly Feasts,* p. 5.

Voice of Youth Advocates, October, 1998, review of *Deadly Feasts,* p. 254.

Wall Street Journal, March 14, 1997, review of *Deadly Feasts,* p. A11.

Washington Post, June 23, 1995, Carolyn See, review of *How to Write,* p. F2.

Washington Post Book World, March 23, 1997, review of *Deadly Feasts,* p. 3; September 5, 1999, review of *Visions of Technology,* p. 11; September 19, 1999, review of *Why They Kill,* p. 6.

Weekly Standard, December 6, 2004, Robert Finch, review of *John James Audubon,* p. 31; July 3, 2006, Robert Finch, review of *The Audubon Reader.*

ONLINE

Richard Rhodes Home Page, http://www.richardrhodes. com/ (February 15, 2007).*

*   *   *

RHODES, Richard Lee
    See RHODES, Richard

RICHELSON, Jeffrey
    See RICHELSON, Jeffrey T.

*   *   *

RICHELSON, Jeffrey T. 1949-
    (Jeffrey Richelson, Jeffrey Talbot Richelson)

PERSONAL: Born December 31, 1949, in New York, NY; son of Herbert H. and Edna Richelson. *Education:* City College of the City University of New York, B.A., 1970; University of Rochester, M.A., 1974, Ph.D., 1975.

ADDRESSES: Home—Alexandria, VA.

CAREER: Writer, educator, policymaker, and consultant. University of Texas at Austin, visiting assistant professor of government, 1976-77; Analytical Assessments Corp., Marina del Rey, CA, research associate, 1977-81; University of California, Los Angeles, senior fellow at Center for International and Strategic Affairs, 1981-82; American University, Washington, DC, assistant professor of government and public administration, 1982-87; writer and consultant, 1987—; National Security Archive, George Washington University, Washington, DC, senior fellow.

MEMBER: Association of Former Intelligence Officers, Naval Intelligence Professionals, National Military Intelligence Association, Committee for the Scientific Investigation of Claims of the Paranormal.

WRITINGS:

NONFICTION

The U.S. Intelligence Community, Ballinger (Cambridge, MA), 1985, 4th edition, Westview Press (Boulder, CO), 1999.

Sword and Shield: The Soviet Intelligence and Security Apparatus, Ballinger (Cambridge, MA), 1985.

(With Desmond Ball) *The Ties That Bind: Intelligence Cooperation between the UKUSA Countries,* Allen & Unwin (Sydney, New South Wales, Australia), 1985.

American Espionage and the Soviet Target, Morrow (New York, NY), 1987.

Foreign Intelligence Organizations, Ballinger (Cambridge, MA), 1988.

America's Secret Eyes in Space, Harper (New York, NY), 1990.

A Century of Spies: Intelligence in the Twentieth Century, Oxford University Press (New York, NY), 1995.

America's Space Sentinels: DSP Satellites and National Security, University Press of Kansas (Lawrence, KS), 1999.

The Wizards of Langley: Inside the CIA's Directorate of Science and Technology, Westview Press (Boulder, CO), 2001.

Terrorism and U.S. Policy, 1968-2002, ProQuest Information and Learning (Ann Arbor, MI), 2003.

Presidential Directives on National Security: Part II: From Harry Truman to George W. Bush, ProQuest Information and Learning (Ann Arbor, MI), 2003.

Spying on the Bomb: American Nuclear Intelligence from Nazi Germany to Iran and North Korea, W.W. Norton (New York, NY), 2006.

Contributor to economic and political journals.

SIDELIGHTS: An expert on government spying and the intelligence community, Jeffrey T. Richelson has written numerous books and articles on espionage and the technology associated with it. His first book, *The U.S. Intelligence Community,* which has been updated in three subsequent editions, is a comprehensive look at the network of intelligence-gathering organizations in the United States. Compiling data and anecdotes via the Freedom of Information Act and numerous interviews, Richelson describes the history of the CIA, FBI, and military intelligence groups and shows how these various organizations work together to form a sophisticated American intelligence system.

"Despite the end of the cold war, there remains a need for a significant intelligence collection and analysis establishment," Richelson once told *CA.* "In addition to understanding the dynamics of individual countries and regions—from Russia to South Africa—there are a variety of problems such as proliferation of advanced weaponry and international terrorism that will require attention from the U.S. and allied intelligence communities."

Although the intelligence community once avoided Richelson as an outsider and a security risk, his scholarly efforts over the years eventually led to his legitimization as an astute scholar of intelligence gathering. As noted by Bruce D. Berkowitz in an *ORBIS* review of Richelson's *A Century of Spies: Intelligence in the Twentieth Century,* "These days the intelligence community cooperates with Richelson by providing unclassified, on-the-record interviews and responding to his Freedom of Information Act requests (Richelson may be one of the largest FOIA users)." Berkowitz added that Richelson "is recognized as a member of the professional community to the extent that he is invited to CIA sponsored conferences."

This acceptance by officials in government intelligence helped Richelson provide an inside history of intelligence gathering in *A Century of Spies.* In the book, Richelson recounts the history of espionage from Czarist Russia and the early British Secret Service to spying in the modern era after the fall of the Soviet Union and the end of the cold war. A reviewer for *Publishers Weekly* noted: "His comprehensive survey explores the impact of spies and their special technology on world events in this century, showing how intelligence gathering and espionage have become a multibillion-dollar enterprise." For example, the book relates how intelligence efforts helped lead to the development of computers and long-distance telegraphs. Calling the book "almost encyclopedic in scope" and "valuable and comprehensive," reviewer David Fromkin, writing in *Foreign Affairs,* commented that "*A Century of Spies* reminds us how central the ordinary business of spying and counterspying has been to the politics, diplomacy, and wars of modern history." A *Publishers Weekly* reviewer concluded: "This decade-by-decade review of key events and breakthroughs in intelligence and espionage is masterly."

Richelson has continued his work through his appointment as a senior fellow with the National Security Archives located at George Washington University. In *America's Space Sentinels: DSP Satellites and National Security,* he provides a comprehensive account of the development of infrared missile-launch detection satellite platforms and includes a discussion of how their use has had a long-term influence on American national security operations. Writing in *Aerospace Power Journal,* Clifford E. Rich noted: "I was impressed that the author's style of writing effectively weaved history, geopolitics, and technical jargon in such a way that this work will appeal not only to people in the space and intelligence career fields but also to a cross section of operators, strategists, and engineers." Echoing these sentiments in the *Bulletin of Atomic Scientists,* James

Bamford praised Richelson for paying "tribute to the thousands of nameless engineers and technicians who developed, launched, and ran America's nuclear-war sentry post in space."

Richelson turned his focus exclusively to America's most famous intelligence organization with his book *The Wizards of Langley: Inside the CIA's Directorate of Science and Technology.* Supplying numerous anecdotes, Richelson provides a historical look of the Directorate of Science and Technology, one of the CIA's three main divisions and the one responsible for developing the modern tools of the spy trade, from misguided efforts to use cats as bugging devices to highly successful U-2 spy planes and reconnaissance satellites. Reviewers noted that, like most of Richelson's books, the heavily detailed *The Wizards of Langley* is primarily for those interested in the spy business. Called a "fine and meticulously researched study" by a reviewer in *Publishers Weekly,* the book has also received praise for its account of the infighting between the CIA and the military over who would control the high-tech spying devices. As noted in a review by Martin A. Lee in the *Washington Post:* "Richelson's book offers a rare glimpse into a vital aspect of U.S. intelligence."

Richelson looks at intelligence gathering from the angle of foreign espionage in *Spying on the Bomb: American Nuclear Intelligence from Nazi Germany to Iran and North Korea.* The book stands as an "authoritative and definitive account of U.S. nuclear espionage from the earliest days of atomic research in WWII to the present," noted a *Publishers Weekly* reviewer. He has "brought together a huge amount of information about Washington's efforts to track the nuclear weapons projects of other countries," stated David Holloway in the *New York Times Book Review.* Beginning with Nazi Germany in World War II, Richelson looks at nuclear projects in fifteen countries, such as China, the Soviet Union, France, Israel, Pakistan, India, Iran, North Korea, Iraq, and elsewhere. He mines information from declassified documents as well as relevant interviews to construct a comparison between what is currently known about the nuclear aspirations of these countries with what was known at the time in history when the assessments were originally made. "This may sound like heavy going, but Richelson writes with admirable clarity. And along the way he has fascinating stories to tell," commented Holloway. He tells how plans were made to assassinate German physicist Werner Heisenberg during World War II. He notes that Presidents Kennedy and Johnson seriously considered attacks on Chinese nuclear installations. And, he covers more recent and more salient controversies on the alleged nuclear capabilities and intentions of Iraq, Iran, and North Korea. Richelson points out the difficulties of gathering reliable nuclear intelligence on foreign countries and relates some measures taken by foreign nations to evade information gathering by satellite, human spies, and other techniques.

Booklist reviewer George Cohen called *Spying on the Bomb* a "searching and informed analysis of our nation's nuclear espionage" programs throughout nuclear history. A *Kirkus Reviews* critic named it "useful for students of nuclear policy and intelligence." All of the case studies addressed by Richelson are a "sobering reminder of how often the professionals in the nuclear-intelligence business have been at least a little wrong in a field where being a little wrong can have catastrophic consequences," observed *Commentary* contributor Patrick J. Garrity.

BIOGRAPHICAL AND CRITICAL SOURCES:

PERIODICALS

Aerospace Power Journal, fall, 2000, Clifford E. Rich, review of *America's Space Sentinels: DSP Satellites and National Security,* p. 122.

American Historical Review, April, 1997, Thomas R. Mockaitis, review of *A Century of Spies: Intelligence in the Twentieth Century,* p. 430; February, 2001, T.A. Heppenheimer, review of *America's Space Sentinels,* p. 214.

Arms Control Today, March, 2006, review of *Spying on the Bomb: American Nuclear Intelligence from Nazi Germany to Iran and North Korea,* p. 47.

Booklist, August, 2001, Gilbert Taylor, review of *The Wizards of Langley: Inside the CIA's Directorate of Science and Technology,* p. 2062; February 1, 2006, George Cohen, review of *Spying on the Bomb,* p. 10.

Bulletin of Atomic Scientists, January, 2000, James Bamford, review of *America's Space Sentinels,* p. 65; September, 2000, Jeffrey T. Richelson, "Shootin' for the Moon," p. 22.

Choice, December, 1999, W.M. Leary, review of *America's Space Sentinels,* p. 744.

Commentary, April, 2006, Patrick J. Garrity, "Guesswork," review of *Spying on the Bomb,* p. 81.

Economist, February 17, 1996, review of *A Century of Spies,* p. S4.

Foreign Affairs, January-February, 1996, David Fromkin, review of *A Century of Spies,* pp. 165-172.

Journal of American History, December, 1998, Nick Cullather, review of *A Century of Spies,* pp. 1146-1149; September, 2000, Andreas Riechstein, review of *America's Space Sentinels,* p. 738.

Kirkus Reviews, January 15, 2006, review of *Spying on the Bomb,* p. 77.

Library Journal, August, 1995, H. Steck, review of *A Century of Spies,* p. 98; August, 2001, Stephen L. Hupp, review of *The Wizards of Langley,* p. 133.

New Scientist, December 9, 1985, Michael Herman, review of *A Century of Spies,* p. 50.

New York Times Book Review, March 26, 2006, David Holloway, "Other People's Nukes," review of *Spying on the Bomb,* p. 19.

ORBIS, fall, 1996, Bruce D. Berkowitz, review of *A Century of Spies,* pp. 653-663.

Publishers Weekly, June 12, 1995, review of *A Century of Spies,* p. 52; September 10, 2001, review of *The Wizards of Langley,* p. 83; December 5, 2005, review of *Spying on the Bomb,* p. 42.

Reference & Research Book News, August, 2006, review of *Spying on the Bomb.*

Washington Post, September 30, 2001, Martin A. Lee, review of *The Wizards of Langley,* p. T04.*

* * *

RICHELSON, Jeffrey Talbot
See RICHELSON, Jeffrey T.

* * *

RITZ, David 1943-
(Esther Elizabeth Pearl)

PERSONAL: Born December 2, 1943, in New York, NY; son of Milton M. (a stockbroker) and Pearl Ritz; married Roberta Plitt (a comedienne); children: Alison, Jessica (twins). *Education:* University of Texas, B.A., 1966; State University of New York at Buffalo, M.A., 1969. *Religion:* Jewish.

ADDRESSES: Home—Los Angeles, CA.

CAREER: Writer. Bloom Advertising, Dallas, TX, copywriter, 1961-70; Houston/Ritz/Cohen/Jagoda (advertising agency), New York, NY, owner, 1971-75; writer, 1975—. Teacher at University of Pennsylvania, 1969.

AWARDS, HONORS: Fulbright scholar, 1968.

WRITINGS:

NONFICTION

(With Ray Charles) *Brother Ray: Ray Charles' Own Story,* Dial (New York, NY), 1978.

(With Marvin Gaye) *Divided Soul: The Life of Marvin Gaye,* McGraw-Hill (New York, NY), 1985, updated and with new introduction, Da Capo Press (New York, NY), 1991.

(With Smokey Robinson) *Smokey: Inside My Life,* McGraw-Hill (New York, NY), 1989.

(With Jerry Wexler) *Rhythm and Blues: A Life in American Music,* Knopf (New York, NY), 1993.

Ray Charles: Voice of Soul, Chelsea House (New York, NY), 1994.

(With Etta James) *Rage to Survive: The Etta James Story,* Villard Books (New York, NY), 1995.

(With B.B. King) *Blues All around Me: The Autobiography of B.B. King,* Avon (New York, NY), 1996.

(With Sinbad) *Sinbad's Guide to Life: Because I Know Everything,* Bantam (New York, NY), 1997.

(With Aretha Franklin) *Aretha: From These Roots,* Villard Books (New York, NY), 1999.

(With others) *The Brothers Neville,* Little, Brown (Boston, MA), 2000.

(With Laila Ali) *Reach! Finding Strength, Spirit, and Personal Power,* Hyperion (New York, NY), 2002.

(With Robert Guillaume) *Guillaume: A Life,* University of Missouri Press (Columbia, MO), 2002.

(With Jimmy Scott) *Faith in Time: The Life of Jimmy Scott,* Da Capo Press (Cambridge, MA), 2002.

(With Walter Yetnikoff) *Howling at the Moon: Confessions of a Music Mogul in an Age of Excess,* Broadway Books (New York, NY), 2004.

(Editor) *Elvis by the Presleys,* still-life photography by Henry Leutwyler, Crown (New York, NY), 2005.

(With Tavis Smiley) *What I Know for Sure: My Story of Growing Up in America,* Doubleday (New York, NY), 2006.

Messengers: Portraits of African American Ministers, Evangelists, Gospel Singers, and Other Messengers of "the Word," photographs by Nicola Goode, Doubleday (New York, NY), 2006.

FICTION

Glory (novel), Simon & Schuster (New York, NY), 1979.

Search for Happiness (novel), Simon & Schuster (New York, NY), 1980.

The Man Who Brought the Dodgers Back to Brooklyn (novel), Simon & Schuster (New York, NY), 1981.

Blue Notes under a Green Felt Hat (novel), Donald I. Fine (New York, NY), 1989.

Barbells and Saxophones, Donald I. Fine (New York, NY), 1989.

Family Blood, Donald I. Fine (New York, NY), 1991.

Passion Flowers, D.I. Fine (New York, NY), 1992.

Take It off, Take It All Off, D.I. Fine (New York, NY), 1993.

(With Mable John) *Sanctified Blues* (novel), Harlem Moon/Broadway Books (New York, NY), 2006.

Also author of novel, *Deeper Than Shame,* under pseudonym Esther Elizabeth Pearl.

SIDELIGHTS: David Ritz is the author of novels and of biographies of celebrity performers such as Ray Charles, Marvin Gaye, and Smokey Robinson of the Miracles. *Brother Ray: Ray Charles' Own Story,* Ritz's biography of the famed soul singer, impressed singer Marvin Gaye to commission a similar book. *Divided Soul: The Life of Marvin Gaye,* informed by the friendship that formed between Ritz and his subject and published after the singer's tragic death, "is a personal history and at the same time a sweeping saga of black music over the past three decades," Norman Richmond observed in a Toronto *Globe and Mail* review. George de Stefano, like other reviewers, found Ritz's presentation balanced between the brilliance of Gaye's musical talent and the darker aspects of his life. Explained de Stefano in the *Nation:* "*Divided Soul* started out in 1979 as a collaboration between Gaye and his longtime admirer. Ritz is sympathetic and loving toward the man whose friend and confidant he was for several years, but he doesn't hide Gaye's dark side, his self-absorption, his cruelties and violence. *Divided Soul* is often startlingly candid, but it manages to avoid lurid sensationalism, no mean feat given the particulars of the story: sex, drugs, child abuse, show-business scandal." This study of Gaye's growth from abused child to rebel to creative popular musician was widely reviewed and generally well received.

Other singers with whom Ritz has collaborated include Aretha Franklin, B.B. King, Etta James, the Neville Brothers, and Jimmy Scott. Reviewing 1999's *Aretha:*

From These Roots for *Booklist,* Donna Seaman maintained that Ritz "is the perfect accompanist, allowing Franklin's speaking voice . . . to flow freely." Mike Tribby, in another *Booklist* review, praised *The Brothers Neville* as "a nice omnibus of information on these beloved performers." Ritz helped jazz singer Scott tell his story in *Faith in Time: The Life of Jimmy Scott*—the story of a man with a haunting, high singing voice caused by Kallman's Syndrome, which, as a *Publishers Weekly* contributor reported, "meant that his testicles never descended and his genitals never fully developed." Coming to fame during the 1940s and 1950s, Scott had been largely forgotten until he was rediscovered in the 1990s. *Library Journal* contributor William Kenz praised the book's balanced presentation, noting that, "refreshingly, Ritz refuses to sensationalize subjects that he could easily hype," and dubbed Scott's autobiography "intriguing and inspiring."

Ritz has also worked on the life stories of other entertainment figures besides singers. Comedian Sinbad, boxer Laila Ali, and actor Robert Guillaume have each been assisted in telling his or her life story by the author. *Guillaume: A Life,* which follows the actor from television to film and the Broadway stage, "reads like a conversation with a close friend," according to *Library Journal* contributor Rosellen Brewer, while in *Booklist* Tribby maintained that, with Ritz's help, Guillaume "comes off as a serious, artful man of notable intellect."

Novels by Ritz have also been favorably reviewed; readers say their plots take some interesting turns. *The Man Who Brought the Dodgers Back to Brooklyn,* for example, is a fantasy in which the Dodgers return to a reconstructed Ebbets Field with a female pitcher, although the story falls just short of a fairy-tale ending. *Blue Notes under a Green Felt Hat,* the story of a jazz-loving hatmaker's son's vocational and romantic choices, "builds to a not-unpredictable trick ending, one [at] which he has dropped a few delectable hints along the way," wrote Leonard Feather in the *Los Angeles Times Book Review.*

Ritz's 1980 fiction offering, *Search for Happiness,* presents the problems that beset a writer of soap operas when he invents a character based on a real-life nun as a means of saving his slipping ratings. Burger King wants to erect a fast-food outlet where the nun's convent stands, and in her fight to save the convent she falls into the tempting arms of a married lawyer—an ethical problem for the real-life nun that sends her TV counterpart's ratings soaring. By the time the soap-opera character is due for some requisite misery, the actress who plays her has identified so closely with the nun that the writer hesitates to create personal problems that will again save the program's ratings. A *Washington Post Book World* contributor commented, "What you got here, Sweetheart, is a soap within a soap, fast, funny, and sad. Also dirty like you wouldn't believe." *Los Angeles Times Book Review* contributor Leslie Raddatz remarked that the writer-protagonist's "epic telling off of the network V.P. and his raffish views on such varied subjects as jogging and love are worth the price of admission."

The author has continued to write both fiction and nonfiction, including helping many coauthors present their memoirs and autobiographies. *What I Know for Sure: My Story of Growing Up in America* is a collaborative effort with Tavis Smiley, a radio and television talk show host. "This surprisingly thoughtful book emphasizes old-school values and the rewards of hard work," wrote Vernon Ford in *Booklist.* Jennifer Johnston, writing in the *Library Journal,* commented: "There are some fantastic stories here . . . and though some are controversial, all are honest and poignant."

Messengers: Portraits of African American Ministers, Evangelists, Gospel Singers, and Other Messengers of "the Word" is a "tribute to contemporary musicians, artists, and ministers who have encouraged him during his journey" toward Christianity, as noted by La Tonya Taylor in *Christianity Today.* A *Publishers Weekly* contributor wrote that "both the words and images that Ritz has pulled together are inspiring." Ritz also served as editor of *Elvis by the Presleys,* which *Booklist* contributor Mike Tribby called "good, clean fun."

Fritz collaborated with musician and minister Mable John to write the novel *Sanctified Blues.* The story focuses on Albertina Merci, a former blues backup singer who now devotes herself to the Bible and imparting its wisdom to others. When a family crisis arises, Albertina is asked to return to her hometown of Dallas, which she does reluctantly since the place brings back many bad memories of racial prejudice. A *Kirkus Reviews* contributor wrote that "many readers will go wild for this gospel-spouting, life-affirming story."

BIOGRAPHICAL AND CRITICAL SOURCES:

PERIODICALS

Black Issues Book Review, May-June, 2003, Clarence V. Reynolds, review of *Faith in Time: The Life of Jimmy Scott,* p. 20.

Booklist, September 1, 1999, Donna Seaman, review of *Aretha: From These Roots,* p. 3; September 15, 2000, Mike Tribby, review of *The Brothers Neville,* p. 201; September 1, 2002, Gordon Flagg, review of *Faith in Time,* p. 38; October 15, 2002, Mike Tribby, review of *Guillaume: A Life,* p. 374; April 15, 2005, Mike Tribby, review of *Elvis by the Presleys,* p. 1412; February 1, 2006, Vanessa Bush, review of *Messengers: Portraits of African American Ministers, Evangelists, Gospel Singers, and Other Messengers of "the Word,"* p. 23; September 1, 2006, Vernon Ford, review of *What I Know for Sure: My Story of Growing Up in America,* p. 35.

Christianity Today, April, 2006, La Tonya Taylor, review of *Messengers,* p. 106.

Ebony, July, 2003, review of *Guillaume,* p. 22; June, 2006, review of *Messengers,* p. 28.

Globe and Mail (Toronto, Ontario, Canada), September 21, 1985, Norman Richmond, review of *Divided Soul: The Life of Marvin Gaye.*

Kirkus Reviews, May 1, 2006, review of *Sanctified Blues,* p. 429; July 15, 2006, review of *What I Know for Sure,* p. 717.

Library Journal, October 1, 2002, William Kenz, review of *Faith in Time,* p. 97; November 15, 2002, Rosellen Brewer, review of *Guillaume,* p. 73; September 1, 2006, Jennifer Johnston, review of *What I Know for Sure,* p. 157.

Los Angeles Times Book Review, October 10, 1980, Leslie Raddatz, review of *Search for Happiness*; August 6, 1989, Leonard Feather, review of *Blue Notes under a Green Felt Hat.*

Nation, October 5, 1985, George de Stefano, review of *Divided Soul.*

Publishers Weekly, July 29, 2002, review of *Faith in Time*; December 12, 2005, review of *Messengers,* p. 60; July 24, 2006, review of *What I Know for Sure,* p. 44.

Washington Post Book World, January 16, 1980, review of *Search for Happiness.**

*   *   *

ROWBOTHAM, David 1924-
(David Harold Rowbotham)

PERSONAL: Born August 27, 1924, in Toowoomba, Queensland, Australia; son of Harold and Phyllis Rowbotham; married Ethel Jessie Matthews (a registered nurse), January 14, 1952; children: Beverly, Jill. *Ethnic-*

ity: "English descent." *Education:* University of Queensland, B.A., 1948 and 1964; attended University of Sydney, 1949.

ADDRESSES: Home and office—Brisbane, Queensland, Australia. *E-mail*—dhrlit@aol.com.

CAREER: Angus & Robertson, Sydney, Australia, member of editorial staff for *Australian Encyclopedia,* 1950-51; *Encyclopaedia Britannica,* London, England, editorial assistant, 1951-52; *Toowoomba Chronicle,* Toowoomba, Queensland, Australia, staff columnist, 1952-55; *Courier Mail,* Brisbane, Queensland, literary and theater critic, 1955-64, chief book reviewer, 1964-69, arts editor, 1969-80, literary editor, 1980-87. Australian Broadcasting Commission, broadcaster for National Book Review Panel, 1957-63; public speaker throughout Queensland. Guest lecturer at universities in California and Hawaii, 1972, and at Japan-Australia Cultural Centre, Tokyo, 1974; founding member of Warana Writers' Festival (now Brisbane Writers' Festival), 1962, and Adelaide Festival of Arts, 1962, *Military service:* Royal Australian Air Force, wireless operator for mobile fighter sector, 1942-45; served in Pacific theater; received commemorative medal, 2005.

MEMBER: International Federation of Journalists, Australian Society of Authors (founding member; member of foundation council and state vice president, 1963—), Fellowship of Australian Writers (Queensland president, 1982), Australian Journalists Association (reserve member), New South Wales Writers Centre.

AWARDS, HONORS: Competition prize, Sydney *Morning Herald,* 1949; Grace Leven Prize for poetry, 1964; Xavier Society Award for poetry, 1969; travel grants from Australian Commonwealth Literary Fund (for the United States), 1972, and Australia Council, 1974 (for Asia), 1976 (for Italy), and 1981 (for the United States); awarded Order of Australia, 1991; emeritus fellowship, Literature Board, Australia Council, 1997.

WRITINGS:

Ploughman and Poet (poetry), Lyre Bird Writers (Sydney, Australia), 1954.
Town and City: Tales and Sketches, Angus & Robertson (Sydney, Australia), 1956.

(Editor) *Queensland Writing,* Fellowship of Australian Writers (Brisbane, Queensland, Australia), 1957.
Inland (poetry), Angus & Robertson (Sydney, Australia), 1958.
All the Room (poetry), Jacaranda Press (Brisbane, Queensland, Australia), 1964.
The Man in the Jungle (novel), Angus & Robertson (Sydney, Australia), 1964.
Brisbane (monograph), University of Sydney (Sydney, Australia), 1964.
Bungalow and Hurricane: New Poems, Angus & Robertson (Sydney, Australia), 1967.
The Makers of the Ark (poetry), Angus & Robertson (Sydney, Australia), 1970.
The Pen of Feathers (poetry), Angus & Robertson (Sydney, Australia), 1971.
Selected Poems, University of Queensland Press (Brisbane, Queensland, Australia), 1975.
Maydays (poetry), University of Queensland Press (Brisbane, Queensland, Australia), 1980.
(With Simon Catling and Tim Firth) *Beginning Outset Geography,* Oliver & Boyd (Edinburgh, Scotland), 1984.
(With Simon Catling and Tim Firth) *Outset Geography,* Oliver & Boyd (Edinburgh, Scotland), 1988.
New and Selected Poems: 1945-1993, Penguin (Melbourne, Australia), 1994.
The Ebony Gates: New and Wayside Poems, Central Queensland University Press (Brisbane, Queensland, Australia), 1996.
Poems for America: New Poems, Interactive Press (Carindale, Queensland, Australia), 2002.
The Brown Island and Other Poems, Picaro Press (Warners Bay, New South Wales, Australia), 2005.
The Cave in the Sky: Poems at Eighty, Picaro Press (Warners Bay, New South Wales, Australia), 2005.

Also author of *The Hammer that Made a Mountain,* 1995. Work represented in anthologies, including *The Indigo Book of Modern Australian Sonnets,* edited by Geoff Page, 2003; and *The Best Australian Poems 2004,* edited by Les Murray, 2004. Contributor to periodicals, including *Newswrite* and *Southerly.*

Rowbotham's papers, diaries, scrapbooks, correspondence, and drafts are collected at the National Library of Australia.

ADAPTATIONS: Readings of some of Rowbotham's poetry were videotaped by Australia's National Sound and Film Archive, 1992; other videotapes include *Penguin Book Poems,* 2004, and *Poems at Eighty,* 2005.

SIDELIGHTS: Australian author and poet David Rowbotham began his writing career after World War II, at a time when his contemporaries were identifying closely with the Australian landscape. Although Rowbotham also has produced poems that link him to his origins, he writes verse that is different in that it is considered more introspective than that of most other modern Australian poets. From his early writings to his present, Rowbotham has celebrated nature and humanity and has become one of Australia's favorite modern poets. In a *World Literature Today* review of *Selected Poems,* Syed Amanuddin noted Rowbotham's "own peculiar idiom and simplicity of diction," and the poet's use of "several themes which suggest the wide range of his knowledge and experience, his love of nature and his humanity." Noting that Rowbotham's poems, unlike many others by Australians, also contain a great deal of social commentary, Amanuddin observed that "no student of Australian poetry can afford to ignore such a poet."

In a *Times Literary Supplement* review of *Selected Poems,* Ronald Tamplin also complimented Rowbotham's work, which he found tends "to hover between landscape and a metaphysical abstraction." Tamplin made special note of poems such as "Dust" and "Prey to Prey," both written in quatrains. According to Tamplin, Rowbotham's "contribution to Australian writing has been constant and painstaking since 1946." Rowbotham's work has transcended the boundaries of his native country as his travels have taken him to other lands, among them America and Asia. Inspired by these journeys, Rowbotham has written collections such as *Maydays,* which contains poems that reflect particular aspects of his homeland and the lands he has visited such as ducks in a Japanese garden and the American theme park Disneyland. An "effective verbal painter," according to Amanuddin, writing about *Maydays* in *World Literature Today,* "Rowbotham outdoes most Australian poets . . . by relating his personal and national experience consciously to global experience."

Rowbotham's early career was associated with the *Bulletin* school of nature poetry, "a school," wrote Thomas W. Shapcott in the sixth edition of *Contemporary Poets,* "that encouraged Australian writers to look more closely at and reaffirm their own regional identity and meaning." Much of the work produced by the school was characterized by "an ever expanding wash of mynah bird and billabong versification," Shapcott explains. Rowbotham's first book, *Ploughman and Poet,* was essentially a collection of lyrics in this vein, although of better quality. So was his second work, *Inland,* which,

said Shapcott, includes "probably his most anthologized—and one of his best—poems, 'Mullabinda.'"

But Rowbotham broke out of the constraints of the nature genre with his third collection, *All the Room.* "From this point on Rowbotham's poetry has struggled its way doggedly, and with considerable effort," Shapcott explained, "into areas of response and experience far removed from the gentle, sunny Darling Downs countryside of the earlier books." The poems in this work left the examination-of-nature theme and turned instead to an examination of interior issues. These issues continued to be explored with *The Makers of the Ark* and *The Pen of Feathers,* Rowbotham's collections from the early 1970s. The best of the poet's later work, Shapcott concluded, "counterpoints a conservative vocabulary and rhythm with an intensely felt response to the poet's own discoveries and concerns, which have been thought through with an almost painful honesty." Rowbotham continued to publish poetry throughout the 1980s and 1990s; his *New and Selected Poems, 1945-1993* is made up of previously uncollected material that had only seen print in literary journals.

Rowbotham once commented in *Contemporary Poets* on his combination of landscape to humanity: "I acknowledge—as a guidance to my earlier work done among my Australian home-countryside, and to my later work done (say) within the sense of surrounding larger worlds—that man and landscape (outer? inner?) cannot be separated, and that it never occurred to me whether or not they could be."

BIOGRAPHICAL AND CRITICAL SOURCES:

BOOKS

Contemporary Poets, 6th edition, St. James Press (Detroit, MI), 1996.

Ewers, John K., *Creative Writing in Australia,* Georgian House (Melbourne, Australia), 1966.

Hadcraft, Cecil, editor, *Australian Literature,* Heinemann (London, England), 1960.

Jaffa, Herbert C., editor, *Modern Australian Poetry: 1920-1970,* Thomson Gale (Detroit, MI), 1979.

Strugnell, John, *Focus on David Rowbotham,* University of Queensland Press (Brisbane, Queensland, Australia), 1969.

PERIODICALS

Antipodes: Journal of the American Association for Australian Literary Studies, December, 2002,

Nicholas Birns, "Invested with Surprise: A Visit with David Rowbotham."

Australian Book Review, April, 1994, review of *New and Selected Poems, 1945-1993,* p. 38; November, 1996, review of *The Ebony Gates,* p. 55.

Australian Weekend Review, March 26, 1994, Martin Duwell, "The Self as Springboard."

Courier Mail (Brisbane, Queensland, Australia), February 5, 1994, Manfred Jurgensen, "Powerful Poetry."

Hollins Critic, April, 2005, Nicholas Birns, review of *Poems for America: New Poems,* p. 18.

Times Literary Supplement, April 9, 1976, Ronald Tamplin, review of *Selected Poems,* p. 443.

Weekend Australian Review, October 25, 2003, Adrian McGregor, "Surviving the Winter of Discontent," p. 4.

World Literature Today, spring, 1979, Syed Amanuddin, review of *Selected Poems,* p. 344; summer, 1981, Syed Amanuddin, review of *Maydays,* p. 526.

ONLINE

David Rowbotham: A Chronicle, http://www.qct.com.au/rowbotham (April 10, 2007).

*   *   *

ROWBOTHAM, David Harold
    See ROWBOTHAM, David

S

SCHMIDT, Lawrence K. 1949-
  (Lawrence Kennedy Schmidt)

PERSONAL: Born October 2, 1949, in Rochester, NY; married Monika Reuss, 1984; children: Kassandra. *Education:* Reed College, B.A., 1972; attended University of Freiburg, 1973-75 and 1976, and University of Madras, 1975; University of New Mexico, M.A., 1978; University of Duisburg, Ph.D., 1983.

ADDRESSES: Office—Hendrix College, 1600 Washington Ave., Conway, AR 72032-3080. *E-mail*—schmidt@mercury.hendrix.edu.

CAREER: Hendrix College, Conway, AR, assistant professor, 1984-89, associate professor, 1989-99, professor of philosophy, 1999—, department chair, 1987-93, 1996-2005. Adult education English teacher in Germany, 1981-83; Marshall T. Steel Center for the Study of Religion and Philosophy, board member, 1984—; Mid-South Philosophy Conference, president, 1986-87.

MEMBER: International Association for Environmental Philosophy, American Philosophical Association, Society for Phenomenology and Existential Philosophy, American Association of University Professors (chapter president, 1987-91, 1996-98; vice president, 1993-96, 1999-2001), Arkansas Philosophical Association, Phi Beta Kappa.

AWARDS, HONORS: Fulbright scholar, 1979-81, senior scholar, 1999.

WRITINGS:

The Epistemology of Hans-Georg Gadamer: An Analysis of the Legitimization of Vorurteile, Peter D. Lang (New York, NY), 1985, 2nd edition, 1987.

(Editor and translator) *The Specter of Relativism: Truth, Dialogue, and Phronesis in Philosophical Hermeneutics,* Northwestern University Press (Evanston, IL), 1995.

(Editor) *Language and Linguisticality in Gadamer's Hermeneutics,* Lexington Books (Lanham, MD), 2000.

Understanding Hermeneutics, Acumen Publishing Limited (Stocksfield, England), 2006.

Contributor to books, including *Phenomenology, Interpretation, and Community,* edited by Lenore Langsdorf and Stephen H. Watson, State University of New York at Binghamton (Binghamton, NY), 1996. Contributor to journals, including *Southern Journal of Philosophy, Southwest Philosophical Review, Philosophy Today,* and *Existentia.*

*   *   *

SCHMIDT, Lawrence Kennedy
  See SCHMIDT, Lawrence K.

*   *   *

SCHRECENGOST, Maity 1938-
  (S. Maitland Schrecengost)

PERSONAL: Surname is pronounced *Shreck*-en-gost; born June 8, 1938, in Scottdale, PA; daughter of Albert Warren and Leona Shirer; married Thomas E. Schrecengost, June 11, 1960; children: Lynda D., Thomas Warren. *Education:* Allegheny College, B.A., 1960; Nova

Southeastern University, M.A., 1994. *Religion:* Christian. *Hobbies and other interests:* Canoeing, birdwatching, crewel embroidery, reading, travel.

ADDRESSES: Home—Summerfield, FL. *E-mail*—tomandmaity@cs.com.

CAREER: Elementary schoolteacher in Murrysville, PA, 1960-62, and Mercersburg, PA, 1980-86; Manatee County School Board, Bradenton, FL, elementary schoolteacher, 1986-2000. Presenter of writing education and research workshops; also works as writing consultant.

MEMBER: Society of Children's Book Writers and Illustrators, National League of American Pen Women, Florida Reading Association, Writers' Bloc.

AWARDS, HONORS: Florida Historical Society, Carolynn Washbon Award, 1998, for *Tasso of Tarpon Springs,* and Patrick D. Smith Prize for Florida Literature, 2000, for *Panther Girl.*

WRITINGS:

Write to Be Read, Highsmith Press (Fort Atkinson, WI), 1992.
Let Them Write! (videotape for teacher training), Title I Media Productions, 1994.
Research to Write, Highsmith Press (Fort Atkinson, WI), 1994.
Researching People, with teacher's guide, Highsmith Press (Fort Atkinson, WI), 1996.
Researching Events, with teacher's guide, Highsmith Press (Fort Atkinson, WI), 1998.
Tasso of Tarpon Springs (juvenile novel), with teacher's guide, illustrated by Rose Stock, Maupin House (Gainesville, FL), 1998.
Panther Girl (juvenile novel), with teacher's guide, illustrated by Sal Salazar, Maupin House (Gainesville, FL), 1999.
Writing Whizardry: 60 Mini-lessons For Teaching Elaboration and Writing Craft, Maupin House (Gainesville, FL), 2001.
Researching Issues, with teacher's guide, Highsmith Press (Fort Atkinson, WI), 2002.
Voice Whizardry: 36 Discovery Activities to Develop Personal Writing Voice, Maupin House (Gainesville, FL), 2004.

High above the Hippodrome (juvenile fiction), SPS Publications (Eustis, FL), 2006.

Contributor to periodicals, including *Florida Living* and *Aglow.*

SIDELIGHTS: Maity Schrecengost once commented: "I was born in 1938 in Scottdale, a small town in southwestern Pennsylvania, the youngest of my parents' four children. It was there, at our small public library, that I fell in love with books. They became my best friends. I began scribbling at an early age, penning my 'last will and testament' at the age of ten. My 'studio' was the roof outside my bedroom window, through which I escaped to avoid detection at dishwashing time.

"Throughout my young adult years, while an at-home mom for our two children, I continued to write, with an occasional publishing success. When I resumed teaching, I became one of a core of teacher consultants for the Pennsylvania Department of Education writing project. As such, I became aware of the need for books to introduce children to the craft of writing. This resulted in the publication of *Write to Be Read, Research to Write, Researching People, Researching Events,* and *Researching Issues.*

"As a fourth-grade teacher in Florida, I also recognized the lack of historical fiction about Florida for young readers. Thus was born *Tasso of Tarpon Springs,* the story of an immigrant Greek boy who stows away to become part of the developing sponge industry in Florida, and *Panther Girl,* the story of a Florida pioneer girl in 1843 and her friendship with a Seminole Indian boy." *High above the Hippodrome* is a historical novel about life on the road with the Ringling Brothers and Barnum and Bailey Circus in 1927.

"Writing for children is a wonderful and terrible responsibility. Children deserve our best. Above all else, they deserve truth. In an era of 'political correctness' and 'revisionist history,' I am ever cognizant of the importance of careful research and accurate portrayal of the historical period represented in my books."

More recently Schrecengost added: "Working with classroom teachers, I was aware of their need for time-efficient, effective mini-lessons for both teaching the writing craft and affording students opportunities to practice writers' devices. *Writing Whizardry: 60 Mini-*

lessons For Teaching Elaboration and Writing Craft, was developed from mini-lessons used in my own classroom. Later as many teachers, unfortunately, turned to 'formula writing' to prepare their students for writing assessment tests, children's strong natural writing voices began to be silenced. *Voice Whizardry: 36 Discovery Activities to Develop Personal Writing Voice* was created to provide activities for teachers and students to rediscover and ultimately use their unique personal writing voices."

*   *   *

SCHRECENGOST, S. Maitland
   See SCHRECENGOST, Maity

*   *   *

SHUMAKER, Peggy 1952-

PERSONAL: Born March 22, 1952, in La Mesa, CA. *Ethnicity:* "Norwegian-American." *Education:* University of Arizona, B.A., 1974, M.F.A., 1979.

ADDRESSES: Office—Fairbanks, AK. *E-mail*—peggy zoe@sprynet.com.

CAREER: Arizona Commission on the Arts, Phoenix, writer in residence, 1979-85; University of Alaska Fairbanks, Fairbanks, visiting assistant professor of creative writing, 1985-86; Old Dominion University, Norfolk, VA, director of creative writing, 1986-88, director of Old Dominion University Literary Festival, 1987-88; University of Alaska Fairbanks, codirector of creative writing, 1988-99, associate professor, 1991-93, professor of English, 1993-99, professor emeritus, 1999—, department head, 1991-93. Arizona State University, faculty associate in creative writing, 1983-85; Pacific Lutheran University, professor at Rainier Writing Workshop, 2003—; featured poet at writers' conferences and other literary gatherings; coordinator of events such as Midnight Sun Writers Conference, 1990, and Alaskan Poetry Festival, 1990; literary judge for Western States Book Awards, 1995, and Pablo Neruda Prize for Poetry from *Nimrod,* 1995. Epoch Universal Publications, managing editor, 1980-81.

MEMBER: Associated Writing Programs (member of board of directors, 1990—; vice president, 1991-92; president, 1992-93).

AWARDS, HONORS: National Endowment for the Arts fellow, 1989.

WRITINGS:

Esperanza's Hair (poetry), University of Alabama Press (Tuscaloosa, AL), 1985.
The Circle of Totems (poetry), University of Pittsburgh Press (Pittsburgh, PA), 1988.
Braided River (poetry chapbook), Limner Press (Anchorage, AK), 1993.
Wings Moist from the Other World (poetry), University of Pittsburgh Press (Pittsburgh, PA), 1994.
Underground Rivers (poetry), Red Hen Press (Los Angeles, CA), 2001.
Blaze (poetry), Red Hen Press (Los Angeles, CA), 2005.
Just Breathe Normally (nonfiction), University of Nebraska Press (Lincoln, NE), 2007.

SIDELIGHTS: The themes of Peggy Shumaker's free verse include surviving abusive relationships, finding an individual identity in relation to contemporary feminism, addressing the half-truths of her past, and protecting the environment. Michael Bugeja of *Writer's Digest* wrote that Shumaker's poetry "is rich with image and viewpoint, meaning that she tries to see the world in insightful and innovative ways, often through the eyes of others." Bugeja speculated that Shumaker may have developed the ability to adopt different perspectives through her community work with inmates, deaf adults, gang members, unwed mothers, and gifted students.

BIOGRAPHICAL AND CRITICAL SOURCES:

BOOKS

Contemporary Poets, 6th edition, St. James Press (Detroit, MI), 1996.

PERIODICALS

Bloomsbury Review, January, 1995, review of *Wings Moist from the Other World,* p. 20.
Kliatt Young Adult Paperback Book Guide, November, 1994, review of *Wings Moist from the Other World,* p. 27.

Publishers Weekly, November 8, 1993, review of *Wings Moist from the Other World,* p. 70.

Writer's Digest, February, 1996, article by Michael Bugeja, p. 12.

ONLINE

Peggy Shumaker Home Page, http://www.peggy shumaker.com (February 12, 2007).

* * *

SOVAK, Jan 1953-

PERSONAL: Born February 13, 1953, in Prague, Czechoslovakia (now Czech Republic); son of Miroslav and Dana Sovak; married Daniela Jerie, 1982; children: Adrianne-Monique. *Ethnicity:* "Czech." *Education:* Attended School of Art, Bechyne, 1968-72, and University of Purkyne, 1972-77.

ADDRESSES: Home—Calgary, Alberta, Canada.

CAREER: Illustrator, conceptual artist, and writer.

AWARDS, HONORS: Award of merit, book illustration category, Canadian Association of Photographers and Illustrators, 1990 and 1992; award for book illustration, Children's Book Centre (of Canada), 1991; Golden Bow Award, Czech Ministry of Culture, Young Readers Literature Society, Children's Book Illustrators Society, and Czech section of International Board on Books for Young People, 1995; Illustrator of the Year Award, Rodokaps (Czech publisher), 1995; Choice awards from Young Readers Association, 1997, and Children's Book Centre, 1998.

WRITINGS:

AUTHOR AND ILLUSTRATOR

Prehistoric Mammals Coloring Book, Dover (Mineola, NY), 1991.

Great Dinosaurs Poster Book, Red Deer College Press (Red Deer, Alberta, Canada), 1992.

Butterflies, Dover (Mineola, NY), 1992.

Zoo Animals, Dover (Mineola, NY), 1993.

Insects, Dover (Mineola, NY), 1994.

Insect Sticker Book, Dover (Mineola, NY), 1994.

Snakes of the World, Dover (Mineola, NY), 1995.

Birds of Prey Sticker Book, Dover (Mineola, NY), 1995.

Realistic Snakes Sticker Book, Dover (Mineola, NY), 1995.

Endangered Animals Sticker Book, Dover (Mineola, NY), 1995.

Desert Sticker Pictures, Dover (Mineola, NY), 1996.

Wild Cats, Dover (Mineola, NY), 1996.

Jurassic Dinosaurs Sticker Pictures, Dover (Mineola, NY), 1997.

Learning about Butterflies, Dover (Mineola, NY), 1997.

Learning about Cretaceous Dinosaurs, Dover (Mineola, NY), 1997.

Learning about Insects, Dover (Mineola, NY), 1997.

(With Phillip J. Currie and Eric P. Felber) *A Moment in Time with: Troodon,* Troodon Productions (Calgary, Alberta, Canada), 1997.

Cretaceous Dinosaurs Sticker Pictures, Dover (Mineola, NY), 1998.

Explore a Coral Reef Sticker Pictures, Dover (Mineola, NY), 1998.

Learning about Forest Animals, Dover (Mineola, NY), 1998.

Learning about Snakes, Dover (Mineola, NY), 1998.

Learning about Tropical Fish, Dover (Mineola, NY), 1998.

(With Phillip J. Currie and Eric P. Felber) *A Moment in Time with: Albertosaurus,* Troodon Productions (Calgary, Alberta, Canada), 1998.

(With Phillip J. Currie and Eva Koppelhus) *A Moment in Time with: Centrosaurus,* Troodon Productions (Calgary, Alberta, Canada), 1998.

Before the Dinosaurs Coloring Book, Dover (Mineola, NY), 1999.

Prehistoric Animals Sticker Book, Dover (Mineola, NY), 1999.

(With Phillip J. Currie and Eva Koppelhus) *A Moment in Time with: Sinosauropteryx,* Troodon Productions (Calgary, Alberta, Canada), 1999.

African Animals Sticker Activity Book, Dover (Mineola, NY), 1999.

Learning about Sharks, Dover (Mineola, NY), 1999.

Seashore Life Sticker Pictures, Dover (Mineola, NY), 2000.

Hummingbirds, Dover (Mineola, NY), 2001.

Lizards, Dover (Mineola, NY), 2001.

Mythological Creatures, Dover (Mineola, NY), 2001.

(With E. Felber) *Predatory Animals,* University of Calgary Press (Calgary, Alberta, Canada), 2001.

Learning about Spiders, Dover (Mineola, NY), 2001.
Realistic Butterfly Stickers, Dover (Mineola, NY), 2001.
Realistic Whales Stickers, Dover (Mineola, NY), 2001.
Learning about Turtles, Dover (Mineola, NY), 2001.
Realistic Dolphins Stickers, Dover (Mineola, NY), 2001.
Realistic Sharks Stickers, Dover (Mineola, NY), 2001.
Colorful Birds Stickers, Dover (Mineola, NY), 2001.
Learning about Farm Animals, Dover (Mineola, NY), 2001.
Learning about Reptiles, Dover (Mineola, NY), 2001.
Rain Forest Animals Stained Glass Coloring Book, Dover (Mineola, NY), 2001.
Common Birds Stickers, Dover (Mineola, NY), 2001.
Fairies and Trolls, Dover (Mineola, NY), 2002.
Exotic Birds, Dover (Mineola, NY), 2002.
Rain Forest Birds, Dover (Mineola, NY), 2002.
Trolls, Elves, and Fairies Coloring Book, Dover (Mineola, NY), 2002.
Lizards Stickers, Dover (Mineola, NY), 2002.
Hummingbirds Stickers, Dover (Mineola, NY), 2002.
Insects Stained Glass Coloring Book, Dover (Mineola, NY), 2003.
Learning about Wild Cats, Dover (Mineola, NY), 2003.
Learning about Swamp Animals, Dover (Mineola, NY), 2003.
Giants and Ogres, Dover (Mineola, NY), 2003.
Prehistoric Animals Magic Book, Dover (Mineola, NY), 2003.
Trolls and Dwarves, Dover (Mineola, NY), 2003.
Learning about Hummingbirds, Dover (Mineola, NY), 2004.
Giants and Ogres Coloring Book, Dover (Mineola, NY), 2004.
Dinosaur Sticker Picture Puzzle, Dover (Mineola, NY), 2004.
Invisible Prehistoric Animals Magic Picture Book, Dover (Mineola, NY), 2004.
Prehistoric Man, Dover (Mineola, NY), 2004.
Dinosaur Scenes, Dover (Mineola, NY), 2006.
Alaskan Wildlife, Dover (Mineola, NY), 2006.
Galapagos Islands, Dover (Mineola, NY), 2006.

Also illustrator of temporary tattoo books, punch-out mask books, bookmarks, and notebooks, all published by Dover.

ILLUSTRATOR; BOOKS PUBLISHED IN ENGLISH

The Palaeoguide, Government of Alberta (Edmonton, Alberta, Canada), 1988.

Junior Encyclopedia of Canada, Hurtig (Edmonton, Alberta, Canada), 1988.
Monty Reid, *The Last Great Dinosaurs: A Guide to the Dinosaurs of Alberta,* Red Deer College Press (Red Deer, Alberta, Canada), 1990.
Currie, *The Flying Dinosaurs: The Illustrated Guide to the Evolution of Flight,* Red Deer College Press (Red Deer, Alberta, Canada), 1991.
Dinosaur World Tour, Ex Terra Foundation (Edmonton, Alberta, Canada), 1991.
Michael Crichton, *Jurassic Park,* Knopf (New York, NY), 1993.
The Audubon Society Pocket Guide: Dinosaurs, Knopf (New York, NY), 1993.
The Land before Us, Red Deer College Press (Red Deer, Alberta, Canada), 1994.
Phillip J. Currie and Zdenek V. Spinar, *The Great Dinosaurs: A Story of the Giants' Evolution,* Sunburst Books (London, England), 1994, Longmeadow Publishing (New York, NY), 1995.
Prehistoric Alaska, Alaska Geographic Society (Anchorage, AK), 1994.
Official Gallery Guide, Royal Tyrrell Museum of Palaentology (Drumheller, Alberta, Canada), 1994.
Colleayn O. Mastin, *Canadian Wild Animals,* Grasshopper Publishing (Kamloops, British Columbia, Canada), 1994.
Colleayn O. Mastin, *Canadian Trees,* Grasshopper Publishing (Kamloops, British Columbia, Canada), 1994.
Colleayn O. Mastin, *Canadian Arctic Animals,* Grasshopper Publishing (Kamloops, British Columbia, Canada), 1994, revised edition published as *Canadian Animals of the Arctic,* 1997.
A. Weismann, *Songbirds,* Dover (Mineola, NY), 1995.
Phillip J. Currie, *Jurassic Dinosaurs,* Dover (Mineola, NY), 1995.
Dinosaur Safari Guide, Voyager Press (Stillwater, MN), 1996.
Phillip J. Currie, *101 Questions about Dinosaurs,* Dover (Mineola, NY), 1996.
Phillip J. Currie, *Cretaceous Dinosaurs,* Dover (Mineola, NY), 1996.
Pacific Rim: National Park Reserve, Blackbird Naturegraphic (Canada), 1996.
M. Jamieson, *Beginnings,* Reidmore Books (Edmonton, Alberta, Canada), 1996.
What Do We Know, World Book (Chicago, IL), 1997.
Colleayn O. Mastin, *North American Endangered Species,* Grasshopper Publishing (Kamloops, British Columbia, Canada), 1997.
Colleayn O. Mastin, *Canadian Ocean Creatures,* Grasshopper Publishing (Kamloops, British Columbia, Canada), 1997.

Colleayn O. Mastin, *Canadian Wildflowers and Emblems,* Grasshopper Publishing (Kamloops, British Columbia, Canada), 1997.

Colleayn O. Mastin, *The Magic of Mythical Creatures,* Grasshopper Publishing (Kamloops, British Columbia, Canada), 1997.

Colleayn O. Mastin, *North American Animals of the Arctic,* Grasshopper Publishing (Kamloops, British Columbia, Canada), 1997.

Ana Adamache, *The Sun King Ray Story,* Astra Books (Calgary, Alberta, Canada), 1997.

Designing Dinosaurs, Bruce County Museum (Southampton, Ontario, Canada), 1997.

Don Lessem, *The Dinosaurs of Jurassic Park,* Universal City Studios (Los Angeles, CA), 1997.

Colleayn O. Mastin, *North American Wild Animals,* Grasshopper Publishing (Kamploops, British Columbia, Canada), 1997.

Colleayn O. Mastin, *Canadian Birds,* Grasshopper Publishing (Kamloops, British Columbia, Canada), 1998.

Colleayn O. Mastin, *Newest and Coolest Dinosaurs,* Grasshopper Publishing (Kamloops, British Columbia, Canada), 1998.

A Walk through Time, Wiley (New York, NY), 1998.

Cornerstones, Gage Educational Publishing (Scarborough, Ontario, Canada), 1998.

Don Lessem, *Dinosaurs to Dodos: An Encyclopedia of Extinct Animals,* Scholastic Inc. (New York, NY), 1999.

Canada Revisited, Arnold Publishing (Scarborough, Ontario, Canada), 1999.

Jerry Hale and Rose Hale, *The Adventures of Muskwa,* Muskwa Trails (Worsley, Alberta, Canada), 1999.

P.A. Arnold, *Canada Revisited,* Arnold Publishing (Scarborough, Ontario, Canada), 2000.

Don Lessem, *Dinosaurs Encyclopedia,* Scholastic Inc. (New York, NY), 2000.

H. Zimmermann, *Beyond the Dinosaurs,* Byron Preiss Publishing (New York, NY), 2000.

Monty Reid, *The Story of Burgess Shale,* University of Calgary Press (Calgary, Alberta, Canada), 2001.

E.H. Colbert, *Age of Reptiles,* Dover (Mineola, NY), 2001.

Arthur Conan Doyle, *Lost Worlds,* Dover (Mineola, NY), 2001.

Tanke and Carpenter, *The Mesozoic Vertebrate Life,* Indiana University Press (Bloomington, IN), 2001.

Lisa Bonforte and others, *Color and Learn Birds, Butterflies and Wild Flowers,* Sagebrush (Minneapolis, MN), 2002.

G. Olshevsky, *Discovering Dinos—Velociraptor,* Smart Apple Media (Mankato, MN), 2002.

G. Olshevsky, *Discovering Dinos—T. Rex,* Smart Apple Media (Mankato, MN), 2002.

G. Olshevsky, *Discovering Dinos—Stegosaurus,* Smart Apple Media (Mankato, MN), 2002.

G. Olshevsky, *Discovering Dinos—Iguanodon,* Smart Apple Media (Mankato, MN), 2002.

G. Olshevsky, *Discovering Dinos—Diplodocus,* Smart Apple Media (Mankato, MN), 2002.

June E. LeDrew, *Girls on the Move,* Ministry of Health (Ottawa, Ontario, Canada), 2002.

Don Lessem, *Scholastic Dinosaurs A-Z: The Ultimate Dinosaur Encyclopedia,* Scholastic Inc. (New York, NY), 2003.

Dinosaurs, Marshall Cavendish (Tarrytown, NY), 2005.

A. Davis, *The House that Edio Wyllt Built,* Trafford Publishing (Victoria, British Columbia, Canada), 2005.

Dinosaur Provincial Park, Indiana University Press (Bloomington, IN), 2006.

Hadrosaurs, 2006.

T. Rex, 2006.

Ankylosaurus, 2006.

Troodon, 2006.

Contributor of illustrations to textbooks, encyclopedias, and other books. Contributor of illustrations to nearly a dozen films, television series, and electronic publications, including *Earth Revealed,* Public Broadcasting Service; *In the Steps of Dragons* and *Trip to China: Feathered Dinosaurs,* both for The Discovery Channel; *Dinosaurs,* The Learning Channel; and *Encarta Yearbook Builder,* Microsoft. Contributor of illustrations to magazines in the United States and Canada, including *Prehistoric Times, Dinosaur, Canadian Geographic, Earth, Cricket,* and *Canadian Rockies.*

ILLUSTRATOR; FOREIGN-LANGUAGE PUBLICATIONS

A. Barkhausen and Z. Geiser, *Elephanten,* Kinderbuchverlag Luzern (Lucerne, Switzerland), 1992.

L. Dossenbach, *Das Lexikon der Tiere,* Kinderbuchverlag Luzern (Lucerne, Switzerland), 1992.

K. Roberts, *Kapitan Rozmysl,* Touzimsky & Moravec (Prague, Czech Republic), 1992.

J. Henson, *Bin Daa! Wer Noooch?,* Motovun/Disney (Lucerne, Switzerland), 1993.

P. Marc, *Mit Livingstone durch Africa,* Bohema Press (Switzerland), 1993.

Jahrbuch der Coburger Landes Stiftung, DNP Coburg (Coburg, Germany), 1993.

J. Moravec (Prague, Czech Republic), *Utek z Onon-dagy,* Touzimsky & Moravec (Prague, Czech Republic), 1994.

J. Slade, *Fiesta Smrti,* Rodokaps (Czech Republic), 1994.

M. Wiliamson, *Navrat Rysaveho Johna,* Rodokaps (Czech Republic), 1994.

J. Slade, *Lassiter a Oregonska Mstitelka,* Rodokaps (Czech Republic), 1994.

J.M. Adam, *Apacsky Mlyn,* Rodokaps (Czech Republic), 1994.

J. Slade, *Supi z Gila Bendu,* Rodokaps (Czech Republic), 1994.

J. Henson, *Willkommen bei den Sinclairs,* Motovun/Disney (Lucerne, Switzerland), 1994.

Evolution: Life and the Universe, Gakken Publishers (Tokyo, Japan), 1994.

Nature Library, Gakken Publishers (Tokyo, Japan), 1994.

Wielkie Dinozaury, Warszawski Dom Wydawniczy (Warsaw, Poland), 1994.

Currie, *Dinosaurs from A to Z,* Yazawa Science Office (Tokyo, Japan), 1995.

From Gaia to Ecopoiesis, Gakken Publishers (Tokyo, Japan), 1995.

O. Janka, *Odvedu te k Siouxum,* Touzimsky & Moravec (Prague, Czech Republic), 1995.

L. Kark, *Sedm z Lancasteru,* Touzimsky & Moravec (Prague, Czech Republic), 1995.

R.H. Douglas, *O Cest Nepritele,* Rodokaps (Czech Republic), 1995.

C. Judd, *Pisen Severu,* Rodokaps (Czech Republic), 1995.

Phillip J. Currie, *Giganten der Lufte: Das Grosse Buch der Flugsaurier,* Arena Verlag (Würzberg, Germany), 1995.

M.H. Bowery, *Cesta Pres Inferno,* Rodokaps (Czech Republic), 1995.

Mass Extinction and Evolution of Life, Gakken Publishers (Tokyo, Japan), 1996.

A Biography of the Dinosaur World, A.G. Tokyo Publishers (Tokyo, Japan), 1996.

O. Collins, *Brianuv Mistrovsky Kousek,* Rodokaps (Czech Republic), 1996.

J. Fabricius, *Plavcici Kapitana Bontekoea,* Touzimsky & Moravec (Prague, Czech Republic), 1996.

J. Moravec, *Cteni z Kameni,* Touzimsky & Moravec (Prague, Czech Republic), 1996.

M.H. Bowery, *Muz Ktery Tam Byl,* Rodokaps (Czech Republic), 1996.

R. Omphalius, *Planet des Lebens,* Motovun Verlagsge-sellschaft (Lucerne, Switzerland), 1996.

M.H. Bowery, *Sewardova Lednice,* Rodokaps (Czech Republic), 1997.

H.H. Isenbart, *Freude mit Pferden,* Motovum Verlags-gesellschaft (Lucerne, Switzerland), 1997.

Gendai Shinsho, Kodansha (Tokyo, Japan), 1997.

Gizem Dolu Afrika Yolculugu, Turkeiye Yayim Haklari (Turkey), 1997.

Science in Crisis, Gakken Publishers (Tokyo, Japan), 1997.

The Dinosaur Handbook, Yazawa Publishing House (Tokyo, Japan), 1997.

Phillip J. Currie and Zdenek V. Spinar, *De Heersers van Toen,* R & B Productions (Netherlands), 1998.

M. Andera, *Vyhubena Zvirata,* Aventinum Publishing House (Tolsteho, Czech Republic), 1998.

V. Hulpach, *Indianske Pribehy,* Aventinum Publishing House (Tolsteho, Czech Republic), 1998.

V. Hulpach, *Indianer Geschichte,* Dausien Verlag (Hanau, Germany), 1998.

Carlsbergfondet Arsskrift, Carlsbergfondet (Copenhagen, Denmark), 1998.

M.H. Bowery, *Dabluv Kolovrat,* Rodokaps (Prague, Czech Republic), 1998.

Scientific Controversies, Gakken Publishers (Tokyo, Japan), 1998.

A. Stevenson, *Ostrov Pokladu,* Touzimsky & Moravec (Prague, Czech Republic), 1999.

Praveka More, Granit Publishers (Prague, Czech Republic), 1999.

Vojtech Turek, *Ztracena more uprostred Evropy* (title means "Vanished Seas in the Center of Europe"), Academia (Prague, Czech Republic), 2003.

Illustrator of several other books published in the Czech Republic, Japan, and Germany. Contributor of illustrations to periodicals.

SIDELIGHTS: Jan Sovak once told *CA:* "I was born in a family of book collectors. For as long as I can remember, my favorite refuge was our attic filled with books and old magazines. There I discovered the importance of illustrations for books. I started to write my own stories, so I could illustrate them. The first book I wrote for this purpose was about a Bengal tiger escaping from a circus and learning how to live as a wild animal. I was eight years old.

"My first and foremost wish is to get children interested in books. I want to open a door for endless adventures of the mind that could lead them on the road to discovery of vast horizons of knowledge and to an understanding of nature and history. Maybe that kind of knowledge could give readers an answer about who we are, where we come from, and what it means to share our planet with other forms of life.

"I am happy to see how important children's book publishing has become in the last few decades. The quality of writers and illustrators is higher than ever, and competition is pushing all of us further yet. As for myself, I love going to bookstores to discover new colleagues with a fresh, new outlook on the illustrating process.

"If writing or illustrating is what you want to do in your life more than anything else, then stick with it! It is not easy, and for most of us it has never been, even for established authors! My favorite comparison is about playing a musical instrument. If you want to become a virtuoso, you must spend many hours every day practicing. It is the same with our craft. My teacher used to tell me: 'If you don't want to work fifteen hours a day on your technique, do something else. Right now there are a lot of people around the world who do exactly that.'"

BIOGRAPHICAL AND CRITICAL SOURCES:

PERIODICALS

Quill and Quire, August, 1991, review of *Great Dinosaurs Poster Book,* p. 21.

*   *   *

SPRINGFIELD, David
    See LEWIS, Roy

*   *   *

STAFFORD, Paul 1966-

PERSONAL: Born September 18, 1966, in Kurrajong, New South Wales, Australia; son of John (an accountant) and Robyn (a language teacher) Stafford. *Ethnicity:* "Australian." *Education:* Charles Sturt University, B.A., 1989. *Hobbies and other interests:* Land care, overseas travel, history and archaeology, bush walking, "canyoning," caving.

ADDRESSES: Home and office—Bathampton, Bathurst, New South Wales, Australia. *E-mail*—pstarr@tpg.com. au.

CAREER: Charles Sturt University, Bathurst, New South Wales, Australia, tutor, 1996—. Literary consultant for primary and secondary schools throughout Australia.

MEMBER: Australians for Native Title.

WRITINGS:

FICTION FOR YOUNG PEOPLE

Blatantly Bogus (short stories), Crawford House (Bathurst, New South Wales, Australia), 1998.
Basically Bollocks (short stories), Crawford House (Bathurst, New South Wales, Australia), 1998.
Ludicrous Lies (short stories), Crawford House (Bathurst, New South Wales, Australia), 1998.
Fully Faked (short stories), Crawford House (Bathurst, New South Wales, Australia), 1998.
Ned Kelly's Helmet (novel), Crawford House (Bathurst, New South Wales, Australia), 1999.
Chronic Crapola (short stories), Crawford House (Bathurst, New South Wales, Australia), 1999.
Heinous Humbuggery (short stories), Crawford House (Bathurst, New South Wales, Australia), 1999.
Totally Toasted (short stories), Crawford House (Bathurst, New South Wales, Australia), 1999.
Hoopy Hoaxes (short stories), Crawford House (Bathurst, New South Wales, Australia), 1999.

FICTION FOR YOUNG PEOPLE; "HORROR HIGH" SERIES

Horror High and the 101 Damnations, Random House (Milsons Point, New South Wales, Australia) 2005.
Horror High and the Interghouls Cricket Cup, Random House (Milsons Point, New South Wales, Australia) 2005.
Horror High and the Feril Peril, Random House (Milsons Point, New South Wales, Australia) 2006.
Horror High and the Great Brain Robbery, Random House (Milsons Point, New South Wales, Australia) 2006.

SIDELIGHTS: Paul Stafford once told *CA:* "I live outside Bathurst, New South Wales, Australia. I studied print journalism at Mitchell College of Advanced

Education, Charles Sturt University, graduating in 1989, but renounced the make-believe world of journalism for the hard and gritty reality of kids' fiction. Although a career in writing has meant abandoning my childhood dream of wealth and respectability, I now get to sleep late, dress scruffy, and gnaw on the skulls of my enemies. It's a trade-off I've learned to live with."

Stafford later commented: "As a kid I loved reading. Now I get paid to write the sort of stuff I would have read. It's the best job in the world (if you don't mind living on bread and water)."

BIOGRAPHICAL AND CRITICAL SOURCES:

PERIODICALS

Magpies, September, 1998, reviews of *Basically Bollocks, Blatantly Bogus, Fully Faked,* and *Ludicrous Lies,* p. 39.

ONLINE

Horror High Books, http://www.horrorhighbooks.com (February 12, 2007).

*   *   *

STEMPEL, Guido H., III 1928-

PERSONAL: Born August 13, 1928, in Bloomington, IN; son of Guido H., Jr. (a research chemist) and Alice (a pianist and music teacher) Stempel; married Anne Elliott (a social worker and mental health volunteer), August 30, 1952; children: Ralph W., Carl W., Jane Stempel Arata. *Ethnicity:* "Caucasian—German/Swiss." *Education:* Attended Carnegie Institute of Technology (now Carnegie-Mellon University), 1945-46; Indiana University—Bloomington, A.B., 1949, A.M., 1951; University of Wisconsin, Ph.D., 1954. *Politics:* Democrat. *Religion:* Methodist.

ADDRESSES: Home—Athens, OH. *Office*—E.W. Scripps School of Journalism, Ohio University, Scripps Hall, Athens, OH 45701. *E-mail*—stempel@ohio.edu.

CAREER: Frankfort Morning Times, Frankfort, IN, sports editor, 1949-50; Pennsylvania State University, University Park, began as instructor, became assistant professor of journalism, 1955-57; Central Michigan University, Mount Pleasant, began as associate professor, became professor of journalism, 1957-65; Ohio University, Athens, began as associate professor, became distinguished professor of journalism, 1965—, also director of School of Journalism and Scripps Survey Research Center. Defense Information School, member of advisory board, 1986-94. West Ohio Conference of the United Methodist Church, member of Board on Higher Education and Campus Ministries, 1996—. *Military service:* U.S. Army, communication specialist, 1954-55.

MEMBER: Athens Rotary Club (president, 1984).

AWARDS, HONORS: Chancellor's Award for Distinguished Service to Journalism and Journalism Education, University of Wisconsin, 1977; Eleanor Blum Award for service to journalism research, Association for Education in Journalism and Mass Communications, 1989; Harold L. Nelson Award for Distinguished Achievement in Journalism Education, University of Wisconsin, 2004; award for "Lifetime of Exemplary Contributions to Journalism and Journalism Education, Newspaper Division," Association for Education in Journalism and Mass Communication, 2005.

WRITINGS:

(Coeditor and contributor) *Research Methods in Mass Communication,* Prentice-Hall (Englewood Cliffs, NJ), 1981.
The Practice of Political Communication, Prentice-Hall (Englewood Cliffs, NJ), 1994.
(Editor and contributor) *Historical Dictionary of Political Communication in the United States,* Greenwood Press (Westport, CT), 1999.
(Coeditor and coauthor) *Mass Communication Research and Theory,* Allyn & Bacon (Boston, MA), 2003.
Media and Politics in America: A Reference Handbook, American Bibliographical Center-Clio Press (Santa Barbara, CA), 2003.

Contributor to professional journals. Past editor, *Journalism Quarterly.*

SIDELIGHTS: Guido H. Stempel III told *CA:* "I write about the research that I do—content studies of presidential campaign coverage and public opinion surveys. I did studies of media coverage of the 1956, 1960, 1964, 1972, 1980, 1984, and 1988 presidential campaigns. All of these dealt with coverage by major newspapers, and three of them also included network television and news magazines. I found virtually no support for the claims of bias in coverage that have come from both sides over the years. Bias is in the eyes of the beholder. My surveys have dealt with media use and with political attitudes. I have found that the Internet is vastly overrated as a news medium, that use of all media except the Internet tends to increase with a person's age, and that use of print media correlates highly with level of education.

"Most of my writing has been articles in research and professional journals. I taught journalism for more than forty years and collaborated with more than thirty faculty members and students in published research. I also was editor of the *Journalism Quarterly* for seventeen years.

"Currently I am director of the Scripps Survey Research Center at Ohio University. We do four surveys a year on a variety of topics. Recent surveys have dealt with topics ranging from the performance of the president and the Iraq war to interest in sports and attitudes about

tattoos. The latter study found that use of tattoos has tripled by generations, going from about three percent for those over sixty-five to nine percent for the next generation to thirty percent for young adults."

BIOGRAPHICAL AND CRITICAL SOURCES:

PERIODICALS

Journalism History, spring, 2000, Louis Liebovich, review of *Historical Dictionary of Political Communication in the United States,* p. 38.

Journal of Broadcasting, winter, 1982, R.C. Adams, review of *Research Methods in Mass Communication,* pp. 508-511.

Reference & Research Book News, August, 2003, review of *Media and Politics in America: A Reference Handbook,* p. 205.

*   *   *

SULLIVAN, Susan
See DUNLAP, Susan

T

TAYLER, Jeffrey 1961-

PERSONAL: Born 1961; married. *Education:* Doctoral study in Russian and East European history, University of Virginia.

ADDRESSES: Home—Russia.

CAREER: Served as a Peace Corps volunteer in Morocco, 1988-90, and as a staff member in Warsaw, Poland, 1990-92, and Tashkent, Uzbekistan, 1992-93; freelance writer and photographer; interpreter; comanager of an American security company operating in Moscow, Russia; commentator for National Public Radio and correspondent for the *Atlantic Monthly.*

WRITINGS:

Siberian Dawn: A Journey across the New Russia, Hungry Mind Press (St. Paul, MN), 1999.
Facing the Congo, Ruminator Books (St. Paul, MN), 2000.
Glory in a Camel's Eye: Trekking through the Moroccan Sahara, Houghton Mifflin (Boston, MA), 2003.
Angry Wind: Through Muslim Black Africa by Truck, Bus, Boat, and Camel, Houghton Mifflin (Boston, MA), 2005, published as *The Lost Kingdoms of Africa: Through Muslim Africa by Truck, Bus, Boat and Camel,* Abacus (London, England), 2006.
River of No Reprieve: Descending Siberia's Waterway of Exile, Death, and Destiny, Houghton Mifflin (Boston, MA), 2006, published as *River of White Nights: A Siberian River Odyssey,* Robson (London, England), 2006.

Contributor to *The Best American Travel Writing,* edited by Jason Wilson and Bill Bryson, Houghton Mifflin (Boston, MA), 2000; contributor to periodicals, including *Condé Nast Traveler, Harper's, National Geographic Magazine, Men's Journal, Smithsonian,* and *Spin.*

SIDELIGHTS: A restless spirit all his life, Jeffrey Tayler has made a name for himself as a travel writer who journeys to the world's most forbidding, oppressive, and inhospitable places. Tayler's yearning to travel, he told Rolf Potts for *Rolf Pott's Vagabonding,* came to him while he was a junior in college: "I developed the conviction that, for me, truths of some exalted and liberating sort resided in foreign lands, and decided that my life would be better led elsewhere." Adept at foreign languages—he speaks Russian, Arabic, Greek, Turkish, and several Romance languages—Tayler decided to travel. First, he traveled to Greece, Italy, Spain, and other European points before ending up in Moscow. For years, Tayler had been fascinated by Russian culture and history. "Ever since I was a teenager," he told John Coyne on the *Peace Corps Writers* Web site, "Russia, Russians, Russian literature, and Russian history have played a role in my life that no one else or nothing ever would equal. Most of my heroes were Russian—Solzhenitsyn and Sakharov among them; many of my favorite writers and works of literature were Russian; my favorite poets and bards were Russian." Having worked for the Peace Corps in Morocco and Warsaw, he moved to Moscow and eventually married a Russian. His respect and admiration for the Russian people led Tayler's desire to know the landscape better, and so he set off on an epic journey that he describes in his first book, *Siberian Dawn: A Journey across the New Russia.*

In a 1993 excursion that extended over eight thousand miles from Magadan in Siberia to the border of Poland, Tayler made a trip that was more ambitious and risky than even most native Russians would dare to hazard. Facing minus-forty-degree temperatures, polluted industrial landscapes, despairing and impoverished people, and frustrating bureaucrats, Tayler records his trip in *Siberian Dawn.* The book is not an ordinary travel guide that would interest aspiring tourists, but rather a deeply felt look into the world of post-Soviet Russia. A *Publishers Weekly* critic described the book as being a "cracker-barrel discussion of who 'won the cold war' and suggestions for reform are left out." "Tayler," asserted *Booklist* writers Thomas Gaughan and Jack Helbig, "is a skilled craftsman who could become a significant new voice in travel literature. Compelling and deeply unsettling reading."

Despite such praise, Tayler initially had a difficult time finding a publisher for *Siberian Dawn.* While the book gathered dust on editors' desks, he decided to go on another excursion that, he hoped, would be a journey of self-discovery. His plan was to recreate the original trip English explorer Henry Morton Stanley took in the nineteenth century. He would go to the Democratic Republic of Congo, formerly Zaire, and take a barge up the Congo River, returning back to the coast in a dugout canoe called a pirogue. As with his Siberian adventure, the trip would be extremely hazardous, though for different reasons. Tayler would have to battle terrible weather, hordes of biting insects, illness, robbers, hostile native people, corrupt soldiers, ferocious crocodiles, and many other dangers. Finally, on his trip back in the canoe, his guide became seriously ill, and Tayler decided to call an end to his voyage. The decision came not only because of the hardships, but also because he had reached an unavoidable conclusion: "I found myself stung by my failure and trying to deny what I would later come to see as obvious: that I had exploited Zaire as a playground on which to solve my own rich-boy existential dilemmas." He admits to himself, as he notes in his book, that his "drama of self-actualization proved obscenely trivial beside the suffering of the Zaireans and the injustices of their past." Thus, Tayler's *Facing the Congo* becomes not just a travel adventure but also a deep exploration into psychological and moral issues. "Eloquent and sincere," stated a *Publishers Weekly* writer, "Tayler brings immense cultural sensitivity to his journey, fully conscious that the poverty and misery are in large part due to Western hegemony." Joshua Kuritzky, writing for *CNN.com,* further noted: "Tayler, a talented writer and astute observer, is constantly aware

of the larger meaning of his trip through Zaire"; the critic added that "observations like this are what make Tayler such an excellent, and underrated, travel writer."

Tayler's next expedition was to another forbidding land, the blistering climate of the Draa Valley of Morocco. Traveling by camel, mule, and foot, he crossed almost six hundred miles of desert to get a better look into the world of nomadic Muslims in a culturally complex land. *Glory in a Camel's Eye: Trekking through the Moroccan Sahara* thus explores the worldview of a people whose religion permeates every aspect of their difficult lives. Reviewers were particularly pleased by the fact that Tayler is not so much interested in the politics of the Arab world as he is in the society itself. "Readers overwhelmed by the many dense texts available on Islamic politics will enjoy this balanced, enlightening memoir," commented a *Publishers Weekly* critic. Tayler, wrote Dennis Drabelle in a *Washington Post Book World* review, "is a sharp observer of natural phenomena, even more so of cultural traits, and his passion for all things Arab is refreshing." *Library Journal* contributor Mari Flynn concluded that "Tayler offers us a memorable picture of a desiccated land and its survivors."

Angry Wind: Through Muslim Black Africa by Truck, Bus, Boat, and Camel was published in England as *The Lost Kingdoms of Africa: Through Muslim Africa by Truck, Bus, Boat and Camel.* It is an account of Tayler's 2002 journey across the Sahel, the Saharan borderlands of Chad, Nigeria, Niger, and Mali, during which he witnessed bureaucratic corruption and extreme poverty. The inhabitants of this region are primarily black but of the Muslim faith, a result of cultural modification that is ongoing. A *Publishers Weekly* contributor who described the volume as being "vividly written and trenchantly observed," noted that Tayler "generally avoids being overwhelmed by either the region's problems or its exotic charms." The trip was a treacherous one that involved unreliable transportation and physical danger from land mines.

Tayler writes of his debates about religion and the foreign policy of President George W. Bush, most of which was negative, and such controversial practices as female genital mutilation. Many blamed all Americans, and even Tayler directly, for their state of suffering. People often queried him as to why he would visit their part of the world, and some assumed he was a CIA agent. A *Kirkus Reviews* contributor noted that "whereas France and England should properly feel their wrath, what the desert-dwellers see on television is America as anti-Islamic crusader." Jo-Anne Mary Benson wrote that Tayler's "balanced coverage examines the region's hospitality and hostility, its beauty and its sordidness." "Lovers of travel literature and those who want to learn more about Islam in Africa should not miss this beautifully written travelogue," concluded Kristine Huntley in *Booklist.*

River of No Reprieve: Descending Siberia's Waterway of Exile, Death, and Destiny was published in England as *River of White Nights: A Siberian River Odyssey.* Tayler recounts his 2004 2,400-mile, two-month voyage on the Lena River by raft with Vadim, a veteran of the Soviet-Afghan war who served as his guide and with whom he shared a volatile relationship during the trip. The difficulty level was very similar to when the trip was made by the Cossacks, who in the sixteenth century annexed much of Siberia for Ivan the Terrible. The river is the third longest in Russia and the only major river that is fully navigable because of the absence of hydroelectric dams. The travelers were plagued by poor weather, heat, and insects as they visited the villages along the way. A *Publishers Weekly* reviewer commented that Tayler, who "is good at describing . . . his thoughts on Russian president Vladimir Putin, who is adored by the very people for whom he provides the least, offers the American reader some borscht for thought about the appeal of their own benighted leader." "This is a good adventure, well-told," wrote Huntley. "That it happens to take place in the depths of Siberia is icing on the cake."

In his interview with Potts, Tayler offered this advice to aspiring travel writers: "Know the place about which you propose to write, or know what you want to research there before you go. You can learn new things along the way, but you should start with a plan and be able to offer an insider's perspective."

BIOGRAPHICAL AND CRITICAL SOURCES:

PERIODICALS

Booklist, February 1, 1999, Thomas Gaughan and Jack Helbig, review of *Siberian Dawn: A Journey across the New Russia,* p. 959; July, 2003, George Cohen, review of *Glory in a Camel's Eye: Trekking through the Moroccan Sahara,* p. 1858; January 1,

2005, Kristine Huntley, review of *Angry Wind: Through Muslim Black Africa by Truck, Bus, Boat, and Camel,* p. 805; April 15, 2006, George Cohen, review of *River of No Reprieve: Descending Siberia's Waterway of Exile, Death, and Destiny,* p. 22.

Bookwatch, August, 2005, review of *Angry Wind.*

Foreign Affairs, March-April, 2005, Nicolas Van De Walle, review of *Angry Wind,* p. 172.

Geographical, November, 2006, Natalie Hoare, review of *River of White Nights: A Siberian River Odyssey,* p. 92.

Kirkus Reviews, December 15, 2004, review of *Angry Wind,* p. 1194; May 15, 2006, review of *River of No Reprieve,* p. 512.

Library Journal, February 15, 1999, Rebecca Miller, review of *Siberian Dawn,* p. 169; July, 2003, Mari Flynn, review of *Glory in a Camel's Eye,* p. 112; January 1, 2005, Jo-Anne Mary Benson, review of *Angry Wind,* p. 137; May 1, 2006, Sheila Kasperek, review of *River of No Reprieve,* p. 110.

Publishers Weekly, January 25, 1999, review of *Siberian Dawn,* p. 82; August 28, 2000, review of *Facing the Congo,* p. 68; May 12, 2003, review of *Glory in a Camel's Eye,* p. 57.

Rocky Mountain News (Denver, CO), July 25, 2003, Ed Halloran, review of *Glory in a Camel's Eye,* p. D30; November 22, 2004, review of *Angry Wind,* p. 45; May 8, 2006, Tom Bissell, review of *River of No Reprieve,* p. 54.

Russian Life, July-August, 2006, Paul E. Richardson, review of *River of No Reprieve,* p. 61.

Spectator, September 23, 2006, Joanna Kavenna, review of *River of White Nights.*

Times (London, England), May 19, 2001, Steve Jelbert, review of *Facing the Congo,* p. 22.

Washington Post Book World, July 22, 2001, Afshin Molavi, review of *Facing the Congo,* p. T7; May 25, 2003, Dennis Drabelle, review of *Glory in a Camel's Eye,* p. T4.

ONLINE

CNN.com, http://www.cnn.com/ (November 23, 2000) Joshua Kuritzky, review of *Facing the Congo.*

Peace Corps Writers Web site, http://www.peacecorps writers.org/ (April 7, 2004), John Coyne, "Talking with Jeffrey Tayler."

Rolf Potts' Vagabonding, http://www.rolfpotts.com/ (February 7, 2007), interview with Tayler.

World Hum, http://www.worldhum.com/ (December 32, 2005), Jim Benning, "Jeffrey Tayler: Facing Africa's 'Angry Wind'" (interview).

*   *   *

TAYLOR, Bill
   See TAYLOR, William C.

*   *   *

TAYLOR, Paul B. 1930-
   (Paul Beekman Taylor)

PERSONAL: Born December 31, 1930, in London, England; son of Edith Taylor; married Alexandra Fatio, May 10, 1958 (divorced October 19, 1977); married Rose-Marie Beauverd (a teacher), January 4, 1978; children: (first marriage) Andrea, Maurice Fatio, Nora Annesley, Paul Guillaume; (second marriage) Gareth Gavin, Aude Aurelia. *Education:* Brown University, A.B., 1954, Ph.D., 1961; Wesleyan University, Middletown, CT, M.A., 1958; postdoctoral study at University of Oslo, 1960-61.

ADDRESSES: Home—Vessy, Switzerland. *Office*—Department of English, University of Geneva, 1211 Geneva 4, Switzerland. *E-mail*—paul.taylor@lettres.unige.ch.

CAREER: Brown University, Providence, RI, instructor, 1961-62, assistant professor of English, 1962-64; University of Iceland, Reykjavik, Fulbright lecturer in English and American literature, 1964-65; University of Geneva, Geneva, Switzerland, professor of medieval English language and literature, 1965-97, honorary professor, beginning 1997, director of department, 1969-78, 1989-92. Yale University, visiting fellow of Berkeley College, 1980-81; University of New Mexico, lecturer, 1987-88, 1998-99; visiting professor at Swiss universities in Lausanne, Fribourg, and Zurich. *Military service:* U.S. Army, 1954-57; became sergeant.

MEMBER: International Association of University Professors of English, International Saga Society, International Society of Anglo-Saxonists, New Chaucer Society, Viking Society for Northern Research, Swiss Association of University Teachers of English.

AWARDS, HONORS: Fulbright fellowship for Norway, 1960-61; fellowship from National Translation Center, 1967-69.

WRITINGS:

(Editor and translator, with W.H. Auden) *Voluspa: The Song of the Sybil* (edition with facing translation), Windhover Press (Iowa City, IA), 1967.

(Translator from the Icelandic and author of critical introduction, with W.H. Auden) *The Elder Edda,* Faber & Faber (London, England), 1969, Random House (New York, NY), 1970.

(Editor, with P.H. Salus) *For W.H. Auden: Essays for His Sixty-fifth Birthday,* Random House (New York, NY), 1972.

(Translator, with W.H. Auden) *Norse Poems,* Athlone Press (London, England), 1981.

Chaucer's Chain of Love, Fairleigh Dickinson University Press (Rutherford, NJ), 1996.

Sharing Story; Medieval Norse-English Literary Relations, AMS Press (New York, NY), 1996.

Chaucer Translator, University Press of America (Lanham, MD), 1998.

Shadows of Heaven: Toomer and Gurdjieff, Samuel Weiser (York Beach, ME), 1998.

Gurdjieff and Orage: Brothers in Elysium, Samuel Weiser (York Beach, ME), 2001.

Gurdjieff's America, Lighthouse Books (London, England), 2004.

Contributor to numerous scholarly books. Contributor of articles and reviews to many scholarly journals, including *American Notes and Queries, Journal of English and Germanic Philology, Journal of Popular Culture, Chaucer Review, Comparative Literature, Scandinavian Studies, Bilingual Review, Journal of the Southwest, Melus,* and *Synthese.*

SIDELIGHTS: Paul B. Taylor once told *CA:* "My major interest has been Germanic language and literature, particularly as an expression of early cultural attitudes. I have studied theories of language use, particularly in Old Icelandic and Old English literature. This interest in language derives primarily from early studies with G.I. Gurdjieff in New York and in Paris (1948-49), and was stimulated by my collaboration with W.H. Auden (1966-72). It has now stimulated writings on American Indian literature."

TAYLOR, Paul Beekman
　　See TAYLOR, Paul B.

*　　*　　*

TAYLOR, William C. 1959-
　(Bill Taylor)

PERSONAL: Born January 26, 1959, in Waterbury, CT; son of Charles Hughes (in business) and Lucille Taylor; married Chloe Mantel, April 1, 1986; children: two daughters. *Education:* Princeton University, B.A. (magna cum laude), 1982; Massachusetts Institute of Technology, M.S., 1987.

ADDRESSES: Home—Wellesley, MA. *E-mail*—bill@ mavericksatwork.com

CAREER: Writer, public speaker, and entrepreneur. *Multinational Monitor,* Washington, DC, cofounder, associate editor, and contributor, 1979-80; *Hartford Advocate,* Hartford, CT, reporter, 1982-83; Center for Study of Responsive Law, Washington, DC, writer and researcher, 1983-85; *Sloan Management Review,* Cambridge, MA, editor, 1986-87; *Fast Company* magazine, cofounder and founding editor; Babson College, Babson Park, MA, adjunct professor.

MEMBER: Phi Beta Kappa.

AWARDS, HONORS: First prize in weekly business and economics reporting, New England Press Association, for "Gold Out of Brass"; Connecticut State Scholarship, 1977-81, and Sigmund Wahrsager Scholarship in political economy, 1981, both from Princeton University.

WRITINGS:

(With Ralph Nader) *The Big Boys: Power and Position in American Business,* Pantheon (New York, NY), 1986.
(With T.J. Rodgers and Rick Foreman) *No-Excuses Management: Proven Systems for Starting Fast, Growing Quickly, and Surviving Hard Times,* Currency/Doubleday (New York, NY), 1993.
(With Alan M. Webber) *Going Global: Four Entrepreneurs Map the New World Marketplace,* Viking (New York, NY), 1996.

(With Polly LaBarre) *Mavericks at Work: Why the Most Original Minds in Business Win,* William Morrow (New York, NY), 2006.

Also author of *Managing across Cultures: Human Resources Issues in Japanese Companies in the U.S.,* 1989. Contributor to books, including *Public Domain, Private Dominion: A History of Public Mineral Policy in America,* by Carl. J. Mayer and George A. Riley, Sierra Books (San Francisco, CA), 1985. Contributor to periodicals, including *Chicago Tribune, USA Today, Harvard Review,* and the *Hartford Advocate.* Contributed monthly column, "Under New Management," to the SundayBusiness section of the *New York Times.*

ADAPTATIONS: Mavericks at Work has been adapted as an audiobook.

SIDELIGHTS: An expert on the future of the business world, William C. Taylor is the coauthor of several books on business and the cofounder of the business magazine *Fast Company.* In the book *No-Excuses Management: Proven Systems for Starting Fast, Growing Quickly, and Surviving Hard Times,* written with T.J. Rodgers and Rick Foreman, Taylor and his coauthors tell how Rodgers turned computer chipmaker Cypress Semiconductor from a Silicon Valley startup in 1983 into a 300 million dollar business. "The book exudes Rodgers's combative style at every turn," wrote Paul H. Weaver in *Reason. No-Excuses Management,* Weaver continued, "offers a candid and engaging picture of the way an unusually thoughtful executive does his job in a challenging industry," and added: "Its outstanding quality is a passionate, almost novelistic sense of reality."

Going Global: Four Entrepreneurs Map the New World Marketplace, written by Taylor and Alan M. Webber, features four business officers—from Whirlpool, McKinsey & Co.'s Tokyo office, Nestle, and Kleiner Perkins—and tells how they helped lead their companies into the global marketplace. "Their stories abound with adventure and conquest," wrote a *Publishers Weekly* contributor. Mary Whaley, writing in *Booklist,* commented that the authors "compare the opening up of the new economy . . . with the discovery of the New World."

Taylor collaborated with Polly LaBarre to write *Mavericks at Work: Why the Most Original Minds in Business Win.* In their book, the authors explain that business leaders should continually look for new challenges and think progressively about their companies. In the process, they discuss a promising new business environment and how many "older" companies, such as IBM and Procter & Gamble, are developing new business models to make their names stand out. In addition, *Mavericks at Work* describes how modern entrepreneurs and businesses, such as Google, Cranium, Whole Foods Market, and ING Direct, have created prosperous companies by being innovative and unconventional. The authors include numerous case studies of business leaders who have ignored tradition and turned to creativity to make their companies successful.

"*Mavericks* offers compelling evidence that differentiation—'strategy as originality,' in the words of Taylor and LaBarre—is crucial to the distinctive customer experiences and breakthrough practices that lead to growth," wrote Jena McGregor in *Business Week*. McGregor went on to call the book "wide-ranging," adding that "Taylor and LaBarre muse on everything from open-source innovation to the value of open-book management." David Siegfried, writing in *Booklist*, noted that, according to the authors, "these new innovators . . . hold the key to reinstituting business as a source of inspiration and progress." An *Economist* contributor referred to *Mavericks at Work* as "a pivotal work in the tradition of *In Search of Excellence*." *Armchair Interviews* Web site contributor Celia Renteria Szelwach wrote: "This book is for corporate executives, entrepreneurs, or anyone desiring to break the mold by applying unconventional ideas and unusual strategies."

BIOGRAPHICAL AND CRITICAL SOURCES:

PERIODICALS

Booklist, June 1, 1996, Mary Whaley, review of *Going Global: Four Entrepreneurs Map the New World Marketplace*, p. 1656; September 15, 2006, David Siegfried, review of *Mavericks at Work: Why the Most Original Minds in Business Win*, p. 12.

Boston Globe, September 24, 2006, Robert Weisman, review of *Mavericks at Work*.

Business Week, October 2, 2006, Jena McGregor, review of *Mavericks at Work*, p. 104.

Economist, November 18, 2006, review of *Mavericks at Work*, p. 86.

Newsweek, October 2, 2006, John Sparks, review of *Mavericks at Work*.

Publishers Weekly, May 20, 1996, review of *Going Global*, p. 247.

Reason, December, 1993, Paul H. Weaver, review of *No Excuses Management: Proven Systems for Starting Fast, Growing Quickly, and Surviving Hard Times*, p. 51.

ONLINE

Armchair Interviews, http://www.armchairinterviews. com/ (March 16, 2007), Celia Renteria Szelwach, review of *Mavericks at Work*.

Mavericks at Work Web site, http://www.mavericks atwork.com/ (March 16, 2007), brief profile of author.

MiamiHerald.com, http://www.miami.com/ (March 16, 2007), Richard Pachter, review of *Mavericks at Work*.

U.S. News & World Report Web site, http://www.us news.com/ (September 17, 2006), Rick Newman, review of *Mavericks at Work*.

World Business, http://www.worldbusinesslive.com/ (January 22, 2007), Morice Mendoza, "The Maverick Mindset," interview with author.*

*   *   *

TEA, Michelle 1971(?)-

PERSONAL: Born c. 1971, in Chelsea, MA.

ADDRESSES: Home—San Francisco, CA.

CAREER: Spoken-word poet and writer.

AWARDS, HONORS: Cable Car Award for Best Critic, 1996, for writing in the *San Francisco Bay Times*; Rona Jaffe Award, 1999; Lambda Award for Best Lesbian Fiction, for *Valencia*; Top Twenty-five Books of 2000, *Village Voice Literary Supplement*, for *Valencia*.

WRITINGS:

The Passionate Mistakes and Intricate Corruption of One Girl in America (novel), Semiotexte (New York, NY), 1998.

Valencia (novel), Seal Press (Seattle, WA), 2000.

The Chelsea Whistle: A Memoir, Seal Press (Seattle, WA), 2002.

(Editor) *Without a Net: The Female Experience of Growing Up Working Class,* Seal Press (Emeryville, CA), 2003.

(Editor, with Clint Catalyst) *Pills, Thrills, Chills, and Heartache: Adventures in the First Person,* Alyson Books (Los Angeles, CA), 2004.

The Beautiful: Collected Poems, Manic D Press (San Francisco, CA), 2004.

Rent Girl (illustrated novel), illustrated by Laurenn McCubbin, Last Gasp (San Francisco, CA), 2004.

Rose of No Man's Land (novel), MacAdam/Cage (San Francisco, CA), 2006.

(Editor) *Baby Remember My Name: An Anthology of New Queer Girl Writing,* Carroll & Graf (New York, NY), 2007.

Author of introduction, *Best Lesbian Erotica 2004,* edited by Tristan Taormino, Cleis Press (San Francisco, CA), 2003. Contributor to periodicals, including *San Francisco Bay Guardian, On Our Backs,* and *Out* magazine.

SIDELIGHTS: Michelle Tea grew up in Chelsea, Massachusetts, and moved to the San Francisco Mission District in 1993. The following year she founded the all-girl spoken word group Sister Spit with Sini Anderson. The group's performances, both in San Francisco and throughout the United States and Canada, have made Tea a fixture on the literary performance scene. Tea has written novels featuring a lesbian protagonist living outside the mainstream. She is also the author of *The Chelsea Whistle: A Memoir,* which depicts Tea's life growing up poor on the East Coast. A reviewer writing in the *Portland Mercury* asserted that the author "is one of the best writers to emerge from a group of young women who use first-person linear narrative and unequivocal language—traditionally thought of as 'male' by feminist theorists—to present the reality of life as a girl."

Tea turned to her life in San Francisco's lesbian subculture for her first book, a stream-of-consciousness novel called *The Passionate Mistakes and Intricate Corruption of One Girl in America.* "I had been writing poems, spoken word stuff, and I was having a good time with it and getting great responses from the open mics I hung out at, but at some point I wanted to shine a wider light on my experiences," Tea said in an interview on the *Venus or Vixen* Web site. She added that she was writing short stories and took one of them and "kind of squished it into a novel." Tea's effort to expand on a short story resulted in a novel focusing on the misadventures of Michelle, a heroine who spends her youth in the Gothic punk scene of Boston, becomes a prostitute, and has an abusive girlfriend. Writing in the *Nation,* Eileen Myles called the book "a gem of endangered narration from a loud and highly marginalized subculture, in particular the third wave of feminism. Tea's work resists categorization, and like all surprising vanguard literature, it's the news—a hunk of lyric information that coolly, then frantically, describes the car wreck of her generation and everything that surrounds it."

In her next novel, *Valencia,* Tea continues to flesh out the life of the fictional Michelle, who the *Portland Mercury* critic described as "a wry girl narrator." According to Tea in an article appearing in the *San Francisco Chronicle,* the novel is based on her first year living in San Francisco. "It's about coming to the city fresh and having nothing to lose," she explained, "arriving already at some kind of bottom, and how instead of that being depressing, it's really freeing." Using what the *Venus or Vixen* contributor called a "rapid-fire, pull-no-punches style," Tea's alter ego describes her life in the girlie-punk culture and her search for a loving mate. As described by Amy Sickels in the *Gay and Lesbian Review, Valencia* "is a fast-paced journey into the bars, streets, and bedrooms of the San Francisco Mission District." Sickels had difficulty with the novel's many characters, pointing out that "the depiction of these women never quite rises above these descriptive tags, and so they remain character types instead of full personalities." However, Sickels continued: "What pulls the reader into Michelle's world is the vividness of the setting against which this fast-paced story is told." Sickels further commented on the novel's anticlimactic ending, but she added that "Tea's energetic language often raises this story above its flaws." A *Publishers Weekly* critic remarked that "Tea's writing is consistently uncommon and textured" but went on to comment that the novel is a "sometimes-superficial, stylized entry." Beth Barnes, writing in the *Lambda Book Report,* was more laudatory: "Despite a conventional narrative and properly placed paragraph breaks, the novel unfolds itself like a lyrical poem, a story that evokes a visceral, emotional response."

Tea's first two novels have autobiographical elements, but her next effort abandons the guise of fiction entirely. *The Chelsea Whistle* recounts Tea's real life growing up in a Boston working-class slum, where many of the youth try to escape through drugs and sex; it describes Tea's determination to leave this depressing world behind. Tea gives honest and frank accounts of life with her scrappy sister, her beleaguered mother, her alcoholic father, and voyeuristic stepfather, as well as of her time dealing with nuns in a Catholic school. "It's mainly about growing up a girl in a poor, weird New England town, feeling unsafe at home and on the street, where girls find safety for themselves or trick themselves into believing they're safe," Tea told Martin Wilson in a *Lambda Book Report* article. A *Publishers Weekly* critic noted that "the writing is well-honed" but also said that the book's "starts and stops, coupled with disappointing ending make her account ultimately unsatisfying." A *Beyond the Closet* reviewer, though, praised Tea's "trademark loose-tongued, lyrical style" in a book that "both celebrates and annihilates one girl's tightrope walk out of a working-class slum and the lessons she carries with her." "Tea writes with unrelenting candor and a lot of wry wit," concluded *Outlook News* contributor Richard Labonte.

Tea has served as editor on several volumes of short fiction or essays, most of which have a sexual and/or feminist sensibility. *Without a Net: The Female Experience of Growing Up Working Class* collects a series of essays that illustrate the ways in which women are affected by poverty, even if they manage to escape the label and rise to a the middle or even upper class. Rachel Pepper, in a review for *Curve,* reported: "This collection contains nary a clunker. You can tell Tea handpicked these writers, cultivated them, and made sure their stories fit together like pieces of a puzzle." Writing for *Herizons,* Jennifer O'Connor remarked that the book "provides honest, insightful and entertaining stories of working-class women." Sheri Whatley, in a review for *off our backs,* wrote: "Within these stories, you hear the voices of women who have lived through the worst and are still surviving," and went on to state: "These are women who are not usually listened to . . . but within their stories lies the core of America."

Pills, Thrills, Chills, and Heartache: Adventures in the First Person is a collection of short stories that Tea edited with Clint Catalyst; the unifying theme is that the fiction is all in the first person. Most of these works tell their stories from the viewpoint of an outsider. Topics range from narrators questioning their sexuality to experiences with rare cancer and reactions to drug and alcohol abuse. "Though wildly uneven, the collection is bound to make a splash with readers seeking edgy fic-

tion," according to a reviewer for *Publishers Weekly.* Writing for *Booklist,* Whitney Scott remarked that the collection offers "life on the fringe, up close and perhaps too personal."

Tea moves on to a new medium with *Rent Girl,* which she refers to as an illustrated novel. This work marks her return to the subject of her own life spent on the street. Jane Ganahl, writing for the *San Francisco Chronicle,* remarked: "Tea's writing is addictive: lyrical yet straightforward, literate yet confessional, with a large helping of ironic humor." With this project, Tea's main objective was to balance her experiences with the raw reality of her situation at the time, particularly her work as a prostitute. She told Ganahl: "I wanted to talk about the reality of it as an occupation, a job." Abe Louise Young wrote in the *Lambda Book Report* that Tea merely scratches the surface of her experiences as a prostitute, commenting that "I want more from the story: more depth, more insight," and calling the book "strangely one-dimensional." *Herizons* reviewer Lisa Foad, however, called Tea's effort "a rich work of art and smarts, one that manages to tackle the difficult terrain of sex work without becoming an apologia, and without victimization or glamorization."

In *Rose of No Man's Land* Tea returns to the more traditional novel format, while instilling her writing with many of the ongoing themes of her earlier work. The book tells the story of life in modern-day American through the eyes of fourteen-year-old Trisha. Trisha seems destined to spend her days working at the local mall with her sister, while her mother lies around watching television with her boyfriend. What many might consider an average suburban life, Trisha somehow turns into a bizarre and unusual existence. In a review for *Lambda Book Report,* Carol Guess remarked: "What's missing from Trisha's life—and the culture Tea captures so adroitly—is authenticity." Guess went on to comment that "there's a loneliness to this life that seems visible only to Trisha and, through Tea's detailed prose, the reader." *Booklist* contributor Michael Cart felt that "too much is predictable," but went on to note that there are "flashes of brilliant writing." Jason Roush, in a review for *Gay & Lesbian Review Worldwide,* concluded: "As Michelle Tea continues to mark her territory as one of today's most important voices in lesbian writing, she's also constructing new realities in which young people can find ways of re-imagining their own lives."

BIOGRAPHICAL AND CRITICAL SOURCES:

BOOKS

Tea, Michelle, *The Chelsea Whistle: A Memoir,* Seal Press (Seattle, WA), 2002.

PERIODICALS

Advocate, November 21, 2000, Matthew Link, review of *Valencia,* p. 58.
Booklist, September 15, 2002, June Pulliam, review of *The Chelsea Whistle,* p. 195; February 15, 2004, Whitney Scott, review of *Pills, Chills, Thrills, and Heartache: Adventures in the First Person,* p. 1038; December 15, 2005, Michael Cart, review of *Rose of No Man's Land,* p. 25.
Curve, June, 2004, Rachel Pepper, review of *Without a Net: The Female Experience of Growing Up Working Class,* p. 64.
Gay and Lesbian Review, fall, 2000, Amy Sickels, "Sleep-deprived in San Francisco," review of *Valencia,* p. 44; July-August, 2006, Jason Roush, "A Time for Speed," review of *Rose of No Man's Land,* p. 44.
Herizons, winter, 2005, Jennifer O'Connor, review of *Without a Net,* p. 42; spring, 2005, Lisa Foad, review of *Rent Girl,* p. 38.
Kirkus Reviews, July 15, 2002, review of *The Chelsea Whistle,* p. 1019; December 1, 2005, review of *Rose of No Man's Land,* p. 1255.
Lambda Book Report, May, 2000, Beth Barnes, "A Dirt-smeared Poetic Perfection," review of *Valencia,* p. 17, and Elizabeth Stark, "Grrl Guide: An Interview with Michelle Tea," p. 18; May, 2001, Martin Wilson, "Very American Obsessions," p. 27; October, 2004, Abe Louise Young, "Room for Reflection," review of *Rent Girl,* p. 11; spring, 2006, Carol Guess, review of *Rose of No Man's Land,* p. 13.
Library Journal, April 15, 2000, Devon C. Thomas, review of *Valencia,* p. 125.
Nation, March 15, 1999, Eileen Myles, review of *The Passionate Mistakes and Intricate Corruption of One Girl in America,* p. 32.
off our backs, January-February, 2005, Sheri Whatley, review of *Without a Net,* p. 50.
Publishers Weekly, March 20, 2000, review of *Valencia,* p. 69; July 1, 2002, review of *The Chelsea Whistle,* p. 66; January 12, 2004, review of *Pills, Chills, Thrills, and Heartache,* p. 37.

San Francisco Chronicle, August 25, 2004, Jane Ganahl, "Michelle Tea Mines Her Colorful Past for a Graphic Memoir," p. E1.

ONLINE

Beyond the Closet, http://www.beyondthecloset.com/ (October 23, 2002), review of *The Chelsea Whistle.*
Fabula Magazine, http://www.fabulamag.com/ (October 23, 2002), Jeff Johnson, review of *Valencia.*
Outlook News, http://www.outlooknews.com/ (October 23, 2002), Richard Labonte, review of *The Chelsea Whistle.*
Portland Mercury Online, http://www.portlandmercury.com/ (October 23, 2002), review of *Valencia;* Ariel Gore, "Nothing but the Truth: A Chat with Valencia Author Michelle Tea."
San Francisco Bay Guardian, http://www.sfbg.com/ (October 23, 2002), review of *Valencia.*
SFstation.com, http://www.sfstation.com/ (October 23, 2002), "Straight Outta Castro, Michelle Tea and Company Take on America."
Venus or Vixen, http://www.venusorvixen.com/ (October 23, 2002), review of *Valencia* and "Interview with Valencia Author Michelle Tea."*

*   *   *

THOMAS, Helen A. 1920-

PERSONAL: Born August 4, 1920, in Winchester, KY; daughter of George and Mary Thomas; married Douglas B. Cornell (a journalist), October 11, 1971. *Education:* Wayne State University, B.A., 1942.

ADDRESSES: Home—Washington, DC. *Office*—National Press Building, Washington, DC 20004.

CAREER: Formerly affiliated with United Press International; wire service reporter in Washington, DC, 1973-74, White House bureau chief, 1974—.

MEMBER: Women's National Press Club (president, 1959-60), American Newspaper Women's Club (former vice president), White House Correspondents Association (president, 1976), Sigma Delta Chi, Delta Sigma Phi (honorary member).

AWARDS, HONORS: Named woman of the year in communications by *Ladies Home Journal,* 1975; L.L.D. from Eastern Michigan State University, 1972, and Ferris State College, 1978; L.H.D. from Wayne State University, 1974, and University of Detroit, 1979.

WRITINGS:

Dateline: White House, Macmillan (New York, NY), 1975.
(With Frank Cormier and James Deakin) *The White House Press on the Presidency: News Management and Co-Option,* edited by Kenneth W. Thompson, University Press of America (Lanham, MD), 1983.
Front Row at the White House: My Life and Times, Scribner (New York, NY), 1999.
Thanks for the Memories, Mr. President: Wit and Wisdom from the Front Row at the White House, Scribner (New York, NY), 2002.
Watchdogs of Democracy? The Waning Washington Press Corps and How It Has Failed the Public, Scribner (New York, NY), 2006.

SIDELIGHTS: Helen A. Thomas is one of the most widely known wire service reporters in the United States. Since 1961 she has covered the White House for United Press International, and in 1974 was named White House bureau chief. In a reporting career spanning five decades she has become a legend, noted for her lively wit, for her tough reporting, and for her position as one of the first women to break into the male-dominated White House press corps. "The daughter of Lebanese immigrants," explained a *Town & Country* contributor, the Detroit native "dreamed of being a reporter and worked hard to realize her goal."

Some of Thomas's biggest leads and stories were provided by Martha Mitchell, the wife of President Richard Nixon's Attorney General John Mitchell. During the Watergate affair, Mitchell would often make revealing telephone calls to Thomas. "Martha loved the press. And any time she spoke out it was usually with a block-buster," Thomas told an interviewer for the *Grand Rapids Press.* "Martha could never give you one, two, three, in sequence, but if you pieced the facts together you found them valid. Listen to the White House tapes and you'll find the proof."

An account of Martha Mitchell, as well as an inside look at the White House during the administrations of Kennedy, Johnson, Nixon, and Ford, is contained in

Thomas's *Dateline: White House.* Godfrey Sperling, writing in the *Christian Science Monitor,* found the book to be filled with "behind-the scenes nuggets and acute observations." Richard Reeves, writing in the *New York Times Book Review,* was equally admiring. He noted that *Dateline* contains "fascinating material on the Johnsons, a touching portrait of Pat Nixon and an interesting portrait of a very tough and very feminine woman named Helen Thomas succeeding in the male world of journalism. More than that, in total, 'Dateline: White House' is a valuable firsthand report on how reporting itself actually works."

Thomas continues the story of her career in *Front Row at the White House: My Life and Times,* and *Thanks for the Memories, Mr. President: Wit and Wisdom from the Front Row at the White House.* "Thomas, known for tough questions and pungent observations," wrote Mary Carroll in *Booklist,* "has covered every president since Kennedy." Her memoirs are littered with stories about the men and women who have occupied the White House during the last forty-plus years. "Kennedy and Reagan were the best at using jocularity to defuse the acrimony often spawned by their policies," explained a *Kirkus Reviews* critic writing about *Thanks for the Memories, Mr. President,* while both Geroge Bushes "inspired as much unintentional as intentional humor" on account of their poor communication skills. *Front Row at the White House,* concluded a *Publishers Weekly* reviewer, is "a sharp chronicle of the nation's recent history—and of the crusade of women reporters to be considered the equal or better of their male counterparts."

BIOGRAPHICAL AND CRITICAL SOURCES:

BOOKS

Biography News, Thomson Gale (Farmington Hills, MI), January-February, 1975.
Thomas, Helen A., *Dateline: White House,* Macmillan (New York, NY), 1975.
Thomas, Helen A., *Front Row at the White House: My Life and Times,* Scribner (New York, NY), 1999.

PERIODICALS

Booklist, March 15, 1999, Mary Carroll, review of *Front Row at the White House,* p. 1259.

Christian Science Monitor, December 30, 1975, Godfrey Sperling, review of *Dateline: White House,* p. 18.

Grand Rapids Press, November 1, 1974, author interview.

Kirkus Reviews, March 1, 2002, review of *Thanks for the Memories, Mr. President: Wit and Wisdom from the Front Row at the White House,* p. 321.

New York Times Book Review, November 30, 1975, Richard Reeves, review of *Dateline: White House,* p. 20.

Publishers Weekly, April 26, 1999, review of *Front Row at the White House,* p. 62; April 8, 2002, review of *Thanks for the Memories, Mr. President,* p. 215.

Town & Country, May, 1999, "First Lady of the Press," p. 70.*

U-W

URSU, Anne

PERSONAL: Born in Minneapolis, MN; married. *Education:* Brown University, graduated.

ADDRESSES: E-mail—anne@cronuschronicles.com.

CAREER: Writer. Worked in a bookstore; *City Pages,* Minneapolis, MN, theater critic; *Phoenix,* Portland, ME, arts writer.

AWARDS, HONORS: Minnesota Book Award, and Bay Area Book Reviewers Award, both for *Spilling Clarence.*

WRITINGS:

NOVELS; FOR ADULTS

Spilling Clarence, Theia (New York, NY), 2002.
The Disapparation of James, Theia (New York, NY), 2003.

"CRONUS CHRONICLES"; YOUNG-ADULT NOVELS

The Shadow Thieves illustrated by Eric Fortune, Atheneum (New York, NY), 2006.
The Siren Song, illustrated by Eric Fortune, Atheneum (New York, NY), 2007.
The Promethean Flame, illustrated by Eric Fortune, Atheneum (New York, NY), 2008.

Contributor of reviews and articles to periodicals, including various newspapers and *Glamour* magazine.

SIDELIGHTS: Anne Ursu began her career writing for adults before turning her attention to a younger reading audience with the "Cronus Chronicles" novels. In the series, Ursu draws readers into a world peopled by characters from Greek myth and legend. There, modern-day characters find themselves embarking on a challenging and sometimes frightening quest that leads them from the depths of Hades' underworld to the heights of Mount Olympus, home of the gods. In addition to several works of adult fiction, she has penned theatre and arts reviews for regional newspapers, and also seen her articles published in national periodicals such as *Glamour* magazine. Discussing her decision to write for younger readers, Ursu noted in an interview for *Powells. com* that, in addition to her own love of reading children's books, younger readers "give you a chance to really be a storyteller. And there are no limits; a kid never tells you what you can and can't do in a book—they just want good stories, no matter where those stories take them."

Ursu begins her "Cronus Chronicles" with *The Shadow Thieves,* which finds thirteen-year-old Charlotte teaming up with her visiting cousin Zee and her English teacher Mr. Metos, to discover the origin of the strange illness that has rendered most of Zee's schoolmates comatose. A trip to the underworld leads the trio to the source of the plague: Philonecron, an immortal demi-demon who has tapped into the students' spirits as a means of animating the shadow army with which he hopes to overthrow Hades, god of the underworld. Battles with animated skeletons, vampires, and harpies provide high points in Ursu's humorous, Greek-inspired story, which

Horn Book contributor Anita L. Burkam deemed a "fast-paced action adventure." Charlotte's "irreverently casual" narration contains "a ridiculous exaggeration that pleasantly leavens the danger," Burkam added, while in *Booklist* Holly Koelling noted that the teen's narrative tone contains "such unabashed cheerfulness and gusto that readers will find much to enjoy." "With a wit and cynicism that will enchant most readers, Ursu weaves an extraordinary tale," concluded *School Library Journal* reviewer Lisa Marie Williams in a review of *The Shadow Thieves,* while a *Kirkus Reviews* writer dubbed the book "a fun and funny tale of youthful heroism." The "Cronus Chronicles," which features illustrations by Eric Fortune, continues with *The Siren Song.*

The first of Ursu's adult novels, *Spilling Clarence,* is set in Clarence, Minnesota, a fictional college town that also boasts a psychopharmaceutical plant. When a fire breaks out in the plant and a chemical cloud is released into the air, town residents are told to stay indoors while men in hazmat suits enter the area. Although an assurance of safety is made, the mind-altering drug deletrium begins to cause the townspeople's forgotten memories to return. In Ursu's story, the focus rests on the experiences of a small group of people stranded at a local bookstore café as a result of this drug. Christine Perkins commented in her *Library Journal* review of *Spilling Clarence* that "Ursu is a writer who cares deeply about her characters." "With compelling, scarred characters and a cleverly rendered setting, Ursu's debut is both thought-provoking and enjoyable," concluded *Booklist* critic Kristine Huntley.

Ursu followed *Spilling Clarence* with *The Disapparation of James.* In this haunting novel, a Midwestern family's outing to a traveling circus results in tragedy when the five-year-old son participates in a clown's disappearing act and consequently vanishes, leaving his parents distraught and his pragmatic older sister determined to solve the mystery. Ursu's story focuses on "the worry and longing, guilt and rage, protectiveness and resentment that characterize parental love," noted a *Publishers Weekly* contributor, and in *Kliatt* Nola Theiss concluded that the novelist "writes with great feeling and empathy for the family members." While noting that the boy's disappearance is never explained, *Booklist* contributor Elsa Gaztamide nonetheless praised *The Disapparation of James* as "a very innovative work of fiction" that focuses on the evolution of a family loss "in a credible and insightful fashion."

BIOGRAPHICAL AND CRITICAL SOURCES:

PERIODICALS

Booklist, December 1, 2001, Kristine Huntley, review of *Spilling Clarence,* p. 631; March 1, 2006, Holly Koelling, review of *The Shadow Thieves,* p. 94.

Horn Book, March-April, 2006, Anita L. Burkam, review of *The Shadow Thieves,* p. 197.

Kirkus Reviews, November 15, 2001, review of *Spilling Clarence,* p. 1578; October 15, 2002, review of *The Disapparation of James,* p. 1502; March 1, 2006, review of *The Shadow Thieves,* p. 241.

Kliatt, May, 2004, Nola Theiss, review of *The Disapparation of James,* p. 24.

Library Journal, November 15, 2001, Christine Perkins, review of *Spilling Clarence,* p. 99.

New York Times Book Review, July 28, 2002, Jeff Waggoner, review of *Spilling Clarence,* p. 17.

Philadelphia Inquirer, January 6, 2002, Carlin Romano, review of *Spilling Clarence.*

Publishers Weekly, November 12, 2001, review of *Spilling Clarence,* p. 34; October 28, 2002, review of *The Disapparation of James,* p. 46.

School Library Journal, April, 2006, Lisa Marie Williams, review of *The Shadow Thieves,* p. 149.

Times-Picayune (New Orleans, LA), June 17, 2002, Susan Larson, review of *Spilling Clarence.*

USA Today, January 30, 2001, Jackie Pray, review of *Spilling Clarence.*

US Weekly, January 7, 2002, Janet Steen, review of *Spilling Clarence,* p. 64.

ONLINE

Anne Ursu Home Page, http://www.anneursu.com (March 15, 2007).

Bookreporter.com, http://www.bookreporter.com/ (January 2, 2002), Kate Ayers, review of *Spilling Clarence* and interview with Ursu.

Powells.com, http://www.powells.com/kidsqa/ (March 15, 2007), "Anne Ursu."*

*   *   *

VINE, Barbara
See RENDELL, Ruth, Baroness of Babergh

WARREN, Nagueyalti 1947-

PERSONAL: Born October 1, 1947, in Atlanta, GA; daughter of Booker Thompson and Frances Anderson Herrin (a registered nurse); married Roy Wright Jr., July 8, 1965 (divorced); married Rueben C. Warren (a dentist and public health administrator), June 14, 1980; children: Alkamessa Dalton, Asha, Ali. *Ethnicity:* "African American." *Education:* Fisk University, B.A., 1973; Boston University, M.A., 1974; University of Mississippi, Ph.D., 1984; Goddard College, M.F.A., 2005. *Politics:* Democrat. *Hobbies and other interests:* Poetry.

ADDRESSES: Home—Lithonia, GA. *Office*—215 White Hall-College Office, Emory University, Atlanta, GA 30322. *E-mail*—nwarren@emory.edu.

CAREER: Northeastern University, Boston, MA, instructor in English, 1977-78; University of Calabar, Calabar, Nigeria, lecturer in English, 1979-80; Fisk University, Nashville, TN, assistant professor of English and department chair, 1984-88; Emory University, Atlanta, GA, professor of African-American studies and associate dean, 1988—. W.E.B. DuBois Foundation, member of advisory board, 1984—; codirector of a mentoring program.

MEMBER: College Language Association, Modern Language Association of America, National Council of Black Studies.

AWARDS, HONORS: Fulbright Fellowship, 1988; Delores P. Aldridge Service Award, 2004.

WRITINGS:

From Uncle Tom to Cliff Huxtable; Aunt Jemima to Aunt Nell: Images of Blacks in Film and Television, Greenwood Press (Westport, CT), 1988.

Coco and George: A Love Dialectic, Sage Publications (Newbury Park, CA), 1992.

Lodestar and Other Night Lights, Edwin Mellen (Lewiston, NY), 1992.

Southern Mothers: Fact and Fiction in Southern Women's Writing, Louisiana State University Press (Baton Rouge, LA), 1999.

Work represented in anthologies, including *American Anthology of Poetry.* Contributor to journals, including *Mississippi Earthworks, CLA Journal, Essence, Gathering Ground,* and *Black Literature in Review.*

SIDELIGHTS: Nagueyalti Warren once told *CA:* "I grew up in the Watts area of South Central Los Angeles and was deeply influenced by the 1965 riots. In college I joined a writer's workshop and continued my interest in both reading and writing by majoring in English. I have written poetry since the age of six, and my first poem was published in a school newspaper when I was in the fourth grade. First influenced by writers like Richard Wright and James Baldwin, in college I discovered the works of Toni Morrison and Maya Angelou. From that point I began to focus on black women writers within the context of the 1970s. Currently I am most intrigued by the works of Alice Walker. My academic research focuses on an analysis of her works."

*   *   *

WEISS, Michael
See WEISS, Mike

*   *   *

WEISS, Mike 1942-
(Michael Weiss)

PERSONAL: Born October 18, 1942, in Washington, DC; son of Harry (an accountant) and Rhoda (a bursar) Weiss; married Carole Rafferty (a writer), June 7, 1985; children: Joshua, Bessie, Nicholas, Casey. *Education:* Knox College, B.A., 1964; Johns Hopkins University, M.F.A., 1965.

ADDRESSES: Home and office—West Sussex, England. *Agent*—International Creative Management, 40 West 57th St., New York, NY 10019. *E-mail*—mikeweiss@sfchronicle.com.

CAREER: Writer and journalist. *San Francisco Chronicle,* reporter. Worked variously as a community organizer, teacher, university lecturer, janitor, cab driver, butcher, encyclopedia salesman, and waterfront laborer.

MEMBER: Author's Guild.

AWARDS, HONORS: Pulitzer Prize nomination for coverage of Baltimore riots, 1968; Edgar Allan Poe Award for best fact crime book, Mystery Writers of America, 1984, for *Double Play: The San Francisco City Hall Killings.*

WRITINGS:

NONFICTION

(Under name Michael Weiss) *Living Together: A Year in the Life of a City Commune,* McGraw-Hill (New York, NY), 1974.
Double Play: The San Francisco City Hall Killings, Addison-Wesley (Reading, MA), 1984.
A Very Good Year: The Journey of a California Wine from Vine to Table, Gotham Books (New York, NY), 2005.

"BEN HENRY" SERIES; MYSTERY NOVELS

No Go on Jackson Street: A Mystery Introducing Ben Henry, Scribner (New York, NY), 1987.
All Points Bulletin, Avon (New York, NY), 1989.
A Dry and Thirsty Ground, St. Martin's Press (New York, NY), 1992.

SIDELIGHTS: Author and journalist Mike Weiss has had a long and varied career as a writer, but much of his work, whether fact or fiction, has focused on modern urban life in America. His first full-length work, published under the name Michael Weiss, was *Living Together: A Year in the Life of a City Commune.* This 1974 nonfiction book chronicles the first year of an experimental residential living arrangement. His next volume, *Double Play: The San Francisco City Hall Killings,* was published in 1984 and won the author an Edgar Allan Poe nonfiction award from the Mystery Writers of America. In it, Weiss chronicles the 1978 shootings of San Francisco mayor George Moscone and city supervisor/gay-rights advocate Harvey Milk. Former supervisor Dan White was convicted of the murders and served five years in prison. Weiss used trial transcripts to compile sections of *Double Play,* and the book details the so-called "Twinkie defense" employed by the defendant. White's lawyer claimed that the San Francisco politician was driven to kill by uncontrollable mood swings brought on by junk food, and as a result, White was convicted of manslaughter—

not murder—and served just five years in prison. Herbert Gold, reviewing *Double Play* for the *Los Angeles Times Book Review,* deemed Weiss's descriptions of the trial "engrossing."

Weiss next turned to fiction, writing detective stories that were set in the San Francisco metropolitan area. His first novel, titled *No Go on Jackson Street: A Mystery Introducing Ben Henry,* revolves around the sleuthing exploits of taxi driver Ben Henry. Weiss weaves elements of urban San Francisco culture into this 1987 whodunit. The plot incorporates murder charges leveled against a dubious acquaintance of Henry's, a gang of mobsters, and a venomous family publishing empire.

All Points Bulletin, Weiss's second Ben Henry novel, appeared in 1989. The author again uses San Francisco as a backdrop for a murder mystery, as cab driver Henry further hones his detective skills on solving the mysterious slayings of three of his colleagues. Weiss continued the series with 1992's *A Dry and Thirsty Ground.* In this work, Weiss moves the now-certified private investigator out of San Francisco and into a rural Northern California setting. Again Henry is occupied in solving a case involving a friend, but this time elements of ecological concern further complicate the plot.

As a reporter for the *San Francisco Chronicle,* Weiss wrote the newspaper series that became his next nonfiction work, *A Very Good Year: The Journey of a California Wine from Vine to Table.* Based on the thirty-nine day series that appeared in 2004, the book describes in detail the creation of a bottle of 2002 Ferrari-Carano Fume Blanc wine. Weiss profiles entrepreneurs and vintners Don and Rhonda Carano, who built the Ferrari-Carano Winery with wealth derived from Nevada gaming concerns. He looks at the work and personalities of the laborers and professionals involved in the creation of the wine, from grape farmer Steve Domenchelli to reserved winemaker George Bursick to the eager, ambitious vineyard workers in El Charco, in Mexico. Weiss also passes along a number of secrets gleaned from a pseudonymous contact called "Deep Cork." Weiss covers the entire winemaking process, from the cultivation and harvest of grapes to the skilled techniques of fermenting and blending wine to the marketing savvy necessary for a successful rollout of a new brand or vintage. *Booklist* reviewer Mark Knoblauch called Weiss's book an "exceptionally readable account of the state of California's wine industry at the start of the new millennium." Weiss "weaves a drama of failures and fears, tragedies and triumphs, births and deaths, ego and jealousy," commented a *Publishers Weekly* contributor, who concluded that the story is a "sweet pleasure."

BIOGRAPHICAL AND CRITICAL SOURCES:

PERIODICALS

Booklist, July, 2005, Mark Knoblauch, review of *A Very Good Year: The Journey of a California Wine from Vine to Table,* p. 1885.
Los Angeles Times Book Review, January 29, 1984, Herbert Gold, review of *Double Play: The San Francisco City Hall Killings,* p. 3.
Publishers Weekly, April 25, 2005, review of *A Very Good Year,* p. 48.

ONLINE

Elevage Web log, http://elevage.blogspot.com/ (July 8, 2005), Vincent Fritzsche, review of *A Very Good Year.*
Winewaves Web log, http://volunteer.blogs.com/winewaves/ (July 18, 2005), review of *A Very Good Year.**

*   *   *

WEST, Carroll Van 1955-

PERSONAL: Born January 29, 1955, in Murfreesboro, TN; son of W.C. (a laborer) and Sara (a teacher) West; married Mary S. Hoffschwelle (a professor), November 29, 1980; children: Owen William, Sara Elizabeth. *Ethnicity:* "White." *Education:* Middle Tennessee State University, B.A., 1977; University of Tennessee, M.A., 1978; College of William and Mary, Ph.D., 1982. *Politics:* "Democrat." *Religion:* Baptist. *Hobbies and other interests:* Travel, sports, photography, music.

ADDRESSES: Home—Murfreesboro, TN. *Office*—Center for Historical Preservation, Middle Tennessee State University, P.O. Box 80, Murfreesboro, TN 37132. *E-mail*—cwest@mtsu.edu.

CAREER: Middle Tennessee State University, Murfreesboro, professor, 1985—, director of Center for Historical Preservation, 2002—. Tennessee Civil War National Heritage Area, director, 2002—; conference participant; consultant to Western Heritage Center.

MEMBER: American Association of State and Local History, National Trust for Historic Preservation, American Historical Association, Organization of American Historians, American Studies Association, Alliance of National Heritage Areas, Western Historical Association, Southern Historical Association, Tennessee Historical Society, Montana Historical Society, Vernacular Architecture Forum.

AWARDS, HONORS: Associate fellow, Center for Great Plains Studies, 1994; American Association of State and Local History, certificate of commendation, 1996, award of merit, 1999; Tennessee History Book Award, 1999; recognition from National Trust for Historic Preservation, 2007.

WRITINGS:

A Traveler's Companion to Montana History, Montana Historical Society Press (Helena, MT), 1986.
Tennessee Agriculture: A Century Farms Perspective, Tennessee Department of Agriculture (Nashville, TN), 1987.
Images of Billings: A Photographic History, Western Heritage Press (Billings, MT), 1990.
Capitalism on the Frontier: The Transformation of Billings and the Yellowstone Valley in the Nineteenth Century, University of Nebraska Press (Lincoln, NE), 1993.
Tennessee's Historic Landscapes, University of Tennessee Press (Knoxville, TN), 1995.
(Editor in chief) *Tennessee Encyclopedia of History and Culture,* Tennessee Historical Society (Nashville, TN), 1998.
(Editor) *Tennessee History: The Land, the People, and the Culture,* University of Tennessee Press (Knoxville, TN), 1998.
Tennessee's New Deal Landscape, University of Tennessee Press (Knoxville, TN), 2000.
(Editor) *Trial and Triumph: Essays in Tennessee's African American History,* University of Tennessee Press (Knoxville, TN), 2002.
(Editor) *A History of the Arts in Tennessee: Creating Traditions, Expanding Horizons,* University of Tennessee Press (Knoxville, TN), 2004.

Contributor to books. Contributor to periodicals. Senior editor, *Tennessee Historical Quarterly*, 1993—.

SIDELIGHTS: Carroll Van West once told *CA:* "I want to explore, document, and interpret the transformation of rural American culture and history since the industrial age, and to convey those events through different media and publications. So, in my Montana work, I have written three books on that theme, one being a statewide study of historical landscapes (with little on the 'cities' of Montana) that came out of a 3,000-plus photographic survey of the state in 1984-85. The other two Montana books focus on Billings and the Yellowstone Valley, with the brief photographic history aimed at a broad audience while *Capitalism on the Frontier: The Transformation of Billings and the Yellowstone Valley in the Nineteenth Century* is an analytical model for exploring rural transformation and its impact on the peoples of a given region.

"As editor of the *Tennessee Historical Quarterly* I have tried to shape new directions in scholarship in addition to my own efforts. Throughout this work, themes of diversity, race, place, change, faith, and continuity are important."

Later West added: "*Capitalism on the Frontier*, in its blending of place and peoples, has informed all of my southern work, especially the more recent focus on my native state of Tennessee. I have had the opportunity of crafting narratives for different audiences from travelers and architectural devotees to college classrooms to reference users and the reading public. Each book is different, but they all share the broad goal of opening up the state's history, both in the topics addressed and in the questions that are asked. *Tennessee's Historic Landscapes* is clearly modeled after the earlier Montana effort, but it better integrates architecture, material culture, and history. My plan is now to update and expand that volume due to the fieldwork of the years from 1995 to 2005, when new significant trends in the landscape of the state emerged from my many field projects, especially the Rural African American Church Survey for the Center for Historic Preservation at Middle Tennessee State University. The strong sense of place gained from the landscapes study, however, clearly influenced the design and content of the *Tennessee Encyclopedia of History and Culture*, both the print version of 1998 and an online edition of 2003, as well as *Tennessee's New Deal Landscape*, a rather fun exploration of how the federal government reengineered the state and its people for the modern era. The encyclopedia was also part of a deliberate strategy of developing new interpretive tools and reference works for the totality of Tennessee history. The editing anthologies of *Tennessee History: The Land, the People, and the Culture* and *Trial and Triumph: Essays in Tennessee's African American History* were also parts of that strategy of placing better texts in the hand of teachers, students, and the reading public who engage with state history. The capstone of this effort was the collaborative production of *A History of the Arts in Tennessee: Creating Traditions, Expanding Horizons*, which is a first-of-its-kind in the literature of Tennessee history and culture.

"A second related, yet different, interest is beginning to shape my work—the impact of mass culture in twentieth-century America. This interest has not yielded any book-length manuscripts, but I have been exploring related questions through various field projects and through a few conference papers and published chapters and articles on such varied topics as Appalachian architecture, Rocky Mountains architecture, northern plains irrigation, and the civil rights movement."

BIOGRAPHICAL AND CRITICAL SOURCES:

PERIODICALS

Business History Review, summer, 1993, Richard S. Kirkendall, review of *Capitalism on the Frontier: The Transformation of Billings and the Yellowstone Valley in the Nineteenth Century*, p. 313.

*   *   *

WHITEHEAD, Colson 1970-

PERSONAL: Born 1970, in New York, NY; son of Arch and Mary Ann Whitehead; married Natasha Stovall. *Education:* Harvard University, graduated 1991.

ADDRESSES: Home—Brooklyn, NY.

CAREER: Writer. *Village Voice*, New York, NY, television critic.

AWARDS, HONORS: Finalist, Ernest Hemingway/PEN Award for First Fiction, and New Voices Award, Quality Paperback Book Club, both 1999, and Whiting Writers' Award, 2000, all for *The Intuitionist;* Editors' Choice, *New York Times,* 2001, and Young Lions Fiction Award, New York Public Library, 2002, both for *John Henry Days;* MacArthur fellowship, 2002; National Book Critics Circle Award finalist and Pulitzer Prize finalist, both for *John Henry Days.*

WRITINGS:

The Intuitionist, Anchor Books (New York, NY), 1999.
John Henry Days, Doubleday (New York, NY), 2001.
The Colossus of New York: A City in Thirteen Parts (nonfiction), Doubleday (New York, NY), 2003.
Apex Hides the Hurt, Doubleday (New York, NY), 2006.

Contributor to periodicals, including *Granta, Harper's,* and the *New York Times.*

ADAPTATIONS: The Intuitionist has been optioned for a movie by director Jonathan Demme.

SIDELIGHTS: Called a "large and vibrant talent" by Adam Begley in the *New York Observer,* author Colson Whitehead has penned several award-winning and critically acclaimed novels, *The Intuitionist John Henry Days,* and *Apex Hides the Hurt.* Writing in the London *Guardian,* Maya Jaggi described *The Intuitionist* as a "thrilling blend of noir and fantasy in the allegorical tale of an elevator inspector in pre-civil rights New York." Jaggi further noted that with *John Henry Days,* Whitehead "has waded into epic" in penning what she described as a "poignant, wittily observed and often gleefully comic" novel juxtaposing a nineteenth-century black folk-hero who defeated a steam drill but died in the process with a modern freelance journalist covering the John Henry Days festival in West Virginia.

Whitehead, a native New Yorker, decided as a young boy that he wanted to be a writer after reading his first Stephen King novel. In 1991 he graduated from Harvard University, and then worked for several years as a television critic for the *Village Voice.* Speaking about his journalism experience with *Salon.com* contributor Laura Miller, Whitehead noted: "I think I got a lot of stuff out of my system. I learned some good habits from

having to produce every other week and trying to make it fresh. *Village Voice* style back then encouraged the first-person—that sort of me-me-me stuff—and I worked through various preoccupations with pop culture." Whitehead also kept busy writing fiction during his *Village Voice* years, and completed a satirical novel of adult life in New York that nobody wanted to publish. "Even my agent dumped me," he admitted to Daniel Zalewski in the *New York Times Book Review.*

Then one night in 1996, while watching a television program about defective escalators, inspiration hit. Whitehead, who had been reading hard-boiled detective novels, wondered if he could fashion an allegory about an equally hard-boiled escalator inspector. Changing the occupation to elevator inspector, Whitehead spent the next nine months writing *The Intuitionist,* the story of Lila Mae Watson, a black elevator inspector whose career is basically sabotaged by white co-workers. "On one level the novel was an homage to Dashiell Hammett," wrote Zalewski, "but its supple racial metaphors earned comparisons to Ralph Ellison." Set in a city that strongly resembles New York, *The Intuitionist* is an allegory dealing with rival schools of elevator inspectors, those who use intuition in their work, such as Watson, the first black woman in the profession, and those who use more hands-on techniques to detect flaws in the system, dubbed the Empiricists. It is election time at the Elevator Guild, and the Empiricists are determined to do whatever it takes to show that the Intuitionists are on the wrong track; their primary tactic is to sabotage one of the elevators in Watson's building. A day after inspection, an elevator in her building goes into free fall, a terrible disaster. In an attempt to clear her name, Watson in turn winds up in a search for the missing notebooks of the Intuitionists' founder, James Fulton, who was working on a "black box": a "perfect elevator" that would allow the city to construct buildings sky-high. Fuller's blueprints for his foolproof elevator are in the missing notebooks, and whoever finds them will control the destiny of the city.

"Deftly and beautifully," wrote Robin Brenner in the online *Rambles,* "the story spins into a subtle exploration of so much more than the predictable points of politics and technology. Reminiscent of post-modern theory, Intuitionism and the debate over the soul and existence of elevators is illuminated as an intriguing argument that echoes the modern yearning for the streamlined sublime." Brenner further noted that Watson's search for the blueprints to the mythical "black box" that will eliminate limits to upward mobility "almost echoes contemporary physicists' search for a Grand Unified Theory of the universe. . . . *The Intuitionist* asks equally piercing and unsettling questions about identity, race, and through this warped mirror, our own less than honorable past."

Critical reception to Whitehead's debut novel largely followed Brenner's assessment. *Booklist* contributor Donna Seaman, while comparing Whitehead's work to that of George Orwell, Ralph Ellison, Kurt Vonnegut, and Thomas Pynchon, also found it "resoundingly original." Calling the story "mesmerizing," Seaman noted that it is the author's "shrewd and sardonic humor and agile explications of the insidiousness of racism . . . that make this such a trenchant and accomplished novel." A reviewer for *Publishers Weekly* similarly called the book "meaty and mythic," and also commented that Whitehead "has a completely original story to tell, and he tells it well, successfully intertwining multiple plot lines and keeping his reader intrigued from the outset." Joining the chorus of praise, *Newsweek* reviewer Veronica Chambers dubbed *The Intuitionist* "the most engaging literary sleuthing you'll read this year," while *Time* contributor Walter Kirn called the book "the freshest racial allegory since Ralph Ellison's *Invisible Man* and Toni Morrison's *The Bluest Eye*."

Whitehead's second novel, a riff on the John Henry myth, is as genre-busting as his first, an attempt to "define the interior crisis of manhood in terms of the entire pop-mad consumer society," according to a reviewer in the *New York Times*. In the novel, the nineteenth-century African-American folk-hero who proved the equal of technology has earned a spot on a postage stamp to be commemorated in 1996. The ceremony, held in a small West Virginia town, draws a crowd of urban media types, including J. Sutter, a freelance journalist who will cover any event in the hope of free food and getting his expenses paid. Sutter is the only black journalist among this pack of hack writers, and he is personally staging his own John Henry-like competition to see how many such events he con consecutively cover. Also among the journalists is Pamela Street, whose father was an avid collector of John Henry memorabilia. Street and Sutter find a focus in one another, and the author even brings John Henry himself into the story as the narrative drifts back in time. Additionally, Whitehead introduces other characters inspired by the John Henry story, including the singer Paul Robeson who played the "steel driving man" on Broadway.

Whitehead's second novel was met by positive critical reaction, most of which applauded the epic scale of his endeavor. Not all reviewers felt, however, that Whitehead was successful in his attempt. Writing in *Esquire*, Sven Birkerts remarked: "We anticipate a full-tilt grappling with myth, but instead Whitehead backs down, leaving us with the clatter and whir of failed connections, the reproachful silence of meanings left unexplored." *Entertainment Weekly* contributor Troy Patterson also had mixed feelings about the novel, calling it an "odd gem—a novel of dazzling facets and glaring flaws," while *Time* critic Paul Gray likewise concluded that *John Henry Days* is "a narrative tour de force that astonishes on almost every page, but it generates more glitter and brilliance than warmth."

Several critics greeted *John Henry Days* with even more praise than they had *The Intuitionist*. Countering the criticism of meanings left unexplored, Zachary Karabell noted in his appraisal for the *Los Angeles Times* that Whitehead's novel "works as a cascade of images and stories that intrigue and engage while remaining opaque, and yet, delicately, meaning emerges." Malcolm Jones, reviewing the title in *Newsweek,* acknowledged that while *John Henry Days* is something of a "mess," it is "a grand mess, one of those stories where the getting there is all the fun. Plundering the past, eviscerating the present, *John Henry Days* is a feast for famished readers." *Booklist* contributor Donna Seaman applauded the novel as an "even more sagacious tale" than Whitehead's debut, calling it "inventive, funny, and bittersweet," as well as "masterfully composed." This "great American novel" explores dualities such as "nature and civilization," "legend and history," "black and white," and "altruism and greed," according to Seaman. A reviewer for *Publishers Weekly* similarly called the book "smart, learned and soaringly ambitious," a novel that "consolidates . . . [Whitehead's] position as one of the leading writers of serious fiction of his generation." Reviewing *John Henry Days* in the *Review of Contemporary Fiction*, Keith Gessen deemed it "an important book," and *New York Times* contributor Jonathan Franzen described Whitehead's second novel as "funny and wise and sumptuously written," as well as an "aleatory fugue on the difficulty of manhood in an age that measures a man by what he buys or what he wears, not by his labor, not even by his human decency."

Whitehead turned to nonfiction in 2003 with *The Colossus of New York: A City in Thirteen Parts,* a collection of short pieces that "mix stream-of-consciousness with observational snapshots," according to *Book* contributor Don McLeese. Drawing comparisons to E.B. White's classic 1949 work *Here Is New York,* Whitehead's volume has "both a loose chronological and a cyclical sense: morning to night, arrival and departure, birth and death," observed a *Kirkus Reviews* critic. According to Philip Lopate, writing in the *Nation,* Whitehead "is treating New York directly as his subject matter, employing some of the classic organizing devices of the urban sketch, such as time of day ('Morning,' 'Rush Hour'), season ('Rain'), place ('Subway,' 'Central Park') and so on. It is moving to watch Whitehead patiently reworking these old tropes, fully conscious of his enterprise's antiquarian aspects. And he writes wonderfully, commanding a lush, poetic, mellifluous prose instrument."

The Colossus of New York earned strong critical praise, with several reviewers paying special attention to the author's complex narrative technique. *Booklist* contributor Donna Seaman remarked that Whitehead "incisively distills the kaleidoscopic frenzy of the city into startlingly vital metaphors and cartoon-crisp analogies." Luc Sante, writing in the *New York Times Book Review,* commented that Whitehead's volume "is a tour de force of voice, restlessly hopscotching from first to second to third person, from observation to speculation to reminiscence to indirect citation, in a staccato rhythm that effectively mimes the noise of the city," adding: "The texture is like the flick of a radio dial across the band, if all the stations had achieved a mysterious unity of subject." In the words of *Library Journal* reviewer Terren Ilana Wein, "this unique treatment of New York is . . . well, it's very New York: beautiful, imaginative, textured, and vibrant."

Whitehead returned to fiction with his 2006 novel *Apex Hides the Hurt,* "a smart tale about who we are under our labels," noted Raina Kelley in *Newsweek.* The work concerns a corporate "nomenclature consultant" who devises names for consumer products, including a series of flesh-toned bandages known as Apex. The melancholic protagonist is called out of his self-enforced retirement to help rename the small Midwestern town of Winthrop. Though a local software entrepreneur favors New Prospera, the African American mayor and members of the city council want the town to revert to its original name, Freedom, in honor of the former slaves who founded it. "The parodically conventional mystery provides the novel's forward motion," observed *New York Times Book Review* critic David Gates, "but—and here's the paradox—what keeps you reading this critique of language is its language, and our perverse delight in the ingenious abuse of words. Corporate-

speak is an easy target, and Whitehead wastes little time on such sport." Seaman, writing in *Booklist,* similarly noted that the author "archly explicates the philosophy of excess and the poetics of ludicrousness, and he incisively assesses the power inherent in the act of naming." In *Apex Hides the Hurt,* remarked a *Kirkus Reviews* contributor, "Whitehead audaciously blurs the line between social realism and fabulist satire."

Speaking with Walter Mosley in *Book,* Whitehead noted: "I feel my ideal reader is me at sixteen, or someone like me, who has just been reading the usual high school stuff and hasn't been exposed to some kind of freaky postwar black literature. . . . Last week I did a thing for this Writers in Schools program in [Washington,] DC. The teacher had taught [*John Henry Days*] two days before and I went and talked about the book and the kids were incredibly smart and thoughtful. They seemed to get the book, they didn't ask the same sort of questions I usually get. . . . They see me as the novelist guy, which I still have a hard time seeing myself as. I guess I am a novelist but they see me as a Novelist with a capital 'N'."

BIOGRAPHICAL AND CRITICAL SOURCES:

PERIODICALS

Atlanta Journal-Constitution, January 24, 1999, Laura Wexler, "*Intuitionist* Rises and Falls, Twisting Clichés with Glee," p. L12; June 3, 2001, Mark Luce, "Regarding 'John Henry,'" p. D4.

Black Issues Book Review, May-June, 2002, Evette Porter, "Writing Home," p. 36; January-February, 2004, Herb Boyd, review of *The Colossus of New York: A City in Thirteen Parts,* p. 58; May-June, 2006, Christopher Jack Hill, "Literary Landscapes," review of *Apex Hides the Hurt,* p. 32.

Bomb, summer, 2001, Suzann Sherman, "Interview with Colson Whitehead," pp. 74-80.

Book, May, 2001, Walter Mosley, "Eavesdropping," p. 44; November-December, 2003, Don McLeese, review of *The Colossus of New York,* p. 82.

Booklist, December 1, 1998, Donna Seaman, review of *The Intuitionist,* p. 651; April 15, 2001, Donna Seaman, review of *John Henry Days,* p. 1536; September 1, 2003, Donna Seaman, review of *The Colossus of New York,* p. 4; February 1, 2004, Donna Seaman, "Walkabout, New York Style," review of *The Colossus of New York,* p. 944; January 1, 2006, Donna Seaman, review of *Apex Hides the Hurt,* p. 64.

Boston Globe, March 19, 2006, Saul Austerlitz, "Identity Crisis," review of *Apex Hides the Hurt.*

Ebony, April, 2006, "Topshelf," review of *Apex Hides the Hurt,* p. 26.

Entertainment Weekly, May 18, 2001, Troy Patterson, review of *John Henry Days,* p. 74; October 24, 2003, Troy Patterson, review of *The Colossus of New York,* p. 111; March 24, 2006, Jennifer Reese, review of *Apex Hides the Hurt,* p. 74.

Esquire, May, 2001, Sven Birkerts, "Carry That Weight," p. 30; March, 2006, Douglas Danoff, "The Talented Mr. Whitehead," p. 78.

Guardian (London, England), June 23, 2001, Maya Jaggi, "Railroad Blues," p. 10.

Houston Chronicle, March 29, 1999, Peter Szatmary, "An Intuitionist's Over-the-Top Elevator," p. 23.

Kirkus Reviews, July 15, 2003, review of *The Colossus of New York,* p. 959; January 1, 2006, review of *Apex Hides the Hurt,* p. 15

Library Journal, October 15, 1999, Dan Bogey, review of *The Intuitionist,* p. 132; April 1, 2001, Ellen Flexman, review of *John Henry Days,* p. 135; August 1, 2003, Terren Ilana Wein, review of *The Colossus of New York,* p. 84; January 1, 2006, Bette-Lee Fox, review of *Apex Hides the Hurt,* p. 106.

Los Angeles Times, May 24, 2001, Zachary Karabell, "Heartache Delicately Circles Old Tale of Man versus Machine," p. E3.

Nation, December 1, 2003, Phillip Lopate, "New York State of Mind," review of *The Colossus of New York,* p. 31.

New Republic, July 24, 2001, Chloe Schama, "The Name Game," review of *Apex Hides the Hurt,* p. 36; August 6, 2001, James Wood, "Virtual Prose," p. 30.

Newsweek, January 11, 1998, review of *The Intuitionist,* p. 66; January 11, 1999, Veronica Chambers, "Love at First Sight," p. 66; May 21, 2001, Malcolm Jones, "Whitehead Hammers out a Hit," p. 59; March 13, 2006, Raina Kelley, "When the Name Game Isn't Just a Game," review of *Apex Hides the Hurt,* p. 61.

New Yorker, May 1, 2006, "Briefly Noted," review of *Apex Hides the Hurt,* p. 87.

New York Observer, July 23, 2001, Adam Begley, "Air Miles and Press Junkets, Consumerism and Coincidence," p. 19.

New York Review of Books, November 2, 2006, Darryl Pinckney, "Branding in America," review of *Apex Hides the Hurt,* p. 56.

New York Times, December 2, 2001, "Editors' Choice."

New York Times Book Review, February 7, 1999, Gary Krist, "The Ascent of Man"; May 13, 2001, Jonathan Franzen, "Freeloading Man," pp. 8-9, Daniel Zalewski, "Tunnel Vision: Interview with Colson Whitehead," pp. 8-9; October 19, 2003, Luc Sante, "Eight Million Reasons," review of *The Colossus of New York,* p. 38; April 2, 2006, David Gates, "You Are Now Entering—," review of *Apex Hides the Hurt,* p. 12.

People Weekly, March 27, 2006, Kyle Smith, review of *Apex Hides the Hurt,* p. 53.

Plain Dealer (Cleveland, OH), May 27, 2001, Frank Bentayou, "PR, Puffery Face off with a Hero of Legend," p. I11.

Publishers Weekly, November 16, 1998, review of *The Intuitionist,* p. 56; March 22, 1999, p. 28; April 16, 2001, review of *John Henry Days,* p. 43; May 26, 2003, review of *The Colossus of New York,* p. 57; January 30, 2006, review of *Apex Hides the Hurt,* p. 40.

Review of Contemporary Fiction, summer, 2001, Keith Gessen, review of *John Henry Days,* p. 155.

San Francisco Chronicle, May 16, 2001, David Kipen, "Whitehead Gives Life to John Henry," p. B1.

Time, January 25, 1999, Walter Kirn, "The Promise of Verticality," p. 78; May 21, 2001, Paul Gray, "A Ballad for All Times," p. 91; March 20, 2006, Lev Grossman, "The Third-Novel Curse," review of *Apex Hides the Hurt,* p. 117.

Times Literary Supplement (London, England), January 15, 1999, Sam Gilpin, review of *The Intuitionist,* p. 21; August 19, 2001, Mark Greif, review of *John Henry Days,* p. 19.

USA Today, March 30, 1996, Bob Minzesheimer, "*Apex* Is the Height of Excellent Writing," p. 5D.

Utne Reader, November-December, 1998, Jon Spayde, "The New Faces of Fiction," pp. 69-75.

Vanity Fair, April, 2006, Elissa Schappell, "Hot Type," review of *Apex Hides the Hurt,* p. 106.

Washington Post Book World, June 21, 1999, Brian Gilmore, "Race to the Top," p. 3; May 20, 2001, Ishmael Reed, "Rage against the Machine," p. 5.

ONLINE

Colson Whitehead Home Page, http://www.colsonwhitehead.com (February 1, 2007).

Powells.com, http://www.powells.com/ (June 14, 2001), Dave Welch, "Interview with Colson Whitehead."

Rambles Web site, http://www.rambles.net/ (April 30, 2002), Robin Brenner, review of *The Intuitionist.*

Random House Web site, http://www.randomhouse.com/
    boldtype/ (April 30, 2002), "Colson Whitehead."
Salon.com, http://www.salon.com/ (January 12, 1999),
    Laura Miller, "The Salon Interview: Going Up."*

*   *   *

WIER, Allen 1946-

PERSONAL: Surname is pronounced like "wire"; born
September 9, 1946, in San Antonio, TX; son of Ralph
A. (a flower wholesaler) and George Ann (a social
worker) Wier; married, wife's name Dara (a poet and
professor), April 2, 1969 (divorced, 1983); married;
wife's name Donnie (a watercolor artist), 1985;
children: (second marriage) Wesley Allen. *Education:*
Baylor University, B.A., 1968; Louisiana State University, M.A., 1970; Bowling Green State University, M.F.
A., 1974. *Politics:* "Usually Democrat." *Religion:*
United Methodist.

ADDRESSES: Office—Department of English, 301 Mc-
Clung Tower, University of Tennessee, Knoxville, TN
37996. *Agent*—Virginia Barber, William Morris Literary
Agency, 1325 Avenue of the Americas, New York, NY
10019. *E-mail*—awier@utk.edu.

CAREER: Writer, novelist, short-story writer, and
educator. Yard clerk for Kansas City Southern Railroad,
1966-67; All-Tex Ranch Supply, Waco, TX, laborer,
1967-68; Longwood College, Farmville, VA, instructor
in English, 1970-72; Carnegie-Mellon University,
Pittsburgh, PA, assistant professor of English, 1974-75;
Hollins College, Hollins College, VA, assistant professor of English, beginning 1975; University of Alabama,
professor of English and director of M.F.A. program,
1980-94; University of Tennessee, Knoxville, member
of English faculty and John C. Hodges Chair for
Distinguished Teaching, 2000-03. University of Texas,
visiting writer, 1983; Florida International University,
visiting writer, 1984-85.

MEMBER: PEN, Associated Writing Programs, Fellowship of Southern Writers (elected to membership, 2001).

AWARDS, HONORS: Creative writing fellowship,
National Endowment for the Arts, 1974; fellow, Bread
Loaf Writers' Conference, 1978; Guggenheim fellow,
1979-80; Dobie-Paisano fellow, University of Texas and

Texas Institute of Letters, 1989-90; named Alabama
travel writer of the year, 1994; Robert Penn Warren
Award for Fiction, Fellowship of Southern Writers,
1997; chancellor's award for outstanding research and
creative achievement, University of Tennessee, 1998;
Most Outstanding Professor in the Classroom Award,
graduate students of University of Tennessee's Department of English, 2005; Texas Institute of Letters Award
in Short Fiction.

WRITINGS:

Things about to Disappear (short stories), Louisiana
    State University Press (Baton Rouge, LA), 1978.
Blanco (novel), Louisiana State University Press (Baton
    Rouge, LA), 1978.
Departing as Air (novel), Simon & Schuster (New
    York, NY), 1983.
(Editor, with Don Hendrie, Jr., and author of introduc-
    tion) *Voicelust: Eight Contemporary Fiction Writ-
    ers on Style,* University of Nebraska Press
    (Lincoln, NE), 1985.
A Place for Outlaws (novel), HarperPerennial (New
    York, NY), 1989.
(Editor and author of introduction) *Walking on Water
    and Other Stories,* University of Alabama Press
    (Tuscaloosa, AL), 1996.
Tehano (novel), Southern Methodist University Press
    (Dallas, TX), 2006.

Contributor to anthologies, including *Carry Me Back,*
Gallimaufry Press (Arlington, VA), 1978; *Studies in the
Short Story,* Holt, Rinehart & Winston (New York, NY),
1984; *A Pocketful of Prose,* Holt, Rinehart & Winston
(New York, NY), 1992; *The Wedding Cake in the
Middle of the Road,* William Morrow (New York, NY),
1992; *That's What I Like about the South,* University of
South Carolina Press (Columbia, SC), 1993; *Best of the
West,* Peregrine Smith, 1998; *The Cry of an Occasion,*
Louisiana State University Press (Baton Rouge, LA),
2001; and *Knoxville Bound,* KWG, 2004.

Contributor of short stories and articles to literary
magazines, including *Texas Review, Ploughshares,
Vanderbilt Review, Idaho Review, New Millennium Writings, Southern Review, Carolina Quarterly, Black Warrior Review, Georgia Review, Window, Shenandoah, Yal-
lobusha Review, Five Points, Metro Pulse, Appalachian
Life, Mid-American Review, Sewanee Review,* and *New
River Review.*

SIDELIGHTS: Allen Wier is a novelist, short-story writer, and educator whose works fall into the category of Southern writing. Born in 1946 in San Antonio, TX, Wier grew up in a world that straddled the relatively conservative mid-twentieth century America and the wilder, less restrained landscape of Mexico. Wier's father, Ralph, was in the wholesale flower business in Mexico, and Wier and his mother George Ann regularly traveled between their home in San Antonio and Ralph's business concerns in Mexico. "What Allen Wier saw, heard, and felt there during those formative years has colored his work since," commented Fred Brown and Jeanne McDonald in *Growing up Southern: How the South Shapes Its Writers.* With such a vivid atmosphere to inhabit in his formative days, "how could Allen Wier have been anything other than a writer?," Brown and McDonald mused. "Those early years in Mexico plunged him into a constantly evolving fairytale whose dreamlike fascination has played out time and again in his work."

Another early influence, Wier told Brown and McDonald, were the Bible stories that his mother shared with him as he grew up. "Those early biblical stories, Wier says, influenced him through both content and style," Brown and McDonald related. "We read the whole Bible from front to back more than once," Wier stated. "We'd read a section and then talk about it. I loved it; it was never punishment in any way." Though his imagination was thoroughly nourished during his youth and teenage years, Wier did not consider becoming a writer until his junior year at Baylor University, Brown and McDonald noted. With the Vietnam war raging and the draft underway, Wier was concerned about being tapped for military service even as he was confused about which direction he should go in life. While considering his options, and deciding whether or not to contribute to the university's literary contest, Wier's house was burglarized. He wrote about the experience in a short story, then wrote a second story based on his summer job on the railroad. He submitted them both to the Baylor literary contest, and won first and second prize with them. He was only permitted to accept first prize, but both stories were published in the campus literary magazine. A revised version of the second story was sold to *Southern Review,* and became Wier's first work accepted for professional publication. He continued to pursue writing, though Baylor had no creative writing program at the time, then went on to graduate study at Louisiana State University and Bowling Green State University.

Wier began to associate his work with the rubric of the Southern writer. "Southerners write family histories,

histories of towns and communities and, even, hollers," he told Brown and McDonald. "There's a great interest in preserving the past, of making local landscapes and their inhabitants immortal. In some southern town you might be a crazy person or behave badly or be alcoholic or on drugs, but you belong, you are *our* crazy person or *our* drunk, so you're okay."

In *Tehano,* Wier presents a complicated and sprawling story of Texas as it develops through the tumultuous years from 1842 to 1866. Told largely by Gideon Jones, a traveling undertaker, aspiring journalist, and lightning rod salesman, the novel concerns the lives and trials of numerous individuals surviving on the rugged edge of the American frontier, in harsh and inhospitable lands often occupied by menacing Comanches, dangerous Mexican outlaws, runaway slaves, and desperate settlers. Among the characters in the book are Portis "Eye" Goar, a cowboy with murderous tendencies who gets shot in the chest by Knobby Cotton, an escaped slave searching desperately for his wife and son, abducted by Indians; Orten Trainer, a one-armed con artist who takes on someone else's identity; a pair of twin boys who find themselves fighting on opposite sides during the Civil War; and Alexander Wesley, an amputee who still carries his detached arm with him and pays dearly for his attachment to the limb. The characters experience violence and bloodshed, Indian attacks, gunfights, and the harshness of the unforgiving Texas countryside. Some survive, some die, and some go on to settle the wildest parts of the Wild West. Wier knits the varied threads of his narrative into an "epic retelling of a pivotal juncture in American history," remarked Margaret Flanagan in *Booklist.* "There are surprises and solid payoffs in the twisting plotline, which weaves the stories of many characters" together into "a leisurely, credible recreation of the Lone Star past," remarked a *Kirkus Reviews* critic. The author offers "a sympathetic picture of Native American life in a time of catastrophic change," commented Ken St. Andre in *Library Journal.*

Wier once told *CA:* "I am especially interested in the possibilities of language—images, textures are important in my work. Thematically much of my work deals with ways in which the imagination, magic, can transform our losses, can hold and share all the dreams and visions and events that must disappear."

BIOGRAPHICAL AND CRITICAL SOURCES:

BOOKS

Brown, Fred, and Jeanne McDonald, *Growing up Southern: How the South Shapes Its Writers,* Blue Ridge Publishing (Greenville, SC), 1997.

PERIODICALS

Booklist, August 1, 2006, Margaret Flanagan, review of *Tehano,* p. 45.
Kirkus Reviews, May 15, 2006, review of *Tehano,* p. 494.
Library Journal, July 1, 2006, Ken St. Andre, review of *Tehano,* p. 73.
Publishers Weekly, May 22, 2006, review of *Tehano,* p. 29.
Texas Monthly, August, 2006, Mike Shea, review of *Tehano,* p. 60.

ONLINE

Allen Wier Home Page, http://www.allenwier.com (March 10, 2007).
University of Tennessee at Chattanooga Web site, http://www.utc.edu/ (March 10, 2007), biography of Allen Wier.
University of Tennessee at Knoxville Web site, http://www.utk.edu/ (March 10, 2007), bibliography of Allen Wier.

* * *

WILLIAMS, Virginia 1940-
(Virginia Parrott Williams)

PERSONAL: Born August 9, 1940, in Nassauadox, VA; daughter of Lloyd Pinckney (in business) and Elva (a homemaker) Parrott; married Redford B. Williams (a physician and researcher), August 12, 1963; children: Jennifer Betts Williams Phillips, Lloyd Carter. *Ethnicity:* "European-American." *Education:* Duke University, A.B., 1962, M.A., 1973, Ph.D., 1980; Brown University, M.A., 1963. *Religion:* Unitarian-Universalist.

ADDRESSES: Home—Hillsborough, NC. *Office*—Williams Life Skills, 2020 W. Main, Ste. 100, Durham, NC 27705. *E-mail*—virginia@williamslifeskills.com.

CAREER: Williams Life Skills, Durham, NC, president, 1996—.

MEMBER: Society of Behavioral Medicine, American Psychosomatic Society.

WRITINGS:

Surrealism, Quantum Philosophy, and World War I, Garland Publishing (New York, NY), 1987.
(With husband, Redford Williams) *Anger Kills,* Times Books (New York, NY), 1993.
(With Redford Williams) *Lifeskills,* Times Books (New York, NY), 1997.
(With Redford Williams) *In Control,* Rodale (Emmaus, PA), 2006.

* * *

WILLIAMS, Virginia Parrott
See WILLIAMS, Virginia

* * *

WOODS, Stockton
See FORREST, Richard

* * *

WRIGHT, Alison 1961-

PERSONAL: Born December 23, 1961, in Summit, NJ; daughter of Frank (a research chemist) and Sonia (a flight attendant) Wright. *Ethnicity:* "Caucasian." *Education:* Attended Pepperdine University; Syracuse University, B.F.A., 1983; University of California, Berkeley, M.A., 1993.

ADDRESSES: Home and office—San Francisco, CA. *E-mail*—awright@alisonwright.com.

CAREER: Photographer and writer, 1980—. Geographic Expeditions, tour leader, 1998—.

MEMBER: Society of American Travel Writers, American Society of Media Photographers, American Society of Picture Professionals.

AWARDS, HONORS: Dorothea Lange Award in documentary photography, 1993, for photographs of child labor in Asia; Lowell Thomas travel journalism award, 2002.

WRITINGS:

The Spirit of Tibet: Portrait of a Culture in Exile (photographs), Snow Lion (Ithaca, NY) 1998.

(Coauthor) *A Simple Monk: Writings on His Holiness the Dalai Lama,* New World Library (Novato, CA), 2001.

Faces of Hope: Children of a Changing World, New World Library (Novato, CA), 2003.

Also contributor of photographs and photographic essays to periodicals around the world.

SIDELIGHTS: Alison Wright once told *CA:* "I am a freelance photojournalist based in San Francisco. I specialize in documenting the traditions and changes of endangered people in remote areas around the world. I want to give a voice to people who otherwise may not have one: children, refugees, land mine victims.

"I have published photographic essays on medicinal healers in the Amazon rain forests, the hill tribes of Southeast Asia, Aung San Suu Kyi in Burma, Burmese refugees in Thailand, Marco Polo's footsteps across the 'silk road' of China and Pakistan, as well as life in the outback of Australia, where I lived for two years. I was based in Nepal for four years, where I documented the plight of children for Unicef and various other aid organizations. I have lived with exiled Tibetans in Nepal and India for over a decade, recording their culture and the challenges which exile has brought. I also lead photographic and cultural tours to Tibet, Nepal, and Bhutan."

BIOGRAPHICAL AND CRITICAL SOURCES:

ONLINE

Alison Wright Photography, http://www.alisonwright.com (April 11, 2007).

Y-Z

YEADON, David 1942-

PERSONAL: Surname is pronounced "*Yee*-don"; born May 29, 1942, in Castleford, England; son of Claude Wade (a grocer) and Margaret Louise Yeadon; married Anne Coultish (a director of rehabilitation services and a writer), March 16, 1968. *Education:* Leeds University, B. City Planning, 1965. *Hobbies and other interests:* Travel, adventure, illustration, photography, budget-gourmet cooking, reading and writing fiction, handmade homes.

ADDRESSES: Home—Mohegan Lake, NY. *E-mail*—david@davidyeadontravel.com.

CAREER: City planner in Wakefield, England, 1959-65; senior city planner in London, England, 1965-67; project coordinator for city of Tehran, Iran, 1968-70; associate city planner in Los Angeles, CA, 1971-72; author and illustrator, 1972—.

MEMBER: Royal Town Planning Institute, Authors Guild.

AWARDS, HONORS: Lowell Thomas Gold and Silver Medals, Society of American Travel Writers, 1993, for best travel book and best foreign travel feature; has received other awards for travel writing.

WRITINGS:

Exploring Small Towns in California, two volumes, Ward Ritchie, 1972.

Hidden Restaurants in California, two volumes, Camaro (San Francisco, CA), 1972.

Wine-Tasting in California, Camaro (San Francisco, CA), 1973.

Sumptuous Indulgence on a Shoestring (cookbook), Hawthorn (New York, NY), 1974.

(With wife, Anne Yeadon) *Towards Independence,* American Federation for the Blind, 1974.

New York Book of Bars, Pubs, and Taverns, Hawthorn (New York, NY), 1975.

Hidden Corners of New England, Crowell (New York, NY), 1977.

Hidden Corners of the Mid-Atlantic States, Crowell (New York, NY), 1977.

When the Earth Was Young: Songs of the American Indian, Doubleday (New York, NY), 1978.

Nooks and Crannies: A Walking Tour Guide to New York City, Scribner (New York, NY), 1979, revised edition published as *New York's Nooks and Crannies: Unusual Walking All Five Boroughs,* Scribner (New York, NY), 1986.

Backroad Journeys of the West Coast States, Harper (New York, NY), 1979.

(With Anne Yeadon) *Living with Impaired Vision,* American Federation for the Blind, 1979.

Backroad Journeys of Southern Europe, Harper (New York, NY), 1981.

Hidden Corners of Britain, Allen & Unwin (London, England), 1981, Norton (New York, NY), 1982.

Offbeat England, Penguin (London, England), 1982.

Island Retreats of America, two volumes, Crown (New York, NY), 1982.

(With Anne Yeadon) *Free New York: 1,500 Free Pleasures and Entertainments,* Free City Books (New York, NY), 1982.

Secluded Islands of the Atlantic Coast, Crown (New York, NY), 1984.

New York: The Best Places, Perennial Library (New York, NY), 1987.

The Back of Beyond: Travels to the Wild Places of Earth, HarperCollins (New York, NY), 1991.

Lost Worlds: Exploring the Earth's Remote Places, HarperCollins (New York, NY), 1993.

The Way of the Wanderer: Discover Your True Self through Travel, Travelers' Tales (San Francisco, CA), 2001.

National Geographic Guide to the World's Secret Places: Escapes to 40 Unspoiled and Undiscovered Earthly Paradises, National Geographic Society (Washington, DC), 2003.

(And illustrator) *Seasons in Basilicata: A Year in a Southern Italian Hill Village,* HarperCollins (New York, NY), 2004.

(And illustrator) *Seasons on Harris: A Year in Scotland's Outer Hebrides,* HarperCollins (New York, NY), 2006.

Contributor to numerous travel and guide books, including *Caribbean Guide,* St. Kitts-Nevis, Insight Guides, 1992; *Philadelphia,* Comcast Pub. Co., 1995; *Chicago,* Comcast Pub. Co., 1995; *New York,* Comcast Pub. Co., 1995; *India,* Travelers' Tales, 1995; *Spain,* Travelers' Tales, 1995; *Hong Kong,* Travelers' Tales, 1996; *The Earth's Last Wild Places,* National Geographic Books, 1996; *Love and Romance,* Travelers' Tales, 1997; *The Road Within,* Travelers' Tales, 1997; *The Gift of Travel: The Best of the Best,* Travelers' Tales, 1998; *America's Hidden Corners,* National Geographic Books, 1998; *The Adventure of Food,* Travelers' Tales, 1999; *The Ultimate Journey,* Travelers's Tales, 2000; *Australia,* Travelers's Tales, 2000; *America's Small Town Escapes,* National Geographic Books, 2000; *Central America,* Travelers' Tales, 2002; *Tuscany,* Travelers' Tales, 2002; *China,* Travelers' Tales, 2004; and *Stories to Live By,* Travelers' Tales, 2005.

Contributor of illustrated articles to periodicals, including the *New York Times, Los Angeles Times, Cue, National Geographic, National Geographic Traveler, Washington Post,* and *America.* Editor, with Anne Yeadon, of eight self-study books on rehabilitation techniques for older blind individuals, Center for Independent Living, 1977-79.

SIDELIGHTS: The backroads of New York, the West Coast states, New England, and of the Mid-Atlantic States are among the many that David Yeadon has traveled. Indeed, since the 1970s, he has made a career of

writing about less-traveled places. In his books as in his journeys, Yeadon downplays major sightseeing attractions and seeks out lesser-known neighborhoods and local landmarks. Typically, he discusses a place's architecture, its parks, its ethnic holdouts, its markets, and its local museums. He sometimes peers into corners so obscure that they are unknown even to many of the region's inhabitants. For the more adventuresome visitor, Yeadon suggests unconventional activities such as traveling desert backroads, attending unusual fairs, visiting out-of-the-way lakes and valleys, discovering unique examples of folk architecture, and losing oneself on forest tracks. He looks at everything from mountain paths to cranberry festivals, and he discusses all types of attractions from uncommon front yards to resident recluses in desert hideouts. Yeadon chats with the inhabitants of backroad communities and collects their folklore to preserve their oral histories.

Yeadon's 1981 book, *Backroad Journeys of Southern Europe,* records fifteen thousand miles of his travels through southern France, Portugal, Spain, Italy, and southern Switzerland. "His book is studded with nuggets of history and quotations from other authors," a *New York Times* critic reported. "But many of his best passages concern small, unplanned-for adventures." The critic further remarked that Yeadon "writes expansively about food . . . markets and festivals, landscape and architecture, people and animals," and called *Backroad Journeys of Southern Europe* "a remarkably sunny-natured book."

Yeadon takes readers further afield in his subsequent books. In *The Back of Beyond: Travels to the Wild Places of Earth* he visits twenty destinations, most located in Asia but a few in the British Isles and the Caribbean. Furthermore, in *Lost Worlds: Exploring the Earth's Remote Places* he treks through locations in Panama, Venezuela, Tasmania, Australia, Fiji, and the Caribbean. According to a *Kirkus Reviews* critic, the latter work is full of the author's "trademark good humor [and] contagious love of wandering," as well as "heavy doses of ecomysticism." With *The Way of the Wanderer: Discover Your True Self through Travel* Yeadon makes the travel diary form a collection of reflective essays on the benefits of visiting the unknown. In it he writes: "To know the world still remains a thing of mystery, silence and secrets—this I find one of the greatest joys of all."

The great appeal of many of Yeadon's travel guides is his dedication to locating and sharing out-of-the-way places that few travelers have seen or read of in other guidebooks. Yeadon goes off the beaten path to give travelers a sense of adventure. In *National Geographic Guide to the World's Secret Places: Escapes to 40 Unspoiled and Undiscovered Earthly Paradises,* he chronicles some of these adventurous journeys. However, in *Seasons in Basilicata: A Year in a Southern Italian Hill Village,* he offers a glimpse of a place that is just as rare and just as much a treasure, though it seems less remote and less unique. Yeadon includes sketches of his visit to the Italian town, providing a warm glimpse of his experiences when he traveled their with his wife. Mary Ann Smyth, reviewing *Seasons in Basilicata* for *Bookloons.com,* called the book "a fascinating tale of a year in another world—divorced from the rest of the universe but still very much a part of it. It's written by a man who has heart and cares about his fellow man." The feeling of Yeadon's "Seasons" books, which will be a series similar to his more adventurous National Geographic travel books, is a much more intimate one. Rather than traveling far and wide, Yeadon will concentrate on some corners of the globe—single locations—and share them with readers on a detailed level.

Yeadon once told *CA:* "After ten years of professional practice, I put aside my city planning career and dabbled. At first an article, a few illustrations, and then came the aroma of that first check, disbelief at the gangling contract, all staples, folds, and formalities. How could anyone be so gullible to pay me for traveling America in a beat-up VW camper with very hazy notions of what I was doing? Not that they paid much at first. I made up the difference on the journey by selling pen sketches of lopsided gold towns and postcards of Victorian gothic fantasy architecture (six for a dollar, custom-backed by Anne in the back of the camper). It was supposed to be a short trip, a sabbatical from designing never-never new towns and solving the unsolvable, a chance to write about real places and people before cashing in the camper for a responsible expense-account-and-Cadillac career. Only it didn't happen that way.

"I never went back. I chose the backroads—thousands upon thousands of miles of them. I explored the hidden corners of America and even came into the big cities searching out the secrets of their nooks and crannies. Occasionally I'd digress for a book on budget gourmet cooking or on the songs of the American Indian. Anne and I collaborated on her work with the aging blind in New York and then set off again together on backroad odysseys of Britain and southern Europe. The books got

longer, the illustrations better, and the themes clearer. Odd adventures and delights of discovery increased. We met wise people out there in quiet places, and they became both part of the book and our lives.

"In an era of mass travel on a global scale, many modern-day explorers overlook the riches of local environments and substitute superficial, fast-paced itineraries through exotic locations for the adventures and surprises of backroad travel closer to home. They miss a lot this way—the hidden places, the little legends, the heritage and the folklore of small communities, people living a quieter way of life reflecting more durable values.

"Further plans? Very vague, just as they should be. More of the same? It's never the same. Each book is a fresh experience, a bevy of new challenges and surprises.

"Yes, I'd like to build our home (an exercise in fantastitecture). I'd like to circle the earth, slowly and on the ground. I'd like to avoid predictability. I'd like to experiment with new writings and illustrations. Most of all, I'd like to keep alive."

BIOGRAPHICAL AND CRITICAL SOURCES:

PERIODICALS

Bloomsbury Review, June, 1991, review of *The Back of Beyond: Travels to the Wild Places of Earth,* p. 27.
Booklist, April 15, 1984, review of *Secluded Islands of the Atlantic Coast,* p. 1146; February 1, 1991, review of *The Back of Beyond,* p. 1111; July, 1993, Joe Collins, review of *Lost Worlds: Exploring the Earth's Remote Places,* pp. 1939, 1953.
Christian Science Monitor, September 7, 1984, reviews of *Secluded Islands of the Atlantic Coast, Hidden Corners of Britain,* and *Backroad Journeys of Southern Europe,* p. B2; January 28, 1991, Mary Warner Marien, review of *The Back of Beyond,* p. 13.
Kirkus Reviews, December 1, 1990, review of *The Back of Beyond,* p. 1663; May 1, 1993, review of *Lost Worlds,* p. 587.
Library Journal, January, 1991, Harold M. Otness, review of *The Back of Beyond,* p. 130; June 15, 1993, Harold M. Otness, review of *Lost Worlds,*

p. 89; April 15, 2001, Ravi Shenoy, review of *The Way of the Wanderer: Discover Your True Self through Travel*, p. 123.

Los Angeles Times Book Review, July 18, 1993, review of *Lost Worlds*, p. 6.

New York Times, August 16, 1981, review of *Backroad Journeys of Southern Europe.*

Publishers Weekly, December 7, 1990, Genevieve Stuttaford, review of *The Back of Beyond*, p. 68.

Quill and Quire, February, 1994, review of *Lost Worlds*, p. 30.

Washington Post Book World, April 14, 1991, review of *The Back of Beyond*, p. 12; July 4, 1993, review of *Lost Worlds*, p. 13.

ONLINE

Bookloons.com, http://www.bookloons.com/ (April 16, 2007), Mary Ann Smyth, review of *Seasons in Basilicata: A Year in a Southern Italian Hill Village.*

David Yeadon Home Page, http://www.davidyeadon travel.com (April 16, 2007).*

*   *   *

YELDHAM, Peter 1927-

PERSONAL: Born April 25, 1927, in Gladstone, New South Wales, Australia; son of Alan (a doctor) and Faith Yeldham; married Marjorie Crane, October 27, 1948; children: one son, one daughter. *Ethnicity:* "Australian." *Politics:* Labor Party.

ADDRESSES: Home—Yarramalong, New South Wales, Australia; fax: 612-43-531448. *Agent*—Nick Quinn, The Agency Ltd., 24 Pottery Ln., London W11 4LZ, England.

CAREER: Writer.

MEMBER: Australian Writers Guild, Australian Society of Authors, British Writers Guild.

AWARDS, HONORS: Sammy Award, best television series in Australia, 1979, for *Run from the Morning;* Writers Guild awards, best adaptation, 1980, for *Ride on Stranger*, 1983, for *1915*, and 1986 for *The Far Country,* and best mini-series, 1989, for *The Alien Years;*

Penguin Award, best script, 1982, for *1915;* Order of Australia Medal, 1991; Centenary Medal, 2003; Australian Logie Award for *Jessica.*

WRITINGS:

NOVELS

Reprisal (thriller), Eldorado (Cremorne, New South Wales, Australia), 1994.

Without Warning (thriller), Pan (Sydney, Australia), 1995.

Two Sides of a Triangle (thriller), Pan (Sydney, Australia), 1996.

A Bitter Harvest (historical), Pan Macmillan (Sydney, Australia), 1997.

The Currency Lads (historical), Pan Macmillan (Sydney, Australia), 1998.

Against the Tide (historical), Pan Macmillan (Sydney, Australia), 1999.

Land of Dreams (historical), Pan Macmillan (Sydney, Australia), 2002.

The Murrumbidgee Kid (historical), Penguin Books (Camberwell, Victoria, Australia), 2007.

Barbed Wire and Roses, Penguin Books (Camberwell, Victoria, Australia), 2007.

PLAYS

Birds on the Wing, Evans Plays (London, England), 1969.

She Won't Lie Down (later known as *"Ready When You Are, Darling"*), Samuel French (New York, NY), 1972.

(With Donald Churchill) *Fringe Benefits* (two-act), Samuel French (New York, NY), 1977.

(With Donald Churchill) *My Friend Miss Flint* (two-act), Samuel French (New York, NY), 1984.

(With Martin Worth) *Lighting up Time* (two-act), Samuel French (New York, NY), 1984.

Seven Little Australians, 1988.

Split down the Middle, 1998.

SCREENPLAYS

The Comedy Man, 1963.

The Liquidator, 1965.

Age of Consent, 1968.
Touch and Go, 1979.

TELEVISION SCRIPTS

Run from the Morning, 1977.
Golden Soak, 1978.
Ride On, Stranger, 1979.
The Timeless Land, 1979.
Tusitala (miniseries), 1985.
Captain James Cook, (miniseries), 1987.
The Heroes, (miniseries), 1989.
Heroes II, (miniseries), 1991.
Jessica (miniseries), 2001.

Author of television plays, including *Reunion Day, Stella, Thunder on the Snowy, East of Christmas,* and *The Cabbage Tree Hat Boys.*

SIDELIGHTS: Peter Yeldham is a versatile Australian writer whose writings include stage plays, scripts for television and film, and novels. His screenplays include *Age of Consent,* director Michael Powell's idyllic film about a middle-aged painter's budding romance with a younger woman. Yeldham's television writings, meanwhile, include such productions as *Run from the Morning,* which J.R. Carroll, writing in the *Australian Book Review,* referred to as "excellent."

Yeldham's first novel, *Reprisal,* concerns three Vietnam War veterans who successfully commit a bank robbery in Sydney, then see their achievement undone when police probe the sudden death of their former getaway driver three years later. While the thieves attempt to prosper in legitimate business, various investigators, including the inspector who handled the original robbery probe, attempt to bring them to justice. *Without Warning* is a thriller in which Megan and David Turner run afoul of a deranged police officer. After a routine pullover results in an argument, lawman Arch Whitelaw determines to wreak havoc on the couple, both of whom are involved in the film business. Whitelaw begins by stalking Megan, then shapes events so that David doubts his wife's fidelity. Megan eventually turns to Whitelaw's superior officer for restitution, but her action only serves to make matters worse. Ultimately the Turners are compelled to retaliate against their mad antagonist. J.R. Carroll described *Without Warning* in an *Australian Book Review* appraisal as "a nightmarish thriller." Carroll added that the novel "builds deceptively, holding the reader and not letting go until the last unexpected . . . twist." In another thriller, *Two Sides of a Triangle,* a disgruntled police officer teams with a beautiful, resourceful woman to topple an Asian drug lord with ties to an English powerbroker.

In his next novel, the historical *A Bitter Harvest,* Yeldham broke from the thriller genre to chronicle the exploits of a former thief, along with his daughter and her husband, throughout pivotal periods in Australian history. Kate Happell wrote in the *Australian Book Review* that *A Bitter Harvest* possesses "an undeniably simple plot and even more simplistic characters," but she added that "it certainly provides entertainment."

The title for Yeldham's next book, *The Currency Lads,* comes from the colloquial phrase for native-born Australians. In the novel, two boys who become friends through a deadly twist of fate grow into enemies as they get older and take opposing sides in Australia's policy of importing cheap, convict labor. In a review for the *Telegraph,* Alister McMillan called *The Currency Lads* "a succulent fable" and praised Yeldham for writing "an epoch rarely visited."

Yeldham's next historical novel, *Against the Tide,* concerns siblings who arrive in Australia toward the end of World War II and find themselves faced with considerable hardship, including the struggle to survive in what Elizabeth Dean, writing in the *Australian Book Review,* called "the inhospitable landscape." Dean deemed *Against the Tide* "a good read for those who like action." In a review of the novel for the *Telegraph,* critic Alan Hill cited Yeldham as "the master of the Australian historical blockbuster."

Yeldham once told *CA:* "When I said I wanted to be a writer at age seventeen, my father said I was insane. He said I should get a safe job in a bank. More than fifty years on, I'm still a writer, enjoying it. The bank would have fired me years ago.

"Having been an expatriate for a third of my life, it was a joy to come home to Australia and absorb myself in writing Australian drama and Australian novels. After being away so long I felt like an immigrant, and so my favorite work, particularly in my novels, has been about immigrants. My feeling is perhaps best summed up by the dedication of my novel *Against the Tide:* 'To the waves of immigrants who made the long journey against the tide, bringing us new visions, this book is dedicated.'"

BIOGRAPHICAL AND CRITICAL SOURCES:

BOOKS

Yeldham, Peter, *Against the Tide,* Pan Macmillan (Sydney, Australia), 1999.

PERIODICALS

Australian Book Review, September, 1994, J.R. Carroll, "Guilt Edge," pp. 62-63; May, 1995, J.R. Carroll, "Crime Past and Present," p. 66; May, 1996, J.R. Carroll, "Cankers," pp. 60-61; June, 1997, Kate Happell, review of *A Bitter Harvest,* pp. 64-65; September, 1999, Elizabeth Dean, review of *Against the Tide,* p. 45.

*   *   *

ZABYTKO, Irene 1954-

PERSONAL: Surname is pronounced "zab-*it*-ko"; born October 19, 1954, in Chicago, IL; daughter of Stanley (a police officer) and Mary (a singer and homemaker) Zabytko. *Ethnicity:* "Ukrainian-American." *Education:* Vermont College of Norwich University, B.A., 1983, M.F.A., 1991; also attended Loyola University Chicago. *Religion:* Eastern Rite Catholic. *Hobbies and other interests:* Singing, drumming, cooking.

ADDRESSES: Home—Apopka, FL.

CAREER: Radio announcer and commercial creator and performer for stations WCWR-AM, Cocoa, FL, and WEZY-FM, Racine, WI, between 1980 and 1981; Community College of Vermont, Montpelier, adjunct professor, 1986; Tupperware, Inc., promotions copywriter, 1990; OdessaPressa Productions, Lyndonville, VT, publisher, 1991-97; Progressive Publishing, Orlando, FL, writer, of MegaBooks, 1998—. Staff writer for the newspapers *Apoka Chief* and *Planter;* WMFE-FM Radio, announcer for "The Arts Connection;" guest on numerous media programs; public lecturer; gives readings from her works. Wheat Street Productions, documentary film producer and writer. Taras Shevchenko State University of Kiev, instructor, 1992; Pedagogical Institute, Drohobych, Ukraine, adjunct

professor, 1993; St., Leo's College, adjunct professor, 1994; University of Central Florida, instructor, 1994-95; Southern College, adjunct professor, 1995; Seminole Community College, adjunct professor, 1996-97; Ball State University, visiting writer and Lilly fellow, 2003; Gotham Writers Workshop (online program), instructor, 2003—; guest lecturer at schools, including Seminole Community College, Calvin College, and Edgewood College; private tutor and substitute teacher of English as a second language. Fellow in residence at Virginia Center of the Creative Arts, 1989, Hambidge Center for the Creative Arts and Sciences, Helene Wurlitzer Foundation of New Mexico, 1991, Dorset Colony, 1992, Edna St. Vincent Millay Colony for the Arts, 1994, Ragdale Foundation, 1995, Mary Anderson Center for the Arts, 1997, 2005, Byrdcliffe Art Center, 1998, Alden B. Dow Creativity Center at Northwood University, 2001, and Leighton Studios for Independent Artists at Banff Centre for the Arts, 2005.

MEMBER: Authors Guild, Authors League of America.

AWARDS, HONORS: Grants from Ludwig Vogelstein Foundation, 1985-86, and Barbara Demming Memorial Fund, 1986; PEN Syndicated Fiction Award, 1988, for the short story "Obligation"; cited among "best books for the teen age," New York Public Library, 2004, for *When Luba Leaves Home;* grant from State of Florida, 2006.

WRITINGS:

The Sky Unwashed (novel), Algonquin (Chapel Hill, NC), 2000.
When Luba Leaves Home (short stories), Algonquin (Chapel Hill, NC), 2003.

Work represented in anthologies, including *Havens for Creatives: IMPACT* (includes short story *"Obligation"*), edited by Char Plotsky, ACTS 1 Creativity Center Anthology Project, 1994; *Literature: An Introduction to Reading and Writing,* 4th edition, edited by Edgar V. Roberts, Prentice Hall, 1995; *New to North America: Writing by Immigrants, Their Children and Grandchildren,* edited by Abby Bogomolny, Burning Bush (New York, NY), 1997; *I've Always Meant to Tell You: Letters to Our Mothers; An Anthology of Women Writers,* edited by Constance Warloe, Pocket Books (New York, NY), 1997; and *From Daughters and Sons to Fathers: What I've Never Said,* edited by Constance

Warloe, Story Line Press (Ashland, OR), 2001. Contributor of more than 150 poems, short stories, essays, and reviews to periodicals, including *Hysteria, Sojourner, NewCollage, Black Cat Mystery, Ukrainian Weekly, Women's Review of Books,* and *Chicago Tribune Sunday Magazine.* Editor, *Vermont Woman,* 1988.

SIDELIGHTS: Irene Zabytko once told *CA:* "Like many other writers, I was an avid reader as child. The magical transformation from reader into writer happened by accident when the Chicago Public Library had a book sale one year. I was twelve or so at the time and remember traveling downtown from my very insular neighborhood expressly for this event. One of the books I spent my allowance on was an autobiography by Edna Ferber, *A Peculiar Treasure.* It was a beautifully printed book with a fancy blue leather cover and several pictures of her with famous people. But what was so amazing was the idea that a woman—a single woman at that—had actually made a living as a successful and well-respected writer. I was also impressed with her penthouse apartment with a rooftop garden where she entertained famous celebrity friends. For a kid who grew up in a very tough inner city neighborhood, her book was a serendipitous revelation that such a life is possible. I still believe in its possibility.

"I write about Ukrainians in America and in Ukraine because I find them fascinating. Early on in my writing life, I wanted to write about 'Americans' whoever they were. I grew up in a very Ukrainian-American neighborhood in Chicago, and attended Ukrainian schools, churches, and summer camps, so that by the time I attended college, I wanted to discard that identity and be a real American. Ironically, everyone else was so charmed by my ethnicity and amazed I was born in Chicago and not in Ukraine. I found that very confusing, and more so when I tried to write stories with characters named Debbie or Ken—which never worked. Then, after reading Flannery O'Connor's *Mystery and Manners,* I realized that, as she said, 'you have to know your people.' I certainly know these Ukrainians, and once I figured that out, the stories about them came easily and I'm still writing about people with names like Yurko and Marusia because they are who I know best to write about.

"Primarily, what influences my work is the story. Ethnicity is important, but even such anthropological observations have to transcend to allow the story to get through for the reader—whoever he or she is in the world—to become involved with and maybe be changed for having read the book or story. For instance, *The Sky Unwashed* is certainly about a very well-known historical catastrophe, Chernobyl, and about a group of old women who return to their deserted village in the contaminated zone around the plant. However, it's my hope that the story also illustrates the tenacity of people surviving cataclysmic events; how they grow despite the odds. That's the transcendence I always hope to find and experience as both a writer and reader.

"There are so many writers who have influenced my work, I hesitate to begin naming them all.

"I have no writing process. I write a lot, and when I don't I become fidgety, and out-of-sorts, and irritating to be around because writing is what I should be doing, and I'm probably not doing it because I'm doing other things that are banal and time-wasters, but which need to be done (like food shopping and bill paying, or updating my resume)."

BIOGRAPHICAL AND CRITICAL SOURCES:

PERIODICALS

Booklist, February 15, 2000, review of *The Sky Unwashed.*

Kirkus Reviews, March 15, 2000, review of *The Sky Unwashed.*

Library Journal, March 1, 2000, review of *The Sky Unwashed.*

Publishers Weekly, February 21, 2000, review of *The Sky Unwashed.*

Ukrainian Weekly, April 23, 2000, "Ukrainian American's Novel Tells Story of Chernobyl's Aftermath," p. 7.